ENCYCLOPEDIA OF
Islam

Encyclopedia of Buddhism
Encyclopedia of Catholicism
Encyclopedia of Hinduism
Encyclopedia of Islam
Encyclopedia of Judaism
Encyclopedia of Protestantism

ENCYCLOPEDIA OF WORLD RELIGIONS

ENCYCLOPEDIA OF
Islam

Juan E. Campo
J. Gordon Melton, Series Editor

An imprint of Infobase Publishing

Encyclopedia of Islam

Facts On File, Inc.
An imprint of Infobase Publishing
132 West 31st Street
New York NY 10001

Library of Congress Cataloging-in-Publication Data

Campo, Juan Eduardo, 1950–
  Encyclopedia of Islam / Juan E. Campo.
    p. cm.— (Encyclopedia of world religions)
  Includes bibliographical references and index.
  ISBN-13: 978-0-8160-5454-1
  ISBN-10: 0-8160-5454-1
  1. Islamic countries—Encyclopedias—Juvenile literature. 2. Islam—Encyclopedias—Juvenile literature. I. Title.
  DS35.53.C36 2008
  297.03—dc22   2008005621

Facts On File books are available at special discounts when purchased in bulk quantities for businesses, associations, institutions, or sales promotions. Please call our Special Sales Department in New York at (212) 967-8800 or (800) 322-8755.

You can find Facts On File on the World Wide Web at http://www.factsonfile.com

Text design by Erika K. Arroyo
Cover design by Cathy Rincon/Takeshi Takahashi
Illustrations by Sholto Ainslie

Printed in the United States of America

VB Hermitage 10 9 8 7 6 5 4 3 2 1

This book is printed on acid-free paper and contains 30 percent postconsumer recycled content.

FOR MAGDA, ANDRÉS, AND FEDERICO
IN MEMORY OF JULIO H. CAMPO (1925–2006)

QUE BONITA ES ESTA VIDA . . .

CONTENTS

ABOUT THE EDITORS AND CONTRIBUTORS

Series Editor

J. Gordon Melton is the director of the Institute for the Study of American Religion in Santa Barbara, California. He holds an M.Div. from the Garrett Theological Seminary and a Ph.D. from Northwestern University. Melton is the author of *American Religions: An Illustrated History*, *The Encyclopedia of American Religions*, *Religious Leaders of America*, and several comprehensive works on Islamic culture, African-American religion, cults, and alternative religions. He has written or edited more than three dozen books and anthologies as well as numerous papers and articles for scholarly journals. He is the series editor for Religious Information Systems, which supplies data and information in religious studies and related fields. Melton is a member of the American Academy of Religion, the Society for the Scientific Study of Religion, the American Society of Church History, the Communal Studies Association, and the Society for the Study of Metaphysical Religion.

Volume Editor

Juan E. Campo, associate professor of religious studies at the University of California, Santa Barbara, holds an M.A. and Ph.D. from the University of Chicago's History of Religions program. He specializes in the comparative study of the cultural formations of Islam in the Middle East and South Asia, sacred space and pilgrimage, and political Islam in the contexts of modernity. His research has taken him to Egypt, where he has lived, studied, or taught for nearly six years, as well as India, Saudi Arabia, Bahrain, Turkey, Malaysia, Singapore, Thailand, and Israel. Professor Campo's first book, *The Other Sides of Paradise: Explorations in the Religious Meanings of Domestic Space in Islam*, won the American Academy of Religion's award for excellence, in 1991. He has edited or contributed articles to a number of leading reference works, including Merriam-Webster's *Encyclopedia of World Religions*, *Encyclopedia of the Qur'an*, and the Macmillan *Encyclopedia of Islam and the Muslim World*. His current projects include a comparative study of modern Muslim, Hindu, and Christian pilgrimage.

Contributors

Fahad A. Alhomoudi holds a Ph.D. from McGill University. He is the vice dean of academic research at al-Imam Muhammad bin Saud Islamic University, Riyadh, Saudi Arabia. He specializes in Islamic thought and Islamic law, with a focus on its origins. He is the author of

Protecting the Environment and Natural Resource in Islamic Law (published in Arabic, 2004). He has presented numerous scholarly papers on topics such as Islamic law and the modern state: conflict or coexistence? and a critical study of the translations of Hadith terminology.

Jessica Andruss earned an M.A. in religious studies at the University of California, Santa Barbara, and is now a Ph.D. candidate at the University of Chicago's Divinity School. Her area of specialization is in medieval Jewish and Muslim scriptural exegesis.

Jon Armajani earned a Ph.D. in religious studies with a focus in Islamic studies and Near Eastern studies from the University of California, Santa Barbara. His areas of expertise include modern Islam and Muslim-Christian relations. He is the author of *Dynamic Islam: Liberal Muslim Perspectives in a Transnational Age* and assistant professor in the Department of Theology at the College of St. Benedict/St. John's University in Minnesota.

Reza Aslan is assistant professor at the University of California, Riverside and author of *No god, but God: The Origins, Evolution, and Future of Islam*. He is also a research associate at the University of Southern California's Center on Public Diplomacy. His commentaries on Islam and the Middle East have appeared in the *Los Angeles Times,* the *New York Times,* the *Washington Post,* and the *Boston Globe*. He has also appeared on a number of major network and cable news programs.

A. Nazir Atassi is assistant professor of history at Louisiana Tech University. He received a Ph.D. from the University of California, Santa Barbara. He specializes in Islamic and Middle Eastern history, with a focus on early Islamic society.

Anna Bigelow is assistant professor of religious studies at North Carolina State University. She received a Ph.D. from the University of California, Santa Barbara, in 2004. Her research focuses on South Asian Islam, especially interreligious relations and shared religious spaces. Her current book project is called *Sharing the Sacred: Devotion and Pluralism in Muslim North India.*

Vincent F. Biondo III is assistant professor of religious studies at California State University in Fresno. He received a Ph.D. from the University of California, Santa Barbara. His specialization is the religious traditions of the West, with a focus on Islam in America and Great Britain. He is author of several articles and coeditor of *Religion in the Practice of Daily Life* (forthcoming).

Stephen Cory received a Ph.D. in Islamic history from the University of California, Santa Barbara. His specialty is the history of North Africa and Islamic Spain during the late medieval and early modern periods. He is currently an assistant professor in history and religious studies at Cleveland State University.

David L. Crawford is assistant professor of sociology and anthropology at Fairfield University. He received a Ph.D. from the University of California, Santa Barbara. He specializes in the study of the societies of North Africa with a focus on the Amazigh people of Morocco. He is the author of *Amazigh Households in the World Economy: Labor and Inequality in a Moroccan Village* and a number of articles and chapters on contemporary Moroccan society and politics.

Maria del Mar Logrono-Narbona received a Ph.D. in history, with a focus on modern Middle Eastern history, from the University of California, Santa Barbara. She specializes in the transnational connections between Syrian and Lebanese diasporas in Latin America during the first half of the 20th century. She is currently visiting professor at Appalachian State University, North Carolina.

Caleb Elfenbein is a Ph.D. candidate in religious studies at the University of California, Santa Barbara. He specializes in Islamic studies, with a focus on Islam in colonial and postcolonial societies.

Kenneth S. Habib is an assistant professor in the music department of the California Polytechnic

State University, San Luis Obispo. His Ph.D. in ethnomusicology is from the University of California, Santa Barbara, with specializations in Middle Eastern and American popular music. He also has taught music at Pomona College and the University of California, Santa Barbara, taught Arabic at Santa Barbara City College, and served as assistant to the director of the Middlebury College Arabic School.

Aysha A. Hidayatullah is a Ph.D. candidate in religious studies at the University of California, Santa Barbara. Her dissertation research examines newly emerging forms of feminist theology in Islam. She has written on a number of topics concerning gender and sexuality in Islam, including the life of Mary the Copt, the prophet Muhammad's Egyptian consort.

Josh Hoffman is a Ph.D. student at the University of California, Santa Barbara, where he specializes in modern Middle Eastern history. His fields of expertise also include premodern Middle Eastern history, global/world history, nationalism, political Islam, international law, and human rights.

Shauna Huffaker is on the history faculty at the University of Windsor, Canada. She holds an M.A. from the School of Oriental and African Studies in London and a Ph.D. from the University of California, Santa Barbara. Her specialization is in Islamic history, with a focus on social history during the Middle Ages.

Amir Hussain holds a Ph.D. from the University of Toronto. He is associate professor in the Department of Theological Studies at Loyola Marymount University. He specializes in the study of Islam, with a focus on contemporary Muslim societies. He is the author of *Oil and Water: Two Faiths, One God.* His commentaries and interviews on contemporary Islam have appeared in the *Los Angeles Times,* the *New York Times,* the *Washington Post,* and the *Christian Science Monitor.*

John Iskander is director of the Near East/North Africa Division of Area Studies at the Foreign Service Institute of the U.S. Department of State in Washington, D.C. He holds a Ph.D. in Islamic studies from the University of California, Santa Barbara. His research interests include medieval Islamic history, Muslim-Christian relations, and modern Egyptian saints.

Linda G. Jones received a Ph.D. in the history of religions from the University of California, Santa Barbara, with a focus on medieval Islam and Christianity in Spain and North Africa. She has edited and coauthored (with Madeleine Pelner Cosman) the *Handbook to Life in the Middle Ages.* She is currently Juan de la Cierva Researcher at the Spanish National Research Council (Department of Medieval Studies) in Barcelona, Spain.

Heather N. Keaney is an assistant professor of history at American University in Cairo. She received a Ph.D. from the University of California, Santa Barbara. She specializes in debates on religiopolitical legitimacy in Islamic history and historiography. She has published "The First Islamic Revolt in Mamluk Collective Memory: Ibn Bakr's (d. 1340) Portrayal of the Third Caliph Uthman" in *Ideas, Images, and Methods of Portrayal: Insights into Classical Arabic Literature and Islam,* edited by Sebastian Gunther.

Jeffrey Kenney received a Ph.D. in religious studies from the University of California, Santa Barbara. He is a specialist in Islam and the author of *Muslim Rebels: Kharijites and the Politics of Extremism in Egypt.* He is currently a professor at DePauw University, Greencastle, Indiana.

Ruqayya Yasmine Khan received a Ph.D. from the University of Pennsylvania. She is a specialist in Islamic studies. Her book *Self and Secrecy in Early Islam* is forthcoming from the University of South Carolina Press (Studies in Comparative Religion). She is currently an associate professor at Trinity University in San Antonio, Texas.

Nuha N. N. Khoury is associate professor of the history of art and architecture at the University of California, Santa Barbara. She specializes in the history of Islamic architecture and urbanism, medieval Islamic iconography, and modern Arab art. Her research has appeared in *Muqarnas: An Annual on Islamic Art and Architecture,* the *International Journal of Middle East Studies,* and the *Journal of Near Eastern Studies.* She also contributed to *Autobiography in Medieval Arabic Tradition,* edited by Dwight Reynolds.

Max Leeming is on the religion faculty of Vassar College, where she teaches Islamic studies and the history of religions, with a focus on sacred space in the Islamic Middle East.

Laura Lohman received a Ph.D. from the University of Pennsylvania and specializes in the music of the Middle East. Her research on Egyptian singer Umm Kulthum appears in *Music and the Play of Power in the Middle East, North Africa and Central Asia* (Ashgate). She is an assistant professor of music at California State University, Fullerton, where she is completing a study of the singer's late career and reception history (Wesleyan University Press).

Gregory Mack is a Ph.D. candidate at the Institute of Islamic Studies at McGill University. He holds an M.A. from the University of Toronto. His specialization is Islamic law; his research presently focuses on legal reforms in the Middle East.

Garay Menicucci is the associate director of the Office of International Students and Scholars at the University of California, Santa Barbara. He has a Ph.D. in Middle East history from Georgetown University. He is a past editorial committee member and author for the *Middle East Report* and teaches an introduction to Middle East studies and Arab cinema at the University of California, Santa Barbara. He has also organized and led several summer seminars in Egypt and Jordan for California K-12 teachers and administrators, funded by Fulbright-Hays Group Projects grants.

Tara Munson is a Ph.D. student in religious studies at the University of California, Santa Barbara. She specializes in the study of Pacific Rim religions, with a focus on the Philippines.

Kathleen M. O'Connor is assistant professor of religious studies at the University of South Florida. She specializes in Islamic studies, with focuses on Islam in the African American community, Islamic medicine, and folk religion. She has published articles and chapters on Islamic healing systems and African American Islam, and contributed to the *Encyclopedia of the Quran.* Her current book project is *The Worlds of Interpretation of African American Muslims.*

Patrick S. O'Donnell holds an M.A. in religious studies from the University of California, Santa Barbara, and is an adjunct instructor in the Department of Philosophy at Santa Barbara City College. He has published articles, reviews, and bibliographies in the following journals: *The Good Society, Globalization, Radical Pedagogy, Theory and Science,* and *Philosophy East & West.* Among the encyclopedias he has contributed to are the *Biographical Encyclopedia of Islamic Philosophers* and the *Encyclopedia of Love in World Religions.*

Kate O'Halloran is a writer and editor specializing in world history. She holds an M.A. in modern literature and languages (French and German) from Trinity College, Dublin, Ireland and has published several books for students.

Sophia Pandya is an assistant professor of religious studies at California State University, Long Beach. She received a Ph.D. from the University of California, Santa Barbara. Her specialization is in the area of women, religion, and the developing world, with an emphasis on women and Islam. She has authored an article on women and religious education in Bahrain.

Firoozeh Papan-Matin is the director of Persian and Iranian studies at the University of Washington, Seattle. She has a master's in English literature and a second master's and a doctorate in Iranian studies from University of California, Santa Barbara. Her dissertation research is on 12th-century Islamic mysticism in Iran.

She has published articles on classical and modern Persian literature. She is the author of *The Love Poems of Shamlu* and *The Unveiling of Secrets Kashf al-Asrar: The Visionary Autobiography of Ruzbihan Baqli.*

David Reeves is a Ph.D. candidate in history at the University of California, Santa Barbara. He specializes in the history of Islam in the Soviet Union, with a focus on Azerbaijan during the Stalin era. He has been awarded a Fulbright-Hayes Fellowship, a University of California, Santa Barbara, Department of History Regent's Dissertation Fellowship, and a Social Science Research Council Pre-Dissertation Fellowship, among others, to conduct his research.

Mehnaz Sahibzada earned an M.A. in religious studies from the University of California, Santa Barbara, and an M.A. in Middle Eastern studies from the University of Texas at Austin. Her areas of interest include Islam in America and Asian American literature. She teaches English at Moorpark High School in Southern California.

Judy Saltzman is emeritus professor of religious studies at California Polytechnic University in San Luis Obispo. Her Ph.D. is from the University of California, Santa Barbara. She specializes in the history of Asian religions, Indian philosophy, Vedanta, and modern German philosophy.

Kerry San Chirico is a doctoral candidate in the Department of Religious Studies at the University of California, Santa Barbara. He specializes in the religions of South Asia, with a focus on Hindu-Christian relations.

Leslie Sargent is a Ph.D. candidate in history at the University of California, Santa Barbara. She specializes in the history of the Russian Empire and the Caucasus in the late 19th and early 20th centuries.

Bhaskar Sarkar is associate professor of film and media studies at the University of California, Santa Barbara. His Ph.D. is from the University of California, Los Angeles. He specializes in postcolonial media theory, Asian cinemas, and Marxist cultural theory. He is the author of *Mourning in the Nation: Indian Cinema in the Wake of Partition* (forthcoming, 2008) and has published essays on philosophies of visuality and Indian and Chinese popular cinemas in anthologies and journals such as *Quarterly Review of Film and Video, Rethinking History: Theory and Practice,* and *New Review of Film and Television Studies.*

Megan Adamson Sijapati is assistant professor of religion at Gettysburg College. She received her Ph.D. in religious studies from the University of California, Santa Barbara. Her specialization is in the religions of South Asia, with a focus on contemporary Islam.

Mark Soileau received a Ph.D. in religious studies, with a focus on Islam, from the University of California, Santa Barbara. He is currently an assistant professor of religious studies at Albion College in Michigan.

Varun Soni is currently a doctoral candidate in the Department of Religious Studies at the University of Cape Town, South Africa. He received a J.D. from the University of California, Santa Barbara, School of Law, an M.T.S. from Harvard Divinity School, and an M.A. from the University of California, Santa Barbara.

Eric Staples received a Ph.D. in history from the University of California, Santa Barbara. He specializes in medieval and early modern Middle Eastern history, and focuses on the social history of early modern Morocco, the maritime history of the Mediterranean and Indian Ocean regions, and underwater archaeology. He is currently involved in a project to build a replica of a medieval Indian Ocean vessel under the auspices of the governments of Oman and Singapore.

Nancy L. Stockdale is assistant professor of history at the University of Northern Texas. She received her Ph.D. from the University of California, Santa Barbara. Her specialization is modern Middle Eastern history, with a focus on the history of Palestine, imperialism, and gender studies. She is the author of *Colonial Encounters among English and Palestinian Women, 1800–1948*.

Jamel Velji is a Ph.D. student in religious studies at the University of California, Santa Barbara. He specializes in Islamic studies, with a focus on Ismaili Shiism and the comparative study of apocalyptic movements.

Michelle Zimney is a doctoral candidate in the Department of Religious Studies at the University of California, Santa Barbara. Her research focuses on the interaction of religion and politics in the Middle Eastern context, including Algeria's civil conflict in the 1990s. Her most recent research is on the Sayyida Zaynab shrine in Damascus.

Z. David Zuwiyya is associate professor of Spanish at Auburn University in Alabama. He received a Ph.D. in Spanish medieval literature from the University of California, Santa Barbara. He is the author of *Islamic Legends concerning Alexander the Great*.

LIST OF ILLUSTRATIONS AND MAPS

Illustrations

Maps

PREFACE

The Encyclopedia of World Religions series has been designed to provide comprehensive coverage of six major global religious traditions—Buddhism, Hinduism, Islam, Judaism, Roman Catholicism, and Protestant Christianity. The volumes have been constructed in an A-to-Z format to provide a handy guide to the major terms, concepts, people, events, and organizations that have, in each case, transformed the religion from its usually modest beginnings to the global force that it has become.

Each of these religions began as the faith of a relatively small group of closely related ethnic peoples. Each has, in the modern world, become a global community, and, with one notable exception, each has transcended its beginning to become an international multiethnic community. Judaism, of course, largely defines itself by its common heritage and ancestry and has an alternative but equally fascinating story. Surviving long after most similar cultures from the ancient past have turned to dust, Judaism has, within the last century, regathered its scattered people into a homeland while simultaneously watching a new diaspora carry Jews into most of the contemporary world's countries.

Each of the major traditions has also, in the modern world, become amazingly diverse. Buddhism, for example, spread from its original home in India across southern Asia and then through Tibet and China to Korea and Japan. Each time it crossed a language barrier, something was lost, but something seemed equally to be gained, and an array of forms of Buddhism emerged. In Japan alone, Buddhism exists in hundreds of different sect groupings. Protestantism, the newest of the six traditions, began with at least four different and competing forms of the religious life and has since splintered into thousands of denominations.

At the beginning of the 19th century, the six religious traditions selected for coverage in this series were largely confined to a relatively small part of the world. Since that time, the world has changed dramatically, with each of the traditions moving from its geographical center to become a global tradition. While the traditional religions of many countries retain the allegiance of a majority of the population, they do so in the presence of the other traditions as growing minorities. Other countries—China being a prominent example—have no religious majority, only a number of minorities that must periodically interface with one another.

The religiously pluralistic world created by the global diffusion of the world's religions has made knowledge of religions, especially religions practiced by one's neighbors, a vital resource in the continuing task of building a good society, a world in which all may live freely and pursue visions of the highest values the cosmos provides.

In creating these encyclopedias, the attempt has been made to be comprehensive if not exhaustive. As space allows, in approximately 800 entries, each author has attempted to define and explain the basic terms used in talking about the religion, make note of definitive events, introduce the most prominent figures, and highlight the major organizations. The coverage is designed to result in both a handy reference tool for the religious scholar/specialist and an understandable work that can be used fruitfully by anyone—a student, an informed lay person, or a reader simply wanting to look up a particular person or idea.

Each volume includes several features. They begin with an essay that introduces the particular tradition and provides a quick overview of its historical development, the major events and trends that have pushed it toward its present state, and the mega-problems that have shaped it in the contemporary world.

A chronology lists the major events that have punctuated the religion's history from its origin to the present. The chronologies differ somewhat in emphasis, given that they treat two very ancient faiths that both originated in prehistoric time, several more recent faiths that emerged during the last few millennia, and the most recent, Protestantism, that has yet to celebrate its 500-year anniversary.

The main body of each encyclopedia is constituted of the approximately 800 entries, arranged alphabetically. These entries include some 200 biographical entries covering religious figures of note in the tradition, with a distinct bias to the 19th and 20th centuries and some emphasis on leaders from different parts of the world. Special attention has been given to highlighting female contributions to the tradition, a factor often overlooked, as religion in all traditions has until recently been largely a male-dominated affair.

Geographical entries cover the development of the movement in those countries and parts of the world where the tradition has come to dominate or form an important minority voice, where it has developed a particularly distinct style (often signaled by doctrinal differences), or where it has a unique cultural or social presence. While religious statistics are amazingly difficult to assemble and evaluate, some attempt has been made to estimate the effect of the tradition on the selected countries.

In some cases, particular events have had a determining effect on the development of the different religious traditions. Entries on events such as the St. Bartholomew's Day Massacre (for Protestantism) or the conversion of King Asoka (for Buddhism) place the spotlight on the factors precipitating the event and the consequences flowing from it.

The various traditions have taken form as communities of believers have organized structures to promote their particular way of belief and practice within the tradition. Each tradition has a different way of organizing and recognizing the distinct groups within it. Buddhism, for example, has organized around national subtraditions. The encyclopedias give coverage to the major groupings within each tradition.

Each tradition has developed a way of encountering and introducing individuals to spiritual reality as well as a vocabulary for it. It has also developed a set of concepts and a language to discuss the spiritual world and humanity's place within it. In each volume, the largest number of entries explore the concepts, the beliefs that flow from them, and the practices that they have engendered. The authors have attempted to explain these key religious concepts in a nontechnical language and to communicate their meaning and logic to a person otherwise unfamiliar with the religion as a whole.

Finally, each volume is thoroughly cross-indexed using small caps to guide the reader to related entries. A bibliography and comprehensive index round out each volume.

—J. Gordon Melton

ACKNOWLEDGMENTS

In publishing the *Encyclopedia of Islam* I am indebted to a great many people. Creating an encyclopedia on any topic is necessarily a group project, requiring the shared knowledge, insights, perspectives, skills, and experiences of many. The task is made even more challenging when it involves religion, which encompasses so many different subjects—ranging from the historical, social, political, and cultural to the spiritual, philosophical, and doctrinal. Moreover, the global nature of Islam and the sometimes intense differences that have arisen among Muslims and between Muslims and non-Muslims during the nearly 1400 years of its history pose additional challenges when seeking to realize the ideals of comprehensiveness, factual accuracy, and fairness.

In order to meet the challenges facing this undertaking, I have made a particular effort to draw upon the wide-ranging and deep scholarly talents of the faculty, postgraduate, and graduate students of the University of California, Santa Barbara, especially those specializing in Islamic and Middle East studies. My editorial assistants, John Iskander (now at the U.S. Department of State) and Michelle Zimney, helped me launch the project and assisted with editing early drafts of many of the contributed articles. Among the more than 40 contributors, I am especially grateful to Garay Menicucci (University of California, Santa Barbara), Nuha N. N. Khoury (University of California, Santa Barbara), Kathleen M. O'Connor (University of South Florida), Amir Hussain (Loyola-Marymount University in Los Angeles), Jon Armajani (College of St. Benedict/St. John's University in Minnesota), Firoozeh Papan-Matin (University of Washington), Mark Soileau (Albion College), Anna Bigelow (North Carolina State University, Megan Adamson Sijapati (Gettysburg College), Aysha Hidayatullah (Emory University), Caleb Elfenbein (University of California, Santa Barbara), Linda G. Jones (Spanish National Research Council in Barcelona), Patrick O'Donnell (Santa Barbara City College), Nancy L. Stockdale (University of North Texas), Stephen Cory (Cleveland State University), Shauna Huffaker (University of Windsor), Heather N. Keaney (American University in Cairo), and Reza Aslan (University of California, Riverside). These individuals wrote a number of articles for the volume, offering fresh perspectives obtained from their recent research in their respective fields of expertise.

Among other colleagues at the University of California, Santa Barbara, who have provided support and inspiration are R. Stephen Humphreys, the holder of the King Abd Al-Aziz ibn Saud Chair of Islamic Studies; Mark Juergensmeyer, director of the Orfalea Center for Global and International Studies; Scott Marcus, associate professor of ethnomusicology; Kathleen Moore, associate professor of law and society; Nancy Gallagher, professor of history; and Professors Dwight Reynolds, W. Clark Roof, Catherine Albanese, and Richard Hecht in religious studies. My approach to this project was also guided by the humanism and spirit of public service exemplified by our late colleague Walter Capps and his wife, Lois. Over the years, Richard C. Martin, Fredrick M. Denny, Richard Eaton, Azim Nanji, Barbara Metcalf, William Shepherd, Steve Wasserstrom, Bruce B. Lawrence, Gordon Newby, Jane D. McAuliffe, Zayn Kassam, Tazim Kassam, and scholars and teachers at other colleges and universities, too many to mention by name, have also provided invaluable inspiration, directly or indirectly.

My deep gratitude also goes to Kendall Busse, Ph.D. student in religious studies, who provided skilled editorial support and helpful feedback along the way, and to several undergraduate research assistants: Maria Reifel Saltzberg, Hassan R. Elhaj, and Hassan Naveed. Their work was funded by the Freshman Seminar Program at the University of California, Santa Barbara. Through the years, my undergraduate students have consistently affirmed my belief that education is an ongoing process with mutual benefits that extend well beyond the classroom.

Funding provided by Fulbright-Hayes Group Projects grants presented me with opportunities to accompany two groups of California K-12 teachers and administrators to Egypt in 2003 and 2004. I benefited greatly from our workshop sessions, travel experiences, and the conversations we shared in Egypt, which enriched my understanding of the K-12 curriculum and the challenges our teachers face in instructing young people about unfamiliar religions, civilizations, and languages. I am especially obliged to Karen Arter, Frank Stewart, and Paul and Ruth Ficken for their encouragement and interest in this publication.

I am also grateful for the hospitality and warmth extended to me by several cultural, interfaith, and religious organizations, including the Turkish-American Pacifica Institute of Los Angeles and Orange Counties, the Interfaith Initiative of Santa Barbara County, the University Religious Center in Isla Vista, and the community of St. Mark's Parish Catholic Church in Isla Vista.

At Facts On File, I owe a great debt to Claudia Schaab and J. Gordon Melton for valuable advice and infinite patience in bringing the publication to completion. Gordon graciously shared photographs of mosques taken during his travels around the world.

Publishing this book would not have been possible without the support of a wide circle of family and friends extending from the United States to Colombia (the land of my birth), Egypt, and India. These include Shafik and Gilane, Galal and Negwa, Amr and Janet, Mahmoud and Suhair, Said and Soraya, Mehran and Nahid, Zaveeni, and Viji and Sujata. Above all, I am indebted to my wife, Magda, to whom this book is dedicated, for her unwavering love and encouragement in good times and bad, and to our sons Andrés and Federico as they begin to follow their own paths in the world.

INTRODUCTION

Among the world's religions, few have attained the historical, cultural, and civilizational stature and diversity that Islam has. Since the seventh century, when it first emerged in the western region of the Arabian Peninsula known as the Hijaz, it has been continuously adapted and carried forth by its adherents, who call themselves Muslims, to new lands and peoples in the wider Middle East, Africa, Asia, Europe, and, more recently, to the Americas, Australia, and New Zealand. Indeed, the new religio-historical syntheses brought about by the back-and-forth interactions of Muslims and non-Muslims, and of the many different cultures to which they belong, have had significant influence for centuries, not only upon the religious experience of a large part of humankind, but also upon the development of philosophy, the arts and sciences, and even the very languages we speak and the foods we eat. European scholars eagerly sought to acquire the wisdom achieved by Muslims in the fields of philosophy, mathematics, astronomy, and medicine during the Middle Ages. The different Islamicate architectural styles developed in a wide variety of locales, ranging from Spain to sub-Saharan Africa, India, Central Asia, and Southeast Asia, were adapted by non-Muslims in many parts of the world. Spanish settlers and immigrants brought "Moorish" (Spanish-Islamic) architectural styles to the New World, beginning in the 16th century, which would later be adapted by European and American architects for our modern homes, hotels, cinemas, concert halls, shopping centers, and amusement parks. Many of our homes are now decorated with beautiful rugs and carpets that bear intricate arabesque designs from Iran, Turkey, Pakistan, or Kashmir. Coffee and sugar, the favored beverages of many Americans and Europeans, are both Arabic in origin and were cultivated and enjoyed in Muslim lands well before they reached the West.

Despite the record of some 14 centuries of such achievements, knowledge about Islam and Muslims has been very limited, especially in the Americas. The modern study of Islam was mostly relegated to a few elite universities until the 1980s, and it was hardly mentioned in social studies textbooks used by secondary school students and teachers. What Americans knew of Muslims was largely confined to those who had lived or traveled in Muslim countries, met Muslim immigrants, or heard about famous African-American Muslims like Malcolm X, the boxer Muhammad Ali, or Karim Abdul Jabbar. What the average person thought or imagined about the Near or Middle East was based on the *Arabian Nights* stories and motion picture images. The situation began to change in the 1980s as a result of the Islamic revolution in Iran of 1978–79, the Lebanese civil war and the 1983 bombing of the United States Marine barracks in Beirut, and the assassination of Egyptian president Anwar al-Sadat, an American ally, by a radical jihadist group in 1981. Even these developments, which were widely reported in the news media, did not have a long-term impact on public awareness or knowledge about Islam and Muslims, although they inspired a number of Hollywood movies based on stereotypes. One important exception, however, was the inclusion of lessons about Islam and the Middle East in secondary school curricula that involved consultations with experts and representatives of local Muslim organizations.

This situation changed dramatically as a result of the terrorist attacks conducted by al-Qaida against the New York World Trade Center and the Pentagon in Washington, D.C., on September 11, 2001. Islam, especially Islamic terrorism, permeated the media—most notably the 24-hour cable news channels and talk radio. Politicians, scholars, policy experts, and religious leaders gave many interviews and talks about Islam, the Middle East, and religious violence. American colleges and universities hired dozens of new lecturers and professors specializing in Islamic studies and the languages and histories of the Middle East. The number of Middle East National Resource Centers based at leading American research universities was increased with the help of additional funding by the U.S. Department of Education, which was committed to enhancing public understanding about the contemporary Middle East and other regions where large Muslim populations live. Increased resources were also provided for teaching Arabic, Persian, Turkish, Urdu, Pashto, and other critical languages.

Today there still exists, despite these significant steps forward, a widespread hunger in the United States and many other countries for even the most basic knowledge about Muslims—their religion, histories, cultures, and politics. One unfortunate consequence of the persistence of this knowledge "gap" is that some have exploited it to spread inaccurate, prejudiced views about Islam and Muslims by citing anecdotal evidence or weaving together scattered bits of factual information, heresay, and even falsehoods. At times this is done to serve some greater ideological objective, but at great cost to the public's ability to make wise judgments of their own, based on accurate information and scholarly expertise. The *Encyclopedia of Islam* is part of a much wider effort undertaken by many scholars and area studies experts to meet the demand for accurate information about Islam, particularly with regard to its place in the contemporary world. This undertaking is based on a growing body of research involving the contributions of people who not only have knowledge and fluency in the relevant languages but have spent extended periods of time in the Middle East and other parts of the world where Muslims live, work, and strive to achieve what we might call "the good life." The reader is encouraged to explore the variety of topics covered by this reference work and follow up with more specialized readings listed at the end of each entry and in the bibliography provided in the back of the book. Before proceeding, however, it will be worthwhile to consider some questions anyone interested in exploring the subject of Islam ought to be asking.

What Is Islam?

This is a question that Muslims have been answering for centuries when it is raised in their homes, schools, and in the circles of gifted scholars, powerful rulers, and wealthy merchants and businessmen. It is also a question posed by many non-Muslims—never more than now, in the first decade of the 21st century. The answers given by Muslims, like those proposed by non-Muslims, have varied greatly, depending on their education, social status, background, and the wider historical and cultural contexts in which they live.

Rather than beginning with a single, definitive response as to what Islam is, a more fruitful approach is to begin with the proposition that Islam is to a large extent what Muslims have made of it based on their different religious sensibilities, cultural identities, social statuses, and historical circumstances. Many of the faithful start with the Quran, the Islamic holy book, which they believe to be a collection of revelations from God (called Allah in Arabic) as delivered in the Arabic language via the angel Gabriel to Muhammad (ca. 570–632) over a 23-year period while he was living in the western Arabian towns of Mecca and Medina (formerly known as Yathrib). It is about the length of the Christian New Testament, consisting of 114 chapters and more than 6,200 verses. About Islam, the Quran itself declares,

> Upholding equity, God, his angels and those with knowledge have witnessed that there is no god but he, the mighty and wise. Indeed, religion [din] in God's eyes is Islam [literally "submission"]. Those who received the book disagreed among themselves out of jealousy only after knowledge had come to them. Whoever disbelieves in God's sacred verses, (let him know that) God is swift in reckoning. (Q 3:18–19).

This passage links Islam, the religion, to belief in one God, in opposition to disbelief (kufr), which will incur God's anger. It also states that the revelation of God's book brings with it both knowledge and disagreement among human beings. The Muslims, therefore, in contrast to disbelievers, are those who believe in God's revelations (the sacred verses) and submit to God's will. The Arabic word *muslim* literally means "one who submits." The Quran promises Muslims rewards both in this world and in the hereafter for their belief and good deeds.

In addition to the Quran, Muslims also look to the hadith—sacred narratives, usually short in length, that contain accounts about what Muhammad and his followers, known as his Companions, said and did. The hadith, which number in the tens of thousands, were systematically collected by Muslims during the early centuries of Islam. One of them, known as the Hadith of Gabriel, provides another, more complex understanding of Islam. According to this story, the angel Gabriel, appearing as a man dressed in a pure white gown, approached Muhammad while he was among his friends and interrogated him about his religion. When Gabriel asked Muhammad about Islam, he replied, "Islam is that you witness that there is no god but God and that Muhammad is God's messenger; that you perform prayer; give alms; fast [the month of] Ramadan; and perform the hajj to the house [of God in Mecca] if you are able to do so."

In this statement, Islam is defined in terms of its Five Pillars, thus underscoring the importance of performing sacred actions, or worship, in this religion. Even the first pillar, known as the *shahada* (witnessing) is regarded as a sacred action, because it involves pronouncing the two foundational tenets of Islam: belief both in one god and in Muhammad as a prophet of God. Recitation of the *shahada* in Arabic occurs throughout a Muslim's lifetime. Muslims repeat it during their five daily prayers, and even at the moment of death, when it should be the last words spoken by a dying person, or spoken by someone else on his or her behalf. Islamic tradition regards the other four of Islam's pillars—prayer, almsgiving, fasting, and hajj—as forms of worship required of all Muslims in order to attain salvation. The fine points of Muslim worship were elaborated as part of the Muslim legal tradition, known as sharia, by qualified religious authorities known as the ulama (sing. *alim*, "one who has knowledge").

The Hadith of Gabriel next takes up the subject of belief, as Gabriel, acknowledging that Muhammad has correctly defined Islam, continues his questioning by asking Muhammad about *iman* (faith, believing). According to the story, Muhammad replies that *iman* involves belief in one God, his angels, his books, his messengers, and the Last Day (Judgment Day), as well as predetermination. Again, Gabriel affirms the correctness of the reply. The Quran mentions *iman* much more than Islam, and even though the two words differ slightly in their root meanings (security for the first, safety for the second), many Muslim commentators have regarded them as being nearly synonymous. It likewise uses a related term, *mumin,* more that it uses the word *muslim.* The aspects of faith Muhammad mentions in his reply to Gabriel were subsequently elaborated and debated for centuries by Muslim theologians, known as the *mutakallims,* or those who practice *kalam* (literally "speech," but more precisely translated as "dialectical theology").

By addressing both Islam and *iman,* the Hadith of Gabriel teaches that religious practice and belief are interrelated aspects of Islamic religion—one cannot be accomplished without the other. But the Hadith of Gabriel is not content with only mentioning these aspects of religion. It introduces a third—*ihsan.* When asked about what this is, Muhammad declares that it calls upon the faithful to be mindful of God's watchfulness and do what is good and beautiful (*hasan*). *Ihsan* adds a spiritual or aesthetic aspect to religion, one that is implicitly connected with its other aspects—practice and believing.

During the Middle Ages, Christian church leaders viewed Islam for the most part as idolatry, or a false religion inspired by Satan. Such prejudiced views can still be encountered in Christian circles, unfortunately, although most Christian leaders today are more likely to want to improve relations with Muslims through inter-religious dialogue and cooperation. Modern scholars specializing in the history and comparison of religions have thought about Islam from a different set of perspectives. In Europe, in the 18th and 19th centuries, when religion began to be studied in terms of the humanities and social sciences rather than theology, some scholars sought to exoticize it as an Eastern religion that stood apart from the West and the religions of Judaism and Christianity. They thought of it as a religion that had been tainted by political despotism and irrationality. Others classed it racially, as a "Semitic" religion, in contrast to the religions of the Indo-Europeans, which included Christianity. Rather than calling it Islam, a term used by Muslims themselves, many scholars in the 19th and 20th centuries decided to call it Mohammedanism, incorrectly assuming that Muhammad's status in Islam was analogous to that of Jesus Christ in Christianity or the Buddha in Buddhism. Despite these missteps, and others, some religious studies scholars concluded that it was more accurate to classify Islam together with Judaism and Christianity as a Western religion, or as monotheistic one, which recognizes a key belief in Islam (belief in one God), as well as its historical relationship with the other two religions. Scholars have even grouped it with Christianity and Buddhism as a "world" religion that has extended its reach globally through missionary work and conversion.

Today many scholars are studying Islam as an Abrahamic religion, in relationship with Judaism and Christianity. This designation is based on the figure of Abraham (Ibrahim), about whom many stories are told in the Bible's book of Genesis and in the Quran. These sacred stories, or myths, as they are called in religious studies scholarship, also talk about Abraham's descendants, whom Jews, Christians, and Muslims regard as the spiritual ancestors of their communities. While Muslims link their religion to Ishmael (Ismail), Abraham's oldest son through Hagar (from Egypt), Jews and Christians relate their religion to Isaac (Ishaq), Abraham's son through Sarah. In addition to sharing a sacred genealogy that connects all three religions with Abraham, there are other important "family resemblances" that they share. These include 1) monotheistic beliefs; 2) beliefs in prophets and supramundane beings such as angels and saints; 3) possession of holy books, revealed through prophets, that serve as the basis for doctrine, worship, ethics, and community identity; 4) a linear view of history from creation to Judgment Day, overlapped by cyclical celebrations of weekly and seasonal holy days; 4) claims to possession of a holy land connected with stories about the origins of each of the religions and the performance of pilgrimages (religious journeys); and 5) belief in human mortality, followed by resurrection, judgment, and reward or punishment in the afterlife.

Identifying the family resemblances shared by the three Abrahamic religions does not mean that they are therefore identical, nor that they have remained unchanged in history. Rather, it draws our attention to their relative degrees of similarity and difference and begs further inquiry concerning how to account for resemblances and degrees of difference, as well as the changes these religions have undergone through time as a result of the mutual interactions. Seen in this light, Islam can be understood relationally, rather than isolated from other religious traditions and communities. Muslims themselves understand their religion relationally, although in many respects their understandings differ from those of non-Muslim students of religion, as defined within modern humanities and social science frameworks.

Who Are the Muslims?

Discussing what Islam is entails additional discussion about who the Muslims are. As is the case with Islam, there are different ways in which this question can be answered too. One way to answer this question is to note that from a basic Islamic point of view, a Muslim is a person who submits to a single, almighty, and merciful God, as delineated in the Quran and sunna (precedent based on the hadith). Collectively, Muslims understand themselves ideally to be members of a single community of believers, known as the *umma*. The original basis for the universal Muslim community was the community founded by Muhammad in Medina after his emigration, or Hijra, from Mecca (about 260 miles south of Medina) with a small group of mostly Arab fol-

lowers in 622. Muslims have come to see this event as being so momentous that they use it to mark the year one on their lunar calendar. The community in Medina became exemplary for succeeding generations of Muslims, especially with regard to matters of piety, worship, and law. The embodiment of the *umma* as a territorial entity ruled by Muslims and following the sharia, or sacred law, was expressed by the concept of the *dar al-Islam,* or "house of Islam." This territorial understanding was superseded by modern nation-states created in Muslim lands during the 19th and 20th centuries.

In addition to viewing themselves as a community united in their belief in God and his prophet, Muslims also identify themselves with different strands of Islamic tradition. The main ones are Sunnism, Shiism, and Sufism. Sunni Muslims are the majority and today make up about 85 percent of the total Muslim population (estimated to be 1.4 million in mid-2007, according to the *Encyclopaedia Britannica*). Their name comes from an Arabic phrase meaning "the people of the sunna and the community of believers" (*ahl al-sunna wa'l-jamaa*). Their Quran commentaries, hadith collections, legal schools (the Hanafi, Maliki, Shafii, and Hanbali schools), and theological traditions are the ones most widely circulated and respected. It is from their ranks that most Muslim rulers and dynasties have arisen. Leading countries with Sunni majorities include Indonesia, Pakistan, Bangladesh, Egypt, Turkey, Morocco, and Nigeria.

The most prominent alternative, or sectarian, form of Islam is that of the Shia, who today constitute up to 15 percent of all Muslims, between 156 and 195 million. Known as the faction of Ali (*shiat Ali*), Muhammad's cousin and son-in-law (d. 661), they are found in many parts of the world, but they constitute majorities in the modern countries of Iran (89 percent of its population), Iraq (60 percent), Bahrain (70 percent), and Azerbaijan (85 percent). Shii Muslims maintain that the most legitimate authorities in all matters are the Imams—select members of Muhammad's family, beginning with Ali ibn Abi Talib (d. 661). Since the seventh century the Shia have vied with the Sunnis about who is best suited to govern the community. In opposition to the Shia, Sunnis favored the caliphs—leaders chosen initially by consensus of community leaders on the basis of their experience and public reputation. In general the Shia believe that 1) their Imams have been divinely appointed and inspired; 2) they are free from sin and error; and 3) they are uniquely qualified to provide religious guidance and insight. According to the Shia, the world itself could not exist without an Imam also being present in it. The largest branch of the Shia, known as the Twelve-Imam Shia, or Imamis, believe that all but one of their 12 Imams suffered martyrdom in defense of their faith and that the 12th will return after a period of concealment (*ghayba*) that began in 872 as a messiah (savior) to inaugurate a reign of universal justice prior to Judgment Day. The teachings of the Imams constitute the core of Shii hadith, and their tombs in Iraq and Iran have become sacred centers where pilgrims assemble to obtain their blessings and intercession.

The Ismailis constitute another division of the Shia, differing from the Twelvers with regard to whom they count among their Imams (beginning with their namesake Ismail, the elder son of Jaafar al-Sadiq [d. 765]), and the deference they give to the authority of the living Imam, rather than to those of the past. Even though they are only about 10 percent of the estimated Shii population overall, they have played a significant role in shaping the course of Islamic history and intellectual life.

Sufism (*tasawwuf*) is a general designation used for the mystical expressions of Islam, wherein experiential knowledge of God and attainment of unity in or with him are primary goals. The term is based on the Arabic word *suf*, or wool, which was worn by Christian and Muslim ascetics in the Middle East. Sufis also explain it in relation to the Arabic word *safa*, which denotes the idea of purity. Although the historical roots of Sufism go back to individual ascetics who lived during the first centuries of Islamic history, most Sufis became organized into groups or orders known as "paths" (sing. *tariqa*) after the 11th century. Each *tariqa* consists of spiritual masters (known as shaykhs and pirs) who attract disciples and initiate them into the mystical teachings and rituals of the group. Sufis turn to the Quran and sunna for inspiration and guidance, and trace the lineages of their doctrines and practices to Muhammad and the first generation of his followers. Most Sufis regard the sharia as a foundational aspect of their spiritual outlook, and their ranks are filled with followers from across the spectrum of the Muslim community—including Sunnis and Shiis, rulers, merchants, scholars, peasants, and ordinary laborers as well. There are many different Sufi orders with branches around the world, although there are no precise statistics for them. They are often credited with having contributed to the spread of Islam, especially through the shrines containing the remains and relics of Sufi saints. These holy places have become the focal points for many forms of popular devotionalism and pilgrimage. Sufism has also produced a rich body of Islamic literature, including mystical poetry, hagiography, and devotional manuals.

In more recent times, other self-identified groupings of Muslims have appeared, sometimes labeled as radical Islamist and jihadist movements. Also known as Islamic fundamentalists, a designation that is declining in use because of its imprecision, these groups are small in terms of actual numbers with respect to the total Muslim population. They have surpassed, however, other Muslim groups in terms of the amount of attention given to them by governments, international organizations, and the global media. This is because of their involvement in activities aimed at fighting perceived enemies of Islam at home and abroad, which can take a heavy toll in terms of civilian casualties and economic damage. The central goal of many of jihadist groups is to establish governments that will enforce Islamic law, uphold public morality, and free Muslims from the control of non-Muslim governments and influence. In justifying their violent actions, they often make use of the traditional Islamic concept of jihad, which is based on an Arabic word meaning "to struggle or make an effort" on behalf of one's religion and community. Many Muslims criticize the way they interpret this concept, which was elaborated in the Islamic legal tradition before the modern era. Some jihadist organizations, despite their violent tactics, win popular support by providing needed social services that legitimate governmental agencies fail to provide. This is the case, for example, with the Palestinian Hamas organization and Hizbullah in Lebanon. Most of these groups act independently, with logistical and economic assistance from foreign sources. Al-Qaida, the organization founded by Usama bin Ladin (b. 1957) and Ayman al-Zawahiri (b. 1951), began in 1984 as a service office for Arabs fighting against the Soviet army in Afghanistan. After the Soviet withdrawal in 1989 and the fall of the Communist-led government, al-Qaida turned its attention to fighting the United States and its allies, especially Israel. To accomplish its objectives, it created a loosely organized global network of cells, which were involved in planning and executing attacks against U.S. embassies in Africa, the USS *Cole*, and the 9/11 attacks on the U.S. mainland. Years later, however, al-Qaida has still not been able to win widespread support among Muslims, and it remains at odds with other Islamist groups in terms of both ideology and tactics.

The estimated number of Muslims in the world today is second only to the number of Christians (about 2.2 million) and larger than other religiously defined communities, including Hindus and Buddhists. Muslims represent more than 20 percent of the world's population (one out of every five people on Earth). Like members of these other religious communities, they also think of themselves in terms of ethnicity and nationality. Indeed, many may put their ethnic and national identity ahead of their religious one,

especially those who are more secular in outlook. Muslims belong to more than 60 different ethnic groups consisting of a million or more members. In addition, there are also 55 nation-states that have Muslim-majority populations. As minorities in countries like the United States, Britain, India, and Australia, many think of themselves in terms of the nationality of the country in which they hold citizenship, or the one from which they have emigrated.

The first generations of Muslims were predominantly Arab, and today Arabs still constitute the single largest Muslim ethnic group. (It should be noted, however, that not all Arabs are Muslims. There are also Arab Christians and Jews.) By the 11th century, large numbers of Berbers, Persians, and Turks had converted to Islam; together with Arabs, they composed much of classical Islamic civilization in the Middle East and North Africa. Today only about one in four Muslims is an Arab, and when all the Middle Eastern ethnic groups to which Muslims belong are added, they amount to less than half of the total of the world's Muslims. Other major ethnic groups include the Javanese of Indonesia, the Bengalis of India and Bangladesh, and the Punjabis of Pakistan and India. Moreover, the nation-states with the largest Muslim populations are located *east* of the Middle East, in Indonesia (207 million), Pakistan (160 million), India (between 138 million and 160 million), and Bangladesh (132.5 million).[1] Large Muslim populations also live in the countries of sub-Saharan Africa (Nigeria, for example has about 67.5 million Muslims) and Central Asia (Afghanistan has about 31.5 million Muslims; Uzbekistan 24.5 million).

Muslims can therefore present themselves as members of a united community of the faithful, as members of particular Islamic subgroups (Sunnis, Shiis, Sufis, etc.), or as members of different

---

[1] These figures are based on 2007–08 estimates in the CIA World Fact Book.

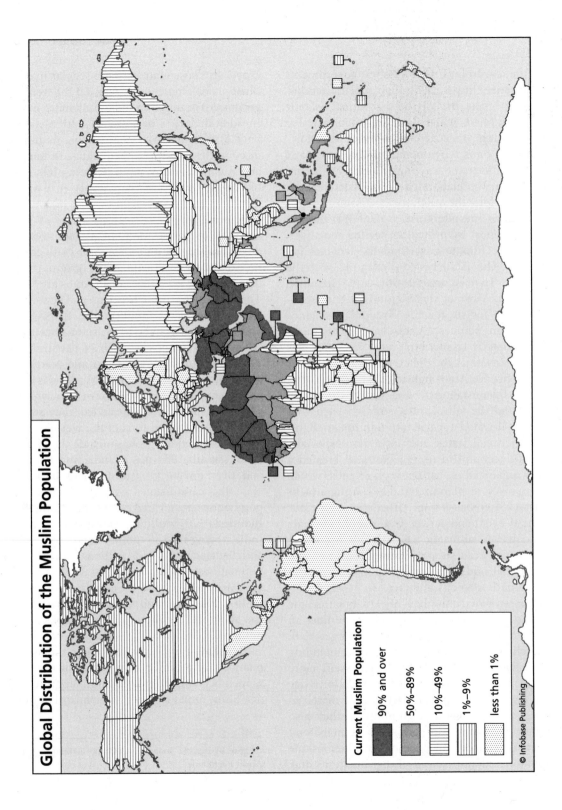

Global Distribution of the Muslim Population

Current Muslim Population

- 90% and over
- 50%–89%
- 10%–49%
- 1%–9%
- less than 1%

© Infobase Publishing

ethnic and national bodies. They may even take pride in tracing their origins to particular regions (like the Hijaz in Arabia), cities and towns, and families and tribes. Education, profession, gender, and social status also contribute to the formation of Muslim identity. The form of Islam by which Muslims live and in which they believe, therefore, is something that is shaped by any combination of these factors. Muslim understandings of themselves and their religion have also been shaped by their ongoing encounters with non-Muslims, peaceful and otherwise, through the centuries.

The Expansion of Islam

Islam has long been a global religion, but this was not the way it began. It first appeared during the seventh century in the Hijaz, a remote mountainous area along the western edge of the Arabian Peninsula, far from the centers of urban civilization. The dominant powers in the Middle Eastern and eastern Mediterranean regions at the time were the Byzantines, heirs to the Roman Empire, and the Persians. These two empires had been fighting continually with each other for control of trade routes, land, and people. Within less than 100 years after Islam's appearance, Arab Muslim warriors had swept out of Arabia into the Middle East and North Africa, bringing about the downfall of Byzantium and Persia and inaugurating a succession of Islamic states that would rule a large part of the known world until the collapse of the Ottoman dynasty after World War I. At its height in the 10th century, Muslim rule extended eastward from Spain (known as Andalusia) and Morocco to the eastern frontiers of Persia and Afghanistan. On the basis of the success of the Muslim conquests, it has become a commonplace to assert that Islam is a violent religion that was spread by the sword. Like all stereotypes, it is based on some truth, mixed with distortion and erroneous conclusions drawn from incomplete evidence. Scholars specializing in the early history of Islam and its transregional expansion have

found that the historical factors involved were much more varied and complex than the "conquest by the sword" thesis would suggest.

Early Islamic historical sources and evidence drawn from the Quran and the hadith indicate that several different religious currents existed in Arabia in the seventh century. These included native Arabian religions, different Jewish and Christian doctrines, and Zoroastrianism—the dualistic religion of ancient Persia. Muhammad ibn Abd Allah (ca. 570–632), the historical founder of Islam, was born in Mecca, a regional shrine town in the Hijaz. After receiving what Muslim sources report were his first revelations at the age of 40 while on Mount Hira outside of Mecca, he drew from these religious currents and launched a religious movement that called for Meccans to worship one God instead of many, perform acts of charity for the weak and the poor, and believe that there would be a final judgment when God would resurrect the dead and hold each person accountable for his or her righteous and wrongful acts. The blessed were promised a place in paradise, the heavenly garden, and the damned would suffer the tortures of hell, the realm of fire. Muhammad attracted a small following of converts from among his relatives, friends, former slaves, and even some non-Arabs. Other Meccans, particularly influential members of the Quraysh clan, became hostile toward him. This opposition resulted in the Hijra (emigration) of Muhammad and his followers to Medina in 622. The community soon grew larger, thanks to the conversion of Medinan clans to Islam. They are remembered as the Ansar (helpers). The earliest expansion of the Muslim community, therefore, occurred peacefully and involved the emigration of the first Muslims from their old home to new ones. Emigration and resettlement subsequently became important factors in the spread of Islam. During this time, the community also had to defend itself from attacks by the Quraysh. After engaging in a successful series of campaigns against his opponents, Muhammad finally achieved the peaceful surrender of Mecca

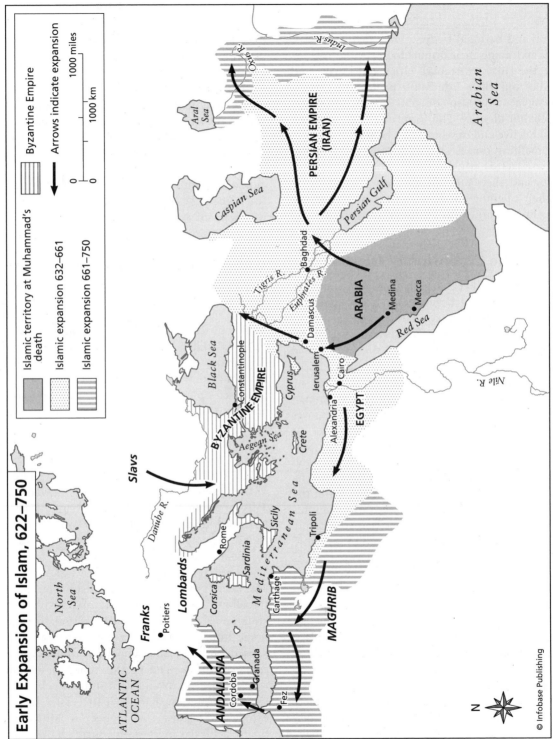

Early Expansion of Islam, 622–750

Islamic territory at Muhammad's death

Islamic expansion 632–661

Islamic expansion 661–750

Byzantine Empire

Arrows indicate expansion

1000 miles

1000 km

ATLANTIC OCEAN

North Sea

Franks

Poitiers

Lombards

Slavs

Danube R.

Rome

Corsica

Sardinia

Black Sea

Constantinople

BYZANTINE EMPIRE

Aegean Sea

Cyprus

Crete

Sicily

ANDALUSIA

Cordoba

Granada

Fez

Carthage

Mediterranean Sea

Tripoli

MAGHRIB

Alexandria

Cairo

EGYPT

Jerusalem

Nile R.

Red Sea

Damascus

Euphrates R.

Tigris R.

Baghdad

Persian Gulf

ARABIA

Medina

Mecca

Arabian Sea

PERSIAN EMPIRE (IRAN)

Oxus R.

Indus R.

Aral Sea

Caspian Sea

N

© Infobase Publishing

in 630. By the time of his death in 632, many of the Arabian tribes had established alliances with him and converted to Islam, setting the stage of the subsequent conquest of Syria, Iran, Egypt, and North Africa.

The rapid defeat of Byzantine and Persian armies, weakened by years of internal dissension and warfare, brought the Arab armies unimagined new wealth and power. Led by the caliphs, successors to the prophet Muhammad, the fledgling Islamic state at first kept its capital in Medina, but it later shifted northward to Damascus, Syria, which remained the seat of the Umayyad Caliphate from 661 to 750. Conquest of territories beyond the Arabian Peninsula did not immediately result in mass conversions to Islam, however. Rather, the evidence indicates that Islam remained a minority religion in these regions for several centuries after the initial waves of conquest. Local populations who accepted Muslim rule were given the choice of either converting or paying special taxes in exchange for accepting the status of "protected" non-Muslim subjects known as *ahl al-dhimma,* or simply *dhimmi*s. The Arab Muslim minority formed an aristocracy that lived in its own cantonments near the communal mosque and the ruler's palace. The offspring of Arab Muslim fathers and non-Arab, non-Muslim mothers were raised as Muslims but held a second-class status among their coreligionists. There were also non-Arab converts called the *mawali* (clients), many of whom had been captured as prisoners of war during the conquests, then granted their freedom upon conversion. The majority of Muslim subjects, however, remained Christians, Jews, and Zororastrians. As *dhimmi*s, they were secure in their property, communal life, and worship as long as they paid taxes, remained loyal to Muslim authorities, and did not either try to proselytize to the Muslims or attack their religion.

Weakened by dynastic conflicts, tribal rivalries, and local uprisings, the Umayyad Caliphate was exterminated in 750 by a coalition of forces, including Shiis and the *mawali,* from Iraq and eastern Iran. A surviving member of the Umayyads was able to escape to Spain, however, where he established the western branch of the Umayyads in Cordoba, inaugurating an era of extraordinary cultural florescence that was due in large part to the fruitful interactions of Muslims, Jews, and Christians. The defeat of the Umayyads in Syria brought the Abbasids to power. They were a party claiming descent from al-Abbas, Muhammad's paternal uncle. The Abbasid Caliphate, which lasted until it was brought down by the Mongol invasion in the 13th century, moved the capital from Damascus to Baghdad, a new garrison city that they had founded on the banks of the Tigris River. It soon became the leading center of commerce, the arts, and Islamic learning of its time. The Arab ruling elite realized that they had to share power with Muslims who came from non-Arab origins, as more of their subjects converted to Islam, intermarried with them, obtained positions in government, and became masters of the Arabic language—the lingua franca of the empire—and Islamic learning. It was during the Abbasid era that Sunni and Shii doctrines and institutions were systematized, Greek and Persian texts were translated and discussed, and sciences such as astronomy, geography mathematics, optics, and medicine flourished.

Each of these developments contributed to the spread of Islam beyond the Middle East to Africa, the Indian Ocean basin, Central Asia, and Southeast Asia during the ensuing seven or eight centuries. Transregional trade south of the Sahara, along the Silk Roads to Asia, and across the Indian Ocean as far as Java resulted in the establishment of Muslim trading communities linked to local cultures through intermarriage as well as commerce.

India is an excellent example of the different ways by which Islam became established in a new land. Peaceful Muslim trading colonies linked to Arabia and Iraq developed along the southern coast around the eighth and ninth centuries. Ismailis from Persia introduced Islam into northern India around the 10th and 11th centuries by winning Hindu converts through their missionary activities. They were followed by Turkish and Afghan warriors who invaded to pillage and conquer but ended up establishing the Delhi Sultanate, which ruled much of the north and the Deccan Plateau between the 13th and 16th centuries. Contrary to the "conquest by the sword" thesis, large numbers of Hindus did not convert to Islam. Rather, scholarly research indicates that there was an inverse relationship between where the centers of Muslim political power were and where the most conversions occurred, which was on the political periphery. The indigenous peoples of Bengal in the northeast, for example, did not convert until the 16th century, when rulers of the Mughal dynasty encouraged the introduction of wet rice agriculture in new land made available when the Ganges River shifted its course eastward. The agents of this development were Sufis and Muslim scholars, who built mosques and shrines that became magnets for the native people, and educational centers for the dissemination of Islamic knowledge and lore. As the historian Richard Eaton has observed, rather than conversion by the sword, Bengalis were converted by the plow.[2]

In summary, conquest was but one among many factors that contributed to the expansion of Islam. Emigration, trade, intermarriage, political patronage, the systematization of Islamic tradition, urbanism, and the quest for knowledge must also be recognized. Sufis, too, played a role in the spread of Islam along trade routes and even to the remotest areas. Pilgrimage should also be recognized as a factor, especially the annual hajj to Mecca, which gathered scholars, mystics, merchants, and ordinary believers from many countries together in one place. After performing the required hajj rituals, pilgrims often took up residence in Mecca to study and meet with scholars and mystics, but eventually they returned home with stories about the Islamic holy land and new insights about Islam to convey to their families and neighbors.

These factors continue to be in effect today, although in modern forms. They have been involved in Islam's spread into western Europe, the Americas, Australia, and New Zealand. Many mosques and Islamic centers have opened in these countries since the 1960s, and the Muslim presence is being increasingly felt in schools, the workplace, and the public sphere. Likewise, global forces are changing the ways Muslims think about themselves and their religion—for better or worse. This includes the colonization of many Muslim lands by European powers during the 19th and 20th centuries. The rapid pace with which such changes have occurred, compared with earlier times, has been assisted significantly by the widespread availability of motorized transportation and the emergence of the new print and electronic media, which have closed the distances that once posed limitations on the movement of people, commercial goods, and, above all, ideas and religious beliefs.

Scope of this Encyclopedia

The purpose of any encyclopedia is to be comprehensive, balanced, and up-to-date. It should also provide readers with new information, familiarize them with foreign concepts and terms, and direct them to additional publications on the subjects presented in it. It is a challenge to meet all of these objectives in any single undertaking, particularly one such as this, which is limited to one volume

---

[2] Richard Eaton, "Approaches to the Study of Conversion to Islam in India." In *Approaches to Islam in Religious Studies,* edited by Richard C. Martin, 108–123 (New York: One World Press, 1987); ———, "Who Are the Bengal Muslims? Conversion and Islamization in Bengal." In *Understanding the Bengal Muslims: Interpretive Essays,* edited by Rafiuddin Ahmed, 25–51 (Oxford and Delhi: Oxford University Press, 2001).

about Islam, one of the world's most important religions. To meet this challenge, the *Encyclopedia of Islam* emphasizes the following subject areas in the entries it contains:

1. *Islam as the religion of Muslims.* This includes entries on aspects of Islamic history, practice, belief, and learning, as well as the major traditions—Sunnism, Shiism, and Sufism. Topics concerning local Islamic religious practices, in addition to expressions of sacred space and time, are also represented.
2. *Islam as an Abrahamic religion.* This area includes entries that take up the interrelationships and intersections that Islam has had with Judaism and Christianity. Entries also deal with Islam's encounters with non-Abrahamic religions, particularly Hinduism and Buddhism.
3. *Islamicate civilizations and cultures,* including articles pertaining to urban life, languages, social and economic life, and the arts and sciences.
4. *Islam in the contemporary world.* This includes entries on most countries with Muslim-majority populations, reform and revival moments, Islamism, regional conflicts (especially the Arab-Israeli conflicts and the Gulf wars), and issues pertaining to civil society (for example, secularism, human rights, democracy, and constitutionalism). Attention has also been given to Muslim minority communities and organizations in the Americas, Europe, Australia, New Zealand, and, to a lesser extent, Asia.

In order to enhance the encyclopedia's appeal for use by students and teachers in secondary schools, a number of entries dealing with educational subjects have been included, as well as articles on animals (camel, cat, dog, horse), children, comic strips and comic books, and the cinema.

Format

Articles are listed alphabetically. Cross-references have been provided within and at the end of each entry in small capitals to assist the reader to explore the variety of relationships the entry has with others. It is also intended to help the reader become more familiar with the many foreign terms encountered in the study of Islam. In some cases an entry and related cross-references are based on native terms (for example, Allah, *fiqh,* and sharia); in other cases they are given in English (for example, abortion, dietary laws, and women). In the entry for Allah, for example, the reader is invited to consult articles such as those on the Quran, *shahada,* prayer, theology, and Muhammad. The entry for abortion refers the reader to articles on topics such as death, afterlife, different schools of Islamic law, children, and birth control and family planning.

Each entry is also accompanied by a bibliography for readers wishing to pursue a topic in more depth. Publications listed in the bibliography are exclusively in English, owing to the intended readership of the encyclopedia, but readers are advised that a significant amount of excellent scholarship is available in other languages, especially French, German, Russian, and, to a lesser extent, Spanish and Italian. These and more specialized publications can be found in the books and articles mentioned in the individual entry bibliographies and in the references listed in the bibliography provided at the back of the book. Works in the primary languages of Islam, such as Arabic, Persian, and Turkish, can also be found in these publications, but Islamic texts in translation have been included in entry bibliographies, where appropriate. The reader is also encouraged to consult the publications listed under the heading "General References and Atlases" in the back of the book. Some entry bibliographies include articles published in *Saudi Aramco World,* a magazine available on the Internet and in print that covers cultural and historical topics relating to the Middle East and Islam. Its format is similar to that of *National Geographic,* and it is especially well-suited for students and the general public. It also provides updated listings for museum exhibits and new publications.

A Note on Terminology, Transliteration, and Translation

Because this *Encyclopedia of Islam* has been written with secondary school students and the general public in mind, I have gone to some lengths to minimize reliance upon academic technical vocabulary and words from foreign languages. When technical terms have been used, it has been to enhance clarity and understanding. An important exception has been my adoption of two terms now widely used by scholars in the fields of Islamic studies and Middle East studies first proposed by Marshall G. S. Hodgson in his monumental three-volume work, *The Venture of Islam.* These are *Islamicate* and *Islamdom.* Occasionally the words *Islam* and *Islamic* are misleadingly or incorrectly applied to phenomena that fall outside the boundaries of the religion itself, resulting in the confusion of social and cultural phenomena with religious ones. While we know that the real-life boundaries between the religious and the nonreligious are always shifting and being negotiated, it is still helpful to recognize that these boundaries nevertheless exist. Using *Islam* and *Islamic* too loosely, moreover, obscures the interrelationships that have developed historically between Muslims, Jews, Christians, Hindus, and others in contexts where Islam was the dominant religion but not the only one.

Therefore, I have adopted Hodgson's term *Islamicate* in order to describe those aspects of "Islamic" society, history, and culture that cannot be attributed exclusively to the religion Islam. For example, *Islamic literature* refers to writing traditions that involve the various religious beliefs, doctrines, practices, laws, and traditions of Islam. *Islamicate literature,* on the other hand, encompasses the variety of writing traditions, Islamic and non-Islamic, that have flourished in contexts where Muslims have held political power or constituted a majority of the population, especially prior to the 19th century. This kind of literature can include secular poetry, philosophy, and scientific writings, as well as the writings of Jews, Christians, and others in Arabic, Persian, and other languages. Likewise, *Islamic architecture* refers to those parts of the built environment connected with Islamic religious practices, such as mosques and madrasas (religious schools), whereas *Islamicate* architecture includes palaces, fortifications, caravanserais, bazaars, dwelling places, and baths. Less frequently, I use *Islamdom* instead of phrases such as *the Islamic world* to refer to social domains where Muslims prevail collectively, especially prior to the 19th century. It is analogous to the term *Christiandom,* which denotes social domains where Christianity prevails.

Following modern standard Arabic pronunciation, which is increasingly being accepted for English transliterations of Arabic words, I use *Quran* instead of *Koran, Muslim* instead of *Moslem, madrasa* instead of *madrassa,* and *Hijra* instead of *Hegira.* I have extended this principle to Arabic names: for example, *Muhammad* instead of *Mohammed, Hasan* instead of *Hassan, Husayn* instead of *Hossein* or *Hussein, Umar* instead of *Omar, Usama* instead of *Osama.* Conventional English spellings for Mecca and Medina have been retained for this publication. Instead of *Shiite,* I use *Shii* (pronounced Shi-i), parallel to the conventional use of *Sunni* (instead of *Sunnite*). *Shii* is used as an adjective (for example, Shii Islam, Shii law) and as a noun for an individual member of the minority *Shii* branch of Islam (for example, "He is a Shii"). The plural in this regard is Shiis (pronounced Shi-is). I use the term *Shia* (pronounced Shi-a), which is based on the Arabic word for "party" or "faction," to refer to Shii Muslims as a group or collectivity—the Shia. *Shiism* is used to refer to the body of beliefs, rituals, doctrines, and traditions that define the Shii branch of Islam (see the entry for this term).

In order to make the *Encyclopedia of Islam* more accessible to the nonspecialist, no diacritical markings have been used for foreign words. Transliterations for ayn (ʻ) and hamza (ʼ) have also been omitted, as has the terminal *h,* sometimes used for the *ta marbuta.* Thus, *shariʻah* is rendered as *sharia, sunnah* is rendered as *sunna,* and *ummah* as *umma.* In cases where an ayn occurs in the middle or end of a word, preceded or followed by the vowel *a,* I have transliterated the word with a double *aa;* thus, *Kaʻba* is rendered as *Kaaba, daʻwa* as *daawa,* and *bidʻa* as *bidaa.*

Dates and Statistical Data

All dates given are according to the Western calendar. Where clarity is required, the abbreviation B.C.E. is used for dates before the common era and C.E. is used for common era dates. These temporal demarcations are considered more suitable than the older ones used for dates in the Western calendar: B.C. (Before Christ) and A.D. (*anno domini;* the year of Our Lord).

Statistical data given in entries for individual countries (for example, Afghanistan, Iraq, Saudi Arabia) are based on the latest 2007–2008 estimates provided by the Central Intelligence Agency of the United States in its World Fact Book (www.cia.gov/cia/publications/factbook/index.html). Other statistics have been obtained from a variety of other sources. Although every effort has been made to provide the most current and accurate statistical information, the reader should be aware that often statistical data is either dated or affected by political, social, or religious biases and circumstances. Care should be taken before making hard comparisons based on statistical data.

CHRONOLOGY

fourth–sixth century

♦ Arabia involved in conflicts between Rome/Byzantium and Persia.

sixth–seventh century

♦ Quraysh tribe rises to prominence in Mecca.

570?

♦ Birth of Muhammad ibn Abd Allah in Mecca.

610

♦ Muhammad receives first revelation at Mt. Hira, near Mecca, and begins career as a prophet.

622

♦ The year of the Hijra: Muhammad and the Muslims migrate from Mecca to Medina.

630

♦ Muhammad wins control of Mecca.

632

♦ Death of Muhammad; death of Fatima, his daughter; election of Abu Bakr as first caliph.

634

♦ Death of Abu Bakr.

635

♦ Conquest of Damascus.

636

♦ Battle of Qadisiyya: Arab army decisively defeats Persian army in Iraq

637

♦ Conquest of Syria and the fall of Jerusalem.

640

♦ Conquest of Persia.

642

♦ Conquest of Egypt; foundation of Fustat (later part of Cairo).

644

♦ Death of Umar ibn al-Khattab, second caliph.

653

- Caliph Uthman authorizes collection and official establishment of the text of the Quran.

655

- Assassination of Uthman, the third caliph.

659

- Muawiya, chief of the Umayyads, conquers Egypt.

661–80

- Damascus becomes new capital of Umayyad dynasty under Muawiya.
- New wave of conquest begins.

661

- Death of Ali ibn Abi Talib, the fourth caliph and first Shii imam.
- Muawiya becomes caliph and founder of Umayyad dynasty.

662

- Revolt of the Khawarij.

680

- Death of Muawiya. Martyrdom of Husayn, third Shii imam, at Karbala, Iraq.

691

- Building of the Mosque of Umar (Dome of the Rock) in Jerusalem.

698

- Arabic becomes official language of government in the Islamic Empire.

700

- Conquest and conversion of Berber tribes in North Africa.

711

- Tariq ibn Ziyad leads conquest of Andalusia (southern Spain).
- Muhammad ibn Qasim initiates Arab conquest of Sind (India).

712

- Muslim armies in Persia begin conquest of Bakhara and Samarqand in Central Asia.

719

- Cordoba becomes administrative capital of Andalusia.

728

- Death of Hasan al-Basri, Muslim ascetic and teacher.

732

- Battle of Tours, France.

749

- Beginning of Abbasid Caliphate.

750

- Abbasids capture Damascus, ending Umayyad rule in Syria; Abu al-Abbas al-Saffah founds Abbasid Caliphate.

754

- Death of al-Saffah; Abu Jaafar al-Mansur becomes second Abbasid caliph.

756

- Establishment of Umayyad rule in Spain.

762–63

- Baghdad founded by Caliph al-Mansur as the capital of the Abbasid Empire.

765

- Death of Jaafar al-Sadiq, sixth Shii imam.

767

- Death of Abu Hanifa, Iraqi jurist and eponym of the Hanafi Legal School.

785–86

- The building of the Great Mosque at Cordoba.

795

- Death of Malik ibn Anas, jurist of Medina and eponym of the Maliki Legal School.

798

- Death of Abu Yusuf, co-founder of Hanafi Legal School.

801

- Death of female mystic Rabia al-Adawiyya.

804

- Death of Shaybani, Kufan jurist and cofounder of Hanafi Legal School.

808

- Foundation of Fez in the Maghrib.

818

- Death of Ali al-Rida, the eighth Shii imam.

820

- Death of al-Shafii, founder of the Shafii Legal School.

827

- Abbasid caliph al-Mamun launches inquisition to impose the Mutazili doctrines as the state religious ideology.

839

- Muslims capture Sicily and southern Italy.

855

- Death of Ahmad ibn Hanbal, hadith scholar and eponym of the Hanbali Legal School.

866

- Death of al-Kindi, early Arab philosopher.

870

- Death of al-Bukhari, author of the most respected Sunni canonical collection of hadith.

874–939

- Period of Lesser Occultation of Muhammad al-Mahdi, the twelfth Shii imam.

909

- Foundation of Fatimid Ismaili Shii dynasty in North Africa.

910

- Death of the Sufi teacher al-Junayd.

912–61

- Golden age of Umayyad rule in Andalusia.

922

- Crucifixion of the Sufi al-Hallaj in Baghdad.

923

- Death of the Quran commentator and historian al-Tabari in Iraq.

929

- Qarmati Shiis attack Mecca and remove the Black Stone from the Kaaba.

935

- Death of al-Ashari, Sunni theologian, in Baghdad.

939

- Twelfth Imam enters Greater Occultation according to Twelve-Imam Shii doctrine.

941

- Death of al-Maturidi, Sunni theologian, in Samarqand.

950

- Death of the philosopher al-Farabi.

951

- Qarmati Shiis return the Black Stone to the Kaaba.

969

- Beginning of Fatimid Ismaili Caliphate in Egypt; Cairo founded.

970

- Fatimids found Al-Azhar mosque-university in Cairo.

997–1030

- Reign of Mahmud of Ghazna, who raids northwest India (Punjab, 1001–21) and puts the conquered territories under Islamic authority in the name of the Abbasid caliph.

1021

- The Fatimid caliph al-Hakim disappears/dies; Druze religion begins.

1037

- Death of Ibn Sina (Avicenna), philosopher and physician.

1062

- Almoravids conquer Morocco.

1064

- Death of Ibn Hazm, Andalusian jurist and scholar.

1067

- Nizam al-Mulk founds the Nizamiyya, a Shafii college, in Baghdad.

1071

- Battle of Manzikert, a decisive defeat of Byzantine armies by Seljuq Turks.

1086

- Almoravids conquer Andalusia.

1091

- Normans recapture Sicily and end Muslim rule there.

1096

- Pope Urban II launches the First Crusade to conquer Jerusalem.

1099

- Crusaders capture Jerusalem, ending the First Crusade.

1111

- Death of Abu Hamid al-Ghazali, philosopher and theologian.

1145

- Almohad dynasty establishes foothold in Andalusia.
- Pope launches Second Crusade.

1166

♦ Death of Sufi master Abd al-Qadir al-Jilani in Baghdad.

1171

♦ End of the Fatimid dynasty; Salah al-Din founds the Ayyubid dynasty in Egypt.

1187

♦ Saladin retakes Jerusalem from crusaders.

1192

♦ Muhammad of Ghur leads Muslim conquest of northern and eastern India.

1193

♦ Death of Salah ad-Din, Ayyubid sultan.

1198

♦ Death of Ibn Rushd (Averroes), Andalusian philosopher and jurist.

1199

♦ Conquest of northern India and Bengal by Ghurids.

1203

♦ Founding of Mongol Empire by Genghis Khan.

1206

♦ Ghurids establish the Delhi Sultanate in India.

1209

♦ Death of Fakhr al-Din al-Razi, theologian.

1215

♦ Mongol invasion of the Middle East begins.

1230

♦ Death of Muin al-Din Chishti, leading Sufi saint in India.

1234

♦ Death of Abu Hafs Umar al-Suhrawardi, Sufi teacher and founder of the Suhrawardi Sufi order.

1240

♦ Death of Ibn al-Arabi, Sufi philosopher, in Damascus.

1250–1519

♦ Mamluk dynasties rule Egypt and Syria.

1258

♦ The Mongols sack Baghdad, ending Abbasid Caliphate.

1260

♦ Mongols are defeated by the Mamluks of Egypt at Ayn Jalut in Syria.

1273

♦ Death of Jalal al-Din Rumi, Sufi poet and teacher, in Konya.

1320?

♦ Death of Yunus Emre, Turkish mystic and poet.

1325

♦ Death of Nizam al-Din Awliya of Delhi, Sufi saint of the Chishti order.

1328

♦ Death of Ibn Taymiyya, Hanbali jurist.

1338

♦ Death of Hajji Bektash, Sufi saint.

1369

♦ Death of Ibn Battuta, famed traveler and Maliki jurist.

1370–1405

♦ Timur (Tamerlane) establishes Timurid Empire in Central Asia, the Middle East, and South Asia.

1380–1918

♦ Ottoman Empire rules much of the Middle East and eastern Europe.

1406

♦ Death of the historian Ibn Khaldun.

1453

♦ Constantinople (Istanbul) falls to Ottomans and becomes the new Ottoman capital; Byzantine Empire ends.

1492

♦ Ferdinand of Aragon and Isabelle of Castile conquer Granada, ending Muslim rule in Andalusia.

1501

♦ Ismail I establishes the Safavid dynasty in Persia.
♦ Twelve-Imam Shiism becomes the state religion of Iran.

1511

♦ The Saadi Sharifs establish Alid power in Morocco.

1517

♦ Ottomans conquer Egypt.

1520–66

♦ Reign of the Ottoman sultan Sulayman the Magnificent.

1526–1858

♦ Mughal dynasty rules India.

1529

♦ Ottomans lift first siege of Vienna and retreat.

1550

♦ Islam spreads to Sumatra, Java, the Moluccas, and Borneo.

1556–1605

♦ Reign of Akbar, Mughal emperor.

1571

♦ Christian fleet defeats Ottoman navy at Lepanto, marking the end of Ottoman dominance in the Mediterranean region.

1596

♦ Shah Abbas makes Isfahan the capital of the Safavid Empire.

1603

♦ Mughal emperor Jahangir begins rule in India.

1605

♦ Death of Akbar.

1609–14

♦ Expulsion of the Muslims from Spain.

1624

♦ Death of Ahmad Sirhindi, Indian mystic and reformer.

1627

◆ Mughal emperor Shah Jahan begins reign.

1640

◆ Death of Mulla Sadra, Persian mystic and philosopher.

1654

◆ Shah Jahan completes construction of Taj Mahal.

1658

◆ Aurangzeb deposes his father, Shah Jahan, and begins reign as Mughal ruler.

1683

◆ Ottomans lift the second siege of Vienna and retreat.

1699

◆ Death of Muhammad Baqir al-Majlisi, leading Shii scholar.

1707

◆ Death of Aurangzeb, inaugurating era of rapid Mughal decline.

1722

◆ Safavid rule in Iran effectively ended by Afghan invasion.

1750

◆ Wahhabi movement, led by Muhammad Abd al-Wahhab, arises in Arabia.

1757–65

◆ English East India Company wins control of Bengal, India.

1762

◆ Death of Shah Wali Allah.

1798–1801

◆ French expedition under Napoleon Bonaparte to Egypt.

1792

◆ Death of Ibn Abd al-Wahhab, founder of the Wahhabi movement.

1801

◆ Wahhabi raiders attack and plunder Karbala in Iraq.

1804

◆ Usman dan Fodio establishes Islamic state of Sokoto in central Sudan.
◆ Wahhabi forces capture Medina.

1805

◆ Muhammad Ali appointed viceroy of Egypt by Ottomans.

1806

◆ Wahhabi forces occupy Mecca.

1812–16

◆ Egyptian troops conduct successful campaign to end Wahhabi control of Arabia.

1816

◆ British withdraw from Indonesia, restoring it to Dutch rule.

1817

◆ Death of Usman dan Fodio, African religious and political leader.

1818

♦ British rule extends throughout India.

1826

♦ Ottomans liquidate the Janissaries and abolish the Bektashi Sufi order.

1830

♦ French forces occupy Algeria, ending 313 years of Ottoman rule.

1832–47

♦ Abd al-Qadir, Algerian religious scholar, leads unsuccessful war against French colonial forces.

1850

♦ Execution of Sayyid Ali Muhammad Shirazi, founder of Babi movement in Iran.

1857

♦ Sepoy Rebellion against English East India Company rule sweeps northern India.

1858

♦ British forces suppress Sepoy Rebellion and end Mughal dynasty; British Crown rule replaces English East India Company rule.

1863

♦ Bahaullah appears in Iraq claiming to be the manifestation of God's will, founding the religious community of the Bahais.

1869

♦ Suez Canal opened.

1870

♦ Muhammad Ahmad ibn Abd Allah appears as the Sudanese Mahdi.

1876

♦ Britain purchases shares of the Suez Canal and becomes involved in Egyptian affairs.

1881

♦ Muhammad Ahmad declares himself Mahdi in northern Sudan.
♦ Death of the first Aga Khan, Ismaili leader in India.

1882

♦ British forces occupy Egypt.

1885

♦ Death of the Sudanese Mahdi.

1891–92

♦ Tobacco revolts against British business interests in Iran.

1897

♦ Death of Jamal al-Din al-Afghani, Muslim reformer and activist.

1898

♦ Death of Sayyid Ahmad Khan, Muslim modernist reformer.
♦ Death of Ghulam Ahmad, founder of the Ahmadiyya movement.

1899

♦ Fall of Mahdist state in the Sudan and its occupation by Anglo-Egyptian troops.

1900–08

♦ Construction of the Hijaz railway to Mecca as a pan-Islamic project.

1901

♦ Abd al-Aziz ibn Saud captures Riyadh.

1901

◈ French forces occupy Morocco.

1905

◈ Death of Muhammad Abduh, Egyptian religious scholar and reformer.
◈ Massacre of Armenians in eastern Turkey.

1905–11

◈ Constitutional revolution in Iran.

1906

◈ All-India Muslim League founded in India.

1909

◈ Establishment of the Anglo-Persian Oil Company.

1912

◈ The beginning of the Muhammadiyya reform movement in Indonesia.

1916

◈ Sykes-Picot agreement signed, defining British and French spheres of influence in the post–World War I Middle East.

1916–18

◈ Sharif Husayn of Mecca leads Arab Revolt against the Ottoman Empire.

1920

◈ Syria and Lebanon become French mandate territories.

1921

◈ Faysal ibn Husayn is made king of Iraq.
◈ Abd Allah ibn Husayn becomes king of Transjordan.

1922

◈ Mustafa Kemal Ataturk abolishes the Ottoman Turkish sultanate.

1922–32

◈ Conquest of Libya by Italy.

1924

◈ The Turkish caliphate is abolished.
◈ Abd al-Aziz and his Wahhabi army conquer Mecca and Medina.

1925

◈ End of the Qajar dynasty in Persia; Reza Khan seizes power in Persia and establishes the Pahlavi dynasty.

1928

◈ Turkey is declared a secular state and adopts Latin alphabet.
◈ Hasan al-Banna founds the Muslim Brotherhood.

1932

◈ Iraq granted independence by League of Nations.
◈ Creation of Kingdom of Saudi Arabia.

1935

◈ Iran becomes the official name of Persia.
◈ Death of Rashid Rida, Syrian religious reformer.

1938

◈ Death of Mustafa Kemal Ataturk, founder of modern Turkey.
◈ Standard Oil of California discovers oil in Saudi Arabia.

1938

- Death of Muhammad Iqbal, Indian intellectual and poet.

1941

- Iran invaded by British and Russian forces, and Reza Khan is forced to abdicate in favor of his son Muhammad Reza Shah in Iran.
- Jamaat-i Islami founded in India by Abu al-Ala Mawdudi.

1942–45

- Japanese occupy Indonesian territories and Malay Peninsula.

1943

- Lebanon becomes independent from France.

1945

- End of World War II. Foundation of the Arab League.

1946

- Jordan, Lebanon, and Syria obtain independence from Britain and France.

1947

- Partition of India results in creation of Pakistan.

1948

- Establishment of the Jewish state of Israel; Arab-Israeli war.
- Death of Muhammad Ali Jinnah, first leader of Pakistan.

1949

- Assassination of Hasan al-Banna, leader of the Muslim Brotherhood.

- Indonesia becomes independent.

1950

- Emirate of Jordan officially renamed the Hashimite Kingdom of Jordan.

1951

- Libya becomes independent.

1953

- Egyptian Free Officers depose monarchy and establish a republic.
- Mossadeq government in Iran overthrown in coup sponsored by the United States and Britain.

1954

- Beginning of Algerian war of liberation against France.
- Jamal Abd al-Nasir becomes president of Egypt.

1956

- Morocco and Tunisia become independent of France.
- Britain, France, and Israel precipitate Suez Crisis by attacking Egypt to control the canal.

1957

- Daawa Party of Iraq founded. Malay Federation wins independence from British rule.

1958

- Revolution in Iraq under Abd al-Karim Qasim overthrows Hashemite monarchy and establishes the Republic of Iraq.

1962

- Algeria becomes independent from France. Muslim World League founded.

1963

♦ Islamic Society of North America founded in Plainfield, Indiana.

1965

♦ Malcolm X, leader of the Nation of Islam, assassinated.

1966

♦ Death of Sayyid Qutb, radical Islamic ideologue.

1967

♦ Israel defeats Egypt, Syria, and Jordan in the Six-Day War.

1969

♦ Colonel Muammar Qadhdhafi overthrows King Idris of Libya and establishes Libyan Arab Republic.
♦ Organization of the Islamic Conference founded.

1970

♦ Egyptian President Jamal Abd al-Nasir dies and is succeeded by Anwar al-Sadat.

1971

♦ Bangladesh (former East Pakistan) becomes independent from Pakistan.

1973

♦ October War (Yom Kippur War) between Israel and a coalition of Arab states, led by Egypt and Syria.

1974

♦ Death of Amin al-Husayni, grand mufti of Jerusalem and Palestinian nationalist.

1975–90

♦ Lebanese Civil War.

1975

♦ Death of Elijah Muhammad, leader of Nation of Islam among African Americans; Warith Deen Mohammad takes charge of the movement and renames it World Community of Islam in the West (changed to American Muslim Mission in 1978).

1977

♦ Death of Ali Shariati, Shii religious thinker.

1978

♦ Anwar al-Sadat, Egypt's president, shares Nobel Peace Prize with Manachem Begin, Israel's prime minister.

1979

♦ Iranian monarchy replaced by a revolutionary Islamic republic with Ayatollah Ruhallah Khomeini as its supreme leader.
♦ Death of Abu al-Ala Mawdudi, founder of the Jamaat-i Islami of India and Pakistan.
♦ Sacred Mosque in Mecca seized by Sunni revivalists proclaiming arrival of the Mahdi.
♦ Soviet Union invades Afghanistan.

1980–89

♦ Iran-Iraq War.

1980

♦ Execution of Ayatollah Muhammad Baqir al-Sadr, leading Shii authority in Iraq.

1981

♦ Assassination of Egyptian president Anwar al-Sadat by radical Islamists.

1982

- Israeli invasion of Lebanon; Hizbullah founded in Lebanon.
- Supreme Council for Islamic Revolution in Iraq founded with Iranian support.

1987–93

- First Palestinian intifada against Israeli occupation.

1987

- Hamas founded in Gaza.

1988

- Naguib Mahfouz, Egyptian author, wins the Nobel Prize for literature.
- Salman Rushdie publishes *The Satanic Verses*, sparking Muslim protests around the world.
- Al-Qaida founded in Afghanistan.

1989

- Death of Ayatollah Khomeini, Shii religious scholar and revolutionary leader; Ayatollah Ali Khamenei becomes supreme leader of Iran.
- Death of Fazlur Rahman, leading Islamic scholar in the United States.
- Soviets withdraw from Afghanistan.

1990

- Iraqi forces at the command of President Saddam Husayn invade and annex Kuwait, causing Gulf War I.

1991

- United States leads international coalition forces in a successful campaign to expel Iraqi forces from Kuwait.

1994

- Yasir Arafat, chairman of the Palestine Liberation Organization, shares Nobel Peace Prize with Yitzhak Rabin and Shimon Peres.

1996

- Taliban, a guerrilla force of Islamist Afghan students, seizes Kabul.

2000–

- Second Palestinian intifada (known as "al-Aqsa Intifada") against Israeli occupation (ongoing).

2001

- Religious militants connected with al-Qaida fly hijacked airliners into the New York World Trade Center and Pentagon; U.S. and coalition forces invade Afghanistan and depose the Taliban.

2003

- U.S. and coalition forces launch Gulf War II by invading Iraq and deposing Saddam Husayn and the Baath Party.
- Shirin Ebadi, Iranian human rights advocate, wins Nobel Peace Prize.

2005

- Iraqi national elections bring Shii political coalition (United Iraqi Alliance) to power.
- Muhammad al-Baradei, director of the International Atomic Energy Agency, wins Nobel Peace Prize.

2006

- Orhan Pamuk, Turkish author, wins Nobel Prize in literature.
- Muhammad Yunus, Bangladeshi banker and economist, wins Nobel Peace Prize.
- Saddam Husayn executed.

2007

- Supreme Council for Islamic Revolution in Iraq changes name to Supreme Iraqi Islamic Council.
- Benazir Ali Bhutto, Pakistan political leader, assassinated.

ENTRIES A TO Z

A

Abbasid Caliphate (750–1258)

The Abbasid Caliphate was a long-lived Sunni dynasty that ruled the Islamicate empire for five centuries and set the standard for Muslim rulers who came later. It took power in a tremendous revolution in 750 that ended the UMAYYAD CALIPH-ATE in Damascus. It was during the Abbasid era, particularly until the 10th century, that the formative elements of Islamicate civilization were put into place. Among the achievements of this era were a massive project of translation, thanks to which Greek philosophy was made available to the Arabs (and later to Latin Europe), the flowering of Arabic prose and poetry, the formation of the major schools of Islamic law, and the consolidation of Shii and Sunni communities with distinctive traditions.

The Abbasids came to power on the back of a masterful propaganda campaign that targeted those elements in the Islamicate empire whom the Umayyads had alienated, especially those who harbored various degrees of loyalty to the family of Ali: the nascent Shia. They put forward the claim, later largely accepted, that a caliph must come from the clan of Hashim, which included Muhammad and Ali, but also Abbas, Muhammad's paternal uncle and the ancestor of the Abbasids.

Only after they had attained power did they make it clear that the revolution they had led was for their own family, not that of Ali, crushing the messianic expectations of those who had awaited a descendant of Ali to come to the throne. The messianic expectations generated by the struggle between the Abbasids and Umayyads, as reflected in HADITHs that can be dated to this period, remain even now an important part of Islamic apocalyptic beliefs regarding portents of the Last Hour and JUDGMENT DAY.

During the heyday of the Abbasid Caliphate, the Islamicate Empire stretched from India and the Central Asian steppes in the east to the western coast of northern Africa. But the heart of the empire was always IRAQ, where they had their capital, BAGHDAD, and what is now IRAN. Iraq, in particular, was extensively irrigated and therefore was a rich source of agricultural produce and the resulting tax revenue. By the ninth century, major parts of the empire were functionally independent, and this gradual breakdown of central rule only increased as time went on. Nonetheless, the provincial rulers, ever anxious to legitimize their rules through official recognition from the CALIPH, largely maintained their symbolic allegiance to him. Even when these rulers were, in fact, much

1

stronger than the caliph, few considered declaring themselves independent outright, in order to maintain an aura of legitimacy as supporters of the traditional caliphate. The clear exceptions to this were the FATIMID DYNASTY (909–1171) and the Umayyads in ANDALUSIA.

The Abbasids thus had little more than symbolic power by the middle of the 10th century, except for a limited revival of their political fortunes in the 12th and 13th centuries. They were finally crushed by the invading Mongols, who took Baghdad in 1258, wiping out most members of the Abbasid family and destroying their legendary capital, Baghdad. While a few of the Abbasids escaped to Egypt, where a figurehead caliphate survived under the tutelage of the MAMLUK DYNASTY, they no longer held even the moral AUTHORITY that they had had when in Baghdad. Today, the Abbasids remain important as a symbol of the former greatness of the Islamicate civilization, and as a model for what a united Muslim community might again attain.

See also ADAB; ARABIC LANGUAGE AND LITERATURE; MAHDI; SHIISM.

John Iskander

Further reading: Paul M. Cobb, *White Banners: Contention in Abbasid Syria, 750–880* (Albany: State University of New York Press, 2001); Tayeb El-Hibri, *Reinterpreting Islamic Historiography: Harun al-Rashid and the Narrative of the Abbasid Caliphate* (Cambridge: Cambridge University Press, 1999); Hugh Kennedy, *The Prophet and the Age of the Caliphates* (Harlow: Longman, 2003); J. J. Saunders, *A History of Medieval Islam* (New York: Barnes & Noble, 1965).

Abd al-Aziz ibn Saud (Ibn Saud) (1880–1953)
charismatic founder of the modern Kingdom of Saudi Arabia and political patron of the conservative Wahhabi sect of Islam

Abd al-Aziz was the descendant of the Al Saud clan of central Arabia that had formed a strategic alliance with the revivalist leader MUHAMMAD IBN ABD AL-WAHHAB (1703–92) and established a tribal state that ruled much of the Arabian Peninsula during the 18th and 19th centuries. In a period of political fragmentation, he revived Saudi control of the peninsula after conducting a raid from neighboring Kuwait in 1902 that resulted in the capture of the town of Riyadh, the future capital of SAUDI ARABIA. He then conquered other regions of the peninsula with the assistance of the Ikhwan (Brotherhood), a Wahhabi fighting force recruited from among Arab tribes. In 1926, after the fall of MECCA and MEDINA, religious authorities recognized Abd al-Aziz as king of the Hijaz and sultan of Najd, the western and central regions of Arabia, respectively. With the support of tribal allies, ULAMA, and the British, he defeated a rebellion among the Ikhwan in 1927–30, and in 1932, he renamed his realm the Kingdom of Saudi Arabia.

Abd al-Aziz was a skillful statesman and leader in times of peace, in addition to being a man of war. He consolidated his power through consultations with close advisers and merchants, intermarriage with influential tribes and clans, and generous disbursements of state revenues. Although he had ruthlessly suppressed the Ikhwan, he maintained solid ties with Wahhabi ulama and gave them control of the country's religious and educational affairs. They were not capable of seriously opposing him as he moved to modernize the kingdom, however. He granted Standard Oil of California OIL exploration rights in 1933, and he persuaded the ulama to allow for the introduction of radio transmissions and the telephone. Oil was first discovered in 1938, and Abd al-Aziz quickly moved to use the new revenues to build family properties and palaces. It was not until after World War II, however, that the Saudi kingdom and the royal family began to fully enjoy the profits of the oil industry. This was when Saudi Arabia became the first Arab country to form close ties with the United States, as signaled by Abd al-Aziz's meeting with President Franklin Roosevelt in 1945 on the deck of the USS *Quincy*. The newly formed Arabian American Oil Company (ARAMCO) then

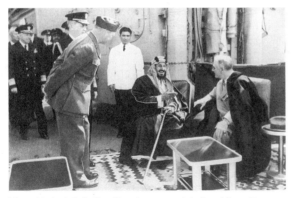

King Abd al-Aziz ibn Saud meets with President Roosevelt aboard the USS *Quincy* in the Suez Canal Zone, February 14, 1945. *(Courtesy of Dr. Michael Crocker/King Abdul Aziz Foundation)*

took charge, with Saudi participation, of building much of the country's infrastructure: roads, airports, communications, electrical power, and water system. When Abd al-Aziz died, he left a country that was about to embark on a rapid and far-reaching modernization program. Since that time, Saudi Arabia has been ruled by his sons, in alliance with the Wahhabi ulama. He is still held in high esteem by his country.

See also AUTHORITY; WAHHABISM.

Further reading: Leslie J. McLoughlin, *Ibn Saud: Founder of a Kingdom* (New York: St. Martin's Press, 1993); Medawi Rashid, *A History of Saudi Arabia* (Cambridge: Cambridge University Press, 2002)

Abd al-Nasir, Jamal *See* NASIR, JAMAL ABD AL-.

Abd al-Qadir al-Jazairi (1808–1883) *Sufi shaykh, leader of Algerian resistance to French colonization, and hero of Algerian independence*
Abd al-Qadir, the son of a Sufi shaykh of the QADINI SUFI ORDER, was chosen by his father Muhyi al-Din to lead the resistance to France's slow-motion colonization of ALGERIA, which had begun in 1830.

From his base in the region of Oran, in the northwest of Algeria, Abd al-Qadir led a fierce and protracted resistance. For about a decade, until 1842, he controlled much of the Algerian hinterland and had de facto recognition as ruler from both the Algerian populace and the French army, which negotiated with him. He implemented a number of reforms during this time, inspired in part by his admiration of Muhammad Ali (r. 1805–48), the founder of modern EGYPT, whose reforms he had witnessed at first hand during a visit to that country. But French determination to conquer the Algerian hinterland led to a brutal policy of depopulation, in which the native Algerians were forced off their land and into camps, with massive destruction of their crops, livestock, and villages. Eventually, in 1847, Abd al-Qadir surrendered to the French in order to stop the catastrophic war. After being exiled to France, he migrated to ISTANBUL and then to DAMASCUS, where he would spend the rest of his life. In Damascus, he became a large landholder and influential personage, dispensing patronage but also teaching Quran and SUNNA at the main Umayyad mosque.

Abd al-Qadir wrote works in which he promoted rationalist explanations of the Quran and Islam, and in this he was in the forefront of Arab and Muslim reformers who sought to understand their religion in light of the changed situation imposed on them by modernity and the supremacy of "science." Toward the end of his life, he began to propound a literalist reading of the scriptures, which, while not contradicting his earlier emphasis on reason, marked a new direction for him. As one of his biographers points out, however, this combination of "rational" and "literal" approaches to Islam and the Quran is typical of Salafi, or neo-traditionalist, Islam. Abd al-Qadir is remembered now, and was honored by Europeans during his life, for his part in stopping a massacre (based on local grievances) of Christians in Damascus in 1860, protecting many himself.

He is remembered by Algerians as the first to mount organized resistance to the colonial

French, who would stay in that country until they were forced out by a widespread revolution in 1962. His position as patriot and early nationalist, but also as an Islamic leader, make him a hero around whom most Algerians can safely unite, and it is largely in Algeria that his memory remains important today.

See also CHRISTIANITY AND ISLAM; COLONIALISM; OTTOMAN DYNASTY; SALAFISM.

John Iskander

Further reading: David Commins, Islamic Reform: Politics and Social Change in Late Ottoman Syria (New York: Oxford University Press, 1990); Raphael Danziger, Abd al-Qadir and the Algerians: Resistance to the French and Internal Consolidation (New York: Homes & Meier, 1977).

Abd al-Qadir al-Jilani (1077–1166) Sufi saint and founder of the Qadiri Sufi Order

Abd al-Qadir was from the Caspian region of Persia and went as a teenager to BAGHDAD to study Hanbali law and THEOLOGY; he was also attracted to the teachings of Sufi masters there. After retreating to the Iraqi desert for several years as an ascetic, he returned to Baghdad, where he became a scholar and a popular preacher who attracted a wide circle of followers, including Jews and Christians whom he had converted to Islam. The center of his activities was a MADRASA, where he taught religious studies and was consulted as a MUFTI. In his sermons, he admonished his listeners to care for the poor and needy, and he sought to harmonize Islam's legal requirements with its spiritual message. When he died in 1166, he was buried in his Baghdad madrasa, which became a popular mosque-shrine that drew pilgrims from the Middle East and India. His followers circulated many stories about his miraculous powers so that within a century after his death he was regarded as one of the leading Sufi saints in the Muslim world. He is considered to be the founder of the QADIRI SUFI ORDER, which now has branches in the Middle East, Africa, South Asia, and Indonesia.

See also HANBALI LEGAL SCHOOL.

Further reading: Khaliq Ahmad Nizami, "The Qadiriyyah Order." In Islamic Spirituality, 2 vols., edited by Seyyed Hossein Nasr, 2: 6–25 (New York: Crossroad, 1991); J. Spencer Trimingham, The Sufi Orders of Islam (New York: Oxford University Press, 1998).

Abd al-Rahman, Umar (1938–) a blind radical Islamic leader who was implicated in the assassination of Egyptian president Anwar Sadat (d. 1981) and the 1993 New York World Trade Center bombing

Umar Abd al-Rahman was born in al-Gamalaya, EGYPT, in 1938, and lost his sight very early in life. After learning Braille as a young child, he excelled at his studies. By age 11, Abd al-Rahman had memorized the QURAN. Having been trained in a series of traditional Islamic learning academies, including al-AZHAR University, he received his doctorate in 1972. He is best known for his work as a preacher and as an Islamist organizer and activist. In this capacity, throughout the 1970s and 1980s, Abd al-Rahman ran afoul of Egyptian authorities, most notoriously for allegedly issuing the FATWA (religious edict) leading to Egyptian president Anwar Sadat's assassination in 1981.

Abd al-Rahman has been linked to two Egyptian Islamist organizations, JIHAD and the Jamaa Islamiyya. As a result of his involvement with these organizations and his criticism of the Egyptian state, Abd al-Rahman was imprisoned a number of times, including after Jamal Abd al-Nasir's death in 1970 and after Sadat's assassination. Through his involvement with Islamist networks, he became active in anti-Soviet resistance in AFGHANISTAN in the early 1980s, raising money and recruiting through his preaching and organizational activities. Abd al-Rahman is said to have established links with the Central Intelligence Agency (CIA), who offered funding and military and logistical support to those fighting the Soviets in Afghanistan.

Making his way to the United States after the Soviet withdrawal from Afghanistan in 1988, Abd al-Rahman continued preaching jihad against non-Muslim powers. Following the Gulf War of 1991, he, like some other veterans of anti-Soviet resistance in Afghanistan, turned his attention to the United States. In 1996, he was found guilty of orchestrating the 1993 attacks on the World Trade Center from his MOSQUE in New Jersey. He is serving life in prison for this crime.

See also JIHAD MOVEMENTS.

Caleb Elfenbein

Further reading: Gilles Kepel, *Jihad: The Trail of Political Islam* (Cambridge, Mass.: Harvard University Press, 2002); Omar Abd al-Rahman, "Umar Abdul Rahman: A Self-Portrait." *Afkar Inquiry* (3 November 1986): 56–57.

Abd al-Raziq, Ali (1888–1966) *liberal Egyptian jurist and political reformer*

A reform-minded judge in Egypt's SHARIA courts, Ali Abd al-Raziq was the author of a controversial book that advocated the separation of Islam from politics. He came from a prominent landholding family in the district of Minya in Upper EGYPT that favored the creation of a constitutional monarchy and other liberal secular reforms. After studying at al-AZHAR and Oxford University, he began his career as a judge in the Egyptian court system. In his book *Islam and the Principles of Government,* published in 1925, he argued that MUHAMMAD's mission was a moral and spiritual one only, and that neither the QURAN nor the HADITH had ever authorized the establishment of a CALIPHATE, or Islamic state. Abd al-Raziq developed his thesis after the new republican government in TURKEY had formally abolished the caliphate in 1924, a time when there were strong secular and nationalist currents in the Middle East. Nevertheless, his book outraged religious authorities and tradition-

ally minded Muslims who wanted to hold on to the ideal of united Muslim polity, even though the caliphate had long before ceased to be an effective political institution in Muslim countries. They were even more offended that he was contesting the role of religious law in public life and traditional doctrines about Muhammad's role as a prophet-ruler. They accused Abd al-Raziq of undermining Islam with European ideas, for which he paid a high price: A council of al-Azhar religious scholars condemned his book, stripped him of his degree, and dismissed him from judicial office. He continued to write but stayed out of public affairs for the rest of his life.

See also ABDUH, MUHAMMAD; GOVERNMENT, ISLAMIC; SECULARISM.

Further reading: Hamid Enayat, *Modern Islamic Political Thought* (Austin: University of Texas Press, 1982); Albert Hourani, *Arabic Thought in the Liberal Age, 1798–1939* (Cambridge: Cambridge University Press, 1983).

Abd al-Wahhab, Muhammad ibn   *See* IBN ABD AL-WAHHAB, MUHAMMAD.

Abduh, Muhammad (1849–1905) *modern Islamic modernist thinker*

Muhammad Abduh was an Egyptian religious scholar, jurist, and leader of a major social reform movement in the Muslim world who advocated a modernist reinterpretation of ISLAM. Known as the "father of Islamic modernism," he was born in 1849 to a modest family in the Egyptian delta. His early education involved traditional QURAN memorization, although Abduh's natural inclinations tended toward SUFISM. In 1877, he concluded his studies in religion, logic, and PHILOSOPHY at AL-AZHAR University and began teaching there as a religious scholar. Simultaneously, he became interested in politics, publishing articles on political and social reform and joining the Egyptian nationalist movement against British occupation of the country. This culminated in Abduh's participation in the unsuccessful 1882 Urabi Revolt and his exile by the Egyptian khedive (ruler).

A major influence in Abduh's life was JAMAL AL-DIN AL-AFGHANI, who had come to CAIRO in 1871. They worked closely together there and later in Paris, where in 1884 they organized a secret society and published *al-Urwa al-Wuthqa* (the strongest link), a newspaper promoting resistance to European expansionism through Muslims' solidarity with one another and through the revival and reform of Islam. Both Abduh and al-Afghani saw stagnation and weakness in Islamicate societies as rooted in the imitation (*taqlid*) of old traditions and called for the use of rational interpretation (IJTIHAD) to incorporate modern ideas into Islam. Abduh in particular saw many parallels between concepts in Islam and ideas associated with the European Enlightenment and drew on these for inspiration. He rejected, however, a wholesale appropriation of western secular values, choosing instead the middle path of an enlightened Islam that valued the human intellect and modern sciences but revered the divine as the source of human morality. He presented his ideas on theology in a series of lectures given in Beirut that were later published as *Risalat al-tawhid* (*The Theology of Unity,* 1942–1943).

In 1888, Abduh returned to Cairo, focusing his energies on educational and institutional reform. After becoming the head (MUFTI) of the nation's SHARIA court system in 1899, he worked to liberalize interpretations of religious law. In this field, he was especially concerned with the status of women and advocated changes in family law and equal opportunities in education, but he was often countered by strong conservative forces.

Muhammad Abduh's ideas were carried on by his associates long after his death. MUHAMMAD RASHID RIDA, a Syrian, published the reformist journal *Al-Manar* (the beacon), which they had started together, until his death in 1935. Qasim Amin (d. 1908) developed further the arguments for women's emancipation as integral to national development and a healthy Muslim society, and he became an inspiration to feminists in the region. HASAN AL-BANNA (d. 1949) would take the spirit of Abduh's activist Islamic ideology and apply it in the founding of the MUSLIM BROTHERHOOD. Abduh died in 1905 near Alexandria, Egypt.

See also EDUCATION; EGYPT; RENEWAL AND REFORM MOVEMENTS; SALAFISM; SECULARISM.

Michelle Zimney

Further reading: Hamid Enayat, *Modern Islamic Political Thought* (Austin: University of Texas Press, 1982); Albert Hourani, *Arabic Thought in the Liberal Age, 1798–1939* (London: Oxford University Press, 1970); Malcolm H. Kerr, *Islamic Reform: The Political and Legal Theories of Muhammad Abduh and Rashid Rida* (Berkeley: University of California Press, 1966).

ablution

Ablution involves the ritual cleansing of the body with pure water in preparation for performance of other acts of worship. Although there are minor differences of opinion among Islamic legal schools, Islamic law generally stipulates two kinds of ablution. One, called *ghusl,* requires an expression of intention, followed by a cleansing of the entire body. It must be performed after sexual activity, menstruation, and childbirth; it is also performed on the body of a dead person to prepare it for funerary PRAYER and burial. The second kind of ablution, *wudu,* involves a partial cleansing starting with an expression of intention, followed by washing of the face, hands up to the elbows, head, and feet. It may also involve washing the ears and nostrils and rinsing the mouth. This method is believed to purify the body after urination and defecation, touching the genitals, sleep, and other activities. Ablution may be performed at home or at the MOSQUE, which has special facilities for this purpose. The numerous communal bathhouses that characterized medieval Islamicate cities also helped to meet this need. In the absence of water, Islamic law allows for the performance of "dry ablution" with sand or a similar substance. Only the hands and face are cleansed if this is the case. Failure to perform the proper ablution prohibits a person from performing prayer, entering a mosque, touching the QURAN, or visiting the KAABA in MECCA.

See also FUNERARY RITUALS.

Further reading: Laleh Bakhtiyar, *Encyclopedia of Islamic Law: A Compendium of the Major Schools* (Chicago: ABC International Group, 1996), 20–61; Marion Holmes Katz, *Body of Text: The Emergence of the Sunni Law of Ritual Purity* (Albany: State University of New York Press, 2002); Arthur Jeffrey, *Reader on Islam* (The Hague: Mouton & Company, 1962), 464–470.

abortion

Abortion is a human intervention to end a pregnancy prior to birth. Although people living in many different societies throughout history have practiced it, abortion has caused considerable reflection and debate about its ethical, legal, religious, social, economic, as well as medical implications. Decisions about abortion involve interrelationships between the woman and her fetus, the woman and her mate or husband, and the wider society—including religious, legal, and medical authorities. At the center of the debate are life and DEATH questions that no individual or society takes lightly.

Muslim religious and legal experts have been involved in discussions about abortion since the 11th century, and they have expressed different points of view on the subject. They often turn to teachings found in the QURAN and HADITH that emphasize the sacredness of human life, such as those that deal with man's creation with a soul (*ruh*) from God (Q 15:29, 32:9), the development of the fetus (Q 23:12-14), and condemnations of murder and the killing of one's own offspring (Q 17:33, 6:151, 81:8-9). Most schools of Islamic law

make a distinction between the first 120 days, when abortion is allowed for a valid reason (for example, to save the life of the mother or a nursing child), and the remainder of the pregnancy, when it is believed that the fetus has received its soul and gains legal status as a person. Abortion thereafter is generally prohibited, unless the mother's health is threatened, since her welfare has precedence over that of the fetus. This is especially true for those who follow the recommendations of the HANAFI LEGAL SCHOOL. On the other hand, most jurists of the MALIKI LEGAL SCHOOL believe that ensoulment occurs at the moment of conception, and they tend to forbid abortion at any point, which puts this school's position closer to that of the Roman Catholic Church. The other schools hold intermediate positions. The penalty prescribed for an illegal abortion varies according to the particular circumstances involved. According to the SHARIA, it should be limited to a fine that is paid to the father or heirs of the fetus. According to Islamic THEOLOGY, there may also be punishment in the AFTERLIFE.

There are no accurate statistics concerning actual abortion rates among Muslims. Most Muslim countries, which often have high birth rates, fall among the group of developing nations, where an estimated 78 percent of the world's abortions are performed. The Muslim countries with the most liberal abortion laws for women are IRAN, Tunisia, and TURKEY. In accordance with the sharia, it is allowed in special circumstances in most other Muslim countries, especially when the health of the mother or a nursing child is involved.

See also ADAM AND EVE; BIRTH CONTROL AND FAMILY PLANNING; CHILDREN; SOUL AND SPIRIT.

Further reading: Jonathan E. Brockopp, ed., *Islamic Ethics of Life: Abortion, War, and Euthanasia* (Columbia: University of South Carolina Press, 2003); especially the chapters by Marion Holmes Katz, Donna Lee Bowen, and Vardit Rispler-Chaim; Basim F. Musallam, *Sex and Society in Islam* (Cambridge: Cambridge University Press, 1983).

Abou El Fadl, Khaled (1963–) *leading scholar of Islamic law, religious reformer, and human rights advocate living in the United States*

Khaled Abou El Fadl was born in Kuwait in 1963 and was raised in both Kuwait and EGYPT. In his youth, he was attracted to the strict, literalist tendency in contemporary ISLAM, but as he matured he came to understand his religion in a less literal way. He credits his parents for helping him to do this. He went to the United States to attend college in 1982 and obtained a bachelor's degree at Yale University in 1986, then a law degree from the University of Pennsylvania (1989), and a doctorate in Islamic studies from Princeton University (1999). He has taught on the faculty of law at the University of California, Los Angeles, since 1998 and lectures frequently to audiences in the United States and abroad.

Abou El Fadl is an outspoken critic of TERRORISM and the puritanical Wahhabi understanding of Islam that is promoted by an influential party of Muslim religious authorities in SAUDI ARABIA and other countries, including the United States and Europe. His views became known to a wider public in the United States after the September 11, 2001, attacks on the World Trade Center and the Pentagon through newspaper editorials, publications, and speeches. He condemns religious fanaticism and supports religious and cultural pluralism, democratic values, and WOMEN's rights. His Muslim opponents accuse him of being a tool of the West, serving the interests of Islam's enemies. What makes Abou El Fadl's ideas so powerful, however, is that he supports many of his opinions with an encyclopedic knowledge of the QURAN and the SHARIA, enhanced further by his training in the secular Western legal tradition. His California home contains thousands of volumes and manuscripts, including many classics on Islamic subjects, which inspired the essays in his *Conference of the Books: The Search for Beauty in Islam*. For him, the search for the truth, or God's law, is an ongoing endeavor, one that involves reasoned argument, the weighing of different points of view, and placement of quranic commandments in their appropriate historical context. Abou El Fadl boldly maintains that this method has been a norm in classical Islamic thought but has been violated by religious fanatics, who base their views on blind imitation and superficial, erroneous interpretations of God's will. In doing this, Abou El Fadl is claiming a place for himself squarely within the reformist tradition in modern Islam. "A careful and reflective synthesis," he writes, "must be worked out between modernity and tradition" (*And God Knows the Soldiers*, p. 115). Through his writings and his public service on behalf of HUMAN RIGHTS, he is impacting both American civil society and Muslim immigrant communities. What remains to be seen is whether he and other progressively minded Muslims will be able to have a profound affect abroad in Muslim-majority countries.

See also RENEWAL AND REFORM MOVEMENTS; SALAFISM; SECULARISM; UNITED STATES; WAHHABISM.

Further reading: Khaled M. Abou El Fadl, *And God Knows the Soldiers: The Authoritative and Authoritarian in Islamic Discourses* (Lanham, Md.: University Press of America, 2001); Khaled M. Abou El Fadl, *Conference of the Books: The Search for Beauty in Islam* (Lanham, Md.: University Press of America, 2001); Omid Safi, ed., *Progressive Muslims: On Justice, Gender, and Pluralism* (Oxford: Oneworld Publications, 2003).

Abraham (Arabic: Ibrahim) *one of the leading Muslim prophets, believed to be the ancestral founder of Judaism, Christianity, and Islam*

One of the most important figures in Islamic sacred history is Abraham, who is considered a patriarchal figure, a close "friend" of God, and, above all, a prophet and founder of the KAABA in MECCA. Western scholars disagree about when the historic Abraham may have lived—some say as early as 2000 B.C.E., others say up to a thousand years later (ca. 1000 B.C.E.). Muslim understandings of Abraham drew significantly from stories found in the book of Genesis in the Bible and related accounts that were circulating among Jews and Christians in the Middle East during the seventh century C.E. These accounts were then adapted to the Arab Muslim environment, as first shown in the QURAN. The fact that Muslims as well as Jews and Christians look to Abraham as an ancestral figure for their respective religions has led some people to call all three religions Abrahamic and their followers "children of Abraham."

Abraham is mentioned in the Quran more than any other prophet except for MOSES. As in the Bible, he is portrayed as an opponent of IDOLATRY (Q 6:74–84), a person who converses with God and the angels (Q 11:69–76), the father of Ishmael (Arabic: Ismail, Q 2:133) and Isaac (Arabic: Ishaq, Q 37:112), a founder of sacred places (Q 2:125–127), and a pious man who was prepared to sacrifice his son at God's command (Q 37:99–111). Islamic traditions emphasize his role as the builder of the ancient Kaaba and his connection with many of the HAJJ rituals. His wife, Hagar, and their son Ishmael are associated with the well of ZAMZAM in the Sacred Mosque and the ritual "running" between the hills of Safa and Marwa. One of the most important memorials in the Sacred Mosque's courtyard is the Station of Abraham, where it is believed he stood while building the Kaaba. Muslims commemorate the attempted sacrifice of his son every year during the ID AL-ADHA (Feast of the Sacrifice), which closes the hajj season. The Quran does not say which of Abraham's two sons he intended to sacrifice, but the consensus reached among Muslims is that it was Ishmael. In Judaism, it is believed to have been his other son, Isaac. Abraham is thought to have been buried in the West Bank town of Hebron, which is called al-Khalil in Arabic in memory of Abraham's reputation as "the friend" of God (see Q 4:125). His tomb there is a place of worship for both Jews and Muslims, but it has become a flashpoint for confrontations between members of these communities in modern times.

See also JUDAISM AND ISLAM; PROPHETS AND PROPHECY.

Further reading: Reuven Firestone, *Journeys in Holy Lands: The Evolution of the Abraham-Ishmael Legends* (Albany: State University of New York Press, 1990); Gordon Darnell Newby, *The Making of the Last Prophet: A Reconstruction of the Earliest Biography of Muhammad* (Columbia: University of South Carolina Press, 1989).

Abu Bakr (573–634) *first of four Sunni "rightly guided" caliphs to rule the early Muslim community after Muhammad's death in 632*

Abu Bakr, the close companion and father-in-law of MUHAMMAD, was elected the first CALIPH of the Muslim community when Muhammad died in 632. Sunni Muslims regard him as one of the four "rightly guided" caliphs, along with UMAR IBN AL-KHATTAB (r. 634–644), UTHMAN IBN AFFAN (r. 644–655), and ALI IBN ABI TALIB (r. 656–661). A native of MECCA, Abu Bakr was a member of a branch of the QURAYSH tribe and made a living as a merchant. He is remembered as the first of Muhammad's associates (excluding family members) to convert to Islam, and he helped protect Muhammad when he departed on the HIJRA to MEDINA in 622. His nickname was *al-Siddiq* (the truthful) because he was the first to confirm the reality of Muhammad's NIGHT JOURNEY AND ASCENT. Abu Bakr was Muhammad's main adviser, and he joined him in all his subsequent battles. His daughter AISHA married Muhammad and became his most important wife. When Muhammad died, Abu Bakr was the candidate favored by the powerful Quraysh and other EMIGRANTS from Mecca to become the Prophet's successor (caliph), against Ali, who was favored by the ANSAR of Medina. Ali and his supporters, however, pledged allegiance to Abu Bakr without conflict. In what were called the "wars of APOSTASY," Abu Bakr was soon forced to suppress rebellions by tribes in outlying regions of the Arabian Peninsula that had refused to pay alms (*zakat*), or had turned away from Islam to follow rival prophets. After successfully prosecuting these wars, he authorized the sending of Muslim and ARAB tribal armies into Syria and Iraq, thus inaugurating the first Muslim conquests outside the Arabian Peninsula. The first collection of the Quran in written form was also initiated at his order.

See also AUTHORITY; CALIPHATE; *FITNA.*

Further reading: Hugh Kennedy, *The Prophet and the Age of the Caliphates* (London: Longman, 1985); Wilferd Madelung, *The Succession to Muhammad: A Study of the Early Caliphate* (Cambridge: Cambridge University Press, 1997).

Abu Hanifa   *See* HANAFI LEGAL SCHOOL.

Abu Zayd, Nasr Hamid (1943–)
influential Egyptian intellectual who was forced to leave his native Egypt because of his secularist approach to interpreting the Quran and other Islamic texts

Nasr Hamid Abu Zayd was born in a small village near Tanta, a city in EGYPT's Nile Delta. His father was a grocer, and his mother was the daughter of a professional QURAN reciter. He graduated from technical school in 1960 and worked as an electrician in a government ministry. In 1968, he moved to Cairo and enrolled at Cairo University, where he obtained a B.A. degree in Arabic language and LITERATURE four years later. He earned a masters degree and a doctorate (1980) in Islamic studies from the same institution. Abu Zayd's master's thesis was on the Mutazili interpretation of the Quran, and his doctoral dissertation was about the famous Sufi MUHYI AL-DIN IBN AL-ARABI (d. 1240) and his mystical interpretations of the Quran. His first academic appointment was to the Department of Arabic Studies at Cairo University. His published works deal with the modern interpretations of the Quran, Islamic law, Ibn al-Arabi, and women's rights. He has studied and taught in the

United States, Japan, and the Netherlands, where he has been a professor of Arabic and Islamic studies at Leiden University since 1995.

The main reason Abu Zayd left Egypt in 1995 was that his secular theories about how to interpret sacred Islamic texts upset influential Muslim conservatives who then caused such a public uproar in the media that he felt his life was in danger. His fears were justified, because Farag Foda, a leading critic of political Islam in Egypt, had been assassinated in 1992 because of his views, and Egyptian Nobel Prize laureate Naguib Mahfouz had barely escaped a fatal stabbing in 1994. Abu Zayd's trouble began in 1992, when he submitted his publications to a tenure review committee at Cairo University. Despite very positive evaluations, the committee recommended that he not be granted tenure, which sparked a national debate over academic freedom and defending Islam and Egypt from the threat of secular values. An influential member of the tenure committee, who also preached at a major mosque in Old Cairo, accused Abu Zayd of "intellectual terrorism" and said that his works were a "Marxist-secularist attempt to destroy Egypt's society" (Najjar, 179). Aside from minor technical flaws, what really upset Abu Zayd's critics was his liberal secularist approach to reading Islamic literature. He argued that in the modern period Muslim extremists and authoritarians promoted misguided understandings about Islam as eternal truths that cannot be disputed. He concluded that such notions were self-serving and did not stand up to the light of rational analysis. A small group of closed-minded zealots, therefore, were preventing foundational Islamic texts such as the Quran and hadith from being debated and understood in terms of context, historical change, and universal values. In an unprecedented action, Abu Zayd's opponents took his case to court and were able to convince the Cairo Appeals Court, backed by the Egyptian Supreme Court, to rule that he was an APOSTATE (a Muslim who had abandoned his religion), and because of this he could no longer remain married to his wife, Ibtihal.

Faced with death threats, forced separation from his wife, and the lack of support from Egyptian civil authorities, he and his wife left the country to live in exile.

See also MUTAZILI SCHOOL; SECULARISM.

Further reading: Fauzi M. Najjar, "Islamic Fundamentalism and the Intellectuals: The Case of Nasr Hamid Abu Zayd." *British Journal of Middle Eastern Studies* 27 (2000): 177–200; Nasr Abu Zaid and Esther R. Nelson, *Voice of an Exile: Reflections on Islam* (Westport, Conn.: Praeger, 2004).

adab

Adab is an Arabic word for refined behavior and good manners that are to be practiced daily. It is also used for areas of knowledge that are today called the humanities, especially literature written in eloquent prose. Both as a code of moral instructions and as a body of knowledge expressed through literature, *adab* has been significantly shaped by the QURAN and the SUNNA of MUHAMMAD, but it has also absorbed local codes of behavior and non-Islamic traditions of learning based in urban social settings. The traditional masters of *adab* were Muslim religious scholars, mystics, and educated elites who served the rulers of Islamicate lands from Spain and North Africa to Southeast Asia, especially between the eighth century and the 20th.

Although mastery of the skills necessary for understanding and producing eloquently written literature was available only to a select minority, training in manners and morals was a life-long process that all members of society were expected to engage in, beginning with childhood education and continuing with individual self-discipline in adulthood. In premodern Islamicate societies, there were written codes of *adab* for specific groups, such as the ULAMA, rulers, nobles, bureaucrats and secretaries, judges, Sufis, tradesmen and artisans, and even musicians. From the general religious perspective of Islam, there are also rules of good conduct that are applicable to all believers. The Quran and the sunna of Muhammad contain these rules, which involve ordinary activities such as eating, dress, grooming, speaking, visitation, and hospitality. Muslim theologians and philosophers saw *adab* as an etiquette or discipline that could help purify the individual's God-given, rational soul by strengthening inner virtues and controlling or even eliminating wrongful behavior such as lying and cheating. Moreover, they thought *adab* could curb worldly passions, for example, sexual desire, greed, anger, jealousy, gluttony, and stinginess. One of the leading medieval theologians, al-Ghazali (d. 1111), linked *adab* to the FIVE PILLARS of Islam (which involve an etiquette for human behavior toward God), Sufi practices, and the attainment of eternal bliss in PARADISE.

Adab is also used as a name for a large and diverse body of literary works that both conveys information *and* demonstrates the creative eloquence of the written word in order to transmit cultural values and entertain readers. It includes books of history, geography, TRAVEL, BIOGRAPHY, poetry, and interesting information about people and natural phenomena. In the early centuries of Islam, much of this literature was written in Arabic and drew upon the styles of expression found in the Quran and hadith. But ancient Greek and Persian learning also inspired and was at home wherever Islamicate civilization flourished. One of the most important contributors to this body of writings was al-Jahiz (d. 869), who may have composed as many as 200 books and essays on a wide range of topics, including animal lore, singing girls, misers, politics, philosophy, and religion.

See also ARABIC LANGUAGE AND LITERATURE; EDUCATION; GHAZALI, ABU HAMID AL-; MORALITY AND ETHICS; SUFISM.

Further reading: Roger Allen, *The Arabic Literary Heritage: The Development of Its Genres and Criticism* (Cambridge: Cambridge University Press, 1998); Barbara Daily Metcalf, ed., *Moral Conduct and Authority: The*

Place of Adab in South Asian Islam (Berkeley: University of California Press, 1984).

Adam and Eve *ancestral parents of all human beings according to Islamic belief*

Muslim understandings of Adam and Eve, the first human beings, are based on the QURAN, the HADITH, and other religious texts. Muslims also regard Adam as the first of a series of prophets that ends with MUHAMMAD. Biblical and later Jewish and Christian stories about Adam and Eve were already familiar to ARAB peoples at the time Islam began in the seventh century, and these stories continued to develop in their new Arabic-Islamic setting thereafter.

According to the Quran, God created Adam from clay (Q 7:12) and gave him life by filling him with his spirit (*ruh*, Q 15:29). God appointed him to be his deputy (CALIPH) on Earth, to which the angels objected because of their fear that he would cause trouble and bloodshed (Q 2:30). God had Adam prove his superiority to them by teaching him the names of everything (Q 2:30–32). The angels finally bowed down to Adam, except SATAN, whom God expelled from heaven for his disobedience (Q 2:34, 7:11–18). The Quran does not mention Eve (*Hawwa*) by name, but it does talk about Adam's "wife" (Q 20:117). She was created from Adam (Muslim commentators say from his rib), and they lived blissfully together in PARADISE, where they were allowed to eat whatever they wished except from the tree of immortality (Q 7:189, 2:35, 20:120). Muslim commentators speculate that this may have been a fig tree, a grape vine, or even wheat. Both Adam and Eve violated God's taboo after being misled by Satan (not a serpent), thus committing the first sin. For punishment, they were expelled from paradise and sent down to Earth, where they and their descendants were to live, die, and be resurrected (Q 7:20–25, 20:121–123, 2:36). Despite this punishment, Muslims do not hold to a doctrine of original sin, which many Christian denominations in the West believe humans have inherited from Adam and Eve. Rather, Islamic tradition holds that God forgave Adam, allowing him to repent and providing him guidance toward salvation (Q 2:37–38).

After the Fall, according to Islamic tradition, Adam landed on Mount Nawdh in India (or Sri Lanka), where he initiated the first crafts; Eve landed in Jidda, Arabia. Some say that the city of Jidda, which means "grandmother," was actually named in memory of Eve. Adam and his wife were reunited when the angel GABRIEL brought Adam to MECCA for the first time to perform the HAJJ. As in the Bible, Eve gave birth to Cain and Abel, and Cain later murdered his brother out of jealousy because God accepted Abel's sacrifice and not his own (Q 5:27–32). Legendary accounts say that Adam and Eve gave birth to 20 sets of girl-boy twins, from which all the world's peoples are descended. According to Shii tradition, Adam and Eve were given a premonition of the martyrdom of their descendant HUSAYN IBN ALI (d. 680), the prophet Muhammad's grandson, and they were the first to express grief on his behalf. Sufis and others, on the other hand, have looked to when, prior to their existence, the children of Adam were brought forth from his loins to testify to God as their lord (see Q 7:171). This was intended to show that worship of one true God was inherent in human nature.

See also ALLAH; ANGEL; PROPHETS AND PROPHESY; SOUL AND SUPPORT.

Further reading: M. J. Kister, "Adam: A Study of Some Legends in *Tafsir* and *Hadith* Literature." *Israel Oriental Studies* (1993): 113–174; Gordon Darnell Newby, *The Making of the Last Prophet: A Reconstruction of the Earliest Biography of Muhammad* (Columbia: University of South Carolina Press, 1989).

adat *See* CUSTOMARY LAW.

adhan (Arabic; also *azan*)

Adhan, the Islamic call to PRAYER, is recited in Arabic before each of the five daily prayers from a MOSQUE. According to traditional accounts, it was first performed by BILAL, one of Muhammad's companions, after the HIJRA to Medina in 622 C.E. The man who performs the call to prayer is called a *muadhdhin* (MUEZZIN), and he should stand facing the QIBLA (toward MECCA) when he does so. Muslims are expected to perform their prayers when they hear the *adhan*. Although the call to prayer may sound melodic, many Muslims object to it being called musical because of its religious meaning.

For Sunni Muslims, the following phrases are chanted (with minor variations in the number of repetitions):

1. *Allahu akbar* (repeated four times) "God is great";
2. *Ashhadu an la ilaha illa Allah* (repeated twice) "I witness that there is no god but God";
3. *Ashhadu anna Muhammadan rasul Allah* (repeated twice) "I witness that Muhammad is the prophet of God";
4. *Hayya ala s-salah* (repeated twice) "Come to prayer";
5. *Hayya ala l-falah* (repeated twice) "Come to safety and prosperity";
6. *Allahu akbar* (repeated twice) "God is great";
7. *La ilaha illa Allah* "There is no god but God."

The *adhan* for the morning prayer adds the following after part 5: *as-salatu khayrun min an-nawm* (repeated twice) "Prayer is better than sleep."

For TWELVE-IMAM SHIISM, the call to prayer can differ slightly with the addition of *ashhadu anna Aliyan waliyu Allah* ("I witness that ALI is the friend of God") after part 3, and *hayya ala khayr al-amal* ("Come to the best of actions," repeated twice) after part 5.

Traditionally, the muezzin chanted the *adhan* from the mosque MINARET, but today he can do it from the mosque floor using loudspeakers. It is not unusual in Muslim cities to hear the *adhan*

coming noisily from several mosques in the same neighborhood, each chanted in a different style. In cities where Muslims are a minority, it may have to be performed quietly or inside the mosque. The call to prayer is also performed on radio and television in Muslim countries, and it can sometimes be heard on radio stations in the United States. The *adhan* may also be chanted softly into the ear of a newborn child, welcoming her or him into the wider Muslim community.

See also MUSIC; SHAHADA; SUNNISM.

Further reading: Hammudah Abd al-Ati, *Islam in Focus* (Beltsville, Md.: Amana Publications, 1998); Scott L. Marcus, *Music in Egypt: Experiencing Music, Expressing Culture* (Oxford: Oxford University Press, 2007); Likayat A. Takim, "From *Bida* to *Sunna*: The *Wilaya* of Ali in the Shii *Adhan*." *Journal of the American Oriental Society* 120 (2000): 166–177.

adultery

Sexual intercourse with someone other than one's marriage partner is called *zina* (adultery) in Arabic. In the SHARIA *zina* encompasses not only adultery but any sexual act among two people who are not married to each other. Pre-Islamic Arabian society may have considered *zina* as one of several acceptable forms of marriage, but Islam brought an end to these multiple forms. For men, the only exception to *zina* concerns sexual intercourse with the female slaves under their ownership, which is allowable (although not common practice today).

Adultery is a grave offense in Islam, as it undermines the basic foundation of Muslim societal organization—the legal contract of marriage by which two partners are bound to each other exclusively by clearly delimited rights and obligations. Among these rights and duties is exclusive sexual access to one's spouse, so as to prevent promiscuity and social disorder. The QURAN includes numerous references on the subject, most notably Q 24:2, which pronounces the fixed *hadd* punishment of 100 lashes for adulterers. Some HADITH accounts go on to specify that this punishment is reserved for unmarried adulterers, while married adulterers are to be stoned to death. The Quran (Q 4:15) insists that four eye witnesses must confirm the act of adultery in order to execute punishment, since unsubstantiated accusations of adultery are an almost equally grave matter. The Quran (Q 24:4) states that anyone who instigates a charge of adultery without the required evidence of four witnesses is punishable by 80 lashes. Because of these stringent requirements of proof, punishment for adultery is rarely executed, although Muslim authorities have tried to enforce it in some modern Muslim countries.

See also CRIME AND PUNISHMENT; DIVORCE; SLAVERY; WOMEN.

Aysha A. Hidayatullah

Further reading: Leila Ahmed, *Women and Gender in Islam: Historical Roots of a Modern Debate* (New Haven, Conn.: Yale University Press, 1992); Abdelwahab Bouhdiba, *Sexuality in Islam.* Translated by Alan Sheridan (London: Routledge & Kegan Paul, 1985); Noel J. Couslon, "Regulation of Sexual Behavior under Traditional Islamic Law." In *Society and the Sexes in Medieval Islam,* edited by Afaf Lufti al-Sayyid-Marsot (Malibu, Calif.: Undena, 1979).

Afghani, Jamal al-Din al- (1838–1897)
leading advocate for Islamic revivalism and Muslim solidarity against European imperialism in the 19th century

Some uncertainty surrounds the origins of Muslim writer, philosopher, and political activist Jamal al-Din al-Afghani, whose name indicates he was from AFGHANISTAN but whose real homeland most scholars identify as Persia, or modern-day IRAN. Born into a Shii family of *sayyids* (descendants of MUHAMMAD), al-Afghani spent his life traveling and teaching in INDIA, the Middle East, and Europe. His main objective was to inspire and organize

a pan-Islamic movement to strengthen Muslims' resistance to the expansion of European, specifically British, power around the world. Among his many prominent disciples were MUHAMMAD ABDUH (d. 1905), with whom he published a newspaper (*al-Urwa al-Wuthqa,* strongest link) in 1884, and Saad Zaghloul (d. 1927), who later led Egypt's independence movement. His major work was a treatise on the role of reason in understanding divine revelation titled *al-Radd ala al-Dahiriyyin* (Reply to the materialists). Many consider him the father of Muslim nationalism.

Al-Afghani's early education in Iran was in THEOLOGY and Islamic PHILOSOPHY, particularly that of ABU ALI AL-HUSSEIN IBN SINA (Latin: Avicenna, d. 1037)). As a youth, he studied modern sciences and MATHEMATICS in India, where he witnessed firsthand the detrimental political and social effects of British imperialism. This contributed to his view that Muslims needed to band together to defend themselves. Muslim solidarity and a revitalized Islam, one that integrated the best of technology and science with traditional Islamic values, were essential if Muslims were to regain control of their lands. He enthusiastically promoted a role for rational interpretation (IJTIHAD) in understanding Islam, a position he debated with European intellectuals, such as Ernest Renan (d. 1892), and Muslim clerics alike.

Al-Afghani's career took him to many countries and into the service of many Muslim governments, including the Ottoman sultan Abd al-Hamid (r. 1806–1909) and Persia's Shah Nasir al-Din (r. 1848–96). However, this did not keep him from directing his criticisms at his patrons, whom he saw as extensions or at least facilitators of European influence in the Middle East. He advocated constitutionalism as a way to check autocratic power, criticized the TANZIMAT reforms in Turkey, and initiated the popular agitation that led to the Tobacco Protests of 1891–92 against British concessions in Persia. In 1896, Nasir al-Din was assassinated by one of al-Afghani's followers, leaving the latter to live out his days in Istanbul under the distrustful surveillance of the sultan. Al-Afghani's influence was seminal to the development of Muslim nationalism and Islamic modernism and to the lives of men such as Muhammad Abduh, MUHAMMAD RASHID RIDA (d. 1935), MUHAMMAD IQBAL (d. 1938), and MUHAMMAD ALI JINNAH (d. 1948), who would carry the Islamic reform movement forward in the 20th century.

See also CONSTITUTIONAL REVOLUTION; PAN-ISLAMISM; RENEWAL AND REFORM MOVEMENTS; SALAFISM.

Michelle Zimney

Further reading: Albert Hourani, *Arabic Thought in the Liberal Age, 1798–1939* (London: Oxford University Press, 1970); Nikki R Keddie, *An Islamic Response to Imperialism: Political and Religious Writings of Sayyid Jamal al-Din "al-Afghani"* (Berkeley: University of California Press, 1983).

Afghanistan

Afghanistan is a mountainous landlocked country with an area of 647,500 sq. km. (comparable in size to the state of Texas) and an estimated population of 32.7 million in 2008. It is situated on the frontier between the Middle East, Central Asia, and South Asia, with IRAN on its western border and PAKISTAN on its eastern and southern borders. A large majority of its people are Sunni Muslim (80 percent), but there are also Shii Muslims (19 percent) and followers of other religions (1 percent). Religious life consists of a mixture of folk religion, SUFISM, and formal Islamic doctrine and practice. Ethnic and tribal loyalties are often stronger than religious and national ones. The major ethnic groups are Pashtun (42 percent, also called Afghans), Tajik (27 percent), Hazara (9 percent), and Uzbek (9 percent). Pushtu and Dari (the Afghani Persian dialect) are Afghanistan's official languages, but there are more than 30 languages and dialects spoken there, most of which belong to the Indo-European and Turkic language families. Its major cities are Kabul (the capital), Qandahar, and Herat, but most of the population still lives in the countryside.

Because of its location, the Afghanistan region has been a crossroads for peoples, merchandise, and empires for centuries. The Arab Muslim armies that arrived in the seventh century were following the routes used previously by Persian and Greek invaders, but none of these empires, or the nearly 20 empires and dynasties that came later, found Afghanistan easy to conquer and control. The Afghan peoples, though internally divided, tend to unite in fierce opposition to outsiders. Islamic rule was not secure there until the late 10th century, when it became the seat of the Ghaznavid dynasty (977–1163), which also governed eastern Iran and launched a series of raids into northern INDIA. Afghanistan then succumbed to invasions by Turks and Mongols during the 13th and 14th centuries. The country's strategic location continued to make it a focal point of conflict between Muslim rulers in Iran and India from the 15th to 18th centuries and a target for the imperial ambitions of Russia and Great Britain in the 19th and early 20th centuries. Despite its turbulent history, medieval Afghanistan saw moments of significant religious and cultural achievement, reflected in its role in the extension of Islamicate architectural forms to India and sponsorship of Firdowsi's Persian epic, the *Shahnama* (ca. 980), and the scientific writings of ABU RAYHAN AL-BIRUNI (973–1048). In addition to being the base from which Muslims invaded northern India, Afghanistan was the birthplace of several important Sufi masters, including IBRAHIM IBN ADHAM (d. 778) and JALAL AL-DIN RUMI (1207–73), and it witnessed the emergence of two of the most important Sufi orders: the CHISHTI SUFI ORDER and the NAQSHBANDI SUFI ORDER.

Afghanistan became a modern independent country in 1919 and evolved into a constitutional monarchy under the influence of the Soviet Union. After fighting off an armed Soviet invasion in 1979–89, the country was torn by a lengthy civil war. Both of these conflicts contributed to the growth of heavily armed guerrilla militias and forced 6 million Afghans to become REFUGEES in neighboring countries. The civil war ended with the establishment of the extremist Islamic government of the TALIBAN in 1996. That government was infamous for its brutal treatment of women, persecution of religious minorities, and destruction of the famed colossal images of the Buddha in Bamian (2001). The Taliban were removed by force in late 2001, when the United States led an international invasion and occupation of the country as a consequence of the war on terror it launched in the aftermath of the September 11, 2001 attacks by the AL-QAIDA organization, which was headquartered in Afghanistan. A constitutionally based transitional government with its capital in Kabul has since been created, but the new regime, known as the Transitional Islamic State of Afghanistan (TISA), faces enormous challenges to its legitimacy from powerful regional warlords, opium drug traffickers, and Muslim guerrilla forces.

   See also AFGHAN MUJAHIDIN; CONSTITUTIONALISM; PERSIAN LANGUAGE AND LITERATURE.

Further reading: Larry P. Goodson, *Afghanistan's Endless War: State Failure, Regional Politics, and the Rise of the Taliban* (Seattle: University of Washington Press, 2001); Ahmed Rasheed, *Taliban: Militant Islam, Oil, and Fundamentalism in Central Asia* (New Haven, Conn.: Yale University Press, 2001).

Afghan mujahidin

The Afghan mujahidin (warriors) are bands of Muslim guerrillas who fought against the Soviet occupation of AFGHANISTAN in 1979–89 and then turned against each other in a bloody civil war that resulted in the creation of the TALIBAN regime in 1996. Informal Islamist parties began appearing in Afghanistan in the mid-1960s, at a time when the radical ideologies of SAYYID QUTB (d. 1966) and ABU AL-ALA MAWDUDI (d. 1979) were becoming a strong presence in neighboring Pakistan. Afghan Islamist parties at the time began adopting the call for JIHAD, which was central to Qutb's and Maududi's programs. It was only with the Soviet invasion of Afghanistan in 1979, however, that these calls were seriously heeded.

   Afghan resistance to the Soviet occupation comprised many different elements, including nationalist parties, pro-China communists, and Islamists. It was the latter group, however, that dominated the fight to expel the Soviets. Based in Afghan refugee camps in Peshewar, Pakistan, Islamist resistance groups, called the mujahidin, quickly began receiving money and arms from SAUDI ARABIA and the UNITED STATES. The dominant force among the Afghan resistance was the Hezb-e-Islami (Islamic Party), led by GULBUDDIN HEKMATYAR (b. 1947?), one of the earliest and most conservative Afghani Islamist activists. Early disunity among as many as seven different Afghan mujahidin groups slowed the progress of the fight against the Soviets, but with foreign assistance, they were able to operate effectively on the battlefield. During this time, the Afghan mujahidin were treated favorably in the Western media as "freedom fighters."

   The Afghan guerrillas were not alone in their fight against the Soviet occupation. Islamists from the entire Muslim world traveled to Afghanistan under the banner of Islam and JIHAD. Among these Islamists were USAMA BIN LADIN (Saudi Arabia), Ayman Zawahiri (EGYPT), UMAR ABD AL-RAHMAN (Egypt), Abdullah Azzam (Palestine), and legions of young men from countries around the Muslim world. The resulting hybrid, transnational network of Islamists advocated an active jihad against foreign powers and a reconstruction of Afghanistan according to an extremely conservative interpretation of Islam. Together, the Afghan and Arab mujahidin forced the Soviet withdrawal in 1989. Hekmatiyar's Hezb-e-Islami and Burhanuddin Rabbani's Jamiat-i-Islami (Islamic Society, based in northern Afghanistan) emerged as the strongest mujahidin groups after the Soviet defeat, but they ended up fighting against each other as well as other groups for control of the country. From bases in Pakistan and central and southern Afghanistan, the Taliban took advantage of this chaotic situation to make their own play for power in 1994–96. *Mujahidin* continues to be a term used by various armed factions that are contending for power and influence in the country since the United States overthrew the Taliban regime in December 2001.

See also JIHAD MOVEMENTS; *MUJAHID*; QAIDA, AL-.

Caleb Elfenbein

Further reading: M. Hassan Kakar, *Afghanistan: The Soviet Invasion and the Afghan Response, 1979–1982* (Berkeley: University of California Press, 1995); Gilles Kepel, *Jihad: The Trail of Political Islam* (Cambridge, Mass.: Harvard University Press, 2002); Ahmed Rashid, *Jihad: The Rise of Militant Islam in Central Asia* (New Haven, Conn.: Yale University Press, 2002).

Africa *See* ALGERIA; EAST AFRICA; EGYPT; LIBYA; MOROCCO; SUDAN; TUNISIA; WEST AFRICA.

African Americans, Islam among

The first African American Muslims were slaves captured in West Africa in the 1700s and brought to the American colonies. The few accounts of them from the early decades of the United States indicate that the Muslims formed somewhat of an elite in the slave community, that many were literate, and that they became known for their resistance to the conditions in which they found themselves. They also resisted attempts by Christians to convert. There remains, however, little evidence to connect Islam within the slave community with a new Islamic movement that developed among African Americans in the urban north in the 20th century.

A new phase for Islam among American blacks began in 1913, when Timothy Drew (1886–1929) assumed the name Noble Drew Ali and founded the Moorish Science Temple of America. This organization can best be seen as an attempt to adapt Muslim themes to the struggle of African Americans for a place of dignity and equality in American life. From his personal research, he concluded that American blacks were descendants of the Moors and that their true homeland was MOROCCO. He suggested that in the founding of the United States, the nationality, freedom, and religion of African Americans had been taken from them. Not having access to an English translation of the QURAN, he adapted a Spiritualist text, the Aquarian Gospel of Jesus Christ, by Levi Dowling, and issued it as the movement's Quran.

The Moorish Science Temple spread among African Americans through the 1930s but declined in the decades after World War II. The thrust it began, however, was picked up by a second organization, the NATION OF ISLAM, dated to 1930, and the activity of a mysterious man known as Wallace Fard Muhammad. He continued Noble Drew Ali's emphasis on African Americans having an African origin and developed an elaborate myth of the primal origin of black people. Leadership of the movement was soon assumed by Elijah Muhammad (1897–1975), who steered it through some controversial years to great success in the 1960s, coinciding with the heyday of the Civil Rights movement.

As the Moorish Science Temple and the Nation of Islam were spreading, the AHMADIYYA movement in Islam sent representatives from India to begin proselytizing. Their greatest success proved to be among black Americans, who for a generation formed the largest community of African-American Muslims. Also competing for the attention of blacks attracted to Islam was a movement formed by Shaykh Daoud, who came from Bermuda in the 1920s.

The shape of the African-American Muslim community began a dramatic transformation in the 1970s. Following the change in U.S. immigration regulations in 1965, a number of Indo-

Pakistani Muslims moved to the United States, many members of the Ahmadiyya movement, who served to reassert its identity as an international Muslim fellowship (while at the same time dealing with its rejection by other Pakistani Muslims as a heretical movement).

The death of Elijah Muhammad led to fights over succession. While his son assumed leadership over the largest segment of the membership, a variety of smaller schismatic groups appeared. Their claim to being the true successor to Elijah Muhammad was strengthened when Warith Deen Muhammad (b. 1933) began to move the Nation of Islam toward Sunni Islam. That move had begun with one of the nation's most prominent leaders, MALCOLM X (1925–65), who had gone on the HAJJ and discovered how different the nation's doctrines were. His advocacy of a move to orthodoxy was among several factors that led to his assassination. In leading the Nation of Islam to orthodoxy, W. D. Muhammad changed the name of the nation several times and in the process lost his most capable lieutenant, LOUIS FARRAKHAN (b. 1933), who moved to reconstitute the Nation of Islam as it was in the early 1970s. The movement led by W. D. Muhammad eventually disbanded as it completely aligned with the larger orthodox community.

By the end of the 20th century, approximately 30 percent of all the mosques in the United States were serving a predominantly African-American constituency. The number of mosques indicated the inroads made into the black community, long dominated by Baptist, Methodist, and Pentecostal Christian churches. It has gained an even greater level of acceptance from the conversion of some outstanding American athletes, such as MUHAMMAD ALI (b. 1942) and Karem Abdul-Jabbar (b. 1947), who adopted Muslim names as their careers soared. There are an estimated 4 to 6 million African-American Muslims in America. Most attend mainstream Islamic mosques, though a significant minority adheres to the Ahmadiyya movement, the several schisms from the Nation of Islam (the largest led by Farrakhan), and other smaller sectarian groups.

See also SLAVERY; SUNNISM.

J. Gordon Melton

Further reading: Steven Barboza, *American Jihad: Islam after Malcolm X* (New York: Image/Doubleday, 1994); Martha F. Lee, *The Nation of Islam, an American Millenarian Movement. Studies in Religion and Society* (Lewiston, N.Y.: Edwin Mellen Press, 1988); Richard Brent Turner, *Islam in the African-American Experience* (Bloomington: Indiana University Press, 1997).

African languages and literature

The variety of Islamic experiences in Africa can be seen in the diversity of languages and literature through which Islam has expressed itself. The most influential literary language has been Arabic. Culturally dominant in North Africa, Arabic has often been the language of religious instruction, devotional practices, and pious writings in sub-Saharan Africa as well. Arab geographers such as al-Bakri (d. 1094) and explorers such as IBN BATTUTA (d. 1368) wrote the oldest existing descriptions of sub-Saharan Africa in Arabic. A couple of centuries after Ibn Battuta's travels in West Africa, the earliest sub-Saharan chronicles were written in Arabic. During the 15th and 16th centuries, the ULAMA of Timbuktu produced original scholarly works in Arabic and copied great Islamic texts from North Africa and the Fertile Crescent in the same language. Religious scholars would continue to use Arabic as the language of instruction into the 19th century.

In the realm of oral tradition, Muslims were more prone to compose and transmit works in the indigenous languages. Storytellers passed down epic tales in the vernacular for hundreds of years. The best known of these is the West African epic, *Sundiata,* which dates from the 13th century. In East Africa, the tradition of Swahili-language poetry developed in both oral and written forms.

A tradition of oral poetry also arose in Somalia, through which poets discussed themes ranging from moral lessons to failed romance. The Somali "praise-singing" tradition provided an avenue through which women could participate, singing songs of praise dedicated to female saints. Other praise songs venerated holy men in languages such as Oromo and Amharic. Epic stories, praise songs, and poetry all combine Islamic and African cultural themes and contain examples of the different elements that create a uniquely African Islamic style.

A larger number of works have been composed in the indigenous languages of African Islam during the modern era. Many languages were first written down during the 19th century, often in the Arabic script. The 19th-century JIHAD states of West Africa produced a considerable amount of literature, much of it in the Fulfide and Hausa tongues, and 19th-century poetry frequently combined religious imagery with anticolonialist themes, as seen in the writings of the great Somali poet Mahammad Abdullah Hasan (d. 1921). Some oral works took longer to find written expression. For instance, Somali epic poems were first written down only in the 1970s.

During the 20th century, African literature expanded in variety and scope, as the short story and the novel gained in popularity. Some of this literature was written in the languages of the colonizers (English and French) but nevertheless expressed anticolonial messages. One popular theme highlighted the tensions in African societies between SECULARISM, mysticism, and scripturalism. Allegorical tales contrasted expressions of pure Islam (often as practiced by simple characters) with the hypocrisy of stern religious figures. Other literature expressed mystical, secularist, socialist, and a variety of other perspectives within the African Muslim community.

See also ALPHABET; ARABIC LANGUAGE AND LITERATURE; EAST AFRICA; WEST AFRICA.

Stephen Cory

Further reading: Albert Gérard, *African Language Literatures* (Washington, D.C.: Three Continents, 1981); Kenneth W. Harrow, "Islamic Literature in Africa." In *The History of Islam in Africa,* edited by Nehemia Levtzion and Randall L. Pouwels (Athens: Ohio University Press, 2000); Kenneth W. Harrow, ed., *Faces of Islam in African Literature* (Portsmouth, N.H.: Heinemann, 1991); John William Johnson, Thomas A. Hale, and Stephen Belcher, *Oral Epics from Africa* (Bloomington: Indiana University Press, 1997).

afterlife (Arabic: *al-akhira*)

Afterlife beliefs are concerned with the question of what happens to a person after physical DEATH. This is one of the enduring subjects of Islamic belief and religious thought, which first developed in the seventh century under the influence of native Arabian religion, Judaism, Christianity, and other Middle Eastern religions. On the basis of the QURAN, hadith, and the teachings of religious scholars, most Muslims believe that God determines when each person will be born and die and that on JUDGMENT DAY he will resurrect everyone in the body and judge each according to that person's beliefs and actions. He will reward good people with eternal life in PARADISE, where they will enjoy heavenly comforts and happiness. Evil people will be sent to the FIRE, where they will endure horrible tortures and punishments. Eventually, many of the people of the Fire will be allowed to join the blessed in paradise.

During the later Middle Ages, people speculated more about what happens in the time between death and resurrection. Popular beliefs about spirits of the dead combined with Muslim theological ideas, which resulted in the development of doctrines about an intermediate stage in the afterlife known as the *barzakh,* where the dead experience a preliminary judgment at the hands of the angels Munkar and Nakir and a preview of their rewards and punishments. The souls of martyrs who died in battle were believed to go directly to paradise during this time. Many

Muslims also believed that the dead remained conscious in the tomb and that their spirits could move about in the world. This was especially true for the saints—holy men and women who could help people who sought their assistance. People claimed to communicate with them in their dreams, and many traveled to their tombs as pilgrims to win their blessings. Such beliefs are still widely held by Muslims today, although proponents of conservative and reformist understandings of Islam argue that they have no basis in the Quran and the teachings of MUHAMMAD.

See also CEMETERY; FUNERARY RITES; INTERCESSION; MARTYRDOM; SAINT; SOUL AND SPIRIT.

Further reading: Juan Eduardo Campo, "Between the Prescribed and the Performed: Muslim Ways of Death." In *Death and Religion in Contemporary Societies,* edited by Kathleen Garces-Foley (Armonk, N.Y.: M.E. Sharpe, 2004); Jane I. Smith and Yvonne Haddad, *The Islamic Understanding of Death and Resurrection* (Albany: State University of New York Press, 1981).

Aga Khan (Agha Khan, Aqa Khan)

Since the early 19th century, *Aga Khan* has been the honorific title used by the official leader (IMAM) of the Nizari Ismaili branch of Shii Islam. The title, which means "lord and master," is hereditary, and its holders claim to be direct descendants of the prophet Muhammad's family through ALI IBN ABI TALIB (d. 661) and FATIMA (d. 633) and their son HUSAYN IBN ALI IBN ABI TALIB (d. 680). The living Aga Khan is considered by his followers to be pure and sinless, and he is their supreme religious AUTHORITY. There can be only one Aga Khan at a time; the present one is Prince Karim al-Husayni, Aga Khan IV (b. 1936). His predecessors were Hasan Ali Shah (d. 1881), Ali Shah (d. 1885), and Sir Sultan Muhammad Shah (d. 1957).

In 1846, Hasan Ali Shah broke with tradition and transferred his residence from IRAN to Bombay, INDIA. Here he received the recognition of British authorities as the legal head of the Ismaili community in 1866, at a time when India was a British colony. However, it was Muhammad Shah, Aga Khan III, who really brought the Ismaili community into the modern era during his 72-year reign. Starting in the early 1900s, he reorganized Ismaili communities in South Asia, the Middle East, and East Africa. He encouraged them to publicly distinguish themselves from other Muslims in terms of their beliefs and practices, instead of trying to conceal them, which had been their custom in order to avoid persecution. Using income from donations given by his followers and from worldwide business enterprises, he promoted religious tolerance and funded public health and social welfare projects for non-Muslims as well as Muslims, including education for women. Aga Khan III also supported the Indian independence movement and promoted the cause of world peace, serving as the president of the League of Nations in 1937. He spent his last years in Geneva, Switzerland, and was buried in Aswan, EGYPT.

Prince Karim al-Husayni, Aga Khan IV, has continued his grandfather's legacy of progressive reform and philanthropy. Unlike his predecessors, he received a Western education and obtained a degree from Harvard University in Islamic history in 1959. Since becoming the Aga Khan at the age of 20 in 1957, he has directed a vast economic network that, together with the Aga Khan Foundation (1967), has financed health, education, and rural development projects in South Asia, Central Asia, and East Africa, as well as the founding of the Institute for Ismaili Studies in London (1977) and Aga Khan University in Karachi, PAKISTAN (1985). The Aga Khan Program for Islamic Architecture (based at Harvard University and the Massachusetts Institute of Technology) and the Aga Khan Award for Architecture have contributed significantly to the study and preservation of the Islamicate architectural heritage around the world as well to the development of new design concepts based on Islamicate patterns.

See also ARCHITECTURE; *AHL AL-BAYT;* EAST AFRICA; ISMAILI SHIISM; ZAYDI SHIISM.

Further reading: Farhad Daftary, *A Short History of the Ismailis* (Princeton, N.J.: Marcus Wiener Publishers, 1998); Willi Frischauer, *The Aga Khans* (London: The Bodley Head, 1970); Renata Holod and Darl Rastorfer, eds., *Architecture and Community: Building in the Islamic World Today* (New York: 1983).

agriculture

Agriculture is farming—cultivating the land to produce crops and raising and caring for livestock. Archaeologists have found the earliest known evidence for the domestication of plants and ANIMALS, which occurred before 8000 B.C.E., in mountainous areas of IRAN, IRAQ, TURKEY, and PALESTINE. Farming, assisted by irrigation technology, contributed to the rise of the first cities in the river valleys of ancient Mesopotamia (Iraq) and EGYPT by 3100 B.C.E., and it shaped significantly the pre-Islamic religious beliefs and practices of these civilizations. Contrary to the stereotype of nomads traveling across vast deserts, during the era of medieval Islamicate civilization (seventh century to 17th century C.E.), settled agriculture was the real basis of the economy and remains so to this day in many countries where Muslims are a majority of the population. Moreover, cotton and many foods consumed today, such as rice, citrus fruits, sugar, and COFFEE, were introduced to Europe and the Americas via Islamicate lands in the Middle East, where they had been transplanted from Asia and Africa during the Middle Ages.

The importance of agriculture in Islamicate societies is reflected in Islamic religion and reli-

Vegetable market, Marrakesh, Morocco *(Federico R. Campo)*

gious law. The QURAN mentions that God is the source of water for plants that yield foods such as dates, grapes, olives, and pomegranates (Q 6:99), and that he has provided humans with animals whose fur supplies material for making houses and furnishings (Q 16:80–83). Also, according to the Quran, the PARADISE that awaits believers in the AFTERLIFE is described as a meadow or lush garden with fruit-laden trees and rivers flowing with water, milk, honey, and wine (Q 47:15). Of all the plants mentioned in the Quran, the date palm, which is emblematic of settled life, is the one that receives the most attention. It is considered a sign of God's generosity toward humans and is said to have provided MARY with shelter and nourishment while she was giving birth to JESUS (Q 19:23–25). In the decoration of mosques, illuminated book manuscripts, and Oriental carpets, Muslims have often used botanic and floral themes inspired not by wild plants and flowers but by cultivated ones. The animals Muslims sacrifice on religious holidays and other ritual occasions are invariably domesticated livestock: sheep, goats, cattle, and camels. Until recently, the amount of income a person was required to pay in fulfillment of the *zakat* (ALMSGIVING) duty in Islam was usually assessed in terms of the size of the harvest and number of heads of livestock owned. Also, according to the SHARIA, non-Muslim subjects were obliged to pay a special tax on their agricultural lands and crops, a requirement that later was extended to Muslim subjects, too. This was an important source of wealth for Islamic empires.

By about 1200, Arab farmers had accomplished what scholars have called a medieval agricultural revolution that changed the food cultures of the Middle East and later of Europe and the Americas. By introducing Eastern irrigation technologies, they enhanced the productivity of the land and brought new areas under cultivation in Iraq, Syria, Egypt, North Africa, Spain, and Sicily. At the same time, they brought new crops from Asia, such as citrus fruits, sugarcane, watermelon, bananas, rice, spinach, eggplants, and perhaps the hard wheat used in the making of semolina and pasta. Botanical gardens where plants could be studied probably assisted the introduction of these crops from Asia into new climates in the Mediterranean region. A significant body of medieval Arabic literature on agricultural science was created in connection with these developments. The increased productivity of the land helped sustain population growth, which contributed to the rise of large medieval CITIES in the Middle East and Spain, such as BAGHDAD, CAIRO, and CORDOBA.

Today, as a result of European colonization in the 19th and 20th centuries and the introduction of modern technologies, agriculture in Muslim lands has undergone a second revolution. New crops (for example, tomatoes, potatoes, corn, and tobacco) and hybrids are being grown, large dams and irrigation systems are being built, and farming is becoming more mechanized, although much human labor is still involved. The traditional agricultural economy has become very commercialized and is affected by global markets more than in the past. It is estimated that agriculture constitutes a significant part of the economy in about 34 Muslim countries and that just under 50 percent of the world's Muslim population is involved in agricultural production, although the trend has been for people to migrate from rural areas to the cities. As a reflection of how important agriculture is, many Muslim countries now have agricultural colleges and government ministries that oversee agriculture and irrigation. Agriculture in many of these countries is nevertheless facing many challenges. Although the Green Revolution in the 1960s helped prevent widespread famine as a result of rapid population growth, a number of countries in the Middle East and Africa have found that urbanization, pollution, soil salinization, government inefficiency and corruption, regional conflicts, and the forces of nature have made it difficult to be agriculturally self-sufficient, making them dependent on imports and aid from international agencies and foreign governments.

See also ARABESQUE; ART; FOOD AND DRINK.

Further reading: Richard C. Foltz, Frederick M. Denny, and Azizan Baharudding, eds., *Islam and Ecology* (Cambridge, Mass.: Harvard University Press, 2003); Andrew Watson, *Agricultural Innovation in the Early Islamic World* (Cambridge: Cambridge University Press, 1983); World Resources Institute, *World Resources* (Oxford, U.K.: Elsevier Science, 2000–01).

ahl al-bayt (Arabic: people of the house)

The *ahl al-bayt* in Islam is a holy family consisting primarily of five members: the prophet MUHAMMAD (d. 632), ALI IBN ABI TALIB (Muhammad's cousin and son-in-law, d. 661), FATIMA (Muhammad's daughter, d. 633), and the two sons of Ali and Fatima, Hasan (d. 669) and HUSAYN (d. 680). It can also include all descendants of Muhammad's clan, the Banu Hashim, and even all Muslims.

Muhammad's family is highly respected by all Muslims, but it is the Shia, followers of the minority branch of Islam, who hold them in highest esteem. They regard the family of Muhammad as pure, sinless, and divinely inspired exemplars of the best worldly and spiritual qualities. Miraculous powers are assigned to members of this family, and it is believed that they will help their devotees enter PARADISE on JUDGEMENT DAY. The Shia also believe that Muhammad's family produces, with God's guidance, the most qualified leaders of the Muslim community, called imams. TWELVE-IMAM SHIISM venerates 12 such leaders, all but one of whom suffered martyrdom at the hands of wayward members of the Muslim community. Like Christians who believe in JESUS as a redeemer, they believe that the suffering and death of these heroic figures, especially of Husayn, the third imam, redeem the sins of the faithful and that the 12th imam, known as MUHAMMAD AL-MAHDI, will arise in the future to combat the forces of evil and inaugurate a golden age at the end of time.

The tombs of *ahl al-bayt* are popular Muslim pilgrimage sites, including those of Ali (Najaf, Iraq), Husayn (Karbala, Iraq, and Cairo, Egypt), Ali al-Rida (the eighth imam; Mashhad, Iran), and of women saints such as Zaynab bint Ali (Damascus, Syria, and Cairo, Egypt). Sufi TARIQAS include members of the holy family, especially Ali, in their lists of spiritual teachers. Rulers of a number of Muslim empires and states have also claimed descent from *ahl al-bayt,* including the FATMID DYNASTY in Egypt (909–1171), the ALAWID DYNASTY of Morocco (1631–present), the HASHEMITE DYNASTY of Iraq (1921–1958) and of Jordan (1923–present), and many of the clerics holding power in Iran since the revolution of 1978–79.

See also AGA KHAN; ALAWI; IMAM; SHIISM; ZIYARA.

Further reading: Mahmoud Ayoub, *Redemptive Suffering in Islam: A Study of the Devotional Aspects of Ashura in Twelver Shiism* (The Hague: Mouton Publishers, 1978); Valerie Hoffman-Ladd, "Devotion to the Prophet and His Family in Egyptian Sufism." *International Journal of Middle East Studies* 24 (1992): 615–637.

ahl al-kitab   *See* PEOPLE OF THE BOOK.

Ahmadiyya

The Ahmadiyya is a controversial Islamic missionary revival movement founded by MIRZA GHULAM AHMAD (ca. 1835–1908) in British INDIA during the 19th century. This movement began in the town of Qadian in northern India in 1889, and it has spread to other parts of the world, including Africa, Southeast Asia, Great Britain, and North America, through the missionary activities of its adherents. Its members, who tend to be economically prosperous, were divided into two separate groups in 1914: the Qadianis (also called the Ahmadiyya Muslim Community) and the Lahoris (also called the Ahmadiyya Association for the Propagation of Islam). Both groups recruit new members by conducting organized missionary programs and active publication activities. The total size of the Ahmadiyya community in 2001 was estimated to be more than 10 million members worldwide, but this figure is disputed. Followers claim that their numbers are growing.

Ahmadiyya members believe that Ghulam Ahmad was a religious renewer sent by God because the religion of Islam was thought to have gone into decline during the 19th century. Like other Muslims, they consider the QURAN to be their holy book and have promoted its translation into many languages. They also practice the FIVE PILLARS of Islam. However, what has made the movement especially controversial are assertions made by Ghulam Ahamad and his followers that other Muslims are unbelievers (*kafirs*) and that Ghulam Ahmad is a prophet, a promised redeemer (MAHDI), a Christlike messiah, and an incarnation of the Hindu god Krishna. Some Christians and Hindus, along with many Muslims, have objected to these beliefs, and the movement was attacked and persecuted by other Islamic groups and conservative religious authorities in India and later in PAKISTAN. As a consequence, the Ahmadiyya experienced internal division into the Qadiani and Lahori branches in 1914.

The larger Qadiani branch of the Ahmadiyya believes that it represents the only true Islam. It emphasizes belief in the prophethood of Ghulam Ahmad and the AUTHORITY of his successors, who carry the title of CALIPH. After the 1947 partition and independence of India and Pakistan, it moved its headquarters to Rabwa, Pakistan. The fourth caliph, Mirza Tahir Ahmad (d. 2003), moved the Ahmadiyya headquarters to London in the 1980s because of heightened opposition faced in Pakistan. The present caliph is his son Mirza Masroor Ahmad (b. 1950), the great grandson of Ghulam Ahmad. The Lahori branch is more moderate in its outlook, affirming Ghulam Ahmad's role as a renewer, but it no longer regards him as a prophet. It also identifies with the wider Muslim community more readily than does the Qadiani branch. Public riots and opposition by Sunni Muslim groups led to an amendment to the Pakistani constitution that declared Ahmadiyya members to be non-Muslims in 1974, followed by an official government ban on group activities in 1984. The name Ahmadiyya has also been used by several Sufi groups, especially that of the Egyptian saint AHMAD AL-BADAWI (ca. 1200–76).

See also CHRISTIANITY AND ISLAM; HINDUISM AND ISLAM; PROPHETS AND PROPHECY; RENEWAL AND REFORM MOVEMENTS.

Further reading: Yohanan Friedmann, *Prophecy Continuous: Aspects of Ahmadi Religious Thought and Its Medieval Background* (Berkeley: University of California Press, 1989); Muhammad Zafrullah Khan, *Ahmadiyyat: The Renaissance of Islam* (London: Tabshir Publications, 1978).

Ahmad Khan, (Sir) Sayyid (1817–1898)
Indian Muslim religious reformer, political figure, and educator

Sayyid Ahmad Khan was among the first to call for the reform of Islam in order to make it more compatible with modern Western thinking, the results of which gave Muslims more of a voice in public life under British rule. When the British put down the Muslim-Hindu uprising against them in 1857 and abolished the MUGHAL DYNASTY, Ahmad Khan felt that the only way for Muslims to recover their influential role in INDIA was to modernize their religion and cooperate with British authorities. While many credit him with inspiring the Muslim nationalist movement that led to the creation of PAKISTAN in 1947, others see him more as a modernizer and educator who valued the idea of Hindu and Muslim cooperation with the British in governing India.

Ahmad Khan was born to a family claiming to be descendants of Muhammad, but of Persian heritage, in DELHI, India. He received a limited formal education in Urdu and Persian in preparation for government service as other members of his family had done for generations. After holding a string of appointments as a minor judge in a number of north Indian towns during his 20s, he began to publish books on Delhi and Mughal history, revealing that despite his inadequate schooling, he had a gift for self-guided learning that allowed him to see things in new ways. When the 1857 uprising occurred, Ahmad Khan remained true to British authorities and subsequently took some pains to demonstrate to them that most Muslims had not supported the rebellion. As part of this effort, he even published a commentary on the Bible in 1862 to promote better understanding between Muslims and Christians. Nonetheless, he also felt that Indians should "honestly, openly and respectfully speak out their grievances" to the British (Gandhi 26).

The real turning point in his career came in 1869, when he journeyed with his two sons to England, where one of them was to be enrolled at Cambridge University with a government scholarship. Ahmad Khan stayed in England for about a year, became familiar with its system of higher EDUCATION, and wrote a number of essays on the life of Muhammad. When he returned to India, he began to publish his ideas for reforming Islam in a new journal, *Tahdhib-i akhlaq* (Refinement of morals). There he criticized areas of FIQH (traditional religious law) that dealt with polygamy, interest, dress, and DIETARY RULES, arguing that many of the traditional rules conflicted with the eternal message of the QURAN, which was in complete conformity with reason, or natural law. He also called for more use of independent judgment (*ijtihad*), especially in relation to modern life. Furthermore, Ahmad Khan implemented what he had learned about British education with the founding in 1875 of the Muhammadan Anglo-Oriental College in the town of ALIGARH, where Muslims and Hindus were to gain a modern education in the arts, science, and law. He also remained involved in Indian politics, opposing the creation of the Indian National Congress in 1885 because he thought that Indians had not yet reached the point at which they could really govern themselves. He believed a status quo arrangement between Indian elites and the British was more realistic,

and he won support for his views from other leading Muslims and Hindus. In appreciation for his efforts, the British awarded him a knighthood in 1888. The Indian nationalist currents prevailed, however, despite Ahmad Khan's dream of cooperative governance of India by British and Indian elites. The last years of his life were spent in Aligarh, continuing his efforts at reform and writing a modernist commentary on the Quran.

See also ALL-INDIA MUSLIM LEAGUE; HINDUISM AND ISLAM; RENEWAL AND REFORM MOVEMENTS.

Further reading: Rajmohan Gandhi, *Eight Lives: A Study of the Hindu-Muslim Encounter* (Albany: State University of New York Press, 1986); Hafeez Malik, *Sir Sayyid Ahmad Khan and Muslim Modernization in India and Pakistan* (New York: Columbia University Press, 1980).

Aisha bint Abi Bakr ibn Abi Quhafa (ca. 614–ca. 678) *one of Muhammad's favorite wives and a leading member of the early Muslim community*

Aisha (Aysha) was born in MECCA to ABU BAKR (d. 634), the close friend of MUHAMMAD and first CALIPH of Islam. Aisha was betrothed to Muhammad in the year 623 in MEDINA, when she was nine years old. Aisha was the only virgin whom Muhammad married, and she never bore any children. She is often remembered as Muhammad's closest and most beloved wife, as the person having the most intimate understanding of the Prophet's practices. As a result, Aisha is credited by Sunnis as the transmitter of more than 2,000 HADITH accounts. After Muhammad's death, she was consulted as an authority on his habits and recommendations.

In 627, Aisha was accused by some Medinan Muslims of committing ADULTERY. During a journey with Muhammad and his caravan, she had become separated from the group while searching for a lost necklace. A young man found her and accompanied her back to Medina safely. Rumors began to circulate, accusing her of engaging in illicit relations with the man. In response to this slander, the QURAN defends Aisha's innocence in Q 24:11–20.

Muhammad died when Aisha was 18 years old; he is reported to have died in her arms in her chambers. After the death of the third caliph, UTHMAN IBN AFFAN in 655, she opposed ALI IBN ABI TALIB's succession to the CALIPHATE, fighting against him in the Battle of the Camel, Islam's first civil war, in 656. For this challenge to Ali, she is often regarded by Shii Muslims with disdain. Although Ali was victorious, Aisha's efforts reflect her defiant and outspoken character as well as the active role she played in political matters. After her military defeat, Aisha returned to MEDINA, spending the remainder of her life transmitting her accounts about the Prophet. She died there in 678 at age 66 and was buried in the al-Baqi CEMETERY.

See also SUNNISM; WOMEN.

Aysha A. Hidayatullah

Further reading: Leila Ahmed, *Women and Gender in Islam: Historical Roots of a Modern Debate* (New Haven, Conn.: Yale University Press, 1992); Denise A. Spellberg, *Politics, Gender, and the Islamic Past: The Legacy of Aisha bint Abi Bakr* (New York: Columbia University Press, 1994).

Ajmer

Ajmer is a major Muslim pilgrimage center located in central Rajasthan in the northwest of INDIA. It has been an urban settlement since at least the 11th century and is located in a region of considerable religious significance to Hindus, Jains, and Muslims. After Muslim armies of the Ghurid dynasty (1149–1206) conquered the Hindu Chauhan dynasty in 1193, Ajmer alternated between Muslim and Hindu rulers until British annexation in 1818.

Ajmer is most famous for being home to the shrine (*dargah*) of Khawaja Muin al-Din (or Muinuddin) Chishti (1135–1229), often called the Prophet of India (*nabi ul-Hind*). Muin al-Din, also known as Gharib Nawaz (the helper of the poor), is undoubtedly the most important and popular of India's many Sufi saints. The Sufi order deriving from him is known as the Chishtiyya, the largest in South Asia, with branches in Southeast Asia, Africa, Europe, and the Americas. The Chishtiyya are known for their advocacy of poverty, avoidance of political power, and meditative practices involving the audition of MUSIC (*samaa*) and devotional songs known as QAWWALI. Pilgrimage to Ajmer is claimed by some to be a substitute for the HAJJ if one is unable to afford the expense of travel to MECCA. All of the Mughal emperors supported the tomb, sponsoring buildings and two giant vessels for the preparation of charitable food offerings to the saint. The tomb of Muin al-Din Chishti remains one of the most important pilgrimage sites in India, drawing Sikhs, Christians, and Hindus as well as Muslims from all over the region, the country, and the world. Since 1955, the shrine has had the distinction of being the only major religious site in India with its own act of parliament specifying its management system. The Dargah Khwaja Saheb Act stipulates an administrator (*nizam*) along with an 11-member oversight board. These officials work with varying degrees of amity with the traditional managers (*khudam*), descendants of the Khwaja's close followers who perform the ritual care of the tomb itself and the council that oversees the *qawwali*. Ajmer is also home to a famous mosque said to have been built by Shams al-Din Iltutmish (r. 1211–36) from the ruins of a temple known as the Two and a Half Day Mosque, or Dhai Din ki Masjid. There are several forts in the area, one predating the Muslim conquest and several built afterward. Among the later mosques is one built by the Mughal emperor AKBAR (r. 1556–1605), who is said to have twice performed the pilgrimage to Ajmer on foot from his capital at Fatehpur Sikri near Agra.

See also DELHI SULTANATE; CHISHTI SUFI ORDER; MUGHAL DYNASTY; SUFISM; ZIYARA.

Anna Bigelow

Further reading: P. M. Currie, *The Shrine and Cult of Muin Al-Din Chishti of Ajmer* (Delhi: Oxford University Press, 1989); Carl W. Ernst and Bruce B. Lawrence, *Sufi Martyrs of Love* (New York: Palgrave Macmillan, 2002).

Akbar (1542–1605) *the most famous emperor of India's Mughal dynasty, known for liberal religious attitudes*

Abu al-Fath Jalal al-Din Muhammad Akbar was the third and most famous ruler of the MUGHAL DYNASTY in INDIA. The son of Humayun (d. 1556) and his Persian wife Hamida Banu, Akbar was born at Umarkot in Sind, northwest India (now part of PAKISTAN). He came to power as a teenager in 1556 and ruled as emperor (*padshah*) until his death in 1605. During his reign, Akbar guided the expansion of the Mughal Empire from its bases in DELHI and Lahore to Rajasthan and Afghanistan in the west, the Himalaya Mountains in the north, Orissa and Bengal in the east, and the northern Deccan Plateau in the south. Akbar's empire dominated India's Indus and Ganges plain. Its centralized government grew wealthy from plunder, tribute, and new tax revenues from agricultural expansion, as well as a significant influx of silver from the New World as a result of trade with European countries.

A flexible attitude toward religion became an important part of Akbar's strategy of governance as he sought to both consolidate his power among fellow Muslims plus win the support of his Hindu subjects. He sponsored the HAJJ to MECCA and patronized Sunni and Shii ULAMA. He included members of the Hindu aristocracy in his government, cancelled taxes imposed on Hindu pilgrims and landholders, and observed Hindu festivals. His HAREM included Christian and Hindu as well as Muslim wives. Akbar performed pilgrimages on foot to the shrine of Muin al-Din Chishti (d. 1236) in AJMER and built a white marble tomb for another Sufi SAINT, Salim al-Chishti, in Fatehpur Sikri, the new capital he constructed near Agra in 1571. Although Akbar himself was illiterate and possibly dyslexic, he funded the translation of Hindu religious texts and held dialogues between representatives of different religions in the House of Worship, a special pavilion in the Fatehpur Sikri palace. Portrayed by his supporters as a sun king and perfect man whose divine light brought peace to the universe, Akbar even attempted to found a new religion for his court known as the Religion of God (Din-i Ilahi). Conservative Sunni ulama opposed Akbar's pluralistic views and innovations, but their reaction did not gain a foothold in the palace until after his death. He was buried in a magnificent tomb near Agra in 1605.

See also CHISHTI SUFI ORDER; HINDUISM AND ISLAM; SIRHINDI, AHMAD.

Further reading: K. A. Nizami, *Akbar and Religion* (New Delhi: Idarah-i-Adabiyat-i-Delli, 1989); John F. Richards, *The Mughal Empire* (Cambridge: Cambridge University Press, 1993).

Akhbari School

The Akhbari School was an influential branch of Shii jurisprudence (*FIQH*) from the 17th century to the 19th century in IRAN, IRAQ, parts of the Arabian Peninsula, and INDIA. Its name comes from the Arabic word *akhbar*, which means "reports" or "traditions," especially traditions about the sayings and actions of any of the 12 Shii Imams (holy men descended from the house of the prophet MUHAMMAD). The Akhbaris, under the leadership of Mulla Muhammad Amin al-Astarabadi (d. 1623), advocated that the SHARIA must be based on the authentic traditions of these infallible Imams and the QURAN. The traditions are found in four books, which were assembled in the 10th and 11th centuries. If there is no reliable or explicit tradition from the imams on a legal matter, then a ruling about that matter is not valid. The Akhbaris rejected the USULI SCHOOL of jurists, who placed emphasis on independent legal reasoning (*IJTIHAD*); they did not require explicit reports from the Imams to make a ruling. The Akhbaris were therefore legal literalists who feared *ijtihad* would corrupt the authentic Islamic tradition. Although the Usulis triumphed over them in the 19th century, they still have a respected place in the wider Shii community of scholars.

See also AHL AL-BAYT; IMAM; SHIISM; TWELVE IMAM SHIISM.

Further reading: Robert Gleave, *Inevitable Doubt: Two Theories of Shii Jurisprudence* (Leiden: E.J. Brill, 2000); Mojan Momen, *An Introduction to Shii Islam* (New Haven, Conn.: Yale University Press, 1985).

Alawi

Technically meaning "pertaining to Ali" in Arabic, *Alawi* is a name for individuals or groups with a special attachment to ALI IBN ABI TALIB (d. 662). The importance of Ali, the cousin and son-in-law of the prophet MUHAMMAD, in Islamic history has led to use of this term for a variety of organizations and groups of people, which are known collectively as *Alawiyya*. Descendants of Ali through either of his sons Hasan (d. 669) and Husayn (d. 680)—and thus descendants of Muhammad (d. 632) through his daughter FATIMA (d. 633)—are often called *Alawi*, in addition to being known as *sharifs* or *sayyids*. Supporters of Ali in the political struggle over the CALIPHATE in early Islamic history are sometimes also referred to as Alawi, though they are more commonly called Shii. Also, claiming descent from Ali and Fatima has been used to legitimate a form of local ruling dynasties, some of which have carried the name Alawi, the prime example being the ALAWID DYNASTY, which has ruled MOROCCO since the 17th century.

Because Ali is considered by most Sufis to represent the esoteric interpretation of the Quran, many Sufi orders trace their spiritual lineages back to him and are known as Alawi orders, as opposed to Bakri orders such as the NAQSHBANDI-YYA SUFI ORDER, which trace their lineages to ABU BAKR (d. 634), the first CALIPH. Other orders were

named Alawi because of their leaders' presumed blood descent from Ali, such as the Alawiyya order of Hadramawt (in the southern region of the Arabian Peninsula) and the Alawiyya branch of the Darqawi order in ALGERIA, which was formed by Ahmad al-Alawi (d. 1934) in the early 20th century.

The two largest religious groups carrying the name Alawi are hereditary groups whose devotion to Ali is so intense that their belief systems are considered heretical by orthodox Sunnis, and they have both been persecuted by them. The Arab Alawis (historically known as Nusayris) of SYRIA, LEBANON, and southern TURKEY and the Turkish and Kurdish Alevis (Turkish rendering of Alawi; historically known as Kizilbash) of Turkey have each preserved esoteric beliefs and secret practices for centuries by living secluded in remote areas in their respective countries. Both see Ali as divine; rather than regarding him as a historical figure, they believe in a cosmic Ali who embodies a manifestation of God.

Alevis in Turkey conduct ceremonies in which mystical songs are sung and a spiritual dance is performed. Numbering several million, they have in recent years become more open about their beliefs and practices and are presently attempting to negotiate a distinctive identity vis-à-vis the nationalist state and Sunni majority. The Arab Alawis limit transmission of their secret beliefs to those who have been formally initiated into their community. Though they constitute a minority in Syria, certain members of the sect have established themselves in important military positions there and have even managed to assume political control over the country through the Syrian BAATH PARTY.

See also AHL AL-BAYT; GHULAT; HUSAYN IBN ALI; SHARIF; SHIISM; SUFISM; TAFSIR; TARIQA.

Mark Soileau

Further reading: Krisztina Kehl-Bodrogi, Barbara Kellner-Heinkele, and Anke Otter-Beaujean, eds., *Syncretistic Religious Communities in the Near East* (New York:

E.J. Brill, 1997); Matti Moosa, *Extremist Shiites: The Ghulat Sects* (Syracuse, N.Y.: Syracuse University Press, 1988); Tord Olsson, Elisabeth Ozdalga, and Catharina Raudvere, *Alevi Identity: Cultural, Religious and Social Perspectives* (Istanbul: Swedish Research Institute in Istanbul, 1998); J. Spencer Trimingham, *The Sufi Orders in Islam* (Oxford, U.K.: Clarendon Press, 1971).

Alawid dynasty (1668–present)

The current ruling dynasty of MOROCCO, the Alawis are one of the few precolonial monarchies to successfully transition into the era of independent nation-states. The dynasty first arose in southeastern Morocco and established its authority throughout the country during the 1660s, under the leadership of Mulay Rashid (d. 1672). Throughout the next 240 years, Alawid sultans ruling from FEZ or Meknes were usually able to control the main urban centers and allied tribes (*bilad al-makhzen*), but they did not receive more than cursory allegiance from the rural hinterlands (*bilad al-siba*).

The situation changed with the establishment of the French protectorate over Morocco in 1912. The French pursued a policy of divide and rule while trying to maintain the illusion of local governance through a compliant Alawid SULTAN (now called "king"). However, King Muhammad V used this approach against them when he rallied nationalist support around his passive resistance to French authority. In 1956, the French administration recognized Moroccan independence under the leadership of its traditional monarchy.

In many ways, the centralizing influence of the French allowed the Alawis to consolidate their control to a degree that was not possible prior to the protectorate. Although the new nation established institutions for participatory government, such as elections and a national assembly, AUTHORITY remained firmly in the hands of the monarchy. Alawid kings (such as Hasan II, r. 1961–99) used their status as *sharifs* (descendants of the prophet MUHAMMAD) to highlight their religiopolitical authority as "Commander of the Faithful." This undercut the rise of radical Islamic challenges to their leadership. The current king, Muhammad VI, seeks to bring much-needed reforms to Moroccan society while retaining ultimate political power. Having ruled Morocco for some 335 years, the Alawid dynasty shows no signs of relinquishing power any time soon.

See also AHL AL-BAYT; COLONIALISM.

Stephen Cory

Further reading: John P. Halstead, *Rebirth of a Nation: The Origins and Rise of Moroccan Nationalism* (Cambridge, Mass: Harvard University Press, 1967); Abdallah Laroui, *The History of the Maghrib: An Interpretive Essay* (Princeton, N.J.: Princeton University Press, 1977).

alchemy (Arabic: *al-kimiya*)

Alchemy is a combination of chemistry and magical knowledge that originated with the Greeks, developed in Islamicate lands, and was transmitted from there to medieval Europe. The outward purpose of alchemy was to transform base metals such as lead into precious ones such as silver and gold. Alchemists engaged in a range of related efforts, such as trying to create life and searching for a medicine to prolong it—an elixir of immortality. Their ideas recognized the ancient Greek division of the natural world into four elements (earth, fire, water, and air) plus four qualities (hot, cold, moist, and dry). They believed in astrology, too, which meant that alchemists thought there was a correspondence between the heavenly world and the earthly world. All matter and spirit, though outwardly different, were really one in essence. Alchemy seeks to play upon this supposed inner unity to change or transform an imperfect or lesser phenomenon into a more perfect, purified one. Not only might lead be transformed into gold, but the human soul itself could be purified of worldly stain. In attempting this, alchemy merges with metaphysics. Muslim alchemists accepted that God was the first creator of the cosmos, but they believed humans could also become creators if they could only unlock the secrets of the universe's elements and qualities and learn how to transform them through their laboratory experimentation.

Although there is a substantial body of medieval Arabic texts on alchemy, the subject is in need of more study before a definitive history can be written. It appears to have become an important topic in Islamicate lands during the ninth and 10th centuries, but some Muslim religious authorities refuted its doctrines because they deviated from what they believed to be true Islam. Early Arabic alchemical literature consisted of translations of Greek texts, especially those associated with Hermes Trismegistos, a mystical figure who was identified with the ancient Egyptian god of writing and wisdom, Thoth. Indeed, EGYPT was thought to be the ancient homeland of the alchemical tradition. To give it a more Islamic stamp, authors constructed a genealogy of sources that included a curious variety of figures such as ALI IBN ABI TALIB (Muhammad's cousin, d. 661), Maria the Copt (one of Muhammad's concubines), Khalid ibn Yazid (an Umayyad prince, d. 683), JAAFAR AL-SADIQ (the sixth Shii imam, d. 765), and a number of Sufis. The grand master of the Islamic alchemical tradition was Jabir ibn Hayyan (d. 815), a shadowy historical figure with Sufi and Shii affinities who was said to have been a friend and disciple of Jaafar al-Sadiq in Baghdad. He was credited with authoring a huge body of alchemical literature, some of which was translated into Latin and transmitted from ANDALUSIA to Europe, where it helped inspire the Renaissance tradition of alchemy. Indeed, modern scholars have concluded that Arab alchemy, with its experimental undertakings and theoretical outlook, played a key role in the development of modern chemistry.

Further reading: S. Nomanul Haq, *Names, Natures, and Things: The Alchemist Jabir ibn Hayyan and His* Kitab al-ahjar (*Book of Stones*) (Dordrecht and Boston: Kluwer Academic, 1994); Donald R. Hill, "The Literature of Arabic Alchemy." In *Religion, Learning and Science in the Abbasid Period*, edited by M. J. L. Young, J. D. Latham, and R. B. Sergeant, 328–341 (Cambridge: Cambridge University Press, 1990).

alcohol   See DIETARY LAWS; FOOD AND DRINK.

Alevi   See ALAWI.

Alexander the Great (356–323 B.C.E.)
youthful conqueror of the ancient world and heroic figure in Islamic tradition

Alexander (Arabic: Iskandar), the youthful king of Macedonia, is considered the greatest conqueror of classical Greek and Roman times (fourth century B.C.E. to fourth century C.E.). He is the heroic subject of the Alexander Romance, a cycle of stories that contributed to the high esteem in which he is held in Islamic tradition.

One should distinguish the legendary content of the Alexander Romance from the historical figure Alexander the Great. The fabulous deeds of the renowned world conqueror are celebrated in medieval literature of the East and the West. There exist romances on Alexander in medieval English, Spanish, French, and German as well as in Ethiopic, Syriac, Armenian, Persian, and Arabic. The first known reference to Alexander in Arabic literature is in the QURAN (Q 18:83–98), where he is called Dhu al-Qarnayn, the "Two-Horned One." The presence of this brief allusion in the sacred book of Islam transforms the Greek pagan Alexander into a Muslim holy man, and Muslim commentators debated over whether he was a prophet. As the Islamic empire spread out from Mecca and Medina into the ancient lands of Mesopotamia (IRAQ) and westward to Spain, quranic exegetes and storytellers of the eighth through 10th centuries from Baghdad to North

Africa sought to elucidate the identity of the Two-Horned One by collecting tales from diverse sources, including Arabic geographical compendiums, local oral literature, the Bible, and the Torah and attributing them to Dhu al-Qarnayn.

By the turn of the first millennium C.E., the romance of Alexander in Arabic had a core centered on the Greek legendary material from a work of the second or third century C.E. known as the *Pseudo-Callisthenes,* wherein the young king and student of Aristotle defeats the Persian army and goes on to take India, China, and lands in between, including the land of the Amazon women, before dying at the age of 32 without making it back home. This material is usually placed in the mouth of the prophet MUHAMMAD, who characterized Dhu al-Qarnayn as one of the faithful whom the Lord had entrusted with the mission of delivering God's message to the remote corners of the earth in preparation for the coming of Islam. Interwoven later into this narrative in the *Tales of the Prophets* literature were episodes of an apparent Arab-Islamic elaboration: the construction of a great barrier to keep the barbarian tribes of Gog and Magog from harassing the people of the civilized world until JUDGEMENT DAY, the voyage to the end of the Earth to witness the sun set in a pool of boiling mud, and Dhu al-Qarnayn's expedition into the Land of Darkness in search of the Fountain of Life accompanied by his companion KHADIR (the Green-One). God veils from Dhu al-Qarnayn the spring of rejuvenating waters because he has become too ambitious in seeking to reveal the secrets of God's creation. For example, he enters forbidden lands inhabited by angels and knocks on the doors of PARADISE itself. The theme of the hero's arrogance is delicately balanced with his piety as seen in his frequent prayer for the strength to complete his mission to call the people of the earth to humble themselves before their creator. Relating numerous encounters with sea serpents, beasts, angels, and enchanted castles, the medieval Islamic versions of the Alexander legend were a favorite among Muslim peoples for many centuries.

See also ARABIC LANGUAGE AND LITERATURE; PROPHETS AND PROPHECY.

Z. David Zuwiyya

Further reading: Wheeler M. Thackston, trans., *Tales of the Prophets* (Boston: Twayne Publishers, 1978); Albert Mugrdich Wolohojian, trans., *The Romance of Alexander the Great by Pseudo-Callisthenes* (New York: Columbia University Press, 1969); Z. David Zuwiyya, *Islamic Legends of Alexander the Great* (Binghamton, N.Y.: Global Publications, 2001).

Algeria (Official name: People's Democratic Republic of Algeria)

One of the largest countries in Africa and the Arab world, Algeria (Arabic: al-Jazair) is located on the Mediterranean coast bordered by TUNISIA and LIBYA to the east, by MOROCCO to the west, and to the south across the Sahara desert by Western Sahara, Mali, Mauritania, and Niger. It is approximately 2.4 million square kilometers, or the equivalent of the continental United States west of the Rocky Mountains. Its population of approximately 33 million (2008) is of mixed BERBER and ARAB ethnicity (except a 1 percent European minority) and largely Sunni Muslim. Religious minorities include Christians and Jews (1 percent). Although the official language of Algeria is Arabic, French and various Berber (Amazigh) languages are also widely spoken. Asserting a distinct Berber language and ethnicity is an important issue for many communities centered in the Kabyle region. Geographically, while the northern regions are mountainous and provide fertile agricultural land, more than 80 percent of the country lies in the Sahara, where rich hydrocarbon and mineral resources are found. The major cities are the capital, Algiers, Constantine, Tlemcen, and Oran.

As early as the fifth century B.C.E., Algeria's indigenous people, Berbers, had established complex economies and within two centuries formed two major kingdoms. The region was then ruled by Romans, Vandals, Byzantines, and ultimately Arabs, who in the seventh century C.E. invaded from the east, initiating a long slow process of Arabization and Islamization of the native population. Political rule of the area for Arabs remained elusive, however, alternating between Berber kingdoms and Arab dynasties until the 16th century, when Ottomans extended their power south from ISTANBUL and took control of Algeria. Throughout this period, North Africa provided a vital corridor for economic and cultural exchanges between the Middle East, Islamicate Spain, and sub-Saharan Africa. Also notable in this period was the development of prominent Sufi (*marabout*) brotherhoods (including the Qadiriyya, Tijaniyya, and Rahmaniyya) that were organized around charismatic spiritual leaders and were renowned for fostering spiritual and political communities that transcended powerful tribal affiliations.

From 1830 to 1962, France occupied and administered Algeria as a colony. Early resistance was led by ABD AL-QADIR, a young man educated in the QADIRI SUFI ORDER, but ended in his defeat in 1847 and exile to DAMASCUS in 1855. Algerians ultimately gained independence from France on July 5, 1962, after a protracted and bloody war lasting eight years. They established a secular socialist state led by the revolutionary FLN (Front de Liberation National) party, which has governed uninterrupted until the present day. During the cold war, Algeria became prominent in the nonaligned movement, a bloc of countries committed to creating a third world force through a policy of nonalignment to the United States and the Soviet Union. Beginning in the 1980s, the state faced an increasingly powerful Islamic opposition movement that resulted in major electoral victories for the FIS (Front Islamic du Salut) in 1990 and 1991. The military responded by nullifying the election results, which touched off years of violence between militant Islamist groups and the Algerian military in which up to 100,000 civil-

ians are believed to have been killed. By 2005, the major violence had subsided, and moderate Islamist groups were brought into the government. Many core issues such as the role of religion in Algerian society, government corruption, and the desire of Kabylie Berbers for more autonomy remain unresolved.

See also ALMOHAD DYNASTY; OTTOMAN DYNASTY; POLITICS AND ISLAM; SUFISM.

Michelle Zimney

Further reading: Robert Malley, *The Call from Algeria: Third Worldism, Revolution, and the Turn to Islam* (Berkeley: University of California Press, 1996); Hugh Roberts, *The Battlefield: Algeria 1988–2002, Studies in a Broken Polity* (New York: Verso, 2003); John Ruedy, *Modern Algeria: The Origins and Development of a Nation* (Bloomington: Indiana University Press, 1992).

Aligarh

A city in Uttar Pradesh (a state in northern INDIA), Aligarh first came under Muslim influence at the end of the 12th century during the rule of Qutb al-Din Aybak (r. 1206–11), the SULTAN at DELHI. IBN BATTUTA (d. 1369), the great Muslim traveler, visited Aligarh during his journeys in India. The region remained under Muslim rule through the Mughal period until 1785, when it was conquered by the Hindu Marathas and eventually annexed by the British in 1803.

The town is most famous for an educational institute founded by Sir SAYYID AHMAD KHAN (d. 1898) in 1871. Beginning as a boys' school in 1878, the Muhammadan Anglo-Oriental (MAO) College was incorporated there. The curriculum incorporated Islamic sciences with instruction in Arabic and modern EDUCATION modeled on the British system with instruction in English. Although the college's mission has always been focused on uplifting the Muslim population of India, the enrollment has also been open to non-Muslims. The goal of the institution was to create an educational center that could produce a progressively educated Muslim population who could excel under the British regime as the Hindus had. Ahmad Khan himself advocated a critical reevaluation of Islamic law in which the Quran and the hadith (to a limited extent) would be considered. He believed true Islam was a wholly rational faith and entirely compatible with modern science. Nonetheless, the Islamic studies curriculum was not confined to Ahmad Khan's idiosyncratic approach. Several faculty members at the college, including an Arabic instructor, have been Europeans. MAO College became Aligarh University in 1920, and in 1925, the women's MADRASA that had been affiliated with it became the Aligarh Women's College. The university now has four areas of study: arts, science, engineering, and THEOLOGY. It became a center for nationalist politics during India's struggle for independence, with some of its students and faculty promoting a united India, while others actively supported the creation of PAKISTAN as a separate Muslim state. Many faculty departed with the partition in 1947, but Aligarh continues to be a top university to the present day.

See also ALL-INDIA MUSLIM LEAGUE; HINDUISM AND ISLAM; RENEWAL AND REFORM MOVEMENTS; SECULARISM.

Anna Bigelow

Further reading: David Lelyveld, *Aligarh's First Generation: Muslim Solidarity in British India* (Princeton, N.J.: Princeton University Press, 1977); K. A. Nizami, *History of the Aligarh Muslim University* (Delhi: Idarah-i Adabiyat-i Delli, 1995).

Ali ibn Abi Talib (ca. 597–661) *cousin and son-in-law of Muhammad, the fourth caliph of the Sunni Muslim community, and first imam of the Shia*

A native of MECCA, he was one of the first persons to accept Islam after Muhammad's wife KHADIJA (d. 619). He grew up in Muhammad's household and married his daughter FATIMA. Ali's courage in battle at Badr (624) and elsewhere converted him into a chivalric hero and warrior saint of Muslim lore.

Ali is the focus of controversy in the succession to leadership of the Muslim community after Muhammad's death in 632. This resulted in the sectarian division between Sunni and Shii Islam. The partisans (*shia*) of Ali believed that MUHAMMAD appointed him his successor following the Farewell Pilgrimage to MECCA a few months before Muhammad's death. Many Shia have considered this a divinely inspired designation that included the descendants of Muhammad's household through Ali.

Following Muhammad's death, ABU BAKR (d. 634) was elected as the first CALIPH. In order to avoid a division in the early Muslim community, Ali recognized Abu Bakr's right to rule and that of the next two caliphs, UMAR IBN AL-KHATTAB (d. 644) and UTHMAN IBN AFFAN (d. 656). Ali was elected the fourth caliph under controversial circumstances following the murder of Uthman. Accused of complicity in the assassination, Ali's period of rule was mired in civil war with his rival, Muawiya ibn Abi Sufyan, leader of the powerful Umayya clan of Mecca. His support dwindled when a faction, the KHAWARIJ (seccessionists), rebelled against him during the Battle of Siffin (657) because he had submitted the conflict with Muawiya to arbitration. Ali's forces succeeded in defeating these rebels at Nahrawan in 658, but one of the Khawarij assassinated him in Kufa, IRAQ, in 661. Muawayya (r. 660–80) became the next caliph and founded the UMAYYAD CALIPHATE in Syria.

While some "extremist" Shiis virtually deify Ali, most consider belief in Muhammad's designation of Ali as his successor a religious duty alongside belief in the oneness of God and the prophethood of Muhammad. The MARTYRDOM of Ali, and especially the massacre of his son al-Husayn and his companions at the Battle of KARBALA (680), made the paradigm of redemptive suffering a characteristic of Shii salvation history.

Shiis and many Sufis regard him as a saint for his renowned ASCETICISM. Indeed, many Sufi orders trace the genealogy of their spiritual descent (*silsila*) directly back to Ali. Ali is remembered as a model of socio-political and religious righteousness that defied worldly corruption and social injustice. His shrine in Najaf, Iraq, is a major pilgrimage site, and the feast of GHADIR KHUMM (18 Dhu al-Hijjah, the twelfth month on the Muslim CALENDAR), which commemorates Muhammad's appointment of Ali as his successor, is an important holiday for Shii Muslims.

See also AHL AL-BAYT; FITNA, SHIISM.

Linda G. Jones

Further reading: S. H. M. Jafri, *The Origins and Early Development of Shia Islam* (London and New York: Longman, 1979); Wilferd Madelung, *The Succession to Muhammad: A Study of the Early Caliphate* (Cambridge: Cambridge University Press, 1977); Abu Jafar Muhammad ibn Jarir al-Tabari, *The History of al-Tabari*. Translated by C. E. Bosworth et al. (Albany: State University of New York Press, 1985–).

Allah

The Arabic term *Allah* is the main one used for the unique deity worshipped in the Islamic religion. It is a contraction that literally means "the God" (Arabic: *al-ilah*), and it occurs about 2,700 times in the QURAN alone. Belief in only one god who is all-powerful and merciful and who has no partners or equals is the most important Islamic doctrine, and Muslims constantly express it in their worship, religious MUSIC, and visual arts. For example, the SHAHADA, the first pillar of Islam, requires that Muslims testify "There is no god but God (Allah)." This phrase is repeated in daily PRAYERS and is written on MOSQUES, banners, and posters in all Muslim communities. Among the most important statements about God in the Quran are those found in the chapter entitled "Sincerity" (Q 112) and in the "Throne Verse" (Q 2:255), which

states, "Allah! There is no god but he, the living, the everlasting. He neither rests nor sleeps." The monotheistic ideal also dominates Islamic THEOLOGY, PHILOSOPHY, law, and even its historical vision. On the basis of the Quran, HADITH, and religious doctrine, Muslims believe that Allah is the same god worshipped by Jews and Christians. It should also be noted that Arabic-speaking followers of Judaism and Christianity in the Middle East use the word *Allah* for God, although their theologies differ from those of Muslims.

Historical evidence indicates that Allah was the name of an ancient Arabian high god in a pantheon of other gods and goddesses like those found in other ancient Middle Eastern cultures. Worshipping him as the only real god may have started before the seventh century in Arabia, but it was in the Quranic revelations delivered by MUHAMMAD as the prophet of Islam between 610 and 632 that the monotheistic ideal received its first clear expression among ARAB peoples. In the Quran, Allah is portrayed as the creator of the universe who brings life and death, never sleeps, and knows, sees, and hears everything. He is both eternal and infinite, and unlike the ancient gods, he does not have parents or children. This belief also rejects Christian notions of God as a father and JESUS as his son. In the Quran, God commands human beings to remember him and to submit to him, but he also shows them his kindness and compassion. He sends prophets such as ABRAHAM, MOSES, JESUS, and Muhammad to guide people to salvation. He can reward them for their faith and good deeds and punish them for their infidelity and sins. As master of JUDGMENT DAY, he will resurrect the dead at the end of time and hold them accountable for what they did in their lives, which means that he can either let them enter the gardens of PARADISE or send them to the FIRE of hell.

According to the prevailing opinion in Islam, God cannot be completely known or perceived by the human mind or the senses; rather than being close by, he stands at great distance from his creation. He also cannot be represented in a picture or statue, which is considered to be IDOLATRY. However, he can be partially known through the Quran, which is his speech, and the "signs" he provides in nature and the course of history. He can also be known through his qualities, many of which are described in the 99 NAMES OF GOD. Muslims through the centuries have nonetheless sought to bridge the gap between God and creation with intermediary figures such as ANGELS, prophets, and SAINTS. Among the Shia, imams (revered descendants of Muhammad's family) play this role. An important part of the Islamic mystical tradition understood the universe to be the result of emanations of light from God, which were embodied most fully by the PERFECT MAN. Some mystics believed this to be the idealized Adam or Muhammad and that those with true spiritual insight might therefore come to know God through this reality. Others anticipated a mystical vision of God in the course of a spiritual ascent or in the afterlife.

See also ANTHROPOMORPHISM; AYA; FIVE PILLARS; MONOTHEISM; PROPHETS AND PROPHECY.

Further reading: Sachiko Murata and William C. Chittick, *The Vision of Islam* (New York: Paragon House, 1994); Fazlur Rahman, *Major Themes in the Quran* (Minneapolis and Chicago: Bilbliotheca Islamica, 1980); W. Montgomery Watt, *Islamic Philosophy and Theology: An Extended Survey.* 2d ed. (Edinburgh: Edinburgh University Press, 1985).

All-India Muslim League (also known as the Muslim League)

Incorporated in December 1906 in Dacca (in modern BANGLADESH), the All-India Muslim League (AIML) played a leading role in the Indian independence movement and the creation of PAKISTAN. It grew out of the ALIGARH movement that had aimed to give Muslims more of a voice in British India. It supported British rule until 1912, when, under the leadership of the journalist and reformer Muhammad Ali (d. 1931), a resolution was passed calling for self-government. During World War I, however, the AIML again supported the British, as did the Indian National Congress (INC), the main Indian nationalist organization. During this period, the INC and AIML worked together, and both organizations passed the Lucknow Pact in 1916 calling for a wider franchise for Indians, larger representations for Indians on councils and in regional governments, and separate electorates for Muslims. During these proceedings, MUHAMMAD ALI JINNAH (d. 1948) emerged as one of the chief figures in the AIML.

Jinnah, a lawyer, had joined the INC in 1896 and the AIML in 1913. In 1920, Jinnah quit the INC in opposition to the management of INC leader Mohandas K. Gandhi's (d. 1948) first anti-British action that ended in some chaos. The break between the INC and the AIML and other Muslim organizations continued to widen as the independence struggle developed. By the 1930's, Muslim demands for protections were increasingly ignored as the INC emerged as the chief Indian negotiator with the colonial government. Up to this point, the AIML's efforts to position itself as the sole voice for India's Muslim population had not been very successful, and a large number of seats in local legislative councils were lost in the 1935 elections. The AIML was widely seen as an urban, elite, Westernized organization out of touch with both the largely rural population and the Muslim religious establishment. After the 1935 electoral losses, Jinnah led the campaign to consolidate the Muslim vote, eventually establishing himself and the AIML as the "sole spokesman" for Indian Muslim interests. In 1940, Jinnah and the AIML met at Lucknow and called for a separate state for India's Muslims. At first, this initiative got a lukewarm reception, especially in Punjab and Bengal, the regions with the largest Muslim populations, where local coalition parties of landlords based in the countryside were more successful. However, due to the INC's apparent Hindu bias, their opposition to significant concessions to Muslims, and the activism of Jinnah and other AIML leaders, the tide was turned. The AIML emerged victorious in the 1945 elections, winning 460 of 533 Muslim legislative seats.

After World War II, the final status negotiations with the British (who were rapidly losing interest in either retaining their authority or seeing through the negotiations to maintain a unified India) led to the 1947 partition of India. Jinnah called the new Muslim majority nation of PAKISTAN "moth-eaten," as the eastern and western halves of the country were hundreds of miles apart, separated by Hindu majority India. As the governor-general of Pakistan, Jinnah attempted to establish a secular CONSTITUTION for the new nation-state. However, following his death in 1948, a resolution was passed in 1950 affirming the Islamic identity of the state in which no law would be passed in violation of the SHARIA. During the era of political turmoil that followed partition and independence, the All-India Muslim League disbanded, reforming as the Muslim League (ML) in the newly independent nations. In Pakistan, the ML failed to establish itself as an effective political party. The lack of infrastructure, financial crises, and the ML's secular stance contributed to its eventual marginalization in Pakistani politics. In Bangladesh (formerly East Pakistan) the ML has not been a major factor in politics because it is viewed as the chief architect of a Pakistan in which the western part of the country dominated the eastern part in terms of language, resources, and authority. In India, the Muslim League no longer has a significant political voice, and only one member of parliament has represented the ML from the state of Kerala in 1999 and 2004.

See also AWAMI LEAGUE; HINDUISM AND ISLAM; SECULARISM.

Anna Bigelow

Further reading: Ayesha Jalal, *The Sole Spokesman: Jinnah, the Muslim League, and the Demand for Pakistan* (Cambridge: Cambridge University Press, 1985); Ian Talbot, *Provincial Politics and the Pakistan Movement: The Growth of the Muslim League in Northwest and Northeast India 1937–47* (Karachi: Oxford University Press, 1988).

Almohad dynasty (1123–1269)

A movement founded in southern MOROCCO by religious reformer and self-proclaimed MAHDI (messianic figure) MUHAMMAD IBN TUMART (1078?–1130), the Almohads managed to unite North Africa and Islamicate Spain under their authority during the late 12th and early 13th centuries. Their name derives from the Arabic *al-muwahhidun,* "those who proclaim the God's oneness."

Upon returning to his native Morocco in 1121 after an extended trip in the Islamicate east, Ibn Tumart recruited followers from among the Masmuda Berbers of the Anti-Atlas Mountains in the region near Marrakesh. Teaching a rigorous doctrine centered on the concept of God's oneness (TAWHID), Ibn Tumart and his disciple Abd al-Mumin (d. 1163) organized the Berbers into an effective fighting force. Abd al-Mumin succeeded Ibn Tumart as caliph upon the latter's death in 1130 and led an extended conquest of North Africa and Islamicate Spain, taking Marrakesh (1147), Seville (1147), TUNISIA (1160), and Tripolitania (1160). Upon securing Almohad power in North Africa, Abd al-Mumin established his family members as heads of state, bequeathing the caliphate to his sons and grandsons.

Under the first four caliphs, the Almohad empire reached the height of its military, political, and cultural influence. Although they initially experienced success in turning back the Christian reconquest (Spanish: Reconquista) in ANDALUSIA, the Almohad army later suffered a disastrous defeat at Las Navas de Tolosa (1212) that left southern Spain open for further Christian advances. The Almohad political-religious system, administered by a BERBER elite, was initially quite cohesive, but the Almohads failed to establish Ibn Tumart's doctrine as a replacement for Maliki Islam, and they began to lose control of the remote regions of their empire by the early 13th century. Later Almohad caliphs would publicly disown the religious doctrines of Ibn Tumart.

Almohad cultural influences included an austere architectural style, of which numerous examples remain in Morocco and Spain. Despite earning a reputation for intolerance toward Christian and Jewish minorities, Almohad openness to philosophical ideas allowed philosophers such as Ibn Tufayl (d. 1185) and IBN RUSHD (Averroës, d. 1198) to expound their teachings. However, Ibn Rushd's works were later banned and burned by the CALIPH Abu Yusuf Yaqub al-Mansur (r. 1184–99). The Sufi movement also expanded under the Almohads, epitomized by the influential mystic IBN AL-ARABI (d. 1240). Nevertheless, the Almohad inability to maintain their vast holdings, win the support of the Maliki ULAMA, defeat Christian opponents in Spain, or subdue competing Berber tribes in North Africa led to their ultimate downfall. In 1269, the only dynasty to successfully unite North Africa perished, as Marrakesh fell before the rising tide of their rivals, the Merinid Berbers.

See also ALMORAVID DYNASTY; MALIKI LEGAL SCHOOL.

Stephen Cory

Further reading: Richard Fletcher, *Moorish Spain* (Berkeley: University of California Press, 1992); Abd al-Wahid al-Marrakushi, *History of the Almohades,* ed. R. Dozy (Leiden: E.J. Brill, 1881); Roger Le Tourneau, *The Almohad Movement in North Africa in the Twelfth and Thirteenth Century* (Princeton, N.J.: Princeton University Press, 1969).

Almoravid dynasty (1042–1147)

A BERBER dynasty that arose from the deserts of southern Mauritania, the Almoravids conquered MOROCCO and Islamicate Spain during the second half of the 11th century. The founder of the Almoravid movement, a teacher of Maliki law named Abd Allah ibn Yasin (d. 1058), was originally brought to the desert by a Berber chief, who was eager for his people to receive proper Islamic instruction. Imposing harsh religious discipline upon the tribesmen, Ibn Yasin developed a core group of followers, whom he later sent to conquer the surrounding lands and enforce his rigorous interpretation of Islam. Although Ibn Yasin was killed in battle in 1058, his successors, Abu Bakr ibn Umar (d. 1087) and Yusuf ibn Tashfin (d. 1106) extended Almoravid rule southward into Ghana and northward throughout Morocco and into Islamicate Spain. After establishing their new capitol of Marrakesh in southern Morocco, Almoravid armies first crossed the Strait of Gibraltar in 1086 to support Muslim princes under siege from the Christian reconquest (Spanish: Reconquista). By the death of Ibn Tashfin in 1106, the Almoravids were supreme rulers over Islamicate Spain.

Ironically, historians since IBN KHALDUN (d. 1406) have speculated that the conquest of Spain was actually the first step in the Almoravid downfall. They argue that when the Almoravids encountered the cultured lifestyle of ANDALUSIA, they eventually abandoned the disciplined ways that had led to their success. Regardless, the Almoravid military bogged down in Spain, and their administrators encountered resistance from the population, who resented domination by what they thought were uncouth desert tribesmen. By the 1140s, much of Andalusia was in open revolt, while the Almohad movement was waging a successful war against the Almoravids in Morocco. The Almohad victory was complete upon the death of the last Almoravid SULTAN in 1147, and the Almoravid dynasty came to an end as suddenly as it had burst upon the political scene less than 100 years earlier. However, the lasting influence of the Almoravids is seen in the continued dominance of the MALIKI LEGAL SCHOOL, which they helped to establish in North Africa.

See also ALMOHAD DYNASTY; WEST AFRICA.

Stephen Cory

Further reading: Richard Fletcher, *Moorish Spain* (Berkeley: University of California Press, 1992); Hugh Kennedy, *Muslim Spain: A Political History of al-Andalus* (London: Longman, 1996); H. T. Norris, "New Evidence on the Life of Abdullah b. Yasin and the Origins of the Almoravid Movement." *Journal of African History* 12 (1971): 255–268.

almsgiving

Almsgiving is a form of charity. It represents an ethical principle, embraced by most societies and religions, that people who enjoy wealth and prosperity have a moral obligation to assist those who are less fortunate and to financially support institutions that serve the needs of individuals and the public. In Islam this obligation is understood to be both a service to God and a service to people. Those who perform this service are promised rewards in this life and in the AFTERLIFE. There are two basic forms of almsgiving in Islam: *zakat,* one of the FIVE PILLARS of worship, and *sadaqa,* a voluntary form of giving. Both are authorized in the QURAN and HADITH, and both are governed by the SHARIA. Other kinds of charitable giving in Islam are perpetual endowments (known as *waqfs*) and a special tithe (*khums*) the Shia give to their religious leaders. Some hadith declare that almost any act of kindness toward another is almsgiving. The linkage of *zakat* with belief and worship is expressed in the Quran:

> Goodness is not that you turn your face to the east or west. Rather goodness is that a person believe in God, the last day, the angels, the book, and the prophets; that he gives wealth out of love to relatives, orphans, the needy, travelers, slaves; that he performs prayer, and that he gives *zakat.* (Q 2:177)

Zakat is based on the Arabic word meaning "to be pure" (*zaka*). Purity is a key concept in Islamic religious thought and practice. It governs the performance of the other religious duties—prayer,

fasting, and the hajj, as well as the dietary laws. In regard to the act of giving *zakat,* the underlying principle is that such an act, done in kindness for the betterment of the needy or the community, purifies the giver and the giver's property. Furthermore, the Quran promises that believers who pay *zakat* will see an increase in their own prosperity (Q 30:39).

According to the sharia, payment of *zakat* is required of adult Muslims each year at the end of RAMADAN, the month of fasting. It is calculated on the basis of one's net income from lawful (*halal*) sources after expenses for food, clothing, and shelter for oneself and dependents have been paid. Traditionally, the tax has been assessed on agricultural yields, livestock production, possession of lawful merchandise, gold, silver, and cash. The general tax rate is 2.5 percent, but there are higher rates for minerals extracted from the ground, war booty, buried property belonging to people who have perished, and property salvaged from the sea. Based on the Quran and hadith, Muslim jurists have also identified those who qualify to receive alms: the hungry and the homeless, the ill, students, recent converts, slaves so that they can be freed, those who struggle "in the way of God," travelers, and those needing assistance in repaying their debts.

Almsgiving became a religious duty after MUHAMMAD established the first Muslim community in MEDINA in 622. It was one of the first obligations to be met by converts. The first serious conflict over APOSTASY occurred when converted Arab tribes refused to pay *zakat* after Muhammad died in 632. As the Muslim empire grew, rulers and religious scholars systematized the rules governing almsgiving, because this was the main form of taxation levied against Muslims for the well-being of the community. Details on how rigorously *zakat* laws were followed are lacking for much of Islam's history. In modern times, Muslims often give alms privately without intervention of the state, and in many communities assistance with payment and calculating the amount due is available to them from *zakat* committees. There are even *zakat* calculators available on the Internet. People may donate to needy individuals or to MOSQUES, charitable organizations, and educational institutions. Only a few modern nations, such as SAUDI ARABIA, Kuwait, Libya, PAKISTAN, and SUDAN, have attempted to administer almsgiving through government agencies. In the aftermath of the September 11, 2001, attacks on the United States, a number of Islamic charitable organizations connected with *zakat* have been investigated or closed down in the United States and abroad because of suspected links with with radical groups engaging in terrorist activities. Muslims living in the United States and Europe have had to look for other ways to fulfill their almsgiving obligations because of this.

Further reading: Laleh Bakhtiyar, *Encyclopaedia of Islamic Law: A Compendium of the Major Schools* (Chicago: ABC International Group, 1996); Azim Nanji, "Ethics and Taxation: The Perspective of Islamic Tradition." *Journal of Religious Ethics* 13 (1985): 161–178.

alphabet

Since Islam is a religion found in many different cultures, its followers speak many different languages, which are written in several alphabets. The most important of these is the Arabic alphabet, consisting of 28 letters written as a script from right to left. This means that there is no separate printed form for individual Arabic letters, as there is in English; it also means that the shape of the letter can be affected by its position at the beginning, middle, or end of the word. All the letters are consonants, but three of them can also represent long vowels: ā, ī, and ū. There are no letters for the short vowels (a, i, and u); they are either not written, or they are represented by optional markings called diacritics written above and below the consonants. Historically, the Arabic alphabet evolved from ancient Semitic scripts that were used by people living in northern Arabia and SYRIA. It gained widespread use only after the

appearance of Islam in the seventh century, however. Nearly all of the most authoritative Islamic religious texts, including the Quran, were originally written in the Arabic cursive script.

Through the centuries, as Islamic religion and civilization spread to new lands, native peoples began to adopt the Arabic language and use its alphabet to write their own languages. Not all of these people were Muslims; Middle Eastern Jews and Christians adopted both the Arabic language and alphabet. By the 10th century, Arabic letters were adapted to write the Persian language and then related dialects such as Kurdish and Pashto, as well as the Turkic languages. To do this, additional consonants were required to represent sounds occurring in those languages but that do not occur in Arabic (for example, *p* as in pony, *ch* as in chair, and *g* as in game). Urdu, which is today the official language of PAKISTAN, is based on a Persianized form of the Arabic alphabet. Arabic letters have also been used to write languages spoken in medieval Spain, Africa, and Southeast Asia. Alongside the Roman alphabet, which is used to write English and other Western languages, the Arabic alphabet is one of the most widely used in the world today. TURKEY, one of the largest Muslim countries in the Middle East, switched from the Arabic alphabet to the Roman in 1928, when its government was being reconstituted along strongly secular lines. However, the Arabic alphabet is still widely used in Arab countries, and (in its Persianized form) in IRAN, AFGHANISTAN, and Pakistan. Moreover, it has been successfully adapted for print media (newspapers, magazines, books, etc.) and the internet, so it continues to play an important role in the communication of religious and secular information, knowledge, and opinions in the modern world.

The Arabic alphabet is especially important in Islam because it was used for writing the words Muslims believe God revealed to MUHAMMAD in the seventh century. Most Muslims attempt to learn the Arabic letters so that they can read the QURAN. Some 29 suras in the Quran begin with letters written separately, and some suras even take their names from these letters, like suras Ta Ha (Q 20) and Ya Sin (Q 36). There has been much disagreement about what the letters mean, but some Muslims explain that their meaning is a mystery known only to God. Muslims also have assigned numerical value to individual letters. For example, many Muslims living in Asia have signs in their businesses and vehicles bearing the number 786, which is the numerical sum of the letters in the phrase *bismillah al-rahman al-rahim* (In the name of God, the most compassionate and most merciful), known as the BASMALA. It is believed to bring good fortune and divert the EVIL EYE. Shii and Sufi Muslims have a long tradition of interpreting the secret meanings of Arabic letters. This can be seen in the interpretation of the the three letters *alif-lam-mim* that begin the second chapter of the Quran. Sufis believed the *alif* represented Allah, that the *mim* represented Muhammad, and that the *lam* represented Gabriel, the angel who acted as the emissary between God and Muhammad in delivering the Quran. In some contexts, the calculation of the numerical values of letters has been used in numerology to foretell the future and write magic spells. This was known as *jafr.*

See also ARABIC LANGUAGE AND LITERATURE; CALLIGRAPHY; PERSIAN LANGUAGE AND LITERATURE; TURKISH LANGUAGE AND LITERATURE.

Further reading: Kristin Brustad, Mahmoud al-Batal, and Abbas Tonsi, *Alif Baa: Introduction to Arabic Letters and Sounds* (Washington, D.C.: Georgetown University Press, 2001); Peter Daniels and W. Bright, eds., *The World's Writing Systems* (New York: Oxford University Press, 1996); Gerhard Endress, *An Introduction to Islam* (New York: Columbia University Press, 1988); Annemarie Schimmel, *Mystical Dimensions of Islam* (Chapel Hill: University of North Carolina Press, 1975).

amulets and talismans

An amulet is a material object believed to protect a person or possession against evil forces.

A talisman is an object believed to provide good fortune or have some benefit for a person or possession, though it can also have a protective function as well. The two terms are often used interchangeably. Amulets and talismans are often small enough to be worn on the body, but they can also be placed in a person's home, workplace, or vehicle. Their use is attested in the religions of the ancient world, in tribal societies, and among the followers of the major religious traditions, including the Abrahamic religions, Judaism, Christianity, and Islam. In the comparative study of religions, scholars have classified the use of amulets and talismans as a form of magic—a way of looking at the world based on a belief that a person can manipulate natural and supernatural forces for good or bad purposes.

Though some Muslim scholars and reformers have criticized the use of amulets and talismans, making and wearing them is a widespread practice in traditional and modern Islamicate societies. They are known by various Arabic terms, the most common being *hijab, hirz, tawiz, tamima,* and *tilsam.* They can be simple objects, such as a bead, stone, piece of jewelry, relic from a holy place, or a drawing of an unusual animal or supernatural being. They often consist of pieces of paper with the NAMES OF GOD, angels, saints, and JINNIS written on them, or select passages from the QURAN, such as the last two chapters (Q 113 and 114), which are called the "protection-seeking ones," and the Throne Verse (Q 2:256). More elaborate amulets and talismans combine these elements with drawings of squares containing magic numbers, astrological symbols, and letters. Such magical objects are placed in a cloth bag, leather pouch, or case made of gold or silver and worn on the body. Small copies of the entire Quran are also commonly used as amulets and talismans.

People believe that amulets and talismans can help channel the power of blessing (BARAKA) to protect a child or valuable possessions, obtain a cure from a physical or mental illness, spark a love affair, facilitate conception and childbirth, induce trees to bear fruit, combat the EVIL EYE, cast out evil spirits, or bring harm to an opponent. There are even amulets that are believed to offer protection from bullets and troublesome government officials. Amulets and talismans are usually obtained from a SHAYKH or some other person claiming specialized knowledge for making ones that are effective, and they are used by Muslims and non-Muslims.

See also CHILDREN; WOMEN.

Further reading: Eleanor Abdella Doumato, *Getting God's Ear: Women, Islam, and Healing in Saudi Arabia and the Gulf* (New York: Columbia University Press, 2000); Joyce B. Flueckiger, "'The Vision Was of Written Words: Negotiating Authority as a Female Muslim Healer in South India.'" In *Syllables of Sky: Studies of South Indian Civilization,* edited by David Shulman, 249–282 (Oxford: Oxford University Press, 1995); Edward W. Lane, *An Account of the Manners and Customs of the Modern Egyptians* (New York: Dover Publications, 1973).

Andalusia

Andalusia (*al-Andalus*) is the name given to regions of Spain and Portugal under Muslim rule between 711 and 1492. It also evokes romantic memories of a "golden age" in that land when culture, learning, and the ARTS flourished and Muslim, Christian, and Jew lived together in harmony. The word *Andalusia* is thought to originally come from the name of a Germanic tribe, the Vandals, who had occupied the Iberian Peninsula and North Africa in the fifth and sixth centuries, before the Muslim conquests. At its greatest extent, Andalusia reached from the Mediterranean shores of southern Spain northward almost to the Pyrenees Mountains. Its northern borders, however, were never secure, as European Christian armies drove southward in what is called the Reconquista, or the "reconquest," of Spain. This started in the 11th century and ended with the fall of Granada, the last Muslim stronghold, to

La Giralda, the minaret for the 12th-century Almohad mosque of Seville, converted into a bell tower for the city's cathedral in the 16th century *(Federico R. Campo)*

the armies of Ferdinand and Isabella in 1492, the same year Columbus landed in the New World.

Muslim armies first crossed from North Africa into Andalusia by way of the Strait of Gibraltar in 711. They soon established themselves in the peninsula's major cities: Malaga, CORDOBA, Toledo, Barcelona, and Zaragosa. The new postconquest society that subsequently arose was dominated by an ARAB Muslim elite and BERBER allies from North Africa who had only recently converted to ISLAM. The Muslims of Andalusia came to be called the Moors by Europeans, but that is not what they called themselves. Most remained loyal to their tribal, family, and regional identities, which contributed to the factionalism that characterized much of the political history of

Andalusia. The indigenous subject populations consisted of Christians (mostly Roman Catholic) and Jews known as the Sephardim (Spanish Jewry). Non-Muslims were treated as *dhimmis* (protected subjects) under the SHARIA, despite sporadic persecution at the hands of some zealous Muslim rulers. The interrelationship between Muslim and non-Muslim in Andalusia produced a unique mix of cultural identities: Arab and Berber immigrants, local converts to Islam (*muwallads*), Christian admirers of Arab culture (Mozarabs), Arabized Jews, MUDEJARS (Muslims living under Christian rule), Conversos (Jews forcibly baptized as Christians during the Reconquista), and Moriscos (Muslims forcibly baptized as Christians after 1492). These groups spoke a mixture of languages—Arabic, Berber, and Latin-based Romance dialects.

Historians have called the golden age of harmonious coexistence shared by Andalusian Muslims and non-Muslims the *convivencia*. It began with the UMAYYAD CALIPHATE, which was transplanted from DAMASCUS to Cordova in 756. The Umayyads ruled Andalusia until 1009, when their CALIPHATE disintegrated and subsequent Muslim leaders turned against each other, while simultaneously they tried to hold off invading Christian armies from the north. The ideal of the *convivencia* nevertheless persisted, as exemplified in Andalusian (Moorish) ARCHITECTURE, poetry, MUSIC, and philosophy. Among the stellar individuals contributing to this unique mix of cultures were religious thinkers and philosophers such as IBN HAZM (d. 1064), IBN RUSHD (d. 1198), and Moses Maimonides (d. 1204, Jewish author of *Guide for the Perplexed*); poets such as Ibn Zaydun (d. 1070) and Judah Halevi (d. 1174, Jewish philosopher-poet); and mystics such as IBN ARABI (d. 1240) and Moses de Leon (d. 1305), author of the *Zohar,* a Jewish mystical text. Some of the great philosophical and literary works of these men eventually were translated into European languages and helped enhance intellectual life in the high Middle Ages and Renaissance. The cultural heritage of the golden age is also reflected in cuisine, as new foods and flavors introduced by the Arabs from the east changed the eating habits of Andalusian peoples. Rice dishes, citrus fruits, and aromatic spices found their way into Andalusian palaces and homes and later enriched the eating traditions of Europe, just as Andalusian learning and the arts enriched the cultural life of Islamicate lands and the west.

See also AGRICULTURE; ALMOHAD DYNASTY; ALMORVID DYNASTY; BERBER; CHRISTIANITY AND ISLAM; EUROPE; JUDAISM AND ISLAM; SEPHARDIC JEWS.

Further reading: Salma Khadra Jayyusi, ed., *The Legacy of Muslim Spain.* 2 vols. (Leiden: E.J. Brill, 1994); Maria Rosa Menocal, *The Ornament of the World: How Muslims, Jews, and Christians Created a Culture of Tolerance in Medieval Spain* (Boston: Little Brown & Co., 2002); W. Montgomery Watt and Pierre Cachia, *A History of Muslim Spain* (Edinburgh: University of Edinburgh Press, 1965).

angel

An angel (from the Greek word for "messenger") is a supernatural being that participates in the relations between God and human beings. Belief in angels usually occurs in monotheistic religions such as Judaism, Christianity and ISLAM, where there is a belief in only one god and there exists a clear separation between this god and the created world. Islamic belief in angels first appears early in the seventh century in the QURAN, and it is based on related beliefs held previously by Zoroastrians, Jews, and Christians in the Middle East. Indeed, according to the Quran and early Muslim theologians, belief in angels is one of the requirements of FAITH. Islamic understandings about angels have developed through the centuries and continue to be part of the spiritual outlook of many Muslims today, although skeptics deny their existence.

According Islamic tradition, angels submit to God's commands and serve as his messengers and helpers. In heaven, they sing his praise, guard his throne, and visit the celestial KAABA, as Muslims visit the earthly one during the pilgrimage to MECCA. They will also greet people when they enter PARADISE. According to the Quran, angels witnessed the creation of ADAM, the first human. All but Iblis (SATAN) bowed down to Adam in respect; God punished Iblis by cursing and expelling him from heaven. Sometimes, Iblis is regarded as one of the JINN, a separate class of supernatural beings, but he is also seen as a fallen angel whose role is to test people's faithfulness to God's commands. Some angels have special functions. For example, GABRIEL is widely regarded as the angel of revelation, Izrail is the angel of death, Malik is the guardian of hell, and Israfil is the one who will blow the trumpet on JUDGMENT DAY. Other angels are responsible for recording people's good and bad deeds, while the angels Mlunkar and Nakir are assigned to conduct interrogations of the dead in their tombs, thus preparing them for their future rewards or punishments in heaven or hell.

Angels are said to be awesome beings made of dazzling light and to have wings, unlike humans, who are made of clay, and the jinn, who are made of fire. But according to some accounts, angels may also appear in human form, as beautiful men and women. Islamic tradition holds that Muhammad encountered Gabriel many times in his adult life: Gabriel transmitted the Quran to him, and he served as his escort through the heavens during the NIGHT JOURNEY AND ASCENT. According to some versions of this story, Muhammad also led the angels in prayer at the AQSA MOSQUE in JERUSALEM. Shia Muslims share many of these beliefs with the Sunnis, but they also claim that their Imams have special knowledge that angels have given to them and no one else and that the angels protect them from harm. In SUFISM and Islamic philosophy, angels were associated with the stars and planets and ranked according to their place in the seven spheres of heaven. Some mystics even thought that humans could perfect their souls enough to become angels themselves.

Further reading: Fazlur Rahman, *Major Themes in the Quran* (Minneapolis and Chicago: Bibliotheca Islamica, 1980); Jane Smith and Yvonne Haddad, *The Islamic Understanding of Death and Resurrection* (Albany: State University of New York Press, 1981); Alford T. Welch, "Allah and Other Supernatural Beings: The Emergence of the Quranic Doctrine of *Tawhid.*" *Journal of the American Academy of Religion* 47 (1979): 733–758.

animals

Animals hold a significant place in the religious beliefs, rituals, ARTS, and FOLKLORE of Muslims. They are discussed in the QURAN and HADITH, mentioned in Islamic legal texts, and depicted in illustrated manuscripts and decorative arts, and stories of them are popular in Islamic religious literature and folklore. Islamic tradition gives humans dominion over animals—people obtain benefits from them such as food and transportation, but people are also responsible for their well-being. In the Quran, where six chapters are named after animals, the most frequently mentioned species are domesticated ones that live in herds, such as sheep, goats, CAMELS, HORSES, and cattle. Wild animals, such as birds, snakes, fish, and insects, are also mentioned, but not in great detail. All creatures are believed to have been created by God for the benefit of humans, and they serve as signs of God's power. The most famous stories in the Quran that involve animals include the raven that showed Cain how to bury his murdered brother (Q 5:31), Noah's ark (Q 23:27), the hoopoe bird that served as a messenger between King Solomon and the queen of Sheba (Q 27:20–28); the staff of MOSES that turned into a serpent (Q 7:107; 26:32), the fish or whale that swallowed Jonah (Q 37:139–145), the birds JESUS created from clay (Q 3:49), the DOG that guarded the seven sleepers in the cave (Q 18:18, 22), and the flock of birds sent by God to destroy "those of the elephant" who were about to attack MECCA (Q 105). The Quran also contains stories about people whom God transformed into pigs and apes because of their wrongful deeds (Q 2:65; 5:60). Quran commentaries and literature about the lives of the prophets added more detail to these stories and also included more animal tales, such as one about the peacock and the serpent who helped SATAN enter the Garden of Eden to seduce ADAM AND EVE. Specific commands in the Quran and hadith concerning food and sacrifice provided the basis for the system of rules about what kinds of animals should be eaten and how they should be slaughtered (*see* DIETARY LAWS). Thus, when an animal is to be sacrificed or slaughtered for food, the act must be done in accordance with detailed rules to make sure that it is permissible to eat the animal and to minimize its pain and suffering. In general, Islamic law does not condone cruelty to animals or blood sports such as cockfighting and bullfighting. Such rules and prohibitions furnish the basis for modern discussions of animal rights in Islam, even though acts of cruelty toward animals do indeed occur in Muslim societies. There is also a belief based on the sayings of Muhammad that people will be held accountable in the AFTERLIFE for the way they treated animals during their worldly existence.

Animals are popular subjects in the literary traditions and folklore of Muslim peoples. Pre-Islamic Arabic poetry is especially rich in references to camels, horses, ostriches, and lions, all animals connected to life in the Arabian Desert. One of the enduring classics of medieval literature is *Kalila wa Dimna,* a collection of fables that was brought to Persia from India and was translated into Arabic by Ibn Muqaffa in the eighth century. This book drew upon animal lore to provide moral lessons and practical advice to rulers. Arabic stories such as the BRETHREN OF PURITY's "Dispute between Animals and Man" (10th century) and Ibn Tufayl's *Hayy ibn Yaqzan* (12th century) underscore the special responsibility humans have in caring for animals. Indeed, according to tales about Muslim saints, showing kindness toward animals was characteristic of

saintly virtue. One of the masterpieces of medieval Persian mystical literature is Farid al-Din Attar's *Conference of the Birds* (*Mantiq al-tayr,* 12th century), an allegorical poem about a flock of different kinds of birds who set out to find their true king, only to discover that their journey is really one of self-discovery. The birds in this poem represent Sufi disciples in quest of God. Middle Eastern lore also has stories about mythological animals, such as the BURAQ (Muhammad's winged riding animal), the SIMURGH (the phoenix), and the Rukhkh (a giant bird mentioned in the legend of Sinbad).

Although conservative ULAMA prohibited the portrayal of humans and animals, both were depicted in illustrated book manuscripts and the decorative arts. Among the most popular books containing illustrations of both domestic and wild animals in the Middle Ages were al-Hariri's *Maqamat,* Ibn Muqaffa's *Kalila wa Dimna,* and the *Shahnama* (the Persian epic of kings). Manuscripts commissioned by the rulers of the Ottoman, Safavid, and Mughal Empires (ca. 16th century to 19th century) often contained illustrations that showed animal and human subjects in exquisite detail. Animals were also portrayed in ceramics, metalwork, carpets, and woodwork. They never appeared, however, in Quran manuscripts and mosque decorations because of the fear that this would violate the Islamic ban on IDOLATRY.

See also ARABIAN NIGHTS; CAT.

Further reading: Esin Atil, *Kalila wa Dimna: Fables from a Fourteenth-Century Arabic Manuscript* (Washington, D.C.: Smithsonian Institution Press, 1981); Farid ud-Din Attar, *The Conference of the Birds,* trans. Afkham Darbandi and Dick Davis (New York: Penguin, 1984); Jonathan Bloom and Sheila Blair, *Islamic Arts* (London: Phaidon Press, 1997); Denys Johnson-Davis, trans., *The Island of the Animals* (Austin: University of Texas Press, 1994); Annemarie Schimmel, *Deciphering the Signs of God: A Phenomenological Approach to Islam* (Albany: State University of New York Press, 1994); Al-Hafiz B.

A. Masri, *Islamic Concern for Animals* (Petersfield, U.K.: Athene Trust, 1987).

Ansar (Arabic: helpers)

The Ansar were early converts to ISLAM from MEDINA who joined in an alliance with MUHAMMAD and the EMIGRANTS from MECCA in 622. They were members of the Arab Khazraj and Aws tribes, the two dominant tribes in Medina at that time, and they served as hosts for the Emigrants. The Ansar participated in the battles against Muhammad's enemies and in the early wars of conquest after his death in 632. Together with other groups that participated in the conquest, they settled in the new garrison towns of Kufa in IRAQ and Fustat (CAIRO) in EGYPT. They also ranked highly on the registries for receiving income from newly conquered territories in the Middle East. As rivals to the QURAYSH tribe of Mecca, they supported the candidacy of ALI IBN ABI TALIB (d. 661) for the CALIPHATE, and in the eighth century, they allied with the Abbasids in their revolt against the UMAYYAD CALIPHATE. As a tribe, they eventually blended in with other members of the Muslim community, but the name continues to be used for mosques and contemporary Muslim organizations.

In Sudan, the Ansar is a significant Islamic movement named after the helpers of the Sudanese MAHDI, Muhammad Ahmad ibn Abd Allah (d. 1885), who ruled the country for a short time in the 1880s. The Mahdis' heirs reorganized the group into a puritanical religious movement in the early 20th century, and it has played a major role in modern Sudanese politics to the present day. The *Ansar* name was also used independently by radical Islamist guerrilla organizations in IRAQ, PAKISTAN, and LEBANON in the 1990s and 2000s.

See also UMMA.

Further reading: Hugh Kennedy, *The Prophet and the Age of the Caliphates: The Islamic Near East from the Sixth to the Eleventh Century* (London: Longman, 1986); W. Montgomery Watt, *Muhammad at Medina* (Oxford: Oxford University Press, 1956).

anthropomorphism

Anthropomorphism is a topic in classical Islamic THEOLOGY. It is concerned with the question as to whether God resembles human beings in his features (attributes), actions, and emotions. Is God completely unlike his creation and distant from it, or not? The issue was raised in debates about statements in the QURAN and HADITH as well as in efforts made by early Muslims to distinguish their religious beliefs from non-Islamic ones, especially those of the ancient Near Eastern cultures and the Greeks, who commonly portrayed their gods and goddesses in human form, and Christians, who held that JESUS was God in the flesh. Political conflicts within the Muslim community in the eighth century may also have intensified the debate.

Muslims who were called anthropomorphists (people who believed that God resembled humans) looked to passages in the Quran that say, for example, "Grace is in God's **hand**" (Q 3:73) and "His **throne** encompasses the heavens and earth" (Q 2:255). They argued that God therefore must have a real hand and that he had a body that could be seated on a throne. The hadith contain even stronger anthropomorphisms, such as the one based on the Bible, which says that God created ADAM "in his image." Their opponents, however, argued that such statements could not be taken literally, but that they were figures of speech intended to help ordinary humans grasp abstract theological concepts. To support their views, the opponents of anthropomorphism quoted the Quran verse that says of God "nothing is like him" (Q 42:11), implying that God lacks resemblance to his creation, including humans.

Anthropomorphic understandings of God were based partly on popular religious piety in the eighth and ninth centuries, and they were articulated by Sunni scholars who held to the literal reading of the Quran and hadith, as well as by followers of extremist Shii doctrines. The extreme rationalist view of God that denied any real resemblance between God and his creation was articulated by the MUTAZILI SCHOOL and supported by the Abbasid caliphs. The middle position in this debate was defined by al-Ashari (873–935) and his followers, who argued that the anthropomorphic descriptions of God based on the Quran and hadith must be accepted as real, but that God remains uniquely different from his creation "without [our] knowing how." This is the doctrine that has prevailed in the Sunni community until the present day. Nevertheless, anthropomorphic understandings of God continue to surface in popular Muslim beliefs and certain strands of SUFISM and speculative thought.

See also ABBASID CALIPHATE; ALLAH; ASHARI SCHOOL; GHULAT; IBN HANBAL, AHMAD; PERFECT MAN.

Further reading: Binyamin Abrahamov, *Anthropomorphism and the Interpretation of the Quran in the Theology of al-Qasim ibn Ibrahim* (Leiden: E.J. Brill, 1996); W. Montgomery Watt, *The Formative Period of Islamic Thought* (Oxford: One World Press, 1998).

Antichrist (Arabic: *al-dajjal,* or *al-masih al-dajjal*)

The Antichrist is a well-known figure who Muslims expect to arrive at the End of Times. Ideas about the *dajjal,* which means "deceiver," do not come directly from the QURAN, although other apocalyptic elements, such as JUDGMENT DAY, Gog and Magog (armies lead by the Antichrist), and the trials and tribulations of the End Times are present. Rather, the term *dajjal*—the Islamic equivalent of the Christian Antichrist—occurs in the HADITH, the second major source of authoritative knowledge in Islam. In many hadith collections, including the authoritative Sunni collections by al-Bukhari and Muslim, the *dajjal* is variously described as being red-complexioned, one-eyed (or blind in one eye), and short (or sometimes enormously large), with bowed legs and curly hair. The name *Unbeliever* will be written on his forehead. It is said that he will perform miracles, attracting many whose faith is weak. However,

true, believing Muslims will not succumb. He will reign for 40 years (or 40 days) before he succeeds in destroying Muslims. Ultimately, the Antichrist will be slain by JESUS, who also plays an important role in Islamic eschatology. The Shia, it should be noted, believe that Jesus and the MAHDI together will slay him, after which the End Times and Judgment Day will come.

The different and sometimes contradictory ways in which the Antichrist is described in Islamic eschatology is a result of early interactions among Muslims and Christians in the Middle East. Muslim scholars are divided on the authenticity of these traditions, which appear to go against the Quranic teaching that Judgment Day will arrive suddenly. Nonetheless, belief in the emergence of the Antichrist is a central aspect of belief for Muslims. There is an active apocalyptic tradition today in which various "Antichrists" are described; some commentators even see the Antichrist embodied in the modern temptations and foreign domination to which Muslims have been subjected.

See also CHRISTIANITY AND ISLAM; DEATH; SHIISM.

John Iskander

Further reading: Bernard McGinn, *Anti-Christ: Two Thousand Years of the Human Fascination with Evil* (New York: Columbia University Press, 2000); Zeki Saritoprak, "The Legend of *al-Dajjal* (Antichrist): The Personification of Evil in the Islamic Tradition." *Muslim World* 93 (2003): 291–308.

anti-Semitism

A term coined in the 19th century, anti-Semitism is used to describe hateful attitudes and hostile actions directed at Jews. It is not to be confused with the persecution of Jews by Christians and others prior to that time, which is better understood as anti-Judaism—the persecution of Jews because of their religious beliefs and practices. The term *Semite* originated in modern history as part of a European scholarly effort to rationally catego-rize the languages and races of the world. It was derived from the name of Shem, a son of NOAH, considered to be one of the ancient ancestors of the Hebrews in the Bible. It acquired negative meaning when white European racists, especially in Germany, asserted that their Indo-European, or Aryan, cultural and biological heritage was supe-rior to that of other races, including that of the "Semites." Both Jews and Arabs were classified as Semitic peoples, but during the late 19th century and early 20th century the term *Semite* came to be used in a deliberate propaganda campaign to dehumanize the Jews of Europe. This campaign culminated in the Holocaust of 1933–45, which involved the mass extermination of millions of Jews and members of other minority groups in concentration camps built by Nazi Germany and its allies in Europe.

Anti-Semitism was imported to Muslim lands from Europe in the 20th century. Prior to that time, Jews in these lands held DHIMMI status, a kind of second-class citizenship, and, except for sporadic outbreaks of violence, they were bet-ter integrated into Islamicate societies than into Christian European ones. Indigenous elites in Muslim countries became influenced by Euro-pean intellectual trends and political ideologies of all kinds—including ant-Semitism—during the decades they were under direct or indirect colonial rule. With the breakup of the colonial empires after World War II, the emergence of new ARAB nation-states, and the creation of ISRAEL, anti-Semitic rhetoric found widespread use in the speeches of Arab leaders and the Middle Eastern media. There were also violent attacks on eastern Jews living in IRAQ, LIBYA, Morocco, and Aden (YEMEN). These attacks, and growing Arab nation-alist rhetoric, together with the desire of Jews to live in their own homeland, caused Jews in many Arab lands to immigrate to Israel.

At first, anti-Semitic hostility in the Middle East was expressed mainly by secular states and political parties. After the 1967 Arab-Israeli war,

however, it was also promoted by radical Islamic movements, beginning with the MUSLIM BROTHER-HOOD in EGYPT and other Arab countries. Publica-tions of this organization repeated dehumanizing caricatures and stereotypes of Jews that had origi-nated in Europe. The demonization of Jews and of Israel intensified in the wake of the IRANIAN REVOLUTION OF 1978–1979, the Israeli invasion of Lebanon (1982), escalation of hostilities in the ARAB-ISRAELI CONFLICTS during the late 1980s and 1990s, and the U.S. and British invasion of Iraq in 2003. Arabic and Persian translations of *The Protocols of the Elders of Zion,* a fraudulent Russian document alleging a Jewish plot to dominate the world, circulated widely in the Middle East, and it continues to be cited in anti-Israeli speeches and even television dramas. Saudi schoolbooks refer to it as if its slanderous allegations were true. Other examples of anti-Semitic ideology in the religiopo-litical rhetoric of the Middle East include iterations of a medieval Christian libel against the Jews and denial of the Holocaust. LOUIS FARRAKHAN, the African-American leader of the NATION OF ISLAM, has also been condemned for making anti-Semitic remarks. In some Jewish circles, anyone who criticizes the policies and actions of the Israeli government, especially with regard to the question of Palestine, is labeled an anti-Semite. Extremist rhetoric appears to be increasing in the first decade of the 21st century among different factions and movements, a development that inhibits the peace-ful resolution of political conflicts in the Middle East. It also undermines efforts to achieve better interfaith understanding.

See also COLONIALISM; JUDAISM AND ISLAM.

Further reading: Jane S. Gerber, "Anti-Semitism and the Muslim World." In *History and Hate: The Dimensions of Anti-Semitism,* edited by David Berger, 73–94 (Philadel-phia: Jewish Publication Society, 1986); Bernard Lewis, *The Jews of Islam* (Princeton, N.J.: Princeton University, 1984); Alexander Cockburn and Jeffrey St. Clare, eds., *The Politics of Anti-Semitism* (Oakland, Calif.: AK Press, 2003).

apostasy

Apostasy, which comes from the Greek word for "defection" or "revolt," is the partial or complete abandonment or rejection of the beliefs and practices of a religion by a person who is a follower of that religion. The charge of apostasy is often used by religious authorities to condemn and punish skeptics, dissidents, and minorities in their communities. This is especially so in religions such as Judaism, Christianity, and ISLAM, where membership in the religious community involves publicly making or consenting to formal statements of belief. Failure to do so may provide grounds for accusations of apostasy and result in severe penalties.

In Islam, apostasy is thought of in two ways: abandoning Islam (*irtidad*) and deviation in religious belief (*ilhad*). In either case, apostasy is regarded as a kind of disbelief, together with HERESY and BLASPHEMY (verbally insulting a religion). The QURAN declares that apostasy will result in punishment in the AFTERLIFE but takes a relatively lenient view toward apostasy in this life (Q 9:74; 2:109). This picture changed significantly during the UMAYYAD and ABBASID CALIPHATES (seventh century to ninth century), when Muslim jurists invoked HADITH that supported the imposition of the death penalty for apostasy, except in cases of coercion. These hadith may well have been a product of the so-called wars of apostasy (the Ridda Wars) that shook the early Muslim community after the death of MUHAMMAD in 632. According to the SHARIA, apostasy is identified with a long list of actions such as conversion to another religion, denying the existence of God, rejecting the prophets, mocking God or the prophets, idol worship, rejecting the sharia, or permitting behavior that is forbidden by the sharia, such as adultery. Muslims disagree over when such actions should be punished, but in the history of Islam, a variety of individuals and groups have been accused of apostasy—atheists, materialists, Sufis, and members of Shii sects. The Sufi mystics MANSUR AL-HALLAJ (d. 922) and Shihab al-Din al-Suhrawardi (d. 1191) were among those in the Middle Ages accused of apostasy and executed, as well many followers of ISMAILI SHIISM. In addition to death, adult male apostates may also be punished by forced separation from their spouses and denial of property and inheritance rights, depending on the legal school. Punishment of female apostates involves not death, but confinement. Punishments may be cancelled if the accused person repents his or her apostasy in public.

In the modern period, conservative Muslim authorities and religious radicals have accused Muslim modernists, intellectuals, and writers of this "crime." Among the most famous to be charged with apostasy or the related crime of blasphemy are the Anglo-Indian writer SALMAN RUSHDIE (b. 1947), the Egyptian intellectual NASR HAMID ABU ZAYD (b. 1943), and the Bangladeshi writer and human rights advocate Taslima Nasrin (b. 1962). In some Muslim countries, apostasy charges have also been leveled against non-Muslims, for example the Bahais in Iran and Christians in Pakistan. International HUMAN RIGHTS advocates, Muslims and non-Muslims, have condemned Islamic apostasy laws in the name of justice and "freedom of thought, conscience, and religion" (Article 18, Universal Declaration of Human Rights).

See also BAHAI FAITH; CHRISTIANITY AND ISLAM; JUDAISM AND ISLAM; HERESY; *KAFIR*.

Further reading: Burhan al-Din Al-Marghinani, *The Hedaya: Commentary on the Islamic Laws.* Translated by Charles Hamilton (New Delhi: Kitab Bhavan, 1994; Rudolph Peters and Gert J. J. De Vries, "Apostasy in Islam." *Die Welt des Islams* 17 (1976–77): 1–25; Abdullah Saeed and Hassan Saeed, *Freedom of Religion, Apostasy and Islam* (Burlington, Vt.: Ashgate Publishing, 2004).

Aqsa Mosque (Arabic: *al-Masjid al-aqsa*)

Regarded by most Muslims as the third most sacred MOSQUE after those of MECCA and MEDINA, the Aqsa Mosque is situated on the eastern edge of the Old City in JERUSALEM. It is part of a complex of buildings and monuments known as the Noble Sanctuary, which stands atop the remains of the Second Temple of ISRAEL, which was destroyed by the Roman army in 70 C.E. Jews and Christians therefore commonly know this area as the Temple Mount. The name of the mosque itself was obtained from a passage in the QURAN that says, "Glory be to him who transported his servant by night from the sacred mosque [in Mecca] to the most distant (aqsa) mosque, the precincts of which we have blessed" (Q 17:1). Though there was some dispute over where the mosque mentioned in the Quran was actually located, the verse was eventually linked by Islamic tradition to the NIGHT JOURNEY AND ASCENT of MUHAMMAD, when he was believed to have been miraculously transported one night from Mecca to Jerusalem, up to heaven, then back down to Mecca. The Aqsa Mosque, therefore, was said to be where Muhammad led the ANGELS and former prophets in PRAYER before his heavenly ascent to meet with God.

Despite this legendary account, the mosque was first constructed after Muhammad's death by the Umayyad caliphs Abd al-Malik (r. 685–705) and his son, al-Walid (r. 705–715). It was designed as a rectangular congregational mosque for Friday prayers, with a dome and a long north-south axis that was aligned with the DOME OF THE ROCK, a separate memorial structure to the north. Mosaics, marble, and carved wood decorated its walls. It had to be reconstructed and expanded several times over the centuries because of earthquakes, and it now can hold up to 400,000 worshippers. When the crusaders seized Jerusalem in 1096, the Aqsa Mosque was converted into a royal palace and later a barracks for the Knights Templar. Muslims believed that these Christians had defiled the mosque; when SALADIN (d. 1193) recaptured the city in 1187, he purified the building so it could once again be used as a place for congregational prayer. After Israel captured east Jerusalem in the 1967 Arab-Israeli war, administration of the mosque remained in the hands of Muslim authorities, and Palestinian Muslims were allowed to continue using it for Friday prayers. Together with the Dome of the Rock, the Aqsa Mosque has since become a symbol for the Palestinian nationalist movement and liberation from Israeli occupation. Indeed, Palestinians call the second intifada (uprising) in the West Bank and Gaza that started in 2000 the al-Aqsa Intifada.

See also ARAB-ISRAELI CONFLICTS; ARCHITECTURE; CHRISTIANITY AND ISLAM; PALESTINE.

Further reading: Oleg Grabar, *The Shape of the Holy: Early Islamic Jerusalem* (Princeton, N.J.: Princeton University Press, 1996); Robert W. Hamilton, *The Structural History of the Aqsa Mosque* (Jerusalem: Oxford University Press, 1949).

Arab
Originally an ethnic designation for the people of Arabia, *Arab* is now commonly used to refer to people who speak Arabic, claim ancestry in North Africa or the Middle East, or consider themselves nationals in one of the recently created Arab nation-states. In its original meaning, Arab applied to several Arabic speaking tribes from the Arabian Peninsula (the area including contemporary SAUDI ARABIA, YEMEN, Oman, United Arab Emirates, Qatar, Bahrain, Kuwait, JORDAN, and parts of SYRIA and IRAQ). Classically imagined as CAMEL-breeding nomads, many Arabs have always lived in CITIES and have been noted for their loyalty to family and hospitality and to a rich poetic tradition. Because MUHAMMAD (d. 632) was a member of the Arab tribe called QURAYSH and he delivered the QURAN in Arabic, the Arabic language became very important to the practice and understanding of ISLAM. Arabs played a crucial role in helping expand the boundaries of Islam beyond the Arabian Peninsula, and today they remain guardians of the most holy Muslim city of MECCA. This has led to some confusion between the terms *Arab* and *Muslim*: Arab is an ethnic category, while Muslim refers to religion.

Arabs are not necessarily Muslim, and indeed there are many Christian Arabs. Moreover, the majority of Muslims (about 80 percent) do not consider themselves to be Arab, and some people who do consider themselves to be Arab—especially the CHILDREN of migrants—do not necessarily speak Arabic. Like all ethnic categories, the definition of Arab is somewhat flexible and depends on context.

See also ARABIC LANGUAGE AND LITERATURE; ARAB LEAGUE.

David Crawford

Further reading: Albert Hourani, *A History of the Arab Peoples* (Cambridge, Mass.: Harvard University Press, 1991); Maxime Rodinson, *The Arabs* (Chicago: University of Chicago Press, 1981).

arabesque

Arabesque is a term meaning *à l'arabe,* or in the ARAB mode, a European designation for ornamental passages in MUSIC, dance, poetry, and visual ART. First used by 17th-century European travelers as an adjective, it began to function as a noun by the later 19th century, when it entered debates

Carved stucco arabesque designs decorate arches in the Court of the Lions in the Alhambra, Granada, Spain (13th/14th century). *(Federico R. Campo)*

on the nature of ornament. The arabesque was understood to represent a paradigmatic way of life—simple and instinctual, close to nature yet profoundly spiritual, unchanging, and stoic. These characteristics were visually apparent in applied decoration of floral scrolls, interlaced and/or overlapping geometric motifs, or stylized writing, sometimes in combination. To European eyes, the two-dimensionality, abstraction, and nonfigural nature of these decorative designs made them perfect expressions of Arab-Semitic abhorrence of representations of living beings (even though some of them included such representations). Their being categorized as ornament underscored their additive and unnecessary nature and their lack of meaning, while their infinite repetition with minute variations expressed a horror of emptiness. By 1900, when the first handbooks on Islamic art were written, the arabesque was cited as the major characteristic of an art whose goal was to express infinite (ethnic or created) variety within unity (of Islam and God). Some Muslim scholars now uphold this concept as an expression of TAWHID (unity) partly as a way of affirming Islamic cultural and political identity.

Recent research demonstrates that the arabesque has complex histories and meanings. On a theoretical level, floral, geometric, or calligraphic arabesques may have acted as carriers of pleasure, mediators between (human) nature and culture. Historically, they first appeared in late 10th-century BAGHDAD, when they were also introduced into the three-dimensional *muqarnas* decoration used for the portals and domes of shrines. The Persian term *girih* (knot) expresses their mathematical and geometrical complexity, and their specific context indicates that they belonged to inter-Islamic philosophical, theological, and political discourses on the nature of God and the universe. The visual appeal of the *girih* mode eventually led to its adoption in a variety of later contexts, even when its original purpose was no longer operative.

See also ARCHITECTURE; CALLIGRAPHY; IBN AL-BAWWAB, ABU AL-HASAN ALI; MATHEMATICS; THEOLOGY.

Nuha N. N. Khoury

Further reading: Terry Allen, *Five Essays on Islamic Art* (Sebastopol, Calif.: Solipsist Press, 1988); Oleg Grabar, *The Mediation of Ornament* (Princeton, N.J.: Princeton University Press, 1992); Ernst Kühnel, *Die Arabesque* (Wiesbaden, 1949); Richard Ettinghausen, *The Arabesque: Meaning and Transformation of an Ornament* (Graz, Austria: Verlag für Sammler, 1976); Gülru Necipoglu, *The Topkapi Scroll—Geometry and Ornament in Islamic Architecture* (Santa Monica, Calif.: The Getty Center, 1995); Yasser Tabbaa, *The Transformation of Islamic Art during the Sunni Revival* (Seattle: University of Washington Press, 2001).

Arabian Nights

The *Arabian Nights* is one of the most famous works of Arabic literature. It consists of several hundred adventure stories, fairy tales, love stories, and ANIMAL fables that storytellers recounted for centuries to audiences living in the Middle East and Asia. Between the 14th and 18th centuries, these stories were written down in Arabic and collected in the book *Thousand and One Nights* (or *Alf layla wa-layla*). It first became known to English readers as *Arabian Nights* in the 18th century. The tales are nested within the overall frame of a story about the fictional king Shahrayar of INDIA who murdered his first wife because she betrayed him and then, continuing his revenge, had each new virgin bride he took thereafter killed. To end the king's killing spree, Shahrazad, the well-educated daughter of the king's minister, offered to marry him, and she was then able to save her own life and bring his killing spree to a halt by entertaining him with a different tale night after night, year after year. With its fanciful and often risqué stories, the *Arabian Nights* is not an example of Islamic religious literature, but it does contain elements—such as references to the

QURAN, the SHARIA, and Sufi dervishes—that draw upon Islamic tradition.

The stories are anonymous, and modern scholars agree that they come from different sources, not all of which are "Arabian." Though the stories are written in Arabic and a number of them refer to BAGHDAD and CAIRO, many of them show strong Indian and Persian influences. Scholars also agree that the *Arabian Nights* circulated in several versions of different lengths during much of its history. The version that first captured the attention of Western readers was based on Arabic manuscripts from SYRIA translated by a French traveler-scholar, Antoine Galland (1646–1715), in collaboration with an Arab Christian named Hanna Diab. Indeed, some of the most beloved stories we now associate with the *Arabian Nights,* such as those about Sinbad, Aladdin, and Ali Baba, circulated as separate stories and were not part of the original 14th-century collection. They were added to the *Arabian Nights* only as a result of Galland and Hanna's collaboration early in the 18th century. Printed translations and adaptations of the *Arabian Nights* quickly became best sellers in Europe and continue to fascinate readers young and old around the world today. Moreover, *Arabian Nights* has inspired modern composers, poets, playwrights, and filmmakers both in the West and the Middle East. However, it has also contributed to the formation of exotic stereotypes about Arabs and Muslims that inhibit cross-cultural communication and understanding, as exemplified in the controversy surrounding the animated Disney feature *Aladdin* (1992).

See also ARABIC LANGUAGE AND LITERATURE; FOLKLORE; ORIENTALISM.

Further reading: Richard F. Burton, trans., *The Arabian Nights.* Edited by Jack Zipes (New York: Penguin Books, 2001; Husain Haddawy, trans., *The Arabian Nights* (New York: W.W. Norton, 1990); Robert Irwin, *The Arabian Nights: A Companion* (London: Penguin Books, 1995).

Arabian religions, pre-Islamic

Before the historical appearance of ISLAM in the seventh century, there were a variety of religions practiced by the peoples of the Arabian Peninsula and its borderlands in southern SYRIA and southern IRAQ. Though the evidence is meager, it appears that in addition to ancient native Arabian religions, there were also three religious traditions that had come into the region from neighboring territories: Judaism, Christianity, and Zoroastrianism. By the middle of the eighth century, Islam had become the dominant religion, and the institutions, practices, and beliefs of the former religions had either been displaced or absorbed by Islamic ones.

Native Arabian religions focused partly on temple cults located in cities and towns, including MECCA, the site of the KAABA, where as many as 360 gods and goddesses may have been worshipped. The temples were ceremonial centers that housed sacred images, which were cared for by ritual experts who conducted ANIMAL sacrifices and transmitted other offerings on behalf of the lay people. Some of these temples attracted pilgrims who came from surrounding regions and had to follow special ritual rules, not unlike those observed during the annual HAJJ. Several of the Arabian deities worshipped were associated with the Sun, MOON, planets, and stars. The main deities in Mecca at the time of Islam's appearance were Hubal (a god of divination), ALLAH and al-Lat (a high god and his wife), al-Uzza (a powerful GODDESS, perhaps Venus), and Manat (a goddess of destiny and another form of Venus). Certain rocks, trees, and springs of water were also believed to be inhabited by spiritual beings, known as JINN. With the exception of Allah only, the QURAN attacked worship of such deities and spirits, and such practices were later formally banned by Islamic law as unbelief (*kufr*) and IDOLATRY (*shirk*)

The Quran contains evidence of the presence of Jewish, Christian, and Zoroastrian religions in the Arabian Peninsula during MUHAMMAD's lifetime (570?–632). Judaism came into Arabia before the first century C.E. but became especially evident after the destruction of the Second Temple in JERUSALEM by the Romans (70 C.E.), which caused a flow of REFUGEES southward. Islamic sources indicate that there was a Jewish community led by rabbis in Yathrib (MEDINA), which existed alongside the settled Arab tribes there in the sixth to seventh centuries. Dhu Nuwas, a Jewish king, ruled southern Arabia for a short time in the sixth century with the support of the Persians. Christianity was familiar to the Arabs in several forms. The Banu Ghassan tribes of Syria were allies of the Byzantine Empire, and were members of the Syrian Church. The Arab Lakhmid rulers of southern Iraq generally held to the Nestorian sect of Christianity. There was also a strong Christian presence in southern Arabia, centered on the city of Najran, which was known for its monasteries, churches, and shrines dedicated to Arab Christian martyrs. Its leaders were allied to the rulers of Byzantium and Ethiopia. Followers of the Zoroastrian religion, the official religion of the Sasanian Persian Empire (224–651), could be found in southern Iraq, along the Arabian coast of the Persian Gulf, and in YEMEN. Most of these Zoroastrians were probably Persians, but there is evidence that some may also have been Arabs. According to early Muslim accounts, one of the first of Muhammad's followers was Salman al-Farisi, a Persian from Iraq who had converted from Zoroastrianism.

See also CHRISTIANITY AND ISLAM; IDOLATRY; *JAHILIYYA*; JUDAISM AND ISLAM.

Further reading: Hisham ibn Kalbi, *The Book of Idols,* trans. N. A. Faris (Princeton, N.J.: Princeton University Press, 1952); Gordon D. Newby, *A History of the Jews of Arabia: From Ancient Times to Their Eclipse under Islam* (Columbia: University of South Carolina Press, 1988); F. E. Peters, *The Arabs and Arabia on the Eve of Islam* (Aldershot, U.K. and Brookfield, Vt.: Ashgate, 1999).

Arabic language and literature

Arabic is the fifth or sixth most widely spoken language in the world today, after Mandarin Chinese, English, Spanish, Hindi, and possibly Bengali. It is the official language of 21 modern countries; nearly 160 million Arabic speakers in the Middle East and abroad use it as their mother tongue. More than 1 billion Muslims around the world regard it as their sacred language because it is the language of the QURAN, the Islamic HOLY BOOK. Many Jews and Christians living in the Middle East also speak it. Arabic has been used continuously as a living, written, and spoken language for nearly 1,400 years and has served as the medium for the creation and transmission of a great number of works on religion, history, PHILOSOPHY, SCIENCE, and MATHEMATICS.

Classified by linguists as a member of the Semitic family of the Afro-Asiatic languages, Arabic is related to Hebrew, Aramaic, and the Akkadian language of ancient Mesopotamia. It originated in the Arabian Peninsula, where it was a poetic language used by the BEDOUIN and townspeople prior to the appearance of ISLAM in the seventh century. The main reason for its rise as a world language is because it is the language of the Quran, which declares itself to be a direct "revelation" from God "in plain Arabic speech" (Q 26:192–196). In addition to being a sacred language, the Umayyad CALIPH Abd al-Malik b. Marwan (r. 685–705) made Arabic the administrative language of the early Arab empire, leading to its codification as a literary language with its own formal grammar by the end of the eighth century. Thus, as lands and peoples from Spain and North Africa to the banks of the Indus River fell under the control of Arab Muslim governments, Arabic became the language of their subjects, Muslims and non-Muslims alike. The languages formerly spoken by the native peoples in these regions became isolated, minority languages, such as Coptic in EGYPT and Aramaic in Mesopotamia (IRAQ), or they were noticeably changed by the introduction of Arabic vocabulary, such as the Persian language. Turkish, Hindi, and Urdu also have an extraordinary number of Arabic loanwords as a result of the spread of Islamic religion and civili-

Arabic Alphabet

Name	Independent	Beginning	Medial	Final	Name	Independent	Beginning	Medial	Final
alif (aa)	ا	ا	ـا	ـا	ḍād (ḍ)	ض	ضـ	ـضـ	ـض
bāʾ (b)	ب	بـ	ـبـ	ـب	ṭā (ṭ)	ط	طـ	ـطـ	ـط
tāʾ (t)	ت	تـ	ـتـ	ـت	dhā (dh)	ظ	ظـ	ـظـ	ـظ
thāʾ (th)	ث	ثـ	ـثـ	ـث	ʾayn (ʿ)	ع	عـ	ـعـ	ـع
jīm (j)	ج	جـ	ـجـ	ـج	ghayn (gh)	غ	غـ	ـغـ	ـغ
ḥāʾ (ḥ)	ح	حـ	ـحـ	ـح	fāʾ (f)	ف	فـ	ـفـ	ـف
khāʾ (kh)	خ	خـ	ـخـ	ـخ	qāf (q)	ق	قـ	ـقـ	ـق
dāl (d)	د	د	ـد	ـد	kāf (k)	ك	كـ	ـكـ	ـك
dhāl (dh)	ذ	ذ	ـذ	ـذ	lām (l)	ل	لـ	ـلـ	ـل
rāʾ (r)	ر	ر	ـر	ـر	mīm (m)	م	مـ	ـمـ	ـم
zayn (z)	ز	ز	ـز	ـز	nūn (n)	ن	نـ	ـنـ	ـن
sīn (s)	س	سـ	ـسـ	ـس	hāʾ (h)	ه	هـ	ـهـ	ـه
shīn (sh)	ش	شـ	ـشـ	ـش	wāw (ww)	و	و	ـو	ـو
ṣād (ṣ)	ص	صـ	ـصـ	ـص	yāʾ (yy)	ي	يـ	ـيـ	ـي

zation. Arabic even found its way into European languages, especially Spanish, which has as many as 4,000 words of Arabic origin (for example, *algodón, arroz, azul, azúcar, alcalde, fulano,* etc.). A number of Arabic nouns have also entered English, such as the words *cotton, rice, sugar, admiral, magazine, sherbet,* and even COFFEE.

There are two basic types of Arabic: formal literary Arabic and everyday spoken (or colloquial) Arabic. The first is subdivided into Classical (or Medieval) and Modern Standard Arabic. It can be comprehended by anyone who has learned to read and write it, no matter what his or her spoken Arabic dialect is, and it is used in books, newspapers and magazines, government documents, SERMONS, and official speeches. Colloquial Arabic is subdivided into a number of regional dialects that can differ significantly from each other. For example, people who speak Egyptian or Iraqi Arabic can understand each other, but they cannot understand the Moroccan Arabic of North Africa. Egyptian colloquial, furthermore, is widely understood throughout the Arab world because of the leading role Egypt plays in the production of movies and the broadcast programming for radio and television. Through the centuries, literary and colloquial Arabic have mutually influenced each other, which is one reason for the language's ongoing vitality.

Arabic literature encompasses a vast range of prose and poetry that deals with both religious and worldly subjects. The body of religious literature in Arabic is massive; beginning with the Quran itself, it includes Quran commentaries, HADITH collections, religious biographies and prophets' tales, texts on religious law, theological treatises, Sufi writings, and religious poetry. Many such works were composed in the Middle Ages, but they have had a lasting impact on Arabic writing, and they are widely available today in print, on compact disks (CDs), and even on the internet. Secular poetry is another major branch of the Arabic literary tradition, especially a type of poem called the *qasida* (a multi-themed ode),

considered to be the most ancient and prestigious form of poetic expression. Classical Arabic poetry addressed themes of love, praise, ridicule, death, and remembrance. It also celebrated wine, hunting, nature, and famous places. Many nonreligious prose works were composed during the Middle Ages as well. They dealt with a variety of topics that were of special interest to rulers and the educated elite: history, geography, government, philosophy, the sciences, differences between various kinds of people, etiquette, proverbs, interesting trivia, and entertaining stories and anecdotes. The most famous works of prose literature are the ARABIAN NIGHTS and the animal fables of *Kalila wa Dimna,* both of which contain stories that have been transmitted from other cultures. There were also popular oral epics about noble Arab warriors such as Antar and Abu Zayd al-Hilali.

The Arabic literary heritage was selectively translated into Hebrew and Latin and transmitted to Europe during the Middle Ages, which enriched intellectual and cultural life there. In modern times, Western learning and literature have influenced Arab writers, creating a fusion of the old with the new. During the 20th century, new generations of Arab authors rose to national and international fame, none moreso than the Egyptian novelist Naguib Mahfouz (b. 1911), who won the Nobel Prize for literature in 1988. In recent decades, an increasing number of women have also made contributions to the Arab literary renaissance, including Nawal al-Sadawi (b. 1930) and Hanan al-Shaykh (b. 1945).

See also ADAB; ALPHABET; ANIMALS; AUTOBIOGRAPHY; BIOGRAPHY; CALLIGRAPHY; FIQH; PERSIAN LANGUAGE AND LITERATURE; TURKISH LANGUAGE AND LITERATURE.

Further reading: Roger Allen, *An Introduction to Arabic Literature* (Cambridge: Cambridge University Press, 2000); Salm K. Jayyusi, *Modern Arabic Poetry: An Anthology* (New York: Columbia University Press, 1987); Kees Versteegh, *The Arabic Language,* 2d ed. (Edinburgh: Edinburgh University Press, 2001).

Arab-Israeli conflicts

Among the most intractable conflicts to emerge in the 20th century are those that developed with the expansion of Zionism (a modern Jewish movement and political ideology) and the establishment of the nation-state of ISRAEL. Israel's ARAB neighbors took offense at the displacement from PALESTINE of more than 700,000 Palestinian Arabs during fighting between Zionist settlers and Arabs in 1947–49 and came to view Israel as a menacing tool of Western expansion in their region. Israelis, meanwhile, viewed their new nation as a necessary haven for world Jewry threatened by ANTI-SEMITISM and saw their new Arab neighbors as unreasonably hostile enemies continuously plotting their destruction. The term *Arab-Israeli conflict* thus does not distinguish between the specific problem of Palestinian displacement and all of its consequences for the Palestinians themselves on the one hand, and the wars and conflicts between Israel and its many Arab neighbors on the other.

Tensions have rarely abated, and formal conflict has broken out between Israel and neighboring Arab states several times. In 1948–49, EGYPT, Transjordan (now JORDAN), LEBANON, SYRIA, and IRAQ invaded the newly declared Israel, hoping to eliminate the new state, but they were repelled by the vastly better equipped and trained Israeli military. In 1956, Israel joined Britain and France in an invasion of Egypt after that nation nationalized the Suez Canal. However, the Soviet Union and the United States forced the alliance to retreat from its invasion, humiliating Israel and bolstering Egypt.

Furthermore, in 1967, after receiving faulty intelligence reports of an imminent Israeli invasion, Egypt, Jordan, and Syria allied in a mutual defense pact, preparing for any potential invasion by Israel with an Egyptian-led blockade of Israeli shipping at the Strait of Tiran. Israel responded by invading the countries, beginning on June 5 and ending on June 11, 1967. The result was a decisive defeat of the Arab armies, the occupation by Israel of the West Bank, the Sinai, the Gaza Strip, and the Golan Heights, and the displacement of at least 300,000 more Palestinians and 80,000 Syrian residents of the Golan.

Israel's occupation of such large areas of Arab territory provoked Egypt and Syria to invade in 1973, and the resulting October War, the cease-fire of which was sponsored by the United States and the Soviet Union, demonstrated the tremendous involvement of the cold war superpowers in the Arab-Israeli conflict. Although peace was eventually brokered between Israel and Egypt in 1977, resulting in a return of the Sinai, tensions did not abate. Israel's 1982 invasion of Lebanon and its continued occupation of Palestinian land guaranteed further hostilities. From 1987 until 1993, the first Palestinian intifada, or uprising, erupted, escalating the tensions between Israel and the millions of Arabs living under its rule as well as those living in neighboring nations. Although an American-sponsored peace plan gained some ground in the mid-1990s, the year 2000 prompted a new intifada from a frustrated, oppressed Palestinian population. Over the years, the conflicts have also fanned the flames of Islamic radicalism in the Middle East, as seen first with the rise of the MUSLIM BROTHERHOOD (1940s), then the Lebanese Shii militia HIZBULLAH (1980s), the Palestinian militant organizations HAMAS and Palestinian Islamic Jihad (1980s), and in the 1990s AL-QAIDA. At the dawn of the new century, Arab-Israeli conflicts appear far from over. Indeed, the American-sponsored "war on terror" that began in 2001 has further pushed Arab-Israeli conflicts to the forefront of world attention.

See also ARAFAT, YASIR; JIHAD MOVEMENTS; JUDAISM AND ISLAM; PALESTINE LIBERATION ORGANIZATION; TERRORISM.

Nancy Stockdale

Further reading: Walter Laqueur and Barry Rubin, eds., *The Israel-Arab Reader* (New York: Penguin, 2001); Avi Shlaim, *The Iron Wall: Israel and the Arab World* (New York: Norton, 2001); Charles D. Smith, *Palestine and the*

Arab-Israeli Conflict (New York: Bedford/St. Martin's, 1995).

Arab League (official name: League of Arab States)

The Arab League was founded in 1945 to serve the collective interests of Arab countries that had achieved their independence from European colonial rule. The founding members were EGYPT, IRAQ, JORDAN, LEBANON, SYRIA, SAUDI ARABIA, and YEMEN. An additional 15 nations have become members since 1945: ALGERIA, Bahrain, Comoros Islands, Djibouti, Kuwait, LIBYA, Mauritania, MOROCCO, Oman, PALESTINE, Qatar, Somalia, SUDAN, TUNISIA, and United Arab Emirates. The Arab League, which has its permanent headquarters in CAIRO, Egypt, is a secular organization that is guided by the ideal of Arab unity and cooperation. It is a forum where Arab states address common issues relating to politics, law, security, transportation, communication, economic development, and social and cultural affairs. The league's charter requires a secretary general as its chief officer, but the supreme authority for the organization is held by its council, which is composed of representatives from the member states. The league convenes summit meetings at least twice a year, which are often attended by heads of state.

Despite the ideal of unity, there are serious divisions within the organization that have been caused by economic inequality, differences in political organization and philosophy, personality clashes among leaders, and various historical and cultural factors. For example, Egypt's domination of the league under the leadership of President Jamal Abd al-Nasir (1918–70), a strong secularist, caused Saudi Arabia to create the MUSLIM WORLD LEAGUE in 1962. Later, Egypt was expelled from the league for signing a peace treaty with Israel in 1979, but it was reinstated in 1987. In another example of disunity, members were unable to peacefully resolve the crisis caused when Iraq invaded Kuwait in 1990. They have also been unable to form a common front for ending the ARAB-ISRAELI CONFLICTS, although they did pass a unanimous resolution in March 2002 that called for recognition of ISRAEL in exchange for Israeli withdrawal from occupied territories in the West Bank, Gaza, and the Golan Heights. Divisions continue to afflict the organization in the aftermath of the invasion of Iraq by the United States and its allies in March 2003 and the Lebanese-Israeli war that erupted in July 2006.

Further reading: Tawfiq Y. Hasou, *The Struggle for the Arab World: Egypt's Nasser and the Arab League* (London and Boston: KPI, 1985).

Arafat (also Arafa)

Arafat is a plain located 12 miles from downtown MECCA where pilgrims come to stand and listen to SERMONS during the HAJJ, the annual Muslim pilgrimage. This gathering, which occurs at midday on the ninth day of the 12th month of the Muslim year (Dhu al-Hijja), is one of the essential requirements of the hajj. If a pilgrim fails to be there on time, her hajj performance is considered to be invalid, and she must perform it again another year in order to satisfy the Islamic pilgrimage requirement. The QURAN mentions Arafat once: "When you pour forth from Arafat, remember God at the sacred monument, and remember how he guided you when previously you had gone astray" (Q 2:198). According to Islamic tradition, Arafat is where ADAM AND EVE were reunited after their expulsion from PARADISE and where GABRIEL taught ABRAHAM the hajj rites.

Among the distinguishing features of the plain are Mount Mercy, also called Arafat, a hill where MUHAMMAD gave a farewell sermon during the hajj he performed just before his death in 632. There is a large MOSQUE nearby called the Namira Mosque, where hajj sermons are delivered today and broadcast throughout the world. There is another mosque at Muzdalifa, the "sacred monument" mentioned in the Quran, where pilgrims camp for the night after standing at Arafat and where they gather the pebbles that they will throw at three pillars in Mina on the way back to Mecca to conclude the hajj rituals. The plain of Arafat is today criss-crossed by paved roads and modern facilities to meet the needs of the more than 2 million pilgrims who gather there each year.

Further reading: Laleh Bakhtiar, *Encyclopedia of Islamic Law: A Compendium of the Major Schools* (Chicago: ABC International Group, 1996); F. E. Peters, *The Hajj: The Muslim Pilgrimage to Mecca and the Holy Places* (Princeton, N.J.: Princeton University Press, 1994).

Arafat, Yasir (1929–2004) *controversial leader of the Palestinian nationalist movement from the 1960s and the first president and prime minister of the Palestinian National Authority*

Yasir Arafat was the foremost political leader of the Palestinian people, an ARAB population that identifies its homeland with PALESTINE (the West Bank, Gaza, and ISRAEL). Educated as a civil engineer, he was a cofounder of the Fatah organization in 1959 (the core unit of the PALESTINE LIBERATION ORGANIZATION [PLO]) and served as chairman of the PLO from 1969 until his death. In 1994, he became president and prime minister of the Palestinian National Authority (PNA), an interim government created in anticipation of the establishment of a legitimate Palestinian nation-state in the West Bank and Gaza. Though many Israelis regarded Arafat as a terrorist because of his involvement in the Palestinian armed struggle for national self-determination, he was also recognized internationally as the legitimate leader of the Palestinian people. He shared the 1994 Nobel Peace Prize with then Israeli prime minister Yitzhak Rabin (1922–95) and Israeli foreign minister Shimon Peres (b. 1923) for his role in negotiating the 1993 Palestinian-Israeli interim peace agreement in Oslo, Norway. He was a controversial figure throughout his career, considered a hero and freedom fighter by some (especially

Palestinians), a corrupt dictator by others (including some Palestinians), and a terrorist (especially by Israelis and many supporters of Israel in the United States).

Arafat was one of the most prominent figures on the Middle Eastern political scene for nearly 40 years. A certain amount of mystery and paradox has surrounded his private and public life, due partly to the mythology that Arafat himself advanced. Although he claimed to have been born in JERUSALEM, he was actually born to Palestinian parents in CAIRO, EGYPT, where he spent much of his early life. His given name was Muhammad Abd al-Rahman Abd al-Rauf Arafat al-Qudwa al-Husayni, but he chose the aliases Yasir (also written as Yasser) and Abu Ammar in honor of Yasir Abu Ammar, one of the heroic companions of MUHAMMAD, the Islamic prophet. A Sunni Muslim, Arafat often quoted the QURAN in his speeches, abstained from pork and alcohol, and followed an ascetic lifestyle. Although he was affiliated with the radical MUSLIM BROTHERHOOD in the 1940s and 1950s, the PLO he headed is a nonreligious entity that favors the creation of a secular state where Muslims, Jews, and Christians alike will have citizenship. The successes that he achieved in his life were matched by serious reversals and failures that have led to the loss of life of many Palestinians and Israelis. After the signing the OSLO ACCORDS, winning the Nobel Peace Prize, and returning to Gaza in triumph in 1994, Arafat's fortunes declined significantly in the face of an internal struggle against the militant Islamic organization HAMAS and the hard-line tactics of an Israeli government headed by his long-time enemy, Ariel Sharon. The United States also challenged Arafat's leadership of the PNA, especially after it launched its global war on terrorism in the aftermath of the September 11th attacks on the World Trade Center and the Pentagon in 2001, with which neither Arafat nor the PLO had any connection whatsoever. In his last years, Arafat's movements were restricted by Israeli armed forces to his compound in Ramallah on the West Bank.

Just before his death from unknown causes, Israeli authorities allowed him to be flown to France for medical care, where he died on November 11, 2004. His remains were flown to Cairo, Egypt, for a state funeral and then to Ramallah for burial.

See also ARAB-ISRAELI CONFLICTS; JUDAISM AND ISLAM.

Further reading: Said K. Aburish, *Arafat: From Defender to Dictator* (New York: Bloomsbury, 1998); Barry Rubin and Judith Colp Rubin, *Yasir Arafat: A Political Biography* (Oxford: Oxford University Press, 2003).

archaeology

Archaeology is the modern study of material remains from the past in order to understand and explain history, culture, and social life. It involves scientific excavation, field surveys, careful recording of data, and critical thinking about what the data mean. Countries in the Middle East and Asia have been centers of archaeological inquiry since the late 18th century, but most of the excavating has been done on the sites of ancient, pre-Islamic, civilizations. Archaeological research in locations associated with Islamicate civilizations has increased in recent years, however. Muslim CITIES, towns, fortifications, way stations, and cemeteries from Spain and Africa to Central Asia and Indonesia provide significant amounts of material evidence about the past, encompassing a time span of nearly 1,400 years. This evidence includes the remains of MOSQUES, palaces, shrines, houses, hostels, burials, ceramics, inscriptions, and coinage.

Even though pre-Islamic history is dismissed by some pious Muslims as a time of pagan ignorance (the JAHILIYYA), Muslim historical writing from the Middle Ages demonstrates an early interest in gathering and preserving information about antiquities, or the material remains of bygone times. These accounts mixed together historical fact, legends from the QURAN, and FOLKLORE about ancient peoples and sites in Arabia, EGYPT,

IRAQ, and IRAN. Nevertheless, when it came to Islamicate cities and buildings, medieval authors did provide richly detailed information about their foundation, design, inhabitants, renovation, and destruction. Much of what we know today about medieval cities such as MECCA, MEDINA, BAGHDAD, CAIRO, DAMASCUS, and CORDOBA comes from the work of these scholars.

Archaeology in the modern study of the Middle East and Asia began with Napoleon Bonaparte's invasion of Egypt in 1798 and continued to develop as European powers competed for colonial dominance in those regions during the 19th and early 20th centuries. Although Europeans engaged in outright plundering of the antiquities of Egypt, PALESTINE (now Israel, Gaza, and the West Bank), and Iraq, they also established research centers and museums that promoted serious archaeological research and the study of ancient and "Oriental" languages. These scholars were mainly interested in uncovering the roots of Western civilization and verifying the historical authenticity of the Bible, so they often ignored archaeological evidence pertaining to Islamic history and society. Toward the end of the 19th century, when Europeans became interested in Islamic ART and religion, they began to excavate sites that dated to the Islamic periods of history (seventh century to 19th century). Among the first places to be excavated were Samarqand in Turkestan (by Russians, 1885), the Qala of Bani Hammad in ALGERIA (by French, 1898–1908), and Samarra in Ottoman Iraq (by Germans, 1911–20). The French conducted the first excavations in Iran from the 1880s to 1931 and in SYRIA after World War I. Meanwhile, the British included Islamic as well as Hindu and Buddhist sites in their Archaeological Survey of INDIA and conducted excavations at Islamic sites in Palestine, Transjordan (now Jordan), and Iraq. Americans became involved in Middle Eastern archaeology in the 1920s, concentrating their efforts in Palestine and Iran. Since World War II, they have focused attention on Islamic sites in Egypt, Jordan, and Yemen. While

Western archaeologists have explored sites in the Arabian Peninsula and the Persian Gulf since the late 1800s, excavations in Mecca and Medina are forbidden because these are holy cities.

Muslims were involved with European and American archaeological activities from the beginning—as authorities who negotiated with them over excavation and ownership rights and as laborers. Moreover, Muslims began to acquire the necessary education and training to participate in joint excavations with Westerners and to conduct their own projects, starting in Egypt, TURKEY, and Iraq. Muslim archaeologists also participated in the founding and administration of national archaeological societies and museums that now exist in nearly all Muslim countries. In cooperation with international organizations, these institutions provide new knowledge about the past, help protect valued monuments and artifacts from destruction as their respective countries undergo rapid modernization, and often encourage tourism to locations of historical importance. In addition, governments in recently independent countries benefit from such institutions in their efforts to forge national identities that link them to their ancient and Islamic heritages.

See also ARCHITECTURE; ORIENTALISM.

Further reading: Timothy Insoll, *The Archaeology of Islam* (Oxford, U.K.: Blackwell Publishers, 1999); Donald Malcolm Reid, *Whose Pharaohs? Archaeology, Museums, and Egyptian National Identity from Napoleon to World War I* (Cairo: American University in Cairo Press, 2002); Stephen Vernoit, "The Rise of Islamic Archaeology." *Muqarnas* 14 (1997): 1–10.

architecture

Architecture is an area of human activity that involves the design, creation, modification, and use of the built environment. The study of Islamic architecture follows the historical development of the study of Islamic ART and is generally included with it by scholars.

As is the case with art, the history of the field gave rise to notions that made use of religious and racial characteristics to capture architectural tendencies. Among these is the idea of the cultivated garden as the PARADISE of former desert nomads and the image of the reward of every good Muslim or of the courtyard house as the type best suited to Islamicate societies intent on secluding their WOMEN. These notions often closed the door on further questioning and investigation and allowed earlier scholars to concentrate on classifying and describing buildings and other structures. In contrast, the courtyard house is currently understood as a shared Mediterranean type that responded to environmental factors ranging from climatic conditions to societal mores. And scholars are beginning to explore the agricultural and economic functions of gardens as well as their organization, cultivation, and imagery. These specialized studies go along with new research in the areas of urbanism, the rise of markets and settlements, and the patterns that are currently creating Islamicate architecture in areas that were not historically populated by Muslims, such as is found in Europe and North America.

As is the case with Islamic art, some historians of Islamic architecture question the linkages

Ibn Tulun Mosque (ninth century) in Cairo, Egypt *(Juan E. Campo)*

The Court of the Lions in the Alhambra, Granada, Spain (13th/14th century) *(Federico R. Campo)*

between a house, a citadel, or a school and the label *Islamic,* and admit as Islamic only those buildings created to house religious activities. The MOSQUE, shrine, tomb, MADRASA, and Sufi enclave are usually included in this category. They are united by their uses, by a general (though not exclusive) avoidance of representations of living beings, and usually by a liberal application of historical and religious inscriptions. Yet even here contradictions arise; the tomb and shrine, for example, may well be deemed un-Islamic within certain Islamic legal and theological positions. These contradictions, which extend to all categories of religious Islamic architecture, arise from the conflation of use and function.

It is the distinction between use and function that moves Islamic architecture (and art) out of the supposed natural systems in which scholars have situated them and places them instead within cultural systems that are capable of producing a multiplicity of arts and architectures under the rubric of Islam. Use refers to the actual situations in which specific buildings or objects are employed, while function is attached to the reasons the building is built and the purposes it serves. Both provoke questions of how, where, when, who, and why, but function focuses mostly on the question

of why. While mosques are built for PRAYER (their use), they may also be intended to commemorate the generosity or enhance the prestige of the person who funded them or to signal the presence of a Muslim community in a new setting (their function). In this sense, Islamic architecture is no different from other architectures. It operates as shelter and as sign, and it is created within relationships that bind clients, designers, architects, builders, suppliers, and users.

See also BAZAAR; CITIES; HOUSES; *MIHRAB*; MINARET; ORIENTALISM; PURDAH.

Nuha N. N. Khoury

Further reading: Oleg Grabar, *The Formation of Islamic Art* (New Haven, Conn.: Yale University Press, 1973); Robert Hillenbrand, *Islamic Architecture: Form, Function, and Meaning* (Edinburgh: University of Edinburgh Press, 1997); Renata Holod and Hasan-Uddin Khan, *The Mosque and the Modern World: Architects, Patrons, and Designs since the 1950s* (London: Thames & Hudson, 1997); George Michell, ed., *Architecture of the Islamic World: Its History and Social Meaning* (London: Thames & Hudson, 1978).

Arkoun, Muhammad (1928–) *noted modern Muslim philosopher and intellectual*

Muhammad Arkoun is one of the most prolific and academically influential liberal Muslim intellectuals of the late 20th and early 21st centuries. He is among the first generation of Muslim intellectuals who have intentionally directed their works towards Western audiences and people living in the majority Muslim world. Most of his works have appeared originally in French and later have been translated into Arabic and other languages.

Arkoun was born on January 2, 1928, in the Berber village of Taourirt-Mimoun in ALGERIA. He has written more than 100 books and articles and has lectured throughout the world. He is a senior research fellow and member of the board of governors of the Institute of Ismaili Studies in London, professor emeritus of the history of Islamic thought at the Sorbonne University in Paris, former director of the Institute of Arab and Islamic Studies there, and editor in chief of the French scholarly journal *Arabica*. He has taught as a visiting professor at several universities in North America and Europe and has earned some of the most prestigious awards in the humanities and Islamic studies.

Arkoun is skeptical about the traditional formulations of Islamic institutions, doctrine, and practice throughout history. He believes that Islamic authorities' fear of societal chaos and their desire for order and obedience helped determine the establishment of Islamic law, thought, and THEOLOGY. According to him, Muslims must free themselves from the oppressive constraints of "orthodox" Islam and work in partnership with members of other religions in creating a world that is rooted in peace, equality, mutual understanding, and intellectual vigor. In such a world, there would be no borders and no core, no sidelined groups and no superior ones. A transformed and open-ended Islam would become the basis for societies where people would seek to understand one another without permitting dogma, ethnic, linguistic, or other differences to block their continued cooperation.

For Arkoun, one way that the powerful sway of Muslim orthodoxy or orthodoxies can be lessened is by means of the creation of a new academic discipline that he calls "applied Islamology." This discipline would be devoted to analyzing and criticizing the ideas and institutions within Islam that have perpetuated discrimination, oppression, and marginalization.

Arkoun's novel and dynamic approach to Islam is also evident in his methodology with respect to the QURAN. The supreme and perfect message of the Quran as a revealed sacred text is a central tenet of Islamic doctrine, and this is one of the ideas that Arkoun criticizes. He believes that the question of whether the Quran was revealed should be suspended pending further academic inquiry, while he contends there is a vigorous Quranic intention. For him, this sacred text does not impose definitive solutions to the practical problems of human existence. It has the capacity to generate within humans a regard for themselves, the world, and the symbols that could potentially provide them with a sense of meaning.

While Arkoun's ideas are thought provoking, their full impact outside scholarly circles remains to be seen. One of the main questions that liberal Muslims such as Arkoun face is the extent to which their ideas may become institutionalized and accepted by the Muslim masses who are not necessarily influenced by intellectual trends in Western colleges and universities. Nevertheless, Arkoun's life and work will continue to be a tremendous force within Islamic studies for many more years.

See also EDUCATION.

Jon Armajani

Further reading: Mohammed Arkoun, *Rethinking Islam: Common Questions, Uncommon Answers,* trans. and ed. Robert D. Lee (Boulder, Colo.: Westview Press, 1989); Mohammed Arkoun, *The Unthought in Contemporary Islamic Thought* (London: Saqi Books, 2002); Robert D. Lee, *Overcoming Tradition and Modernity: The Search for Islamic Authenticity* (Boulder, Colo.: Westview Press, 1997).

Armenians

Armenians are an ethnic-religious group of people whose origins date back at least to the middle of the second millennium B.C.E. Some scholars believe that Armenians, whose language is Indo-European, are descendants of populations that migrated from southeastern Europe to eastern Anatolia, or the Armenian plateau, as it is sometimes called. This region, located between the Mediterranean, Black, and Caspian Seas, was a battleground in which powerful ancient empires, including Medes, Assyria, Persia, Hellenistic Greece, Parthia, and Rome fought to expand their territories. An inscription on a rock attributed to Persia's King Darius refers to Armina, showing that Armenia was known to its neighbors as early as the sixth century B.C.E. Native dynasties ruled Armenia for five centuries until the area was conquered by the Romans. In the fourth century C.E., Christianity, to which many Armenians had already voluntarily converted, became the state religion of the Roman Empire and as such was imposed on all Armenians.

From the seventh to the 11th centuries, ARAB, Mongol, and Turkic peoples conquered the territories inhabited by Armenians, a transformation that made many Armenians the subjects of Muslim rulers. However, Christianity, together with the unique Armenian language, helped Armenians resist assimilating to the cultures of those who ruled them over them. With the fall of Constantinople to the Ottomans in the 15th century, all Armenians in western Asia (the Middle East) became subjects of Muslim rulers, either Ottoman or Persian. In the early 19th century, Russia successfully conquered much of the South Caucasus, including Georgia, eastern Armenia, and northern Azerbaijan. Many Armenians left IRAN and Anatolia and moved to Russian controlled territories, believing that their status and living conditions would improve in the Orthodox Christian Russian Empire. Some Armenians living in the Ottoman Empire during the TANZIMAT reforms also hoped that their status would improve.

However, many Armenian intellectuals believed that Armenians' security and status would improve only with autonomy and that they would have to fight to obtain it. The revolutions that occurred in the early 20th century in Russia, Persia, and the Ottoman Empire inspired many Armenians to join in armed struggle against their imperial leaders. Armenian solidarity strengthened after the Young Turks orchestrated the extermination of the Armenian population in 1915. Their systematic campaign to expel Armenians through forced migration caused the deaths of an estimated 1 million to 1.5 million Armenians. Many survivors emigrated, increasing the numbers of Armenians living in the diaspora. A number of countries they migrated to are in the Arab Middle East: SYRIA, LEBANON, PALESTINE, and EGYPT. In the chaotic conditions created by World War I and the Bolshevik revolution in Russia, Armenians established an independent republic in eastern Armenia, one that survived only briefly until the Bolsheviks extended their control in the South Caucasus. For 70 years, Armenia was a socialist republic within the framework of the Soviet Union under the leadership of the Communist Party in the Kremlin.

In the late 1980s, Gorbachev's glasnost inspired many Armenians to push for change, and Armenia declared independence from the Soviet Union in 1990. In 1991, a political dispute between Armenia and Azerbaijan over the region of Nagorno-Karabagh escalated into a military conflict. This war lasted until 1994, when a cease-fire was in place, leaving Armenians in control of Karabagh. Armenians have successfully established the independent Republic of Armenia. However, like other republics of the former Soviet Union, Armenia suffers from economic stagnation, corruption, and inadequate development of democratic institutions.

See also CHRISTIANITY AND ISLAM; OTTOMAN DYNASTY.

Leslie Sargent

Further reading: George A. Bournoutian, *A History of the Armenian People* (Costa Mesa, Calif.: Mazda Publishers, 1994); Richard G. Hovannisian, ed. *The Armenian People from Ancient to Modern Times* (New York: St. Martin's Press, 1997); Ronald Grigor Suny, *Looking toward Ararat: Armenia in Modern History* (Bloomington and Indianapolis: Indiana University Press, 1993).

art

Pop artist Andy Warhol (1928–87) defined art as whatever the artist deemed it to be by affixing his signature to it. Swiss painter Paul Klee (1879–1940) likened the artist to a tree trunk that absorbs nutrients from the roots to produce a different image in the branches and leaves, making the artist the intermediary between nature and culture. During the 19th and early 20th centuries some art historians still championed Academic painting, which codified styles and stipulated that they had to coincide with content, resulting in art that was edifying as well as aesthetically pleasing. These Euro-American views tell us that art is a changeable concept; its definitions differ according to time, place, and school of thought. Whether we consider medieval Europe or modern China, we should expect art to reflect the perceptions of its creators, consumers, and scholars.

From the 19th century on, the Islamicate world produced art that is part of the general history of modern art. Historically, however, the definition and material of what we know as Islamic art are different. Indeed, only in moments of tension is there a sense of an art that is considered primarily Islamic in its content and intentions (as, for example, in the case of CALLIGRAPHY in 10th-century Iraq), and in those cases it is because the visual formulas followed rules that were viewed as more "orthodox" than others. As elsewhere in the world before the dissemination of the idea of the artist as creative genius, art itself was not understood in the same ways in the past as it is today. Rather, artistic value was seen in the expenditure of surplus—whether surplus skills and talent or money and material—to produce objects that performed beyond their immediate uses (for instance, ceramic plates) by eliciting pleasure from the viewer or user. As such, a variety of richly decorated objects in different media (as opposed to canvas painting and three dimensional sculpture), wall paintings (properly also part of ARCHITECTURE), and illustrated books form the bulk of historical Islamic art.

Islamic art is first of all a subdiscipline of art history concerned with the study of a variety of visual cultures collected under the rubric Islam. The designation of the field was in place by 1900 when the first publications titled *Islamic*

Ceramic artist, Turkey *(Juan E. Campo)*

Art replaced ones dedicated to the ethno-racial/regional categories ARAB, Persian, Turkish, Moresque, and Indian art. The earlier trend followed the model of the Napoleonic invasion and exploration of EGYPT in 1798, with its agenda of knowing, ordering, controlling, and colonizing. Recent scholarship has made great strides in overcoming this legacy and its Orientalizing offshoots, but its effects continue to dominate views of the field and its contents.

Despite excellent work by archaeologists, paleographers, epigraphers, and historians, Islamic art was understood up to the mid-20th century as the material reflection of unchangeable religious essences and racial characteristics. Among its stereotyped features was the supposed Semitic-Arab abhorrence of the representation of living beings, which coincided with Islamic injunctions against the making of images. The infinite ARABESQUE, with its floral, geometric, and calligraphic varieties, compensated for this lack while repeating the formula of the essential oneness of God. The ornamented objects, and especially the rugs and carpets that were much in demand by collectors and museums, reflected the Arab Muslim's nomadic desert heritage, which did not encourage great works of painting or sculpture, the types of work that populated European art. An updated version of such Orientalist views surfaced in London's World of Islam Festival in 1976. The films, exhibitions, and publications that accompanied the festival ensured the wide dissemination of its views, and some of these were adopted by some young Arab states in constructing their national identities.

Islamic art is now conventionally defined as art made for Muslims by Muslims in primarily Islamic contexts. The new definition allows for possibilities of differentiation in place and time and facilitates the organization of the material into the chapters of survey books. Nonetheless, it is not without problems. It locates Islamic art outside the processes of art production and consumption studied by art historians. And it endorses chronological and regional divisions at the expense of intellectual, philosophical, economic and other (including religious) developments. Some of these problems arise from the huge amount of material in different media studied in the field and from its temporal and geographic scope: India to Spain from 650 to 1800 (which still leaves out large areas with an Islamic presence and interrupts the temporal range at the point when the field came into being).

These problems may begin to dissipate once we realize that Islamic art is a modern Euro-American construct based on otherness and difference. Once that happens, the material will be opened up to new theoretical and critical considerations that will place it more properly within the processes and histories of human creativity.

See also ORIENTALISM.

Nuha N. N. Khoury

Further reading: Sheila S. Blair and Jonathan M. Bloom, "Art and Architecture: Themes and Variations." In *The Oxford History of Islam*, edited by John L. Esposito, 215–267 (Oxford: Oxford University Press; Robert Hillenbrand, *Islamic Art and Architecture* (New York: Thames & Hudson, 1999); Donald Malcolm Reid, *Whose Pharaohs? Archaeology, Museums, and Egyptian National Identity from Napoleon to World War I* (Cairo: The American University Press, 2002); Stephen Vernoit, ed., *Discovering Islamic Art: Scholars, Collectors and Collections* (New York: I.B. Tauris, 2000).

asceticism

Asceticism involves a variety of religious practices that seek to control or manipulate the body and bodily desires in order to perfect one's mental or spiritual condition. The word comes from Greek *askesis,* which means "training" or "exercise." Although it has often been used in connection with the monastic practices of medieval Christianity (abstinence, fasting, poverty, vigils, and retreats), historians of religion now use the term to study asceticism comparatively in a variety of religions and cultures. It is a defining characteristic of Hinduism, Buddhism, and, to a lesser extent, ISLAM.

Extreme asceticism and celibacy are officially refuted in Islam, because the ULAMA emphasized moderation in religious practice. Nevertheless, a number of practices Muslims engage in have ascetic features, such as the duties of fasting during RAMADAN and doing the HAJJ to Mecca. In fasting, Muslims are required to completely avoid food, drink, and sexual activity during the daytime for 30 consecutive days every year. Many also accompany these practices with PRAYER and late-night vigils. Participants in the hajj are required to maintain ritual purity, wear simple garments, abstain from sex, avoid harming ANIMAL life, and avoid incurring violence. Shaving, haircuts, nail clipping, and wearing perfume or make-up are also banned during the hajj, which lasts about six days annually. Even ALMSGIVING (*zakat*) has an ascetic quality, because it obliges Muslims to render some of their wealth (but not all of it) for the welfare of the community. A concept of purification is associated with this activity, as reflected in the word *zakat* itself, which is based on an Arabic word for "pure" or "sinless" (*zaki*).

The virtuosos of asceticism in Islam, however, are Sufis, those who follow its mystical path. Indeed, the name *sufi* is thought to be a reference to the frock of wool (*suf*) worn by early ascetics. Sufis claimed to have been inspired by the example of MUHAMMAD and early members of the Muslim community, although historically their techniques and beliefs seem to have been influenced by pre-Islamic ascetic traditions found in the religions of the Middle East and Asia. Muhammad was remembered for his simple lifestyle, frequent vigils, spiritual retreats, and extra fasting. Later, in the aftermath of the early Arab Muslim conquests (seventh and eighth centuries), ascetics such as HASAN AL-BASRI (d. 728) were repulsed by the wealth and luxurious lifestyle enjoyed by Muslim rulers. They felt that this worldliness distracted people from keeping their focus on God, obeying his laws, and reaching PARADISE. Other early ascetics were IBRAHIM IBIN ADHAM (d. ca. 778) and RABIA AL-ADAWIYYA (d. 801). With the appearance of organized Sufism after the 10th century, a member of a brotherhood (TARIQA) of Sufis was called a *faqir,* "poor man," or its Persian equivalent, DERVISH, because of his adherence to a spiritual life of poverty. Sufis used ascetic practices to control the impulses and passions of the lower soul (*nafs*), and they identified them with stations on the path to spiritual perfection: poverty, repentance, seclusion, withdrawal, abstinence, renunciation, and hunger. Special fasting practices, prayer postures, nighttime vigils, self-mortification, and extended periods of seclusion were developed by many of the Sufi brotherhoods, which provided manuals to their members to guide them in their practices. Some groups in India, such as the Shattariyya, adopted yogic forms of asceticism, but this was not widespread. Others, such as the Qalandars,

engaged in what some call deviant ascetic practices, such as taking hallucinogenic drugs, walking about nearly naked, and practicing forms of self-mutilation.

See also ABLUTION; BAQA AND FANA; SUFISM.

Further reading: Carl W. Ernst, *Teachings of Sufism* (Boston: Shambala, 1999); Ahmet T. Karamustafa, *God's Unruly Friends: Dervish Groups in the Islamic Later Middle Period, 1200–1550* (Salt Lake City: University of Utah Press, 1994).

Ashari School

The Ashari School is the foremost school of THEOLOGY in Sunni ISLAM. It is named after Abu al-Hasan al-Ashari (873–935), who sought to define and defend core doctrines about God, the QURAN, and FREE WILL in terms of rational philosophy. Although we lack details about his life, we know he was from the southern Iraqi town of Basra and that he was a member of a respected family that claimed descent from one of Muhammad's earliest followers. He was first an enthusiastic supporter of the MUTAZILI SCHOOL, which, armed with Greek rationalism, refuted traditional religious beliefs and argued instead that 1) the attributes assigned to God in the Quran (such as hearing and seeing or having face and hands) were not part of his essential being; 2) the Quran was created; and 3) humans could exercise free will independent from that of God. However, by the time he was 40 years old, al-Ashari had become convinced that these positions and related ones were wrong. Switching course, he used the Mutazili tools of rational disputation against them to argue instead that 1) God's attributes were real, even if we do not know how they are so; 2) the Quran was God's speech and therefore eternal and uncreated as he is; and 3) human free will is impossible because God creates everything, including individual human actions.

The Ashari School grew in Basra and Baghdad, drawing its inspiration from al-Ashari's theology and method of rational argumentation. By the late 12th century, it had become the dominant Sunni theological tradition and was officially taught as a subject in Sunni centers of learning. Among the most prominent members of this school were al-Baqillani (d. 1013), al-Baghdadi (d. 1037), AL-GHAZALI (d. 1111), and al-Razi (d. 1209). For centuries, the Ashari School gave a rational basis to Sunni faith and provided an intellectual defense against speculative philosophy and Shii doctrines. During the 19th and 20th centuries, it gave way to currents of Islamic modernism and secularism that swept the Muslim world as a result of European colonial expansion and the influx of new ideas from the West. Many Ashari tenets, however, continue to hold an important place in contemporary Muslim religious thought.

See also ALLAH; ANTHROPOMORPHISM; MADRASA; THEOLOGY.

Further reading: Richard M. Frank, *Al-Ghazali and the Asharite School* (Durham, N.C.: Duke University Press, 1994); W. Montgomery Watt, *The Formative Period of Islamic Thought* (Oxford: One World Press, 1998).

Ashura

Ashura is the 10th day of the first Islamic month, MUHARRAM, and the most important holiday of the year for the Shia. It had been a day of FASTING for pre-Islamic Arabs and for Jews (identified with Yom Kippur) and was recognized by Muhammad (d. 632) as an Islamic day of fasting, though when the month of RAMADAN was made the holy month of fasting for Muslims, the fast of Ashura became voluntary rather than mandatory. Islamic tradition has associated this important day with biblical events recognized by Jews and Christians: It has been considered to be the day when Noah's ark landed after the Flood and when Jonah was freed from the fish that had swallowed him.

A more documented event occurred on this day in the year 680, one that was to have serious implications for Islamic history. HUSAYN IBN ALI,

the grandson of the PROPHET, was killed in the desert of KARBALA in IRAQ by the UMAYYAD caliph Yazid's (r. 680–683) forces. This event has come to symbolize in sacred history and ritual the rift between Shiis and Sunnis and led to the development of MARTYRDOM as a definitive value of SHIISM. So, for the Shia the first 10 days of the month of Muharram, leading up to the day of Ashura, are a time of mourning for the death of Husayn. In IRAN and other Shii-dominated areas (for example, Lebanon, Bahrayn, and Shii communities in PAKISTAN, INDIA, AFGHANISTAN, Tajikistan, as well as immigrant communities in Europe and North America), mourners express their sorrow in a complex of public and private ceremonial gatherings, street processions, and morality plays. Public lamentations sometimes reach a frenzy in which men beat their breasts or slash their heads to draw blood in commemoration of the spilling of Husayn's BLOOD at Karbala. Theatrical performances reenact the events of the Karbala tragedy. Another rite performed during Ashura in Iran and areas influenced by Persianate culture is the *rowzeh khani* (also known as a *qiraya,* "reading," in Arabic-speaking IRAQ), which consists of lamentations, moving sermons, and improvised readings about events that transpired at Karbala. The name *rowzeh* is derived from a book of Karbala narratives, *The Garden of the Martyrs* (*Rawdat al-shuhada*), written by Husayn Waiz Kashifi around 1503, in connection with the establishment of the Shii SAFAVID DYNASTY in Iran. People of all classes participate in these gatherings, including Sunnis, and, in India, Hindus and Buddhists. Women often organize Ashura gatherings in their homes.

See also CALENDAR; HOLIDAYS; HUSAYNIYYA; TWELVE-IMAM SHIISM; UMAYYAD CALIPHATE.

Mark Soileau

Further reading: Kamran Scot Aghaie, ed., *The Women of Karbala: Ritual Performance and Symbolic Discourses in Modern Shii Islam* (Austin: University of Texas Press, 2005); Peter Chelkowski, ed., *Taziyeh: Ritual and Drama in Iran* (New York: New York University Press,

1979); Elizabeth Warnock Fernea, *Guests of the Sheik* (New York: Anchor Books, 1995); David Pinault, *The Shiites: Ritual and Popular Piety in a Muslim Community* (New York: St. Martin's Press, 1992).

Assassins

In the 12th century, Europeans gave the name *Assassins* to a group of ruthless killers they had heard about during their CRUSADES and travels in the Middle East. One of the most famous accounts about them is found in the writings of world traveler Marco Polo (1254–1324). He described the Assassins as agents recruited by a leader called Old Man of the Mountain, who kept them drugged and entertained in hidden GARDENS patterned after those of the Islamic PARADISE as described in the QURAN. When the leader wanted them to do his bidding, which included the assassination of rulers and officials, he would send them out with the promise that when they accomplished their tasks ANGELS would carry them back to paradise as a reward. By the 14th century, Europeans were using the term *assassin* more generally for anyone who murdered a ruler or high-ranking official, which is the meaning it still has today. The name is originally from the Arabic *hashishi*, someone addicted to hashish (a narcotic made from Indian hemp).

The actual Assassins, as distinguished from the ones imaginatively described by Europeans, were Nizari Isamaili Shia—devoted followers of Hasan-i Sabbah (d. 1124), a charismatic Shii leader who announced the coming of a new religious era and led an uprising against Sunni Muslim rulers in the Middle East. His trained fighters, who were willing to sacrifice their lives for him, operated out of fortresses in the remote mountains of SYRIA and Persia (IRAN), the most famous of which was Alamut, located in the Elburz Mountains near the Caspian Sea. These fighters would infiltrate towns and palaces to carry out their assignments, which included political assassinations as well as other disruptive actions. They inspired fear and hatred in the hearts of Sunni authorities, who were also contending with European crusader armies in Syria and Palestine at that time. Sunnis usually called the Nizaris "apostates," but they also tried to insult them by calling them *hashishis*. Legends about the Assassins began to circulate among European crusaders and travelers in the Middle East at this time. The Mongols from the steppes of Central Asia finally put an end to Nizari rule in Persia in 1256, and the MAMLUK rulers of EGYPT did the same in Syria by 1273. The violent activities of the Assassins ceased, and the history of the Nizari branch of Islam took a different turn as its members retreated from politics and killing to live more peacefully in widely scattered communities where some followed the path of SUFISM and engaged in new missionary activities, especially in Persia and INDIA.

See also AGA KHAN; APOSTASY; FATIMID DYNASTY; *FIDAI*; ISMAILI SHIISM.

Further reading: Farhad Daftary, *The Ismailis: Their History and Doctrines* (Cambridge: Cambridge University Press, 1990); Bernard Lewis, *The Assassins: A Radical Sect in Islam* (Oxford: Oxford University Press, 1967).

Ataturk, Mustafa Kemal (1881–1938)
founder and first president of the modern Republic of Turkey

Mustafa Kemal was born in Salonica, then part of the Ottoman Empire. He attended military schools in the Balkans, where Greek and Slavic nationalist movements were active, and went on to graduate from the military academy in ISTANBUL, the Ottoman capital. During his early military appointments, he worked to organize opposition to the despotism of the Ottoman SULTAN Abdulhamid, though he was not directly involved in the Young Turk revolution of 1908. He gained military fame as commander of the Turkish troops that repelled the invasion of Allied forces at Gallipoli in 1915.

Dissatisfied with the Ottoman regime's compliance with the British, who occupied Istanbul after

World War I, Mustafa Kemal left Istanbul in 1919 to gather support for a resistance movement in Anatolia, eventually settling in Ankara, where the Grand National Assembly was opened in 1920. When Turkish troops under Mustafa Kemal's command defeated the Greek troops that had invaded western Anatolia in 1921, the nationalist forces earned enough bargaining power to reject the terms of the Sèvres treaty (the World War I peace agreement that would have divided the country) and to abolish the Ottoman sultanate, which had reigned for 600 years. In 1923, a new treaty ensuring Turkey's borders was agreed to at Lausanne (in Switzerland), and the republic was proclaimed with Mustafa Kemal as its president.

Mustafa Kemal's regime was autocratic, which allowed him to push through a series of reforms designed to rebuild TURKEY as a modern, Western,

Mustafa Kemal Ataturk *(Juan E. Campo)*

secular nation. In 1924, he abolished the CALIPH-ATE, which Ottoman sultans had assumed since the 16th century, and closed religious schools. He closed the DERVISH lodges, which were seen as threatening to the secular regime, and banned the wearing of religious dress outside of places of worship. He had a new civil code adopted, bringing equal rights to WOMEN. He had the Arabic ALPHABET replaced with a modified Latin alphabet and encouraged the replacement of Arabic and Persian words in the language with "pure" Turkish words, even if they had to be invented.

In 1934, a law was passed requiring all citizens to adopt a surname, and Mustafa Kemal chose for himself that of Ataturk, meaning "Father of the Turks." Ataturk died in 1938 in Istanbul after having served four terms as president, but his legacy has continued until today. His mausoleum in Ankara continues to be visited regularly; his image appears on every banknote and in every public building, and his statues stand prominently in every city and town. Boulevards, universities, towns, and Istanbul's international airport are named after him. The ideas he brought to fruition—constituting an ideology known as Kemalism—also continue to make up the dominant ideology of the Turkish state.

See also OTTOMAN DYNASTY; SECULARISM.

Mark Soileau

Further reading: Lord Kinross, *Atatürk: The Rebirth of a Nation* (London: Weidenfeld & Nicolson, 1964); Andrew Mango, *Atatürk: The Biography of the Founder of Modern Turkey* (New York: Overlook Press, 1999).

Aurangzeb (1618–1707) *Indian Muslim ruler who led the Mughal Empire when it controlled the greatest amount of territory on the Indian subcontinent*

The great grandson of AKBAR (r. 1556–1605) and son of Shah Jahan (r. 1628–58), Aurangzeb came to power during a bloody civil war for succession in 1657. After killing all of his brothers, his rivals for power, and imprisoning his father, he secured control in northern INDIA and engaged in a series of ongoing military campaigns to conquer independent kingdoms in the south. When he died in 1701, his empire stretched from the Himalayas in the north to the southern edge of the Deccan Plateau and from Bengal in the east to AFGHANISTAN in the west. His successors were unable to maintain control over such a vast territory, so the Mughal Empire began to break up into smaller states again after his death, setting the stage for the onset of British colonial influence in the mid-1700s.

Aurangzeb is remembered for his religious conservativism and his intolerant attitude toward his non-Muslim subjects, in contrast to Akbar and other Mughal rulers. He promoted strict adherence to the SHARIA, enhanced the influence of the Sunni ULAMA in the court, and actively encouraged CONVERSION to ISLAM. One of his most important contributions to the Muslim community was his sponsorship of the *Fatawa-i Alamgiri* (completed in 1675), a comprehensive compilation of Sunni legal rulings. His religious conservativism had serious drawbacks, however. Imperial patronage of MUSIC, ART, and ARCHITECTURE decreased, and even though Hindus continued to serve as officials and allies of the Mughal government, their status declined. Active opposition to Aurangzeb, which included Muslims, grew as a result of his destruction of Hindu temples, the imposition of special taxes and restrictions, and his persecution of the growing Sikh community in northern India, which resulted in the martyrdom of one of their leaders, Guru Tegh Bahadur (d. 1675). The legacy of Aurangzeb's policies has continued to fuel Hindu-Muslim tensions in South Asia since independence and partition in 1947.

See also DARA SHIKOH; HINDUISM AND ISLAM; MUGHAL DYNASTY.

Further reading: Gordon Johnson, *Cultural Atlas of India* (New York: Facts On File, 1996); John F. Richards, *The Mughal Empire* (Cambridge: Cambridge University Press, 1993).

Australia

The continent of Australia joins neighboring islands of INDONESIA and NEW ZEALAND in demarcating the southwestern extent of the Pacific Ocean and the eastern extent of the Indian Ocean. Australia is separated from Indonesia by the Aratura Sea and from New Zealand by the Tasmania Sea. Also part of the country of Australia is the large island of Tasmania, off the continent's southeast coast. The country has a total land area of some 2,967,100 square miles.

The Aboriginal peoples, Australia's original inhabitants, settled the land as early as 40,000 years ago. They created a diversity of cultures across the continent. They seem to have migrated from Southeast Asia. Europeans made note of Australia's existence in the 17th century, but only in 1770 did Captain James Cook (1728–79) claim it for Great Britain. British settlement began less than two decades later, the first settlement being the infamous penal colony at Botany Bay. Over the next two centuries, the descendants of British settlers became the dominant force in Australia, making up two-thirds of its 19 million inhabitants. The remaining third constitutes an extremely diverse ethnic spectrum that includes many people from former British colonies from India and Southeast Asia.

The original Muslims in Australia were from AFGHANISTAN, men employed as CAMEL drivers. Many settled in central Australia, and the contemporary town of Alice Springs was at one time referred to by local residents as MECCA. That original Afghan community did not perpetuate itself and eventually died out. (Some Muslims point to evidence of even earlier Muslims coming to Australia from MALAYSIA and Indonesia to settle in fishing villages along the northern coast.) Over the next decades, the number of Muslims grew slowly and fluctuated widely. From a low point in the early 1930s (around 2,000), the community reached more than 10,000 by 1970. Since that time, it has grown at a much more rapid rate. It was approaching 150,000 by the time of the 1991 national census and today includes some estimated 315,000 residents. It constitutes about 1.5 percent of Australia's 21 million citizens.

The Muslim community has an extremely diverse ethnic makeup, its members deriving from more than 50 countries, including those in western Africa, the Middle East, and southern Asia. The largest group of Australian Muslims comes from Lebanon and TURKEY. Its members have concentrated in the major urban centers in the southeastern part of the continent. Through the last decades of the 20th century, regional councils of Muslims were formed, leading to the creation of the Australian Federation of Muslim Councils, the primary national Islamic organization. The growth of the community has allowed a variety of regional and national organizations, such as the United Muslim Women Association, to emerge.

The Australian Federation appoints a titular spiritual head of the Islamic community who bears the title MUFTI of Australia and New Zealand. The current mufti, Egyptian-born Taj Al-Din Hamid Abd Allah Al-Hilali (b. 1941), has become well known for his outspokenness, especially in his defense of the Muslim community in the wake of recent bombings in the United States, Bali, and London, the commitment of Australian troops to Afghanistan and Iraq, and government efforts to suppress possible terrorist acts in Australia.

Nationally, Muslims have concentrated on the education of the next generation and where possible have opened Islamic schools for youths at the primary and secondary levels. Leaders have expressed concern about the secular atmosphere in the country and laws promoting the liberation of youths in their mid-teens.

Today there are more than 100 MOSQUES and PRAYER halls in Australia. Most are Sunni in orientation, with no one legal school or ethnic membership dominating. The largest number of mosques and Islamic schools are found in the Sydney and Melbourne urban areas. Al Zahra College,

the first Islamic institution of higher learning, is located in Sydney.

See also EUROPE; UNITED STATES; WEST AFRICA.

J. Gordon Melton

Further reading: A. H. Johns and A. Saeed, "Muslims in Australia: The Building of a Community." In *Muslim Minorities in the West, Visible and Invisible,* edited by Yvonne Haddad and Jane I. Smith, 192–216 (Walnut Creek, Calif.: Altamira Press, 2002); Abdullah Saeed, *Australian Muslims: Their Beliefs, Practices and Institutions* (Melbourne: Department of Immigration and Multicultural and Indigenous Affairs, Australian Multicultural Foundation, University of Melbourne, 2004). Available online. URL: www.amf.net.au/PDF/religion-CulturalDiversity/Resource_Manual.pdf. Accessed on December 27, 2005; Wafia Omer and Kirsty Allen, "The Muslims in Australia." In *A Yearbook of Australian Religious Organizations,* edited by Peter Bentley and Philip J. Hughes, 114–115 (Kew, Victoria: Christian Research Association, 1997).

authority

Authority is the basis by which power is legitimately used to bring about compliance and obedience. In secular terms, it is often connected with how leaders and governments justify their right not only to exist, but also to rule others with their consent. In a hereditary monarchy, for example, authority is vested in the person of the king and his dynasty. In a liberal DEMOCRACY, authority is vested in the people, who then consent to be legally subject to those they elect to governmental office. In either case, the exercise of authority displaces the need to rely upon only brute force to obtain compliance. Max Weber (d. 1920), one of the founders of modern sociology, identified three basic types of authority that are generally accepted by modern scholars: 1) traditional authority based on the sanctity of the past, 2) charismatic authority involving the sanctity of individuals, and 3) rational-legal authority involving bureaucratic organizations. These three ideal types of authority

Genealogy of Muhammad, the Caliphs, and the Shii Imams

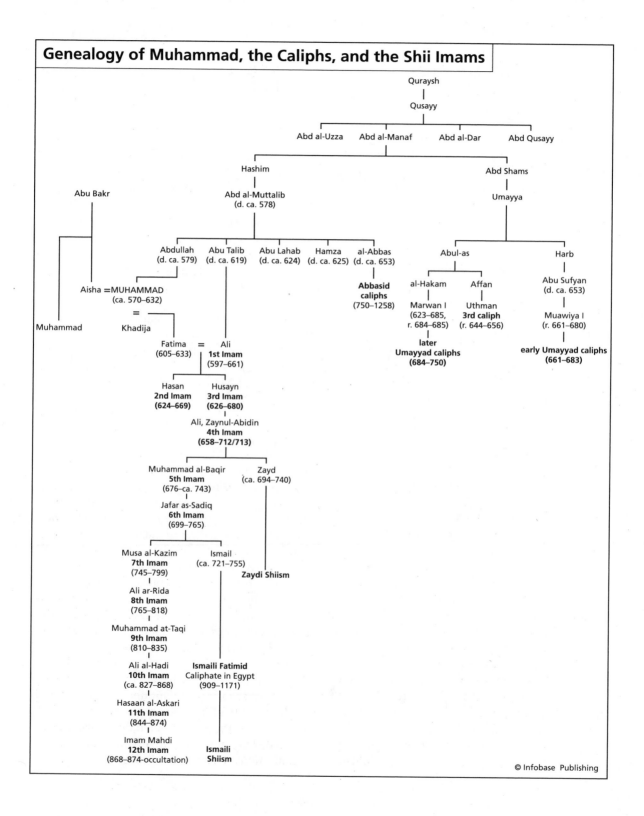

Quraysh
|
Qusayy

Abd al-Uzza — Abd al-Manaf — Abd al-Dar — Abd Qusayy

Hashim — Abd Shams

Abu Bakr

Abd al-Muttalib
(d. ca. 578)

Umayya

Abdullah
(d. ca. 579)
Abu Talib
(d. ca. 619)
Abu Lahab
(d. ca. 624)
Hamza
(d. ca. 625)
al-Abbas
(d. ca. 653)

Abul-as

Harb

Aisha =MUHAMMAD
(ca. 570–632)
=

Abbasid
caliphs
(750–1258)

al-Hakam

Affan

Abu Sufyan
(d. ca. 653)

Muhammad

Khadija

Marwan I
(623–685,
r. 684–685)

Uthman
3rd caliph
(r. 644–656)

Muawiya I
(r. 661–680)

Fatima
(605–633)
=
Ali
1st Imam
(597–661)

later
Umayyad caliphs
(684–750)

early Umayyad caliphs
(661–683)

Hasan
2nd Imam
(624–669)
Husayn
3rd Imam
(626–680)

Ali, Zaynul-Abidin
4th Imam
(658–712/713)

Muhammad al-Baqir
5th Imam
(676–ca. 743)
Zayd
(ca. 694–740)

Jafar as-Sadiq
6th Imam
(699–765)

Musa al-Kazim
7th Imam
(745–799)
Ismail
(ca. 721–755)

Zaydi Shiism

Ali ar-Rida
8th Imam
(765–818)

Muhammad at-Taqi
9th Imam
(810–835)

Ali al-Hadi
10th Imam
(ca. 827–868)
Ismaili Fatimid
Caliphate in Egypt
(909–1171)

Hasaan al-Askari
11th Imam
(844–874)

Imam Mahdi
12th Imam
(868–874–occultation)
Ismaili
Shiism

© Infobase Publishing

apply both to secular and religious social institutions, and they help us to understand the complex networks of authority that have formed in the history of ISLAM and that are evident in Islamicate societies today.

Sacred authority in Islam begins with God, the QURAN (God's word), and MUHAMMAD (the conveyer of God's word). The Quran declares that God is lord of all CREATION (Q 1:2) and that he holds sovereignty over the heavens and the earth (Q 5:40). Humans, therefore, are destined to be his "servants" or "worshippers." Indeed, the human acknowledgment of God's authority is expressed in Islam's FIVE PILLARS, which are collectively called *ibadat,* "duties of worship/servitude." The Quran alludes to its own authority as a sacred scripture when it states "That is the book in which there is no doubt, a guidance for the God-fearing" (Q 2:2). As the "command" (*amr*) revealed by the "lord of the worlds" (Q 56:80), the Quran is connected with the qualities of divine sovereignty, such as nobility (Q 56:77), glory (Q 50:1), might (Q 15:87), and wisdom (Q 36:2). In THEOLOGY, the Quran is regarded as God's speech and is one of his eternal attributes. Muslims turn to it for guidance with respect to matters of belief and religious practice, and it is the first of the four roots of religious law (FIQH). Among humans, God's authority (SULTAN) is entrusted above all to his prophets and messengers, the recipients and transmitters of God's word (Q 11:96) whom people must obey (Q 4:64). It is Muhammad in particular who is to be followed, for the Quran declares, "Whoever obeys the messenger obeys God" (Q 4:80). His authority is based on his personal charisma, but it also involves the authority of a sacred tradition of prophets that reaches back to Adam, the first human being, and the creation. Aside from the Quran itself, Muhammad's authority in the early Muslim community is reflected in a separate document known as the Constitution of MEDINA, which stipulates that if the early community is ever in disagreement, it should refer the matter to God and to Muhammad. The long-term importance of Muhammad as an authority for the Muslim community was assured with the collection of hadiths about his sayings and actions and the establishment of Muhammad's SUNNA (rules for belief, worship, and moral conduct) as a basis for law in the ninth century. Inheritance of Muhammad's personal charisma was to become an important aspect of Muslim rulers' authority, as it was for the Abbasids, the Fatimids, and the contemporary monarchies of MOROCCO and JORDAN. Among the various divisions of the Shia, descent from Muhammad through Ali and Fatima is a necessary qualification of the divinely guided Imams, people the Shia have regarded as the ideal rulers and religious figures for Muslims.

With the passage of time and the rise of Islamic empires, the networks of authority became more complex. The Quran acknowledges this complexity when it states, "obey God, the messenger, and those in authority (*amr*) among you" (Q 4:59). Though Muhammad's successors, the caliphs, first saw themselves mainly as tribal chieftains, after the rise of the Islamic empire they claimed primary authority in both spiritual and worldly affairs. This can be seen in the formal titles they took: "God's deputy" (*khalifat Allah*), rather than "deputy/successor of God's messenger" (*khalifat rasul Allah*), or even "commander (*amir*) of the faithful" and "God's authority (*sultan*) on earth." Several of the early Abbasid caliphs (eighth to ninth centuries) attempted to claim the exclusive right to decide matters of religious doctrine. By the 10th century, in the face of growing challenges to their authority in religious matters, rulers had negotiated a division of legitimate power with the ULAMA, the experts in Islamic law and tradition. Caliphs, sultans, and kings exercised authority in worldly affairs, while the ulama claimed mastery in the realm of religion. The actual division of labor between the rulers and ulama was rarely so clear, however, for the rulers were expected to uphold and enforce SHARIA as well as patronize the ulama. On the other hand, the ulama, in addition to interpreting the sharia, could exercise moral authority over rulers by either upholding or contesting their legitimacy. Only in the 20th century did the ulama ever act to overthrow a ruler and replace him with one of their own—the establishment of the Islamic Republic of Iran under Ayatollah RUHOLLAH KHOMEINI in 1979 was the exception rather than the rule.

Select WOMEN also held positions of authority among both rulers and religious scholars. Women in the ruling elites were occasionally involved in making decisions of state and influencing the selection of rulers, and they would also make donations to fund mosques and religious schools. Women from scholarly families even became famous as teachers, particularly in the science of hadith during the Middle Ages. Muhammad's wife AISHA (d. ca. 678) is an exemplary figure, because she is remembered for her leading role in the political and religious affairs of her time.

In addition to the rulers and the ulama, Sufi brotherhoods also developed their own concepts of authority. The Sufis consider themselves to be disciples of a master Sufi, known as a SHAYKH or *pir.* This Sufi master is to be obeyed absolutely because of the power of his personal charisma, or holiness, but his authority is also recognized because of his inclusion within a spiritual lineage of saints that links him to ALI IBN ABI TALIB (d. 661) or ABU BAKR (d. 634) and ultimately to Muhammad. Recognition of the master's status is expressed in Sufi rituals and prayers. Sainthood is a related type of charismatic authority recognized in SUFISM, where even though the SAINT was thought to be completely obedient to God, he or she was also God's intimate friend (WALI) and an embodiment of God's wisdom and blessing power in the world. There are many women counted among the saints, but as Sufi masters, they are a minority. In any case, the Sufis had to negotiate their own spheres of authority with those of the rulers and the ulama; they were often tied to both by bonds of kinship, loyalty, and patronage.

Since the mid-18th century, the networks of authority that formed during the Middle Ages have been fragmented by a variety of historical forces. Two of the decisive forces for change were the breakdown of the Ottoman, Safavid, and Mughal Empires that once ruled millions of people between the Mediterranean and the Bay of Bengal, and the invasion of Muslim lands by European colonial empires. The major shifts in political power caused by these changes led in turn to profound changes in the traditional military, political, legal, educational, and economic institutions. The authority of the ulama became increasingly circumscribed as Western-style institutions and values were adopted by reform-minded Muslims and colonial administrators. Moreover, the introduction of the printing press to Muslim lands during the 19th century not only made it possible for the transmission of new ideas and visions to more people, but it also enabled more Muslims to become literate and consult their own sacred scriptures, commentaries, histories, literature, and books of religious law than ever before. The ulama had to contend with emerging national aspirations among Muslims and imported Western secularist ideals, while at the same time debating with ordinary Muslims who wanted to consult and interpret their religious heritage on their own. Later, the introduction of broadcast media and the internet accelerated these processes. The overall result is that multiple and frequently contending notions of authority are at play in Muslim communities, not always with the best results. In some cases, sacred authority has been mobilized to counteract and resist Western involvement in Muslim countries; in other cases, it has been manipulated by tyrants and Muslim radical groups to consolidate power and suppress pluralistic and democratic forces. The result is the creation of authoritarian regimes that hold a number of Muslim countries in their grip today, often with the approval and support of Western powers, especially in countries where OIL is a major resource.

See also ABBASID CALIPHATE; *AHL AL-BAYT*; ALLAH; CALIPH; IMAM; SHIISM.

Further reading: Arthur F. Buehler, *Sufi Heirs of the Prophet: The Indian Naqshbandiyya and the Rise of the Mediating Sufi Shaykh* (Columbia: University of South Carolina Press, 1998); Patricia Crone and Martin Hinds, *God's Caliph: Religious Authority in the First Centuries of Islam* (Cambridge: Cambridge University Press, 1986); Dale F. Eickelman and James Piscatori, *Muslim Politics* (Princeton, N.J.: Princeton University Press, 1996); Carl W. Ernst, *The Shambhala Guide to Sufism* (Boston: Shambhala, 1997); Ann K. S. Lambton, *State and Government in Medieval Islam: An Introduction to the Study of Islamic Political Theory: The Jurists* (Oxford: Oxford University Press, 1981); Max Weber, *The Theory of Social and Economic Organization* (New York: Macmillan Company, 1964).

autobiography

Autobiography is a kind of literature in which authors write primarily about their own lives and about the people, places, ideas, and events that affected them. It is sometimes also called self-narrative. In the 20th century, most European and American scholars held that autobiography was a product of individual self-consciousness that originated uniquely in "Western civilization" inspired by a Christian outlook and that it rarely occurred anywhere else in the world or in other religious communities before the modern period. This view has been seriously questioned in recent years as the literature of other civilizations has been further studied and translated. Scholars are now finding significant evidence for traditions of premodern autobiographical writing in non-Western cultures, especially in Islamicate ones.

Islamic autobiographical literature before the 20th century was written mainly in Arabic, Persian, and Turkish, the three leading literary languages of Muslims during the Middle Ages. The first Muslim autobiographies that we know anything about were written by ninth-century historians, mystics, and officials. In later centuries, this list grew to include religious scholars, jurists, philosophers, poets, physicians, scientists, rulers, politicians, soldiers, and converts. Pre-Islamic autobiographies that had been translated from Persian and Greek may have influenced some of these authors, but many were more inspired by the biographies of MUHAMMAD (d. 632) and the first Muslims, who were regarded as ideal role models. Later writers, in their turn, wanted to set examples of themselves for their readers. Others wanted to use their life stories to show how God had blessed them. In Sufi literature, autobiographical narratives recounted the spiritual journeys of the authors, including their dreams and visions. Among the most famous Sufi autobiographical writings are those of ABU HAMID AL-GHAZALI (d. 1111), RUZBIHAN BAQLI (d. 1209), IBN AL-ARABI (d. 1240), and Shah Wali Allah (d. 1762). Other prominent Muslims who have left autobiographies are the physician and philosopher IBN SINA (d. 1036), the Syrian warrior-poet Usama ibn Munqidh (d. 1188), the historian IBN KHALDUN (d. 1406), and Babur (d. 1530), the founder of the MUGHAL DYNASTY in INDIA. Much later, several West Africans brought to the UNITED STATES as slaves in the 19th century wrote short autobiographies in Arabic, much to the surprise of the American public.

When authors in Islamicate lands fell under the influence of European literary traditions during the 19th and 20th centuries, indigenous autobiographical traditions underwent significant changes. The number of autobiographies published in Muslim countries increased with the introduction of the printing press, they were written in many different modern languages (including English), and they included new secular and national perspectives, as well as more traditional ones. Egyptian author and educator Taha Husayn's (d. 1973) autobiography, which recalls his village childhood and his student days at al-Azhar University in CAIRO, embodies the fusion of the traditional with the modern, and it is still regarded as a landmark in the history of modern Arabic literature. Another impact of modernity has been the publication of women's autobiographies, including those of feminists such as HUDA AL-SHAARAWI (1879–1947) and FATIMA MERNISSI (b. 1940) as well as Islamic activists such as ZAYNAB AL-GHAZALI (d. 2005). For many, the *Autobiography of Malcolm X* (first published in 1964), which recounts the author's journey from a life of street crime to leadership in the African-American Muslim community, is the most important work of its kind to come from the North American context.

See also ARABIC LANGUAGE AND LITERATURE; BIOGRAPHY; MALCOLM X; PERSIAN LANGUAGE AND LITERATURE; TURKISH LANGUAGE AND LITERATURE.

Further reading: Taha Husayn, *An Egyptian Childhood*, trans. E. H. Paxton (London: Heineman, 1981); Fatima Mernissi, *Dreams of Trespass: Tales of Harem Girlhood* (Reading, Mass.: Addison Wesley, 1994); Dwight F. Reynolds, ed., *Interpreting the Self: Autobiography in the Arabic Literary Tradition* (Berkeley: University of California Press, 2001).

Averroës *See* IBN RUSHD, ABU WALID MUHAMMAD IBN AHMAD.

Avicenna *See* IBN SINA, ABU ALI AL-HUSAYN.

Awami League

The Awami (People's) League is one of the two most powerful political parties in BANGLADESH, together with its rival, the Bangladesh National Party (BNP). It is an important example of the secular currents in modern Muslim politics. The league was founded in 1949 by Husayn Shaheed Suhrawardy (1892–1963) and other members of the Bengali branch of the ALL-INDIA MUSLIM LEAGUE in what was then called East Bengal (after 1955 it was called East Pakistan), a province of

PAKISTAN created as a result of the partition of INDIA in 1947. Earlier, Suhrawardy and his colleagues had been active in the Indian nationalist movement against British colonial rule. Created after partition, the East Pakistan Awami Muslim League (later renamed the Awami League) gave voice to Bengali Muslims opposed to West Pakistan's domination of the new country. Bengali nationalists wanted greater self-rule in a loosely knit federation, inclusion of Hindus and Sikhs in the national polity, and recognition of Bangla, their national language, as an official state language. The West Pakistani leadership, however, wanted to preserve its privileged position, retain Pakistan's distinct Muslim identity, and keep Urdu as its only official language.

Suhrawardy was eclipsed in the 1960s by the charismatic Sheikh Mujibur (Mujib) Rahman (1920–75), who expanded the Awami League's appeal to the Bengali masses with his "Six Point Program" for more equality in Pakistani affairs. Advocating a secular parliamentary democracy, the Awami League won a landslide victory in the 1970 national elections. Its triumph was short-lived, however, because the Pakistani military intervened in 1971 to declare martial law, and it imprisoned Mujib for treason, which precipitated a war for independence from Pakistan. With the assistance of Indian troops, East Pakistan thus became Bangladesh in 1971, and Mujib, released from prison, became its first prime minister. The new government's constitution was based on "four pillars" advocated by Mujib and the Awami League: democracy, socialism, secularism, and nationalism. The league's popularity soon declined, however, in the face of a famine in 1974 and political and economic failures that resulted in a series of coups after Mujib's death in 1975. It regained its parliamentary majority in the 1996 elections, and Mujib's daughter, Shaikh Hasina Wajid, became Bangladesh's prime minister (1996–2001). The league remains strongly secular in outlook. As one observer has noted, the Awami League upholds the idea that "Bangladeshis are Bengalis who happen to be Muslims," while its rival, the BNP (created in 1978), considers "Bangladeshis to be Muslims who happen to be Bengalis" (Baxter, p. xiii).

See also DEMOCRACY; JINNAH, MUHAMMAD ALI; HINDUISM AND ISLAM; SECULARISM.

Further reading: Craig Baxter, *Bangladesh: From a Nation to a State* (Boulder, Colo.: Westview Press, 1997); Charles P. O'Donnell, *Bangladesh: Biography of a Muslim Nation* (Boulder, Colo.: Westview Press, 1984).

aya

Aya is the Arabic word for a verse in the QURAN or more generally a "sign" or "wonder." In both senses, Muslims believe that an *aya* contains a message from God for human beings to heed. The verses, or phrases and sentences of different lengths and styles, are grouped into chapters in the Quran, called suras. Of the more than 6,000 verses in the Quran, the shorter ones tend to be poetic and occur in chapters in the second half of the book, most of which are associated with MUHAMMAD's years as a prophet in MECCA (610–622). Verses in the first half, which date to the years Muhammad lived in MEDINA (622–632), tend to be longer and lack both rhyme and rhythm. In handwritten copies of the Quran, a floret or some other decorative marking is often inserted at the end of each verse to facilitate reading, since punctuation such as periods and question marks is not used in old Arabic script. In modern printed copies, the decorative inserts usually contain the verse number, thus reflecting the influence of printed Bibles in the West. Muslim commentators distinguish between two kinds of verses: those that are clear and unambiguous (*muhkamat*) and those that are obscure or mysterious (*mutashabihat*). The former are generally those to which the ULAMA turn when making religious law (FIQH), while the latter, including the mysterious letters that begin a number of chapters, have attracted the attention of speculative thinkers and mystics.

Pilgrimage mural showing Quran verses and other religious sayings, Qurna, Egypt *(Juan E. Campo)*

In addition to denoting verses of scripture, the Quran uses the word *aya* to denote "signs" and "wonders" revealed by God in nature and in narratives of sacred history associated with the lives of prophets who lived before Muhammad's time. The signs in nature include the CREATION of heaven and Earth, the alternation of day and night, rainfall, sea wind, the beginning and ending of life, the growth of plants, and the benefits ANIMALS provide to humans (for examples, see Q 36:33–45; 41:37–39; 42:29, 33). In sacred history, the destruction of unbelievers and the rescue of believers from peril are included among God's signs, as exemplified by the story of Noah's ark (Q 54:9–15). Other prophets who performed signs and wonders according to the Quran are MOSES (Q 20:17–24) and JESUS (Q 3:49). Muhammad's opponents in Mecca challenged him to produce similar signs (Q 6:37), for which his response was the recitation of Quranic verse (Q 31:7; 45:6), which brings the two meanings of *aya* together, both as a verse and a miraculous sign.

See also ALLAH; *BASMALA*; *TAFSIR*.

Further reading: Farid Esack, *Quran: A Short Introduction* (Oxford, U.K.: Oneworld, 2001); W. Montgomery Watt and Richard Bell, *Introduction to the Quran* (Edinburgh: Edinburgh University Press, 1970).

ayatollah (Arabic: sign of God)

Ayatollah is a title bestowed on the most highly esteemed religious scholars in TWELVE-IMAM SHI-ISM since the 19th century. It is held by experts of Islamic law, especially members of the USULI SCHOOL based in IRAN and IRAQ. Religious education in the Shii MADRASA system and expertise in the practice of legal reasoning (*IJTIHAD*) are minimum qualifications for becoming an ayatollah, but there are no other formal requirements. The madrasas of Qum (Iran), Mashhad (Iran), and Najaf (Iraq) are where ayatollahs have received their training and where many of them have taught. Ayatollahs gain their status by popular acclamation, which is demonstrated by their ability to collect religious taxes. They claim that they are representatives of the Hidden IMAM, and the highest ranking among them are called "sources of emulation," meaning that other Shia should follow their rulings. These supreme leaders can also be called a "grand ayatollahs." Ayatollahs have become especially powerful since the IRANIAN REVOLUTION OF 1978–79.

See also AUTHORITY; KHOMEINI, RUHOLLAH; *MUJ-TAHID*; ULAMA.

Further reading: Moojan Momen, *An Introduction to Shii Islam* (New Haven, Conn.: Yale University Press, 1985); Michael M. J. Fischer, *Iran, from Religious Dispute to Revolution* (Cambridge, Mass.: Harvard University Press, 1980).

Ayodhya

A Hindu pilgrimage center in Uttar Pradesh, north INDIA on the river Sarayu, Ayodhya is now most famous as the home of a site contested by Hindus and Muslims as the birthplace of the Hindu god Rama or the location of an early 16th-century MOSQUE known as the Babri Masjid. Modern day Ayodhya is closely linked with the mythical city of the epic *Ramayana*, the capital of the god-king Rama, an incarnation of Vishnu from an earlier epoch of Hindu history. Historical and archaeological evidence indicates that the two cities are not the same, but a vast number of the more than 800 million Hindus in India do not make this distinction. It is clear that Ayodhya has been an important pilgrimage city for centuries, noted in particular as a base for several orders of Hindu ascetic *sadhus* (holy men) and for its exceptionally powerful Hanuman temple. The popularity of Ayodhya as a pilgrimage destination grew under Mughal patronage in the 16th and 17th centuries, and until the 19th century the religious conflict in the town was limited to struggles between rival orders of Hindus. The Babri Masjid was inaugurated in 1528 under the sponsorship of Mir Baqi, a general in the service of the first Mughal emperor, Babur (r. 1526–30). In 1859, the British government erected a fence following several incidents, and it was determined that Hindus would no longer be allowed to freely enter the mosque as had been the custom. Then in 1949, idols of Rama appeared in the mosque, and it was claimed that a security guard had had a vision of Rama himself. From that time until 1992, the shrine was closed for all worship except for an annual Hindu ceremony to maintain the idols that had been installed. Dereliction in the courts and on the part of the government allowed the situation to fester until in the 1980s the issue was raised by several Hindu nationalist organizations, in particular the World Hindu Council (VHP) and the political party Bharatiya Janata Party (BJP). On December 6, 1992, this movement was successful in drawing an enormous crowd of activists who destroyed the mosque, triggering Hindu-Muslim riots across India in which more than 3,000 were killed. After 1992, there was little change in the situation as the courts failed to rule decisively, and the BJP, which came to power in 1998, allowed the instigators of the violence to take up cabinet-level positions in the government. The question of the temple has continued to be a triggering issue for Hindu-Muslim violence, most recently setting off a series of riots in the western state of Gujarat in spring 2002 resulting in more than 2,000 deaths and more than

100,000 people displaced from their homes. In both 1992 and 2002, the victims were overwhelmingly Muslim, making the identity of the site one of the most critical, yet intransigent, challenges to India's multireligious polity. In 2003, the Indian Supreme Court ordered the Archaeological Survey of India (ASI) to conduct excavations of the site, but the results have proved too indefinite to bring about any resolution.

See also HINDUISM AND ISLAM; MUGHAL DYNASTY.

Anna Bigelow

Further reading: Sarvepalli Gopal, ed., *Anatomy of a Confrontation: The Rise of Communal Politics in India* (London: Zed Books, 1993); Sushil, Srivastava, *The Disputed Mosque: A Historical Inquiry* (New Delhi: Vistaar Publications, 1991); Peter Van der Veer, *Gods on Earth: Religious Experience and Identity in Ayodhya* (Delhi: Oxford University Press, 1997).

Azad, Abu al-Kalam (1888–1958) *Indian Muslim intellectual and nationalist leader*

Abu al-Kalam Azad was a leader in INDIA's struggle to gain independence from Britain in the early 20th century, and he served as the country's first minister of education from 1947 until his death in 1958. His most important religious work was *Tarjuman al-Quran* (1931), a two-volume Urdu language translation and commentary on the QURAN, which he wrote while in prison.

Azad was born in MECCA to an Indian father and Arab mother and moved with his parents to Calcutta, India, when he was around 10 years old. His father, Khairuddin Dihlawi (1831–1908), was a religious man who chose to give his son a traditional Islamic education at home. Azad proved to be a gifted student who was attracted to the modern ideas of SAYYID AHMAD KHAN (1817–98), which conflicted with the traditional Sufi outlook of his father. His thinking was further affected by his travels in the Middle East in 1908–09, when he met with nationalists and religious reformers in IRAN, IRAQ, TURKEY, and EGYPT. After returning to

India, he established a weekly Urdu journal in 1912 called *Al-Hilal* (crescent moon), in which he called upon India's Muslims to unite and join with other Indians in a nonviolent campaign for independence from Britain. After the British imprisoned Azad for three and a half years, he joined with the great Indian nationalist leader Mohandas K. Gandhi (1869–1948) in the KHILAFAT MOVEMENT in 1920 and then continued as a leader in the Congress Party, where he worked to bring Muslims and Hindus together in the independence movement. He used his knowledge of the Quran and Islamic history to win support for this effort, as can be seen in his *Tarjuman al-Quran,* but many Indian Muslims felt that they had to work separately from Hindus to create their own state. The British imprisoned him several more times in the 1930s and 1940s, but from 1940 to 1946 he served as president of the All-India National Congress, after which he became India's first minister of education. Azad was completely against the division of India into two states and was deeply disappointed when PAKISTAN and India were partitioned in 1947.

See also ALL-INDIA MUSLIM LEAGUE; HINDUISM AND ISLAM; JINNAH, MUHAMMAD ALI.

Further reading: Ian Henderson Douglas, *Abul Kalam Azad: An Intellectual and Religious Biography,* eds. Gail Minault and Christian W. Troll (New Delhi: Oxford University Press, 1988); Syeda Saiyidain Hameed, *Islamic Seal on India's Independence: Abul Kalam Azad, A Fresh Look* (Karachi: Oxford University Press, 1998).

al-Azhar (Arabic: the brilliant one)

Al-Azhar is now the most important center of Islamic learning in and the institution most symbolic of the world of Sunni Islam. It was built by the Fatimid rulers of EGYPT (r. 969–1171) as the primary MOSQUE and center of missionary outreach in their new capital of CAIRO. With the rise to power of the Ayyubid dynasty under SALADIN in 1171, al-Azhar lost much of its prestige, particularly to other MADRASAS that arose at this time.

Scholars at al-Azhar taught the Islamic precepts of QURAN, hadith, and law (FIQH) but also such fields as PHILOSOPHY and SCIENCE. In the 13th century, under the Mamluks, al-Azhar slowly regained its prominence and was rebuilt and refurbished. But it was under the OTTOMAN DYNASTY, which conquered Egypt in 1517, that al-Azhar became again the dominant religious institution in Egypt, especially in the 18th century.

The graduates of al-Azhar were the most highly educated in Egypt as that country began to confront the challenges of modernity in the 19th century. Napoleon Bonaparte, during his brief conquest of Egypt (1798–1801), looked to the scholars of al-Azhar as potential leaders in the Egypt he intended to create, but the university was also the site of much resistance to the French presence. As Egypt was brought under the firm rule of Muhammad Ali (d. 1848), like Napoleon, it was to the graduates of al-Azhar that he turned to find men who would lead the country in its modernization. Among those he sent to Europe in the 19th century to acquire modern scientific learning, many were Azharites. In fact, until the founding of the modern University of Cairo in 1908, al-Azhar was the only institution of higher learning in the country.

Because al-Azhar combined a great deal of religious prestige with a formidable, if traditional, academic program, successive governments have striven to reduce its power or to turn its power to their own ends. The religious endowments that had made al-Azhar financially independent have been under governmental control since 1812. The state also controls the appointment of the rector of the university, a powerful and influential position in Egypt. In the 1960s, the Egyptian national government under President Jamal Abd al-Nasir (r. 1954–70) reformed and modernized the educational program, expanding its teaching to such fields as engineering and medicine. While this broadened and expanded the university, it also had the effect of weakening its religious character.

Al-Azhar Mosque in Cairo, Egypt *(Juan E. Campo)*

Nonetheless, al-Azhar, which is not a strictly hierarchical institution, retains a certain tradition of independence from the government and can influence government decisions in some areas. The government of Egypt has, thus, recently granted al-Azhar an expanded role in the censorship of films and books. More problematic for the government, however, are the independent scholars within the institution who condemn specific government policies, such as Egypt's peace with ISRAEL or the United States. On the whole, however, the government-appointed rector and his associates tend to have national and international prestige, and when they speak for al-Azhar, they often claim to be speaking for the Muslim community as a whole.

See also EDUCATION; SUNNISM.

John Iskander

Further reading: Chris Eccel, *Egypt, Islam, and Social Change: Al-Azhar in Conflict and Accommodation* (Berlin: K. Schwarz, 1984); Tamir Moustafa, "Conflict and Cooperation between the State and Religious Institutions in Contemporary Egypt." *International Journal of Middle East Studies* 32 (2000): 3–22.

B

Baath Party

The Baath Party has been the ruling political party in SYRIA since 1963, and it was the party that governed IRAQ briefly in 1963 and then again from 1968 until its removal by U.S. and coalition forces in spring 2003. Two Syrian schoolteachers who had studied at the Sorbonne in Paris during the 1920s founded it in the 1940s: Michel Aflaq (1910–89), a Greek Orthodox Christian, and Salah al-Din al-Bitar (1912–80), a Sunni Muslim. These men envisioned the Baath Party as a modern revolutionary movement that would unite ARABS and liberate their lands from British and French colonial control, which had become more entrenched in the region as a result of the creation of their mandate territories in Syria, Transjordan, and Iraq after World War I. The Baath message of pan-Arab unity held great appeal to the peoples living in these territories in the 1940s, and by the 1960s, the party had become the major player in Syrian and Iraqi politics.

The name of the Baath Party, officially known as the Arab Socialist Baath Party, is based on the Arabic word for resurrection or renewal. The name refers to the rebirth of the glories of Arab self-rule that the party has sought to bring about after centuries of being governed by foreigners, especially Turks and Europeans. The party rec-ognizes ISLAM as the authentic spiritual force that can make this happen but not as the source for specific institutions, laws, and policies. Muhammad is looked to as an exemplary Arab leader, not as an object of religious devotion. In other words, Baathists conceive of religion in secular terms, not as a system of eternal truths to be used in actually running a government or drafting legislation. In fact, however, party ideology has drawn more upon elements of European fascism and communism than upon Islamic ideals and values. This SECULARISM is reflected in the party's official motto: "Unity, Freedom, and Arab Socialism."

In the party's early years, it sought to create a base of support among the Arab masses. Failing in this, the party allied itself with the military in the 1960s and built hierarchical networks of political and security units that infiltrated all levels of society down to the neighborhood and tribal levels in the 1970s. In Iraq, the size of the army was increased until it became one of the largest in the region. In 1966, the Syrian and Iraqi branches of the party divorced, and control of both fell into the hands of local ethnoreligious minorities—ALAWI Shia in Syria, led by Hafiz al-Asad (1930–2000), and Arab Sunnis from Tikrit in Iraq, led by SADDAM HUSAYN (1937–2006). These two authoritarian rulers used their large security forces to coerce and brutalize their real or imagined opponents and to monopolize power in their respective countries. This led to the massacre of thousands of members of the MUSLIM BROTHERHOOD in Syria during the 1980s. In Iraq, tens of thousands of communists, Kurds, Shiis, and others considered disloyal by the Baathists fell victim to the state terror apparatus during Husayn's long rule. At the same time, the party leadership promoted the modernization of schools, agriculture, industries, health care, and the national infrastructure through investment of public funds and limited privatization. Syria's involvement in the ARAB-ISRAELI CONFLICTS and Iraq's involvement in wars with Iran, Kuwait, and Western powers in the 1980s and 1990s had disastrous consequences for both countries, especially Iraq. Although the Iraqi branch of the party was officially disbanded after the U.S.-led invasion in 2003, it is thought that many former Baath members, together with former Iraqi soldiers, have played a leading role in the Iraqi insurgency against American forces and any Iraqis who cooperate with them. They have formed a loose alliance with Muslim guerrilla forces in this context.

Further reading: Eberhard Kienle, *Baath v. Baath: The Conflict between Syria and Iraq, 1968–1989* (London: I.B. Tauris & Co., 1990); Kanan Makiya (Samir al-Khalil), *Republic of Fear: The Inside Story of Saddam's Iraq* (New York: Pantheon Books, 1990); Marion Farouq-Sluglett and Peter Sluglett, *Iraq since 1958: From Revolution to Dictatorship* (London: I.B. Tauris & Co., 2001).

Babism

Babism was a 19th-century Shii messianic movement based in IRAQ and IRAN that announced the immanent return of the Hidden Imam, a redeemer sent by God, and thereby challenged the legitimacy of powerful religious and political authorities at the time. As a result, it was violently suppressed, but it gave birth to a new movement, which became the BAHAI FAITH. The name Babism (*Babiyya*) was based on the Arabic word *bab*, "gate" or "door," indicating a living man inspired by God who provides access to the Hidden Imam.

Ali Muhammad (1819–50), a young merchant from Shiraz, Iran, launched the movement. As a student pilgrim at the Shii holy cities of KARBALA and Najaf in Iraq, he was attracted to the Shaykhis, a Shii sect that had arisen earlier in the century. After returning to Shiraz, he gained a following of disciples, and in 1844, he proclaimed that he was the *bab*, offering as proof an inspired interpretation of a chapter in the QURAN (Q 12). He sent his followers throughout Iran and Iraq to win converts, one of whom was Mirza Husayn Ali Nuri (1817–92), who would later be known as Baha Ullah, the founder of the Bahai Faith. Ali Muhammad's growing popularity and criticism of the AUTHORITY of the traditional Shii ULAMA soon caused them to look at him with disfavor, and he was imprisoned in a remote mountain fortress in Azerbaijan in 1847. He wrote many religious tracts in his prison cell, the most famous of which was the *Bayan* (exposition), which claimed to be a holy book with a new universal law that replaced other religious laws, including the SHARIA. Some followers regarded him as a new prophet, and at the end of his life, before being executed for APOSTASY in 1850, he proclaimed that he was the Qaim (one who will arise)—the Hidden Imam himself.

Babi leaders, including an influential woman named Qurrat al-Ayn (d. 1852), decided to break the movement's ties with the Islamic religion and lead a revolt against authorities in northern Iran. Thousands of Babis were reported to have died at the hands of government troops, especially after a failed assassination attempt against Nasir al-Din Shah (d. 1896), the ruler of Iran, in 1852. Most of the movement's survivors turned to the religion of Baha Ullah (the Bahai Faith) in 1863, but others stayed loyal to Ali Muhammad's designated heir, Mirza Yahya (or Subh-i Azal, d. 1912), and this group of Babis became known as Azalis. Azali Babism survived a period of exile in Iraq and Turkey, and its adherents participated in the Iranian

CONSTITUTIONAL REVOLUTION of 1906. A very small number of Babis survive today in the Central Asian republic of Uzbekistan.

See also IMAM; MAHDI; SHIISM.

Further reading: Abbas Amanat, *Resurrection and Renewal: The Making of the Babi Movement in Iran* (Ithaca, N.Y.: Cornell University Press, 1989); Denis MacEoin, *Rituals in Babism and Bahaism* (London: British Academic Press, 1994).

al-Badawi, Ahmad (ca. 1200–1276) *one of the most popular Sufi saints in Egypt; honored every year by two commemorative festivals*

According to reverential accounts of his life, Ahmad al-Badawi (the BEDOUIN) was born to a family in FEZ, MOROCCO, that traced its ancestry back to the AHL AL-BAYT, MUHAMMAD's family. This is why many Egyptians call him *al-SAYYID* (master), which implies descent from the Prophet. Legends portray him in two different ways in his youth: as a saintly child who memorized the entire QURAN and studied Islamic law and as a noble Bedouin horseman. Together with his parents, he traveled on pilgrimage from Morocco to MECCA. After being instructed by a mysterious voice, he went to IRAQ with his brother to visit the tombs of two leading Sufi SAINTS, ABD AL-QADIR AL-JILANI (d. 1166) and Ahmad al-Rifai (d. 1182). On his way back to Mecca, according to legend, he defeated a beautiful genie and her demon army and converted her into a pious devotee, thus demonstrating his superior saintly power. While he was in Mecca in 1238, a voice once again spoke to him while praying in a cave as Muhammad used to do. This time the voice told him to go to the delta town of Tanta, EGYPT, where he resided for the rest of his life, claiming to receive guidance from Muhammad himself. In Tanta, Ahmad al-Badawi surpassed all other rivals in his acts of ASCETICISM and demonstrations of his *BARAKA* (saintly power). Egypt's rulers honored him, and it is even said that he battled Christian crusaders. After his death in

1276, his followers organized themselves into a Sufi brotherhood known as the Ahmadiyya, one of the largest in Egypt today, and they converted his tomb into a shrine. He is considered to be one of the four primary holy men (*qutb*s) of Egypt, and he has been the subject of Egyptian folktales, novels, and television dramas.

Every year millions flock to his shrine to participate in his *mulids* (commemorative festivals). Prior to the modern period, the main festival was in August, at the height of the Nile flood season. Now that dams and levees have ended the annual inundation, it is in October, at the end of the harvest season. The second festival is held in the spring. Sufi brotherhoods gather in Tanta to perform their *dhikr*s (religious chants) and other rituals, while ordinary pilgrims come to seek his blessing to cure an illness, become successful in school or business, gain debt relief, or satisfy some other personal need. Many have their sons circumcised in booths near the Ahmadi Mosque hoping to alleviate the danger of infection. Visitors return home with mementos of their pilgrimage, such as trinkets, sweets flavored with rosewater, and chickpeas. These are distributed to friends and relatives in the belief that they contain some of Sayyid Ahmad's *baraka*. The Egyptian government closely regulates the shrine and its festivals, and despite the saint's widespread popularity, reform-minded and conservative Muslims condemn the *mulids* and the practices associated with them because they think it is BIDAA, a corruption of what they believe is the true Islam.

See also CIRCUMCISION; CRUSADES.

Further reading: Edward B. Reeves, *The Hidden Government: Ritual, Clientelism, and Legitimation in Northern Egypt* (Salt Lake City: University of Utah Press, 1990).

Baghdad

Baghdad, the capital of IRAQ, is situated on the Tigris River near the Euphrates River in the center of a region that used to be known as Mesopotamia, the site of Babylon and other ancient cities. It has a population of approximately 5 million people in a country composed of 28 million. Most of the city's residents are ARAB Muslims, but it is also home to small numbers of other Iraqi ethnic and religious groups: Kurdish Muslims, Turkomans, Arab Christians (including Assyrians and Chaldeans), Mandeans, and Jews. There are at least 2 million Shii Muslims living there, many in Sadr City, a low-income neighborhood on Baghdad's northeastern perimeter.

According to early Muslim histories, in 762 Abu Jafar al-Mansur, the second CALIPH of the ABBASID CALIPHATE (750–1258), traced the foundations of the city of Baghdad with flaming cotton seeds and eventually built, through the labor of 100,000 builders, architects and engineers from around the empire, a perfectly round city, a form unprecedented in Islamicate ARCHITECTURE. This new capital, called the Madinat al-Salam (City of Peace), housed within its three concentric circles of baked brick walls the caliph, his court, soldiers, citizens and markets. Within a decade, the growing population and its palaces and markets had spilled outside the original walls, and the legendary city of GARDENS, canals, and floating pontoon bridges rapidly became the cultural and religious center of Islamdom. The medieval city boasted a host of famous personages in Islamic history. HARUN AL-RASHID (r. 786–809), a figure made famous by the *ARABIAN NIGHTS,* and his son Abu al-Abbas Abd Allah al-Mamun (r. 813–833), helped build a thriving intellectual center where scholars gathered from around the world in a library called the House of Wisdom. There, in addition to the development of the sciences such as engineering, MATHEMATICS, and astronomy, foreign works of philosophy and literature were translated into Arabic. The Nizamiyya MADRASA at its height had a population of 10,000 to 20,000 students seeking higher EDUCATION from noted scholars, jurists, and philosophers, including ABU HAMID AL-GHAZALI (d. 1111), who, before retiring into a mystical life and writing his famous *The Revival of the Religious*

Sciences, was the principal of that school. The oldest, most liberal, and currently largest of the four Islamic law schools, the HANAFI LEGAL SCHOOL, was founded in Baghdad by Abu Hanifa (d. 767).

Beginning as early as the ninth century, a series of citywide upheavals, political and religious power struggles, floods, and plagues left the city vulnerable to the Mongol attack of 1258, which decimated much of the population and urban infrastructure. The 14th through the early 20th centuries were punctuated by foreign occupations and leadership changes, most notably by the Safavids (1507 and 1623), the Ottomans (1534 and 1638), and finally the British in 1917.

In 1932, Iraq gained its independence, and the University of Baghdad, one of three modern universities in Baghdad, opened in 1957. During the 1970s and 1980s, OIL revenues were allocated to a building campaign of new city monuments, palaces, and ceremonial avenues. Three of the most noted monuments are the Hands of Victory arch, the Monument of the Unknown Soldier, and the Martyr's Monument, with its split turquoise dome 190 meters in diameter that recalls the famous green dome that once towered over al-Mansur's original city. All three were designed to commemorate the country's war against Iran (1980–88) and the Iraqi soldiers who died in it. For more than three decades, Baghdad also served as the headquarters for the Arab Baath Socialist Party, which governed the country until it was overthrown when the United States and its coalition forces invaded Iraq in March 2003. The Republican Palace of the deposed Iraqi leader, SADDAM HUSAYN (r. 1978–2003), which stands on the west bank of the Tigris not far from where Mansur's round city once stood, now serves as the headquarters of the American occupation.

See also BAATH PARTY.

Margaret A. Leeming

Further reading: Jacob Lassner, *The Shaping of Abbasid Rule* (Princeton, N.J.: Princeton University Press,

1980); Kanan Makiya [Samir al-Khalil], *The Monument: Art, Vulgarity and Responsibility in Iraq* (Berkeley: University of California Press, 1991); Paul Wheatley, *The Places Where Men Pray Together: Cities in Islamic Lands, Seventh through the Tenth Centuries* (Chicago: University of Chicago Press, 2001).

Bahai Faith

The Bahai Faith is a new religion that grew out of the Shii environment in IRAN in the mid-19th century. It presents itself as a new universal FAITH that believes in world peace, religious tolerance, and unity and equality among all people. It has its own scriptures in Persian and Arabic, but it also recognizes the fundamental truths expressed in the sacred writings of other religions. There are currently about 6.8 million Bahais, or followers of this religion, of whom about 300,000 still live in Iran. In that country, they have been treated as apostates and subjected to persecution, especially since the creation of the Islamic Republic in 1979.

The founder and prophet of the Bahai Faith was Mirza Husayn Ali Nuri (1817–93), who took the surname Baha Allah, "splendor of God," from which the religion gets its name. Baha Allah (or Baha Ullah) was born to an influential family in Tehran, the capital of Iran, and joined the Babi movement with his half-brother Mirza Yahya in the 1840s. BABISM was a radical Shii sect that challenged religious and political authorities in Iran and IRAQ and preached the coming of the Hidden IMAM, who would initiate a golden age with a new universal religious law that was to surpass the SHARIA. The Babis were violently suppressed as heretical by the Iranian government with the backing of the Shii ULAMA, and Baha Allah and other surviving Babis were forced into exile in Baghdad, Iraq, in 1853. In 1863, he announced to associates that he, Baha Allah, was the awaited imam of the Babis. The majority of Babis who followed him became the Bahais; those who did not but continued to follow his brother Mirza Yahya (known as Subh-i Azal) became the Azalis. In 1867, after being forced to move to Ottoman TURKEY, Baha Allah publicly proclaimed his divine mission by sending letters to many of the world's leaders, thus formally renouncing Islam and launching the Bahai Faith. Ottoman authorities, concerned by the trouble he might cause with such claims, imprisoned him near Akka, Palestine (now in Israel), where he died in 1892. He was succeeded by his son Abd al-Baha (d. 1921), a gifted leader who helped both organize and internationalize the religion after Baha Alla's death. He won new converts from Christianity in Europe and America, where the Bahai Faith soon established branches. The Bahais now have nearly 20,000 local spiritual assemblies in some 233 countries.

Baha Allah's writings are the most important sacred scriptures for the religion. They are believed to be divine revelations, replacing the QURAN and Islamic law. The most important of his books are *The Book of Certainty* (*Kitab-i iqan*) and *The Most Holy Book* (*al-Kitab al-aqdas*). Both uphold the idea of God's oneness as well as the values of equality, social justice, learning, and the unity of all people. Like Islam, there is no clergy in the Bahai Faith, and all adherents are expected to perform specific ritual obligations, which include an annual fast, abstention from alcohol and nonmedicinal drugs, and daily prayers. Women hold equal status with men, and, unlike Islam, marriage is monogamous. Not unexpectedly, the Bahai Faith has flourished in modern secular societies. On the other hand, the persecution and discrimination Bahais are experiencing in Iran and other Muslim countries is due partly to the fact that their religion is seen as APOSTASY by Muslim authorities and also because it is thought to be too much under the influence of Western countries and Israel, where its main religious center is now located.

See also SHIISM.

Further reading: Mojan Momen, *The Bahai Faith: A Short Introduction* (Oxford, U.K.: Oneworld Publications, 1999); Peter Smith, *The Babi and Bahai Religions:*

From Messianic Shiism to a World Religion (Cambridge: Cambridge University Press, 1987).

Bahrain   *See* GULF STATES.

Bamba, Ahmadu (Ahmad Bamba) (1850–1927) *Senegalese mystic and founder of the Muridiyya Sufi order*

Ahmadu Bamba (also known as Ahmad Bamba) was born to a family of scholars in Kayor, Senegal, in WEST AFRICA. He became a devotee of the QADIRI SUFI ORDER, which he taught among his native Wolof people. French colonial officials grew alarmed over increasing support for Bamba's teaching and sent him into exile in Gabon in 1895. Although they allowed him to return to Senegal in 1902, Bamba was exiled again later that year, this time to Mauritania. French authorities hoped that removing Bamba would limit his popularity, which they perceived as a threat to their colonial interests despite the nonpolitical nature of his teaching. Instead, Bamba's support only continued to grow, and he was able to establish his own distinctive PRAYER ritual (*wird*) and Sufi order while in Mauritania. Upon returning to Senegal in 1912, Bamba made his home in Diourbel. During World War I, he reluctantly supported the French with troops and money. However, after his death in 1927, his tomb was moved to Touba, a city he founded in 1887 and that remains the main pilgrimage site and hub of the Muridiyya Sufi Order.

Bamba established the Muridiyya as an economic and religious community during the 1880s, developed a new Islamic pedagogy that emphasized action, work, and loyalty, and attracted followers from many different backgrounds. The Muridiyya work ethic has made the order an important contributor to the Senegalese economy during the past century.

See also COLONIALISM.

Stephen Cory

Further reading: Lucy C. Creevey, "Ahmad Bamba 1850–1927." In *Studies in West African Islamic History.* Vol. 1, *The Cultivators of Islam,* edited by John Ralph Willis (London: Frank Cass, 1979); Donald B. Cruise O'Brien, *The Mourides of Senegal: The Political and Economic Organization of an Islamic Brotherhood* (Oxford, U.K.: Clarendon Press, 1971).

Bangladesh (Official name: People's Republic of Bangladesh)

Bangladesh (Hindi: land of the Bengalis) is a country in South Asia bordered by INDIA on all sides but the extreme southeast, where it shares a border with Myanmar (Burma). Situated at the northern end of the Bay of Bengal, it straddles the delta of the Ganges, Brahmaputra, and Meghna Rivers, which leaves much of the country subject to destructive annual floods. The population is estimated to be 154 million, of whom about 83 percent are Muslim and 16 percent are Hindu. This makes it the fourth largest Muslim country in the world, after Indonesia, PAKISTAN, and India. Even though Bangladesh's official state religion is Islam, it is also the Muslim country with the largest Hindu minority population. Most of the Muslims are Sunnis who follow the HANAFI LEGAL SCHOOL. Two major Muslim social classes can be differentiated: the nobles (*ashraf*) who migrated from northern India (especially from nearby Bihar) and use the Urdu language to set themselves apart, and the commoners (*ajlaf*) who belong to the indigenous Bengali population. Most of the Hindus are affiliated with the Scheduled Castes, formerly called Untouchables or Harijans (children of God). Many Bengali Hindus, especially those belonging to the upper castes, migrated to India after the 1947 partition, and they now reside in the Indian state of West Bengal.

Bangladesh is part of what had formerly been the northeast Indian province of Bengal. For much of its history, this had been a densely forested frontier region that fell beyond the reach of direct Hindu, Buddhist, and Muslim rule. In eastern Bengal, people lived mostly in small hunting and gathering communities and adhered to local tribal religions. In the western region, small states rose and fell, the most important being the Pala dynasty (ca. 750–1159), which subscribed to Buddhism, and the Sena dynasty (ca. 1095–1223), which followed Brahmanic Hinduism. The first Muslims in Bengal were Afghanis, Persians, and Turks who came into the area as conquerors during the reign of the DELHI SULTANATE (1206–87). Local Muslim states arose subsequently in the western part of Bengal, but full-fledged Islamization did not begin until the MUGHAL DYNASTY won control of the region during the reign of AKBAR (r. 1556–1605).

CONVERSION of the Bengali populations to Islam did not occur by the sword, as has been alleged. Historian Richard Eaton argues that Mughal elites in Bengal (the *ashraf*) did not promote Islam as a state religion; they maintained a social and cultural distance from the native population. Widespread conversion in Bengal began only in the 17th century as a result of several factors: 1) the gradual eastward shift of the Ganges River, which opened up forest lands to the outside world and to intense agricultural development, 2) the influx of pioneer holy men who built mosques and shrines that formed the nuclei of hundreds of new agricultural communities and spread Islamic influence to the indigenous peoples, and 3) economic prosperity under Muslim rule brought about by the region's integration into the world economy through the export of textiles. These socioeconomic and cultural factors not only resulted in religious conversion in a region where the Hindu religion had also only recently been introduced, but they also gave Bengali Islam a distinctive stamp. Hindu gods and scriptures were not rejected but adapted to Islamic understandings of God, the prophets, and their holy books. At the same time, Islamic doctrines and practices were recast into Hindu forms. The divine name ALLAH, for example, was used interchangeably in Bengali Islamic literature with the Sanskrit terms for Hindu gods, such as

Great Person (Pradhanpurusha), the One Without Color (Niranjan), and God (Ishvar). The prophets, particularly Muhammad, were called *avatars,* a Sanskrit designation for the Hindu god Vishnu's different manifestations. Bengal Muslims were also familiar with the popular Hindu epics the *Mahabharata* and the *Ramayana.* Amalgamations of Islamic with Hindu beliefs and practices cut across communal boundaries and produced a distinctive Bengali religious literature as well as devotional movements such as that of Satya Pir, who was venerated as a Sufi saint by Muslims and as a god by Hindus. Sufi orders and the veneration of Muslim saints at their shrines continue to play an important role in the popular religion of Bengal today.

While Mughal officials struggled to solidify their control of Bengal by forming an Urdu-speaking elite oriented westward to the imperial courts in Delhi, Agra, and Lahore, and as more and more Bengalis became Muslims, Europeans appeared on the scene to compete for access to the region's economic wealth. The Portuguese appeared first in 1517, followed by the Dutch in 1602, the British in 1650, the French in 1690, and the Danes in 1755. It was the British, however, who prevailed, ruling Bengal first through the agency of the English East India Company (1757–1857) then directly through the British Crown in the era of the Raj (1857–1947).

Foreign colonial presence gave rise to two important kinds of movements in Bengal: religious revival movements among both Hindus and Muslims and anticolonial nationalist movements. The two major religious revival movements among Muslims were the FARAIZI MOVEMENT, which advocated strict adherence to the FIVE PILLARS of Islam, and the Tariqa-i Muhammadiyya (Muhammadan Movement) inspired by SAYYID AHMAD BARELWI (d. 1831), which sought to establish a community governed by the SHARIA. Both of these 19th century movements were reacting to the decline of Muslim influence, which they hoped to reverse by purifying Islam of what they perceived to be wrongful practices and Hindu influences. They also were opposed to British rule. Even though they were short-lived, in the long run these movements helped set the foundations for the Muslim nationalist movement of the 20th century, which had broad appeal across all strata of Bengali society. Bengalis were active in the ALL-INDIA MUSLIM LEAGUE, a political party formed to give Indian Muslims a greater voice in their own affairs. Its first meeting was convened in 1906 in Dhaka, the capital of Bengal. However, Urdu speakers from northern India and the Punjab dominated the Muslim League, thus marginalizing the Bengalis.

After India was partitioned in 1947, Bengal was reconstituted as the East Bengal Province of Pakistan, under the governance of West Pakistan, which was located more than 1,000 miles away, across northern India. The secularist AWAMI LEAGUE political party was created to give voice to East Bengal's grievances against West Pakistan. In the following years, the league gained widespread support among Bengali Hindus as well as Muslims, advocating a more democratic government and more power at the local level. After the league scored an overwhelming victory in the 1970 national elections, East Pakistan (the official name of East Bengal since 1955) declared independence from West Pakistan, which caused the central government to invade the country to end the Bengali revolt. Hundreds of thousands were killed as a result, but Indian troops joined with the Bengalis to defeat the Pakistani forces. East Pakistan was then renamed Bangladesh, and the Awami League led the country with its socialist development policies until it was removed by a military coup in 1975. Since 1978, the country's political life has been dominated by the Bangladesh Nationalist Party (BNP), founded by General Ziaur Rahman, who served as president from 1976 to 1981. Today the Awami League is the main opposition party in the country. Despite the growing influence of the Islamist party, the JAMAAT-I ISLAMI, Bangladesh still considers itself to be a moderate, democratic country. One reflection of this is in roles women have played in public life there,

including Khaleda Zia (Ziaur Rahman's widow), Bangladesh's prime minister from 1991 to 1996; and Sheikh Hasina (Mujibur Rahman's daughter), head of the Awami League and prime minister from 1996 to 2001, and from 2009 to the present.

See also COLONIALISM; HINDUISM AND ISLAM.

Further reading: Craig Baxter, *Bangladesh: From a Nation to a State* (Boulder, Colo.: Westview Press, 1997); Richard M. Eaton, "Who Are the Bengal Muslims? Conversion and Islamization in Bengal." In *Understanding the Bengal Muslims: Interpretive Essays,* edited by Rafiuddin Ahmed, 25–51 (Oxford and Delhi: Oxford University Press, 2001); Asim Roy, *The Islamic Syncretistic Tradition in Bengal* (Princeton, N.J.: Princeton University Press, 1983); Tony K. Stewart, "Satya Pir: Muslim Holy Man and Hindu God." In *Religions of India in Practice,* edited by Donald S. Lopez, Jr., 578–597 (Princeton, N.J.: Princeton University Press, 1995).

Banna, Hassan al- (1906–1949) *Egyptian founder and intellectual leader of the Society of Muslim Brothers*
Born in Mahmudiyya, EGYPT, al-Banna was greatly influenced by his father, an AL-AZHAR graduate who served as the village imam and religious instructor. Al-Banna exhibited a propensity toward religious activism at an early age, joining several organizations that fought against British colonial influence and "un-Islamic" trends in Egypt. Following primary school, he completed teacher training at Damanhur and then Dar al-Ulum in CAIRO, after which (in 1927) he accepted a teaching position in Ismailiyya, a city in the Suez Canal Zone with a heavy British presence. His passionate interest in religious and social affairs quickly drew the attention of a group of disaffected locals who appealed to him to become their leader, and the result, in 1928, was the founding of the Society of Muslim Brothers, also known as the MUSLIM BROTHERHOOD. In 1932, al-Banna transferred to Cairo, where he established a branch of the society and began to expand its purpose and structure, positioning it to

become the premier Islamist organization in the Muslim world.

From the outset, al-Banna viewed the society as a broad-based movement, encompassing intellectual, moral, and practical goals. Unlike earlier reformers, such as JAMAL AL-DIN AL-AFGHANI (d. 1897) and MUHAMMAD ABDUH (d. 1905), who had provided the intellectual Islamic legitimacy for accommodating the changes brought about by contacts with the West, al-Banna wanted to create an Islamic order (*nizam islami*) that encouraged modern Muslims to live according to what he deemed to be their tradition. And, for al-Banna, there was a desperate need for such an order because Egyptians, along with other Muslim peoples, had adopted the secular ways of their colonial occupiers and subsequently lost their identity. The society, under al-Banna's direction, operated on a grassroots level—through the founding of schools, clinics, factories, and publishing houses—to demonstrate the strength of the Islamic alternative to a people who had become enamored with Western nationalist ideologies, such as communism, capitalism, and liberal democracy

Political conflict, and occasionally political violence, was the order of the day in Egypt throughout the 1930s and 1940s, as nationalist movements fought for independence from the British and vied for power among themselves. The society played an important role in the proindependence fight, and al-Banna participated in the political process, even running for election once. In the end, however, the society's Islamic agenda put the organization on a collision course with Egypt's more secular establishment, including government authorities. Implicated in the murder of several government officials, the society was dissolved in late 1948, and, in what most observers regard as an act of government retribution, al-Banna himself was assassinated in February 1949.

Al-Banna's legacy within the Islamist movement in Egypt and the Muslim world is that of father of the movement and martyr to the cause. His life story exemplifies the Islamist struggle to establish an authentic Muslim society, ruled by and for Islam, a struggle that continues to this day.

See also ISLAMISM; POLITICS AND ISLAM; RENEWAL AND REFORM MOVEMENTS.

Jeffrey T. Kenney

Further reading: Richard P. Mitchell, *The Society of the Muslim Brothers* (London: Oxford University Press, 1969); M. N. Shaikh, trans., *Memoirs of Hasan Al Banna Shaheed* (Karachi: International Islamic Publishers, 1981); Charles Wendell, trans., *Five Tracts of Hasan al-Banna'* (Berkeley: University of California Press, 1978).

baqa and *fana* (Arabic: abiding and annihilation)

Baqa and *fana* are key concepts in SUFISM. They are employed by Sufis in their discussions about mystical experience and union with God. At issue is whether any aspect of a mystic's individuality (or selfhood) really remains or abides (*baqa*) when mystical union or annihilation (*fana*) is experienced, and whether true self-annihilation can really be attained. A common teaching story used in connection with this subject is that of the moth that is drawn to the light of a candle only to perish in the flame: Does the moth completely perish, or does something of the moth continue to exist in a transformed state after it is consumed by the flame? The roots of such discussions are based partly in human speculation about life (existence) and DEATH (the end of existence; nonexistence). When people are born into the world, are they born into true life? When they die, does life truly come to an end? Pre-Islamic Neoplatonic thinkers in the Middle East, among whom were many Christian mystics, identified the living God with true existence and viewed worldly existence as a kind of nonexistence. Therefore, for a Sufi influenced by Neoplatonism, to be truly alive meant finding a way out of this corrupt world, which he considered to be a kind of death or prison, and returning to a mystical union with God, the source of life. Sufis heeded a saying of MUHAMMAD, which stated "Die before you die." For them, this meant not that they should physically die, but that they should strive to purify themselves of worldly existence so that all that remains is God. Some Sufis maintained that the attributes of the individual are thereby replaced by those of God. Such discussions about *baqa* and *fana* also addressed questions concerning the relation between body and soul and whether the soul was divine and immortal.

Formal Islamic doctrine has tended to affirm life in this world as a gift from God and to anticipate an AFTERLIFE of immortal existence in PARADISE or hell, based on a final judgment of one's beliefs and actions. However, Neoplatonic ideas surfaced early in the history of the Muslim community. The QURAN itself emphasizes the distinction between the transitory nature of life in this world (*al-dunya*) and eternal life in the hereafter (*al-akhira*), which is qualitatively better. Moreover, an oft-quoted passage in the Quran states, "Everything on [the Earth] is transitory; all that subsists is the face of your lord (God), the one of majesty and generosity" (Q 55:26–27). This statement implies that life is fleeting and that only God subsists permanently.

In the ninth century, as Neoplatonism became more influential among Muslim intellectuals, Sufis promoted the idea of the relationship between *baqa* and *fana* as states of mind or consciousness that were not limited to physical life and death. The first Sufi to be credited with developing such a doctrine was Abu Said al-Kharraz of Baghdad (d. 899). He taught that *baqa* meant abiding in the contemplation of God's divinity, thus stressing the difference between the mystic and God, while *fana* meant the annihilation of one's awareness of being an imperfect human. Al-Hujwiri (d. ca. 1077), a Persian mystic, went further to say that annihilation comes by way of a vision of God's

majesty, which so overwhelms the visionary that he becomes "dead to reason and passion alike, dead even to annihilation itself" (al-Hujwiri, 246). This line of thought characterizes the attitude of AL-JUNAYD (d. 910) of BAGHDAD and other "sober" Sufis toward mystical experience. They believed that the mystic continued to experience a perfected awareness of the self after annihilation in God.

Others, known as the "intoxicated" Sufis, took a different tack. They maintained that the mystic could completely shed his or her human attributes by following the mystical path and ultimately achieve ecstatic union with God. ABU YAZID AL-BISTAMI (d. ca. 875) and MANSUR AL-HALLAJ (d. 922) were important Sufi visionaries who were included in this group. Al-Hallaj was also credited with introducing the idea that the mystical quest was comparable to that of the lover seeking union with his or her Beloved (God), a theme that lies at the heart of the rich poetic traditions associated with Sufism.

One of the most beautiful expressions of a sober Sufi understanding of the relation between *baqa* and *fana* occurs in Farid al-Din Attar's *Conference of the Birds* (composed ca. 1177). This Persian poem tells the story of a flock of birds who gave up their worldly attachments in order to find Simurgh, their king. After traversing seven valleys, each valley representing a different spiritual station, they are finally admitted to the inner chamber of Simurgh, where they discover that they are identical to their king and surrender themselves to annihilation, only to abide once again in their individual selfhoods at the end of their quest. In later Sufi thought, the way to union with God required prior annihilation in the Sufi master and Muhammad, both of whom were believed to be reflections of God's light.

See also ALLAH; HAL; MAQAM; PERSIAN LANGUAGE AND LITERATURE; *TARIQA*; SOUL AND SPIRIT.

Further reading: Farid Ud-Din Attar, *The Conference of the Birds,* trans. Afkham Darbandi and Dick Davis (New York: Penguin Books, 1984); Ali bin Uthman al-

Hujwiri, *The* Kashf al-Mahjub: *The Oldest Persian Treatise on Sufism.* Translated by R. A. Nicholson (Delhi: Taj Company, 1997); R. A. Nicholson, *The Mystics of Islam* (New York: Schocken, 1975); Annemarie Schimmel, *Mystical Dimensions of Islam* (Chapel Hill: University of North Carolina Press, 1975).

Baqli, Ruzbihan (1128–1209) *leading mystic of 12th-century Iran, famed for his accounts of his visionary experience and controversial ecstatic sayings*

Ruzbihan Abu Muhammad ibn Abi Nasr al-Baqli al-Fasawi was born in Fasaa, a province in the south of IRAN. When older, he moved to the nearby city Shiraz, where he delivered sermons at the town's famous old MOSQUE and enjoyed a large following among the townfolk, as well as some of the local rulers. In his AUTOBIOGRAPHY, Ruzbihan explains that his spirituality is unrelated to his upbringing because he was born and raised in a family that was ignorant about God and was unable to understand him. He defines his call to mysticism in terms of his special relationship with God. Ruzbihan had spiritual experiences as early as age three. At age 15, he was addressed by voices from the unseen world (*ghayb*) calling him a PROPHET. One day around this time, as he was leaving his shop for afternoon prayers, he heard an extraordinary voice and followed it to a nearby hill. There he saw a handsome SHAYKH telling him about God's oneness (*TAWHID*). Ruzbihan describes this event as a turning point in his spiritual awakening. For the rest of his life, he experienced mystical states, and secrets were disclosed to him.

Ruzbihan's writings are in Persian and in Arabic. They describe the visionary events that constituted the life of the author and the knowledge that he acquired by these events. Best known today as the author of *Abhar al-ashiqin* (The jasmine of lovers), *Kashf al-asrar* (The unveiling of secrets), and *Sharh-i shathiyat* (An exegesis of ecstatic sayings), Ruzbihan also wrote on a range of subjects including *TAFSIR* (interpretation), HADITH, and *FIQH* (Islamic jurisprudence).

Sharh-i shathiyat is a classical reference on Islamic mysticism. It is a compilation of sayings by entranced mystics as they were experiencing spiritual states. *Abhar al-ashiqin* is a masterpiece in Persian belles lettres. It provides a geography of love whence God's attributes of "might" (*jalal*) and "beauty" (*jamal*) come into view. Ruzbihan's autobiography, *Kashf al-asrar,* which he began writing at age 55, is a unique document in the genre of Muslim AUTOBIOGRAPHY. While similar to many Muslim biographies and autobiographies, *Kashf al-asrar* concerns the inner spiritual life of the author/protagonist, but unlike most of them, its plot is not centered on the external events that advance the story of his life. In this respect, *Kashf al-asrar* differs from the works that constitute the canon in the medieval Islamic biographical and autobiographical literature.

Today, Ruzbihan's shrine is a pilgrimage site in his hometown, Shiraz.

See also SUFISM.

Firoozeh Papan-Matin

Further reading: Ruzbihan Baqli, *Abhar al-ashiqin,* eds. Henry Corbin and Muhammad Muin (Tehran: Ketabkhane-ye Manuchehri, 1987); Carl Ernst, *Ruzbihan Baqli: Mysticism and the Rhetoric of Sainthood in Persian Sufism* (Richmond, Va.: Curzon Press, 1996).

baraka

Baraka is an Arabic term for blessing used by peoples of the Middle East and followers of Islam. It has been understood both as a specific force that emanates from God and as a more impersonal power that brings about prosperity or good luck at the same time that it counteracts evil forces. According to the QURAN, *baraka* is a power that God can both bestow and withhold, a notion similar to that of *berakhah* in Judaism. If people are mindful of God and do good things, they qualify to receive divine blessing and prosperity; if not, they will not receive it. PROPHETS, as God's agents, can also bestow blessings, as ABRAHAM and MOSES do in the Quran. Like a kind of electricity, it was thought to emanate primarily from God to his creation through the Quran and intermediary prophets and SAINTS. Once ISLAM became a fully institutionalized religion in the ninth century with hierarchies of political and religious power and AUTHORITY that involved rulers, soldiers, ULAMA, administrators, commoners, and slaves, then *baraka* itself was also thought of as a sacred power that flowed from God through a hierarchy of supermundane beings. Today the ordinary person still has simply to hear or see the Quran to benefit from its *baraka*. It can also be obtained by touching a saint, a saint's relic, or even a person who has visited the KAABA, a shrine, or similar holy place. Indeed, obtaining *baraka* is one of the main reasons people perform pilgrimages.

As an impersonal force, *baraka* is supposed to be present in certain stones, trees, natural springs, or manufactured objects—especially in pre-Islamic cultures, among the BEDOUIN, and in rural populations. Egyptian peasants still believe that the antiquities of the ancient Egyptians have this power, and they take scrapings from the pyramids and temples to place in amulets or to mix into a potion with other substances to cure a disease. The idea of blessing also has become diffused in the everyday speech of Muslims and non-Muslims in the Middle East, who use words derived from the Arabic word *baraka* to wish each other a happy holiday and to congratulate someone upon marriage or some other success in life.

See also EGYPT; MIRACLE; *WALI*; *ZIYARA*.

Further reading: Michael Gilsenan, *Recognizing Islam: Religion and Society in the Modern Arab World* (New York: Random House, 1982); Edward Reeves, *The Hidden Government: Ritual, Clientelism, and Legitimation in Northern Egypt* (Salt Lake City: University of Utah Press, 1990); Edward Westermarck, *Ritual and Belief in Morocco*. 2 vols. (New York: University Books, 1968).

Barelwi, Sayyid Ahmad (Bareilly, Brelwi) (1786–1831) *militant religious revivalist leader in North India*

Sayyid Ahmad Barelwi was born to a prominent family of SAYYIDs (descendants of MUHAMMAD) in Awadh province in northern INDIA. After moving to DELHI, where he studied with the son of the Muslim reformer Shah Wali Allah (d. 1762), he served in the cavalry of a Muslim ruler in central India for seven years (1811–18). In 1822, Sayyid Ahmad went on the HAJJ to MECCA. When he returned to India, he combined reformist Islamic ideas with his military experience to launch a movement that quickly migrated from Delhi to Bengal and ultimately to AFGHANISTAN, Kashmir, and the Punjab in northwest India.

At a time when the Mughal Empire was in its death throes, Sayyid Ahmad and his disciples sought to bring Muslims back to what he thought was the true Islam and lead them to greatness by way of a JIHAD against the British, who were becoming more and more powerful at this time. In his teachings, he called upon Muslims to give up un-Islamic idolatrous practices and return to the simple monotheism of the QURAN and Muhammad. He condemned Muslim participation in Hindu social and religious practices, worship at saint shrines, and Shii veneration of the imams. He and his followers thought of themselves as following the path of the first Muslims under Muhammad's leadership, and many believed that Sayyid Ahmad was the "renewer" (*mujaddid*) of the age. Some even considered him to be the awaited MAHDI (Muslim messiah). Sayyid Ahmad's opponents labeled him a "Wahhabi," a follower of the puritanical Saudi form of Islam, but he did not consider himself as such. He was more a follower of the teachings of Shah Wali Allah of Delhi than Muhammad ibn Abd al-Wahhab (d. 1792), the founder of the so-called Wahhabi movement in Arabia during the 18th century.

Sayyid Ahmad decided to mount his jihad against the British from a base in northwest India. In 1826, after gathering recruits from the region of what is now Afghanistan and Baluchistan, he set out for the Punjab, where the population was a mixture of Muslims, Hindus, and Sikhs. There he attempted to displace the local Sikh governor, Sher Singh (d. 1843), and after several battles and skirmishes he was killed at Balakot (near Kashmir) in 1831. His movement was put into disarray, but it reorganized itself and became a nonjihadist reform movement known as the Path of Muhammad, based in Patna. Sayyid Ahmad is still remembered by many Pakistani and Indian Muslims as a martyr (*shahid*), and his shrine still stands in the town of Balakot, Pakistan, along with memorials to those who died in battle with him.

The movement launched by Sayyid Ahmad in the early 19th century is distinct from a movement the emerged later in the 1880s called the Barelwi Movement, under the leadership of Ahmad Riza Khan (1856–1921) of Barelwi, a scholar of the SHARIA. Members of this movement strongly believed that they were the Indian heirs of Muhammad and his companions in MEDINA, and they opposed the reformist ideas of SAYYID AHMAD KHAN (d. 1898) and ABU AL-KALAM AZAD (d. 1958). Instead they espoused a combination of Sufi devotionalism and pilgrimage to saint shrines with a reformist attitude toward the SHARIA. Their understanding of Islam was also at odds with that of Sayyid Ahmad's "Wahhabi" movement and the conservative school based in DEOBAND. Although the Barelwi Movement began in rural areas, it has since gained a strong following among educated Muslims in urban areas of India and Pakistan.

See also HINDUISM AND ISLAM; MUGHAL DYNASTY; RENEWAL AND REFORM MOVEMENTS; WAHHABISM.

Further reading: Mohiuddin Ahmad, *Saiyid Ahmad Shahid: His Life and Mission* (Lucknow: Academy of Islamic Research and Publications, 1975); Ghulam Mohammad Jaffar, "Teachings of Shah Wali Allah and the Movement of Sayyid Ahmad Shahid of Bareilly." *Hamdard Islamicus* 16, no. 4 (1993): 69–80; Barbara D. Metcalf, *Islamic Revival in British India: Deoband, 1860–1900* (Princeton, N.J.: Princeton University Press, 1982).

Basmachi

Basmachi, a Turkic word translated as "bandit," was a derogatory term used by Bolshevik and Soviet authorities to refer to almost all forms of violent indigenous Central Asia resistance to Russian power following the Russian Revolutions of 1917. This resistance grew in response to the economic and social dislocation resulting from Russian campaigns of land confiscation and looting. The largest movement labeled Basmachi was led by Enver Pasha (d. 1922), one of a number of former Turkish military officers who fought in the region under the banner of pan-Turkism (a nationalist movement among Turkic peoples). Although he commanded 15,000 to 20,000 troops by spring 1922, he and the other Turkish officers were seen as outsiders, and they failed to gain a real following among the population. The Soviets made effective use of their greater military force, and in 1923, the government offered amnesty to those rebels who would give up the fight and surrender their weapons. Revolts continued, however, with one large Basmachi group holding out for seven months in 1924.

Numerous so-called Basmachi revolts continued into the 1930s with varying intensity in Tajikistan, Uzbekistan, and Turkmenistan. These revolts were different from those of the 1920s, as they were unorganized, peasant-based movements with less of a coherent ideology. Soviet collectivization of AGRICULTURE, their campaign to root out "class enemies" in the countryside, as well as an escalated struggle against Islam caused the number of these uprisings to increase. Most of the fighting men came from the peasantry, and their leaders were village elders, tribal heads, and Sufi shaykhs. Basmachi revolts were firmly rooted in local communities, so that organizationally and objectively they could never coalesce into a mass uprising large enough to dislodge the Soviets. The revolts also remained immune to calls to join the larger national or pan-Turkic struggle. By the late 1930s, through military force and political and economic concessions, Basmachi-style revolts had been quashed.

See also BUKHARA; TURKEY.

David Reeves

Further reading: Edward Allworth, *The Modern Uzbeks from the Fourteenth Century to the Present* (Stanford, Calif.: Hoover Institution Press, 1990); Shoshana Keller, *To Moscow, Not Mecca: The Soviet Campaign against Islam in Central Asia, 1917–1941* (Westport, Conn.: Praeger, 2001).

basmala

The *basmala*, also known as the *tasmiya*, is an Arabic word for the phrase *bi-smillah ir-rahman ir-rahim*, "In the name of God most compassionate, most merciful." This is the first verse of the QURAN; it begins all of its chapters but one (Q 9), and it is recited before reading any part of the Quran. According to religious authorities, people should pronounce it before any worthwhile activity, such as a formal speech, a meal, taking medicine, using the toilet, slaughtering an ANIMAL for food, sexual intercourse with one's spouse, and traveling. Many recite it when they awake each day and before going to sleep. It is believed that whoever repeats the *basmala* will be granted his or her wishes, and it is also supposed to keep SATAN away. Important documents and religious books begin with the *basmala*, and Muslim students write it at the beginning of their homework and exams. Also, Quran inscriptions on the walls of MOSQUEs and other buildings begin with this phrase. Indeed, it is perhaps the most frequently used verse in Arabic CALLIGRAPHY, where it is written in many styles and forms. According to the HADITH, "Whoever writes the *basmala* beautifully will obtain many blessings" or "enter PARADISE." Because its words are believed to be so powerful and beneficial, it is frequently used in amulets to help people obtain a blessing or protect them from harm. Car bumper stickers and decals often feature it or its numerical equivalent, 786, which is popular in INDIA, PAKISTAN, and BANGLADESH.

The *basmala* has been accorded special status in Islamic stories and commentaries, too. For example, it is said that GABRIEL once told Adam, the first human being, that the *basmala* was "the word whereby the heavens and the earth came to be, by which the water was set in motion, by which the mountains were established steadfast and the earth made firm, and whereby the hearts of all creatures were strengthened" (Jeffrey, 556). Sunni Quran commentaries mention that the *basmala* contains all of the SHARIA in it, because in it God gives both his essence and attributes. The Shia respect a hadith which says that all of the Quran is contained in the *basmala* and that Ali represents the dot under the Arabic letter *b* in that word, meaning that Ali, the first Shii Imam, embodies not only the *basmala*, but the entire Quran.

See also ALLAH; *BARAKA*; NAMES OF GOD; SUNNISM; TRAVEL.

Further reading: Arthur Jeffrey, *A Reader on Islam* (The Hague: Mouton & Co., 1962); Moshe Piamenta, *Islam in Everyday Arabic Speech* (Leiden: E.J. Brill, 1979).

batin (Arabic: inward, hidden)

The idea of an inner or secret truth is one that has intrigued religious thinkers and mystics in many different religious traditions. In ISLAM, this idea is captured by the term *al-batin*. It is particularly important in relation to the interpretation of scripture. Sunnis are known for being in favor of interpreting the QURAN to bring forth its conventional, outward (*zahir*) meanings, a procedure called TAFSIR. Many Shii scholars, on the other hand, have contended that although the Quran has outward meanings that change with the passage of time, it also has inward (*batin*), esoteric ones that contain eternal truths. Indeed, they have supported key doctrines in their understanding of Islam by a process of scriptural interpretation they call *tawil,* which allows them to extract the Quran's inward, symbolic meanings.

In their debates over the Quran's outward and inward meanings, Muslims have invoked the following verse:

> (God) sent down upon you this book in which are some clear verses—they are the mother of the book—and others that are ambiguous. Those whose hearts are devious follow what is ambiguous in it to cause discord when they interpret it. Only God knows how to interpret it and those who are firm in knowledge, they say: "We believe in it; all comes from our lord." (Q 3:7)

Sunnis say that only God and Sunni religious scholars are qualified to interpret the Quran, especially the clear verses, while other interpretations are troublesome. The Shia maintain that, to the contrary, God endowed the infallible Shii IMAMS with the gift of interpreting both the clear and ambiguous verses to extract their inward meaning. They teach that verses referring to the "straight path" (Q 1:6), the "light of God" (Q 64:8), and the "truthful ones" (Q 9:119) are secret references to their Imams. Even the Sun and the moon, mentioned in Q 91:1–4, are interpreted to represent Muhammad and Ali, while "day" stands for the imams and "night" for the enemies of the imams. Moreover, the Shia see the story of Abraham's sacrifice (Q 37:100–110) as a secret prefiguration of Husayn's martyrdom at KARBALA in 680. Most Sunnis would reject such interpretations.

The Ismailis, or Seven-Imam Shia, were the first major Shii sect to propagate the idea of inward meanings of the Quran, starting in the eighth century. They maintained that Muhammad, as the prophet of Islam, was sent to transmit the outward meanings of the Quran, and that the Imams were charged with transmitting its inward meanings. Most branches of the Ismailis accepted the coexistence of the two kinds of interpretation, as did the Twelve-Imam Shia. They also required

that members become knowledgeable about the Quran's outward meanings before delving into its hidden ones. Ismailis maintained that there were ascending levels of inward meanings that students had to comprehend in order to arrive at the supreme truth. Sufis also have sought to elicit the inward meanings of the Quran, but they do so with the guidance provided by divine inspiration or a Sufi master (SHAYKH or *pir*), rather than an Imam.

See also HAQIQA; ISMAILI SHIISM; TWELVE-IMAM SHIISM.

Further reading: Moojan Momen, *An Introduction to Shii Islam* (New Haven, Conn.: Yale University Press, 1985); David Pinault, *The Shiites: Ritual and Popular Piety in a Muslim Community* (New York: St. Martin's Press, 1992).

Bawa Muhaiyaddeen Fellowship

The Bawa Muhaiyaddeen Fellowship was founded by the American followers of Sri Lankan Sufi mystic Muhammad Raheem Bawa Muhaiyaddeen. Little is known of the early life, not even the birth date, of Bawa Muhaiyaddeen. He emerged from obscurity in the 1930s when he began to teach in Colombo, where the Serendih Study Group was formed. Here he was discovered by an American spiritual seeker, and in 1971, he accepted an invitation to move to the United States. Once in Philadelphia, a group of disciples formed around him, the Bawa Muhaiyaddeen Fellowship was organized, and he decided to stay in the West, though he periodically returned to Sri Lanka to teach.

Through the 1970s and until his death in 1986, Bawa Muhaiyaddeen was credited with a number of books, many developed from his talks, as he could not read or write, and the fellowship grew slowly but steadily. Additional centers were opened across the United States and one in England before his death. Subsequently, the fellowship has expanded to AUSTRALIA.

While a Muslim, Bawa Muhaiyaddeen tried to emphasize the universal quality of his message that transcended religious labels. He centered his message on the unity of God and human unity in God and tried to so communicate the experience of God as to speak to people of all religious backgrounds. He understood a Sufi to be one who had lost the self in the solitary oneness that is God. The individual's soul is the point of contact, where the realization of God is possible. Bawa Muhaiyaddeen, who died in 1986, recommended that his disciples constantly affirm that nothing but God exists, try to eliminate all evil from their lives, inculcate the Godlike qualities of patience, tolerance, peacefulness and compassion, and try to treat all lives as one's own life. These actions should lead naturally to the practice of remembering God, the DHIKR.

The fellowship makes numerous books, audiotapes, and videotapes of Bawa Muhaiyaddeen's presentations available to seekers through Fellowship Press. Its headquarters complex in Philadelphia includes a building for public meetings, a MOSQUE, and a press. Bawa Muhaiyaddeen's tomb, located outside of Philadelphia, was dedicated in 1987. An estimated 5,000 adherents attend meetings across the UNITED STATES and in CANADA, the United Kingdom, NEW ZEALAND, AUSTRALIA, and Colombo, Sri Lanka. The Fellowship's internet site is found at http://www.bmf.org/.

See also SUFISM.

J. Gordon Melton

Further reading: M. R. Guru Bawa Muhaiyaddeen, *God, His Prophets and His Children* (Philadelphia: Fellowship Press, 1978); M. R. Guru Bawa Muhaiyaddeen, *Truth and Light* (Philadelphia: Fellowship Press, 1974); M. R. Guru Bawa Muhaiyaddeen, *The Truth and the Unity of Man* (Philadelphia: Fellowship Press, 1980).

bazaar (Persian: marketplace)

One of the most important public spaces in Islamicate lands is the urban district known as the bazaar or marketplace (called a *suq* in Arabic-speaking lands), the center of business and commerce. Found in CITIES from North Africa to INDIA and Central Asia, it consists of small shops, warehouses, handicraft centers, banks, public bathhouses, bakeries, cafes, street vendors, and inns. People from all walks of life cross paths there—the wealthy and beggars, men and WOMEN, seniors and CHILDREN, farmers and soldiers, natives and foreigners, nomads and sailors, the literate and the illiterate, the skilled and the unskilled, men of religion and the laity, Muslims and non-Muslims. The bazaar can be open air, but Islamicate cities are also famous for their covered marketplaces, with massive gateways that can be closed at night for security. The bazaar is typically subdivided into zones defined by craft or trade. Thus, all of the spice shops are close together, as are those of the goldsmiths and silversmiths, coppersmiths, sword makers, carpenters, cloth merchants, booksellers, tent makers, and so on. Businesses that do not make large profits tend to be located in secondary bazaars and peripheral areas, as are the ones that pollute, such as tanneries, slaughterhouses, and pottery workshops.

Among the distinct buildings of the bazaar in premodern cities is the caravanserai (also known as the *khan, funduq,* or *wikala*), a large rectangular structure with an open courtyard, storerooms, and stables on the ground level and lodgings for traveling merchants above. It is estimated that in the 17th century CAIRO had as many as 20,000 shops and 360 caravanserais in its marketplace, but most premodern cities had smaller commercial zones. In rural areas, bazaars have not usually been permanent parts of the landscape. Rather, they have operated on a periodic basis according to the days of the week, the most popular market days being Thursdays and Fridays.

Islamic religious institutions have evolved in close relationship to the marketplace. Grand MOSQUES for communal PRAYER are typically located where the main business districts are. The income from commercial properties in bazaars can be set aside by the owners as charitable bequests (*waqf*) to provide charity in perpetuity to the poor and

Public market in Marrakesh, Morocco *(Federico R. Campo)*

to pay for the building, maintenance, and staffing of mosques, MADRASAS, QURAN schools, Sufi hospices, hospitals, and public fountains. These revenues have also been used to maintain holy sites in MECCA and MEDINA and to care for the needs of Muslims performing the HAJJ. A substantial part of Islamic jurisprudence (FIQH) is concerned with regulating commercial transactions, and the ULAMA considered the bazaar an important arena for enforcing public morality. ABU HAMID AL-GHAZALI (d. 1111), for example, drew attention to market practices that were violations of the Islamic moral code, such as usury, price gouging, selling defective merchandise, cheating with the scales, and trading in forbidden goods (e.g., wine, musical instruments, and silk clothing for men). Following a fundamental ethical principle, when

they encounter such wrongdoing, good Muslims are obliged to command what is right and forbid what is wrong. Indeed, the medieval office of the market inspector (*muhtasib*) was specifically charged with regulating conduct in the marketplace, commercial and otherwise.

Religious authorities have been linked to the bazaar in other ways, too. Many have come from the merchant class, and even if they have not, a considerable amount of their income has. They have customarily managed funds from the charitable bequests. Studies of the ulama in IRAN and IRAQ reveal that they have been supported by donations received from lay members of the community, especially the *bazaaris*, or merchants. The economic relations between these two groups are further cemented by their intermarriage.

In the modern period, the traditional bazaars have adapted to the new global consumer economy. Many have become centers of tourism, such as the old marketplaces of FEZ, Cairo, JERUSALEM, DAMASCUS, Aleppo, ISTANBUL, Jeddah, Delhi, and Hyderabad (in southern INDIA). But even in these changed circumstances, the heritage of the traditional bazaar can still be felt when one walks down their streets. Also, as it has in the past, the contemporary marketplace can become a flashpoint for political protest, as happened in IRAN, where *bazaaris* joined with the Shii ulama to spearhead the revolution that brought about the downfall of the monarchy in 1978–79.

See also HISBA.

Further reading: Michael Cook, *Forbidding Wrong in Islam: An Introduction* (Cambridge: Cambridge University Press, 2003); Yitzhak Nakash, *The Shiis of Iraq* (Princeton, N.J.: Princeton University Press, 1994); Andre Raymond, *The Great Arab Cities in the 16th–18th Centuries: An Introduction* (New York: New York University Press, 1984); Lewis Werner, "Suq—4,000 Years Behind the Counter in Aleppo." *Saudi Aramco World* 55 (March/April 2004): 24–35; Paul Wheatley, *The Places Where Men Pray Together: Cities in Islamic Lands, 7th through the 10th Centuries* (Chicago: University of Chicago Press, 2001).

Bedouin

The Bedouin are ARAB dwellers of the desert who traditionally follow a nomadic lifestyle. Their name is based on an Arabic word meaning to be plain, to be open (*badaa*), from which the word desert (*badiya*) is formed, which suggests that deserts are thought of as wide-open lands or plains. The meaning of the word *Bedouin* stands in contrast to the Arabic word for civilized town dwellers (*hadar*). *Bedouin* is often, but not always, used as a synonym for *Arab*. Bedouin peoples have historically lived in the desert regions of the Arabian Peninsula, SYRIA, JORDAN, ISRAEL and PALESTINE, IRAQ, EGYPT, North Africa, and outlying areas of Africa and Central Asia. People living in CITIES and towns stereotype the Bedouin as an uncultured lot, yet the Bedouin are also recognized for their strong sense of tribal honor, egalitarianism, generosity, courage, and poetic eloquence. Medieval Muslim scholars thought the "pure" Arabic of the QURAN was closely related to the Bedouin dialect of the QURAYSH tribe, but most modern scholars believe it was a common poetic language used throughout western Arabia. Several have noted that values of Bedouin culture are embedded in the religious language of the Quran. Bedouin traditionally make their living by herding pastoral ANIMALS (sheep, goats, CAMELS, HORSES, and cattle), which they lead to different grazing areas and water sources within their tribal territories on a seasonal basis. Because of their seasonal migrations and lifestyle, they dwell in tents that can be easily transported from place to place.

Historical and ethnographic studies reveal that pastoral peoples such as the Bedouin live in a symbiotic relationship with town dwellers. For example, they trade animal products for agricultural products and goods produced by settled populations. In times of drought, Bedouin take up residence in urban lands until conditions improve. On the other hand, town dwellers have relied on Bedouin warriors for their defense and to guide caravans to their destinations. Bedouin warriors were also known for their raids on other nomadic tribes, caravans, and settlements. Today the Bedouin, like other nomadic peoples in the Middle East and elsewhere, are being forced to become more sedentary by extensive conversion of lands to agricultural development and government settlement policies. In the kingdoms of SAUDI ARABIA and Jordan, however, the Bedouin have been recruited to form elite corps in their royal armed forces. Bedouin ideals still color the cultural life of peoples living in the Arabian Peninsula, as can be seen in styles of dress, social customs, and fondness for camping in the desert.

The religious outlook of the Bedouin is recognized for its simplicity. In pre-Islamic Arabia, the features of the landscape (rocks, trees, and springs) and religious shrines were the focal points of their religious activity, which included pilgrimage and animal sacrifice. In addition, four specific months of the year were held to be sacred times when warfare was prohibited for Arabs living in the vicinity of MECCA. The early Muslim community in MEDINA built alliances with Bedouin tribes and won their CONVERSION to ISLAM, which was expressed by performance of Islamic PRAYER and ALMGSGIVING. However, Bedouin also allied with MUHAMMAD's opponents, and when he died in 632, many tribes that had converted to Islam when he was alive attempted to abandon it. This led to the Wars of APOSTASY, in which the Muslim forces under the leadership of the caliph ABU BAKR (r. 632–634) proved victorious. The rebellious tribes were reincorporated into the Muslim community, and they played an important role in the early Arab Muslim conquest of the Middle East, North Africa, and Spain. Indeed, the conquest was really conducted as an extension of Bedouin-style warfare involving small-scale raids rather than massive troop movements.

The Arab historian IBN KHALDUN (d. 1406) developed a theory of the rise and fall of civilizations based on his knowledge of the involvement of Bedouin Arabs in the early conquests and the subsequent emergence of Islamicate civilization in the Middle East and North Africa. This theory rested on the thesis that civilizations originate with tribal solidarity (asabiyya) and the ability of one tribe to dominate others. Eventually, this dominance leads to the accumulation of wealth and power and the birth of urban institutions. Religion reinforces the moral basis of urban civilization and tempers the destructiveness of social forces, but eventually civilization succumbs to the onslaught of new, more vigorous tribal groups. A recent example of this pattern can be seen in the rise of Saudi Arabia, which began in the 18th century when the Saudi clan formed a multitribal fighting force motivated by the religious ideology of MUHAMMAD IBN ABD AL-WAHHAB (d. 1792).

See also AGRICULTURE; FOOD AND DRINK; HONOR AND SHAME.

Further reading: Leila Abu Lughod, *Veiled Sentiments: Honor and Poetry in a Bedouin Society* (Berkeley: University of California Press, 2000); Donald P. Cole, *Nomads of the Nomads: The Al Murrah Bedouin of the Empty Quarter* (Chicago: Aldine Publishing Company, 1975); Dale F. Eickelman, *The Middle East and Central Asia: An Anthropological Approach.* 4th ed. (Englewood Cliffs, N.J.: Prentice Hall, 2001); Jibrail Jabbur, *The Bedouins and the Desert: Aspects of Nomadic Life in the Arab East* (New York: State University of New York Press, 1995).

Bektashi Sufi Order

The Bektashi Order, which is based in TURKEY, was formed by disciples of the 13th-century SAINT Haji Bektash Veli (*WALI*), who is said to have migrated to Anatolia from Khorasan. He settled in a village in central Anatolia and exerted a strong influence over the Turkish peasants and wandering dervishes living in the region. After his death, the site of his tomb attracted followers, who eventually formed a coherent order, which was firmly institutionalized by Balim Sultan in the early 16th century. The order spread through lands occupied by the Ottomans, especially in the Balkans. Bektashis were affiliated with the JANISSARY corps of the Sultan's army, for whom they served as chaplains. It was this relationship that led to their suppression when Sultan Mahmud II abolished the Janissaries in 1826. Bektashis later reappeared but were again officially closed down along with all other dervish orders in Turkey in 1925. Nevertheless, Bektashis have continued to exist in Turkey, and there are also communities in Bulgaria, Bosnia, Macedonia, and Albania.

Like the Shia, Bektashis revere Ali and the Twelve Imams but also Haji Bektash and other saints. They seek spiritual perfection through correct behavior and disguise their beliefs through a complex symbolism that pervades all Bektashi ritual, clothing, ART, and poetry. Disciples are initiated in an elaborate ceremony by a spiritual guide called a *baba* (father), who continues to direct their spiritual progress by instructing them in Bektashi beliefs through the use of poetry, stories, and even jokes. Bektashis meet in a ceremony (closed to outsiders) known as *meydan,* which is followed by a ritual meal in which food is shared, poetry is sung to the accompaniment of MUSIC, and disciples are instructed by the *baba.* The feast also includes the consumption of alcohol, which has symbolic significance. Because of their use of alcohol and their lack of compliance with Islamic practices such as PRAYER in MOSQUES and FASTING during RAMADAN, Bektashis have often been condemned by orthodox authorities, yet they are also known for their wisdom, humor and tolerance.

See also ALI IBN ABI TALIB; IMAM; SHIISM; SUFISM.

Mark Soileau

Further reading: John Kingsley Birge, *The Bektashi Order of Dervishes* (London: Luzac & Co., 1937); F. W. Hasluck, *Christianity and Islam under the Sultans* (Oxford: Oxford University Press, 1929); Frances Trix, *Spiritual Discourse: Learning with an Islamic Master* (Philadelphia: University of Pennsylvania Press, 1993).

Berber

Berber is a term for the most ancient known culture, people, and language in North Africa. Berbers, or Imazighen, once lived from south of the Sahara all the way from the Mediterranean and from EGYPT in the east to the Canary Islands in the far west. During their long history, Berber-speaking peoples have been influenced by a number of religious traditions, including paganism, Christianity, and Judaism, but the most profound debt is to ISLAM. Today Berbers are overwhelmingly Sunni Muslims.

Berbers were introduced to Islam in the eighth century when some joined ARAB Muslims in conquering Spain (ANDALUSIA), but the conver-

sion of more remote Berbers took hundreds of years. Relations between Arabs and Berbers were not always harmonious, particularly when Arabs treated Berber speakers as inferiors. In the 12th century, Berber groups formed the core of the Almoravid and then the ALMOHAD DYNASTY that ruled much of Spain and North Africa, and Berbers were central to the Marinid (1196–1464) and Fatimid dynasties (909–1171) also. Today Berbers continue to inhabit small communities in EGYPT, LIBYA, and TUNISIA, but most live in ALGERIA, Mauritania, Niger, and especially MOROCCO, where they are thought to constitute 40 percent of the population. There are also large communities of migrant Berbers in Europe, especially in Belgium, the Netherlands, and France.

The term *Berber* relates to the Greek and Roman word for *barbarian,* and thus many contemporary scholars and activists prefer the terms *Amazigh* (singular) or *Imazighen* (plural) to describe what most English speakers know as Berbers. One thing that makes Imazighen distinctive is their language, which seems to be remarkably similar over a vast territory and has persisted for a very long time despite the political dominance of written languages such as Latin, French, and Arabic. Today *Berber* usually refers to someone who speaks some variety of Berber (Tamazight) as their first or only language, though there are Imazighen who do not speak the language but remain passionately attached to Amazigh culture and identity.

See also ALMORAVID DYNASTY; FATIMID DYNASTY.

David Crawford

Further reading: Michael Brett and Elizabeth Fentress, *The Berbers* (Oxford: Blackwell Publishers, 1996); Ernest Gellner and Charles Micaud, *Arabs and Berbers: From Tribe to Nation in North Africa* (Lexington, Mass.: Heath, 1972).

Bible   *See* HOLY BOOKS.

bidaa (Arabic: innovation)

Bidaa is a term used by Muslim jurists and the legally minded to classify beliefs, activities, and institutions accepted by Muslims that are not mentioned by either the QURAN or the SUNNA. The most literalist jurists, following IBN TAYMIYYA (d. 1328), such as members of the HANBALI LEGAL SCHOOL and the Wahhabi movement in SAUDI ARABIA and elsewhere overtly reject anything they determine to be such an innovation. Most jurists and many Muslims, however, follow the views of AL-SHAFII (d. 820), one of the founding figures of the Islamic legal tradition, who drew a distinction between innovations that are good (*hasan*) and those that are bad (*sayya*) or blameworthy (*madhmuma*). Permissible innovations include study of Arabic grammar, building schools, wearing nice clothing, and serving good food to guests. Widespread practices such as using ARABESQUE to beautify MOSQUES and Quran manuscripts have been classed as "disapproved" (*makruh*) innovations but have not been subject to any penalty or prohibition. Innovations that would lead to IDOLATRY and HERESY are classed as disbelief (KAFIR [or *Kufr*]), and may incur penalties. Sunni jurists have included in this last class of innovations popular religious practices associated with SAINT shrines, Shii doctrines about the IMAMS, and the sectarian beliefs of the AHMADIYYA sect of ISLAM.

In the modern period, the idea of *bidaa* has become more a part of Muslim religious discourse and argumentation than ever before. Literalists use it to condemn not only popular religious practices but also secular customs in pluralistic societies, such as celebrating birthdays, keeping pets, listening to popular MUSIC, and saluting a country's flag. Paradoxically, they also have embraced the use of modern technology never mentioned in the Quran and sunna in their daily lives, to run their institutions, and to disseminate their Islamic message. Progressive Muslims for their part promote the idea of the good innovation in their efforts to reconcile medieval Islamic tradition with the vicissitudes and ambiguities of a rapidly changing world. Many are in agreement with thinkers such as KHALID ABOU EL FADL (b. 1963), who maintains that whatever is based on moral insight cannot be condemned or dismissed as a blameworthy or corrupt innovation.

See also FIQH; SHAFII LEGAL SCHOOL; SHIISM; WAHHABISM.

Further reading: Muhammad Umar Memon, *Ibn Taymiyya's Struggle against Popular Religion* (The Hague: Mouton, 1976); Yusuf al-Qaradawi, *The Lawful and the Prohibited in Islam* (Al Halal Wal Haram Fil Islam), trans. Kamal El-Helbawy et al. (Indianapolis: American Trust Publications, [1980]); Vardit Rispler, "Toward a New Understanding of the Term *bidaa*." *Der Islam* 68 (1991): 320–328.

Bilal (d. ca. 641) *African slave and early convert to Islam who was freed and chosen to be the first person to call people to prayer*

Bilal ibn Rabah was a man of Ethiopian ancestry born in MECCA as a slave to one of the powerful branches of the QURAYSH tribe, the Banu Jahm. According to Muslim sources, he was one of the early converts to ISLAM, but his owner would torture him to try to force him to give up his new religion and return to the worship of MECCA's old GODDESSes, Al-Lat and Uzza. He refused and would utter the words, "One, one!" in reference to the one God, ALLAH, while under torture. ABU BAKR, MUHAMMAD's close associate, was moved by Bilal's steadfast courage and purchased his freedom by exchanging one of his own slaves for him. Bilal later joined other Mecca Muslims in the HOJRI to MEDINA in 622. Muhammad appointed him to be the community's first MUEZZIN, the man who makes the call to PRAYER, because of his melodious and powerful voice. He also served as Muhammad's personal attendant. In his last years, Bilal participated in the conquest of SYRIA, where he spent the rest of his life.

Today there is a shrine for Bilal in the cemetery of DAMASCUS, and his memory is kept alive for

Muslims around the world in oral traditions and in children's literature about Muhammad's companions. He is especially honored among African-American Muslims, who consider him an ancestral figure. Warith Din Muhammad (b. 1933), leader of the American Muslim Mission, called his followers "Bilalians," and he changed the name of the Nation of Islam's newspaper to *Bilalian News*. Several MOSQUES in African-American communities are named after him, too.

See also AFRICAN AMERICANS, ISLAM AMONG; NATION OF ISLAM.

Further reading: Muhammad Abdul-Rauf, *Balal ibn Rabah: A Leading Companion of the Prophet Muhammad* (Indianapolis, Ind.: American Trust Publications, 1977); Martin Lings, *Muhammad: His Life Based on the Earliest Sources* (New York: Inner Traditions International, 1983).

biography

A biography is a written account about someone's life story. The author has to make a choice about what to include and exclude, how to organize the narrative, and exactly how to represent the person to the reader. Some biographies can be very detailed; others may provide only a brief sketch of a person's life. In the vast field of Islamic literature, biography is one of the most enduring genres, encompassing a cumulative body of texts that span nearly 1,400 years in Arabic, Persian, Turkish, and other languages. It was used to commemorate important people and to highlight their praiseworthy qualities for the instruction of others. A special kind of Islamic biography, called hagiography in English, was composed to emphasize the holiness of SAINTS, recount their blessings and miracles, and portray their superiority over their enemies and rivals.

The most important biographies of Muslim religious figures are those written about Islam's foremost prophet, MUHAMMAD. The prototype for this group of biographies is *The Way of God's Messenger* (*Sirat rasul Allah*), written by MUHAMMAD IBN ISHAQ (d. 767) and later edited by Ibn Hisham (d. 833). The purpose of this work was to authenticate Muhammad's status as a true prophet. It contains details about his ancestry and family life, where he lived, relations with companions and opponents, how he received revelations of the QURAN, his alliances and battles, and miraculous events in his life, especially his NIGHT JOURNEY AND ASCENT. This book has been the main source to which Muslims (and non-Muslims) have turned through the centuries for knowledge about Muhammad, although many other Muslims have written biographies about him, too. His personal traits and accounts about specific events in his life have been celebrated in poetry, song, and folklore in all Muslim societies. One of the most widely known modern biographies of Muhammad by a Muslim is *The Life of Muhammad* by the Egyptian writer Muhammad Husayn Haykal (d. 1956). There have also been film and cartoon versions of his life, although he cannot be shown because of the formal Islamic prohibition against portraying the Prophet in figural form. Since the 19th century, many secular scholars in Western countries have written biographies about Muhammad, such as W. Montgomery Watt, Frants Buhl, Maxime Rodinson, and F. E. Peters. Most of the Western studies have sought to explain the historical origins of Islam and critically assess Muhammad's role as a leader, rather than portray him as an exemplary prophet or holy man.

Muslim scholars have also excelled in producing biographical dictionaries, one of the most characteristic kinds of Islamic literature. The standard for such dictionaries was set by Ibn Saad's *Book of the Classes* (*Kitab al-tabaqat al-kabir*), which was written in IRAQ during the early ninth century to help establish the authenticity of the HADITH. It contains 4,250 biographies about the men and WOMEN of the early Muslim community, including Muhammad, his family, and the first CALIPHS. Later dictionaries told about the lives and accomplishments of hadith specialists, QURAN reciters, jurists, judges, poets, rulers, bureaucrats, and physicians. In the 13th century, Ibn Khallikan (d. 1282) compiled the first comprehensive dictionary of prominent people from all walks of life who lived after the first generations of Muslims. Its 800 articles were organized alphabetically. Some dictionaries were organized according to tribe; others limited themselves to telling about the famous men of a single city or region, such as Nishapur (in IRAN), BAGHDAD, DAMASCUS, CAIRO, Yemen, or ANDALUSIA (Islamic Spain). Dictionary-like biographical entries were also embedded in historical chronicles and literary works. An entry could range in length from a few lines to many pages. One of average length typically provided information about the subject's family lineage, names and titles, EDUCATION, places lived in and visited, writings, areas of expertise, employment history, birth, and death. Because these books were compiled by educated elites for their peers, they neglected to include information about the common people. Biographies about famous women were also included in these dictionaries—Ibn Saad's dictionary has entries for 600 women—but seldom if ever were a famous man's female relatives mentioned, unless they were also famous.

Muslim hagiographies focused on praiseworthy characteristics (*manaqib*), miracles, and teachings of Sufi saints—the "friends (*awliya*) of God." These accounts were first compiled in Arabic dictionaries at the end of the 10th century, just as the Sufi brotherhoods were beginning to play a more visible role in Islamic society. The first Sufi biographical dictionary was that of the al-Sulami of Nishapur (d. 1021). It originally contained 1,000 biographies, but only 105 of these accounts survive in a very abbreviated version called *Classes of the Sufis* (*Tabaqat al-sufiyya*). The largest surviving collection of Sufi biographies is the *Adornment of the Saints* (*Hilyat al-awliya*) by Abu Nuaym al-Isfahani (d. 1038), which has 649 entries. Beginning in 13th century, Sufi biographical dictionaries were also written in Persian, as exemplified by Farid al-Din Attar's (d. 1220) entertaining *Memorial of the Saints* (*Tadhkirat al-awliya*) and, later, in India, Dara Shikoh's (d. 1659) *Ship of the Saints* (*Safinat al-awliya*). Similar works were compiled in Turkish after the 16th century.

The introduction of mechanized print technology in the 19th century and computers in the 20th century has given new life to the Islamic biographical tradition. Printed editions of medieval biographical dictionaries are widely available, as are biographies of Muhammad, the first caliphs, and other revered Muslims of the past. Some of these have been translated from their original Arabic or Persian language into modern Urdu, Indonesian, English, and other languages. Moreover, new biographies that reflect modern points of view are being produced in great numbers. These works often show the influence of western styles of writing, but their purpose is to reinterpret the accomplishments of prominent Muslims in light of contemporary interests and concerns in the wider Muslim community: the search for authenticity, refutation of Western ORIENTALISM, religion and nationalism, religious and political reform, and the status of WOMEN. ALI SHARIATI (d. 1977), for example, wrote about the lives of early Shii holy figures to inspire Iranians in the decade prior to the IRANIAN REVOLUTION OF 1978–79. Several books have been written about important women in Islamic history in order to counter Western and traditional Muslim stereotypes of women as historically inconsequential and lacking social or cultural agency. Among the leading Muslim women biographical writers are the Egyptian Aysha Abd al-Rahman (also known as Bint al-Shati, d. 1998) and the Moroccan FATIMA MERNISSI (b. 1940). Another important recent development is the publication of biographies in newspapers and magazines and, most recently, the placement of them on compact disks and the internet for even wider circulation.

See also ARABIC LANGUAGE AND LITERATURE; AUTOBIOGRAPHY; DARA SHIKOH; PERSIAN LANGUAGE AND LITERATURE; SUFISM; ULAMA; *WALI*.

Further reading: Carl Ernst, "Lives of Sufi Saints." In *Religions of India in Practice,* edited by Donald S. Lopez, Jr., 495–512 (Princeton, N.J.: Princeton University Press, 1995); R. Stephen Humphreys, *Islamic History: A Framework for Inquiry* (Princeton, N.J.: Princeton University Press, 1991), 187–208; F. E. Peters, *Muhammad and the Origins of Islam* (Albany: State University of New York Press, 1994); Widad al-Qadi, "Biographical Dictionaries: Inner Structure and Cultural Significance." In *The Book in the Islamic World: The Written Word and Communication in the Middle East,* edited by George N. Atiyeh, 93–122 (Washington, D.C.: Library of Congress, 1995).

birth control and family planning

Birth control and family planning are significant issues in many Muslim countries today. Statistical surveys indicate that Muslim countries have among the highest population growth rates in the world. While the rate in Western countries such as Great Britain is .2 percent, .39 percent in France, and .89 percent in the UNITED STATES, in Muslim countries it can reach nearly 3.5 percent. For example, it is 1.49 percent in INDONESIA, 1.98 percent in PAKISTAN, 2.08 percent in BANGLADESH, 2.44 percent in SAUDI ARABIA, and 3.44 percent in YEMEN. The governments of most of these countries as well as regional and international organizations realize that such growth rates pose serious challenges to social and economic development programs. Many governments do not have the resources to meet the needs of their own people, and even those that have ample resources—particularly oil-producing countries such as Saudi Arabia—have difficulty dealing with the challenges of population growth due to inefficient or unequal distribution of the wealth, corruption of officials, or political instability. With growing populations and inadequate resources, people are not able to obtain adequate schooling, health care, and employment. Even though governments realize that family planning and birth control programs can help alleviate these problems, other factors, including religion, affect the extent to which they are willing and able to implement them.

Muslims have looked to the QURAN and HADITH for guidance on birth control and family planning, as they do for other issues of importance in their lives. It is important to realize, however, that their sacred scriptures are ambiguous on the subject, therefore leaving room for different interpretations. Two verses in the Quran forbid slaying CHILDREN because of inability to provide for them (Q 17:31; 6:151). The Quran also implicitly condemns the killing of female infants (Q 60:12; 81:8–9), a practice observed by some ARAB tribes in western Arabia at the time of ISLAM's appearance. Such verses are used to promote a "right-to-life" approach to birth control. Opponents of birth control also quote verses that refer to children as being a divine gift (Q 16:72; 18:46; 25:74). They find additional support in the Quran and hadith for the view that contraception is wrong because only God has the power to determine life and sustain it (Q 67:1–2; 56:57–74; 11:6). Humans, therefore, should not act against his will. On the other hand, advocates of birth con-

Egyptian newlyweds with family members *(Juan E. Campo)*

trol quote hadiths that they believe support the opposite position. One of these hadiths states that MUHAMMAD did not object to the practice of coitus interruptus (Arabic: *azl*), a form of contraception involving withdrawal of the penis from the vagina before ejaculation. Many Muslim jurists argue that this provides a precedent that allows for modern forms of birth control. Another hadith states that a man should not practice *azl* unless he has permission from his wife, which is interpreted as permission for WOMEN to have a say in their reproductive rights. ABORTION is also allowed by most jurists, but only under specific conditions.

Even though birth control and family planning programs have been inaugurated by many governments and nongovernmental organizations, their success has been hampered because economic resources are lacking and because most Muslim countries still have large proportions of their populations making their livings by AGRICULTURE, a way of life in which having large families is traditionally an advantage. Furthermore, deeply embedded traditions in male-dominant societies, reinforced by conservative ULAMA, have encouraged parents to have many children. There are also political factors that have affected family planning efforts. Some Muslim nationalist leaders and religious authorities have urged families to have many children as a way to resist domination by non-Muslim governments. In this light, birth control and family planning are portrayed as part of a Western conspiracy to limit the size of the Muslim population. This was the case with the growth of the Palestinian population in the West Bank and Gaza and in IRAN, where the population exploded from 34 million to 50 million between 1979 and 1986.

Ironically, the Islamic Republic of Iran has one of the most successful family planning programs in the world today. After a long, costly war with IRAQ (1980–88), the Iranian ulama realized that they needed to curb Iran's population growth rate. As a result, new family planning programs were launched, and birth control devices were made widely available. Now, when an Iranian couple wants to get married, they are required to attend a course on family planning that includes instruction in the use of intrauterine devices (IUDs), birth control pills, and condoms. Birth control devices are often distributed for free by government health centers. For couples with children who want to make sure they have no additional pregnancies, voluntary vasectomies and female sterilizations are allowed. In general, the government now encourages people to have small families rather than large ones.

Further reading: Basim Musallam, *Sex and Society in Islam* (Cambridge: Cambridge University Press, 1983); Abdel Rahim Omran, *Family Planning in the Legacy of Islam* (London: Routledge, 1992); Robin Wright, *The Last Great Revolution: Turmoil and Transformation in Iran* (New York: Random House, 2000): 160–187.

birth rites

Birth rites are observed in most religions and cultures. They celebrate the addition of a new member to the family and the community, express feelings of gratitude toward the gods (or God), and also involve practices intended to protect the infant and mother from the harm of supernatural forces. In ISLAM, there are no formally required birth rites or sacraments, but Muslims everywhere may engage in one or more traditional ritual practices when a child is born.

Most of the ULAMA concur that several ritual practices related to childbirth are permitted. The foremost of these is the *aqiqa* rite, which involves animal sacrifice, shaving the infant's head, and performing acts of charity. Usually one sheep, goat, or ram is sacrificed in thanksgiving for a girl (two for a boy) on the seventh day after birth. The act is believed to commemorate the near-sacrifice of Ishmael (Ismail) by his father, ABRAHAM (Ibrahim). This is also when a child receives his or her given name, a festive event that may include QURAN recitation and readings of the birth story of MUHAMMAD. In early Islam, the naming ceremony was connected with a ritual called *tahnik*, which involved rubbing the infant's palate with a date. This practice was based on the example of Muhammad, who gave the first child born to the Muslim community a date that he had chewed and mixed with his saliva. Another practice is whispering the call to PRAYER (ADHAN) into the newborn's right ear and the second call to prayer, (*iqama*, or the SHAHADA) in its left ear. Islamic law exempts the mother of the newborn from fulfilling daily prayers and fasting while nursing and experiencing postpartum bleeding, but before she can resume her daily acts of worship, she is required to perform a complete bodily ABLUTION to purify herself.

Muslim authorities also approve of the practice of male CIRCUMCISION, considered to be a rite of purification and a symbol of membership in the Muslim community. It does not have the theological significance it is given in Judaism, in which it symbolizes the COVENANT between God and the people of ISRAEL. In Islam, circumcision was a greatly celebrated rite of passage that usually occurred when a boy was seven, 10, or 13. For most Muslim boys today, however, it is done at birth in a clinic or hospital. Female circumcision (excision of the clitoris) is a controversial practice that does not receive the endorsement of all religious authorities and is not widely performed.

There are many ritual practices related to childbirth that are not endorsed by the SHARIA and that ulama regard as harmful innovations (BIDAA). In many cultures, the mother observes taboos, or ritual avoidances, for 40 days after birth, while the midwife and the mother's female relatives and friends assist her in performing rites to appease or repel evil spirits and to ensure the mother's continued fertility. In Upper EGYPT and Nubia, the placenta, or afterbirth, may be taken to the Nile as an offering to the river spirits. In PALESTINE, it was customarily buried to keep domestic animals from eating it and to ensure the well-being of the infant. In many Muslim cultures, the umbilical cord may be placed in a cloth bag to be worn around the neck of the child as a kind of amulet, or it may be buried in the house. Of course, many such practices have been forgotten with modernization and the impact of Islamic reform movements. Nonetheless, some traditional practices prevail. Today many parents still decorate the infant's body or clothing with colorful beads or small pieces of jewelry to deflect the EVIL EYE.

Lastly, mention should be made of birthday celebrations. Until recently, they were held only for prophets and SAINTS. However, a holy person's birthday (*mawlid*) is usually interpreted to be the anniversary of his or her death, when they go to the invisible world, rather than birth in the material world. Ordinary Muslims living in modernized societies now emulate Europeans and Americans by celebrating birthday anniversaries with cards, gifts, and sweets.

See also CHILDREN.

Further reading: Winifred S. Blackman, *The Fellahin of Upper Egypt* (1927. Reprint, Cairo: American University in Cairo Press, 2000), 64–89; Jonah Blank, *Mullahs on the Mainframe: Islam and Modernity among the Daudi Bohras* (Chicago: University of Chicago Press, 2001): 54–60; Avner Giladi, "On *Tahnik*—An Early Islamic Childhood Rite," *Children of Islam: Concepts of Childhood in Medieval Muslim Society* (New York: St. Martin's Press, 1992): 35–41; Hilma Granqvist, *Birth and Childhood among the Arabs* (Helsingfors: Söderström, 1947); Jafar Sharif, *Islam in India, or the* Qanun-i Islam: *The Customs of the Musalmans of India*, trans. G. A. Herklots (1921. Reprint, Delhi: Low Price Publications, 1997): 21–40.

Biruni, Abu Rayhan, al- (ca. 973–1051) *Persian scholar famous for his books on Indian religion and civilization, history, mathematics, astronomy, pharmacology, and medicine*

Al-Biruni was born near the city of Khwarazm (modern Khiva in Uzbekistan) and gained his early EDUCATION from scholars in this region of Central Asia. When the Turkish ruler Mahmoud of Ghazna (r. 998–1030) conquered Khwarazm in 1017, he drafted al-Biruni into service as his court astronomer and astrologer in AFGHANISTAN. Between 1022 and 1030, al-Biruni accompanied Sultan Mahmoud in a series of attacks he launched into northern INDIA, which provided the scholar with an opportunity to study Hindu religion and philosophy for a period of about 10 years. He met with Brahmins and even studied Sanskrit, the sacred language of Hindus. The result of these studies was his unprecedented book, the India Book (*Kitab al-Hind*), which he finished writing in 1031 after he returned to Ghazna. The book described in detail Hindu religious beliefs, ritual practices, philosophy, the caste system and marriage, as well as India's accomplishments in MATHEMATICS and SCIENCE. He wrote it from a comparative perspective that privileged his own Islamic religion and culture but acknowledged the accomplishments of the Hindus at the same time. Al-Biruni also translated Sanskrit texts on Hindu cosmology and philosophy into Arabic. Scholars estimate that he wrote nearly 180 books on different subjects in his lifetime, mostly in Arabic, but many of these have been lost.

See also HINDUISM AND ISLAM.

Further reading: Al-Biruni, *Alberuni's India: An Account of the Religion, Philosophy, Literature, Geography, Chronology, Astronomy, Customs, Laws and Astrology of India about A.D. 1030*, ed. and trans. Edward C. Sachau (Delhi: Low Price Publications, 1989); Seyyid Hossein Nasr, *An Introduction to Islamic Cosmological Doctrines* (Boulder, Colo.: Shambhala, 1964): 107–174; George Saliba, "Al-Biruni and the Sciences of His Time." In *Religion, Learning and Science in the Abbasid Period*, edited by M. J. L. Young, J. D. Latham, and R. B Serjeant, 405–423 (Cambridge: Cambridge University Press, 1990).

Bistami, Abu Yazid al- (Bayazid) (d. ca. 875) *early Persian Sufi known for his ecstatic sayings and mystical experiences*

Little is known about Abu Yazid al-Bistami's life except for the statements attributed to him by Sufi tradition that reflect his intense religious experiences of passing away (*fana*) in God and mystical flight. He is thought to have come from a Zoroastrian family living in the El Burz mountain area south of the Caspian Sea in Persia (today's IRAN). He led an ascetic lifestyle, seeking detachment from the world. Later, when he had ecstatic experiences of union with God, he would make statements such as "Glory be to me," as if God were speaking through him. This, of course, roused the anger of conservative religious authorities, who considered such statements to be BLASPHEMY. However, Sufi scholars defended Abu Yazid by attesting to his good standing as an observant Muslim and by explaining that statements made while in a mystical state differ from those made while engaged in ordinary conversation, arguing that he may simply have been quoting God rather than speaking as God. Abu Yazid also spoke of becoming a bird and flying through the realms of the universe to the divine throne, like the NIGHT JOURNEY AND ASCENT that MUHAMMAD was reported to have made. According to one account, when he reached God, he heard his voice and melted like lead, sensing that he was so close to him that he "was nearer to him than the spirit is to the body" (Sells, 244). Because of such utterances, he was classed as one of the first "intoxicated" Sufis, in contrast to "sober" ones whose experiences were more attuned to maintaining a distance between the self and God. Reports of Abu Yazid's sayings spread through Persia to IRAQ, Central Asia, and TURKEY. They were recorded in writing by the 10th century, when he had become so venerated as a SAINT that learned scholars visited his tomb to gain his blessing (BARAKA). The Mongol ruler of Persia further embellished his shrine in the early 14th century. Abu Yazid was also memorialized by having been included in the teaching lineages of prominent Sufi brotherhoods.

See also ASCETICISM; BAQA AND FANA; TARIQA.

Further reading: Carl W. Ernst, *Words of Ecstasy in Sufism* (Albany: State University of New York Press,

1985): 212–250; Michael Sells, *Islamic Mysticism: Sufi, Quran, Miraj, Poetic and Theological Writings* (New York: Paulist Press, 1996).

Black Muslims   *See* AFRICAN AMERICANS, ISLAM AMONG; NATION OF ISLAM.

Black Stone

The Black Stone is a sacred rock encased with silver that has been placed in the southeastern corner of the KAABA in MECCA. Though it is not mentioned in the QURAN, it is discussed in the HADITH, commentaries, and historical literature. Its exact origins are uncertain, though it was probably one of the sacred objects worshiped in Mecca in pre-Islamic times. Western scholars assert that it may have originally been a meteorite. Early Muslim accounts say that it was originally a radiant white sapphire brought by GABRIEL to Adam after his expulsion from PARADISE. It turned to black as a result of being touched by idolaters who were ritually impure. Another early story says that Gabriel brought it to Ismail from a nearby mountain when he and his father, ABRAHAM, were constructing the Kaaba and that they were the ones who inserted the stone into the building's southeastern corner. When the QURAYSH tribe was rebuilding the Kaaba early in the seventh century, MUHAMMAD is reported to have been entrusted to put the Black Stone back in its place when tribal factions could not agree which one among themselves should do so. Some traditions state that the Black Stone will develop the ability to speak on JUDGMENT DAY in order to testify on behalf of those who have kissed or touched it in good faith.

Despite the uncertainty of its origins, it is indeed a focus of ritual activity on the part of pilgrims who go to Mecca for the HAJJ and UMRA. The pilgrims' seven circumambulations of the Kaaba should begin and end at the corner where the Black Stone is, and each time they pass it they are supposed to kiss, touch, or salute it with their right hands. This practice is controversial because to an outsider it appears to be a form of IDOLATRY. Muslims deny this and refer to a hadith wherein the caliph UMAR IBN AL-KHATTAB (d. 644) says, "By God, I am kissing you knowing that you are a stone and that you can neither do any harm nor good. If I had not seen God's Prophet [Muhammad] kissing you, I would not have kissed you." Thus, Muslims understand that they are respectfully imitating the actions of their PROPHET rather than worshipping the stone itself.

See also ADAM AND EVE.

Further reading: Arthur Jeffrey, *A Reader on Islam* (The Hague: Mouton & Company, 1962); Muslim, *Sahih Muslim.* Translated by Abdul Hamid Siddiqi. 4 vols. (Lahore: Sh. Muhammad Ashraf, 1972), 1:641–643; Francis E. Peters, *The Hajj: The Muslim Pilgrimage to Mecca and the Holy Places* (Princeton, N.J.: Princeton University Press, 1994), 14–15.

blasphemy

Blasphemy is from a Greek word that means speaking evil. In the history of religions, it refers to disrespectful or irreverent statements about cherished or officially approved religious beliefs, doctrines, institutions, and practices. It is usually considered to be a product of biblical tradition and the history of organized Judaism and Christianity, in which speaking against God has been severely condemned and occasionally punished. Blasphemy laws still exist in many Western countries, though they are gradually being repealed. Concern with blasphemy also occurs in Islamic societies, where it is closely linked with such serious transgressions as APOSTASY (*irtidad*), disbelief (*KAFIR*), and IDOLATRY. Muslim jurists have used statements in the QURAN that condemn MUHAMMAD's opponents for their outright denial (*takdhib*) of the truth of his religious message (e.g., Q 54, 5:10) or their fabrication (*iftira*) of false beliefs (Q 11:18; Q 39:32) to justify imposing harsh penalties against anyone they thought had verbally insulted sacred Islamic beliefs or values. Insulting Muhammad or asserting that there will be no physical resurrection are but two of the many verbal actions considered blasphemous. Muslims and non-Muslims alike could be held liable on blasphemy charges, which, if proven and not retracted, could result in punishments ranging from public censure, to disinheritance, to mandatory divorce, to death.

Muslim jurists have enforced blasphemy laws only occasionally in the past. There were several significant instances during the Middle Ages involving Muslim philosophers and Sufis. The most famous of these involved the mystic MANSUR AL-HALLAJ (d. 922), who was accused of saying, "I am the truth," (i.e., God). In more recent times, blasphemy charges have been made against followers of the BAHAI FAITH and of the AHMADIYYA branch of Islam in PAKISTAN. There was also the famous case of SALMAN RUSHDIE (b. 1937), who was condemned by Muslims around the world in 1988–89 for his imaginative novel Satanic Verses. Rushdie's opponents, led by the ayatollah RUHOLLAH KHOMEINI in Iran, said it slandered Muhammad and his wives, and Khomeini issued a FATWA (an advisory ruling based on the SHARIA) calling for his death. Today, as governments in recently independent Muslim nation-states increasingly try to centralize their power and as Islamic activism escalates, some states and radical Islamic groups are using the charge of blasphemy to gain legitimacy and popular support at the expense of intellectuals, Muslim liberals, and non-Muslim minorities. This has given new life to the idea of blasphemy in Islam, while at the same time more and more Muslims are embracing the ideals of liberalism, pluralism, and individual freedom of belief and expression.

See also ABU ZAYD, NASR HAMID; CRIME AND PUNISHMENT.

Further reading: Carl W. Ernest, *Words of Ecstasy in Sufism* (Albany: State University of New York Press, 1985); Rudolph Peters and Gert J. J. De Vries, "Apostasy in Islam." *Die Welt des Islams* 17 (1976–1977): 1–25; Abdullah Saeed and Hassan Saeed, *Freedom of Religion, Apostasy and Islam* (Burlington, Vt.: Ashgate Publishing, 2004).

blood (Arabic: *dam*)

The vital bodily fluid of blood has special significance in the QURAN, and in Islamic practice it is the subject of ritual laws that are discussed at length in the SHARIA.

The Quran regards blood as vital for human life, as reflected in its condemnation of killing as the shedding of blood (Q 2:30, 84). The Quran also gives special importance to the blood clot (*alaq*), which is considered the substance out of which God created humans. The chapter titled "Clots of Blood" (Q 96 *al-Alaq*) begins: "Recite in the name of your Lord who created—created man from clots of blood," thus stressing the power of God in creating humans from such a humble substance. In other verses, the *alaq* is a particular stage in the development of the human (Q 22:5; Q 23:12–14). Some modern interpreters have compared these Quranic revelations to current medical understandings of the development of the human embryo and point to the similarities as proof that the Quran contains biological knowledge unknown to humans until recent scientific discoveries.

Another indication of the importance of blood in the Quran is the prohibition against ingesting it, which is mentioned four times, along with carrion, pork, and meat not consecrated in the name of God (Q 2:173; Q 5:3; Q 6:145; Q 16:115). Because of this prohibition, all ANIMALS to be consumed must be slaughtered by slitting their throats and draining the blood completely. This procedure must likewise be followed when animals are sacrificed, as in the annual Feast of Sacrifice, in which Muslims commemorate ABRAHAM's willingness to sacrifice his son upon God's command. Though the Islamic version of the story of Abraham is similar to that in the Old Testament, Muslim scholars agree that the purpose of sacrifice in ISLAM is not the atonement of sins, as in the Old Testament; rather, what is important is Abraham's submission to God's will. The Quran states that with animal sacrifices, "It is not their meat nor their blood that reaches Allah; it is your piety that reaches him" (Q 22:37).

Lastly, in the sharia menstrual blood is considered to be a source of major impurity, and WOMEN are exempted from PRAYER and FASTING as long as their monthly period lasts, as are women experiencing postpartum bleeding. When a woman's period ends, she must perform a complete ABLUTION before engaging in an act of worship or entering a sacred place, such as a MOSQUE. Rules about menstruation and ritual purity are a major topic in the HADITH and FIQH literature.

See also DIETARY LAWS; ID AL-ADHA.

Further reading: Laleh Bakhtiar, *Encyclopedia of Islamic Law: A Compendium of the Major Schools* (Chicago: ABC International Group, 1996); Somaiyah Berrigan, ed., *An Enlightening Commentary into the Light of the Holy Quran.* 2 vols. (Isfahan: Amir-al-Momineen Ali Library, 1994), 2:121–128; Maurice Bucaille, *The Bible, the Quran and Science: The Holy Scriptures in the Light of Modern Knowledge.* Translated by Alastair D. Pannell and Maurice Bucaille (Indianapolis: American Trust Publications, 1979), 198–210.

boat

Boats have been a primary means of transportation on the waters in Islamicate lands. The QURAN mentions NOAH's ark, a boat made of planks and nails (Q 54:13), and to this day the benediction God gave to Noah when he launched it—"Embark! In the name of God be its course and mooring" (Q 11:41)—is written on boats and ships owned or used by Muslims. The Quran also mentions ships boarded by Jonah (Q 37:140) and MOSES (Q 18:71). Muslims have used boats and ships since the inception of ISLAM as vehicles of commerce, TRAVEL, and military conflict. Seafaring Muslim merchants have been a vital part of both

Egyptian feluccas docked in Aswan *(Juan E. Campo)*

the Mediterranean and Indian Ocean maritime trading networks and were responsible for the initial spread of Islam along the coasts of South and Southeast Asia. Muslim navies controlled much of the Mediterranean for centuries and took part in such famous naval battles as the Battle of the Masts, when a newly formed Islamic fleet first defeated its Byzantine counterpart in 655.

There were a wide variety of types of boats in medieval Islamdom, but there were two basic methods of construction: the Mediterranean method and the West Indian Ocean method. In the Mediterranean, boats were built frame first, constructing a wood skeleton and then attaching the planking over it with metal nails. In the Indian Ocean, boats were built shell-first, from the outside in, and sewn together completely with palm fiber cord without the use of nails. After the intrusion of the European navies in the 16th century, the Indian Ocean tradition gradually faded as boat builders adopted European methods, which were better suited to modern weaponry such as cannon. Today a rich tapestry of traditional boats still exists in Muslim lands, from the fishing felucca of the Nile to the merchant dhow of the Gulf, plying the waters side by side with their more modern fiberglass and metal counterparts.

Eric Staples

Further reading: George F. Hourani, *Arab Seafaring in the Indian Ocean in Ancient and Early Medieval Times* (Princeton, N.J.: Princeton University Press, 1995); Dionisius A. Agius, *In the Wake of the Dhow* (London: Ithaca Press, 2002).

Bohra

Bohras, whose name comes from the Gujurati verb "to trade," are members of an Ismaili Shia community founded in Gujurat, INDIA, in the late 11th century. The seat of the FATIMID DYNASTY, then in CAIRO, dispatched the *dawat,* or religious mission, to western India to increase membership in this tradition of Islam. Early in the process, a disagreement concerning the identity of the 19th IMAM divided Ismailism; the Bohras believe that Mustali billah (d. 1101) was designated as the 19th Imam, while the Nizari Ismailis believe that this authority was invested in Nizar (d. 1095). In 1132, the 21st Imam from the line of Mustali billah, al-Tayyibi, became hidden from public. This line of Imams continues in secret to this day. Since al-Tayyibi's concealment (GHAYBA), the community has been led by a series of chief *dais* (religious propagandists, missionaries); these leaders possess the title of *dai al-mutlaq* (cleric of absolute authority). The *dai al-mutlaq* is the chief religious figure of the Bohra community. He guides his followers in both spiritual and worldly matters and is thought to be in contact with the Hidden Imam.

The largest community of Bohras is the Daudi Bohras, named after their 27th *dai,* Daud ibn Qutb Shah (d. 1612). They number about 1 million, live throughout South Asia, East Africa, the Middle East, and the west, and are led by the 52nd *al-dai al-mutlaq,* Muhammad Burhan al-Din (b. 1915), whose headquarters are in Bombay. Since succeeding his father to the office of *dai* in 1965, Burhan al-Din has initiated a number of changes in the religious and administrative aspects of the faith, emphasizing the congruence between Islam and modernity. He has built an extensive network of Bohra schools whose curricula include the combination of Islamic and non-Islamic subjects, he has mandated a distinctive dress code for the community, and he has helped to restore Fatimid relics and architectural sites in EGYPT.

The Daudi Bohras retain a religious hierarchy similar to that of their Fatimid ancestors. The *dai al-mutlaq,* who is appointed by his predecessor, is responsible for filling positions in the *dawat.* Local religious functions are performed by *amils* (deputies/priests), community representatives of the *dawat.* The Daudi Bohas also follow seven (rather than five) pillars of Islam, as articulated by Fatimid jurists. These are: WALAYA (love and allegiance) to God, the Prophets, the *dais,* and the Imams; *tahara* (ritual purity); *salah* (PRAYER); *zakat* (ALMSGIVING); *sawm* (FASTING); HAJJ (pilgrimage to Mecca); and JIHAD (struggle).

Other Bohra communities retain doctrinal beliefs similar to those of the Daudi Bohras. The Sulaymani Bohras, who have approximately 74,000 adherents, mostly in India and Yemen, follow a different line of *dais* and are named after their 27th *dai,* Suleyman ibn Hasan (d. 1597). The Aliya Bohras are named after Ali ibn Ibrahim (d. 1637) and have approximately 5,000 adherents.

See also DAAWA; ISMAILI SHIISM.

Jamel Velji

Further reading: Jonah Blank, *Mullahs on the Mainframe: Islam and Modernity among the Daudi Bohras* (Chicago: University of Chicago Press, 2001); Farhad Daftary, *A Short History of the Ismailis: Traditions of a Muslim Community* (Princeton, N.J.: Markus Wiener Publishers, 1998).

books and bookmaking

The 10th-century royal of CORDOBA (one of more than 70 in the Umayyad capital of Spain) had a catalog of 44 volumes listing more than 400,000 titles. The catalog volumes alone outnumbered the total number of books in medieval France, despite such important universities as those of

Paris and Chartres. Adelard, a 12th-century English-man from Bath who traveled through SYRIA, PALESTINE, Sicily, and Toledo (where many of the Cordoban books and scholars resided after the city fell to the northern kings during the Reconquista) brought back two treasures: an Arabic translation and commentary on Euclid's *Geometry* and rationalism. "The further south you go," he said, "the more they know. They know how to think. From the Arabs I have learned one thing: if you are led by authority, that means you are led by a halter." The lesson took root slowly, but a few hundred years later Europe entered its Age of Reason and the Enlightenment.

The wealth of knowledge and habits of reasoning encountered by Adelard and numerous European travelers resulted from practical and intellectual undertakings that were supported by, and in turn enabled, a number of activities and industries, from bookmaking to administration and international trade. The major medium involved was paper, whose technology was available in the eastern parts of Islamdom (Samarqand in Central Asia) and that was quickly adopted by the Abbasids in the eighth century. Paper was invaluable for official documents and bank drafts because it was difficult to change once the ink was

Cairo bookbinder Hisham proudly exhibits his craftsmanship *(Juan E. Campo)*

absorbed (unlike vellum, which could be scraped clean). Paper was also relatively cheap to make, as it was manufactured from rags produced from flax. This made it part of the agricultural and textile industries, as well as recycling and garbage collecting activities. The flax grown in EGYPT was used in making linen, which could be reused in making paper (a by-product was cheap flaxseed lamp oil). A single excavation campaign at Fustat (CAIRO's medieval industrial and commercial hub) produced hundreds of thousands of rags that were earmarked for recycling into paper, a process that required the water of the nearby Nile for pulping and milling. (Today in Cairo the old community of garbage collectors is once again recycling scrap rag into paper products that are sold to tourists.) Paper was also part of the informal economy of Egypt; graverobbers sold linen shrouds to manufacturers who then recycled them into paper. In 10th-century Egypt, as elsewhere, paper and books depended on cities whose schools produced the literate consuming public and whose shops, banks, and take-out restaurants required paper as a primary or packaging material.

Collecting raw materials was only the first step in paper- and bookmaking. Sheets of paper were made in molds, then sized (sealed) and polished to produce an adequate writing surface. Sheets were either stacked or folded four times to produce quartos that were then sewn together. Inks, pens, and bindings of different materials (not to mention metal inkwells, wood bookstands, and other paraphernalia) were part of the writing craft, and professional scribes usually made their own inks and pens. Luxury editions (often commissioned or produced in royal workshops) demanded another crew of specialists that included painters (for illustrations), illuminators (for marginal decoration), and gilders, as well as overseers who coordinated the work. The finished pages were polished again with a smooth stone (preferably an agate) before they were bound in tooled leather or papier maché covers. Sometimes the bound book was slipped into a case with folding flaps to protect the edges. Books were then stacked on top of each other on library shelves (which saved them from bending and warping).

Paper was sold at specialty shops or by booksellers whose shops were usually close to mosques and madrasas, since the scholars who studied and taught there were major consumers. Booksellers acted as publishers and distributors of books and conducted searches for rare works on demand. They were one link in the chain of knowledge dissemination that began with authors. An author published his work either by writing the first copy himself or dictating it to scribes or STUDENTS. Scribes compared copies to ensure accuracy before selling them. A student had to read the book back to the teacher-author (sometimes in the presence of witnesses) before obtaining an *ijaza* (permission; certificate) to teach and publish the work himself. The *ijaza* and its circumstances were always noted on the manuscript copy, so that copyright and accuracy were maintained through combined oral-written means. In teaching and dictating the book to his own students, the original student became part of the chain of authorized transmitters of the author's work.

Scholars sometimes traveled to find an authoritative transmitter of a specific work. Alternatively, visiting scholars dictated or authorized readings of their own works during their travels. In these ways, knowledge was exchanged, shared, and passed down for generations, often with commentaries that were either published separately or added to a book as marginalia (notes written in the margins of the book). Commentaries were often as important as the original works. They corrected scribal errors, provided cross-references, or glossed terms, names, and concepts that were no longer familiar (and so aid us in understanding the originals today). They also sometimes questioned the content, thereby providing written records of the processes of reasoning and disputation among scholars. Reasoning and questioning (which required additional proof) were applied in all areas, from MATHEMATICS to religious law (FIQH),

thereby always advancing the state of knowledge in any field by eschewing blind dogma—the "halter" mentioned by Adelard of Bath.

The first great boom in paper and book production in Islamdom occurred in ninth- and 10th-century IRAQ, when the Abbasids realized paper's potential in administering their vast empire, collecting past knowledge, and disseminating their own laws and histories. This boom revolved around BAGHDAD, the capital and cultural center. It resulted in changes that ranged from the format of books, to scripts, to the conduct of everyday life. These processes continued to develop over centuries before the wide adoption of print. Despite great losses due to time, fire, or recycling of paper and books into new works, thousands of written works have survived. Aside from many QURAN manuscripts and books on Islamic religion and history, they also include translations and commentaries on Greek works in philosophy, medicine, and geography that would not have survived or reached Europe (or reached it in understandable form) otherwise. Nor would we have the glimpses of daily life that we have from the thousands of scraps of paper that were discovered in an old synagogue in CAIRO (the Geniza). From the paper and book industries, we know the bases of the maps that aided European voyages in the 15th century, as well as how a brother and sister consoled each other in letters that traveled across great distances in the 10th.

See also CALLIGRAPHY; EDUCATION; LITERACY; MADRASA.

Nuha N. N. Khoury

Bibliography: Jonathan M. Bloom, *Paper before Print: The History and Impact of Paper in the Islamic World* (New Haven, Conn.: Yale University Press, 2001); James Burke, *The Day the Universe Changed*. Rev. ed. (Boston: Little, Brown & Company, 1995); Brinkley Messick, *The Calligraphic State: Textual Domination and History in a Muslim Society* (Berkeley: University of California Press, 1993); Johannes Pederson, *The Arabic Book*. Translated by Geoffrey French (Princeton, N.J.: Princeton University Press, 1984).

Bosnia and Herzegovina

Bosnia and Herzegovina is a predominantly Muslim country in the southern Balkan mountains. With an area of nearly 20,000 square miles (the size of New Hampshire and Vermont combined), it is bordered on the north and west by Croatia (a predominantly Catholic country), on the east by Serbia (a predominantly Eastern Orthodox Christian country), and on the south by Montenegro (also a predominantly Orthodox land). It has a small outlet to the Adriatic Sea providing it with less than 15 miles of coastline.

Ethnically, Bosnia and Herzegovina is home to three main groups: Bosniaks (a modern designation for South Slovaks who are mostly Muslim, 48 percent), Serbians (14.3 percent), and Croatians (14.3 percent). In addition to Islam (40 percent), the chief religions are Eastern Orthodoxy (31 percent) and Roman Catholicism (15 percent). The Bosnians and Herzegovinans do not form separate groups ethnically so much as religiously, being defined by their religious affiliation since the 15th century. There is no separate language for the country; its 4.6 million residents speak either Serbian or Croatian.

At the end of the 12th century, Bosnia gained its independence from its neighbors, the Hungarians (including the Croatians) to the north and the Serbians to the east. The Kingdom of Bosnia was a religiously divided land. Its people were partly Catholic and partly Orthodox, but many were adherents of an independent third religion, the Bosnian Church, which held to an esoteric religion called Bogomilism, with roots in Manicheanism. Originating in Macedonia, Bogomilism had appeared in the 10th century and spread across the southern Balkans. In Bosnia, where its had its greatest support, it became identified with the Bosnian national spirit and came to define the people in contrast to the Eastern Orthodox faith radiating from Constantinople and the Catholic faith of the Hungarian.

Then at the end of the 15th century, Turkish forces swept over the southern Balkans, and Islam was introduced into Bosnia and Herzegovina. Because of the use of the Inquisition by the Catholic Church against the Bogomils, it appears that given the choice, the Bogomils supported the Turks over their former Catholic rulers and assisted their conquest. Many Bogomils saw themselves as closer to Islam in belief than Christianity and rather quickly converted to Islam, while the remainder made the conversion through the next decades. As Bosnian elites affirmed their Islamic beliefs, many of their number rose to positions of prominence in the empire, several serving as the grand vizer in the sultan's court in Constantinople (ISTANBUL) in the late 16th century. Under Turkish rule, a governor (pasha) was appointed who made his headquarters in Sarajevo. The land was divided into eight districts (*sanjaks*). Islam in the land adhered to the HANAFI LEGAL SCHOOL, the school favored by Ottoman rulers.

In the 19th century, the Bosnians became critical of what they saw as corruption coming to dominate the Ottoman Empire, and a new spirit of independence swept the land. A half century of conflict resulted in the Austro-Hungarian Empire pushing the Ottomans out of the area. Rather than achieving independence, however, Bosnia and Herzegovina came under Habsburg rule. At the end of the 19th century, Bosnian Muslims made a new effort to mobilize in the cause of national independence with a focus for a time in the Muslim National Organization. In 1909, the Austrian authorities created a new office of Reis-ul-ilema, the supreme leader of the Muslim community. Austria continued to exercise its hegemony throughout World War I, after which Serbia came to control Bosnia and Herzegovina.

Through the 20th century, Muslims existed as the largest group in Bosnia and Herzegovina, but the land was successively incorporated into larger political structures—Serbian, Nazi, and Yugoslavian Communist—that repeatedly forced the Muslims into a minority status. Successive governments also continued policies that set different ethnic and religious communities against each other, an expedient means of keeping control of the often restless population. During World War II, Serbians and Croats massacred Muslims, and the latter retaliated in kind. Muslims suffered additionally under the antireligious policies adopted by the Marxist Yugoslavian regime of Marshall Tito (Josip Broz, 1892–1980). For a period, mosques were closed, children were denied religious instruction, and no teachers of Islam could be trained. In reaction, a Muslim revival was noticeable in the 1960s identified with nationalistic aspirations as much as religious sentiments.

The Yugoslavian Federation fell apart in 1991. Bosnia and Herzegovina declared its independence. However, the effort to build a Bosnian state was opposed by Serbians residing in the north and eastern parts of the country. In attempting to avoid the dissolution of the country, the Bosnian president Alija Izetbegovic (1925–2003) promised that the new country would not evolve into an Islamic state (in contradiction to a position he had earlier advocated) and assured the rights of the Christian minorities. The guarantees, however, did not stop Serbians allied with troops of the former Yugoslav Federation from starting a civil war. The Bosnian war became one of the bloodiest experiences of the region. Serbian forces, with the support of the government in Belgrade, which had publicly disavowed its involvement, carried out a number of massacres in pursuit of a policy of "ethnic cleansing." The worst of the massacres occurred in 1995 in Srebrenica, where thousands of Muslims were slaughtered. Such actions led to the postwar arrest of many of the Serbian leaders as war criminals.

The war ended in December 1995 with the signing of the Dayton Agreement, which included a new constitution for the country recognizing the three distinct groups within its borders and assigning to each a set of specific rights and representations in the new government.

See also CHRISTIANITY AND ISLAM; EUROPE; OTTOMAN DYNASTY.

J. Gordon Melton

Further reading: Norman Cigar, *Genocide in Bosnia: The Policy of 'Ethnic Cleansing'* (College Station: Texas A&M University Press, 1995); Robert Donia and John Fine, *Bosnia and Herzegovina: A Tradition Betrayed* (New York: Columbia University Press, 1994); John Fine, *The Bosnian Church: A New Interpretation* (Boulder, Colo.: East European Quarterly, 1975); H. T. Norris, *Islam in the Balkans: Religion and Society between Europe and the Arab World* (Columbia: University of South Carolina Press, 1993); Mark Pinson, ed., *The Muslims of Bosnia-Herzegovina: Their Historic Development from the Middle Ages to the Dissolution of Yugoslavia* (Cambridge, Mass.: Harvard University Press, 1993).

Brethren of Purity

The Brethren of Purity (Ikhwan al-safa), or True Friends, were a group of 10th-century Muslim intellectuals who compiled a remarkable philosophical and scientific encyclopedia in Arabic known as Essays of the Brethren of Purity (*Rasail ikhwan al-safa*). According to some accounts, the original author was supposed to be a venerated figure such as ALI IBN ABI TALIB (d. 661) or JAAFAR AL-SADIQ (d. 765), but scholars are skeptical about this. Rather, there is general agreement among scholars that the encyclopedia was the product of a philosophical movement in Basra, IRAQ, that was influenced by Ismaili (Seven-Imam) Shiism and SUFISM. The members of this movement were from the elite learned class in Abbasid society. What is most notable about the encyclopedia is that it contains a synthesis of major traditions of learning that flourished in the Middle East at the time when the culture of the ABBASID CALIPHATE (750–1258) was at its height. It combined Islamic thought with other traditions of knowledge that had originated in the cultures of the ancient Mediterranean region and in ancient India and Persia and that were later inherited by Muslims. Thus, the work recognized the previous intellectual and ethical achievements of Greek, Jewish, Christian, Hindu, and Buddhist cultures. Because of its cosmopolitan outlook, conservative Sunni ULAMA condemned it.

The encyclopedia is divided into four parts: 1) MATHEMATICS, which includes essays on astronomy, geography, and Aristotle's logic; 2) natural SCIENCE, including theories of matter, botany, biology, body and soul, death and resurrection; 3) psychological and rational sciences; and 4) religious sciences. The Neoplatonic theory of creation by emanation from a single creator, together with the notion that all creation was organized according to a hierarchical pattern (an idea that had circulated widely in the pre-Islamic Middle East), was a dominant theme in the encyclopedia. Indeed, the encyclopedia's avowed purpose was to teach people how to purify their souls of bodily and worldly attachments and ascend back to the divine source from which they had come. The most famous section of the encyclopedia is the lengthy debate between ANIMALS and humans, which questioned the moral right humans had to exploit animals as slaves. The debate ended by affirming that animals indeed were inferior to humans, but they had their own intrinsic worth as God's creatures, requiring humans to treat them humanely.

See also ADAB; ARABIC LANGUAGE AND LITERATURE; ISMAILI SHIISM.

Further reading: Lenn Evan Goodman, trans., *The Case of the Animals versus Man before the King of the Jinn: A Tenth-Century Ecological Fable of the Pure Brethren of Basra* (Boston: Twayne Publishers, 1978); Sayyed Hossein Nasr, *Islamic Cosmological Doctrines* (Boulder, Colo.: Shambhala, 1978), 25–104; Ian Netton, *Muslim Neoplatonists: An Introduction to the Thought of the Brethren of Purity* (London: George Allen & Unwin, 1982).

Buddhism and Islam

Buddhism and Islam are two of the world's major religious traditions, and they have influenced each other at points throughout history. Both religions came into being in part through the isolated meditations and subsequent spiritual insights of the respective movements' founders, Siddhartha Gautama (known later as the Buddha) in the sixth century B.C.E. on the southern border of Nepal, and Muhammad in seventh-century C.E. Arabia. After the seventh century, significant interactions between Buddhists and Muslims took place along trade routes through Central Asia known as the Silk Road. Through these routes, Islam made significant inroads into Central Asia and China beginning in the seventh century. Though Buddhism in Central Asia started to decline with the political expansion of Islam at this time, the region retained Buddhist influences, and the Mongol invasions of the 13th century helped to further bring Buddhist influences from the east into this largely Muslim region. Accompanying Muslim political expansion eastward, Islam spread from Iran and AFGHANISTAN into South Asia, where its eventual political ascendancy coincided with the 12th-century disappearance of Buddhism in the regions of Afghanistan and PAKISTAN, where it had existed in its "Serindian" form, and in INDIA, its birthplace.

Over the centuries, Buddhists and Muslims have influenced each other in the fields of medicine, art, architecture, and literature, evidenced, for example, in the blend of Muslim and Buddhist ideas in the Tibetan Muslim literary classic *The Autobiography of Kha che Pha lu.* Another example of such mutual influence is the life story of the great Sufi IBRAHIM IBN ADHAM (d. 778), whose hagiography bears striking thematic resemblance to that of the Buddha, for he renounced his life as the prince of Balkh—a region of present day Afghanistan, where Buddhism flourished in the early centuries C.E. prior to the arrival of Islam in the eighth century—for a pious, ascetic life. Significant cultural contact between Muslims and Buddhists is also evidenced in the 13th-century world history called *Jami al-tawarikh,* written by a Persian official named Rashid al-Din (d. 1318), which includes a biography of the Buddha in its chapter on India, discusses Buddhist concepts in Islamic terms, and documents the presence of 11 Buddhist texts circulating in Persia in Arabic translation. The destruction in 2001 of the Bamiyan Buddha statues in Afghanistan by the

TALIBAN, who viewed the statues as idols, brought international attention to the shared geographic and cultural history of these two religious traditions. Today there are Muslim communities in regions with significant Buddhist populations, such as CHINA, Tibet, Cambodia, Myanmar, Sri Lanka, Thailand, and Vietnam. Also, MALAYSIA is a Muslim country that has a significant Buddhist population (20 percent), mostly ethnic Chinese.

See also HINDUISM AND ISLAM.

Megan Adamson Sijapati

Further reading: Ainslee T. Embree, *Sources of Indian Tradition, Volume One: From the Beginning to 1800* (New York: Columbia University Press, 1988); Gray Henry, ed., *Islam in Tibet, Tibetan Caravans* (Louisville, Ky.: Fons Vitae, 1997).

Bukhara

Bukhara is a city dating to the fifth to fourth century B.C.E. and is now located in the Republic of Uzbekistan. The principal city in a desert oasis, Bukhara came under the rule of the Arab UMAYYAD CALIPHATE in 709. Over the next 700 years, Bukhara switched hands between Arabs, Persians, Turks, and Mongols and came under the control of TAMERLANE in the 14th century. Bukhara became a famous center of Islamic learning, with the NAQSHBANDI SUFI ORDER taking its name from Baha al-Din Naqshband, who lived in Bukhara in the 14th century. Bukhara became a principal stop on the great Silk Road caravan routes. The Timurid dynasties ruled from Samarqand until the invasion of Uzbek tribes early in the 16th century. In 1557, Abd Allah ibn Iskander Khan (d. 1598) made Bukhara his capital, from which his state took its name. During the period of the Bukhara Khanate, the city reached its historical zenith and featured some of the most magnificent examples of Islamicate ARCHITECTURE of the time. However, internal feuding eventually weakened the khanate, and in 1740, Bukhara fell to the Persians, only

to regain its independence in 1753, though greatly reduced in size and power.

Bukhara was conquered by the Russians in 1868 and made a protectorate, allowing the ruling dynasty to continue in power. With the turn of the century, there arose a Muslim intellectual reform movement, and these "Young Bukharans" struggled against the conservative ULAMA for influence, only to be rebuffed by the ruling emir. With the Russian Revolution of 1917, Russian control disappeared, only to reappear in 1920, when, with the help of many of the Young Bukharans, Soviet forces gained control, and the last emir fled into exile. The Bukhara People's Soviet Republic was established and lasted until 1924, when it was dismembered and divided between the Uzbek, Tajik, and Turkmen Soviet Socialist Republics. Over the years of Soviet rule, Bukhara lost its political and economic importance, though it continues to be a regional seat of Islamic learning.

See also CENTRAL ASIA AND THE CAUCASUS.

David Reeves

Further reading: Audrey Burton, *The Bukharans: A Dynastic, Diplomatic and Commercial History 1550–1702* (New York: St. Martin's Press, 1997); Adeeb Khalid, *The Politics of Muslim Cultural Reform* (Berkeley: University of California Press, 1998); Attilio Petrocciolli, ed., *Bukhara: The Myth and the Architecture* (Cambridge, Mass.: The Aga Khan Program for Islamic Architecture, 1999).

Bukhari, Muhammad ibn Ismail *See* HADITH.

Bumiputra

Bumiputra is an official designation for the native, majority population of MALAYSIA (about 58 percent). A Sanskrit-Malay word meaning son of the Earth, it is applied to ethnic Malays, although there is some dispute as to exactly which of Malaysia's different indigenous groups are actually included under it. The use of the designation *Bumiputra* was part of an effort to form a new national Malaysian identity in the wake of independence from British colonial rule in 1957. Also, this usage seems to have been influenced by the Islamic resurgence in the country. For a Malay to convert from ISLAM to another religion not only entails being accused of APOSTASY, it also means giving up one's national identity. According to the 1957 Malaysian Federal Constitution, a Malay (Bumiputra) is defined as a follower of Islam who "habitually speaks the Malay language" and "conforms to Malay custom." Malay Muslims, therefore, not only stand apart from the Hindu and Chinese Buddhist immigrant communities, they are also distinct from immigrant Muslims.

In the 1970s, laws were passed to give Malay Bumiputras special advantages. The king of the country, for example, was charged with safeguarding their privileges with regard to EDUCATION and employment. The result has been discriminatory (some say racist) government policies that give Malays more access to subsidized housing, state universities, and government-contracted projects. In a practice known as Ali Baba, a non-Bumiputra company (Baba) must join in a partnership with one owned by a Bumiputra (Ali) in order to receive government business. Since 2000, under pressure from non-Bumiputra groups, the government has taken steps to allow for a more egalitarian treatment of members of these groups.

See also RENEWAL AND REFORM MOVEMENTS.

Further reading: Janet A. Nagata, *The Reflowering of Asian Islam: Modern Religious Radicals and Their Roots* (Vancouver: University of British Columbia Press, 1984); William Roff, *The Origins of Malay Nationalism* (New Haven, Conn.: Yale University Press, 1967).

Buraq, al-

Al-Buraq (an Arabic name possibly meaning "lightning") is the fabled animal ridden by the prophets that is most famous for having carried MUHAMMAD

Al-Buraq, the legendary mount of the prophets *(printed poster)*

from MECCA to JERUSALEM and then up through the seven heavens during his NIGHT JOURNEY AND ASCENT. According to Islamic tradition, it was brought to him by GABRIEL already saddled and bridled. In appearance, it was a winged white steed, smaller than a mule, with long ears. It reportedly flew through the air like the wind. Starting in the 14th century, al-Buraq was depicted in manuscript illustrations with a woman's head and a crown. This is the way it continues to be depicted, sometimes even with the tail of a peacock, in Egyptian pilgrimage murals, Islamic religious posters, and colorful painted trucks that ply the roads of AFGHANISTAN, PAKISTAN, and INDIA. Al-Buraq is also the popular name Palestinians have given the Western Wall in JERUSALEM, where it is believed Muhammad tethered the animal when he prayed at the AQSA MOSQUE. There is even said to have been a small MOSQUE dedicated to al-Buraq in that spot. More recently, the name has been adopted by modern cargo airlines and internet companies because of the animal's association with speedy movement through the air.

See also ANIMALS; FOLKLORE; HORSE.

Further reading: Juan Eduardo Campo, *The Other Sides of Paradise: Explorations into the Religious Meanings of Domestic Space in Islam* (Columbia: University of South Carolina Press, 1991); Arthur Jeffery, *Reader on Islam* (The Hague: Mouton & Company, 1962).

burial   *See* CEMETERY; FUNERARY RITUALS.

burqa (also burka)

From the Arabic term *burqu,* a burqa is a type of partial or complete face covering worn by some WOMEN in various Muslim cultures, at least since the Abbasid period (c. ninth to 10th century) and varying by locale and time period. It is most often a "cloth covering the entire face below the eyes" (Stillman, 147), but because the term *burqu* is often used interchangeably with *niqab* and other local terms for face coverings, it may also involve different regional variations, such as a mesh cloth over the whole face or an opaque cloth with holes for the eyes.

No explicit religious injunction for the burqa is found in the QURAN or HADITH, and the ULAMA generally agree that it is not required dress for women. In contemporary contexts, Muslim women wearing modest dress most often choose to cover the entire body except the face and hands. Therefore, it may be said that forms of face covering such as the burqa are less commonly worn by Muslim women than other types of modest garments.

Reasons for wearing the burqa must be understood within social contexts. Contrary to stereotypical depictions, there exists no singular meaning to explain why women may wear the burqa. Rather, the burqa in its many forms may be worn for a multitude of reasons, varying from one context to another. Among countless other meanings, it might make specific statements about a woman's piety, her values regarding sexual modesty, her resistance to Western notions of sexuality, her desire for privacy or mobility in male-dominated environments, or her membership in a political or national movement.

Conservative and radical Islamist movements such as the TALIBAN in AFGHANISTAN have recently contributed to an increase in the numbers of women donning the burqa. In this regard, the Western mass media have helped make the term familiar throughout the world, and for many, it has come to symbolize the controversial Taliban regime's abuse of Afghan women.

See also HIJAB; VEIL.

Aysha A. Hidayatullah

Further reading: Leila Ahmed, *Women and Gender in Islam: Historical Roots of a Modern Debate* (New Haven, Conn.: Yale University Press, 1992); Dawn Chatty, "The Burqa Face Cover: An Aspect of Dress in Southeastern Arabia." In *Languages of Dress in the Middle East,* edited by Nancy Lindisfarne-Tapper and Bruce Ingham, 127–148 (London: Curzon and the Centre of Near and Middle Eastern Studies, School of Oriental and African Studies, 1997); Fadwa El Guindi, *Veil: Modesty, Privacy and Resistance* (Oxford: Berg, 1999); Yedida K. Stillman, *Arab Dress: From the Dawn of Islam to Modern Times,* ed. Norman A. Stillman (Leiden: E.J. Brill, 2000).

C

Cairo (Arabic: al-Qahira; Misr al-Qahira; or Misr)

The capital of EGYPT, Cairo is a global metropolis of about 16.8 million residents (est. 2008), the largest Muslim city in the world. It straddles the Nile River near the ancient pyramids of Giza and occupies an area of 82.6 square miles (214 square kilometers) at the southern tip of the Nile Delta in northern Egypt. Most Cairenes (Cairo residents) are Sunni Muslims who follow the SHAFII LEGAL SCHOOL, but it is also home to a sizeable Coptic Orthodox Christian population of several million as well as immigrant communities from the wider region of the Mediterranean basin, Africa, and the Middle East. It hosts international businessmen, diplomats, REFUGEES, scholars, and technical personnel working for foreign companies. AL-AZHAR, the foremost Sunni university, is located there, as are dozens of remarkable mosques, churches, and other monuments that date back to as early as the seventh century. It is also the seat of the patriarchate of the Coptic Orthodox Church and has cathedrals belonging to several other Eastern Orthodox churches. A thriving Jewish community once lived there, but most Egyptian Jews emigrated to ISRAEL after its creation in 1948. Cairo has played such an important role in the cultural, social, economic, and political life of the country and the region that the nation itself is officially known as Misr, one of the Arabic names for Cairo. In colloquial Arabic, Egyptians like to boast, "Masr (colloquial for Misr) is the mother of the world"—the center of civilized life. Despite its prestige and the influence it holds in Arab and Muslim countries, Cairo is beset by the same problems faced by many other large, crowded modern cities—urban crowding, housing shortages, pollution, unemployment and underemployment, and a stressed infrastructure.

The history of Cairo begins with a garrison town named Fustat that was built on the east bank of the Nile by the Muslim army of about 10,000 soldiers that invaded Egypt in 641. Fustat was situated next to an old Roman fortress known as Babylon. At the town's center was the governor's residence and a small congregational MOSQUE, called the Mosque of Amr after the Muslim commander Amr ibn al-As (d. ca. 663). This mosque-government complex was surrounded by markets and residential quarters for the different Arab tribal groups that had formed the core of the invading Muslim army. Fustat served as the first capital of Egypt during the UMAYYAD CALIPHATE (661–750), based in DAMASCUS, and the ABBASID CALIPHATE (750–1258), based in BAGHDAD. By

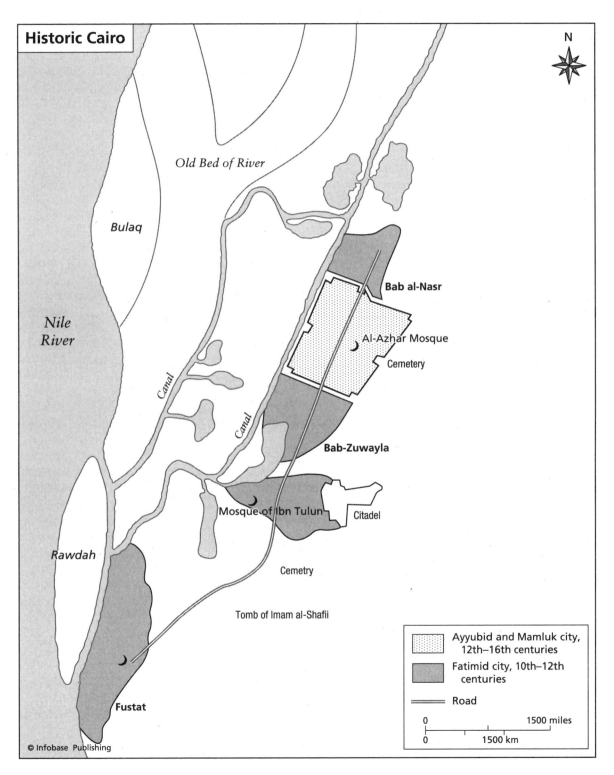

Historic Cairo

N

Old Bed of River

Bulaq

Nile
River

Canal

Canal

Bab al-Nasr

Al-Azhar Mosque

Cemetery

Bab-Zuwayla

Mosque of Ibn Tulun

Citadel

Rawdah

Cemetry

Tomb of Imam al-Shafii

Fustat

© Infobase Publishing

Ayyubid and Mamluk city,
12th–16th centuries

Fatimid city, 10th–12th
centuries

Road

0   1500 miles

0   1500 km

the 10th century, it had developed into a thriving commercial center linking the Mediterranean region and sub-Saharan Africa with the Red Sea and Indian Ocean trade networks. It took several centuries for Fustat to reach its peak as an urban center, but once it did, visitors compared it to legendary Baghdad because of its large markets, parks, and beautiful GARDENS. Al-Muqaddasi, a 10th-century geographer, called Fustat "the glory of Islam and the commercial center of the universe" (Raymond, 30). Among the products it was known for were textiles, refined sugar, paper, glass, and ceramics. Its population, estimated to be 175,000, was large for CITIES of that time. The rich tended to live alongside the poor, and some of the people were housed in large multistory apartment buildings that could hold 350 residents. In addition to a growing population of Muslims, Fustat also had Christian and Jewish inhabitants. An area now known as Old Cairo had several antique churches, one of which was believed to stand on the spot where the infant Jesus and his family had stayed when they fled Palestine during the reign of Herod the Great (r. 37–34 B.C.E.). The Ben Ezra synagogue was one place of worship for Jews in Fustat, and it became famous late in the 19th century because of the large cache of papers, known as the Geniza documents, that were discovered there. These documents shed light on the social and economic life of the medieval city and on relations between Jews, Christians, and Muslims. Fustat's CEMETERY was situated to the east of the city, and it later became the site of many of Cairo's major funerary monuments, as well as an important center of social life, as families went there to remember the dead, worship at the tombs of SAINTS, and give charity to the poor.

The story of Cairo, however, is really a tale of *two* cities—one for the common people and one for the rulers. As Fustat grew, officials moved the center of government outside the populated quarters to vacant hills just beyond the northeast edge of the city. The first of these governmental cities was call al-Askar ("cantonment"), built in 751,

Medieval Cairo *(Source: unknown)*

which was replaced by another called al-Qatai ("wards") in 869. In 969, a Shii dynasty known as the Fatimids (r. 909–1171) arrived from North Africa and founded a new governmental city that replaced al-Qatai. They named it al-Qahira ("conqueror"), from which comes the English name *Cairo,* and they wanted it to serve as the new capital for their CALIPHATE, which rivaled that of the Abbasids in Baghdad. The original Cairo was built about three miles northeast of Fustat; it was rectangular in shape, enclosed by a strong defensive wall, and oriented toward Mecca. Inside lived the Fatimid caliph, his household, officials, and the army. The most prominent architectural features were al-Azhar (the rulers' congregational mosque), a large palace complex, and a street that bisected the city lengthwise from the southwest to the northeast. The city soon developed its own commercial district to serve the needs of its residents, and increased prosperity caused it to grow beyond the limits of the original walled city. Additional mosques and public areas were built, and special attention was given to establishing shrines for AHL AL-BAYT, descendants of Muhammad. The most famous of these shrines are those of HUSAYN IBN ALI (located within Cairo's walls), and the tombs of the women saints Ruqayya and Nafisa (located in the open area south of Cairo and east of Fustat). The two cities, Fustat and Cairo, thus became symbiotically connected, but distinct urban centers.

During the 11th century, famines and fires contributed to a decline in Fustat's population, while Cairo grew and became more prosperous. Common people were allowed to live there starting in 1073, and its population began to occupy new residential areas just outside the city gates. Under the Kurdish Ayyubid dynasty (r. 1173–1250), it entered a new phase in its history. In terms of religion, the Ayyubid conqueror SALADIN (r. 1174–1193) and his heirs put an end to the Fatimid Shii missionary activities that had not been very successful in Egypt, and they promoted Sunni Islam instead. They sponsored a building program that involved erecting 25 MADRASAS to propagate Sunni religious learning, especially jurisprudence (FIQH), in addition to a number of congregational mosques and Sufi hospices. They also built a mausoleum for Imam al-SHAFII (d. 820), the founder of one of the four Sunni legal schools, and an adjacent madrasa. To enhance Cairo's defenses and to reinforce their control of the city, the Ayyubids built a massive citadel on a rocky spur overlooking Cairo and Fustat on the east side, and they built a single defensive wall that enclosed both cities and the citadel. During the Mamluk era (1250–1517), this large urban conglomeration grew in size, with more markets and residential areas, palaces, mosques, hospices,

and hospitals. This was also when Cairo became the most important center for Islamic learning in the world, especially after the Mongol invasions destroyed many of the cities of Persia and IRAQ in the 13th century. The city played host to many scholars and mystics from the East as well as from North Africa and Andalusia, despite the political turmoil it endured at the hands of the Mamluk rulers at this time.

After the Ottoman Empire conquered Egypt in the early 16th century, Cairo functioned as its administrative capital for the region, and it continued to be a major intellectual and commercial center. Its population actually grew from less than 200,000 to about 263,000 during this time. As they had done in previous eras, the ULAMA served as intermediaries between commoners and the ruling elites, who were foreigners. Al-Azhar dominated religious life as the main congregational mosque and madrasa in Egypt, and it even rivaled the religious institutions of Istanbul, the Ottoman capital.

Cairo was briefly occupied by Napoleon's French expeditionary force from 1798 to 1801. The French scholars who accompanied the army produced a detailed account of Egypt at the time, the massive 23-volume *Description de l'Égypte,* which included important information about Cairo and its institutions. The construction of modern Cairo, however, did not begin until later in the 19th century, when Egypt was ruled by the Turko-Albanian dynasty of Muhammad Ali (1805–1952). Bolstered by increased revenues from the Suez Canal and cotton exports, Khedive Ismail (r. 1863–1879) laid the foundations for a new planned city on vacant land between the old caliphal city of Cairo and the east bank of the Nile River. He had been inspired by the geometric pattern of streets and boulevards he discovered during his travels in Europe, especially by those conceived by the French planner Baron Haussmann (d. 1891). This newly developed area soon became the political, economic, and cultural heart of the city, graced by parks and European-style buildings, including the first opera house built in the Middle East. Today it is where many of the embassies, international hotels, banks, department stores, and cinemas are located. Thus, visitors to Cairo will find a modern city and its suburbs coexisting with what remains of its medieval architectural core. Fustat has virtually disappeared except for an archaeological park and a district called Old Cairo, where the Mosque of Amr, several churches and monasteries, and the Ben Ezra Synagogue still stand.

See also CHRISTIANITY AND ISLAM; DHIMMI; FATIMID DYNASTY; JUDAISM AND ISLAM; MAMLUK; OTTOMAN DYNASTY.

Further reading: S. D. Goitein, *A Mediterranean Society: An Abridgement in One Volume.* Edited by Jacob Lassner (Berkeley: University of California Press, 1999); Andre Raymond, *Cairo.* Translated by Willard Wood (Harvard, Mass.: Harvard University Press, 2000); Max Rodenbeck, *Cairo: The City Victorious* (London: Picador, 1998); Caroline Williams, *Islamic Monuments in Cairo: The Practical Guide* (Cairo: American University in Cairo Press, 2002).

calendar

The Islamic calendar is comprised of 12 lunar months, based on the cycles of the moon rather than upon those of the Sun, which forms the basis of the Western Gregorian calendar. Each month in the Islamic calendar lasts from one first sighting of the crescent moon to the next. The 12 months of the Islamic calendar in order are Muharram, Safar, Rabi al-Awwal, Rabi al-Thani, Jumada al-Ula, Jumada al-Thaniyya, Rajab, Shaban, RAMADAN, Shawwal, Dhu al-Qada, and Dhu al-Hijja.

The Islamic calendar, comprised of 354 days, shifts with respect to the solar calendar, with each month in the former beginning 10 or 11 days earlier every year. Since the sighting of the moon sometimes varies with respect to longitude and latitude, the Islamic calendar may vary from one part of the world to another. Because the Islamic calendar shifts, solar calendars are often used in addition to Islamic calendars. In IRAN, for instance, three calendars are in common use: the Persian solar, the Islamic, and the Gregorian.

Muslims mark the first year of their calendar (sometimes called the HIJRA calendar) with the establishment of the first Islamic community and governmental structure in the city of MEDINA (in modern-day SAUDI ARABIA), following MUHAMMAD's and the early Muslims' emigration from MECCA in 622 C.E. Muslims designate this year as 1 A.H. (i.e., anno Hegirae, or "hijra year"). Two of Islam's most significant months are Ramadan and Dhu al-Hijja. During Ramadan, Muslims abstain from food, drink, and sexual relations from sunup to sundown. They mark the end of this month by ID AL-FITR, which celebrates the final breaking of this fast. Dhu al-Hijjah is the month of the HAJJ, or pilgrimage to Mecca, and at the end of the hajj, Muslims commemorate ID AL-ADHA, which celebrates Abraham's readiness to offer his son Ismail as a sacrifice.

While the above rituals are celebrated by Sunnis and Twelve-Imam Shiis, there are others that are celebrated exclusively by the Shia, or that they emphasize more than the Sunnis. These holidays include the birth and DEATH anniversaries of Muhammad, his daughter FATIMA, and the Twelve Imams (or sacred leaders) of SHIISM. The Shia also celebrate other significant occurrences, such as Muhammad's public declaration of Ali as successor at GHADIR KHUMM near Mecca during the Prophet's final pilgrimage; the meeting between Muhammad, his family, and the Christians from Najaran at Mubahila; and most significant for Shia, ASHURA, or the 10th of Muharram, which is the day Husayn, one of the Prophet's grandson's, was martyred at KARBALA in modern-day Iraq. The annual rituals in which Shia engage on this day and their related meanings form a cornerstone of their collective identity and worldview.

The Islamic calendar is also punctuated by the weekly Friday congregational prayers that involve

Muslims going in large numbers for noon PRAYER at a MOSQUE. This prayer service is typically longer than others during the week because it includes a sermon based on the QURAN. Finally, astronomy and the Muslim calendar are significant for Muslims because they help them calculate precisely when during each day they must perform the five obligatory prayers.

See also FIVE PILLARS; HOLIDAYS; SUNNISM.

Jon Armajani

Further reading: Ahmad Birashk, *A Comparative Calendar of the Iranian, Muslim Lunar, and Christian Eras for Three Thousand Years: 1260 BH–2000 AH; 639 BC–2621 C.E.* (Costa Mesa, Calif.: Mazda Publishers, 1993); David A. King, *Astronomy in the Service of Islam* (Aldershot, U.K. and Brookfield, Vt.: Variorum, 1993); Ahmad Hussein Sakr, *Feast, Festivities and Holidays* (Lombard, Ill.: Foundation for Islamic Knowledge, 1999).

caliph (Arabic: *khalifa,* deputy, vicegerent)

Caliph is the title of the ruler of the Islamic community after the DEATH of MUHAMMAD in 632 and was claimed by many pretenders to that leadership. Another title given the caliph was "commander of the faithful" (*amir al-muminin*).

As a prophet, Muhammad had been a unique leader exercising absolute religious and political AUTHORITY. The caliphs were not prophets and therefore could not exercise this dual authority in the same way, and yet the community was accustomed to leadership that was both political and religious. The first four caliphs, known as the Rashidun, or rightly guided, exercised some religious authority as COMPANIONS OF THE PROPHET, but over time, the position came increasingly to be a political one.

The majority Sunni view among Muslims is that Muhammad did not appoint a successor, and so his companions and leaders within the community agreed upon ABU BAKR (r. 632–634). There was no consensus, however, on whether a caliph should be appointed or elected and by whom, on what basis the selection should be made, nor on the precise duties and responsibilities of the caliph. These questions would continue to plague Islamic GOVERNMENT throughout the period of the CALIPHATE. Abu Bakr appointed UMAR IBN AL-KHATTAB (r. 634—644) as his successor, and it was during his caliphate that many of the early Arab Muslim conquests took place. Due in part to the legacy of the conquests, but even more to Umar's ability to combine egalitarian leadership and religious piety, he came to symbolize the ideal caliph. His status was heightened by the fact that the reigns of UTHMAN IBN AL-AFFAN (r. 644–656) and ALI IBN ABI TALIB (r. 656–661) that followed him were marked by internal strife and civil war. These events led to the permanent division of the Muslim community into Shii and Sunni Islam and brought about the end of the Rashidun caliphate. Subsequently, few caliphs could be held up as ideal Islamic rulers. Rather, they inherited and exercised their power in a way similar to that of the kings and emperors in neighboring non-Islamic lands.

After the 10th century, the caliph's power was overshadowed in the political realm by the SULTANs, and in the area of religion by the ULAMA. The caliph's strength and significance was based primarily on his role as the symbolic head of the Islamic community. It was for this reason that the Ottoman sultan Selim (r. 1512–1520), upon conquering the Islamic heartlands in the early 16th century, adopted the title of caliph in order to strengthen his religious legitimacy and authority.

As Ottoman power waned in relation to that of European rulers from the 18th century onward, Ottoman sultans sought to retain some authority by claiming to be the spiritual leaders of the Muslims and defenders of Islam. The Ottoman defeat in World War I, which led to the rise of the new Turkish Republic, meant the end of the caliphate. The founder of the new secular state of TURKEY, MUSTAFA KEMAL ATATURK, formally abolished it in 1924.

See also FATIMID DYNASTY; IMAM; GOVERNMENT, ISLAMIC; OTTOMAN DYNASTY; SUNNISM; UMAYYAD CALIPHATE.

Heather N. Keaney

Further reading: Patricia Crone and Martin Hinds, *God's Caliph* (Cambridge: Cambridge University Press, 1986); Hugh Kennedy, *The Prophet and the Age of the Caliphates: The Islamic Near East from the Sixth to the Eleventh Century* (London: Longman Press, 1986); Wilfred Madelung, *The Succession to Muhammad* (Cambridge: Cambridge University Press, 1997).

caliphate

The caliphate is the office of religious and political ruler in Islamdom. It went through several stages of historical development. The first four CALIPHS make up what is regarded by Muslims as the Rashidun, or the caliphate of the rightly guided (r. 632–661). These caliphs were all early converts to ISLAM and close COMPANIONS OF THE PROPHET Muhammad. For the most part, they continued to model the ideals of Islamic government: upholding proper religious practice and social justice. It was during this period that Islam experienced its most rapid expansion into SYRIA, IRAQ, PERSIA, and North Africa

The period of the rightly guided caliphate ended in civil war, and the capital of the Islamic empire and the caliphate moved from Medina to DAMASCUS. There the UMAYYAD CALIPHATE (r. 661–750) became increasingly secular, exercising authority based on the power of the military rather than moral or religious AUTHORITY. The tension between religious legitimacy and secular authority eventually led to the overthrow of the Umayyads in the eighth century by the Abbasids, who moved the capital to BAGHDAD, Iraq. The early ABBASID CALIPHATE (750–1258) is regarded as the golden age of Islamicate civilization.

In addition to its wealth and power, the caliphate symbolized the united Muslim community (UMMA), living proof that despite bloodshed and civil war, God had not abandoned his community. When the caliphate's political power began to decline, the Muslim community held even more tightly to the symbolic significance of the caliphate. Starting in the 10th century, a series of military commanders seized control of the military and political workings of the empire. Eventually, authority was divided up among these commanders, who were known as amirs or SULTANS. Due to the symbolic and religious significance of the caliphate, however, sultans claimed to rule on its behalf. Throughout the medieval period, the caliphate and sultanate complemented each other, with the former lending religious legitimacy to the latter, while the sultanate provided the political and military power to defend Islamdom.

The sultans proved incapable, however, of defending Islam and the caliphate from the Mongols, who destroyed Baghdad and the Abbasid Caliphate in 1258. Even though the MAMLUK sultans of EGYPT attempted to continue the caliphate in CAIRO through an Abbasid survivor, the caliphate no longer carried the same religious significance. When the Ottoman Turks defeated the Mamluks in 1517, they absorbed the caliphate into their sultanate.

When the Turkish nationalist MUSTAFA KEMAL ATATURK (d. 1938) dismantled the Ottoman Empire and established TURKEY as a modern, secular nation-state, he formally abolished the caliphate in 1924. This marked the symbolic end of an era and made official what had in many ways been a longstanding reality. Today there are still reformers who call for a restoration of the caliphate, believing that it is necessary for enforcing SHARIA and establishing God's government on Earth.

See also IMAM; FATIMID DYNASTY; KHILAFAT MOVEMENT; OTTOMAN DYNASTY.

Heather N. Keaney

Further reading: Halil Inalcik, *The Ottoman Empire: The Classical Age 1300–1600* (London: Phoenix Press,

2000); Hugh Kennedy, *The Armies of the Caliphs: Military Society in the Early Islamic State* (New York: Routledge, 2001); Donald Quataert, *The Ottoman Empire, 1700–1922* (New York: Cambridge University Press, 2000); David Wasserstein, *The Caliphate in the West: An Islamic Institution in the Iberian Peninsula* (Oxford: Clarendon Press, 1993).

calligraphy

The term *calligraphy* comes from Greek *kalligraphia,* meaning beautiful writing, or the visual elaboration of written scripts known in Arabic as *khatt* (line).

Within the field of Islamic ART, calligraphy refers to stylized scripts in languages that use (or used) the Arabic ALPHABET, among them Arabic, Persian, Urdu, and Ottoman Turkish. The word that designates the practice and the forms of stylized writing is *khatt,* whose basic meaning as line associates it with both architectural planning and geometry. As calligraphy, *khatt* means penmanship or an individual hand, and *khattat* applies to a master practitioner of *khatt* as a visual art form (but also to sign painters).

The status of Arabic as the shared language of Islamic scriptures led Orientalist historians to associate stylized scripts exclusively with religious values and, at the same time, to consider this writing a subset of (meaningless) ARABESQUE ornamentation. The practice of stylized writing, in fact, has a number of internal histories that governed forms, aesthetic criteria, and contextual meanings. These histories show that changes in the forms of letters indicate historical disruptions rather than continuities; the adoption or rejection of particular scripts was a conscious means of expressing desired meanings through form.

The rationalization of scripts in 10th- and 11th-century IRAQ produced a new canon of writing in which clarity, legibility, and harmony defined aesthetic quality in *khatt*. But this writing reform also allowed its Abbasid sponsors to order and control the output of scribes and to create a visual system that immediately expressed loyalty to them as opposed to rivals such as the Fatimids, who continued the use of angular forms. This example demonstrates that the much romanticized art of Islamic calligraphy neither follows an evolutionary line in which angular letters naturally mutated into rounded ones, nor reflects identical and unchanging Islamic ideals, but rather highlights distinctions among them. Qazi Ahmad's 17th-century Persian treatise on calligraphy similarly illustrates views governed by a different time, place, and group ideology and ascribes the invention of beautiful writing to Imam Ali (d. 661), patron saint of Iranian calligraphers of the time.

Finally, the United States postal stamp designed by *khattat* Muhammad Zakariya (whose training comprises a spiritual content) illustrates the use of calligraphy to symbolize the presence of Muslims in the country. In this instance, an official document again embraces *khatt* as a sign of a particular community but deploys it as an item of identity politics in a new cultural and historical setting that reinterprets it to fit this context.

See also ARABIC LANGUAGE AND LITERATURE; FATIMID DYNASTY; IBN AL-BAWWAB, ABU AL-HASAN ALI IBN HILAL; IBN MUQLA, ABU ALI MUHAMMAD.

Nuha N. N. Khoury

Further reading: Oleg Grabar, *The Mediation of Ornament* (Princeton, N.J.: Princeton University Press, 1992); Qazi Ahmad bin Mir Munshi al-Husayni, *Gulistan-i Hunar,* trans. V. Minorsky, *Calligraphers and Painters: A Treatise by Qadi Ahmad, Son of Mir Munshi (circa A.H. 1015/A.D. 1606)* (Washington, D.C.: Smithsonian Institution, 1959); Yasin Safadi, *Islamic Calligraphy* (Boulder, Colo.: Shambhala Publications, 1978); Yasser Tabbaa, *The Transformation of Islamic Art During The Sunni Revival* (Seattle: University of Washington Press, 2001).

call to prayer *See ADHAN.*

camel

The camel is a large humpbacked mammal with a long neck that has become the symbol of the Arab BEDOUIN way of life. There are two kinds: the dromedary, or one-humped, camel of ARAB lands, North Africa, IRAN and INDIA; and the Bactrian, or two-humped, camel of Central Asia and parts of Iran and AFGHANISTAN. The dromedary was originally from Arabia and was domesticated by 2500 B.C.E. It was essential for the subsistence of Arab nomadic tribes, who used it for transport, clothing, and food. Because of its strength and ability to traverse great distances, the Arabs have called it "the ship of the desert." It is mentioned in the Hebrew Bible, the New Testament, and the QURAN. Historical evidence indicates that the camel gradually replaced preexisting wheeled forms of transport in the Middle East after the first century C.E. as a result of the growing influence of camel-herding Arab traders on the economy of the cities and the animal's efficiency in desert transportation and warfare. These developments may actually have caused changes in the layouts of Middle Eastern cities, where the straight streets of the ancient Roman era gave way to narrow and winding ones during the Middle Ages.

Camels were a favorite subject for the pre-Islamic Arab poets, but among the most legendary ones were the she-camels of Salih, an early Arabian prophet, and MUHAMMAD. Salih's camel was miraculously brought forth from a rock to prove to the people of Thamud (in northwestern Arabia) that Salih was a prophet. The camel provided abundant milk for the people, some of whom became Muslims, but others who refused to believe slaughtered the camel and threatened to kill Salih. According to early Islamic stories, God destroyed them for their disbelief as a consequence. The Quran also tells a short version of this story (Q 7:72–79, 11:61–68). Muhammad's she-camel, according to early biographical accounts, was allowed to wander in MEDINA until it stopped and rested, thus determining the site where Muhammad would build his home and mosque. Another famous dromedary carried AISHA, Muhammad's widow, during the Battle of the Camel, when she and other leading COMPANIONS OF THE PROPHET led an unsuccessful rebellion against the caliph ALI IBN ABI TALIB in 656.

Because the camel chews its cud but does not have cloven hoofs, its meat is forbidden by Jewish dietary law. This is not the case in Islamic law. However, camel meat is not eaten as often as mutton because the animal is more valuable as a beast of burden and as a source of milk. In some areas, such as the Nile Valley, it is used for plowing fields and other agricultural tasks. Camels also serve as sacrificial ANIMALS for Islamic HOLIDAYS and saint festivals. Muslim rulers from the 13th century until the 20th century would send a camel-borne palanquin to MECCA as a symbol of their authority during the annual HAJJ. The camel is still a popular theme in Egyptian pilgrimage murals and folk art.

See also DIETARY LAWS; HORSE.

Further reading: Richard W. Bulliet, *The Camel and the Wheel* (Cambridge, Mass.: Harvard University Press, 1975); Gordon Darnel Newby, *The Making of the Last Prophet* (Columbia: University of South Carolina Press, 1989).

Camp David accords

The Camp David accords were signed by Egyptian president ANWAR AL-SADAT, Israeli prime minister Menachem Begin, and U.S. president Jimmy Carter on September 17, 1978, and created a general framework for Israeli withdrawal from the Sinai Peninsula, taken by ISRAEL in 1967, in exchange for a formal peace treaty between the two countries. The 13 days of negotiations mediated by the U.S. president were notoriously acrimonious, and the two negotiating teams were held virtual prisoners at the U.S. presidential retreat at Camp David, Maryland, until they reached agreement. Even in the hours leading up to the official televised signing ceremony, Begin balked at putting his name to a document that also included provisions that would have led, if implemented, to an eventual end to the Israeli occupation of Palestinian land in the West Bank and Gaza based on UN Security Council Resolution 242. An Egyptian-Israeli peace treaty was signed by Begin and Sadat in Washington on March 26, 1979. Subsequently, Begin and Sadat received the Nobel Peace Prize for their agreement, but the Middle East was left in turmoil.

The Camp David accords were the result of a lengthy political opening to Israel initiated by Anwar Sadat. After Sadat's surprise attack on Israeli forces in the Sinai in October 1973 and the resulting military stalemate, Sadat indicated through secret diplomatic channels that he was willing to negotiate a comprehensive peace agreement with the Israeli government. For the next four years, Sadat's overtures to Israel fell on deaf ears until November 20, 1977, when he made an astounding visit to JERUSALEM and addressed the Israeli Knesset. Despite Sadat's bold initiative, the Israeli government conducted substantive negotiations only under pressure from the Carter administration.

Significantly, the Camp David accords placed the Palestinian question at the heart of the Middle East conflict. EGYPT, Israel, and JORDAN were summoned to negotiate an agreement to establish a "self-governing authority" to represent the Palestinian population in the occupied West Bank and Gaza. When the Palestinian authority was established, a transitional five-year period would commence, the end of which would bring an Israeli withdrawal from the occupied territories, Palestinian elections, and Palestinian "autonomy." The Palestinian section of the accords was never addressed and never implemented.

The Camp David accords resulted in a peace treaty between Egypt and Israel as well as the final withdrawal of Israeli troops from the Sinai Peninsula in the spring of 1982. However, the imperfections in this separate peace agreement led not only to a rather "cold peace" between Egypt and Israel but also to a profound crisis in the Middle East region. Even before the final Israeli withdrawal from Sinai, Sadat was gunned down by Islamist opponents of the treaty on October 6, 1981. Arab governments initiated a diplomatic boycott of Egypt. The Begin government embarked on a full-scale invasion of LEBANON in June 1982, just weeks after the Sinai withdrawal. Israeli public outrage at the massacre of Palestinian civilians in Beirut in September 1982 and the rising Israeli military casualties resulting from its occupation of Lebanon led to Begin's resignation in 1983 and his self-imposed withdrawal from public life until his death in 1992. The Camp David accords, while successful in achieving a negotiated peace between Egypt and Israel, set an unfortunate precedent of unfulfilled transitional phases and left the question of Palestinian sovereignty unresolved. These problems have since plagued every other attempt to reach a truly comprehensive settlement of the Arab-Israeli conflict.

See also ARAB-ISRAELI CONFLICTS; PALESTINE.

Garay Menicucci

Further reading: Irene Beeson and David Hirst, *Sadat* (London: Faber and Faber, 1981); William L. Cleveland, *A History of the Modern Middle East* (Boulder, Colo.: Westview Press, 2004); William Quandt, *Camp David: Peacemaking and Politics* (Washington, D.C.: Brookings Institution, 1986).

Canada

There has been a Muslim presence in Canada since very early times, with the first national census for 1871 showing 13 Muslims. It was not until the 20th century that Islamic institutions became established in North America. The first MOSQUE in Canada was the al-Rashid Mosque in Edmonton, Alberta, built in 1938. June 28, 1952, saw the first national Muslim conference in Cedar Rapids, Iowa, with 400 Muslims from Canada and the United States in attendance. In July, 1954, the Federation of Islamic Associations of the United States and Canada (FIA) was formed. The first conference of the FIA was held in London, Ontario, in 1955.

With the growth of the Muslim community in North America and the migration of Muslim students from other countries (particularly the ARAB world, but also IRAN, INDIA, PAKISTAN, and TURKEY) to study in North America, the MUSLIM STUDENTS ASSOCIATION (MSA) was formed in 1963. Today there are active chapters of the MSA in most major colleges and universities in North America. In 1981, the ISLAMIC SOCIETY OF NORTH AMERICA (ISNA) was created. It is the largest Islamic organization in North America, with its Canadian headquarters in the Toronto suburb of Mississaugua, Ontario. There are, of course, many other Muslim communities in North America, representing such groups as the Shia (both Twelve-Imam and Ismaili) and Sufi societies, the NATION OF ISLAM (and all of its splinter groups such as the Nation of Five Percenters), the Dar ul-Islam, and others.

There is no accurate count of the Muslim population in Canada or the UNITED STATES. The Canadian census does ask the question of religious affiliation. The 1981 Census of Canada was the first to recognize Islam as a separate, distinct religious category. According to the 1981 census, there were 98,165 Muslims in Canada. The overwhelming majority (77 percent) of Canadian Muslims were foreign-born, with only 23 percent being born in Canada. In 1981, more than half (53.1 percent) of Canadian Muslims lived in Ontario. The figures from the 1991 census show 253,260 Muslims in Canada, an increase of more than 2.5 times the number from 1981.

The figures from the 2001 census list 579,600 Muslims in Canada, an increase of almost 2.3 times the number from the 1991 census. The estimate of 579,600, however, may be low. The main reason is that most Muslims are recent immigrants who are reticent to self-identify as members of a minority religious group for reasons ranging from personal privacy, to a perception of discrimination, to a desire to fit in. This is particularly true with the recent immigration of REFUGEES into Canada from countries such as Somalia, Bosnia, and Albania. On the other hand, estimates of population numbers are often linked with self-worth, that is, minorities often tend to prefer higher estimates for their own group and lower estimates for others.

The ways in which Islam is lived and practised in Canada can best be seen in the Toronto area, which has the largest population of Canada's Muslims. Three umbrella organizations represent various communities there: the Islamic Society of North America (ISNA), the Canadian Council of Muslim Women (CCMW), and the Council of the Muslim Community of Canada (CMCC). There is a strong Shii presence in Toronto, both in its Twelve-Imam and Ismaili forms. Sufis, including members of the Chishti, Alawi, Qadiri, Jerrahi, Rifai, Naqshbandi, and Nimatullahi orders are quite active in Toronto. The Ahmadis are actively involved in proselytizing and have built the largest mosque in the Toronto area. This mosque, named the Bait-ul-Islam (House of Islam), is actually the largest mosque in all of Canada. It was designed in 1987 by Gulzar Haider, a professor of architecture at Carleton University in Ottawa, Ontario, and the same architect who in 1979 was asked to design the mosque for the headquarters of the Islamic Society of North America in Plainfield, Indiana.

While Islam is a minority tradition in Canada, Sunni Muslims constitute the majority of Toronto's Muslims. However, there are substantial minority communities who practice their own forms of Islam. Shi'i traditions are quite well represented in Toronto. One estimate is that Shiis make up at least 30 percent of the total Muslim population of North America, about twice that found generally among Muslims, and attributable to immigration patterns. The Shii community in Canada increased dramatically after the expulsion of South Asians from Uganda in 1972 and the subsequent arrival of Muslims from other East African countries such as Kenya or Tanzania. Seven years later came the revolution in Iran, resulting in another wave of Iranian Shii immigration into North America. There is also a substantial Ismaili community in Canada (predominantly of South Asian and EAST AFRICAN origin), self-estimated to consist of some 30,000 members in the Greater Toronto Area alone. Another minority is the Ahmadi community in Toronto, which has experienced major difficulties from other Muslims.

Amir Hussain

Further reading: Sheila McDonough, "Muslims of Canada." In *South Asian Religious Diaspora in Britain, Canada, and the United States,* edited by Harold Coward, John R. Hinnels, and Raymond Brady Williams, 173–189 (Albany: State University of New York Press, 2000); Rheem A. Meshal, "Banners of Faith and Identities in Construct: The Hijab in Canada." In *The Muslim Veil in North America: Issues and Debates,* edited by Sajida Sultana Alvi, Hooma Hoodfar, and Sheila McDonough, 72–104 (Toronto: Women's Press, 2003); Regula Qureshi, "Transcending Space: Recitation and Community among South Asian Muslims in Canada." In *Making Muslim Space in North America and Europe,* edited by Barbara Metcalf, 46–64 (Berkeley: University of California Press, 1996); A[sma] Rashid, *1981 Census of Canada: The Muslim Canadians, A Profile* (Ottawa: Statistics Canada, 1992).

cat

During his travels in SYRIA, the American Romantic poet and journalist Bayard Taylor (1825–78) encountered an unprecedented sight: a hospital where cats roamed freely and were sheltered, cared for, and fed. This institution was funded by a private endowment (waqf) that supplied veterinary care, food, and caretakers' wages. The British Orientalist and sometime denizen of Cairo Edward W. Lane (1801–76) described a cat garden that was originally endowed by the 13th-century ruler al-Zahir Baybars (r. 1260–77). At a time when European town dwellers ate cats or killed them by papal decree (which led to rising rat populations that may have hastened the spread of plagues), cats enjoyed life in ARAB cities in ways that signal their special relationship with Arabs generally and Muslims in particular.

The cat is the quintessential pet in Islam. According to a HADITH, "Love of cats is an aspect of faith." Other hadiths prohibit the persecution and killing of cats. But it is because the cat is considered pure that it is welcomed in homes; a Muslim may eat food that cats have sampled or perform ABLUTIONS with water from which they have drunk. Such rulings are often accompanied by biographical snippets that demonstrate MUHAMMAD's fondness for cats. He took care of the kittens that a cat was allowed to have on his cloak, and he cut off his sleeve rather than disturb a sleeping cat when he had to rise for prayers. His own cat was purportedly named Muizza, and he invented the nickname of the famous companion and hadith transmitter Abu Hurayra (Father of the Kitten) because the latter was always accompanied by his cat. According to legend, it was this cat that saved Muhammad from a snake. Until recently, Arab farmers also told of cats that warned or protected them against snakes.

Cats were guardians of food stores and granaries and, consequently, important members of the environmental network that sustained cities. In the text- and paper-based cultures of Arab-Islamicate cities, they protected books against mice and became friends to bibliophiles and scholars with whom they sometimes appear in paintings. The cat's symbiotic relationship with people and (crowded) cities is reflected in the account of the cat's creation in al-Damiri's (ca. 1341–1405) *Book of Animals:* when the ANIMALS on Noah's Ark complained of mice, God caused the lion to sneeze and so created the first cat. Cats continue to play this role in modern cities, where they prowl the streets in pest patrols and keep impurities outside the home. The cat's enemy is the lofty skyscraper, which is transforming the street hunters into indoor pets.

See also FOLKLORE.

Nuha N. N. Khoury

Further reading: *Cats of Cairo,* Photographs by Lorraine Chittock, Introduction by Annemarie Schimmel (New York: Abbeville Press, 2001); Bayard Taylor, *Lands of the Saracen* (New York: Putnam, 1855).

cemetery

A cemetery is a plot of land dedicated to the burial of the dead. It is usually set apart from residential and commercial areas and contains distinctive monuments, religious buildings, and gravestones that memorialize those who are buried in it. Beyond serving the practical end of providing a place for the disposal of the bodies of the deceased, cemeteries often are regarded as sacred ground in connection with the AFTERLIFE beliefs of a community. This is especially evident for the Abrahamic religions, which believe in the resurrection of the body for a final judgment. For followers of Judaism, Christianity, and ISLAM, therefore, cemeteries are regarded as places of rest for the dead until that time.

Cemeteries form part of the communal landscape wherever Muslims reside. In rural areas, they are located in fields or elevated areas adjacent to villages. Urban cemeteries are usually placed outside the city limits. Cemeteries in medieval

Cairo's City of the Dead (al-Qarafa) *(Juan E. Campo)*

Islamicate cities were usually located outside the city gates, where they could be easily reached by funeral processions and people who wanted to visit the gravesites of family, friends, or holy people. Some urban historians have noted that cemeteries may have actually inhibited the expansion of some cities, but many cemeteries have also been engulfed by urban growth or simply abandoned or forgotten with the passage of time. Jews and Christians living in Muslim countries bury their dead in their own cemeteries.

Visiting the dead and pilgrimages to the tombs of Muslim SAINTs are important aspects of life for many Muslims to this day, even though such practices are condemned by followers of the most conservative schools of Islamic law, such as the Wahhabis of SAUDI ARABIA. During Ramadan, on major feast days, and during the mourning period after someone dies, families visit the cemetery together, and women prepare food to distribute to the needy on behalf of the dead. In Cairo's largest cemetery, the City of the Dead (also known as al-Qarafa), there are family mausoleums that look like houses where people pass the holiday near their deceased relatives. Cemeteries may have trees and gardens, which make them popular places for strolling, picnicking, and other forms of socialization. They were also known as places where people could meet secretly to conduct illicit activities, so secular and religious authorities have periodically sought to control or ban people from using cemeteries for anything other than their intended purposes. In the popular imagination, they are believed to be places where the JINNI and demons may lurk.

Among the most famous cemeteries in Islamic lands are the medieval ones found in MEDINA, DAMASCUS, CAIRO, and BAGHDAD, where the COMPANIONS OF THE PROPHET, his relatives and descendants, and other important figures from early Islamic history are buried. NAJAF, Iraq, where the Shii shrines of Muhammad's cousin ALI IBN ABI TALIB (d. 661) is buried, has the Valley of Peace, a vast cemetery where many of the Shia lay their

dead to rest. The nearby shrine city of KARBALA, where Ali's son Husayn (d. 680) is buried, has another important Shii cemetery, known as the Valley of Faith. In Iran, the shrine of the eighth Shii IMAM Ali al-Rida (d. 818) at Mashhad is surrounded by cemeteries that began to develop when TWELVE-IMAM SHIISM became the religion of the Safavid state in the 16th century. Tehran's Behesht-i Zahra cemetery has recently become famous as the burial place of Ayatollah RUHOLLAH KHOMEINI (d. 1989) and Iranian martyrs of the 1978–79 revolution and the eight-year war with IRAQ (1980–88). Also, powerful Muslim rulers have left spectacular funerary complexes that they built for themselves from MOROCCO to Cairo, Tabriz (Iran), BUKHARA (Uzbekistan), Delhi, Agra, and Hyderabad (INDIA). These constructions contain some of the best surviving examples of medieval Islamicate architecture in the world.

Small cemeteries can be found on the grounds of MOSQUES and MADRASAS located within city precincts, such as the MAMLUK madrasas of Cairo, Ottoman mosques in Turkey, and the Mecca Mosque in Hyderabad. Sufi hospices may also have burial grounds on the premises for a Sufi saint, SHAYKHS, dervishes, family members, and important patrons. For example, the shrine of Nizam al-Din Awliyya (d. 1325) contains, in addition to the graves of his family and disciples, those of Amir Khusraw (d. 1325), a leading Persian poet and friend of Nizam al-Din, and Jahanara (d. 1681), an influential Mughal princess and patron of the CHISHTI SUFI ORDER.

Since the 1970s, Muslim immigrants to EUROPE and the UNITED STATES have purchased lots within existing non-Muslim cemeteries for the burial of their dead. Some prefer, however, to transport the bodies of their deceased back to their homelands for burial.

See also DEATH; FUNERARY RITUALS; JINNI; SUFISM.

Further reading: Raymond Lifchez, ed., *The Dervish Lodge: Architecture, Art, and Sufism in Ottoman Turkey* (Berkeley: University of California, 1992); Muhammad

Umar Memon, *Ibn Taymiyya's Struggle against Popular Religion* (The Hague: Mouton, 1976); Christopher C. Taylor, *In the Vicinity of the Righteous: Ziyara and the Veneration of Muslim Saints in Late Medieval Egypt* (Leiden: E.J. Brill, 1999).

Central Asia and the Caucasus

The former Soviet republics of Central Asia are overwhelmingly Muslim (the exception being Kazakhstan, which continues to have a large non-Kazakh population), while of the new republics of the South Caucasus, only Azerbaijan has a Muslim majority. However, there is a large Muslim population in the North Caucasus that is still within the Russian Federation. Present-day Kazakhstan, Uzbekistan, Turkmenistan, Kyrgyzstan, and Tajikistan as well as the North Caucasus are predominantly Sunni, while Azerbaijan is in the main Shii.

Islam came to Central Asia and the Caucasus in the middle of the seventh century along with Arab conquest (ca. 639–643). Throughout the Middle Ages, Central Asia grew wealthy from the Silk Road, which made its cities major centers for the propagation of Islamic learning and culture, even during the era of the Mongol Empire (13th century to 15th century), which provided a degree of political unity. SUFISM also played a very important role in the development of Islam in the region, both in the Middle Ages and modern times. Sufis such as Ahmad al-Yasavi (d. 1166) were particularly instrumental in Islamizing Turkmen and Kazakh nomads. Sufism was also of the utmost importance in establishing Islam in the North Caucasus. Unlike Central Asia and the North Caucasus, Azerbaijan was ruled by various Persian states, and its people became Shia with the emergence of the SAFAVID DYNASTY at the beginning of the 16th century.

The Russian conquest of Central Asia and the Caucasus over the course of the 19th century took many forms and engendered many different responses. In the North Caucasus in particular, Sufi-led Islamic movements were able to fend off Russian advances for nearly 30 years. The official Russian policy, however, was to keep their hands off the religious affairs of the two regions. Nevertheless, under the increased influence of both European ideas and wider Islamic intellectual trends, there developed in the cities of Central Asia and Azerbaijan the Jadid movement, a group of young local intellectuals who sought to "modernize" Islam. They came into conflict with traditional religious authorities, and after the Russian Revolution, they allied with the Bolsheviks. Many became part of the Soviet administration. This alliance did not last long, however—the last of the former Jadids perished in Joseph Stalin's Great Terror of 1936–38.

The fragile Bolshevik hold on the two regions in the early to mid-1920s necessitated a cautious approach to Islam, though party ideology called for the abolition of all religion. In 1927, with the rise of Stalin, this changed, and there commenced a full assault on Islam both as a religion and as a way of life. Women were forcibly unveiled, polygamy was attacked, and bride price was outlawed. Islamic social institutions were closed, religious leaders arrested, and mosques destroyed. This fight against perceived "backwardness" did not run smoothly, as large-scale revolts appeared throughout both regions. By the early 1930s, only through the mass use of force was resistance broken.

With the coming of World War II, the Soviet fight against religion lessened, and the overt repression of religious leaders and places of worship declined. An officially sanctioned Islam was promoted, with clergy and MOSQUES under the direct control of Soviet administrators. This forced nonofficial Islam to push practices further underground. The Soviet Union was never able to destroy Islam, and with its collapse in 1991, Islam regained its importance in local societies.

Since the collapse of the Soviet Union, Islam has become politicized throughout the two regions, though the extent of this varies. The continuity of leaders in the new republics has led to a continuation of certain Soviet policies toward Islam. In Turkmenistan and Uzbekistan, state-sanctioned Islam is all that is allowed. Especially in Uzbekistan, authorities have used the fight against "fundamentalism" and "TERRORISM" to crush any political opposition. Immediately following the collapse in Tajikistan, a civil war broke out between central secular authorities and self-proclaimed Islamists. This war lasted until 1997, with some Islamists brought into government and a moderate Islamist party allowed. A politicized Islam has also been prominent in the North Caucasus, particularly in CHECHNYA.

See also BASMACHI; BUKHARA; COMMUNISM; ISLAMISM; KARIMOV, ISLAM; NAQSHBANDI SUFI ORDER; SHAMIL.

David Reeves

Further reading: Devin DeWeese, *Islamization and Native Religion in the Golden Horde* (University Park: Pennsylvania State University Press, 1994); Ahmed Rashid, *Jihad: The Rise of Militant Islam in Central Asia* (New Haven, Conn.: Yale University Press, 2002); Anna Zelkina, *In Quest for God and Freedom: The Sufi Response to the Russian Advance in the North Caucasus* (New York: New York University Press, 2000).

chador   See BURQA; *HIJAB*; PURDAH; VEIL.

charity   See ALMSGIVING.

Chechnya

Chechnya is located on the northeastern slopes of the Caucasus Mountains, within the internationally recognized borders of the Russian Federation. The most recent Russian census placed Chechnya's population at nearly 1.1 million, but many estimates place the actual number between 600,000 and 780,000 people.

In the late 18th century, the Russian Empire started serious military incursions into the North Caucasus, and from the beginning, the fiercest resistance came from the people of Chechnya and neighboring Dagestan. The first major leader of this resistance was Shaykh Mansour, who combined Islamic preaching with military struggle. The most successful uprising against the Russians, however, took place from the 1830s to 1859 and was led by Imam SHAMIL (1796–1871). A Naqshabandi Sufi leader, Shamil for a period was able to create an Islamic proto-state in most of present-day Chechnya and Dagestan. With Shamil's defeat, the region passed into Russian control and relative stability, though outbreaks of violence did occur. With the Russian Revolution of 1917 and the demise of central control, the Chechens declared their independence and were briefly a part of a federation of North Caucasian peoples called the Mountain Republic. The Bolsheviks were able to reestablish some control only after much costly fighting in the early 1920s, though sporadic resistance continued. The Chechens were deported to Central Asia in 1944 for alleged collaboration with the Nazis, and as a consequence a quarter to a half of the population died. They were not allowed to return home until the 1950s.

With the demise of the Soviet Union, tension returned to the region. In 1991, the President of Chechnya, Jokhar Dudayev (1944–96) declared Chechnya independent and, though not recognized by any foreign government or Russia, was de-facto independent until the Russians launched full military operations on New Year's Eve 1994. An extremely bloody war ensued, with Russia initially making significant gains, but the Chechens launched a major counteroffensive in 1995. By 1996 the Russians were defeated and agreed to a cease-fire. Altogether, there were an estimated 70,000 casualties. The end of the war, however, did not bring political or economic stability to Chechnya. In 1999, following unexplained terrorist bombings in Russia, which were blamed on Chechens, and a Chechen military incursion into Dagestan, Russia invaded Chechnya again, sending almost 100,000 troops and creating approximately 250,000 REFUGEES. Though Russia has claimed victory and has set up a pro-Russia political administration, they do not control all of Chechnya, and a war of attrition has continued to the present.

See also COMMUNISM; CENTRAL ASIA AND THE CAUCASUS; NAQSHABANDI SUFI ORDER.

David Reeves

Further reading: Thomas de Waal and Carlota Gall, *Chechnya: Calamity in the Caucasus* (New York: New York University Press, 1998); Sebastian Smith, *Allah's Mountains: The Battle for Chechnya* (New York: I.B. Taurus, 2001).

children

Children are a vital part of society. They embody a people's heritage and its future, and although children are often expected to contribute to household tasks and work to support their parents, families and societies usually invest significant resources and care in their upbringing, EDUCATION, and marriage.

Islamic views of children and childhood are expressed in religious literature and the SHARIA, and they are formed in the lived culture of the Muslim family and the local community. In general, Islamic perspectives on childhood reflect norms commonly found in patrilineal societies, in which sons are often favored over daughters. The QURAN teaches that sons and material wealth are evidence of the favor God has shown to humans, but it also teaches that such worldly blessings can divert people from seeking God and the rewards of the hereafter (Q 17:6; 8:28). On the other hand, the Quran also teaches that believers be kind to their parents, speak to them with respect, and call upon God to bless them for taking care of them during childhood (Q 17:23–24). The SHARIA addresses legal issues concerning children that are inspired by the ethical message of the Quran. These include an explicit ban on killing infants, including girls, and rules concerning adoption

and foster parentage. MUHAMMAD (d. 632) was orphaned at an early age (Q 93:6), and this very likely helped make care for orphans and respect for their rights to property foundational Islamic values. The Quran instructs believers to do good to orphans as well as parents and others in need (Q 4:36), and it promises that those who do not treat orphans well will be punished in the AFTERLIFE (Q 4:10). Another facet of the sharia protects the rights of breastfeeding infants and their mothers in event of DIVORCE (Q 2233; 65:6), and it permits resort to the services of wet nurses, following the example set by Muhammad, who was nursed by a BEDOUIN woman in his infancy.

Biographies of famous men and WOMEN have little to say about their childhood years, but substantial evidence for medieval Muslim understandings of children and childhood can be found in legal, medical, and ethical literature. These sources indicate that childhood was recognized as a distinct stage in the formation of the individual and that children were fully incorporated into the moral, legal, intellectual, and emotional life of medieval Islamicate societies. They recognized that children had their own distinct personalities and abilities, which form in the period between birth and puberty. How a child has been cared

Three generations of an American Muslim family *(Juan E. Campo)*

for, raised, and educated was thought to have a direct bearing on his or her physical, mental, and spiritual growth. Parents were instructed to teach their children to do all things in moderation, including good eating habits, since excess was a source of bodily, psychological, and social ills. They were also charged with encouraging moral qualities such as honesty, generosity, and control of the passions.

Medieval Muslim authors urged parents to be gentle and compassionate with their children and to exercise restraint in punishing them for misbehavior. Of course, parents were expected to inculcate their children with knowledge about Islam and the performance of its religious duties, particularly after the age of seven. A widely held view was that children were by nature born to be Muslims but that they learned their religion by imitating their fathers and teachers. In regard to their emotional development, children were to be protected from traumatic experiences, and parents were advised to comfort them immediately after any painful or frightening event.

The DEATH of a child, particularly during the first two years of life, was a reality that many families had to face. Common causes of death were gastrointestinal diseases, malnutrition, famine, and plagues. Except for extraordinary situations, Muslim jurists ruled that children were to be accorded all the formalities of a proper Muslim burial. Theological texts dealt with the fate of children in the afterlife, and the deep emotions caused by the loss of a child inspired authors to write books and poems in order to comfort bereaved parents.

Modernization projects launched during the last 150 years by Western colonial governments and reform-minded rulers of Muslim lands have contributed significantly to improving the quality of life for children in many of those countries. Primary and secondary schools were opened in cities and towns, allowing more girls and working-class children to gain knowledge and skills necessary to improve their social and economic status. Even children living in rural areas have gained access to education, and many have migrated to cities when schools were lacking in the countryside. Such changes have enabled many to loosen the bonds of dependence that linked them to their natal families. Better health and nutrition have helped lower infant mortality rates. Muslim majority countries in the Middle East, Asia, and Africa consequently experienced significant population growth in the latter half of the 20th century. For example, as infant mortality rates in countries such as EGYPT, IRAN, and BANGLADESH declined from around 200 per 1,000 in 1955 to around 35 per 1,000 in 2005, their populations increased dramatically. Egypt's population during this period jumped from 23 million to 77.5 million, Iran's from 19 million to 68 million, and Bangladesh's from 45.8 million to 144.4 million. At the same time, the populations of Muslim-majority countries have grown increasingly younger, unlike those of Europe and North America. In Egypt and Bangladesh, 33 percent are under the age of 14, while this number in Iran is 27 percent (compared to 20 percent in the United States and 18.4 percent in France). According to World Bank estimates, 36 percent of the population in the Middle Eastern and North African region as a whole is under the age of 15, compared to 16 percent among the countries of the European Union.

Although children have often benefited greatly from the changes modernization has brought to Muslim-majority countries, they have also suffered from them. They have become the innocent victims of the national, regional, and global conflicts that have shaken countries such as Iraq, Lebanon, Palestine, and Afghanistan. It is estimated that 500,000 Iraqi children died as a result of the economic sanctions leveled against SADDAM HUSAYN's government in the 1990s by the United Nations. On the other hand, radical Islamic organizations have recruited children and unemployed youths to serve as fighters or suicide bombers in some countries. Moreover, population growth, limited economic resources, and government inefficiency and corruption have also had detrimental effects on children in Muslim countries. International agencies and relief organizations, including a number of Islamic ones, have sometimes intervened to help children faced with the harmful effects of such developments, but the resources of these organizations are limited.

See also ABORTION; BIOGRAPHY; BIRTH RITES; CIRCUMCISION; FUNERARY RITUALS; *KUTTAB*.

Further reading: Hamid Ammar, *Growing Up in an Egyptian Village: Silwa, Province of Aswan* (1954. Reprint, London: Routledge & Kegan Paul, 1966); Elizabeth Warnock Fernea, ed., *Children in the Muslim Middle East* (Austin: University of Texas Press, 1995); Avner Giladi, *Children of Islam: Concepts of Childhood in Medieval Muslim Society* (New York: St. Martin's Press, 1992).

China

The People's Republic of China includes within its borders a substantial Muslim population. According to the 1990 census, there were 17,587,370 Muslims in China. Chinese-speaking Muslims, or Hui, numbered 8,602,978 and are the largest percentage of the Muslim population. The Hui can be found throughout China—there are large communities on the southern Chinese coast, in Guangdong and Fujian provinces, which had very early contact with Muslim sea traders. In Yunan province in southeast China, there is also a sizeable Muslim population. There are some quite different variations of belief and practice between these and the other Hui communities that live in close proximity with Han Chinese society and the Hui of Gansu and Ningxia provinces in the north. In these two provinces, Muslims constitute the majority of the population, and therefore Islamic social and cultural characteristics are stronger and more visible. Xinjiang, in Chinese Central Asia, is also a majority Muslim province. However, the Hui constitute a minority there, while mostly Turkic-speaking peoples dominate. In this last group, the majority are the Uyghurs, who numbered about 7,214,431 in 1990. There are also a large number of Kazakh, Kirghiz, Uzbek, and other Muslim ethnic groups in Xinjiang.

The influence of ISLAM spread in China following the conversion of the Mongol rulers of the 13th century. With the rise of the Qing dynasty in the 18th and 19th centuries, discrimination and persecution increased along with greater outside political, economic, and social control. During this period, there were prominent Muslim rebellions and attempts to create an Islamic state in Yunan as well as Xinjiang and Gansu. Sufi brotherhoods, in particular the Naqshabandis, played a large role in the rebellions. With the end of any central state control following the Nationalist Revolution in 1911, there were once again large-scale uprisings in Xinjiang, Gansu, and Ningxia, often pitting one Muslim ethnic group against another, with the Hui allying more often with the Han than with other Muslims. These uprisings ended as the Chinese Communist Party consolidated control over the region in the late 1940s and 1950s. The Communist state has recognized 10 separate Muslim nationalities that enjoy a greater degree of autonomy in areas where they are a minority. However, in Xinjiang, Han immigration has increased significantly, which has hindered the economic development of the indigenous population. This has brought some unrest to the region, leading to increased repression by the Chinese Communist authorities in their "war against terrorism."

See also CENTRAL ASIA AND THE CAUCASUS; COMMUNISM; NAQSHABANDI SUFI ORDER.

David Reeves

Further reading: Linda Benson, *The Ili Rebellion: The Moslem Challenge to Chinese Authority in Xinjiang 1944–1949* (Armonk, N.Y.: M. E. Sharpe, 1990); Dru C. Gladney, *Ethnic Identity in China: The Making of a Muslim Minority Nationality* (Fort Worth, Tex.: Harcourt Brace College Publishers, 1998).

Chiragh Ali (1844–1895) *19th-century Indian religious reformer and secularist thinker*

Chiragh Ali was a Kashmiri Muslim who served in the British government of north INDIA in his early career. In 1877, he was appointed to the court of the nizam (ruler) of Hyderabad, where he served as the revenue and political secretary. He was a close ally of SAYYID AHMAD KHAN (d. 1898), the leading advocate for modern Islamic reform in India after the 1857 uprising against British rule that resulted in the end of the MUGHAL DYNASTY and marked the demise of Muslim rule in that land. Ali is best known for books and essays that articulated the Aligarh program for Islamic modernization in the late 19th and early 20th centuries. He maintained that the QURAN was authoritative in matters of worship and morality but denied that it provided an infallible blueprint for government or legislation. He objected to British Orientalists, Christian missionaries, and Muslim traditionalists who claimed that Islam endorsed theocratic government (the combination of religion and the state) and that Islamic law was unchangeable. Instead, he insisted that Islamic government and the SHARIA were largely human creations that adapted to changing historical circumstances in different localities. His interpretation of JIHAD was that it was a defensive strategy used by MUHAMMAD and the first Muslims when threatened with attack; it was never intended to legitimate aggression in the name of religion. He was critical of British colonial rule in India, for he charged them with having turned the country into a great prison—a situation that would only bring about the "decay" of the people. He called for political liberty and thought it could best be achieved under the sovereignty of the Ottoman SULTAN, who at that time was trying to resuscitate the Ottoman Empire in order to hold off the European powers. This does not mean that he wanted a return to the old ways of Muslim rule in India, however. He charged that traditional Islamic legal rulings concerning government, slavery, concubinage, marriage, divorce, and the status of non-Muslims were not suited to the needs of modern Muslims, and he called for their revision or elimination. Ali recognized that his views were controversial but believed they provided a basis upon which Muslims could erect a platform for progressive change and freethinking in the modern era. His life's work, therefore, contributed significantly to the formation of the modern Islamic liberal tradition in South Asia.

See also ORIENTALISM; OTTOMAN DYNASTY; RENEWAL AND REFORM MOVEMENTS; SECULARISM.

Further reading: Aziz Ahmad, *Islamic Modernism in India and Pakistan, 1857–1864* (London: Oxford University Press, 1967); Chiragh Ali, "The Proposed Political, Legal, and Social Reforms." In *Modernist Islam, 1840–1940: A Source-Book,* edited by Charles Kurzman, 277–290 (New York: Oxford University Press, September 2002).

Chishti Sufi Order

The Chishtis are one of the largest Sufi brotherhoods in South Asia (INDIA, PAKISTAN, and BANGLADESH) and help give Islam in this region its distinctive identity. They take their name from a remote village called Chisht, which had been a Sufi center as early as the 10th century. It was Muin al-Din Chishti (d. 1236), a man from Chisht, who established the brotherhood in India. In genealogies of their Sufi masters, however, they trace their ancestry all the way back to MUHAMMAD (d. 632), ALI (d. 661), and the 11 other Shii imams and include such famous non-Indian Sufis as IBN AL-ARABI (d. 1240), RUZBIHAN BAQLI (d. 1209), and JALAL AL-DIN RUMI (d. 1273). After Muin al-Din and his contemporary, Bakhtiyar Kaaki (d. 1235), the Chishti spiritual lineages consist predominantly of Sufi masters born in India, which makes this order distinct from most other Sufi groups in the region.

The foremost Chishti ritual practice is the DHIKR (*zikr* in local dialects), as it is in other Sufi orders. The Chishti *dhikr* combines repeated pronouncements of the NAMES OF GOD (especially ALLAH,

Tomb of Shaykh Salim Chishti, Fatehpur Sikri, India (16th century) *(Juan E. Campo)*

samii "hearer," *basir* "seer," and *alim* "knower") with yogic forms of breath control, meditation, and other ascetic practices. The Chishtis included Hindi, Punjabi, and Persian formulas in their *dhikrs,* unlike other Sufi orders, particularly the Naqshbandis, who stress Arabic recitations. The most public forms of Chishti worship are musical audition (*samaa*) and pilgrimage to shrines of Chishti SAINTS. Unlike other Sufis who were suspicious of music's legality and influence on the soul, Chishtis embraced listening to MUSIC as a core practice for the attainment of spiritual ecstasy, if not a state of enduring ecstasy itself. Some have combined audition with bodily movement and dance. As a result of Chishti acceptance of musical audition as a legitimate spiritual practice, other Sufi brotherhoods in South Asia have also allowed

it. During the Middle Ages, these auditions were meant only for initiated Sufis, but in modern times both Sufis and non-Sufis attend them. They are called QAWWALI performances, and they are regularly held at the tombs of Chishti saints. These shrines are the focal points of pilgrimage, attracting pious visitors, men and WOMEN, Muslims and non-Muslims, from throughout India. The most celebrated shrine is that of Muin al-Din in AJMER, considered by many to be the MECCA of Indian Islam. Other major Chishti shrines are those of Farid al-Din Ganj-i Shakar (d. 1265) in Pakpattan, Pakistan, and NIZAM AL-DIN AWLIYA (d. 1325) in DELHI.

Since its foundation in 13th century India, the Chishti order has intentionally distanced itself from political authorities and dependence upon state patronage. Despite close ties to members of the MUGHAL DYNASTY, the ideal of separation from the state has prevailed, contributing to the order's ability to flourish in modern, secular India and to establish new roots in South Africa, Europe, and America. Today people around the world enjoy the musical heritage of the Chishtis through recordings of *qawwali* performances by artists such as Nusrat Fateh Ali Khan and the Sabri Brothers.

See also KHAN, INAYAT; NAQSHBANDI SUFI ORDER; SUFISM; *TARIQA; ZIYARA.*

Further reading: P. M. Currie, *The Shrine and Cult of Muin al-Din Chishti of Ajmer* (Delhi: Oxford University Press, 1989); Carl W. Ernst and Bruce B. Lawrence, *Sufi Martyrs of Love: The Chishti Order in South Asia and Beyond* (New York: Palgrave Macmillan, 2002).

Christianity and Islam

Islam was born into a world in which Christianity was quite dominant, although the Hejaz, where MECCA and MEDINA lie and where MUHAMMAD lived his life (ca. 570–632), apparently had more Jews than Christians. Polytheism, of course, was the most common religious characteristic of all in that specific environment, and it was primarily against that polytheism and idol worship that the QURAN, the message given to Muhammad, preached. JESUS, called "Isa" or al-Masih (the messiah), and the Christians are both mentioned repeatedly in the Quran. Jesus is affirmed as a divinely appointed messenger (*rasul*) who was given a message like that of the Quran. In the Quran, Christians are spoken of favorably in some contexts, as in Q 2:62, which says, "Those who believe, and those who follow Judaism, and the Christians (al-Nasara, the Nazarenes) and the Sabians, any who believe in God and the Last Day, and work righteousness, shall have their reward with their Lord; on them shall be no fear, nor shall they grieve."

But other verses suggest a polemical relationship, although that is much more in evidence with regard to the Jews, a situation made sensible by the significant Jewish population of Medina at the time that Muhammad and the early Muslims went to that town, and the fact that most of these Jews appear not to have been convinced of Muhammad's prophetic mission. Thus, in Q 2:120, we find the verse, "And the Jews will not be pleased with you, nor the Christians until you follow their religion. Say: Surely God's guidance is the [true] guidance. And if you follow their desires after the knowledge that has come to you, you shall have no guardian from God, nor any helper."

The Quran claims a direct link between Islam and ABRAHAM, thus bypassing Jewish and Christian claims to be linked to that great forebear of the monotheistic religions. For example, the Quran challenges Jews and Christians, saying, "You people of the Book, why are you so argumentative about Abraham, seeing that the Torah and the Gospel were only revealed after his time? Abraham was not a Jew, nor was he a Christian. He was a man of pure worship and a Muslim [or a submitter]" (Q 3:65, 67). More assertively, other verses state that the cultic worship around the KAABA in Mecca was founded by Abraham (Q 2:125).

The strongest Quranic polemic against Christian dogma concentrates on the Christian belief in the Trinity and the death and resurrection of Jesus. The Quran considers the Trinity to be an expression of polytheism and utterly rejects any ascription of divinity to Jesus. Christian belief in Christ's divinity is understood in the Quran to be in direct contradiction to the message preached by Jesus. Equally important, the Quran denies Jesus' death, saying, "They did not kill him, nor did they crucify him, but it was made to appear to them as such" (Q 4:157). Because these objections to the doctrines held by most Christians in the seventh century were so familiar from the previous centuries of Christological controversy, it appeared to John of DAMASCUS (d. ca.749), one of the fathers of the Greek church, that Islam was essentially a Christian "heresy," and he placed Islam at the end of the section on heresies in his great work, *De*

Fide Orthodoxa. The Quran also rejects monasticism, which had become a major expression of Christian piety and asceticism in the Middle East by that time.

Other than the adherents of Arabian polytheism, who were fought until they converted to Islam, non-Muslims within lands controlled by Muslim governments have historically been dealt with as *dhimmi*s, protected by the government and allowed freedom of religion so long as they paid a poll tax (JIZYA) and did not publicly offend Muslim sensibilities. Where Christianity had been deeply rooted before the coming of Islam, it generally has retained a presence. Thus, in the countries of the Fertile Crescent, such as IRAQ, SYRIA (including JORDAN, PALESTINE, and Lebanon), but also in EGYPT, there are strong Christian communities with historical ties to the Christian churches and communities that were present in the Middle East before the rise of Islam. This is also true of India, which has a Christian community tracing itself back to the first century and which has had an uninterrupted presence there. North Africa west of Egypt, on the other hand, witnessed a relatively quick, complete CONVERSION to Islam within a few centuries of its appearance, although Jewish communities continued to thrive there until the mid-20th century. In ANDALUSIA (Spain), Christians continued to thrive and partake of public life during the period of Muslim rule (711 to the final conquest of Granada in 1492). The Christian Arabs of Andalusia as well as Jews provided an important conduit for transferring the scientific and philosophical knowledge of Islamdom—far more sophisticated than that of Europe at the time—to the north.

In most Muslim-majority countries today, there are numerous Catholic, Orthodox, and Protestant churches. Even leaving aside the Protestant churches, there are as many as 20 Apostolic churches, depending on how they are counted. This is largely because, as a result of missionary efforts and splits along the way, a single, formerly "national" church may split numerous times.

Thus, for instance, the Assyrian Church of the East (found mainly in northern Iraq, southern TURKEY, Syria, IRAN, southwest INDIA, and now the United States), which has its own rite and independent hierarchy, has a Catholic counterpart, named the Chaldean Catholic Church. The Coptic Orthodox church of Egypt similarly has several counterparts, including the Melkites (in union with Constantinople), Coptic Catholics (Rome) and Protestant Coptic (Presbyterian). When, as in the last example, Protestant churches are included, the number of churches becomes extraordinarily difficult to count. In general, however, one can say that the churches divide as follows: 1) those that come out of the Assyrian Church of the East; 2) those that can be called the Orthodox churches of the East, who recognize the patriarch of Constantinople as *primus inter pares* (first among equals); 3) the Oriental Orthodox churches, such as the Coptic and Armenian, which share theological orientation and mutual recognition; 4) the various Catholic churches and Catholic counterparts of other churches (mainly quite recent in origin); and 5) Protestants of various denominations. Depending on how one defines the "Islamic world," there are as many as 47 million Christians today living in lands that are Muslim majority or have been historically vital centers of Islamic government and civilization, including India. The largest populations are in INDONESIA (19 million), followed by SUDAN (9.5 million) and Egypt (at least 4.5 million).

Thus, Christians have survived and sometimes thrived under Muslim rule, and in many cases, Christians were able to attain positions of great power and wealth in Muslim-majority lands. Two periods since the rise of Islam have seen Christians conquer Muslims within their heartlands. The first period is that of the CRUSADES and Reconquista. The Crusades were a series of expeditions (1095–1291) by European Christians to retake Jerusalem for Christianity and to fight Muslims in the Holy Land as part of a holy war blessed by the Catholic pope. The Crusades met with limited success and eventually led to the mobilization of a Muslim JIHAD to expel the "Franks." With their foreign ways and crudities so acutely observed by Muslim scholar-warriors such as Usama ibn Munqidh (d. 1188), the crusaders were always unlikely to survive, as indeed they did not. The Reconquista, on the other hand, succeeded in defeating the Arabo-Islamic statelets that took root in Andalusia and expelling Muslims and Jews for whom Andalusia was home. Those who stayed behind were forced to convert to Christianity.

In the modern period, beginning in the 18th century, Europeans, mainly Christians, came to rule over vast territories in which Muslims lived and that had formerly been ruled by Muslims. These included much of the Middle East, all of North Africa west of Egypt, the Indian subcontinent, and almost the entire continent of Africa, the eastern, western, and northern parts of which had large Muslim populations. For nearly 200 years, Muslims thus lived either in lands directly controlled by European countries or in ostensibly independent nations whose freedom was often held in check by European power (the Ottoman Empire, for example, or Iran). In every case, these colonial empires were undone by the end of World War II, but their impact remains profoundly felt in such things as their legal and political institutions, economic orientations, as well as the radical Islamist ideologies that have developed in part as a response to the European imperial project. While the Europeans did not always encourage missionary efforts, they also did not stop such activities, and thus one of the main encounters between Christianity and Islam in the modern period has been largely destructive. For one thing, this resulted in mutual animosities and divisions that have, ironically, made it more difficult (but not impossible) for Muslims to engage in the kind of critical examination of religious authority and knowledge that has had such radical effects on the relations between religion, society, and the state in the West. The Europeans often justified their rule on the basis of their superior scientific

St. Catherine's Monastery at Mount Sinai, Egypt. A mosque minaret stands behind the bell tower. *(Juan E. Campo)*

knowledge. The implicit or explicit blaming of Islam for the "backwardness" of Muslims has both led to increased Islamic radicalism and to fruitless apologetics. But this Christian missionary effort from the West has also made the situation of the native Christian communities of Muslim-majority countries more tenuous than it previously was.

Part of the modern condition is the rootlessness and change brought about by emigration, both voluntary and forced. A great many African Muslims were brought to the New World as slaves, and the wounds of this (at least partially) Muslim-Christian encounter have not properly healed. Voluntary emigration for the sake of economic opportunity and religious freedom has also been a part of the encounter, however, and this has been much more positive. Large communities in the Americas and even more significant ones in Europe are having the effect of changing the way Muslims experience and understand their religion as well as creating greater opportunity for interreligious communication and DIALOGUE (or conflict in some cases). New to interpreting approaches Islam and interpretations that take these new experiences into account are enriching the Muslim intellectual repertoire in ways that will almost certainly have great impact in the years to come. In light of this ongoing and increasing mingling of peoples and religions, a "clash of civilizations" between Islam and the West is actually very unlikely, although conflicts based on specific grievances in Muslim-majority countries are likely to continue to have an impact on interreligious relations.

See also COLONIALISM; *DHIMMI;* EUROPE; JUDAISM AND ISLAM; UNITED STATES; LATIN AMERICA.

John Iskander

Further reading: Talal Asad, *Formations of the Secular: Christianity, Islam, Modernity* (Stanford, Calif.: Stanford University Press, 2003); Richard W. Bulliet, *The Case for Islamo-Christian Civilization* (New York: Columbia University Press, 2006); Norman Daniel, *Islam and the West: The Making of an Image* (Oxford: Oneworld, 1993); Hugh Goddard, *A History of Christian-Muslim Relations* (Chicago: New Amsterdam Books, 2000); Tarif Khalidi, *The Muslim Jesus: Sayings and Stories in Islamic Literature* (Cambridge, Mass.: Harvard University Press, 2001).

cinema

Although motion picture technology first developed in EUROPE and the UNITED STATES during the late 19th and early 20th centuries, film production rapidly became a global phenomenon. It was first introduced into Muslim lands by Westerners, but by the 1930s and 1940s, native entrepreneurs had developed their own film industries, which really began to flourish after World War

II with the rise of newly independent nation-states. Except for SAUDI ARABIA, where movie theaters are banned because of the puritanical outlook of the Wahhabi Islam practiced there, the cinema became a popular pastime in many countries, especially among city dwellers. EGYPT, IRAN, and TURKEY have become major centers of film production in the Middle East. LEBANON, ALGERIA, Tunisia, INDONESIA, and MALAYSIA have also developed their own film industries. INDIA, where secular-minded Muslims are active in the cinema, produces more films than any country in the world. The following article discusses the Arab, Iranian, and Indian cinemas as well as representations of Arabs and Muslims in American and British films.

ARAB CINEMA

CAIRO is the Hollywood of the Arab world. Nearly 3,000 films have been produced in Egypt. No other Arab country comes close to this number. The first screenings of the French Lumière brothers' films took place in Alexandria in 1896. Egypt began producing its own films as early as 1909, but film production during the colonial period was dominated by European capital and often by European directors as well. Egypt was the only Arab country to establish a national film industry prior to its formal independence in 1952. Most other Arab countries did not develop a national cinema until the period of decolonization after World War II.

Arab cinema has been greatly influenced by Hollywood. American-made movies early on captured local markets in many Arab countries, Egypt included—as much as 80 percent of the screen time is monopolized by American film exports. However, Arab cinema also developed its own cinematic idioms and cultural nuances even as it adapted Hollywood plots and churned out low-budget comedies, musicals, and romantic dramas. The great Arab comic film actors such as Egyptians Ismail Yasin and Adel Imam and Syrian Durayd Laham were masters at slapstick humor, but they all employed their comic talents in films

Movie billboards in Cairo, Egypt. The billboard on the far left is for *Al-Mansi (The forgotten one),* featuring Adil Imam and Yusra. *(Juan E. Campo)*

that had a nationalist edge and socially critical content, which directly appealed to Arab popular audiences that had living memories of colonialism and foreign domination.

Arab cinema also developed a star system. Popular singers such as UMM KULTHUM, Shadya, and Abd al-Halim Hafiz promoted their musical artistry through cinema from the late 1930s through the 1960s and broadened their appeal throughout the Arab World. Egypt had its equivalent of Marilyn Monroe in Samya Gamal (1960s) and even its equal to actor-political activist Susan Sarandon in Yusra, who has fought censorship and championed Arab causes such as opposing foreign aggression against Iraq in the 1990s and supporting Palestinian rights.

The Arab world has produced an impressive array of directors who have mastered film language in a way that has created a body of serious artistic production that is of world-class quality. Perhaps the most renowned of these artist-directors is Egyptian Youssef Chahine (d. 2008), a Christian by heritage, whose work in the early 1950s launched the career of Omar Sharif and who continues to be prolific to this day (*Alexandria. . . . New York,* 2004). Since the 1980s in the era of globalization, European financing (especially French) has lent new life to an ailing Arab film industry and cultivated talented new directors such as Yousri Nasrallah (*Gate of the* Sun, 2004, Egypt), Nouri Bouzid (*Man of* Ashes, 1986, Tunisia), Moufida Tlatli (*Silence of the Palaces,*

1994, Tunisia), and Palestinian Elia Suleiman, whose film *Divine Intervention* won the Grand Jury Prize at the Cannes Film Festival in 2002.

Although Arab cinema, as elsewhere, is predominantly secular in outlook, Islamic subjects and themes often do occur in dramas and films on historical topics. Dramatic films usually affirm social virtues such as marital fidelity, respect for the FAMILY, charity, making an honest living, and defending the weak, while they also condemn immorality and criminal behavior. They include scenes of people at PRAYER, reciting the QURAN, visiting MOSQUES or shrines, and celebrating religious holidays. Moreover, a number of films have addressed hot-button socioreligious issues such as polygamy and divorce, criticizing aspects of Islamic family law as practiced in countries such as Egypt. Since the 1990s, Islamic radicalism has been critically examined in films such as Nader Galal's *The Terrorist* (Egypt, 1994) and Atef Hetata's *Closed Doors* (Egypt, 1999). Historical films have dealt with topics such as the CRUSADES (Youssef Chahine's *Al-Nasir Salah al-Din,* 1963) and the lives of famous Muslims, such as RABIA AL-ADAWIYYA (Egypt, 1955) and IBN RUSHD (Youssef Chahine's *Destiny,* Egypt, 1997).

IRANIAN CINEMA

The advent of cinema in Iran can be traced to the beginning of the 20th century with the inauguration of the first movie house in 1907. It was in the 1930s that cinema became a more serious enterprise with the establishment of the first film studio and the release of movies such as *The Brother's Revenge, Abi and Rabi,* and the *Lor Girl.* During this time, cinema aimed at entertaining city dwellers and concerned itself with topics such as the migration of villagers into the city and the transformation of traditional ethics into bourgeois values. For instance, *Rapacious,* released in 1934, was about a peasant who left his wife for a city woman. This decade witnessed the first Persian-language sound newsreel with Prime Minister Muhammad Ali Furughi (1887–1942) and

MUSTAFA KAMAL ATATURK (1881–1938). Another significant production in the 1930s was an adaptation from Ferdawsi's national epic the *Shahnamah,* "The Book of the Kings," which has traditionally fostered national pride among Iranians. It is safe to say that the birth of Iranian cinema is inseparable from the advent of modernity and its cultural manifestations in Iranian society.

In the next decades, Iranian cinema developed into a primarily commercial industry with a limited "art film" cinema that operated in its shadows. A favorite theme for this commercial cinema was Iranian patriarchal attitudes toward life, tradition, and gender. This was expressed in the genre *film jaheli,* a genre that was initiated by Ismail Kushan. In these films, the character of the working class or petit bourgeoisie was explored and celebrated. The male protagonist provided a caricature of the medieval practice of chivalry, in which honor was based on the chastity of a man's female relatives (sister, daughter, female cousins, etc). This theme dominated Iranian cinema of the 1960s. Another important theme at this time was the relationship between Iranians and Westerners. *Ibram in Paris* (1964) highlighted the difference between Iranians and Europeans.

The intellectual response to this commercial cinema is not limited to the production of art films. In 1971, Masoud Kimiai (b. 1941) undertook the production of *Dash Akul,* based on a modern classic short story with the same title by the acclaimed Iranian prose writer Sadiq Hidayat. The story is a psychological evaluation of the themes of chivalry, which are also expressed in the film's more commercial counterparts. In the 1960s, other art filmmakers such as Furugh Farrukhzad (1935–67) and Daryush Mehrjui (b. 1937), inspired by international cinema, made great contributions in their documentaries and surrealistic films. These filmmakers, along with others, developed the New Iranian Cinema as an alternative to commercial cinema.

With the establishment of the Islamic Republic of Iran in 1979 and its puritanical attitudes toward the arts, the prospects for Iranian cinema seemed murky and pessimistic. More than half the country's nearly 500 movie theaters were confiscated or closed down. Contrary to expectations, however, Iranian cinema in the past two and a half decades has developed into an international cinema with claims on artistic novelty. Today, filmmakers such as Abbas Kiarostami (b. 1945), Muhsin Makhmalbaf (b. 1957), and his young daughter Samira are familiar names to Iranian film viewers across the globe. Perhaps the religious revolution, followed by unforeseen conditions of strict censorship and oppression, actually inspired and compelled the creative work of these filmmakers and many others. The topics explored by the filmmakers of the post-1979 revolution era tackle the subtleties in the controversies that define the sociocultural life of Iranians today, such as war, the relations between the sexes, and the status of women. Furthermore, the vital and dynamic relationship between this cinema and its audience abroad has produced a range of new possibilities for artistic expression that was not evident in the decades before the revolution.

INDIAN CINEMA

The place Muslims occupy in Indian cinema is something of a conundrum, reflecting their vexed affiliations within South Asian modernity. If one focuses on the supposedly Hindi-language cinema based in Bombay, it is necessary to underscore the extensive influence of Urdu literature on both film dialogue and song lyrics. Before the partition of the country at the point of its independence from British rule in 1947, Lahore was also an important center for the production of Hindi-Urdu films. Already in the 1940s, Muslim producer-directors such as A. R. Kardar and Mehboob Khan had come into prominence in these two centers. As Bombay cinema was securing its genres and audiences and consolidating a national cinematic idiom, composers Ghulam Haider and Naushad were instrumental in laying down the conventions of a musical style that became the most identifiable trait of the industry.

The 1940s were also marked by a steady mounting of communal tensions and brutal riots, eventually leading to the creation of PAKISTAN. In the course of the mayhem, millions of people became homeless refugees; the early skirmishes over Kashmir in the late 1940s compounded the atmosphere of hatred and suspicion. Some Muslim actors took on Hindu names to ensure their acceptability. Thus, Mumtaz Jehan came to be known as Madhubala, while Yusuf Khan became famous as Dilip Kumar. Nargis, on the other hand, did not suffer any loss of popularity due to her openly Islamic identity, went on to play the title role in the landmark film *Mother India* (1957), and became a member of parliament in the 1970s. Other luminaries of the Bombay industry, including Ghulam Haider and singer Nurjehan, chose to move to Pakistan. Contemporary popular discourse, for instance in the anglophone magazine *Filmindia,* reflected the deep anxieties and ambivalences of a wounded social matrix, mourning the loss of creative agents and simultaneously denouncing them for their "betrayal."

Muslims who stayed on in India as part of a minority community faced prejudice and wariness. Even someone as respected as Dilip Kumar had to contend with aspersions and periodic witch hunts. The plight of the Muslim citizenry is thoughtfully documented in M. S. Sathyu's film *Garam Hawa* (1973), which, after initial difficulties with the censors, went on to win the highest national awards. At the end of this film, the young protagonist, Salim, chooses to stay on in India and finds his community in a leftist group. The narrative resolution clearly upholds a secular, class-based political agenda over communal politics founded on religious affiliations. The author of the original story, Ismat Chugtai, and the scriptwriter, Kaifi Azmi, were both associated with the Progressive Writers' Association and were stalwarts of modern Urdu literature. Azmi was also responsible for many superb song lyrics; his daughter, Shabana Azmi, became an important face of the so-called Indian New Wave of the 1970s (and is currently the most revered actress of the Indian screen and a social activist of international repute). Thus, Muslims maintained a strong creative presence in postpartition Indian cinema. The late Shahir Ludhianvi continues to be the most influential lyricist, and the late Mohammed Rafi remains, arguably, the most beloved male "playback singer."

Two major genres have focused primarily on Muslim life and culture: the Muslim "socials," which range from the reformist *Elaan* (1947) to the swooningly romantic *Chaudvin ka Chand* (1960); and spectacular historicals, which look back nostalgically to a glorious Islamic past (the caliphate, as in *Judgment of Allah* [1935]; the Delhi Sultanate, as in *Razia Sultan* [1983]; and the Mughal Empire, as in *Mughal e Azam* [1960]). In general, though, Muslim characters occupy peripheral roles in mainstream Bombay films: as sidekicks, smugglers, pimps, courtesans, and frequently blind fakirs, or minstrels. Of course, one can locate a few significant exceptions to this cinematic marginalization, such as *Coolie* (1983), starring the great Amitabh Bachchan.

In the late 1980s, as a resurgent right-wing nationalism centered on *hindutva,* or an essential Hinduness, gathered force, it became imperative for a relatively new group of filmmakers to explore the place of the *mussalman* within Indian society and polity. Saeed Mirza and Khaled Mohammed, for instance, addressed the perplexing question of Muslim-Indian identity in the aftermath of the destruction of the Babri mosque in December 1992 by the votaries of *hindutva* and the subsequent riots in Bombay in lyrical yet incisive films such as *Naseem* (1995) and *Fiza* (2000). Meanwhile, the community continues to be an indispensable and enigmatic presence in Bombay cinema. The three most popular actors of the past decade—Shah Rukh Khan, Salman Khan, Amir Khan—happen to be Muslims.

MUSLIMS IN BRITISH AND AMERICAN CINEMA

Arabs and Muslims have been represented in American and British films since the days of the silent movies. Although they have been stereotyped as villains, they have also been depicted as romantic leads (*The Sheik* [1921]), ARABIAN NIGHTS heroes (*The Thief of Baghdad* [1924 and 1940], *The Seventh Voyage of Sinbad* [1958], and *Aladdin* [1992]), victims of prejudice or senseless warfare (*A Passage to India* [1984], *Three Kings* [1999]), and harem princesses and bellydancers (*Lost in a Harem,* 1944). They have appeared as important secondary characters in adventure films such as *The Crusades* (1935), *Lawrence of Arabia* (1961), and *Robin Hood: Prince of Thieves* (1991). The depictions of Arabs and Muslims in these films often conform to romantic Western stereotypes about peoples of the Orient that began in the 19th century. In the late 1970s and 1980s, as the Middle East became a major focal point of American interests and suffered several intense regional wars, Arabs and Muslims began to be increasingly dehumanized and portrayed as terrorists, kidnappers, and greedy and corrupt OIL shaykhs. This is evident in such films as *Protocol* (1984), *Delta Force* (1986), *Not without My Daughter* (1990), *Navy SEALs* (1990), and *True Lies* (1994). However, there have also been a few English-language international films that present more favorable views of Arabs and Muslims, such as *The Message* (1976), an account of the life of Muhammad, and *Lion of the Desert* (1981), about the Libyan resistance to Italian occupation during the 1930s. These were both produced by Moustapha Akkad (d. 2005), a Syrian filmmaker.

See also HINDUISM AND ISLAM; ORIENTALISM.

Juan E. Campo, Firoozeh Papan-Matin (Iranian cinema), Garay Menicucci (Arab cinema), Bhaskar Sarkar (Indian cinema)

Further reading: General: Roy Armes, *Third World Film Making and the West* (Berkeley: University of California Press, 1987); John C. Eisele, "The Wild East: Deconstructing the Language of Genre in the Hollywood Eastern." *Cinema Journal* 41, 4 (2002): 68–94; Jack G. Shaheen, *Reel Bad Arabs: How Hollywood Vilifies a*

People (New York: Olive Branch Press, 2001); Arab Cinema: Walter Armbrust, *Mass Culture and Modernism in Egypt,* (Cambridge: Cambridge University Press, 1996); Ibrahim Fawal, *Youssef Chahine* (London: BFI Publications, 2001); Viola Shafik, *Arab Cinema: History and Cultural Identity* (Cairo: American University in Cairo Press, 1998); Iranian Cinema: Hamid Dabashi. *Close Up: Iranian Cinema, Past, Present, and Future* (New York: Verso, 2001); Richard Tapper, ed., *The New Iranian Cinema: Politics, Representation and Identity* (London: I.B. Tauris Publishers, 2002); Indian Cinema: Akbar S. Ahmed, "Bombay Films: The Cinema for Indian Society and Politics." *Modern Asian Studies* 26 (1992): 289–320; Tejaswini Ganti, *Bollywood: A Guidebook to Popular Hindi Cinema* (New York: Routledge, 2004); Ashish Rajadhyaksha and Paul Willemen, *Encyclopedia of Indian Cinema,* 2d ed. (New Delhi: Oxford University Press, 1999).

circumcision (Arabic: *khitan* for males; *khafd* for females; *tahara* for both males and females)

Male circumcision is a surgical procedure that involves removing the foreskin of the penis. It has been widely practiced among indigenous tribal peoples of Africa and AUSTRALIA and among members of specific religious communities, especially Jews, Christians, and Muslims. Today many people think it is done for purposes of hygiene, but this explanation is disputed, and it does not withstand empirical scrutiny in most instances. Ethnographic evidence suggests that, in fact, it is performed for various reasons, depending on context. In many tribal societies, it is done at puberty as a male rite of passage into adulthood. In biblical tradition, circumcision is the sign of a COVENANT (contract) between God, ABRAHAM, and his descendants, the Hebrews. In Islam, male circumcision is almost universally practiced as a form of bodily purification. Only in some Muslim cultures is it a rite of passage to adulthood. Also, in contrast to the Judaic form, it is never mentioned in the Muslim HOLY BOOK, the QURAN,

nor is it considered to be the sign of a covenantal relationship between God and Muslims.

Scholars have found evidence that Arabs practiced circumcision before Islam's appearance and think that it later continued as an accepted practice in the early Muslim community. This explanation by itself does not account for the persistence of the custom nor its acceptance by non-Arab Muslims, who now constitute perhaps 80 percent of the world's Muslim population. Although circumcision is not mentioned in the Quran, it is mentioned in the HADITH, oral reports about what MUHAMMAD and his companions said and did that were transmitted, collected, and studied by pious Muslims in order help regulate Muslim affairs in the newly emerging Islamic empire. What the hadith do is establish male circumcision as an acceptable Muslim practice. According to one hadith, circumcision is one of five acts (along with trimming the mustache, shaving pubic hair, plucking hair from the arm pits, and clipping fingernails) for which humans have a natural predisposition (*fitra*). Other hadiths report that Abraham, the sacred ancestor of Jews, Christians, and Muslims, had circumcised himself. In the context of the SHARIA, Muslim jurists have ruled that it is either a required (*wajib*) or a recommended practice (SUNNA). In legal manuals, it is treated as a form of ritual purification, called *tahara*, that puts the body of the individual into the proper condition for worship.

Circumcision is performed by doctors at birth in hospitals and clinics today, but in many Muslim cultures a barber traditionally performs it at some time between the seventh day after birth and puberty, depending on local practice. In TURKEY, there are clinics where circumcisers are trained in the appropriate surgical techniques, and boys are circumcised at the age of six or seven. Large family celebrations with feasting, MUSIC, Quran recitation, and visits to nearby saint shrines often accompany the event. In cases in which the family has a limited income, the circumcision celebration may be combined with a marriage ceremony so as to minimize expenses. The circumcision may even be called a "wedding" or be understood as a milestone on the road to marriage. Uncircumcised converts to Islam may be required to be circumcised, but there are different opinions about this.

Female circumcision, or clitoridectomy, is called "female genital mutilation" (FGM) by HUMAN RIGHTS advocates because of the physical and emotional damage it can do to the patient. It is not as widely practiced among Muslims as is male circumcision, but it appears to be an ancient custom that is especially prevalent in sub-Saharan and northeast Africa. Christians and followers of other religions in that region as well as Muslims practice it. The minimal form of female circumcision, which is ruled to be obligatory by some Muslim jurists, involves removal of the tip of the clitoris. There are more extreme forms, however, that involve the entire female genital area. These procedures are not endorsed by most jurists and appear to be governed by local customs. Midwives, barbers, and female healers usually perform female circumcision with the approval of female relatives of the patient. Infection rates are high, and there can be serious complications. Like male circumcision, the procedure is considered by its practitioners to be a kind of purification that helps prepare girls for their eventual marriage. Unlike male circumcision, however, it is not accompanied by large family celebrations.

See also BIRTH RITES; WOMEN.

Further reading: Abu Bakr Abd al-Razzaq, *Circumcision in Islam.* Translated by Aisha Bewley (London: Dar al-Taqwa, 1998); John G. Kennedy, "Circumcision and Excision Ceremonies." In *Nubian Ceremonial Life,* edited by John G. Kennedy, 151–170 (Cairo: American University in Cairo Press, 1978); Nahid Touba, *Female Genital Mutilation: A Call for Global Action* (New York: Women, Inc., 1993).

cities

The history of ISLAM as a religion and a civilization is one that is centered on urban life and institu-

tions, contrary to stereotypes that exaggerate the importance of deserts and nomadic pastoralism. Muslims based their first empires in the same lands where the ancient Mesopotamians and Egyptians built the first cities in history and where Hellenistic cities flourished after the conquests of ALEXANDER THE GREAT in the fourth century B.C.E. The lives of MUHAMMAD and the first Muslims were lived primarily in the towns of MECCA and MEDINA, located in the Hijaz region of the arid Arabian Peninsula. The impact of these two cities on Islam is reflected in the QURAN itself, which distinguishes between Meccan and Medinan chapters. Mecca's importance is also underscored in the FIVE PILLARS of Islam, which require that Muslims face toward that city's Sacred Mosque when they do their daily prayers and that they must perform the *hajj* there at least once in their lifetimes if they are able.

During their early conquests, Arab Muslim armies occupied ancient cities and towns of the Middle East, such as JERUSALEM, DAMASCUS, and Aleppo in SYRIA, Alexandria in EGYPT, Nishapur and Balkh in IRAN, and Samarqand in Central Asia. They did the same when they penetrated the Iberian Peninsula, where they settled in the old Roman cities of CORDOBA, Seville, and GRANADA. In many regions of the empire, they built new garrison towns, some of which grew into major urban centers such as Fustat in Egypt, Tunis and FEZ in North Africa, Basra and Kufa in Iraq, and Shiraz in Iran. They built the legendary city of BAGHDAD in IRAQ in the eighth century, and later, when Muslim armies invaded northern India in the 12th century, they founded the fortress city of DELHI. All of these cities served as important political, cultural, religious, and economic centers. People of different ethnicities, religions, and social classes interacted in them on a daily basis.

In an important 10th-century topographic encyclopedia, al-Muqaddasi (also known as al-Maqdisi, d. ca. 990) described hundreds of cities and towns in Muslim lands from ANDALUSIA to Central Asia. These urban systems were connected by trade routes that spanned mountains, deserts, river lands, and sometimes seas, forming complex spatial hierarchies, organized vertically from the local fortress or commercial center to the district capital, the provincial capital, and transregional metropolis. Some of these cities had specialized functions, such as the holy cities of Mecca, Medina, Jerusalem, and KARBALA; the commercial centers of Aleppo (in Syria) and Fustat; and the palace cities of Baghdad, Samarra (in Iraq), CAIRO, and Madinat al-Zahra (next to Cordoba). A number of cities became famous as centers of learning and scholarship, such as Baghdad, Nishapur, Cairo, and Cordoba. Najaf in Iraq and Qumm in Iran became major centers of learning for the Shia. All cities were dependent on nearby agricultural lands and water systems, and they benefited from symbiotic relations with BEDOUIN and other nomadic peoples who provided pastoral animal products, caravan transport, and often warriors for the army. Urban populations varied in size from a few thousand for the smaller settlements to nearly a million in medieval Baghdad, Cairo, and Cordoba at their height, far exceeding the populations of European cities at the time. Famines, plagues, droughts, wars, and invasions severely affected city life, causing population levels to fluctuate; smaller towns and cities were often abandoned in such situations. IBN KHALDUN (d. 1406), the famous medieval philosopher of history, pointed out that city dwellers became unhealthy because of their luxurious diets and lack of exercise compared to nomadic peoples, who were more abstemious and physically fit.

Typical features in the medieval Islamicate urban landscape were the Friday MOSQUE, permanent marketplace, palace complex or fortress, public bath, and residential quarters. Other important architectural features were shrines containing relics of holy men and women, public fountains, caravanserais, religious colleges, and Sufi hospices. Most cities also had non-Muslim religious structures such as churches and synagogues. Streets were typically narrow and winding. Cem-

eteries were usually located on the outer edges of the inhabited areas. Unlike the Greco-Roman Hellenistic cities that preceded them, Islamicate cities did not have theaters, coliseums, or gridlike street patterns.

Cities in Muslim lands have undergone major transformations in the modern era. Colonization resulted in the creation of European-style quarters and suburbs that contrasted greatly with the old medieval cities. New street patterns, architectural styles, and building materials were introduced by colonial architects and native ones who emulated the West. Electric lighting, motorized transport, and modern communications enhanced the quality of life for many urban dwellers during the 20th century. Several of these cities, such as Cairo, ISTANBUL, and New Delhi have become cosmopolitan centers of global reach and importance, where modern skyscrapers stand next to medieval heritage sites and buildings displaying modern revivals of traditional architectural styles. On the other hand, new educational and employment opportunities, improved health services, land reform, and mechanization have resulted in major population shifts from the countryside to the city. As a consequence, urban populations increased dramatically during the latter part of the 20th century, placing great strains on the urban infrastructure and city services. Millions of people living in densely populated urban shanty towns attached to the older quarters or juxtaposed to upper-income and business districts find themselves faced with low incomes or no jobs, substandard housing and infrastructure, and poor schooling and health care. These slums can be found in such major cities as Rabat (Morocco), Cairo, Beirut, Baghdad, Tehran, Karachi, and Dhaka and contribute to the population of disaffected youths who become recruits for Islamic organizations and extremist movements.

The metropolitan areas with the largest populations in Muslim countries today are greater Cairo (est. 16.8 million, 2008), Jakarta (Indonesia) (13.1 million, 2005), Dhaka (Bangladesh)

(12.5 million, 2005), Karachi (Pakistan) (11.8 million, 2005), Istanbul (Turkey) (9.8 million, 2005), and Tehran (Iran) (8.6 million, 2005).

See also ARCHITECTURE; BAZAAR; CAMEL; CEMETERY; COLONIALISM; HOUSES; MADRASA.

Further reading: Albert Hourani, *A History of the Arab Peoples* (Cambridge, Mass.: Harvard University Press, 1991), 109–146; F. E. Peters, *Jerusalem and Mecca: The Typology of the Holy City in the East* (New York: New York University Press, 1986); Shams al-Din al-Muqaddasi (al-Maqdisi), *The Best Divisions for Knowledge of the Regions,* trans. Basil A. Collins (Reading, U.K.: Garnet, 2001); Paul Wheatley, *The Places Where Men Pray Together: Cities in Islamic Lands, Seventh through the Tenth Centuries* (Chicago: University of Chicago Press, 2001)

citizenship

The idea that identity is inextricably linked with a given territory or land develops with the appearance of the modern nation-state of 17th-century Europe. Being French or Spanish, for example, began to reflect not only a certain lineage or a set of cultural habits, but most importantly the simple fact of having been born in a given geographic space. As the model of the modern state spread to other parts of the world through European colonization of parts of Africa, Asia, and the entire Western hemisphere, traditional identities and affiliations began to change. This is especially true in lands where the majority of inhabitants were Muslim. In fact, the effects of changing identities and affiliations in the Muslim lands brought by COLONIALISM are still felt today, as seen in the transnational composition of many Islamist movements. Central to these changes is the idea of citizenship, or the bestowal of an official national identity on an individual by a government.

Prior to the postcolonial states found in many parts of the Muslim world, identity hinged on kinship relations and the idea of the UMMA, or the community of Muslims. For the majority Sunni Muslims, after MUHAMMAD's death in 632 a CALIPH led the community, at least symbolically, until the office's abolition in 1924. Regardless of where an individual is born or what language they speak, as long as they are born as a Muslim or convert to Islam they are part of the UMMA. Historically, in most cases only members of the *umma* were subject to Islamic law, even if non-Muslims—or *dhimmis*—lived in areas ruled by Muslim leaders. Otherwise, non-Muslims, and particularly Jews, Christians, and in some cases Hindus, lived according to their own legal traditions. Although a territorial element can be found in the Islamic legal designations *dar al-Islam* (abode of Islam) and *dar al-harb* (abode of war), these came into effect only when Muslims came into contact with large non-Muslim populations, such as occurred through conquest or trade. Individual identity, however, depended on one's religious affiliation. As bounded political territories, modern states of the Muslim world in general and, more particularly, the idea of citizenship, changed not only local political organization but also grounds for legal AUTHORITY and for individual identity.

See also DAR AL-ISLAM AND DAR AL-HARB; LAW, INTERNATIONAL.

Caleb Elfenbein

Further reading: Benedict Anderson, *Imagined Communities* (New York: Verso, 1991); John L. Esposito, *Islam: The Straight Path* (New York: Oxford University Press, 1998); Albert Hourani, *A History of the Arab Peoples* (Cambridge, Mass.: Harvard University Press, 1991).

civil society

Civil society is located between the intimate-private spheres of familial life and the various organs of the state: administrative, legislative, judicial, and economic. In large measure, it is beholden to those selfsame institutions, for the state serves to "frame" or structure social relations outside its immediate purview (for example, through the legal system). The nature, complexity, and differentiation of power relations, nodes, and networks account for the ongoing interdependence between the state and civil society. The institutions, associations, organizations, gathering places, and social movements on the terrain of civil society act as a kind of schoolhouse for DEMOCRACY or as a dress rehearsal for more traditional forms of political participation. While authoritarian regimes routinely attempt to "depoliticize" or "privatize" relations within society, the modern state finds it difficult to implement this divide-to-conquer strategy. It does not have the capacity to become truly totalitarian, to manipulate and control the entire spectrum of activities and dialogue constitutive of the various "publics" in civil society.

The moral, political, and cultural capacities of actors in civil society are based on norms of trust, reciprocity, friendship, commitment, and the like that are metaphorically termed "social capital." The strength and circulation of this social capital signals both the desire and potential for democratization and may be the very locus of "democracy" in societies with governments that suffer from democracy deficits.

In the Middle East, civil society consists of "a mélange of associations, clubs, guilds, syndicates, federations, unions, parties and groups [that] come together to provide a buffer between state and citizen." (Norton, 1:7). Professional associations of doctors, lawyers, engineers, and teachers are particularly strong in EGYPT, TUNISIA, MOROCCO, SUDAN, and among the Palestinians. These syndicates are often the leading edge of civil society owing to the high level of education, political awareness, and financial resources of their members. In Egypt, members of the MUSLIM BROTHERHOOD are elected majorities on the boards of most of these associations.

Among the Arab GULF STATES, Kuwait's civil society deserves mention, with its fairly free press, professional associations, and cultural clubs. In particular, the reception areas (*diwaniyyah*) in peoples' homes function as gathering places where men socialize and discuss a variety of topics, political and otherwise. Kuwaiti women have started their own *diwaniyyahs*, and it was the *diwaniyyah* that gave birth to the country's prodemocracy movement in the 1990s. While Kuwait's constitution provides the framework for its civil society, the state has never recognized independent voluntary organizations. TURKEY, with its secular state, has a yet more energetic civil society, much of it Islamic. Still, its Islamist members possess "contradictory motivations and goals and sometimes radically differing interpretations of fundamental religious principles and political platforms" (White, 6). When the Turkish military regime crushed the left in the early 1980s, Muslim activists filled the void; they conducted charitable, humanitarian, and educational projects while agitating for economic and social justice. The electoral success of the Islamic Justice and Development Party provides evidence of the ability of Muslims to effectively organize and mobilize others in civil society.

Finally, note should be made of the attraction of militant Islamist groups such as HIZBULLAH and HAMAS. These groups draw young recruits and galvanize popular support for several reasons, not the least of which is their "provision of substantial social services and charitable activities, from education to housing and financial support of the members of families killed, wounded, or detained by authorities." (Esposito and Burgat, 76)

See also AUTHORITY; CONSTITUTION.

Patrick O'Donnell

Further reading: John L. Esposito and François Burgat, eds., *Modernizing Islam: Religion in the Public Sphere in Europe and the Middle East* (New Brunswick, N.J.: Rutgers University Press, 2003); John Keane, *Civil Society: Old Images, New Visions* (Stanford, Calif.: Stanford University Press, 1998); Augustus Richard Norton, ed., *Civil Society in the Middle East.* 2 vols. (Leiden: E.J. Brill, 1995–1996); Jenny B. White, *Islamist Mobilization in Turkey: A Study in Vernacular Politics* (Seattle: University of Washington Press, 2002); Carrie Rosefsky Wickham, *Mobilizing Islam: Religious Activism and Political Change in Egypt* (New York: Columbia University Press, 2002).

clitoridectomy   *See* CIRCUMCISION.

coffee

Coffee is one of the most widely consumed brewed beverages in the world today, especially by adults. It is a stimulating drink made from husks and kernels obtained from berries of the coffee tree that are dried, roasted, ground, mixed with water, and then lightly boiled. Its story is interwoven with the history of Islamic religion, the cultures of the Middle East and Africa, and their early encounters with modern Europe. The story is partly reflected in the English word *coffee* itself, which came into the language in the 17th century from Arabic *qahwa* by way of Turkish *kahveh* (the Arabic letter w is pronounced as a v in Turkish). The word *café* came into English via Arabic, Turkish, and then French. Even the scientific name for the tree that produces the most commonly used coffee berry, *Coffea Arabica,* suggests the beverage's historical connection to the Arabian Middle East. The tree was originally native to Ethiopia in Northeast Africa, but it began to be cultivated in Arabia during the 14th or 15th century. In order to better understand the history of coffee, one must trace how a berry native to Africa came to be cultivated and used by ARABS to make a tasty beverage called *qahwa,* which then became a favorite drink in Ottoman TURKEY and EUROPE, and then a global commodity grown in tropical regions of Southeast Asia, Africa, the Caribbean, and especially in LATIN AMERICA (the center of coffee production today).

There are several imaginative accounts about the discovery of coffee. The most familiar tale among Europeans and Americans is that of the Ethiopian goatherd who one day observed his goats dancing about after eating coffee berries. He tried the beans himself, found them to be invigorating, and shared his discovery with a "monk," who then roasted them and concocted a brew that allowed him and other monks to stay awake for their nightly PRAYERS. A more historically valid account is provided by Abd al-Qadir al-Jaziri, a 16th-century Muslim jurist, in a book he wrote about coffee drinking. He mentioned reports about a 15th-century Sufi shaykh known as al-Dhabhani from YEMEN who observed people using *qahwa* for medicinal purposes during a visit to Ethiopia. Upon returning to Yemen, he also benefited from using it, and he recommended it as a beverage to his Sufi brothers. They found that it gave them more vigor and helped them stay awake on nights when they had long prayer vigils and DHIKR rituals. There are yet more accounts about coffee's origins, but they generally agree that cultivating and drinking it began with the Sufis of Yemen. By 1511, it had reached the holy cities of MECCA and MEDINA, and then Yemeni Sufis introduced it to students and scholars at AL-AZHAR in CAIRO. In the mid-1500s, coffee became a popular beverage in the cities of SYRIA and Turkey, especially in the Ottoman capital, ISTANBUL. It later reached IRAQ, IRAN, and INDIA with the help of pilgrims returning home from the HAJJ to Mecca.

The coffee prepared in most of the Middle East is served very black with the grounds still in it; they are allowed to settle to the bottom of the cup before drinking. The first places to serve it to paying customers appear to have been taverns where wine was also available. In the 16th and 17th centuries, it began to be served at coffeehouses and streetside stalls in many Middle Eastern cities, where European travelers first began to notice it. According to an 18th-century French travel account, "All sorts of people come to these places, without distinction of religion or social position; there is not the slightest bit of shame in entering such a place, and many go there simply to chat with one another" (Hattox, 94). Storytellers and poets entertained coffeehouse customers with folk tales and epics about famous Muslim warriors or, in the case of Iran, Persian kings and princes. Today Middle Eastern men still frequent neighborhood coffeehouses to do business; join friends to play cards, backgammon, and chess; listen to the radio; and watch soccer matches on television. At home, Middle Eastern women prepare and serve coffee to guests and friends. Also, in almost any gathering of women, there are several who offer to tell friends' fortunes by reading the patterns of the fine black coffee sediment created when the empty cups are turned upside down, then right side up again.

Some Muslim religious and political authorities attempted to either outlaw coffee drinking or close coffeehouses as they became more and more popular in the 16th century. There were suspicions that coffee was an intoxicating beverage and that it should therefore be banned like alcoholic drinks, which are forbidden according to Islamic DIETARY LAWS. Religious conservatives also wanted it banned because they believed it was a harmful innovation (BIDAA), not explicitly permitted by the QURAN and HADITH. Coffeehouses were suspect because immoral activities reportedly occurred there. Also, some government officials became concerned because of the seditious talk and plots that might be hatched when men gathered to drink coffee. None of these efforts to prohibit coffee succeeded, however, as any visitor to the Middle East today can see with his or her own eyes.

The coffee trade was originally in the hands of Muslim merchants working out of the port of Mocha (al-Mukha) in Yemen, from which the best coffees originally came. Some types of coffee still carry the name *mocha*. Before the end of the 18th century, two things happened to end the Muslim monopoly on coffee cultivation and trade. First, the Europeans had not only acquired a taste for coffee themselves, but they had successfully introduced coffee cultivation to their colonies in the New World and tropical Asia. Muslim merchants lost access to the European market, and they had to compete against the lower prices offered by European merchants. Second, more and more of the world's maritime commercial traffic fell into the hands of Europeans; even the port of Mocha was opened to Dutch, French, and British sailing vessels. Although coffee is still produced in Yemen, most of the coffee consumed in the Middle

Umm Kulthoum Café, Cairo, Egypt *(Juan E. Campo)*

East and other parts of the world comes from Latin America (especially Brazil). Coffee drinking in the United States began in the days of the British colonies, but it did not become a popular beverage until after the Boston Tea Party of 1773, when Americans boycotted British tea and drank coffee instead.

See also FOOD AND DRINK; SUFISM.

Further reading: Eric Hansen, "Yemen's Well-Traveled Bean." *Saudi Aramco World* 48, no. 5 (September/October 1997): 2–9; Ralph S. Hattox, *Coffee and Coffeehouses: The Origin of a Social Beverage in the Medieval Near East* (Seattle: University of Washington Press, 1985); Bennett Alan Weinberg and Bonnie K. Bealer, *The World of Caffeine: The Science and Culture of the World's Most Popular Drug* (New York: Routledge, 2001).

colonialism

Colonialism is a historical process whereby one state subdues another state or territory for political and economic advantage. In addition to the use of armed force, colonialism usually involves the establishment of a colonial government and migration to the new territories by settlers who occupy the most productive land and control important sectors of the region's society and economy. Ancient empires such as those of Greece and Rome engaged in colonial practices, and so did medieval ones, including the Islamicate empires. But historians more often associate colonialism with the establishment of modern European empires around the world between the 16th and 20th centuries. Colonial acts of conquest and exploitation of foreign lands and peoples have been justified by colonizers in terms of higher principles or values, such as a "civilizing mission" or a "white man's burden" to improve life for colonized people, reason (over tradition and superstition), and liberty from despotism. As a consequence, colonized peoples may find themselves driven out of their homelands, absorbed into the new colonial order, or compelled to adopt anticolonial and revolutionary strategies of resistance. In colonial contexts, religion has proven to be a tool for both the colonizing powers, who use it to convert and control their colonial subjects, and their indigenous supporters and opponents, who find it a source of strength and inspiration in defense of their values and ways of life.

In Muslim lands, colonization occurred when successive waves of European explorers, soldiers, merchants, administrators, and missionaries arrived between the 16th and 20th centuries. Superior weapons technology helped facilitate their colonial undertakings. By the mid-20th century, some 90 percent of the Muslim world had fallen under direct colonial control. People living in other regions, such as the Hijaz in western Arabia, TURKEY, PERSIA, and AFGHANISTAN, witnessed indirect forms of European colonial involvement. Aside from the conquest of ANDALUSIA in the 15th century, one of the earliest instances of colonization occurred when the army of the Russian czar overran the Tatar khanate (principality) of Kazan on the Volga River in 1552. Tatar Muslims were uprooted from their homes, fertile lands were transferred to Russian settlers, and the region was opened to evangelization by Orthodox Christian missionaries. The conquest of other Muslim territories in Astrakhan and western Siberia soon followed. By the end of the 19th century, the Russian empire had extended its control to the Caucasus and Central Asia.

Many European powers competed with each other to establish colonies in Muslim lands. After Napoleon tried and failed to establish a French presence in Egypt in 1798, the French turned to North Africa, where ALGERIA, TUNISIA, and MOROCCO became French colonial territories between 1830 and 1900. By 1914, France had won footholds in western and equatorial Africa. The English East India Company, a merchant venture, was the instrument by which Great Britain was able to gain nearly total hegemony in South Asia (greater INDIA and Sri Lanka) and the Persian Gulf by the end of the 19th century. The British Crown established direct rule in India after smashing the uprising of 1857, and it created protectorates with all the major GULF STATES (excluding Iran) by 1900. Britain occupied EGYPT in 1882 to guarantee access to the newly constructed Suez Canal, its lifeline to India. In 1914, Nigeria became a British colony and protectorate, as did part of the Horn of Africa. At the end of World War I, France and Britain took control of former Ottoman territories in SYRIA and IRAQ, including what is now Lebanon, ISRAEL, PALESTINE, and JORDAN. Not to be outdone, Italy attempted to establish colonial footholds in Libya and the Horn of Africa in the 1930s, but these efforts were cut short by World War II.

Desire to control the spice trade drew both Britain and the Netherlands to Southeast Asia in the 17th century. After first obtaining trading privileges from local Muslim rulers, they competed with each other to monopolize the region's economic and political affairs. The Dutch completed their hegemony over what is now Indonesia during the 18th century, while the British colonized the Malay Peninsula in the 19th century. The Spanish, following upon the success of their New World conquests, began colonizing the Philippines in the late 16th century. They halted the Islamization this island region was undergoing at that time and retained the Philippines as a

Crown colony until it became a possession of the United States in 1898.

It is difficult to overestimate how deeply European colonialism changed life wherever it reached in the world. Native and traditional forms of government, subsistence, commerce, and education were replaced and transformed. Social institutions and cultural practices were reshaped and often redefined in new frameworks of thought and action acquired from the West. Western powers such as the French attempted to rule their colonies with their own administrators, as the Spanish and British had done in the New World. Greatly outnumbered by the African and Asian populations, however, Europeans realized that they would have to shift to a policy of ruling in cooperation with native leaders. This is the way the British governed India and Egypt. Native elites served as bridgeheads for introducing Western reforms into their countries and for transferring natural resources and wealth away from them. They were educated in local schools featuring new Western curricula, and they studied abroad in European schools and academies. Such changes caused deep cleavages in colonial societies, which were once defined by close ties of language, kinship, reciprocity, and patronage. Colonial cities such as CAIRO, FEZ, and New DELHI reflected these new divisions in their layouts. Traditional residential and commercial quarters were separated from and surpassed by new urban districts with their European-style buildings and broad boulevards. Indigenous peoples nevertheless benefited from colonization as health and housing conditions improved, new employment opportunities arose, and LITERACY spread from the select few to the populace at large. Such developments helped pave the way for participation of more people in public life and self-governance.

Colonialism also had a marked impact on Islam. Muslim religious leaders led anticolonial resistance movements in French Algeria, the Russian Empire's Caucasus region, Dutch Indonesia, the Anglo-Egyptian Sudan, British Somalia, and Italian LIBYA. These movements failed in the short run, but they were incorporated into the histories of the nation-states that emerged in the formerly colonized territories during the 20th century. Pan-Islamism, an attempt to reunite Muslims under a revived Ottoman CALIPHATE in the late 19th century, was another way in which Muslims attempted to oppose colonial incursions into their territories. This movement died when the caliphate was officially abolished by the secular government of the new Republic of Turkey in 1924. One of the most famous modern Islamic movements was the MUSLIM BROTHERHOOD of Egypt. It began as a social and religious revitalization movement in 1928, but it became a militant opponent of the British and Zionist Jews who created Israel in 1948. The brotherhood joined with secular Arab nationalists to overthrow the British-backed monarchy in 1953, which resulted in the creation of the Egyptian Republic.

The success of European colonization—together with the decline of the Ottoman, Persian, and Mughal Empires—created a sense of crisis in Muslim societies. The age-old privileges of their religious authorities, the ULAMA, were undermined by the creation of secular schools, the spread of literacy and European languages, and the introduction of Western law codes bypassing the SHARIA. In response, religious revival and reform movements, supported and led by the ulama, swept through much of the Muslim world. Revivalists sought to uphold and defend essential Islamic teachings, emphasizing literalistic interpretations of the Quran and hadith, together with adherence to the FIVE PILLARS, family law, and other prescribed religious practices. Meanwhile, reform-minded modernists, often with the approval of colonial authorities, sought to demonstrate that Islam conformed to the principles of Western reason and science. Revivalists and reformers alike declared war on religious beliefs and practices they considered to be corrupt innovations (BIDAA) and superstitions. For many of them, this meant turning against popular Sufism and the worship of saints. It also meant questioning the validity of traditional FIQH (jurisprudence), and turning to IJTIHAD (individual legal reasoning) for the interpretation of Islam's legal requirements and prohibitions. Such developments not only helped Muslims adapt to the rapid changes their societies were undergoing, but they also helped defend them from Christian missionaries and foreign governors who wanted to convert and rule them.

None of these developments escaped notice of the Europeans. A new branch of knowledge about Middle Eastern and Islamicate societies called ORIENTALISM was born in the colonial era. It involved the study of the languages, institutions, history, and religions of colonized subjects in order to understand them and govern them more effectively. In India, the British studied Muslim and Hindu laws in order to codify them and use them to help administer the country. The French collected extensive information about Sufi brotherhoods in North Africa in order to identify resistance leaders and enlist cooperation of religious authorities. Likewise, the Dutch monitored the flow of Indonesian pilgrims to and from Mecca, suspecting they were involved in anticolonial movements. The scientific study of the Middle East and Islam, however, was not only for the pragmatic purpose of colonial governance. It also was driven by a curiosity about the origins of Western civilization. Gaining knowledge about the Orient was a way for Europeans to create knowledge about themselves and, aided by theories of race and civilizational progress, to represent themselves as better and as more advanced than non-Europeans.

The golden age of European colonialism was brought to an end in 1945 by World War II, which had devastated the populations of Europe and loosened the hold of the colonial powers over African, Asian, and Middle Eastern peoples. Nevertheless, colonialism has left a profound imprint on the world and on Muslims, one that is still very much in evidence in the early 21st century. Many Muslims today consider themselves to be citizens of nation-states that were created in the 20th century, and the boundary lines that define these countries were drawn by the colonial powers or by native elites to whom they delivered the reigns of government. Moreover, many of the major conflicts that have shaken the world since 1945 have roots in the colonial era: the ARAB-ISRAELI CONFLICTS, wars between India and Pakistan, and the GULF WARS involving Iraq and Iran. It is also widely recognized that the currents of religious radicalism, reform, and revival present in Muslim societies today were born during that era. Today the economic life and security of many of the former colonized regions remain dependent upon Europe and the United States as well as multinational corporations. Some historians and political scientists have therefore coined the term *neocolonialism* to describe the new system of global and international relations that emerged during the cold war (post-1945). The invasion of Iraq by the United States and Britain in 2003 is but one example of this new form of international power relations, and it has already demonstrated an impact on political Islam and the ways Muslims understand and practice their religion.

See also AFGHANI, JAMAL AL-DIN AL-; AHMAD KHAN, SAYYID; CHRISTIANITY AND ISLAM; CIVIL SOCIETY; DEOBAND; EDUCATION; ISLAMISM; POLITICS AND ISLAM; RENEWAL AND REFORM MOVEMENTS; WAHHABISM.

Further reading: Albert Hourani, *A History of the Arab Peoples* (Cambridge, Mass.: Harvard University Press, 1991); Rashid Khalidi, *Resurrecting Empire: Western Footprints and America's Perilous Path in the Middle East* (Boston: Beacon Press, 2004); Charles Kurzman, et al., eds. *Modernist Islam, circa 1840–1940: A Sourcebook* (New York: Oxford University Press, 2002); Thomas Metcalf, *Ideologies of the Raj* (Cambridge: Cambridge University Press, 1998); Michael Rywkin, ed., *Russian Colonial Expansion to 1917* (London: Mansell Publishing, 1988).

comic strips and comic books

Comic strips are a popular art form consisting of a sequence of framed cartoons that tell a story, usually accompanied by speech bubbles and narrative text boxes. Comic books are expanded versions of comic strips published as a magazine or book. The publication of comic strips began in Germany and the UNITED STATES in the latter part of the 19th century. Mass-market production of comic strips and comic books first began to prosper in the United States during the 1930s. Many countries around the world also developed this form of popular literature during the last century, including Britain, France, Italy, and Japan. It has spread widely because of the growth of print culture, increased literacy rates, demand for popular forms of entertainment, and development of a global consumer economy. From the beginning, comics have been created for both CHILDREN and adults, but the popularity of adult comics increased during the closing decades of the 20th century.

Comics are popular in the Middle East and elsewhere where there are large Muslim populations. Illustrated book manuscripts were produced in Islamicate societies during the Middle Ages that contained pictures of ANIMALS, heroic warriors, holy figures, mythological creatures, ANGELS, and other extraordinary beings. These books were created by professional calligraphers and painters who worked for a few powerful and wealthy patrons and did not enjoy widespread circulation. The introduction of comics in the modern sense did not occur until the 20th century as a result of European influence in Muslim lands. In the Middle East, most early comics were in English and French, but by the mid-1960s they began to be rendered in local languages, such as Arabic. Disney cartoon characters such as Mickey Mouse and Donald Duck became popular in the Arab world with the publication of the weekly Egyptian comic magazine *Miki*. It was not long before these characters were adapted to native cultures and shown wearing *galabias* (Egyptian-style robes), carrying prayer beads, and celebrating RAMADAN. Likewise, Superman's alter ego, Clark Kent, was changed to Nabil Fawzi, while Batman and Robin became Subhi and Zakkour.

Aside from the conversion of imported comic book characters into local ones, rising nationalist politics in newly independent countries led to the search for culturally authentic subjects and characters. Some comics featured folkloric figures such as the wise Egyptian fool Juha, known in other parts of the Middle East as Nasr al-Din Khoja or Mullah Nasr al-Din, while others retold ARABIAN NIGHTS stories, such as "Sinbad the Sailor." Historic subjects portrayed in Arab comics include the medieval traveler IBN BATTUTA, Salah al-Din (SALADIN), and the crusaders and guerrillas who fought against the French and the Israelis. Even WOMEN, such as the Syrian queen Zenobia of Palmyra (third century C.E.), have found a place in the comics. Comics in TURKEY have recounted the story of that nation's founding father, MUSTAFA KEMAL ATATURK (d. 1938). In Iraq, comics were used to lionize SADDAM HUSAYN, the country's former president, and promote the ideology of the BAATH PARTY. Egypt's charismatic president, JAMAL ABD AL-NASIR (d. 1971), and Hafiz al-Asad (d. 2000) of Syria have also been comic book subjects. In INDIA, which has one of the largest Muslim populations in the world (although they represent only about 12 percent of the country's population), the Mughal emperors AKBAR (d. 1605) and Jahangir (d. 1627) have been subjects of Amar Chitra Katha comics, a very popular line of comic books celebrating favorite topics in Indian history, religion, literature, and folklore since 1967. Although this series often favors Hindu subjects at the expense of Muslim ones, it did publish an issue on Nur Jahan, the gifted and influential wife of Jahangir and mother of Shah Jahan (d. 1666), the builder of the Taj Mahal.

There are also comics with mainly Islamic religious content. This would seem to contradict the Islamic prohibition against the portrayal of human beings, especially of holy people. It should be remembered, however, that this ruling has not prevented the creation and reproduction of figural images in premodern manuscript illuminations, traditional folk art, modern print publications, and commercial art. Islamic comics have several different kinds of themes. Some involve holy figures mentioned in the QURAN or famous people in early Islamic history. Muslim prophets such as ABRAHAM and MUHAMMAD are never portrayed in human form in these publications. Rather, such comics depict a landscape or a burst bubble accompanied by a speech bubble or narration box containing the prophet's words, while the prophet himself remains invisible. Other people are shown in human form, however. Another kind of Islamic comic seeks to teach the importance of performing one's ritual obligations, living a pious life, or adhering to the ethical values of Islam. Muslim periodicals published in Europe and North America contain comics for children that address similar issues. These are also intended to help youth learn about their religious heritage in secular societies where they are in the minority. On the other hand, anti-Islamic comics have been published in the United States and Europe by individuals and groups seeking to convert Muslims or criticize or insult their beliefs and practices. Such activity, while it is allowed in the name of freedom of the press, has provoked angry responses, as witnessed in Europe in 2006 when the publication of unsympathetic cartoon images of Muhammad in Denmark and other countries sparked demonstrations by immigrant Muslims in Europe and outraged Muslims in other parts of the world.

See also BOOKS AND BOOKMAKING; CALLIGRAPHY; EUROPE; FOLKLORE.

Further reading: Allen Douglas and Fedwa Malti-Douglas, *Arab Comic Strips: Politics of an Emerging Mass Culture* (Bloomington: Indiana University Press, 1994); "It's a Bird! It's a Plane! It's . . . Nabil Fawzi!" *Saudi Aramco* 21 (March/April 1970): 18–25; Frances Prichett, "The World of Amar Chitra Katha." In *Media and the Transformation of Religion in South Asia,* edited by Lawrence A. Babb and Susan S. Wadley, 76–106 (Philadelphia: University of Pennsylvania Press, 1995).

communism

One of the most important expressions of political ideology, social organization, revolutionary action, and economic development to appear in the 19th and 20th centuries was communism. Its founding figure was Karl Marx (d. 1883), a German intellectual and journalist, who argued that history was an ongoing struggle between the haves and the have-nots (the rich and the poor) over control of wealth. He believed that history would end with the triumph of the working class over the exploitative holders of capital, bringing about a peaceful, classless society in which wealth was shared communally. Communism, also known as Marxism, inspired social and revolutionary movements in EUROPE, Asia, Africa, and the Americas. Several of these movements were able to establish centralized dictatorial regimes run by communist parties in Russia (known as the Soviet Union from 1917 to 1991), Yugoslavia, CHINA, North Korea, Vietnam, and most of the countries in Eastern Europe. These governments were strongly opposed to organized religion, because they believed that religion represented the established interests of the old order and that it perpetuated false ideas about human nature, economy, and society. By the end of the 20th century, the majority of governments under communist control had fallen except those of China, Vietnam, North Korea, and Cuba. The decline of communism at the end of the century coincided with the resurgence of political Islam, and some scholars have seen a causal relationship between the two phenomena.

During the 20th century, Islam encountered communism in three ways: 1) intermittent subjugation of Muslim populations by communist governments in the Soviet Union, Eastern Europe, China, YEMEN, and AFGHANISTAN; 2) overt opposition by conservative Islamic states such as Saudi Arabia to communist governments and parties; and 3) competition among rival Islamic and communist party organizations in their opposition to undemocratic and authoritarian right-wing governments and occupying powers. Many Muslims see communism as being incompatible with their core Islamic values and teachings, such as their belief in God, performance of obligatory acts of worship, and acquisition of religious instruction as a part of one's moral development. Muslims in the Middle East in particular have also rejected communism because of the Soviet Union's quick recognition of ISRAEL in 1948 and the support French Marxists showed for their government in its bloody war against the Algerian independence movement in 1954–62.

The governments of the Soviet Union and other communist nations pursued policies to organize subject Muslim populations in Central Asia into discreet nationalities based on ethnicity (for example, Uzbek, Tajik, and Kirghiz) and cut them off from their ties to Muslims and Islamic centers in the Middle East. Mosques and Islamic schools were closed or converted into cultural sites, while the overt practice of Islam was largely forced to go underground. The dissolution of the Soviet Union in 1991, however, spurred the revival of Islam, including militant Islamism, in the former Central Asian republics. In China, Muslims enjoyed religious freedom after World War II because they sided with the Communists in their campaign against the Nationalists for control of the country. This relationship disintegrated during the Chinese Cultural Revolution (1966–76), when Islam was outlawed. Since that time, however, Muslim communities have been allowed to rebuild their institutions, and their situation has improved.

The Islamic governments of SAUDI ARABIA and the Iranian republic both took clear stands against the spread of communist influence. During 1960s and 1970s, Saudi king FAYSAL IBN ABD AL-AZIZ (r. 1964–75) urged Muslims to oppose the spread of atheism in their lands, by which he meant not only communism but also Zionism and ARAB socialism. Saudi Arabia and PAKISTAN helped the UNITED STATES provide covert support in the 1980s to the AFGHAN MUJAHIDIN in their guerrilla war against the People's Democratic Party of AFGHANISTAN, a communist party that had seized power in 1979 with the backing of the Soviet army. Indeed, the United States regarded both Saudi Arabia and Pakistan as staunch allies during the cold war (1945–91). Meanwhile, after the Islamic revolution in IRAN (1978–79), the new Khomeini regime violently eliminated the Marxist Tudeh (communist) Party, the Fedaiyan-i Khalq, and other leftist groups that had formed earlier in opposition to the Iranian monarchy.

Elsewhere, Islamic opposition movements competed with small groups of communists and leftists attempting to gain political power in countries ruled by conservative or secular authoritarian governments. This was the case in Iran, EGYPT, and Iraq. The Palestinian nationalist movement against Israeli occupation also reflects this factional rivalry. Several leading 20th-century revivalists and reformers who were overtly opposed to communism nonetheless seized upon Marxist rhetoric concerning social justice, class struggle, revolution, and liberation and reshaped it in an Islamic mold. ABU ALA AL-MAWDUDI (d. 1979), SAYYID QUTB (d. 1966), and ALI SHARIATI (d. 1977) were in the forefront of this group. The Islamic movement that has most fully embodied the combination of Marxism with revivalist Islamic ideology is the MUJAHIDIN-I KHALQ, which opposed Iran's monarchy and was violently suppressed after the creation of the Islamic Republic in 1979.

See also CENTRAL ASIA AND THE CAUCASUS; *FIDAI*; MUSLIM BROTHERHOOD; POLITICS AND ISLAM.

Further reading: Alexandre Bennigsten and Chantal Lemercier-Quelquejay, *Islam in the Soviet Union* (London: Praeger, 1967); Ernest Gellner, "Islam and Marxism: Some Comparisons." *International Affairs* 67 (1991): 1–6; Dru C. Gladney, *Muslim Chinese: Ethnic Nationalism in the People's Republic* (Cambridge, Mass.: Harvard University Press, 1991); Ali A. Mazrui, "The Resurgence of Islam and the Decline of Communism." *Futures* 23 (1991): 273–289.

community   *See* UMMA.

Companions of the Prophet (Arabic: *al-sahaba; ashab al-nabi*)

The Companions of the Prophet are the Muslims who joined with MUHAMMAD (d. 632) in MEDINA during the seventh century to form the first Islamic community. They are highly esteemed by Sunni Muslims not only because of the roles they played in early Islamic history but also because of their involvement in the preservation and transmission of the QURAN after Muhammad's death and in the definition and consolidation of the SUNNA itself. In fact, the HADITH upon which the sunna is based include lists of transmitters that invariably give the names of companions who had witnessed what Muhammad said or did or who are themselves considered to have been virtuous exemplars of authentic Islamic practice.

Sunni tradition recognizes several groups among the companions, with some overlap among them. They are the first four "rightly guided CALIPHS" (Abu Bakr, Umar, Uthman, and Ali); the EMIGRANTS (*muhajirun*) from MECCA; the Helpers (ANSAR) from Medina, veterans of Badr, Uhud, and other early battles against Muhammad's enemies; and the People of the Bench. The last-named was a group of poor and pious Muslims who gathered at a bench (*suffa*) in Muhammad's MOSQUE in Medina. They are highly respected in Sufi tradition. The companions also included WOMEN, especially the "Mothers of the Believers," among whom Muhammad's wife, AISHA, was foremost. On the other hand, the companions whom Sunnis revere (except Ali) are reviled by many Shii Muslims. The Shia contend that individuals such as Abu Bakr, Umar, and Aisha actually corrupted the pristine Islamic community by preventing Ali, the first Shii Imam, from becoming Muhammad's successor after his death in 632.

See also SHARIA; UMMA.

Further reading: Fuad Jabali, *The Companions of the Prophet: A Study of Geographical Distribution and Political Alignments* (Leiden: E.J. Brill, 2003); Muslim ibn al-Hajjaj, *Sahih Muslim,* trans. Abdul Hamid Siddiqi, 4 vols. (Lahore: Sh. Muhammad Ashraf, 1975).

consensus   *See* IJMAA.

Constantinople   *See* ISTANBUL.

constitutionalism

Minimally, constitutionalism means government can and should be legally limited in its powers and that AUTHORITY is derived from and depends upon those limitations. Such constitutionalism, in principle, even if not in practice, has become part and parcel of Islamic history. Indeed, the Charter (or Constitution) of MEDINA, MUHAMMAD's compact with the Muslim and Jewish community (*umma*) that constituted the first Islamic polity after the HIJRA in 622, has been regarded as an early foundation for constitutionalism in modern Muslim-majority countries.

Sociologically speaking, a constitution is a "coordinating convention" that establishes "self-regulating" institutions that both "enable" and "constrain" democratic behavior. Social contract theories are misleading inasmuch as "agreement" or "tacit consent" is *not* a condition for accepting the constitutional order; mere acquiescence suffices. This renders the Western conception of "popular sovereignty" a rhetorical contrivance or metaphor, which, in turn, has important consequences for Islamic political theory. One oft-cited reason for Muslim hostility to liberal constitutionalism is the notion of popular sovereignty, which is seen as infringing upon or contradicting the sovereignty that properly belongs to God. Nevertheless, the idea of sovereignty may have still have a role to play in constitutionalism if God's conferral of "vice-regency" (or deputation of authority) to humans implies some sort of individual sovereignty. Here, sovereignty (in a distributive or shared sense) entails according human beings theological and metaphysical freedom, which is logically prior to any notion of rights and liberties found in a constitution. The citizen-sovereign would thus make the laws, be bound by those laws, and yet somehow remain "above" the law in acts of civil disobedience, amending or reforming the constitution, or in a constitutional revolution. Conceding this conception, the literal meaning of popular sovereignty in a collective sense commits the informal logical fallacy of composition.

Among the criteria for a liberal constitution are limits on majority decision making; recognition of human and civil (and increasingly, social and economic) rights and liberties; an independent and impartial judiciary to guarantee and protect these rights (including judicial review); and separation of executive, legislative, and judicial powers. Among the concepts within the Islamic tradition suggestive of or compatible with constitutionalism are *shura* (consultation), IJMAA (consensus), IJTIHAD (as independent legal reasoning), *maslaha* (public welfare), *majlis* (tribal council; public audience granted the caliph), *bayaa* (an unwritten contract or pact involving the recognition of, and allegiance to, political authority), and *wilaya* (custodianship, guardianship, trusteeship).

In the 19th century Ottoman Empire, EGYPT, and TUNISIA, constitutions were honored in the breach. Autocracy, patrimonialism, tribalism, and colonialism have left their indelible marks on efforts at liberal reform and the democratic aspirations of Muslims. In the second half of the 20th century, socialist and nationalist ideologies were added to the mix. That said, and keeping the Muslim Middle East and North Africa in mind, one can endorse Noah Feldman's remark "that the world is littered with beautifully drafted constitutions that have been ineffective or ignored in practice" (Feldman, 186). The Iranian CONSTITUTIONAL REVOLUTION (1905–11) prefigured much of the potential and some of the problems that were to attend later democratic experiments, most conspicuously the IRANIAN REVOLUTION OF 1978–79. The constitution of the Islamic Republic of Iran contains ostensibly democratic features—in Malise Ruthven's words, it is a "hybrid of Islamic and western liberal concepts" (Ruthvin, 372). But Ayatollah Khomeini's conception of the "guardianship of the jurist"

(*wilayat-i faqih*), expressed in the constitution in terms of the "chief juriconsult" and the 12-member Council of Guardians, has blocked democratic methods and processes, enshrining an insidious form of religious authoritarianism. Feldman contends the constitutional monarchies of JORDAN and MOROCCO "represent the best hope for the development of Islamic democracy in the Arab world" (Feldman, 50) The machinations of the military in Pakistan, Algeria, and—less frequently and less confidently—TURKEY, make mincemeat of constitutional law. Nonetheless, Turkey is rightly described as an "emerging democracy." The constitutional monarchy of MALAYSIA is betwixt and between authoritarianism and democracy, while Indonesia's democratic evolution has relied on well-crafted and well-timed constitutional reform.

Constitution making is today in process in IRAQ, AFGHANISTAN, and the Palestinian occupied territories, with the assistance or support of the U.S. government or local political organizations, such as the Palestinian National Authority. After enacting the proto-constitutional and provisional Basic Law, a constitutional committee has completed its third draft of the constitution for an independent and sovereign Palestinian state (subject to further amendments). Islam is declared the official religion of the future Palestinian state, while the constitution guarantees "equality in rights and duties to all citizens irrespective of their religious beliefs." The "principles" of "Islamic SHARIA" are termed "a major source of legislation," not unlike the way in which the principle(s) of natural law have functioned in a number of Western constitutions.

See also CIVIL SOCIETY; DEMOCRACY; PALESTINE.

Patrick S. O'Donnell

Further reading: Hamid Enayat, *Modern Islamic Political Thought* (Austin: University of Texas Press, 1982); John L. Esposito and John O. Voll, *Islam and Democracy* (New York: Oxford University Press, 1996); Noah Feldman, *After Jihad: America and the Struggle for*

Islamic Democracy (New York: Farrar, Straus & Giroux, 2003); Russell Hardin, *Liberalism, Constitutionalism and Democracy* (Oxford: Oxford University Press, 1999); Malise Ruthven, *Islam in the World,* 2d ed. (Oxford: Oxford University Press, 2000).

Constitutional Revolution

The Iranian Constitutional Revolution of 1905–11 "represents the first direct encounter in modern IRAN between traditional Islamic culture and the West" (Enayat, 166). It had a lasting effect on Iranian politics and helped to form Ayatollah RUHUL-LAH KHOMEINI's formulation of Islamic governance, crystallized in his conception of the "guardianship of the jurist" (*wilayat-i faqih*), which was to have a decisive impact on the religious, democratic, and constitutional character of the 1979 revolutionary republic.

Western powers had been meddling in Iran since the Napoleonic wars in the 19th century. Britain and Russia, in particular, had geopolitical designs and economic interests that left Iran only partly independent. The QAJAR DYNASTY's survival, in fact, depended on these two European powers. Treaties, terms of trade, and foreign concessions fundamentally restructured the Iranian economy, decimating craft production, while the importation of cheap consumer goods "did not necessarily bring a better life to most Iranians. More sugar, tea, tobacco and especially opium were consumed . . . while prices of basic foodstuffs rose" (Keddie 1981: 57). At the same time, Western philosophical and political ideas such as liberalism, representative government, and CONSTITUTIONALISM began to circulate among workers, merchants, and elites alike. The Tobacco Protest of 1891–92 was a prelude to the Constitutional Revolution, as the Muslim modernist and pan-Islamist JAMAL AL-DIN AL-AFGHANI persuaded key ULAMA to mobilize merchants of the BAZAAR alongside their fellow Iranians to boycott tobacco products.

Periodic protests over customs (tax) reforms, a series of strikes, and the operation of secret societies signaled widespread dissatisfaction with the regime's capitulation to foreign powers. Japan's victory in the 1904–05 Russo-Japanese War and the Russian Revolution of 1905 further emboldened the protesters. The actual catalyst for the Constitutional Revolution was the caning (of the feet) of two sugar merchants for raising their prices. Mullahs, merchants, and protesters took sanctuary (*bast*) outside Tehran and called for, among other things, a "house of justice." The ruler, Muzaffar al-Din Shah (r. 1896–1907), issued a decree consenting to the request but failed to act on it. A growing coalition of forces shared a nationalist identity: leftist social democrats, secular and religious reformers, orthodox ulama, Freemasons, merchants, shopkeepers, students, and guild members. Nationalist slogans and calls for a constitutional monarchy rallied the opposition taking *bast* in Qom and at the British legation's compound in Tehran.

In August 1906, the shah's royal proclamation permitted the formation of a *majlis* (national assembly or parliament) and the drafting of a constitution. The first *majlis* convened in October 1906, and a new constitution, modeled in part on the Belgian constitution of 1831, was ratified on December 30, 1906, just prior to the death of Muzaffar al-Din. Supplementary constitutional laws were signed the following year by the new shah, Muhammad Ali (r. 1907–09). With minor amendments, this constitution remained legally in effect until the 1978–79 revolution.

Prominent Shii mullahs were proponents of a constitution recognizing TWELVE-IMAM SHIISM as the official religion of the country, including Sayyid Muhammad Tabatabai, Sayyid Abdullah Bihbihani, Mulla Muhammad Kazim Khurasani, and Muhammad Husayn Naini. An early supporter of the revolution, Shaykh Fadlullah Nuri, turned against the constitution and the *majlis* when he realized the ulama were not to be accorded the final say as to whether legislation was in keeping with Islamic tenets, particularly the sharia. Nuri led the anticonstitutionalist clerics at the same time the Anglo-Russian Convention of 1907 was dividing Iran into respective spheres of British and Russian influence. Not long after an unsuccessful coup attempt by the anticonstitutionalists, reflecting deep divisions among the elites and in the larger society as well, the Cossack Brigade helped shut down the *majlis* in June 1908. Constitutionalists, nationalists, and revolutionary Social Democrats regained control in July 1909 and deposed the shah. Dissatisfaction on many fronts descended into rounds of assassination and terrorism, while public discontent with an increasingly conservative constitutional government grew from 1910 to 1911.

With the consent of the British, the Russians offered an ultimatum to the government when the American financial adviser Morgan Shuster was brought in to help the country out of its financial morass. Fortified by antiimperialist demonstrations, the *majlis* rejected the ultimatum. By the end of 1911, the Russians were bombing Tabriz and Gilan, massacring revolutionaries in Azerbaijan, and executing and deporting constitutionalists. A coup led by Nasir al-Mulk and the cabinet ended the second *majlis* and the revolution that brought it to power. However, future revolutionary forces would look back to Iran's first Constitutional Revolution to learn from its lessons and inspire their own efforts to oppose tyrannical regimes.

See also COLONIALISM; DEMOCRACY; POLITICS AND ISLAM.

Patrick S. O'Donnell

Further reading: Janet Afary, *The Iranian Constitutional Revolution, 1906–1911* (New York: Columbia University Press, 1996); Mangol Bayat, *Iran's First Revolution: Shiism and the Constitutional Revolution of 1905–1909* (New York: Oxford University Press, 1991); Hamid Enayat, *Modern Islamic Political Thought* (Austin: University of Texas Press, 1982); Nikki R. Keddie, *Modern Iran: Roots and Results of Revolution* (New Haven, Conn.: Yale University Press, 1981); Nikki R. Keddie, ed., *Religion and Politics in Iran: Shiism from Quietism to Revolution* (New Haven, Conn.: Yale University Press, 1983).

conversion

Conversion to Islam is a remarkably simple process, normally entailing no more than saying, with the proper intent, the SHAHADA: I declare that there is no god but God, and that MUHAMMAD is the messenger of God. The QURAN explicitly rejects imposition of religious belief, and Islam has historically allowed other religions great freedom.

Islam has always been a proselytizing religion; Muhammad converted his earliest followers in the seventh century from the pagan ways of MECCA to the worship of a single God, ALLAH. After suffering Meccan persecution, the small community moved to MEDINA, where the small band of Muslims grew to form the nucleus of the Islamic community, or UMMA. After the death of the Prophet in 632, the Arab Muslim armies burst out of the Arabian Peninsula, conquering enormous swathes of territory of the Byzantine Empire and utterly destroying the Persian empire of the Sassanians. In the resultant Islamicate empire, Islam was the religion of the state, but members of other religious groups were allowed freedom of worship as DHIMMIs, or "protected subjects." As a result of the military expansion of the Islamicate empire, the erroneous notion of "conversion by the sword" has historically taken root among non-Muslims. In fact, there was little attempt to convert non-Muslims during the early conquests. In some cases, conversion was actively discouraged, for it deprived the state of a source of revenue, as *dhimmi*s were taxed differently from Muslims. The empire itself, however, clearly emerged through the use of military power, and the dominance of Muslims within that empire should be considered a major, if partial, motivation for later conversion. Nonetheless, it is important to note that non-Muslims living in Islamicate polities generally had freedoms and rights that non-Christians could only dream of in medieval Europe.

Among scholars, debate has centered on the question of when conversion to Islam primarily took place, especially in the Islamicate heartlands of the Middle East. The consensus, that the majority of such conversions took place during the ninth century, is probably more correct for some areas, such as Iran, than for others, such as Egypt, where evidence points to a considerably later turning point. A more interesting question, however, is why and how conversion occurred; this question has yet to be taken up in a serious manner.

In the outlying areas of Islamdom, particularly in Southeast Asia and Central Asia, but also in South INDIA and Bengal, conversion to Islam came about as a result of different factors, largely the role of traders and SUFIS, who were able to offer a different and convincing system of belief and worship that attracted followers. Conversion to Islam continues to contribute significantly to the growth of the community, with major, organized efforts now underway in Africa, where Muslim and Christian missionaries are in direct competition, but also in Europe and North America.

See also APOSTASY; CHRISTIANITY AND ISLAM; COPTS AND THE COPTIC CHURCH; JUDAISM AND ISLAM; LATIN AMERICA.

John Iskander

Further reading: Richard Bulliet, *Conversion and the Poll Tax in Early Islam* (Cambridge, Mass.: Harvard University Press, 1979); Daniel Dennett, *Conversion and the Poll Tax in Early Islam* (Cambridge, Mass.: Harvard University Press, 1950); Richard Eaton, *The Rise of Islam and the Bengal Frontier, 1204–1760* (Berkeley: University of California Press, 1993); Michael Gervers and Ramzi Bikhazi, eds., *Conversion and Continuity: Indigenous Christian Communities in Islamic Lands, Eighth to Eighteenth Centuries* (Toronto: Pontifical Institute of Medieval Studies, 1990).

Copts and the Coptic Church

The Copts are members of the native Christian church of EGYPT. The name *Copt*, like the name *Egypt*, comes from the Greek word *Aegyptos*. Thus, *Coptic* was used to mean *Egyptian*. When the Arab Muslims conquered Egypt in 641–42, they continued to use the word *Copt* to refer to the indigenous Christian population, the descendants of the ancient Egyptians. Today Egypt is 85 percent to 90 percent Muslim, and all its residents consider themselves Egyptians, while the term *Copt* refers specifically to a member of the country's native Christian population.

The Christian community in Egypt traces its origins to the Apostle Mark (first century). Although the Egyptian church suffered many persecutions under the Roman emperors, when Christianity became the dominant religion of the Roman Empire in the early fourth century, the church flourished and Alexandria was the center both of religious and intellectual life. Egypt was also the birthplace of monasticism.

Despite the contributions of the Coptic Church, by the fifth century, theological differences and political tensions were straining the relationship between the Copts and the other Christians of what was then the Byzantine Empire. In the seventh century, Islam arose in Arabia, and a Muslim army invaded Egypt under the leadership of Amr ibn al-As (d. ca. 663), one of the COMPANIONS OF THE PROPHET.

Relations between the Christian Coptic population and the Arab Muslim rulers ranged from antagonism to cooperation depending on social, economic, and regional factors. The Copts were granted DHIMMI status as a protected community under Islam but were also expected to pay an additional tax. Muslim rulers relied on the Copts to continue the administration of the country, and Copts held important positions in government throughout the medieval era. Although Coptic remained the language of administration for about a century after the arrival of Islam, Arabic language and Islamicate culture gradually came to dominate in Egypt, and Copts began to convert to Islam in increasing numbers. This was especially true during a time of persecution in the 14th

The Virgin Mary Coptic Church in Zamalek, Cairo, also called the Maraashly Church *(Juan E. Campo)*

century, such that by the 15th century the Coptic language had all but disappeared except for liturgical purposes.

In the medieval period, despite the Copts' protected status and service in the government, they suffered from periodic popular discrimination and waves of persecution during times of famine or hardship. This continued into the modern era. Egypt now has a constitution promising equal rights to all citizens regardless of their religion, but many Copts feel they are victims of discrimination as a religious minority in a predominantly Muslim country.

The last hundred years have witnessed a revival among the Copts. This is most clearly evidenced by the greater focus on "Sunday school" instruction and renewed interest in the monastic way of life. At the same time, however, the number of Copts within Egypt continues to dwindle, primarily as a result of emigration to the West.

See also CHRISTIANITY AND ISLAM.

Heather N. Keaney

Further reading: Barbara L. Carter, *The Copts in Egyptian Politics* (London: Croom Helm, 1986); Jill Kamil, *Coptic Egypt: History and Guide* (Cairo: American University in Cairo Press, 1987); Otto F. A. Meinardus, *Two Thousand Years of Coptic Christianity* (Cairo: American University in Cairo Press, 1999); John Watson, *Among the Copts* (Brighton, U.K.: Sussex Academic Press, 2000).

Cordoba (Córdoba, Cordova)

Cordoba is a large city that was once the leading center of Muslim political power and culture in ANDALUSIA in medieval Spain. It is located on the banks of the Guadalquivir River, which flows between the Sierra Morena range to the north and the Sierra Nevada range to the south before it enters the Atlantic Ocean. Its location has made it an important center of commerce since ancient times. The Romans seized and colonized it in the second century B.C.E. and ruled it until they were replaced by Germanic invaders from central Europe, who controlled it for most of the time between the fifth and eighth centuries C.E. It surrendered to Muslim armies from North Africa in 711 and achieved the height of its greatness during the reign of the Umayyad caliph Abd al-Rahman III (r. 912–961). It is estimated to have had about 300,000 inhabitants at that time, making it the largest city in medieval EUROPE. Medieval Arab historians remembered Cordoba as "the bride of al-Andalus," and even Hroswitha (d. ca. 1002), a Christian nun in Germany, called it "the ornament of the world." After the 10th century, its fortunes declined because of political strife, and it finally fell to the armies of the Christian Reconquista in 1236. Today its population still stands at about 300,000, and it serves as the capital of the Spanish province of the same name.

Islamicate Cordoba's most famous architectural landmarks were its grand MOSQUE and palace cities. The mosque is thought to have been founded on the site of an ancient church by prince Abd al-Rahman I (r. 756–788), the last surviving member of the Umayyad dynasty of SYRIA that had been massacred by the Abbasids in 750. By the 10th century, it had become the largest mosque of its kind in any of the Muslim lands, and it was renowned for its great beauty. The mosque's design recalled that of Umayyad mosques in Syria to the extent that even its prayer niche (MIHRAB) faced south rather than southwest, the actual direction of MECCA. When it was later captured by the Christians, they built a Gothic cathedral and several chapels within its walls, thus symbolizing the religious and political displacement of Islam by Christianity.

Cordoba's first Muslim rulers built the Alcazar, the main government palace, next to the grand mosque, following the urban palace-mosque pattern used in cities of the Islamicate Middle East. When Christian forces captured Cordoba in 1236, they occupied the Alcazar and later built a royal palace and church on its grounds. This was where Christopher Columbus came to get permission to sail to the Indies in 1492. Muslim rulers also erected luxurious palaces and palace cities on the city's outskirts. The most legendary of these was Abd al-Rahman III's Madinat al-Zahra, which boasted exquisite ARABESQUE ornamentation and paradisiacal gardens. Unfortunately, it was destroyed by rebellious BERBER troops in 1013.

As a center of learning, Cordoba had dozens of Muslim and Christian schools. It also had as many as 70 libraries, including the famous Alcazar library of the caliphs, which housed 400,000 books—substantially more than any other library in Europe in the 11th century. Among Cordoba's great creative artists and thinkers were poets such as Ibn Abd Rabbihi (d. 940) and Ibn Zaydun (d. 1071), jurist and religious scholar IBN HAZM (d. 1064), and IBN RUSHD (also known by his Latin name Averroës, d. 1198), the famed Muslim author of books on philosophy, THEOLOGY, law, and medicine. Cordoba was also the birthplace of Maimonides (also known as Moshe ben Maimun, d. 1204), who became the most important Jewish philosopher and religious scholar of the Middle Ages.

See also CHRISTIANITY AND ISLAM; CITIES; UMAYYAD CALIPHATE.

Further reading: Robert Hillenbrand, "'Ornament of the World': Medieval Cordoba as a Cultural Centre," in *The Legacy of Muslim Spain,* ed. Salma Khadra Jayyusi. 2 vols. (Leiden: E.J. Brill, 1994), 1:112–135; Maria Rosa Menocal, *The Ornament of the World: How Muslims, Jews, and Christians Created a Culture of Tolerance in Medieval Spain* (New York: Little, Brown, 2002).

cosmology   *See* CREATION.

Council on American-Islamic Relations (Acronym: CAIR)

CAIR is the largest Islamic civil liberties group in the UNITED STATES. It is headquartered in Washington, D.C., and has 28 regional offices in the United States and Canada. It was founded in June 1994 by Omar Ahmad, a computer engineer from the San Francisco Bay area. He is currently the chairman of its board of directors, which has six other members to promote a positive image of Islam and Muslims in America. CAIR publishes reports for the media, government, and local law enforcement, including an annual civil rights report documenting cases of discrimination. Handbooks for local Muslim leaders demonstrate how to safely participate in the public sphere by holding MOSQUE open houses and developing interfaith relationships. In addition to monitoring anti-Muslim hate crimes, CAIR publishes action alerts on its Web site and by e-mail to promote local activism.

On the national level, CAIR has sponsored public relations campaigns showing Muslims as fully American as well as organizing a voter registration drive. To help educate Americans about Islam, CAIR has also assembled a package of books and other resource materials that can be purchased and donated to public libraries. It also publishes a handbook that explains Islam to law enforcement officials, a "community safety kit" to help Muslims deal with religious and ethnic profiling and hate crimes, a survey of mosques in the United States, and annual reports on the status of Muslim civil rights. CAIR swiftly issued a condemnation of the attacks of September 11, 2001 and has organized interfaith memorial services on subsequent anniversaries.

CAIR has also emerged as the leading Islamic community service organization on the local level. Local CAIR chapters spend the majority of their time dealing with individual cases of discrimination by advocating workplace, hospital, and school accommodation of religious practices. Since September 11, 2001, CAIR has become increasingly involved in hosting conferences, seminars, and town hall meetings to bring together American Muslims, non-Muslims, and government officials.

In addition to its primary goals of promoting a positive image of Muslims in America, reducing ignorance about Muslims, and protecting Muslim citizens from discrimination and criminal violence, CAIR works with related organizations such as the MUSLIM PUBLIC AFFAIRS COUNCIL (MPAC) and the American Muslim Council (AMC) to lobby Congress on domestic issues and in doing so attempts to promote Muslim unity on a local and national level.

See also CIVIL SOCIETY; DEMOCRACY; DIALOGUE.

Vincent F. Biondo III

Further reading: Organization Web site: Available online. URL: http://www.cair-net.org. Council on American-Islamic Relations, *A Rush to Judgment: A Special Report on Anti-Muslim Stereotyping, Harassment and Hate Crimes Following the Bombing of Oklahoma City's Murrah Federal Building, April 19, 1995* (Washington, D.C.: Council on American-Islamic Relations, 1995); Yvonne Yazbek Haddad, ed., *Muslims in the West: From Sojourners to Citizens* (New York: Oxford University Press, 2002); Mohamed Nimer, *The North American Muslim Resource Guide,* (New York: Routledge, 2002); Jane I. Smith, *Islam in America* (New York: Columbia University Press, 1999).

Council on Islamic Education (acronym: CIE)

The Council on Islamic Education is a nonprofit American Muslim organization founded in 1990 to provide curricular advice and to assess instructional materials used in K–12 public schools in the UNITED STATES. It is based in Fountain Valley, California, and its founding director is Shabbir Mansuri, who first came to the United States in 1969 to study chemical engineering. A group of highly qualified Muslim scholars, most of whom hold tenured appointments at leading American universities, provides CIE with the expertise needed to undertake its mission. Although it understands itself to be an organization that provides advice for curricular planning and textbook development in a variety of K–12 subject areas, it is primarily concerned with ensuring that Muslims and Islam are represented in a fair and balanced manner in textbooks and other instructional material used in world history and religion classes. Seeking to operate in conformity with the decision of the U.S. Supreme Court in the First Amendment case of *Abington Township v. Schempp* (1963), the CIE favors teaching *about* religion in public schools as an aspect of human history and culture and *not* teaching religion for devotional purposes, which is not allowed in public schools by the First Amendment. In addition to consulting with textbook publishers, the CIE conducts pedagogical workshops and participates in regional and national social studies and educational conferences. Together with the First Amendment Center, which has offices at Vanderbilt University in Tennessee and in Arlington, Virginia, it published a study in 2000 entitled "Teaching about Religion in National and State Social Studies Standards." Among its other publications are teachers' guides on Muslim HOLIDAYS, Muslim WOMEN, Islamic literature, the CRUSADES, and Islam's contributions to the formation of Western civilization. The CIE has rejected charges made by critics who say that the organization promotes a negative view of the United States and Western civilization as well as an overly favorable view of Islam, its peoples, and its history.

See also EDUCATION; STUDENT.

Further reading: Elizabeth Barrow, ed., *Evaluation of Secondary-Level Textbooks for Coverage of the Middle East and North Africa.* 3d ed. (Ann Arbor, Mich.: Middle East Studies Association and the Middle East Outreach Council, June 1994); Charles Haynes, *A Teacher's Guide to Study about Religion in Public Schools* (Boston: Houghton Mifflin, 1991); Charles C. Haynes, Sam Chaltain, et al., *The First Amendment in Schools: A Guide from the First Amendment Center* (Alexandria, Va.: Association for Supervision and Curriculum Development, 2000).

covenant

A covenant is a contractual agreement or commitment that states the mutual duties and obligations of the parties involved. In the Abrahamic religions of Judaism, Christianity, and Islam, it has considerable theological significance because it expresses the relation between God and humans at specific moments in sacred history. Sometimes it is understood as a bilateral agreement involving mutual concord between God and his people, and in other cases, it is given by God alone. According to the doctrines of these religions, God will reward humans for heeding his commands and punish them for forgetting or disobeying them. The TORAH of Judaism expresses the covenants between God, humankind, and the people of ISRAEL that occurred in the times of Noah, ABRAHAM, Isaac, Jacob, and DAVID. The most important such agreement in Judaism is the covenant established at Sinai, which MOSES conveyed to the Israelites from God. Christians have regarded this as the old covenant, or "testament," which has been succeeded by a new one given by JESUS in the GOSPELs.

In Islam, as in Judaism and Christianity, God is believed to have established covenants with both humankind and with sacred individuals (the

prophets) and their followers. The covenant mentioned most often in the QURAN is the one between God and the people of Israel, which they are blamed for breaking (for example, Q 2:83). The key division expressed in the quranic agreements is between those who honor God's commands as believers and those who do not—the forgetful and the disbelievers. The most universal covenant is the primordial one God established on the Day of *Alastu,* when he brought forth all of Adam's future progeny and they acknowledged his oneness and sovereignty (Q 7:172). Muslims are told that if they remember to keep God's covenant and fulfill other conditions, they can return in the AFTERLIFE to the PARADISE from which Adam had been expelled for violating his agreement with God (Q 2:35–36, 13:20–23). Those who do not will face God's curse and the fires of hell (Q 13:25). Aside from Adam, other prophets who were party to covenants with God were Abraham, MOSES, JESUS, and MUHAMMAD. In regard to Muhammad, the Quran states that the prophets have all agreed with God to believe in and help his future messenger, the prophet of Islam (Q 3:81). In SHIISM, the idea of covenant has been shaped to promote belief in its doctrines concerning Muhammad's holy family (the AHL AL-BAYT) and the IMAMS.

See also ADAM AND EVE; CHRISITIANITY AND ISLAM; HOLY BOOKS; JUDAISM AND ISLAM; SHARIA.

Further reading: John Wansbrough, *Quranic Studies: Sources and Methods of Scriptural Interpretation* (Oxford: Oxford University Press, 1977), 8–12; Bernard Weiss, "Covenant and Law in Islam." In *Religion and Law: Biblical, Judaic, and Islamic Perspectives,* edited by E. B. Firmage, B. Weiss and J. W. Welch, 49–83 (Winona Lake, Ind.: Eisenbrauns, 1990).

creation

Historians of religion have noted that most religions and traditional societies have creation myths—stories about the origins of the world, plants and ANIMALS, human beings, and important aspects of social life. The events these nonscientific accounts describe purportedly took place during the primordium, at the beginning time of the world and human history. People hold them to be true in literal and symbolic ways, and the stories contain reflections about human mortality, good and evil, and even the end of the world. Creation accounts are usually recited, remembered, or performed in rituals on important HOLIDAYS, usually linked to the seasons.

Islamic stories and beliefs about creation are to be found in the QURAN and a wide array of writings in Arabic, Persian, and other languages in the Muslim world. These writings include the HADITH, histories, philosophical essays, mystical texts, and poetry. Creation myths have also been incorporated into the oral traditions of Muslim peoples from Africa to Southeast Asia. They contain themes and beliefs that were once part of the indigenous religious and cultural life even before Islam arrived on the scene. With Islamization, the native themes were reshaped to uphold the Quran's chief teaching that everything in existence was created by one sovereign God (ALLAH) and that he had no partners in this. As a consequence, all creation, especially human beings, was obliged to submit to him and serve him.

The Quran's creation accounts drew from those that originated in the ancient civilizations of the Middle East, especially those found in the book of Genesis in the Hebrew Bible, which date to at least the seventh century B.C.E. However, because it was organized according to different rules than those used for the Hebrew Bible, the Quran's creation passages were not presented as a continuous story. It has verses that discuss God's creation of the universe (the *cosmogony*), the creation of Adam and his wife (the *anthropogony*), and the story of their fall from grace and expulsion from Paradise, but they are dispersed and repeated in different chapters, starting with the second chapter, "Al-Baqara" (The cow). Indeed, details from the biblical accounts were omitted, suggesting that either they were not familiar to

Muhammad and his audience or they were not deemed to be relevant to the message Muhammad wished to convey. One consequence of this is that the quranic creation stories were not celebrated in rituals or on particular holidays, in contrast to creation stories in other religions and cultures. By the eighth century C.E., Muslim scholars were reassembling the quranic creation passages and combining them with biblical material and Jewish rabbinic lore to write continuous narratives about God's creative activities. These creation myths were included in books about the PROPHETS who preceded MUHAMMAD, such as those written by IBN ISHAQ (d. 767), al-Thaalabi (d. 1036), and al-Kisai (ca. 13th century). They were also included in al-Azraqi's (d. 837) history of Mecca and the famous world history written by Abbasid historian and Quran commentator al-Tabari (d. 923).

In the Quran, as in the Bible, God creates by two methods: through craftsmanship and through speech. The doctrine of creation from nothing (Latin, *creation ex nihilo*) as a way of proving God's absolute transcendence and power is not clearly stated in the Quran, but it was taken up by Jewish, Christian, and Muslim theologians later in the Middle Ages. Most of the Arabic words used in the Quran to describe God's creative actions suggest they resembled human activities such as leather working, making pottery, building, and growing, which implies that formless matter already existed. The most common word for creation is based on the root consonants *kh-l-q,* which the Quran uses more than 200 times in relation to God. Indeed, one of his 99 names is *al-Khaliq* (the creator), as stated in this verse: "He is God the Creator, the Maker, the Shaper of Forms. He has the most beautiful names. All that are in heaven and earth glorify him. He is the Almighty, the Wise" (Q 59:24).

In refutation of polytheistic beliefs, the Quran proclaims that it was God alone who raised the heavens and spread out the earth below them, making it stable and placing rivers on it (Q 13:2–3). Pagan gods, ANGELS, and other beings had no inherent powers in creation. God created day and night, the Sun, the MOON, and the signs of the zodiac (Q 21:33; 25:61–62). The Quran also states in several places that God created the heavens and Earth in six days and then established his throne (Q 7:54; 10:3, 11:7). Unlike the Genesis account, however, the Quran refutes the idea that God ever took the seventh day as a day of rest (Q 2:255), which Jews and Christians have celebrated as the holy Sabbath day. God is also praised for creating GARDENS with different kinds of fruits and vegetables for people to eat, and he is the source of the water that nourishes them (Q 6:141; 21:19). Moreover, he is even remembered for having provided people with houses and clothing (Q 16:80–81). The absolute creative power attributed to God in the Quran later became the basis for the theological claim that God did not just create the world "in the beginning," but that he is active as a creator at each moment in time as long as the world exists. It also was invoked in support of the prohibition against making statues and paintings of living beings, for in doing so the artist was thought to be attempting to assume God's creative power.

In addition to craftsmanship, God was also believed to be able to create through speech. Once he decides to create something, according to the Quran, all he has to do is say, "Be!" and it is so (kun fa yakun) (Q 2:117). This kind of creation is not as common as the craftsman type, but it is said to have been involved with the creation of the heavens and Earth, Adam, and Jesus (Q 3:59).

The Quran describes the creation of human beings in two ways. One concerns the origin of the first human being, ADAM. He was fashioned by God from dust or wet clay (Q 30:20; 6:2; 7:12); the commentaries likened the process to making a hollow clay pot. Some early writings said God used different colors of dust from different places on Earth, thus explaining the variety of skin colors and personalities that distinguish people from one another. Alternately, they mentioned that the dust was taken from the KAABA, JERUSALEM, YEMEN, the Hejaz, EGYPT, the east, and the west. As in the

biblical account, God then breathed his spirit (ruh) into Adam, thus giving him life (Q 15:29). Also, as indicated above, the Quran says that Adam was created when God conceived a design and spoke to the dust, saying, "Be!" (Q 3:59). It does not detail the creation of Eve other than in very general terms (Q 4:1). Nonetheless, the commentaries, drawing upon biblical lore, reported that she was created from one of Adam's ribs while he slept.

The second way in which the Quran describes God's involvement in creating humans is in terms of human reproduction. God created humans from sperm (Q 16:4; 36:77) in the wombs of mothers (Q 3:6; 39:6). The very first verses many Muslims believe were revealed to Muhammad were those at the beginning of Sura 96, which declare, "Recite in the name of your lord who created, created the human being from clotted blood" (vv. 1–2). This passage links God's creative power to the formation of the embryo.

The idea that God's creation is designed for the material and spiritual benefit of human beings is central to the Quran. Indeed, God created them to be his deputies (khalifa) on Earth (Q 2:30). Materially, the Earth provides people with what they need to live and enjoy their appointed time on Earth. Spiritually, everything in creation is intended to be a reminder that God was the source of all and that people should worship him. To be ungrateful and forgetful of God were equivalent to disbelief and infidelity (kufr). This idea is connected to the quranic concept of signs (ayat), which are manifest both in the created world and in the sacred book, for ayat also means verses of scripture. The interwoven signs of the world and the holy book, if they are recognized and heeded, lead to God and salvation. If they are rejected and ignored, they lead to suffering and damnation (Q 2:164–165; 50:6–8). Although the world of everyday existence is essentially true and good, the Quran emphasizes that humans must be more attentive to the affairs of the next world in anticipation of JUDGMENT DAY. Recognizing that human beings are mortal and that the world will end one day, the Quran attributes to God the power not only to create, but also to create *again*. The resurrection of the dead is portrayed as a new creation (Q 17:49–51).

The concept of creation by emanation was an alternative belief expressed in later Islamic writings, but not in the Quran. It first developed in pre-Islamic times among mystics known as Gnostics and Neoplatonist philosophers. Both groups exercised a profound impact on the religions of the Middle East, especially among Christians after the third century, and later among Muslims. According to this belief, the manifest universe is the product of a series of emanations issuing like waves of light from a single absolute source or godhead. In Islam, this belief was embraced by illuminationist philosophers inspired by IBN SINA (d. 1037), mystics who followed the ideas of IBN AL-ARABI (d. 1240), and certain schools of Shii esoteric thought, especially Iranian ones. Many who supported this belief quoted a famous holy hadith (*hadith qudsi*), in which God declares, "I was a hidden treasure that desired to be known, then I created the world so that I would be known." The infinite, eternal, unmanifest God desired to become self-aware, so he created a cosmos that reflected to a greater or lesser degree his attributes. In other words, the universe was created as God's mirror. The human being was the highest being in God's creation because he, like God, was capable of self-awareness and most fully reflected his attributes, especially in the inner heart. With knowledge of this hidden reality, Sufis believed they could free themselves from the prison of the created world, overcome the veils that separated them from God, and return to the condition of primal unity with him. They embellished this concept with a doctrine of mystical love, saying that God created the universe out of love, that human existence was a painful separation from him, and that SUFISM provided the key for attaining a reunion of the lover with the divine beloved. Also, many followers of this school of mysticism conceived of MUHAMMAD as the most perfect human being, created by God's light at the beginning of

time, and through him the rest of creation became possible. According to a 16th-century Hindavi mystical poem written in northern INDIA, "This lamp of creation was named Muhammad! For him the Deity fashioned the universe. . . . His name is Muhammad, king of the three worlds. He was the inspiration for creation" (Manjhan 5). Moreover, in INDIA, the Islamic emanationist theory of creation assimilated aspects of Hindu cosmology, so that God was spoken of as a Hindu god: the unmanifest Brahma, Vishnu the preserver of the universe, and Shiva the destroyer of the universe. His ability to create by speech was identified with the sacred Hindu mantra of creation, Om.

Today Muslims hold to quranic and emanationist beliefs about creation as matters of faith. But many are also familiar with scientific theories of cosmogony and the origin of humans. While there are those who reject modern scientific theories, many have accepted them without feeling that they undermine quranic truths. Indeed, Muslim modernist thinkers in the tradition of SAYYID AHMAD KHAN (d. 1898), JAMAL AL-DIN AL-AFGHANI (d. 1897), and MUHAMMAD ABDUH (d. 1905) have sought to demonstrate not only that Islamic beliefs are compatible with Western science, but that medieval Muslim scholars actually contributed to the formation of modern science. Associations and institutes of Islamic science have arisen that seek to demonstrate how Quranic cosmology is compatible with modern scientific theories about creation and other scientific topics.

See also AYA; IDOLATRY; NAMES OF GOD; PERFECT MAN; SOUL AND SPIRIT.

Further reading: Maurice Bucaille, *The Bible, the Quran and Science: The Holy Scriptures Examined in the Light of Modern Knowledge.* Translated by Alastair D. Pannell and Maurice Bucaille (Indianapolis: American Trust Publications, 1979); Jan Knappert, *Islamic Legends: Histories of the Heroes, Saints and Prophet of Islam.* 2 vols. (Leiden: E.J. Brill, 1985), 1:23–41; Manjhan, *Madhumalati: An Indian Sufi Romance* (Oxford: Oxford University Press, 2000); Thomas J. O'Shaughnessy, *Creation and* the *Teaching of the Quran* (Rome: Biblical Institute Press, 1985); Annemarie Schimmel, "Creation and Judgment in the Koran and in Mystico-Poetic Interpretation." In *We Believe in One God*, edited by Annemarie Schimmel and Abdoljavad Falaturi, 149–177 (New York: Seabury Press, 1979); Ahmad ibn Muhammad al-Thalabi, *Arais al-majalis fi qisas al-anbiya, or "Lives of the Prophets."* Translated by William M. Brinner (Leiden: E.J. Brill, 2002).

crescent   *See* MOON.

crime and punishment

A criminal act is one that involves a serious violation of social or moral laws and requires the state or some other official authority to hold legal proceedings and punish the guilty person or persons. The laws may be based on social norms and customs, legislation by political authorities, or interpretations of commandments attributed to a supramundane power or deity. A crime can therefore be defined as a threat to the social and political order or even as an offense against God.

In Islamic jurisprudence (*FIQH*)—based on Quranic revelation, the SUNNA (custom) of MUHAMMAD and the first Muslims, the consensus of religious jurists, and legal reasoning—there are only six crimes that warrant punishment as offenses against God: 1) ADULTERY, 2) false accusation of adultery, 3) drinking wine, 4) theft, 5) highway robbery, and 6) APOSTASY (opinion is not unanimous on this crime, however). The punishments for anyone found guilty of these crimes by a qualified Muslim judge are severe; they are not left for God to decide, as is the case for lesser sins and transgressions, nor can they be reduced. Adultery is to be punished by flogging or death by stoning, false accusation of adultery and drinking wine by flogging, and theft by amputation of a hand or foot. According to most legal schools, apostasy and highway robbery involving homicide require the death penalty, but highway robbery without homicide is punished as a theft would be.

Such corporal punishments were called "God's boundaries" (*hudud Allah*), a term borrowed from the QURAN, where it was used in reference to marriage and family laws that should not be transgressed (Q 2:187). In Islamic jurisprudence, the meaning expanded to include these corporal punishments, indicating that such punishments had the force of divine will behind them, not society's. But classifying them as "boundaries" suggests that jurists had a sense that *hudud* cases had to meet stringent standards of justice before a judgment of guilt could be pronounced. Thus, in cases of adultery, four male witnesses were stipulated, which made proving that such an offence had occurred difficult. Also, the penalty of flogging for bearing false witness in adultery cases legally protected the accused. In cases of theft, the punishment of amputation was not to be enforced when the perpetrator stole to stay alive or when the stolen property was of little value or illegal.

Homicide was condemned in the strongest terms in both the Quran and hadith, but it has not been classed as a crime that was subject to the *hudud* penalties. Premeditated murder was classed as a major sin forbidden by God that would be punished on JUDGMENT DAY (Q 4:93; 17:33; 25:68–69). In addition, relatives of the victim were given the right of retaliation on the basis of the principle of "a life for a life," and they were given the right to grant clemency, which could not be done when the crime was subject to the *hudud* penalties. In cases of manslaughter or unintentional homicide, the guilty party was required to compensate the family of the deceased for their loss by freeing a slave and paying a fine, or "blood money" (Q 4:92). For other offenses, judges were allowed to impose punishments at their discretion, but in theory, punishment should not exceed the least of the *hudud* penalties in severity.

Most nations with Muslim-majority populations today have adopted criminal codes and penal systems that are based on Western models. A few selectively apply the prescribed Islamic punishments, usually in conjunction with government

Islamization policies. These countries include SAUDI ARABIA, IRAN, PAKISTAN, and SUDAN. Islamist groups and movements usually place the enforcement of Islamic laws and punishments at the top of their agendas for radical political and social change. At the same time, attempts at enforcing Islamic penalties have provoked protests from both Muslims and non-Muslims because they are seen as being either unjustly applied or in violation of international HUMAN RIGHTS principles.

See also CUSTOMARY LAW; ISLAMISM; PALESTINE; RENEWAL AND REFORM MOVEMENTS; SHARIA.

Further reading: Muhammad Abdel Haleem, Adel Omar Sherif, and Kate Daniels, eds., *Criminal Justice in Islam: Judicial Procedure in the Sharia* (London: I.B. Taurus, 2003); Rudolph Peters, "The Islamization of Criminal Law: A Comparative Analysis." *Die Welt des Islams* 34 (1994): 246–253; Joseph Schacht, *An Introduction to Islamic Law* (Oxford: Oxford University Press, 1964).

Crusades (1095–1291)

The Crusades were a series of military campaigns conducted by European Christians in the lands of Asia Minor (Byzantium), SYRIA, PALESTINE, and EGYPT. They were more a product of events in Europe than of those in the Middle East. The Catholic Church was undergoing a period of reform in the 11th century and wanted to exert more authority over secular government. The church also wanted to limit the amount of fighting within Europe. Thus, in 1095, when Pope Urban II (r. 1088–99) called for what would be the first of many crusades, he described the crusade as a pilgrimage (for which the sins of the crusaders would be forgiven) and a defensive war to take back the Holy Land, especially JERUSALEM. Considering the fact that the Muslims had been controlling the Holy Land for 450 years, during which time Christian pilgrims had unhindered access to the holy sites, it seems clear that the pope wanted to assert his authority to forgive sins and wage war rather than to respond defensively to any Muslim aggression

The First Crusade achieved its goal of capturing Jerusalem from the Muslims in 1099. The crusaders' indiscriminate slaughtering of men, WOMEN, and CHILDREN, done in the name of God, has made the Crusades live in infamy for Muslims and would later become an embarrassment for the Catholic Church and Christianity in general.

The level of violence decreased after the First Crusade. The crusaders divided up Palestine and Syria into city-states ruled by European lords. With the establishment of the Crusader States, the need to govern the people peacefully and profitably overshadowed the zeal for holy war. Christian and Muslim princes made various alliances with one other, and traders traveled between both communities.

Nevertheless, the crusaders continued to try to take more territory, while the Muslims tried to take back what they had lost. As the crusaders lost territory to the Muslims, they called for new crusades. During the Third Crusade, the English king Richard the Lion-Hearted (also known as Richard I, d. 1199) waged a long campaign against the Muslim leader SALADIN (r. 1174–93). The mutual respect that characterized their rivalry has made them the subject of legend.

The Crusades produced numerous geopolitical consequences. In Europe, they strengthened the church and deflected internal political rivalries—for a time. In the Middle East, they encouraged political unification and religious renewal, which ultimately enabled the Muslims to defeat the crusaders. The Crusades have come to symbolize confrontation between East and West, Islam and Christianity, and as such continue to evoke strong feelings and memories, particularly among Muslims, for whom European colonialism and the foundation of ISRAEL have revived previously dormant memories of the medieval wars between Christians and Muslims.

See also ASSASSINS; COLONIALISM; CHRISTIANITY AND ISLAM; ISTANBUL; JIHAD.

Heather N. Keaney

Further reading: Francesco Gabrieli, *Arab Historians of the Crusades* (Berkeley: University of California Press, 1984); P. M. Holt, *The Age of the Crusades: The Near East from the Eleventh Century to 1517* (New York: Longman, 1986); Amin Maalouf, *The Crusades through Arab Eyes.* Translated by Jon Rothschild (London: Al Saqi Books, 1984). Reprint, Cairo, Egypt: The American University in Cairo Press, 1990); Kenneth Setton, ed., *A History of the Crusades.* Vols. 1–6 (Madison: University of Wisconsin Press, 1969).

customary law (Arabic: *ada, urf;* also *adat*)

Customary law in Islam consists of traditional customs and practices on the local level that are not directly based on the QURAN and HADITH but that still have legal weight. Before the modern era, it was largely unwritten and uncodified. Customary law pertains to matters of marriage, DIVORCE, inheritance, murder, honor crimes, the status of WOMEN, and land tenure.

Historically, when a town, country, or region fell under Muslim rule, the unwritten local laws and customs were never completely swept away and replaced by those of the SHARIA, or Islamic law. Rather, they coexisted alongside Islamic law, or they were assimilated and continued to be honored in the new Islamicate society. Historians of Islamic law have noted that local traditions were not as a rule formally recognized as one of the sources of law (Quran, SUNNA, IJMAA [consensus], and *qiyas* [analogy]), but Muslim jurists did discuss them and legitimate them as sunna or *ijmaa*. On the other hand, a custom or practice that conservative ulama determined to be blatantly un-Islamic could be condemned as an illegal BIDAA (innovation). Customary law was also invoked in advisory opinions, or fatwas. By such means, local custom contributed to the formation of the major Islamic legal traditions. Thus, the MALIKI LEGAL SCHOOL embodied the local customs of Medina, while the HANAFI LEGAL SCHOOL embodied those of southern Iraq, a much more cosmopolitan region than the Arabian Peninsula. Western scholars, moreover, have maintained that both the Quran and the sunna embody customary laws present in the Hijaz *prior* to the appearance of Islam. If their theory is correct, therefore, what eventually became the universal sharia originated in the local customary law of western Arabia and was later continuously shaped by the indigenous legal traditions of the wider Middle East and beyond. Muslims of conservative outlook may refute this theory by claiming that Islamic law is based more on revelation from God, but they must still account for the differences between the Islamic legal schools and the variety of local customs that have acquired legal legitimacy in different parts of the Muslim world.

In the Middle East and perhaps even more so in Africa and Asia, customary law has coexisted with religious law. Before the modern era, it may even have surpassed it on the level of the locality, especially among tribal populations and settled communities living in remote areas. During the 19th and 20th centuries, Dutch colonial officials attempted to use customary law (*adat*) as a way to weaken the authority of Muslim jurists and the influence of the sharia in Indonesia. Modern Islamic reform movements and Islamic revivalism do not yet appear to have directed their energies against customary law in most countries, however. They are more directed against colonial and postcolonial Western laws and institutions. Customary law appears to still be widely valued as part of the indigenous cultural heritage.

See also ADULTERY; AUTHORITY; CRIME AND PUNISHMENT; FATWA; *FIQH.*

Further reading: Noel James Coulson, "Muslim Custom and Case Law." In *Islamic Law and Legal Theory,* edited by Ian Edge, 259—270 (New York: New York University Press, 1996); Wazir Jahan Karim, *Women and Culture: Between Malay Adat and Islam* (Boulder, Colo.: Westview Press, 1992); Gideon Libson, "On the Development of Custom as a Source of Law in Islamic Law." *Islamic Law and Society* 4, no. 2 (1997): 131–155.

D

daawa (Arabic: invitation, religious call, summons) (also dawa, Persian dawat, or Indonesian/Malaysian dakwah)

Daawa is a term that has acquired a number of meanings in the history of Islam, but it is mainly thought of as religious outreach for purposes of CONVERSION or bringing lapsed Muslims back into the faith. In the QURAN, it is God's invitation to humans to worship and believe in him (Q 14:10; 10:25) and humans' calling upon God to hear their prayers (Q 14:33; 7:180). In the Quranic view, the PROPHETS are the ones who effectively transmit God's call to their peoples to sway them from praying to false gods or idols and to guide them on the monotheistic path to salvation. Prophets and others who undertake the challenging task of conveying God's daawa are called dais ("inviters" or "summoners"). Moreover, according to the Quran, the whole community of believers is charged with "calling to goodness, commanding the right and forbidding the wrong" (Q 3:104). In other contexts, Muslims used the word daawa as a synonym for the call to prayer (ADHAN) and as an alternate name for the first chapter of the Quran, the FATIHA (Q 1), which is a verbal prayer for God's assistance, guidance, and mercy.

During the eighth century, leaders of the Abbasid movement in IRAQ and IRAN gave daawa an overt political meaning by making it a form of religious propaganda. They called upon faithful Muslims to help them bring the community back to the "true" Islam by overthrowing the UMAYYAD CALIPHATE in SYRIA. Their efforts proved successful; they ended Umayyad rule and created the ABBASID CALIPHATE (750–1258) in BAGHDAD. At about the same time as the Abbasid movement, early Shii groups, several of which had supported the Abbasids until the Abbasids turned against them, called upon Muslims to accept the authority of their imams, the descendants of Muhammad's family (AHL AL-BAYT) whom the Shia believed to be the divinely chosen leaders of the Muslim community. The Ismailis, a minority sect of the Shia, used daawa to challenge the claims of their rivals, the TWELVE-IMAM SHIA, undermine Sunni rulers, and win support for their own leaders, whom they believed to be divinely guided and possessors of secret knowledge (BATIN) from God. The Ismaili rulers of the FATIMID DYNASTY (909–1171) in North Africa and EGYPT organized a daawa movement to promote their claims to divine authority and to oppose the Abbasid Caliphate with one of their own. Their dais (missionaries) were sent from CAIRO to far reaches of the DAR AL-ISLAM, where they spread Ismaili doctrines publicly and covertly, recruiting support for the imams. The

Nizari Ismailis in Iran, known as the ASSASSINS, also made extensive use of *daawa* on behalf of their leaders. Today, some branches of the Ismailis even call themselves "the Dawat."

In the modern period, the meaning of religious outreach has undergone further development. *Daawa* has become a keystone for many contemporary Islamic organizations and institutions in countries with Muslim majorities and also in those where they are minorities. The collapse of the last Islamicate empires (the Ottomans, Safavids, and Mughals) after the 17th century, combined with the onset of European colonial domination in many Muslim lands, led Muslims to use religious outreach in order to achieve unity among themselves, to convert others, and to engage non-Muslims in intercultural and interfaith DIALOGUE, especially in Europe and North America. The Ottoman sultan Abdulhamid II (r. 1876–1901) and other promoters of PAN-ISLAMISM used *daawa* in an attempt to unify all Muslims under his religious and political authority. The Ottoman Empire came to an end after World War I, but the task of fostering Muslim unity through *daawa* has been taken up anew by organizations such as the MUSLIM WORLD LEAGUE and the ORGANIZATION OF THE ISLAMIC CONFERENCE.

The increased Christian missions in Muslim lands that accompanied European colonization caused Muslims to organize their own missionary activities in response. Since the early decades of the 20th century, significant effort has been dedicated to educating Muslims about the core elements of their religion so as to encourage an internal religious revival and help them contend either with Christian missionaries or with the influence of modern ideas and non-Islamic lifestyles and customs. The governments of SAUDI ARABIA, Kuwait, Libya, Egypt, and Pakistan have created institutions to train imams and community leaders, develop modern methods for propagating Islam, hold conferences, and publish *daawa* literature. Their outreach campaigns have been conducted in African countries and the newly

independent Central Asian republics of the former Soviet Union, as well as the Middle East and parts of Asia. Activist Islamist organizations, such as the MUSLIM BROTHERHOOD, also regard outreach as an important part of their strategy for achieving their religious and political goals. The DAAWA PARTY OF IRAQ was created by Shii religious leaders to oppose the spread of COMMUNISM and secular Arab nationalism. After the fall of SADDAM HUSAYN'S BAATH PARTY government in 2003, it became one of Iraq's leading political parties. The TABLIGHI JAMAAT, founded in 1927 in India, is a very popular nongovernmental Sunni missionary movement that carries its message of simple religious piety door-to-door in many parts of the world.

Like Christian missions, Muslim *daawa* organizations engage in charity and relief efforts. Their mission also includes building neighborhood mosques, opening medical clinics, and establishing printing presses. Pious WOMEN, many of them veiled, have been increasingly visible in such activities. Mosque-based organizations in non-Muslim countries undertake *daawa* activities in their communities to attract lapsed Muslims and to educate non-Muslim leaders, officials, and the wider public about Islam. Such efforts have been particularly successful in pluralistic countries such as the United States. Muslim organizations have made extensive use of publications, electronic media, and most recently the Internet to conduct their outreach campaigns.

See also AHMADIYYA; ALMSGIVING; CHRISTIANITY AND ISLAM; *DAR AL-ISLAM* AND *DAR AL-HARB*; DIALOGUE; EDUCATION; IMAM; MADRASA; SHIISM.

Further reading: Thomas Arnold, *The Preaching of Islam: A History of the Propagation of the Muslim Faith,* 3d ed. (London: Luzac, 1935); Farhad Daftary, *A Short History of the Ismailis* (Princeton, N.J.: Marcus Weiner, 1998); Saba Mahmood, *Politics of Piety: The Islamic Revival and the Feminist Subject* (Princeton, N.J.: Princeton University Press, 2005), 57–78; Larry Poston, *Islamic Dawah in the West: Muslim Missionary Activity and the Dynamics of Conversion to Islam* (Oxford:

Oxford University Press, 1992); Jane I. Smith, *Islam in America* (New York: Columbia University Press, 2000), 160–167.

Daawa Party of Iraq (Religious Call Party [Arabic: Hizb al-Daawa al-Islamiyya]; also Dawa, Islamic Dawa Party)

The Daawa Party is one of the two leading Shii political parties in IRAQ. It was founded in the holy city of Najaf by Muhammad Baqir al-Sadr (d. 1980) and other members of the Shii clergy in 1957. Its original purpose was to oppose communist and Arab nationalist movements that were gaining strength in Iraq and to reverse the declining influence of the Shii ULAMA. It drew its first recruits from the religious colleges of Najaf and KARBALA, but traditional-minded ulama did not approve of the party's innovations. To avoid detection, the Daawa formed secret cells of party members, resembling those of Iraqi communists and Baathists. From 1964 to 1968, after the fall of the leftist government of Abd al-Karim Qasim (d. 1963), Daawa was able to operate more openly and recruited new members from college students and intellectuals in other Iraqi cities. Many new recruits also came from the Thawra district on the northeastern edge of BAGHDAD, a low-income quarter (now known as Sadr City) of Shii immigrants from the countryside. Outside Iraq, it established branches in LEBANON, SYRIA, IRAN, AFGHANISTAN, and Britain. Strengthening its grip on the country in the late 1960s, Iraq's Baath government launched a repressive campaign against the Shia, forcing Shii groups to go underground.

Daawa leaders were executed by the government during the 1970s, but the party was still able to organize antigovernment demonstrations on major Shii religious holidays. Party activism intensified in the aftermath of the IRANIAN REVOLUTION OF 1978–79, which was inspired by Ayatollah RUHOLLAH KHOMEINI (d. 1989), a senior Iranian cleric who had lived and taught in Najaf from 1964 to 1978. The goals and tactics of

Daawa became more radical. It called for establishing an Islamic government in Iraq, created a terrorist operations unit, and conducted armed attacks against the Baathists and their allies in other Persian GULF STATES during the Iran-Iraq war of 1980–88. It attempted to assassinate Iraq's president, SADDAM HUSAYN, and other government officials, and it was allegedly involved in the bombing of the U.S. embassy in Kuwait in 1983. The Iraqi government officially outlawed Daawa in 1980 and declared that party members would be subject to execution. Muhammad Baqir al-Sadr and other Shii leaders were arrested and put to death. Many members fled to Iran, where they set up a headquarters in exile, supported by that country's revolutionary government. Although the party has preached peaceful coexistence between Sunnis and the Shia, together with Iraqi national unity, the leadership and ideology of the party has largely been shaped by Shii doctrines and symbols. For example, party tracts at the time stated that the highest levels of leadership should be held by *mujtahids*, a designation for Shii religious authorities. Nevertheless, during their exile in Iran, effective leadership of the party shifted to lay members, such as Ibrahim Jaafari (b. 1947), a physician who had joined the party in the 1960s.

The party remained a staunch opponent of the government of Saddam Husayn but shifted to improve its relations with Western countries after the Gulf War of 1990–91, when an international coalition army drove Husayn's Iraqi forces out of Kuwait. After Husayn's government was overthrown by the United States in 2003, the Daawa Party reestablished itself in Iraq, and party members joined the new provisional government. In January 2005, it became a leading member of the United Iraqi Alliance, a coalition of political parties elected to govern the occupied country until a constitutional government could be formed. Daawa members won control of important government ministries, and Ibrahim al-Jaafari, the head of Daawa, became the country's new prime minister. He was succeed by another party loyal-ist, Nouri al-Maliki (b. 1950), in May 2006. The Daawa Party favors the creation of a government based on Islamic law but no longer requires that it be ruled by Shii ulama. Its major partner (and rival) is the Supreme Council for Islamic Revolution in Iraq (SCIRI, changed to Supreme Islamic Iraqi Council in 2007), a Shii party that was established in Iran by Iraqi exiles during the 1980s. Like the Daawa Party, its followers had also returned to Iraq as soon as Husayn's government had fallen. The strongholds of support for both parties are located in the Shii cities of southern Iraq, and both enjoy cordial relations with the Islamic Republic of Iran.

See also BAATH PARTY; COMMUNISM; POLITICS AND ISLAM; SHIISM.

Further reading: T. M. Aziz, "The Role of Muhammad Baqir al-Sadr in Shii Political Activism in Iraq from 1958 to 1980," *International Journal of Middle East Studies* 25 (1993): 207–222; Amatzia Baram, "Two Roads to Revolutionary Shii Fundamentalism in Iraq: Hizb al-Dawa al-Islamiyya and the Supreme Council of the Islamic Revolution in Iraq." In *Accounting for Fundamentalisms: The Dynamic Character of Movements*, edited by Martin E. Marty and R. Scott Appleby, 531–586 (Chicago: University of Chicago Press, 1994).

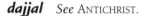

dai   *See* DAAWA; ISMAILI SHIISM.

dajjal   *See* ANTICHRIST.

Damascus

Damascus has been the capital of the Arab Republic of SYRIA since 1946. It is densely populated, with about 3.5 million inhabitants, or about 19 percent of the total population of the country. About 40 miles from the Mediterranean coast, it is situated on the edge of the desert at the foot of Mount Qassioun, one of the massifs of the eastern slopes of the Anti-Lebanon. The Barada River

The Great Umayyad Mosque of Damascus, Syria *(Juan E. Campo)*

crosses the city and provides water to the rich agricultural area known as the Ghuta, which Muslim tradition regards as one of the three earthly PARADISES, along with Samarkand (in modern Uzbekistan) and al-Ubulla (in IRAQ).

The exact date of the foundation of the city remains unclear, although archaeological evidence suggests the fourth millennium B.C.E. as the beginning date for continued human habitation. The first historical mention of the city refers to its conquest by the Egyptian pharaoh Thutmoses III in the 15th century B.C.E. Damascus was later inhabited by Assyrians, Babylonians, Achaemenids, Greeks, Nabateans, Romans, and finally the

Byzantine Empire up until the Muslim conquest in 635 C.E. During the rule of the UMAYYAD CALIPHATE (662–750), Damascus became the capital of this, the first Islamic dynasty, and an important cultural and economic center of the region. They built the beautiful congregational MOSQUE that still stands in the heart of the old city. In 750, the Abbasids defeated the Umayyads and installed their capital in BAGHDAD. Damascus then became a provincial town subject to the rule of different Islamic dynasties that conquered the area. Only in the 12th century did Damascus regain its splendor under the rule of the Zenkid Turkish prince Nur al-Din (d. 1174) and his Ayyubid successor, SALADIN (r. 1174–93). It became a center of religious learning and literary production. In 1260, the city was devastated by the same Mongol invasion that had obliterated the ABBASID CALIPHATE OF BAGHDAD in 1258.

By 1517, the Ottoman Turks had conquered all the territory from SYRIA to EGYPT. Under the Turkish dynasty, the city of Aleppo, in the north of Syria, became the most important economic center of the region. Nonetheless, Damascus still played an important economic and religious role, as is attested to by the numerous *khans* (trade centers and rest houses) and the proliferation of religious sites. Along with CAIRO and Baghdad, it was used as one of the main staging points for caravans that conveyed pilgrims to Mecca for the annual HAJJ.

During World War I, under the British promise of the creation of an Arab Syrian state, British troops commanded by General Allenby entered the city in October 1918 and established the Syrian Kingdom of Amir Faysal ibn Husayn ibn Ali (r. 1918–20), whom the British would later make king of Iraq. The British occupation violated the terms of the Sykes-Picot agreement signed with France in 1916, according to which Syria and Lebanon were to remain under French influence. On July 25, 1920, France entered Damascus and occupied Syria and Lebanon, establishing a colonial mandate system in the area. In 1925, Damas-

cus became the capital of the federal state of Syria under French mandate, and it remained the capital after Syria's independence in 1946.

See also CITIES; OTTOMAN DYNASTY.

Maria del Mar Logrono

Further reading: Afif Bahnassi, *Damascus: The Capital of the Umayyad Dynasty* (Damascus: Dar Tlass, 2002); Lynn Theo Simarski, "Visions of Damascus." *Saudi Aramco World* 42, no. 2 (March/April 1991): 20–29.

Daoud Ahmed (1891–1980) *pioneer American Muslim*

Sheikh Al-Haj Daoud Ahmed Faisal led one of the early successful efforts to spread Islam in America. Born in MOROCCO, he moved with his family to Bermuda at the age of 10. He subsequently migrated to the UNITED STATES in 1907. He attended the Juilliard School in Manhattan, where he mastered the violin and specialized in both classical and jazz music. In 1920, he married Dakota Station, later known as Sayidah Khadijah.

Through the 1920s, he associated with several Muslim groups, including the AHMADIYYA, but in 1928, with his wife's assistance, he founded the Islamic Propagation Center of America in Brooklyn. Located at 143 State Street, it came to be known informally as the State Street Mosque. From Brooklyn, he spread Sunni Muslim teachings, somewhat in competition with the effort of Noble Drew Ali, to propagate his form of sectarian Islam. In 1934, he purchased the Talbot Estate in East Fishkill, Dutchess County, New York, and turned it into a Muslim community known as Madinah al-Salaam (City of Peace). He was able to sustain the community for eight years, but it finally folded for financial reasons.

At some point, he made the HAJJ to MECCA, possibly at the end of the 1930s. In 1943, he added the title sheikh (Arabic *SHAYKH*) to his name as a sign of a relationship with King ABD AL-AZIZ IBN SAUD (d. 1953), who had a decade earlier consolidated his control of modern SAUDI ARABIA.

Both Abd al-Aziz and Shaykh Khalid of JORDAN gave Daoud a charter to establish Islamic work in North America. By this time, he had opened centers in several American cities, but in 1944, he incorporated his following as the Muslim Mission in America.

Sheikh Daoud offered Islam as the rightful and original FAITH of African Americans and a means of their throwing off their self-understanding as Negroes. At the same time, however, he refused to slant his presentation and opposed the racial theories of both Noble Drew Ali and Elijah Muhammad and the NATION OF ISLAM. He saw Islam as a way to the establishment of human equality and human rights as the means of reaching ultimate peace.

Sheikh Daoud continued to lead his movement, soon eclipsed by the Nation of Islam, until his death in February 1980. Along the way, he authored one book, *Islam the True Faith, the Religion of Humanity* (1965), a broad survey of Muslim teachings, leaders, and history. Since his death, the Muslim Mission has been absorbed into the larger Muslim community.

See also AFRICAN AMERICANS, ISLAM AMONG; DAAWA; RENEWAL AND REFORM MOVEMENTS.

J. Gordon Melton

Further reading: Sheikh Al-Haj Daoud Ahmed Faisal, *Islam the True Faith, the Religion of Humanity* (Brooklyn, N.Y.: Islamic Mission of America, 1965); Adib Rashad, *Islam, Black Nationalism & Slavery: A Detailed History* (Baltimore: Writer's Inc., 1995); Malachi Z. York, *Shaikh Daoud vs. W. D. Fard* (Eastonton, Ga.: Holy Tabernacle Ministries, n.d.).

dar al-Islam and *dar al-harb* (Arabic, House of Islam and House of War)

Dar al-Islam and *dar al-harb* are concepts used in medieval Islamic legal and political thought to differentiate territories under Muslim rule where the SHARIA is followed from those that are not. In the *dar al-Islam*, the sharia was observed, and non-

Muslim residents were to be given "protected" (DHIMMI) status as long as they paid their taxes and did not act to subvert the Islamic religious and political order. Non-Muslims were allowed to enter Islamic territories temporarily from the *dar al-harb* for peaceful purposes, such as commerce and diplomacy, after they had received a guarantee of security from a Muslim in the *dar al-Islam*.

Any territory where Muslim rule and the sharia did not prevail was classified as the *dar al-harb*. According to jurists, Muslims were obliged to bring it under Islamic rule, either through surrender by treaty or through conquest in JIHAD. CONVERSION was not the primary intent of this doctrine, however. The concept was not expressed in the QURAN and HADITH, but it was grounded in the early historical experience of the Islamic community (UMMA) as it expanded by conquest under the leadership of MUHAMMAD from its base in MEDINA into the rest of the Arabian Peninsula. Under his successors, this expansion extended to the rest of the Middle East and North Africa, ANDALUSIA, and significant parts of Asia. At the height of the ABBASID CALIPHATE (10th century), the *dar al-Islam* was a broad swath of territory that reached more than 4,000 miles from the Atlantic coasts of Spain and northwest Africa in the west to the eastern borderlands of IRAN and AFGHANISTAN. The world outside this territory, therefore, was considered the *dar al-harb*.

The ULAMA adapted this polarized concept of the world to changing historical realities. For example, Shafii jurists recognized a House of Truce (*dar al-sulh*), which allowed for peaceful relations with non-Muslim powers as long as they agreed to pay taxes to Muslim authorities. When Muslim lands fell under the control of non-Muslims, jurists instructed Muslims living there to either fight or remove themselves to the *dar al-Islam*. This was what Maliki jurists recommended to Muslims in the territories of Andalusia that had been taken by Christian armies during the Reconquista. It was also the view held by leaders of revivalist movements in British India, such as the Tariqa-i Muhammad (Muhammadan Path) led by SAYYID AHMAD BARELWI (d. 1831). Other jurists, however, ruled that as long as Muslims were secure and allowed to fulfill their religious duties, they could accept non-Muslim governments and consider themselves to still be in the *dar al-Islam.*

With the end of the last Muslim empires and the rise of new nation-states in the 20th century, the concepts of the *dar al-Islam* and the *dar al-harb* have been replaced by international laws, treaties, and conventions governing relations between states. Nonetheless, they still have their place in the Islamic legal heritage, and they are invoked from time to time in Muslim political rhetoric.

See also LAW, INTERNATIONAL; POLITICS AND ISLAM; WEST AFRICA.

Further reading: John Kelsay, *Islam and War: A Study in Comparative Ethics* (Louisville, Ky.: Westminster/John Knox Press, 1993); Majid Khadduri, *War and Peace in the Law of Islam* (Washington, D.C.: Middle East Institute, 1955).

Dara Shikoh (Dara Shukoh, Dara Shikuh) (1615–1659) *Mughal prince known for his writings on Sufism and liberal attitudes toward other religions, especially Hinduism*

Dara Shikoh was the first son of one of the most powerful sovereigns of India's MUGHAL DYNASTY, Shah Jahan (r. 1628–58). In his AUTOBIOGRAPHY, Dara wrote that his father longed for an heir to the throne and prayed that Sufi SAINT Muin al-Din Chishti would fulfill his wish. The next year, Queen Mumtaz Mahal gave birth to Dara near the saint's shrine in AJMER. Dara spent his early years in the palace and then was assigned command of an army when he was 17 years old. His father also gave him administrative appointments and high state honors to qualify him to be his successor and avoid dynastic conflict. Nevertheless, when Shah Jahan became ill in 1657, Dara and three younger brothers, Muhammad Shuja, Murad, and AURANGZEB, engaged in a life-and-death struggle for their father's Peacock Throne. Aurangzeb and Murad accused Dara of being an apostate because of his involvement with Hindu yogis and ascetics. Never very adept at war, Dara was defeated on the battlefield, tried by the ULAMA for APOSTASY, and executed in 1659. Aurangzeb took the throne for himself and did away with his remaining brothers.

Dara Shikoh, like his great-grandfather Akbar (d. 1605), is usually placed within the liberal wing of South Asian Islam, in juxtaposition to hardline religious conservatives such as his brother Aurangzeb. His interest in religion first became evident in 1640, when he was 25 years old. It was at this time that he compiled a biographical dictionary about MUHAMMAD, the Prophet's wives and family, the first CALIPHs, the Shii IMAMS, and hundreds of Sufis, particularly those of the Qadiri, Naqshbandi, Chishti, Kubrawi, and Suhrawardi orders. During the same year, he and his older sister, Jahanara (d. 1681), were initiated into the Qadiri Sufi Order by Mullah Shah, a prominent Sufi master who had been serving as their spiritual guide. Dara wrote several books and tracts on Sufi doctrine and practices, reflecting the stages of his journey on the Sufi path. His most important comparative work was *Majmaa al-bahrayn* (The confluence of the two oceans), in which he sought to prove that Islam and the Vedanta tradition in Hindu religious thought shared the same essential truths. For example, he equated the great names of God in Islam with those given by Hindus to their absolute cosmic being. He also identified the Islamic idea of resurrection with Hindu notions of liberation. Shortly before his death, Dara translated chapters of the Sanskrit philosophical commentaries on the Vedas known as the *Upanishads* into Persian. Indeed, it was through his translation, in which he had the assistance of Hindu pandits and ascetics, that the *Upanishads* became familiar to scholars of Indian language and literature in the West. Dara also was involved with the translation of the *Bhagavad Gita*, the most well known sacred text in the Hindu religion.

See also HINDUISM AND ISLAM; PERSIAN LANGUAGE AND LITERATURE; SUFISM.

Further reading: Muhammad Dara Shikuh, *Majmaa al-bahrayn, or The Mingling of the Two Oceans.* Edited and translated by M. Mahfouz ul-Haq (Calcutta: Asiatic Society, 1929); John F. Richards, *The Mughal Empire* (New Delhi: Cambridge University Press, 1993); Saiyid Athar Abbas Rizvi, *A History of Sufism in India,* 2 vols. (Delhi: Munshiram Manoharlal Publishers, 1983).

Dar ul-Arqam (Arabic: House of Arqam)

The Dar ul-Arqam is the most influential and popular Islamic renewal movement to have originated in Southeast Asia. It was founded in MALAYSIA in 1968 by Shaykh Ashaari Muhammad at-Tamimi (b. 1938), a member of the Awrad Muhammadiyya Sufi Order based in MECCA. Dar ul-Arqam took its name from al-Arqam ibn Abi al-Arqam, one of the COMPANIONS OF THE PROPHET who gave refuge to MUHAMMAD in his home. A number of early conversions to Islam took place there. The Dar ul-Arqam movement began in the Malaysian capital Kuala Lumpur, where members used a home to conduct grassroot religious education classes. Shaykh Ashaari encouraged his followers to study the QURAN and Islamic teaching to make religion part of their everyday lives. The focus of his movement was on individual self-improvement in conformity with Islamic values, not on trying to seize political power and impose Islamic religious law. The movement grew to a membership of about 10,000 in the 1980s, with up to 100,000 supporters. This was the outcome of an effective missionary (DAAWA) program involving public lectures, print and visual media, and even concerts. Dar ul-Arqam opened villages and schools throughout Malaysia, as well as branches elsewhere in Southeast Asia and in countries as far away as China, Australia, and the United States. It also had branches in the Middle East. Aside from its active outreach program, it successfully invested its resources in agricultural and commercial projects geared toward the emerging capitalist economy. The creation of the Al Arqam Group of Companies, composed of more than 400 businesses, was announced in 1993.

Dar ul-Arqam's extraordinary successes in the worlds of religion and business had serious political repercussions. Its increased influence among wealthy and powerful members of Malaysian society caused the government of Prime Minister Mahatir (r. 1981–98) to take measures against it. In 1994, it was deemed to be a "deviant cult" by the National Fatwa Council, the Islamic arm of the state. Shaykh Ashaari, who was accused of claiming to have had direct contact with God and the Prophet, was arrested and held without trial. After a televised confession broadcast from the National Mosque, he was released from prison and placed under house arrest for 10 years. The movement was officially disbanded in 1994, but it was allowed to reconstitute itself as a multinational business called Rufaqa Corporation, for which an ailing Shaykh Ashaari has served as the chief executive officer. Early in 2005, he published a book, *Civilizational Islam,* in which he expressed his support for Malaysia's new prime minister, Abdullah Ahmad Badawi.

See also FATWA; RENEWAL AND REFORM MOVEMENTS; SUFISM.

Further reading: Ahmad Fauzi Abdul Hamid, "Sufi Undercurrents in Islamic Revivalism: Traditional, Post-Traditional and Modern Images of Islamic Activism in Malaysia." *Islamic Quarterly* 45 (2001): 177–198; *25 Years of Darul Arqam: The Struggle of Abuya Syeikh Imam Ashaari Muhammad at-Tamimi* (Kuala Lumpur: Penerbitan Abuya Dengan Izin Asoib International Limited, 1993).

darwish   *See* DERVISH.

David (Arabic: Dawud, Daud) *biblical king of Israel and Judah who is revered by Muslims as a prophet of God*

David is known to the followers of all three Abrahamic religions. Modern scholars of the Bible estimate that he lived during the late 11th and early 10th century B.C.E. According to the narratives given in 1 Samuel, 2 Samuel, and 1 Kings of the Hebrew Bible, David rose from humble origins to become a legendary man of war and king of Israel and Judah. He made JERUSALEM his capital, which came to be known as "the city of David." He was the father of Solomon, who succeeded him to the throne and built the city's first temple for the god of the Israelites on Mount Zion. David is also remembered for having been the author of many of the poetic compositions contained in the biblical book of Psalms. In both Jewish and Christian scriptures, the idea developed that God's future messiah, or anointed savior, would come from David's descendants. The GOSPELs of Matthew (Mt. 1:1–17) and Luke (Lk. 3:23–83) clearly link JESUS' heritage to the royal household of David, and in Matthew, he is called "the son of David."

The QURAN mentions David 16 times in verses that present him as a biblical figure, as well as in passages that present him as a Muslim PROPHET. Thus, there are brief statements about his slaying Goliath (Q 2:251), receiving a kingdom and wisdom from God (Q 38:20), and being associated with Solomon (Q 27:15). More important, he is said to have received the book of Psalms (*zabur*) from God (Q 4:163; 17:55), which qualifies him as a prophet in Islamic tradition. David is also called God's CALIPH (*khalifa*) on Earth (Q 38:26), meaning his deputy. The biblical stories about his relations with Saul, Jonathan, and his son Absalom; his wars with the Philistines; the capture of Jerusalem; and his affair with Bathsheba and the death of her husband Uriah are completely omitted from the quranic narratives. The HADITH concentrated on his dedication to prayer and fasting, but not on the biblical stories.

More developed portrayals of David were provided in Quran commentaries (*TAFSIR*) and legendary stories (*qisas*) about the prophets, such as those collected by al-Tabari (d. 911) and al-Thalabi (d. 1036). These narratives drew upon rabbinic traditions that circulated among Jewish communities of the Middle East centuries prior to the appearance of Islam. This was where Arabic versions of the stories of Saul, Goliath, and Bathsheba ("that woman") were recounted. Such stories gave readers more details about how David received the Psalms and how pleasant his voice was when he recited them. He was also shown to be a God-fearing man who repented for his affair with Uriah's wife. Sufis would later remember him especially for his ASCETICISM and repentance. David's connection with Jerusalem is not mentioned in the Quran, hadith, commentaries, or *qisas* literature but is included in a specific genre of medieval Arabic literature that dealt with the sanctity of the city.

See also HOLY BOOKS; JUDAISM AND ISLAM; PROPHETS AND PROPHECY.

Further reading: Gordon Darnell Newby, *The Making of the Last Prophet: A Reconstruction of the Earliest Biography of Muhammad* (Columbia: University of South Carolina Press, 1989); Ahmad ibn Muhammad al-Thalabi, *Arais al-majalis fi qisas al-anbiya, or "Lives of the Prophets."* Translated by William M. Brinner (Leiden: E.J. Brill, 2002).

death

Islamic discussions on death and the AFTERLIFE are based on the teachings of the QURAN and the HADITH. The Quran refers to death in 36 chapters and the JUDGMENT DAY in 29 chapters. Notwithstanding the diversity of the contexts in which death is discussed, the themes of returning to God and taking responsibility for one's actions are essential in these discussions. The Quran and hadith explain that a person has only one life and one chance to prepare him- or herself for the afterlife. Therefore, death is the terminus that gives purpose and meaning to the life of the individual who is on a journey back to God. The dead are resurrected on Judgment Day for an evaluation of how they lived their lives and whether they will go to heaven or hell.

Varied interpretations of death by Muslims throughout the centuries have produced a complex ESCHATOLOGY that can be divided into the majority Muslim and the gnostic mystical views. The majority perspective adheres to the teachings of the Quran as they were transmitted through MUHAMMAD. These teachings warn and guide believers away from sin and remind them of the rewards and punishments of the afterlife. The gnostic mystical view upholds an esoteric understanding of death that is direct, personal, and unmediated. This kind of understanding is attained by means of mystical practices and through visionary discoveries. The mystics, who claim they have experienced death while alive, describe how their souls departed from their bodies and the world of matter and journeyed into the realm of death. There they have seen the mysteries of Judgment Day and have experienced God's attributes of might and majesty. Thus, their belief in the Quran and the teachings of the Prophet is based on the personal insights they have gained through the death journey. Some Muslims interpret death as self-sacrifice and as an expression of FAITH. They refer to the Quran, which considers those who die on the path of Islam and for the sake of other Muslims to still be alive. Such a person (martyr, or *shahid*), similar to innocent children, escapes the intermediary stage between death and resurrection (*barzakh*) and goes to PARADISE. The culture of valorizing martyrs—those who die on the path of Islam—has been enforced among the Shii Muslims for centuries. Their paradigm martyr is the grandson of Muhammad, Imam HUSAYN IBN ALI, who died in battle at KARBALA at the hands of his political rivals in 680. Imam Husayn is the central figure in the mourning plays that are annually held in commemorating his death and in celebrating the fate and faith of the Muslim martyrs. In the final analysis, for Muslims, life and death are interconnected through one's susceptibility to the realities of the unseen that are transmitted by the Prophet or experienced by the individual mystic.

See also BAQA AND FANA; CEMETERY; FUNERARY RITUALS; MARTYRDOM; SHIISM; SUICIDE.

Firoozeh Papan-Matin

Further reading: Muhammad Abu Hamid al-Ghazali, *The Remembrance of Death and the Afterlife, Kitab dhikr al-mawt wa-ma badahu,* Book XL of *The Revival of the Religious Sciences, Ihya ulum al-Din.* Translated by T. J. Winter (Cambridge: The Islamic Texts Society, 1995); Jane Idleman Smith and Yvonne Yazbeck Haddad, *The Islamic Understanding of Death and Resurrection* (Oxford: Oxford University Press, 2002).

Delhi

The capital of modern INDIA, greater Delhi is situated on the west bank of the Yamuna River in the northern part of the country. It encompasses an area of about 572 square miles, which includes the modern city of New Delhi, and is home to nearly 14 million people. Today, the majority of the city's inhabitants are Hindus from northern India, and Muslims constitute its largest minority. There are also a large number of Sikhs, many of whom fled to the city from the Punjab at the time of the violent 1947 partition, when India became an independent country. Delhi is also home to Buddhists, Jains, Christians, and an international diplomatic corps that serves at embassies in New Delhi, the southern part of the city.

The history of Delhi is actually one of at least eight different fortress cities built in close proximity to each other over many centuries, each designed to satisfy the needs and tastes of a different group of rulers. The earliest is thought to have been Indraprastha, a Hindu city that existed 3000 years ago. Muslims from AFGHANISTAN invaded at the end of the 12th century and located the capital of the DELHI SULTANATE there in 1193. The dynasties of the sultanate situated their fortress cities on lands on the south side of modern Delhi. Later rulers transferred the capital to Agra or Lahore, but eventually they returned to Delhi. The Mughal ruler Shah Jahan

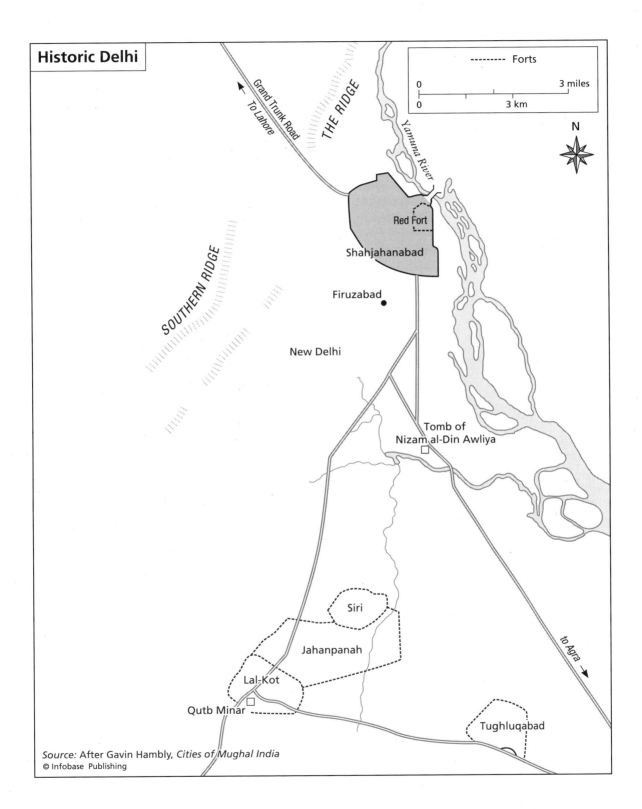

Historic Delhi

Forts

0   3 miles
0   3 km

N

Grand Trunk Road
To Lahore

THE RIDGE

Yamuna River

Red Fort

Shahjahanabad

Firuzabad

SOUTHERN RIDGE

New Delhi

Tomb of
Nizam al-Din Awliya

Siri

Jahanpanah

to Agra →

Lal-Kot

Qutb Minar

Tughluqabad

Source: After Gavin Hambly, *Cities of Mughal India*
© Infobase Publishing

(r. 1628–58) built Delhi's most spectacular Islamicate urban complex, which he called Shahjahanabad (Shah Jahan City). It was located north of the previous city sites, on the west bank of the Yamuna.

Among Delhi's most important Islamic monuments are the Qutb Minar complex, comprised of a towering MINARET and the Quwwat al-Islam communal MOSQUE. Construction of these buildings began in 1193 and continued intermittently for several centuries. They were built where a Hindu temple once stood and incorporate sections from the temple walls and local architectural features, symbolically demonstrating both that the Hindu religion was being subordinated to Islam and that Islam was adapting itself to its Indian environment. About three miles northeast of this site, Sultan Ala al-Din Muhammad Khilji (r. 1296–1316) built the fortress city of Siri, near which the Chishti saint NIZAM AL-DIN AWLIYA (d. 1325) located his mosque and Sufi hospice. Nizam al-Din's shrine is still considered to be one of the most sacred centers in Delhi for Indian Muslims. Other rulers sponsored the construction of communal mosques, domed tombs, and religious schools, which combined Middle Eastern architectural traditions with indigenous ones. At Shahjahanabad, the most impressive structures that still stand are the Jama Masjid, the largest communal mosque in India, and the Red Fort, with its palaces, gardens, kiosks, audience halls, administrative offices, and private mosque for the ruler.

Delhi was besieged by British forces during the 1857 rebellion, and significant areas of the city were razed to the ground. The British not only eradicated the MUGHAL DYNASTY but also rebuilt the city to serve their needs as India's new sovereigns. Military cantonments were situated in strategic areas, and a residential neighborhood known as the Civil Lines for British administrators was established on the north side of Shahjahanabad. This is where Delhi University was also built early in the 20th century. New Delhi, designed by Edwin Lutyens and Herbert Baker to be the capital of British India after 1911, is distinguished by a dazzling complex of Mughal–British-style government buildings, monuments, gardens, and a central business district. In addition to serving the practical purposes of government, it was also intended to symbolize Britain's political and cultural mastery over India. Today, it is where the official business of an independent India is conducted. The residence of the former British viceroy is now where India's president conducts official receptions. The Indian parliament is located nearby in the same complex of buildings.

Delhi has functioned as a center of Islamic religion and culture through much of its history. In addition to Nizam al-Din Awliya, other famous Muslims who were born there or who spent significant parts of their life there were the Chishti saints Qutb al-Din Bakhtiyar Kaaki (d. 1235) and Nasir al-Din Chiragh-i Dihli (d. 1356); the great Indo-Persian poet Amir Khusraw (d. 1325); the Mughal prince and student of Muslim and Hindu philosophy and mysticism DARA SHIKOH (d. 1659); Dara's sister Jahanara, also a Sufi devotee (d. 1681); the early modern revivalist Shah Wali Allah (d. 1762); the religious reformer SAYYID AHMAD KHAN (d. 1898); and the renowned Urdu poets GHALIB (d. 1869) and Altaf Husayn Hali (d. 1914). Delhi is also the location of the official memorials for many of modern India's great non-Muslim leaders, such as MOHANDAS K. GANDHI (d. 1947), Jawaharlal Nehru (d. 1964), and Indira Gandhi (d. 1984).

See also ARCHITECTURE; CHISHTI SUFI ORDER; CITIES; HINDUISM AND ISLAM.

Further reading: Sheila S. Blair and Jonathan M. Bloom, *The Art and Architecture of Islam, 1250–1800* (New Haven, Conn.: Yale University Press, 1994); William Dalrymple, *City of Djinns: A Year in Delhi* (London: Penguin, 2003); R. E. Frykenberg, ed., *Delhi through the Ages: Essays in Urban History, Culture, and Society* (New York: Oxford University Press, 1986).

Delhi Sultanate (1211–1526)

The Delhi Sultanate is the collective name given to the first rulers and dynasties to conquer and establish direct Muslim rule in northern INDIA. They made DELHI, or the cluster of fortress CITIES that succeeded each other and eventually became Delhi, their capital. The rulers were Turks and Afghans who formed an elite class that emulated the cultural and political traditions of the Persians. As Muslim sovereigns, however, they derived their legitimacy from the Abbasid CALIPH in BAGHDAD, who recognized Iltutmish (r. 1211–36), the Turkish MAMLUK commander in India, as the SULTAN for that region in 1229. Muslim rulers in India thereafter kept the title, which identified its holders as powerful sovereigns who served as defenders of the CALIPHATE.

The five main phases of the Delhi Sultanate were

Mamluk dynasty	1211–1290
Khalji dynasty	1290–1320
Tughluqi dynasty	1320–1413
Sayyid dynasty	1413–1451
Lodi dynasty	1451–1526

The Delhi Sultans conquered much of northern India, including west Bengal and the Deccan region of central India. With the passage of time, despite persistent and spirited resistance from Hindu Rajput kings, the ranks of the Muslim ruling elite grew by intermarriages and alliances with Hindus and the recruitment of Hindu converts and Indian-born Muslims. Hindu states in southern India paid tribute to the Delhi Sultans when they were strong enough to exercise influence southward. The Delhi Sultanate suffered a terrible reversal when the Mongol conqueror Timur (TAMERLANE, d. 1405) invaded India and sacked Delhi in 1398–99. He did not stay long, but he left behind a shattered sultanate. In 1526, Timur's great grandson, Babur, returned to found the MUGHAL DYNASTY and absorb the remnants of the Delhi Sultanate.

It is not an accident that the Delhi Sultanate first arose at the same time that the Mongols were invading the Middle East from their bases in Central Asia. Indeed, the building of Delhi's fortifications was done in large part to defend against Mongol invaders from the northwest. These defensive efforts were successful, so that as Muslim cities in Persia were being razed to the ground, Muslim refugees, including religious scholars and mystics, were able to find a new home in India.

The Delhi sultans built MOSQUEs and religious schools and employed Hanafi judges and legal scholars to serve in them. The 13th century was also when the Chishti, Suhrawardi, and Kubrawi Sufi orders established their centers in India. On the other hand, the Delhi sultans, who were Sunnis, attempted to eradicate Ismaili Shia rulers and communities that had earlier settled in northwestern areas of India. Also, in their wars of expansion, they plundered and desecrated Hindu temples, as previous dynasties had done from bases in AFGHANISTAN. This appears to have been a method of enhancing state revenues and undermining the legitimacy of rival Hindu monarchs rather than an outright assault against the Hindu religion. Once the Delhi sultans consolidated their hold on territories in India, they generally took a more pragmatic approach toward their Hindu subjects, who far outnumbered them. Many Hindu temples and religious sites were left alone; Muslim rulers endorsed protecting them and even allowed demolished temples to be repaired and new ones to be built. This policy continued to be observed by the Mughals.

See also CHISHTI SUFI ORDER; HANAFI LEGAL SCHOOL; HINDUISM AND ISLAM; ISMAILI SHIISM.

Further reading: Richard Eaton, "Temple Desecration and Indo-Muslim States." In *Beyond Turk and Hindu: Rethinking Religious Identities in Islamicate South Asia,* edited by David Gilmartin and Bruce B. Lawrence, 246–281 (Gainesville: University Press of Florida, 2000); Andre Wink, *Al-Hind: The Making of the Indo-Islamic*

World, Vol. 2, *The Slave Kings and the Islamic Conquest, 11th–13th Centuries* (Leiden: E.J. Brill, 1997); Stanley Wolpert, *A New History of India,* 5th ed. (New York: Oxford University Press, 1997).

democracy

Democracy, or "rule by the people," is a term that has been used to describe a number of different kinds of government. In the modern sense, it is usually connected to the idea of government by popularly elected officials who legislate and enforce the laws in accordance with notions of individual liberties and civil rights. Historically, Islamic political thought has legitimated many kinds of governance, from the despotic to the benign. The bountiful intellectual fruits of Islamic traditions—philosophical, theological, jurisprudential, mystical—are capable of justifying a wide array of political models and forms of political behavior, including models and forms of democratic provenance. Professors, pundits, policy makers, and the public in their wake have argued or assumed that ISLAM and democracy are inherently incompatible, that cultural and political properties intrinsic to Islamicate civilization preclude the birth of anything remotely resembling "Islamic democracy." Yet empirical studies conclude that such cultural explanations do not account for the emergence and success or failure of democracies.

Today, a clarion call from Muslims around the world is heard on behalf of the virtues of democratic values and principles, methods, and processes. The overwhelming preference of the "Arab street" and the majority of non-Arabic Muslims is for ballots ("paper stones"), not bullets, as militant, jihadist Muslims prove the exception to the rule. In short, Islamic democracy is not an oxymoron.

Minimalist or thin theories of democracy focus on the electoral components of the democratic process, the desiderata being free and fair, multiparty elections by secret and universal ballot. An electoral democracy is a constitutional order in which the chief executive (for example, president or prime minister) and legislative offices are filled through regular and competitive elections. By this standard, for example, TURKEY, BANGLADESH, and INDONESIA are democratic, as are several states of the former Soviet Union. EGYPT and MALAYSIA are quasi- or semi-democratic, JORDAN and MOROCCO are democratic by fits and starts, and ALGERIA has democratic pretensions, as do Kuwait and Bahrain. Interestingly, IRAN also scores high on this electoral scorecard. Even SAUDI ARABIA has been unable to resist the reformist clamor for electoral democracy: The kingdom's cabinet held its first elections for municipal councils in early 2005. As various forums of dialogue or "talking shops" are essential forms of democratic participation, the fact that the Saudi leaders (in particular, former crown prince and now king Abd Allah ibn Abd al-Aziz [b. 1923]) are talking about reform with "reform groups" portends changes on the desert horizon, however distant. Post-Saddam IRAQ entered the early stages of forming a democratic polity in 2004–05, where Shii political parties have prevailed. HAMAS, the Islamic radical resistance organization, won in Palestinian elections in 2006. In the previous year, after the withdrawal of Syrian troops, the radical Shii organization HIZBULLAH won seats in the Lebanese election, plus two cabinet posts. The results of these elections provoked an escalation of armed conflict between Israeli forces and Hamas in PALESTINE and Hizbullah in LEBANON.

Other problems persist. Executive offices are often uncontested, and opposition parties face unwarranted if not unreasonable government restrictions (and not a few parties are "banned" for this or that reason), with often limited access to media. In addition to voting fraud, authoritarian elites do not hesitate to resort to insidious forms of "electoral engineering" to achieve favorable electoral outcomes. In this case, the maxim "something is better than nothing" holds. Perchance international election monitoring can play a more effective part in preventing or discouraging attempts at electoral manipulation.

As a consequence of electoral participation, some of the more militant Salafi Islamists have formed alliances and coalitions with both Islamic and "secularist" parties and movements, often renouncing the methods of violence in ending the campaign for an "Islamic revolution." Denying Islamists participation in electoral politics can have deleterious results, as in Algeria, when the Islamic Salvation Front (FIS) resorted to rebellion and violence. At other times, the denial of participation simply compels Islamists to engage in the politics of CIVIL SOCIETY, as with the MUSLIM BROTHERHOOD in Egypt during the 1980s and 1990s. Islamist parties demonstrating some level of commitment to democratic principles and procedures are found, for example, in Tunisia, Algeria, Morocco, Egypt, Jordan, Lebanon, Malaysia, and Indonesia, as well in most of the republics of the former Soviet Union.

The growth and consolidation of democracy in Muslim-majority countries face enormous obstacles: authoritarian political traditions and communalist orientations (including recalcitrant ULAMA with medievalist responses to the conditions of modernity); histories of colonialist rule and imperialist interference; the need to implement economic reforms by way of integration into the global economy; the effects of anticolonial nationalist struggles that lacked democratic priorities; and economically bloated and inefficient states with excessive military expenditures, to list the more egregious difficulties. Fortunately, the level of economic development provides little information about the chances of transition to democracy, although per capita income does correlate with the sustainability of democratic regimes. Political economists and democratic theorists alike well know that rentier states, such as the Persian Gulf oil-producing countries, pose peculiar problems for democratic development. Of course, more substantive participatory and deliberative democratic theories elaborate a variety of different social and institutional conditions that serve as prerequisites of, or that are at least conducive to, full-fledged democratic consolidation and flourishing. When or if the various forms of Islamic democracy do arise, the corresponding criteria of assessment will be more stringent than those that take into account only electoral forms of democracy.

See also CONSTITUTIONALISM; GOVERNMENT, ISLAMIC; ISLAMISM; POLITICS AND ISLAM.

Patrick S. O'Donnell

Further reading: Khaled Abou El Fadl, Joshua Cohen, and Deborah Chasman, eds., *Islam and the Challenge of Democracy: A Boston Review Book* (Princeton, N.J.: Princeton University Press, 2004); Robert A. Dahl, Ian Shapiro, and Jose Antonio Chiebub, eds., *The Democracy Sourcebook* (Cambridge, Mass.: MIT Press, 2003); John L. Esposito and John O. Voll, eds., *Islam and Democracy* (New York: Oxford University Press, 1996); Noah Feldman, *After Jihad: America and the Struggle for Islamic Democracy* (New York: Farrar, Straus & Giroux, 2003).

Deoband

Located in Saharanpur District in Uttar Pradesh, INDIA, Deoband town contains MOSQUEs and buildings from the 15th and 16th centuries and is mentioned in the *Ayn-i Akbari* of Abu'l Fazl (d. 1602). It is famous for the Dar al-Ulum (House of Sciences) school, which was founded in 1867 by a group of highly learned ULAMA. Principal among them was Mohammad Qasim Nanautawi (1832–77), who was trained by teachers in the lineage of Shah Wali Allah (1703–62), the great Sufi reformer and intellectual in DELHI. The goal of the institution was to create a new Indian body of ulama that could provide spiritual and legal guidance to Indian Muslims, rather than continuing to depend on scholars from the Arabian Peninsula or having to travel to the Middle East for instruction. Another paramount objective in the founding of the school was to counteract the growing influence of Christian missionaries.

The Deoband curriculum follows the HANAFI LEGAL SCHOOL and provides advanced training in religious law. The original Deoband center has spawned more than 8,000 schools and institutes for all levels of instruction. Deoband is one of several major centers of Islamic learning in India, including the Nadwat ul-Ulama and ALIGARH Muslim University. The curriculum at Deoband incorporates three prevalent schools of Islamic learning in India: those of Delhi, Lucknow, and Khayrabad. The Delhi school had focused on TAFSIR (QURAN commentary) and HADITH, Lucknow emphasized FIQH (jurisprudence), and Khayrabad gave precedence to theology and philosophy. Deoband's ideological approach combined these and gave it its signature twist by focusing on Shah Wali Allah and his idiosyncratic hadith scholarship. Wali Allah regarded hadith as often unreliable. Indeed, in his view all revelations other than the Quran could at best be regarded as *hadith qudsi,* or "holy speech." Wali Allah regarded Malik ibn Anas's *Muwatta* (eighth century) as the pinnacle of hadith collections, as it was the earliest and closest in time to the Prophet. He was a proponent of IJTIHAD (independent legal reasoning) and a critic of *taqlid* (blind adherence to legal scholars), viewing imitation of any model other than Muhammad as suspect.

The influence of Deoband has been far reaching, and its curriculum is standard throughout Muslim South Asia. The early years of study in the basic curriculum focus on Arabic language, the BIOGRAPHY of MUHAMMAD, recitation of the Quran, and jurisprudence. The eighth, and final year focuses solely on hadith. Master's degrees are offered in law, Quranic interpretation (TAFSIR), theology, and ADAB literature. Legal opinions, or fatwas, are obtainable upon solicitation from the center at Deoband. Deobandi schools known as MADRASAS are also centers for DAAWA (proselytization). Deoband publishes books by its ulama past and present and issues a newspaper, *al-Dai* (the call). Dar al-Ulum Deoband has counted among its vice chancellors and principals many luminaries of South Asian ulama such as Shaykh al-Hind Maulana Mahmood Hassan (1851–1920), Maulana Muhammad Anwar Shah Kashmiri (1875–1933), and Maulana Syed Hussain Ahmed Madani (1879–1957). Although there is no political party directly linked to Deoband, the school has had a profound impact on Muslim politics, having trained many of the key members of political groups such as JAMIYYAT AL-ULAMA-I HIND, Jamiyatul Ulama-i Pakistan, and JAMIYYAT AL-ULAMA-I ISLAM.

Through the use of its curriculum and the proliferation of its graduates, Deoband is often linked to the spread of extremist ideologies most vividly exemplified by the TALIBAN. To some degree, this influence is real. In other cases, it is merely nominal, as the authority inherent in the name of Deoband is invoked to legitimate all kinds of Islamic conservatism. Although Deoband remains one of the most important institutes of Islamic learning, in India it may be soon be eclipsed by the increasing influence of Nadwat ul-Ulama, where enrollments have outstripped Deoband's since the mid-1990s.

See also EDUCATION.

Anna Bigelow

Further reading: Barbara Daly Metcalf, *Islamic Revival in British India: Deoband, 1860–1900* (Princeton, N.J.: Princeton University Press, 1987); Muhammad Qasim Zaman, *The Ulama in Contemporary Islam* (Princeton, N.J.: Princeton University Press, 2002).

dervish (Persian: *darvish,* also spelled *darwish, darwesh*)

A dervish is an individual who has chosen the Sufi path. The origin of this Persian word is unclear, but it is generally taken to refer to someone who is poor or a beggar. In SUFISM, the term, like the Arabic term FAQIR (poor), refers to someone who is humble and who has renounced the world in order to follow the Sufi path. While this often involves actual poverty and a renunciation of material possessions, which may necessitate begging for subsistence, a more spiritual sense of poverty suggests the control of desires, so that the dervish can focus on God. Many Sufi guides, in fact, warn dervishes against extreme poverty, since poverty itself must be forgotten, as it is only a stage on the path and can distract one from focusing on God.

In early Islamic history, piety was often expressed through individual ASCETICISM. Inevitably, some ascetics gained fame, followers were attracted to their example, and in this way schools developed. By the 12th century, Sufi orders such as the Qadiris had begun to take definite shape around the person or the tomb of a famous master, with formal rules and special buildings designed to accommodate and feed resident dervishes and provide space for rituals. Each order developed its own forms of worship, including chanting the names of God or special formulas (DHIKR); the singing of mystical poetry to music, often accompanied by dancing; and sometimes ecstatic practices, which might include, as with the RIFAI SUFI ORDER, dervishes eating hot coals or piercing their bodies with spikes. *Dervish* thus came to refer to a member of such an order, and in some orders, such as the Mevlevis and Bektashis, it refers to a particular rank in the hierarchy of the order. *Whirling dervishes* is a name used by Westerners for members of the MEVLEVI SUFI ORDER, who perform circular dances as part of their musical ceremonies. Some orders, such as the Qalandaris, were more loosely organized, and their disciples traveled constantly from place to place, being known as wandering dervishes.

See also BEKTASHI SUFI ORDER; SAINT.

Mark Soileau

Further reading: Ahmet T. Karamustafa, *God's Unruly Friends: Dervish Groups in the Islamic Later Middle Period 1200–1550* (Salt Lake City: Utah University Press, 1994); Annemarie Schimmel, *Mystical Dimensions of Islam* (Chapel Hill: University of North Carolina Press, 1975); Spencer Trimingham, *The Sufi Orders in Islam* (Oxford: Clarendon Press, 1971).

Devil   *See* SATAN.

dhikr (zikr, zikir)

Dhikr is Arabic for recollection, or remembrance. The QURAN calls upon humans to recollect God and not to forget him: "O you who believe! Remember God often" (Q 33:41); "O people! Remember the blessing God has given you" (Q 35:2); and "Remember your lord when you forget. Remembrance causes people to discover the real reason they were created to begin with—to serve God. Indeed, people will be held accountable on the Judgment Day if they forget God (Q 18:24)." The Quran also calls upon believers to remember God's PROPHETs, the bearers of previous revelations. The Quran itself is called a "remembrance" (*dhikra*), and its verses are signs (*ayat*) revealed so that people recall God and his sovereignty over heaven and earth. Muslims believe that the obligation of remembrance rests upon a primordial COVENANT that God established with Adam's progeny (all humans), wherein they recognized him as their lord (Q 7:172).

Occasions for remembering God arise throughout a Muslim's life—a birth and death, before eating a meal, beginning a journey, on feast days, and in the performance of the FIVE PILLARS of Islamic worship. During the month of Muharram and at other times of the year, the Shiis remember their holy imams, who were martyred for their belief in God. The idea of remembrance has assumed an especially important place in SUFISM, in which *dhikr* refers both to a word or phrase pronounced repeatedly during their ritual practices and to the ritual practices themselves. Among the sacred words and phrases used most commonly by Sufis in this regard are ALLAH, or one of God's other divine names; *la ilaha illa Allah* "there is not god but God"; *Allahu akbar* "God is greater"; *al-hamdu lillah* "Praise God"; and simply *hu* "He." For some Sufi orders, a single litany may be repeated 70,000 times.

The introduction of *dhikr* performances into the life of the Sufi orders began around the 11th

"Remember God" says the sign posted on a stand with clay jugs containing water for thirsty passersby in downtown Cairo. *(Juan E. Campo)*

century. Each Sufi order developed its own distinctive code of *dhikr* practices, which it ascribed to its founding Sufi masters. By regulating the practices, they not only fostered the embodiment of the spiritual teachings of the order, but also disciplined the behavior of its members and actualized the AUTHORITY of the order's leadership. *Dhikr* activities are conducive to ecstatic outbursts and unpredictable behavior, so the code helps provide a degree of decorum.

Dhikr rituals have been performed in solitude and in group gatherings, silently or audibly (by heart or by tongue). Most frequently, they occur at Sufi hospices (the *khanqah, tekke,* or *rabita*) and at saint shrines. Performance of the litanies is accompanied by breath control techniques and rhythmic movements of the body, which can induce a trancelike state of consciousness (HAL) or ecstatic experience (*wajd*). Participants have been said to visualize colored lights, or flashes, which they believe emanate from the realm of the unseen. The atmosphere of *dhikr* performances may be enhanced by MUSIC, drums, and dancing, as exemplified by the *sema* of the MEVLEVI SUFI ORDER. On the other hand, Naqshbandi Sufis are known to refrain from such outward performances and promote silent *dhikr* instead. In the past, conservative Muslim authorities may have criticized such activities, but today religious conservatives, Islamists, and secular Muslims who hold rational-scientific worldviews vehemently oppose them. Nonetheless, in the world of the Sufis and their many supporters, the *dhikr* is seen as a way to gain spiritual enlightenment and achieve union (*ittisal*) or annihilation (*fana*) in God. In this regard, remembering God entails forgetting oneself and the world, even if only for the moment.

See also ADAM AND EVE; *AYA; BAQA AND FANA;* NAMES OF GOD; NAQSHBANDI SUFI ORDER; SHIISM; *TARIQA.*

Further reading: Michael Gilsenan, *Saint and Sufi in Modern Egypt: An Essay in the Sociology of Religion* (Oxford: Oxford University Press, 1973), 156–187; J. Spencer Trimingham, *The Sufi Orders in Islam* (1971. Reprint, New York: Oxford University Press, 1988), 194–217; Pnina Werbner, "Stamping the Earth with the Name of Allah: Zikr and the Sacralizing of Space among British Muslims." In *Making Muslim Space in North America and Europe,* edited by Barbara Metcalf, 167–185 (Berkeley: University of California Press, 1996).

dhimmi (from the Arabic *ahl al-dhimma,* people of the treaty)

*Dhimmi*s are the non-Muslims who live within Islamdom and have a regulated and protected status. The term as such does not appear in the QURAN but is found in HADITH related to MUHAMMAD's treatment of Jews and Christians within the territories controlled by the nascent Islamic state. The relevant quranic verse in that regard commands the Muslims to "fight those who have previously received revelation and do not believe in God or in the Last Day, who do not forbid that which God and his Prophet have forbidden, and who do not believe in the true religion, until they agree to pay the JIZYA in humility." (Q 9:29) Thus, *dhimmi* status is not accorded to all members of religions recognized as having had previous divine revelation. Rather, it is the status of members of those religions living within an Islamic polity (the *dar al-Islam*) who have submitted to the political dominance of the Islamic state. Much of the modern demagoguery around this topic is therefore entirely irrelevant, insofar as Muslims, who constitute small minorities in the West, could not (and generally would not) attempt to make others submit to their religiopolitical authority.

Historically, *dhimmi* status has been applied quite broadly to various non-Muslims living in lands controlled by Muslims. Thus, for instance, Zoroastrians, who did not have a "previously received revelation" or scripture, were accorded this protected status, as were Hindus and many others. Being treated as a *dhimmi* in such circumstances carried certain benefits as well as potential liabilities. The benefits were clear: *Dhimmis* were allowed to practice their religions freely and without constraint, except in cases in which a public practice might openly conflict with Muslims' sensibilities or in which they insulted Islam. Moreover, *dhimmis* were granted most of the protections due to Muslims, could not be arbitrarily harmed, and could not be forced to convert or emigrate from Muslim-ruled territories. The liabilities were potentially numerous, but generally only one was of any import: paying the *jizya*, or poll tax—a tax on individual members of the community in question. *Jizya* was regularly collected, and it appears to have been onerous for impoverished *dhimmis*, as evidenced especially in Goitein's work on Jews in medieval CAIRO. In some cases, the wealthy *dhimmis* might pay the tax for

others of the community who were indigent, but this was not universal by any means. Other than the tax, there were numerous regulations, often cast as the so-called Pact of Umar, referring to the second CALIPH, but most likely from the 11th century or so, at least in its present form. Nonetheless, from the eighth century, certainly, one could find occasions when rulers imposed restrictions on the *dhimmi*s, including forcing them to wear certain prescribed clothing different from that of Muslims (perhaps originally to forestall espionage), forbidding their building of new places of worship or even repairing existing ones, requiring that all high officials be Muslims (they very often were not), and so on.

However, historical evidence makes abundantly clear that the *dhimmi* rules were never systematically applied and were most often applied temporarily by rulers who lacked legitimacy and tried to gain it by dressing themselves in the garb of piety. While restrictions governing non-Muslims were generally not applied, others, such as those prohibiting non-Muslim men from marrying Muslim women (but not the inverse), as well as rules against APOSTASY from Islam (but not the inverse), were broadly applied. While these restrictions do not amount to persecution, they likely made CONVERSION to Islam more attractive. On the other hand, compared to the virulent anti-Judaism that arose in Europe in medieval times, the situation of *dhimmi*s was quite enviable. The picture, in other words, was complex.

In the modern period, this term has occasionally been resuscitated, but it is generally obsolete. AFGHANISTAN's TALIBAN wanted to impose the legally prescribed *dhimmi* dress codes on non-Muslims and did so to some extent. But this has not been the case elsewhere, and most Muslims worldwide appear to have regarded this action incredulously. As ideas about nationalism and CITIZENSHIP take precedence over those of religiously determined identity, many Islamic groups such as the MUSLIM BROTHERHOOD have recognized the equality of Muslims and non-Muslims in a putative Islamic state, thereby emptying *dhimmi* status of any real meaning.

See also CHRISTIANITY AND ISLAM; *DAR AL-ISLAM AND DAR AL-HARB*; EMIGRANTS; HINDUISM AND ISLAM; JUDAISM AND ISLAM.

Further reading: Khaled Abou El Fadl, "Islamic Law and Muslim Minorities: The Juristic Discourse on Muslim Minorities from the Second/Eighth to the Eleventh/Seventeenth Centuries," *Islamic Law and Society* 1 (1994): 141–187; Patricia Crone, *God's Rule* (New York: Columbia University Press, 2004), 358—392; S. D. Goitein, *A Mediterranean Society,* 6 vols. (Berkeley: University of California Press, 1967–1993).

Dhu al-Qarnayn   *See* ALEXANDER THE GREAT.

dialogue

Interreligious (or interfaith) dialogue is a form of positive interaction between known followers of different religious traditions or different denominations and sects within a single religious tradition. It is done on different levels, from the individual and local to the institutional and global. Dialogue topics include THEOLOGY, worship, ethics, interfaith relations, and worldly issues. The goals of dialogue can vary, but they often involve efforts to achieve mutual understanding and tolerance, identify shared values, establish interfaith bonds, overcome prejudice and religious fanaticism, and, perhaps most importantly, avert conflict or foster healing where conflict has occurred. Dialogue may also result in a reexamination of one's own religious convictions. One thing dialogue does not intend to do is convert people from one religion or one denomination to another, nor does it seek to create a new religion. Muslim leaders and organizations engage in dialogue with non-Muslims, including Christians, Jews, Hindus, and Buddhists. There have also been some efforts to promote mutual understanding among Sunni and Shii Muslims.

Muslims have been in close contact with people belonging to other religions for all of their history, beginning with MUHAMMAD's encounters with polytheists and Jews in MECCA and MEDINA in the seventh century. There is substantial evidence for exchanges and discussions between Muslims, Christians, and Jews in the first centuries of Islamic history in SYRIA, IRAQ and EGYPT. These exchanges have left their imprint on Islamic religious tradition, philosophy, the sciences, and monumental architecture. They also enriched religious and cultural life in medieval ANDALUSIA. Figures such as AL-BIRUNI (d. 1048), AKBAR (d. 1605), and DARA SHIKOH (d. 1659) are remembered for their learned engagement with Hindu pundits and representatives of other religious communities in INDIA. On the other hand, conservative religious authorities, Muslims and non-Muslims, wrote polemical literature refuting the religious claims of other religions. Muslim rulers employed non-Muslims in the courts as ministers and physicians, which is how the great Jewish philosopher Maimonides (d. 1204) made his living in Egypt. Non-Muslims were legally protected subjects (DHIMMIs) under the SHARIA, but they held subordinate status and periodically fell victim to Muslim tyrannical rulers.

Continuing interfaith dialogue activities by organized religious associations, whereby all participants had relatively equal footing, did not really begin to develop until the early 20th century, with the onset of a new ecumenical spirit in the West. The 1893 Parliament of World Religions in Chicago signaled new, more tolerant attitudes among some Christian churches toward non-Christians. The parliament included at least two people who represented the "Mohammedan" faith (Islam). Major Christian churches began to consider interreligious communication to be a more valued goal than conversion. They also had the benefit of more accurate knowledge about Islamic beliefs and history, thanks to the efforts of European and American scholars, the Orientalists. Muslims, for their part, were reluctant to participate in interreligious dialogues for several reasons. Language posed a barrier initially, because most Muslim religious authorities were not conversant in the European languages. Many thought dialogue might be a disguised missionary effort by European Christian churches, and they were wary of connections between their conversation partners and the European colonial powers that had occupied their countries. However, the creation of new nation-states in the 20th century, growing knowledge of European languages and cultures, and increased global travel, immigration, and communication helped overcome these barriers. Since the 1960s, catastrophic violence in the Middle East and attacks by Muslim radicals in Europe and the United States, especially the September 11th assaults in 2001, have also provided incentives for Muslims to engage more actively in dialogue with non-Muslims.

The World Council of Churches and the Roman Catholic Church began to actively embrace interreligious dialogue in the 1950s and 1960s. They organized international and regional conferences and published books and papers that promoted dialogue among Christians, Jews, and Muslims. Joined by countless other organizations on local and global levels, they continue to promote interreligious dialogue today. Their efforts have prompted Islamic organizations such as the MUSLIM WORLD LEAGUE and the WORLD MUSLIM CONGRESS to participate in and sponsor similar activities, beginning in the 1980s and 1990s. Dialogue among Jews, Christians, and Muslims has been further enriched by a growing recognition that more than being monotheistic religions, they are Abrahamic, which emphasizes a common religiocultural heritage as "children of Abraham," the ancestral biblical figure who is also highly esteemed by Muslims. Muslim-Jewish dialogue, however, has been negatively affected by the ongoing violence in Israel-Palestine, but this conflict has made the need for such dialogue even

more urgent. As a consequence, leading Muslim and Jewish organizations in the United States are making concerted efforts to sponsor dialogue activities, often with the encouragement and support of Christian groups.

Interreligious dialogue is also occurring on college and university campuses in the United States and Europe, helping to build friendships, mutual understanding, and acceptance among Muslims, Jews, Christians, and secularists. Progressive Muslim scholars raised and educated in Europe and the United States such as Tariq Ramadan (b. 1962) and KHALED ABOU EL FADL (b. 1963) represent a significant new force that is contributing to greater understanding between Muslims and non-Muslims. On a global scale, another noteworthy development is the formation of groups promoting dialogue, tolerance, and understanding that have been inspired by Sufi ideals. These include the Naqshbandi-Haqqani Sufi Order and followers of the modern Turkish thinker FETHULLAH GÜLEN (b. 1941). These groups have strong followings among young people, many of whom are college educated and cosmopolitan in outlook.

See also BUDDHISM AND ISLAM; CHRISTIANITY AND ISLAM; COUNCIL ON AMERICAN-ISLAMIC RELATIONS; *DHIMMI;* AL-HAQQANI, MUHAMMAD NAZIM; HINDUISM AND ISLAM; JUDAISM AND ISLAM; MOHAMMEDANISM; MUSLIM PUBLIC AFFAIRS COUNCIL.

Further reading: M. Darol Bryant and S. A. Ali, eds., *Muslim-Christian Dialogue: Promise and Problems* (St. Paul, Minn.: Paragon House, 1998); M. Fethullah Gülen, *Toward a Global Civilization of Love and Tolerance* (Somerset, N.J.: The Light, Inc., 2004); Yvonne Y. Haddad and Wadi Z. Haddad, eds., *Muslim-Christian Encounters* (Gainesville: University Press of Florida, 1995); Hans Küng, *Islam: Past, Present and Future* (Oxford: Oneworld, 2007); Tariq Ramadan, *Western Muslims and the Future of Islam* (New York: Oxford University Press, 2004); Gerard Sloyan, ed., *Religions of the Book* (Lanham, Md.: University Press of America, 1996).

dietary laws

Many religions and cultures define themselves not only by what they believe, but also by what they eat and how they prepare it. Food brings people together and separates them from others, it links them to the natural and sacred worlds, it fills their memories and imaginations, and it helps to mark their places in time and space. The rules that influence peoples' food practices can be a matter of social customs that are passed from generation to generation, or they can be construed as having issued from sacred beings through a revelation or a mythical story that may involve themes of sacrifice and DEATH. Sometimes, dietary laws and customs can be both a matter of social custom and religion. This is the case for Islamic dietary laws, which are less rigorous than dietary laws in Orthodox Judaism.

In Islamic dietary laws, foods are classified into groups—those that are lawful (HALAL) and forbidden (HARAM), and those that are pure (*tahir, tayyib*) and impure (*rajis, najis*). This division into lawful-pure and forbidden-impure groups of food is based on the QURAN and HADITH, the Islamic sources of revelation. Jurists in the different schools of Islamic law have elaborated upon it further. The most general statement in the Quran about food is one that was intended for all "children of Adam": "Eat and drink, but do not be wasteful, for God does not like wasteful people" (Q 7:31). The Quran instructs people to eat only lawful and good things from the Earth and not to "follow in Satan's footsteps" (Q 2:168). Both of these verses indicate that eating raises ethical issues. The Quran also identifies specific foods that God has provided for people to eat: dates, grapes, olives, pomegranates, grains, and the flesh of domestic cattle, sheep, goats, and CAMELS (Q 6:99, 141–145; 80:25–32). For Muslims, any meat that is consumed must come from an animal that has been slaughtered or sacrificed in accordance with specific rules: The name of God (the BASMALA) must be invoked (Q 6:118, 121), and a deep incision with a sharp knife must be made across the throat. Most seafood can be eaten (Q 5:96; 16:14), as well as hunted animals as long as the name of God has been pronounced when the hunting weapon is discharged (Q 5:4). The Quran permits Muslims to share the lawful and pure food of Jews, Christians, and other PEOPLE OF THE BOOK (Q 5:5), but jurists rule that the food of known heretics, apostates, idol worshippers, and atheists is forbidden. If there is any doubt about the source of the food, a Muslim is usually allowed to eat it as long as the name of God has been pronounced over it before being eaten.

The Quran expressly forbids believing Muslims from eating carrion (meat from unsacrificed dead things), spilt blood, pork, and food that has been offered to idols instead of God (Q 5:3; 6:145). The HADITH expands this list to include other forbidden food, especially the flesh of predators (animals with fangs or talons). As for any meat from an animal that has not been correctly slaughtered, Muslim jurists maintain that it must be considered as carrion, making it inedible. This includes animals that have been strangled, beaten to death, killed by a fall, or gored to death (Q 5:3). Wine (*khamr*) is also prohibited (Q 5:90–91), and jurists have applied this rule to other intoxicating substances. All such forbidden foods and bever-

Turkish family offers hospitality to visitors from America (*Juan E. Campo*)

ages are said to be impure and can prevent Muslims from fulfilling their religious duties unless avoided or removed. Only in cases of dire necessity are exceptions made to these prohibitions (Q 2:172–173).

Specific dietary rules may also apply to worship and other activities in Muslim life. PRAYER, FASTING during RAMADAN, ALMSGIVING, and the HAJJ all involve restrictions and procedures concerning food that participants are required to observe. Offering food is one of the most important acts of charity, but the act is invalid if the food offered is forbidden. There are also rules of etiquette recommended for occasions involving FEASTING and hospitality as well as ordinary meals (for example, pronouncing the *basmala,* taking food and drink with the right hand, and not reclining while eating). Sufi brotherhoods have developed rules for eating and fasting that apply exclusively to their members.

In the modern age of large-scale movements of people around the world, science, and fast-food franchises, Muslim dietary rules have taken on new significance. Many educated Muslims, for example, attempt to explain their ancient dietary laws to non-Muslims in terms of modern concepts of health and science. Others use them to maintain their distinctive identities in foreign lands or as their own Muslim cultures undergo far-reaching changes. Studies of Muslim immigrants in Europe and the United States have shown that adherence to dietary laws concerning pork, alcohol, and animal slaughter are among the most common aspects of their religious tradition they are likely to observe. Practicing African-American Muslims are also careful to observe Muslim dietary laws. In Muslim countries, many of which are quite secular, governments issue laws that seek to win compliance for dietary rules and control the availability of alcohol. SAUDI ARABIA, LIBYA, SUDAN, IRAN, and AFGHANISTAN have officially banned the sale and public consumption of alcohol, although there is often a black market trade in such banned beverages.

See also ANIMALS; APOSTASY; FOOD AND DRINK.

Further reading: Valerie J. Hoffman, "Eating and Fasting for God in Sufi Tradition." *Journal of the American Academy of Religion* 63 (Fall 1995): 465–484; Yusuf al-Qaradawi, *The Lawful and the Prohibited in Islam* (Al-halal wal-haram fi al-Islam). Translated by Kamal El-Helbawi, M. Moinuddin Siddiqui, and Syed Shukry (Indianapolis: American Trust Publications, 1960), 39–78.

disbelief   *See* KAFIR.

divorce

Divorce is a formal separation between a husband and wife by custom or by law. In Islam, it falls within the sphere of jurisprudence (FIQH), which is concerned with family law and also includes the laws of marriage and inheritance. Divorce (*talaq*) is therefore legally recognized in the Islamic legal tradition, where it is based on detailed rulings given in the QURAN (Q 2:226–232, 236–237, 241; 65:1–7) and HADITH and further elaborated in the schools (*madhahib*) of religious law. Moreover, Islamic divorce law is not monolithic—it embodies differences of opinion among the legal schools and reflects local customs found within the world's various Muslim communities. Muslim family law did not begin to be formally codified until the 20th century, but even with this codification there are still significant differences among the divorce laws instituted by countries with Muslim majority populations.

Although divorce is permitted in Islam, Muslims have noted that the Quran and hadith contain statements that recommend against it. The Quran urges that the husband and wife seek arbitration in order to preserve their relationship (Q 4:35). According to a hadith cited in the collection of Abu Daud (d. 889), Muhammad said, "None of the things permitted by God is more hated by him than divorce." As a permitted practice, however, Islamic law gave men the exclusive right to initiate divorce, which could be accomplished by simply stating "I divorce you" three times. The woman need not even be present when he pronounced divorce, and no formal judicial process was required. Medieval Islamic divorce law put WOMEN at a significant disadvantage, but it was partly mitigated by 1) the recommendation that the three proclamations of divorce be performed on three separate occasions, 2) the requirement that the husband pay the woman all or part of her dowry, and 3) the requirement that the husband provide her with lodging and support for a waiting period of up to three menstrual cycles (about three months). The husband could revoke the divorce during this period as long as he had not pronounced the divorce declaration a third time. If the woman was pregnant, he was obliged to support her for the duration of her pregnancy, and both mother and child had to be maintained for up to two years while the child was being nursed. The divorce was irrevocable once the three-month waiting period had ended and the pronouncement had been made a third time. A woman could not initiate a divorce, but in special circumstances she had the right to petition a judge to annul the marriage. The MALIKI LEGAL SCHOOL of Sunni Islam is considered to have been the most liberal in this respect, for it allowed a woman to request an end to the marriage because of the husband's cruelty, inability to support her, desertion, or contracting an illness that could be harmful to her. APOSTASY could also be grounds for divorce. Shii law concerning divorce was similar to that of the Sunnis. In actual practice, a divorcee was often at the mercy of her former husband's willingness to fulfill his legal obligations and a judge's willingness to intervene if he did not.

During the 20th century, Muslim reformers sought to change traditional divorce law to give women a more equitable footing in initiating divorce and to protect them from its arbitrary use by their husbands and ad hoc judicial rulings. New legislation concerning divorce was adopted by many newly created countries to make this possible. Among Muslim-majority countries in the forefront of reform were TUNISIA, EGYPT, TURKEY,

ALGERIA, JORDAN, and LIBYA. In some instances, traditional Islamic law has collided with secular law, as occurred in the controversial 1985 case of Shah Bano Begum, an impoverished divorcee in INDIA. The Indian Supreme Court ruled on the basis of that country's civil law code that Shah Bano was entitled to receive alimony after her husband of 43 years divorced her to take a second wife. The decision sparked widespread demonstrations by India's Muslim minority, who saw it as an affront to their religion by Hindus. The result was the passage of the 1986 Muslim Women Act, which upheld the traditional Islamic law that limited the obligation of the husband to pay for the divorcee's maintenance for only the duration of the three-month waiting period. In Western countries, most Muslims adhere to local civil codes governing marriage and divorce.

See also CHILDREN; HINDUISM AND ISLAM; RENEWAL AND REFORM MOVEMENTS.

Further reading: Peter Awn, "Indian Islam: The Shah Bano Affair." In *Fundamentalism and Gender,* edited by John Stratton Hawley, 63–78 (New York: Oxford University Press, 1994); John L. Esposito and Natana Delong-Bas, *Women in Muslim Family Law.* 2d ed. (Syracuse, N.Y.: Syracuse University Press, 2001); Ziba Mir-Hosseini, *Marriage on Trial: A Study of Islamic Family Law: Iran and Morocco Compared* (London: I.B. Taurus, 1993).

dog

The dog is a descendant of the wolf and was one of the first domesticated ANIMALS. Archaeological evidence indicates its domestication first occurred in the Middle East around 10,000 B.C.E. Despite the ancient and close association between humans and dogs, Middle Eastern cultures have formed mixed attitudes toward them. A common insult used by people in the region, no matter whether they are Muslim, Jew, or Christian, is to call someone a dog or the offspring of one. Yet these same cultures have also accepted dogs as living creatures worthy of humane treatment and valued for their usefulness in guarding property, hunting, and herding sheep.

The ambivalent feelings Middle Eastern peoples have held for dogs is especially evident in Islamic contexts. The QURAN, for example, employs the dog as a simile for disbelievers (Q 7:176). The HADITH advise Muslims not to stretch out their arms like dogs when they prostrate themselves in PRAYER. Most jurists maintain that dogs and pigs alike are inherently impure (*najis*) animals, meaning that contact with them or their secretions invalidates a person's prayer. They can also profane a MOSQUE or prayer place by their presence. In either case, the defilement can be corrected by physically removing the animal and symbolically washing the places they touched with earth and clean water. Several reasons have been given for regarding dogs as a source of such impurity. Muslim authorities invoke hadith that say ANGELS do not enter houses in which there are dogs. Al-Jahiz (d. ca. 868), a famous Iraqi literary figure, proposed that dogs are reviled because they have a mixed nature—neither wild nor domestic, neither human nor demonic, but combinations of these qualities. In the philosophical story of the debate between humans and animals related by the BRETHREN OF PURITY, dogs as well as cats are condemned by other animals for associating too closely with humans and assuming human qualities.

Nonetheless, Islamic literature also expresses favorable attitudes toward dogs. MUHAMMAD is reported in the hadith to have said that when a man or woman gives water to a thirsty dog, that person would be rewarded by God and enter paradise. He once ordered the killing of black dogs in MEDINA but relented, saying, "The black dog was one of the communities (created by God). Thus it was not created but for some good purpose, so the obliteration of its kind must create some deficiency in nature." The SHARIA permits the use of dogs in hunting wild game (see Q 5:4) as well as for herding flocks and protecting property,

but not keeping them as pets. The most famous Middle Eastern canine breed is the Saluki, an Arabian hound known for its prowess in hunting down gazelles and rabbits. Moreover, not all jurists agreed that dogs were impure animals, and al-Jahiz recounted their virtues as well as their deficiencies. Muslim commentaries on the Quran mention a dog named Qitmir that kept company with the Companions of the Cave (see Q 18:9–26), a group of youths who proclaimed their belief in God but had to retreat to a cave where God let them sleep for centuries in order to escape persecution from disbelievers. The commentators regarded Qitmir as a protective and loyal canine who would be allowed to enter paradise. Rumi (d. 1273), the Persian poet and mystic, even acknowledged that Qitmir and other dogs had an inner awareness of God's love for his creation. Despite such support for the virtues of dogs, cats tend to be held in higher esteem in Islamic tradition than dogs.

See also CAT; DIETARY LAWS.

Further reading: Lenn Evan Goodman, ed. and trans., *The Case of the Animals versus Man before the King of the Jinn: A Tenth-Century Ecological Fable of the Pure Brethren of Basra* (Boston: Twayne Publishers, 1978); Ibn Marzuban, *The Book of the Superiority of Dogs over Many of Those Who Wear Clothes*. Translated and edited by G. R. Smith and M. A. S. Abdel Haleem (Warminster, U.K.: Aris & Phillips, 1978); Yusuf al-Qaradawi, *The Lawful and the Prohibited in Islam* (Indianapolis: American Trust Publications, n.d.); Ahmad b. Muhammad al-Thalabi, *Arais al-majalis fi qiṣaṣ al-anbiya, or, Lives of the Prophets*. Translated by William M. Brinner (Leiden: E.J. Brill, 2002).

Dome of the Rock

The Dome of the Rock is the most prominent architectural feature in the urban landscape of JERUSALEM and is one of the most exquisite works of Islamic ART and ARCHITECTURE in the world. The building is located in the middle of a spacious plaza atop a hill on the eastern edge of the city where the ancient Israelite temple of Solomon used to stand. This sacred precinct is known today as the Temple Mount (Hebrew: *Har ha-Bayit*) and as the Noble Sanctuary (Arabic: *al-Haram al-Sharif*). The physical structure of the building itself shelters a legendary rock that in Jewish tradition is believed to be where ABRAHAM's sacrifice occurred and where Muslims believe MUHAMMAD stood before ascending to heaven. The building consists of a large golden dome that crowns an eight-sided building and is supported by a cylinder resting on a complex of piers, arches, and columns. Beautiful Arabic inscriptions and mosaics with vegetal motifs, crowns, and jewel designs decorate the monument inside and out.

The Umayyad CALIPH Abd al-Malik ibn Marwan (r. 685–705) built the Dome of the Rock between 691 and 693. The Haram area had been largely abandoned in the centuries between the destruction of the Second Temple in 70 C.E. and the arrival of the Muslims in 638. Abd al-Malik's project was but part of a larger one to develop the area and Islamize the city. Scholars have several explanations for the dome's unique design and decorations. The prevailing view is that it represents an Umayyad effort to claim Jerusalem as a holy city for Muslims and to express the triumph of Islam over the Byzantine Empire and the Christian Church. Indeed, as art historian Oleg Grabar has pointed out, the Arabic inscriptions that decorate the building contain verses from the QURAN that recognize JESUS as a prophet and refute the Christian doctrine of his divinity. Moreover, the structure incorporates features that echo those of the nearby Church of the Holy Sepulcher (known to Eastern Christians as the Basilica of the Anastasis), which it overlooks on the western side, not those of a MOSQUE. The main mosque in the Haram area is the AQSA MOSQUE, located south of the Dome of the Rock.

The building has withstood centuries of political and religious turmoil, neglect, and change. It has undergone numerous repairs, and restorations have been done to it. When Jerusalem fell to the crusaders in 1099, Godrey of Bouillon, one of their leaders, had it converted into a church called the Temple of the Lord. When SALADIN (d. 1193) retook the city in 1187, he personally joined with his troops in purifying the Haram and removing Christian images and inscriptions from the Dome of the Rock. During the 20th century, the Dome of the Rock became a symbol of Palestinian nationalism and Islamic activist movements. It is still frequented by Muslims living in the West Bank, Israelis, and foreign visitors. Occasionally, it has also served as a flashpoint for confrontations between Palestinians and Israeli security forces.

See also CHRISTIANITY AND ISLAM; CRUSADES; ISRAEL; JUDAISM AND ISLAM; NIGHT JOURNEY AND ASCENT; UMAYYAD CALIPHATE.

Further reading: Amikam Elad, *Medieval Jerusalem and Islamic Worship: Holy Places, Ceremonies, Pilgrimage* (Leiden: E.J. Brill, 1993); Oleg Grabar, *The Shape of the Holy: Early Islamic Jerusalem* (Princeton, N.J.: Princeton University Press, 1996).

dreams

Dreams and visions (Arabic: *ruya* or *manam*) occupy a special place in Islam as in many ancient Near Eastern religions, since such experiences are considered intimately linked to prophecy. In the QURAN (as in the Bible), God communicates to his PROPHETS through dreams and visions, and many prophets are endowed with the power of dream interpretation. Several HADITH manifest MUHAMMAD's affirmation of the relation between dreams and prophethood; for example, "The divine revelation comes to prophets in waking as well as in sleep." Given the quranic precedent and the importance that Muhammad attached to dreams, the early Muslims greatly esteemed oneiromancy, the pre-Islamic science of dream classification and interpretation. The belief in the divinely inspired "good dream" (*ruya hasana*)—as distinguished from demonic-inspired "muddled dreams" (*adghath al-ahlam*)—has provided a paradigm for the social acceptance of dreams and visions as authoritative in Islamicate societies up until the modern period. The proliferation of dream narratives in Islamic (auto)biographical writings, historical chronicles, belles-lettres, and philosophical treatises demonstrates that they fulfill the social functions of arbiters of contested religious and political AUTHORITY and sources of communal or individual guidance. Traditionally, oneiric accounts have predominated in Sufi (auto)biographies.

Quranic narratives of the dreams and visions of prophets and kings follow the biblical accounts. ABRAHAM's vision (*manam*) ordering him to sacrifice his son (Q 12:102), the dreams of JOSEPH, and the "muddled, confused dreams" of Pharaoh (Q 12:44), among others, are recorded. The Islamic inheritance of this oneiric legacy is seen in the scriptural references to Muhammad's dreams and visionary experiences, which prefigure critical events in his life. Prior to the Battle of Badr, God granted Muhammad a dream of the victory (Q 8:43). His triumphal entrance into MECCA is described as the fulfillment of the vision (*ruya*) of God's apostle (Q 48:27). The narrative of Muhammad's Night Journey to JERUSALEM (*isra*) and heavenly ascension (*miraj*) reads "We [God] granted the vision [*ruya*] which we showed thee, but as a trial for men" (Q 17:60). Despite this quranic attestation of a vision, most Muslims believe that the ascension was an actual physical journey manifesting Muhammad's charismatic powers.

The science of oneiromancy flourished under Islam due to the interest in interpreting Muhammad's dreams and his declaration that in the absence of further prophecies after him, God would continue to guide human beings through "good dreams." The most renowned systematic oneirocritics of the Islamic period include Ibn Sirin (d. 728), al-Dinawari (alive in 1006), al-Shahin (15th century), and al-Nabulusi (d.

1731). Treatises on the subject by the latter three authors still survive and show the influence of Artemidorus's *Oneirocritica,* which was translated into Arabic by Hunayn ibn Ishaq (d. 873), the Christian transmitter of Greek philosophy to the Arabs. Such treatises typically expound definitions and procedures of dream interpretation, the duties of the oneirocritic, and elaborate systems of dream classification.

For Islamic philosophers such as IBN SINA (d. 1037) and IBN RUSHD (d. 1198), dreams were manifestations of ultimate reality, instruments through which God (the divine intellect) transmitted knowledge to mankind. In Sufi narratives, spiritual progress is often recounted in ascending stages patterned on Muhammad's heavenly ascension. Autobiographical accounts of Sufis' dreams authenticate the authors' own piety and charisma vis-à-vis their peers. Often, as with AL-GHAZALI (d. 1111), a dream could be a liminal experience marking a conversion to a new spiritual state. Medieval historical chronicles often exploited the symbolic nature and authority of dreams to surreptitiously reveal an ostensibly neutral author's true opinion about a communal dispute.

In the modern period, dreams continue to function as loci of power for Sufis and as alternative sources of authority for political or religious reformers. Thus, Shah Wali Allah of Delhi (d. 1762) became convinced of his mission to reform the Islamic UMMA after dreaming of Muhammad and his grandsons. The Fulani leader USMAN DAN FODIO (d. 1817) justified his JIHAD against social corruption in response to a dream of the prophet Muhammad. Nevertheless, some contemporary Arabs and Muslims have exhibited skepticism toward the authority of dreams. This is true of Salafi reformers seeking to purify Islam from the "innovations" of popular and Sufi religious practices, such as MUHAMMAD ABDUH (d. 1905) and MUHAMMAD RASHID RIDA (d. 1935), who had studied European ideas on skepticism and rationality.

See also BIDAA; NIGHT JOURNEY AND ASCENT; SALAFISM; SUFISM.

Linda G. Jones

Further reading: Toufic Fahd, "The Dream in Medieval Islamic Society." In *The Dream in Human Societies,* edited by Gustav E. von Grunebaum and R. Caillois, 351–379 (Berkeley and Los Angeles, University of California Press, 1966); Marsha K. Hermansen, "A Cognitive Approach to Visionary Experience in Islamic Sufi Thought." *Religion* 27 (1997): 25–43; Linda G. Jones, "Dreams and Visions: A Comparative Analysis of Spiritual Gifts in Medieval Christian and Muslim Conversion Narratives." In *Medieval Cultures in Contact,* edited by R. F. Gyug, 105–138 (New York: Fordham University Press, 2003); Elizabeth Sirriyeh, "Dreams of the Holy Dead: Traditional Islamic Oneirocriticism versus Salafi Scepticism." *Journal of Semitic Studies* 45, no. 1 (Spring 2000): 115–130.

Druze

The Druze are Arabic-speaking followers of a religion of the same name that originated in the 11th century. They call themselves "the Unitarians" (*muwahhidun*). There are an estimated 1 million members of this religious community, and they live mainly in the mountains and rural areas of LEBANON, SYRIA, and ISRAEL.

The Druze religion began in EGYPT during the reign of al-Hakim bi-Amr Allah (r. 996–1021), a CALIPH of the Ismaili FATIMID DYNASTY, who promoted his dynasty's doctrines through a well-organized system of religious outreach called the DAAWA. Al-Hakim, who was known for his extraordinary eccentricities, allowed himself to be declared not just the divinely appointed Ismaili imam, but God himself. This caused a split among Ismailis, and the group favoring al-Hakim's divinity formed the new religion in 1017 under the leadership of Muhammad ibn Ismail al-Darazi (d. 1019), after whom the Druze were named, and Hamza ibn Ali ibn Ahmad. Al-Darazi disappeared or was assassinated, so it was Hamza who orga-

nized the religion and its missionary activities, which quickly won converts among peasants in the mountains of Lebanon and Syria.

Hamza presented himself as the IMAM of the Druze, and he developed the doctrine that al-Hakim, like JESUS in Christianity, was the embodiment of God the creator in history. Those who followed him were the Unitarians—worshippers of the one God as revealed in the person of al-Hakim. Furthermore, Hamza formed a scriptural canon for the new religion: six books of letters known as *Al-Hikma al-sharifa* (The noble wisdom). The SHARIA was abrogated, which meant, among other things, that the FIVE PILLARS of Islamic worship were no longer required, polygamy was forbidden, and DIVORCE was discouraged. Instead, the Druze were expected to honor seven duties, which included belief in al-Hakim's divinity, rejection of SATAN and non-Druze beliefs, submission to God, truthfulness, and solidarity among the Druze community. Members of the religion were encouraged to conceal their belief by practicing *taqiyya* when among Muslims and other non-Druze peoples. Other important tenets of the Druze religion are belief in reincarnation immediately after death and belief that the soul lives through multiple lives in order to attain perfection.

Al-Hakim had disappeared mysteriously in the Muqattam Hills of CAIRO in 1021, and Hamza disappeared around 1043. It was believed that both had entered a period of concealment (GHAYBA), and they were expected to return at some time in the future to establish universal justice. Meanwhile, no more conversions were accepted, and leadership was eventually assumed by a group of religious authorities known as shaykhs, who were drawn from an elite segment of people initiated into the secrets of the religion. These Druze initiates were called the *uqqal,* "enlightened ones." Women as well as men were allowed to be members of this group. The lay members of the Druze community were called the *juhhal,* "ignorant ones." Group loyalty and solidarity were very strong among the Druze, and this is still the case today. Among the leading Druze families are the Jumblats of Lebanon, the Atrashes of Syria, and the Tarifs of Galilee in Israel.

See also ISMAILI SHIISM.

Further reading: Robert Brenton Betts, *The Druze* (New Haven, Conn.: Yale University Press, 1988); Talal Fandi and Ziyad Abi-Shakra, eds., *The Druze Heritage: An Annotated Bibliography* (Amman: Royal Institute for Inter-Faith Studies; London: Druze Heritage Foundation, 2001); Marshall G. S. Hodgson, "Al-Darazi and Hamza in the Origin of the Druze Religion." *Journal of the American Oriental Society* 82 (1962): 5–20.

dua *See* PRAYER.

E

East Africa

The Islamic religion first appeared in East Africa during the lifetime of MUHAMMAD (ca. 510–632), when he sent some of his followers to Abyssinia (in modern Ethiopia) in order to escape Meccan persecution. By the 10th century, Muslim merchants had introduced their faith into Somalia. During the next 500 years, Muslims carried their religion down the East African coast along the trade routes. Muslim communities were established in many of the trading towns along the coast and on several nearby islands. Because of their involvement in international trade, coastal Islamic communities often included Muslims of Arab, Persian, and South Asian origin who belonged to Shafii, Ibadi, Shii, and several other Islamic groups.

Prior to the modern era, East African Islam was mostly limited to the coast due to its association with Muslim merchants, who did not tend to travel inland. This limitation did not apply to the northeastern regions, where small Muslim principalities arose as buffer states between Muslim Egypt and Christian Ethiopia, and in the region of the modern nation of SUDAN, where the sultanates of Wadai, Dar Fur, and Sinnar held sway. In these areas, Islam became the religion of the rul-

ing class but spread more slowly among common people, who also clung to pre-Islamic practices. Increasing ties with the Middle East and the rising influence of Sufi orders led to a more widespread Islamic adherence by people of the region between the 16th and 18th centuries.

European colonial powers began to exert their influence with the arrival of the Portuguese on the East African coast during the 16th century. Portuguese support for Christians in the region led to increased tensions with the Muslims. This situation was exacerbated by the triumph of European COLONIALISM at the end of the 19th century. Colonial rule actually served to spread Islam throughout societies in which Muslim communities had predated colonialism. Europeans extended trade into the interior, opening new fields for Islamic expansion. They also promoted Muslims into positions of influence and created urban conditions that favored the spread of Islam. However, in areas that had been largely untouched by Islam prior to the colonial era, Christian missionaries experienced considerable success.

As a result, East Africa entered the era of independent states as a region divided among Muslim, Christian, and "traditional," or indigenous, religious communities. This has often led to tension between the different religious communities, as evidenced by the long-standing civil war in Sudan between the Islamic north and non-Muslim rebels in the south. In other countries, interfaith relations have been more peaceful. For example, Muslims in Kenya, Tanzania, and Malawi have used a variety of nonviolent means to advance their interests as minority religious communities within secular nation-states. Tensions between Sufi orders and various revivalist groups have also affected the development of East African Islam, with revivalists accusing Sufis of promoting non-Islamic practices. In summary, Islamic communities in East Africa are marked by their diversity and include Muslims from a wide variety of ethnic backgrounds, sectarian loyalties, educational levels, economic statuses, and political viewpoints.

See also CHRISTIANITY AND ISLAM; WEST AFRICA.

Stephen Cory

Further reading: H. B. Hansen and M. Twaddle, *Religion and Politics in East Africa* (London: Currey, 1995); John Middleton, *The World of the Swahili, an African Mercantile Civilization* (New Haven, Conn.: Yale University Press, 1992); Randall L. Pouwels, *Horn and Crescent: Cultural Change and Traditional Islam on the East African Coast (800–1900)* (Cambridge: Cambridge University Press, 1987); J. S. Trimingham, *Islam in East Africa* (London: Oxford University Press, 1964).

education

Muslims, like all peoples, have sought skills and knowledge in all aspects of life from different kinds of teachers to suit their various needs, aspirations, and values. Until the modern era, much of their education was obtained orally and by memorizing or by imitating skills demonstrated by others. In traditional Muslim societies, parents and other elders provided CHILDREN with their first lessons in morality and good manners. They trained them to help perform household chores such as food preparation, caring for and feeding ANIMALS, fetching water, and collecting fuel for the domestic hearth. While boys learned to farm and tend the flocks, girls typically learned to bake bread, cook rice, care for children and the elderly, and weave textiles. Craftsmen such as potters, tanners, glass-makers, carpenters, smiths, and builders taught their skills to apprentices, while would-be merchants learned to buy and sell in the BAZAAR. Soldiers trained in military garrisons and barracks, often located on the outskirts of a city.

Formal education for Muslims before the 19th century consisted of a curriculum based on the QURAN. Developing basic reading and writing skills was interwoven with learning how to submit to God's will, worship him, and obey his commands and prohibitions. The importance of religious education in Islam is conveyed by what many accounts say was the first quranic verse revealed to Muhammad, "Recite, for your lord is most noble; who taught by the pen; he taught the human being what he did not know" (Q 96:3–5). In other words, God is the supreme educator. Elementary education involved memorizing the Quran and hadith, learning the Arabic ALPHABET, simple arithmetic, and beginning to read Arabic prose and poetry. CALLIGRAPHY was sometimes taught, and Persian poetry was included in the curricula of schools in IRAN, AFGHANISTAN, and Central Asia. At first, instruction occurred in homes and MOSQUES, but eventually it shifted to the Quran school (a KUT-TAB, *maktab*, or *pesantren*), which was located in or near a mosque. A male teacher called a *mudarris* or *muallim* presided in the classroom. He was a person who had obtained at least some advanced knowledge in the religious sciences. He taught between 10 and 20 students, sometimes with the help of an assistant teacher or an advanced STUDENT. During class, students sat on the floor with legs crossed in a semicircle (*halaqa*) facing the teacher. Discipline could be very strict, with corporal punishment used when students misbehaved or failed their lessons. Rote learning was standard in the Quran school; independent thinking and creativity were not encouraged.

Around the age of 15, students who had completed two or three years in a Quran school, or the equivalent with tutors, could obtain higher levels of education from religious experts who taught at the congregational mosques (sing. *jami*), mosque-colleges (sing. *masjid*), and colleges of law (sing. MADRASA). The colleges and other places of religious education developed from local learning circles of teachers and students and became the dominant centers of higher learning during the 11th and 12th centuries as a Sunni response to philosophical rationalism and growing Shii power and influence. The Shia also developed institutions of higher education. In the early period, major centers of learning were located in the cities of Kufa, Basra, BAGHDAD, Nishapur, Shiraz, Balkh, CAIRO, DAMASCUS, JERUSALEM, MEDINA, GRANADA, and CORDOBA. Later ones emerged in Isfahan, Qom, Mashhad, Najaf, and ISTANBUL. In INDIA, the leading centers of Islamic education were in DELHI, Jawnpur, Bijapur, and Lucknow. The salaries of the professors, their assistants, and the expenses for founding, maintaining, and operating the schools were traditionally financed by private donations from wealthy and powerful individuals, including WOMEN. As a rule, Islamic schools were not funded directly by the government or public taxes. They often housed manuscript libraries, and there were usually copyists and booksellers nearby, making it convenient for students to acquire learning materials and texts. Madrasas usually had residential quarters for leading professors and students, but additional housing was available at nearby hostels.

The purpose of the college was to teach the SHARIA and related subjects. It usually specialized in a particular school (*madhhab*) of Islamic law. Sunni madrasas specialized in teaching the jurisprudence (*FIQH*) of one of the four major Sunni schools—Hanafi, Shafii, Maliki, or Hanbali. Shii colleges emphasized Jaafari jurisprudence and the teachings of the Twelve IMAMS. A few colleges offered courses in more than one legal tradition as well as in comparative *fiqh*. The curriculum typically included courses in the Quranic sciences (*TAFSIR* and alternative readings of the Arabic text), HADITH studies, ARABIC LANGUAGE AND LITERATURE, and the biographies of MUHAMMAD and his companions. Theology, history, and ethics were also taught, but as secondary subjects. Philosophy, mysticism, the natural SCIENCES, and advanced MATHEMATICS were studied by only a select few; they were more commonly studied outside the college. Students who obtained higher education became members of the ULAMA: judges, jurists, preachers, or teachers of Islamic knowledge. Although girls could attain an elementary education, they were not allowed into the religious colleges. They could obtain a higher education only in a limited way at the mosque, or, if they were from the family of a great male scholar, at home. Indeed, some of the most noted hadith scholars in medieval Cairo and Damascus were the daughters of famous male scholars.

Medieval madrasa education depended on the development of informal, face-to-face relations between students and teachers. Students joined the learning circle of a scholar (SHAYKH) known for his mastery of a particular field of Islamic scholarship. Learning at this level still involved significant amounts of memorization, but it also required cultivating the skills of intellectual conversation and disputation. Serious students might take years to master the different areas of knowledge and the relevant intellectual skills. At the same time, they formed long-lasting networks of associations with their teachers and fellow students. When they had demonstrated mastery of a teacher's book or subject area, they would receive a certificate (*ijaza*) that authorized them to teach what they had learned to others. They did not get a degree from the college as today's students do, but collected certificates from individual professors with whom they had studied. This authorization incorporated them into traditions of scholarship that had been transmitted over many generations. Moreover, students often had to travel abroad in order to further their education. The importance of educational travel was recognized early in Islamic history, as expressed in a well-known hadith that commanded, "Seek knowledge, even unto China." Indeed, the Arabic word for student is *talib,* which literally means "seeker." Traditions and practices of learning, therefore, contributed to the creation of a cosmopolitan Islam that transcended local geographic, ethnic, and cultural boundaries.

Today the medieval Islamic tradition of learning has been largely displaced by modern systems of education and knowledge. Survivals of the past can still be found, but in fragmented and altered forms. This transformation was caused by several significant developments. It started when far-reaching educational reforms were introduced during the 19th century as a result of European invasions of Muslim lands in eastern Europe, the Middle East, North Africa, and South Asia. Muslim rulers realized that they had to create modern armies that could stand up to those of Europe and reform governmental institutions to make them operate more effectively than in the past. They recruited advisers and teachers from Europe to open modern schools based on Western knowledge, and they sent delegations to study in Europe. With the new schools came the printing press to produce books and other instructional materials in European languages. Arabic ceased to be the universal language of learning; it was replaced by French and English and later by local languages, such as Turkish in TURKEY and Persian in Iran. European ideas about democracy, freedom, nationalism, capitalism, liberalism, socialism, fascism, and SECULARISM were introduced to Muslim lands along with the new schools and languages.

The first Western-style schools were opened in Istanbul, Cairo, and Tunis. Graduates went on to serve as officers, doctors, engineers, and government officials. They were in the forefront of modernizing Middle Eastern and North African states, forming what scholars have called "bridgehead elites" for European powers. By the middle of the 19th century, ministries of education were created to operate centralized school systems based on French models. When the Republic of Turkey was created in 1923, all Islamic schools there were closed down. In India, educational reform was introduced by British colonial authorities, because they needed literate, skilled natives to help govern the country and serve in the army. Their larger goal was to transform India into a modern, liberal country like England. Indians, they believed, would have to shed their own cultural heritage in the process, which aroused strong anticolonial nationalist feelings among the Indians.

Christian missionaries arrived from Europe to found schools that offered education in modern subjects in LEBANON, PALESTINE, SYRIA, and EGYPT. These schools were attended by Muslims and Jews as well as Christians. At Catholic missionary schools, the language of instruction was usually French, and all students were required to attend Mass, whether they were Christians or not. Muslims also attended schools established by American Protestants and Russian Orthodox missionaries. In some of these schools, speaking Arabic was discouraged if not completely forbidden. Other schools, such as the American University of Beirut, founded by Protestant missionaries from the United States, have played a significant role in the modern Arabic literary renaissance.

Reform-minded Muslims responded to the creation of schools based on European models and Christian missionary influence by devising models that combined Western with Islamic learning. These efforts were spearheaded by Muslim modernists such as SAYYID AHMAD KHAN (d. 1898) in India and JAMAL AL-DIN AL-AFGHANI (d. 1897) and MUHAMMAD ABDUH (d. 1905) in the Arab Middle East. The reformed curricula emphasized modern letters and sciences. The study of Islam or the Quran was no longer dominant but altered to fit with the teaching of secular subjects such as history, literature, and "religion." With the emergence of new nation-states in the 20th century, secular education prevailed in the public schools and universities of most Muslim countries. School

Girls' school in Upper Egypt *(Juan E. Campo)*

curricula were designed to inculcate students with a sense of patriotism as well as knowledge and training needed to find employment in a modern society. Nevertheless, the teaching of traditional Islamic subjects continued on the elementary levels at Quran schools and at select colleges and universities, such as AL-AZHAR in Cairo, Islamic University in Medina, and the Shii madrasas in Najaf and Qom. Even at these institutions, however, modern influences were strongly felt. Al-Azhar University, for example, has added colleges of medicine, agriculture, and engineering.

The establishment of modern schools and universities by secular governments, missionaries, and Muslim reformers has improved the overall educational level of people living in the countries of the Muslim world. There are now hundreds of state-run universities and a growing number of private universities, many of them with professors who have been educated, at least in part, in Europe and North America. Nevertheless, the quality of the educational experience varies widely. Many schools and universities are overcrowded and lack adequate funding for teachers' salaries, libraries, textbooks, audio-visual equipment, computers, and building maintenance. Girls have had access to modern education since the 19th century but often to a lesser extent than boys because of fam-

ily obligations, cultural traditions, and socioeconomic factors.

Some observers have also asserted that schools and universities have served as breeding grounds for radical Islamic movements. While this may be true in certain instances, such as the Islamic revolutionary movement led by Ayatollah RUHOL-LAH KHOMEINI (d. 1989) and some groups inspired by Wahhabi doctrines in Saudi-funded madrasas, it is probably not as widespread as some have proposed. Other factors are likely to be more important in the proliferation of such movements. On the other hand, it can be argued that modern education has also improved the quality of life for many, stimulated democratic forces, and fostered a cosmopolitan, pluralistic outlook in many Muslim countries.

See also ALIGARH; AUTHORITY; BOOKS AND BOOK-MAKING; DEOBAND; LITERACY; MUFTI; *MURID;* SHIISM.

Further reading: Jonathan P. Berkey, *The Transmission of Knowledge in Medieval Cairo: A Social History of Islamic Education* (Princeton, N.J.: Princeton University Press, 1992); Noura Durkee, "Recited from the Heart." *Saudi Aramco World* 51 (May/June 2000): 32–35; George Makdisi, *The Rise of Colleges: Institutions of Learning in Islam and the West* (Edinburgh: University of Edinburgh Press, 1981); Roy Mottahedeh, *Mantle of the Prophet* (New York: Random House, 1985); Charles Michael Stanton, *Higher Learning in Islam: The Classical Period,* A.D. *700–1300* (Savage, Md.: Rowman & Littlefield, 1990); Gregory Starrett, *Putting Islam to Work: Education, Politics, and Religious Transformation in Egypt* (Berkeley: University of California Press, 1998).

Egypt (Official name: Arab Republic of Egypt)

Today's Arab Republic of Egypt is the most populous country in the Arab world at 81.7 million residents (2008 est.), of whom probably 90 to 94 percent are Sunni Muslims, with the remaining 6 to 10 percent Christians, mainly Orthodox Copts. It has an area of 386,258 square miles, which makes it about the size of Texas and New Mexico combined. Egypt is said to be "the gift of the Nile," the great African river that bisects the country from south to north. The Nile drains into the Mediterranean Sea via the delta, which fans out northward from CAIRO. Egypt shares borders with SUDAN to the south, LIBYA to the west, and ISRAEL and Gaza to the northeast. Its eastern limits are defined by the Red Sea and the Gulf of Aqaba.

Modern Egypt's government is based in the capital city of Cairo and consists of a very strong presidency, a parliament made up of a more important lower people's assembly and a less significant advisory council, as well as a fairly independent judicial system. Islam, according to the constitution amended in 1980, is the official religion of the state, and Islamic law (SHARIA) is proclaimed to be "the principle source of legislation" (Article 2). Egypt's economy is heavily reliant on agriculture, most of which goes to the domestic market. The major earners of hard currency are tourism, remittances from Egyptians working abroad, and oil exports.

In ancient times, Egypt was one of several cradles of world civilization and one of the major world powers. Egypt was part of the Roman Empire, ruled from Constantinople, when it was conquered by the Muslim armies in 641–642. For the first several centuries, Egypt's prime importance for the Islamicate empire, with its capital in MEDINA, DAMASCUS, or BAGHDAD, was as a source of grain and of surplus wealth to be extracted in taxes. By the 10th century, however, the Abbasid Empire was weakening, and Egypt was becoming more independent. The foreign FATIMID DYNASTY of Ismaili Shiite persuasion, conquered Egypt in 969, founded Cairo in 970, and made Egypt the center of a CALIPHATE to rival that of Baghdad. Two dynasties followed, the Ayyubids (1171–1250) and the MAMLUKs (1250–1517), both contributing greatly to making Egypt a great center of learning, culture, and power. AL-AZHAR, originally founded by the Fatimids as the center of their missionary efforts, eventually came to be the foremost center

of Sunni learning. The first Ayyubid ruler, SALA-DIN (d. 1193), was responsible for defeating the crusaders and retaking JERUSALEM. The Mamluks saved Egypt and Syria from the onslaught of the Mongols, who had already destroyed Baghdad and many of the cities in eastern Islamicate lands. In 1517, however, Egypt came under the control of the Ottomans, the last universal Islamicate empire.

Napoleon wrested Egypt from the largely nominal rule of the Ottomans in 1798. His dominion lasted only three years, but the shock of the massive defeat suffered by the Ottoman troops

Downtown Cairo and the Nile River, as seen from the Jazira Tower, looking southward. The Cairo Opera is in the foreground. (Juan E. Campo)

was to change Egypt's history. Muhammad Ali (r. 1805–49), determined to build a European-style military to defend his rule, began the process of centralization, institutionalization, and discipline that would eventuate in an independent Egyptian nation later in the century, although this was not his intent. His grandson Ismail (r. 1863–79) did much to modernize Egypt ("civilize" was the term he used), changing the architectural face of its cities, expanding education, and allowing the development of journalism.

Great Britain, looking after its financial interests in Egypt and eager to control this strategic location, invaded in 1882, remaining in the country, under one guise or another, until 1954. British rule set back reform and development in most respects, although freedoms of the press and religion were probably greater during this period than most others in recent memory. The revolution of 1952, which was to usher in complete independence, changed Egypt tremendously, ending the monarchy imposed by the British, breaking up the enormous landholdings that came to characterize Egypt in the 19th century, and reorienting Egypt away from British influence to leadership in the nonaligned movement. JAMAL ABD AL-NASIR, Egypt's president from 1954 to 1970, was the charismatic former army officer who spearheaded these efforts while also attempting to realize the unification of all the Arab peoples. With the support of the United States, Nasir successfully defended the country against an invasion by the armies of Israel, Britain, and France in the 1956 Suez War, which was sparked when he placed the canal under Egyptian sovereignty. Modern Egyptian history has played out in the shadow of the Arab-Israeli struggle, which has proved much more devastating to the Arabs, including the Egyptians, than to Israel. Egypt fought unsuccessful wars against Israel in 1948, 1967, and 1973. Economic development, educational reform, and democratization all were put off in the name of the greater struggle. The CAMP DAVID ACCORDS that Abd al-Nasir's successor, MUHAMMAD ANWAR AL-SADAT (r. 1970–81) signed with Israel in 1978 inaugurated a welcome era of relative peace and stability that allowed some attention to be paid to these crucial issues. Al-Sadat shared the Nobel Peace Prize with Israeli prime minister Menachem Begin for his role in negotiating and implementing the accords. Another result of the agreement was that Egypt became a close ally of the United States.

Religious ferment in Egypt has been important to the entire region. The MUSLIM BROTHERHOOD, founded in 1928 by HASAN AL-BANNA, has helped in a variety of ways to consolidate the Islamization of society in Egypt and elsewhere. The radical ideologue SAYYID QUTB (d. 1966) has been crucial in providing an intellectual underpinning to the Islamist movements that arose after the 1967 Arab-Israeli War. But Egyptian intellectuals such as Taha Hussein (d. 1973) and NASR HAMID ABU ZAYD (b. 1943) have sought innovative ways of integrating textual criticism into the study of Islam, and in this respect Egyptian thinkers are often ahead of their times. In other cultural spheres, too, such as literary production, the CINEMA, MUSIC, and the broadcast media, Egypt is the most important nation in the Arabic-speaking world. Its most famous novelist and short story writer, Naguib Mahfouz (1911–2006), won the Nobel Prize in literature in 1988 for his moving portrayals of life in Egypt and his enlightened treatment of contemporary political and religious subjects.

See also ARAB-ISRAELI CONFLICTS; COPTS AND THE COPTIC CHURCH; OTTOMAN DYNASTY.

John Iskander

Further reading: Geneive Abdo, *No God but God: Egypt and the Triumph of Islam* (Oxford and New York: Oxford University Press, 2000); Khaled Fahmy, *All the Pasha's Men: Mehmed Ali, His Army, and the Making of Modern Egypt* (Cambridge and New York: Cambridge University Press, 1997); Timothy Mitchell, *Rule of Experts: Egypt, Techno-Politics, Modernity* (Berkeley: University of California Press, 2002).

Eid *See* HOLIDAYS; ID AL-ADHA; ID AL-FITR.

Emigrants (Arabic: *muhajirun*)

The emigration, or HIJRA, of MUHAMMAD and his first followers from MECCA to MEDINA is considered to be the foundational event in the history of the early Muslim community. Beginning in 622 and continuing until the conquest of Mecca in 630, small groups of supporters, men and WOMEN alike, abandoned their old homes to escape persecution and took up residence in Medina (then known as Yathrib). These people are remembered in Islamic tradition as the Emigrants. They were converts from different tribes and classes in Mecca and tribes outside Mecca who joined Muhammad in Medina. Aside from members of Muhammad's immediate family, the Emigrants also included his cousin and son-in-law ALI IBN ABI TALIB (d. 661) and the other men who would become the first caliphs after Muhammad's death—ABU BAKR (d. 634), UMAR IBN AL-KHATTAB (d. 644), and UTHMAN IBN AFFAN (d. 656). According to early historical sources, not every Emigrant was of Arabian descent; one was BILAL, a former slave from Ethiopia, and another was Salman, a Persian convert. It is estimated that the total number of Emigrants was less than 400.

Together with the ANSAR (helpers), Arab converts to Islam from Medina, the Emigrants held a place of honor in early Islamic society. Muhammad formed a brotherhood between them when they first arrived in Medina, and he soon concluded a series of agreements with other Arab and Jewish groups that ensured that the Emigrants would enjoy protection and solidarity in their new home. They participated in the early battles against Muhammad's opponents in Mecca and Medina and were given priority in the distribution of the booty. Both the Emigrants and the Ansar would later be remembered for the roles they played in collecting, reciting, and commenting on the QURAN. They also played an important role in the transmission of the HADITH. Although the status of the Emigrants remained high after Muhammad's death, their political influence in the community shifted to leaders of the QURAYSH tribe in Mecca, who had once led the opposition against Muhammad. Abu Bakr (r. 632–634) relied on the Quraysh, who had converted to Islam after 630, for support in his claim to become the first CALIPH and for assistance in keeping the community unified. This laid the basis for the eventual rise of the UMAYYAD CALIPHATE, which was led by descendants from the Banu Umayya, a leading Quraysh clan.

In the 20th century, other Muslims would be called Emigrants. These included those who moved to Turkey from Russia and southeastern Europe to avoid being ruled by non-Muslim governments, as well as Indian Muslims who moved to PAKISTAN as a result of the 1947 partition of INDIA.

See also CALIPHATE; COMPANIONS OF THE PROPHET.

Further reading: Michael Lecker, *Muslims, Jews, and Pagans: Studies on Early Islamic Medina* (Leiden: E.J. Brill, 1995); W. Montgomery Watt, *Muhammad: Prophet and Statesman* (Oxford: Oxford University Press, 1964).

emigration *See* HIJRA.

Enoch *See* IDRIS.

eschatology (Greek *eschatos*, "last")

In the comparative study of religions, *eschatology* is a term used for beliefs and doctrines concerning last things—DEATH, the end of the world, and the AFTERLIFE. Muslims all share certain expectations for the end times, but there are significant differences between Sunni and Shiite expectations, as well as cases of difference between scholarly and popular interpretations within the same sect. All Muslims believe that time is linear, having begun with God's creation of the universe, and all expect an end to human history to come at a time of God's choosing. The end, according to the QURAN, will arrive suddenly but will be accompanied by dramatic signs. At that time, the dead will be raised physically, and all will be judged according to their FAITH and deeds. All Muslims believe that there is life after death.

The Quran has a good deal to say about the coming end. That humans will be called to account for their good and bad deeds on that day is affirmed repeatedly. The last day will be accompanied by a great trumpet blast, when "the mountains are lifted up and crushed with a single blow" (Q 69:14). Humans will be reunited with their bodies and will await judgment in great fear. The day of reckoning is usually presented as a matter of receiving a book with one's accumulated deeds. Those to whom the book is given in the right hand will enter PARADISE (generally called the GARDEN), while the others will enter the fires of hell (often simply the FIRE). Both the rewards and the punishments are rather graphically depicted in the Quran and are given substantial elaboration in HADITH and other traditional materials.

Before the day of reckoning, however, Muslims expect that several events not mentioned in the Quran will occur. Many traditions speak of a time of inversions to precede the end, in which "normal" social relations will be turned on their head: sons will not obey their fathers, slave girls will give birth to their own masters, and the poor and the weak will become leaders. While there is no unanimity on this point, the general thrust of popular Sunni eschatological belief is that the end times will see the rise of a deceptive leader, or ANTICHRIST (Dajjal), who will be fought and vanquished by either the MAHDI or JESUS, ushering in a millennial period before the JUDGMENT DAY. Being extra-Quranic, however, this popularly accepted narrative is highly contested by Muslim scholars. IBN KHALDUN (d. 1406), for instance, rejected the entire luxuriant set of traditions that purport to prophecy the coming of the Mahdi, which would

also raise doubts as to his belief in the rise of the Dajjal and the reappearance of Jesus.

For the Twelve-IMAM Shia, a belief in the Mahdi comes to be an article of faith and is thus much more central than it is for Sunnis. According to Shii histories, the 12th IMAM, or descendant of Ali through his son Husayn, disappeared from view after 874 but is still present in the world and will return at the end of time to fill the earth with justice as it is filled now with corruption and injustice. To be a true believer, one must have this belief in the presence and eventual reemergence of the imam Mahdi. In this sense, Shii THEOLOGY indicates that humanity is always on the threshold of the millennial age.

See also AFTERLIFE; CREATION; FAITH; ISMAILI SHIISM; TWELVE-IMAM SHIISM.

John Iskander

Further reading: David Cook, *Studies in Muslim Apocalyptic* (Princeton, N.J.: Darwin Press, 2002); Muhammad Abu Hamid al-Ghazali, *The Remembrance of Death and the Afterlife, Kitab dhikr al-mawt wa-ma badahu, Book XL of The Revival of the Religious Sciences, Ihya ulum al-Din.* Translated by T. J. Winter (Cambridge: Islamic Texts Society, 1995); F. E. Peters, *Judaism, Christianity and Islam: The Classical Texts and Their Interpretation,* vol. 3, *The Works of the Spirit* (Princeton, N.J.: Princeton University Press, 1990); Jane I. Smith and Yvonne Y. Haddad, *The Islamic Understanding of Death and Resurrection* (Albany: State University of New York Press, 1981).

ethics and morality

Ethics and morality are concerned with how humans should live their lives in accordance with what they know to be right and wrong. The two terms are often used interchangeably. However, when scholars distinguish them, they understand ethics to mean philosophical reflection upon moral conduct, while morality pertains to specific norms or codes of behavior. Questions of ethics, therefore, involve such subjects as human nature and the capacity to do good, the nature of good and evil, motivations for moral action, the underlying principles governing moral and immoral acts, deciding who is obliged to adhere to the moral code and who is exempted from it, and the implications of either adhering to the moral code or violating it. Morality encompasses the values and rules that govern human conduct, such as the Golden Rule, which holds that a person should treat others as he or she would be treated.

There is no necessary relation between ethical beliefs and religion; people in many times and places engage in moral action without having to adhere to a particular religion. Nevertheless, most religions promote moral teachings and engage in ethical reflection. Religions also provide motivations for acting in accordance with moral principles by promising rewards and punishments from a god or some other supramundane power in this world or in the AFTERLIFE. Religions can also criticize individual and communal morality. This "prophetic" function is most evident among the Abrahamic religions (Judaism, Christianity, and Islam), but it is present in other religions too. Lastly, it should be noted that the close relationship between religion and morality can have negative aspects. When a religious AUTHORITY, normally expected to embody moral virtues, is believed to have committed criminal, tyrannical, or other immoral acts, it can provoke resentment or opposition and engender sectarian and reform movements.

Ethical awareness has been a defining feature of Islam, even though engaging in moral PHILOSOPHY per se has not. Rather than being a formal area of knowledge, ethics in Islam has been a topic addressed more often in a practical sense within a variety of contexts, including ones in which it was engaged with non-Muslim ethical traditions, both religious and nonreligious. Indeed, Islamic morality has formed internally among Sunnis, Shiis, Sufis, and rationalists while also being shaped by interactions with pre-Islamic Arabian, Greek, Persian, Jewish, Christian, and other ethical traditions on the local and global levels. This process has continued in the modern period as a result of encounters with Western powers and modern secular moral systems.

The word *islam* implies a moral outlook, since it is understood to mean submission to God's will, which is seen as a good that brings a person into harmony with the "natural" order of CREATION. Submission and performing good deeds, the QURAN teaches, are done because they are prescribed by God, they reciprocate God for the blessings he provides, and they are rewarded, whereas rebellious and wrongful acts are punished. Muslims believe that performing the required FIVE PILLARS of Islam is "worship" or "service" (*ibada*), and they have given it moral meaning. Therefore, they associate the virtue of keeping bodily hygiene with prayer ablutions, overcoming selfishness with fasting, and promoting equality among believers with pilgrimage. Islamic morality is clearly involved in the duty of ALMSGIVING, a charitable redistribution of wealth for the benefit of the needy and the community as a whole. Participants in the annual HAJJ to MECCA, the fifth pillar, are prohibited from being violent, acting rudely, and harming most plants and ANIMALS. According to the HADITH, those who perform the hajj properly are forgiven their sins and rewarded with PARADISE. Furthermore, in a famous hadith, called the Hadith of GABRIEL, *islam* and FAITH (*iman*) itself are closely associated with *ihsan*, "doing the good." *Ihsan,* the hadith states, means doing what is good and beautiful in worshipping God, knowing that he is aware of what a person does, even if he (God) is not visible.

Muslims look primarily to the Quran and the SUNNA of Muhammad, "customary practice" expressed in the hadith, for moral guidance. The Quran's chief moral instruction, one that echoes throughout the history of Islam, is for people to "command what is known to be right (*maaruf*) and forbid what is reprehensible (*munkar*)." This is stated, for example, in the third chapter: "Let a people from among you invite (others) to goodness. Let them command what is known to be right and forbid what is reprehensible. They are the ones who will prosper" (Q 3:104, cf. 9:7). Such statements are closely connected to obeying God and worshipping him.

The question of what is "known to be right" has been an important subject of debate among Muslims. One position is that whatever God commands is what is right. The problem with this is that the Quran offers more in the way of general principles than specific rules (most of these rules are found only in the first few chapters of the Quran). The principles in question include justice, goodness, kindness, forgiveness, honesty, and piety. This has led some to take the position that humans are born with an instinctive or innate knowledge of what is right and wrong, but because of their wayward and fickle nature, they do not always choose to act morally. The purpose of the Quran, therefore, is not so much to dictate specific commandments, but to "remind" people of what they should already know by nature and to guide them to do the right thing. If they disobey, they will pay a price for it, if not here and now, then in the hereafter.

The most commonly used Islamic term for morality, the Arabic word *akhlaq,* is not found in the Quran, but the root *kh-l-q* from which it is derived occurs frequently in connection with the act of creation. From a Muslim perspective, therefore, human morality is part of the created order of the world, intimately connected with God the creator. The "signs" (sing. AYA) of God are evident in the natural world, in events, and in verses of scripture. The verses provide moral guidance, as does the wider world. Humans, as part of God's creation, are called upon to contemplate these signs to discover the truth and know what is best.

The other major source of Islamic moral wisdom, the sunna of MUHAMMAD, is based on the hadith. Muslims consider Muhammad's sunna to be a body of norms that should be followed in worship and in everyday life. The idea of Muhammad as an exemplary figure comes from the remembered experience of the first Muslims, and it is also supported by the Quran, which regards him as a "beautiful model" (Q 33:21). Hadith collections had chapters about the virtues that he embodied. These included respect for parents and elders, maintaining strong family ties, being good to neighbors, caring for children, avoiding abuse of servants and slaves (a social institution until the 19th and 20th centuries), being well-mannered, offering hospitality to guests, visiting the sick, showing mercy to animals, being patient and sincere, greeting people correctly, asking permission before entering a house, dressing modestly, and avoiding lying and rude speech. These were all taken to be demonstrations of Muhammad's moral character, called *akhlaq* or ADAB. Likewise, Sufis drew upon the hadith about Muhammad, too, to emphasize the virtues of generosity, poverty, humility, and concern for others, including the poor.

From the eighth century onward, Muslim legal scholars, the ULAMA, consulted and debated with each other over how to systematize the quranic commandments and Muhammad's sunna so as to be able to effectively implement the SHARIA, or sacred law, in a complex, multicultural, and historically changing Islamicate society. In doing so, they were not satisfied with determining only what was legally required (HALAL) and what was forbidden (HARAM), nor did they trust individuals to know what the right thing to do was. Rather, they devised a five-step scale for classifying human acts according to their conformity to God's will: obligatory, recommended, permitted, disapproved, and forbidden. The ulama then detailed all sorts of human activities, rule on their permissibility, and on what kinds of rewards and penalties, if any, such acts entailed. Sunni as well as Shii jurists engaged in this activity, but other Muslims were familiar with it, too, especially among the educated elites living in urban areas. In addition to courts of law, Muslim authorities created the office of *muhtasib* to enforce the moral code in public places and oversee transactions conducted in the marketplace. Alongside this, the juridical construction of morality, there was also a culture of refined behavior (*adab*) that shaped the ethical outlook of urban Muslims. This was expressed in writings that set forth the virtues for different classes and groups to honor, including the ulama, rulers, bureaucrats, merchants, and craftsmen.

Moral philosophy was an important subject for Muslim intellectuals, even if it did not have equal weight with sharia and FIQH in the eyes of the ulama. The scholars who contributed to this area of ethics during the Middle Ages were Abu Yusuf Yaacub al-Kindi (d. 870), Abu Bakr Muhammad al-Razi (also known as Rhazes, d. ca. 925), ABU NASR AL-FARABI (also known as Alfarabius, d. 950), and ABU ALI AL-HUSAYN IBN SINA (also known as Avicenna, d. 1037), MUHAMMAD IBN RUSHD (also known as Averroës, d. 1198), and Nasir al-Din Tusi (d. 1198). Perhaps the most noteworthy of all were Miskawayh (d. 1040), the Persian author of *Refinement of Morality;* ABU HAMID AL-GHAZALI (d. 1111), Persian mystic and author of *Revival of the Religious Sciences;* and the Andalusian man of letters ALI IBN HAZM (d. 1064). Originally sparked by the rationalist theology of the Mutazila in the eighth century and further influenced by Aristotelian ethics, this area of Muslim scholarly discussion declined after the 12th century, but it experienced revived interest among Muslims in the 19th and 20th centuries.

Today Islamic ethics and morality are receiving close scrutiny in Muslim lands and beyond as never before. The encounters of traditional Islamic moral laws and values with modern secular laws and values have raised urgent questions about whether and how the sharia in whole or in part requires preservation, reform, adaptation, or rejection. Respect for HUMAN RIGHTS, individualism, religious freedom, and women's rights has caused Muslims to search their ethical heritage to find where there is compatibility and where there is not. Violent actions performed in the name of Islam against public officials and civilians by militant organizations have given added urgency to this search. While it is true that many Muslims have condemned violent acts in the name of religion, they have also sought to make moral arguments in favor of violence (JIHAD) and revolution in the face of oppression, tyranny, and attacks against core beliefs and practices. As in the past, given the many ways in which Muslims understand and practice their religion, views on these and many other issues diverge widely within the worldwide Muslim community.

See also ABORTION; CRIME AND PUNISHMENT; CUSTOMARY LAW; FATE; *HISBA;* ISLAMISM; MUTAZILI SCHOOL; SUICIDE; WOMEN.

Further reading: Muhammad ibn Ismail al-Bukhari, *Imam Bukhari's Book of Muslim Morals and Manners.* Translated by Yusuf Talal DeLorenzo (Alexandria, Va.: Al-Saadawi Publications, 1997); Michael Cook, *Forbidding Wrong in Islam: An Introduction* (Cambridge: Cambridge University Press, 2003); Frederick M. Denny, "Ethical Dimensions of Islamic Ritual Law." In *Religion and Law: Biblical-Judaic and Islamic Perspectives,* edited by Edwin B. Firmage, Bernard G. Weiss, and John W. Welch, 199–210 (Winona Lake, Ind.: Eisenbrauns, 1990); Richard G. Hovannisian, ed., *Ethics in Islam* (Malibu, Calif.: Undena, 1985); Toshihiko Izutsu, *Ethico-Religious Concepts in the Quran* (Montreal: McGill University Press, 1966); Gary E. Kessler, *Philosophy of Religion: Toward a Global Perspective* (Belmont, Calif.: Wadsworth Publishing, 1999); Kevin Reinhart, *Before Revelation: The Boundaries of Muslim Moral Thought* (Albany: State University of New York Press, 1995).

Europe

Although often misperceived as alien to Europe, Islam has had a long and varied presence in that part of the world. It first entered Europe with the Arab and BERBER armies that conquered the Iberian Peninsula (modern Spain and Portugal) from the Goths in 711. Muslims later entered Gaul but suffered defeat at Poitiers in 732 and in the Pyrenees passes in 748. Successive Islamic dynasties ruled

Sicily, Malta, and Syracuse from 827 until the Norman conquests in 1090–91. Islamic rule lasted longest in Iberia, reaching its zenith during the UMAYYAD CALIPHATE (912–1031) and ending with the fall of GRANADA (1492). Felipe III expelled the remaining Moriscos (forcibly baptized Muslims who remained in Spain after 1492) from Spain in 1609–14. In eastern Europe, Anatolian Turks invaded the Balkans during the mid-13th century, and Islam continued to spread with the Ottoman conquests of the 14th century. The Ottomans captured Constantinople (later ISTANBUL), the capital of the Byzantine Empire, in 1453, and Poland, Lithuania, Hungary, and Budapest came under Muslim rule during the 15th to the 17th centuries. The collapse of the Ottoman Empire early in the 20th century, the two World Wars, the dissolution of Yugoslavia, and the more recent Balkan wars decimated Muslim populations in Poland and Hungary, but significant numbers remain in the Balkans. In western Europe, Islam has grown since the 1950s due to conversion and immigration from the Indian subcontinent, Africa, and the Middle East to Britain, France, Germany, the Netherlands, Italy, and Spain.

CORDOBA, the capital of ANDALUSIA, was the largest, wealthiest, and most advanced city in medieval Europe. It had paved, illuminated streets, running water, textiles, paper and glass factories, public baths, numerous libraries, and free schools. The Great Mosque of Cordoba rivaled its counterparts in CAIRO and BAGHDAD and was Europe's

Suburban London mosque, formerly a church *(J. Gordon Melton)*

first university. The Muslim rulers of Andalusia and Sicily lavishly patronized artists, philosophers, and scientists. Muslims were innovators in mathematics, philosophy, medicine, botany, astronomy, and agriculture, and they recovered Greek philosophical and scientific works lost to Christian Europe. Hydraulic technology used and developed by Muslims revolutionized traditional Mediterranean AGRICULTURE.

The Arabo-Islamic cultural and intellectual heritage has been enormously important to Latin Europe. These traditions were transmitted via the Mozarab (Arabized) Christians, trade and diplomatic relations, oral performances of Arabic poetry and stories, and especially the translation schools in Toledo and elsewhere. Iberian and Norman monarchs sponsored translations of Muslim philosophical, scientific, and literary works, including the commentaries of IBN SINA (Avicenna, d. 1037) and IBN RUSHD (Averroës, d. 1198) on Aristotle and the medical compendia of Ibn Sina and al-Razi (Rhazes, d. ca. 935)—standard medical texts in Western Europe until the 16th century. Translated mathematical treatises introduced calculation with Arabic numerals, algebra, trigonometry, and advanced geometry into the West. Arabic literature and lyric influenced or anticipated European literary genres. Romance lyric-songs and Provençal courtly love poetry are historically related to the Arabic *muwashshah* (a form of Andalusian love poetry). Dante's renowned *Divine Comedy* (14th century) borrowed motifs from accounts of Muhammad's NIGHT JOURNEY AND ASCENT. Boccaccio incorporated translated Arabic fables into *The Decameron* (14th century). In the 16th century, the mystical symbolism of John of the Cross and Teresa of Avila echoed the earlier Spanish Sufi writings of IBN AL-ARABI (12th century), Ibn Abbad of Ronda (14th century), and others. Arabic loan words in the Romance languages and English reflect the Arabo-Islamic cultural legacy. Finally, many Arabic words entered Spanish and, though written in Latin letters, the Maltese language spoken on the Mediterranean island nation of Malta today is considered a dialect of Arabic.

It is estimated that between 44 million Muslims (6 percent of Europe's total population) live in Europe as of 2008. In southeastern Europe, Albania and BOSNIA AND HERZEGOVINA have the largest percentages of Muslims: 70 percent and 40 percent, respectively. Among the countries of western Europe, France has the largest Muslim population (about 5 million, mostly from North Africa), followed by Germany (about 2 million, mostly from Turkey) and the United Kingdom (about 1.5 million, mostly from India-Pakistan and the Arab Middle East). Significant numbers also live in Spain, Italy, and the Netherlands. Many of these Muslims arrived after 1950 as guest workers to help rebuild Europe after the devastation caused by World Wars I and II. In recent decades, many immigrants have come as REFUGEES from strife-ridden countries such as LEBANON, SUDAN, and IRAN. Muslim scholars and intellectuals have gone to Europe for their education or as immigrants and refugees. Among the most prominent are FAZLUR RAHMAN (from Pakistan), MUHAMMAD ARKOUN (from ALGERIA), Bassam Tibi (from SYRIA), NASR HAMID ABU ZAYD (from EGYPT), and Taslima Nasrin (from BANGLADESH). Award-winning authors of Islamic heritage living in Europe include SALMAN RUSHDIE (from INDIA) and Tariq Ali (from PAKISTAN). Tariq Ramadan (b. 1962) is a leading representative of the new generation of reform-minded Muslim intellectuals who were born in Europe. Immigrant Muslims have established MOSQUES and community organizations in all European countries. A major institute for the study of ISMAILI SHIISM was founded by the AGA KHAN in London. Although many immigrants maintain close contact with their homelands, all are required to follow the civil laws of their adopted countries of residence.

While immigrants, converts, and native-born Muslims have made significant contributions to contemporary European society and culture, there have also been times of significant tension and cultural confrontation. Veiling and the status of Muslim WOMEN in secular society have been particularly divisive issues. To varying degrees, European societies have discriminated against Muslim immigrants and citizens, which was a factor behind the eruption of riots in French cities in 2005. One of the Al-Qaida cells involved in the 9/11 attacks on the World Trade Center and the Pentagon in 2001 was based in Hamburg, Germany. As a consequence of cultural animosities and recent wars in AFGHANISTAN, IRAQ, and Israel-Palestine, radical Islamic groups have launched terrorist attacks on civilian targets in Madrid and London.

See also ANTI-SEMITISM; CHRISTIANITY AND ISLAM; JANISSARY; JUDAISM AND ISLAM; SECULARISM; SUFISM.

Linda G. Jones and Juan E. Campo

Further reading: Jack Goody, *Islam in Europe* (Cambridge: Polity Press, 2004); Shireen Hunter, ed., *Islam, Europe's Second Religion: The New Social, Cultural and Political Landscape* (Westport, Conn.: Praeger Publishers, 2002); Salma Khadra Jayyusi, ed., *The Legacy of Muslim Spain* (Leiden: E.J. Brill, 1994); María Rosa Menocal, *The Arabic Role in Medieval Literary History: A Forgotten Heritage* (Philadelphia: University of Pennsylvania Press, 1987); Tariq Ramadan, *Western Muslims and the Future of Islam* (Oxford: Oxford University Press, 2004).

Eve *See* ADAM AND EVE.

evil eye

Belief that the eye has the power to cause evil or misfortune is found in many cultures. It forms but one part of a magical worldview that attempts to explain the accidents and illnesses that afflict people. Rather than being a generalized theory of misfortune, it is always concerned with explaining specific instances: What caused a particular person or possession to suffer harm at this or that time and place while others nearby or in a

Evil eye poster, with medallions containing the name of God (r.) and Muhammad (l.), framed by protective verses from the Quran *(printed poster)*

similar situation remained unaffected? In other words, belief in the evil eye is but one way of trying to account for why bad things happen to good people, and it may even conflict with other explanations. Religious conservatives object that it contradicts the belief that ultimately it is God who determines what happens for good and evil. People with a modern scientific outlook, on the other hand, may refute evil eye beliefs as irrational superstitions. But for the many who hold to a magical worldview, identifying the evil eye as the cause of an affliction allows them to take steps to deflect it or minimize its effect, even if it cannot be completely eliminated. The fact that people think that they can take preventive measures against it provides them with a sense that they can exercise control over otherwise unpredictable and painful events in life. This helps explain the acceptance and persistence of evil eye beliefs in so many parts of the world.

In Islamicate cultures, evil eye beliefs are especially pronounced among peoples living in lands from MOROCCO to INDIA, including the eastern Mediterranean region and the Arabian Peninsula. Many non-Muslims living in these areas also share these beliefs, including Christians, Jews, and Hindus. There are several names given to the evil eye in the languages of these cultures. In Arabic, it can be *al-ayn,* "the eye," *al-nazra,* "the look," or *al-hasad,* "envy." In Persian, it is known as *chashm zakhm,* "the eye that wounds," or *chashm shur,* "the salty eye." A child, a nursing mother, a valuable farm ANIMAL, a fruitful agricultural field, a plate of good food, or a valuable possession (such as a car or truck, a machine used in making a living, a business, or a home) can provoke feelings of jealousy or inadvertently attract envious glances from passersby, neighbors, friends, or competitors and opponents. Once such a person's envious eye looks at or "hits" its target, it can cause it serious harm. If the victim is a person, especially a male child, it can cause illness, an accident, or even death. The milk of a lactating woman, a goat, or a cow may stop flowing. A field can suffer crop damage. A car or machine might be destroyed or damaged in an accident or suffer a breakdown. One's business or home might burn down. Praising someone or something, even with the best of intentions, is thought to make the object of praise even more susceptible to the malevolent effects of the envious eye.

Within such a belief system, a number of preventive devices and remedies are available. The most common is to place a colorful piece of jewelry, often a blue and white bead, on the person or possession to deflect "the look." An amulet containing the name of God or a verse from the QURAN also has apotropaic power. Many people hang or paint verses of the Quran in their businesses and homes or on their cars and trucks. Among the parts of the Quran usually employed for such purposes are the BASMALA (Q 1:1), the FATIHA (Q 1), the Throne Verse (Q 2:255), and the last two chapters of the Quran, known as "the protection-seeking ones" (Q 113 and 114). In fact, Q 113 implores God's protection "from the evil of the envier when he envies."

A copy of the whole Quran is also believed to offer protection.

Similarly, in everyday speech, people utter formulaic phrases containing God's name, such as *smallah,* "in the name of God," *ma shaa Allah,* "whatever God wills," or *Allah akbar,* "God is greater." One popular incantation used against the evil eye states, "In the name of God I cast a spell to protect you from everything that may harm you; from every envious eye. In the name of God I cast a spell to protect you, and may God heal you from every harmful person or eye." There are many other methods used for deflecting the eye. Among them is "dispraise." For example, instead of praising a cute or beautiful baby, well-wishers instead will tell the parents how ugly the child is. Proud parents will interpret such expressions as compliments. Other protective measures include disguising male infants as females, leaving them unwashed, and calling them by unflattering names. Images of outstretched hands are also thought to provide protection. With a new home, business, vehicle, or machine, it is not unusual for the owners to sacrifice an animal and make hand imprints with its blood in a visible place on the new possession. Burning incense and consulting with male and female magicians are other measures people use for protection from the evil eye.

See also AMULETS AND TALISMANS; ANIMALS; BARAKA; CHILDREN.

Further reading: Alan Dundes, ed., *The Evil Eye: A Casebook* (Madison: University of Wisconsin Press, 1981); Amitav Ghosh, "Reflections of Envy in an Egyptian Village." *Ethnology* 22 (1983): 211–233; Edward Westermarck, *Ritual and Belief in Morocco,* 2 vols. (New York: University Books, 1968).

exegesis *See* TAFSIR.

F

Fadlallah, Muhammad Husayn (1935–)
militant Shii religious leader and spokesman for the Hizbullah organization in Lebanon

Shaykh Fadlallah was born in Najaf, IRAQ, where his Lebanese father was a Shii religious scholar. At the Shii MADRASA in Najaf, he pursued advanced Islamic studies in order to become one of the Shii ULAMA. He also became politically involved by opposing the growing influence of the Communist Party in the Iraqi government during the 1960s. Among the most influential people in his early career were Grand Ayatollah Abu al-Qasim Khui (d. 1992), one of the most prominent scholars of Shii jurisprudence (*FIQH*) in Iraq, and Shaykh Muhammad Baqir al-Sadr (d. 1980), a politically active member of a prominent family of Iraqi religious scholars. In 1966, Fadlallah was appointed by Khui to serve the needs of Shia living in the low-income neighborhoods of Beirut, LEBANON.

During the devastating Lebanese civil war, which lasted from 1975 to 1990, Shaykh Fadlallah emerged as a leading community activist. Inspired by the success of the Islamic revolution in IRAN of 1979, he played an instrumental role in organizing Shii militants in the early 1980s and became the head of HIZBULLAH in 1985. He continues to be this organization's chief spokesman. Fadlallah holds strongly anti-Israeli and anti-American views and combines them with an ideology of Islamic revolution and political JIHAD. During the 1980s, he was implicated in assassinations and kidnappings in Lebanon, the bombings of the U.S. embassy and of the U.S. and French military headquarters in Beirut, and the Lebanese Shii resistance to the Israeli occupation forces. Consequently, both Israel and the United States regard him as a terrorist leader, and there is some suspicion that the United States was involved in a failed assassination attempt against him in 1985. Although he has been supportive of Iranian ayatollah RUHOLLAH KHOMEINI and religious hardliners in Tehran, he has broken with them over their notions of Islamic government under the absolute authority of a religious expert (*faqih*). Instead, he has expressed support for a division of political power among religious and secular leaders. Much of his work in Lebanon has focused on charitable organizations and social services, which has won widespread support for Hizbullah among the Lebanese Shia. He approves of the participation of women in public life, and he has also been a strong supporter of militant Palestinian Islamist organizations, although not of Yassir

Arafat's PALESTINE LIBERATION ORGANIZATION. In recent years, he has come to be regarded by many as the "spiritual leader" of the Lebanese Shia, and he appears to have shifted from radical militancy to grassroots social and political activism.

See also COMMUNISM; ISRAEL; SHIISM; TERRORISM.

Further reading: Talib Aziz, "Fadlallah and the Making of the Marjaiyya." In *The Most Learned of the Shia: The Institution of the Marja Taqlid,* edited by Linda S. Walbridge, 205–215 (New York: Oxford University Press, 2001); Martin Kramer, "The Oracle of Hizbullah: Muhammad Husayn Fadlallah." In *Spokesmen for the Despised: Fundamentalist Leaders in the Middle East,* edited by R. Scott Appleby, 83–181 (Chicago: University of Chicago Press, 1997).

faith (Arabic: *iman,* security)

In general, Western usage of *faith* is as a synonym for religion—an organized system of beliefs concerning a supreme being and that being's relations with creation, especially with humans. Thus, people speak of the "Christian faith" or the "Islamic faith." The term also has a more specific meaning—trust in God and his promise for salvation. This concept is based on the books of the Bible, and it achieved further development in the histories of Jewish and Christian religious thought in the Middle East, the Mediterranean basin, and Europe. The ancient Hebrew *aman* (to be true or trustworthy), related to the Arabic *iman,* is used in the Old Testament to express the mutual commitment between God and his chosen people as it was embodied in their covenantal relationship. In other words, the God of the Israelites promised to remain faithful to his promise of blessings for Israel as long as they maintained their love for him and kept his commandments (for example, Deuteronomy 7:9). In times of difficulty, people were expected to still hold fast to the hope that God would strengthen them and come to their rescue. For Christians, the focus of faith is on the figure of JESUS as the son of God and how his death and

resurrection are believed to offer hope and salvation for the faithful. It is seen as something that comes as a gift from God and that people render toward him in love.

The heart of Islamic faith is unconditional belief in God's oneness; that he is universal, eternal, all-knowing, all-seeing, compassionate; and that he has no rivals or partners. From this core belief follow others—that there will be a resurrection and final judgment, and that God communicates with humans through his ANGELS, PROPHETS, and HOLY BOOKS (for example, Q 4:136). The FIVE PILLARS, required of all able Muslims (submitters), routinize these beliefs through performance of the ritual actions of testifying that God is one and Muhammad is his messenger, prayer, almsgiving, fasting, and pilgrimage. The QURAN suggests a close interrelationship between faith and works (for example, Q 2:177), and this relationship is usually considered to be a fundamental one in the religion. According to the HADITH, faith is sometimes regarded as distinct from *islam* (submission), but it is also seen as synonymous with it or as a facet of it. In the well-known Hadith of GABRIEL (cited in the authoritative collections of Muslim, Bukhari, and IBN HANBAL), a stranger who later turns out to be Gabriel, the angel of revelation, poses questions to MUHAMMAD about both *islam* and *iman.* Muhammad responds by listing the Five Pillars and the key elements of faith outlined above, suggesting that although *islam* and *iman* may differ, they are closely connected nevertheless. Islam thus involves an inner belief, while faith entails an outward expression. In one of many passages concerning the faithful (*mumin,* pl. *muminun*), the Quran states that they are the ones whose faith is strengthened when they hear God's revelations *and* that they are those who pray and perform acts of charity (Q 8:2–3). The faithful are also those who have fear (TAQWA) of God and place their trust in him. Moreover, from the quranic perspective, faith stands in clear opposition to disbelief (*kufr*) in God and his revelation and in opposition to the hypocrisy (*nifaq*) of those who only pretend to be true believers (for example, Q 3:90–91, 167; 4:60–61). Those who believe and do good works are promised a reward in the AFTERLIFE, while those who do not believe will be punished.

As Islamic religious thought developed, Muslim theologians and philosophers pursued the discussion of faith in more depth. Among the topics they debated, apart from that of faith and action, were those of differences in degree of faith, whether faith remains constant or increases and decreases, and the relation of reason and faith. The Shia, meanwhile, extended the content of faith to include belief in the infallibility and moral perfection of the IMAMS, and, among the Twelve-Imam Shia, the rise of the messianic Imam MAHDI. They also argued that JUSTICE was an attribute of God. Sunnis disagreed and even went so far as to label such beliefs heretical. In the modern era, Sunni and Shii religious thinkers have sought to demonstrate the compatibility of faith and reason in order to defend Islam against secular rationalism. At the same time, intensive religious outreach (DAAWA) programs have been directed as much at enhancing the faith of Muslims as at winning new converts.

See also ALLAH; COVENANT; *KAFIR*; THEOLOGY; TWELVE-IMAM SHIISM.

Further reading: Toshihiko Izutsu, *Ethico-Religious Concepts in the Koran* (Montreal: McGill University Press, 1966); Fazlur Rahman, *Major Themes of the Quran* (Minneapolis: Bibliotheca Islamica, 1980).

fana *See* BAQA AND FANA.

faqih *See* FIQH.

faqir *See* DERVISH.

Farabi, Abu Nasr al- (ca. 870–950)
prominent Muslim philosopher of the Middle Ages known for his interpretations of Aristotle and Neoplatonism

The first systematic thinker in Arab-Islamic PHILOSOPHY, al-Farabi penned the tradition's first political treatise and was the first true logician in Islamic history. The currents of Peripatetic-Neoplatonic thought (Peripatetic does not here denote an exclusively Aristotelian legacy) he set in motion reverberate in our own time with Ismaili philosophy and in the renewed interest in both the Illuminationist tradition (for example, Shihab al-Din Abu Hafs al-Suhrawardi, d. 1191) and the School of Isfahan (for example, MULLAH SADRA, d. 1640).

As his name suggests, al-Farabi was from the district of Farab in Transoxiana, being of probable Turkish or Turkoman origin. Little information is available on his early life. He worked as a night watchman in a garden in DAMASCUS before moving to BAGHDAD. In the turbulence of 10th-century Baghdad, al-Farabi mastered Arabic, becoming conversant in a number of other languages as well. He studied with Christian Aristotelians of the Syriac tradition, considered among the greatest logicians of his time. He soon surpassed these exemplars by virtue of his treatment of the entire corpus of Aristotelian logic. His educational regimen included not only the various branches of philosophy, but took in MATHEMATICS, physics, astronomy, and MUSIC. Indeed, in addition to penning a handful of treatises on music, al-Farabi was an accomplished musician.

One of the animating purposes of al-Farabi's writings on logic was the need to distinguish the discipline of philosophical logic from the rules (or logic) of grammar, the former akin to a universal grammar that provides the rules necessary for reasoning in any language, while the latter relies on rules generated by convention and is thus relative to a particular language. In his view, the logical and grammatical "sciences" complement each other. Logic likewise pertains to the arts (poetics), politics, religion, and jurisprudence, as it lays down the rules of reasoning peculiar to these respective domains (hence, there are types of rationality and different modes of discourse and argumentation).

Al-Farabi's cosmological and metaphysical doctrines are the foundations upon which he builds—like Plato (d. ca. 347 B.C.E.)—the political philosophy explicated in his books *The Virtuous City* (al-Madina al-fadila) and the *Civil Polity* (al-Siyasa al-madaniyya). He uses a Neoplatonic emanationist theory crafted within the structure of Ptolemaic cosmology to account for God's power of CREATION. However, God, or the First Being (al-awwal), does not, like "the One" of the ancient philosopher Plotinus (d. 270 C.E.), utterly transcend being and thought. Rather, it is conceived largely along the lines of Aristotle's Unmoved Mover, albeit with emanationist properties. God's principal activity is, as it were, intellectual, "echoing Aristotle's conception of God's activity as 'thinking of thinking' (nōesis noēseos). It is God's intellectual activity which underlies God's role as the creator of the universe" (Black, 189). In effect, al-Farabi's First Being cleverly combines a Neoplatonic metaphysics of emanation, Aristotle's Unmoved Mover, and the Quranic conception of God. It is clever insofar as it attempts to fuse the absolute transcendence and unity (TAWHID) of God with a rational account of the world's creation, albeit one at odds with the doctrine of creation from nothing (ex nihilo).

Al-Farabi's political philosophy is more straightforwardly Platonic, outlining a gradation of different kinds of polities at the apex of which is the ideal city dedicated to good and happiness. For al-Farabi, philosophy provides us with the highest form of knowledge or wisdom (hikma). But philosophy must endeavor to be practical. For example, the ruler(s) of the ideal polity arduously and artfully unites the arts and sciences of philosophy and prophecy, or political and religious leadership. In addition, the polity aims at realizing the virtues and happiness of its citizens, as the best form of life is within a properly ruled polis.

Al-Farabi valued philosophy as the highest form of knowledge, owing in part to its reliance on "scientific demonstration," whereas he confined THEOLOGY to "imaginative representations," resorting to the rational methods of rhetoric and dialectic. However rational such methods may be, they are not on par with the demonstrative method of philosophy. Moreover, the "acquired intellect" of the philosopher is a different medium from the "imaginative faculty" of the prophet, for prophetic revelations are the truths of philosophy put in understandable form for commoners. The rhetorical, dialectical, and political arts, in other words, permit wisdom to be put in a communicative form congenial to the masses. After all, philosophers are few and far between, but their wisdom and understanding should and can benefit everyone.

Deemed the "second teacher" (after Aristotle, d. 322 B.C.E.) and the "second master" (after Abu Yusuf Yaqub ibn Ishaq al-Kindi, d. ca. 866 C.E.), al-Farabi was a great synthesizer of philosophical and theological traditions. Renowned for an ascetic demeanor, near the end of his life he returned to Aleppo in SYRIA following a trip to EGYPT. There he was associated with Sayf al-Dawla (918–967), a prince known for his generous patronage of the arts. At 80 years of age, he died in Aleppo. Al-Farabi's philosophy left a decisive impression on IBN SINA (d. 1037) and was deeply cherished by Islamic and Jewish philosophers, affecting even the Latin Scholasticism of 13th-century Europe. The great Muslim theologian ABU HAMID AL-GHAZALI (d. 1111) found much to contend with in the subsequent development of Islamic Neoplatonism.

See also CREATION; POLITICS AND ISLAM.

Patrick S. O'Donnell

Further reading: Deborah L. Black, "Al-Farabi." In *History of Islamic Philosophy,* edited by Seyyed Hossein Nasr and Oliver Leaman, 178–197 (London: Routledge,

1996); Majid Fakhry, *Al-Farabi: Founder of Islamic Neo-platonism* (Oxford: Oneworld, 2002); Oliver Leaman, *An Introduction to Classical Islamic Philosophy.* 2d ed. (Cambridge: Cambridge University Press, 2002); Ian Richard Netton, *Al-Farabi and His School* (London: Routledge, 1992).

Faraizi movement (Persian spelling; Arabic, Faraidi movement)

The Faraizis were a religious renewal and anti-British protest movement that arose in the Bengal region of INDIA in the early 19th century. Their name is based on the Arabic for "religious duties" (*faraid*), which emphasizes their advocacy of a return to the core requirements of Islamic practice. The movement's founder was Hajji Shariat Allah (ca. 1781–1840), who performed the HAJJ from eastern Bengal in his late teens and resided in MECCA for about 20 years. It is likely that he was influenced by WAHHABISM and other revivalist Islamic ideas while in residence there, for it was after his return to Bengal from Arabia in the early 1800s that he launched the movement. From the 1760s, Bengal had been under the control of the English East India Company, whose economic and agricultural policies were having devastating effects on the indigenous textile industry and the livelihood of the region's farmers. The local population, which was mostly Muslim, had grown restive under the British administration's exploitative land and taxation policies that favored the British and Hindu landholders and speculators. Bengali Muslims were therefore receptive to the formation of a resistance movement.

Shariat Allah told Bengali Muslims to return to what he considered to be the true Islamic practices and to give up Shii and Sufi saint worship and certain marriage and funerary customs. Furthermore, he taught that Muslims should not perform communal prayers as long as they did not have a legitimate Muslim ruler governing them. At the same time, he supported landless Bengali peasants in their protests against wealthy landlords by urging them to reject forced labor and to not pay their taxes. With its reformist and egalitarian message, the Faraizi movement he launched was then able to establish a base of popular support in rural eastern Bengal, particularly under the leadership of Shariat Allah's son, Dudu Miyan (1819–63). The latter even declared India to be a *dar al-harb* (house of war) as long as it was ruled by non-Muslims such as the British and came into open clashes with British authorities. Landlords and the British rallied to oppose the movement and accused Shariat Allah and his son of trying to create their own kingdom. The Faraizis were held in check by their opponents, and they lost support among many Muslims because of their rejection of popular religious practices and their condemnation of Muslims who did not agree with Faraizi doctrines. With the imprisonment of Dudu Miyan at the time of the great 1857 uprising against British rule, the Faraizi movement ceased to be politically active. Nevertheless, it continued to exist as a religious revival movement until the early 20th century.

See also BANGLADESH; COLONIALISM; *DAR AL-ISLAM AND DAR AL-HARB*; RENEWAL AND REFORM MOVEMENTS.

Further reading: Nurul H. Choudhury, *Peasant Radicalism in 19th Century Bengal: The Faraizi, Indigo, and Pabna Movements* (Dhaka: Asiatic Society of Bangladesh, 2001); Muin-ud-Din Ahamd Khan, *History of the Faraidi Movement in Bengal, 1818–1906* (Karachi: Pakistan Historical Society, 1965).

Farrakhan, Louis (1933–) *controversial African-American leader of the Nation of Islam from 1977*

Born Louis Eugene Walcott, the son of a domestic worker and immigrant, Farrakhan grew up in Boston. As a youth, Farrakhan played the violin, excelled academically in high school, and became actively Episcopalian. In 1955, during a trip to Chicago for a musical performance, Farrakhan attended one of the Nation of Islam's conventions. Greatly influenced by the founder, Elijah Muhammad's, teachings, Farrakhan put his musical interests aside and became an active member of the nation, changing his name to Louis X, which later became Louis Haleem Abdul Farrakhan. Following Elijah Muhammad's death in 1975, his son, Wallace Deen Muhammad, began leading the nation and shifted away from Elijah's teachings, declaring his father's extreme views racist. Wishing to return to Elijah's original message, Farrakhan formed a competing organization in 1977, which is among several other groups that claim the name NATION OF ISLAM.

Farrakhan has caught public attention since the mid-1980s for allegedly making anti-Semitic remarks, accusations that Farrakhan denies, claiming that the media is biased. Such allegations aside, Farrakhan's leadership of the nation has led to many positive reforms. Farrakhan has diminished the number of drug dealers in public housing projects, has permitted WOMEN to become public leaders in the nation, and has played a key role in the development of Islam in America. He has also built MOSQUES in several U.S. cities. Farrakhan has traveled to various parts of the Middle East and North Africa, allegedly attacking the U.S. government and Jewish groups during his trips abroad. In 1999, claiming to have a near-death experience with prostate cancer, Farrakhan began preaching racial and religious unity. Farrakhan appears widely on television and speaks on radio. He and his wife, Khadijah (Betsy), have 11 children, several of whom are actively involved in the nation.

See also AFRICAN AMERICANS, ISLAM AMONG.

Mehnaz Sahibzada

Further reading: Robert Dannin, *Black Pilgrimage to Islam* (New York: Oxford University Press, 2002); Mattias Gardell, *In the Name of Elijah Muhammad: Louis Farrakhan and the Nation of Islam* (Durham, N.C.: Duke University Press, 1996); Eric C. Lincoln, *The Black Muslims in America* (Trenton, N.J.: Africa World Press, 1994); Jane I. Smith, *Islam in America* (New York: Columbia University Press, 1999).

Farsi   *See* PERSIAN LANGUAGE AND LITERATURE.

fasting (Arabic: *sawm* or *siyam*)

The primary fast in Islam, and one of its FIVE PILLARS, takes place during the month of RAMADAN, when observant Muslims refrain from eating, drinking any liquids, smoking, or having sexual intercourse during daylight hours. The beginning and end of the fast each day are marked by calls to PRAYER: before dawn, when a white string can be distinguished from a black one, and again at sunset. Muslims generally break their fast with a drink of thick fruit juice and a date, after the custom of MUHAMMAD (d. 632). Some will then pray before a large meal (*futur*), consisting of dishes special to the month, is served. These meals are occasions for families to gather and for neighbors and friends to visit one another. Indeed, it is not unusual for large quantities of food to be consumed at night during Ramadan, despite the daylight fasting requirements. The end of the month and of the fast is marked by the ID AL-FITR, or "feast of fast-breaking."

Muslims look to the quranic chapter "The Cow" (Q 2:183) as the injunction from God to fast. It reads, "O you who believe! Fasting is prescribed for you, as it was prescribed for those before you, so that you may guard against evil." Although children often participate for a few hours a day or a few days in the month, all Muslims who have reached puberty are expected to fast. Temporary exceptions are made for those who are in poor health, for those who are traveling, or for menstruating and pregnant women, with the idea that these missed fast days will be made up at a later date.

Outside the month of Ramadan, fasting is also observed on the day before the ID AL-ADHA, which marks the end of the formal HAJJ season. Some

Muslims, mostly Shia, also fast on Tuesdays and Thursdays throughout the year, but especially during the months of Shaaban and Rajab.

In addition to fulfilling a religious requirement, fasting is associated with a variety of other benefits. For some, it presents an opportunity to focus on one's spiritual life. Indeed, many Sufis are known to include extended fasts in their religious practice. For others, the feelings of hunger are an important reminder of the plight of less fortunate members of the community. For still others, fasting may be performed as an act of expiation for a broken promise. Finally, fasting is seen as providing beneficial health effects.

See also ASCETICISM; DIETARY LAWS; FEASTING; FOOD AND DRINK.

Michelle Zimney

Further reading: Hammudah Abdalati, *Islam in Focus* (Indianapolis: Islamic Trust Publications, 1996); Marjo Buitelaar, *Fasting and Feasting in Morocco: Women's Participation in Ramadan* (Oxford: Berg, 1993).

fate

Fate is a power or force that is thought to determine in advance what happens in the world, particularly to human beings. It is opposed to pure accident or chance and is often equated with the idea of fortune or destiny in this world and in the AFTERLIFE. Fatalism is a worldview that upholds the belief that all events are predetermined and that it is useless for anyone to try to change them. In ancient Mesopotamia, fate was believed to be in the hands of the gods, whom human beings were created to serve. In ancient Greece, it was personified in the form of three women or was said to be something controlled by the god Zeus. Christian thinkers reinterpreted ancient beliefs about fate by associating it with Divine Providence, which they qualified by also asserting a human capacity for choosing between good and evil. Christian theology has struggled, therefore, with reconciling belief in God's omnipotence with human free will.

Although Islam is often represented as a fatalistic religion, two different trends of thought developed within the Muslim community in regard to the issue of God's predetermination of events and human freedom. The competing Muslim theological discussions of this topic all quote quranic verses to support the positions they have taken. Speaking of God's incomparable majesty and power, the QURAN states, "God guides to truth whom he wills and leads astray whom he wills" (Q 14:4), and "When he decrees a thing, he says to it 'Be' and it is" (for example, Q 2:117). Verses such as these have been used by those who argued that God determines all that happens to people, whether good or evil. This view is also reflected in the popular Arabic expression, "*In sha Allah*" (If God wills it so), which people often say when planning a future activity. In a similar vein, the Quran declares, "Nothing will happen to us except what God has written for us" (Q 9:51), implying that human destiny has been preordained in a divine book or tablet. Moreover, the Quran states that all created things have been assigned a fixed term of existence (*ajal*). Even a person's DEATH was thought to be predetermined (see Q 6:2, 39:42, 40:68). God's power to determine everything that happens became a formal aspect of Sunni THEOLOGY, especially in the ASHARI SCHOOL, and it had the approval of early Muslim rulers, who sought to protect their own power by arguing that it was God-given, despite their own moral failures as Muslims.

Nonfatalist advocates of free will sought to give human beings more responsibility in deciding how to conduct their lives and shape their own destinies. They pointed to the many verses in the Quran that spoke of the Final Judgment and maintained that God's judgment would be just only if humans were righteous or sinful by choice rather than by fate. According to one such verse, "Truth is from your Lord, so whoever wills, let him believe, and whoever wills, let him disbelieve. Indeed, we have prepared a Fire for the disbelievers . . . and for those who believe and do good works, we will not let go astray the reward of those who do beautiful things" (Q 18:29–30). AL-HASAN AL-BASRI (d. 728), remembered in part for being an early free will advocate, tried unsuccessfully to explain to the Umayyad CALIPH Abd al-Malik (r. 685–705) the correctness of this belief. In developing his argument, he maintained that God commanded only the good and that evil was caused by humans or SATAN. He and others like him in IRAQ, SYRIA, Arabia, and YEMEN were called the Qadariyya (the party favoring human self-determination). This early trend in Islamic religious thought developed into the Mutazili tradition of Islamic theology and contributed significantly to the formation of the rationalist school of thought in Shii theology, as opposed to the Ashari school of the Sunnis.

Since the 19th century, Orientalists, missionaries, and travelers from Europe and North America have attributed fatalistic beliefs to ordinary Muslims, particularly in regard to their explanations of illness and misfortune. Some have reported that critical medical care was refused out of a belief that the fate of the patient was in God's hands. However, Muslims have indeed sought out remedies and cures for illnesses when they were available, and fatalistic acceptance is only one option, used when hope is lost. This is true even where conservative predeterminist Islamic doctrines prevail, such as among Wahhabis in SAUDI ARABIA. One should remember that medicine was one of the foremost applied sciences in medieval Islamicate civilization. In a different regard, modern Islamic reformers in many Muslim lands have been incorporating notions of free will into their thinking, further loosening the hold of the Ashari brand of predeterminism and promoting progressive change among Muslims.

See also ALLAH; JUDGMENT DAY; MUTAZILI SCHOOL.

Further reading: Fazlur Rahman, *Major Themes of the Quran* (Minneapolis: Bibliotheca Islamica, 1989); Helmer Ringgren, *Studies in Arabian Fatalism* (Uppsala: Lundequistska Bokhandeln, 1955); W. Montgomery Watt, *The Formative Period of Islamic Thought* (Edinburgh: University of Edinburgh Press, 1973).

Fatiha (Arabic: The Opening, or the Opening of the Book)

The Fatiha is the first of the QURAN's 114 chapters. It is the one most widely memorized by Muslims and is used in their worship and daily life. Unlike most of the other chapters, which have mixed contents such as apocalyptic visions, sermons, dialogues, stories, commandments, and PRAYERS, the Fatiha is strictly a verbal prayer. It consists of seven verses:

1. In the name of God, the merciful, the compassionate.
2. Praise be to God, the lord of the worlds (or beings),
3. The merciful, the compassionate,
4. Master of the Day of Judgment.
5. It is you whom we worship, and it is you to whom we turn for help.
6. Guide us on the straight path,
7. The path of those on whom you have bestowed your blessing, and not of those who have incurred your anger and have gone astray.

Muslim and non-Muslim scholars generally agree that this chapter dates to the time when MUHAMMAD was still living in MECCA (ca. 619), although it was probably not widely used until the Islamic religion became more organized after the HIJRA to MEDINA in 622. Some have argued that it is comparable to the Jewish Shema prayer (Deut. 6:4–9) and the Lord's Prayer (Mt. 6:9–13) in Christianity and that it was probably originally intended for use in worship. Indeed, since as early as the seventh century, it has been a required part of the five daily ritual prayers (*salat*), the weekly communal prayers, and the two annual Id prayers (ID AL-FITR and ID AL-ADHA). Muslim jurists have ruled that performance of a *salat* is invalid if recitation of the Fatiha is omitted. The fact that practicing Muslims around the world have consistently memorized and recited it (usually in Arabic) for centuries, regardless of their ethnic or religious outlook, means that it has become an identifying characteristic of membership in the wider Muslim community (UMMA).

According to the HADITH and Quran commentaries, the Fatiha is "the mother (essence) of the Quran" and its "greatest chapter." One widely circulated hadith declares, "God has revealed nothing like [it] in the Torah and the Gospel." Aside from using it in their daily prayers, Muslims also recite it during BIRTH RITES, weddings, and funerals, and to inaugurate new buildings, businesses, and formal gatherings. Muslims in northern INDIA have developed a funerary ritual called the Fatiha, which involves reciting the chapter and making food offerings on behalf of the dead in a sacralized room of the house. The page of the Quran on which the Fatiha is written has been the most beautifully decorated page in Quran manuscripts and printed editions. It is often displayed in homes, businesses, and MOSQUES as an expression of religiosity and as a means of ensuring God's blessing for those places.

See also AMULETS AND TALISMANS; BASMALA; FUNERARY RITUALS.

Further reading: Laleh Bakhtiyar, *Encyclopedia of Islamic Law: A Compendium of the Major Schools* (Chicago: ABC International Group, 1996); S. D. Goitein, "Prayer in Islam." In *Studies in Islamic History and Institutions,* edited by S. D. Goitein 73–89 (Leiden: E.J. Brill, 1966); Moshe Piamenta, *Islam in Everyday Arabic Speech* (Leiden: E.J. Brill, 1979).

Fatima (ca. 605–633) *daughter of Muhammad, wife of Ali, and mother of Shii Imams, the Shia regard her as a saint, the only woman they count among the five "pure" members of the Prophet's household*

Fatima was the youngest daughter born to MUHAMMAD and his wife KHADIJA. Early historical sources provide few details about her, except to indicate that she married Muhammad's cousin ALI IBN ABI TALIB (d. 661) shortly after the HIJRA to MEDINA, when she was about 18 years old. Like other Muslim families at that time, they lived in poverty until more lands and property were acquired by the early community as a result of the early conquests under Muhammad's leadership. She bore Ali two sons who lived to adulthood: Hasan (624–669) and Husayn (626–680). Accounts say that in his last days, Muhammad drew Ali, Fatima, and their two sons together under his cloak and said, "God wishes to remove impurity from you, O People of the House [AHL AL-BAYT], and to thoroughly purify you" (Q 33:33). This confirmed the holy status of all five members of Muhammad's household, and as a result of this incident they are also known as the People of the Cloak. Fatima also gave birth to two daughters, Umm Kulthum and Zaynab. When Muhammad was on his deathbed in 632, Fatima and Ali tended to him, while the leadership of the community was being decided elsewhere by Muhammad's associates ABU BAKR (d. 634), UMAR IBN AL-KHATTAB (d. 644), and their allies. Thus, she was implicated in the events that led to the split between the Sunni and Shii branches of Islam. Fatima died at a young age, within a year of her father. Accounts differ as to where she was buried. Some say she was buried in Baqi cemetery, near Muhammad's house; others say she was buried on the grounds of his MOSQUE.

Fatima is greatly revered by Muslims, especially the Shia. Among the other names by which she is known are al-Zahra, "the Radiant," al-Mubaraka, "the Blessed," and al-Tahira, "the Pure." According to medieval Shii hagiographies, her marriage with Ali was celebrated in heaven and on Earth, and all the Shii imams have descended from this couple. It is also said that because of her purity, she did not menstruate like other women, and her pregnancies lasted only nine hours. Moreover, she will be the first to enter PARADISE after the Resurrection, and, like MARY in Catholic Christianity, she will intercede for those who honor her and her offspring and descendants, the Imams. Indeed, in Shii literature, Fatima is compared to Mary the mother of JESUS because of the violent deaths suffered by each of their sons. Although Fatima's name is not mentioned in the QURAN, Shii commentaries point out passages they believe contain hidden references to her, such as Q 55:19, where the two oceans of water that flow together are interpreted as the reunion of Ali and Fatima after a dispute. In popular Islamic practice, an image of an outstretched hand, called the Hand of Fatima, is used as an amulet to deflect the EVIL EYE, and the Shia display it in ASHURA processions in India.

During the 1970s, Fatima gained a modern importance through the lectures and writings of the Iranian intellectual ALI SHARIATI (d. 1977), who portrayed her as a symbol of the total woman—daughter, wife, mother, freedom fighter, and defender of the oppressed. Although Fatima was likened to the Virgin Mary in Islamic tradition, she should not be confused with Our Lady of Fatima, the name given to the apparitions of Mary near the town of Fatima in Portugal in 1917.

See also IMAM; SHIISM; WOMEN.

Further reading: Marcia K. Hermensen, "Fatimeh as a Role Model in the Works of Ali Shariati." In *Women and Revolution in Iran,* edited by Guity Nashat, 87–96 (Boulder, Colo.: Westview Press, 1983); Jane Dammen McAuliffe, "Chosen of All Women: Mary and Fatima in Quranic Exegesis." *Islamochristiana* 7 (1981): 19–28; Susan Sered, "Rachel, Mary, and Fatima." *Cultural Anthropology* 6, no. 2 (1991): 131–146.

Fatimid dynasty (909–1171)

The Fatimids were a medieval Ismaili Shii dynasty that ruled over a band of territory that stretched from TUNISIA in North Africa to EGYPT, the Red Sea region (including MECCA and MEDINA), PALESTINE, and SYRIA. They rivaled the Sunni dynasties of the Abbasids in IRAQ (750–1258) and the Umayyads of ANDALUSIA (756–1009), both of which they unsuccessfully attempted to overthrow. Their first capital was Mahdiyya, on the Tunisian coast, but

in 969, they shifted eastward and founded a new capital in Egypt, next to the flourishing commercial city of Fustat. The name they gave to their new royal city was CAIRO (Qahira, "conqueror"). The name of the dynasty itself was derived from that of Muhammad's daughter FATIMA (d. 633), and they traced their lineage to the Prophet's household through the seventh IMAM, Ismail (d. ca. 762), the son of JAAFAR AL-SADIQ, the sixth Shii Imam. The first Fatimid Imam or CALIPH was Abd Allah (r. 909–934), who was considered to be the MAHDI, the promised deliverer sent by God. Sunnis did not accept this claim and instead remembered him by the derogatory name of Ubayd Allah, "little servant of God."

The Fatimids sponsored an active program of religious outreach and propaganda (DAAWA) throughout North Africa, the Middle East, and northwest India to promote their cause but failed to win large numbers of followers, even in Egypt. Nonetheless, Egypt prospered for nearly a century under Fatimid rule. Ismailis were able to practice their tradition of Islam in public, while other Muslims and non-Muslims enjoyed relative tolerance. Jews and Christians as well as Sunni Muslims held high positions in government. The famed Geniza documents, a collection of medieval writings recovered from Cairo's Ben Ezra synagogue, have yielded valuable details about the daily life of Jews and their social and economic relations with non-Jews at this time. Intellectual life also thrived, in part a result of Ismaili efforts to articulate their messianic doctrines and refute Sunni attacks. Important works on PHILOSOPHY, religion, history, BIOGRAPHY, and the SCIENCES were composed and collected in private libraries. The Fatimid palace alone had a House of Knowledge that contained a reading room, a meeting place for scholars, and a library containing several hundred thousand scholarly books. Rulers also supported the formation of a distinct tradition of Ismaili religious law, which was explained in public sessions after Friday PRAYER at AL-AZHAR and other major MOSQUES in the capital.

The mosque of al-Hakim bi-Amr Allah (early 11th century), Cairo, Egypt *(Juan E. Campo)*

The Fatimid dynasty's most memorable ruler was the caliph al-Hakim bi-Amr Allah (r. 996–1021), who built a monumental mosque and gateways in Cairo and founded the House of Knowledge. In 1009, however, he destroyed the Church of the Holy Sepulcher, the burial place of Jesus, which contributed to the launching of the First Crusade at the end of the century. Al-Hakim has also been charged with abusing his power by arbitrarily ordering the execution of members of his court, confining women to their homes, persecuting Christians, Jews, and Sunni Muslims, banning popular recreational activities, having Cairo's dogs killed because their barking annoyed him, and outlawing the game of chess. Al-Hakim died under mysterious circumstances in 1021, but Ismaili claims about his divinity gave rise to the Druze religion in Syria. Later, after 1094, a schism in the dynasty led to the creation of the two major branches of the Ismaili Shia, the Mustalis and the Nizaris. The Yemeni and Indian Bohra Ismailis trace their origins to the first of these branches; the latter is associated with the sect known in the West as the Assassins and the modern-day Aga Khan Ismailis. The Fatimid dynasty suffered from a number of damaging internal and external crises, including natural catastrophes, dynastic disputes, ethnic and religious factionalism, opposition from powerful Sunni rulers in Syria and Iraq, and the invasion of the first crusaders from Europe in

1096. In 1171, the last Fatimid caliph, al-Adid, was overthrown by a Kurdish commander, SALA-DIN (1174–93), who became the SULTAN of Egypt and the founder of the Ayyubid dynasty (1174–1250). This Sunni dynasty effectively put an end to Ismaili influence in Egypt.

See also ABBASID CALIPHATE; CHRISTIANITY AND ISLAM; ISMAILI SHIISM; UMAYYAD CALIPHATE.

Further reading: Farhad Daftary, *A Short History of the Ismailis* (Princeton, N.J.: Marcus Wiener Publishers, 1998); Heinz Halm, *The Empire of the Mahdi: The Rise of the Fatimids.* Translated by Michael Bonner (Leiden and New York: E.J. Brill, 1996).

fatwa

Most legal systems have a tradition that allows experts to state their opinions with respect to questions of law. In Islamic law, one way this is done is by issuing a fatwa, which is an opinion based on knowledge of the QURAN and the SUNNA of Muhammad. It is given orally or in writing in response to a question asked by a man or woman. The legal AUTHORITY who answers the question is called a MUFTI, an author of fatwas. He should be knowledgeable in the sacred scriptures of Islam and the SHARIA, though he is not required to follow the rulings of a specific Islamic legal school (*madh-hab*). The fatwa is different from a decision made in a court of law by a judge (*qadi*) because it does not require review of evidence and testimony from two parties in the context of a legal hearing or trial. Rather, it is an informed response to a question that may concern, for example, a matter of worship, marriage and divorce, inheritance, business and finance, crime, APOSTASY, or daily behavior. Thus, a person might request a fatwa for something as seemingly trivial as to whether one can brush his teeth in the daytime during the RAMADAN fast (which might invalidate the fast for that day), or as important as to whether a Muslim can live in a country ruled by non-Muslims (which might require a JIHAD). The fatwa is only advisory, which is underscored by the phrase "and God knows best" (*Allah aalam*) that often occurs at its conclusion. Indeed, fatwas may contradict each other, in which case the questioners are left to decide for themselves. Although many are given orally, those that are issued by a powerful or influential mufti may be written, collected, and published. In the past, most fatwas addressed questions coming from local Muslim communities, and this is still often the case, as it is among Muslims living in the United States and Europe. Since the introduction of the modern print and electronic media, however, fatwas can reach a global audience. Many leading Islamic organizations and religious authorities now have Internet sites where people can submit questions, receive advisory opinions, and review opinions given in answer to questions asked previously by others online.

See also FIQH; IJTIHAD; RUSHDIE, SALMAN.

Further reading: Muhammad Khalid Masud, Brinkley Messick, and David S. Powers, *Islamic Legal Interpretation: Muftis and Their Fatwas* (Cambridge, Mass.: Harvard University Press, 1996); Rudolph Peters, *Islam and Colonialism: The Doctrine of Jihad in Modern History* (The Hague: Mouton, 1979).

Faysal ibn Abd al-Aziz Al Saud (King Feisal) (1906–1975) *king of Saudi Arabia from 1964 to 1975 who inaugurated a significant program of economic, governmental, and social modernization and strove to unite Muslims against the spread of socialism and communism during the cold war era*

Faysal was the fourth son of Saudi Arabia's first king, Abd al-Aziz ibn Saud (r. 1926–53) and a direct descendant on his mother's side of MUHAMMAD IBN ABD AL-WAHHAB (d. 1792), the founder of the puritanical Wahhabi movement. Faysal was himself a religiously minded man, no doubt shaped by his early upbringing in the household of his maternal grandfather, a leading Wahhabi authority. At the age of 14, he was the first member of the Saudi family to visit England and

Europe and was named foreign minister after his return in 1919. Faysal played an active role in the Saudi conquest of the Arabian Peninsula in the 1920s and 1930s and served as governor of the Hijaz, the western part of Arabia where MECCA and MEDINA are located. At the end of World War II, he represented SAUDI ARABIA at the United Nations. In 1953, he was named the country's crown prince and foreign minister and contended with his brother King Saud ibn Abd al-Aziz for the upper hand in Saudi affairs. With the help of the ULAMA, he successfully forced Saud to step down from the throne, and he became the kingdom's third monarch in 1964.

Saudi Arabia experienced a great increase in OIL revenues during Faysal's reign. This helped to finance a far-reaching program of modernization. He expanded the state bureaucracy and centralized planning and decision making in the hands of the royal family. Faysal made substantial improvements in the country's roads, communications, electrical supply, and social services. He also modernized the country's educational system, opening new universities and vocational centers in the kingdom's major cities and towns. With the encouragement of his wife, Iffat, he opened more than 100 schools for girls, despite opposition from religious and social conservatives. Faysal was a staunch opponent of EGYPT's Arab nationalist leader, JAMAL ABD AL-NASIR (r. 1954–70) and sought to unite Muslim nations against the influence of the Soviet Union and the spread of Arab socialism. He also participated, with some reluctance, in the oil embargo against the United States because of its support for ISRAEL in the October 1973 Arab-Israeli war. In 1975, he was assassinated by a nephew and was succeeded by his brother, Crown Prince Khalid ibn Abd al-Aziz (r. 1975–82). A major research center for Islamic studies in Riyadh and a university in the eastern region of Saudi Arabia have been named in his honor.

See also ABD AL-AZIZ IBN SAUD; ARAB-ISRAELI CONFLICTS; COMMUNISM; ORGANIZATION OF THE ISLAMIC CONFERENCE; WAHHABISM.

Further reading: Madawi al-Rasheed, *A History of Saudi Arabia* (Cambridge: Cambridge University Press, 2002); Nadav Safran, *Saudi Arabia: The Ceaseless Quest for Security* (Cambridge, Mass.: Harvard University Press, 1985).

feasting

Feasting is a celebratory cultural activity that involves the sharing of quantities of food and drink by families, social groups and classes, and entire communities. It is known to many societies—tribal, agricultural, and industrial—and religions. As Caroline Walker Bynum has noted, feasting and FASTING often link members of communities to each other and to the rhythms of nature, with its times of plenty and times of famine and drought (Bynum, 34). Periods of feasting and fasting tend to complement each other, even if they do not always coincide with the seasonal patterns of nature.

There are two major times of feasting recognized in Islam. One is ID AL-ADHA, the Feast of Sacrifice, a three- to four-day holiday that commemorates the sacrifice of ABRAHAM and the conclusion of the HAJJ rites in MECCA. The other is ID AL-FITR, the Breakfast Feast, a three- to four-day holiday that marks the end of the month-long RAMADAN fast. These HOLIDAYS are celebrated by Muslims around the world; they involve visiting among families, neighbors, and friends and the preparation of savory foods and desserts. Families often schedule engagements and weddings during Id holidays in order to keep overall expenses down, because people have more free time to attend, and because BARAKA (divine blessing) is believed to be especially strong at such times of the year. Families also visit cemeteries on these days to donate food to the poor on behalf of the souls of deceased loved ones. The idea of feasting, moreover, has been incorporated into Islamic visions of the AFTERLIFE. In PARADISE, the blessed are rewarded with heavenly dishes and beverages, which are served endlessly in luxurious settings.

The MAWLID of the prophet MUHAMMAD, which commemorates the days of his birth and death, is observed in many Muslim countries with the enjoyment of nuts and sweets (especially in the Middle East) or cooked stews and milk and rice dishes (in INDIA). The anniversaries of the birth or death of other Muslim SAINTS provide occasions for feasting in many Muslim communities, especially for pilgrims who visit the saints' shrines, where they often share food with each other, even if they are total strangers. At shrines in South Asia, such as that of Muin al-Din Chishti (d. 1236) in AJMER, specially blessed food is cooked and distributed to pilgrims and the poor from community kitchens (langar khanas) affiliated with the shrines.

The Shia hold feasts in honor of the birthdays of their IMAMS and women descended from Muhammad, such as FATIMA and her daughter ZAYNAB BINT ALI IBN ABI TALIB. For many of the Shia, the most important feast day is that of GHADIR KHUMM (observed shortly after Id al-Adha), which celebrates Muhammad's designation of Ali as his successor in 630. Even with the ASHURA rites of the month of MUHARRAM, a time of sadness and fasting for the devoted, subdued feasting occurs in Iraqi and Iranian homes, where people gather to hold readings of lamentations in honor of the martyrdom of HUSAYN IBN ALI and his followers at KARBALA in 680. For many South Asian Muslims, Shab-i Barat (the night of commission), which occurs in the middle of the month of Shaban, before Ramadan, is another important time of feasting. At that time, people share dishes consisting of stews, curries, and sweets with friends and relatives in remembrance of the dead.

Most Muslim feasts are set according to the Islamic lunar CALENDAR, which means that they do not coincide with the seasons of the solar year (spring, summer, fall, winter). For example, if Id al-Adha falls on June 25 one year, the next year it will come 11 days earlier, on June 14, and so on from one solar year to the next. Some Muslim mawlid celebrations, however, are observed according to the solar calendar. For example, that of AHMAD AL-BADAWI of Tanta, EGYPT, occurs annually at the time of the fall harvest, when food is plentiful. Ancient spring fertility and first fruits feasts occur in many Muslim countries, although they are not usually recognized as Islamic holidays per se. NAVRUZ is the spring holiday most widely observed by Iranians and others living in eastern Islamicate lands. In Egypt, the spring holiday is called Shamm al-Nasim (smelling the breeze). It occurs on the Monday after the Coptic Christian Easter and involves picnics in the countryside and city parks or family meals at home.

All Muslims engage in feasting at important moments in the human life cycle. These occur when a child is born, when a boy is circumcised, when a couple is engaged and married, and when a person dies. Such occasions are usually not restricted to the nuclear family but often involve many others—extended family, neighbors, and friends. Non-Muslims may also participate in these celebrations. Other feasts may be held when someone recovers from an illness or returns home safely from a long journey or pilgrimage to Mecca.

See also BIRTH RITES; CIRCUMCISION; FOOD AND DRINK; FUNERARY RITUALS; SHIISM.

Further reading: Caroline Walker Bynum, *Holy Feast and Holy Fast: The Religious Significance of Food to Medieval Women* (Berkeley: University of California Press, 1987); Elizabeth Fernea, *Guests of the Sheik: An Ethnography of an Iraqi Village* (1965. Reprint, New York: Anchor Books, 1989), 116–125; John Kennedy, ed., *Nubian Ceremonial Life: Studies in Islamic Syncretism and Cultural Change* (Berkeley and Cairo: University of California Press and American University in Cairo Press, 1978); Jafar Sharif, *Islam in India, or the Qanun-i Islam: The Customs of the Musalmans of India.* Translated by G. A. Herklots (1832. Reprint, Delhi: Low Price Publications, 1997), 151–217.

fedayeen *See* FIDAI.

Federation of Islamic Associations (acronym: FIA)

One of the first organizations created to link different Muslim groups in North America was the Federation of Islamic Associations. It started in 1952 in Cedar Rapids, Iowa, under the name of the International Muslim Society. Its membership consisted mostly of people of Syrian and Lebanese descent living in the Northeast and Midwest. The MOSQUES represented by its early members were those of Cedar Rapids, Iowa, Dearborn, Michigan, Michigan City, Indiana, and Quincy, Massachusetts. The group's purpose was to promote Muslim self-awareness and to help Muslims adapt to life in the UNITED STATES and CANADA. At its third annual meeting in Chicago in 1954, the group's name was changed to Federation of Islamic Associations. During that year, it appealed to the American president, Dwight Eisenhower (r. 1952–60), for recognition of Islam as a religion by the U.S. armed forces. As it grew, the FIA offered information about Islam to non-Muslims, organized social events where Muslim youths could meet future spouses, monitored media coverage of Islam and Middle Eastern politics, and established full-time accredited schools for Muslims. The main publication of the FIA was the *Muslim Star.* In the 1960s and 1970s, it worked together with the MUSLIM STUDENTS ASSOCIATION (MSA), which was based on college and university campuses in the United States and Canada. The FIA attempted in the 1970s to conduct a census of Muslims living in the United States and to standardize the curriculum for religious education classes held at mosques and Islamic centers, but these efforts were not successful. There is still no widely accepted estimate of the number of Muslims living in the United States. The FIA's effectiveness has diminished greatly since the 1970s. The MSA and the ISLAMIC SOCIETY OF NORTH AMERICA (ISNA) have largely replaced it, and publication of the *Muslim Star* has ceased.

Further reading: Kambiz Ghanea Bassiri, *Competing Visions of Islam in the United States: A Study of Los Ange-* les (Westport, Conn.: Greenwood Press, 1997); Jane I. Smith, *Islam in America* (New York: Columbia University Press, 1999).

Fez

Fez is a city in northern MOROCCO that has been the country's political and intellectual capital for much of its history and remains famous for its old city (medina), declared a world heritage site by the United Nations Educational, Scientific and Cultural Organization (UNESCO) in 1981. Today it has a population of nearly 1 million (2004), composed of mostly ethnic Arabs and Berbers. The majority of residents are Sunni Muslims, though there is a sizeable Jewish community that has lived there for centuries. The MALIKI LEGAL SCHOOL is the predominant one in the city, as it is in most of the rest of North Africa.

The history of Fez began in the late eighth century, when the first leaders of the Idrisid dynasty (789–926) established the city at the edge of the Saiss valley. Possessing a strategic location in the western corridor between the Mediterranean Sea and the Sahara, Fez became the northern terminus for the Saharan caravan trade and also benefited from its location near one of Morocco's richest agricultural regions. Over the centuries, Fez was ruled by a number of different dynasties, none of which left their mark on the city to the same extent as the BERBER Marinid dynasty (1196–1464). Between 1248 and 1465, the Marinids embellished their capital with many of the exquisite architectural monuments for which it is known. In addition, Fez was the country's intellectual capital, largely due to the presence of the Qarawiyyin University, which became the center of learning for western Islamdom. During this same period, the Spanish Reconquista drove Andalusian Muslims to North Africa, where many settled in Fez, making it the repository of the legacy of Hispano-Islamicate culture.

After the fall of the Marinids, Fez's fortunes declined, although it has retained its reputation

The old city of Fez, Morocco *(Federico R. Campo)*

as the country's cultural center. During the 20th century, the city's political prominence was eclipsed by Rabat, and its economic dominance was claimed by Casablanca. The establishment of a modern university in Rabat has even robbed Fez of its distinction as Morocco's intellectual center. Much of the historic Medina has fallen into disrepair, despite attempts by various groups to restore it. Debate continues over what lies ahead for this "jewel of Spanish-Arabic civilization" and whether Fez can make a future for itself to rival its glorious past.

See also ANDALUSIA; CITIES.

Stephen Cory

Further reading: Titus Burckhard, *Fez, City of Islam.* Translated by William Stoddart (Cambridge: Islamic Texts Society, 1992); Roger Le Tourneau, *Fez in the Age of the Merinids.* Translated by B. A. Clement (Norman: University of Oklahoma Press, 1961).

fidai (Arabic, also *fidawi*, plural: *fedayeen, fidayin;* Persian *fedaiyan*)

A *fidai* is one who is willing to sacrifice his life for a cause, which can be religious or political or a combination of both. The term is based on an Arabic word meaning ransom or redemption (*fida*). A verbal form of this word occurs in the QURAN, where God redeems Abraham's son with a sacrificial animal (Q 37:107), thus freeing ABRAHAM from sacrificing his own son, which is what God had previously demanded of him. In Islamic law, paying ransoms was permitted in order to free

Muslim prisoners from their Christian captors. Later in the Middle Ages, the fedayeen were the dedicated followers of Hasan-i Sabbah (d. 1124), the leader of the Nizari branch of the Ismaili Shia in IRAN, IRAQ, and SYRIA. Known to the West as the ASSASSINS, the fedayeen would infiltrate enemy towns in order to publicly assassinate prominent leaders, even at the risk of their own lives. One of their most important victims was the Seljuk vizier Nizam al-Mulk (d. 1092), the political head of the Abbasid Empire at the time. Such actions earned them the hatred of many Muslims, who called them heretics and hashish smokers (thus the name *Assassin*).

In more recent times, several groups of guerrilla fighters have been called fedayeen. These include Arab volunteers from EGYPT, JORDAN, and Syria who fought on behalf of the Palestinians against the Israelis between 1948 and 1967. They became the dominant elements in the formation of the PALESTINE LIBERATION ORGANIZATION in the 1960s. In Iraq, the Fedayeen Saddam was created in 1995 to serve as SADDAM HUSAYN's paramilitary force. When Anglo-American forces invaded and occupied Iraq in 2003, it constituted the core of the resistance the coalition forces encountered. The most overtly religious fedayeen in the modern period were the Fedaiyan-i Islam, a radical Shii terrorist group in Iran. Formed during the 1940s in close association with Shii clerics, it was composed mostly of young men living on the margins of Iran's major cities. Through assassinations of secular government officials, they sought to bring about a new political system based on the SHARIA. Violently suppressed by the shah's government in the 1950s, the organization reemerged after the 1978–79 revolution, only to dissolve when the Khomeini government was formed and most of the radicals' objectives were achieved. The secular counterpart to the Fedaiyan-i Islam was the Fedaiyan-i Khalq (the people's fedayeen), a Marxist movement that sought to overthrow the Shah's government during the 1970s.

See also ISMAILI SHIISM; JIHAD; SUICIDE.

Further reading: Farhad Daftary, *The Ismailis: Their History and Doctrines* (Cambridge: Cambridge University Press, 1990); Farhad Kazemi, "The Fadaiyan-e Islam: Fanaticism, Politics, and Terror." In *From Nationalism to Revolutionary Islam*, edited by Said Amir Arjomand (Albany: State University of New York Press, 1984); Yezid Sayegh, *Armed Struggle and the Search for State: The Palestinian National Movement, 1949–1993* (Oxford: Oxford University Press, 1997).

fiqh (Arabic: understanding)

Fiqh is a term for Islamic law, particularly as it is interpreted and implemented by legal experts from among the ULAMA. Whereas the SHARIA is ideally the comprehensive body of law ordained by God, *fiqh* involves Muslims' commitment to understand God's law and make it relevant to their lives. As such, it is a religious form of what is called "jurisprudence" in the West, and it extends its reach from matters of worship to detailed aspects of everyday conduct. A member of the ulama who is trained in *fiqh* is called a *faqih* (jurist).

When the first Arab-Muslim empires arose during the eras of the UMAYYAD CALIPHATE (661–750) and the ABBASID CALIPHATE (750–1258), Muslims were compelled to create a legal system for the conduct of their own affairs and their relations with their non-Muslim subjects. Administering new territories from Spain and North Africa to northwest India with their diverse peoples presented challenges to Muslims that Muhammad and the first Muslims had not contemplated in seventh-century Mecca and Medina. The Umayyads and Abbasids looked to the preexisting legal traditions of the Byzantine and Persian Empires, Jewish and Christian laws, and local custom. Religiously minded Muslim jurists used the QURAN, community customs, and their individual opinions to arrive at legal decisions during this early period. Many held that Muslim laws should be based as much as possible on the Quran and the SUNNA (authentic practice) of Muhammad and his Companions

Encyclopedia of Islam / Juan

31318020890736

p11482618

Mon Apr 30

7789 S

as recorded in the HADITH. By the ninth century, Muslim jurists had developed a coherent Islamic legal tradition that was held to be applicable to matters of worship as well as more worldly affairs, especially in towns and cities. Out of numerous local legal traditions, four major *fiqh* schools (sing. *madhhab*) came to be recognized as authoritative among Sunni Muslims: the HANAFI LEGAL SCHOOL, the MALIKI LEGAL SCHOOL, SHAFII LEGAL SCHOOL, and the HANBALI LEGAL SCHOOL. The Hanafis began in Kufa (Iraq), the Malikis in MEDINA, the Shafiis in Fustat (Egypt), and the Hanbalis in BAGHDAD. Several Shii legal schools also arose, but the principal one is the Jaafari Legal School of TWELVE-IMAM SHIISM.

All of these traditions of *fiqh* continue to be followed today by Muslims, especially in matters of worship, personal status, and family law. The Hanafi School now prevails among Muslims in TURKEY, IRAQ, Central Asia, AFGHANISTAN, CHINA, PAKISTAN, and INDIA. The Maliki School is followed mainly in North Africa, the SUDAN, WEST and Central AFRICA, and Kuwait. The chief legal school in EGYPT, SYRIA, EAST AFRICA, South India, Sri Lanka, Southeast Asia, and the PHILIPPINES is that of the Shafiis. The Hanbali School prevails in SAUDI ARABIA and Qatar, and it has had a significant influence on many Muslims around the world. The Jaafari tradition of *fiqh* is followed by the Shia of IRAN, southern Iraq, southern LEBANON, and parts of India and Pakistan.

The different legal schools have come to agree that there are four fundamental sources, or "roots," of *fiqh*. Ranked in order of importance, they are the Quran, the sunna, consensus (IJMAA), and analogical reasoning (*qiyas*). This ordering of the sources for law was developed by the great jurist MUHAMMAD IDRIS AL-SHAFII (d. 820). In the Quran itself, there are only a few dozen legislative commands, found mostly in the Medina chapters (for example, Q 2, 3, 4, and 5). Much of the law is drawn from the HADITH, which contains accounts of what Muhammad said and did. The sunna, or normative practice, is derived from these accounts.

Not all hadith were considered to be authentic, however. Muslims had to decide which ones were valid, based on who had transmitted them and whether they conformed to the Quran. During the ninth century, hadith regarded as the most authentic were arranged by subject and collected into books, which made them more available for study and consultation by students, scholars, and legal experts throughout Muslim lands. The two leading hadith collections for Sunnis are those of al-Bukhari (d. 870) and Muslim (d. 875).

Al-Shafii and other jurists recognized that the Quran and hadith did not address all of the legal issues Muslims faced in the widespread Islamicate empire, so they accepted laws based on communal consensus to supplement those based on revelation. This, the third root of *fiqh*, was endorsed by a hadith ascribed to Muhammad, which stated, "My community will never agree on error." Eventually, the consensus was understood to be that of the jurists themselves, not of the community at large. The fourth root, *qiyas*, allowed for the limited use of personal reasoning by qualified jurists, but it was subordinated to REVELATION, the hadith, and communal tradition. Analogical reasoning helped jurists make rulings concerning such issues as determining the direction of prayer, the minimum amount of money a groom owed to his bride's family at marriage, and varieties of food and drink not mentioned in the Quran and hadith that were forbidden to Muslims. A more inclusive form of legal reasoning, known as IJTIHAD, also played a significant role in the development of the Islamic legal tradition, although it met with considerable resistance from conservative jurists who were concerned that too much independent reasoning, or personal opinion, would cause Muslims to stray from the sharia.

Most areas of life were thought to be governed by *fiqh,* at least in theory. These included worship (ritual purity, PRAYER, ALMSGIVING, FASTING, and the HAJJ), social life (marriage, DIVORCE, inheritance, and business transactions), and crimes (ADULTERY, theft, use of alcohol, brigandage, and APOSTASY).

According to jurists, the legal correctness of any activity was to be judged according to a scale of values. On the positive side were acts deemed to be required or recommended by God and the Prophet; on the negative side were forbidden and reprehensible ones. Between these two groups were acts and relations that were simply permitted, without special merit or fault. Adherence to Islamic law was a matter of personal responsibility, endorsed by the quranic commandment of "commanding the right and forbidding the wrong" (Q 3:104). Ultimately, divine reward and punishment awaited Muslims in the hereafter according to their righteousness or sinfulness. In society, however, the law was enforced by the state and its designated officials, such as the judge (*qadi*) and public censor (*muhtasib*). People also obtained advisory opinions (sing. FATWA) from a *fiqh* specialist known as a MUFTI. Basic knowledge about the law and its "roots" was gained by living in a Muslim society, but those who were to become experts had to become literate in Arabic and study with legal scholars at Islamic colleges (sing. MADRASA). There, *fiqh* was the core subject of the curriculum.

In the 19th and 20th centuries, *fiqh* and the authority of jurists were seriously weakened with the introduction of Western legal systems as a result of colonization and the creation of modern nation-states. In most Muslim countries, *fiqh* was confined to matters of personal law, and efforts were made to reduce a legal tradition in which differences of opinion were accepted to one concretized in formal legal codes. Jurists have since responded by engaging in their own legal reform efforts and creating schools for preserving and propagating their religious traditions within increasingly secular societies. In some countries, moreover, Islamic jurisprudence and Muslim jurists have assumed positions of significant influence, such as Saudi Arabia and Iran. Indeed, in the 1970s, the Iranian revolutionary leader Ayatollah RUHOLLAH KHOMEINI (d. 1989) promoted a theory of Islamic government ruled by jurists called *wilayat al-faqih,* "the jurist's government," which served as the basis for the drafting of the Islamic Republic of Iran's constitution in 1979.

See also COLONIALISM; EDUCATION; *HISBA*; SECULARISM; WAHHABISM.

Further reading: Ignaz Golziher, *Introduction to Islamic Theology and Law.* Translated by A. and R. Hamori (Princeton, N.J.: Princeton University Press, 1981); Wael Hallaq, *The Origins and Evolution of Islamic Law* (Cambridge: Cambridge University Press, 2004); Fazlur Rahman, *Islam.* 2d ed. (Chicago: University of Chicago Press, 2002); Joseph Schacht, *An Introduction to Islamic Law* (Oxford: Clarendon Press, 1964).

Fire (Arabic: *al-nar*)

Fire is not just an element of nature in Islam, it is also the equivalent of hell. Belief in a place of punishment for wrongdoers in the AFTERLIFE is widespread among the world's religions. In Islam, belief in a fiery hell, together with belief in a heavenly PARADISE for the righteous, is regarded as an important component of FAITH. Muslims base their afterlife beliefs on the QURAN and the HADITH, where there are numerous statements about both the Fire and paradise. Historically, however, these beliefs were developed from afterlife ideas that had originated earlier among the ancient civilizations of the Middle East, Zoroastrianism and early Judaism and Christianity.

According to the Quran, the Fire was a horrific "home" or "dwelling" where the sinful and unbelievers were forced to wear clothing of fire, drink scalding water, and eat poisonous fruit (Q 37:62–68; 22:19–21). Another Quranic name for the Fire was Gehenna (*jahannam*), a term for hell used in Judaism and Christianity. The Quranic depiction of the Fire was greatly enhanced in later medieval accounts about the afterlife that occur in the hadith, theological works, and visionary literature. According to some imaginative traditions, the realm of the

Fire was composed of seven levels, each with its own distinctive name, such as "abyss," "blaze," and "furnace." People were assigned to the level that suited the degree of their sinfulness, together with the corresponding punishments that were administered by the angel Malik and his assistants. Some accounts described the Fire as a living creature—a monster with thousands of heads and mouths. According to Muslim theologians, wrongdoers would not necessarily be punished in the Fire for eternity. Rather, punishment was finite, and wrongdoers might eventually be admitted to paradise once their sins had been atoned.

Belief in the Fire helped focus the attention of Muslims on holding fast to their faith and performing their religious obligations. Some medieval Sufis, however, held that too much concern with the Fire and paradise could distract spiritually minded mystics from achieving union with God. Others saw fire as a metaphor for the passion of the spiritual lover that ended with his or her annihilation in the beloved, God, or they interpreted it as the intense pain experienced as a result of one's separation from God. In more recent times, modernist thinkers and reformers have attempted to explain the Fire and paradise as psychological or spiritual conditions rather than actual places where people would live in the afterlife. Nonetheless, the prevailing view among Muslims today, as with most Muslims in the past, is that punishment in the fires of hell is a reality that awaits all wrongdoers and unbelievers.

See also ANGEL; DEATH; ESCHATOLOGY; SATAN.

Further reading: Abu Hamid al-Ghazali, *The Remembrance of Death and the Afterlife (Kitab dhikr al-mawt wa-ma bdahu): Book XL of the Revival of the Religious Sciences (Ihya ulum al-din).* Translated by T. J. Winter (Cambridge: Islamic Texts Society, 1995); Jane Idleman Smith and Yvonne Yazbeck Haddad, *The Islamic Understanding of Death and Resurrection* (Albany: State University of New York Press, 1981).

fitna (Arabic: punishment by trial, temptation)

The term fitna has several meanings. In the context of early Islamic history, it refers to one of several armed conflicts, or civil wars, that occurred within the Muslim community (UMMA) during the seventh and eighth centuries. These wars led to the establishment of the UMAYYAD CALIPHATE in DAMASCUS, the rise of the KHAWARIJ sectarian movement, the schism between the Sunnis and the Shiis, and the founding of the ABBASID CALIPHATE in BAGHDAD. The first *fitna* occurred when the caliph UTHMAN IBN AFFAN was assassinated in 656 by a group of dissidents from EGYPT who were angry with the favoritism he had shown to members of his clan, the Abd Shams, a prominent branch of the QURAYSH tribe in MECCA. Uthman's successor, ALI IBN ABI TALIB, MUHAMMAD's cousin, declined to avenge his death, which earned him the enmity of Uthman's supporters, including Muhammad's wife AISHA BINT ABI BAKR and some leading COMPANIONS OF THE PROPHET. Ali defeated these opponents at the Battle of the Camel that same year, but this only led to a clash with Muawiya ibn Abi Sufyan (d. 680), a close relative of Uthman, and Muawiya's Syrian Arab supporters at the Battle of Siffin in 657. This confrontation ended with an arbitrated peace that left the question of leadership in the Muslim community unresolved until 661, when Ali was assassinated by the Khawarij, a dissident faction that had opposed Ali's peace agreement with Muawiya at Siffin. The first *fitna* ended in 661, with Muawiya becoming CALIPH, inaugurating the reign of the Syrian-based Umayyad Caliphate (661–750).

The second *fitna* occurred when HUSAYN IBN ALI, grandson of Muhammad, rebelled against the Umayyads and was killed with a group of loyal supporters at KARBALA, Iraq, in 680. The tragic story of his death as a martyr has since assumed a place of central importance in the religious life of the Shia, and it is remembered by them annually during their ASHURA rituals. Other factions in the early Muslim empire also rebelled at this time, including one led by Ibn Zubayr, who created a rival caliphate in Mecca that lasted from 681 to 692, when it was destroyed by Umayyad forces from Damascus. The third major *fitna* began in 744–745, when Shia in Iran and Iraq rebelled against the Umayyads. In 750, these opposition forces defeated the Umayyad armies and replaced their caliphate with a new one led by the Abbasids, rulers who claimed descent from Muhammad's uncle Abbas. Other, more localized *fitna*s occurred, but these three not only determined the course of early Islamic history but also shaped the development of the doctrines, practices, and institutions of Sunni and Shii Islam. Indeed, one of the chief justifications for having a strong ruler was to prevent *fitna* from bringing chaos to the community of Muslims. Also, the major HADITH collections included chapters devoted to traditions about the great *fitna* that would beset the community leading up to the end of the world and the final judgment.

Likewise, the QURAN uses *fitna* in the negative sense of a trial or punishment that God inflicts upon humans or has allowed them to undergo, usually to test their FAITH. Thus, God tested the prophets MOSES and DAVID (Q 9:126; 38:24) as well as ordinary people (Q 21:35) and permitted SATAN to tempt the evil-minded (Q 22:53). Evildoers will be punished with the *fitna* of being forced to eat the bitter fruit of the Zaqqum tree in hell (Q 37:62–66). Children and property are worldly temptations that test the faith of believers (Q 8:28).

In modern times, *fitna* has become a very politically charged term. Conservative Muslim authorities accuse WOMEN who go without veiling in public of being embodiments of *fitna* (sexual temptation), thus undermining the moral fabric of society. FATIMA MERNISSI (b. 1940) and other Muslim feminists argue that such men are invoking medieval understandings of *fitna* to justify the segregation of women and the curtailment their freedoms. In ALGERIA, SYRIA, EGYPT, IRAQ, SAUDI ARABIA, and elsewhere, political demonstrations, popular uprisings, and insurrections have often been labeled with the term *fitna* by leaders and official media sources who hope thereby to quell the dissent or violence and maintain public order.

See also ESCHATOLOGY; SHIISM; SUNNISM.

Further reading: Marshall G. S. Hodgson, *The Venture of Islam*. Vol. 1, *The Classical Age of Islam* (Chicago: University of Chicago Press, 1974); Wilferd Madelung, *The Succession to Muhammad: A Study of the Early Caliphate* (Cambridge: Cambridge University Press, 1997); Fatima Mernissi, *The Veil and the Male Elite: A Feminist Interpretation of Women's Rights in Islam* (Philadelphia: Perseus Books, 1992).

Five Pillars

The Five Pillars are five ritual acts required of all Muslims, based on injunctions in the QURAN and elaborated in the SUNNA of the Prophet MUHAMMAD and in law (FIQH) developed by the principal legal schools of Islam. The pillars nurture two primary relationships for individual Muslims: the relationship with God and with the entire community of Muslim believers, the UMMA. The first pillar, the SHAHADA, is a verbal witnessing of the unity of God and of Muhammad's position in Islam as the bearer of the final revelation, with the words "There is no god but God, and Muhammad is the messenger of God." Shia add, "and Ali is the friend of God," in reference to their first IMAM, ALI IBN ABI TALIB (d. 661). Uttering the *shahada* sincerely in the presence of two Muslim witnesses is all that is necessary to become a Muslim. The central and possibly most visible pillar is *salat*, translated as PRAYER, but here referring specifically to five daily cycles of prostrations after sunset, during the evening, at dawn, at midday, and at mid-afternoon. Prayer is performed anywhere ritual purity can be maintained. Muslim men are required to attend a congregational MOSQUE (*masjid*) for Friday prayers. Friday prayer in a mosque is not a required activity for Muslim women or for Shia. The third pillar, *zakat*,

Friday prayer at al-Husayn Mosque in Cairo, Egypt *(Juan E. Campo)*

usually translated as ALMSGIVING, asks Muslims to give as charity a percentage of their wealth attained from profit on certain kinds of income and represents part of a larger attitude of charity (*sadaqa*) encouraged by the *umma*. Muslims who are not ill, traveling, menstruating, or nursing fast from dawn to dusk during RAMADAN, the ninth month of the Islamic lunar CALENDAR, to fulfill the fourth pillar of Islam. The prohibition on eating, drinking, smoking, and sexual activity during the day acts as a social leveler that is enhanced by the communal activities and sharing of FOOD AND DRINK in the evening. Finally, the fifth pillar, the HAJJ, takes place as an annual pilgrimage to MECCA and the surrounding area, including a series of ritual acts required of every Muslim one time during his or her lifetime if physically and fiscally possible.

See also ADHAN; FASTING; HOLIDAYS; SHIISM.

Margaret Leeming

Further reading: Frederick Denny, *An Introduction to Islam* (New York: Macmillan, 1994); Sachiko Murata and William C. Chittick, *The Vision of Islam* (St. Paul, Minn.: Paragon House, 1994).

flag

All modern countries use flags as national symbols, and many of these national flags—including those of secular nations—display designs that have a recognized connection with a religious tradition. The

Flags

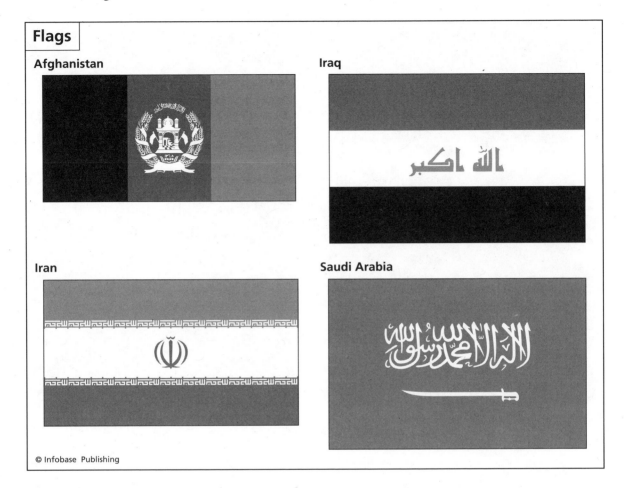

Afghanistan

Iraq

Iran

Saudi Arabia

© Infobase Publishing

flags of the United Kingdom (Britain), Switzerland, Sweden, Denmark, and Greece, for example, have crosses on them, which links them with the Christian religion. The ISRAELI flag has the Star of DAVID, who was an ancient Israelite king and has traditionally been regarded as the composer of the biblical book of Psalms. The flag of Japan has a sun disk, which is a symbol of the sun goddess Amaterasu, ancestor of the Japanese imperial household. Flags and banners have been used to rally Muslims since the days of MUHAMMAD in the seventh century. Today, among the countries with Muslim-majority populations, several have flags with features that link them to the religion of Islam. SAUDI ARABIA's flag combines the Arabic SHAHADA (the declaration "There is no god but God and Muhammad is his messenger") and a sword on a field of green. The sword stands for the Saudi royal dynasty that established the country, while green is regarded as a holy Islamic color. The flag of the Islamic Republic of IRAN consists of the name of ALLAH artfully presented as a flower or juxtaposed crescent moons in the center, framed by two horizontal bands containing repeated geometric renderings of the expression *Allah akbar,* "God is greater." The use of red in the flag represents the Shii virtue of martyrdom. In 1990, the Iraqi leader SADDAM HUSAYN added the same phrase to the flag of his country, and it remained on Iraq's flag even after the fall of his government in 2003. The new flag of AFGHANISTAN consists of the *shahada* inscribed over a mosque. The flags of 11 countries with Muslim-majority populations contain a form of the new MOON (*hilal*) and star design, including ALGERIA, Azerbaijan, PAKISTAN, and TURKEY. This symbol has traditionally been used to represent states governed by Muslims, especially since the 18th century, but it is not seen as an aspect of Islamic worship, unlike the *shahada*.

See also GOVERNMENT, ISLAMIC; POLITICS AND ISLAM.

Further reading: William G. Crampton, *Smithsonian Handbooks: Flags* (New York: DK Publishing, 2002).

folklore

Folklore in the Islamicate lands encompasses a rich and varied body of oral and written literature. In the QURAN, several terms are used to denote the narrative accounts of prophets and other didactic tales: *qassa, haka, haddatha, khabara,* and *naba-a.* These words indicate the relating of news or passing on of information, often with specific reference to the sayings and doings of exemplary figures. The word *ustura* also appears in the Quran with the pejorative connotation of the superstitious tales believed by the credulous and sinful. The same semantic range appears in the HADITH literature. It seems clear that there were active storytelling traditions extant in the Hijaz (the western region of the Arabian Peninsula) from before the time of MUHAMMAD (d. 632) that may have accompanied the rich tradition of pre-Islamic poetry. In addition to early Arabian traditions, Islamic folklore has been profoundly influenced by the storytelling traditions in other parts of the world, particularly those linked to the region via the Silk Road. Indian, Chinese, Turkish, and Persian stories have greatly enriched Arabic folklore. Since at least al-Muhassin ibn al-Tanukhi's 10th-

century collection of anecdotal tales, *al-Faraj baad al-shidda* (Joyous Relief after Hardship), there have been efforts to compile and classify the various types of Arabic narratives. Another famous work was Muhammad Awfi's *Jawami al-hikayat wa-lawami al-riwayat* (Collection of stories and illustrious tales), a 13th-century collection of some 2,000 Persian narratives.

Among the classificatory categories, *hikaya* is perhaps the most common term used to denote the range of fictional narratives, encompassing didactic tales with ethical and moral functions, etiological tales and fables, heroic ballads and legends, and fanciful stories of the supernatural. These works include the *Tutinama* and *Kalila wa Dimna,* two cycles of fable that were translated into Arabic from Sanskrit literature. The *Gulistan* of Saadi (d. ca. 1291) is perhaps the greatest example of Persian *hikaya* literature. The *sira* denotes a biographical account that may range from the life of Muhammad to the *Sirat Bani Hillal,* a long oral epic poem describing tribal wars and genealogical heroes of BEDOUINS that remains one of the most popular tales in EGYPT and the Middle East. The *qissa* came through Persian and Turkish literature to signify biographical legends such as the *Hamzanama* (The tale of Hamza), love stories such as *Layla wa Majnun* and *Shirin-Farhad,* and hagiographical tales of PROPHETS and SAINTS such as the *Qisas al-anbiya* or the *Menaqib-i Haji Bektash.* The most famous collection of Arabic folklore is, of course, *Alf Layla wa-Layla* (*The Thousand and One Nights,* or ARABIAN NIGHTS), a tremendous gathering of tales with Asian, Middle Eastern, and European origins. However, this collection was actually reimported to the Middle East from the French traveler Jean Antoine Galland's publication *Les mille et une nuits,* which he began to publish in 1704. Some of the tales are of Arab origin, but many also appear to be the inventions and collections of Galland and later editors. The cycle was reintroduced into the Arab world in the early 19th century and has gained popularity.

See also ANIMALS; ARABIC LANGUAGE AND LITERA-
TURE; MAJNUN AND LAYLA; PERSIAN LANGUAGE AND
LITERATURE.

Anna Bigelow

Further reading: Dwight Reynolds, *Heroic Poets, Poetic
Heroes: The Ethnography of Performance in an Arab
Epic Oral Tradition* (Ithaca, N.Y.: Cornell University
Press, 1995); John Seyller, *The Adventures of Hamza:
Painting and Storytelling in Mughal India* (Washington,
D.C.: Freer Gallery of Art, Arthur M. Sackler Gallery,
Smithsonian Institution, and London: Azimuth, 2002);
Ahmad ibn Muhammad al-Thalabi, *Arais al-majalis fi
qisas al-anbiya, or "Lives of the Prophets."* Translated by
William M. Brinner (Leiden: E.J. Brill, 2002).

food and drink

Food is a fundamental requirement for all living
things, yet how it is selected, grown, prepared,
served, and eaten are uniquely human activities.
Humans also have the ability to imagine and
manipulate symbolic meanings for food, incorporating them into their religious and cultural
life. The natural environment sets some limits
on the kinds and quantities of food that might be
available, grown, and harvested, but the cultural
environment is able to exploit these limitations
to the maximum, creating elaborate cuisines for
bodily pleasure, display on the table, and mental contemplation. Food and drink also occupy
important places in memory and history, allowing
people to recall significant moments in the life of
their family, community, or nation and to express
their individual and collective identities.

Muslim social and religious life reflects these
different aspects of culinary culture. The QURAN
provides a general framework with respect to the
religious and symbolic dimensions, as reflected
in its depictions of PARADISE, descriptions of God's
creative power, and legislation of DIETARY LAWS.
ADAM AND EVE, the first humans, lived in a garden, enjoying all its fruits except those of the tree
of immortality, which was forbidden to them (Q
7:189; 2:35). When they disobeyed God and ate
from it, they were denied their place in the garden.
As creator of the universe, the Quran declares that
God is the one who sends rainwater to nourish the
earth's vegetation, including foods for people to
eat such as grain, date palms, grapes, olives, and
pomegranates (Q 6:99). More than being purely
natural phenomena, the growth of food plants and
animals is presented as a system of signs designed
to remind the faithful to submit and worship the
one God, ALLAH. According to the Quran, he created all manner of food for humans to consume
(Q 6:14; 26:78), commanding the faithful, "Eat
of the good things that we have granted you"
(Q 2:172). Moreover, in the AFTERLIFE, righteous
believers are promised lush gardens through
which rivers of water, milk, honey, and wine flow
where they will consume food and drink served
by youthful servants and beautiful servant girls,
the houris (sing. HOURI).

The command to "eat of the good things"
is linked to admonitions not to follow in the
way of SATAN, but to be thankful to God and
eat only what is permitted. Eating, therefore, is
symbolically associated with moral action, since
the Quran relates eating permitted foods with
thanking God, who provided them. The dietary
laws of what is permitted (HALAL) and forbidden
(HARAM) are given in some detail in the Quran and
elaborated further in the HADITH and juristic literature. While most foods are allowed, Muslims are
obliged to abstain from consuming swine flesh,
blood, carrion, and wine. Meat must be properly
slaughtered in the name of God. Muslims are
permitted to eat lawful and pure food prepared
by other People of the Book, particularly Jews
and Christians. Adherence to the dietary laws
expresses the relation of Muslims with God and
establishes their identity as a distinct religious
community among other peoples.

For centuries, Muslims have drawn inspiration from MUHAMMAD, the founding prophet of
Islam, for many aspects of their life, including

Flatbreads hot from the baker's oven in Alexandria, Egypt *(Magda Campo)*

their culinary practices. According to the HADITH, he exemplified the ideal of moderation, expressed in a quranic admonition for all people, "Eat and drink, but do not be wasteful, for [God] does not like those who are wasteful" (Q 7:31). In a similar vein, MUHAMMAD is remembered to have said, "A believer eats with one intestine, while a disbeliever eats with seven intestines," meaning that Muslims should consume only what is sufficient for their needs and not overeat. He is said to have recommended that everyone sitting at a meal eat small amounts so that there is food for all, including unexpected guests. Moreover, he also advocated giving food to the hungry, even if it meant that one's own family had to forgo a meal. Such practices reflected and upheld Arab hospitality customs.

There is a body of lore in Islam about the relation between good health and good food. Greek medical science (with Indian and Persian elements) was transmitted to Muslims during the eighth and ninth centuries, but they also developed their own distinctive body of medical knowledge known as "the medicine of the Prophet" (*al-tib al-nabawi*) in the ninth century. According to a book on the subject by Ibn Qayyim al-Jawziyya (1292–1350), Muhammad provided guidance on how to maintain bodily health, which was seen as a gift from God. Among the basic dietary facts Ibn Qayyim wanted his readers to know was that eating too little, overeating, eating only one type of food, and nutritional imbalances were major causes of illness. Muhammad's eating and drinking habits as described in the hadith showed the way to a healthy life, as stories about his other teachings and deeds showed the way to salvation after death.

Following the example of the Prophet, Muslims were taught that it was preferable to sit down and invoke the name of God before eating, eat and drink with the right hand only (the left was associated with Satan), and take food only from the serving dishes nearest to where one was seated. Also, food should be passed to the right, not to the left. It was also reported that when Muhammad liked a food, he ate it, but if he disliked it, he kept silent and left it on his plate. Reflecting his Arabian cultural heritage, Muhammad's favorite beverage, aside from water, was fresh milk. In addition to its nutritional value, milk was thought to reduce depression and help people who suffered from lung diseases. Muhammad's other preferred foods included a meat and bread stew called *tharid,* which Muslims in many parts of the world still prepare in a variety of ways. Meat was thought by some commentators to be the preferred food of paradise. Muhammad used vinegar as a condiment with bread, but he also liked to eat fruits, honey, and sweets. Vinegar was thought to help with digestion, while figs were good for the liver and spleen and an antidote for poison.

In accordance with Muslim scriptures and customs, culinary practices play an important role in ritual life and in FEASTING traditions. This is most evident in the month-long RAMADAN fast, when Muslims are required to abstain from all food and drink during the daylight hours. The fast is broken at the end of each day, when traditional Ramadan dishes are usually prepared. Dates and water are favorites for breaking the fast. People of the Arabian Peninsula have a favorite Ramadan dish called *ramadaniyya,* a mixture of dried fruits and nuts that has been soaked overnight in water. There is also a major feast that marks the end of Ramadan called ID AL-FITR (Feast of Fast-Breaking), when sweets are customarily consumed. The other major feast on the Muslim calendar is ID AL-ADHA (Feast of the Sacrifice), which is held at the conclusion of the annual HAJJ to Mecca. This holiday features the sacrifice of pastoral animals (lambs, goats, cattle, and CAMELS) and consumption of meat dishes in memory of the piety of ABRAHAM, who nearly sacrificed his own son at God's command but was allowed to substitute a ram instead. Even fulfilling the obligation of ALMSGIVING (*zakat* and *sadaqa*), another of Islam's FIVE PILLARS, involves food, since calculation of the amount required to be given in charity was originally based on crop production and livestock holdings. Many Muslims still fulfill their charitable obligations by providing food for the hungry and needy.

Aside from the two Ids, one of the most widely observed Islamic holidays is the birthday (MAWLID) of Muhammad, which occurs during the third month of the Islamic lunar calendar. Muslims in many parts of the world, especially children, celebrate it with the consumption of sweets. Followers of Shiism and Sufism observe holiday feasts and fasts connected with SAINTS particular to their traditions—the Shii IMAMS and Sufi *awliya,* or "friends of God." Life cycle observances such as circumcision, marriage, and DEATH also involve distinctive culinary practices in accordance with local food traditions.

There is no distinctively Islamic cuisine that is embraced by all Muslims, however. Dietary laws set some limitations, but they still allow a great deal of latitude with regard to the kinds of food and drink allowed and the ways they can be prepared, combined, and served. Distinctive culinary cultures, therefore, have developed in different parts of the Muslim world. Among the most notable are those of the Persians, Arabs, and Turks. Other major cuisines are those of South Asia and Southeast Asia. Among the Middle Eastern peoples, lamb is the favorite meat, and wheat bread and rice compete with each other as the basic staples. Rice becomes increasingly important as one travels eastward from the Persian Gulf region to Southeast Asia. All cuisines in Muslim countries benefit from the widespread use of savory spice mixtures, herbs, and peppers. Favorite beverages are tea, fruit drinks (*sharbat*), and COFFEE for special occasions. Cooling yogurt-based drinks are popular in TURKEY, IRAN, and INDIA.

Persian culinary culture has ancient pre-Islamic roots and is distinguished by its variety of rice dishes (especially pilafs), its mild sweet and sour flavor combinations, its preference for fresh herbs, and its soups. Persia greatly influenced the culinary cultures of the Arabs, the Turks, and the peoples of northern India.

Arab cuisine, which has pre-Islamic BED-OUIN origins, is noted for its spicy lamb dishes, vegetable and meat kabobs, meat stews, stuffed vegetables, and tasty condiments and salads such as hummus (a mashed chickpea and sesame paste dip) and tabbouleh (a parsley, cracked wheat, and tomato salad flavored with onion, lemon, mint, and olive oil). The high culture of medieval BAGHDAD played a major role in the interweaving of Arab food traditions with those of Persia and the East. A popular fried and stuffed appetizer known as *sanbusak* was introduced to the Arab Middle East there. Among North African peoples, the most typical staple food is couscous, which consists of little grains of semolina wheat dough that are steamed and served like rice with meats, vegetables, and savory sauces.

Turkic peoples, like the Arabs, started out as nomads. Their food traditions developed gradually as a result of interactions with Persians, Arabs, Greeks, and peoples of eastern Europe. The palace kitchens of the Ottoman sultans in Istanbul contributed significantly to the creation of a cosmopolitan cuisine in east Mediterranean lands and eastern Europe after the 15th century that continues today. Typical elements in Turkish cuisine include kabobs, meat casseroles and pastries made with fine layers of filo dough, and widespread use of yogurt and cheeses. They rival the Persians in the variety of elegant rice dishes they prepare, especially pilafs and dolmas (vegetables stuffed with rice and meat). The most common staple for Turks, however, is bread, which they also call "the food of friendship."

The culinary traditions of South Asia are both ancient and diversified, with deep pre-Islamic roots that extend geographically throughout India to Persia and AFGHANISTAN, the Indian Ocean basin, and Southeast Asia. South Asia is home to great Hindu and Buddhist civilizations, and Islamicate civilization flourished there with them after the 12th century. The historical interrelations between these civilizations are reflected in the region's culinary cultures. Typical elements found on north Indian and Pakistani Muslim tables include wheat bread (naan or chapatti) as a basic staple, a variety of tasty lentil and bean dishes called dal, batter-fried vegetable and meat appetizers (pakoras), curries, and spicy dishes of layered or mixed meat, rice and vegetables called biryanis. Masala, a combination of dry spices, is used to flavor meats and vegetables, while spicy mint and sweet mango chutneys are used as condiments. In southern India (Kerala and Tamil Nadu), molded rice dumplings served with a fiery chili soup called *sambar* is very popular, as are *dosas*, a pancake made of a mixture of lentil and rice flour. Shrimp and fish dishes are also favorites. Coconut milk is used in cooking, and coconut chutney is the preferred condiment in the region. For the people of West Bengal and BANGLADESH, the favorite foods are local rice and fish dishes, but they are also fond of north Indian cuisine. Indeed, historical scholarship has shown that the Islamization of this region was partly a result of the conversion of its forest lands east of the Ganges to wet rice agriculture in the 17th and 18th centuries by Muslims and Hindus who immigrated from north India.

There are many different regional culinary cultures in Southeast Asia, too, where the largest Muslim population in the world is located today. The influence of Indian and Chinese culinary cultures can be found there, but there are also indigenous ones that have distinctive dishes, especially those featuring taro and cassava root products, sago palm flour, and seafood. Rice has lately become an important food staple, however, for many people in the region. In both INDONESIA and MALAYSIA, people also like to eat a type of kabob called *satay,* which has thin strips of meat, fish, or chicken that are skewered, grilled, and served with dipping sauces. Hot chilis, originally from the New World, and sweet coconut milk are used along with other spices and peanut sauces to add flavor to rice and fish dishes.

Muslim culinary cultures have continued to change and evolve in the modern period. Colonization of Muslim lands by Europeans led to the introduction of new foods, restaurants, and industrialized food production. With the creation of nation-states in the 20th century, national cuisines began to appear, as reflected in cookbooks featuring "Lebanese," "Palestinian," "Turkish," "Moroccan," "Saudi," and even "Kuwaiti" recipes. During the last decades of the 20th century, American soft drinks flooded local markets, followed by fast food chains featuring hamburgers, French fries, fried chicken, and pizza. These were locally owned franchises, however, which had to adhere to Islamic dietary laws. They also allowed limited use of local flavorings and adaptations of indigenous recipes.

During the 1990s and 2000s, opposition to U.S. Middle East policies sparked boycotts of U.S.-based food chains and a return to more traditional indigenous foods in many countries. It also led to the creation of alternative "Islamic" commodities, such as Mecca Cola and ZAMZAM Cola. On the other hand, the influx of Muslim immigrants into Europe and North America led to the establishment of *halal* food businesses that served the immigrant communities in those parts of the world. It also helped introduce new foods there, as can be seen in the popularity of Turkish *doner* kebab sandwiches in Germany, North African foods in France, South Asian foods in Great Britain, and Arab (especially Lebanese and Palestinian) and Persian foods in the United States.

See also AGRICULTURE; ANIMALS; *BASMALA;* COLONIALISM; CREATION; FASTING; OTTOMAN DYNASTY.

Further reading: Peter Heine, *Food Culture in the Near East, Middle East, and North Africa* (Westport, Conn.: Greenwood Press, 2004); Ibn Qayyim al-Jawziyya, *Healing with the Medicine of the Prophet.* Translated by Jalal Abual Rub (Riyadh: Darussalam, 2003); Claudia Roden, *The New Book of Middle Eastern Food* (New York: Random House, 2001); Maxime Rodinson, A. J. Arberry, and Charles Perry, *Medieval Arab Cookery* (Devon, U.K.: Prospect Books, 2001); David Waines, *In a Caliph's Kitchen* (London: Riad El-Rayyes, 1989); Sami Zubaida and Richard Tapper, eds., *A Taste of Time: Culinary Cultures of the Middle East* (London: Tauris Parke Paperbacks, 2001).

free will and determinism   *See* ASHARI SCHOOL; FATE; MUTAZILI SCHOOL; THEOLOGY.

fundamentalism   *See* ISLAMISM; POLITICS AND ISLAM; WAHHABISM.

funerary rituals

Funerary rituals are concerned with the disposal of the dead and provide the living with ways to channel deeply felt emotions caused by the loss of a loved one. They are occasions when a society's beliefs about life and DEATH and the sacred and profane are most visible and when the bonds that hold people together as families and communities are affirmed and tested. In Islamic communities, as in Jewish and Christian ones, funerary rituals involve different kinds of activities: preparations for death and burial, interment of the body, mourning, and memorialization. These rites combine practices prescribed by religious tradition, local cultural customs, and improvised actions called forth by the specific circumstances present when a death or a funeral occurs.

FIQH literature, composed by experts in Islamic law, sets forth the formal ritual requirements and taboos that Muslims are expected to observe.

According to these texts, which are based on interpretations of the QURAN, HADITH, and the consensus of the ULAMA, funerary rites should include: 1) pronouncing the testimony of faith (SHAHADA) prior to death and turning the dying person's face toward Mecca; 2) ritually washing and shrouding the corpse; 3) performing funeral prayers; 4) conducting the body to the CEMETERY; 5) burial of the corpse on its right side, with the face turned to MECCA; 6) mourning; and 7) visiting the grave. The corpse may be dressed in ordinary but not expensive clothing. Burial should be performed at a nearby cemetery within 24 hours of death. Men usually preside in the funeral prayers and ceremonies, but in many cultures WOMEN also participate. The body is placed in the grave without a coffin, and extra room is left in the grave out of a belief that the deceased will be compelled to sit up and undergo an interrogation by two angels of death known as Munkar and Nakir. To prepare the dead for this interrogation, basic articles of faith are recited at the time of burial. This is called the *talqin*. People usually take turns throwing dirt into the grave, and they pronounce prayers on behalf of the deceased, especially the verse "From it [the earth] we created you, then we put you back into it, and from it we will bring you forth again" (Q 20:55). Other funerary prayers include the FATIHA (Q 1) and the chapter "Ya Sin" (Q 36) of the Quran as well as supplications drawn from the hadith and other religious texts. Once the grave is filled, it is leveled. The ulama have strongly disapproved of decorating the grave site or erecting a building over it. Nonetheless, many Muslim cemeteries have gravestones, mausoleums, MOSQUES, and SAINT shrines. Indeed, some of the most impressive examples of Islamicate art and architecture are connected with housing and memorializing the dead.

Muslim jurists have also attempted to curb many lamentation and mourning practices because of their belief that too much grief for the dead is an affront to God, the giver of life and death. They are also wary of the assimilation of what they regard as un-Islamic innovations (BIDAA); excessive grieving, public displays of emotion, singing, and dancing are considered to be reprehensible or forbidden. Despite such regulations, in actual practice people may mourn for up to 40 days, or even a year, after death, especially for husbands, wives, or parents. Somber Quran recitations are conducted during the mourning period, during which families customarily keep a solemn public demeanor, wear black clothing, and avoid festive occasions such as weddings and parties. Relatives, friends, neighbors, and acquaintances are expected to visit, bring gifts of food, and offer their condolences as soon as they can after a death has occurred. Often, meals are shared in memory of the dead; in rural societies, such feasts may bring a whole village together. In many Muslim cultures, an animal is sacrificed, with the meat shared among the mourners and the poor. Each year, especially on major HOLIDAYS, family members visit the graves of loved ones, and in some cultures they distribute food to children, strangers, and the needy in remembrance of the dead.

Of course, prescribed and culturally determined funerary practices may be waived or circumvented in exceptional situations. Soldiers who die in battle can be interred in their blood-soaked garments without ritual cleansing or funerary prayers. People who die on an ocean voyage may be buried at sea. Victims of wars or natural catastrophes—earthquakes and tidal waves, for example—may be buried in mass graves. In modern times, Muslims who have migrated to Western countries may be buried in coffins in accordance with local burial and sanitation ordinances. Some immigrant mosques have their own mortuary facilities and purchase plots of land in existing cemeteries for the burial of Muslims. Some Muslims, however, prefer to have their dead transported back to their native lands for burial.

See also ABLUTION; AFTERLIFE; FOOD AND DRINK; MARTYRDOM; SOUL AND SPIRIT; SUICIDE.

Further reading: Ahmed Abd al-Hayy Arifi, *Death and Inheritance: The Islamic Way; A Handbook of Rules Pertaining to the Deceased.* Translated by Muhammad Shameem (New Delhi: Kitab Bhavan, 1995); Laleh Bakhtiar, *Encyclopedia of Islamic Law: A Compendium of the Major Schools* (Chicago: ABC International Group, 1996), 40–53; Juan Eduardo Campo, "Muslim Ways of Death: Between the Prescribed and the Performed." In *Death and Religion in a Changing World,* edited by Kathleen Garces-Foley, 147–177 (New York: M.E. Sharpe, 2005); Timothy Insoll, *The Archaeology of Islam* (Oxford: Blackwell Publishers, 1999), 166–200.

Funj Sultanate

The Funj Sultanate was an Islamic dynasty that ruled the Upper Nile region of the SUDAN for 300 years, from 1504 to 1821. Originally a pastoral people, the Funj established a state based in Sinnar under the leadership of Amara Dunqas after the latter defeated the Christian kingdom of Alwa in 1504. Although Muslim monarchs ruled the sultanate, the Funj developed a hierarchical society headed by a semidivine king and a caste-like ruling elite. The kings prided themselves on their Islamic credentials, encouraged the presence of Muslim scholars and holy men within their kingdom, and provided support for pilgrims to go to MECCA. However, in order to heighten a sense of their separation from the common man, these monarchs withdrew from public view, leaving the high court officials to take functional leadership of the kingdom.

The Funj were active in the caravan trade, establishing business relationships with EGYPT and the wider Ottoman Empire. Maliki law and Sufi orders both expanded considerably under Funj rule. However, the Funj system broke down during the late 18th century, when the SULTANS lost political control to regional warlords, economic control to a new merchant class, and spiritual authority to the local holy men. Muhammad Ali of Egypt finally brought the kingdom to an end, conquering the region in 1820–21.

See also EAST AFRICA; MALIKI LEGAL SCHOOL.

Stephen Cory

Further reading: P. M. Holt, *The Sudan of the Three Niles: The Funj Chronicle, 970–1288/1504–1871* (Leiden: E.J. Brill, 1999); R. S. O'Fahey and J. L. Spaulding, *Kingdoms of the Sudan* (London: Methuen, 1974); Jay Spaulding, *The Heroic Age in Sinnar* (East Lansing: African Studies Center, Michigan State University, 1985).

Fyzee, Asaf Ali Asghar (1899–1981) *Indian Muslim intellectual and a leading scholar of Ismaili Shiism and Islamic law*

A. A. A. Fyzee was born near Poona, INDIA, to a prominent family of Ismaili Shii merchants. His family favored the British educational system, so after he obtained his college education, they sent him to study at Cambridge University, where he studied with several of the best Orientalist scholars of the early 20th century, including A. A. Bevan and R. A. Nicholson. After 1926, he was employed at the High Court of Bombay. Fyzee continued with his scholarly interests, however, publishing studies and translations pertaining to Islamic and Anglo-Islamic jurisprudence (FIQH). As a reflection of the quality of his scholarly ability, he was appointed a professor of Islamic jurisprudence at Government College in Bombay. In 1949, he was appointed India's ambassador to EGYPT and then served in several other ambassadorial and government posts. He received many academic honors in his later career and taught Islamic studies at McGill University in Canada and at the University of California at Los Angeles. One of Fyzee's most esteemed contributions to scholarship is his *Outlines of Muhammadan Law* (1949). At the end of his career, he devoted himself to a critical edition of a medieval Ismaili *fiqh*, Qadi Numan's *Pillars of Islam* (originally written in the 10th century).

Fyzee's views of Islamic religion and law (SHARIA and *fiqh*) were very modern and progressive, like those of MUHAMMAD IQBAL (1877–1938) and ABU AL-KALAM AZAD (1888–1958), other major Indian Muslim intellectuals whom he admired. He acknowledged the eternal truth contained in the QURAN but also maintained that the interpretation of the Quran and God's law had to adapt to changing historical circumstances. Reflecting his secular Western education and the influence of ORIENTALISM, Fyzee argued for the construction of a modern Islam. Thus, he proposed that what he called the "reinterpretation" of Islam required not only knowledge of traditional Islamic sacred texts and the conditions in which they were produced but also the study of the history of religions, the comparative study of "Semitic" religions (Judaism, Christianity, and Islam) and languages (Hebrew, Aramaic, and Arabic), and knowledge about modern SCIENCE. Islamic THEOLOGY (kalam) should be reformed in light of contemporary European thought and even recognize the insights of Protestant theologians and Jewish thinkers. Moreover, Fyzee argued that reinterpretation of Islamic law involved making critical distinctions between essential moral principles and detailed laws that were suited only to limited historical circumstances. Among the areas where he felt that immediate reform was needed was that of women's rights, where he pointed out the contradictions between the rights given to them by the Quran in matters of marriage and inheritance, and the de facto denial of these rights to WOMEN in many Muslim-majority countries in the 20th century.

See also ISMAILI SHIISM; SECULARISM.

Further reading: Kenneth Cragg, *Troubled by Truth: Life Studies in Interfaith Concern* (Edinburgh: Pentland Press, 1992), 187–202; A. A. A. Fyzee, *Outlines of Muhammadan Law* (Delhi: Oxford University Press, 1999); Ismail Poonawala, "In Memorium: A. A. A. Fyzee, 1899–1981," *International Journal of Middle East Studies* 14, no. 3 (1982).

G

Gabriel (Hebrew: man of God; Arabic: Jibril)

Gabriel is the ANGEL of revelation in Islamic belief and is counted among the archangels. His name first appears in the pre-Islamic period in two late books of the Bible—the book of Daniel (8:15–26, 9:21–27) in the Old Testament and the Gospel of Luke (1:11–20, 26–38) in the New Testament. Gabriel is also mentioned in the extra-biblical book of 1 Enoch (9:1–10, 40:6) and in rabbinic Bible commentaries. In these texts, he is portrayed as a divine messenger and as an intercessor on behalf of God's people. In the QURAN, Gabriel's name occurs three times as one of God's angels; he is the bringer of revelation (Q 297–98) and MUHAMMAD's supporter (Q 66:4). Though not specifically mentioned in other parts of the Quran, medieval commentators identified Gabriel with the angelic spirit (*ruh*) that appeared to MARY as a perfectly formed man to announce to her that she would give birth to JESUS (Q 19:17–21). He was also thought to be the spirit that descended on the NIGHT OF DESTINY (*laylat al-qadr*), when the Quran was first revealed (Q 97), and in Q 27:192–194 he was said to be the "trustworthy spirit" who brought God's revelation to Muhammad's heart.

Gabriel plays a bigger role in later accounts of Muhammad's life. He is one of the angels involved in cutting open Muhammad's breast and cleansing his heart so as to prepare him for his prophetic mission. In Ibn Ishaq's BIOGRAPHY of Muhammad (eighth century), Gabriel confronts the prophet on Mount Hira and commands him to recite the Quran's first verses. According to IBN ISHAQ (d. 767) and Quran commentators, he guided Muhammad on his miraculous journey from MECCA to JERUSALEM, then through the seven heavens, where he had visions of heaven and hell, former prophets, and God. According to the HADITH, Gabriel once appeared to Muhammad and his companions in the form of a man with black hair, dressed in white garments, and interrogated him about Islam, FAITH (*iman*), and right action (*ihsan*). He also was linked to the events surrounding Muhammad's HIJRA to MEDINA in 622, having warned him that his life was in danger.

In collections of legends about the prophets who preceded Muhammad, such as al-Thalabi's *Lives of the Prophets* (11th century), Gabriel's role in human history was greatly expanded. For example, Gabriel taught Adam the skills he needed in order to survive after being expelled from PARADISE. He also came to the aid of ABRAHAM, JOSEPH, and MOSES. The Shia link Gabriel to key events in their versions of the lives of Muhammad, ALI IBN ABI TALIB, FATIMA, and other Shii Imams. Thus, Gabriel was present when Fatima and Ali were married. He also conveyed to Muhammad a testament that was to be transmitted to the Imams, and he announced to Muhammad that his grandson Husayn (d. 680), the foremost of the martyrs, would be killed by fellow Muslims.

Accounts differ as to Gabriel's appearance. As an angel, he was a being of pure light. According to some traditions, he had a human form (as in Q 19:17–21) and could even ride a horse into battle as a turbaned warrior. RUZBIHAN BAQLI (d. 1209), the Persian mystic, saw Gabriel as "a bridegroom, like a moon among the stars," wearing a red garment with green silk trim (Baqli 47). Persian and Turkish illustrated manuscripts of the 15th to 18th centuries usually portray Gabriel in a human form with wings, elegant garments, and a crown, surrounded by flames. In some of the early hadith and other texts, he was given a more awesome appearance—a being with six wings, each of which had 600 wings that could stretch across the horizons of the earth.

See also ADAM AND EVE; HOLY BOOKS; HUSAYN IBN ALI; IMAM; NIGHT JOURNEY AND ASCENT; SHIISM.

Further reading: Ruzbihan Baqli, *The Unveiling of Secrets: Diary of a Sufi Master.* Translated by Carl W. Ernst (Chapel Hill, N.C.: Parvardigar Press, 1997); F. E. Peters, *A Reader on Classical Islam* (Princeton, N.J.: Princeton University Press, 1994), 51–53, 65–66; Abu Ishaq Ahmad ibn Muhammad ibn Ibrahim al-Thalabi, *Arais al-Majalis fi Qisas al-Anbiya, or "Lives of the Prophets."* Translated by William M. Brinner (Leiden: E.J. Brill, 2002).

Gandhi, Mohandas Karamchand (1869–1948) *political and spiritual leader of Indian nationalist movement for independence from British colonial rule*

Known as Mahatma (Sanskrit, "great soul"), Gandhi was instrumental in the successful struggle for Indian independence from British imperial rule through his methods of nonviolent resistance. Gandhi was born in the Indian state of Gujarat in 1869 into the *vaishya* caste (merchants, traders, and farmers) and was influenced by a variety of Indian religions, including Jainism. From 1888 to 1891, he studied law in London, where he was exposed to the Theosophical movement and influenced by the writings of Leo Tolstoy (d. 1910). In 1893, he began practicing law in South Africa, where he was deeply influenced by the political oppression of Indians by the British and, as a result, began developing his unique strategies of pacifist tactics based on the Indian religious principles of satyagraha (Skt., truth-force) and ahimsa (Skt., nonharm, nonviolence). Gandhi returned to INDIA in 1914 and garnered mass support for the independence movement's political party, the Indian National Congress. Through his Satyagraha campaigns of 1920–22 and 1927–34 and in other strategies of nonviolent noncooperation such as the Salt March in 1930, in which he mobilized a diversity of Indians and brought their struggle for independence to the world's attention, Gandhi's methods of passive resistance exposed the moral untenability of British colonial rule in India. Gandhi remained formally affiliated with the Congress Party only through the mid-1930s but continued to serve as the independence movement's symbolic leader up through India's independence in August 1947.

Gandhi saw each of India's religious traditions as encompassing similar truths and believed that each religious community of India deserved political representation in a future independent India. Nonetheless, he articulated his political vision for an independent India in Hindu symbolism, which cultivated distrust among India's largest religious minority, its Muslims, who were represented politically by the Muslim League led by MUHAMMAD ALI JINNAH (1876–1948). Unlike Jinnah, who represented the position that Muslims were a unique cultural, religious, and social entity deserving of political autonomy in a future state called PAKISTAN, Gandhi believed in an independent India that would be religiously diverse but unified in essence under a pluralistic style of Hinduism. Gandhi was deeply opposed to the idea of the partition of India into Muslim and Hindu states and was devastated by the violent partition of British India into Pakistan and India that took place upon India's independence. Gandhi was assassinated on January, 30, 1948, by a Hindu extremist. His tragic death brought to the nation's attention the anger of Hindu extremists at Gandhi's concern for Indian Muslims. Since his death, Gandhi has become a worldwide icon for the power of passive resistance to political oppression, influencing such major leaders as Martin Luther King, Jr.

See also ALL-INDIA MUSLIM LEAGUE; COLONIALISM; HINDUISM AND ISLAM; KHILAFAT MOVEMENT.

Megan Adamson Sijapati

Further reading: Judith Brown, *Gandhi and Civil Disobedience, 1928–1934* (Cambridge: Cambridge University Press, 1977); Mohandas K. Gandhi, *An Autobiography: The Story of My Experiments with Truth* (Boston: Beacon Press, 1957); Barbara D. Metcalf and Thomas R. Metcalf, *A Concise History of India* (Cambridge: Cambridge University Press, 2002); Rudrangshu Mukherjee, ed., *The Penguin Gandhi Reader* (New York: Penguin Books, 1993).

garden (Arabic: *bustan* or *janna;* Persian: *bagh*)

Gardens have played a central role in Islamdom as locations of revenue production, display, scientific exploration, entertainment, and relaxation. Medieval poetry from throughout Islamdom, inscriptions on garden pavilions and palaces, medieval botanical manuals, and travel literature all attest to the central role of the garden in public and private ARCHITECTURE.

CALLIGRAPHY adorning religious architecture within or adjacent to gardens indicates that patrons consider these spaces as earthly representations of the heavenly PARADISE. Both the QURAN and HADITH literature contain numerous descriptions of paradise as a tree-filled, pleasantly perfumed, and peaceful place in which the righteous and pure followers of Islam will dwell after JUDGMENT DAY. One of the most often-repeated Quranic phrases about paradise mentions gardens of eternity beneath which four rivers flow (Q 4:57; 5:85; 9:72; 18:31). The inhabitants of paradise (also referred to as Eden and al-Firdaus) will live in complete comfort with their loved ones in palaces built of silver and gold. These descriptions of paradise in the Quran and hadith are often paired with descriptions of hell (the FIRE).

Paradisal garden in Chefchaouen, Morocco *(Federico R. Campo)*

While the iconography of 17th-century gardens such as the Taj Mahal complex in India certainly suggests paradise, it is difficult to make the same argument for all gardens in Islamicate realms. Archaeological studies of garden remains and medieval Arabic and Persian literature suggest that gardens served many roles, especially within the imperial palatial complexes of the Islamic empires. Ninth-century palace gardens of Samarra and BAGHDAD, for example, were showplaces of hydraulic engineering. Hidden waterworks caused mechanical birds to whistle and sing from tree branches in one such garden, dazzling foreign ambassadors. The 10th- and 11th-century gardens of Andalusian Spain contained experiments in irrigation and botanical science. The 15th-century Topkapi Palace gardens in ISTANBUL provided revenue for the SULTAN, and large parks housed exotic animals from throughout the realm for hunting and display.

The most ubiquitous and well-known garden form is the *chahar-bagh* (four-part garden), a garden crossed by water channels separating tree or flower beds within which is placed a centrally positioned pavilion. This form was probably influenced by pre-Islamic Roman and Sasanian gardens. Gardens also exist in a linear format and as larger unstructured parklands.

While descriptive studies abound on gardens in Islamic history, more analytical work on contextual meanings associated with these gardens needs to be carried out. Similarly, contemporary garden design deserves further attention. Private gardens abound in inward-facing urban residential areas, and green spaces have become essential elements of land use and landscape design in expanding urban centers such as CAIRO, Istanbul, and Riyadh.

See also AFTERLIFE; AGRICULTURE; ANDALUSIA; CITIES.

Margaret Leeming

Further reading: Jacob Lassner, *The Topography of Baghdad in the Early Middle Ages* (Detroit: Wayne State University Press, 1970); Gulru Necipoglu, *Architecture, Ceremonial, and Power: The Topkapi Palace in the Fifteenth and Sixteenth Centuries* (New York: Architectural History Foundation, 1991); D. Fairchild Ruggles, *Gardens, Landscape, and Vision in the Palaces of Islamic Spain* (University Park; Pennsylvania State University Press, 2000).

Gaza   *See* PALESTINE.

genie   *See* JINNI.

Ghadir Khumm

Ghadir Khumm is one of the most important religious holidays for the Shia. It is named after a spring located between MECCA and MEDINA in the Hijaz (western Arabia) where MUHAMMAD stopped with his companions after performing his farewell pilgrimage to Mecca in 632. At that location, Muhammad stood next to his cousin and son-in-law ALI IBN ABI TALIB (d. 661) and told his listeners to consider Ali their master (*mawla*). This event is recounted in Sunni and Shii sources, but there are different versions of it; each community interprets it differently. According to accounts favored by the Shia, Muhammad delivered a sermon in which he stated that he would soon depart this world and that he was leaving his followers two things: the QURAN and the AHL AL-BAYT, his family. Taking Ali by the hand, he asked his audience if he, Muhammad, did not have priority over other believers. When they agreed that he did, Muhammad then declared, "Ali is the master [*mawla*] of whomever I am the master." The Shia therefore understand this declaration as the divinely inspired transfer of AUTHORITY to Ali and the other holy IMAMs, whom they consider to be the true leaders of the Muslim community. It also serves as a precedent for their belief in *nass*, the God-given power that an imam has to designate his successor. The Sunnis, however, do not accept this interpretation of what happened at Ghadir

Khumm, nor do they recognize it as a holiday of any significance. Rather, they view the event as a call for Muslims to respect Ali because of his close relationship with Muhammad but not as a designation of leadership commanded by God.

Shii observance of the holiday of Ghadir Khumm began during the 10th century in EGYPT and IRAQ, both of which were ruled by the Shii dynasties at that time. It is celebrated by Shia around the world on the 18th day of the 12th month (Dhu al-Hijja) on the Islamic lunar calendar, a few days after the end of the annual HAJJ. In IRAN, it is a public holiday, and Iraqi Shiis perform pilgrimages to KARBALA on that day.

See also FATIMID DYNASTY; HOLIDAYS; SHIISM; SUNNISM.

Further reading: Paula Sanders, *Ritual, Politics, and the City in Fatimid Cairo* (Albany: State University of New York Press, 1994), 121–134; John Alden Williams, *The World of Islam* (Austin: University of Texas Press, 1994), 170–172.

Ghalib, Mirza Asad Ali Khan (1797–1869)
leading Indo-Pakistani author famed for his Persian and Urdu poetry and prose

Ghalib was born into a prominent Muslim family closely connected to the court of the MUGHAL DYNASTY in INDIA. He spent his early childhood in Agra, the former capital, but at the age of 15 he moved to DELHI, the location of the imperial court, where he lived for most of his life. His poetic gifts were recognized by the ruler of Awadh in north India and by Bahadur Shah II (d. 1857), the last Mughal emperor. Ghalib lost his royal patrons (and nearly his life) with the great Indian "mutiny" against the British in 1857, but he soon overcame his financial troubles with the help of a pension from the new British government in India. He wrote in both Persian, the literary language of the elite, and Urdu, the "camp" language of the Muslim court. His poetry expressed emotions of sorrow and suffering and

echoed mystical themes, but it was not overtly religious. Indeed, he was a humanist in outlook who regarded Muslims, Hindus, and Christians as brothers. He employed classical Arabic and Persian poetic forms: the GHAZAL (love lyric), *qasida* (ode), and *mathnavi* (rhymed couplet). Today, he is remembered best for his Urdu poetry, collected in his *Diwan*. He wrote more poetry in Persian, however, and this has been collected in his *Kulliyyat*. Among Ghalib's prose writings are a history of the Mughals and essays on the Persian language. In 1969, the Ghalib Academy was opened to commemorate the centenary of Ghalib's death. It is located in New Delhi near the tomb of the Chishti Sufi saint NIZAM AL-DIN AWLIYA (d. 1325) and houses a museum and library.

See also PERSIAN LANGUAGE AND LITERATURE.

Further reading: Ralph Russell, *Ghalib: The Poet and His Age* (London: Allen & Unwin, 1972); ———, *The Oxford India Ghalib: Life, Letters, and Ghazals* (New Delhi: Oxford University Press, 2003).

Ghannoushi, Rashid al- (1941–) *leading Tunisian activist and founder of the Islamic Tendency Movement, now known as the Renaissance Party (Hizb al-Nahda)*

Rashid al-Ghannoushi advocates a modernist interpretation of Islam and the use of nonviolent means toward establishing Islamic rule. He is also the leading political opposition figure to the Tunisian government. Born in 1941 in the village of al-Hama in southeastern TUNISIA, al-Ghannoushi was the youngest of eight children. His father informally taught the QURAN and sent his son to the prestigious Zaytuna University, where he received a traditional religious education. Later, at the University of DAMASCUS, he earned a master's degree in philosophy and began his involvement in politics, briefly joining a secular nationalist party. However, any enchantment he may have had with these ideas dissipated with the Arab defeat by Israel in 1967 and the unfolding of massive student protests in France against the secular government there in 1968, something he witnessed firsthand as a philosophy student at the Sorbonne.

At the core of his ideas is the conviction that the adoption of nationalism and SECULARISM by Arabs has weakened their countries and led to a general crisis of identity in the region. He believes that the only way for Arabs to enter modernity is by following the path set by their own religion, history, and civilization. This was an idea being espoused by the MUSLIM BROTHERHOOD, with whom he had had contact in Damascus, and one that he would subsequently develop in the Tunisian context. Al-Ghannoushi spent much of the 1970s working as a high school philosophy teacher, meeting with the government-sponsored Quranic Preservation Society and spreading the teachings of Islamist thinkers such as ABU AL-ALA MAWDUDI (d. 1979), HASAN AL-BANNA (d. 1949), and SAYYID QUTB (d. 1966). To their ideas he added an emphasis on the practical solutions Islam offers for the spiritual, economic, and political problems of the day and the necessity for Muslims to pursue those solutions through activism and innovation. His message attracted a broad spectrum of people, including students, leftists, and workers.

With a program of political liberalization initiated in April 1981 by Tunisia's president Habib Bourguiba, al-Ghannoushi attempted to translate his following into a political party—the Islamic Tendency Movement—that could pursue political change through peaceful participation in the country's democratic process. However, his goal of Islamizing Tunisian society, as well as his broad appeal, were perceived as a threat by the authorities and resulted in the repeated imprisonment of al-Ghannoushi and his followers. Al-Ghannoushi was given a life sentence in 1987 but released and granted amnesty the following year with the change of government in Tunis. Throughout the 1990s, relations between the Tunisian state and its Islamist opposition continued to deteriorate, with many parties, including al-Nahda, banned

from participation in elections. This was a fate shared by his contemporaries Ali Abbasi Madani (b. 1931) of ALGERIA and Abd al-Salam al-Yasin (b. 1928) of MOROCCO, whose own Islamic reform movements have also been excluded from official representation. Al-Ghannoushi now lives in Britain as a political refugee and continues to be influential in Islamist thought and politics.

See also ARAB-ISRAELI CONFLICTS; DEMOCRACY; ISLAMISM; POLITICS AND ISLAM; RENEWAL AND REFORM MOVEMENTS.

Michelle Zimney

Further reading: Francois Burgat and William Dowell, *The Islamic Movement in North Africa* (Austin: University of Texas Press, 1997); Linda G. Jones, "Portrait of Rashid al-Ghannoushi," *Middle East Report* 153 (July–August 1988): 19; Charles Kurzman, ed., *Liberal Islam: A Sourcebook* (New York: Oxford University Press, 1988).

ghayba (Arabic: absence)

In Shiism, *ghayba* refers to the withdrawal, or occultation, of an individual—most frequently the IMAM, or holy leader—from human sight. This Imam's life can be miraculously elongated while in this absence, when he is thought to be close to God. The concept first appeared in Shii circles in the early eighth century and became connected to eschatological beliefs concerning the return of the imam preceding the end time. Among the various branches of SHIISM, the largest group, Twelve-Imam Shia, believe in a lesser and greater *ghayba* of their 12th imam, MUHAMMAD AL-MAHDI (b. 868). Four deputies successively represented this Imam over the span of about 70 years during his "lesser *ghayba.*" Immediately preceding the death of the fourth deputy in 941, this Imam is believed to have inaugurated "the greater *ghayba,*" which will continue until shortly before the end of the world. Until that time, the 12th Imam remains alive on this earth, concealed. Then, at a time appointed by God, he will arise as the Islamic messiah, the MAHDI, to rule and establish justice on earth until JUDGMENT DAY. Although the death of the fourth deputy signaled a cessation of formal contact between the imam and his community, the Hidden Imam is thought to be in contact with many of his followers miraculously, through dreams or visions. In his absence, authority is exercised by his representatives, the ULAMA, who are masters of religious law and the traditions of the imams. The most influential group of Shii ulama in recent times are the Mujtahids, those who can practice IJTIHAD, or independent reasoning based on the principals of FIQH, or Islamic jurisprudence.

The concept of *ghayba* is shared by other Shia groups, including the DRUZE. This religious group, which developed from ISMAILI SHIISM, believes in a lesser and greater *ghayba* that began with the disappearance of their caliph-imam al-Hakim, whom they consider to be divine, in 1021.

A doctrine resembling that of *ghayba* exists among other Shia groups. This doctrine, known as *satr,* refers to the concealment of a continuing line of imams. The BOHRA Shiis of India believe that their imams are in *satr.*

See also AKHBARI SCHOOL; AUTHORITY; TWELVE-IMAM SHIISM; USULI SCHOOL.

Jamel Velji

Further reading: Seyyed Hossein Nasr, Hamid Dabashi, and Seyyed Vali Reza Nasr, eds., *Shi'ism: Doctrines, Thought, Spirituality* (Albany: State University of New York Press, 1988); Wilferd Madelung, "Authority in Twelver Shiism in the Absence of the Imam." In *La notion d'authorité au Moyen Âge: Islam, Byzance, Occident* (Paris: Presses Universitaires de France, 1978), 163–173.

ghazal (Arabic; also *ghazel, gazal*)

A *ghazal* is a love poem about eternal desire never fulfilled, in which unrequited and unattainable love drives the loyal lover to misery. Often, the lover will be likened to a moth near a candle, while the beloved is beautiful and inaccessible, off gallivanting with another or drinking from a wine goblet. The *ghazal* can be interpreted both as a love poem and a devotional poem, for the pain of separation that one feels from one's lover is analogous to the pain of separation one feels from God.

The *ghazal* is originally a Persian poetic form that came to INDIA in the 12th century with Muslim rule and flourished in India during the MUGHAL DYNASTY (1526–1708). The rise of Urdu as the popular poetic language of north India gave birth to the Urdu *ghazal,* which is between five and 15 couplets long and uses the same rhyme and refrain throughout the poem. Although an Urdu *ghazal* is a single poem, each couplet within the *ghazal* is considered a poem in and of itself, like a pearl in a necklace.

In India, the popularity of the *ghazal* led to the development of the *mushaira,* which is a gathering of poets who recite *ghazal* couplets to one another. The *ghazal* also evolved into its own musical form, as *ghazal* singers began performing with semiclassical musicians. Early Indian CINEMA incorporated *ghazal* MUSIC into its commercial films, making *ghazal* music popular and accessible to a larger audience.

Although the *ghazal* has historically been associated with Islam, it is now an ecumenical form of poetry adopted by different religious communities. The Urdu *ghazal* is still the most famous form and remains popular in PAKISTAN and India, but *ghazal* traditions have emerged in other South Asian languages as well as in Spanish, Italian, and English. Among the most famous *ghazal* poets are Amir Khusrau (d. 1325), Hafiz (d. 1389), Mir Taqi Mir (d. 1810), MIRZA GHALIB (d. 1869), and Faiz Ahmed Faiz (d. 1984).

See also PERSIAN LANGUAGE AND LITERATURE.

Varun Soni

Further reading: Agha Shahid Ali, ed., *Ravishing Disunities: Real Ghazals in English* (Middletown, Conn.:

Wesleyan University Press, 2000); K. C. Kanda, trans., *Masterpieces of Urdu Ghazal: From the 17th Century to the 20th Century* (New Delhi: Sterling Publishers, 1990); Frances Pritchett, *Nets of Awareness: Urdu Poetry and Its Critics* (Berkeley: University of California Press, 1994).

Ghazali, Abu Hamid al- (also al-Ghazzali; Latin: Algazel) (1058–1111) *one of the most famous Muslim intellectuals of the Middle Ages, he wrote important works on Islamic mysticism, theology, and philosophy that had a lasting effect on medieval Muslim religious thought*

Al-Ghazali was born in the town of Tus, IRAN, where he received his early education before moving to Nishapur, a major Iranian center of Sunni learning in the 11th and 12th centuries. Among his most famous teachers in Nishapur was al-Juwayni (d. 1085), a renowned scholar of Ashari THEOLOGY and Islamic jurisprudence (FIQH). Al-Ghazali remained in Nishapur until al-Juwayni died. Then he joined the circle of scholars patronized by Nizam al-Mulk (d. 1092), the powerful Seljuk Turkish VIZIER of the Abbasid Empire. He soon became one of the leading scholars of BAGHDAD, and in 1091, he was one of the first teachers appointed to the faculty of the new Nizamiyya College (MADRASA) there, where he taught Shafii law. It is reported that some of his lectures attracted up to 300 students, an unusually large number for a medieval school. Al-Ghazali's public success as a scholar and teacher caused him to question his motives and the sincerity of his faith, so that in 1095, he found himself unable to speak or carry on with his work. This spiritual crisis led to his resigning his position, leaving his family, and setting out on an 11-year sabbatical in SYRIA. During this time, his explorations focused on the ways and teachings of SUFISM. In his spiritual AUTOBIOGRAPHY, al-Ghazali wrote about what he discovered during this lengthy retreat: Of all the various schools of religion in Islam, "I knew with certainty that the Sufis are uniquely those who follow the way to God Most High, their mode of life is the best of all, their way the most direct of ways, and their ethic the purist" (Ghazali, 56). He returned to teaching briefly at the Nishapur madrasa and founded a Sufi hospice (*khanqah*) in his hometown, Tus, where he spent his last days.

Al-Ghazali acquired deep knowledge of many areas of Islamic religious thought and approached his subjects in a systematic manner. Scholars have identified him as the author of about 60 books. His most famous one was *The Revival of the Religious Sciences* (ca. 1097), a wide-ranging work that sought to wed Islamic practice with theological and mystical truths. Written during his long retreat, it is organized into four parts: 1) the FIVE PILLARS of Islam and their spiritual significance; 2) how to morally conduct one's daily affairs—such as dietary practices, marriage, work, traveling, and listening to MUSIC—so as to come closer to God; 3) how to discipline the self to eliminate human weaknesses such as desire, slander, envy, and greed that lead to damnation; and 4) how to purify the human soul and pursue the path toward God and salvation. The last part also includes vivid descriptions of DEATH and the AFTERLIFE, the ultimate destiny of all humans.

Two other well-known books, *The Incoherence of the Philosophers* (ca. 1095) and *The Deliverer from Error* (ca. 1108), display al-Ghazali's knowledge both of the theological and philosophical traditions of his times and of the differing points of view held by scholars and men of religion. In these works, he sought to demonstrate logically what he thought were the fallacies and shortcomings of the philosophers and Ismaili theologians. Defending the ASHARI SCHOOL of theology to which he belonged, he maintained that religious truths pertaining to God, creation, and the soul could not be adequately fathomed by the rational mind apart from revelation. In al-Ghazali's opinion, the arguments of Muslim philosophers such as AL-FARABI (d. 950) and IBN SINA (d. 1037) against the existence of individual souls and belief in a bodily resurrection were in conflict with quranic truths, as was their position on the eternity of the world. Al-Ghazali's main critique of the Ismaili Shia, who were posing a serious threat to Sunni hegemony during the 11th and 12th centuries, was that they gave too much AUTHORITY to their IMAMS. Believers only had to recognize God's existence and adhere to the SUNNA of MUHAMMAD to conduct their lives. Moreover, al-Ghazali cautioned against allowing commoners to engage in theological or philosophical speculation because it would harm their chances for salvation. He also criticized the exaggerated claims of Sufi mystics, who spoke of divine knowledge and complete annihilation of the self in God. Only God can fully know himself, he wrote, and annihilation, if achieved at all, was only for the moment.

Al-Ghazali's contributions to the history of Islamic thought and mysticism are still being debated today. Many recognize that his writings helped give new meaning to Muslim practices by conjoining them to Sufi values and insights. The use of logical argumentation in his theological writings set a standard for later Muslim theologians to follow. Al-Ghazali's bold criticisms of Muslim philosophers echoed throughout the Muslim intellectual world and obliged IBN RUSHD (d. 1198), the Andalusian philosopher-jurist, to write a retort entitled *The Incoherence of the Incoherence.* On the negative side, he may have contributed to the decline of Islamic philosophical reflection by the forcefulness of his theologically based arguments against many of its main tenets.

See also ALLAH; ETHICS AND MORALITY; ISMAILI SHIISM; PHILOSOPHY; SHAFII LEGAL SCHOOL.

Further reading: Massimo Campanini, "Al-Ghazzali." In *History of Islamic Philosophy,* edited by Seyyed Hossein Nasr and Oliver Leaman, 258–274 (London: Routledge, 1996); Abu Hamid al-Ghazali, *Al-Ghazali's Path to Sufism: His Deliverance from Error, al-Munqidh min al-dalal.* Translated by R. J. McCarthy (Louisville, Ky.: Fons Vitae, 2000); W. Montgomery Watt, *The Faith and Practice of al-Ghazali* (London: George Allen & Unwin, 1953).

Ghazali, Zaynab al- (1917–2005) *the most important female leader in the Egyptian Muslim Brotherhood during the 20th century and founder of the Society of Muslim Ladies*

Zaynab al-Ghazali was the daughter of a merchant and Islamic teacher who was educated at the famous AL-AZHAR University in CAIRO, EGYPT. She studied the QURAN, quranic commentary (TAFSIR) and HADITH at home in her youth but never attained more than a secondary school EDUCATION. She became a member of Huda Shaarawi's Egyptian Feminist Union, the country's first organized WOMEN's rights movement. Dissatisfied with the liberal, secular orientation of this movement, in 1936, she quit it when she was 18 years of age and launched the Society of Muslim Ladies, which sought to promote piety among women and address social problems within an Islamic framework. As part of its DAAWA (Muslim outreach) activities, this organization conducted religious classes for women at MOSQUES, trained them to preach, and provided social services to the needy. It also published a journal for Muslim women from 1954 to 1956 called *al-Sayyidat al-Muslimat* (Muslim women). Al-Ghazali said that when the Egyptian government forced her to disband the organization in 1964, the association's membership had grown to 3 million throughout the country. In 1949, she joined the MUSLIM BROTHERHOOD at the invitation of its founder, HASAN AL-BANNA (d. 1949), and her society worked in cooperation with the Muslim Sisters to help families who suffered from the campaign ABD AL-NASIR, Egypt's president from 1956 to 1970, was waging against the brotherhood in the 1950s and early 1960s. She conducted secret meetings with the brotherhood and their supporters to study Islamic literature and discuss plans for bringing about ISLAMIC GOVERNMENT. She is credited with helping to disseminate the writings of the Islamic ideologist SAYYID QUTB (d. 1966), which were composed during the years of his imprisonment for engaging in antigovernment activities.

She was sentenced to 25 years of prison in 1965 for conspiring to overthrow Egypt's government but served only six. Al-Ghazali's memoirs about her prison years were published in 1977 (published in English as *Return of the Pharaoh: Memoirs in Nasir's Prison*). In this autobiographical account, she described how her faith helped her withstand the horrible tortures she suffered at the hands of government agents, and she denied charges that the brotherhood had ever conspired to overthrow the government violently. ANWAR AL-SADAT (r. 1970–81) freed al-Ghazali and other members of the brotherhood after he became president as part of a strategy to win support of Muslim activists. He needed them to consolidate power and undermine the influence of the late Abd al-Nasir's supporters, many of whom were Arab socialists. After her release, al-Ghazali continued an active career of teaching and writing for Islamic periodicals. Her articles on women and family life urged women to educate themselves about what she held to be Islam's true values, arguing that the religion offers both women and men all their rights and that they do not have to turn to the West to obtain them. She hoped that by cultivating Islamic values at home, women could contribute to the moral and political transformation of the wider society. In her later years, al-Ghazali avoided overt political activity but worked on a Quran commentary. Al-Ghazali was married twice, divorcing her first husband because he had interfered with her JIHAD and marrying the second only after he had agreed not to interfere with her *daawa* activities. She never had children.

See also ISLAMISM; SHAARAWI, HUDA.

Further reading: Zainab al-Ghazali, *Return of the Pharaoh: Memoirs in Nasir's Prison*. Translated by Mokran Guezzou (Broughton Gifford, U.K.: Cromwell Press, 1994); Valerie J. Hoffman, "An Islamist Activist: Zaynab al-Ghazali." In *Women and the Family in the Middle East,* edited by Elisabeth Warnock Fernea, 233–254 (Austin: University of Texas Press, 1985); Saba Mahmood, *Poli-*tics of Piety: The Islamic Revival and the Feminist Subject (Princeton, N.J.: Princeton University Press, 2005).

Ghulam Ahmad (ca. 1830–1908) *the self-proclaimed Mahdi and founder of the Ahmadiyya movement of Islam in colonial India*

Ghulam Ahmad, also called Mirza Ghulam Ahmad Qadiani, founded an Islamic missionary revival movement in British INDIA known as the AHMADIYYA in 1889. He came from a prosperous family of Sunni Muslim landowners in the small town of Qadian in the Punjab region of northern India. He received a good EDUCATION but resisted his father's wishes that he become a lawyer or work for the British colonial government. Instead, Ghulam Ahmad pursued a religious life—for a period of about 20 years he claimed to receive revelations from God, and through his writings and missionary efforts he attracted a following that grew to about 20,000 members by the time of his death in 1908.

At the end of the 19th century, several Muslim empires were coming to an end. Muslim lands were increasingly falling under the direct or indirect control of European colonial powers, and Christian missionaries from Europe were seeking converts among Muslims. Ghulam Ahmad was among those Muslims who felt that their religion needed to be revived and reformed in order to survive. He saw himself as "the light of this dark age," a "rightly guided one" (MAHDI), and the peaceful renewer of the religion, who was expected to appear at the beginning of the 14th century on the Islamic CALENDAR (1300 A.H. coincided with 1882 on the Western calendar). His followers, especially the Qadiani branch of the Ahmadiyya movement, also think that Ghulam Ahmad claimed to be a PROPHET, which has offended other Muslims because a central Islamic belief is that there can be no prophets after MUHAMMAD (d. 632). In response to this criticism, the Qadianis have argued that there are two kinds of prophet: those who bring God's law and those who make it work.

Muhammad, they claim, was the last to bring God's law, but Ghulam Ahmad was among the prophets chosen to revive it and make it work. Another of his controversial teachings was that JESUS did not die on the cross but survived the crucifixion and escaped to KASHMIR (northern India), where he died and was buried. Thus, the promised messiah was Ghulam Ahmad, not Jesus, a claim that offended Christian missionaries in British India as well as Muslim authorities. Also, members of the Hindu community in northern India objected to his assertion that he was an incarnation of the Hindu god Krishna. Despite strong opposition and persecution, the movement Ghulam Ahmad launched has now reached many countries around the world and has an estimated membership of more than 10 million. His male heirs continue to serve as the leaders of the Qadiani branch of the Ahmadiyya. Their current leader is Mirza Masroor Ahmad (b. 1950), Ghulam Ahmad's great grandson, who became the Ahmadiyya CALIPH after his father, Mirza Tahir Ahmad, died in 2003.

See also AUTHORITY; CHRISTIANITY AND ISLAM; COLONIALISM; HINDUISM AND ISLAM; RENEWAL AND REFORM MOVEMENTS.

Further reading: Yohanan Friedmann, *Prophecy Continuous: Aspects of Ahmadi Religious Thought and Its Medieval Background* (Berkeley: University of California Press, 1989); Muhammad Zafrullah Khan, *Ahmadiyyat: The Renaissance of Islam* (London: Tabshir Publications, 1978).

ghulat (Arabic "to exaggerate," "to exceed the proper bounds")

The *ghulat* were early radical Shii groups known for their exaggerated beliefs about God, ALI IBN ABI TALIB (d. 661), and other Shii Imams. Ali was the cousin and son-in-law of MUHAMMAD, whom the Shia consider to have been the rightful heir to the leadership of Islam after the Prophet's death. The *ghulat* deified Ali and believed that he was a superhuman being with miraculous powers. The term *ghali* (pl. *ghulat*) was used disparagingly by mainstream Muslims to refer to supporters of these beliefs. Such doctrines were considered heretical to Sunni and later moderate Shii authorities, who consider God to be one and not incarnate in human beings.

When these extremist doctrines about Ali spread to newly Islamized areas such as IRAQ, IRAN, Anatolia, and Central Asia during the eighth century, they were mixed with pre-Islamic and Christian beliefs, such as reincarnation, resurrection, and the Christian Trinity (God, JESUS, and the Holy Spirit). A variety of sects that applied such views to the veneration of Ali and the 12 Imams arose, many of which survive today, such as the Alawis (Nusayris) in SYRIA, the Ahl-i Haqq (People of the Divine Truth) in Iran, the Alevis in TURKEY, and the Shabak in northern Iraq. While some believers within these groups may equate Ali with God, it is more common for them to place Ali in a spiritual trinity along with ALLAH and Muhammad or to see Ali as a manifestation of God. These sects have been influenced by SUFISM in their beliefs and ritual practices, and most require members to undergo an initiation ceremony.

Since these sects are considered heretical by orthodox Muslim authorities, they have often been persecuted. They therefore practice in secret and often resort to concealing or even denying their true beliefs from outsiders, employing the Shii tactic of *taqiyya* (dissimulation).

See also ALAWI; *BATIN*; IMAM; SHIISM.

Mark Soileau

Further reading: Krisztina Kehl-Bodrogi, Barbara Kellner-Heinkele, and Anke Otter-Beaujean, eds., *Syncretistic Religious Communities in the Near East* (New York: E.J. Brill, 1997); Matti Moosa, *Extremist Shiites: The Ghulat Sects* (Syracuse, N.Y.: Syracuse University Press, 1988).

ghusl   See ABLUTION.

God   *See* ALLAH.

goddess

A goddess is a female form of deity found in many of the world's religions. She is usually paired with a male god and commonly included within a polytheistic religious system. The goddesses of ancient EGYPT and Mesopotamia were associated with the natural world—earth, fertility, plants, animals, the sky, and the planets. Some, such as Ishtar of IRAQ and Isis of Egypt, were worshipped as protectors of the king and his household. When Islam appeared in the seventh century, most forms of goddess worship had either disappeared or been assimilated by Christianity. The Virgin MARY and JESUS, for example, were portrayed like Isis holding the infant Horus in the iconography of early Christian Egypt. Nevertheless, traditional goddess worship did continue in the more remote regions of the Middle East, including the Arabian Peninsula, where it disappeared after it encountered the new religion of Islam.

The three most popular goddesses in pre-Islamic Arabia were al-Lat, Manat, and al-Uzza, sometimes called the daughters of ALLAH. Al-Lat (possibly the female counterpart of the Arabian high god Allah) was worshipped by Arab tribes in much of the peninsula. Her main temple was located in Taif, a town in the mountains southeast of MECCA, where she was worshipped in the form of a rock that was shaped like the KAABA. Manat, a very ancient goddess, was worshipped by the Arabs of Mecca, MEDINA (Yathrib), and the surrounding territories. She may have been a local form of the goddess Ishtar, and her name suggests that she had power over human fortunes and destinies. A sacred site for her statue was created in a coastal town near Medina, and members of Medina's leading tribes would go there to shave their heads on their return from pilgrimage to Mecca. Al-Uzza (the mighty one) was worshipped in northern Arabia and SYRIA, perhaps as a local version of the ancient Greek goddess Aphrodite. Her shrine

was located on the road between Mecca and Taif, where there was a grove of sacred trees. People went there on pilgrimage to conduct sacrifices and consult oracles. Just before MUHAMMAD began his mission, the QURAYSH tribe, the most powerful in Mecca, consolidated the worship of all three goddesses at the Kaaba. After 630, once Muslims had won control of western Arabia, they destroyed the images and shrines of these goddesses.

The idea of the woman as an embodiment of holiness did not end with the coming of Islam, however. The veneration of female SAINTS, particularly those descended from the House of the Prophet (AHL AL-BAYT), such as FATIMA and ZAYNAB BINT ALI IBN ABI TALIB, is found in many Muslim lands among both Sunnis and Shiis. Moreover, the female beloved portrayed in Sufi literature was a symbol of the beautiful qualities of God, even though she was not explicitly called a goddess. Lastly, Muslims in certain parts of INDIA participate in rituals held at the temples of Hindu goddesses. Such beliefs and practices are strongly condemned by strict followers of Islam, particularly those influenced by Wahhabi doctrines and Islamic modernism.

See also ARABIAN RELIGIONS, PRE-ISLAMIC; SATANIC VERSES; WAHHABISM; WOMEN.

Further reading: Hisham ibn Kalbi, *The Book of Idols.* Translated by N. A. Faris (Princeton, N.J.: Princeton University Press, 1952); Manjhan, *Madhumalati: An Indian Sufi Romance.* Translated by Aditya Behl and Simon Weightman (Oxford: Oxford University Press, 2000); F. E. Peters, *The Arabs and Arabia on the Eve of Islam* (Aldershot, U.K., and Brookfield, Vt.: Ashgate, 1999).

good and evil   *See* ETHICS AND MORALITY.

Gospel (Arabic: *injil*)

The QURAN and Muslims refer to the entire New Testament as the Gospel, not just the first four books of that section of the Bible. The Quran could be interpreted as suggesting that the Gospel is a sacred text that God revealed to JESUS, as he revealed the TORAH to MOSES and the Quran to MUHAMMAD. This relationship with other sacred scriptures is evidenced by the fact that nine of the 12 times the Gospel is mentioned in the Quran, it occurs in relation to the Torah (Arabic: *al-tawrat*), the Jewish sacred text. However, Muslims have also maintained that the Torah and the Gospel, as Jews and Christians have received them, contain errors and omissions, while the entire Quran is absolutely perfect and complete.

While there are four Gospels in the New Testament and, according to Christians, they constitute one of several kinds of literature in that section of the Bible, the Quran uses the Arabic singular of Gospel. There is another significant difference between Christian and Muslim understandings of Gospel or Gospels. Christians view the Gospels as the proclamation of the "good news" of salvation that God offers to human beings through Jesus, while Muslims understand Gospel as containing God's laws and ethics, together with prophecies concerning Muhammad's coming.

In terms of similarities and differences regarding the Quran's view of the Gospel and the Gospels as they appear in the New Testament, several Quranic verses overlap significantly with material in all or some of the four New Testament Gospels. Other quranic passages contain ideas and symbols that are similar to noncanonical gospels and other Christian texts. A number of other statements that the Quran attributes to Jesus as well as stories about him do not have any substantial similarity to the Gospels or any other Christian texts. Thus, textually there are numerous similarities and differences in terms of ideas and symbols in the Quran's representation of the Gospel and the Gospels as they appear in the New Testament.

See also CHRISTIANITY AND ISLAM; HOLY BOOKS; JUDAISM AND ISLAM.

Jon Armajani

Further reading: Kenneth Cragg, *A Certain Sympathy of Scriptures: Biblical and Quranic* (Brighton, U.K., and Portland, Ore.: Sussex Academic Press, 2004); John C. Reeves, ed., *Bible and Quran: Essays in Scriptural Intertextuality* (Leiden and Boston: E.J. Brill, 2004).

government, Islamic

Only about 10 percent of the QURAN deals with government or legislative matters. Therefore, Muslims have relied on the words and actions of MUHAMMAD (d. 632) as transmitted in the HADITH literature to provide much of the basis for Islamic law (SHARIA and FIQH) and government. Since Muhammad was both a religious and political leader, Muslims generally agree that government and law should be Islamic. There is a large degree of consensus over what constitutes Islamic law, but much less over what qualifies as Islamic government. Consequently, many governments, past and present, base their claim to be Islamic on the degree to which they support and enforce sharia.

After Muhammad's death, the government was led by his key companions, who became the first four CALIPHS and were able to continue to model religious and political AUTHORITY based on their close relationship with Muhammad. But with the rapid expansion of the Arab-Islamicate empire, the CALIPHATE became more political and secular. At the same time, the first generation of Muslims was passing away. Both events highlighted the need for greater systemization of the sharia in order to guide the ruler and the community. In the process, the ULAMA (religious scholars) greatly increased their authority as the definers of Islamic law but also supported the caliph for the sake of unity and continuity. In the medieval period, most people accepted that the government could claim to be Islamic as long as it supported and defended the sharia, regardless of the character of the ruler himself or his administration.

In order to strengthen their religious legitimacy, rulers have often claimed to support Islamic law while all the while encroaching on its authority. In the medieval period, rulers established a parallel system of courts that enabled them to side-step the SHARIA. Many Muslim countries in the modern period have based the primary law code of the land on Western models. Sharia is limited to the arena of personal status laws, those dealing with divorce, inheritance, marriage, and the family. The degree to which people are satisfied with this or desire a greater application of the sharia often depends on the political and economic conditions in a particular country.

While a few reformers call for a return of the caliphate, many argue that Islamic principles such as *shura* (consultation) and *maslaha* (general welfare) support the ideal of an Islamic DEMOCRACY. Most activists and reformers who call for Islamic government are concerned primarily with the sharia becoming the law of the country—at least for its Muslim citizens. This is based on a belief that the sharia is divinely ordained and when properly interpreted and applied will bring about just and equitable society. However, Islamic political theorists are still debating the key question of who should have the authority to interpret and enforce sharia.

See also IRANIAN REVOLUTION OF 1978–1979; ISLAMISM; POLITICS AND ISLAM; SAUDI ARABIA.

Heather N. Keaney

Further reading: Antony Black, *The History of Islamic Political Thought: From the Prophet to the Present* (New York: Routledge, 2001); Mohammad Asghar Khan, *Islam, Politics, and the State: the Pakistan Experience* (London: Zed Books, 1985); Ann Lambton, *State and Government in Medieval Islam* (1981. Reprint, Oxford: Oxford University Press, 1995).

Granada

The city of Granada (Arabic: *Gharnata*) is the capital of the province of Granada in ANDALUSIA and has a population of 250,000. Its strategic location at the confluence of the Darro and Genil Rivers and at the foot of the Sierra Nevada Mountains accounts for its continuous settlement since prehistoric times. During the early period of Islamic rule, Granada's population was largely Jewish (hence the Arabic epithet "Granada of the Jews"). Granada gained prominence as an Islamicate city following the fragmentation of the UMMAYYAD CALIPHATE into petty kingdoms after 1013. A BERBER general, Ibn Ziri (d. 1025), founded the Zirid kingdom, making Granada its urban center and the Alhambra its royal capital.

The ALMORAVID DYNASTY deposed the Zirids in 1090 and ruled until their defeat by the ALMOHAD DYNASTY in 1166. Spanish Muslims, led by Ibn al-Hud, overthrew the Almohad leader al-Mamun (ca. 1232). Subsequently, Muhammad Ibn al-Ahmar wrested power from Ibn al-Hud, establishing the Nasrid dynasty in 1238.

Ibn Ziri founded Granada's Great Mosque, whose beauty rivalled those of Seville and CORDOBA. He also built the Old Casbah (fortress), which enclosed the royal palace and the commercial and residential quarters. Granada was surrounded by orchards of pomegranate (Granada means pomegranate in Spanish) and other trees, and the soil was so fertile it yielded crops biannually. The most lucrative industries were textiles (silk, wool, linen, cotton) and gold- and silver-smithing.

The 13th-century Christian conquests reduced Andalusia to the tiny kingdom of Granada, which extended from Algeciras to Almeria. Surrounded by enemies, the Nasrid kingdom owed its longevity to its vassalage to Castile, its astuteness in pitting one foe against another (Castile, Aragon, North Africa), and Christian dynastic wars (1350–1412). Weakened by decades of internal strife, Abu Abd Allah (Boabdilla) finally surrendered Granada to Ferdinand and Isabella in 1492.

The Nasrid period is justifiably called the golden age of Islamicate culture in Spain. The Maliki and Sufi underpinnings of the Nasrid dynasty are especially noteworthy. Muhammad I deployed Sufi symbols to legitimate his authority and consolidated his rule on the edifice of the

MALIKI LEGAL SCHOOL. The Nasrid slogan "those who make [Islam] victorious through God" (in Arabic *Nasr* means victory) mitigated Granada's vassalage to Castile and epitomized the ideology of a frontier territory threatened by Christian (and Muslim) enemies.

The architectural expression of Nasrid "victory" is the Alhambra fortress (Arabic: *al-Hamra* "the red," referring to its reddish hue). Perched atop Sabika Hill, the Alhambra was a fortress and royal capital. Muhammad I began the construction of the Alhambra complex, and it was completed during the reign of Muhammad V (d. 1391). Nasrid Granada's population was overwhelmingly Muslim since most native Christians and Jews had migrated to Christian Iberia. The capitulation agreement of 1492 allowed the Muslims to retain their customs, but these rights were successively rescinded. Granada's MOSQUES were confiscated, and some 70,000 Muslims were forcibly baptized and prohibited from using Moorish dress, language, and customs. In the wake of Muslim revolts in 1501 and 1568 and the evidence of their continued Islamic practices, Felipe III decreed their expulsion from Spain, which transpired between 1609 and 1614.

See also CITIES; CHRISTIANITY AND ISLAM; SUFISM.

Linda G. Jones

Further reading: Abd Allah b. Buluggin, *The Tibyan: Memoirs of Abd Allah b. Buluggin, the Last Zirid Emir of Granada.* Translated and edited by Amin T. Tibi (Leiden: E.J. Brill, 1986); L. P. Harvey, *Islamic Spain, 1250 to 1500* (Chicago: University of Chicago Press, 1992); Bernard F. Reilly, *The Medieval Spains* (Cambridge: Cambridge University Press, 1993).

Gülen, Fethullah (1941–) *leading Islamic reformist thinker and preacher from Turkey*

Born in a farming village near Erzurum in eastern TURKEY, Fethullah Gülen, affectionately known to his followers as Hoja efendi (a Turkish title of respect), obtained his early EDUCATION at home, at primary school, and from religious teachers. He regards his mother as his first teacher and credits his father, Ramiz Gülen, for teaching him Arabic. He is reported to have memorized the QURAN at an early age. Although Sufi organizations had been banned in Turkey by MUSTAFA KEMAL ATATURK in 1925, his teachers included several who had been affiliated with the reformist NAQSHBANDI SUFI ORDER. He also studied nonreligious subjects such as modern SCIENCE, PHILOSOPHY, and history.

Gülen began to give sermons in local settings when he was 16 and was greatly influenced by the teachings of Said Nursi (d. 1960), a prominent Muslim modernist thinker of Kurdish heritage who was advocating the compatibility of modern science and knowledge with Islam in Turkey. A pious young man, Gülen received his first appointment in 1959 as the IMAM at the prominent Ucserefeli Mosque in Edirne, western Turkey. He served there for two and a half years, then performed his Turkish military service. When he got out, he held various positions and gave talks on religious and political subjects throughout the country, concerned at the time with growing communist influence. Inspired by Said Nursi and the Nurcu movement, he favored the development of an ideological alternative to the secular Turkish nationalism of Ataturk (called Kemalism). His tape-recorded sermons gained wide circulation and were especially well received by university students. After a military coup in 1971, Gülen was sentenced to prison for three years for his outreach activities. But this did not curtail his popularity, and, in 1975, he organized conferences dealing with the QURAN, science, and Darwinism. It is said that young people from throughout Turkey flocked to hear his sermons and lectures. During the 1980s, after another military coup, Turkish authorities continued to monitor his activities, even raiding his home. He was able to act more openly in the 1990s because of mainstream acceptance of religious parties such as the REFAH PARTY in Turkish politics. Gülen had public meetings with high government officials in Turkey and was instrumental in the establishment of the Journalists and Writers Foundation in 1994. He also gained the attention of the international media due to his involvement in Turkish politics and his endorsement of DEMOCRACY, pluralism, and interreligious DIALOGUE. His outreach to other religious communities is evident in the meetings he has held with leading representatives of Turkey's Jewish and Christian communities and his audience with Pope John Paul II in 1998. He is credited with having written more than 60 books, mostly in Turkish, published frequent journal and magazine articles, and recorded many audio and video cassettes.

Gülen has performed the HAJJ several times since his first visit to MECCA in 1968. He has also visited Europe and the UNITED STATES, where he has lived since 1999. He receives medical care there but continues to serve as an inspiration for his followers in Turkey and around the world. He has taken a strong stand against radical ISLAMISM. In the aftermath of the September 11, 2001, attacks in the United States, he issued a statement to the media declaring, "Terror can never be used in the name of Islam or for the sake of any Islamic ends. A Muslim can only be the representative and symbol of peace, welfare, and prosperity" (Gülen, 2002).

The Gülen movement (also known as the Fethullahcilar) has achieved remarkable advances since the 1990s. It has established 250 schools in Turkey, southeastern Europe, Turkic parts of Central Asia, and other parts of the world. The curricula of the movement's schools, which enroll large numbers of children from rural and working-class backgrounds, emphasize a progressive attitude to modernity and religion with the objective of making the world a better place for all. In 1997, the movement opened Fatih University, a private university on the outskirts of ISTANBUL, which has faculties in the humanities, social sciences, business, sciences, engineering, and vocational studies. A branch in Ankara, Turkey's capital, has schools

of medicine, nursing, and vocational studies. The movement's members have opened centers in several American cities, where they conduct interfaith activities, lectures, conferences, and Turkish cultural programs. Many of the movement's male members, who call each other "brother" (abi), are involved in international education, business, and professional careers. WOMEN in the movement, who typically wear headscarves, are well educated and play visible and active roles in community life. It also operates Zaman (Time), a leading Turkish newspaper, and a satellite television station that produces educational and entertainment programming in Turkish that reflects Gülen's religious and ethical ideals.

See also DAAWA; RENEWAL AND REFORM MOVEMENTS; SECULARISM.

Further reading: Bulent Aras and Omer Caha, "Fethullah Gülen and His Liberal 'Turkish Islam' Movement," Middle East Review of International Affairs 4, no. 4 (2000): 30–42; Mucahit Bilici, "The Fethullah Gülen Movement and Its Politics of Representation in Turkey," Muslim World 96, no. 1 (2006): 1–20; Fethullah Gülen, Essays, Perspectives, Opinions. Rev. ed. (Somerset, N.J.: The Light, 2004); ———, The Statue of Our Souls: Revival in Islamic Thought and Activism. Translated by Muhammad Çetin (Somerset, N.J.: The Light, 2005); M. Hakan Yavuz and John L. Esposito, eds., Turkish Islam and the Secular State: The Gülen Movement (Syracuse, N.Y.: Syracuse University Press, 2003).

Gulf States

The Persian Gulf (also called the Arabian Gulf, especially by Arabs) is a strategic body of water about 93,000 square miles in area (slightly less than the size of Oregon) separating the Arabian Peninsula from IRAN. Its northwestern shore receives the outflow from the Tigris and Euphrates Rivers, and it opens to the Indian Ocean at the Strait of Hormuz, located 615 miles to the southeast. The gulf is surrounded by eight countries— Iran, IRAQ, SAUDI ARABIA, Kuwait, Bahrain, Qatar, the United Arab Emirates (UAE), and Oman. The landmass occupied by these states collectively is 1.8 million square miles, or half the landmass of the United States. The individual Persian Gulf countries range in size from the smallest, Bahrain (the size of Washington, D.C.) and Qatar (the size of Connecticut), to the largest, Iran (the size of Alaska) and Saudi Arabia (one-third the size of the United States). The total population of the region is about 130 million, or slightly less than half that of the United States. Iran, with 65.8 million people (2008 estimate), has the largest population by far of all the Gulf countries, followed by Iraq (28.2 million) and Saudi Arabia (28.1 million, including 5.6 million nonnationals).

This is a very diverse region with respect to religion, culture, politics, and economics. It has been home to several civilizations plus a major crossroads for others, linking Asia with the Middle East and Europe and the Indian Ocean with the Mediterranean. It is populated by city dwellers, nomads, farmers, and, in modern times, immigrants from many parts of the world. The immigrants come especially from South Asia, attracted by employment opportunities in the OIL industry that developed there in the latter part of the 20th century or by jobs in the commercial sector. Previously best known for its AGRICULTURE, spices, pearl fisheries, cities of commerce, and pilgrimage networks, the Gulf region today is the center of the petroleum industry. It has more than half the world's proven oil reserves, and it produces about a third of the world's oil. The native population is mainly Persian speaking on the eastern side of the Gulf and Arabic speaking on the western side. The majority belongs to the Twelve-Imam branch of Shii Islam, especially in Iran, Iraq, and Bahrain, but there is also a significant Sunni Muslim presence. The IBADIYYA, an off-shoot of the KHAWARIJ, the earliest Muslim sect, are a majority in Oman. All the major Islamic legal schools are present in the Gulf region, led by the Jaafari Legal School among the Shia and the HANBALI LEGAL SCHOOL among the Sunnis, as well as a significant number

of Hanafis and Malikis. WAHHABISM, a particularly puritanical branch of the Hanbali tradition based in Saudi Arabia, is very influential among Sunni populations in the Gulf region. The Gulf is home to several of Islam's most treasured holy cities— MECCA and MEDINA in Saudi Arabia, Najaf and KARBALA in Iraq, and Mashhad in Iran. Non-Muslim religious communities are also found there, including Christians, Hindus, Bahais, Buddhists, Sikhs, Zoroastrians, and Jews.

The modern Gulf states all arose during the 20th century. Prior to that time, the most important countries with a long history of state control were Iran and Iraq, which were ruled by Muslim dynasties such as the Umayyads, Abbasids, Seljuks, Ottomans, and Safavids. An Indian Ocean empire based on trade was commanded by the rulers of Oman during the 19th century. Yet much of the Arabian Peninsula, and even significant parts of Iran and Iraq, have been controlled by different tribal groups and confederations. Today the major regional powers are the Islamic Republic of Iran, the Republic of Iraq, and the Kingdom of Saudi Arabia (treated elsewhere in this volume). The smaller Arab Gulf states are the Kingdom of Bahrain, the State of Kuwait, the Sultanate of Oman, the State of Qatar, and the UAE. All of these states took present form after a period of British hegemony during the 19th century, when local tribal SHAYKHS became British clients protected by the Royal Navy. Britain essentially ran the foreign affairs and defense of these countries until it acceded to their independence after World War II. Even with their formal independence, however, the smaller Gulf States have continued to rely on alliances with greater powers, such as the UNITED STATES, for their survival. Oil has given them a great deal of economic security, but it has also made them vulnerable to international political forces and regional insurgencies. Since 1981, one major revolution and three major wars have been fought in the Gulf region. Therefore, to improve their strategic security, affirm their common interests, and coordinate their relations, the five smaller Arab Gulf States, plus Saudi Arabia, formed the Gulf Cooperation Council (GCC) on May 25, 1981. For political and strategic reasons, Iran and Iraq are conspicuously absent from this regional alliance.

BAHRAIN

The smallest of the Gulf States, the island nation of Bahrain has a population of 718,306 (2008 est.), more than 235,000 of whom are nonnationals. The majority (70 percent) consists of followers of TWELVE-IMAM SHIISM who maintain close ties to Shii religious centers in Iraq and Iran. The government is controlled by the Sunni Al Khalifa, a merchant family. Bahrain has been subject in the past to Portuguese and British rule, but it achieved independence in 1971, when it became officially known as the State of Bahrain. At that time, a constitution was approved and an elected national assembly was created, but it was disbanded in 1975. It was then ruled as a conservative shaykh-dom (emirate) until 2002, when the government was reclassified as a monarchy and the national assembly was reconstituted in response to Shii demands for more participation in governance.

KUWAIT

Situated on the western side of where the Shatt al-Arab waterway empties into the Persian Gulf, Kuwait is bordered by Iraq to the north and Saudi Arabia to the south. Its population is 2.6 million (2008 est.), of whom as many as 60 percent are nonnationals. Most of the people are Sunni Muslims and followers of the MALIKI LEGAL SCHOOL. About 25 percent are adherents of Twelve-Imam Shiism; many of the country's wealthy merchants are Shiis with roots in Iraq and Iran. There is a mixed population of non-Muslim residents, including Christians, Hindus, Buddhists, and Sikhs. Kuwait's ruling family is the Al Sabah, who are Sunni Arabs. They have played a leading role in Kuwaiti affairs since the 18th century, when Kuwait City, the capital, emerged as a regional commercial center. Once closely allied to Otto-

man authorities in southern Iraq, they agreed to become a British protectorate in 1899. The country achieved independence in 1961, and its government is classified as a constitutional monarchy, which consists of a ruling emir from the Al Sabbah and a national assembly. In reaction to opposition and criticism from the assembly, however, the emir has intervened to disband it several times since the 1960s. Shiis in Kuwait became politically active in the aftermath of the IRANIAN REVOLUTION OF 1978–1979. Some Shii radicalism was stirred up by pro-Iranian agents, but activism has also come about as a result of Shii frustration with the lack of a proportional voice in national affairs. The government has occasionally resorted to harsh countermeasures, and eruptions of violence have occurred. Sunni Islamist groups, some affiliated with the MUSLIM BROTHERHOOD, have also formed there. The government, as a result, has made some concessions to such groups, such as supporting conservative Islamic legislation with respect to WOMEN's rights and alcohol consumption.

From August 1990 to March 1991, Iraq invaded and annexed Kuwait on the orders of SADDAM HUSAYN, Iraq's president. Although the Al Sabah were able to escape, many Kuwaitis and nonnationals suffered. The occupation was ended by an armed international coalition of forces authorized by the United Nations. During the 1990s, Kuwait supported efforts to contain Husayn's regime, and it allowed the country to be used as a staging area for the 2003 invasion and occupation of Iraq by a second armed coalition, led by the United States and Britain.

OMAN

Located at the southeastern end of the Arabian Peninsula at the Strait of Hormuz and on the shores of the Gulf of Oman and the Arabian Sea, the Sultanate of Oman is the third-largest country in the region. The UAE borders it in the northwest, Saudi Arabia in the west, and Yemen in the southwest. The country, whose capital is Musqat, is ruled by a member of the Al Bu Said family, which has been in power since the 18th century. The ruler was originally called a *SAYYID,* but this title was later changed to SULTAN. Until the 1950s, the country's interior was ruled by a more religious figure, also from the Al Bu Said, called an IMAM. Like other parts of the Arabian Peninsula, Oman was Islamized during the seventh century. Early in the 19th century, it became a commercial empire that dominated the Indian Ocean trade. It gained possessions on the coasts of EAST AFRICA, the Persian Gulf, Iran, and present-day PAKISTAN. The coming of European steam-powered ships, growing British influence in the region, and internal political disputes brought this empire to an end by the end of the 19th century. Thereafter, Omani rulers relied heavily on the British for assistance in consolidating and keeping their control of the country. In more recent times, it has developed close relations with the United States.

Most of Oman's 3.3 million (2008 est.) inhabitants are Arabs, but there are significant numbers of peoples from outside the country, especially Baluchis from Iran, South Asians, and Africans. More than 16 percent of Oman's inhabitants are nonnationals, many of whom are engaged by the country's oil industry. Islam is its dominant religion, with 75 percent belonging to the Ibadiyya sect. Other Muslims belong to the Sunni and Shii branches of Islam. Christians and Hindus also live in Oman, and the sultan has granted them lands for their churches and temples.

QATAR

The second-smallest state in the Middle East, Qatar is located on a small peninsula bordered by Saudi Arabia and the nearby island nation of Bahrain. Doha is the nation's capital, and it is ruled by a member of the Al Thani, a Sunni Arab clan that migrated into the peninsula from central Arabia and came to power with British assistance in 1868. Although it became a province of the Ottoman Empire in the latter part of the 19th century, it became a British protectorate after World War I and attained independence in 1971. The Al Thani developed friendly relations with ABD AL-AZIZ IBN SAUD, the founder of the Kingdom of Saudi Arabia, and, as a result, the leading form of Sunnism followed in Qatar is that of the Wahhabis, albeit in a more liberalized form. Followers of Twelve-Imam Shiism are a small minority. The country's population of 824,789 (2008 est.) is 95 percent Muslim, but it is made up of diverse ethnic groups (Arab 40 percent, South Asian 36 percent, Iranian 10 percent, and other 14 percent). This diversity is a reflection of the changes the country has undergone from once having an economy based on pastoralism, pearling, and fishing to one based on oil, which began to be exported in significant quantities in the 1950s. Qatar has become a close ally of the United States, and, under the present emir, Hamad bin Khalifa Al Thani (r. 1999 to the present), local elections have been held, and women have been given the right to vote and run for office. The headquarters of the Al Jazeera broadcasting network, one of the freest in the Middle East, is also located there.

UNITED ARAB EMIRATES

The UAE, formerly known as the Trucial States, is a federation of seven small states (Abu Dhabi, Ajman, Dubai, Fujaira, Ras al-Khaima, Sharja, and Umm al-Qaiwain) located near the Strait of Hormuz on the southeastern shore of the gulf. It is bordered by Qatar to the west, Saudi Arabia to the south, and Oman to the east. The leaders of the UAE come from its most powerful or wealthy Arabian tribes, particularly the Al Nahayyan of Abu Dhabi, the Al Maktoum of Dubai, and the Qasimis of Ras al-Khaima and Sharja. Prior to independence in 1971, the individual emirates had established exclusive treaty relations with Great Britain. Overall authority is now exercised by the Supreme Council of emirs from each of the seven states, with a president from the Al Nahayan and vice president from the Al Maktoum. The country is home to an estimated 4.6 million (2005) people, of whom at least 47 percent are nonnationals, mainly from South Asia and Iran.

By some estimates, nonnationals may even outnumber UAE citizens. The majority of the country's populace follows Sunni Islam (80 percent) and the Maliki tradition of law. The Shia are a minority (16 percent). The rest includes Christians, Hindus, Buddhists, Bahais, and Sikhs, who have freedom of worship. Christians, Hindus, and Sikhs have their own churches and temples, while others conduct their religious practices at home. Oil has brought the country great prosperity since its discovery there in 1958, and its per capita income is now comparable to that of countries in western Europe. The UAE has also become a flourishing center of international commerce and a modern architectural showcase; buildings there reflect Islamic and Western motifs.

See also GULF WARS; ORGANIZATION OF PETROLEUM EXPORTING COUNTRIES.

Further reading: Helen Chapin Metz, *The Persian Gulf States: A Country Study* (Washington, D.C.: Federal Division, Library of Congress, 1994); Rosemarie Said Zahlan, *The Making of the Modern Gulf States: Kuwait, Bahrain, Qatar, the United Arab Emirates, and Oman* (London: Unwin Hyman, 1989).

Gulf Wars

Between 1980 and the present (2008), the Persian Gulf region was subject to three major conflicts that pitted country against country, Muslim against Muslim, and Muslims against the UNITED STATES, Great Britain, and their allies. Although religion was not the cause for these conflicts, it nonetheless was an important factor. The conflicts, in turn, affected the ways in which religion was used by the various parties involved to serve their short- and long-term strategies and policy objectives. In addition, competition for control of the world's largest OIL fields was a key element in each of the conflicts.

THE IRAN-IRAQ WAR OF 1980–1988

This, the first of the modern Gulf wars, began on September 22, 1980, when Iraqi forces invaded IRAN by crossing the Shatt al-Arab waterway into southwestern Iran. A major cause of the conflict was a long-standing dispute between the two nations over control of this vital waterway, which is used for transporting oil to global markets via the Persian Gulf. IRAQ had been obliged by a United Nations resolution in 1975 to share the waterway jointly with Iran, a development that SADDAM HUSAYN (d. 2006), Iraq's president, saw as an insult to his country's sovereignty. Another area of contention was Iraq's historic claim to the Iranian province of Khuzistan (also known as Arabistan), where there was a large population of Arabs whom Iraq felt needed its protection. In 1980, Husayn perceived that the overthrow of the Pahlavi monarchy in 1979 by an Islamic revolution led by Ayatollah RUHOLLAH KHOMEINI (d. 1989), the charismatic Shii leader, had left Iran's defenses weak and in disarray. Husayn concluded that this was a situation he could exploit to make Iraq the dominant power in the Persian Gulf. At the same time, Husayn was angered by efforts undertaken by Iranian agents to stir up resistance against his government among Iraqi Shia, the country's majority population, who live in the southern part of the country, where many of Iraq's oil fields are located.

Religion was used in the war to win popular support domestically and appeal to the wider Muslim community. After initial losses on the battlefield, Iranian forces rallied, with the backing of thousands of youthful volunteers called the Basij, who were encouraged to become holy martyrs by dying for their country in imitation of Imam Husayn, the heroic grandson of Muhammad who perished in the battle of KARBALA in 680 fighting the forces of tyranny and injustice. By 1982, Iran had regained much of the territory initially lost to the Iraqi offensive. Saddam Husayn, on the other hand, attempted to mobilize Iraqi patriotism by recalling the Battle of Qadisiyya (ca. 636), in which Arab Muslim armies were thought to have decisively defeated the Sassanian Persian army, opening all of Iran to conquest. He also invoked, with little success, the symbolism of the Shii Imams ALI IBN ABI TALIB (d. 661) and Husayn in order to maintain the loyalty of Iraq's Shii majority. Iran and Iraq soon became locked in a long war of attrition, during which Iraq bombed Iranian towns and CITIES and used chemical weapons to lethal effect in battle.

Iraq was supported by other Arab countries and received logistical support from Europe and the United States through secret third-party transfers. The United States in particular followed a policy of containment (strategic isolation) first of Iran, then later of Iraq, in order to secure greater influence in the region and control the spread of revolutionary SHIISM. The war came to an end in 1988 with assistance from the United Nations, but without a formal peace treaty. Fervor for war was also reduced following Khomeini's death in 1989, allowing Iran to take concrete steps toward making peace with its neighbor. It was not until after Iraq had invaded Kuwait in 1990, when it needed to be on good terms with Iran, that Iraq withdrew from all occupied Iranian territory, conducted prisoner exchanges, and agreed to reopen the Shatt al-Arab to commercial traffic.

The war exacted a terrible price on both countries: A total of about 1 million lives were lost at the cost of billions of dollars to the infrastructure and economy of each country. Nevertheless, the war allowed Khomeini to eliminate domestic opponents of his Islamic revolution, and it gave the government an independent militia, the Basij, which still plays a leading role in helping the government maintain its power.

THE GULF WAR OF 1990–1991 (ALSO CALLED THE FIRST GULF WAR)

This short war was precipitated when Iraq invaded Kuwait on August 2, 1990. Iraq had long claimed sovereignty over Kuwait, which was made a British protectorate in 1899. In the late 1980s, at the end of the Iran-Iraq war, Saddam Husayn came to resent the close relationship Kuwait had formed with the United States, which was impeding his ambitions to make his country the chief power in the Gulf region. At the same time, Iraq held a large national debt because of its war with Iran, and it resented the fact that the other major Arab oil-producing countries were not willing to keep oil prices high so that it could pay off this debt. Moreover, Husayn complained that Kuwait had been illegally tapping into the Rumayla oil field that lies on the Iraqi-Kuwaiti border. When regional and international mediation efforts failed to satisfy Iraqi demands, Iraq's forces took the country by force. In the ensuing months, an international coalition of 34 countries, led by the United States, formed first to protect incursion into SAUDI ARABIA, then to compel Iraq's withdrawal from Kuwait. United Nations resolutions authorized these actions, in addition to several resolutions that imposed economic sanctions and condemned Iraq for human rights violations.

The world was deeply concerned that the looming conflict would affect oil supplies, and many observers worried that Iraq might resort to the use of chemical or biological weapons against the coalition. While serious diplomatic efforts were being made to resolve the crisis, the coalition assembled its forces in the Gulf region in what was called Operation Desert Shield, the first phase of the war. This was the defensive phase, but the second phase involved attacking Iraq in order to force it to withdraw from Kuwait. The United Nations gave Iraq until January 15, 1991, to withdraw peacefully, but it resisted, hoping to rally the support of the Muslim world and find a diplomatic alternative. On January 17, 1991, the United States launched the offensive phase of the war, known as Operation Desert Storm, with a crippling aerial bombing campaign. Iraq responded by launching missiles with conventional warheads at targets in ISRAEL and Saudi Arabia. The missiles inflicted minor damage, except for one that hit a U.S. military barracks in Dhahran, Saudi Arabia, killing U.S. military personnel there. On February 22–23, Iraq began to set fire to Kuwait's oil fields, causing serious environmental damage.

With the air campaign well under way, a ground attack, known as Desert Saber, was launched from Saudi Arabia into Kuwait and southern Iraq on February 24. Iraqi troops were quickly overcome and driven out of Kuwait in less than six days, and on March 3, 1991, Iraq agreed to a cease-fire and to abide by previous UN resolutions. President George H. W. Bush (r. 1988–93) and his advisers agreed not to try to advance to BAGHDAD and overthrow Saddam Husayn because of the tremendous costs in life and resources this would involve. Instead, on April 3, the UN Security Council passed Resolution 687, which set terms for a permanent cease-fire and required Iraq to allow on-site inspections for weapons of mass destruction, renounce terrorism, and pay reparations from its oil revenues. The coalition withdrew its forces from southern Iraq, but later, in 1992–93, the United States and Great Britain created zones in the airspace over the northern and southern thirds of the country where Iraqi military aircraft were not allowed to fly (known as no-fly zones). These were to protect the Kurds, an ethnic group in northern Iraq, and the Shia from Husayn's forces, but they also gave the United States and Britain the ability to strike at his forces whenever necessary.

The religious dimensions of this war were complex. Many Muslim authorities and Islamic activist groups quickly reacted to the invasion of Kuwait by condemning Husayn and Iraq. EGYPT, SYRIA, and Saudi Arabia joined the U.S.-led coalition. Although some Islamic leaders favored using non-Muslim troops to protect Saudi Arabia and expel Iraq from Kuwait, most leading voices advocated letting Muslim countries resolve the conflict among themselves. Also, some Islamist groups objected that the stationing of non-Muslim troops in Saudi Arabia would profane the holy cities of MECCA and MEDINA, and many were suspicious of American and Israeli hegemonic designs on the region. Saddam Husayn himself appealed to the support of Muslims on such grounds, even though many in the region regarded him as a religious hypocrite and disbeliever. In an effort to enhance his Islamist credentials, Husayn added the religious phrase Allah akbar (God is greatest) to the Iraqi flag.

The MUSLIM BROTHERHOOD in Egypt and its counterpart in PAKISTAN, the JAMAAT-I ISLAMI, joined those who first condemned Saddam Husayn's actions, but as the war progressed, they voiced their opposition to the coalition force, fearing that it secretly wanted to recolonize Muslim lands. Many North African Muslim leaders held similar views. Public opinion in JORDAN was strongly pro-Iraqi, and the Muslim Brotherhood effectively mobilized to win seats in parliament and in King Husayn ibn Talal's (r. 1950–99) cabinet. Iran's Shii revolutionary government opposed both Saddam Husayn's invasion of Kuwait and the dispatching of American troops to the region, even going so far as to call for a JIHAD against the United States. They proceeded to finalize a cease-fire with Iraq and offered sanctuary to Iraq's air force so that it would not be destroyed.

The response of Iraqi Shia to the war was especially noteworthy. Shii opposition groups such as the Supreme Council for Islamic Revolution in Iraq (SCIRI) and the Daawa Party, which had been forced into exile by Husayn's government, hoped that the regime would fall, but they did not want to see their country destroyed by a full-scale war. They also began to favor the creation of a more democratic government. Shii leaders joined leaders of secular Iraqi opposition groups in calling for a popular uprising against Husayn during the war. When it was evident that Iraq would be defeated, these calls intensified. Further incitement for a rebellion was provided by President Bush on February 15, 1991, when he called on "the Iraqi military and the Iraqi people to take matters into their own hands" (Sifry and Cerf, 96). Their rebellion actually started during the first week in March in southern Iraq, quickly spreading to Kurdish areas in the north. It included disaffected members of the regular armed forces as well as civilians. However, when it became evident that the United

States was not going to help the rebels, Husayn's elite Revolutionary Guard acted with deadly force to end the rebellion. In less than two weeks, it was completely smashed. Estimates indicate that as many as 100,000 Kurds and 130,000 Shiis had been killed in the uprising alone. Great damage was done to Shii cities, towns, and shrines in the south as well as to Kurdish population centers in the north.

THE GULF WAR OF 2003– (ALSO CALLED THE SECOND GULF WAR AND OPERATION IRAQI FREEDOM)

This war, which is ongoing at this writing (August 2008), consists of two phases. Although targets in southern Iraq were subject to periodic aerial bombings by American warplanes in 2002, the first phase of the war proper began on March 20, 2003. It opened with massive "shock-and-awe" aerial attacks and a full-scale ground invasion northward from Kuwait by a coalition force composed mainly of U.S. and British troops. Kurdish militias joined with U.S. Special Forces to secure territory in northern Iraq. The invasion force achieved a quick victory on the battlefield and took control of Baghdad on April 9, overthrowing the BAATH PARTY–controlled government of Saddam Husayn. The second phase of the conflict involved a U.S.-led occupation of the country and a largely low-intensity war against loosely organized Iraqi resistance fighters and a small but deadly force of foreign radical Muslims who infiltrated the country during the occupation to fight the Americans. During this phase, governance of the country shifted from a Provisional Coalition Authority headed by an American administrator (Paul Bremer) to an interim Iraqi government and then to an elected government based on a new democratic constitution. The new government had majority Shii representation for the first time in Iraq's modern history. However, significant numbers of Iraqis, most of them disenfranchised Sunni Arabs, did not accept the legitimacy of this government. There have been numerous attacks on civilians by a variety of militias and Muslim jihadists, leading some observers to conclude that this second phase of the war has actually become a civil war between the Sunni Arab minority and the Shii majority. Altogether, the war and occupation have exacted a high toll from the Iraqi people—more than 100,000 lives lost, many more injured, up to 4 million Iraqi REFUGEES, and billions of dollars of damage done to the infrastructure and the economy.

This war, unlike the previous Gulf wars, was not caused by an overt act of Iraqi aggression. Rather, it was caused by a combination of several factors, including a perceived threat that Iraq *might* act aggressively (it had violated 17 UN Security Council resolutions). A small group of U.S. policy makers and commentators, now known as the Neocons (an abbreviation of "Neoconservatives"), were unhappy with the outcome of the 1990–91 Gulf War because they had wanted to see Saddam Husayn's government completely removed from power in order to create a Middle East that was more favorable to American strategic interests. They met periodically with a group of Iraqi exiles, known collectively as the Iraqi National Congress (INC), and lobbied in Washington for bringing about "regime change" in Iraq during the latter part of the 1990s. As part of their strategy, they promoted continuation of the UN-authorized embargo, even though many countries favored normalizing relations with Iraq and a UN human rights agency estimated that as many as 500,000 Iraqi children had died as a result of the embargo during the first 10 years that it was in effect.

The election of George W. Bush as president in 2000 brought many of the Neocons into power, so immediately after the terrorist attacks of September 11, 2001, concrete steps were taken for going to war against Iraq as part of a global "war against terrorism." Even though there was no Iraqi involvement in the 9/11 attacks, Bush administration officials argued that with its weapons of mass destruction, it posed an imminent threat to the United States and its allies, despite the absence of conclusive evidence that Iraq, in fact, still had such weapons. Weapons inspections and intelligence assessments conducted before and after the war have shown that most, if not all, of Iraq's arsenal of lethal weapons had been destroyed or significantly degraded since the mid-1990s as a result of the UN inspections.

Alternatively, the Bush administration argued that the replacement of Husayn's government by a democratic government would help spread the cause of freedom in the region, provide its people with greater security, and help resolve the Israeli-Palestinian conflict. Consequently, the invasion was called Operation Iraqi Freedom. On a more practical level, having a friendly government in Baghdad that allowed American troops to be stationed in the country would assure U.S. control of the world's oil supply at a time of growing demand by newly industrializing nations, especially CHINA and INDIA. Iraq has the fourth-largest proven oil reserves in the world and a strategically dominant location vis-à-vis other oil-producing nations in the Middle East.

The third Gulf War has had a significant impact on the dynamics of Islamic politics and radicalism in the early 21st century. Above all, it has brought Shii Muslims into power where there had previously been a secular Arab regime consisting mostly of Sunnis. Instead of the Baath Party, the dominant parties in the government now are the Daawa Party and the Supreme Council of Islamic Revolution in Iraq (renamed Supreme Islamic Iraqi Council in May 2007), both of which are Islamic organizations that had been opposed to Saddam Husayn's regime and had received protection, support, and training from the revolutionary Shii government in Iran. In addition, two Shii religious figures have risen to national prominence in the country—the venerable Ayatollah Ali Sistani (b. 1930), an expert in the SHARIA, and Muqtada al-Sadr (b. 1973), who comes from a prominent family of Shii religious authorities and controls a Shii militia. Despite U.S. military presence in the country, the war has also given Iran the opportunity to influence Iraqi affairs in a way that it has not been able to do since the days of the SAFAVID DYNASTY in the 17th century, when it was part of the Safavid Empire. Leaders of Saudi Arabia and Jordan, meanwhile, have expressed concern that the war has allowed the Shia to exercise more influence throughout the Middle East, from LEBANON to the Persian Gulf, creating what some observers have called a "Shii Crescent."

At the same time, radical Sunni Muslim organizations, led by AL-QAIDA, have declared a jihad on U.S. and British troops in Iraq, using the foreign occupation of a Muslim country in their propaganda to win new recruits. In addition to attacking U.S. and British troops, they have also been held responsible for killing Shii civilians in suicide bombings and assassinations. Inspired by WAHHABISM, they regard Shiism as a form of unbelief and oppose the cooperation of Shii officials in the Iraqi government with U.S. authorities. Their actions have contributed significantly to sectarian violence between Iraqi Shiis and Sunnis. Radical Islamic groups and overt Shii-Sunni sectarian violence were not present in Iraq when it was under Baath control prior to Operation Iraqi Freedom. Experts have expressed concern that these forces may further destabilize the entire region and put the world's oil supply in jeopardy.

See also DAAWA PARTY OF IRAQ; GULF STATES; ISLAMISM.

Further reading: George Packer, *Assassin's Gate: America in Iraq* (New York: Farrar, Strauss & Giroux, 2005); James Piscatori, ed., *Islamic Fundamentalisms and the Gulf Crisis* (Chicago: The Fundamentalism Project, American Academy of Arts and Sciences, 1991); Anthony Shadid, *Night Draws Near: Iraq's People in the Shadow of America's War* (New York: Henry Holt, 2005); Micah L. Sifry and Christopher Cerf, eds., *The Iraq War Reader: History, Documents, Opinions* (New York: Simon & Schuster, 2003).

H

hadd *See* CRIME AND PUNISHMENT.

hadith (Arabic: speech, report, narrative)

A hadith is a short report, story, or tradition about what MUHAMMAD (d. 632), the historical founder of the Islamic religion, said or did and about what he did *not* say or do. The word *hadith* is also used with reference to the body of such reports, known as *the hadith*. There were literally thousands of hadith circulating in the Muslim community in oral and written form in Islam's first century. These were eventually collected into books during the ninth and 10th centuries. These reports are part of a very large corpus of such accounts that govern Islamic law, religious practice, belief, and everyday life. Most Muslims believe that the hadith should complement the QURAN. As such, it embodies one kind of revealed truth that defines the SUNNA, or the authentic code of action approved by Muhammad as the foremost prophet of Islam. Throughout Islamic history, each of the major Islamic traditions—SUNNISM, SHIISM, and SUFISM—has looked to the hadith for guidance and inspiration.

In its classic form, a hadith is composed of two parts, a chain of transmitters (the *isnad*) and the main text (*matn*) of the report. A hadith from the chapter on beverages in the collection of Muslim ibn al-Hajjaj states:

> Abd Allah ibn Muadh al-Anbari told us that he was told by Shuba on the authority of Abu Ishaq on the authority of al-Bara who said that Abu Bakr the Truthful said, "When we went from Mecca to Medina with the Prophet, we passed by a shepherd. God's Messenger had become thirsty, so I milked [an animal] and brought some milk to him. He drank it until his thirst was quenched."

The list of transmitters here goes back in time from Muslims in the ninth century to Muhammad in the seventh century. ABU BAKR, a close companion of Muhammad and the first CALIPH (r. 632–634), was the witness. The sunna, or religious norm, is contained in the main text, which upholds the permissibility of drinking milk fresh from an animal, no doubt a widespread practice in Arabia at the time. Hadith can also express prohibitions. In the same chapter on beverages, Muslim includes a hadith transmitted by AISHA, Muhammad's wife, which prohibits intoxicating drinks. According to this hadith, Muhammad said, "Every beverage that intoxicates is forbidden

[HARAM].". It thus complements and expands upon the Quran's ban against drinking wine. In addition to matters of belief and practice, the hadith also contain historical information and Quran commentary (TAFSIR).

A very special kind of hadith is the *hadith qudsi* (holy hadith). This is one that contains a saying attributed to God by Muhammad but not found in the Quran. Although it is a divine saying, it is not regarded with the same authority as a verse from the Quran, and modern scholars think that many holy hadith originated late in the eighth century, long after Muhammad's time. This kind of hadith usually narrates a teaching about God, the virtues of piety, and the end of the world. In one of the most popular holy hadith discussed by Sufis, God says, "I was a hidden treasure that wished to be known, so I created the universe so that I might be known." In another, found in several Sunni collections, God says, "Spend [in charity], O son of Adam, and I shall spend on you." This one promises blessings for the generous.

The earliest of the major Sunni collections was the *Musnad* of IBN HANBAL (d. 855). It was organized according the names of the COMPANIONS OF THE PROPHET, who were originally credited in the *isnad* with having transmitted the hadith. He started with reports attributed to the first four caliphs (Abu Bakr, UMAR, UTHMAN, and ALI) and concluded with hadith transmitted by women, most notably Aisha and other wives of the Prophet. The renowned traditionist of Baghdad reportedly gathered a total of about 700,000 hadith, narrated by more than 900 companions, of which he selected 30,000 for his *Musnad*. Ibn Hanbal's staunch defense of the hadith at a time when others wanted to base religion and law on human reason and personal opinion made him the leader of the *ahl al-hadith* (Hadith partisans) movement in Abbasid Iraq during the ninth century, which contributed significantly to the formation of the Islamic legal tradition.

The six most authoritative and canonical hadith collections recognized by Sunnis are those of al-Bukhari (d. 870), Muslim ibn al-Hajjaj (d. 874), Abu Daud (d. 888), al-Tirmidhi (d. 892), Ibn Maja (d. 892), and al-Nasai (d. 915). Of these, the first two are considered to be the most correct and are thus called "the two correct ones" (*al-sahihan*). All six are arranged by subject, like the Jewish Talmud (the oral TORAH of MOSES). Muslim's collection, for example, is organized into "books" on the following topics: matters of FAITH, ritual purity, PRAYER, ALMSGIVING, FASTING, HAJJ, commercial transactions and oaths, criminal punishments, JIHAD, government, sacrifice, drinks, dress, greeting and visitation, and miscellany, including accounts about the AFTERLIFE and Quran commentary. Muslim is reported to have gathered some 300,000 hadith in his lifetime, of which only an estimated 3,000 were included in his collection.

The Shia developed their own authoritative hadith collections by the 10th century. These collections were based on statements attributed to the imams, starting with ALI IBN ABI TALIB (d. 661), and they generally upheld Shii doctrines about them. They did not include hadith transmitted by the first three caliphs and many of the companions because the Shia authorities considered these individuals corrupt usurpers who prevented members of Muhammad's household from assuming leadership of the Islamic UMMA. Among the leading Shii collections are those of al-Kulayni (d. 939), Ibn Babuya al-Qummi (d. 991), and Muhammad al-Tusi (d. 1067). Perhaps the most comprehensive later Shii hadith collection is Muhammad Baqir al-Majlisi's *Bihar al-anwar* (Oceans of Lights), completed around 1674. The modern printed edition of this book consists of more than 110 volumes.

Sufis also valued the hadith, especially those that endorsed their spiritual disciplines and teachings. They were not averse to using narratives of questionable authenticity, but they also knew how to win the approval of literal-minded ULAMA by citing hadith from the canonical collections. Thus, in his book of Sufi biographies, called The

Generations of the Sufis (*Al-Tabaqat al-sufiyya*), al-Sulami (d. 1091) links the sayings of prominent mystics to the hadith of Muhammad.

Muslim scholars recognized very early on, certainly by the middle of the eighth century, that some of the hadith had been forged or transmitted carelessly. Hadith transmitters and collectors even attacked each other for doing so. Moreover, because so much of law and doctrine was founded on hadith, they needed to be assessed according to their *degree* of authenticity or lack thereof. Such concerns led to the development of a science of hadith criticism (*ilm al-hadith*). The focus of this science was on the names of transmitters listed in the *isnad*. Hadiths were basically judged according to how continuous the line of transmitters was. Hadith with the most continuous lines were called *sahih* (correct, sound), as long as the content did not contradict the Quran. If an *isnad* was discontinuous or had unreliable transmitters, then the hadith was called *hasan* (good). If a hadith had transmitters known to be unreliable or if the content was not in conformity with the Quran and had unacceptable content, then it was called *daif* (weak). The need to know who the transmitters were, where they lived, when they converted to Islam, and so forth helped spark the writing of biographical encyclopedias, which became a major genre of Islamic and Arabic literature.

Since the late 19th century, Western scholars of Islamic studies, especially those known as Orientalists, have treated the hadith with even more skepticism than medieval Muslim scholars. They have argued that the hadith were either verbalized survivals of pre-Islamic custom, legitimated during the Islamic period by attributing them to Muhammad and his companions, or they were fabricated a century or more after Muhammad's death to legitimate practices and beliefs that emerged after the seventh century. Scholarly consensus in recent decades has moved closer to the position accepted by most Muslims—that many, if not most, of the hadith are authentic, but they still demand critical assessment. Beyond the question of authenticity, however, the most critical question facing Muslims today is whether and how the hadith can still inform Muslim life in the age of globalization and profound social and cultural change.

See also AKHBARI SCHOOL; AUTHORITY; BIOGRAPHY; *FIQH*; ORIENTALISM; SHARIA.

Further reading: Hadith translations: Husayn al-Baghawi, expanded by Wali al-Din al-Khatib al-Tribizi, *Mishkat al-Masabih* (*The Niche for Lamps*). Translated by James Robson, 4 vols. (Lahore: Sh. Muhammad Ashraf, 1964–1966); Muslim ibn al-Hajjaj, *Sahih Muslim: Being Sayings and Doings of the Prophet Muhammad as Narrated by His Companions and Compiled under the Title al-Jami al-Sahih by Imam Muslim*. Translated by Abdul Hamid Siddiqi (Lahore: Sh. Muhammad Ashraf, 1971–1973); John Alden Williams, *The Word of Islam* (Austin: University of Texas Press, 1994), 36–65. **Secondary works:** Frederick Mathewson Denny, *An Introduction to Islam* (Upper Saddle River, N.J.: Pearson/Prentice Hall, 2006); William A. Graham, *Divine Word and Prophetic Word in Early Islam* (The Hague and Paris: Mouton, 1977); Etan Kohlberg, "Shii Hadith." In *The Cambridge History of Arabic Literature*. Vol. I, *Arabic Literature to the End of the Umayyad Period*, edited by A. F. L. Beeston et al., 299–307 (Cambridge: Cambridge University Press, 1983); Muhammad Zubayr Siddiqi, *Hadith Literature: Its Origin, Development and Special Features* (Cambridge: Islamic Texts Society, 1993).

Hagar (Arabic: Hajar) *biblical maidservant of Abraham and mother of his son Ishmael, whom Muslims include in the ancestry of the Arab peoples and the prophet Muhammad*

Islamic understandings of Hagar are based on two stories found in the book of Genesis, the first book of the Hebrew Bible, or Old Testament. According to the first of these stories, Hagar was the Egyptian servant girl whom Sarah, the wife of ABRAHAM, gave to her husband to bear his child because she herself was barren. After Hagar became pregnant, Sarah exiled her to the desert, where she encountered an ANGEL who told her to return to Abraham's household to give birth to their son Ishmael (Gen. 16:1–16). The second story takes place after Sarah gave birth to her own child, Isaac, and expelled Hagar and Ishmael into the desert once again because Sarah did not want Ishmael to share Abraham's inheritance with her son. When Hagar and Ishmael ran out of food and water, the angel of God provided them a well of water and promised to make the descendants of Ishmael "a great nation" (Gen. 21: 8–21). Modern scholars think that these stories were an attempt by Hebrew authors living in the 10th century B.C.E. to explain the origins of the BEDOUIN nomads of Syria-Palestine. These stories were later commented and expanded upon by Jewish rabbis.

Islamic narratives about Hagar were included in QURAN commentaries (but not in the Quran itself), "tales of the prophets" literature (*Qisas al-anbiya*), and early histories of MECCA. These stories were transposed to the Arab-Islamicate milieu from rabbinic Judaism between the eighth and 11th centuries C.E. Reflecting this new context, Hagar, for example, was called both an Egyptian and a Copt (an Egyptian Christian). The wilderness where Hagar and Ishmael were exiled was identified with the ancient site of Mecca in Arabia and the angel of God with GABRIEL, the angelic messenger to Muslim prophets. According to Islamic accounts, Hagar, in her search for water, ran between Safa and Marwa, two hills adjacent to the future site of the KAABA in Mecca, before Gabriel provided her and her son with water from the spring of ZAMZAM. Hagar's search was memorialized in the seven runnings performed by pilgrims to Mecca between Safa and Marwa during the Greater and Lesser Pilgrimages (the HAJJ and the UMRA). In a similar manner, the location of the sacrifice of Abraham was transferred to the Mecca territory, and in one Islamic version of the story, SATAN attempted to recruit Hagar to dissuade Abraham from sacrificing his son. She steadfastly refused. Both Hagar and Ishmael reportedly died in Mecca and were buried next to the Kaaba in a place called the Hijr, which remains part of the Sacred Mosque precinct today.

Both Hagar and Ishmael were included in the genealogies of the Arab peoples and the prophet Muhammad, thus making them part of the Abrahamic heritage. Muhammad was once reported to have said to one of his companions, "When you conquer EGYPT, be kind to its people, for they have the covenant of protection and are your kinfolk." This was because Hagar, the mother of Ishmael, was an Egyptian.

See also ARABIC LANGUAGE AND LITERATURE; CHILDREN; COPTS AND THE COPTIC CHURCH.

Further reading: Reuven Firestone, *Journeys in Holy Lands: The Evolution of the Abraham-Ishmael Legends* (Albany: State University of New York Press, 1990); Ahmad ibn Muhammad al-Thalabi, *Arais al-majalis fi qisas al-anbiya, or "Lives of the Prophets."* Translated by William M. Brinner (Leiden: E.J. Brill, 2002).

hajj

The fifth pillar of Islam is the annual pilgrimage to MECCA, called the hajj, which all Muslims are required to perform at least once in their lifetimes if they are able to. This religious journey, which is forbidden to non-Muslims, involves a series of ritual activities that pilgrims called hajjis must perform over a period of six days during the 12th month of the Muslim CALENDAR, Dhu al-Hijja ("pilgrimage month"). The rituals are performed in a sacred landscape that includes the Sacred Mosque in Mecca, the town of Mina (about three miles east of the Grand Mosque), and the plain of ARAFAT (about seven miles east of Mina). In addition, many pilgrims visit MUHAMMAD's MOSQUE in MEDINA on their way to or from Mecca.

The QURAN and SUNNA provide authorization for the hajj rituals, which are believed to have been initiated by sacred figures in Islamic history: ADAM, ABRAHAM, HAGAR (Abraham's wife), and especially Muhammad. The essential hajj rituals

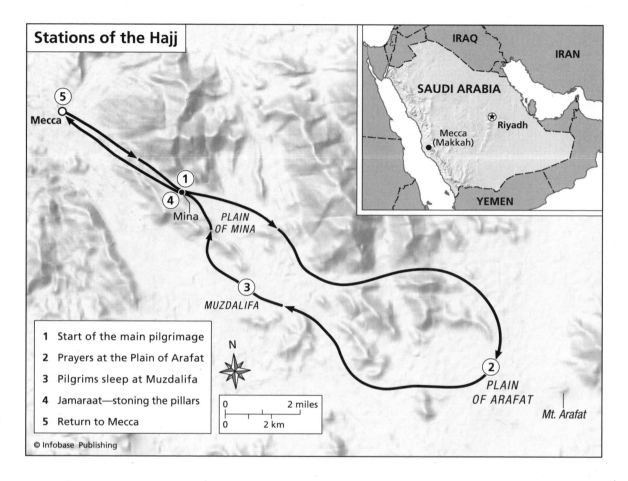

Stations of the Hajj

1 Start of the main pilgrimage
2 Prayers at the Plain of Arafat
3 Pilgrims sleep at Muzdalifa
4 Jamaraat—stoning the pillars
5 Return to Mecca

© Infobase Publishing

are performed in and around the city of Mecca. They include 1) statement of intention and purification of the body, 2) inaugural circumambulation of the KAABA seven times, 3) running between the hills of Safa and Marwa seven times, 4) encampment at Mina, 5) standing at the plain of Arafat at midday on 9 Dhu al-Hijja, 6) spending the evening at Muzdalifa (between Arafat and Mina), 7) stoning the three "satanic" pillars at Mina, 8) ANIMAL sacrifice, and 9) farewell circumambulation of the Kaaba. Standing at Arafat is the most important of these rites, and if it is missed, the hajj is disqualified. The animal sacrifice is celebrated worldwide by Muslims as a HOLIDAY, known as ID AL-ADHA. *FIQH* literature spells out the details

of each of these rituals, and most pilgrims must rely on expert guides and handbooks in order to complete the requirement successfully. Muslims believe that the hajj is an expression of repentance and obedience to God as well as a demonstration of their unity. Many consider the assembly of pilgrims in their simple white garments at Arafat to be a rehearsal for the resurrection of the dead and JUDGMENT DAY.

The hajj has its origins in ancient Middle Eastern religious practices that were performed in western Arabia well before the appearance of Islam. Muhammad's Farewell Hajj, which occurred shortly before his death in 632, is the model that all other Muslims follow when they perform the pilgrimage. Later Muslim rulers were responsible for supporting the pilgrimage and maintaining the holy sites in Mecca. They helped supply provisions and organize pilgrim caravans that traveled overland via the cities of CAIRO, DAMASCUS, BAGHDAD, Basra, and Sanaa or by boat to the Red Sea port of Jidda. Before modern times, the journey to Mecca could be quite hazardous; pilgrims might be attacked by thieves or die of disease. Only a few thousand were usually able to go, but today, with the availability of motorized transportation such as the automobile and the airplane, as many as 2.5 million Muslims perform the hajj each year. To accommodate such large numbers of pilgrims, the government of SAUDI ARABIA has spent more than $100 billion dollars since the 1950s to modernize and expand the pilgrimage facilities. To make the pilgrimage safer and more manageable, it has cooperated with the governments of other Muslim countries to set quotas for the number of pilgrims each of them is allowed to send. Other Muslim governments, such as those of EGYPT, PAKISTAN, TURKEY, INDONESIA, and MALAYSIA, play important roles in the regulation of the pilgrimage, which helps demonstrate their support for Islam to their citizens.

See also FIVE PILLARS; UMRA; ZIYARA.

Further reading: Robert R. Bianchi, *Guests of God: Pilgrimage and Politics in the Islamic World* (Oxford: Oxford University Press, 2004); David Long, *The Hajj Today: A Survey of the Contemporary Pilgrimage to Makkah* (Albany: State University of New York Press, 1979); F. E. Peters, *The Hajj: The Muslim Pilgrimage to Mecca and the Holy Places* (Princeton, N.J.: Princeton University Press, 1994); Michael Wolfe, *The Hadj: An American's Pilgrimage to Mecca* (New York: Grove Press, 1993).

hal (Arabic: condition, state of being)

Religious experience is seen by many as a defining feature of religion itself. Scholars of religion hold different points of view as to whether it constitutes an extraordinary type of experience or whether it is conditioned by language, culture, and perception—in other words, by ordinary human existence in the world. In the comparative study of religions, a dual classification of religious experience has been proposed—theistic and nontheistic. The first involves personal encounters with a god that are discontinuous with everyday lived experience, such as those attributed to MOSES, Paul, MUHAMMAD, and Teresa of Avila. The second is based on impersonal encounters with a more abstract force or principle of order, such as those found in esoteric Hinduism and Buddhism. Some scholars make a differentiation between profoundly powerful external experiences and contemplative inward experiences.

Hal is a term the Sufis have used in their discourses to describe a kind of theistic, inward religious experience. They adapted it from the technical vocabulary of early Muslim scholars of Arabic language, medicine, and philosophy. Al-Muhasibi (d. 857) of Basra, a contemplative mystic, is thought to have been the first to have employed it in relation to mystical experience. The *hal* was understood as an inner state or spiritual "encounter" that descends from God into the heart of the mystic. Most Sufi thinkers considered it to be a spontaneous state of grace, or "flash of lightning," that was one of many possible states in the quest for higher consciousness, or intimate knowledge of God. Unlike the MAQAM, or spiritual "station," the *hal* could *not* be attained as a result of the Sufi's own intentions or efforts. Although in theory it was discontinuous with everyday lived experience, the language Sufis used to describe the different kinds of states they experienced reflected the wider world in which they lived. Among the states they identified were those of "repentance," "longing," "love," "intimacy," "contraction," "expansion," "delight," and even "terror." The leading writers who contributed to the development of the idea of the spiritual state among Sufis were al-Sarraj of Tus (d. 988), al-Hujwiri of Lahore (d. ca. 1072), al-Qushayri of

Nishapur (d. 1074), al-Ansari of Harat (d. 1089), and AL-GHAZALI of Tus (d. 1111).

See also ALLAH; SUFISM.

Further reading: Ali ibn Uthman al-Hujwiri, *The Kashf al-Mahjub: The Oldest Persian Treatise on Sufism.* Translated by R. A. Nicholson (1959. Reprint, New Delhi: Taj Printers, 1997); Michael Sells, *Early Islamic Mysticism: Sufi, Quran, Miraj, Poetic and Theological Writings* (New York: Paulist Press, 1996).

halal (Arabic: permissible, lawful)

Islam is a religion that assigns significant attention to practice. This is evident in the priority Muslims have given to performing the FIVE PILLARS of ritual worship and observing the SHARIA. Practice is an aspect of religious identity and social life, and, in Islamic belief, it affects a person's FATE in the AFTERLIFE. From the start, Muslims relied on a convenient set of categories for classifying lawful and unlawful practices. *Halal* was one of these categories, used for classifying "permissible," lawful practices in accordance with the QURAN, the SUNNA, and the doctrines of the different schools of Islamic law (*FIQH*). Its counterpart for designating unlawful, forbidden practices was HARAM. Both terms contribute to defining the ethical standards that Muslims are enjoined to follow in the conduct of their lives.

The binary categories of *halal* and *haram* (and related terms based on the Arabic consonantal roots *h-l-l* and *h-r-m*) were established by the Quran, where they were used in connection with ritual acts of worship, DIETARY LAWS, and family law. They are therefore believed to have been created by God. Moreover, Muslims believe that the range of things that God has made lawful is much more inclusive than what he has forbidden. After MUHAMMAD's death in 632, during the early centuries of the Arab Islamicate empire, religious scholars and jurists seem to have found the binary classification of practices too inflexible to regulate everyday life, so they devised an alter-

native scheme of five categories (*ahkam*), placed on a scale of acts as follows: obligatory (*wajib/ fard*), recommended (*mandub*), merely permitted (*mubah*), disapproved (*makruh*), and forbidden (*haram*). *Halal* was therefore replaced by three different degrees of lawfulness, or permissibility. Jurists ruled that performance of obligatory acts was rewarded by God, and their omission was punishable. Recommended acts were rewarded but not punishable for their omission. Acts that were merely permitted were neutral, subject neither to reward or punishment, and acts disapproved were reprehensible but not subject to punishment. This schema gave jurists more flexibility when debating sacred law and issuing judgments and advisory rulings (fatwas). In recent times, when Muslims have had to deal with different kinds of value systems and legal traditions and when some Islamic movements have sought to reformulate Islam into an ideology for mobilizing the masses, many have resorted to assessing practices once again in terms of the simpler binary categories of *halal* and *haram*.

Muslims have used *halal* most widely to categorize foods that conform to Islamic dietary laws. Meat from domesticated ANIMALS (for example, sheep, cattle, CAMELS, poultry) that have been correctly slaughtered and drained of all blood is considered to be *halal*. Other prepared foods and beverages, as long as they do not contain alcohol, blood, carrion, or other impure substances, are also classified as *halal*. Groceries and restaurants that sell food to Muslims in countries where they are a minority, such as in Europe and the Americas, often advertise that they offer *halal* foods. As the term *kosher* is used on food product labels for Jews, the designation *halal* can also be found on some food products for Muslims. Such labeling has become the subject of consumer protection laws in the United States. The usage of *halal*, moreover, extends well beyond the dining table and the grocery store. In the most widely published book on the subject, Egyptian religious scholar Yusuf al-Qaradawi (b. 1926) employs it in discussions of clothing, hair, home furnishings, pets, employment, business, bathing, male and female relations, child rearing, toys, recreational activities, social relations, and relations with non-Muslims.

See also AUTHORITY; FATWA; FOOD AND DRINK.

Further reading: Laleh Bakhtiar, *Encyclopedia of Islamic Law: A Compendium of the Major Schools* (Chicago: ABC International Group, 1996); Yusuf al-Qaradawi, *The Lawful and the Prohibited in Islam (Al-halal wal-haram fi al-Islam)*. Translated by Kamal El-Helbawi, M. Moinuddin Siddiqui, and Syed Shukry (Indianapolis: American Trust Publications, 1960).

al-Hallaj, al-Husayn ibn Mansur (857–922) *controversial early Sufi remembered for his proclamation "I am the Truth" and for the martyr's death he suffered at the hands of Muslim authorities in Baghdad*

Born in the Fars region of southern Iran, al-Husayn ibn Mansur al-Hallaj moved with his family to Wasit, a town in central Iraq. His father probably worked in the textile industry (*hallaj* is Arabic for a person in the cotton or wool carder profession). In his youth, al-Hallaj memorized the QURAN and studied SUFISM with Sahl al-Tustari (d. 896), but he was not initiated as a Sufi until he was 20 years old. Marriage did not sway him from his spiritual quest, and, traveling between IRAN, IRAQ, and MECCA, he reportedly gained a following of 400 disciples. He was also said to have visited INDIA, Central Asia, and the tomb of JESUS in Jerusalem. After performing the HAJJ to Mecca for the third time, he returned to his family in BAGHDAD and created a model of the KAABA in his house. Al-Hallaj's affiliations with rebels, Shiis, and non-Muslims eventually aroused the suspicions of conservative Sunnis and political authorities. Some of his former Sufi associates even accused him of magic and witchcraft. Moreover, while engaged in his spiritual quest for God, he made public sermons and statements that angered his opponents. In one of these, he said that Muslims could fulfill the hajj duty by performing circum-ambulations in their hearts and giving charity to the poor at home. His most famous utterance was, "I am the Truth," which his enemies interpreted to be an assertion of his own divinity. In the Islamic worldview, Truth (*haqq*) was regarded as an attribute of God. Sufis made such statements (*sha-thiyyat*) while in a state of ecstasy, implying that they were speaking in God's voice, not their own. Al-Hallaj soon became implicated in the religious and political intrigues of 10th-century Baghdad and was imprisoned for nine years. Finally put on trial by his enemies in 922, he was charged with BLASPHEMY, beaten, and crucified. His remains were burned and thrown into the Tigris River, preventing his family and friends from giving him a proper Muslim burial or from venerating him as a saint. Al-Hallaj consequently has a mixed legacy, remembered by some as a heretic and by others as a martyred SAINT. His sayings were written down and collected by his followers. He is also credited for having written *Kitab al-Tawasin*, an assemblage of meditations on MUHAMMAD, the prophet's NIGHT JOURNEY AND ASCENT, and SATAN's dialogues with God and MOSES.

See also APOSTASY; FUNERARY RITUALS; *HAQIQA*; JUNAYD, ABU AL-QASIM IBN MUHAMMAD; MARTYRDOM.

Further reading: Louis Massignon, *The Passion of al-Hallaj: Mystic and Martyr of Islam*, 4 vols. Translated by Herbert Mason (Princeton, N.J.: Princeton University Press, 1982); Michael Sells, *Early Islamic Mysticism: Sufi, Quran, Miraj, Poetic and Theological Writings* (New York: Paulist Press, 1996), 266–280.

Hamas

Hamas, an Arabic acronym for the "Islamic Resistance Movement," emerged from the MUSLIM BROTHERHOOD during the first Palestinian intifada (uprising of the West Bank and Gaza territories against Israeli occupation). With charitable, political, and militant wings, Hamas became a controversial and pervasive force among Palestinians in the late 20th century.

The Palestinian Muslim Brotherhood had a history of opposition to the secular PALESTINE LIBERATION ORGANIZATION (PLO) in the years preceding the intifada of 1987. Active in the Occupied Territories as well as EGYPT and JORDAN, the Muslim Brotherhood encouraged a rejection of secularity among Palestinians, in opposition to the nonreligious nationalism of the PLO. In the early 1980s, spiritual leaders in the brotherhood, such as Shaykh Ahmad Yassin (d. 2004), created a financial and military infrastructure that could challenge the PLO for leadership of the Palestinians. This framework became the basis of Hamas, an organization that was initially supported by the Israeli government, which hoped to undermine the PLO.

In 1987, however, Hamas unleashed itself onto the Israeli occupation of the West Bank and Gaza Strip, becoming one of the most important forces of leadership in the intifada. Indeed, Hamas claimed that it had initiated the intifada, although that is still a point of debate among historians. Hamas developed a political and theological understanding of the occupation that appealed to many Palestinians while at the same time organizing charitable, educational, medical, and housing outreach programs to Palestinians living in the dire conditions of refugee camps and under Israeli occupation. Unlike the PLO, which viewed the Palestinian condition in secular nationalist terms, Hamas expressed itself in Islamic terms. Theologians such as Yassin argued that the occupation of Palestine was an affront to all Muslims and that the presence of the Zionist Israeli state needed to come to an end for religious as well as political reasons. Hamas proposed the destruction of ISRAEL and the institution of a Muslim government in PALESTINE that ruled according to the SHARIA. This was a message that inspired many Muslim Palestinians but also alienated moderate Muslims as well as Christian and secular Palestinians and those who preferred the leadership of the PLO.

As the PLO entered into negotiations with Israel during the era of the peace initiatives of the 1990s, Hamas continued to gain in popularity among Palestinians who felt less connected to the PLO as it grew closer to Israel. The Palestinian Authority assured Israel that it would restrict the activities of Hamas's militant factions, but the emergence of a new intifada in 2000 demonstrated that Hamas was still very popular among many living under Israeli occupation. At the beginning of the 21st century, Hamas continued to be one of the most active, militant participants in the intifada against Israeli occupation and, in the eyes of many, too important a player to be excluded from negotiations. Like their counterparts in the ultra–right wing Israeli camp, Hamas became a powerful social and political force, largely existing outside the channels of public diplomacy, yet striking at the heart of the Palestinian-Israeli conflict. An indication of the movement's growing influence among Palestinians is that it won a majority of seats in the Palestinian legislative election of January 2006, a development that complicated relations with the PLO and ended any chance for reaching a negotiated peace agreement with Israel.

See also ARAB-ISRAELI CONFLICTS; ISLAMISM; POLITICS AND ISLAM; TERRORISM.

Nancy L. Stockdale

Further reading: Ziad Abu-Amr, *Islamic Fundamentalism in the West Bank and Gaza* (Bloomington: Indiana University Press, 1994); William L. Cleveland, *A History of the Modern Middle East* (Boulder, Colo.: Westview Press, 2000); Mark Juergensmeyer, *Terror in the Mind of God: The Global Rise of Religious Violence* (Berkeley: University of California Press, 2003).

Hanafi Legal School

The Hanafi Legal School (*madhhab*) is one of the four Sunni traditions of Islamic law, and it is considered to be the most widespread. It was named after Abu Hanifa (d. 767), an Iraqi of Persian heritage, who was credited by later generations of legal scholars to be its founder. The school originated in the turbulent southern Iraqi city of Kufa, one of the earliest centers of Islamic learning outside the Arabian Peninsula. Iraqi legal scholars began to formulate a legal tradition based on the assertion that their understanding of the SUNNA (authoritative practice) of MUHAMMAD was authenticated by the fact that it had been transmitted to them by the COMPANIONS OF THE PROPHET who had come to IRAQ when it was first occupied by Arab Muslim forces in the seventh century. After the QURAN, Abu Hanifa and his circle favored using individual informed opinion (ray) based on precedent and reason (IJTIHAD) rather than strict reliance on the HADITH, about which they were more cautious than their counterparts in MEDINA. In fact, the Hanafis were known as the "People of Opinion" and were opposed by the "People of Hadith." Abu Yusuf (d. 798) and al-Shaybani (d. 804) were key members of Abu Hanifa's circle of disciples who contributed significantly to the formation of the Hanafi School. The Abbasid caliphs heeded calls to create a more formal legal system and turned to men of religion to help them do this, which placed the Iraqi followers of Abu Hanifa in a position of great influence. Abu Yusuf was appointed to be the caliph Harun al-Rashid's legal adviser and chief judge of Baghdad, and he wrote a book on taxation and fiscal matters. Al-Shaybani was likewise appointed by Harun to be a judge but spent most of his career as a teacher in BAGHDAD, where he wrote a number of legal works, which formed the original core of Hanafi teachings. With the full support of the Abbasids, the Hanafi School evolved into an official legal tradition. Abu Hanifa was given the honorific title "IMAM" and credited not only for his own teachings and doctrines but also for those of his predecessors *and* successors. The school has been called the most liberal of the Sunni *madhhab*s, especially for the legal doctrines it espoused in its early years, but it became more conservative in the later Middle Ages.

From their base in Iraq, the Hanafis established new branches in the cities and towns of IRAN, AFGHANISTAN, and Central Asia during the ninth century. They were not as successful in SYRIA and EGYPT until the Ayyubid dynasty came to power in the 12th century. In North Africa and ANDALUSIA, they failed to gain any lasting footholds. However, after the precedent set by the Abbasids, the Hanafi School enjoyed the patronage of later Sunni dynasties, such as the Seljuks (1030–1307), Ottomans (ca. 1300–1922), and Mughals (ca. 1526–1857). Islamic colleges (MADRASAS) were established for the teaching of official Hanafi doctrines and those of the other major Sunni schools. Such efforts also resulted in the production of authoritative handbooks, manuals, commentaries, and compendia of Hanafi law, such as Ali al-Marghinani's *Hidaya* (12th century), Ibrahim al-Halabi's *Multaqa al-abhur* (16th century) in Ottoman lands, and the *Fatawa-i Alamgiri* (17th century) in Mughal INDIA. Governmental support, coupled with a long tradition of legal learning and commentary, helps explain the widespread influence the school has gained in Muslim lands from the eastern Mediterranean region to Central and South Asia. When these lands were colonized by European countries in the 19th and 20th centuries, their legal traditions were seriously undermined by the secular civil laws promulgated by these new powers. Nevertheless, Hanafi law was subsequently incorporated into the civil codes of many modern Muslim countries, particularly in the areas of family law and ritual. Among the places where Hanafi law is still operative, even if only in reduced form, are TURKEY, Syria, LEBANON, Israel-Palestine, JORDAN, Iraq, Egypt, eastern Europe, the Caucasus, South and Central Asia, and Muslim regions of China.

See also ABBASID CALIPHATE; COLONIALISM; EDUCATION; FIQH; SHARIA.

Further reading: Wael B. Hallaq, *The Origins and Evolution of Islamic Law* (Cambridge: Cambridge University Press, 2005), 150–177; Joseph Schacht, *An Introduction to Islamic Law* (Oxford: Oxford University Press, 1966).

Hanbali Legal School

The Hanbali Legal School (*madhhab*) began in BAGHDAD during the ninth century. It was the last of the four major Sunni legal schools to appear and was distinguished by its preference for making law based on literal interpretations of the QURAN and HADITH. The school was named after AHMAD IBN HANBAL (d. 855), the famed Iraqi hadith scholar and theologian. It grew from his circle of students, which included two of his sons, in reaction to rationalist methods and doctrines being advocated by the HANAFI LEGAL SCHOOL and the MUTAZILI SCHOOL. Hanbalis believed that they were defenders of the faith and of God's law, the SHARIA. In addition to narrow readings of the Quran and hadith, Hanbali law was also derived from the rulings (FATWAS) of the COMPANIONS OF THE PROPHET that conformed to the Quran and SUNNA and analogical reasoning (*qiyas*), but only when absolutely necessary.

Abu Bakr al-Khallal (d. 923) played a major role in creating the Hanbali School. He traveled throughout the Middle East, collecting the legal teachings and rulings of Ibn Hanbal's followers. He was also credited with writing books on theological topics and an early history of the Hanbali School. Other leading Hanbali scholars were Ibn Aqil (d. ca. 1120) and Ibn al-Jawzi (d. 1200), both of whom wrote on literary and theological topics as well as religious law. The most famous Hanbali scholar was IBN TAYMIYYA (d. 1328), who wrote copiously on all major areas of medieval Islamic learning and attempted to revive Islam by calling on Muslims to restore the original religion of MUHAMMAD and his companions. The stringent Sunni outlook of Ibn Taymiyya and other Hanbalis was reflected in their attacks on SHIISM and aspects of SUFISM, especially SAINT worship. Nevertheless, many Hanbalis were initiated into Sufi brotherhoods, and one, ABD AL-QADIR AL-JILANI (d. 1166), was even credited with founding a Sufi brotherhood, the Qadiri Sufi Order.

The Hanbali School flourished in Baghdad from the 11th to the 13th century, when it contrib- uted to the strengthening of SUNNISM and defending the legitimacy of the ABBASID CALIPHATE against its rivals. During this time, the Hanbalis also established branches in IRAN and AFGHANISTAN, but their most important new base was in Syria, which replaced Baghdad as the center of Hanbali activity after it was destroyed by the Mongols in 1258. By the 16th century, there were 10 Hanbali religious colleges (MADRASAS) in Damascus alone. The Hanbali tradition continued under Ottoman rule (16th to 20th century), even though the Ottomans favored the Hanafis. It enjoyed a major revival when the Wahhabi movement formed an alliance with the Al Saud of Arabia in the 18th century. Today the Hanbali School is the official form of Islamic law in SAUDI ARABIA and Qatar. Saudi funding and the annual gathering of pilgrims in MECCA for the HAJJ have helped make it very influential among conservative Islamic RENEWAL AND REFORM MOVEMENTS in EGYPT, Syria, INDONESIA, and parts of South Asia. Modified forms of Hanbali law and doctrine have also been embraced by radical Islamic movements in many parts of the world.

See also BIDAA; FIQH; ISLAMISM; OTTOMAN DYNASTY.

Further reading: Wael B. Hallaq, *The Origins and Evolution of Islamic Law* (Cambridge: Cambridge University Press, 2005), 150—177; Nimrod Hurvitz, *The Formation of Hanbalism: Piety into Power* (London: Routledge Curzon, 2002); George Makdisi, "The Hanbali School and Sufism," *Huminora Islamica* 2 (1974): 61–72.

haqiqa (Arabic: truth, reality)

The term haqiqa is used in many contexts in Islam with a variety of significations. It is related to the word haqq (the true, the real), which is one of the names by which God is known. *Haqiqa* is thus often used in a more abstract way than *haqq*. Unlike *haqq*, which is mentioned many times in the QURAN, *haqiqa* does not appear in Islam's holy book. Nevertheless, it has developed as an important concept in Islamic PHILOSOPHY and mysticism.

In Arabic and Islamic rhetoric, *haqiqa* refers to the essential meaning of a word or expression, as opposed to its metaphorical meaning (*majaz*). Islamic philosophy has made much use of the term in a variety of ways, but the basic understanding of *haqiqa* is as the nature or essential reality of a thing.

The concept has also been taken up by Sufis, for whom *haqiqa* is so important that it can be considered the ultimate goal of the mystic path, which is attainment of true knowledge through experience of the divine mysteries. It usually refers to hidden, as opposed to manifest, meaning, and is often used in contrast to SHARIA, the formal outward practices and laws of Islam. While Sufis often focus on the inner meaning (*haqiqa*) of a practice, most agree that the formal practice should not, however, be neglected. Sharia and *haqiqa* have, in fact, been compared to the body and spirit of religion and are said to operate together as two sides of the same coin. Other Sufis have made these concepts stages in a series of mystical development, beginning with sharia (formal practices of Islam), moving through TARIQA (mystical practices of Sufism), leading to *maarifa* (divine knowledge, wisdom), and then culminating in *haqiqa* (immediate experience of the essential reality), though the exact order of these may vary for other Sufis.

See also BAQA AND FANA; SUFISM.

Mark Soileau

Further reading: R. A. Nicholson, *Studies in Islamic Mysticism* (1921. Reprint, Cambridge: Cambridge University Press, 1978); Annemarie Schimmel, *Mystical Dimensions of Islam* (Chapel Hill: University of North Carolina Press, 1975).

al-Haqqani, Muhammad Nazim

(1922–) *mystic and spiritual teacher who pioneered the establishment of Naqshbandi Sufi orders in Europe, Asia, Africa, and the Americas*

Shaykh Muhammad Nazim Adil al-Haqqani was born and raised in Larnaca on the island of Cyprus in the eastern Mediterranean Sea. He claims descent from MUHAMMAD (d. 632) on both sides of his family, from the prominent 11th-century Iraqi Sufi ABD AL-QADIR AL-JILANI on his father's side and from the famous 13th-century Perso-Turkish Sufi master JALAL AL-DIN RUMI (d. 1273) on his mother's side. Al-Haqqani received a secular EDUCATION as a child and learned about the Qadiri and Mevlevi Sufi Orders from relatives. After graduating from high school in 1940, he went to TURKEY for his university education, receiving a degree in chemical engineering from Istanbul University. His brother's death during World War II caused him to turn to religion for solace and understanding. His religious studies focused on Arabic, Islamic jurisprudence (*fiqh*), and SUFISM. His spiritual guide at that time in Istanbul was Shaykh Sulayman Arzurumi, who initiated him into the NAQSHBANDI SUFI ORDER. In some circles, this SHAYKH was considered to be one of the leading Sufi masters in the world. Al-Haqqani's spiritual quest led him to SYRIA and LEBANON, and in 1945 he became the disciple of the Naqshbandi shaykh and visionary Abd Allah al-Daghistani, who had immigrated from the Caucasus region of southern Russia. This discipleship was to last until al-Daghistani died in 1973. Al-Daghistani instructed al-Haqqani to return to Cyprus, his homeland, and establish a branch of the Naqshbandi order. Despite opposition from secular authorities, he succeeded in building up a following there immediately after World War II and returned for visits to Syria and Lebanon. Later, he traveled to more distant destinations in Central Asia, MALAYSIA, INDONESIA, South Asia, and Russia. He began to make regular visits to Europe in 1973 and visited the UNITED STATES and CANADA for the first time in 1991 to promote his teachings and win followers. It is also said that he has performed the HAJJ to MECCA 27 times as leader of the Cypriot pilgrims. Al-Haqqani has reportedly won thousands of converts to his teachings around the world. In recognition of his commitment to resolving modern conflicts, he was elected copresident of the World Conference of Religion for Peace in 1999 and was a delegate to the United Nations Millennium Peace Summit in 2000.

The Haqqani Naqshbandi order now claims to have some 70 centers and branches in North America, South America, Europe (including Russia), Africa, Sri Lanka, Southeast Asia, Australia, and Japan. The order has small followings in Syria, EGYPT, and PAKISTAN. Its U.S. headquarters is located in Washington, D.C., and it is directed by his deputy Muhammad Hisham Kabbani, chairman of the Supreme Islamic Council of America. Despite his global journeys, Al-Haqqani still calls Cyprus his home.

Al-Haqqani was given the title "cosmic axis" (*qutb*) by Shaykh al-Daghistani, but he has since acquired other honorific titles from his followers that underscore his saintly status, including "Sultan of Saints" (*Sultan al-Awliya*), "Unveiler of Secrets," and "Keeper of Light." He is also called the religious "renewer" (*mujaddid*) of the technological age. Moreover, the Haqqani-Naqshbandi order considers him to be the 40th sufi shaykh of the Naqshbandi sacred lineage, which they believe was inaugurated by Muhammad in the seventh century. Al-Haqqani lectures widely, and his talks are recorded and published in books and pamphlets and on the Internet. In addition to teaching about Sufi understandings of love, faith, compassion, wisdom, and spiritual practices, he has also included controversial statements about the coming of a third world war and the return of JESUS and the MAHDI, the Muslim messiah. This apocalyptic strand of thinking can be traced to Shaykh Daghistani, his spiritual guide.

See also DIALOGUE.

Further reading: Ron Geaves, "The Haqqani Naqshbandis: A Study of Apocalyptic Millennialism with Islam." In *Faith in the Millennium,* edited by Stanley E. Porter, Michael A. Hayes and David Tombs, 215–231 (Sheffield, U.K.: Sheffield Academic Press, 2001); Muhammad Hisham Kabbani, *Classical Islam and the Naqshbandi Sufi Tradition* (Washington, D.C.: Islamic Supreme Council of America, 2003).

haram

The great French sociologist Emile Durkheim (d. 1917) proposed that religious life was based on an absolute division between the sacred and the profane. The sacred, he argued, encompasses those things "which are protected and isolated by prohibitions." In Islam, the term that most nearly conveys this meaning of the sacred is haram and other words formed from the Arabic root *h-r-m*. It is used to describe the sacred quality of the Grand Mosque in MECCA and the KAABA as well as other sacred places, such as the Prophet's Mosque in MEDINA and the Noble Sanctuary (*al-haram al-sharif*) in JERUSALEM. Performing the HAJJ rituals in Mecca requires that pilgrims enter into a sacred condition called *ihram* before entering the city. They must desacralize themselves when they complete the pilgrimage. In many Muslim cultures, such as EGYPT, even a family's home is said to have its sacredness (*hurma*). This means that such places are considered to be set apart from others and that access to them is restricted and governed by rules and prohibitions designed to uphold their sacred or forbidden character. Its significance extends to female family members and spouses who are considered to be legally forbidden to others. This idea is reflected in the word harim, which refers to either a sacred place or WOMEN. The English word *harem* is related to it etymologically. Haram is also used with respect to sacred months in the year, such as RAMADAN, the month of fasting, and Dhu al-Hijja, the month of the HAJJ to Mecca.

In Islamic law and ethics, *haram* has been used to classify forbidden and unlawful practices, in contrast to *HALAL*, which is used for lawful and permitted ones. The QURAN established the scriptural basis for this distinction, mainly in regard to ritual, DIETARY LAWS, and family law. Muslims therefore hold that the determination of what is permitted and what is forbidden originates from God. According to the Quran, for example, among the things God forbids people to eat are pork, carrion, blood, and food offered to other gods (Q 2:173). With respect to family law, it was forbidden to marry members of the immediate family or their spouses (Q 4:22–24). On the other hand, Muslim men were permitted to marry women of the PEOPLE OF THE BOOK—mainly Jews and Christians (Q 5:5). Muslim jurists later refined the absolute division between *halal* and *haram* by devising a five-fold scale of categories (*ahkam*) to classify all human activities: *wajib/fard* (required), *mandub* (recommended), *mubah* (permitted), *makruh* (disapproved), and *haram* (forbidden). The ULAMA have often differed and debated among themselves about how to classify specific acts according to these categories. Acts classified as *haram* were those that could be punished. These included adultery, theft, highway robbery, apostasy, idolatry, consumption of alcohol, and murder. Usury, gambling, and making money related to illicit activities and substances have also often been classified as *haram*. Some Muslims regard listening to MUSIC and dancing as forbidden activities, while some may merely disapprove of them, regard them as neutral, or see them as permissible according to the context. In the modern era, debating what is lawful and unlawful has become one of the foremost aspects of Muslim religious life, one in which more Muslims are participating now than ever before. These debates range from basic questions about owning pets and how to dress to more complex ethical and moral issues such as ABORTION, euthanasia, and warfare.

See also CRIME AND PUNISHMENT; FOOD AND DRINK; HAREM; SUICIDE.

Further reading: Laleh Bakhtiar, *Encyclopedia of Islamic Law: A Compendium of the Major Schools* (Chicago: ABC International Group, 1996); Juan E. Campo, *The Other Sides of Paradise: Explorations into the Religious Meanings of Domestic Space in Islam* (Columbia: University of South Carolina Press, 1991); Yusuf al-Qaradawi, *The Lawful and the Prohibited in Islam (Al-halal wal-haram fi al-Islam)*. Translated by Kamal El-Helbawi, M. Moinuddin Siddiqui, and Syed Shukry (Indianapolis: American Trust Publications, 1960).

harem (Arabic: *harim* and *haram*)

A harem is a separate quarters for WOMEN in a palace or upper-class house. It is also a way of referring to the women, particularly when they are a man's legal wives, concubines, female servants, and other attendants. The word itself is a rendering in Western languages of the Arabic *harim* (a sacred or forbidden place or woman) and its synonym, HARAM. The harem is also known as a *zenana* in Persian and Indian contexts and as a *seraglio,* an Italian version of a Turkish word for palace (*sarai*).

Although often associated with the Islamic religion and society, the history of the harem is complex and varied, going back to the pre-Islamic times of the ancient Mesopotamians, Persians, and Greeks. The subordination of women to their fathers, husbands, and masters appears to have been a long-standing aspect of the patriarchal organization of these societies, particularly among rulers and other elites. By veiling his womenfolk and keeping them in seclusion, a man could demonstrate his wealth, status, and power. During the first millennium B.C.E., Assyrian kings are thought to have had special quarters in their palaces for women and concubines, and the wives of nobles were required to wear veils in public. The Achaemenid and Sassanian dynasties of Persia (sixth century B.C.E. to seventh century C.E.) were renowned for the size of their harems. For example, Darius III (380–330 B.C.E.) was said to have had one with nearly 400 women. ALEXANDER THE GREAT (356–323 B.C.E.), the Macedonian conqueror, defeated Darius in battle and took control of his harem as well as his empire in 333 B.C.E. Royal harems are thought to have become even larger in the days of the Sassanians, who ruled Persia and Iraq for several centuries before the arrival of Muslim armies in the seventh century. Khusrau I (r. 531—579 C.E.) reportedly had as many as 12,000 women in his harem, probably an exaggerated figure. In contrast, Greeks and Romans practiced monogamous marriage, but honorable women were still expected to care for the home and their children, a notion supported by the philosopher Aristotle (d. 322 B.C.E.). Greek and Roman law excluded women from public life, and they were regarded as children by nature in relation to men.

The harem in early Muslim society reflected the influences of the ancient civilizations that preceded it. Pre-Islamic marriage practices in Arabia were diverse, and scholars have found evidence for both polygyny (having more than one wife) and polyandry (having more than one husband). In general, women were becoming more subordinate to their fathers and husbands in MUHAMMAD'S time, and polygyny displaced polyandry. Muhammad had a number of wives and concubines who were called upon to veil and live in at least partial seclusion at a distance from others, reflecting, perhaps, his status as prophet and commander of the believers. Nevertheless, the hadith and early historical accounts indicate that women could play roles of central importance in the early Muslim community, such as Muhammad's wives KHADIJA (d. 619) and AISHA (d. 678). Muhammad's son-in-law ALI BIN ABI TALIB (d. 661), the fourth CALIPH and first Shii IMAM, is reported to have had nine wives after the death of his first wife, FATIMA (d. 633), as well as a number of concubines, while his son Hasan (d. 669) is said to have married up to 100 women. Such practices were followed in other Muslim households, especially in the following century as wives and children of the defeated Persians were taken captive and adopted into the postconquest Arab Muslim society. Persian harem practices were probably adopted by Arab rulers at this time.

The image of a palace harem of seductive women, dancing girls, and slaves as depicted in *ARABIAN NIGHTS* fantasies is partly a product of the royal court of the ABBASID CALIPHATE (750–1258). Royal wives and daughters had their own palaces in BAGHDAD in the early days of the caliphate, but, by the 10th century, they became secluded in the palace of the ruler, out of the public eye. They were attended by slave girls, entertainers, and eunuchs; intruders could be put to death. Reports that harem women intrigued against each other to win the heart of the ruler or secure the throne for one of their sons fed the imaginations of Europeans in the 18th and 19th centuries, further contributing to the invention of exotic fantasies about harem life that found their way into fictional writings and Hollywood films during the 20th century.

New historical studies of Ottoman, Mughal, and Persian harems of the 16th and 17th centuries have yielded valuable insights about what harem life was actually like and helped dispel myths that have captured the Western imagination. This research has shown that royal harems were highly organized complex communities that assumed different characteristics at different moments in history, depending on local circumstances, personalities, and configurations of power. They often included non-Muslims as well as Muslims. Upper-class women and children were educated and trained in arts and crafts there. Harem women exercised considerable political influence in dynastic affairs and were not always secluded from the wider society. A ruler's mother, wives, concubines, daughters, and servants were involved in raising his sons and participated in the politics of arranging royal marriages and the succession. Indeed, some harem mothers and wives, such as Hurrem (also known as Roxelana, d. 1558) in Ottoman ISTANBUL, Pari-Khan Khanum (d. 1578) in Safavid Isfahan, and Nur Jahan (d. 1645) in Mughal DELHI, played central roles in affairs of state.

Harem institutions came to an end with the passing of the last Islamicate empires and the dynasties that ruled them in the 19th and 20th centuries. Nevertheless, they survive in the imaginations of the West and in the palaces of a handful of autocratic Muslim kings and SULTANs.

See also CINEMA; *HIJAB;* HOUSES; MUGHAL DYNASTY; OTTOMAN DYNASTY; SAFAVID DYNASTY; VEIL.

Further reading: Leila Ahmed, *Women and Gender in Islam* (New Haven, Conn.: Yale University Press, 1992), 17–19, 79–84; 116–123; Sarah Graham Brown, *Images of Women: The Portrayal of Women in Photography of the Middle East 1860–1950* (New York: Columbia University Press, 1988), 70–85; Ruby Lal, *Domesticity and Power in the Early Mughal World* (Cambridge: Cambridge University Press, 2005); Fatima Mernissi, *Dreams of Trespass: Tales of a Harem Girlhood* (New York: Perseus Books, 1994); Leslie P. Peirce, *The Imperial Harem: Women and Sovereignty in the Ottoman Empire* (Oxford: Oxford University Press, 1993).

Harun al-Rashid (766–809) *Abbasid caliph of Baghdad who achieved legendary status in the stories of the* Arabian Nights

Harun al-Rashid was the fifth ruler of the ABBASID CALIPHATE and ruled its vast empire from 786 to 809. A son of the third Abbasid CALIPH, al-Mahdi (r. 775–85), he was born in the city of Rayy, located near the modern Iranian capital of Tehran. His mother, al-Khayzuran, was a former slave girl from YEMEN. She was known as a woman of strong personality who greatly influenced affairs of state in the reigns of her husband and sons until her death in 789. While still a teenager, Harun was appointed to lead attacks on Byzantine armies in the West, which allowed the Abbasid forces to reach the Bosporus Strait, near the city of Constantinople, the Byzantine capital. Later, his father appointed him to be the governor of some of the wealthiest provinces of the empire, including EGYPT and SYRIA. He became caliph in his early 20s, inaugurating a great medieval Islamicate golden age. BAGHDAD, the Abbasid capital, began its rise to preeminence during Harun's reign. The empire's economic prosperity and its openness to learning from all parts of the known world contributed significantly to the flourishing of the arts and literature, Islamic learning, and the development of medicine and the sciences. Harun corresponded with rulers in CHINA and Europe. He was also a learned man who patronized artists and scholars. A man of great personal piety, he put the weight of his authority behind proponents of the emerging Sunni tradition and maintained the anti-Shii policy of his predecessors. Harun is also remembered for having performed the HAJJ nine or 10 times. He appointed followers of Abu Hanifa (d. 767), founder of the HANAFI LEGAL SCHOOL, to serve as legal advisers and judges. Abu Nuwas, the foremost Arabic poet of the Abbasid era, lived in Baghdad during much of Harun's life. The caliph's wife, Queen Zubayda (d. 831), sponsored many charitable works, most memorably a water system for pilgrims going to MECCA on the annual hajj.

Harun's portrayal in the *ARABIAN NIGHTS* is largely fictional, but it serves as a tribute to him and the splendor of his court. He conducted campaigns against the Byzantine Empire, but his rule was marred by political unrest in SYRIA and IRAN. Also, ANDALUSIA fell under Umayyad rule during his reign. In his last years, Harun ordered that the Abbasid Empire be divided between his two sons, al-Amin (r. 809–813) and al-Mamun (r. 813–833), which led to a devastating civil war. Harun died during a campaign to quell a rebellion and was allegedly buried in the city of Tus. His son al-Mamun reunited the empire after defeating his brother in battle. The height of the Abbasid golden age was reached during al-Mamun's reign.

See also ADAB; ARABIC LANGUAGE AND LITERATURE; SUNNISM; UMAYYAD CALIPHATE.

A. Nazir Atassi

Further reading: Andre Clot, *Harun al-Rashid and the World of the Thousand and One Nights.* Translated by J. Howe (London: Saqi Books, 1989); Tayeb El-Hibri, *Reinterpreting Islamic Historiography: Harun al-Rashid and the Narrative of the Abbasid Caliphate* (Cambridge: Cambridge University Press, 1999); Hugh Kennedy, *When Baghdad Ruled the World: The Rise and Fall of*

Islam's Greatest Dynasty (Cambridge, Mass.: Da Capo Press, 2005); al-Tabari, *The Early Abbasid Empire*. Vol. 2. Translated by John A. Williams (London: Cambridge University Press, 1989).

al-Hasan al-Basri (642–728) *ascetic and theologian of Basra who defended belief in free will and human responsibility for good and evil acts*

Al-Hasan al-Basri was born in MEDINA, the son of a free Persian war captive. Little is known about his life, but some accounts say that he moved to Basra (in southern IRAQ) from Medina when he was about 15 years old. He participated in the Muslim conquest of IRAN but spent most of his life in Basra, where he became a famous preacher known for his ASCETICISM and profound piety. His sermons called on people to renounce the world and fear God's wrath in the AFTERLIFE. One of his most famous teachings was, "Be with this world as if you had never been there, and with the otherworld as if you would never leave it." Indeed, al-Hasan was reputed to be the most knowledgeable man of his time in matters of religion. When the Umayyad CALIPH Abd al-Malik (r. 685–705) asked him to explain his views about FREE WILL (*qadar*) AND DETERMINISM (*qada*), he composed a brilliant defense of the free will position. Drawing on the QURAN, he argued that God had given people the ability to perform an act or not do so. If God had already predetermined people's acts, the mission of the prophets and their warnings about JUDGMENT DAY would make no sense. This was a controversial position to take, for it held people responsible for what they did or did not do. Some men of religion argued that this diminished God's transcendent power over CREATION. Rulers did not like such views, either, because belief in free will meant that they, too, could be held accountable for their sins.

Al-Hasan was honored in later generations as a founder of the MUTAZILI SCHOOL and the ASHARI SCHOOL of theology. His teachings and stories were mentioned in many works of medieval Islamic literature. He was also embraced by the Sufi tradition. His name was listed in the spiritual genealogies of most Sufi brotherhoods after that of ALI IBN ABI TALIB (d. 661), Muhammad's cousin. The Persian poet Farid al-Din Attar (d. ca. 1230) included several legends about him in his collection of stories about Sufi SAINTS, Memorial of the Friends of God (*Tadhkirat al-awliya*). These depicted him as a contemporary of RABIA AL-ADAWIYYA (d. 801), the famous female mystic of Basra, even though the two probably never really met. In one account, she rejected al-Hasan's offer of marriage by declaring that she was already tied to God. Another story tells of his throwing a rug onto the waters of the Euphrates River and inviting her to join him on it for prayer. Rabia countered by throwing her rug into the air and inviting him to join her up there instead, hidden from the sight of others. A shrine dedicated to al-Hasan stands on the outskirts of Basra today.

See also FATE; SUFISM; *TARIQA*; THEOLOGY.

Further reading: Michael Sells, *Early Islamic Mysticism: Sufi, Quran, Miraj, Poetic and Theological Writings* (New York: Paulist Press, 1996); David Waines, *An Introduction to Islam.* 2d ed. (Cambridge: Cambridge University Press, 2003).

Hashimite dynasty (also known as the Hashemites)

Descendants of the Islamic prophet MUHAMMAD, the Hashimites have played a crucial role in Middle Eastern history for centuries. Muhammad was a member of the clan of Hashim, whence the name Hashimite. This term became important during the rule of the ABBASID dynasty (750–1258), as the CALIPHATE used it to trace their lineage to the Prophet and thus secure political and spiritual AUTHORITY. However, in the modern period, the name *Hashimite* most often refers to the long-standing custodians of MECCA (until it came under Saudi control in 1924) and the modern rulers of JORDAN.

Rulers and custodians of the Hijaz and its holy CITIES from 1201 until 1925, the Hashimites' power base shifted to the newly formed nation of Jordan once they were driven from Arabia by the Saudi confederation. Through a combination of their wealth, location, symbolic importance, and political authority, the Hashimites have exercised considerable influence in modern Middle Eastern history.

The Hashimites of Jordan trace their lineage to Muhammad through his daughter FATIMA and her husband ALI (d. 661), the fourth Islamic CALIPH. Rulers of Mecca from 1201 until the Ottoman conquest of 1517, the Hashimites nonetheless maintained their custodianship of the holy city until 1924. Their status as sharifs, or descendants of the Prophet, and their long guardianship over the holy cities gave the Hashimites a certain authority among Muslims.

In 1916, HUSAYN IBN ALI (d. 1931), then sharif of Mecca, organized an army that successfully pushed the Ottomans out of their remaining Arab territories. Led by his son Faysal and assisted by the legendary British adventurer T. E. Lawrence (d. 1935), otherwise known as Lawrence of Arabia, the troops operated under the assumption that a British promise made to Husayn would be fulfilled: that, at the end of World War I, a united, independent Arab state would be created. However, the British did not honor this promise. Instead, they encouraged the League of Nations to create several new mandate territories out of the former Ottoman lands that they and the French could incorporate into their empires.

The Hashimites, soon to be displaced from their traditional leadership in Arabia, were given command of some of these new mandate proto-nations. After a brief stint ruling SYRIA, Faysal was driven out of DAMASCUS by the French and declared by the British to be king of the new nation of IRAQ in 1921, while his brother Abdullah was given control of the newly formed nation of Transjordan. Hashimite rule in Iraq ended violently in 1958, but by 1946, Transjordan received its independence and became the Hashimite Kingdom of Jordan.

Since establishing themselves in Jordan, the Hashimites have worked to create a legitimate and unified state in a region with severe tensions. The Arab-Israeli conflict has brought hundreds of thousands of Palestinian refugees to Jordan, and the Israeli victory in the war of 1967 deprived the Hashimites of their custodianship of the holy city of Jerusalem. Cast out of their traditional leadership of the holy cities of the Hijaz for nearly a century and unable to rule over the holy sites of Jerusalem since 1967, the Hashimites nevertheless entered the 21st century as important political players in the Middle East, controversial yet often-consulted rulers of a small nation wedged between contentious neighbors.

See also COLONIALISM; OTTOMAN DYNASTY.

Nancy L. Stockdale

Further reading: Beverly Milton-Edwards and Peter Hinchcliffe, *Jordan: A Hashemite Legacy* (London: Routledge, 2001); Mary Christina Wilson, *King Abdullah, Britain and the Making of Jordan* (Cambridge: Cambridge University Press, 1990).

heaven   *See* GARDEN; PARADISE.

Hegira   *See* HIJRA.

Hekmatyar, Gulbuddin (1947–   ) *Afghan Mujahidin leader and head of the Hizb-i Islami (Islamic Party); although he received significant support from Pakistan and the United States in the 1980s, he was officially recognized as a terrorist after the events of September 11, 2001*

Gulbuddin Hekmatyar is an ethnic Pushtun who studied engineering in Kabul, AFGHANISTAN, in the 1960s. Although he may have once been attracted to Marxism, he fell under the spell of the Islamic revolutionary ideology of the Egyptian SAYYID QUTB (d. 1966) and helped organize Muslim students against the growing influence of Marxist political parties in Afghanistan. After being imprisoned for his political activities in 1972–73, he joined other Afghan radicals in Peshawar, PAKISTAN, to plot a violent coup against the Afghan government with the backing of the Pakistanis. He was put in charge of recruiting support within the army. When the coup failed in July 1975, Hekmatyar escaped capture and execution and proceeded to create the Hizb-i Islami, a radical organization consisting of former university students and ethnic Pushtuns.

Between 1978 and 1992, Hekmatyar and his group conducted a ruthless JIHAD against Afghanistan's Marxist government, its Soviet allies, and rival AFGHAN MUJAHIDIN groups. He proved to be a charismatic leader known for his strategic skills and merciless treatment of his enemies. Pakistan's Inter-Services Intelligence Directorate (ISI) helped equip and train his forces during this time, and he became the chief recipient of covert support from America's Central Intelligence Agency, which was using the Afghan mujahidin in its proxy war against the Soviet Union during the closing decade of the cold war. After the Soviet withdrawal and the downfall of the Marxist government in 1992, Hekmatyar established bases south of Kabul from which he conducted attacks against his Afghan rivals. The civil war between Hekmatyar and other Afghan warlords continued even after he became prime minister in 1993. His most consistent opponents were Burhan al-Din Rabbani, Tajik leader of the Jamiat-i Islami (Islamic Society), and Ahmad Shah Massoud, leader of the Tajik mujahidin. Kabul suffered heavy civilian casualties as a result of the conflict. Meanwhile, the TALIBAN, a well-organized force of Afghan refugees and war veterans, was gaining control of much of the country with the support of the Pakistani ISI. When they finally seized Kabul in September 1996, Hekmatyar and the other warlords were forced to flee the city. After AL-QAIDA attacked the UNITED STATES on Sep-

tember 11, 2001, he sided with USAMA BIN LADIN but was forced to flee to IRAN when the United States invaded Afghanistan in October of that year. Iran expelled him and the Hizb-i Islami in 2002, and he has since gone into hiding. Hekmatyar has consistently called for attacks against U.S. and international armed forces and is considered to be a terrorist by the governments of the United States and Afghanistan.

See also COMMUNISM; ISLAMISM; TERRORISM.

Further reading: Steve Coll, *Ghost Wars: The Secret History of the CIA, Afghanistan, and Bin Ladin, from the Soviet Invasion until September 10, 2001* (New York: Penguin Books, 2004); Oliver Roy, *Afghanistan: From Holy War to Civil War* (Princeton, N.J.: Darwin Press, 1995).

hell   *See* FIRE.

Helpers   *See* ANSAR.

heresy

A heresy is a doctrine or belief that authorities believe to be false or that deviates from what is accepted by the mainstream or orthodox community. In early Islam, emergence of heresies paralleled the competition over power and AUTHORITY that followed the death of MUHAMMAD (ca. 570–632). Muhammad's dual role of prophet and tribal leader set the stage for the fusion of "right religion" (orthodoxy) and righteous rule that subsequently defined the office of his successor, the CALIPHATE. The holders of this office, CALIPHs, justified their rule in religious terms and often dismissed their opponents as religious deviants. Heresies, then, were born in conflict and received their stigma from the winning faction, which by virtue of its power established the operational norms of society.

It was the first civil war (656–661), or *FITNA*, that gave rise to the earliest heresies in Islam: the

KHAWARIJ and the Shia. Both groups diverged from what became the Sunni orthodox view of rulership. In fact, it was the divergence of these groups that led to the military and intellectual assertion of Sunni dominance. The first civil war produced only temporary political unity, but it introduced permanent religious division into the community of Muslims. Over time, the Khawarij and the Shia evolved into full-scale minority sects, with defining ideologies, mythic histories, and legal systems. And within the regions that fell under their military control, these sects had the power to create societies that reflected their worldviews, like the majority Sunnis.

Along with heresies rooted in political opposition, there were heresies of pure religious belief. In fact, the number of heresies based solely on belief multiplied exponentially as the Sunni tradition refined its views in relation to the range of religious opinion voiced within the expanding empire. Medieval Muslim sources list some 72 heretical sects in Islam. While exaggerated, this number captures the diversity and richness of intellectual engagement in early and medieval Islam. Sunni attempts to police Muslim belief by labeling opponents as heretical demonstrate the extent to which religious unity was viewed as essential to the health and welfare of the community as a whole.

In the modern period, the idea of heresy has largely fallen out of favor, though factional disputes remain. When the label of heretic is now wielded, it tends to be with the purpose of polemic rather than prosecution, although in the very recent period this latter, too, has emerged as Muslims struggle to reconcile the Islamic heritage with the intellectual challenges presented by modernity. Nonetheless, what medieval thinkers once labeled as heresies modern Muslims tend to think of as alternative schools of thought.

See also APOSTASY; BLASPHEMY; IBADIYYA, *KAFIR*; SHIISM; SUNNISM; *UMMA*.

Jeffrey T. Kenney

Further reading: Ignaz Goldziher, *Introduction to Islamic Theology and Law.* Translated by Andras and Ruth Hamori (Princeton, N.J.: Princeton University Press, 1981); Wilferd Madelung, *Religious Schools and Sects in Medieval Islam* (London: Variorum, 1985); Muhammad al-Sharastani, *Muslim Sects and Divisions.* Translated by A. K. Kazi and J. G. Flynn (London: Kegan Paul International, 1984).

Hezbollah   *See* HIZBULLAH.

Hidden Imam   *See* GHAYBA; IMAM; TWELVE-IMAM SHIISM.

hijab (Arabic: cover, partition, barrier)

The practice of *hijab,* or veiling, among Muslim WOMEN varies throughout the world. In modern discussions, *hijab* usually refers to a VEIL that is worn to cover a woman's hair, neck, and ears but not her face. The issue of *hijab,* especially as it relates to women's veiling, is one of great debate. The QURAN uses the word seven times, mostly with the meaning of screen or partition (for example, Q 19:17; 38:32; 17:45). The word is often interpreted, especially by Sufis, in the sense of a veil or barrier that stands between God and the created world. *Hijab* is further elaborated upon in the HADITH. However, the tradition of modest dress and particularly of veiling women predates the rise of Islam. Indeed, veiling was a common practice in the pre-Islamic Near East, acting as a marker of class, faith, ethnicity, and age in many cultures.

While the practice has varied through time and place, *hijab* has become a point of debate in the modern era. Non-Muslim imperialists often used *hijab* as an example of the "inferiority" of nations they wished to conquer, claiming it was a discriminatory practice that should be abolished. In the early 20th century, supporters of Westernization in nations such as TURKEY and IRAN used the formal banning of the *hijab* as a symbolic way of demonstrating that their nations were modern and progressive. However, postcolonial nationalist and religious movements have embraced the *hijab* as a symbol of Islamic piety and cultural potency.

The contemporary debate about the *hijab* reflects the complex nature of identity in a postcolonial world. Those who reject the *hijab* often argue that it is a symbol of patriarchal domination over women's bodies, a socially enforced indicator of women's submission to men. However, for many women who choose to wear some form of modest dress, *hijab* is a marker of propriety, faith, and freedom. They argue that wearing the *hijab* allows them to be recognized as "respectable" women, giving them greater freedom of movement in social situations where they may have otherwise been subjected to sexual innuendo. They embrace it as a way of rejecting the objectification of women's bodies as well as a marker of their piety. Also, they adopt the *hijab* as a symbol of their Islamic identity and view it as a historical connection to generations of Muslim women preceding them.

See also BURQA; COLONIALISM; HAREM; PURDAH.

Nancy L. Stockdale

Further reading: Leila Ahmed, *Women and Gender in Islam: Historical Roots of a Modern Debate* (New Haven, Conn.: Yale University Press, 1992); Margot Badran and Miriam Cooke, eds., *Opening the Gates: A Century of Arab Feminist Writing* (London: Virago, 1990); Fadwa el Guindi, *Veil* (New York: Berg, 1999); Fatima Mernissi, *The Veil and the Male Elite: A Feminist Interpretation of Women's Rights in Islam* (Reading, Mass.: Addison-Wesley, 1991).

Hijaz *See* MECCA; MEDINA; SAUDI ARABIA.

Hijra (Arabic: emigration, abandonment; also spelled Hijrah, Hejira)

The theme of an epic journey from home into the world can be found in the myths and sacred histories of many cultures and religions. It occurs in the origin myths of Australian aborigines and the Indian tribes of the American Southwest. The Hebrew Bible narrates the journeys of the patriarch ABRAHAM from Mesopotamia to Canaan and EGYPT and the famous exodus of MOSES and the Israelites from slavery in Egypt to Sinai and then to the "land flowing with milk and honey"—the Holy Land. The exodus is remembered every year during the Jewish feast of Passover. The New Testament Gospels describe the journeys of JESUS in PALESTINE, culminating with his Last Supper, crucifixion, and resurrection in JERUSALEM. The book of Acts tells the story of how Paul and other apostles carried the Gospel throughout the Holy Land and then to Asia Minor and Greece. Among the Asian religions, one of most famous events in the life of the Buddha was his Great Going Forth—his abandonment of wealth, home, and family in search of enlightenment. The Islamic "exodus" or "great going forth" is the Hijra, the emigration of MUHAMMAD and about 70 of his fellow Muslims from MECCA to MEDINA in 622. This event was considered so important that Muslims have designated it to be year one on their official lunar CALENDAR. The 15th century of the Hijra began in 1982.

The word *hijra* is Arabic for emigration or abandonment, but it was also given other meanings in medieval Arabic dictionaries, including "forsaking one's home or country and moving to another place." English dictionaries often mistranslate *hijra* as "flight." That the journey of Muhammad and his followers was more of an emigration than a flight is supported by the details of the accounts about the event provided by Ibn Ishaq's BIOGRAPHY of the Prophet (mid-eighth century) and other early Islamic historical sources. According to these accounts, as Muhammad gained more followers from different classes of Mecca's society, he also attracted the attention of the city's leading authorities, particularly dominant clans of the QURAYSH tribe. They were angered by the Quran's attacks on their polytheistic religion and worldly attachments, which caused them to neglect widows, orphans, and the poor. Some were outraged by the prediction that those who did not believe in ALLAH would be punished in the AFTERLIFE for their disbelief. The Quraysh tried to impose a boycott against Muhammad's clan, the Banu Hashim, to cut them off from intermarriage with other Meccans and from the city's commercial life. The boycott failed, but Muhammad's safety was seriously threatened in 619 when his chief protectors died—his wife KHADIJA and his uncle Abu Talib.

To secure the position of himself and his religious movement, Muhammad sought new alliances with tribes in nearby towns and soon completed one with the Aws and Khazraj tribes of Yathrib, an oasis town located about 275 miles north of Mecca. In return for their conversion to Islam and sheltering and protecting his followers, he agreed to serve as the town's peacemaker, a role customarily assumed by holy men in Middle Eastern societies. Muhammad also sent one of his companions to Yathrib to teach the Quran and win more converts. The new Muslims of Yathrib were called the Helpers (ANSAR). Meanwhile, persecution of Muhammad and his followers in Mecca by the Quraysh intensified; the weaker ones were physically tortured or imprisoned. Muhammad ordered his followers to emigrate to Yathrib in small groups, while he remained in Mecca with his friend ABU BAKR and his loyal cousin ALI IBN ABI TALIB. The Quraysh plotted to murder Muhammad and invaded his house only to find Ali sleeping in his bed. Muhammad had secretly escaped with Abu Bakr, and the two of them hid in a cave for three days before making their way to Yathrib. After they arrived, Muhammad built the city's first two MOSQUES and established an agreement, also known as the Constitution of Medina, that called for mutual support among the Helpers, the EMIGRANTS from Mecca, the Jews, and non-Muslim Arabs. The agreement also recognized Muhammad as the leading AUTHORITY of the new community, the UMMA. Thereafter Yathrib became

known as Madinat al-Nabi (City of the Prophet), or simply Medina.

Muslim sources also speak of an earlier hijra of Muslims to Abyssinia (Ethiopia) between 615 and 622. Muhammad may have sent some Muslims there to receive the protection of the country's Christian king, the Negus. Some of them returned to Mecca before the Hijra to Medina, but most seem to have rejoined their coreligionists in Medina after 622.

The caliph UMAR IBN AL-KHATTAB (r. 634–644) signaled the importance of the Hijra in Islam when he declared that it would be used to set the official Muslim calendar in 638. Its importance was also reflected in the division of the Quran into Meccan (pre-Hijra) and Medinan (post-Hijra) chapters. The Medina chapters contain most of the Quran's ritual rules and social laws, which originally applied to the governance of the new community Muhammad had created after the Hijra. Most of the authentic HADITH are thought to have started to circulate during this era. In Islamic law, the issue of emigration was debated by jurists when Muslims in ANDALUSIA and later other Muslim lands found themselves being ruled by non-Muslims. Some jurists, especially those of the MALIKI LEGAL SCHOOL, said that Muslims were obliged to emigrate to Muslim territories, as the Prophet had done. Others said that residence in non-Muslim lands was permissible as long as Muslims were allowed to fulfill their religious duties. In a similar vein, sectarian groups such as the KHAWARIJ called for true Muslims to emigrate from territories ruled by corrupt Muslims.

The ideal of the Hijra has continued to be an important one for Muslims in more recent centuries. Reform and revival movements in WEST AFRICA and South Asia used it to organize opposition to colonial rule. ABD AL-AZIZ IBN SAUD (d. 1953) established settlements called hijras in central Arabia, where BEDOUINS were indoctrinated with Wahhabi teachings. When INDIA and PAKISTAN were partitioned in 1947, the Muslim migration into Pakistan was called a hijra. More recently, leaders of radical Islamic movements have called upon their followers to abandon JAHIL-IYYA society, the society of infidelity, and prepare for JIHAD against disbelievers in imitation of the first Muslims of Medina. One of the most famous of these groups was the Egyptian Jamaat al-Muslimin (Muslims Group), which was known to the international media as Jamaat al-TAKFIR WA'L-HIJRA (the Excommunication and Emigration Group). It was founded in the mid-1970s but quickly suppressed by the Egyptian government. Hijra has been used in a more secular sense by Arabs and Muslims to describe their migrations to Europe and the Americas to find employment.

See also CHRISTIANITY AND ISLAM; DAR AL-ISLAM AND DAR AL-HARB; JUDAISM AND ISLAM; RENEWAL AND REFORM MOVEMENTS; SHARIA; USMAN DAN FODIO.

Further reading: Zakaria Bashier, *Hijra: Story and Significance* (Leicester, U.K.: The Islamic Foundation, 1983); F. E. Peters, *Muhammad and the Origins of Islam* (Albany: State University of New York Press, 1994); W. Montgomery Watt, *Muhammad: Prophet and Statesman* (Oxford: Oxford University Press, 1964).

hilal See MOON.

Hinduism and Islam

Prior to the advent of Islam in South Asia, the subcontinent was home to a wide variety of religious traditions, including Hinduism, Buddhism, Jainism, and small populations of Christians and Jews. By far the numerically and geographically largest of these was the complex of traditions grouped under the rubric of Hinduism, a geographical term designating the religion of the peoples who inhabited lands east of the Indus River valley, which runs through modern-day PAKISTAN. The Hindu traditions developed from the encounter between indigenous religions devoted to particular places and deities and the Vedic traditions brought by the migration of the

Aryans into the region, which began around 1500 B.C.E. The Vedic religion of the Aryans emphasized reciprocity between humans and gods, the importance of sacrifice, and precise recitation of the sacred scriptures to ensure ritual efficacy. The Aryan social structure was highly stratified, and caste hierarchy remains an element in many Hindu traditions. The Hindu belief in a multiplicity of deities contrasts sharply with Islamic monotheism. However, it should be remembered that some forms of philosophical Hinduism are monist in doctrine, a fact acknowledged by Muslim travelers to the subcontinent such as AL-BIRUNI (d. 1051).

The classical period of Hinduism that preceded significant Muslim presence in South Asia saw the consolidation of cults dedicated to the great gods Shiva and Vishnu and the goddess (Devi) in her myriad forms (for example, Lakshmi, Sita, Durga, and Parvati). By the 10th century, the major philosophical schools had emerged, the epic tales *Mahabharata* and *Ramayana* were compiled, legal and sacrificial manuals abounded, and the development of a huge corpus of devotional literature to particular deities was well under way. Hindu traditions pervaded the subcontinent. Buddhism was strong in the northeast and along the Silk Road but was waning in influence in the subcontinent as it waxed in Central, East, and Southeast Asia. This was the world encountered by the first significant influx of Muslims.

Islam first entered INDIA through long-established trade routes from the Middle East: the Silk Road in the north and ocean passages in the south. There are signs of early communities along the coast, where Muslims intermarried with local people. In the north, the first area to fall under direct Muslim rule was the Sind, conquered by Muhammad ibn Qasim in 711. The next major invasion was that of Mahmud of Ghazni (r. 998–1030), who plundered the northwest region and attacked Ismaili Muslims who had settled there during the 10th century. Accompanying him to India was the Arab polymath al-Biruni, who stud-

Tomb of Chishti saint Qutb al-Din Bakhtiar Kaki in Mehrauli, New Delhi, India *(Juan E. Campo)*

ied Indian languages, sciences, customs, and religions. His record is the first textual evidence that the ballyhooed antipathy of Hindus and Muslims is overstated. Al-Biruni's writings reveal a rich and nuanced appreciation for a great deal about Hindu culture. From the 10th century onward, the north of India was dominated by kingdoms whose ruling dynasties were Turks and Mongols. However, research reveals that the greatest CONVERSION to Islam was in the regions of South Asia, where Hinduism was least firmly entrenched. This would dispel commonly held views that conversion was either the result of force or a desire to escape an oppressive caste structure.

For most of the thousand years of Muslim dominance in South Asia, relations between Hindus and Muslims were largely peaceful, with Hindu and Muslim rulers employing high-level ministers from other religions and ethnic groups, patronizing each other's buildings and festivals, and visiting each other's holy places. This reached an apex under the Mughal emperor AKBAR, who briefly introduced a new religious system called the Din-i Ilahi, or Religion of God, inspired by his conversations with scholars and mystics from Muslim, Hindu, Buddhist, Zoroastrian, Jain, and Christian traditions. Also popular in this period and to the present day are the shared devotional practices associated with Muslim SAINTS, most notably of the CHISHTI SUFI ORDER, which is centered at AJMER, Rajasthan.

Religious differences, however, have in the past been contentious in South Asia, as they continue to be to the present day. In spite of 1,000 years of rule, Islam never became the majority faith in the region; at the time of the completion of the British conquest in 1857, Muslims made up approximately 25 percent of the population. As the Indian independence movement grew and the British prepared to depart from the subcontinent, Muslims sought guarantees of representation in government and civil services. The nationalists of the Indian National Congress under MOHANDAS KARAMCHAND GANDHI (d. 1948) and Jawaharlal Nehru (d. 1964) opposed the schemes put forward by MUHAMMAD ALI JINNAH (d. 1948) and the ALL-INDIA MUSLIM LEAGUE for a strong federated state system. As a result, when the British rapidly departed in 1947, the subcontinent was partitioned into India and East and West Pakistan. In a seismic population shift, 15 million people moved between the northwest and northeast regions, and estimates of those who lost their lives in the violent transition range from 200,000 to 1 million. The legacy of Partition in terms of Hindu-Muslim relations in India has been traumatic. Indian Muslims today remain vulnerable, less educated, poorer, and politically marginalized, despite being about 13 percent of the population, or about 130,000,000 people (the third-largest Muslim population in the world after INDONESIA and PAKISTAN).

See also AYODHYA; BUDDHISM AND ISLAM; MUGHAL DYNASTY; SUFISM.

Anna Bigelow

Further reading: David Gilmartin and Bruce Lawrence, eds., *Beyond Turk and Hindu: Rethinking Religious Identities in Islamicate South Asia* (Gainesville: University Press of Florida, 2000); Peter Gottschalk, *Beyond Hindu and Muslim* (New Delhi: Oxford University Press, 2001); Andre Wink, *The Making of the Indo-Islamic World.* 2 vols. (New Delhi: Oxford University Press, 1999).

hisba (Arabic: counting, reckoning, regulating)

The *hisba* was both the state institution for promoting good and forbidding evil and the personal responsibility of Muslims to do the same. Though the word literally means counting, it came to be accepted as shorthand for the injunction from the QURAN and the SUNNA requiring the promotion of good and the forbidding of evil, which was the subject of extensive debate in Islamic law. Although the Quran suggests that every Muslim must engage in this practice (Q 3:104), considerable difference of opinion existed concerning whom, how, and under what circumstances a person should actively pursue forbidding wrong in particular. In most cases,

Traditional public fruit and vegetable market in Cairo, Egypt *(Juan E. Campo)*

scholars wrote that the duty applied only within the Islamic community; women and disabled Muslim men were exempt, and individuals were not obligated to place themselves in danger in order to suppress any evils of which they were aware. The same verse was also understood to mean that promoting good and forbidding evil was a communal responsibility, which came to be more commonly interpreted as empowering the state to enforce the injunction.

In the early Islamic period, persons appointed to enforce the *hisba* in the community were responsible for ensuring that prayers were performed properly, MOSQUES were maintained, and market dealings were kept honest. The *hisba* was institutionalized during the reign of the Abbasid caliph Abu Jaafar al-Mansur in 773 through the establishment of the office of *muhtasib,* or market controller, in the religious hierarchy of the state. From this period, the *muhtasib* role in maintaining public morality was largely confined to ensuring proper conduct in the markets. Duties included guaranteeing uniform weights and measures and occasionally currency, keeping a record of prices and preventing hoarding in times of famine, and maintaining safe and clear roads through the city. Though the office declined in prestige after the Middle Ages, in many Muslim lands, these remained the duties of the *muhtasib* until the governmental reforms of the 19th and early 20th centuries.

Where the rise of political Islam has led to the establishment of an Islamic state or the introduction of a law code based on the SHARIA, the reintroduction of the state institution of the *hisba* has also often occurred. SAUDI ARABIA has a government department called the General Presidency of the Promotion of Virtues and the Prevention of Vices, the most public face of which is the *mutawain,* or religious police, charged with upholding morality in the kingdom. The state established by the TALIBAN in AFGHANISTAN also maintained a similar department and police force. The governors of states in northern Nigeria that adopted laws based

on the sharia in the 1990s have established sharia implementation committees or sharia monitoring police, both of which are known as *hisba,* in order to assist the government in encouraging the population to conform to the new legal code.

See also BAZAAR; ETHICS AND MORALITY; IBN TAYMIYYA, TAQI AL-DIN AHMAD.

Shauna Huffaker

Further reading: Ahmad ibn Abd al-Halim ibn Taymiyah, *Public Duties in Islam: The Institution of the Hisbah, Al-Hisba fi al-Islam.* Translated by Muhtar Holland (Leicester, U.K.: Islamic Foundation, 1982). Michael Cook, *Commanding Right and Forbidding Wrong in Islamic Thought* (Cambridge: Cambridge University Press, 2000).

Hizb al-Daawa al-Islamiyya *See* DAAWA PARTY OF IRAQ.

Hizb al-Tahrir al-Islami (Arabic, also spelled Hizb ut-Tahrir; Islamic Liberation Party)

Hizb al-Tahrir is a revolutionary Sunni Islamist party, an early offshoot of the MUSLIM BROTHERHOOD. It was founded in Jerusalem in 1952 by Taqi al-Din al-Nabhani (1909–77), a Palestinian teacher and judge who had graduated from AL-AZHAR University. In the first years of its existence, Hizb al-Tahrir opened branches in a number of Arab countries, including JORDAN, SYRIA, LEBANON, IRAQ, PALESTINE, and Kuwait. During the 1970s, its belief that Arab governments were un-Islamic led it to engage in subversive activities, including coup attempts against nationalist regimes in Iraq, EGYPT, and Syria. Guided by its unbending authoritarian religious ideology, Hizb al-Tahrir has organized itself into networks of small, secretive cells that have recruited followers in many parts of the world. It looks for new members in MOSQUES, religious gatherings, and university campuses. Its close-knit organization helps foster solidarity among its members and insulates it against outside government surveillance and arrests. Some observers have remarked that it resembles the Communist Party in organization more than other Islamist movements, even though it is overtly anticommunist and antisocialist in its ideology.

During the 1990s, increased Western military presence in the Middle East, the fall of the Soviet Union, the break up of Yugoslavia, and the Palestinian-Israeli conflicts provided Hizb al-Tahrir with opportunities to extend its reach into Europe, Pakistan, Central Asia, MALAYSIA, and INDONESIA. It currently maintains a public relations office in London, and its governing council is thought to have headquarters in Lebanon. It disseminates its ideas via numerous publications and Arabic- and English-language Web sites. However, it is banned as a terrorist organization in most Arab countries, Germany, Russia, and all the Central Asian republics, where it has gained many followers in recent years. British authorities have been monitoring it carefully, especially after the London Metro bombings in July 2005. According to one estimate, Hizb al-Tahrir has more than 20,000 members, including recent converts to Islam. Another asserts that it may have as many as 80,000 members in Uzbekistan alone (Benard, 345).

The ideology of the party centers on the goal of reuniting all Muslims into a single community under an Islamic government called the CALIPHATE, which once ruled the early Islamicate empire. This government is obligated to rule in accordance with the SHARIA, the law of God. All other political systems that govern Muslims are illegitimate and must be overcome by winning public opinion. Only by doing this will Muslims at last be free of the burdens imposed by centuries of colonial rule. Hizb al-Tahrir professes to be a nonviolent Islamic activist movement. Its British branch, for example, has joined with other Muslim community organizations to raise funds for charity and to combat drugs. However, police and security agencies suspect that its members pose a terrorist threat. Its publications purportedly equate prayer with JIHAD and TERRORISM, and it has allowed for the killing of apostates, or "those who commit aggression against the sanctities of the Muslims" (Benard, 347). It has also been condemned for being anti-Semitic and supporting suicide attacks in Israel.

See also ANTI-SEMITISM; COMMUNISM; ISLAMISM; RENEWAL AND REFORM MOVEMENTS.

Further reading: Cheryl Benard, "Central Asia: 'Apocalypse Soon' or 'Eccentric Survival?'" In *The Muslim World after 9/11,* edited by Angel M. Babasa, et al, 321–366 (Santa Monica, Calif.: Rand Corporation, 2004); Shereen Khairallah, "The Islamic Liberation Party: Search for a Lost Ideal." In *Vision and Revision in Arab Society,* Center for the Study of the Modern Arab World, 87–95, CEMAM Reports. Vol. 2 (Beirut: Dar al-Mashreq, 1975); Ahmed Rashid, *Jihad: The Rise of Militant Islam in Central Asia* (New Haven, Conn.: Yale University Press, 2002).

Hizbullah (Hezbollah)

Hizbullah is a Lebanese Shii Islamist party led by Sayyid Hassan Nasrallah (b. 1960). Its name means Party of God in English, a phrase from the QURAN describing those who will triumph over disbelievers and enter PARADISE because of their faith (Q 5:56; 58:22). The modern Lebanese Hizbullah grew out of religiously based Shii militant movements in the late 1970s and early 1980s aimed at fighting Israeli incursions into LEBANON. Throughout the 1980s and 1990s, it led the armed resistance to Israel's invasion and occupation of a significant portion of southern Lebanon and is widely credited with forcing Israel's withdrawal in May 2000. The party is committed to the eventual establishment of an Islamic state in Lebanon based on the theory of Wilayat al-Faqih, or guardianship of the religious jurist, developed and executed by Ayatollah RUHOLLAH KHOMEINI in IRAN. However, despite the theory's theological implications that all Muslims belong first and foremost to a transnational UMMA (community of Muslims), Hizbullah has in recent years taken great efforts to emphasize its Lebanese and nationalist identity.

Since the end of the country's civil war in 1989, Hizbullah has participated in elections, assuming a prominent position in Lebanese politics while maintaining an armed presence in the south near Lebanon's border with ISRAEL. While the movement claims its roots in the period prior to the IRANIAN REVOLUTION OF 1978–1979, it is generally acknowledged that Hizbullah coalesced as a fighting force only with organizational and military aid from Iran's postrevolutionary government. Other factors leading to its emergence include the historical underrepresentation of Shii Muslims in Lebanese politics as well as their economic and social marginalization, both of which contributed to a general mobilization of Shia throughout the 1950s and 1960s. In 1974, the Shii cleric imam Musa al-Sadr founded the populist Shii Movement of the Deprived and a year later its military wing, Amal. In the wake of al-Sadr's mysterious disappearance in 1978 and the increasingly discredited secular Arab nationalist ideologies with which Amal and its new leader, Nabih Berri, were associated, Hizbullah's religious message gained salience. In the early 1980s, ex-members of Amal such as Nasrallah and Hizbullah's first secretary general, Shaykh Subhi al-Tufayli, joined forces with clerics and other supporters of the Iranian Revolution to create an umbrella organization to defend Shii interests. On February 16, 1985, Hizbullah published an open letter announcing its ideological and social visions and marking its transition from a secret resistance movement to an open political one.

Today, Hizbullah maintains close ties with Iran and SYRIA, holds roughly 10 percent of the seats in the Lebanese national parliament, and controls many municipalities in southern Lebanon and the Bekaa Valley. Additionally, it provides a wide variety of social services for its constituent communities, including job training, education, and medical care. It also owns a satellite channel called al-Manar (the Beacon), over which it broadcasts a variety of religious, political, and entertainment programs.

Since May 2000, disputes over prisoners, land mines, and the Shebaa Farms have continued to fuel low-grade conflict and frequent incursions by both Israel and Hizbullah along the Israeli-Lebanese border, or "blue line." In July 2006, the conflict intensified once again against a backdrop of increasing tensions between the UNITED STATES, Syria, and Iran over implementation of UN Resolution 1559 and Iranian nuclear activities. Much of Lebanon's infrastructure was destroyed by Israeli air attacks, and heavy casualties were incurred on both sides. Ensuing diplomatic efforts focused on integrating Hizbullah's military wing into Lebanon's national forces and promoting a sustainable long-term peace agreement. Despite that conflict and efforts by the U.S. government to marginalize Hizbullah, notably through its designation as a terrorist organization, the party is likely to figure prominently in Lebanese politics for many years to come.

See also ARAB-ISRAELI CONFLICTS; SHIISM; TERRORISM.

Michelle Zimney

Further reading: Ahmed Nizar Hamzeh, *In the Path of Hizbullah* (Syracuse, N.Y.: Syracuse University Press, 2004); Naim Qassim, *Hizbullah: The Story from Within* (London: Saqi Books, 2005); Magnus Ranstorp, *Hizb'Allah in Lebanon: The Politics of the Western Hostage Crisis* (New York: St. Martin's Press, 1996); Amal Saad-Ghorayeb, *Hizbullah: Politics & Religion* (London: Pluto Press, 2002).

holidays

The two most important holidays observed by Muslims are the ID AL-ADHA (Feast of the Sacrifice), held at the conclusion of the HAJJ during the 12th month of the Muslim CALENDAR (Dhu al-Hijja), and the ID AL-FITR (Feast of Breaking the Fast), held at the end of RAMADAN during the first days of the 10th month (Shawwal). These holidays are observed with special communal prayers in the morning hours, FEASTING, gatherings of family and friends, and performance of charitable acts. Aside from these celebrations, every Friday in the year is considered to be an especially holy day because it is the day of communal PRAYER. However, it is not regarded as a day of rest like the Sabbath is in Judaism (Saturday) and Christianity (Sunday). Another important day for many is Laylat al-Qadr (NIGHT OF DESTINY), which falls in the latter part of Ramadan. It commemorates the first revelation of the Quran to MUHAMMAD. Most Muslims, with the exception of the followers of the Wahhabi sect, also celebrate the day of Muhammad's birth (*Mawlid* al-Nabi), which falls on the 12th of Rabi al-Awwal, the third lunar month. Another event celebrated by many Muslims every year is the NIGHT JOURNEY AND ASCENT of Muhammad.

In addition to these major holidays, which are observed by all Muslims, the Shia observe holy days commemorating the deaths of the IMAMS (sacred leaders descended from Muhammad) and other members of Muhammad's family (*AHL AL-BAYT*). The most important of these holy days is ASHURA, which remembers the martyrdom of HUSAYN IBN ALI (d. 680) on the 10th day of the 12th month (Dhu al-Hijja). The Shia also observe the anniversary of GHADIR KHUMM on the 18th of the same month, which is associated with Muhammad's designation of ALI IBN ABI TALIB (d. 660), their first imam, as his successor to lead the community. Members of Sufi brotherhoods celebrate the major religious feasts observed by other Muslims. In addition, they participate in pilgrimages and festivals connected with saintly men and women, especially members of Muhammad's family and their descendants. These are usually popular religious gatherings that occur at local shrines at different times of the year. Some attract millions of celebrants from far and wide, such as the *mawlid* of AHMAD AL-BADAWI of Tanta (EGYPT) and ZAYNAB of CAIRO or the *urs* of Muin al-Din Chishti in AJMER (INDIA).

Muslims share some holidays with non-Muslims. The most important seasonal holiday celebrated by people living in Muslim lands, NAVRUZ, is connected with the advent of spring. It is observed in IRAN, AFGHANISTAN, Azerbaijan, and Kurdish areas of IRAQ and TURKEY on March 21. Egyptians celebrate spring on Shamm al-Nasim (Smelling the Breeze), which falls on the first Monday after the Coptic Christian feast of Easter. Moreover, secular national holidays are observed in many countries with Muslim majorities. These usually commemorate the country's independence from colonial control, a political revolution, or a victory in war. Some countries honor the memory of their founders with holidays, such as MUSTAFA KEMAL ATATURK (d. 1938) in Turkey and MUHAMMAD ALI JINNAH (d. 1948) in PAKISTAN. Most Muslims recognize the religious holidays of non-Muslims, wishing them well on these occasions and participating in feasts and parades. Non-Muslims, likewise, often recognize Muslim holidays. Such reciprocal interfaith activities occur both in countries where Muslims are majorities and where they are minorities. In the UNITED STATES, there has been growing recognition by community leaders and the media of Muslim observance of the Ramadan fast. On the other hand, followers of radical and puritanical Islamic doctrines have denounced the observance or recognition of non-Muslim holidays by Muslims because of the belief that they are unauthorized innovations that may lead Muslims astray. Outside of SAUDI ARABIA, however, such views are in the minority.

See also BIDAA; MOON; WAHHABISM.

Further reading: Johan Blank, *Mullahs on the Mainframe: Islam and Modernity among the Daudi Bohras* (Chicago: University of Chicago Press, 2001); Tanya Gulevich, *Understanding Islam and Muslim Traditions* (Detroit: Omnigraphics, 2005); Gustav E. von Grunebaum, *Muhammadan Festivals* (1951. Reprint, London: Curzon Press, 1976).

holy books

One of the most important features common to the Abrahamic religions of Judaism, Christianity, and

Islam is the primacy their adherents give to holy books, scriptures believed to have been revealed or inspired by the one God. Jews look to the TORAH (Hebrew: "teaching" or "law"), the revelation given by God in Hebrew to MOSES at Sinai, which consists of written and oral components. The written Torah includes the five books of Moses (the Pentateuch), the Prophets, and the Writings (for example, the books of Psalms and Proverbs). The oral Torah, known as the Talmud, is said to have been inherited by the rabbis, Jewish sages, from Moses. It consists of the Mishnah (Hebrew: "repetition"), a collection of legal prescriptions plus extensive rabbinic commentaries. Scripture for Christians is the Old Testament, which includes the books of the Hebrew written Torah, and the New Testament, composed of the four Gospels of Matthew, Mark, Luke, and John, letters of Paul and other early church authorities, an early history of the church (Acts of the Apostles), and the concluding book of Revelation. In Islam, the holy book is the QURAN (Arabic: "recitation"), which Muslims believe to be the word of God as communicated to MUHAMMAD during the last 23 years of his life (between 610 and 632 C.E.). It is complemented by the HADITH, accounts of Muhammad's deeds and sayings transmitted and assembled into books by his followers after his death. Both Sunni and Shii Muslims look to the Quran and hadith for guidance, but the Shia prefer to interpret both in light of the teachings of the IMAMS (divinely inspired descendants of Muhammad).

Jewish, Christian, and Muslim holy books have historically defined communities of religious belief and action, serving as the basis for their understandings of God and his CREATION, ritual life, ethics and law, history, and ways to salvation in this world or in the AFTERLIFE. Indeed, membership in the Abrahamic communities is defined, in part, by believing what is taught in them. The communities, however, are not passive recipients of scriptures, blindly following their teachings. Rather, Jews, Christians, and Muslims continually preserve and infuse them with new life from gen-

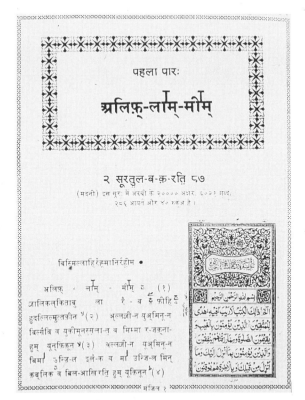

Page from modern print edition of the Quran showing the first verses of Sura 2, with Arabic text on the right and Hindi transliteration on the left (*Quran majid, New Delhi, 1987*)

eration to generation by studying and memorizing them, using them in worship, and interpreting and debating their meanings in accordance with lived experience and changes in the world around them. The ways communities give life to scripture are represented, for example, by the Jewish rabbi, a "master" of the Torah, who is charged with teaching and upholding its commandments. His counterpart in Islam is the *alim* (pl. ULAMA), "one who knows" the Quran, hadith, and the SHARIA (Islamic law). Any person who has memorized the Quran is called *hafiz,* "one who preserves" the sacred text. Muslims are obliged to recite short passages from the Quran during their five daily prayers. In Christianity, Bible readings are central to Protestant life and worship, and the Roman Catholic Mass includes a Liturgy of the Word, which consists of readings from the Old and New Testaments prior to the priest's sermon and celebration of the Eucharist. Incorporating holy books into worship helps communities maintain their meaning through the generations.

Another way in which holy books are shaped by religious communities is through canonization, the process whereby religious writings are formally selected, organized, and given authority. When religious authorities establish a scriptural canon, its contents usually become fixed. They cannot be changed or removed, and new material cannot be added. A canon of holy writings can be elaborated only through traditions of commentary and interpretation. Most Bible scholars maintain that the Hebrew texts of the Torah had been fixed by Palestinian rabbis by the end of the first century C.E., while the Talmud, sometimes called a second Torah, was fixed later in the sixth or seventh century C.E. by the rabbis of Babylonia (Iraq). Officials of the Christian church fixed the New Testament canon by the end of the fourth century. Islamic studies scholars generally agree that the Quran achieved its canonical form during the reign of the caliph UTHMAN IBN AFFAN (r. 644–656), who commanded that variant copies be collected into a single official version.

In addition to being attributed to a divine source and having a fixed canonical text, other factors have contributed to giving a holy book its holiness or sacrality. One is the assertion that it came down from heaven. This belief is most clearly expressed in relation to the Quran, which is thought to have descended with angels on the NIGHT OF DESTINY (Q 97) from an archetypal book (Q 43:4 "mother of the book," and Q 85:22 "preserved tablet") in the seventh heaven to the lowest heaven, from which GABRIEL brought it to Muhammad. The heavenly origin of scripture is often connected to the notion that even though revealed in history, it is in some sense ancient or primordial. Rabbinic

commentaries assert that God consulted the Torah when he created the world. In Christianity, JESUS is the "word" (*logos*) that existed in the beginning and then became flesh (John 1). According to the influential ASHARI SCHOOL of Islamic *kalam* (dialectical THEOLOGY), the Quran is the uncreated speech of God and is coeternal with him. Another important aspect of a book's holiness involves the belief that the language in which it is written itself is sacred, and therefore the scripture must be copied and recited according to precise rules. This is especially the case with the Hebrew language in Judaism and the Arabic language in Islam. On this basis, conservative Muslims also maintain that the Quran should not even be translated, because that would corrupt and distort God's word. Moreover, anyone who even touches the Quran should be in a condition of ritual purity.

The identification of holy books with communities is expressly recognized in Islam. The Quran declares that every community has a prophet who conveys God's word (Q 10:47). It commands its readers and listeners to declare, "We believe in God and what was revealed to us, to Abraham, Ishmael, Isaac, Jacob, and the tribes [of Joseph and his brothers], and to Moses and Jesus, and what was given to the prophets by their lord. We do not make any differentiation between them and we all submit to him" (Q 2:136). It therefore associates Jews, the Children of Israel, with the Torah of Moses and Christians with the GOSPEL of Jesus. Jews and Christians are known collectively as PEOPLE OF THE BOOK (*ahl al-kitab*), or recipients of sacred revelations from God. In the Quranic view, however, these communities ignored or corrupted the books they received, as evidenced in their failure to recognize Muhammad as a prophet and the Christian doctrine of the divinity of Jesus, which contradicted the quranic assertion of God's absolute oneness and transcendence (for example, Q 5:12–19). This made them disbelievers, although the Quran also recognizes the common ground they share with Muslims for also being recipients of a holy book.

Just as Christians had to define their beliefs in relation to the Torah (the Old Testament), Muslims had to do so in relation to both the Torah and the Gospel. Because the received form of the earlier scriptures has been altered, or corrupted, however, Muslims must look primarily to the Quran for guidance. With a few exceptions, they have not consulted the Old and New Testaments either in matters of religious belief or practice. Nevertheless, as a result of being People of the Book, Jews and Christians were allotted legal rights under Islamic law as "protected" subjects (*ahl al-dhimma*). When Muslims encountered other peoples in the Middle East and Asia, despite wars and confrontations, they eventually came to recognize Zoroastrians, Hindus, and Buddhists as also being religious communities that had received holy books. In today's global culture, traditional Islamic belief in a universal book from which all holy books are ultimately derived has provided a basis for engaging in DIALOGUE across religious and cultural boundaries.

See also ARABIC LANGUAGE AND LITERATURE; BUDDHISM AND ISLAM; CHRISTIANITY AND ISLAM; *DHIMMI*; JUDAISM AND ISLAM; SHIISM; *TAFSIR*.

Further reading: John Corrigan et al., *Jews, Christians, Muslims: A Comparative Introduction to Monotheistic Religions* (Upper Saddle River, N.J.: Prentice-Hall, 1998); Frederick M. Denny and Rodney L. Taylor, *The Holy Book in Comparative Perspective* (Columbia: University of South Carolina Press, 1985); William A. Graham, *Beyond the Written Word: Oral Aspects of Scripture in the History of Religion* (Cambridge: Cambridge University Press, 1987); F. E. Peters, *A Reader on Classical Islam* (Princeton, N.J.: Princeton University Press, 1994).

holy war   *See* JIHAD.

honor and shame

Cultural anthropologists have maintained that honor and shame are a set of cultural norms and expectations that characterizes Mediterranean societies, including Arab Muslim ones, but not exclusively so. In the Mediterranean region, the "honor and shame complex" stresses the value of dignified comportment, generosity, and family loyalty as well as bravery and independence for men and self-control and modesty for women. In Muslim societies, honor and shame are imagined to involve the application of reason (*aql*) to control base instincts (*nafs*), though parallel concepts may be found in other Mediterranean countries such as Greece and Italy. Where notions of honor and shame exist, family and tribal identity is very important, and honor killings, in which male family members murder a female relative who has transgressed a particularly serious moral boundary, involve attempts to reclaim the honor of the larger family group. Some scholars have argued that the paired ideals of honor and shame are too general to capture the important subtleties and differences among Mediterranean societies. Others have argued that these are European concepts that do not adequately capture the cultural perspectives of the non-European Mediterranean.

See also CUSTOMARY LAW; WOMEN.

Further reading: Lila Abu-Lughod, *Veiled Sentiments: Honor and Poetry in a Bedouin Society* (Berkeley: University of California Press, 1999); J. G. Peristiany and J. Pitt-Rivers, eds., *Honor and Grace in Anthropology* (Cambridge, Cambridge University Press, 1991).

horse

Horses were treasured ANIMALS in the Islamicate societies of the premodern Middle East, where they served as mounts for warriors and became symbols of chivalry and manliness. The most famous breed is the Arabian horse, a small, swift riding animal known for its beauty and intelligence. Its strength and maneuverability made it a valuable asset in battle, and it is credited with having been an important factor in the successful Arab conquest of the Middle East, North Africa, and ANDALUSIA during the seventh and eighth centuries. Arabians were also used in the sport of horse racing, and many race horses today have Arabian blood.

Experts disagree about their origin. Some say Arabians developed during the fourth or fifth century in the Arabian Peninsula from horses that had migrated from Central Asia. Others say the breed originated in North Africa. Arabians were introduced into Europe during the Middle Ages, where they contributed to the development of some of the best European breeds. They declined in the Arabian Peninsula when modern transportation and weapons technologies arrived in the 19th century, but meanwhile they became favorites among breeders in Europe and North America. In recent times, the practice of breeding Arabians has been revived in SAUDI ARABIA and JORDAN. An Arabian horse is the central figure in Walter Farley's, *The Black Stallion,* a popular children's novel (1941) and film (1979). Another famous breed from Islamicate lands is the Akhal Teke (also known as the Persian or Parthian horse), indigenous to Central Asia and considered by many to be one of the oldest breeds in existence. It has been embraced by the Turkmen culture, which has strong nomadic roots.

The horse is held in high esteem in Arabo-Islamicate literature. It was said to be the animal closest in nature to humans because of its noble demeanor. In the QURAN, horses are described as creatures that God created for men to ride (Q 16:8); elsewhere they are identified with WOMEN, children, stores of precious metals, and land as being among the beautiful things to be enjoyed in life (Q 3:14). According to commentators, having a horse in the house is a way to keep SATAN and the JINN from harming its owner. In Islamic lore, Ishmael (Ismail) the son of ABRAHAM was the first human to tame a horse for riding, and King Solomon was said to have ridden a winged horse, like Pegasus in Greek mythology. The HADITH indicate that MUHAMMAD rode horses and that he even approved the holding of horse races (with-

out betting) in MEDINA. Also, he is said to have used a magical horselike animal named BURAQ when he traveled from MECCA to JERUSALEM and ascended into heaven during his NIGHT JOURNEY AND ASCENT. Among the Shia, the most famous horse is the one belonging to HUSAYN IBN ALI IBN ABI TALIB (d. 680). This animal carried him to KARBALA, where he was martyred. It is also said that at the end of time it will be resurrected from the Euphrates River to carry Husayn once again into battle against wrongdoers.

Horses were a favorite subject for poets, and it is estimated that more than 100 books about horses and horsemanship circulated in Islamdom during the Middle Ages. These books often have detailed descriptions of a horse's physical features and markings, which are interpreted as omens affecting the fortunes of its rider. Technical knowledge about breeding, training, and veterinary care is also provided, but it differs considerably from modern methods of horse care and training.

See also ARABIC LANGUAGE AND LITERATURE; CAMEL.

Further reading: Walter Farley, *The Black Stallion* (New York: Random House Books for Young Readers, 1991); David James et al., "The Arabian Horse." *Saudi Aramco World* 37 (March/April 1986); Jonathan Maslow, "The Golden Horses of Turkmenistan." *Saudi Aramco World* 48 (May/June 1997): 10–19; David Pinault, *Horse of Karbala: Muslim Devotional Life in India* (New York: Palgrave, 2001).

houri

Houris are beautiful wide-eyed virgins who are believed to await good Muslims in PARADISE. They are mentioned only four times in the QURAN, which describes them as being pure, modest, and like hidden pearls in appearance (Q 55:56; 56:23; 37:49). Much more is said about them in medieval commentaries and stories about DEATH and the AFTERLIFE, where they are portrayed in sensuous detail, living in luxurious mansions and palaces.

Believers, especially pious men and martyrs, are promised two, 72, 500, or even thousands of houris as wives when they enter paradise in reward for their virtues and sacrifices. Sufi commentators interpret them as symbols of heavenly bliss rather than providers of sexual pleasure. Although there is no consensus on the issue, some traditions hold that believing WOMEN who go to paradise are 70,000 times better than the houris and that with their youth restored, they will enjoy reunion with their faithful husbands. The linkage of paradise virgins with MARTYRDOM on the battlefield during JIHAD first occurred in the eighth century and was elaborated in the following centuries. It was revived in the 20th century by preachers and militant Islamic organizations. Radical groups in LEBANON, PALESTINE, IRAN, and IRAQ have interwoven vivid accounts of heroic death in war and descriptions of sensuous rewards in paradise in an effort to recruit young men for battle and suicide operations against enemies.

Further reading: Maher Jarrar, "The Martyrdom of Passionate Lovers: Holy War as a Sacred Wedding." In *Myths, Historical Archetypes, and Symbolic Figures in Arabic Literature: Towards a New Hermeneutic Approach,* edited by A. Neuwirth et al., 87–107 (Beirut: In Kommission bei Franz Steiner Verlag Stuttgart, 1999); Franz Rosenthal, "Reflections on Love in Paradise." In *Love and Death in the Ancient Near East: Essays in Honor of Marvin H. Pope,* edited by J. H. Marks and R. M. Good, 247–254 (Guilford, Conn.: Four Quarters Publishing, 1987).

houses

The house is not only a material object, it is a place and idea where society, culture, and the environment intersect. The human dwelling provides shelter from the elements, but it embodies important cultural distinctions, such as inside and outside, public and private, self and other (or family and nonfamily), nature and culture, male and female, and young and old. In some cultures, the house becomes a symbol for order against chaos, or it reflects the intersections of cosmic polarities, such as heaven and earth or sacred and profane. People invest significant amounts of labor and wealth in their dwellings and domestic furnishings, but they also invest them with their sympathies and emotions. This sense of attachment or emotional ownership makes a house into a home.

The houses Muslims have constructed and imagined embody all these possibilities, ranging from the material to the symbolic and religious. They have inherited the architectural traditions of pre-Islamic indigenous societies, just as they have appropriated many of the cultural and religious institutions of these societies. In doing so, Muslims have also redefined their homes in conformity with their own distinctive values and preferences. This process of redefinition has been an ongoing one from the time of Islam's first historical appearance to the modern era, with all of the latter's revolutionary changes and ruptures, global migrations, and technological innovations.

Traditional Muslim domestic ARCHITECTURE has usually employed materials that are readily available. Nomadic peoples make their tents from

Rural home in Qurna, Upper Egypt, embellished with images and calligraphy celebrating the hajj to Mecca, as well as protecting the home from evil *(Juan E. Campo)*

the tanned skins and fabrics woven from the hair of goats, sheep, and CAMELS as well as from palms, reeds, and grasses. Houses in villages, towns, and CITIES in many parts of the Middle East, North Africa, and Asia have traditionally been made of raw or baked mud brick reinforced by stone or wood if available. In rocky areas of YEMEN, western Arabia, and the Levant (SYRIA, Israel-Palestine, LEBANON, and JORDAN), local stone is used for house construction. The urban palaces and mansions of medieval Muslim rulers in EGYPT, TURKEY, Persia, and INDIA were made of professionally cut stone, together with baked brick and wood. Houses made mostly of wood are limited to forestlands, such as those of eastern Europe, the Caspian Sea region, the Hindu Kush, INDONESIA, and MALAYSIA. The Industrial Revolution and colonization of Muslim lands by European powers brought the introduction of new manufactured materials, such as steel-reinforced concrete, aluminum, glass, and plastics. This has resulted in the creation of housing that is often alienated from its natural setting. Manufactured materials and modern designs have also made it possible to erect multistory apartment blocks capable of accommodating hundreds if not thousands of people in a single residential area.

The stereotypical "Islamic" dwelling is often said to be the Middle Eastern courtyard house, a complex of rooms situated around a courtyard that is open to the sky but closed to the outside. Entrance is provided by a single doorway or gate that leads into the courtyard. Windows may be lacking or are placed high enough so that passersby cannot look inside the house. The courtyard is a work area and provides access to guest rooms, private living quarters, storerooms, and a stable. It also allows for air circulation, an advantage in regions that have a hot climate. Yet the association of the courtyard house with Islam is a tenuous one at best. Courtyard houses existed in the Middle East and Mediterranean regions for centuries before Islam's appearance. Moreover, after Muslims had established their

religion in the Mediterranean and Middle Eastern regions, both they and their non-Muslim neighbors continued to use this house form as well as others. As Muslims migrated beyond the Middle East, they usually adopted the local domestic architectural traditions of Africans, Asians, and Europeans. Whatever traditional architectural forms Muslims have used for their housing have generally allowed for the accommodation of extended families and varying degrees of interaction between public and private spheres of social life. There has been little evidence for an *absolute* separation of public and private spaces, and the same is true with respect to the segregation of men and women within the house. Rather, such divisions are situational, depending on temporal, social, and economic factors. The HAREM—a segregated domestic area for WOMEN—is a creation of wealthy landholders and urban elites, not a product of Islamic religion per se.

The symbolic and legal significance of houses in Islam can be situated, to an extent, in the QURAN and HADITH, where Arabic words such as *bayt* and *dar* are used both for ordinary human dwellings and for sacred places and dwellings in the AFTERLIFE. The Quran asserts that God created ordinary dwellings and furnishings to demonstrate his grace to people so that they would "submit" to him (Q 16:80–83). On the other hand, it also states that God has punished disbelieving and immoral people by destroying them and ruining their houses (for example, Q 7:74–79, 27:45–52). Believers who give up their homes and emigrate to God and MUHAMMAD are promised great rewards (Q 4:100).

The Grand Mosque in MECCA is called "God's sacred house," and the KAABA is called "the first house created for people" (Q 3:96–97, 5:97, 5:2). The hadith state that the Kaaba is an earthly replica of "the frequented house" in heaven, which is visited by thousands of ANGELS each day. In addition to these sacred places, there is the house of Muhammad in MEDINA, which consisted of the private apartments of his wives facing toward an open courtyard. This house became a sacred center, and Muhammad is reported to have said, "Whoever visits my house deserves my intercession [on JUDGMENT DAY]." It was also a place of communal prayer that served as a model for other mosques in Syria, IRAQ, EGYPT, and North Africa. In popular Islamic usage, all mosques can be called "houses of God."

The chapters of the Quran associated with the latter part of Muhammad's career (622–632) contain ritual commandments and rules concerning houses, both human and divine. The most important pilgrimage command in the Quran urges "people to perform a HAJJ *to the house* [the Kaaba] if they are able to do so" (Q 3:97). With respect to ordinary houses, believers are instructed to request permission before entering a person's house (Q 24:27–29), and they are to permit a divorced woman to keep her house, at least until it can be determined whether she is pregnant (Q 65:1, 6).

Nearly one-third of the references to houses in the Quran pertain to the rewards and punishments that await people in the afterlife. PARADISE is called the "house of peace," the "house of the god-fearing," or simply "the house" (*dar*). The people of PARADISE are promised dwellings and lofty apartments among its gardens and flowing rivers. Evildoers, on the other hand, will go to the FIRE (hell), which is also called the "evil house" and the "house of perdition." Their shelters there will be made of fire.

Even though Muslims do not adhere to religious building codes with respect to their housing, they do employ religious symbols and amulets to sanctify their dwellings. Many place verses of the Quran, the names of God, or pictures of mosques in Mecca, Medina, or JERUSALEM on their house walls. These forms of "decoration" are intended to secure God's blessing for the household and to repel evil forces. In rural and working class neighborhoods of Egypt, families decorate the walls of their homes with religious inscriptions and images when members of the family perform

the hajj. These pilgrimage murals often express symbolic relations between the pilgrim's home and the sacred houses of Mecca, Medina, and paradise. Shii homes in Lebanon, Iraq, and IRAN often display prayers for the People of the House (AHL AL-BAYT) and the 12 IMAMS, or portraits of beloved Shii SAINTS and shrines. The use of religious symbols and talismans, combined with efforts to adhere to codes of etiquette, hospitality, and morality in the home, are believed to make it a center of blessing with its own sacred character (*hurma*).

See also AMULET; HARAM; HAREM; MOSQUE.

Further reading: Juan Eduardo Campo, *The Other Sides of Paradise: Explorations into the Religious Meanings of Domestic Space in Islam* (Columbia: University of South Carolina Press, 1991); Timothy Insoll, *The Archaeology of Islam* (Oxford: Blackwell Publishers, 1999); Guy T. Petherbridge, "Vernacular Architecture: The House and Society." In *Architecture of the Islamic World: Its History and Social Meaning,* edited by George Michell, 176–208 (New York: Morrow, 1978).

hudud   *See* CRIME AND PUNISHMENT.

hujja (Arabic: proof, convincing argument; also spelled *hujjat*)

The idea of a *hujja*, or proof, is expressed in the QURAN, where God provides true arguments (proofs) through revelation against the false ones raised by humans (Q 4:165; 42:16). Also, according to the Quran, PROPHETS can provide proofs against those who disbelieve (Q 6:77). In other contexts, *hujja* has been used most widely among the Shia with reference to prophets, IMAMS (sacred leaders descended from Muhammad), and high-ranking religious authorities. In this sense, a *hujja* is a living proof of God's existence in human form. One Shii sect, the Ismailis, has used it for esteemed leaders who claimed access to the hidden MAHDI and engaged in missionary activities

(*DAAWA*) on behalf of the Ismaili movement. The term has also been adopted as a title to honor Twelve-Imam Shii ULAMA, who may be called *hujjat Allah* (or *hojjatollah*), "proof of God." Among Muslim theologians and philosophers, *hujja* has been used in the technical sense of a convincing or rational proof in a theoretical argument, such as in debates over the immortality of the soul or the createdness of the Quran.

See also AUTHORITY; SHIISM.

Further reading: Farhad Daftary, *The Ismailis: Their History and Doctrines* (Cambridge: Cambridge University Press, 1990), 127–128, 561.

human rights

The relationship between Islam and human rights is the subject of much contention in modern political and religious discussions. Individual rights such as freedom of speech, freedom of assembly, and freedom of religion that found early expression in the U.S. Bill of Rights, the French Revolution, and more recently in the 1948 United Nations (UN) Universal Declaration of Human Rights form the basic framework of internationally recognized principles of human rights. Together with additional covenants on political, economic, and social rights, the rights of children, and declarations against torture and discrimination based on race and gender, these documents aim (some would say claim) to represent a set, albeit incomplete, of universal principles applicable to all persons everywhere.

However, some question whether these rights are really achievable or desirable for everyone, particularly in Islamic contexts. Those who see Islam as an impediment to human rights often focus on gender inequalities found in the SHARIA, Islamic law, and the poor human rights records of many governments in Muslim-majority lands. They cite these as evidence that some essential quality of Islam prevents the realization of human rights for its believers. The vast majority of Muslims and many non-Muslims argue, however, that human rights are not only compatible with Islam but integral to its core values of justice, equality, and freedom. They criticize the cultural bias of the current UN framework as placing too much emphasis on the individual and call for a deeper understanding of the rich cultural and religious heritage Islamicate societies have to contribute to the discussion.

The Arabic word for right, *haqq* (pl. *huquq*), also means truth. Muslims agree that the ultimate expression of truth for Islam is found in its holy book, the QURAN, and that God (ALLAH) is the final arbiter of justice. Human rights then are given to humanity and guaranteed by God. They are universal and for all time. The Quran discusses freedom of religion (Q 2:256), justice and equality (Q 5:8), the right to a basic standard of life (Q 51:19), the right to participate in governance (Q 42:38), and rights of inheritance (Q 4:7–9), among others. It should be noted that interpretations of these verses are not fixed. Rather, they often reflect the liberal and conservative views of different sectors of society. One can say broadly, however, that rights in Islam are conceptualized as belonging to the individual and to the community, and the community's right to function in harmony takes precedence over those of an individual. In addition to this major difference, some Islamic scholars (ULAMA) also promote a vision of gender relations built on the idea of complementarity, which refers to different but equal and complementary rights and roles for each of the genders. This differs significantly from secular and feminist emphasis on strict equivalence of gender roles.

The public discussion of human rights in Islam has traditionally taken the form of legalistic debates between ulama as to the meaning of the Quran. While this continues to the present day, additional forums appeared in the latter half of the 20th century. They include the Universal Islamic Declaration of Human Rights issued in 1981 and the Cairo Declaration on Human Rights in Islam adopted in 1990. The latter expressly asserted rights to EDUCATION, equality before the law, marriage, ownership of property, work, freedom from unlawful arrest, and freedom to express one's opinions freely to the extent that these all fall within the sharia.

Muslims are currently confronting human rights problems throughout the Muslim world, in Europe, and in the UNITED STATES. Many of the measures enacted to strengthen security after the attacks of September 11, 2001, in the United States have disproportionately targeted Muslims within the country as well visitors and students coming from the Muslim world. In Europe, Muslims face issues ranging from the wearing of the HIJAB in French public schools to discrimination in employment and housing aimed at growing immigrant populations. In many countries in the Middle East, notably ALGERIA, EGYPT, and SYRIA, Islamic organizations opposing secular governments through both peaceful and violent means have been brutally repressed. IRAN as a formal Islamic state is often criticized for its dogmatic approach to Islamic law. Critics of the government are often jailed, and WOMEN are required to conform to "Islamically proper" dress codes. At the same time, Iranian women enjoy broad representation in the national parliament, and the non–state-sponsored press in the country is lively. Across the region, efforts to create civil society organizations (JORDAN and LEBANON are notable exceptions) are often thwarted. This affects human rights organizations in general but also groups that advocate for specific issues such as women's rights. The latter has included in recent years efforts to modify marriage and divorce laws, promote women's suffrage, and bring attention to inadequate public services for poor women and children. The prominent Iranian human rights activist Shirin Ebadi (b. 1947), a Muslim writer, lawyer, and judge, was awarded the Nobel Peace Prize in 2004 for her work on many of these issues. Other leading contemporary Muslim human rights advocates include Abdullahi An-Naim (United States and SUDAN), Abd al-Karim Soroush (Iran), FATIMA MERNISSI (MOROCCO); KHALED ABOU EL FADL (United States), Taslima Nasrin (BANGLADESH), and MUHAMMAD ARKOUN (France and Algeria).

See also DEMOCRACY; GOVERNMENT, ISLAMIC; SECULARISM.

Michelle Zimney

Further reading: Abdullahi Ahmad An-Naim, *Toward an Islamic Reformation: Civil Liberties, Human Rights and International Law* (Syracuse, N.Y.: Syracuse University Press, 1996); Kevin Dwyer, *Arab Voices: The Human Rights Debate in the Middle East* (Berkeley: University of California Press, 1991); Ann Mayer, *Islam and Human Rights* (Boulder, Colo.: Westview Press, 1999).

Husayn, Saddam (Saddam Hussein)
(1937–2006) *dictatorial president of Iraq from 1979 until being deposed by American and allied forces on April 9, 2003*

Saddam Husayn was the most influential figure in IRAQ's modern history since King FAYSAL I (d. 1933). He was a leading member of the Iraqi BAATH PARTY during the late 1960s, and, after becoming president of the country in 1979, he maintained power through the Iran–Iraq War (1980–88) and Gulf War of 1991. He was deposed in 2003 by coalition forces led by the United States and Great Britain.

Husayn was born to a poor peasant family in the village of al-Awja near the ancient city of Tikrit, an important center for nationalist and anti-British policies. His father, Husayn Abd al-Majid, died before he was born, and he was raised by his strong-willed mother, Sabha Tulfah al-Mussallat, and his paternal uncle, Ibrahim al-Hassan. He experienced a harsh childhood, which had a lasting impact on Husayn. At about the age of 10, Husayn fled his immediate family to live with his maternal uncle, Khayrallah Talfah, in Tikrit and later BAGHDAD. Talfah was an Arab nationalist army officer who might had had the greatest influence on Husayn's developing political consciousness, infusing him with nationalist, anticolonialist, and antiregime sentiments.

Husayn attended primary and secondary school in Baghdad, where he became active in student politics and was attracted to the pan-Arab vision of JAMAL ABD AL-NASIR (d. 1970) and the Baathist ideas of Michel Aflaq (d. 1989). He joined the Baath Party in 1957 and was sent to jail after becoming involved in antiregime activities. Husayn later participated in a failed plot to assassinate ruling general Abd al-Karim Qasim (d. 1963) soon after fleeing to SYRIA and EGYPT, where he completed his secondary education and entered Cairo University to study law.

Husayn returned to Iraq when the Baath Party seized power in February 1963 and was soon in charge of the party's military organization and the Peasant Bureau, which helped him build an important constituency. But the Baathists were ousted from power nine months later, at which time Husayn married his cousin Sajida Talfah and politically reestablished close ties with senior Baathists. He was arrested again for antiregime activity and sentenced to two years in jail, where he continued his political activities and resumed his education. This period left an important impression on his tactics, forcing him to become self-reliant, wary of opponents, and intolerant of internal party divisions.

After escaping from prison in 1966, Husayn played a major role in reorganizing and rebuilding the Baath Party in Iraq, leading to the overthrow of the regime in 1968. During the early years of the second Baath government, Husayn gradually strengthened his power base, championing party unity, a strong military, an end to the Kurdish rebellion, and a modernized society. He played a major role in the nationalization of the Iraqi oil industry, securing its income to finance his reform policies. In 1979, Ahmad Hasan al-Bakr (d. 1982) relinquished the presidency to Husayn, who quickly purged his party and executed a number of top officials.

Aware of the ethnosectarian structure of Iraqi society, Husayn adopted a secular domestic policy that avoided any politicization of religion, emphasized Iraq's unique character and history, and developed a cult of personality as a modern populist. Focus was placed on absorbing modern technology and linking military and industrial production. In terms of foreign policy, Iraq signed an aid pact with the Soviet Union in 1972, which lasted until 1978, at which time Iraq settled within the American sphere of influence until 1991. However, Husayn sought a leading role in the Middle East for Iraq, opposing a policy of dependence on either the Soviet Union or the United States, and favored establishing close cooperation with Europe, particularly France, to balance international relations.

After the IRANIAN REVOLUTION OF 1978–1979, relations rapidly deteriorated between the two countries. Husayn believed the new regime posed a serious threat to Iraq's internal stability and favored confrontation. Soon, the two countries entered into eight years of bloody and costly war. Iraq ultimately emerged as the victor, albeit an exhausted one. In the meantime, the regime waged a harsh campaign against Kurdish insurgents, which culminated in the destruction of villages, forced resettlements, and the use of chemical weapons at Halabja. Husayn came to believe that the UNITED STATES and its allies were unhappy with Iraq's victory over IRAN and wanted to punish him for Iraq's independent posturing and the enlargement of its military arsenal. In the post–cold war era, he began to warn other Arab states about the need to resist American imperial ambitions in the Middle East.

The invasion of Kuwait in 1990 was spurred on by Husayn's need to finance debt incurred during the war with Iran, his belief that Kuwait was historically an integral part of Iraq, and conflicting signals he received from the United States. This event revealed Husayn's high ambition and self-confidence, which allowed him to consult widely while ultimately making decisions alone and sometimes taking gambles. The invasion resulted in a devastating loss against a 30-state coalition led by the United States. Over the following decade, Husayn fought for the survival of his regime and to maintain Iraq's territorial unity and sovereignty. He ultimately lost the battle to stay in power following the 2003 U.S.-British invasion of Iraq. After his capture by the U.S. military, he continued to deny that Iraq had weapons of mass destruction. In 2005, he and a number of former Baathist associates were placed on trial by a special Iraqi tribunal for genocide, crimes against humanity, and war crimes. Saddam Husayn was sentenced to death and hanged on December 30, 2006.

See also GULF STATES; GULF WARS; SECULARISM.

Gregory Mack

Further reading: Shiva Balaghi, *Saddam Hussein: A Biography* (Westport, Conn.: Greenwood Press, 2006); Kanan Makiya, *The Monument: Art and Vulgarity in Saddam Hussein's Iraq* (New York: I.B. Tauris, 2004); Judith Miller and Laurie Mylroie, *Saddam Hussein and the Crisis in the Gulf* (New York: Times Books, 1990).

Husayni, Muhammad Amin al- (Husseini)
(1895–1974) *influential Mufti of Jerusalem and Palestinian nationalist leader*

Perhaps the most influential spiritual and political leader of the Palestinians before the "calamity" (*nakba*) of 1948, Hajj Amin al-Husayni used his position to attempt to thwart Zionist plans to establish a Jewish state in PALESTINE. Born into one of Jerusalem's most notable Muslim families, al-Husayni was educated at AL-AZHAR in EGYPT and ISTANBUL's Ottoman War College. An officer in the Ottoman Army in Anatolia during World War I, he was appalled by the creation of the British mandate over Palestine and especially the 1917 Balfour Declaration, which established the British desire to create a national home for Jews in Palestine.

By 1920, al-Husayni was very active in his public opposition to Zionist settlement in Palestine. Despite his activism, however, when the British mandatory powers established the country's Supreme Muslim Council in 1921, Herbert Samuel, Britain's high commissioner of Palestine, declared al-Husayni its leader and grand MUFTI of JERUSALEM. The Supreme Muslim Council was made responsible for managing all of the *waqfs* (religious endowments) of Palestine, as well as the SHARIA courts and Islamic schools. With his prominent new post, al-Husayni became the most prominent religious authority for Palestine's Muslims.

As mufti, al-Husayni used his power to focus on two crucial goals. The first was to organize the Palestinian population against the creation of a Jewish state, and the second was to promote the centrality of Jerusalem as a sacred Muslim city. Throughout the 1920s, the Supreme Muslim Council raised money throughout Muslim lands for the renovation of the Haram al-Sharif (Noble Sanctuary/Temple Mount), promoting the prominence of Jerusalem as an Islamicate city under attack by the Zionists, who were not only Jews but also largely secular. He also hosted two important pan-Islamic conferences in 1928 and 1931 at the AQSA MOSQUE, spreading his fame far beyond Palestine's borders.

With his extensive family connections and the power granted his position as mufti, al-Husayni was able to transform his religious leadership into political authority. When cooperation with the British mandate failed and the Arab revolt of 1936–39 broke out, al-Husayni declared his support for the uprising. The British responded by issuing a warrant for his arrest and dismissing him from his position as the leader of the Supreme Muslim Council in September 1937. Al-Husayni spent the next decade working against the British, first in BAGHDAD trying to foment uprising against their authority, and then, during World War II, working in Germany as an adviser to the Nazi regime.

When the United Nations announced its partition plan for Palestine in 1947, al-Husayni, still in exile, rejected it and called for Muslims to rise up in support of the Palestinians and against a Zionist state in the Muslim holy land. In the wake of the defeat of the Palestinians, al-Husayni spent the rest of his life traveling throughout Muslim-majority lands speaking on behalf of the Palestinian nationalist cause and denouncing the creation of ISRAEL.

See also ARAB-ISRAELI CONFLICTS.

Nancy L. Stockdale

Further reading: William L. Cleveland, *A History of the Modern Middle East* (Boulder, Colo.: Westview Press, 2000); Philip Mattar, *The Mufti of Jerusalem: Al-Hajj Amin al-Husayni and the Palestinian National Movement* (New York: Columbia University Press, 1992).

Husayn ibn Ali, Sharif of Mecca (1854–1931) *ruler of Mecca who allied with Great Britain and led the Arab revolt against Ottoman rule during World War I*

A dynamic but ultimately flawed political leader, Husayn ibn Ali was a fundamental player in the breakdown of Ottoman AUTHORITY over Arabia. Self-declared CALIPH of the Arabs, he lost his family's centuries-old custodianship of MECCA and MEDINA yet lived to see his sons take control of new Arab nations carved from the Ottoman Empire.

Husayn ibn Ali was born around 1854 in the Ottoman capital of ISTANBUL (Constantinople). A member of the Hashimite clan, his family had either ruled or held guardianship as sharifs (descendants of MUHAMMAD) over the holy cities of Mecca and Medina since 1201. In 1908, Husayn himself became emir (commander, ruler) of Mecca. As the sharif and emir, he used his descent from the prophet Muhammad to legitimate his authority over the holy cities and worked to keep the peace of the Hijaz for the ruling Ottoman Empire. Despite his privileged position under the Turks, however, Husayn gained international attention with a variety of anti-Ottoman policies during World War I. In a series of letters between himself and Britain's high commissioner of Egypt, Sir Henry McMahon, written between July 1915 and March 1916 (known as the McMahon-Husayn correspondence), Husayn pledged to raise an army against the Ottomans in exchange for British assistance in establishing an independent Arab state after the war. Claiming to be the king of the Arabs, Husayn disagreed with McMahon about the boundaries of a future state but nevertheless raised an army that successfully displaced the Ottomans from most of the Hijaz in 1916.

The Arab revolt continued to the Red Sea at Aqaba in 1917 and on to DAMASCUS in 1918. Led by his son Faysal (d. 1933), Husayn's army was a decisive factor in bringing the Ottomans to their knees in the region. However, at the San Remo Conference, Britain and France divided the Arab territories of the now-defunct Ottoman Empire between themselves, destroying Husayn's idea of a united Hashimite Arab kingdom. His son Faysal was eventually made king of the newly created IRAQ, while his son Abd Allah (d. 1951) became king of the new nation of Transjordan (now JORDAN).

Despite the new political landscape, Husayn declared himself caliph in March 1924 from his base in Mecca. However, by October of that year, he was forced to flee by the Saudi forces. Defeated, he made his way to Cyprus, where he lived in exile until 1930. For his final year of life, Husayn lived in Amman, the capital of Transjordan. It was there that he died, exiled from his family's traditional place as custodians of the holy cities, in 1931.

See also COLONIALISM; HASHIMITE DYNASTY; OTTOMAN DYNASTY; SAUDI ARABIA.

Nancy L. Stockdale

Further reading: Haifa Alangari, *The Struggle for Power in Arabia: Ibn Saud, Hussein and Great Britain, 1914–1924* (New York: Ithaca Press, 1998); William L. Cleveland, *A History of the Modern Middle East* (Boulder, Colo.: Westview Press, 2000); David Fromkin, *A Peace to End All Peace: The Fall of the Ottoman Empire and the Creation of the Modern Middle East* (New York: Henry Holt, 1989).

Husayn ibn Ali ibn Abi Talib (also Husain and Hussein) (626–680) *grandson of the prophet Muhammad and third imam of the Shia, martyred at Karbala*

MUHAMMAD, the PROPHET of Islam, left no sons and only two grandsons, Hasan and Husayn, who were born of his daughter FATIMA (d. 633) and his trusted cousin ALI IBN ABI TALIB. Muhammad is remembered to have been remarkably affectionate toward his grandsons, especially the younger, Husayn, who was six years old when his grandfather died.

Husayn was born in MEDINA in 626. Along with his brother, he accompanied his father, Ali, on military campaigns. After the death of Ali (the fourth CALIPH, though his followers thought he should have been the first) in 661, Hasan claimed the CALIPHATE but soon renounced his claim under pressure from Muawiya, who had gathered military support in order to take over the caliphate for himself. Obedient to his brother, Husayn also acknowledged Muawiya as caliph and continued to do so even after Hasan's death in 669. He refused, however, to recognize Muawiya's son Yazid (r. 680–683), who was known as an immoral tyrant, as heir apparent.

When Muawiya died in 680, the governor of Medina attempted to force Husayn to pay homage to Yazid, but Husayn fled to MECCA. There he received word from citizens of Kufa in Iraq, who were sought to oppose the UMAYYAD CALIPHATE with Husayn as their leader. Despite warnings of the dangers of such a revolt, Husayn left Mecca with a small group of family and supporters to meet with his followers in Kufa. On the way, he was confronted by Umayyad forces, and attempts at negotiation failed. Husayn's party eventually camped at a site in the desert known as KARBALA. Husayn had learned that his followers in Kufa had abandoned him, and, being trapped in the desert and cut off

from water, he gave his supporters the opportunity to flee during the night, but they remained by his side, knowing that they were greatly outnumbered and had little chance of surviving. On 10 Muharram (ASHURA), Husayn again refused to surrender, and fighting began. Though they fought courageously, the men of Husayn's party were massacred, and Husayn too was killed. His head was cut off and sent to Yazid in Damascus along with the WOMEN and CHILDREN of his party, including his sister ZAYNAB and his son Ali, who would become the fourth IMAM, Zayn al-Abidin (d. 713).

The spilling of the blood of the Prophet's last grandson was an emotional event that touched all Muslims, but for the Shia it was a tragedy that dramatically symbolized injustice and oppression. With this event, MARTYRDOM became a distinctive characteristic of SHIISM and Husayn the archetypal martyr. His death at Karbala has been recounted in countless books and poems and is reenacted every year on 10 Muharram in emotional theatrical dramatizations often accompanied by mourners beating and slashing their bodies with razors to commemorate the shedding of the blood of Husayn.

See also AHL AL-BAYT; TWELVE-IMAM SHIISM.

Mark Soileau

Further reading: Mahmoud Ayoub, *Redemptive Suffering in Islam: A Study of the Devotional Aspects of Ashura in Twelver Shiism* (The Hague: Mouton, 1978); Peter Chelkowski, ed., *Taziyeh: Ritual and Drama in Iran* (New York: New York University Press, 1979); Moojan Momen, *An Introduction to Shii Islam: The History and Doctrines of Twelver Shiism* (New Haven, Conn.: Yale University Press, 1985); Allamah Sayyid Muhammad Husayn Tabatabai, *Shiite Islam.* Translated by Seyyed Hossein Nasr (Albany: State University of New York Press, 1975).

Husayniyya (Arabic, based on the name Husayn; also spelled Hosayniyya)

A Husayniyya is a ritual hall, room, or building where the Shia gather to commemorate the

MARTYRDOM of the third IMAM, HUSAYN IBN ALI (d. 680), who died on the battlefield of KARBALA in IRAQ. Historically, it began in 10th-century Iraq with tents that were erected temporarily for ASHURA observances at the beginning of Muharram, the first month on the Islamic CALENDAR. Later, these observances were conducted in palaces, houses, or open spaces. In the era of the SAFAVID DYNASTY (1501–1722), when the name *Husayniyya* was first coined, Iranian and Iraqi Shii Muslims made it a more fixed structure attached to a house or a self-standing building.

The idea of creating a special ritual gathering place for Ashura observances subsequently spread beyond Iraq and IRAN to Shii communities in other parts of the world. As a consequence of its growing popularity and adaptation to different Shii localities, it became known under a variety of other names, such as *takiya* (place of piety) and *zaynabiyya* (in honor of Husayn's sister Zaynab)

in Iran; *matam* (funeral house) in Bahrain and Oman; and *imambarah* (enclosure of the Imam), *imambargah* (Imam building), *azakhana* (mourning house), *ashurkhana* (Ashura house), and *taaziyakhana* (condolence house) in INDIA, BANGLADESH, and PAKISTAN. These constructions were financed by donations from wealthy Muslim merchants, landlords, or nobles, and by *waqfs*, which were income-producing properties set aside by the donor as perpetual endowments for the benefit of the community. As a form of Islamic ARCHITECTURE, the Husayniyya assumed a variety of forms. It does not resemble the MOSQUE so much as it does the *khanqah* and TEKKE, where Sufis gather at appointed times to remember God and honor the memories of MUHAMMAD and the Sufi SAINTs and spiritual masters. Although some are of considerable size, most are modest structures.

The size and number of Husayniyyas have been affected by the degree of prosperity in the

Husayniyya in Bahrain *(Juan E. Campo)*

local community and the attitudes of the rulers. For example, it is estimated that in the early 19th century, the north Indian city of Lucknow had as many as 8,000 Husayniyyas and *takiya*s under its pro-Shii rulers, the Nawwabs, while the region of Khorasan in Iran today has some 2,000 such structures. Sunni Wahhabis, on the other hand, destroyed Husayniyyas in the past and strictly control their proliferation in the Eastern Province of SAUDI ARABIA today. Shii immigrant communities living in North America and Europe have built their own Husayniyyas.

The ritual practices conducted at the Husayniyya have varied, often depending on local community custom. Generally, they are governed by what one scholar has called the "Karbala paradigm," which involves the commemoration of events surrounding the martyrdom of Husayn and his loyal followers. Rituals include long, moving recitations of elegiac poems (sing. *marthiyya*) that employ themes of divine justice and worldly injustice, death, and suffering. Such recitations often provoke outbursts of weeping among participants. The Husayniyya, often decorated with banners, religious portraiture, emblems, and Karbala models, is where ritual objects used in Ashura processions are stored, and affiliated members organize the Ashura processions and related ritual performances. In many communities, participants in Husayniyya rituals beat their chests in rhythmic unison or afflict their bodies by self-flagellation, which can induce copious bleeding—a demonstration of one's piety, devotion, manliness, and atonement for one's sins. Theatrical reenactments, including musical performances and costumed actors, of moments in Shii sacred history, culminating with Husayn's death, are staged at Husayniyyas and *takiya*s in Iran. Husayniyyas are also where people gather for PRAYER, other religious HOLIDAYS, and funerals.

Traditionally, Husayniyyas have been religious places for men, while WOMEN have conducted their Ashura rites at home, although they also watch and participate in public processions.

In recent years, women in some countries have established their own Husayniyyas, using them as centers of EDUCATION and political activity, as has happened in Bahraini *matam*s in recent years. The modern transformation of Husayniyyas into political focal points occurred in Iran in the 1960s and 1970s, when Iranians became actively involved in antigovernment activities that eventually led to the IRANIAN REVOLUTION OF 1978–1979. The most famous example is the Husayniyya-i Irashad, founded in 1965 in the Iranian capital, Tehran. It had male and female members and offered films and a forum for the expression of new religious and political ideas. It engaged ULAMA and laity alike and featured the lectures of ALI SHARIATI (d. 1977), whose revolutionary talks rallied people against the government.

See also SHIISM; WAHHABISM.

Further reading: Kamran Scot Aghaie, ed., *The Women of Karbala: Ritual Performance and Symbolic Discourses in Modern Shii Islam* (Austin: University of Texas Press, 2005); Juan R. I. Cole, *Roots of North Indian Shiism in Iran and Iraq: Religion and State in Awadh, 1722–1859* (Berkeley: University of California Press, 1988); Vernon James Schubel, "Karbala as Sacred Space among North American Shia: 'Every Day Is Ashura, Everywhere Is Karbala.'" In *Making Muslim Space in North America and Europe,* edited by Barbara Metcalf, 186–203 (Berkeley: University of California Press, 1996).

hypocrites

A hypocrite is someone whose actions contradict his or her outwardly stated beliefs or values. In early Islamic history, the "hypocrites" (Arabic *munafiqun,* fem. *munafiqat*), also called "dissemblers" and "dissenters," were originally Muslims in MEDINA who opposed or disagreed with MUHAMMAD. In other words, they were regarded as a disloyal faction within the Muslim community. According to Ibn Ishaq's eighth-century BIOGRAPHY of Muhammad, the *Sira,* they were mostly from the tribes of Aws and Khazraj, from which many early Medinan converts had come. They appear to have had ulterior motives when they first became Muslims and did not disclose their real beliefs. They avoided helping Muhammad in his battles against his Meccan opponents, and some of them spread a slanderous rumor about his wife AISHA BINT ABI BAKR. They were also accused of being loyal to his rivals and conspiring with Jewish tribes in Medina against him.

The QURAN mentions hypocrites 32 times, and one of its chapters even bears the name as its title (Q 63). It associates them with the worst enemies of Islam—the disbelievers (sing. *KAFIR*) and the polytheists (sing. *mushrik*); all will be punished in hellfire (Q 4:140; 33:73). It accuses them of violating one of the chief moral imperatives of Islam; instead of commanding what is known to be right and forbidding what is reprehensible, "they command what is reprehensible and forbid what is known to be right" (Q 9:67). In the HADITH, the hypocrites are condemned as liars and promise breakers.

During the later Middle Ages, jurists allowed for treatment of hypocrites as Muslims under religious law as long as they kept their true beliefs to themselves. They were eligible to marry Muslim women and be buried as Muslims. However, Sunnis and Shiis accused each other of being hypocrites, reflecting internal rivalries within the Muslim community as each group tried to discredit the other. Some modern Muslim political ideologues have attacked various groups and movements in their writings by calling them hypocrites. Those attacked may be Muslims who belong to secular or leftist organizations or Jews and other non-Muslim groups. Islamist and other opposition groups have used the term to criticize leaders of wealthy Arab oil countries who do not care for the poor, Muslims who assist Western governments in their battle against Islamic radicalism, and Muslims who refuse to join them in conducting JIHAD against the enemies of Islam.

See also ANSAR; COMMUNISM; EMIGRANTS; IDOLATRY; ISLAMISM; JUDAISM AND ISLAM; SHIISM; SUNNISM.

Further reading: Muhammad ibn Ishaq, *The Life of Muhammad: A Translation of Ibn Ishaq's Sirat Rasul Allah.* Translated by Alfred Guillaume (Oxford: Oxford University Press, 1955), 242–270; W. Montgomery Watt, *Muhammad at Medina* (1956. New edition, Oxford: Oxford University Press, 1981).

I

ibada   *See* FIVE PILLARS.

Ibadiyya

The Ibadiyya sect of Islam is one of several Muslim Kharijite movements that declared war against the wider Muslim community in the seventh and eighth centuries because of what they considered to be gross moral shortcomings of its leadership. It is named after one of the leaders in these movements, Abd Allah ibn Ibad (d. late seventh century or early eighth century) of Basra, known as "IMAM of the Muslims" and "imam of the people" in Ibadi sources. The Ibadis also hold the Omani scholar Jabir ibn Zayd al-Azdi (d. ca. 722) in high esteem. Ibadis have adopted a moderate stance toward nonmembers and dissociated themselves from extremist Kharijis, who called unrepentant Muslims who had committed a grave sin (*mushrikun*). On the other hand, they also claim to be distinct from Sunni and Shii Muslims. The Ibadi sect today has its largest following in the Persian Gulf country of Oman (about 75 percent of the population), but branches also exist in EAST AFRICA, LIBYA, TUNISIA, and ALGERIA. During the Middle Ages, it also had followers who lived along old routes of conquest and trade in IRAQ, EGYPT, the SUDAN, the Hijaz, YEMEN and Hadramawt, IRAN, and perhaps INDIA and CHINA.

Ibadi doctrine about God is similar to that of the Mutazila in several respects. They affirm the createdness of the QURAN, and they interpret anthropomorphic references to God in the Quran symbolically rather than literally. On the other hand, with respect to the question of free will versus predeterminism, their belief is like that of the Sunni ASHARI SCHOOL, with its affirmation of God's power to determine events while leaving human beings with the capacity to acquire the consequences of their actions, whether good or evil. Ibadis differentiate between inward belief in God's oneness, outward declaration of this belief, and implementing this belief in practice. This is an outcome of their historical experience as an Islamic sect that witnessed moments when concealment of belief (*kitman*) was a key to survival in the face of persecution by enemies. In this respect, they are like the Shia, who developed the analogous doctrine of pious dissimulation (*taqiyya*). Like the Shia, they have also witnessed times when they were strong enough to defend themselves. They have even developed a concept of MARTYRDOM, which Ibadis call *shira* (purchase)—the willingness to sacrifice one's life on behalf of the community in order to gain entrance into PARADISE. A minimum force of 40 men is required before *shira* is permitted, however. Generally, in contrast to extremist Kharijites, the Ibadis do not consider other Muslims to be disbelievers who must be fought and killed. Rather, their relations with outsiders range from peaceful association to neutrality to hostile avoidance. In their ritual life, Ibadis practice the same duties of worship as do other Muslims, with some minor differences.

Ibadis heed the AUTHORITY of their own imam, an office of leadership that began in 730. Unlike the Shia, whose imams are descended from the household of Muhammad, Ibadi imams attain office through election by a body of ULAMA and tribal leaders. The Ibadi imam may also be deposed for errant behavior. Moreover, in contrast to the Shia, there can be more than one imam at a time among the different Ibadi communities, and there may also be times when there is no official imam. In Ibadi history, the elective tradition of leadership has competed with a dynastic one. In recent times, their imams have been members of the Al Bu Said dynasty in Oman, which has held power since the 17th century. However, they now prefer to call themselves SULTANS, which emphasizes their temporal power. Oman, therefore, is called a sultanate.

See also FREE WILL AND DETERMINISM; GULF STATES; KHAWARIJ; MUTAZILI SCHOOL; SHIISM; SUNNISM.

Further reading: Dale F. Eickelman, "From Theocracy to Monarchy: Authority and Legitimacy in Inner Oman." *International Journal of Middle East Studies* 17 (1985): 3–24; ———, "Ibadism and the Sectarian Perspective." In *Oman: Economic, Social, and Strategic Developments*, edited by Briam R. Pridham, 31–50 (London: Croom Helm, 1987); Valerie J. Hoffman, "The Articulation of Ibadi Identity in Modern Oman and Zanzibar." *Muslim World* 94 (2004): 201–216.

Iblis *See* SATAN.

Ibn Abd al-Wahhab, Muhammad (1703–1791) *conservative religious reformer who launched the Wahhabi movement and helped found the first Saudi state*

Ibn Abd al-Wahhab was born in Uyayna, an oasis town located in the Najd, the central region of what is now SAUDI ARABIA. He was raised in a family of Hanbali jurists and religious scholars and demonstrated an early interest in studying the QURAN and other areas of Islamic learning, especially HADITH studies. His father, a Hanbali judge and teacher of hadith and FIQH, provided him with his early education in the religious sciences. Further details about Ibn Abd al-Wahhab's early career are anecdotal, but it appears that he began to advocate a strict Islamic reformism while in his early 20s. He gained a following in his hometown, but political opposition forced him to go to MECCA and MEDINA, where he met and studied with other reform-minded ULAMA. He became familiar with the writings of the medieval Hanbali reformer Ibn Taymiyya and excelled in his knowledge of Hanbali law. Later he traveled to Basra, a port town in IRAQ, where he encountered Shii doctrines and practices that met with his disapproval because they departed from the Islam of the Quran and the SUNNA.

After Basra, Ibn Abd al-Wahhab moved to Huraymila, the Najdi town where his father lived. This was where he wrote *The Book of Unity (Kitab al-tawhid)*, which expressed many of his key teachings. Copies of it were circulated throughout the Najd. After his father died in 1740, his mission became more public. He promoted the doctrine of TAWHID, belief in God's absolute uniqueness and rejection of polytheism (SHIRK), IDOLATRY, and unbelief. His belief that *tawhid* included following God's commandments and prohibitions meant that he also sought to address moral issues in his society and culture. He favored strict enforcement of the SHARIA, including performing PRAYER, giving *zakat* (ALMSGIVING), and enforcing punishments for ADULTERY. Those who failed to heed his teachings were seen as unbelievers (KAFIRS) and could be subdued through JIHAD. Tribal leaders and ulama in Huraymila decided that they did not want Ibn Abd al-Wahhab to undermine their AUTHORITY, so they conspired against his life, forcing him to return to Uyayna, his hometown. Uthman ibn Hamid ibn Muammar (d. 1749), the ruler of Uyayna, at first welcomed the reformer, even arranging for him to marry his aunt. The situation changed, however, when he cut down one of the town's sacred trees, demolished a shrine belonging to Zayd ibn al-Khattab (one of the COMPANIONS OF THE PROPHET), and, above all, condemned a woman to death by stoning after she confessed to adultery. The outcry these actions stirred caused Uthman to withdraw support from Ibn Abd al-Wahhab, who had to flee Uyayna in 1744.

He settled in Diriya, about 40 miles from Uyayna, near Riyadh. The small town was ruled by the clan of the Saud, led by Muhammad ibn Saud. That same year, "the two Muhammads" reached a mutual agreement: Ibn Saud would protect Ibn Abd al-Wahhab from his enemies and make him the IMAM of Diriya, while Ibn Abd al-Wahhab would collect *zakat* for the Saudi ruler and help him extend his control over the Najd region through his preaching and declaring jihad against Saudi enemies. These included "infidels" who did not heed Ibn Abd al-Wahhab's call (DAAWA) to accept his version of Islam, as well as tribes who would not submit to Saudi rule. The agreement turned out to be more fruitful than the two might have imagined. From it they were able to create a confederation of tribal groups, both settled and nomadic, that provided the basis for a new state in central Arabia.

When Muhammad ibn Saud died in 1765, Ibn Abd al-Wahhab continued the alliance with his son Abd al-Aziz ibn Muhammad (d. 1803). He maintained his base in Diriya, where he taught and wrote, seeking to win others to his cause. His strategy included assigning Wahhabi judges to the towns and oases that had submitted to Saudi

rule. By the time of his death, Saudi-Wahhabi rule reached Riyadh (the future Saudi capital) and the shores of the Persian Gulf. A few years later, it encompassed most of the Arabian Peninsula, including the holy cities of Mecca and Medina.

Ibn Abd al-Wahhab's legacy was carried on by his descendants and disciples. His son Abd Allah wrote works against Shiism and endorsed the Wahhabi forays into southern IRAQ in early 1801. His grandson Sulayman (d. 1818) served as judge in Diriya until executed by Ottoman-Egyptian forces sent from EGYPT into Arabia to destroy the early Saudi state. Today, his teachings form part of the official ideology of the Kingdom of Saudi Arabia, which arose from the ashes of the first Saudi state under the leadership of King Abd al-Aziz ibn Saud (d. 1953) in the early 20th century. Ibn Abd al-Wahhab's heirs, known as the Al al-Shaykh (the family of Shaykh Ibn Abd al-Wahhab), now hold powerful positions in the Saudi government and intermarry with members of the Saudi royal family. His works are widely available in printed form, and his ideas hold sway among conservative religious reformers and radicals in many Sunni countries. Among those influenced by Ibn Abd al-Wahhab's teachings is USAMA BIN LADIN, leader of the AL-QAIDA organization responsible for the attacks on the World Trade Center and the Pentagon in 2001. Many Muslims, Sunnis, and Shiis alike reject Ibn Abd al-Wahhab's puritanical understanding of Islam, nevertheless.

See also BIDAA; RENEWAL AND REFORM MOVEMENTS; WAHHABISM.

Further reading: Natana J. DeLong-Bas, *Wahhabi Islam: From Revival to Global Jihad* (Oxford: Oxford University Press, 2004); Madawi al-Rasheed, *A History of Saudi Arabia* (Cambridge: Cambridge University Press, 2002), 14–23; John O. Voll, "Muhammad Hayat al-Sindi and Muhammad Ibn Abd al-Wahhab: An Analysis of an Intellectual Group in Eighteenth Century Medina." *Bulletin of the School of Oriental and African Studies* 38, no. 1 (1975): 32–39.

Ibn al-Arabi, Muhyi al-Din (Ibn Arabi)

(1165–1240) *prominent medieval mystic and visionary who enriched the Sufi tradition of Islam with his numerous and profound spiritual writings*

Ibn al-Arabi, known as "the greatest shaykh," was born in the town of Murcia in ANDALUSIA (Muslim Spain) at a time of great change in the wider Mediterranean region. The puritanical ALMOHAD DYNASTY was attempting to fend off the Christian Reconquista from northern Spain, and Muslim and Christian armies were competing for control of the Holy Land in the eastern Mediterranean region. Meanwhile, fearsome Mongol armies were expanding their conquests in Asia and were on the brink of invading IRAN. It was also the era of many of the great Sufi masters, including Shihab al-Din Abu Hafs al-Suhrawardi (d. 1234) and JALAL AL-DIN RUMI (d. 1273).

Although details about his youth are disputed and surrounded by pious legend, recent research has found that Ibn al-Arabi may have come from a family of soldiers and that he himself had served the Almohads in this capacity before turning to the spiritual path. His formal education began after he moved with his family to Seville, a major center of learning, where he spent the first part of his life. He studied the QURAN and its commentaries, HADITH, grammar, and *FIQH* (jurisprudence). According to his own account, his promise as a man of mystical leanings seems to have been in evidence even as a teenager, when he met with IBN RUSHD (1196–98), the renowned Andalusian philosopher and jurist. Ibn al-Arabi was also said to have sought the guidance of known masters of the spiritual path in southern Spain, including two women, Shams of Marchena and Fatima of Cordoba, who proclaimed herself his "spiritual mother."

Ibn al-Arabi left home for the first time in the 1190s, when he went to North Africa in search of spiritual guidance. This launched a career of traveling that he continued to pursue throughout his life. In 1202, inspired by a vision, he went to MECCA for the HAJJ, stopping in Alexandria and CAIRO en route. While in Mecca, where he had spiritual inspirations and visions, he began to write one of his most important works, *The Meccan Revelations (Al-Futuhat al-Makkiya)*. About two years later, he visited BAGHDAD, then returned to EGYPT, where his teachings were condemned by the literal-minded ULAMA. Ibn al-Arabi resumed his residence in Mecca for a year to continue his spiritual pursuits, then traveled to Konya, the capital of a Turkish dynasty, where he was embraced by Sufi disciples. One of them was Sadr al-Din al-Qunawi (d. 1274), who became one of Ibn al-Arabi's foremost interpreters and played a major role in the spread of his teachings.

Ibn al-Arabi traveled widely in Asia Minor, IRAQ, SYRIA, and PALESTINE until 1223, when he finally settled in DAMASCUS. There he finished The Meccan Revelations, assembled a collection of poetry, and had a vision of MUHAMMAD in 1229 that he claimed inspired his most influential work, *The Bezels of Wisdom (Fusus al-hikam)*. Altogether, he estimated that he had written as many as 289 books and treatises, most of which remain untranslated and unpublished. This makes him the most prolific of all Sufi authors. Ibn al-Arabi was buried on Mount Qassioun, just outside the city limits. Reportedly destroyed by his enemies, his tomb was rebuilt and embellished with a MOSQUE and Sufi hospice by the Ottoman sultan Selim I in 1516–17, when Damascus was incorporated into the Ottoman Empire.

Ibn al-Arabi became famous only after his death, when pious biographies about him and commentaries on his writings gained wide circulation in Islamdom. He was known for the depth and complexity of his mysticism, ranging from his understanding of God, the universe, nature, and humanity to the human soul. His knowledge was based on a scholarly command of Islamic tradition (including Sunni *fiqh* [jurisprudence]), the teachings of other mystics and visionaries, and the originality of his own religious experiences and visions. Despite his knowledge of the Quran and hadith, some of his ideas, or at least the ways they were construed by others, outraged literal-minded ulama such as IBN TAYMIYYA (d. 1328) and even some leading Sufis. His main insight concerned the "oneness of being" (*wahdat al-wujud*): the belief that all created things were tangible reflections of God's hidden essence, *al-Haqq* (truth, reality), which filled the universe. This idea was inspired by a HADITH *qudsi* (holy hadith) favored by Sufis, wherein God said, "I was a hidden treasure who wished to be known, so I created the universe so that I would be known." Ibn al-Arabi, like mystics before him, understood CREATION as a mirror wherein God, the Truth, sought to know himself. His opponents accused him of pantheism (equating God with creation)—an affront to the doctrine that God was transcendent and independent of creation. Ibn al-Arabi recognized, however, that God was both present in the world and beyond it.

Moreover, he maintained that God's desire to know himself through creation was matched by man's yearning to know himself through God and nature. Although man was a servant of God, he also had been created with God's spirit. God and man, therefore, longed to be with each other, a longing that Ibn al-Arabi and his followers associated with love (*mahabba*). A form of this love was reflected in the mutual attraction between a man and a woman. Indeed, Ibn al-Arabi even taught in *The Bezels of Wisdom* that man's knowledge of God was completed and perfected in contemplating how a woman reflected God's transcendent reality. He recognized, nonetheless, that humans often became too attached to worldly concerns and desires, so they had to strive to sever these attachments and return to the source. Drawing on anecdotes from his own life experience, he often talked about detachment from the world and seeking God as an ascent or spiritual journey to the world of the unseen.

In addition to the themes of the unity of being, desire for reunion, and the spiritual journey, a fourth major theme found in Ibn al-Arabi's writings is that of the PERFECT MAN (*al-insan al-kamil*).

He saw the world, both physical and spiritual, as organized into hierarchies, such as those between the one and the many, the invisible and the visible, God and servant, man and woman. As humans were superior in rank to other creatures in the visible world, there were qualitative differences among human beings, too. The highest rankings among them were the prophets and SAINTS, or "friends of God." Unlike ordinary men, these were the ones who were most taken with spiritual ascents and mystical journeys. In this, they, and Muhammad being the foremost among them, came closest to the ideal of the Perfect Man, the image and reflection of God through whom the known universe came into being.

Although he never founded a Sufi order (TARIQA), Ibn al-Arabi's teachings and those of his disciples were widely embraced by Sufis in TURKEY, Persia, INDIA, and INDONESIA. Sufis in Egypt and YEMEN also found them attractive, but to a lesser extent than elsewhere. Translations and interpretations of Ibn al-Arabi's work by modern scholars in Europe and the UNITED STATES have helped spread his influence in the West. In 1977, the Muhyidin Ibn Arabi Society was founded in London to promote better understanding of his work and that of his disciples. Aside from Ibn Taymiyya, his many critics have included the historian IBN KHALDUN (d. 1406), Sufi shaykh AHMAD SIRHINDI (d. 1624), members of the Wahhabi sect of SAUDI ARABIA and beyond, and an array of modern Muslim revivalists and modernists. Controversy over his teachings flared again in 1979 when the Egyptian parliament attempted to ban the republication of the print edition of The Meccan Revelations. The attempt failed due to public outcry.

See also ALLAH; *HAQIQA*; PROPHETS AND PROPHECY; SUFISM; WAHHABISM; *WALAYA*.

Further reading: Claude Addas, *Quest for the Red Sulphur: The Life of Ibn Arabi* (Cambridge: Islamic Texts Society, 1993); William C. Chittick, *Ibn Arabi: Heir to the Prophets* (Oxford: Oneworld Publishers, 2005); Th. Emil Homerin, "Ibn Arabi in the People's Assembly:

Religion, Press, and Politics in Sadat's Egypt." *Middle East Journal* 40, no. 3 (Summer, 1986): 462–477; Ibn al-Arabi, *The Bezels of Wisdom*. Translated by R. W. J. Austin (Mahwah, N.J.: Paulist Press, 1980); Annemarie Schimmel, *Mystical Dimensions of Islam* (Chapel Hill: University of North Carolina Press, 1975), 259–286.

Ibn al-Bawwab, Abu al-Hasan Ali

(unknown–1022) *copyist of the earliest extant Quran manuscript using all elements of 10th-century calligraphic reforms*

Ibn al-Bawwab worked as librarian for the Shii Buyid rulers in Shiraz (in IRAN) and was later buried in BAGHDAD, the city that gave rise to the calligraphic *khatt* (Arabic script) reforms and the *girih* mode of geometric ornamentation that in the 11th century suppressed variant readings of the QURAN. He produced a copy of the Quran in 1000–01 that is now preserved at the Chester Beatty Library in Dublin. Ibn al-Bawwab's use of the proportioned scripts and accompanying geometric designs soon after their creation indicates that he was loyal to the Sunni Abbasids (r. 750–1258) as opposed to the Buyid dynasty (932–1062).

Ibn al-Bawwab occupies a special place among medieval commentators on *khatt* as the person who perfected, through the elegance of his writing, the proportioned script invented by ABU ALI MUHAMMAD IBN MUQLA (d. 940). His is the first surviving copy (and one of the very first such copies) of a Quran in cursive scripts, or what were originally considered secular scripts (the six pens of Ibn Muqla). His signed and dated manuscript provides a rare instance of a preserved work that exemplifies major shifts in the processes of copying and producing these manuscripts.

Earlier, making copies of the Quran was the domain of specialists who used gold ink on vellum, often employing brushes to fill in the outlines of stylized, extended, and difficult to read letters. Each horizontally disposed page carried a few lines of about seven to nine words, resulting in expensive, multivolume products of limited circulation. In contrast, Ibn al-Bawwab's copy is a small volume (ca. 13.5 × 17.8 cm) in a vertical paper format in which the text is written with pen. The body of the text is entirely vocalized and written in a clear, rounded *naskhi* script, while chapter headings, verse counts, and other statistics are in *thuluth* script. The text itself follows the approved Abbasid version, while the use of reform scripts and geometric (*girih*) decoration in the frontispieces similarly expresses Abbasid dogma on the accessibility of the divine message and eternity of universal order.

See also ABBASID CALIPHATE; ARABESQUE; BOOKS AND BOOKMAKING; CALLIGRAPHY; FATIMID DYNASTY; MADRASA.

Nuha N. N. Khoury

Further reading: D. S. Rice, *The Unique Quran Manuscript of Ibn al-Bawwab in the Chester Beatty Library* (Dublin: E. Walker, 1955); Yasser Tabbaa, *The Transformation of Islamic Art during the Sunni Revival* (Seattle: University of Washington Press, 2001).

Ibn al-Farid, Abu Hafs Umar (1181–1235)

leading poet of the Arabic language and a widely recognized Sufi saint of Egypt

Umar Ibn al-Farid was born and lived most of his life in EGYPT. He spent 15 years in MECCA, where he went after the death of his father. It is not clear how he supported himself, but he probably made a living teaching poetry and literature as well as having a sinecure teaching HADITH, in which he was trained.

Ibn al-Farid's poetry has long been highly esteemed for its beauty. His poems often bear multiple meanings and can be read as poems of love and pleasure or of the mystical path of SUFISM. During his life and in the first generations after his death, Ibn al-Farid was mostly known as a mystically inclined poet, and it was very much his poetry that defined his early reputation. He was an active member of the literary society of his time, and contemporary poets studied at his feet. He appears to have avoided close links to rulers and the perks derived therefrom.

Ibn al-Farid's greatest poetry took themes present in Arabic poetry and used them in innovative ways that expressed the longing of the mystic for the divine beloved. Thus, the theme of a lover drinking in memory of the beloved is transformed, in the justly famous opening line of Ibn al-Farid's "Wine Ode" (*Khamriyya*), to an allusion to the Islamic belief in a primordial COVENANT between God and humanity in which humans, before time began, recognized God's supremacy and oneness. Thus, he says, "We drank in memory of the beloved a wine; We were drunk with it before creation of the vine" (Homerin, *Arab Poet* 11). Here the beloved is God, while drunkenness refers to the spiritual state of intoxication, a state known and recognized by Sufis. The fact that this drunkenness occurs before the vine was even created reinforces the metaphorical nature of this allusion and draws the listener's mind to the primordial covenant. Much of his poetry is of this sort; in Arabic it is often piercingly beautiful and deeply resonant.

Within a century of his death, Ibn al-Farid's renown evolved from that of a great poet of mystical inclination to a great Sufi whose poetry would guide those on the mystical path of Sufism. Stories began to circulate about his supernaturally given knowledge and of his ability to induce mystical states in those around him. Early on, commentators began to read Ibn al-Farid's verse in light of the monistic doctrine of IBN AL-ARABI (d. 1240), in which the only reality that beings have lies in their relationship to the Absolute Being (God). This doctrine was very controversial, for it appeared to break, or at least blur, the line of distinction between God and humanity. Thus, Ibn al-Farid's poetry, which is not so clear on this point, came to be lumped with Ibn al-Arabi's more explicit monism. For those who followed Ibn al-Arabi, of course, this was positive. But Ibn al-Arabi was always controversial, and thus Ibn al-Farid came to be associated with and seen through the hotly contested issue of monism.

In the centuries after his death, Ibn al-Farid was periodically charged with infidelity for allegedly having espoused this doctrine of monism. But he was also treated with increasing veneration by members of the populace and by the elite of the MAMLUK dynasty (1250–1517). Sober scholars, too, were among his public supporters in later times, asserting his orthodoxy and refuting his opponents. Ibn al-Farid's grandson was in part responsible for transforming him into a SAINT, especially by publishing a BIOGRAPHY in which MIRACLES were prominently recounted, for miracles were the sine qua non of a Muslim saint. His burial site in the hills just outside CAIRO was already a recognized place of pilgrimage by Mamluk times. It continued as a popular shrine through Ottoman times, declining as new modern habits began to develop in the 19th century and as Sufism became increasingly suspect among reformist and modernizing Muslim intellectuals. While Sufism is still regarded somewhat warily by many Muslims, it experienced a modest revival in Egypt in the late 20th century that continues today. Ibn al-Farid's tomb is now the scene of one of the major saint festivals (sing. MAWLID) on the religious calendar of Cairo. Egypt's most famous singer of religious songs, Shaykh Yasin al-Tihami comes to the festival most years, drawing large and devoted crowds. His songs include those based on the poetry of Ibn al-Farid, whom locals refer to as "our master Umar."

See also ARABIC LANGUAGE AND LITERATURE; AUTHORITY; *BIDAA*; SALAFISM.

John Iskander

Further reading: Th. Emil Homerin, *From Arab Poet to Muslim Saint: Ibn al-Farid, His Verse and His Shrine* (Cairo: American University in Cairo Press, 2001); ———, *Umar ibn al-Farid: Sufi Verse, Saintly Life* (New York: Paulist Press, 2001); R. A. Nicholson, *Studies in Islamic Mysticism* (Cambridge: Cambridge University Press, 1921).

Ibn Battuta, Abu Abd Allah Muhammad al-Lawati (1304–1377) *famous Muslim world traveler from Morocco*

Ibn Battuta was arguably one of the most well-traveled figures of the medieval period, whose journey spanned almost 30 years and covered three times the distance of his more famous European counterpart, Marco Polo (d. 1324). He traveled from WEST AFRICA to CHINA, receiving patronage, hospitality, and occasionally employment from local rulers and Sufi orders. His extended travels effectively demonstrate the links that tied together premodern Islamicate lands, where a Muslim scholar could work and wander in many different regions in a world without firm borders.

Born in Tangiers, Ibn Battuta began his travels with a pilgrimage to MECCA in 1325. From there, his wanderlust took him throughout most of Islamdom, through the Arabian Peninsula, EGYPT, IRAQ, Persia, EAST AFRICA, Anatolia, the Asian steppes, AFGHANISTAN, and INDIA. He also ventured beyond the realms of Islam, exploring Southeast Asia, China, Spain, and West Africa before ultimately retiring to the court of the Marinid ruler in MOROCCO, Abu Inan (r. 1348–58). There the SULTAN commissioned the Andalusian scholar Ibn Juzayy to commit Ibn Battuta's story to paper, and the book was completed by 1357. In spite of certain sections borrowed from a previous traveler's account and its tendency to exaggerate, this work marks a new style within the travel literature genre, expanding on the traditional descriptions of pilgrimage to include more personal information and a much larger geographical scope. It is also a testament to the rich diversity of Islam in this period, with its verdant blend of Islamic mysticism, religious law, and local custom. For these reasons, it is considered a historical treasure trove of information for Islamicate societies in the 14th century.

Eric Staples

Further reading: Douglas Bullis, "The Longest Hajj: The Journeys of Ibn Battuta." *Saudi Aramco World* 51 (July/August 2000): 7–39; Ross Dunn, *The Adventures of Ibn Battuta* (1986. Reprint, Berkeley: University of California Press, 2004); Hamilton A. R. Gibb, *The Travels of Ibn Battuta 1325–1354.* 5 vols. (Cambridge: Hakluyt Society at the University Press, 1954–2000).

Ibn Hanbal, Ahmad (780–855) *leading Sunni hadith scholar and theologian remembered as the founder of the Hanbali legal school; a popular defender of traditional Islamic piety against Muslim rationalists and the Abbasid Caliphate*

Ahmad ibn Hanbal was born in Abbasid BAGHDAD and lived there most of his life. His family's ancestors had participated in the Arab conquests of Iraq and northeastern Iran, where his grandfather had served as a governor and his father as a soldier. He studied Arabic and Islamic law (FIQH), but his real passion was for the HADITH. Beginning in 795, when he was 14 years old, Ibn Hanbal went to study hadith with scholars in Kufa and Basra (leading Iraqi centers of learning). He also studied in YEMEN, SYRIA, MEDINA, and MECCA. A pious man, he had made the HAJJ to Mecca five times before he turned 33, and he performed several religious retreats in Medina. Because of his expertise in the area of hadith studies, he was one of the leading People of Hadith, a group of traditionalist religious scholars who opposed the People of Opinion (*ray*), religious scholars who preferred individually reasoned legal thinking over strict adherence to precedents expressed in the hadith.

Ibn Hanbal's most celebrated work was the *Musnad*, a multivolume collection of an estimated 27,000 hadith that has been ranked among the six most authoritative Sunni books of hadith. Unlike other hadith collections, which were organized by subject, the *Musnad* was organized according to the names of the earliest known transmitters of each hadith. It began with hadith attributed to the first four caliphs (ABU BAKR, UMAR, UTHMAN, and ALI), then other leading COMPANIONS OF THE PROPHET, the ANSAR, Meccans, Medinans, people of Kufa and Basra, Syrians, and female authorities such as AISHA and Hafsa (two of Muhammad's wives). Ibn Hanbal has also been credited for having written on theological, legal, and ethical topics.

In 833, the Abbasid caliph al-Mamun (r. 813–833) attempted to impose the theological doctrines of the rationalist MUTAZILI SCHOOL and ran into the staunch opposition of Muslim traditionalists, the foremost of whom was Ibn Hanbal. The hadith scholar objected to the Mutazili view that the Quran was created, holding instead to the more popular view that it was uncreated and eternal, thereby affirming its sacred character. Al-Mamun died, but the Abbasid "inquisition" (*mihna*) was continued by his successors, al-Mutasim (r. 833–842) and al-Wathiq (r. 842–847). Ibn Hanbal was imprisoned for two years, and, after being beaten, he was allowed to go home, where he remained in retirement until 847. At the end of the Abbasid persecutions, he resumed his teaching and was even entertained as a guest of the new caliph, al-Mutawakkil (r. 847–861). When he died of an illness in 855, it was reported that thousands attended his funeral. His tomb in Baghdad's Martyr's Cemetery became one of the city's most popular shrines. His teachings were preserved and transmitted by his circle of disciples, including his sons, Salih (d. ca. 880) and Abd Allah (d. 828).

Ibn Hanbal had a profound effect on the history of Islam. His legacy is embodied not only in the *Musnad* and the legal school that bears his name, but also by the generations of Sunni ULAMA who have shaped Islamic tradition through the centuries. He helped make hadith the centerpiece of Islamic law and THEOLOGY and strengthened the religious AUTHORITY of the ulama against state interference.

See also ALLAH; IBN TAYMIYYA, TAQI AL-DIN AHMAD; SUNNISM; WAHHABISM.

Further reading: Michael Cooperson, *Classical Arabic Biography: The Heirs of the Prophets in the Age of al-Mamun* (Cambridge: Cambridge University Press, 2000); Nimrod Hurvitz, *The Formation of Hanbalism: Piety into Power* (London: Routledge Curzon, 2002).

Ibn Hazm, Ali ibn Ahmad ibn Said (994–1064) *leading Andalusian religious scholar and poet*

Ibn Hazm was born in Cordoba, the capital of ANDALUSIA. He lived in a politically turbulent time when the UMAYYAD CALIPHATE was collapsing. Little is known of his family's background except that they may have been Iberian Christians who converted to Islam. His father served the Umayyad court, and he himself relied on their patronage. Ibn Hazm spent his youth in the HAREM, where he gained intimate knowledge of life among the Andalusian elite and the roles WOMEN played in society. He received formal EDUCATION in Arabic language arts, religious sciences, PHILOSOPHY, and history. His gifts placed him in the circle of the best intellects of his time. He had a critical temperament and was a nonconformist in many respects. For example, instead of following the MALIKI LEGAL SCHOOL, the prevailing one in Andalusia, Ibn Hazm was the leading advocate of the Zahiri Legal School, which upheld literal interpretation of the QURAN and HADITH and opposed subjective opinion. He was imprisoned more than once for the political intrigues in which he became implicated. A prolific writer, his biographers credit him with some 400 books on many different topics. Only a few dozen of these have survived. He spent his last years in exile from his beloved Cordoba.

One of Ibn Hazm's most famous books was *Kitab al-fisal fi al-milal wa'l-ahwa wa'l-nihal* (*The book of distinguishing between religions, heresies, and sects*), a comparative look at religions and philosophical schools from the point of view of a believing Muslim intellectual. It provided a rational defense of key tenets of Islamic belief against the truth claims of the Muslim philosophers, challenged Jewish legal doctrines, and refuted Christian teachings about the authenticity of the Gospels and the divinity of JESUS. It also levied cutting criticisms against SHIISM and other Islamic sects and theological schools. Scholars credit Ibn Hazm with being informed about the doctrines he attacked, but they also recognize that he was adamant about the ultimate truth of his own beliefs, particularly the absolute unity of God and the authenticity of the Quran as the word of God. Another of his famous works is *Tawq al-hamama* (Neck-ring of the dove), a fascinating essay on Andalusian Arab understandings of love, enriched by colorful anecdotes drawn from his personal experiences and those of his acquaintances. It began with discussions of how couples fall in love and communicate with each other and then their unions, separations, and betrayals. The religious message Ibn Hazm sought to convey to his readers in this work was that people must try to overcome the carnal appetites of their bodies and follow God-given reason and religious law to win salvation.

See also ADAB; ARABIC LANGUAGE AND LITERATURE; THEOLOGY.

Further reading: Ghulam Haider Aasi, *Muslim Understanding of Other Religions: A Study of Ibn Hazm's Kitab al-fasl fi al-milal wa al-ahwa wa al-nihal* (Islamabad: International Institute of Islamic Thought and Islamic Research, 1999); Lois A. Giffen, "Ibn Hazm and the *Tawq al-hamama.*" In *The Legacy of Muslim Spain,* edited by Salma Khadra Jayyusi, 420–442 (Leiden: E.J. Brill, 1994); Maria Rosa Menocal, *The Ornament of the World: How Muslims, Jews, and Christians Created a Culture of Tolerance in Medieval Spain* (Boston: Little Brown & Co., 2002).

Ibn Idris, Ahmad (ca. 1750–1837) *19th-century reformist Sufi leader*

Ahmad ibn Idris was an influential Sufi teacher in the 19th century. Born in MOROCCO, Ibn Idris received a religious EDUCATION at the Qarawiyyin MOSQUE in FEZ and established himself as an important Sufi teacher there. In 1798, he left Morocco and spent the remainder of his life in the

Hijaz (western Arabia), Upper EGYPT, and YEMEN, where he died at the advanced age of 87.

Ibn Idris focused his work on preaching and teaching. He was an excellent organizer and trainer of disciples, but he did not leave a coherent corpus of writings. Apart from prayers, litanies, and personal letters, most of what remains are summaries of his teachings assembled by his disciples. Profoundly mystical yet humble, Ibn Idris influenced the lives of many Sufis who passed through Arabia during nearly 40 years in the region. He is well known for his defense of the Sufi way in a debate with two Wahhabi scholars near the end of his life. His legacy was to point Sufi movements toward a moderate path and away from the controversial practices and doctrines that earned the criticism of literalist groups such as the Wahhabis. Although Ibn Idris did not found his own TARIQA, his disciples established influential Sufi orders that have spread his teachings beyond Africa to the Middle East, eastern Europe, and Southeast Asia. The term *Idrisiyya* refers both to his school of thought and to the Sufi order that looks to him as its founder.

See also RENEWAL AND REFORM MOVEMENTS; SUFISM; WAHHABISM.

Stephen Cory

Further reading: R. S. O'Fahey, *Enigmatic Saint: Ahmed Ibn Idris and the Idrisi Tradition* (Evanston, Ill.: Northwestern University Press, 1990); ———, "The writings by, attributed to, or on Ahmad Ibn Idris." *Bibliotheca Orientalis* 43, nos. 5/6 (1986): 660–669; John O. Voll, "Two Biographies of Ahmad Ibn Idris al-Fasi (1769–1837)." *International Journal of African Historical Studies* 6 (1973): 633–645.

Ibn Ishaq, Muhammad (704–767) *author of the leading biography of Muhammad*

Details about the early years of Ibn Ishaq's life are lacking, other than that he was born in MEDINA to an Arab family and that his grandfather had converted to Islam after having been taken captive in southern IRAQ. His father and uncle were known as early collectors of Islamic oral tradition. As an adult, Ibn Ishaq lived both in Medina and EGYPT, becoming famous for his mastery of HADITH and accounts of Muhammad's battles and raids (*maghazi*). He returned to Medina where MALIK IBN ANAS (d. 795), the eponymous founder of the MALIKI LEGAL SCHOOL, became his enemy, possibly because of Ibn Ishaq's Shii sympathies, his use of HADITH transmitted by Jewish converts, or his questioning of Malik's authority as a hadith expert. Another respected scholar in Medina, perhaps defending his wife's reputation, accused Ibn Ishaq of citing her falsely as one of his hadith informants. In this stormy climate, he moved on to BAGHDAD, the new capital of the ABBASID CALIPHATE, where he became a tutor to the son of the caliph al-Mansur (r. 754–775).

While in BAGHDAD, Ibn Ishaq wrote his famous BIOGRAPHY of MUHAMMAD, known as *Sirat rasul Allah* (The biography of God's prophet), or simply *Al-Sira* (The biography). It appears to have been part of a larger project on the history of the world that was intended for the edification of the caliph's son. The larger work, known as The Book of the Beginning (Kitab al-Mubtada), included accounts about the creation of the world and the lives of the pre-Islamic prophets and culminated with the biography of Muhammad. Ibn Ishaq may also have wanted to add a history of the caliphate up to his own time, but this part of the project was never completed. The *Sira* emphasized the campaigns Muhammad conducted against his opponents during the Medina phase of his career (622–632), but it also provided valuable information on Muhammad's ancestry, the history of MECCA before Islam, his life before the HIJRA of 622, his encounters with pagan Arabs, Jews, and Christians, the occasions when the QURAN was revealed, and the conversion stories of his early followers. The *Sira* was later edited by Ibn Hisham (d. 833), who removed material he believed to be objectionable to the emerging Sunni consensus, but some of the censored material can be gathered from later

sources. There was no other early source for the life of Muhammad like Ibn Ishaq's Sira, and all other biographies of the Prophet have had to rely on it, including biographies written by modern scholars.

Ibn Ishaq attracted many students of early Islamic biography and history during his years in Baghdad. They transmitted his work to later generations after his death in 767.

See also ARABIC LANGUAGE AND LITERATURE.

Further reading: Muhammad ibn Ishaq, *The Life of Muhammad: A Translation of Ibn Ishaq's Sirat Rasul Allah.* Translated by Alfred Guillaume (Oxford: Oxford University Press, 1955); Gordon Darnell Newby, *The Making of the Last Prophet: A Reconstruction of the Earliest Biography of Muhammad* (Columbia: University of South Carolina Press, 1989).

Ibn Kathir, Imad al-Din Ismail ibn Umar
(1301–1373) *leading Syrian historian, Quran commentator, and scholar of hadith*

Ibn Kathir was born in Busra, SYRIA, and educated in the MAMLUK MADRASAS of DAMASCUS. One of his most prominent teachers was TAQI AL-DIN AHMAD IBN TAYMIYYA (d. 1328), the foremost Hanbali jurist of the Middle Ages, but he considered himself a follower of the SHAFII LEGAL SCHOOL. Ibn Kathir became one of a circle of leading ULAMA who were consulted by Mamluk rulers and held several minor appointments at local MOSQUES and madrasas. He is famous among Muslims around the world today for his TAFSIR (QURAN commentary), which uses HADITH to illuminate meanings of the scripture. He also authored a compendium of hadith, which assembled the six major Sunni collections plus additional hadith in one work. Among scholars of medieval Islam, his book on Islamic history, *Al-Bidaya wa'l-Nihaya* (The beginning and the end) is held in high esteem. It is 14 volumes long in its modern print edition and provides a lengthy biography of MUHAMMAD, a history of the UMAYYAD and ABBASID CALIPHATES, an account of the Mongol invasions, and a history of Damascus. Ibn Kathir became blind at the end of his life and was buried in the Sufiyya Cemetery near the grave of his teacher Ibn Taymiyya.

Further reading: Ibn Kathir, *The Life of the Prophet Muhammad.* 4 vols. Translated by Trevor Le Gassick (London: Garnett Publishing, 1998–2000); ———, *Tafsir Ibn Kathir.* 10 vols., abridged. English translation by Safiur-Rahman Al-Mubarakpuri (Riyadh, Saudi Arabia: Dar-es-Salam Publications, 2000).

Ibn Khaldun, Abd al-Rahman ibn Muhammad (1332–1406) *medieval scholar famed for his philosophy of history and insights into the rise and fall of civilizations*

Ibn Khaldun was born in Tunis to a family of court officials and religious scholars that had emigrated from Seville in Islamicate Spain (ANDALUSIA) during the 13th century. His father, Muhammad, was a jurist who saw to it that his son acquired a thorough EDUCATION in the traditional religious sciences, including QURAN studies, HADITH, and *FIQH* (jurisprudence)—especially that of the MALIKI LEGAL SCHOOL. This was a time when intellectual and cultural life in Tunis prospered under the rule of the Marinids, a BERBER dynasty that ruled parts of North Africa and Andalusia from 1196 to 1464. After the Black Death took the lives of both his parents in 1348–49, Ibn Khaldun left to work in the Marinid court in FEZ. He became deeply involved in political affairs there but continued to further his formal education as well. In 1362, he joined the court of the Nasirid dynasty (1212–1492) in Granada, Spain, and led a peace delegation to the Christian ruler Pedro the Cruel in Seville in 1364. At this time in his career, his chief mentor, Ibn al-Khatib (d. 1374), described him as a man who "commands respect, is able . . . unruly, strong-willed, and full of ambitions for climbing to the highest position of leadership" (Mahdi, 40).

Leaving Andalusia to further enhance his career, Ibn Khaldun traveled to ALGERIA, where he was briefly employed as an adviser to the Hafsid ruler there and as a preacher and jurist. However, these were turbulent times in the Maghrib (North Africa), and after repeated attempts to secure long-term employment, he retired to a desert oasis near Oran in 1374, where he and his family lived under the protection of a friendly Arab desert tribe. Renouncing a career in politics, he dedicated himself to a scholar's life and began to write the famous introduction, known as the "Muqaddima," to his universal history of the Arabs and Berbers (*Kitab al-Ibar*). In 1378, Ibn Khaldun returned to his native Tunis, but, in 1382, he went to CAIRO, EGYPT, where his scholarly reputation earned him several appointments as a teacher of Maliki law and as the city's chief Maliki jurist. In his AUTOBIOGRAPHY, he called his new home "the metropolis of the world . . . illuminated by the moons and stars of its learned men." He was to spend the remaining years of his life there, completing and revising his multivolume history (seven volumes long in its Arabic printed edition) and offering advice to the Mamluk rulers of Egypt and his former royal patrons in Tunis. When the Mongol armies of TAMERLANE (d. 1405) invaded SYRIA in 1400, Ibn Khaldun reluctantly accompanied the MAMLUK army to DAMASCUS to oppose the invasion. During the siege, he was invited to a lengthy audience with the Mongol conqueror. According to the scholar's account, the two men discussed their respective views of history and the rise and fall of civilizations for 35 days, and Ibn Khaldun provided Tamerlane with information about the peoples and lands of Egypt and North Africa. Tamerlane's forces plundered Damascus, but Ibn Khaldun negotiated his own freedom and returned to Cairo, where he held several posts as a Maliki judge and scholar. He also finished writing his autobiography and made the final revisions in his universal history before his death in 1406.

The Muqaddima is encyclopedic in scope; it expresses Ibn Khaldun's philosophy of history and brilliant understanding of society and religion. It is divided into a preface and six substantive chapters. The chapters address the following subjects: society and nature, tribal society, politics and government, urban society, economics, and religious knowledge and the sciences. In these chapters, he proposes what he calls a "new science" of history and civilization. Ibn Khaldun argues that at the beginning of human culture, kin-based groups banded together to overcome the forces of nature, with the most successful ones developing a strong feeling of group solidarity, which he called *asabiyya*. Competition and conflict between groups in time ended with some groups becoming more powerful than others, forming political states. Eventually this led to the establishment of the institutions of government, the building of great cities and civilizations, and the development of learning. Ibn Khaldun acknowledges that the laws established to restrain human violence and ensure justice could be either natural (man-made) or God-given. Revealed law, he argues, especially in a religion such as Islam, not only contributes to worldly security but also offers salvation in the AFTERLIFE. Drawing on his own life experience and knowledge of history, however, Ibn Khaldun also recognizes that ruling dynasties, cities, and civilizations fall and that morality and justice become corrupted. Indeed, he believes that civilizations possess the seeds of their own destruction, for with prosperity and luxury, the bonds of social solidarity weaken, leaving them vulnerable to collapse from within and invasion from without. Tribal groups possessing a more profound degree of group solidarity then arise and form new states and civilizations, thus inaugurating another phase in the cycle of history. Ibn Khaldun sought to convey to the rulers under whom he served the secrets of history that, if mastered, would assure long-lasting peace and security for their subjects and preserve the civilizational heritage they enjoyed.

Ibn Khaldun's philosophy of history had a mixed reception in his own time and was favorably viewed by reform-minded Ottoman historians in the 18th century. However, it has been most deeply appreciated by modern scholars in the West and in Muslim countries; many see it as an exemplary attempt to explain history, society, and religion in terms of human reason.

Further reading: Frances Carney Gies, "The Man Who Met Tamerlane." *Saudi Aramco World* 29 (September/October 1978): 14–21; Ibn Khaldun, *The Muqaddimah: An Introduction to History.* Translated by Franz Rosenthal. Edited and abridged by N. J. Dawood (Princeton, N.J.: Princeton University Press, 2004); Muhsin Mahdi, *Ibn Khaldun's Philosophy of History* (Chicago: University of Chicago Press, 1964).

Ibn Muqla, Abu Ali Muhammad (886–940) *chief minister of three Abbasids and inventor of the proportioned scripts used in Arabic calligraphy*

Born in BAGHDAD at the height of its power and influence, Ibn Muqla was responsible for inventing or implementing a number of administrative reforms. These included the regularization of scripts necessary for documentation and for copying historical and other cultural tracts and that were later used for copying the QURAN. Recent research shows that these reforms disrupted preexisting systems and eliminated the class of professional Quran copyists. These findings revise Orientalist views of Arabic CALLIGRAPHY as an evolutionary process and as an Islamic art form that merely compensated for the supposed absence of figural representation.

Ibn Muqla's writing system, known as *al-khatt al-mansub,* enabled the letters of any given script to be in proportion to one another. It required a well cut pen (*qalam*) with a deep slit for holding ink. The nib produced a rhombus-shaped dot that became the basic unit of a geometric letter design system. Writing an *alif* (the long, vertical Arabic A) required a number of dots one on top of the other, resulting in the maximum height of any other letter. The *alif* acted as control: its total height was the diameter of a circle that enclosed all letters of a particular script. Accordingly, letters were in proportion to one another inasmuch as they were proportional to the circle produced by the *alif*. The proportions held regardless of letter size, which resulted from the actual size of the nib. Ibn Muqla applied this system to six modes of writing, producing the six pens (*al-aqlam al-sitta*) of what is known as Arabic calligraphy or, more accurately, *khatt*.

The reform produced a new aesthetic canon; later medieval scribes and connoisseurs judged the beauty of writing according to the degree of clarity and harmony produced through the new system. Although the reforms may have been originally intended for secular texts, their adoption for copying scripture was complete within two generations. The change in the visual appearance of the holy text reflected controversies over the nature of the Quran and its message, which the Abbasids considered eternal and accessible to all. The clarity and legibility of proportioned writing mirrored this ideological position and combated proponents of an esoteric message accessible only to a chosen elite.

Ibn Muqla, too, fell victim to the politics of the Abbasid court at the end of his life. He was imprisoned, suffered the amputation of his right hand, and died in disgrace.

See also ALPHABET; ART; IBN AL-BAWWAB, ABU AL-HASAN ALI; ORIENTALISM.

Nuha N. N. Khoury

Further reading: Yasin Safadi, *Islamic Calligraphy* (Boulder, Colo.: Shambhala Publications, 1978); Yasser Tabbaa, *The Transformation of Islamic Art during the Sunni Revival* (Seattle: University of Washington Press, 2001).

Ibn Rushd, Muhammad (also known in the West by his Latinized name, Averroës) (1126–1198) *a leading philosopher in the Middle Ages famed for his learned commentaries on Aristotle and his refutation of Muslim theological teachings*

Ibn Rushd was born in CORDOBA, one of the major centers of Islamicate culture and learning in ANDALUSIA. At that time, it was ruled by the ALMOHAD DYNASTY of North Africa, known for its puritanical adherence to Islamic law and interest in PHILOSOPHY. Both his grandfather and father had been leading judges of the MALIKI LEGAL SCHOOL, and as a youth he also studied Maliki law, THEOLOGY, medicine, MATHEMATICS, and astronomy. It is not known exactly when he took up the study of philosophy, but it may have been through his teacher of medicine and mathematics, Abu Jaafar ibn Harun. (In medieval Islam, medicine, mathematics, and philosophy were seen as related areas of learning.)

At the age of 27, Ibn Rushd was retained by the Almohad court in Marrakesh, the Almohad capital in what is now Morocco, as an astronomer. Around 1169, the prominent court physician and philosopher Ibn Tufayl (d. 1185) introduced him to the caliph Abu Yaaqub Yusuf (r. 1163–84), who engaged him in a discussion about whether heaven was created or eternal, a controversial question because it pitted conventional Muslim theological doctrine about God's unique eternity against the philosophical view that the world was eternal. Ibn Rushd, reportedly a modest and discreet man, made a favorable impression on the caliph with his answers, and this helped him obtain coveted appointments as a judge in Seville and Cordoba and as successor to Ibn Tufayl as court physician in 1182. He began to write the philosophical works and commentaries during this time, prompted, perhaps, by the caliph's complaint that the works of Aristotle (384–322 B.C.E.), the ancient Greek philosopher, were difficult to understand. Ibn Rushd enjoyed the favor of Abu Yaaqub Yusuf's successor, Yaaqub al-Mansur (r. 1184–99), until 1195, when he was banished to Lucena, a small town south of Cordoba. This may have been for political reasons, but it led to an order by Cordoba's city council to have his philosophical works burned because they were thought to undermine the faith. He was restored to favor a few years later but died shortly thereafter in 1198. Ibn Rushd was buried in Marrakesh, but his body

Statue commemorating Ibn Rushd in Cordoba, Spain *(Federico R. Campo)*

was later transferred to Cordoba, his hometown, for burial.

Ibn Rushd is estimated to have written more than 100 books and treatises in his lifetime. He is best known for his commentaries on Aristotle, whose works had been translated into Arabic in SYRIA during the eighth century. Ibn Rushd's commentaries were written in Arabic, translated into Hebrew and Latin, and then transmitted to Europe in the 13th and 14th centuries. Indeed, it was mainly through Ibn Rushd's commentaries that European intellectuals and theologians (known as the Scholastics) discovered Aristotle. Even though it met with strong opposition from the Catholic Church, his work contributed significantly to the advancement of the Western philo-

sophical tradition during the High Middle Ages. Thomas Aquinas (d. 1274), the foremost Catholic theologian of the time, consulted and contended with Ibn Rushd's interpretation of Aristotle in composing his major theological works, *Summa Theologica* and *Summa contra Gentiles.*

Another one of Ibn Rushd's major works was a treatise that argued against the views of ABU HAMID AL-GHAZALI (d. 1111), the famous Baghdadi scholar who adhered to the ASHARI SCHOOL of Sunni theology and was held in high esteem by the Almohads. In a book titled *The Incoherence of the Philosophers* (*Tahafut al-falasifa*), al-Ghazali had opposed the Neoplatonist philosophical views of AL-FARABI (d. 950), IBN SINA (d. 1037), and others who argued that the world was eternal, that God had no knowledge of the particulars of his CREATION, and who denied a bodily resurrection and final judgment. Instead, al-Ghazali maintained that philosophy and religion were incompatible and that philosophers should be condemned as infidels. Ibn Rushd, defending Aristotle and the Islamic philosophical tradition, entitled his refutation of al-Ghazali *The Incoherence of the Incoherence* (*Tahafut al-tahafut*) and asserted that reason and revelation were indeed compatible, it was only that they differed in language and interpretation. Some of those who read his work alleged that he held to a belief in "two truths"—that there was one truth that could be known by human reason and another that could be known by revelation from God. A fuller reading of Ibn Rushd, however, does not support this claim. In addition to his philosophical and theological works, he also wrote books on Islamic law, politics, and astronomy. His medical encyclopedia, *The Book of Generalities (Kitab al-kulliyat)*, dealt with a variety of topics, including anatomy, disease, diet, and healing. It was translated into Latin and read by medical students in medieval Europe.

The persecution and condemnation Ibn Rushd suffered in his last years, combined with the political and cultural decline of Islamicate Spain, dampened the impact of his work in Islamicate lands.

Aside from his sons, he had few followers until the modern period. In the 20th century, Arabic publishers in Beirut and Cairo issued print editions of several of his books on law, theology, and medicine. This was a result of renewed interest in his thought that came with increased interaction with Europe and a movement to reform Islam in conformity with modern notions of rationality. A revived interest in Ibn Rushd is also reflected in the feature film *Destiny* (al-Masir, 1997), directed by the Egyptian filmmaker Youssef Chahine (b. 1926). The film depicts Ibn Rushd as a respected scholar and family man contending with political authoritarianism and religious fanaticism, a reality faced by many in the world today.

Further reading: Iysa A. Bello, *The Medieval Islamic Controversy between Philosophy and Theology: Ijma and Tawil in the Conflict between al-Ghazali and Ibn Rushd* (Leiden: E.J. Brill, 1989); Oliver Leaman, *Averroes and His Philosophy* (Oxford: Oxford University Press, 1988); Caroline Stone, "Doctor, Philosopher, Renaissance Man." *Saudi Aramco World* 54 (May/June 2003): 8–15.

Ibn Saud   See ABD AL-AZIZ IBN SAUD.

Ibn Sina, Abu Ali al-Husayn (Latin as Avicenna) (979–1037) *gifted Persian philosopher and physician whose writings were widely studied in the Middle East and Europe*

More is known about Ibn Sina's early life than about most other medieval Muslim scholars because he wrote an AUTOBIOGRAPHY about his youth, supplemented with details about his adult career contributed by later Muslim biographers. He was born in a village near BUKHARA (now in Uzbekistan) and educated under the supervision of his father, a learned man with Ismaili affiliations. Ibn Sina is thought to have had a remarkable memory. He claims that by the age of 10 he had memorized the QURAN and large amounts of

Arabic poetry. Soon thereafter, he studied several highly complex subjects, including logic, Islamic law (FIQH), and the metaphysics of Aristotle, as explained by the Turkish philosopher AL-FARABI (d. 950). He also studied Neoplatonic PHILOSOPHY, which was held in high esteem by Ismaili scholars such as the BRETHREN OF PURITY. Because he was allowed free access to the royal library of the Samanid dynasty (819–999), he was able to educate himself so well that he boasted of becoming a teacher to the tutors hired by his father to educate him. By the time he had turned 21, he had already become famous for his medical knowledge and healing skills and had written his first book on philosophy.

When his father died in 1002, Ibn Sina left Bukhara and traveled westward, finding temporary employment in the courts of several local rulers. He continued to teach and write while serving in government posts. Around 1020, Ibn Sina became a court physician to the Shii ruler Shams al-Dawla (r. 997–1021) in Hamadan in western IRAN. He was imprisoned in 1022 as a result of political intrigues but managed to escape to Isfahan in the south, where he was protected by Ala al-Dawla Muhammad (r. 1008–41), the local ruler. Isfahan was his home for 15 years, where he continued his scholarly activities and completed writing his major works. He died in the company of Ala al-Dawla while on a military expedition. He was buried in Hamadan, where a monumental tomb memorializes his contributions to Islamic philosophy, medicine, and SCIENCE.

Estimates concerning the number of books and treatises he wrote range from 100 to 250. Most of them were written in Arabic, even though his native language was Persian. Among the most exhaustive of his works on philosophical and religious subjects was *Kitab al-shifa* (*The Book of Healing*). It dealt with four chief topics: logic, physics, MATHEMATICS, and metaphysics. The chapters on physics included substantial discussion about the nature of the human soul and its relation to mind and body. He argued that all human souls were immortal and thus not subject to a bodily resurrection. In his discussion of metaphysics, he attempted to show that all beings had their origin in what he called the Necessary Existent, the first cause, or God. Ibn Sina's God represented the highest beauty, lacking any defect; he was both the essential lover and the beloved. Inspired by Neoplatonism, Ibn Sina supported the idea that the rest of CREATION flowed from God in waves, or emanations. Such ideas were highly offensive to literally minded Muslims. He developed these ideas further in a group of writings concerned with mysticism and "Oriental Wisdom." Ibn Sina also wrote an encyclopedic book on the healing arts titled *The Canon of Medicine* (*Al-Qanun fi al-tibb*), which drew extensively on Greek and Arab medical literature and even some of his own personal experience. It included his recommendations on caring for infants, raising CHILDREN, and EDUCATION.

Ibn Sina's genius inspired and challenged philosophers, men of religion, mystics, physicians, and scientists in the Middle East and Europe for centuries after his death. In Islamicate lands, these included luminaries such as AL-GHAZALI (d. 1111), IBN RUSHD (d. 1198), IBN AL-ARABI (d. 1240), Abu Hafs al-Suhrawardi (d. 1294), and MULLA SADRA (d. 1640). Latin translations of *The Book of Healing* and *The Canon of Medicine* were read in European universities as early as the 12th century and were studied there for centuries. The Catholic theologian Thomas Aquinas (d. 1274), like his counterparts in the east, also benefited from Ibn Sina's learning while arguing against some of his ideas about God, the soul, and creation. Even today Ibn Sina's work is being read in many centers of learning around the world. In 1979–80, the 1,000-year anniversary of his birth was celebrated in many countries. Hospitals in the Middle East and South Asia bear his name, including one in Baghdad. Iranians regard him as a national hero. The United Nations Educational and Social Organization (UNESCO) established a prize for groups and individuals in the fields of ethics and science in his honor in 2004.

Further reading: William Gohlman, *The Life of Ibn Sina: A Critical Edition and Annotated Translation* (Albany: State University of New York Press, 1974); Dimitri Gutas, *Avicenna and the Aristotelian Tradition: Introduction to Reading Avicenna's Philosophical Works* (Leiden: E.J. Brill, 1988); Shams Inati, "Ibn Sina." In *History of Islamic Philosophy*, edited by Seyyed Hossein Nasr and Oliver Leaman, 231–246 (London: Routledge, 1996); David Tschanz, "The Arab Roots of European Medicine." *Saudi Aramco World* 48 (May/June 1997): 20–31.

Ibn Taymiyya, Taqi al-Din Ahmad (Ibn Taymiya, Ibn Taimiya) (1263–1328)

prominent Hanbali jurist and theologian who inspired Islamic revivalist movements, especially Wahhabism

Ibn Taymiyya was born in the ancient city of Harran in what is now southeastern TURKEY. He came from a family of scholars affiliated with the HANBALI LEGAL SCHOOL. When he was only six years old, his family fled to DAMASCUS in order to escape the Mongols who had invaded the Middle East from Central Asia, plundering cities and killing many in their path. He obtained his EDUCATION at a Hanbali MADRASA directed by his father.

At the age of 21, Ibn Taymiyya succeeded his father as director and began to teach and write books. In his work, he advocated a literal interpretation of the QURAN and HADITH and called on Muslims to follow the example set by the COMPANIONS OF THE PROPHET, the *salaf*. He condemned many of the teachings of Muslim philosophers, theologians, and Shiis. He was also outraged by popular belief in saints and visiting saints' tombs. Arguing that this was not condoned by the early Muslim community, he ruled that it was BIDAA (unorthodox innovation) and therefore forbidden. He did not reject Sufi piety and asceticism, however, as long as God remained the focus of worship. He is reported to have been a member of the Qadiri Order of Sufis. Ibn Taymiyya also opposed traditionalist approaches to the understanding of the SHARIA and favored the use of IJTIHAD (independent legal reasoning) by qualified jurists.

When the Mongols invaded SYRIA in 1300, he was among those calling for JIHAD against them and ruled that even though they had recently converted to Islam, they should be considered unbelievers. He went to EGYPT to win support to this cause and became embroiled in religio-political disputes there. Ibn Taymiyya's enemies accused him of ANTHROPOMORPHISM, a view that was objectionable to the teachings of the ASHARI SCHOOL of Islamic THEOLOGY, and he was imprisoned for more than a year in 1306. Upon release, he condemned popular Sufi practices and the influence of IBN AL-ARABI (d. 1240), earning him the enmity of leading Sufi SHAYKHS in Egypt and another prison sentence. He was released by the Egyptian sultan in 1310.

The sultan allowed Ibn Taymiyya to return to Damascus in 1313, where he worked as a teacher and jurist. He had supporters among the powerful, but his outspokenness and nonconformity to traditional Sunni doctrine and Sufi ideals and practices continued to draw the wrath of the religious and political authorities in Syria and Egypt. He was arrested and released several more times, although he was usually allowed to continue writing FATWAS (advisory opinions in matters of law) and defenses of his ideas while in prison. Despite the controversy that surrounded him, Ibn Taymiyya's influence reached well beyond Hanbali circles to members of other Sunni legal schools and Sufi groups. Among his foremost students were IBN KATHIR (d. 1373), a leading medieval historian and Quran commentator, and Ibn Qayyim al-Jawziya (d. 1350), a prominent Hanbali jurist and theologian who helped spread his teacher's influence after his death in 1328. Ibn Taymiyya died a prisoner in the citadel of Damascus and was buried in the city's Sufi cemetery.

Hanbali influence subsequently declined in Syria and Egypt, especially after the region fell under Ottoman control in the 16th century. In the 18th century, Ibn Taymiyya's teachings influenced the revivalist movement led by MUHAMMAD IBN ABD AL-WAHHAB (d. 1792) in the Arabian Peninsula. His books are today widely read in SAUDI ARABIA, Egypt, Syria, JORDAN, South Asia, and Southeast Asia. In addition to inspiring religious revivalists and reformers, some of his rulings have also been used to justify acts of violence committed by followers of radical Islamic groups. One of these was the Jihad Group responsible for the assassination of Egyptian president ANWAR AL-SADAT (d. 1981).

See also SAINT; SALAFISM; SUFISM; WAHHABISM.

Further reading: George Makdisi, "Ibn Taimiya: A Sufi of the Qadiriya Order," *American Journal of Arabic Studies* 1 (1974): 118–129; Abd al-Hakim ibn Ibrahim Matroudi, *The Hanbali School of Law and Ibn Taymiyyah: Conflict or Conciliation* (London: Routledge, 2006); Muhammad Umar Memon, *Ibn Taymiya's Struggle against Popular Religion* (The Hague: Mouton, 1976).

Ibn Tumart, Muhammad (ca. 1078–1130) *12th-century religious reformer, self-proclaimed mahdi (messianic figure), and founder of the North African Almohad dynasty*

Born in the Anti-Atlas Mountains in southern MOROCCO, Ibn Tumart left for an extended trip to the Muslim East in 1106. While there he studied FIQH (Islamic jurisprudence) and became convinced that the dominant MALIKI LEGAL SCHOOL of Morocco was leading Muslims astray through its elaborate rules based upon human reasoning. Instead, Ibn Tumart emphasized the original Islamic sources of the QURAN and HADITH and taught a strict doctrine based on the Muslim doctrine of TAWHID (unity). On his way home in 1117, Ibn Tumart created a stir in a number of locations through his preaching and aggressive treatment of those he considered to be unbelievers.

Having raised the ire of the Almoravid government in Marrakesh, Ibn Tumart retreated to his own people, the Masmuda BERBERS of the Anti-Atlas Mountains, in 1121. There he laid the foundations for the future ALMOHAD DYNASTY, claiming the title of MAHDI (messianic deliverer) and implementing a rigorous religious ethic among his Berber following. Posing as a holy man and miracle worker, Ibn Tumart rallied the Masmuda against the ruling ALMORAVID DYNASTY. Although he failed in his attempt to take Marrakesh (1124), the city would eventually fall to his successor, Abd al-Mumin (r. 1133–63), along with the rest of North Africa and Islamicate Spain after Ibn Tumart's death in 1130.

See also ANDALUSIA.

Stephen Cory

Further reading: M. Kisaichi, "The Almohad Social-Political System or Hierarchy in the Reign of Ibn Tumart." *Memoirs of the Research Department of the Toyo Bunko* 48 (1990): pp. 81–101; Roger Le Tourneau, *The Almohad Movement in North Africa in the Twelfth and Thirteenth Century* (Princeton, N.J.: Princeton University Press, 1969).

Ibrahim   *See* ABRAHAM.

Ibrahim Ibn Adham (730–777) *early Sufi saint who was a model for piety in Sufi tradition and whose conversion story mirrors that of the Buddha*

Ibrahim ibn Adham was born a prince in Bactria, Balkh (present-day AFGHANISTAN)—where Buddhism flourished until the 11th century—in a recently created Arab settlement. Legend tells that Ibn Adham's conversion to the Sufi path began when out hunting in the forest one day he was confronted by a voice prompting him to examine his true calling in life. Like the Buddha, to whom Ibn Adham is frequently compared, he thereupon chose to renounce his claim to kingship and set off

for MECCA, leaving an infant son and wife behind, to spend the rest of his life in saintly devotion to ALLAH. In 748, he migrated from MECCA to SYRIA, where for the following few decades he lived the life of a wandering Sufi in the desert. It is believed that he died around 777 in Syria while participating in raids against Byzantine Christians. He is reported to have transmitted several HADITH and is remembered for his extreme ASCETICISM and generosity.

One of the earliest Sufis, Ibrahim ibn Adham's legend grew and developed in the centuries following his death as he became a frequent model of piety in Sufi treatises written in communities from Arabia to East Asia. Early sources on Ibrahim ibn Adham include hagiographies written in the 11th century by al-Sulami and in the 13th century by Farid al-Din al-Attar. Ibrahim ibn Adham's story was told in the oldest Persian treatise on SUFISM, the classic *Kashf al-mahjub* by Al-Hujwiri in Lahore, Pakistan. A 17th-century Malay text, *Bastanu's-salatin,* written by an Indian Muslim named Ar-Raniri, presented Ibrahim ibn Adham as one of the greatest early SAINTS of Islam. He stands out as a paradigm of saintly devotion in such hagiographies, like the most famous and earliest of known WOMEN Sufis, RABIA AL-ADAWIYA (d. 801). But as he embodied the ideal of unsurpassed piety and asceticism, Rabia stood for the ideal of passionate love for God. One famous story described Ibn Adham's 14-year journey to Mecca and his frequent stops for prayer at holy sites along the way, only to discover upon reaching Mecca that the KAABA had to meet Rabia.

See also BUDDHISM AND ISLAM.

Megan Adamson Sijapati

Further reading: Russell Jones, *Nuru'd-din ar Rahini Bastanu's-Salatin, bab IV, fasal 1: critical edition and translation of the first part of Fasal 1, which deals with Ibrahim ibn Adham* (Kuala Lumpur: Dewan Bahasa dan Pustaka, 1974); John Alden Williams, ed. *Themes of Islamic Civilization* (Berkeley and Los Angeles: University of California Press, 1971).

Id al-Adha (Arabic: Feast of Sacrifice)

The most important yearly festival HOLIDAY of the Islamic CALENDAR is Id al-Adha, or al-Id al-Kabir (Great Feast). It is also known as Id al-Qurban (Feast of Sacrifice), as well as Qurban Bayrami (Sacrifice Feast) in Turkic lands, Bakar Id (Goat Feast) in INDIA, and Reraya Qurben (Sacrifice Holiday) in INDONESIA. In Muslim-majority countries today, it has been declared a public holiday. The festival begins on the 10th day of the 12th month (Dhu al-Hijja) of the Islamic lunar year, at the conclusion of the annual HAJJ rites in MECCA, and lasts for up to four days. According to Islamic law, Muslims around the world who are able are obliged to sacrifice an unblemished sheep, goat, cow, or CAMEL. They are also expected to attend a special communal PRAYER, traditionally held in open air or at a MOSQUE, where they listen to a holiday sermon. Unlike other prayer times, there is no ADHAN (call to prayer) performed. Muslims believe that the festival represents complete obedience to God, as ABRAHAM obeyed him when commanded to sacrifice his son. According to the story, which has biblical roots and is retold in the QURAN and Islamic exegetical literature, a ram was substituted in place of Abraham's son. Among the Shia, this story is associated with themes of MARTYRDOM and redemption.

The sacrificial feast allows all Muslims, pilgrims and nonpilgrims alike, to experience a sense of community at the conclusion of the hajj. Men customarily perform the sacrifice with their own hands according to ritual slaughtering procedures approved by Islamic law, but meat can also be obtained from qualified butchers. In Mecca, there are special slaughtering facilities in the pilgrim town of Mina, just outside the holy city. Muslims living in the UNITED STATES or Europe obtain their meat from a HALAL butcher, or they go to a farm where they can purchase an animal and slaughter it themselves, as they would in a Muslim country. WOMEN participate by preparing dishes made from the meat of the sacrificed animal. Everywhere Id al-Adha is a very festive time when people gather together with family and friends. CHILDREN wear bright new clothing. Muslim girls in India and PAKISTAN show off fresh henna designs on their hands and arms. In many communities, the holiday affirms ties to deceased loved ones and the poor, because people distribute food to the needy in memory of the dead. Women usually visit cemeteries during the Id to do this. Meat may also be distributed through mosques and Islamic charities, making Id al-Adha one of the few times in the year when the needy eat meat. In modern times, the internet has made it possible for people to make donations online by credit card so that needy Muslims anywhere in the world can join in the FEASTING.

See also ALMSGIVING; ANIMALS; FOOD AND DRINK; FUNERARY RITUALS.

Further reading: Jonah Blank, *Mullahs on the Mainframe: Islam and Modernity among the Daudi Bohras* (Chicago: University of Chicago Press, 2001); 104–110; John R. Bowen, "On Scriptural Essentialism and Ritual Variation: Muslim Sacrifice in Sumatra and Morocco." *American Ethnologist* 19 (Nov. 1992): 656–671; Hava Lazarus-Yafeh, "Muslim Festivals." *Numen* 25 (April 1978): 52–64.

Id al-Fitr (Arabic: Feast of Fast-Breaking)

The second most important yearly festival on the Islamic CALENDAR after ID AL-ADHA is Id al-Fitr, or al-Id al-Saghir (Little Feast). This holiday is also known as Kuchuk Bayram (Little Feast) in Turkic lands and Hari Raya Puasa (Fasting Day of Celebration) in MALAYSIA. The festival celebrates the end of the RAMADAN fast and begins with the sighting of the new moon on the eve of the first day of the 10th month (Shawwal) of the Islamic lunar year. It usually lasts for up to three days. In Muslim-majority countries today, it has been declared a public HOLIDAY, like Id al-Adha. To prepare for the holiday, each person is obliged to offer charity for the needy during the closing days of Ramadan. This is called *zakat al-fitr* or *zakat Ramadan*, and it is comparable to the animal sacrifices performed for the Id al-Adha. It is supposed to earn forgiveness for wrongs done during Ramadan and help provide assistance to the poor so that they can enjoy the holiday too. Muslims who are able are expected to attend a special communal PRAYER in the early morning, traditionally held in open air or at a MOSQUE, where they listen to a holiday SERMON. When prayers end, people go home to break their fast with a daytime meal.

Like other major feasts during the year, Id al-Fitr enhances the sense of community among believers. People gather together with family and friends; CHILDREN go outdoors to play wearing brightly colored new holiday clothes. Girls in INDIA and PAKISTAN show off fresh henna designs on the hands and arms. Gifts are exchanged between family members. Each local Muslim culture has its own holiday food traditions. In many countries, sweet pastries are a favorite food, traditionally prepared by WOMEN at home during the last days of Ramadan. Rice and vermicelli dishes are also popular.

See also ALMSGIVING; FEASTING; FOOD AND DRINK.

Further reading: Marjo Buitelaar, *Fasting and Feasting in Morocco: Women's Participation in Ramadan* (Oxford: Berg, 1993); Riadh El-Droubie, "Muslim Festivals." In *Festivals in World Religions,* edited by Alan Brown, 211–233. (New York: Longman, 1986); Hava Lazarus-Yafeh, "Muslim Festivals." *Numen* 25 (April 1978): 52–64.

idolatry

Idolatry (Arabic: SHIRK) in Islam is mentioned in the QURAN in a variety of forms whose root (sh-r-k) meaning is "sharing, participating, associating," in the context of "associating" anything other than God with God. "Associationism" in Islamic tradition has been applied in two basic contexts. The primary meaning is usually understood as actual polytheism or the worship of images, both overt infringements of Islam's cardinal principle,

TAWHID, declaring in life and thought "the oneness of God." The secondary and polemic sense involves accusations by some Muslims against other Muslims for being insufficiently "pure" in thought or practice, even though those accused of *shirk* might consider themselves monotheists in good standing.

The early quranic contexts for *shirk,* meaning polytheism and idolatry, identify "opponents" of Muhammad and the early UMMA, or religious community of Muslims, among the pagan Meccans. According to one of the earliest postquranic Arabic sources on pre-Islamic religion, *Kitab al-asnam* (The book of idols) attributed to Hisham ibn al-Kalbi (d. 821), the Prophet's pagan contemporaries among the QURAYSH, who dominated the social, political, economic, and religious life of his hometown, MECCA, had images of plural divinities and sacred powers within the center of tribal worship for the region, the KAABA, including such deities as Hubal, Shams, Sin, and, among others, a triple GODDESS associated with Arabian star-worship of Venus as the morning-evening star who is named briefly (Q 53:20) in the Quran as Allat (fem. of Allah, lit. "the Goddess"), al-Uzza (fem. "the Mighty One"), and Manat.

According to a highly problematic narrative known later as the SATANIC VERSES, the triple goddesses were alluded to in the eighth- to mid-ninth-century biography of the prophet (*Sirat rasul Allah*) as well as described by Muslim historian al-Tabari in his early tenth-century History of the prophets and kings as "the high flying cranes (*gharaniq*) whose intercession is to be hoped for." In other words, the early Meccans could continue to have recourse to the triple goddess alongside recourse to ALLAH. This reference to the "satanic verses," which do not actually appear in the Quran as we have it today, is usually explained in Islamic exegesis as an occasion of abrogation (*naskh*) in the Quran wherein God sent down a later revelation (Q 53:19–23) to supersede and "abrogate" the authority of the earlier narrative suggested in the *Sira.* The quranic verses as they stand in canonical Islamic revelation absolutely deny both divine plurality and femininity as well as any powers of intercession outside Allah's will.

The *mushrik* (one who associates) in broader polemic understanding *acts* as if there were divine beings other than God and may be viewed as a polytheist as well as an idolater, even though he is a Muslim. The accusation of "associationism" applied to Muslims views with suspicion objects of popular devotion, especially the veneration of saints and other supermundane beings, as potential rivals for the sole worship the Muslim owes to God. Later and modern Islamic interpretation view the two contexts of *shirk*—polytheist-idolater and popular intercessionist—as virtually synonymous. Such popular devotion, however, became a large part of the belief and practice of the ordinary person as opposed to the theoretical rigor and almost ascetic purity of practice espoused by Muslim jurists and theologians. The devotions of the vast majority of Muslims from the lifetime of MUHAMMAD down to modern times have included ritual propitiation of a wide array of spiritual beings (such as astral spirits and angels, believed in medieval Islam to inhabit planetary bodies; the JINN; and the invocation, direction, and exorcism of spirits of the dead, whether familial or spirits of local saints and holy persons), manipulation of elemental and divinely created powers of natural objects (planets and stars, lightning, rain, wind, fire, the ocean, as well as sacred trees, springs, and stones), ritual use of objects or images of sacred power (the verbal and material use of sacred texts in quranic CALLIGRAPHY and recitation), or even people and institutions *treated* as objects of sacred power and recourse (prophets and saints as in Muhammad and his family, the Shii imams, Sufi saints, great teachers and healers, and religious institutions such as famous MOSQUES and MADRASAS [legal colleges], which were at the same time burial sites of local saints used as foci of ZIYARA (pilgrimage, intercessory prayer, divinatory and healing rituals). In modern times, belief in and practice of such popular devotions have

significantly declined, especially in highly urbanized and educated milieus. However, the underlying belief in God's presence in the world and in his material instrumentality through nature and revelation is still a core of the Islamic worldview. Examples of popular devotion and intercessory aid can still be found in living contexts in many Muslim countries, whether modern jurists continue to think it "idolatrous" or not.

See also ANGEL; ARABIAN RELIGIONS, PRE-ISLAMIC; AUTHORITY; *BIDAA;* HINDUISM AND ISLAM; INTERCESSION; SAINT; THEOLOGY.

Kathleen M. O'Connor

Further reading: Gerald R. Hawting, *The Idea of Idolatry and the Emergence of Islam: From Polemic to History* (New York: Cambridge University Press, 1999); Hisham ibn al-Kalbi, *The Book of Idols: Being a Translation from the Arabic of the Kitab al-asnam.* Translated by Nabih A. Faris (1952. Reprint, Princeton, N.J.: Princeton University Press, 1972); Elizabeth Sirriyeh, "Modern Muslim Interpretations of *shirk.*" *Religion* 20 (1990): 139–159; Muhammad I. H. Surty, *The Quranic Concept of al-shirk (Polytheism)* (London: Ta Ha Publishers, 1982); Alford T. Welch, "Allah and Other Supernatural Beings: The Emergence of the Quranic Doctrine of *tawhid.*" *Journal of the American Academy of Religion,* Thematic Issue: Studies in Quran and *Tafsir* 47, no. 4 (1979): 733–753.

Idris *Islamic prophet, usually identified with the biblical Enoch*

Idris is an unusual prophet briefly mentioned twice in the QURAN (Q 19:56–57; 21:85–86), where he is described as trustworthy and patient. The Quran adds that God had "raised him up to a high place" (Q 19:57), a statement that most Muslim commentators believe meant that God let him enter PARADISE without first dying. This made him a unique human being. Even his name is an unusual one; it probably originated as a term in ancient Hebrew for "interpreter" (*doresh*) of the

TORAH. This is an early Jewish reference to Enoch, who is mentioned in the Bible as a descendant of ADAM and an ancestor of Noah who had "walked with God." Likewise, Islamic tradition regards Idris as a prophet who lived between the time of Adam and Noah. Eighth-century Muslim sources explicitly mention that Idris's true name is Enoch and that he is called Idris in Arabic because of his devotion to the study (*dars*) of the sacred books of his ancestors Adam and Seth (a son of Adam). In the line of legendary prophets who preceded MUHAMMAD (d. 632), he is credited with being the first person to write with a pen, to sew clothes, and to study astronomy. According to one prophet story, Idris's great piety attracted the attention of the angel of death, who visited him for three days in his human form and then rewarded him with a tour of heaven, hell, and the gardens of paradise. Muhammad is said to have met Idris in the fourth heaven during his NIGHT JOURNEY AND ASCENT. Sufi masters such as RUZBIHAN BAQLI (d. 1209) and MUHYI AL-DIN IBN AL-ARABI (d. 1240) also mention that they encountered him in their visionary journeys.

See also JUDAISM AND ISLAM; PROPHETS AND PROPHECY.

Further reading: Yoram Erder, "The Origin of the Idris in the Quran: A Study of the Influence of Qumran Literature on Early Islam." *Journal of Near East Studies* 49 (1990): 339–350; Ahmad ibn Muhammad al-Thalabi, *Arais al-majalis fi qisas al-anbiya, or "Lives of the Prophets."* Translated by William M. Brinner (Leiden: E.J. Brill, 2002), 83–85.

ifrit   *See* JINNI.

ijmaa (Arabic: consensus, agreement)

A technical term used in Islamic law (FIQH), *ijmaa* was the third authoritative source after the QURAN and the SUNNA considered by Sunni jurists when they made a ruling or advisory opinion (FATWA). In contrast to IJTIHAD (individual reasoned opinion), *ijmaa* recognized the social and practical basis of law. Also, unlike *ijtihad,* it was thought to be free of error. The ULAMA justified using consensus as a source in their interpretations of the SHARIA by invoking a HADITH attributed to MUHAMMAD that said, "My community will never agree in an error." They also used quranic verses for support, such as Q 2:143: "We have made you a middle community [UMMA] so that you may be witnesses before humankind." Thus, jurists linked *ijmaa* to an idealized concept of Islamic community using the words of sacred scripture and the Prophet.

Ijmaa was originally rooted in pre-Islamic Arabian custom, which continued to develop in the Arabian Peninsula and in newly conquered towns and settlements throughout the Middle East in the wake of the Arab-Islamic conquests of the seventh and eighth centuries. It gradually evolved from being a sociocultural practice to a religious one. Early scholars, judges, and administrators based their judgments on the Quran and sunna (customary practice) of localities, such as MEDINA and Kufa in southern IRAQ. When they needed to recommend what the correct sunna for Muslims to follow should be, they looked to the *ijmaa* of the local community. Even the selection of hadith to substantiate what was sunna was done in conformity to consensus. After al-Shafii's efforts to systematize the science of Islamic jurisprudence in the early ninth century, consensus was increasingly identified with the practice of the Muslim community during Muhammad's lifetime as established by the jurists who constituted the chief authorities of the different law schools. Defined largely in religious terms, it gained a kind of perfection or infallibility in the eyes of Sunni jurists that *ijtihad* and analogical reasoning (*qiyas*) never had. The assertion of infallibility for Muslim consensus helped give coherence to the legal schools, make them more inclined to accept each other's authority, and accept or reject customs and practices originating in non-Muslim societies and other religions. Jurists belonging to the Twelve-

Imam branch of Shiism rejected the idea of the infallibility of *ijmaa*. Instead, it was the 12th Imam alone who could guarantee infallibility, which means that Shii jurists had to strive to determine what his opinion was for a particular question.

See also AUTHORITY; MUJTAHID; SHAFII, MUHAM-MAD IBN IDRIS AL-; TWELVE-IMAM SHIISM.

Further reading: Wael B. Hallaq, "On the Authorita-tiveness of Sunni Consensus," *International Journal of Middle East Studies* 18 (1986): 427–454; ———, *The Origins and Evolution of Islamic Law* (Cambridge: Cam-bridge University Press, 2005).

ijtihad (Arabic: striving, exerting)

A technical term employed in Islamic jurispru-dence (FIQH), *ijtihad* refers to the use of indepen-dent judgment to arrive at legal rulings in matters that are not explicitly addressed in the QURAN and SUNNA. A scholar who engages in *ijtihad* is known as a MUJTAHID. Both terms are related to the Arabic word JIHAD (struggle, effort), suggesting that, like jihad, not all people are qualified to undertake it, that the effort must be directed to meet a specific end, and that it is regarded as a virtuous endeavor even if it should fall short of its goal.

For most of its history, Islamic law has been an ongoing process of scholarly study, reflec-tion, debate, and critical reasoning grounded in dynamic historical and social contexts, rather than a code of timeless, inflexible rules. Although modern scholars have claimed that the so-called gate of *ijtihad* was closed as long ago as the 10th century, *ijtihad* has, in fact, been a key aspect of Islamic jurisprudence for centuries thereafter. It is often contrasted with *taqlid* (imitation, tradition), which refers to acceptance of rulings reached in the past by ULAMA belonging to a particular legal school or tradition, such as one of the four chief Sunni legal schools. The two tendencies, *ijti-had* and *taqlid*, have sometimes worked together and sometimes in opposite directions. Both have played significant roles in the development of the

Islamic legal tradition. *Taqlid* helped preserve the Muslim community's memory of the sacred past, while *ijtihad* helped it adapt to change and new issues arising in the present.

In the first centuries of Islam, when the legal tradition was only beginning to take shape in an era of Arab-Islamic conquests, migrations, and conversions, *ijtihad* was synonymous with *ray*, individual opinion. Because the Quran did not address all matters of consequence facing the Muslim community after the death of MUHAMMAD in 632, and because the HADITH were only begin-ning to be collected and used for legal purposes, Muslim leaders and judges often had the freedom to resolve legal questions with their own indi-vidual reason and discretion. These questions per-tained to many areas of religion and life: worship, family law, criminal penalties, commerce, and warfare. The early legal authorities who supported this method of jurisprudence were called People of Opinion (*ray*). This relatively free *ijtihad* resulted in the formation of localized legal tradi-tions in the new Islamicate empire. Some legal authorities feared that the basis of law in religion might be lost if opinion (or *ijtihad*) was relied on too much. Consequently, by the early ninth century, the People of Opinion found that they were opposed by the People of Hadith, who, after the Quran, wanted to give priority to the sunna of Muhammad and his companions, which was derived from the hadith. The most famous leader of the tradition-minded People of Hadith was the Baghdadi jurist AHMAD IBN HANBAL (d. 855).

By the 10th century, *ijtihad* had gained a place in all four of the major Sunni legal schools, but it was more limited than in the earlier centuries. It was considered a religious duty that had to be hon-ored by jurists, but it was to be used only if there was no precedent in the Quran, the sunna, or the consensus (IJMAA) of the school in which they had been trained. Within each school, the jurists were ranked according to reputation, expert knowledge in the law, and experience. Only the ones who excelled in these qualifications, the *mujtahids*, could exercise *ijtihad.* The lower-ranking jurists were not qualified to use *ijtihad;* they were only to follow the traditional rulings honored by their own school and those authorized by *mujtahids.* Even so, Sunni jurists recognized that *ijtihad* did not have the certainty that the Quran, sunna, and consensus had and that it could lead to an imperfect or incorrect ruling. Jurists in TWELVE-IMAM SHIISM accept the priority of the Quran when they make rulings, but then they look to the infallible pronouncements of the imams. In their view, particularly in the USULI SCHOOL of Shii *fiqh,* the *mujtahid* is a highly esteemed jurist who makes rulings on behalf of the Hidden Imam until his messianic return. Their rulings tend to hold more AUTHORITY, therefore, among the Shia than the rulings of Sunni *mujtahids* hold among Sunnis.

When the great Muslim empires of the 16th and 17th centuries—the Ottomans, Safavids, and Mughals—weakened and fragmented in the face of a series of internal and external challenges, reform-minded ulama sought ways to reverse the process and restore Muslim governments and societies to their former grandeur. In part, they blamed the sorry state of affairs in Muslim lands on what they considered the rigidity and irrationality of the traditional law schools and overemphasis on *taqlid.* Proclaiming that the "gate of *ijtihad*" had been closed in the 10th century, they wanted it reopened so that it could play a more important role in adapting the SHARIA to modern life and restoring Islam to its original form. Among those calling for such legal reform were early Salafis such as Muhammad Abduh (d. 1905) and a variety of later jurists and intellectuals. Leading obstacles preventing such reformers from realizing their goals have been a lack of agreement about guidelines for how to conduct *ijtihad* and the introduction of law codes based on Western law. Nevertheless, many educated Muslims today support the idea of using *ijtihad* to adapt the sharia to modern life, even if it means turning away from rulings preserved in the traditional legal schools. Some very independently minded

reformers argue that it should be the right for any educated Muslim to use *ijtihad* to bypass legal tradition and construct an Islam suited to individual values and spiritual outlook.

See also MUFTI; RENEWAL AND REFORM MOVEMENTS; SALAFISM.

Further reading: Shaista P. Ali-Karamali and Fiona Dunne, "The Ijtihad Controversy." *Arab Law Quarterly* 9, no. 3 (1994): 238–257; Wael B. Hallaq, "Was the Gate of Ijtihad Closed?" *International Journal of Middle East Studies* 16 (1984): 3–41; Rudolph Peters, "Ijtihad and Taqlid in 18th and 19th Century Islam." *Die Welt des Islams* 20 (1989): 132–145.

Ikhwan al-Muslimin, al- *See* MUSLIM BROTHERHOOD.

Ikhwan al-Safa *See* BRETHREN OF PURITY.

imam (Arabic: leader, guide, a person to be imitated)

Imam is a term that has several meanings in Islamic belief and practice. Its basic meaning for Sunnis is "leader of group PRAYER" (*salat*), literally the one "in front of" the congregation, standing before the MIHRAB (niche indicating the QIBLA, direction of prayer, facing the KAABA in MECCA). A leader of prayer can be any qualified adult with sufficient knowledge of the prayer ritual. Although "prayer leader" is the basic meaning of the term *imam,* in practice an imam's function also includes giving the SERMON (*khutba*) from the pulpit (MINBAR) as part of Friday noon prayer, relating interpretation of Islamic religious and legal texts (for example, QURAN, HADITH, *FIQH,* THEOLOGY) to current events and issues in the local Muslim community. Customarily, men must lead mixed or male-only prayer gatherings, and WOMEN lead only women's prayer groups. This traditional exclusion of women from the imam's function in mixed group prayer gatherings is beginning to be challenged by liberal Muslim organizations and communities, such as the Progressive Muslim Union. Also, women have begun to be trained as imams at a recently established MADRASA (legal college) in MOROCCO. Having women imams is still considered problematic by the majority of Muslim scholars and conservative Muslims worldwide.

Sunnis also use the term *imam* as an honorific title for the eponymous founders of the chief schools of Islamic law. Thus, AHMAD IBN HANBAL, the namesake for the HANBALI LEGAL SCHOOL, is known as Imam Ahmad. In such contexts, the title indicates that he is an exemplar, or leader to be followed in matters of law.

For Shii Muslims *imam* is associated with a fundamental doctrine concerning charismatic male leadership that comes from MUHAMMAD via his daughter, FATIMA, and son-in-law and cousin, ALI, through his twin grandsons, Hasan and HUSAYN, and their descendants (known collectively as the AHL AL-BAYT, "Family of the House"). Muslims who follow the guidance of these Imams are known as *shiat Ali* (the party of Ali). Forming a dissenting minority after the death of Muhammad, the party of Ali believed that only a descendant of Muhammad could lead the UMMA with the necessary grace and spiritual AUTHORITY. There are three major groups of Shia who divide according to the number of descending Imams they follow, Twelve-Imam Shia (or the Imamiyya), Seven-Imam Shia (or the Ismailiyya), and Five-Imam Shia (or the Zaydiyya). Of the three groups, the Twelve-Imam Shia is the largest community, today found principally in IRAN and IRAQ. Ismaili Shiis are numerous in northern INDIA, while Zaidi Shiis are a significant minority in YEMEN.

The doctrine of *imama,* the Shii THEOLOGY concerning the Imams, institutionalizes the prophetic authority and charisma of Muhammad and his family. Spiritual attributes of the Shii Imams include divinely inspired knowledge, or knowledge of the unseen (*ilm al-ghayb);* divine investiture (*nass*) rather than human election;

sinlessness (*isma*) and infallible judgment; and divine intimacy and friendship (WILAYA). These superhuman qualities make the Imams spiritual mediators who are described in Shii hadith as "pillar[s] of light" between Earth and heaven and "witnesses for God to his creation." Imams provide the esoteric interpretation of revelation (*tawil*) that guides the Shii community toward salvation.

See also ISMAILI SHIISM; SUNNISM; ZAYDI SHIISM.

Kathleen M. O'Connor

Further reading: Farhad Daftary, *The Ismailis: Their History and Doctrines* (New York: Cambridge University Press, 1990); Moojan Momen, *An Introduction to Shii Islam: The History and Doctrines of Twelver Shiism* (New Haven, Conn.: Yale University Press, 1985); Barnaby Rogerson, *The Heirs of Muhammad: Islam's First Century and the Origins of the Sunni-Shia Split* (Woodstock, N.Y.: Overlook Press, 2007); Abdulaziz Abdulhussein Sachedina, *Islamic Messianism: The Idea of the Mahdi in Twelver Shiism* (Albany: State University of New York Press, 1981); W. Montgomery Watt, *The Formative Period of Islamic Thought* (Edinburgh: Edinburgh University Press, 1973).

imambarah See HUSAYNIYYA.

imambargah See HUSAYNIYYA.

iman See FAITH.

India (Official name: Republic of India)

Located in South Asia, the modern country of India extends 1,000 miles east and west and 1,000 miles north and south at its widest points. It has an area of nearly 1.3 million square miles, about one-third the size of the United States. It is composed of five chief geographical regions: the Himalayan Mountain Range along its northern border, the Indus and Ganges River Plains, the Thar Desert in the west near the PAKISTAN border, the Deccan Plateau that defines peninsular India, and a 4,350 mile coastline (including island territories) that meets the Arabian Sea, the Bay of Bengal, and the Indian Ocean. It shares its longest border with BANGLADESH in the east, followed by Pakistan in the west, China and Nepal in the north, and Burma and Bhutan in the northeast. Sri Lanka lies just 18.5 miles off the southern coast of India. India has several sizeable cities: Kolkata (formerly Calcutta), Delhi, Mumbai (formerly Bombay), Chennai (formerly Madras), and Bangalore. The national capital is New Delhi, a modern extension to the old city of DELHI; it is situated on the banks of the Yamuna River in the Indo-Gangetic plain.

The government of India is a federal parliamentary DEMOCRACY—the largest in the world. It has a multiparty political system, with the two leading parties being the Indian National Congress Party and the Baharatiya Janata Party (BJP, Indian People's Party). The majority party alliance in the parliament selects the prime minister, who chairs a council of ministers and holds executive power. India also has an elected president, but this is a ceremonial office. The president's term is five years. Each of India's 28 states has its own elected state legislature and chief minister. There are also seven union territories, four of which are located in outlying areas. The others are the territories of Delhi (like Washington, D.C.), Chandigarh in the Punjab, and Pondicherry (Puducherry), a former French colony located in southern India.

India's population is estimated to be nearly 1.15 billion (2008). Hindus are by far the majority (80.5 percent). Sikhs make up about 2 percent of the population, and other minority religions include Zoroastrians, Christians, Buddhists, and Jews. Muslims make up about 13.4 percent of the total, or about 160 million. This means India has one of the largest Muslim populations in the world after INDONESIA and Pakistan. Prior to the 1947 partition of India that resulted in the cre-

ation of Pakistan, it is estimated that about 24.3 percent of the country's population was Muslim (1941 census). According to the 2001 census of India, 97 percent of the country's Muslims live in 13 states. The states with the highest percentages are Jammu and KASHMIR (67 percent), West Bengal (25.2 percent), Kerala (24.7 percent), Uttar Pradesh (18.5 percent), Bihar (16.5 percent), and Karnataka (12.2 percent). Several of the union territories also have large percentages of Muslims: Lakshadweep (95 percent), Assam (30.9 percent), and Delhi (11.7 percent). About 61 percent of India's Muslims today are involved in AGRICULTURE, whereas those living in cities tend to be

Visitors flock to the shrine of Hajji Ali, Bombay (Mumbai), India. (*Juan E. Campo*)

self-employed in traditional professions. Muslims are underrepresented in salaried professions and high-tech industries. Muslims also tend to have higher rates of illiteracy than Hindus or Christians, especially among WOMEN.

Muslims tend to be labeled as outsiders by members of other Indian groups, yet intermarriage and conversion have brought about a significant degree of indigenization. The Indian census does not recognize racial or ethnic groups, but it does recognize language populations. There are 22 official languages that belong to two main language families—the Indo-European (in the north) and the Dravidian (in the south). Muslims speak the local languages of the regions where they live. The greatest number speaks Hindi-Urdu, but there are also many who speak Kashmiri, Bengali, Marathi, Sindhi, Malayalam, Gujarati, and Kannada. Punjabi is another language spoken by Indian Muslims, but more so in nearby Pakistan than in India. Like other Indians, most speak more than one language, including English, another of India's official languages. Within a particular language-speaking domain, Muslims may distinguish themselves from Hindus and others by greater use of Arabic and Persian loanwords, and, in some areas, the use of Urdu script (a modified version of Perso-Arabic script) instead of Devanagari, the Sanskritic script. Also, many Arabic and Persian loanwords have entered into the languages spoken by non-Muslims through the centuries. This process is slowly being reversed, however, as non-Muslims attempt to replace these loanwords with Sanskritic ones.

All of the major expressions of Islam are present in India, in addition to several that developed on Indian soil. Although many of these expressions came from the Middle East and Central Asia, they have been shaped by centuries of Hindu-Muslim interaction, both on the level of popular religion and on the level of formal institutions and doctrines. In terms of formal Islamic tradition, especially in urban India, most Muslims are Sunnis affiliated with the HANAFI LEGAL SCHOOL.

The SHAFII LEGAL SCHOOL prevails in southern India, especially in the states of Kerala, Tamil Nadu, and somewhat less so in Karnataka. In recent years, Hanbali law may be gaining some influence through workers returning to India after living or studying in SAUDI ARABIA and through the dissemination of Hanbali ideas via the print and electronic media. About 10 percent of Indian Muslims are Shii. TWELVE-IMAM SHIISM is especially strong in Hyderabad in the south and the region of Awadh in the north (centered on Lucknow in Uttar Pradesh). Followers of ISMAILI SHIISM, known as Bohras and Khojas, are found today mainly in Mumbai (Bombay), but they have been historically influential in a wider area encompassing the Sind (now in Pakistan), Gujarat, and Maharashtra. The number of Ismailis is much smaller than that of the Twelve-Imam Shiis. India is also the birthplace of the AHMADIYYA sect, which was founded by GHULAM AHMAD (d. 1908) in the Punjab during the last decade of the 19th century. Moreover, Islam's presence in South Asia contributed significantly to the emergence of Sikhism, a separate religious tradition, in the Punjab during the 16th and 17th centuries.

The shape Islam has taken in India and South Asia generally has been greatly influenced by SUFISM. The leading Indian Sufi orders are the Chishtis (since the 13th century), the Suhrawardis (since the 13th century), the Qadiris (since the 15th century), and the Naqshbandis (since the 16th century). Of these four orders, the Chishti is the one that has become most grounded in the Indian context, with major SAINT shrines located in AJMER, Delhi, Ahmedabad, and Gulbarga (other important Chishti shrines are located elsewhere in India and modern Pakistan). The other Sufi orders originated in the Middle East and Central Asia. They all benefited from official patronage during the eras of the DELHI SULTANATE and the MUGHAL DYNASTY. Membership of the orders has been recruited from among the Sunni populace at large, but the festivals held at Sufi shrines (called *dargah*s in eastern Islamicate lands) in honor of their saints (*pirs*) can attract hundreds of thousands from across a wide spectrum of religious traditions. The Shiis, for their part, have directed their piety toward the imams and their descendants. They hold large gatherings and processions during ASHURA, the annual commemoration of the martyrdom of Imam Husayn. Ismailis have similar observances in honor of their Imams and *pirs*, and in difficult times, they have employed Sufi ideas and symbols to avoid persecution by literally minded Sunni jurists and judges.

When Muslim rule was declining and British colonial control was increasing, Islamic RENEWAL AND REFORM MOVEMENTS began to arise in India. AHMAD SIRHINDI (d. 1624) and Shah Wali Allah (d. 1762) were among the early pioneers in these reform movements. After the suppression of the 1857 Muslim-Hindu uprising (known in British history as the Sepoy Mutiny) against the government of the English East India Company, Sunni ULAMA at the DEOBAND MADRASA near Delhi sought to bolster Islamic EDUCATION among Indian Muslims in order to preserve their tradition. Deobandi schools have since spread throughout South Asia, and the ulama continue to be active in adapting their religious traditions to the rapid changes brought with modernity. Another consequence of the 1857 uprising was the founding of the Mohammedan Anglo-Oriental College in Aligarh by Sir SAYYID AHMAD KHAN (d. 1898), which was designed to educate Muslims in the modern sciences and prepare them for leadership in colonial India. From 1919 to 1924, Muslims in northern India participated in the KHILAFAT MOVEMENT in an unsuccessful effort to revive a pan-Islamic CALIPHATE. Other important movements that originated in India that have since had global impact are the Deobandi missionary movement known as the TABLIGHI JAMAAT (founded in the late 1920s) and Abu al-Ala Mawdudi's JAMAAT-I ISLAMI (founded in 1941), an Islamic political movement that became an increasingly important political force in Pakistan after its creation in 1947.

ISLAM IN SOUTH ASIA: A HISTORICAL SKETCH

The conventional understanding found in modern India and often outside India is that its history consists of three phases: an ancient Hindu Vedic golden age from around 1200 B.C.E. to 1000 C.E., an Islamic age of foreign conquest and despotism from around 1000 to 1600, and a British colonial age that laid the foundations for modern independent India from 1600 to 1947. An assortment of facts can be brought forth in support of this view of history. Such a view, however, tends to treat Islam in monolithic terms, exaggerating the role of religion at the expense of social, political, and economic processes in Indian history. It relies on the misleading idea of irreconcilable gaps between Muslims and Hindus as well as between Muslims and the British. These perceived gaps are the results of India's experience with COLONIALISM and communal politics since the 1930s and 1940s, rather than a reflection of precolonial historical realities in South Asia. In recent years, the three-phase model has been given new life by Hindu nationalists and Muslim radicals, as well as Western scholars such as Samuel P. Huntington, who has proposed a post–cold war world of civilizational "clashes" based largely on religious identity. Now, however, some scholars are questioning the validity of the model, arguing that it is a gross oversimplification and that nowhere is it more oversimplified than in its conceptualization of the "Islamic age." It overlooks the variety of ways that Muslims used to indigenize their religion in India during the more than 1,000 years they have lived there, the complex array of forms that Islam took there (as described above), and how Indian Muslim rulers and the English engaged in various sorts of cooperation and power sharing even after the 1857 uprising. Conflicts and acts of violence did occur and still do, but they were not confined to the eras of Muslim rule, nor did they always occur along religious or cultural "fault lines" between Muslims and non-Muslims.

Although the Arabs may have maritime connections with India prior to the appearance of Islam, the first recorded contact between Arab Muslims and the people of the Indus Valley did not occur until the campaign led by Muhammad ibn Qasim al-Thaqafi (d. 715), who invaded Sind on behalf of the UMAYYAD CALIPHATE in 711 and reached as far north as the city of Multan. Although maligned by later British historians and Indian nationalists, the only early Islamic account indicates that the raid was prompted by an attack on a ship carrying Muslim pilgrims near the coast of Sind (the lower region of the Indus River). The non-Muslim subjects were Hindus and Buddhists whom al-Thaqafi treated as "protected" peoples (dhimmis), like Jews and Christians who accepted Muslim rule and paid a special tax called the JIZYA. There is little evidence that they were forced to convert, as some later historians assert. Sind became a province in the early Muslim empire.

The next major incursions by Muslim armies did not occur until the turn of the 10th century, when the controversial Turkic ruler Mahmud of Ghazni (r. 998–1030) launched up to 17 raids into Sind and adjacent regions from Ghazni, his capital in AFGHANISTAN. Mahmud, a defender of SUNNISM, conducted these raids partly to eradicate Ismaili Shia who had settled in the Sind region. But he also wanted to control the region to secure its trade routes and plunder its wealth in order to enhance revenues for his growing empire and building projects in Ghazni. Hindu temples were especially good targets because they contained gold and precious gems. The most noteworthy of the temples Mahmud attacked was Somnatha, a Shiva temple located near a major regional port. Such temple raids were common in the ancient world and were also conducted by rival Hindu kings against each other. Mahmud's raids paved the way for direct Muslim rule deep in the Indo-Gangetic plain. In 1192, the state that Mahmud had created was destroyed by a short-lived Persian dynasty known as the Ghurids. The commanders they assigned to rule in Delhi became independent and established the Delhi Sultanate, which was to rule northern India until the arrival of the Mughals in the early 16th century.

The first Delhi sultan was Qutb al-Din Aybek (r. 1206–10), who initiated the building of the Quwwat al-Islam (Power of Islam) Mosque and the Qutb Minar, a monumental complex on the southern outskirts of Delhi. It was built on the site of a Hindu temple with stones taken from destroyed temples. Aybek wanted the world to know that Muslims were the new rulers in the land. Interestingly, early Hindu sources and inscriptions suggest that the new rulers were not seen as Muslims by the local populace. They were referred to instead in social or ethnic terms as mlecchas (barbarians), Turushkas (Turks), Shakas (Central Asians), or Yavanas (Greeks) in remembrance of those other foreigners who had invaded India centuries before the Muslims. Conservative ULAMA of the Delhi Sultanate and later chroniclers considered the Indians to be unbelievers (KAFIRS) and polytheists (mushriks) who must be fought and subdued. However, this outlook was not the prevailing one at the time. The practical necessities of organizing and ruling an expanding state government meant that the Muslim Afghans, Turks, and Persians, as minority rulers, had to find ways of winning the cooperation of the population. These included collaborating with Hindu Rajputs (local kings), bringing non-Muslims into government service, and treating the populace not as disbelievers but as dhimmis. Intermarriage between Muslims and Hindus also occurred. Historians of this period have found that there was no widespread program of forced conversion to Islam, nor was there wanton destruction of Hindu places of worship, as is the conventional view nowadays. Rather, Muslim rulers desecrated only those temples that were closely identified with rival Hindu rulers. They also patronized Hindu temples. During the mid-13th century, the Delhi Sultanate was home to religious scholars and Sufis seeking refuge from the Mongol onslaught that was sweeping through Middle Eastern lands, destroying many of its grandest cities. This made India a new center for Islamic learning and the pursuit of Sufism. It was at this time that the CHISHTI SUFI ORDER was founded in India, with generous support from the Delhi Sultanate.

In southern India, Islam arrived with Arab traders from southern Arabia rather than Turkic and Persian warriors from Afghanistan and Central Asia. They established trading outposts along the Konkan (modern Karnataka) and Malabar (modern Kerala) coasts as part of the wider Indian Ocean trading system, perhaps as early as the eighth century. These merchants received guarantees of security from local Hindu rulers and intermarried with the native population, giving rise to the indigenous Mappila people. Later histories of this era even suggest that they were able to convert one of the local rulers and obtain permission from him to build the first mosque in Malabar, the Cheraman Juma Masjid, which resembled a south Indian Hindu temple in its design. For centuries, the Mappila have maintained connections with their Arabian roots, many of them going to work in the Persian Gulf region. The vitality of these people is reflected in the fact that they continue to grow in number, constituting one of the largest Muslim populations by ratio to non-Muslims in India today.

At the beginning of the 14th century, the Delhi Sultanate was ruling all of northern India from the Punjab to the mouth of the Ganges in Bengal. It then extended its reach southward into the Deccan Plateau. Sultan Muhammad ibn Tughluq (r. 1325–51) temporarily (1313–23) moved the capital 700 miles southward from Delhi to Daulatabad (formerly known as Devagiri) to better integrate the region under his rule and to avoid the Mongol threat from the northwest. By the end of his reign, Muslim rule had extended to the banks of the Kaveri River deep in southern India. The sultanate was unable to maintain centralized rule over this vast area for long. Regional kingdoms emerged throughout India, including the Hindu kingdom of Vijayanagar in the south, which emulated many

of the political and cultural attributes of the Muslim court. There were even Shii dynasties in the central Deccan region created by Persian warrior immigrants. The Deccan thus became an area of dynamic cultural interaction and sociocultural genesis, mixing not only Muslim and Hindu but also Turkic and Persian with Dravidian and Arab influence from the Konkan and Malabar coastal areas.

The next configuration of Muslim power in India was that of the MUGHAL DYNASTY, which displaced the remnants of the Delhi Sultanate in the early 16th century and ruled until the British military eradicated it in the aftermath of the 1857 rebellion. The Mughals, a family of rulers claiming descent from the Mongol conquerors Genghis Khan (d. 1227) and TAMERLANE (d. 1405), built upon the foundations of the Delhi Sultanate and created a highly centralized bureaucratic state that at its height in the late 1600s controlled much of what now encompasses the modern nation-states of India, Pakistan, and Bangladesh. From the reign of AKBAR (r. 1556–1605) to that of his great grandson AURANGZEB (r. 1657–1707), the Mughal era was one of great cultural florescence and economic prosperity. The capital cities of Delhi, Agra, and Lahore were embellished with breathtaking palaces, GARDEN tombs, and MOSQUES, the foremost of which was the Taj Mahal, a tomb built by Shah Jahan (r. 1627–66) for Mumtaz Mahal (d. 1631), his beloved wife. Mughal artists produced magnificently illustrated epics and dynastic histories. Akbar even commissioned illustrated Persian translations of the Hindu sacred epics the *Ramayana* and the *Mahabharata*. The Mughals also promoted the cultivation of new agricultural lands in Punjab and Bengal, a development that led to the conversion of the populations of those areas to Islam, not by force but through everyday interactions with Muslim judges and holy men at their mosques and shrines. Indeed, as Richard M. Eaton has noted, there was an inverse relationship between conversion to Islam and political power. The areas with the largest proportions of Muslims—Bengal, the Punjab, Kashmir, and Malabar—were those that were most distant from the political centers of the Mughal empire.

Europeans became interested in India during the 15th century because of the thriving spice trade that involved Asia, India, the Middle East, and Africa in a global system of maritime commerce. Columbus's first voyage of discovery to the New World in 1492 was to find an alternate route to the "Indies" for the Spanish monarchs. Shortly thereafter, in 1498, Vasco de Gama sailed to India via the Cape of Good Hope, opening an era of European colonial expansion in Asia that would last for four and a half centuries. The Dutch, the French, and the English followed the Portuguese, competing for market access and lucrative trade agreements with Indian merchants and creditors. Europeans found that in addition to spice, India also had other sorts of goods that would bring a profit in European markets, especially cotton and silk textiles. The English East India Company, created in 1600, opened trading "factories" (warehouses) at several Indian ports during the 17th century to purchase and transport such goods to market, but they found that the most lucrative profits were to be made in Bengal, where the Ganges River provided good access to production centers inland. This was also an area that was thriving as a result of the Mughal policy of promoting agricultural production on newly reclaimed lands on the eastern side of the Ganges delta.

The Mughals gave the British free trade rights so that by 1750 Bengal was providing 75 percent of the company's goods. Meanwhile, the company had created its own fortifications and standing militia to protect warehouses and agents from attacks by the French or local opponents and thieves. The company also formed alliances with local Mughal governors, providing them with military assistance when it promised to be advantageous. Before long, these governors, called nawabs, found that by allying themselves with the British they could win greater independence from Mughal overlords in distant Delhi. This was an era when there was a mingling of cultures as British agents became Indianized, some converting to Islam and living like Mughal royalty. The situation changed significantly after company troops defeated the forces of the nawab of Bengal at the Battle of Plessey near Calcutta in 1757. With this victory, the British began to select the local Muslim governors themselves, and they were able to levy taxes on the local population to pay for goods that they shipped to England, rather than use funds from British investors. They formed a regular army with Indian recruits, mainly uppercaste Hindus, called sepoys (from the Persian *sipahi,* "infantryman"). This evolved into one of the largest armies in the world by the end of the 18th century, replacing the forces of the Mughals and local rulers. Bolstered by victories on the battlefield, the British developed an air of superiority over the native populations. Company officials and employees became more and more corrupt and greedy in their dealings, and in 1765, their tax collecting privileges in Bengal, Bihar, and Orissa were legalized by a dispensation from the Mughal emperor. British control in India increased in the ensuing decades as they operated from headquarters in Calcutta, Bombay, and Madras. Mughal rulers became British minions, with very little independence beyond the walls of their imperial palace at the Red Fort in Delhi.

In 1773, the British Crown appointed a governor general to oversee company operations and combat corruption among company officials. One of the first governor generals was Lord Charles Cornwallis (d. 1805), who had come to India in 1786 after the defeat of his army by American and French forces in America. The governor generals inaugurated a series of land and tax reforms and created an administrative organization that became what is now known as the Indian Civil Service. Although civil servants initially had to learn Arabic, Persian, Hindustani, and other native languages to conduct business, English eventually was made the official language of administration. English-language schools were established to train

Indians for employment in the civil service and to serve as a new native elite to help the British rule the land.

Company officials took an interest in India's antiquities and the Sanskrit language as their power increased. One of them, William Jones (d. 1794), founded the Royal Asiatic Society of Bengal in Calcutta (1784), an early center of Orientalist scholarship. The research its scholars conducted enhanced knowledge about Sanskrit language, literature, and ancient Indian religion, but it was done in a way that portrayed contemporary Indians as inferior to modern Europeans and highlighted differences between Hindus and Muslims. Thomas Macaulay (d. 1859), a leading colonial official, declared in 1835 that after having consulted with Orientalist scholars, he had concluded, "a single shelf of a good European library was worth the whole native literature of India and Arabia" (Metcalf and Metcalf, 80–81). Jones's scholarship also furthered the process of transferring Indian law from the hands of Muslim and Hindu jurists to those of British-style civil courts, with the ulama and pandits demoted to simply being court advisers. The ethnocentric zeal of reforming-minded British administrators even led to banning the children of mixed Anglo-Indian parentage from employment in the civil service. The division between the British and Indians increased in the 19th century with the invention of racist theories of culture and the arrival of evangelical Christian missionaries who eagerly sought to convert Indian Hindus and Muslims from their "heathen" ways. Even Indians educated in English schools were treated with derision and contempt. The antagonisms caused by the shortcomings of British officials and their policies finally exploded in 1857 with a rebellion that spread beyond the ranks of the company army to the general population in the cities of northern India. The violent suppression of this "mutiny" brought an end to company rule as well as to the Mughal dynasty. India was placed under the direct rule of the British Crown, represented by the governor general,

who was reclassified as the viceroy of India. This phase of Indian history now became known as that of the British Raj (from the Hindi word for "kingdom," "rule").

The 1857 rebellion was a clear sign that a nationalist spirit was stirring in India. Native elites had obtained English-language proficiency and education in the history and liberal secularist ideals of modern Europe. They used this knowledge to organize themselves and argue for more egalitarian treatment from British officials. The railroad system created by the British after 1850, the expansion of the postal service, and newspapers made it possible for them to effectively communicate with each other across the great expanse of India. At the same time, supporters of religious reform arose in both the Hindu and Muslim communities, many taking the route of liberalism, others having strong separatist sympathies.

The desire for independence coalesced in the creation of the secularly oriented Indian National Congress (INC), convened originally in Bombay in 1885 by English-educated Indians who wanted to lobby for greater participation in the civil service and local legislative councils. This organization had majority Hindu membership, but it reached out to English-educated Muslims in the name of a united Indian nation. Most Muslim leaders, including the reformer Sayyid Ahmad Khan, declined to participate. The INC, however, did attract MUHAMMAD ALI JINNAH (d. 1948), a Muslim lawyer who had been admitted to the bar in London and practiced law in Bombay. He joined the INC in 1895 and remained active until differences with MOHANDAS K. GANDHI caused him to resign in 1920. Jinnah was also a member of the ALL-INDIA MUSLIM LEAGUE (AIML), an organization founded in 1906 to win a greater role for Muslim elites in the British colonial government. AIML, under Jinnah's leadership, joined with the INC to pursue mutual interests, resulting in the Lucknow Pact of 1916. This agreement called for majority representation in government, extending voting rights to more Indians, and separate electorates for Muslims. AIML and INC also agreed to support the British in World War I; more than 1 million Indians served in the British armed forces during this war.

After the war, both organizations participated in the Khilafat movement (1919–24), but their relations grew more strained when the movement failed. Muslims continued to participate in the effort to achieve self-government, but AIML leadership became increasingly concerned about their minority status in a democratic republic where Hindus would be in the majority. They knew that not only were they in the minority, but also that the Muslim populace was scattered across India, speaking different languages and having different social statuses. Instituting the SHARIA or an Islamic government was not on their agenda. Rather, they sought ways to create a sense of common purpose among India's Muslims to protect their political interests. Whereas the leadership in Congress favored creating a centralized federal government elected by the majority with no guaranteed reservations for Muslims, AIML leaders wanted more provincial autonomy in parts of India where Muslims were in the majority. They also wanted at least a third of the seats in the legislature reserved for Muslims. Not all Muslim leaders, however, favored Muslim political advocacy. Indian ulama, especially the Deobandis, envisioned a Muslim community who were educated in Islam and its moral principles living together with other Indians. Indeed, many supported the INC, as did several prominent secular Muslims.

As Hindu and Muslim approaches to self-government diverged internally as well as externally, many Indians joined in opposing British reluctance to surrender power to the Indian people. In the forefront of those opposed to Indian independence was Winston Churchill (d. 1965), an imperialist and political conservative who would become England's heroic prime minister during World War II. Regarding Indians as children who needed to be disciplined, the British resorted on several occasions to the use of brute force to quell acts of civil disobedience and nonviolent demonstrations. Nevertheless, Indian political parties achieved greater voting rights and were able to hold elections in 1937. This brought the INC to power for the first time. The AIML had a weak showing in these elections; even where Muslims were in the majority, local parties based on class rather than religious identity did better than the AIML. The INC, on the other hand, failed to bring about meaningful changes in the aftermath of the election, thus limiting its ability to win skeptical Muslim voters to its ranks.

World War II brought further division between the two parties. The INC, departing from its pro-British stance in World War I, refused to support the British. Subhash Bose (d. 1945), a two-term INC president, even raised an army with Japanese support to fight against them, hoping to achieve independence by bringing about a British defeat. The mainstream INC leadership, led by Gandhi, won widespread popular support by mobilizing large-scale acts of civil disobedience against the British, known as the Quit India Movement. Many of the party's leaders spent the war in prison as a consequence, but they triumphed after the war by sweeping the elections of 1945–46. The AIML, on the other hand, decided to support the British war effort in the hope that their political position would improve with the war's conclusion. In the postwar elections, it, too, could claim victory. It won all reserved seats in the national legislature, plus most of the Muslim seats in local legislatures.

The AIML's success was a result of a strategy of reaching out to rural voters through Sufi *pirs* and taking advantage of divisions among local political parties. Jinnah's party also gained popular support among Muslims by invoking the ideal of Pakistan, a "pure land" for all Indian Muslims where they could be free to realize their ideals to the fullest. The idea of a political entity to protect Muslims from domination by non-Hindus had been articulated earlier by MUHAMMAD IQBAL (d.

1938), a leading Indian intellectual, past president of AIML, and close associate of Jinnah. In the election's aftermath, Jinnah claimed to be the "sole spokesman" for India's Muslims, but he was still undecided about whether that state would be within the boundary of an Indian nation or outside it. Most Muslims, in fact, were not calling for a two-state partition but a self-governing Muslim entity in a united India. Hindu-Muslim communal rioting and the inability to find a compromise solution with INC leadership, particularly with its chairman, Jawaharlal Nehru (d. 1964), eventually convinced Jinnah that a separate Muslim state in areas where Muslims were in the majority was indeed necessary. Such an entity would have to consist of grouped provinces, not fragmented states scattered across India as some were proposing. The two provinces that would form the new Muslim state were the Punjab in the west and Bengal in the east.

The British realized that in their weakened postwar position they could no longer hold nationalist forces at bay in India or anywhere else in the world where they still had colonies or mandate territories. In March 1946, therefore, they sent a high-level delegation to India to try to mediate the differences between the contending Indian nationalist parties, hoping to prevent a two-state partition. This is what Gandhi desired, too, and he even proposed that Jinnah be named India's first prime minister, an idea that was ignored. Hindu nationalists assassinated him in January 1948 because of their anger over his efforts to achieve reconciliation between Muslims and Hindus. In the end, the British delegation failed, and Lord Mountbatten, the Crown's last viceroy, was appointed in February 1947 to oversee the drawing of political boundaries and the smooth transfer of power to the leaders of India and Pakistan no later than June 1948.

The Punjab region straddled the western border between the two newly created countries and became the site where intercommunal hatreds exploded in a frenzy of mass murder, rape, and flight during the summer of 1947. Terrified Sikhs and Hindus fled eastward to India, and terrified Muslims fled westward to Pakistan. Although statistics in such turbulent conditions are often imprecise, it is widely accepted that as many as 10 million were uprooted and 1 million died in the violence. The reverberations of this painful moment in Indo-Pakistani history can still be felt in the streets and byways of both countries. Pakistani Muslims remember this event as a HIJRA, recalling the Hijra of MUHAMMAD from MECCA to MEDINA in 622.

On August 15, 1947, India's first prime minister, Jawaharlal Nehru, stood before a large crowd and proclaimed India's independence. It was a bittersweet moment, because it combined the thrill of independence with the pains of partition. Nehru chose to raise India's new flag that day in front of Old Delhi's Red Fort, the former seat of the Mughal rulers. The previous evening, speaking before the Constituent Assembly in New Delhi, he had declared, "The past clings on to us still." The choice of the site and Nehru's words indicate that the founding of the new republic was done with a keen awareness of how it had taken shape during a long history of Hindu, Muslim, and British interaction. It is also worth noting that not all Indian Muslims migrated to Pakistan. About half of them stayed, declaring that India was their true home.

On August 15, 2007, India celebrated its 60th anniversary. The intervening years were ones that saw Muslim participation in Indian politics, including three Muslims who served as president. They were also a time marked by several conflicts and near-conflicts with Pakistan. The two countries still have not reached a settlement on the question of Kashmir, a borderland Muslim majority state that was officially made part of India at the time of partition. Nevertheless, Indians and Pakistanis continue to share a common history and culture, including a love for romantic poetry, popular music, curried foods, Bollywood films, and, above all, the sport of cricket. The rise of religious radicalism among Hindu and Muslim militants has torn at the fabric of the Indian polity, with violent outbursts at AYODHYA and Mumbai in 1992 and Gujarat in 2002. Such communal violence is very likely to cause further trouble at home in the foreseeable future, and it may also spill over the Indo-Pakistani border. Since both countries have recently acquired arsenals of nuclear weapons, the need for intercommunal peacemaking and conflict resolution on the local and regional levels is more important now than ever before.

See also AZAD, ABU AL-KALAM; BARELWI, SAYYID AHMAD; BIRUNI, ABU RAYHAN AL-; BOHRA; CINEMA; *DHIMMI;* FARAIZI MOVEMENT; GHALIB, MIRZA ASAD ALI KHAN; *GHAZAL;* GOVERNMENT, ISLAMIC; HINDUISM AND ISLAM; JAMIYYAT ULAMA-I HIND; NEPAL; ORIENTALISM; *QAWWALI.*

Further reading: Jackie Assayag, *At the Confluence of Two Rivers: Muslims and Hindus in South India* (New Delhi: Manohar, 2004); Fred W. Clothey, *Religion in India: A Historical Introduction* (New York: Routledge, 2006); Richard M. Eaton, ed., *India's Islamic Traditions, 711–1750* (Oxford: Oxford University Press, 2003); ———, "Temple Desecration and Indo-Muslim States." In *Beyond Turk and Hindu: Rethinking Religious Identities in Islamicate South Asia,* edited by David Gilmartin and Bruce B. Lawrence, 246–281 (Gainesville: University Press of Florida, 2000); John Norman Hollister, *The Shia of India* (1953. Reprint, New Delhi: Oriental Books Reprint Corporation, 1979); Gordon Johnson, *Cultural Atlas of India: India, Pakistan, Nepal, Bhutan, Bangladesh and Sri Lanka* (New York: Facts On File, 1996); Bruce B. Lawrence, "The Eastward Journey of Muslim Kingship: Islam in South and Southeast Asia." In *The Oxford History of the Muslim World,* edited by John L. Esposito, 395–431 (Oxford: Oxford University Press, 1999); Barbara Metcalf and Thomas Metcalf, *A Concise History of India* (Cambridge: Cambridge University Press, 2002); David Pinault, "Shiism in South Asia." *Muslim World* 87, nos. 3–4 (July–October 1997): 235–257.

Indonesia (Official name: Republic of Indonesia)

The modern nation of Indonesia has the largest population of Muslims in the world. It was formally established in 1950 as the culmination of several steps following World War II in which the Dutch gave up control of what had previously been the Dutch East Indies. Indonesia is a democratic republic whose 20th-century history was greatly influenced by its two presidents, Sukarno (r. 1945–67) and Suharto (r. 1967–98). It has also had a woman president, Megawati Sukarnoputri (2001–04), Sukarno's daughter. Administratively, Indonesia is divided into 33 provinces, several of which have special religious status. Hinduism is protected in Bali, and the SHARIA has been instituted in Aceh (on Sumatra).

Consisting of some 17,000 islands, Indonesia stretches from Sumatra in the west to the island of New Guinea (which Indonesia shares with the nation of Papua New Guinea) in the east. It includes the islands of Java, Borneo (which it shares with the nations of MALAYSIA and Brunei), Bali, and Sulawesi. The entire island of Timor was for a brief period (1975–2002) part of Indonesia, but its eastern half (formerly under Portuguese rule) voted to separate in 2002 and emerged as an independent nation. Indonesia's capital is Jakarta, the largest city in the country with more than 8.8 million residents (2005). Located on the island of Java, it is home to the Istiqlal (Independence) Mosque, which, built in 1975, is the largest in Southeast Asia.

Indonesia is multiethnic in the extreme, with about 300 different ethnic groups. The largest is Javanese (40.6 percent), followed by the Sundanese (15 percent) and the Madurese (3.3 percent). There is also a significant Han Chinese minority (2 percent), which dominates the privately owned business sector. This ethnic diversity is celebrated in the country's motto, *Bhinneka tunggal ika,* or "unity in diversity." The country recognizes the diversity, but in the face of the splintering effect such diversity can produce, it has promulgated several unifying principles. The state philosophy of *Pancasila* (Sanskrit: five principles) promotes the idea of finding unity in the belief in one God, the first of the five principles. The other four principles are belief in a just and civilized humanity, national unity, democracy, and social justice. The government recognizes six major religious communities—Muslim, Hindu, Buddhist, Confucian, Roman Catholic, and Protestant—while privileging Islam somewhat as the majority religion.

The present religious diversity of the islands began with the traditional folk religion of the original inhabitants. Hinduism came to Sumatra and Java as early as the second century C.E., and it grew in importance for the next millennium. Hinduism's hegemony was briefly challenged by Buddhism, which found its major support in Java in the ninth century. The ninth-century Mahayana stupa at Barobudur is a reminder of this phase of the country's history. It was renovated by the United Nations Educational, Scientific and Cultural Organization (UNESCO) in 1973 and is now an international tourist site as well as a place of worship and pilgrimage. A Hindu kingdom, the Majapahit, founded in the 13th century, grew to include much of what is modern Indonesia. After the spread of Islam in the 16th century, Buddhism disappeared, and Hinduism was pushed back to a few enclaves, of which the island of Bali is the most notable. Buddhism was reintroduced in the 20th century. Christianity came to Indonesia as early as the seventh century but made real progress only with the arrival of European colonial powers in the 15th century. Three centuries of Dutch control allowed the Reformed Church to establish centers throughout the islands.

Islam was originally brought to the Indonesian islands during the first millennium C.E., but only in the 13th century did settled Muslim communities appear as a result of maritime trade networks that linked Southeast Asia with the Indian Ocean basin and the Middle East. The first Muslims may have come from Gujarat and Malabar on the west coast of INDIA, followed by Arabs from Hadramaut on the Arabian Peninsula. In 1297, Sultan Malik al-Salih (d. 1297) became the first Muslim ruler in what is now Indonesia. His kingdom was in Aceh, which occupies the northern tip of Sumatra. Islam spread during the heyday of the Majapahit kingdom in eastern Java and made gains as local rulers adopted the new faith. During the 15th century, the sultanate of Malacca (what is now Malaysia) supported the spread of Islam through Sumatra and Java. At the same time, the Majapahit kingdom was suffering from severe inner fragmentation. The Islamic kingdom of Demak founded on Java in 1478 would, with a victory in 1527, claim to have finally succeeded Majapahit rule. From this point on, Islam would steadily come to dominate the islands, but often infused with native, Hindu, and Buddhist elements.

The fragmentation of Hindu rule in the 15th century and the rise of Islam coincided with the coming of the Portuguese (1512) and then the Dutch (1602). The Dutch East India Company dominated the islands for two centuries but fell into bankruptcy. In 1800, it yielded control to the government of the Netherlands. There were several revolts against Dutch rule, which was ended in World War II when the Japanese occupied the islands and nationalist forces prevailed at the end of the war in 1945. Since that time, rule by the central government has been challenged by Islamic groups in Aceh and the Darul Islam (House of Islam) movement.

The early Muslims followed the SHAFII LEGAL SCHOOL, and to the present almost all Indonesian Muslims are Shafiis. Islam is especially strong in Aceh and Java due to the high esteem communities give to the ULAMA and religious boarding schools, the *pesantren* (Javanese: place of students). Traditional learning focuses on Arabic language, quranic studies, Islamic jurisprudence (FIQH), and SUFISM, but modern secular EDUCATION and vocational training are also available. Sufism formed a significant stream of Muslim practice and was especially significant in Java. According to traditional accounts, Sunan Ampel, a Muslim saint (WALI) and ruler of a small province of the Majapahit kingdom, formed the Walisongo (or Wali Sanga), a council composed of nine saints, in the late 15th century. The saints engaged in missionary activities, founding centers and MOSQUES at Demak and Giri. Centers associated with their names continue to provide spiritual guidance for Indonesians. More than two dozen different Sufi orders have established themselves in the country, some originally from South Asia and others from the Middle East. The Naqshbandis and Qadiris are two of the leading orders in Indonesia. The tombs of some of the early Javanese Sufi saints have become pilgrimage sites. Indonesians have also participated in the annual HAJJ to Mecca, especially after the introduction of modern forms of transportation in the 19th century and independence in 1945. Contact with religious scholars in MECCA and MEDINA has contributed significantly to Islamic reform movements and DAAWA activities in Indonesia. Since the 1980s, Indonesia regularly sends about 200,000 pilgrims per year, more than any other country. Another distinction is that more women than men participate, unlike other Muslim countries.

Today more than 86 percent of the Indonesian population identify as Muslims (2000), making the country the home to the largest number of Muslims in the world, in excess of 200 million. Included in the larger Muslim community, along with followers of scriptural Islam and Sufis, is a significant number of followers of a variety of Islamic-inspired syncretistic religions. Many mix Islam with native Indonesian religions, often characterized by the inclusion of ancestor veneration. Others are new spiritual movements such as SUBUD and Sumarah.

On December 26, 2004, much of Aceh and other parts of coastal Sumatra were devastated by a tsunami that killed more than 200,000 Indonesians. Much of the damage was centered on Banda Aceh, the provincial capital. An international effort was launched to help the Indonesian government bring emergency relief to the survivors and rebuild affected areas. Islamic Relief, a London-based nongovernmental organization, was one of the agencies that participated in this effort.

See also BUDDHISM AND ISLAM; COLONIALISM; HINDUISM AND ISLAM.

J. Gordon Melton

Further reading: Greg Barton and Greg Fealy, eds., Nahdlatul Ulama, Traditional Islam and Modernity in Indonesia (Clayton, Aust.: Monash Asia Institute, 1996); B. J. Boland, The Struggle of Islam in Modern Indonesia (The Hague, Netherlands: H. H. I. Smith, 1970); Bahtiar Effendy, Islam and the State in Indonesia (Singapore: Institute of Southeast Asian Studies, 2003); R. S. Kipp and S. Rogers, Indonesian Religion in Transition (Tucson: University of Arizona Press, 1987); Karen Petersen, "The Pesantren at Surialaya." Saudi Aramco World 41 (November/December 1990): 8–15.

infidel   See IDOLATRY; KAFIR.

Insan al-Kamil, al-   See IBN AL-ARABI, MUHYI AL-DIN; PERFECT MAN.

intercession

Belief in intercession involves the theological principle that PRAYERS and practices on another's behalf have the power to bring salvation or blessing. Several terms in Arabic signify the idea of intercession, principally shafaa and wasila (or tawassul), the former emphasizing the substitutionary aspect and the latter the mediating aspect of intercession.

In the QURAN, the term shafaa appears 24 times, and its significance is ambivalent. The Quran clearly indicates that there will come a time when no intercessory power will avail. This is confirmed in the canonical HADITH texts of al-Bukhari, Muslim, and al-Tirmidhi, which contain traditions indicating that due to the prayers of MUHAMMAD, no one will remain left in the FIRE except those specifically named in the Quran. Less clear is whether prior to JUDGMENT DAY, prayer on another's behalf will have any efficacy. Several passages indicate that God grants intercessory power to those whom he chooses (Q 2:255, 10:339; 19:87; 20:109; 21:28; 34:23; 40:7; 42:5; 53:26). There are also hadith describing Muhammad's practice of praying in cemeteries on behalf of the dead. This tradition is continued in the standard funeral prayers (*salat al-janaiz*), which include a communal supplication to God and the Prophet on behalf of the deceased. However, several other verses in the Quran emphasize the futility of appealing to intercessors of any kind on the part of the wrong-doers (Q 6:94; 7:53; 21:28; 30:13; 36:23; 39:43; 40:18; 74:48) and that the privilege of intercession is the sole province of Allah (Q 6:51; 6:70; 10:18; 32:4; 39:44).

Such passages give ground to a host of later commentators, such as the famous 14th-century scholar IBN TAYMIYYA (d. 1328), who vehemently opposed the practice of prayer and supplication at the tombs of the dead for their intercession with God. Among many Sunnis, however, belief in the ability of Muhammad and the SAINTS, those who are closest to God (the *awliya*), to bring the prayers of the common people closer to God is nearly universal. The practice is defended by many on the grounds that these saints are models of piety, that they are better able to communicate directly with God, and that contemplation at any grave provides an important reminder of the ephemerality of life. However, such prayers are equally universally challenged by absolute monotheists who claim that such prayers commit *SHIRK* (assigning partners to God) and appear to question the omnipotence and omnipresence of God. Among the Twelve-Imam Shia, the intercessory power of the IMAMS is affirmed, and prayer at their tombs and those of other members of the AHL AL BAYT (the house of the Prophet) is canonical.

See also AFTERLIFE; BIDAA; FUNERARY RITUALS; SHIISM.

Anna Bigelow

Further reading: Muhammad Hisham Kabbani, *Intercession* (Chicago: Kazi Publications, 1998); Shaun Marmon, "The Quality of Mercy: Intercession in Mamluk Society." *Studia Islamic* 87 (1998): 125–139; David Pinault, "Shia Lamentation Rituals and Reinterpretations of the Doctrine of Intercession: Two Cases from Modern India." *History of Religions* 38, no. 3 (1999): 285–305; Annemarie Schimmel, *And Muhammad Is His Messenger: The Veneration of the Prophet in Islamic Piety* (Chapel Hill: University of North Carolina Press, 1985).

intifada   See ISRAEL; PALESTINE.

Iqbal, Muhammad (1877–1938) *leading Indian poet, intellectual, and statesman*

Muhammad Iqbal, a remarkably brilliant Muslim intellectual who initially articulated the idea of modern PAKISTAN, was born in Sialkot, a town north of Lahore. His father owned a tailor shop. He received both his B.A. (1897) and M.A. (1899) degrees from the Government College in Lahore. An outstanding student, he excelled in Arabic, Urdu, Persian, and English and emerged from the university as a poet of note in both Urdu and Persian. In 1903, while a faculty member at his old school, he published his first book, a study of economics.

In 1905, he traveled to Europe for postgraduate studies and completed a Ph.D. at Munich two years later after completing a dissertation on Persian metaphysics. He came to know some of the most brilliant scholars in Europe at the time, including the Orientalists Thomas Arnold, E. G. Brown, and R. A. Nicholson. He taught for a year at London University, was admitted to the bar, and in 1908 returned to what then was INDIA. For the next years, Iqbal practiced law, taught part time in Arabic and English literature, and wrote the Urdu and Persian poems that would make him famous. In 1915, he quit his teaching post to spend time promoting humanistic Islamic reform. In 1923, he received a knighthood from the British government.

Iqbal entered politics in 1926 and was elected to the Punjab Legislative Council, where he served for three years (1926–29). A close ally of MUHAMMAD ALI JINNAH (d. 1948), he became president of the ALL-INDIA MUSLIM LEAGUE in 1930. From this post, he moved from previous ideas about the coexistence of Islam and Hinduism in India and began to advocate the idea of establishing an independent Muslim state to be carved out of Indian territory. For this idea, he is known as the "thinker of Pakistan" (*mufakkir-i Pakistan*). Inspired by the reformist legacy of the ALIGARH movement, he also called for a "reconstruction" of Islamic thought, and the majority of his writing, including his poetry, was to this end. Although Iqbal opposed the secular nationalism of Europe, he believed that the formation of an independent state on the Indian subcontinent would somewhat reverse the disasters faced by the Muslims in the early years of the 20th century, including the fall of the Ottoman CALIPHATE. Iqbal did not live to see the realization of his dream, as he passed away in 1938. His tomb is located in Lahore, Pakistan.

See also HINDUISM AND ISLAM; RENEWAL AND REFORM MOVEMENTS.

J. Gordon Melton

Further reading: Muhammad Iqbal, *The Reconstruction of Religious Thought in Islam* (Lahore: Institute of Islamic Culture, 1986); ———, *Tulip in the Desert: A Selection of the Poetry of Muhammad Iqbal* (Montreal: McGill-Queens University Press, 1999); Annemarie Schimmel, *Gabriel's Wing: A Study into the Religious Ideas of Sir Muhammad Iqbal* (Pakistan: Muhammad Suheyl Umar, 2000); Dieter Taillieu, Francis Laleman, and Winand M. Callewaert, *Descriptive Bibliography of Allama Muhammad Iqbal (1877–1938)* (Brussels: Peeters, 2000).

Iran (Official Name: Islamic Republic of Iran, formerly Persia)

Located in southwest Asia (the Middle East), Iran, comparable in size to the state of Alaska, covers an area of 628,000 square miles. Deserts constitute a large portion of this area, and two major mountain ranges, Alburz and Zagros, cover about 50 percent of the entire land. The Caspian Sea in the north, Persian Gulf in the south, and more than a dozen major rivers throughout the country are its main water resources. Iran shares borders in the north with the Republics of Armenia, Azerbaijan, and Turkmenistan; in the east with AFGHANISTAN and PAKISTAN; and in the west with IRAQ and TURKEY. Its capital city is Tehran, near the Caspian Sea in the north.

Iran's population is estimated at 65.8 million (2008 est.), with an equal divide between men and women. Persians make up 51 percent of the population. Azeris, a Turkic people, are the largest non-Persian minority and constitute 24 percent of the population. They are followed by the Gilaki and Mazandaranis (8 percent), Kurds (7 percent), Arabs (3 percent), Lurs (2 percent), Baluchis (2 percent), and Turkmen (2 percent). Iran is a multiethnic and multireligious country with an 89 percent Shii Muslim majority. Sunni Muslims make up 9 percent of the population, mostly Baluchis and Kurds. The remaining 2 percent are Zoroastrian, Jewish, Christian, and Bahai. The major language spoken is Persian (Farsi), an Indo-European language.

Iran is an ancient country with more than 2,500 years of recorded history. The Greeks called it Persia after the southwestern region Fars, which was the home of the founders of the Achaemenian dynasty (559–330 B.C.E.). The Achaemenians established a powerful and sophisticated Persian empire in the ancient world. The Sassanian dynasty (224–651 C.E.) was the last Persian empire before the Muslim Arab conquest that began in 637 and was finalized by 651. Within two centuries of the conquest, Islam had largely replaced Zoroastrianism, which had been the ancient religion of Persia and the official religion of the Sassanian Empire. Iran remained mostly Sunni until the coming of the SAFAVID DYNASTY (1501–1722), which patronized TWELVE-IMAM SHIISM and made it the official religion of the state. In the 19th century, Britain and Russia competed for influence in Iran, thus exposing it to increased Western influence.

The CONSTITUTIONAL REVOLUTION of 1905–11 declared the advent of modernity by challenging the absolute rule of the monarch. At the same time, William Knox D'Arcy, a wealthy English investor, discovered OIL in southwestern Iran in 1908, and in 1909, the Anglo-Persian Oil Company was founded. This company was renamed the Anglo-Iranian Oil Company in 1935, and it became British Petroleum in 1954. Oil revenues helped finance Iran's modernization during the 20th and 21st centuries.

The Pahlavi monarchy (1925–78) emerged as a result of the social and political turmoil of the constitutional era. The first Pahlavi monarch, REZA SHAH PAHLAVI (1878–1944) established a despotic, centralized modern state. Emulating what MUSTAFA KEMAL ATATURK (d. 1938) was doing in Turkey in the 1920s, he sought to introduce modern industry and implement economic and social reforms. It was during his reign, also, when the country's ancient name *Persia* officially became *Iran,* a name based on Aryan, the name of an ancient Indo-European people. In time, due in part to the impact of oil wealth, the Pahlavis produced drastic economic and cultural discrepancies among the people. In 1941, Reza Pahlavi was deposed by British and Soviet forces who occupied the country fearing he would become an ally of Nazi Germany. They replaced him with his young son, MOHAMMAD REZA SHAH PAHLAVI (r. 1941–78), who allowed Iran to become a close ally of the United States after World War II. In 1951, nationalist democratic elements were strengthened by the election of Muhammad Mossadegh (d. 1967) as prime minister. When he moved to nationalize Iranian oil production, British and American covert operatives arranged for him to be removed from office in 1953, thereby strengthening the Shah's hold on the country. During the 1960s, with U.S. support, he introduced the White Revolution, a large-scale modernization program that surpassed anything his father had done. This pro-

Iranian youth reads Quran at home. Framed pictures on mantle (left to right): Ayatollah Muhammad Beheshti, the *Shahada,* Ayatollah Ruhollah Khomeini (National Geographic Magazine)

gram angered elements of the Iranian populace, especially the Shii religious authorities, the traditional merchant class (the *bazaaris*), and leftists.

Pahlavi rule was brought to an end in 1979 as a result of massive public demonstrations and national strikes that were held for more than a year. The demonstrators were ordinary people from all walks of life and varied political and religious affiliations. Their undisputed demand was democratic rights and an end to the Pahlavi monarchy. This notwithstanding, the religious faction of the revolutionary movement under the leadership of Ayatollah RUHOLLAH KHOMEINI (1901?–89) established itself as the state authority by eliminating opposition groups and intellectuals who posed a challenge to them and by holding a national referendum that imposed a choice between monarchy and an Islamic republic. The constitution of the Islamic Republic of Iran, adopted in 1979, is organized on the basis of Islamic law (SHARIA) and gives supreme authority to the Shii leader (*faqih,* religious jurist). The constitution describes the responsibilities of the three branches of the government (the legislative power, the executive power, and the judiciary power), while emphasizing that their operations are subject to the authority of the leader and the guardian council. Any attempt to introduce social change through legal and parliamentary channels and by means of public participation in national referenda is accordingly monitored by the authority of the religious elite who rule Iran.

Revolutionary Iran has had to contend with a number of serious crises since the 1979 revolution. The first arose when revolutionary youths seized the American embassy in Tehran and took its personnel hostage for 444 days in 1979–80. This ended with the release of the hostages and the closing of the U.S. embassy in 1980. The United States proceeded to penalize Iran by launching an economic embargo as part of a policy of containment to limit its influence in the region. In September 1980, Iran was invaded by Iraq, which, under the leadership of SADDAM HUSAYN (r. 1968–2003), sought to gain control of access to the Gulf through the Shatt al-Arab waterway and to check the spread of Khomeini's Shii revolution to Iraq and other Arab Gulf countries. To the surprise of many, Iranians rallied to halt the invasion, but a bloody nine-year war of attrition ensued that resulted in the deaths of as many as a million Iranians and Iraqis. The war ended in a cease-fire brokered by the United Nations. Iran's troubles continued in the 1990s, with a rapidly growing population, economic stagnation, growing demands for liberalization by the postrevolution generation, corruption, political chaos in neighboring Afghanistan, and the proliferation of nuclear weapons in Israel, Pakistan, and India. At the same time, however, Iran encouraged radical Shii groups to take up arms against Sunni-led governments in Iraq, SAUDI ARABIA, Kuwait, and Bahrain. It also supported HIZBULLAH in LEBANON, a Shii guerrilla movement that had formed when Lebanon was invaded by Israel in 1982.

A short-lived period of cultural liberalization occurred in 1998–2002, represented by such figures as Muhammad Khatami (b. 1942), who served as president from 1997 to 2005, Abd al-Karim Soroush (b. 1945), a philosopher and intellectual critic of Islamic radicalism, and human rights activist Shirin Ibadi (b. 1947), who won the 2003 Nobel Peace Prize. The liberal currents these figures represented were especially popular with women and young Iranians, but they were strongly opposed by hard-line supporters of the revolutionary Shii ideology of Khomeini and his successors. This party regained significant popular support when U.S. president George W. Bush identified that country as part of an "axis of evil" responsible for terrorism around the world. Reactionary elements were further energized when the United States and Britain invaded neighboring Iraq to remove Saddam Husayn in 2003. The invasion helped bring about the election of Mahmoud Ahmadinajad (b. 1956), the hard-line former mayor of Tehran, as president in 2005. His government played an active role in supporting Shii political groups in post-Saddam Iraq, opposing Israel, and seeking close ties with Syria. Also, under his leadership, Iran accelerated efforts to become a nuclear power, which provoked the United States and European countries to take diplomatic and military countermeasures.

See also CONSTITUTIONALISM; GULF STATES; GULF WARS.

Firoozeh Papan-Matin

Further reading: Ervand Abrahamian, *Iran between Two Revolutions* (Princeton, N.J.: Princeton University Press, 1983); W. B. Fisher, *The Cambridge History of Iran.* Vols. 1–7 (Cambridge: Cambridge University Press, 1968); Nikki Keddie, *Modern Iran: Roots and Results of Revolution* (New Haven, Conn.: Yale University Press, 2003).

Iranian Revolution of 1978–1979

The overthrow of the shah of IRAN, MOHAMMAD REZA PAHLAVI (1919–80), in 1979 by populist forces led by Ayatollah RUHOLLAH KHOMEINI (1902–89) established the Islamic Republic of Iran. This revolution has been regarded as one of the most significant in modern history, along with the French Revolution of 1789 and the Russian Revolution of 1917. What makes the Iranian Revolution unique is the important role played by religion. Even though antishah sentiments were held by a wide spectrum of urban Iranians, Islamic revolutionary symbolism, together with anti-Western sentiments, played a major role in uniting the opposition. Moreover, the creation of a Shii revolutionary government under Khomeini's leadership inspired radical Islamic groups in many Muslim countries during the 1980s and 1990s. The revolution was also a factor in several Persian Gulf wars during this period. Many Iranians emigrated to the United States as a result of the revolution.

Bolstered by development assistance from the United States and increased OIL revenues, the shah's government pushed a program of aggressive social and economic reforms in the 1960s and 1970s to make Iran a modern nation in accordance with Western standards of progress. These reforms sought to promote industrialization and land reform, improve WOMEN's rights, and support the establishment of Western-style coeducational institutions. It was reminiscent of MUSTAFA KEMAL ATATURK's modernization program in TURKEY during the 1920s. The program was implemented in an authoritarian manner without seeking popular support and was plagued by inflation, land speculation, and spiraling unemployment. Jalal Al-e Ahmad (d. 1969), an Iranian writer, condemned the increased Westernization of his country and called it a disease—*gharbzadegi* (Westoxication). The United States, through its widely acknowledged support for the shah, was increasingly seen as being the source of this "malady." Iranians objected to the land reforms, rapid sexual integration in schools and the workforce, compulsory Western dress in public contexts while traditional religious forms of dress such as the veil or chador were banned, using the pre-Islamic Achaemenid solar calendar in place of the Islamic lunar CALENDAR, and giving preferential treatment to Western—first British, then American—business and diplomatic interests. The more the resistance to the shah's modernization projects grew, the more the shah's secret police force, SAVAK (notorious for illegal and violent methods), compelled compliance and repressed dissent. Growing disaffection with the shah's rule among diverse sectors of Iran's population testified to the increasing sense of internal corruption of the Iranian national character, expressed in Shii terms as seduction by the West for ephemeral material benefits. Many Iranians felt they were losing their Islamic identity and culture.

Intellectuals such as ALI SHARIATI (d. 1977), imprisoned by the shah in 1964, and religious authorities such as Ayatollah Khomeini, forced into exile by the shah in 1964, gave religious shape to the political forces aligning in opposition to the shah. Both Shariati and Khomeini maintained that Islam must play a revolutionary role against tyranny, capitalism, corruption, and Western influence. Khomeini in particular was speaking as a leading member of the Twelve-Imam Shii ULAMA, who believed that they acted as representatives of and deputies for the last Shii Imam (the 12th divinely appointed descendant of the prophet MUHAMMAD) until his messianic return from Occultation (GHAYBA) at an undefined time in the future to eradicate injustice and corruption, inaugurating an age of universal Islam before JUDGMENT DAY. Moreover, the Twelver jurist who was acknowledged by his juridical peers and the rest of the Shii community (UMMA) to be the supreme AUTHORITY was believed to have divine investiture (*nass*) and infallibility (*isma*) in matters of religious law and everyday life. An ayatollah so recognized was known as the *marjaa al-taqlid,* or "source of imitation." Further, Khomeini, in a series of declarations issued from his exile in IRAQ argued that the *marjaa* was not only the chief religious authority, but also the ideal ruler. He called for the overthrow of the shah's regime and its replacement with a theocracy based on the SHARIA.

The resulting revolution of 1978–1979 involved massive demonstrations in Iran's cities on major Shii holy days or days of mourning for "martyrs" killed during the demonstrations. One of the slogans that echoed through the streets declared, "Every day is ASHURA, every place is KARBALA," in memory of Imam Husayn's MARTYR-DOM at Karbala in 680. These strikes and demonstrations, many of which were organized by local revolutionary *komiteh*s (committees) and MADRASA students, together with lack of U.S. political support, forced the ailing shah and his queen to flee the country on January 15, 1979. Khomeini returned in triumph from his 15-year exile on February 1 and was greeted by millions of cheering Iranians, some thinking that the messianic age had arrived and others thinking the ayatollah would support the creation of a democratic government, then step back from the political arena. Instead, Khomeini moved quickly to create an interim government, and Iran was declared an Islamic republic by national referendum in March 1979. An Islamic constitution was drafted by the interim government and passed by another referendum. It included an article that designated the chief Shii jurist the supreme leader of the republic, thus making Khomeini's doctrine of government of the jurist (*vilayet-i faqih*) a reality. Khomeini remained both the supreme leader and *marjaa-i taqlid* until his death in 1989.

The revolutionary government of the new Islamic Republic implemented draconian measures to undo the shah's program of modernization, Westernization, and secularization that had so distressed traditional and sharia-minded Iranians. In its place were reassertions of "traditional" Islamic gender roles and spheres (public sphere as male space, and private as female); the resumption of mandatory "modest" dress for women; the

gradual removal of women from professional and public employment, particularly in the legislature and judiciary; expansion of the sharia court system to all spheres of law (not just family law); the closure of Western-style educational institutions and programs with the exception of medicine and some of the technical professions, and reconstitution of Islamic educational institutions using traditional religious curricula and pedagogical methods emphasizing memorization and recitation. Enforcement of these laws and others was undertaken by morals police who increasingly intimidated Iranians in the streets and at home. The Revolutionary Guard, a special armed force, was created to protect the republic from enemies foreign and domestic. The new government imprisoned, tried, and executed members of the shah's government. It also turned against the People's Warriors (MUJAHIDIN-I KHALQ), a rival, left-leaning revolutionary organization that had recruited members from Iran's middle-class youth. On November 4, 1979, pro-Khomeini students seized the U.S. embassy in Tehran and took embassy personnel as hostages for more than a year (1979–80). This event not only helped Khomeini consolidate his power but also brought down the then American president, Jimmy Carter, who lost his reelection bid in 1980 largely for failing to resolve the hostage situation.

Although there continue to be hard-line "revolutionaries" in Iran, the social, political, artistic, and intellectual, as well as religious pendulums showed signs of swinging back toward more moderate, reform-minded expressions of the Iranian spirit in the generation since Khomeini and his supporters toppled the shah's regime. This trend suffered a setback, however, in 2005, when religious hardliners seeking to keep the spirit of Khomeini's revolution alive prevailed in national elections.

See also BAZAAR; CONSTITUTIONALISM; CONSTITUTIONAL REVOLUTION; GULF WARS; TWELVE-IMAM SHIISM; USULI SCHOOL.

Kathleen M. O'Connor

Further reading: Hamid Algar, trans., *Islam and Revolution: Writings and Declarations of Imam Khomeini* (Berkeley, Calif.: Mizan Press, 1981); Said A. Arjomand, *The Shadow of God and the Hidden Imam: Religion, Political Order and Societal Change in Shiite Iran from the Beginning to 1990* (Chicago: University of Chicago Press, 1984); Juan R. Cole and Nikki R. Keddie, eds., *Shiism and Social Protest* (New Haven, Conn.: Yale University Press, 1986); John L. Esposito, ed., *The Iranian Revolution: Its Global Impact* (Gainesville: University Presses of Florida, 1990); Nikki Keddie, *Modern Iran: Roots and Results of Revolution* (New Haven, Conn.: Yale University Press, 2003); Roy Mottahedeh, *The Mantle of the Prophet: Religion and Politics in Iran* (New York: Simon & Schuster, 1985); Abdulaziz A. Sachedina, *The Just Ruler in Shiite Islam: The Comprehensive Authority of the Jurist in Imamite Jurisprudence* (New York: Oxford University Press, 1988).

Iraq (Official Name: Republic of Iraq)

Located in the heart of the Middle East, Iraq covers an area of nearly 169,000 square miles, comparable in size to the state of California. This area consists of mountain ranges to the east and north and vast desert plains to the south and west, with the Tigris and Euphrates Rivers traversing it diagonally from northwest to southeast. The confluence of the Tigris and Euphrates Rivers in the southeastern part of the country forms the Shatt al-Arab, a 120-mile long river that drains into the Persian Gulf. Iraq shares its longest border with IRAN (formerly known as Persia) to the east, followed by SAUDI ARABIA to the south, TURKEY to the north, SYRIA to the west, Kuwait to the southeast, and JORDAN to the west. It has the fourth-largest proven OIL reserves in the world (2006), with fields located in the southeast near the Shatt al-Arab and the Kuwaiti border, and in the north.

The capital of Iraq is BAGHDAD, located in the central part of the country. The government operated as a dictatorial one-party political system until 2003, when it was overthrown by a U.S.-led invasion. The current government has a constitution and is technically classified as a parliamentary democracy consisting of a multiparty national assembly, or parliament. Iraq's head of state is the prime minister. It also has a president, but this is mainly a ceremonial office.

Iraq's population is estimated to be about 28.2 million (2008), nearly equally divided between males and females. Arabs make up about 75 percent and Kurds 15 percent to 20 percent, with the remainder being small minorities such as Turkomans, Assyrians, and Persians. Most of the Kurds, Turkomans, and Assyrians live in the northern part of Iraq. The main languages spoken in Iraq are Arabic and Kurdish (closely related to Persian). A small minority speaks Turkoman, a Turkic language. Many educated Iraqis speak English as a second language. The majority of the population are adherents of TWELVE-IMAM SHIISM (60 to 65 percent), who follow either the USULI (rationalist) or Akhbari (traditionalist) SCHOOLS of Shii jurisprudence. Most of Iraq's Shiis live south of Baghdad. The rest are mainly Sunnis (32 to 37 percent), most of whom follow the Hanafi School of Sunni jurisprudence. The largest Sunni populations are in the central and northern parts of the country, including the Kurdish areas. There are several small religious communities, including Christians (3 percent) as well as Mandeans and Yazidis, who adhere to ancient pre-Islamic religions. The Sunnis include both Arabs and Kurds, while the Shia are mainly Arabs. Christians follow either the Assyrian Orthodox Church or the Chaldean Church, which is in communion with the Roman Catholic Church. Historically, the country's cultural coherence has been challenged not only by its ethnic and religious diversity but by internal tribal divisions and the pull of greater Syria to the west, Turkey to the north, Iran to the east, and the Arabian Peninsula to the south.

ANCIENT IRAQ

Iraq has been called the "cradle of civilization" because it is one of the first places where domestication of plants and ANIMALS occurred and cities with monumental ARCHITECTURE and writing were constructed. The ancient civilizations that flourished there between the fourth millennium and the first millennium B.C.E. were those of the Sumerians, Akkadians, Assyrians, and Babylonians. Their religious life emphasized the worship of multiple gods and goddesses whose images were housed in great temples and shrines in the major cities. Many of these deities represented cosmic and natural forces, such as Anu, the god of the heavens, Antu, the earth goddess and wife of Anu, Enlil, the lord of the winds, and Ea (Enki), the god of the sweet waters. There was also Inanna (Ishtar), a youthful goddess associated with the planet Venus and fertility, and Erishkigal, goddess of the underworld. Ancient Mesopotamian deities also governed aspects of human culture, such as kingship, warfare, writing, childbirth, and magic. One of the most important works of Mesopotamian literature was the creation hymn "Enuma elish" (When on High), written on clay tablets in the Akkadian language. Another important literary work of the Mesopotamians was the *Epic of Gilgamesh,* which related the adventures of a king named Gilgamesh and his companion Enkidu. The *Code of Hammurabi* is one of the earliest compilations of law in history and may have influenced the law codes of the Hebrew Bible. Mesopotamian civilization produced a vast number of other cuneiform writings, from economic records and histories to incantations and religious hymns.

In addition to its agricultural wealth, Iraq benefited from its location along major trade routes that linked it to Central Asia, INDIA, Africa, and the Mediterranean world. It prospered from this trade, but its prosperity and strategic location also made it a prize for conquest by outside powers throughout its history. During the first millennium B.C.E., Iraq was ruled by a succession of large empires, some of them native, others foreign. The first of these was that of the Neo-Assyrians, based in northern Iraq (tenth to seventh

centuries B.C.E.). This was followed by that of the Neo-Babylonians (seventh to sixth centuries B.C.E.), or the Chaldeans, which is remembered for its destruction of the temple of Yahweh in JERUSALEM in 586 B.C.E. and removing its Israelite population into captivity in Babylon, the imperial capital in southern Iraq. The land of the Tigris and Euphrates Rivers became part of the great Persian empire of the Achaemenid dynasty, based in Iran, during the sixth to fourth centuries B.C.E. One of the things this dynasty is remembered for is allowing the Israelite Jews to return to Jerusalem and rebuild their temple in 538. The empire fell when the Middle East was conquered by the armies of ALEXANDER THE GREAT of Macedon (d. 323 B.C.E.) during the last decades of the fourth century B.C.E. The Seleucid dynasty, heirs of one of Alexander's generals, ruled Iraq between 312 and 141 B.C.E. They built a capital city called Seleucia on the Tigris about 20 miles southeast of where Baghdad would later be built by Muslim rulers. Parthian armies from Iran invaded Iraq during the second century B.C.E. and swept the Seleucids away. They began to use Ctesiphon, a town next to Seleucia, as their regional capital. During the second century B.C.E., the Parthians began to engage with Roman armies for control over Middle East trade routes, and the two empires continued to battle with each other intermittently for more than two centuries.

ISLAMIC IRAQ

Early in the reign of the caliph UMAR IBN AL-KHATTAB (r. 634–644 C.E.), a series of skirmishes between Arab Muslim and Persian forces ended with a complete defeat of the Persian army at the Battle of al-Qadisiyya (ca. 636), changing the course of Iraq's history for centuries to come. The Sasanian dynasty that had ruled Iraq and Persia since it had deposed the Parthians in 226 never recovered from the blow. When the last Sasanian king finally died in 651, Muslims had become the undisputed rulers of the region. Several garrisons built for immigrant Arab Muslim armies in Iraq evolved rapidly into major new towns: Basra, Kufa, and Wasit. They were bolstered by an indigenous Arab population (mostly Christian) based in Iraq's older cities and in rural areas. A new postconquest Iraqi society emerged consisting of a mixed population of Arabs, Jews, Kurds, Christians, Zoroastrians, Africans, Indians, and tribal groups, all subject to Muslim rulers. Iraqi Arabs and non-Arabs who converted to Islam became clients of Arab Muslim tribes and clans, gaining second-class status. Other groups acquired DHIMMI (protected) status, which allowed them to maintain their own communal organization and religious laws as long as they bowed to the authority of Muslim government, paid their taxes, and did not engage in proselytizing. Adherence to ancient polytheistic forms of religion, already in decline, virtually came to an end in postconquest Iraq with loss of political patronage and conversion to monotheistic religions, especially Islam.

Ruled by governors appointed by the CALIPHS in MEDINA and later by the Umayyad dynasty in DAMASCUS, Iraq was a major source of wealth for the early Muslim empire and a gateway to Persia and lands beyond. It had a large, diversified population and productive agricultural lands and developed into an important political center. ALI IBN ABI TALIB (d. 661) was able to become the fourth caliph with the support of Kufa's population, and it was near Basra that he defeated rivals at the Battle of the Camel (656). Ali made Kufa the capital, but after his assassination there, the first Umayyad caliph, Muawiya (r. 661–680), moved it to Damascus. Years later HUSAYN IBN ALI sought to rally his father's old supporters in his campaign to become the Muslim head of state, but he and his supporters were massacred on the way to Kufa at KARBALA by Umayyad troops. Early Shii movements and other anti-Umayyad sentiments continued to stir in Iraq and beyond to the distant plains of Persia until they coalesced into the Abbasid Revolution, which ended Umayyad rule in Syria in 750 and brought forth the new ABBASID CALIPHATE.

The Abbasids ruled much of Islamdom from Iraq until the 10th century, when they had to bow to various regional soldier dynasties who paid them nominal allegiance. They ruled from Baghdad, originally a round city founded in 762 by Mansur, the second Abbasid caliph (r. 754–775), as a royal fortress. It grew rapidly, however, into a center of medieval urban civilization that outshone all the cities of the Middle East–Mediterranean region in its cultural importance, opulence, and power. Under Abbasid rule, the major branches of Islamic law and learning flourished in Iraq, while the Sunni and Shii branches of Islam crystallized. SUFISM grew from Iraqi soil through the contributions of legendary ascetics, teachers, and visionaries such as AL-HASAN AL-BASRI (d. 728), RABIA AL-ADAWIYYA (d. 801), Maaruf al-Karkhi (d. ca. 815), al-Muhasibi (d. 857), MANSUR AL-HALLAJ (d. 922), ABU HAMID AL-GHAZALI (d. 1111), and ABD AL-QADIR AL-JILANI (d. 1166). Iraq's CITIES were also famous for their poets, philosophers, and scientists. Even when the Abbasid political power waned, the intellectual and cultural achievements that had been realized in Iraq had a lasting impact that extended far beyond the frontiers of the Muslim Middle East.

The Abbasid era was brought to an end by the Mongols, nomadic warriors who rode in from Central Asia and ravaged cities in Persia and Iraq, finally plundering Baghdad in 1258. Although the Mongol rulers, known as the Ilkhanids, converted to Islam, they relegated Iraq to provincial status and divided it into a northern and a southern district. While Persia prospered under Mongol rule, Iraq's urban populations declined, and neglect of its irrigation systems led to a marked decrease in its agricultural production. Baghdad was plundered for a second time in 1401 by TAMERLANE, a Mongol warrior king. In the following century, the country experienced further political fragmentation as it fell into the hands of local rulers—Arabs, Kurds, and Turkomans. During the 16th and 17th centuries, it became a frontier between the expansionist projects of the Persian

Safavid and Ottoman Turkish empires and was often controlled by local clients of these powers. Although Najaf and Karbala prospered as centers of Shii learning and pilgrimage, the region as a whole continued to stagnate until the Ottomans initiated far-reaching administrative reforms in the 19th century.

IRAQ IN THE 19TH AND 20TH CENTURIES

The Ottomans divided Iraq into three provinces—Mosul in the north, Baghdad in the center, and Basra in the south; repaired and expanded the irrigation system; and legislated land tenure reforms that promoted the settlement of Arab pastoral tribes in the south. These changes fostered urban growth and enhanced the status of Shii religious authorities in their shrine cities. Ottoman rulers, upholders of SUNNISM, wished to placate Iraq's Shii ULAMA and their supporters in order to keep rival powers at bay, including Persians and Europeans. The ulama seized the opportunity to win the CONVERSION of southern Iraq's tribal population. Consequently, the majority of Iraq's population became Shii by the early 1920s. Ottoman dominion over Iraq ended because of their alliance with Germany during World War I, which was defeated by the Allied Powers, including Britain and France, in 1918. Britain ruled Iraq as a mandate territory from 1918 to 1932 under the authority of the secret Sykes-Picot Agreement it had made with France during the war, later upheld at the postwar international San Remo Conference (1920). The Shia of southern Iraq led a tribal uprising (*intifada*) that was decisively ended by the British the same year. Attempting to legitimate their mandate, the British installed Faysal ibn Husayn (d. 1933), the son of the ruler of Hijaz, as monarch. In fact, they only succeeded in creating a Sunni monarchy that failed to win the loyalty of most Iraqis. It survived a number of coup attempts and demonstrations until 1958, when it was violently ended by a revolt led by Iraqi Free Officers under the command of Brigadier Abd al-Karim Qasim.

The BAATH PARTY, which had established a branch in Iraq in the 1950s, first came to power in Iraq in 1963, when it deposed Qasim's government and executed him. It conducted a bloody purge of Qasim's supporters, particularly leftists and communists. The first Baath regime lasted only a few months before it was in turn overthrown by non-Baath Arab nationalist officers. In 1968, after the stunning defeat of Arab forces by Israel in 1967, the Baath Party returned and was quickly able to gain nearly absolute control of the country. One of the most prominent figures in the new regime was SADDAM HUSAYN (d. 2006), who had risen through the ranks of the party, often by violent means. He became Iraq's president in 1979. The Baath government, composed mostly of Sunnis, espoused a secular Arab identity. With growing revenues from oil exports, it was able to modernize and expand Iraq's infrastructure and educational system as well as its military. The cost of this was dear, however, as the Shii majority was denied full political participation, leftist movements were eradicated, Jews were persecuted, and Kurds were repressed. Shii political movements, such as the DAAWA PARTY (founded in the late 1950s) and the Supreme Council for Islamic Revolution in Iraq (SCIRI, founded in the early 1980s), arose, but their leaders were imprisoned, assassinated, or driven into exile. Iran's Ayatollah RUHOLLAH KHOMEINI was granted asylum from the shah's security forces in 1964, but he was forced to leave Iraq by Saddam Husayn in 1978.

Beginning in 1980, Iraq became involved in a continuous series of GULF WARS of national, regional, and global scope that have continued to afflict it in the first decades of the 21st century. In 1980, it went to war with Khomeini's newly established Islamic Republic of Iran to gain control of the Shatt al-Arab and Iran's oil fields nearby. That conflict ended only after more than eight years with a truce when Khomeini died in 1989. During the war, Iraqi forces used chemical weapons against Iranians and against their own Kurdish population in the north. It was a very costly conflict in terms of loss of life and economic damage for both countries. Iraq then invaded Kuwait in 1990 because of a dispute over oil, precipitating the next major Gulf War. In 1991, after an extended campaign of aerial bombing that destroyed much of Iraq's infrastructure, an international coalition of forces led by the United States expelled Iraq from Kuwait. Thinking they might be able to overthrow the government, Shiis in the south and Kurds in the north revolted. The coalition powers allowed Iraq's military to quell the uprisings. However, they forced the government to give up its high-grade weapons programs and stockpiles of weapons of mass destruction. A UN-sponsored embargo was also imposed to gain Iraq's compliance, at great cost to ordinary Iraqis. U.S. and British warplanes enforced no-fly zones over the northern and southern parts of the country and periodically bombed Iraqi military installations during the 1990s.

EARLY 21ST-CENTURY IRAQ

Saddam Husayn's Baath dictatorship finally fell in April 2003 when U.S. and British forces invaded Iraq on the premises that Iraq was stockpiling weapons of mass destruction and supporting radical Islamic terrorism. With the fall of Baghdad, the army was disbanded, Baath Party members were dismissed from their jobs, and the occupying powers created an interim government to rule the country. It was led by a council composed of representatives from different sectors of Iraq's population. The Arab Shia and the Kurds took advantage of the situation to maximize their political interests against those of the Arab Sunnis, who had controlled the country since the days of Ottoman rule. The Daawa Party and the Supreme Council for Islamic Revolution in Iraq (SCIRI; now called the Supreme Islamic Council) returned from exile in Iran, while many Shiis turned to the ulama in Najaf for guidance. Three religious figures became particularly prominent at this time—Ayatollah Ali Sistani (b. 1930), a senior Iranian-born cleric; Abd al-Aziz al-Hakim (b. 1950), head of SCIRI and a

cleric; and Muqtada al-Sadr (b. 1973), a militant young cleric and member of the widely beloved Sadr family. The U.S.-led invasion of 2003, therefore, helped give Iraq's Shia a dominant position in the government. Their position was confirmed in the January 2005 elections, when a coalition of Shii parties gained a parliamentary majority, and the first two prime ministers they appointed were members of the Daawa Party. Moreover, in refutation of the previous Baath regime's secular outlook, the new Iraqi constitution stipulated that Islam was the national religion and the basis of the country's laws, although freedom of religion was also recognized.

Since the U.S. and British occupation began in 2003, many parts of the country have seen increasing levels of violence. Indeed, some experts have observed that Iraq has become afflicted with at least five wars, often overlapping with each other. These are the war of Iraqi opposition to U.S. occupation forces and their allies; the war between government and Baathist militias; the war of foreign jihadis affiliated with AL-QAIDA against occupation forces and the Shia (who are seen as infidels); the war between rival Shii militias; and the border war between Kurdish guerrillas and Turkey. Iran is also reported to be involved in these conflicts by providing support for Shii militias and Shii blocs in the government. According to some estimates, more than half a million Iraqis have lost their lives in this violence, and about 4 million have become REFUGEES. Many observers are pessimistic about the chances for an end to the violence in the near future. As a solution, some recommend that the country be partitioned into three semiautonomous states—Kurdish in the north, Shii in the south, and Sunni in the middle.

See also AKHBARI SCHOOL; COLONIALISM; GULF STATES; OTTOMAN DYNASTY; SELJUK DYNASTY; SHIISM.

Further reading: Thabit Abdullah, *A Short History of Iraq: From 636 to the Present* (London: Pearson/Longman, 2003); Hugh Kennedy, *When Baghdad Ruled the*

World: The Rise and Fall of Islam's Greatest Dynasty (Cambridge, Mass.: Da Capo Press, 2005); Kanan Makiya, Republic of Fear: The Politics of Modern Iraq (Berkeley: University of California Press, 1998); Yitzhak Nakash, The Shiis of Iraq (Princeton, N.J.: Princeton University Press, 1994); Georges Roux, Ancient Iraq (London: Penguin Books, 1992); Vali Nasr, The Shia Revival: How Conflicts within Islam Will Shape the Future (New York: W.W. Norton, 2006).

Isa   See JESUS.

islah   See RENEWAL AND REFORM MOVEMENTS.

Islam

The name for the second-largest religion in the world after Christianity, *Islam* is a word formed from the Arabic consonants *s-l-m*. It is related to the Arabic word for "peace," *salam,* which is one of the 99 most beautiful NAMES OF GOD and also a cognate of the Hebrew word *shalom.* One of the names for PARADISE in Arabic is *Dar al-Salam,* House of Peace. Using these consonants to form the verbal noun *islam* creates the meaning "to enter into a state of peace," which is conventionally translated into English as "surrender" or "submission." The word *muslim* is an active participle based on the same word; hence, a Muslim is literally "one who enters a state of peace," "one who surrenders," or "one who submits." Islam, therefore, is an action that brings two parties into a peaceful relationship, the one who surrenders and the one to whom one surrenders. In most contexts, it describes a relationship between humans and one sovereign God, but it can also describe a relationship between all creation and the divine creator. According to Islamic teachings, surrender to God leads to eternal salvation.

Unlike names of other major religions such as Hinduism and Buddhism, which were coined by Western scholars in the 18th and 19th centuries, *Islam* has been used by Muslims as a name for their own religion since the early centuries of their history. The term occurs seven times in the QURAN in passages usually dated to the Medinan period of MUHAMMAD's career (between 622 and 632), when he and his followers increasingly had to differentiate their religious beliefs and practices from those associated with others, especially Jews, Christians, and polytheists. The most well-known verse where Islam occurs in the Quran is Q 5:3:

> Today those who have disbelieved in your religion [*din*] are miserable, so do not fear them. Fear me. Today I have perfected your religion for you, bestowed my grace upon you, and chosen Islam for you as your religion.

These words were accompanied by commandments concerning dietary laws, HAJJ rituals, and relations with people of other religions. They indicate that toward the end of Muhammad's life, probably when he performed the farewell pilgrimage (ca. 632), Islam was being represented as a set of specific religious practices legislated by God. These practices placed Muslims in juxtaposition to those who practiced disbelief, the *kafirs.*

The idea of submission to God through outward actions was linked in the Quran not only to fearing God but also having FAITH (*iman*). Indeed, the Arabic words for faith-belief (*iman*) and believer (*mumin*) and related terms occur much more frequently in the Quran than the words *islam* and *muslim. Iman* alone occurs 44 times, and the term for believers (*muminun-muminin*) occurs 179 times. The meanings of these words sometimes overlap in quranic usage, but in the HADITH they become more distinguishable. In the Hadith of GABRIEL, for example, *islam* was expressly identified with the FIVE PILLARS (testimony of faith, PRAYER, ALMSGIVING, FASTING, and hajj), while *iman* was identified with belief in God, ANGELS, HOLY BOOKS, prophets, and JUDGMENT DAY. The specifics of Islam as practice were subsequently developed primarily in the contexts of religious law, the SHARIA, which sought to encompass all facets of life in the Muslim community. The cornerstones of Islamic belief were captured in the SHAHADA: "There is no god but God and Muhammad is his messenger." Other aspects of faith were expressed in the Quran, the hadith, and later creedal statements. The inward and experiential aspect of Islam was explored in more depth by Sufi mystics. THEOLOGY, however, never attained the prominence in Islamic religion that it held in Christianity. Muslims were held more answerable for their wrongful acts than for unorthodox beliefs.

Although Muslims see Islam as a unique monotheistic religion, they also believe that it is one of a group of Abrahamic religions interlinked through a common mythic lineage to the ancient biblical patriarch and quranic prophet ABRAHAM. The Quran, for example, mentions the *millat Ibrahim*, the religion of Abraham, eight times. It states, "Who is better in religion than he who submits himself completely to God while doing what is right and follows, as a believer in one God, the religion of Abraham?" (Q 4:125). This verse links Abraham's religion with performing an act of submission. Elsewhere in the Quran, Abraham asks God to make him, his son, and their descendants his submitters (or Muslims, Q 2:128). Islam, therefore, is seen as the one true religion proclaimed by Abraham and all the other prophets until Muhammad. Jews and Christians are considered to be PEOPLE OF THE BOOK who, like Muslims, believe in one God and possess sacred scriptures that came from the same heavenly source, the "mother of the book" (Q 43:4).

One consequence of this belief concerning other religions was that wherever Muslims ruled, People of the Book were guaranteed "protected" (DHIMMI) status under the sharia, as long as they paid their taxes, recognized the authority of the Muslim ruler, and did not proselytize Muslims. Muslim authorities in INDIA even recognized Hindus as People of the Book with their own prophets and scriptures. Of course, history has shown that these protections were not always observed, however. Muslims understood that their religion could not accept disbelief and IDOLATRY, but they also recognized that Islam obliged them to establish relations with followers of other religions. This outlook was also reflected in a concept the ulama called the *dar al-Islam* (house of Islam), a designation for territories ruled by Muslims but that included protected non-Muslim resident communities. This realm was opposed to the *dar al-harb* (house of war), which was not under Muslim rule and which under certain conditions could be made a target for JIHAD.

ISLAM IN WESTERN EYES

Understandings of Islam among Europeans and Americans have been shaped by the historical interactions of Muslims and non-Muslims through the centuries. During the Middle Ages—the era of the CRUSADES and the Christian conquest of Spain—many Europeans saw Islam as the heretical or idolatrous religion of the enemy. They regarded Muhammad as a demon named Mahound, a false prophet or a magician and charlatan. In his *Divine Comedy,* the famed Italian poet Dante Alighieri (d. 1321) placed Muhammad and his cousin Ali in the level of hell reserved for people who caused religious division and dissent. Other Christian writers called Muslims pagans, gentiles, Saracens, or Moors, terms that usually connoted the superiority of Christianity, which they saw as the one true religion. Admittedly, a handful of medieval scholars sought a deeper, more accurate understanding of Islam, but others studied it to refute its truth claims and to convert Muslims. Negative European understandings of Islam continued in the 15th and 16th centuries, when Europe was confronted with the threat of invasion by the Ottoman Empire. Turkish armies seized Constantinople (ISTANBUL) in 1453 and soon gained control of much of eastern Europe and the eastern Mediterranean. The words *Turk* and *Muslim* became synonymous, usually with negative connotations.

Different understandings of Islam arose during the 18th and 19th centuries as Western scholars began to study the Middle East using the methods of Enlightenment rationality. Islam, like other religions, was studied in the light of the new sciences of history, language, and culture instead of traditional theology. Critical editions of Arabic and Persian texts, including the Quran, were translated and published in modern European languages. Scholars such as Sylvestre de Sacy (d. 1838), Edward W. Lane (d. 1876), W. Robertson Smith (d. 1894), Ignaz Goldziher (d. 1921), and Theodor Noeldeke (d. 1930), who specialized in these studies, called themselves Orientalists, based on the belief at the time that the Orient began east of Greece in the Near/Middle East. They began to present their findings in Orientalist journals and societies in the mid-1800s. One of these organizations was the American Orientalist Society, which was founded in 1842 and still publishes a highly respected scholarly journal. For all the advances the Orientalists made in the study of Islam and the Middle East, the objectivity of their research was colored by different degrees of bias and self-interest. Some looked to the East to explain the origins of European civilization, while many sought to demonstrate the superiority of European culture at the expense of non-European cultures and civilizations. ORIENTALISM also became involved with actual European colonization of Muslim lands and was used to help administer colonial territories from North Africa to India and INDONESIA. Consequently, Europeans viewed Islam in various ways: sometimes as a backward, violent religion; sometimes as an *ARABIAN NIGHTS* fantasy; and sometimes as a complex and changing product of history and social life.

Scholars engaged in the scientific study of religion, having broken free of the restrictions of the Christian church, no longer were satisfied with treating Islam as a heretical religion. Orientalists began to treat it as a Semitic religion, along with Judaism, in contrast to Indo-European and "primitive" religions. Some even renamed Islam MOHAMMEDANISM and called Muslims Mohammedans. This was done in conformity with the classification of other religions, such as Christianity (named after Christ), Buddhism (named after the Buddha), and Zoroastrianism (named after the ancient Persian sage Zoroaster). Most Muslims have rejected Mohammedanism as a designation for their own religion because they argue that submission to God is the focus of their religion, not Muhammad. Islam has also been classified with Judaism and Christianity as a monotheistic religion, as a "revealed" religion, and as one of the "Western" religions. Other scholars have regarded it as one of the world religions, which, like Buddhism and Christianity, made a home for itself in many countries and actively sought converts. More recently, it has been understood as an Abrahamic religion.

Today, understandings of Islam continue to be shaped by the interactions, debates, and overt conflicts between Muslims and non-Muslims. The growing strategic and economic importance of OIL and the introduction of secular law codes and ideologies into lands where Islam is the majority religion during the colonial era and after World War II have intensified these interactions. Many of the world's proven oil reserves are located in newly independent Muslim countries, with the mixed blessing of greater per capita incomes but also more social and political instability. Western-style SECULARISM has brought great advances in terms of EDUCATION and political participation, but it has also confined religion to the private sphere. While many Muslims have come to understand their religion in secular terms, many others have rejected this understanding as they look to their religion for solutions to problems and crises facing their society, politics, and culture in a time of rapid changes. Slogans such as "Islam is a religion and a state" and "Islam is the solution" have gained wide currency in many Muslim countries. Since the 1970s, when many Muslims started calling for a "return" to Islam after experiencing the shortcomings of their national governments and political ideologies, some Western scholars and many journalists have portrayed Islam as a threat to the West, often equating it with "fundamentalism," "TERRORISM," and, most recently, "fascism." ARAB-ISRAELI CONFLICTS, the IRANIAN REVOLUTION OF 1978–79, GULF WARS, and AL-QAIDA's attack on the World Trade Center and the Pentagon on September 11, 2001, have only escalated the level of this sort of rhetoric, which neither advances knowledge nor facilitates effective national and international policy making. The anti-Western rhetoric coming from radical Muslim ideologists such as Egypt's SAYYID QUTB (d. 1966) and their supporters has also had harmful consequences.

Defining Islam is an undertaking that, to a significant extent, has occurred in the context of Muslim and non-Muslim historical interactions, whether they be framed in terms of believers and disbelievers, People of the Book and polytheists, jihadists and crusaders, Easterners and Westerners, secularists and theocrats, or insiders and outsiders. Islam is what Muslims have made of it, what non-Muslims have made of it, and what they have made of it together. There is ample evidence to show that defining Islam is a highly polarized and confrontational enterprise involving civilizational "clashes." But more careful consideration shows that this has not always been the case, as is evident in the pluralistic contexts of medieval Spain, CAIRO, BAGHDAD, and in various parts of Africa and Asia. Thoughtful and learned men and women in these contexts found a common ground on which to learn about each other, debate issues of mutual interest and concern, and, above all, live together. Modern migrations of Muslims to Europe and the Americas, the reach of the Internet, interreligious dialogue on local and transnational levels, and the increased participation of Muslim and non-Muslim scholars jointly in the study of Islam and Muslims promise to ameliorate and correct the angry and distorted definitions that have been produced and reproduced in recent years. The possibility awaits of once again understanding Islam on the basis of mutual interests and shared commitment so that people may face together challenges that stand before global society in the 21st century.

See also ALLAH; ANDALUSIA; ARABIC LANGUAGE AND LITERATURE; CHRISTIANITY AND ISLAM; COLONIALISM; *DAR AL-ISLAM AND DAR AL-HARB*; DIALOGUE; EUROPE; ISLAMISM; JUDAISM AND ISLAM; *KAFIR*; and the introduction to this volume.

Further reading: Norman Daniel, *Islam and the West: The Making of an Image* (Oxford: Oneworld, 1993); Sachiko Murata and William C. Chittick, *The Vision of Islam* (St. Paul, Minn.: Paragon House, 1994); Andrew Rippin, *Defining Islam: A Reader* (London: Equinox Publishing, 2007); Maxime Rodinson, "The Western Image and Western Studies of Islam." In *The Legacy of Islam.* 2d ed. Edited by Joseph Schacht and C. E. Bosworth, 9–62 (Oxford: Oxford University Press, 1974, 9–62); Edward W. Said, *Orientalism* (New York: Pantheon Books, 1978); Jane I. Smith, *An Historical and Semantic Study of the Term 'islam' as Seen in a Sequence of Quran Commentaries* (Missoula, Mont.: Scholars Press, 1975).

Islamic Society of North America

The Islamic Society of North America (ISNA) is an association of Muslim organizations and individuals concerned with social and educational development, outreach programs, and public relations in the United States and Canada. It was formed in 1981, evolving from the MUSLIM STUDENTS ASSOCIATION (MSA), in order to serve the religious and social needs of Muslim graduates from American colleges and universities. ISNA serves as an umbrella organization for the MSA and approximately 300 other affiliated community and professional organizations, including the Association of Muslim Social Scientists (AMSS), the Association of Muslim Scientists and Engineers (AMSE), the Islamic Medical Association of North America (IMANA), and the Council of Islamic Schools in North America (CISNA). A diversity of Muslim communities, MOSQUES, and other institutions belong to ISNA, varying in size, membership, ethnicity, and styles of leadership. Despite this diversity, constituent members are perceived by local Muslims as representing ISNA.

ISNA headquarters lie in Plainfield, Indiana, in a complex of buildings, which includes a mosque, library, and offices. It is a notable example of contemporary Islamic architecture, designed by Gulzar Haidar and built in 1979 with funds donated by the United Arab Emirates. The Office of the General Secretariat oversees all departments and services, is involved in administration and management of offices and facilities, and is accountable to the elected president of ISNA. Subsidiary units include Conventions and Conferences, Membership, Community Outreach, Leadership Development, Youth Coordination, Community Development, Publications, and the ISNA Development Foundation.

The executive council and the board of directors (*Majlis al-Shura*) are the two policy-making bodies recognized within the constitution of ISNA. The latter body presently consists of 23 members, including representatives elected by the general body of ISNA and others elected by the presidents of regional chapters and affiliates. The society has a membership and support base of about 400,000 Muslims, with its leadership drawn predominantly from immigrant communities, although native-born Americans are increasingly prominent. Members receive *Islamic Horizons,* the bimonthly flagship publication of ISNA edited by Omer Bin Abdullah, which addresses national and international affairs. Annually, ISNA hosts a major convention in addition to numerous regional and specialty events.

See also COUNCIL ON AMERICAN–ISLAMIC RELATIONS; MUSLIM PUBLIC AFFAIRS COUNCIL; UNITED STATES.

Gregory Mack

Further reading: Yvonne Y. Haddad, *The Muslims of America* (New York: Oxford University Press, 1991);

Islamic Society of North America, *2004 Annual Report* (Plainfield, Ind.: ISNA, 2004); Sulayman S. Nyang, *Islam in the United States of America* (Chicago: Kazi Publications, 1999).

Islamism

Since the 1990s, *Islamism* has been used by Western scholars and some journalists as a term covering a variety of modern Islamic revolutionary groups and ideologies that have the goal of implementing Islamic law (SHARIA) as the absolute basis for every aspect of life in majority-Muslim countries.

Typically, Islamist groups strive to overthrow governments that are secular or that the Islamists believe are not properly implementing Islamic principles. Islamists seek to replace such regimes with governments they believe would embody what the Islamists perceive to be genuinely Islamic ideals. Some examples of many Islamist groups are the MUSLIM BROTHERHOOD, which has chapters in EGYPT and many other countries, HAMAS among the Palestinians in the West Bank and Gaza, HIZBULLAH among Shiites in LEBANON, JAMAAT-I ISLAMI in PAKISTAN, and AL-QAIDA globally.

Islamists believe that the Islamic governments they institute must give their financial and political support exclusively to Islamic schools and universities and ban all other forms of EDUCATION, establish economic systems wholly free of dependence on Western countries, create societies where wealth is distributed equitably among all groups and where the large gaps that exist between the rich and poor are reduced, and enable the availability of health care and a wide array of social services, including orphanages and welfare services for all individuals in the Islamic state.

Islamists also have the objective of establishing Islamically based moral codes that involve men and WOMEN being required to dress in accordance with the Islamists' interpretation of Islamic law, the legally enforced separation of men and women who are not part of the same family, a complete prohibition of sex outside marriage, and the banning of alcohol, prostitution, gambling, and virtually all forms of Western movies, television shows, magazines, books, images, and music. Islamists believe that these cultural products should be forbidden because they are anti-Islamic in that they often promote sex outside marriage, alcohol consumption, selfishness, and materialism, all of which contradict Islam.

Islamism is one of the most potent religious, social, and political forces in the world today and will have a substantial impact on many aspects of global politics for the foreseeable future.

See also GOVERNMENT, ISLAMIC; JIHAD MOVEMENTS; MAWDUDI, ABU AL-ALA; POLITICS AND ISLAM; QUTB, SAYYID; TERRORISM.

Jon Armajani

Further reading: John L. Esposito, *The Islamic Threat: Myth or Reality?* 3d ed. (New York: Oxford University Press, 1999); Fawaz A. Gerges, *The Far Enemy: Why Jihad Went Global* (New York: Cambridge University Press, 2005); Bruce B. Lawrence, *Shattering the Myth: Islam beyond Violence* (Princeton, N.J.: Princeton University Press, 2000); Ali Rahnema, *Pioneers of Islamic Revival* (London: Zed Books, 2005); Malise Ruthven, *A Fury for God: The Islamist Attack on America* (London: Granta, 2004).

Ismaili Shiism (Sevener Shiism and Seven-Imam Shiism)

SHIISM is a sectarian form of Islam, and Ismaili Shiism is one of its major subdivisions. It is named after Ismail (ca. 721–755), the elder son of JAAFAR AL-SADIQ (699–765), the sixth Shii IMAM. Ismailis believe that Ismail was the rightful heir to the imamate after Jaafar's death, instead of Jaafar's son Musa al-Kazim (ca. 745–799), who is regarded as the seventh Imam by the Twelve-Imam Shia. The doctrines and law of the Ismailis are similar to those of other major Shii sects, but they differ significantly in their concepts of AUTHORITY. They are also known for the emphasis they place on the difference between outward (*zahir*) and inner secret (BATIN) meanings of the QURAN and other religious texts and symbols. Because of periods of persecution in the past, they practiced *taqiyya* and disguised themselves as Sunnis, Twelve-Imam Shiis, Sufis, and Hindus. Although precise statistics are lacking, some estimates say there are about 15 million Ismailis (compared to about 150 million Twelve-Imam Shiis and about 1.2 billion Muslims total). Prior to the 19th century, they resided mainly in the Indian subcontinent, YEMEN, IRAN, AFGHANISTAN, and mountainous areas of Central Asia. They established merchant communities in EAST AFRICA during the 19th century. Now they can be found in many countries of the world, including immigrant communities in the United Kingdom, CANADA, and the UNITED STATES.

Four major forms of Ismaili Shiism developed during the Middle Ages. They all spread secret Ismaili teachings by means of missionaries known as *dais* who challenged the authority of Sunnis and Twelve-Imam Shiis. The first form was that of the Qaramatians, which appeared in southern IRAQ in the late ninth century and spread to eastern Arabia, Bahrain, and Yemen. It was named after Hamdan Qaramat, who, together with his aides, announced that Ismail's son Muhammad was the promised MAHDI (a messianic savior) who would abrogate the SHARIA and rule the world in JUSTICE. Claiming they acted on his behalf, they recruited converts from among the BEDOUIN tribes and organized small communities that practiced collective ownership of property. Challenging the legitimacy of the ABBASID CALIPHATE in the early 10th century, they attacked cities in SYRIA and Iraq as well as pilgrim caravans. The Qaramatians plundered MECCA in 930 and carried away the KAABA'S BLACK STONE. The second form of Ismailism was that of the Fatimids, a movement based in North Africa that broke with the Qaramatians on the basis of their claim that Abd Allah (also known as Ubayd Allah, d. 934), a leading Ismaili missionary, was related to Muhammad ibn Ismail through a line of "hidden Imams." Abd Allah proclaimed that he was the Mahdi in 899 and later established the FATIMID DYNASTY, which ruled from CAIRO, EGYPT, between 969 and 1171. The Fatimid DAAWA made converts in different parts of North Africa and the Middle East, especially in Syria, Persia, and the region of Sind in INDIA.

The Fatimid form of Ismaili Shiism suffered a schism stemming from a succession dispute after the death of the eighth caliph-imam, al-Mustansir (r. 1036–94). Egyptian Ismailis supported the candidacy of al-Mustali (r. 1094–1101), the younger son of al-Mustansir, but Ismailis in Syria and Persia supported his older son Nizar. The Mustali branch of the Ismailis continued in Egypt until the end of the Fatimid dynasty in 1171, when it moved to Yemen and eventually India. With the end of their caliphate, they claimed that Mustali's baby grandson Tayyib had become a hidden imam who would return at some time in the future.

The third form of Ismaili Shiism was the one that developed from supporters of Nizar's claim to the imamate, the Nizaris. Nizar was executed in a Cairo prison, but his *dai* in Persia, Hasan-i Sabbah (ca. 1056–1124), became the head of his sect. Hasan was both a scholar and a man of action who established fortresses on mountaintops in Persia and Syria, the main one being Alamut in the Elburz Mountains near the Caspian Sea. He continued the Ismaili challenge to Sunni Abbasid rule in the Middle East and was known for his use of assassination as a tactic against Sunni leaders. Hasan and his successors claimed that they governed the Nizari state on behalf of the hidden Imams. In 1162, a second *dai* named Hasan became the Nizari leader. Claiming to be the imam, Hasan announced during the month of RAMADAN in 1164 that he had been instructed by the hidden imam to announce that the resurrection had come. This was the beginning of a new spiritual age in which the sharia was abolished for the Nizaris. Hasan claimed to be the hidden Imam's CALIPH, and all members of the

community were told that they were to follow his spiritual teachings and commands instead of the sharia. This doctrine remained in effect until a later caliph-imam, Jalal al-Din Hasan (r. 1210–21), declared that the resurrection was not the final one and that his followers should respect the sharia. He did this to establish better relations with the Sunni caliphate in BAGHDAD. Nizaris continued to rule their own states in Persia and Syria until the Mongol invasions of the mid-13th century destroyed them, and Nizari communities became fragmented.

The fourth form of medieval Ismaili Shiism was the philosophical one. Neoplatonist PHILOSOPHY appears to have been embraced by the early Ismailis in Iraq and Syria. This included a respect for human knowledge as a manifestation of divine truth (HAQIQA), the distinction between outer and inner levels of reality, and a conceptualization of God as the supreme Intellect from which the universe had come forth through emanations. A famous example of the Ismaili respect for knowledge and learning was the Fatimid House of Wisdom (*ilm*) in Cairo, which accumulated a library of several hundred thousand books on subjects ranging from the Quran and HADITH to logic, astronomy, and MATHEMATICS. Many of the *dai*s and Ismaili caliph-imams were reputed to be learned in these subjects, in addition to having mystical insights into divine truth. Leading Ismaili scholars in the Middle Ages included the North African Qadi al-Numan (d. 974), who wrote the leading compendium of Ismaili law; the Persian traveler, Ismaili *dai,* and philosopher Nasir-i Khusraw (d. ca. 1075); and Nasir al-Din al-Tusi (d. 1274), the Persian theologian, philosopher, and scientist.

Today the major branches of Ismaili Shiism are the Khojas and the Bohras. The Khojas belong to the Nizari form of the sect and the Bohras to the Mustali. Both are the result of Ismaili *daawa* activities in the Indus Valley region of modern Indo-Pakistan that may date to the time of the Fatimid dynasty in Egypt. The Khojas, the larger of the two groups, are led by the AGA KHAN, a descendant of the Nizari caliph-imams, whom they call "the Imam of the Age" (*Imam-i zaman*). As a result of their need to conceal themselves and their missionary activities in times of persecution, Khoja religious language has adapted many terms and concepts from Sufism and devotional Hinduism (*bhakti*), evident in terms such as *pir* and guru (Sufi master), DHIKR and *samaran* (remembrance of God), TARIQA and *sath panth* (Sufi order, "true path"). God was known as ALLAH and Alakh (a Sanskritic name for the transcendent God), or as Rahman (the most merciful) and Ram (an avatar of the Hindu god Vishnu). The key religious texts for the Khojas are the *ginans*, which contain sacred hymns that are sung at their religious gatherings. The Ismaili Bohras, who are mainly from the region of Gujarat in India, are led by a man known as the *dai mutlaq* (the absolute *dai*), who maintains continuous contact with the hidden imam. Their main headquarters since the 19th century has been in Mumbai.

Khojas and Bohras are typically involved in business and finance. They tend to avoid politics, but they embrace EDUCATION and scholarship. The Institute of Ismaili Studies in London was founded in 1977 by the Aga Khan in order to support research on Shiism and enhance interfaith understanding. Both communities have supported projects relating to the preservation of the Islamicate architectural heritage and adapting it to meet the needs of Muslim communities today. They have also contributed significantly to humanitarian causes.

See also AHL AL-BAYT; ASSASSINS; BOHRA; BRETHREN OF PURITY; DRUZE; FYZEE, ASAF ALI ASGHAR; HINDUISM AND ISLAM; SUFISM; TWELVE-IMAM SHIISM.

Further reading: Ali S. Asani, *Ecstasy and Enlightenment: The Ismaili Devotional Literature in South Asia* (London: I.B. Taurus, 2002); Jonah Blank, *Mullahs on the Mainframe: Islam and Modernity among the Daudi Bohras* (Chicago: University of Chicago Press, 2001); Farhad Daftary, *A Short History of the Ismailis* (Edinburgh: Edinburgh University Press, 1998); John Norman Hollister, *The Shia of India* (1953. Reprint, New Delhi: Oriental Books Reprint Corporation, 1979).

isra* and *miraj   *See* NIGHT JOURNEY AND ASCENT.

Israel

The modern country of Israel was created in 1948 as a homeland for the Jewish people. Located on the eastern shores of the Mediterranean Sea, it covers an area of 8,017 square miles not including the occupied territories of PALESTINE (the West Bank and Gaza). It is comparable in size to the state of New Jersey and smaller than Los Angeles County, California. The western limit of the country is defined by a coastline that extends from north to south, with the land sloping eastward across a coastal plain up to the Judean Hills. East of the Judean Hills lie the Jordan Rift Valley and the Dead Sea. The southern part of the country is desert, including a narrow corridor leading down to the tip of the Gulf of Aqaba in the Red Sea. The countries that border Israel are LEBANON and SYRIA to the north, JORDAN to the east, and EGYPT to the west-southwest. The Palestinian Authority has legal jurisdiction of the West Bank, a large area between JERUSALEM and the Jordan Valley, and Gaza, a narrow coastal strip on the Israeli-Egyptian border. Israel also occupies the Golan Heights, a border area that is claimed by Syria.

Israel's political capital is in the modern city of Tel Aviv. Although Israel lacks a formal constitution, it does have a set of Basic Laws that provide guidelines for governance. Establishing a constitution has been delayed because of disagreements between Jewish secular and religious parties over the nature of the nation's laws. The country is ruled by an elective parliamentary democracy led by a prime minister. Israeli Arab citizens, like its Jewish citizens, have voting rights and representation in the parliament, known as the Knesset, but there is no Palestinian representation from the occupied territories.

Israel's population is estimated to be 7.1 million, including nearly 383,000 Israelis living in West Bank settlements, East Jerusalem, and the Golan (2008 estimate). It is 76.4 percent Jewish, mostly native-born, and 23.6 percent non-Jewish, mostly Arab (2004). Judaism is the religion of the majority, 16 percent are Muslims, about 2 percent are Christians, and 1.6 percent are followers of the DRUZE religion (2004). Although many of Israel's citizens are practicing members of their religious communities, many have secular worldviews. The combined population of the West Bank and Gaza is approximately 3.5 million (2004 estimate). Islam is the religion of most citizens of the Palestinian Authority: 90.1 percent in the West Bank and 98.7 percent in Gaza (2007 estimate). Most are Sunni Muslims historically affiliated with the HANAFI LEGAL SCHOOL. The size of the Arab Christian population has been declining steadily since the 1967 Arab-Israeli War. They make up less than 10 percent of the population in the West Bank and Gaza and belong to a number of different denominations, including Greek, Syrian and Armenian Orthodox, Greek Catholic, Roman Catholic, and Protestant.

The land where modern Israel is now located was the setting for many of the stories and events related in the Bible. It lies at a major crossroads for the peoples of the Mediterranean region, the Nile Valley, Arabia, and beyond. The ancient Israelites were but one of several different groups that lived there. They established kingdoms during the first half of the first millennium B.C.E. known as Samaria and Judah. The former, the Northern Kingdom, was destroyed by the Assyrian Empire in 721 B.C.E. Judah (later Judea), the Southern Kingdom, was brought to an end by the Babylonian Empire in 586 B.C.E. The Babylonians took Judah's rulers into exile in Mesopotamia and destroyed the temple in Jerusalem. It was after this time that many of the books of the Hebrew Bible (Old Testament) were compiled. The religion of Judaism

is also said to have appeared in this period, when it replaced ancient Israelite religion. Cyrus II (r. 539–530 B.C.E.), Achaemenid emperor of Persia, defeated the Babylonians and allowed the captive Jews to return home. He also gave them permission to rebuild the Second Temple in Jerusalem. In the following centuries, the region became either a province or client of several powerful empires, including those of ALEXANDER THE GREAT and his successors (333–67 B.C.E), Rome (67 B.C.E–330 C.E.), and Byzantium, the continuation of the Roman Empire in the East (330–640).

Byzantine control over the province of Palestine came to an end when Arab Muslim armies defeated the Byzantines in a series of battles between 632 and 637. Taking greater Palestine and Syria, where there were several large Arab tribal confederations, had been one of MUHAMMAD's top priorities, but it was not until the reign of the caliph UMAR IBN AL-KHATTAB (r. 634–644) that the Muslim conquest occurred. In 638, he went to Jerusalem personally to accept the peaceful surrender of the city. Historical sources indicate that the new Muslim rulers did not encounter serious opposition, for the local populace and the region's economy prospered. Jews were able to move back to Jerusalem after having been previously banned and restricted to living in the Galilee by the Romans and Byzantines. Both the region's Christian majority and the Jews were obliged to accept DHIMMI (protected) status, which granted them legal rights under Muslim law as long as they paid taxes and did not revolt, slander the Islamic religion, or attempt to convert Muslims.

From the QURAN, Muslims knew Israel more as a people rather than a land or kingdom. Jacob was a biblical figure who was also known as Israel. He is mentioned once in the Quran by this name. His offspring, the children of Israel, are mentioned 42 times as recipients of the TORAH of Moses. Kings DAVID and Solomon are both mentioned, but more as prophets than as rulers of a holy land. Later Quran commentaries and Muslim stories about the biblical prophets attempted to identify sacred events with specific locations in Palestine. Several verses in the Quran were interpreted as references to the holy land, or Syria. For example, according to one such statement, "We made the people (the children of Israel) who were weak inherit the land where we placed our blessing east and west" (Q 7:137, compare 5:21 and 21:71). By the 10th century, the sacredness of Palestine-Syria was discussed in detail by Muslim geographers such as al-Maqdisi (also known as al-Muqaddisi, d. ca. 990). Jerusalem was the focal point of this sacred land, for it was the first QIBLA (prayer direction) and the place where Muhammad went on his famous NIGHT JOURNEY AND ASCENT. This sacredness achieved architectural expression in the DOME OF THE ROCK and the AQSA MOSQUE, located on the site of the ancient Israelite temple. Al-Maqdisi listed dozens of other associations between the Palestine (Filistin) and sacred history—how its topography memorialized ABRAHAM, Isaac, MOSES, David, Solomon, John the Baptist, JESUS, and MARY. Gaza, he noted, was known for being the burial place of Muhammad's great grandfather Hashim and the birth place of al-Shafii (767–820), the founder of the SHAFII LEGAL SCHOOL. He also mentioned how Palestine would serve as the future site of the resurrection and final judgment. Such sites were visited by Muslim pilgrims, along with Christians, who had been making the Holy Land a pilgrim destination since the fourth century.

Palestine, as part of greater Syria, flourished under the Umayyad caliphs, who ruled from nearby DAMASCUS. Its fortunes declined somewhat when the UMAYYAD CALIPHATE came to an end in 750 and power shifted eastward to IRAQ, where the ABBASID CALIPHATE ruled. When Abbasid power weakened in the 10th century, this area of the empire became a battlefield for religious movements, regional powers, and tribal groups. Among the primary participants in these conflicts were the Byzantines, the FATIMID DYNASTY in Egypt, and the Seljuk Turks, who swore allegiance to the Abbasids in Baghdad. The Fatimid caliph al-Hakim bi-Amr Allah (r. 996–1021), known for his eccentricities, ordered the destruction of the Church of the Holy Sepulcher in Jerusalem in 1009 and took various punitive measures against both Christians and Jews as well as officials who earned his displeasure and ordinary Muslims. News of the fate of the Church of the Holy Sepulcher eventually reached Europe and became one of the causes for the launching of the First Crusade by Pope Urban II in 1095 to take back the Holy Land in the name of Christianity. The entire region from Egypt to Constantinople was the scene of crusader wars for nearly 200 years. The armies from Europe took Jerusalem in 1099 after massacring Muslims and Jews living in the city. It remained under crusader control until 1187, when the warrior prince SALADIN (d. 1193) established Muslim rule once again. During the 13th century and again in the early 15th century, Palestine was threatened by Mongol invasions from the east, but Muslim armies were able to repel them. Palestine stayed in the hands of Muslim rulers throughout the reigns of the Mamluk sultans of Egypt and Syria (1250–1517) and of the OTTOMAN DYNASTY (1517–1917).

During the Ottoman period, Palestine was governed from Damascus, except for a brief period in the 1830s when it was controlled by Egypt. It returned to Ottoman control in 1840, then, during an era of far-reaching Ottoman political and economic reforms in the 1880s, it was divided administratively into three districts: Nablus, Acre, and Jerusalem. Britain, France, Austria, and Russia competed against each other for influence in the region, and Europeans began to go there not just as pilgrims but as settlers, too. SEPHARDIC JEWS (also known today as Mizrahim "Easterners") had lived in Palestine continuously for centuries, but during the latter part of the 19th century, new Jewish immigrants went from Europe to settle there. Most of these were Ashkenazi (European) Jews who belonged to an international movement known as Zionism, which aspired to establish a homeland for diaspora Jews in Palestine. It was based partly on the nationalist movements that were sweeping Europe during the 19th century, and it was partly a reaction against increasing ANTI-SEMITISM there. Although modern Zionism was mainly secular, it was also mindful of the biblical view that Canaan (an ancient name for Israel) had been promised to the Jews as descendants of Abraham (Gen. 17).

During World War I, Palestine was the main scene of the Arab Revolt, an armed insurgency of Arab forces, supported by the British, against Ottoman troops. Arabs hoped to be able to govern themselves after the war. Instead, with the defeat of Germany and the breakup of the Ottoman Empire in 1918, the British took control of Palestine as a mandate territory, in accordance with the secret Sykes-Picot Agreement of 1916 and approval of the League of Nations. In 1917, the British Foreign Office issued the Balfour Declaration, which stated it "viewed with favour the establishment in Palestine of a national home for the Jewish people" and affirmed "that nothing shall be done which may prejudice the civil and religious rights of existing non-Jewish communities in Palestine." Until they gave up their mandate in 1948, the British tried unsuccessfully to mediate between these two competing and increasingly hostile nationalist movements, one Jewish, one Arab Palestinian. Jewish immigration from Europe increased in the 1930s, as many fled from Nazi Germany. A key figure for the Palestinian cause was Hajj AMIN AL-HUSAYNI (d. 1974), the MUFTI of Jerusalem who organized strikes and attacks against British troops and Jewish settlers, culminating in the Arab Revolt of 1936–39. He was unable, however, to unify the different factions involved on the Palestinian side of the struggle. On the side of the Zionists, David Ben Gurion (d. 1973), who had immigrated to Palestine from Poland in 1906, emerged as a prominent and effective political leader.

The end of the British mandate precipitated an all-out Arab-Israeli war in 1948, the first of several such major regional conflicts. When the United Nations approved a resolution for creating two states (General Assembly Resolution 181) in 1947, one for Jews and one for Arabs, Jewish leaders declared their support for it, while Palestinian Arabs, backed by other Arab states, rejected it. When the last British troops left in 1948, Israel declared its independence and was recognized by the Soviet Union, the United States, and other countries. Arab armies consisting of troops from the ARAB LEAGUE states of Egypt, Syria, Lebanon, and IRAQ were defeated in the ensuing war. Approximately 800,000 Palestinians fled or were driven from their homes and forced to live in refugee camps in Syria, Jordan, Lebanon, and Egypt. Their abandoned property was seized by the victorious Israelis. Israeli Jews remember this as their war of independence, but Arabs call it "the catastrophe" (al-nakba). Once Israel became independent, Jewish immigration from abroad increased, including survivors of the Nazi death camps in Europe. Middle Eastern Jews also immigrated to Israel after experiencing anti-Jewish discrimination and violence in several newly independent Arab countries during the 1950s. Israel, for its part, encouraged this immigration, which helped ensure that Jews became the majority population.

Israel has had several more wars with Palestinians and Arab neighbors since that time. The second Arab-Israeli war, known as the Six-Day War, occurred in 1967. It resulted in the shattering defeat of Arab armies and occupation of the West Bank, East Jerusalem, Gaza, and Egypt's Sinai Peninsula. More Palestinian refugees were created, and the secular PALESTINE LIBERATION ORGANIZATION (PLO) led by YASIR ARAFAT (d. 2004) became internationally recognized as the embodiment of the Palestinian nationalist cause. Another major war was the Yom Kippur/October War of 1973, which led in 1978 to a peace agreement with Egypt and return of the Sinai to that country. The

United States became Israel's greatest ally during this time, providing it with large amounts of foreign aid and weaponry as well as diplomatic backing in the UN and elsewhere.

In 1982, Israel invaded Lebanon to eliminate Palestinian guerrilla bases and then occupied southern Lebanon until it withdrew its forces in 2000. Another form of conflict occurred in 1987, when Palestinian civilians living in the West Bank and Gaza protested against the Israeli occupation. This "uprising," known as the First Intifada, ended in 1993 with the signing of the OSLO ACCORDS by Yitzhak Rabin (d. 1995), the Israeli prime minister, and Yasir Arafat, chairman of the PLO. Both men received the Nobel Peace Prize for this agreement. A second uprising, known as the Al-Aqsa Intifada, erupted in 2000 as a consequence of defects in the Oslo Accords, expansion of Israeli settlements on the West Bank, and deteriorating relations between Palestinians and Israelis. It ended with an uneasy truce in 2006.

Although religion was not the primary cause for these conflicts, religious politics and radicalism increased with the failure to find a lasting solution for the basic issue of Palestinian statehood. During the First Intifada, the radical Islamic movement HAMAS emerged in Gaza to challenge both the Israelis and the PLO leadership. It sought to liberate Palestine and establish an Islamic government, asserting that the land was a permanent Islamic bequest (*waqf*) that could never be transferred to non-Muslims. Since 1987, Hamas has achieved widespread support among the Palestinians and won the 2006 Palestinian legislative elections. Israel's 1982 invasion and occupation of southern Lebanon gave rise to HIZBULLAH, a Shii militant organization with close ties to Iran. It engaged in an intense but short border war with Israel in the summer of 2006. Israel, for its part, witnessed the rise of radical Zionist groups and parties that wanted to expand Israeli settlements in the West Bank and Gaza and opposed making any territorial concessions as part of any Israeli-

Palestinian peace agreement. In 1995, a member of one of these groups assassinated Israeli prime minister Yitzhak Rabin at a Tel Aviv peace rally because of the latter's signing of the Oslo Accords. The U.S.-led "war on terror" and its occupation of Iraq have further complicated efforts to peacefully resolve the Israeli-Palestinian crisis and increased religious radicalism and terror strikes in the region. Christian Zionists in the United States have also become engaged in the politics of war and peace in the Middle East and have shown strong support for Israel and right-wing Israeli Zionist parties.

See also ARAB-ISRAELI CONFLICTS; CHRISTIANITY AND ISLAM; COLONIALISM; CRUSADES; JUDAISM AND ISLAM; TERRORISM.

Further reading: Moshe Gil, *A History of Palestine, 634–1099* (Cambridge: Cambridge University Press, 1992); Walter Laquer and Barry Rubin, *The Israel-Arab Reader: A Documentary History of the Middle East Conflict.* 6th ed. (New York: Penguin Books, 2001); Bernard Reich, *A Brief History of Israel* (New York: Facts On File, 2004); Paul Wheatley, *The Places Where Men Pray Together: Cities in Islamic Lands, 7th through the 10th Centuries* (Chicago: University of Chicago Press, 2001), 112–126.

Istanbul (Constantinople)

The present-day city of Istanbul is the largest in TURKEY and once was the capital of both the Byzantine and Ottoman Empires. It straddles both sides of the Bosporus, the narrow strait connecting the Black Sea to the Marmara Sea and from there to the Mediterranean. It separates Europe from Asia, thus making Istanbul the only city in the world to sit astride two continents. Its unique position has also given the city strategic importance throughout history.

The city was founded in the seventh century B.C.E. as Byzantium and, after falling under Roman rule, eventually became the capital of the Roman Empire under Constantine the Great in

The magnificent Süleymaniye Mosque (16th century), as seen from the Golden Horn, Istanbul, Turkey *(Juan E. Campo)*

330 C.E., when it was renamed Constantinople. The city remained the capital of the ensuing Byzantine Empire and the center of the Byzantine Orthodox Church (now known as the Greek Orthodox Church) for 1,000 years. One of the most spectacular churches in the East, the Hagia Sophia (or Aya Sofia) Basilica, was built there on the site of an older church and dedicated by the Byzantine emperor Justinian (r. 527–565) in 537. Constantinople was on the route crusaders took from Europe to SYRIA and PALESTINE between the late 11th century and the 13th century, and it was plundered and occupied by European soldiers during the Fourth CRUSADE (1202–04). It became the capital of the Latin Empire until 1261, when the Byzantines recaptured it. The Fourth Crusade has remained a bitter memory for many Orthodox Christians and still affects their relations with the Roman Catholic Church.

Attracted by Constantinople's wealth, strategic importance, and prestige as a center of culture and learning, and inspired by a HADITH calling on Muslims to conquer the city, Arab armies besieged Constantinople between 674 and 678 and again in 717–718, but they were unable to take it. The Byzantine Empire suffered substantial losses of land in Anatolia and Thrace when Muslim Turkish armies invaded beginning in the 11th century, and the city was finally taken by the Ottomans under Sultan Mehmed II (the Conqueror) in 1453. It was then resettled with people from other parts of the empire and developed as an Ottoman Muslim city through the construction of MOSQUES and Islamic economic and social institutions. The Hagia Sophia Basilica was converted into an Ottoman state mosque. Nonetheless, the city was never exclusive to Muslims; significant numbers of Christians and Jews continued to live there. It remained the seat of the Ottoman government until the dynasty was overthrown by MUSTAFA KEMAL ATATURK in 1922, after which time Ankara was proclaimed capital of the nascent Republic of Turkey. The Aya Sofia Mosque was converted into a museum in 1935, reflecting the strong secular outlook of the new Turkish republic. While the city was referred to by many different names through the Ottoman period (Istanbul, Kostantiniye, Der Saadet, Islambol), it was not until 1930 that it was officially named Istanbul, the Turkish rendering of a Greek phrase meaning "in the city."

With 11.3 million residents (2007 estimate), Istanbul remains the largest city in Turkey. It has the largest port and is the commercial and cultural center of the country. It is the fifth-largest city in a Muslim-majority country, after CAIRO, Jakarta (INDONESIA), Dakha (BANGLADESH), and Karachi (PAKISTAN). Like other major urban areas, it suffers from air and water pollution and overcrowding due to mass migrations from rural areas of the country. Istanbul is also a major tourist destination. Roman and Byzantine remains include the Hippodrome, underground cisterns, and many churches, including the Aya Sofia. Ottoman monuments include many mosques, such as Süleymaniye and Sultan Ahmed, palaces such as the Topkapi Palace, and the Grand Bazaar.

See also CITIES; OTTOMAN DYNASTY.

Mark Soileau

Further reading: Zeynep Celik, *The Remaking of Istanbul: Portrait of an Ottoman City in the Nineteenth Century* (Berkeley: University of California Press, 1993); John Freely, *Istanbul the Imperial City* (London: Viking, 1996); Bernard Lewis, *Istanbul and the Civilization of the Ottoman Empire* (Norman: University of Oklahoma Press, 1963); Orhan Pamuk, *Istanbul: Memories and the City* (New York: Vintage, 2006).

J

Jaafar al-Sadiq (ca. 699–765) *early Shii scholar recognized as the sixth Imam by Ismaili and Twelve-Imam Shiis*

Abu Abd Allah Jaafar ibn Muhammad, also known as Jaafar al-Sadiq, was born in the holy city of MEDINA and was the son of the fifth Shii Imam, Muhammad al-Baqir (676–ca. 743). Both are held to be among the AHL AL-BAYT, descendants of the prophet MUHAMMAD through ALI IBN ABI TALIB (d. 661) and his wife FATIMA. Umm Farwa, his mother, was a descendant of ABU BAKR (d. 634), Muhammad's close companion and the first caliph. According to traditional accounts, Jaafar performed the HAJJ with his father and accompanied him when he was summoned to DAMASCUS by the Umayyad caliph Hisham ibn Abd al-Malik (r. 723–743) for questioning. Some accounts state that Hisham later poisoned Muhammad al-Baqir, who was buried in Medina. Jaafar succeeded his father as Imam and has been credited for establishing the doctrine of *nass* (designation of an imam by God or a previous imam), theoretically reducing disputes over succession to the imamate by limiting the number of claimants. He lived at a time when there was a great struggle occurring among Muslim factions contending for leadership in the UMMA. Indeed, he witnessed both the violent end of the UMAYYAD CALIPHATE at the hands of the Abbasids in the mid-eighth century and the Abbasid suppression of its former Shii allies in the aftermath of their victory over the Umayyads. He was also well aware of factional disputes among the Shia themselves over the question of leadership. When the Abbasids came to power, Jaafar was interrogated and imprisoned as a potential threat to their rule. It is not surprising, therefore, to learn that he endorsed practicing *taqiyya* (pious dissimulation) to avoid persecution at the hands of Sunni rulers. He was also credited with having set forth the doctrine of the Imams' infallibility (*isma*) because of their esoteric knowledge.

The Shia have regarded Jaafar as one of the leading imams, but he has been cited as an authority in many different strands of Islamic learning and tradition. He was remembered as a master teacher of HADITH among both Sunnis and Shiis. He was famous for being a hadith transmitter in both branches of the Muslim community, and several prominent Muslim scholars were said to have studied with him, including Abu Hanifa (d. 767) and MALIK IBN ANAS (d. 795). These were the eponymous founders of the Sunni Hanafi and Maliki Legal Schools. Likewise, Jaafar was remembered as the eponymous founder of the Jaafari Legal

School of the Shia. In addition to law, he was also embraced as an authority in the fields of THEOLOGY, Arabic grammar, ALCHEMY, and fortune telling. Sufis included him in their genealogies of spiritual authority, and an early QURAN commentary with mystical overtones has been ascribed to him.

According to Shii tradition, Jaafar, like his father, was poisoned to death by an enemy; in Jaafar's case it was the caliph Mansur (r. 754–775). Jaafar was buried in Medina's Baqi Cemetery, and his tomb was an object of pilgrimage until destroyed by the Wahhabis centuries later. After his death, there was a dispute among Shii factions over succession to the imamate. Those who claimed that the seventh Imam was his eldest son, Ismail (d. 760), eventually became the Ismaili branch of SHIISM. Those who supported the candidacy of Jaafar's son Musa al-Kazim (d. 799) and his heirs later became the Twelve-Imam branch of Shiism. One Shii faction, no longer extant, claimed at the time that Jaafar was not really dead, but that he had gone into a state of concealment (GHAYBA) and would return as the Mahdi, or Muslim messiah. This claim was attributed to other imams in both branches of Shii tradition.

See also ABBASID CALIPHATE; AUTHORITY; IMAM; ISMAILI SHIISM; TWELVE-IMAM SHIISM.

Further reading: Marshall G. Hodgson, "How Did the Early Shia Become Sectarian?" Journal of the American Oriental Society 75 (1955): 1–13; Moojan Momen, An Introduction to Shii Islam (New Haven, Conn.: Yale University Press, 1985), 37–39, 154–156; Michael Sells, Early Islamic Mysticism: Sufi, Quran, Miraj, Poetic, and Theological Writings (Mahwah, N.J.: Paulist Press, 1996), 75–88; Liyakat M. Takim, The Heirs of the Prophet: Charisma and Religious Authority in Shiite Islam (Albany: State University of New York Press, 2006).

Jahiliyya (Arabic: era of ignorance, barbarism)

The state of affairs in Arabia and much of the rest of the world before the rise of Islam in the seventh century is known to Islamic tradition as the Jahiliyya era, or the time of ignorance. Beginning in the 13th century, some Muslims came to apply this term to non-Muslims of later times.

The term has often been used to connote the pagan polytheism of the Arabian Peninsula before the revelation of the QURAN. Muslims view this period with particular disdain because polytheism, or assigning partners to God (SHIRK), is viewed as absolutely contradictory to Islam's own strict MONOTHEISM (TAWHID). They believe that Islam brought humanity true and ultimate knowledge through the Quran and HADITH, founded on the recognition that there is one God and MUHAMMAD is his prophet. In contrast, Muslims associate Jahiliyya with total spiritual darkness.

A significant figure who developed the Muslim understanding of the term Jahiliyya was the 13th- and 14th-century Muslim intellectual TAQI AL-DIN AHMAD IBN TAYMIYYA (d. 1328). As the Mongol armies swept westward toward the central lands of Islam, including Syria and Egypt, and as they became Sunni Muslims over time, many people living in those and other central lands faced a dilemma. If the Muslims living in these regions fought the Mongols, they would have been in violation of the SHARIA's injunctions forbidding Muslims from killing each other. If those Muslims did not engage in battle against the Mongols, their regions would be conquered by this foreign group. Supporting the Mamluk rulers of Egypt and Syria against the Mongols, Ibn Taymiyya wrote that any professed Sunni Muslim ceases to be one—and automatically becomes part of jahili culture— when he, among other things, breaks major Islamic injunctions concerning life, limb, and property. For Ibn Taymiyya, their offensive war against other Muslims clearly made the Mongols part of jahili culture, and as such the Muslims of Syria and Egypt were justified—even obliged—to wage war against them, even though they may have adhered to other aspects of the sharia.

In the 20th century, certain Islamists, such as SAYYID QUTB (d. 1966), a Muslim intellectual who played a leading role in Egypt's MUSLIM BROTHER-HOOD, adapted Ibn Taymiyya's ideas and viewed all modern secular governments (among other non-Muslim entities) as part of *jahili* culture and as legitimate targets for militant attacks. The Jihad Group of Egypt, under the leadership of Muhammad Abd al-Salam Faraj (d. ca. 1981), drew explicitly on Ibn Taymiyya's writings to justify the assassination of President ANWAR AL-SADAT (d. 1981), whom they accused of not being a true Muslim, like the Mongols of the past.

See also ARABIAN RELIGION, PRE-ISLAMIC; IDOLATRY; JIHAD.

Jon Armajani

Further reading: G. R. Hawting, *The Idea of Idolatry and the Emergence of Islam: From Polemic to History* (New York: Cambridge University Press, 1999); Sayyid Qutb, *Milestones* (Chicago: Kazi Publications, 2003); Emmanuel Sivan, *Radical Islam: Medieval Theology and Modern Politics* (New Haven, Conn.: Yale University Press, 1990).

Jamaat-i Islami (Urdu: Islamic Group)

The Jamaat-i Islami is an Islamic political party in PAKISTAN founded in 1941 by ABU AL-ALA MAWDUDI (1903–79), the most widely influential Muslim thinker of South Asia in the 20th century. It is an ideological movement that has aimed to create an Islamic state in which all aspects of social and political life would be governed according to Islamic standards and law. The Jamaat initially rejected the Pakistan independence movement and remained apart from political participation, believing that Islam is a universal system not to be encompassed by the boundaries of a nation-state and choosing to focus instead on developing its ideological support base. But upon the creation of Pakistan in 1947 based on religious identity, but not religious law, the Jamaat mobilized into a political party to work toward making Pakistan an ideal Islamic state founded on an Islamic constitution based on the QURAN and SUNNA and a

legal system based on SHARIA, mirroring the socio-religious system as established by MUHAMMAD (d. 632) and the first four CALIPHS.

The Jamaat believes in peaceful political progress toward an Islamic state through democratic process and works toward the development of a large Islamic base in society, attempting to effect social change through state institutions. It believes that technological modernization is required for the development of Islamic society but is opposed to what it views as Western-style modernization with its marginalization of religion and its moral corruption evident in HUMAN RIGHTS, WOMEN's advancement outside the home, birth control, and bank interest. Like its founder, most of the Jamaat's members and leaders are educated laymen rather than trained ULAMA, and their focus is often more on political concerns than religious ones. The Jamaat is supported by an elected council, has varying levels of membership, and is led by a president who is elected by party members for a five-year term. Alongside the ulama of Pakistan, the Jamaat participated in the violent anti-Ahmadi movement in 1953, which resulted in the declaration of Pakistan's AHMADIYYA community as a non-Muslim minority. It has survived as a political party during Pakistan's periods of martial law and political turbulence by operating as a religious organization. Outside of Pakistan, the Jamaat has branches in INDIA, KASHMIR, and BANGLADESH, and it publishes a monthly Urdu-language magazine out of Lahore called the Tarjuman al-Quran. Its active student wing is called the Islami Jamiat-i Talaba (Islamic Association of Students, IJT). The Jamaat had associations with the Islamic revolutionary government in IRAN and is known to have ties to SAUDI ARABIA.

See also DEMOCRACY; GOVERNMENT, ISLAMIC; ISLAMISM; RENEWAL AND REFORM MOVEMENTS.

Megan Adamson Sijapati

Further reading: Mumtaz Ahmad, "Islamic Fundamentalism in South Asia: The Jamaat-i-Islami and the Tablighi Jamaat of South Asia." In *Fundamental-*

isms Observed, edited by Martin E. Marty and R. Scott Appleby, 457–531 (Chicago: University of Chicago Press, 1991); Kalim Bahadur, *The Jamaat-i-Islami of Pakistan: Political Thought and Political Action* (New Delhi: Chetana Publications, 1977); Seyyed Vali Reza Nasr. *Mawdudi and the Making of Islamic Revivalism* (Oxford: Oxford University Press, 1996).

jami *See* MOSQUE.

Jamiyyat al-Ulama-i Hind (Association of Indian Ulama, also spelled Jamiyatul Ulama-i Hind; acronym: JUH)

Founded in 1919 by a group of religious scholars (ULAMA) under the leadership of the respected Deobandi scholar Mawlana Mahmud Hasan (1851–1920), the JUH sought to unify India's Muslim population and to solidify its Muslim scholars. It was composed of ulama from several major centers of Islamic learning in India, especially the Dar-ul Ulum DEOBAND, but also Farangi Mahal and Nadwat ul-Ulama of Lucknow, INDIA.

Extremely active in the fight for India's independence from British rule, the JUH was formed in the 1920s at the height of the KHILAFAT MOVEMENT, which sought to reestablish the Ottoman caliphate. This movement was also supported by MOHANDAS K. GANDHI (d. 1948) and the Indian National Congress (INC). The JUH advocated abstaining from engaging in political activism in favor of the pan-Islamic view that the religion could not be confined to or defined by a particular nation-state. Nonetheless, the JUH joined with the INC in order to press for independence from the British, under whom religious freedom was severely curtailed. The majority of the JUH ulama likewise looked askance at the Muslim League's secular, modernist leadership and opposed their efforts to establish a Muslim state. Under the charismatic leadership of Mawlana Hussain Ahmad Madani (d. 1957) in the 1930's, the agenda of the JUH focused on cultural and religious issues such as strong advocacy of the Dissolution of Muslim Marriages Act of 1939, which set up a separate legal code that provided for Muslim divorce to be adjudicated according to SHARIA principles. Other Indian Muslim leaders, such as MUHAMMAD IQBAL (d. 1938) and ABU AL-ALA MAWDUDI (d. 1979), criticized Madani and the JUH for their collaboration with the Hindu-dominated INC.

The JUH saw themselves as working on behalf of autonomy for Muslims *within* the greater Indian polity, not outside of it. As Madani put it, Islam was one *millat* (religion) within the Indian *qawm* (nation). However, many Indian ulama found this position increasingly untenable. In 1945, there was a schism that led to the establishment of the JAMIYATUL AL-ULAMA-I ISLAM in order to accommodate those with separatist views. Since 1947, the JUH has focused on religious and cultural issues and has remained aloof from politics.

See also ALL-INDIA MUSLIM LEAGUE; COLONIALISM; SECULARISM.

Anna Bigelow

Further reading: Yohanan Friedmann, "The Attitude of the Jamiyyat-i Ulama-i Hind to the Indian National Movement and the Establishment of Pakistan." *Asian and African Studies* 7 (1971): 157–183; Muhammad Qasim Zaman, *The Ulama in Contemporary Islam: Custodians of Change* (Princeton, N.J.: Princeton University Press, 2002).

Jamiyyat al-Ulama-i Islam (Association of the Ulama of Islam, also spelled Jamiyatul Ulama-i Islam, acronym: JUI)

The JUI broke off from the Jamiyyat al-Ulama-i Hind (JUH), an association of DEOBANDI ULAMA, in 1945 over the JUH's support for the Hindu-dominated Indian National Congress and their opposition to the call for the creation of a separate Muslim state, PAKISTAN. There are currently Pakistani and Bangladeshi branches of this group, including several subgroups under different leadership. Since the establishment of these Muslim states, the JUI has been active as a political party and has pressed for the implementation of the SHARIA. In Pakistan, the JUI was active in the anti-AHMADIYYA riots in 1953 and 1974 and anti-Shia agitations. Part of the JUI's agenda has also been to establish a "pure" Islam in Pakistan. In particular, the JUI has sought to eliminate the worship of saints and other practices they regard as un-Islamic.

As a political party, the JUI held political control of the Northwest Frontier Province (NWFP) in the 1970's under the leadership of Maulana Mufti Mahmud (1919–80), who was chief minister from 1971 to 1973. In addition to pursuing populist policies regarding land reform, public education, and health care, during this period several "Islamic" laws were instituted and remain, including the prohibition of alcohol, a reform of inheritance laws, and the mandatory observance of Ramadan. The JUI opposed the regimes of Zulfiqar Ali Bhutto (r. 1973–77) and Benazir Bhutto (r. 1988–90, 1993–96), gave lukewarm support to Nawaz Sharif (r. 1990–93, 1997–99), and has been an active critic of the regime of Pervez Musharraf (r. 1999–2008). Currently, under the leadership of Mahmud's son Fazlur Rahman, the JUI is again influential as part of the Muttahida Majlis-i Amal (MMA) coalition of religious parties that came to power in the NWFP in 2002. The JUI is also popular in Baluchistan.

See also ISLAMISM; POLITICS AND ISLAM; SHIISM.

Anna Bigelow

Further reading: Jamal Malik, *Colonialization of Islam: Dissolution of Traditional Institutions in Pakistan,* 2d ed. (New Delhi: Manohar Publications, 1998); Muhammad Qasim Zaman, *The Ulama in Contemporary Islam: Custodians of Change* (Princeton, N.J.: Princeton University Press, 2002).

Jammu and Kashmir   *See* KASHMIR.

Jannisary (Turkish *yeniçeri*: new troops)

The elite standing army corps of the Ottoman Empire, the Janissaries originated in the 14th century as a corps of soldiers made up of Christian prisoners of war. They developed into a regular standing infantry through the institution known as *devşirme*—the levying of boys from the Christian peoples conquered by the Ottomans. The recruits were converted to Islam, taught the Turkish language, and trained for specific functions in the Ottoman palace and military. Though they received regular salaries, the Janissaries were considered slaves, and other Muslims were thus excluded from their ranks. The Janissaries were subject to strict discipline and were forbidden to marry. Their organization was steeped in tradition, and each regiment was independent, with its own symbol and flag. Their loyalty to the regiment and to the SULTAN gave them strength in battle, making them an effective force in Ottoman conquests. In peacetime, they served important functions in Ottoman CITIES, including fire-fighting, maintaining law and order, and ensuring fair trade. They became a force in internal politics known for revolting against and overthrowing viziers and even sultans, symbolically announcing their mutinies by overturning their large soup cauldrons. The Janissaries had an affiliation with the BEKTASHI SUFI ORDER, whose *baba*s (spiritual leaders) served as chaplains to the troops.

Because of their regular salary and the privileges and distinctions they received, Muslims began to seek admission to the Janissary corps through patronage and bribery. This led to a decline of discipline, which worsened when Janissaries were allowed to have outside careers while still garnering their wages. By the 18th century, the Janissaries were widely seen as a nuisance, and they resisted attempts at reform. Finally, when Sultan Mahmud II (r. 1808–39) created a new regular corps in 1826, the ensuing mutiny was put down, and the Janissaries were destroyed.

See also CHRISTIANITY AND ISLAM; CONVERSION; EUROPE; OTTOMAN DYNASTY; SLAVERY; TANZIMAT.

Mark Soileau

Further reading: Geoffrey Goodwin, *The Janissaries* (London: Saqi Books, 1994); David Nicolle and Christa Hook, *The Janissaries* (Oxford: Osprey, 1995)

Jerusalem (known in Arabic as al-Quds [Holy] and Bayt al-Maqdis [House of the Holy])

Jerusalem is a holy city for followers of the three Abrahamic religions—Judaism, Christianity, and Islam. For each, however, it is holy for different reasons. For Jews, it is the location of Mount Zion, the center of the world where the ancient Israelite Temple of Solomon once stood. For Christians, it is where JESUS convened the Last Supper with his disciples and where he endured the Passion, was crucified, died, resurrected, and ascended to heaven. For Muslims, it is where MUHAMMAD prayed and entered into the heavens on his NIGHT JOURNEY AND ASCENT. Most Muslims consider it to be Islam's third most sacred city after MECCA and MEDINA, although they also recognize it is not exclusive to them alone as the other two cities are. Through the centuries, devout members of all three religions have lived and journeyed to Jerusalem on pilgrimage. They go to visit and worship at places that are held sacred by each of these religions. The Western Wall of the ancient Temple is a major focus of Jewish prayer and piety. For Christians, its most holy places are the Church of the Resurrection (also called the Church of the Holy Sepulcher) and the Mount of Olives, where they believe Jesus ascended to heaven. Muslims visit and pray at the AQSA MOSQUE and the DOME OF THE ROCK in the Haram al-Sharif (Noble Sanctuary, known as the Temple Mount to Jews and Christians). All three religions have traditions stating that Jerusalem will be the focal point of cataclysmic events that will signal the endtimes and the arrival of JUDGMENT DAY.

Aerial view of Jerusalem's Old City showing the Dome of the Rock and the Haram al-Sharif (top), and the Church of the Holy Sepulcher (the domed structure at the bottom) *(National Geographic Magazine)*

PRE-ISLAMIC JERUSALEM

Jerusalem is among the oldest cities in the world. Archaeological evidence suggests human settlement in its environs as early as the fourth millennium B.C.E. Its early name, Rushalimum (or Urusalim), appears in ancient Egyptian and Syrian texts dated to the 19th and 14th centuries B.C.E. This name may have meant "foundation of the god Salim"; only much later, after the biblical period, was its name interpreted to mean "City of Peace." Between 2000 and 1500 B.C.E., Jerusalem developed into a walled city located on the hill of

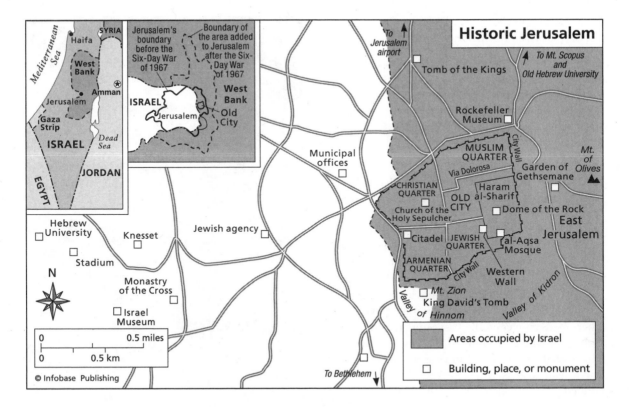

Historic Jerusalem

Areas occupied by Israel

☐ Building, place, or monument

© Infobase Publishing

Ophel (Mount Zion), protected on three sides by the Central Valley and the Kidron Valley, which met at its southern tip. During the reigns of the Israelite kings DAVID (r. ca. 1010–970 B.C.E.) and Solomon (r. ca. 970–928 B.C.E.), Jerusalem became a royal capital and the center of the cult of Yahweh (the Lord God), the supreme deity of the Hebrews who was worshipped in Solomon's Temple. The city was barely 188,000 square yards in area, or about the size of a large shopping mall in the United States today. This was not an unusual size for an ancient town or city, however. After Solomon's time, ancient Israel was divided into two kingdoms, with Jerusalem as the capital of Judah (the Southern Kingdom) and Samaria the capital of ISRAEL (the Northern Kingdom). The Northern Kingdom fell to the Assyrian army in 722 B.C.E., and the Southern Kingdom was destroyed by the

Babylonians in 686. The Babylonians plundered and destroyed the city and its temple, carrying the leading inhabitants into captivity in southern Mesopotamia. These events were related in the historical books of the Hebrew Bible (2 Kings, 1 & 2 Chron.), and they inspired the revelations and visions of the biblical prophets (for example, Isaiah, Jeremiah, and Ezekiel).

A remnant remained in Jerusalem after the Babylonian conquest until Cyrus the Great of Persia defeated the Babylonians and allowed the Israelite exiles to return in 538 B.C.E. The Second Temple was built around 515 B.C.E., but the restoration of the city and its walls was not completed until the governorship of Nehemiah (mid-sixth century B.C.E.). The city grew to twice the size it had been during the time of the First Temple. When Alexander the Great's armies swept through the Middle East in the fourth century B.C.E., Jerusalem fell into the hands of his general Seleucus I Nicator (r. 312–281 B.C.E.) and his heirs, the Seleucids. Under the influence of Hellenistic culture, the city was embellished with a stadium and gymnasium, and worship of Hellenistic gods was introduced in the Temple. Jewish rule was restored by the Hasmoneans (or Maccabees) around 166 B.C.E. The last Hasmoneans were subjugated by Rome about a century later in 63 B.C.E., and Jerusalem became part of the Roman Empire, governed by Rome's clients, the Herodian Dynasty (63 B.C.E.–50 C.E.). Herod the Great (r. 40 B.C.E.–4 B.C.E.), under the patronage of Julius Caesar and other prominent Romans, conducted major building projects in Jerusalem. He rebuilt the Temple, enlarged the Temple Mount, and enhanced the city's fortifications. Herod's successors ruled Judaea during the ministries of Jesus and his disciples and were implicated in their persecution. The Hellenization of the city continued during this time, as reflected in its theater, temples to Greco-Roman deities, and luxurious homes for the wealthy on the hillsides west of the Temple Mount. Tensions among Jews opposed to Hellenization and Roman rule erupted into an outright revolt in 66 C.E., resulting in the destruction of the Second Temple, the slaughter of the civilian population, and the devastation of much of the city in 70. Jewish religious life found fertile soil elsewhere in PALESTINE, the east Mediterranean region, and Mesopotamia. Jesus' followers, who came to be known as Christians, followed their Jewish brethren into towns and cities of Palestine and the east Mediterranean region.

During the second century, another Jewish uprising, known as the Bar-Kochba Revolt, broke out when the Romans decided to build a temple to Jupiter on the Temple Mount in 130. The revolt was violently crushed, and Jews were banned from living in the city. Jerusalem was transformed into a Roman garrison named Aelia Capitolina after the family of the emperor Hadrian (r. 117–138) and the Temple Mount became a place of desolation.

The city continued to languish under its Roman overlords until the emperor Constantine (r. 306–337) converted to Christianity and, with the help of his mother Helena, gave new life to it. Helena identified the site of Jesus' crucifixion, burial, and resurrection on Golgotha, the hill situated west of the Temple Mount. She was authorized by her son to construct a church there to house the relic of the True Cross. This was the Church of the Resurrection (or Holy Sepulcher). She also had basilicas built on the Mount of Olives and in Bethlehem. During the reign of the emperor Justinian (r. 527–565) the "new" (Nea) Church of the Theotokos was built near the Church of the Resurrection in honor of MARY as the "mother of God." Jerusalem and environs then became a major focus of early Christian pilgrimage activity. By the late sixth century, the city had at least 17 churches. It was one of the major patriarchates in the Byzantine Empire, where Christianity had become the religion of state. At about the same time, though often excluded from the city by Christian authorities, Jews were assembling traditions (found in the Talmud and rabbinic midrash) about the sacredness of the Temple Mount and its Stone of Foundation, identifying it as the location of the biblical creation account, the place from underneath which the floodwaters came in the time of Noah, the location of Abraham's near-sacrifice of his son Isaac, and where the Messiah would stand to proclaim the new messianic age.

During the first half of the seventh century, Jerusalem underwent ongoing political and religious turbulence. Sassanian armies invaded the region from Persia, defeating Byzantine forces. They captured Jerusalem in 614, which led to considerable loss of life and destruction in the city, and they carried the relic of the True Cross back to their capital, Ctesiphon, in Mesopotamia. Persians left the city temporarily in the hands of the Jews, who anticipated the onset of a new age. Meanwhile, the Byzantine emperor Heraclius (r. 610–641) launched a counterattack against the Persians, finally returning to Jerusalem in triumph with the True Cross in 629. Jews were accused of conspiring with the Persians and implicated in the killing of Christians and destruction of churches. Once again, Christian authorities banned them from the city. They were prohibited from public worship, and in 634 Heraclius ordered that all the Jews in his empire be baptized.

ISLAMICATE JERUSALEM

Arabs appear to have lived in Jerusalem in the first century, for they are mentioned in the New Testament's Acts of the Apostles (Acts 2:5–11). There is also evidence that there were Christian Arabs in the city when it was ruled by the Byzantine Empire. Jerusalem was not mentioned by name in the QURAN, but several verses have been understood by later Muslim commentators as references to it. The most important of these was the "farthest mosque" (al-masjid al-aqsa) mentioned in Q 17:1, which was identified in Islamic commentaries with the place where Muhammad prayed in Jerusalem on his miraculous Night Journey. The Aqsa Mosque in the Noble Sanctuary (al-haram al-sharif), or Temple Mount platform, commemorated this event. The other verse most commonly associated with Jerusalem is Q 2:142–153, where commentators maintain that Muhammad was commanded to face toward the QIBLA of Mecca, instead of Jerusalem, the first qibla of the Muslims of Medina. Later texts elaborated on both Muhammad's Night Journey and the changing of the qibla. Indeed, a distinct literary genre concerned with the praiseworthy qualities (fadail) of Jerusalem would arise around the time of the CRUSADES (12th to 13th century) that sought to place the city on a par with Mecca and Medina and identify it as the site where important events were expected to occur on Judgment Day.

Muslim political control over Jerusalem was established in 638, when Arab armies accepted the peaceful surrender of the city by the Byzantines. This was during the reign of the caliph UMAR IBN AL-KHATTAB (r. 634–644), who, according to some accounts, was received by the city's Christian patriarch Sophronius. Umar has also been credited with having the neglected Temple Mount cleared of debris and building a small mosque near where the Aqsa Mosque would later be erected. There was no forced conversion of Jews and Christians to Islam. Generally faring better than under their former Roman, Persian, and Byzantine rulers, they were treated as "protected" (DHIMMI) communities because they were PEOPLE OF THE BOOK. During the UMAYYAD CALIPHATE (661–750), which had established its capital in nearby DAMASCUS, Muslim rulers greatly embellished the Noble Sanctuary by reconstructing and expanding the Aqsa Mosque and erecting the Dome of the Rock, a strikingly beautiful edifice that symbolized the advent of the new Umayyad political order and promoted Islamic doctrines about God and Jesus against those of Christianity.

As the centuries passed, Arabic replaced Greek as the language of the populace. Jerusalem's prosperity declined when the Abbasids ended Umayyad rule and transferred the capital eastward from Damascus to BAGHDAD in the mid-eighth century. As Abbasid power weakened in the 10th century, rival powers contended for control over Jerusalem and its environs. It remained a city where the Christian majority lived together with Jews and their Muslim rulers until the era of the CRUSADES (11th to 13th centuries). Intercommunal tensions were intensified when the Fatimid caliph in CAIRO, al-Hakim bi-Amr Allah (r. 996–1021), ordered the destruction of the Church of the Resurrection in September 1009. Historians have offered different explanations for these and other actions taken against Jews, Christians, and even Muslims. Some explanations point to al-Hakim's unstable personality or to his concern that the Christian holy site was too wealthy and attracting too many pilgrims, especially during the Easter holidays. Others posit that he suspected Christians of colluding with rival rulers and BEDOUIN chieftains to undermine Fatimid rule in Syria-Palestine. Earthquakes, warfare, and a poor economy further contributed to Jerusalem's decline. Moreover, in contrast to Cairo, Mecca, Damascus, and Baghdad, it lacked significant centers of learning and famous scholars.

Eventually, word of al-Hakim's harsh measures against Christians in Jerusalem reached Europe and provoked the launching of the First Crusade in 1099, which sought to place Jerusalem and the Holy Land under European Christian rule. The crusaders took the city on July 15, 1099, with much loss of life and destruction of property. Eyewitness accounts describe the wholesale slaughter of men and women, Muslims and Jews alike, by the crusader warriors. City streets were said to have run red with blood. In the aftermath of the crusader victory, Muslims and Jews were banned from the city, and even Eastern Christians (Greeks, Armenians, Nestorians, Georgians) were expelled from its holy places. The crusaders converted the Aqsa Mosque into a palace and the Dome of the Rock into a church that they named the "Temple of the Lord."

The Latin Kingdom of Jerusalem the crusaders founded lasted until 1187, when the Kurdish Muslim warrior prince SALADIN (d. 1193) reconquered the city and pushed the crusaders to the coastal areas of Palestine and Syria. Saladin, who founded the Ayyubid dynasty (1169–1260), restored the Muslim holy sites in the Noble Sanctuary and reopened Jerusalem to Muslims, Jews, and Eastern Christians. Some of the churches and convents built by the crusaders were transformed into mosques, MADRASAS, and Sufi hospices, which attracted Muslim scholars, students, and mystics belonging to many of the leading Sufi orders to the city. Christians were permitted to maintain control of the Church of the Resurrection, and even Latin pilgrims were allowed to come. In 1229, during a time of political feuding within Muslim ranks, the sultan al-Kamil (r. 1218–38), Saladin's nephew, allowed Latin crusaders to reoccupy Jerusalem under the command of Frederick II (d. 1250), the Holy Roman Emperor and enlightened monarch from Sicily. Once again, non-Christians had little if any access to the holy city. This interlude was

short-lived, however. After Frederick II departed, Turkish troops allied with the Ayyubids attacked both Damascus and Jerusalem in 1244, bringing death and ruin in their wake. The crusading came to an end, but one of its significant outcomes was to enhance Jerusalem's importance as a sacred symbol among Muslims, Christians, and Jews. This is when much of the Muslim devotional literature concerning Jerusalem's praiseworthy qualities was composed and when pious Jews dreamed of returning and reclaiming their sacred land. Despite its holiness, or perhaps partly because of it, Muslim rulers did not allow the city to have its own defensive walls, a standard feature for cities that had political or strategic importance. The three religious communities were intermingled; there was little if any ghettoization of religious minorities.

After the fall of the Ayyubids, Jerusalem came under the control of the Mamluks, a dynasty of slave-soldiers that ruled from Cairo and Damascus between 1250 and 1517. The city prospered under their patronage. It is estimated that only about 70 Jewish families, divided into Sephardic (Spanish and "Oriental") and Ashkenazi (European) communities, lived there at this time, while many Jews lived in the Galilee to the north. Mamluk control was ended in 1517, when Ottoman armies conquered the region and incorporated it into their expansive empire, which was based in the city of ISTANBUL (Constantinople), the former capital of the Byzantines that the Ottomans had taken in 1453. Jerusalem enjoyed the patronage of the Ottomans, who built the great wall known as Suleyman's Wall in 1537–41, which now defines the "Old City," and continued to support the funding of its Islamic institutions. The Ottoman *millet* system of governance, which favored the formation of communities on the basis of religious and ethnic identity, led to the appearance of religiously aligned neighborhoods in Ottoman cities. This explains the division of Jerusalem into 18 quarters divided among 4 groups: Jewish (2 quarters), Muslim (4 quarters), Armenian Christian (4 quarters), and other Christians (Greeks, Latins, and Copts) before the end of the 18th century. By 1850, Jerusalem had an estimated total population of 15,000, with Jews becoming the largest group (6,000) for the first time since the Roman period. By the turn of the century, the city had 55,000 residents, including a large Jewish majority (35,000).

CONTEMPORARY JERUSALEM

As the Ottoman Empire collapsed from internal and external forces, Jerusalem became subject to increasing involvement by European powers and growing tensions among the different communities that lived in it. European governments opened consulates there, and missionaries opened schools and churches to win converts. European Jewish philanthropists such as the Montefiores and the Rothschilds supported the building of schools, clinics, and hospitals for the city's Jewish population. Meanwhile, Jerusalem had become the focal point of a worldwide Zionist movement that sought to create a modern national homeland for all Jews. After World War I, the Ottoman Empire collapsed. Its holdings in Syria, Transjordan (later Jordan), and Palestine were divided between France and Britain, the two main victors in the war. Transjordan and Palestine (including Jerusalem) fell under the British mandate, which remained in effect until 1948, when the modern state of Israel was created. During the mandate period, Palestinian Arab nationalism was also stirred, and Jerusalem became a major center for the Palestinian nationalist movement, a largely secular movement that included Arab Christians as well as Muslims.

Conflict between Jewish and Arab nationalisms led to the division of Jerusalem into two parts in the war of 1947–48. Although the United Nations recommended that the city be internationalized, Jews claimed control of West Jerusalem and Arabs claimed East Jerusalem. The dividing line ran north to south in line with the western wall of the Old City. Israel made West Jerusalem its capital, despite international objections. Jordan ruled East Jerusalem until the 1967 Arab-Israeli war, when the entire city came under Israeli control. Today Jerusalem remains a much-contested holy city—a focal point of religious violence, nationalist aspirations, and messianic expectations that extend all the way to the evangelical Christian communities of the United States. Its status as Israel's capital remains controversial. Calls for its internationalization continue, but there is also support for making it the shared capital of both Israel and a Palestinian state that has yet to be realized. Meanwhile, the city has grown in size and population. It is Israel's largest city, followed by Tel Aviv-Jaffa and Haifa. In 2007, according to the Israeli Central Bureau of Statistics, it had more than 732,000 inhabitants (65 percent Jews, 32 percent Muslims, and 2 percent Christians), including those living in outlying towns and settlements.

See also ABBASID CALIPHATE; ARAB-ISRAELI CONFLICTS; CHRISTIANITY AND ISLAM; FATIMID DYNASTY; JUDAISM AND ISLAM; MAMLUK; OTTOMAN DYNASTY.

Further reading: Karen Armstrong, *Jerusalem: One City, Three Faiths* (New York: Random House, 1996); Meron Benvenisti, *City of Stone: The Hidden History of Jerusalem* (Berkeley: University of California Press, 1996); Oleg Grabar, *The Shape of the Holy: Early Islamic Jerusalem* (Princeton, N.J.: Princeton University Press, 1996), F. E. Peters, *Jerusalem* (Princeton, N.J.: Princeton University Press, 1995); ———, *Jerusalem and Mecca: The Typology of the Holy City in the Near East* (New York: New York University Press, 1987); A. L. Tibawi, "Jerusalem: Its Place in Islam and Arab History." *The Islamic Quarterly* 12, no. 4 (1968): 185–218.

Jesus (Arabic: Isa) *the first-century Jewish teacher who Christians believe to be a savior and who Muslims believe was a prophet who brought the Gospel, which contained part of God's message for humanity*

Jesus' name appears in 15 quranic chapters and 93 verses. Known as "the Messiah Jesus, the son of Mary" (for example, Q 3:45), Muslims believe that Jesus was born of a virgin named MARY and that he taught the true religion of God, many aspects of which Christians later misinterpreted (for example, Q 5:17; 19:16–37). Following the quranic narrative, they hold that while he was not crucified, he was raised to heaven and will return at the end of time to defeat the ANTICHRIST (al-Dajjal). Muslims also believe that Jesus was a prophet (rasul, nabi) who foretold the coming of MUHAMMAD. Additional accounts about Jesus were later included in the HADITH, *Lives of the Prophets* literature, and Sufi poetry and hagiographies.

One of several mistakes Muslims believe Christians have made about Jesus is their claim that he was divine. Because a key belief in Islam is an absolute MONOTHEISM (TAWHID), Muslims believe it is blasphemous to maintain that any human being can have divine attributes. For Muslims, God is perfect and holy and as such cannot be captured in any human form. The idea that Jesus was human and not divine does not detract from his important role as a prophet. The message he preached to humanity was as meaningful as the prophets who preceded him. Muslims also reject the Christian notion of the trinity because they believe it is a form of IDOLATRY that undermines God's oneness.

The QURAN's assertions about Jesus suggest that he and Muhammad had similar experiences, and, as such, Muslims believe that there were some parallels between the lives of these figures. God gave each of them the task of proclaiming his message to humanity. They both had companions who attempted to understand their message, encountered opponents who severely criticized the ideas they declared, and gave prophecies about the future. Muslims believe Jesus foretold the coming of Muhammad, while in the hadith, Muhammad declared the day of judgment that would come at the end of time.

Muslims believe that when Jesus' enemies attempted to crucify him, God intentionally deceived them by projecting Jesus' likeness onto someone else whom they mistakenly crucified (Q 4:157–158). However, Muslims do believe that Jesus ascended into heaven. For them, neither divinity nor crucifixion is necessary to authenticate the enormous value of Jesus' life and teachings. The Arabic name Isa (Jesus) is used by Muslims as a personal name, and it is thought that the mixing of Muslims and Christians in ANDALUSIA (Islamic Spain) helped make Jesus a common name among Spanish-speaking Christians as well.

Followers of one of the branches of the AHMADIYYA sect, unlike the majority of Muslims, maintain that Jesus survived crucifixion and migrated to KASHMIR under the name Yuz Asaf, where he survived to old age and was buried.

See also CHRISTIANITY AND ISLAM; GOSPEL; HOLY BOOKS; PROPHETS AND PROPHECY.

Jon Armajani

Further reading: Kenneth Cragg, *Jesus and the Muslim: An Exploration* (London and Boston, G. Allen & Unwin, 1985); Tarif Khalidi, *The Muslim Jesus: Sayings and Stories in Islamic Literature* (Cambridge, Mass.: Harvard University Press, 2001); Javad Nurbakhsh, *Jesus in the Eyes of the Sufis* (London: Khaniqahi-Nimatullahi Publications, 1983); Edward Geoffrey Parrinder, *Jesus in the Quran* (Oxford: Oneworld, 1995); Neal Robinson, *Christ in Islam and Christianity: The Representation of Jesus in the Quran and the Classical Muslim Commentaries* (London: Macmillan, 1991); Ahmad ibn Muhammad al-Thalabi, *Arais al-majalis fi qisas al-anbiya, or "Lives of the Prophets."* Translated by William M. Brinner (Leiden: E.J. Brill, 2002), 622–680.

jihad

Literally, the Arabic word *jihad* means to strive or struggle (in the path of God); it often refers to religiously sanctioned warfare. The QURAN advocates jihad to extend God's rule (Q 2:192, 8:39), promising reward in the AFTERLIFE for those who are killed in battle (Q 3:157–158, 169–172) and punishment for those who do not participate (Q

9:81–82, 48:16). Other quranic verses deal with exemption from military service (Q 9:91, 48:17), fighting during the holy months (Q 2:217) and in the holy lands (Q 2:191), prisoners of war (Q 47:4), safe conduct (Q 9:6), and truce (Q 8:61).

The classical doctrine of jihad, developed during the eighth and ninth centuries, delineated between *dar al-Islam* (house of Islam) and *dar al-harb* (house of war, i.e., those who did not submit to Islamic rule). Islamic law presumed an ongoing state of warfare between the two, except for limited truces under specific circumstances. Legal scholars defined who was obligated to participate in jihad and who was a legitimate target (noncombatants such as WOMEN, CHILDREN, and the elderly were protected). A recognized Muslim government could declare jihad for legitimate reasons (defense or propagation of the faith), but jurists generally agreed that not all Muslims were required to go to war; a limited force could perform the duty on behalf of others. Before launching jihad, Muslims must offer unbelievers the chance to submit to Islamic rule without fighting, either by converting to Islam or by paying a poll tax. Jihad was conducted only if unbelievers refused to submit.

After the conquest era (mid-seventh century to mid-eighth century), truce between Muslim and non-Muslim states became the norm. Sometimes Muslims allied with non-Muslims against other Muslim states. In fact, jihad has historically most often been launched against other professing Muslims or else has been defensive in nature. Governments used jihad to legitimize their reigns, labeling opponents as apostates, rebels, or unbelievers and thus legitimate targets for jihad. Jihad during the modern era has been mostly an anticolonialist enterprise.

Jihad has not always meant actual warfare. Since the 12th century, Sufis and others have defined it from a spiritual point of view, referring to an individual's inner struggle against unbelief and sin or to society's struggle to bring Islamic community in line with God's laws. Some invoke a HADITH in which MUHAMMAD addressed soldiers returning from battle: "You have come for the best, from the lesser jihad to the greater jihad." When asked what the greater jihad was, he replied, "The servant's struggle against selfish desire." This pacifistic view is also supported by a verse in the Quran (Q 22:78). Modernists often argue that jihad is allowed only as defensive warfare or the foundation for Islamic international law. They maintain that Islamic law is superior to Western international law due to its venerable age of 13 centuries, its humane principles, its foundation in divine dictates, and its clear-cut notions of just war and unjustifiable aggression.

Radical Islamists use jihad to challenge the status quo, which they accuse of selling out to Western dominance. After SAYYID QUTB (d. 1966), revivalists increasingly believed that society could not be changed from within. Rather, the oppressive secularist regimes must be brought down so that true Islamic society could be established. By defining Egyptian society as JAHILIYYA (in a state of ignorance), Qutb opened the door for declarations of jihad against Muslim rulers who were perceived as hypocrites for failing to establish proper Islamic societies. Radical Islamic groups have recently differentiated between the jihad against these rulers, whom they call "the near enemy," from Western powers, including the United States, whom they call "the far enemy." They have also reinterpreted Islamic law to justify terrorist attacks on individuals (including women and children) historically excluded as targets and to avoid the restriction that only a recognized Islamic government could launch jihad.

See also COLONIALISM; *DAR AL-ISLAM* AND *DAR AL-HARB*; ISLAMISM; MARTYRDOM; TERRORISM.

Stephen Cory

Further reading: David Cook, *Understanding Jihad* (Berkeley: University of California Press, 2005); Majid Khadduri, *War and Peace in the Law of Islam* (Baltimore: Johns Hopkins University Press, 1962); Rudolph Peters,

Islam and Colonialism: The Doctrine of Jihad in Modern History (The Hague: Mouton, 1979); Rudolph Peters, *Jihad in Classical and Modern Islam* (Princeton, N.J.: Markus Weiner Publishers, 1996).

jihad movements

Jihad is one of the most contested terms in Islam. The term's basic Arabic meaning yields words generally meaning striving or struggle, whether in the more general sense of striving for correct practice or, more particularly, striving for interpretive clarity in reading the QURAN and HADITH. Jihad, however, has been widely understood, by both Muslims and non-Muslims, as religiously sanctioned warfare. The Islamic legal schools formalized jihad doctrines of warfare in the wake of the early conquests, based on statements in the Quran and hadith. Radical Islamist movements active in modern times have given the term renewed significance, often significantly changing traditional understandings formulated in the premodern Islamic legal traditions. Claiming to act in the name of Islam, these movements have strived to fight what they see as imperialist anti-Muslim agents and apostates, both at home and abroad.

Jihad movements appeared in a number of different Muslim societies in the 18th and 19th centuries, coinciding with the onset of the second millennium of the Islamic CALENDAR. Some were Mahdist in nature, following the lead of self-proclaimed MAHDIS (Islamic messianic leaders) and the onset of a new age. Promoting Islamic revival and reform, these movements established Islamic states in West Africa. The movement of the Sudanese Mahdi Muhammad Ahmad (d. 1885) opposed European imperialism, a trend that a number of jihad movements followed in North Africa, the Caucasus region, INDIA, Sumatra, and Java. The Wahhabi movement in Arabia attacked what its leaders considered un-Islamic practices and created the Saudi state using a jihadist ideology and tribal warriors. After World War II, as Muslim lands became decolonized, jihad movements and militias arose in opposition to Israeli occupation of the West Bank and Gaza territories. They also appeared in LEBANON in response to ISRAEL's occupation of the country in 1982. Egyptian president ANWAR AL-SADAT (d. 1981) was assassinated by the Jihad Group, which considered him to be an un-Islamic leader because of his pro-Western policies, despotism, and peace agreement with Israel. The Soviet occupation of AFGHANISTAN between 1979 and 1989 gave birth to an array of anti-Soviet militias that included jihad groups composed of Afghan and foreign guerrilla fighters supported by the UNITED STATES and SAUDI ARABIA. These included a loosely organized group of Arab fighters led by USAMA BIN LADIN and Ayman al-Zawahiri that came to be known as AL-QAIDA (The Base). The success of the jihadist militias against the Soviet army inspired bin Ladin's group to engage in other militant activities. It also gave new motivation to jihad movements in other Muslim lands.

Following the events of September 11, 2001, many Muslims have actively sought to distance themselves—and Islam in general—from jihadist interpretations of Islam. Nonetheless, movements such as the Jamaa al-Islamiyya (Islamic Group) in EGYPT and al-Qaida have made their mark, creating an association of Islam with violence that has proved difficult to break. It is important to note, however, that there are Muslim movements that carry out "jihadist" work in the name of Islam that is explicitly nonpolitical and nonviolent. The TABLIGHI JAMAAT, which began in India in the early 20th century and has spread throughout the world, is one such movement. Jihad in this context has come to mean the struggle to keep Muslims within the Islamic fold in the face of Western-style modernity and SECULARISM, a task accomplished through personal piety and proselytizing.

See also ABD AL-RAHMAN, UMAR; AFGHAN MUJAHIDIN; FARAIZI MOVEMENT; BARELWI, SAYYID AHMAD; HAMAS; HIZBULLAH; RENEWAL AND REFORM

MOVEMENTS; SHAMIL; TERRORISM; WAHHABISM; WEST AFRICA.

Caleb Elfenbein

Further reading: Fawaz A. Gerges, *Journey of the Jihadist: Inside Muslim Militancy* (Orlando, Fla.: Harcourt, 2006); Gilles Kepel, *Jihad: The Trail of Political Islam* (Cambridge, Mass.: Harvard University Press, 2002); Ahmed Rashid, *Jihad: The Rise of Militant Islam in Central Asia* (New Haven, Conn.: Yale University Press, 2002); William R. Roff, "Islamic Movements: One or Many?" In *Islam and the Political Economy of Meaning: Comparative Studies of Muslim Discourse* edited by William R. Roff, 31–52 (London: Croom Helm, and Berkeley: University of California Press, 1987).

Jinnah, Muhammad Ali ("the greatest leader": Qaid-i Azam, Quaid-i Azam)

(1876–1948) *leading Muslim politician in prepartition India and first governor-general of Pakistan*

Muhammad Ali Jinnah was born in Karachi (now in Pakistan) to a successful Ismaili Khoja family from Gujarat. In his youth, he attended a Muslim school, but he obtained his high school EDUCATION from a Christian missionary school in Karachi. At the age of 17, instead of attending the University of Bombay, Jinnah was sent by his family to London to work as an apprentice in an international trading firm that did business with his father, Jinnahbhai (d. 1901). He never completed his apprenticeship but was drawn to study law at Lincoln's Inn instead. At the age of 19, he became the youngest Indian ever to be admitted to the English bar. He also took an interest in British politics, attending sessions of the House of Commons during his sojourn in London and helping an Indian politician become the first member from that country to be elected to this legislative body. In 1896, he was obliged to return to INDIA because his father's business had failed.

The Jinnah who came back to India had become Anglicized—his austere demeanor, dress,

and personal habits were more English than Gujarati. He earned a good reputation as a civil attorney in Bombay (now known as Mumbai), one of India's most important ports and commercial centers. He became caught up in the nationalist movement that was seeking to win a greater role for Indians in the British colonial government as well as a greater share of the civil service jobs. The most important body of nationalists was the Indian National Congress (INC), which had been established in Bombay in 1885, and Jinnah became an active member starting in 1906. As the Indian nationalist movement shifted to seeking actual independence from British rule, Muslim elites in northern India became increasingly concerned about their eventual minority status in a nation that would be dominated by a Hindu majority,

Muhammad Ali Jinnah with his sister Fatime on his 72nd birthday (1947), Karachi, Pakistan *(Corbis/Bettmann)*

even if it was secular and democratic in outlook. It was in this context that the ALL-INDIA MUSLIM LEAGUE (AIML) was formed in 1906. Jinnah, who was not a very devout Muslim, deferred joining it until 1913 and became its president in 1916. His strategy was to maintain Muslim-Hindu cooperation in the nationalist cause, but he quit the INC in 1920 because of his concern that MOHANDAS K. GANDHI (d. 1948), a fellow-Gujarati and rising star in the INC, was giving the movement a more Hindu character than he could accept. He was unhappy both with Gandhi's support of the KHILA-FAT MOVEMENT and with his strategy of mobilizing the masses to participate in nonviolent acts of civil disobedience. He, on the other hand, preferred to work through the existing political system that was dominated by India's educated elites, operating within the limits of British colonial law.

During the 1920s, Jinnah struggled to keep AIML united, obtain assurances from the INC that Muslims would be guaranteed representation in any future local and national legislatures, and win recognition for Muslim representation in Muslim majority regions of Northwest India (Sindh and the Punjab). He left India in frustration in 1930 and stayed in London until 1935, when he returned to reunite the AIML and renew its participation in the nationalist cause. The league suffered a surprising defeat in India's first national election in 1937. It failed to win in Muslim-majority provinces, while the INC, on the other hand, achieved impressive victories and gained control of the parliament. Jinnah did not give up but changed tactics to gain popular support for AIML by mobilizing India's Sufis and campaigning in the countryside. Moreover, unlike the INC, the AIML under his leadership declared its support for the British during World War II, which placed it in a favorable position vis-à-vis the British when the war ended in 1945. As a result, AIML swept all the seats reserved for Muslims in the parliamentary election of 1946.

The elections, however, rather than leading to an intercommunal consensus for national unity, exacerbated tensions between Hindus and Muslims in northern India. AIML and its supporters called for a separate homeland for Muslims—PAKISTAN (Pure Land). This idea had been first proposed by MUHAMMAD IQBAL (d. 1938), an Indian intellectual and poet, in 1930, when he was inaugurated as president of AIML. Iqbal urged Jinnah after the 1937 elections to support self-determination for the Muslims of northwest India and Bengal. Jinnah was not enthusiastic about a separate homeland, but, in 1940, he declared that Hindus and Muslims constituted two different nations that had never been united and never would be. In the postwar climate, he pushed more forcefully for an independent Pakistan, believing that Congress under the leadership of Gandhi and Jawaharlal Nehru (d. 1964) would never agree to share power with AIML or give Muslims a guaranteed percentage of seats in parliament. Democracy would only bring about a Hindu raj (rule) in place of the British one. In 1946, a British proposal to make India into a loose federation of provinces grouped according to religious affiliation failed to win support from either AIML or INC. Jinnah called for Muslims to take "direct action" on behalf of the idea of an Indian Muslim homeland by going on strike and conducting public protests, but this led to outbreaks of communal violence in different parts of India, especially in Bengal, Calcutta, and Bihar. Pakistan emerged as an independent state with Jinnah as its first leader, or governor-general, on August 14, 1947, while India proclaimed independence from Britain on August 15, 1947.

Jinnah's career as leader of the newly independent country was short-lived. He died of tuberculosis and lung cancer on September 11, 1948. His burial place on a hill in Karachi, Pakistan's provisional capital, has become a national monument. He has also been memorialized on Pakistan's currency, and one of its most prominent universities, the Qaid-i Azam University (also known as Quaid-i Azam University) in Islamabad, has been named after him.

See also COLONIALISM; DEMOCRACY; HINDUISM AND ISLAM; ISMAILI SHIISM; POLITICS AND ISLAM; SECULARISM.

Further reading: Akbar S. Ahmed, *Jinnah, Pakistan, and Islamic Identity* (London: Routledge, 1997); Ainslie Embree and Stephen Hay, eds., *Sources of Indian Tradition.* Vol. 2, *Modern India and Pakistan.* 2d ed. (New York: Columbia University Press, 1988); Dominique Lapierre and Larry Collins, *Freedom at Midnight.* 2d ed. (New Delhi: Vikas Publishing, 1997); Stanley Wolpert, *Jinnah of Pakistan* (Oxford: Oxford University Press, 1984).

jinni (Arabic singular of jinn, or English genie)

The jinn are intelligent beings capable of doing good and evil. They were first known to the inhabitants of pre-Islamic Arabia as a kind of nature spirit or minor deity. Poets and seers were believed to have magical powers in part owing to being possessed by, or having a special relation with, them. Indeed, MUHAMMAD's seventh-century opponents accused him of being possessed by these spirits rather than being in communion with the one God, ALLAH. The jinn are mentioned frequently in the QURAN, which even has a chapter about them that bears their name (Q 72). As creatures created from smokeless fire or vapor, they stand in contrast to ANGELS, who were created from light, and humans, who were created from clay. Iblis, or SATAN, is one of the jinn (Q 18:50), but the Quran also portrays him as a rebellious angel (Q 38:73–76), a belief that had arisen in Judaism and Christianity previously. The jinn can have human qualities; their knowledge is limited and they have moral agency. They can either submit to God and become Muslims, or they can slander and disobey him, for which God will judge them. The demonic jinn are called satans (Arabic *shayatin*). There are many tales about the jinn, and some even hold that they can marry people and have children. Unlike humans, however, they can change shapes so that they can appear as ANIMALS such as cats, dogs, and goats. Belief in them is an accepted aspect of official Islamic doctrine.

When Islam spread outside of Arabia, belief in the jinn was assimilated with local beliefs about deities and spirits, from Africa to IRAN, TURKEY, INDIA, and Southeast Asia. In folk religion, they are spirits often held responsible for extraordinary events, even miracles, as well as many kinds of illness. Special amulets are made to control them or keep them from doing harm. During the 19th century, a WOMEN's religious movement known as the Zar cult emerged in the Nile Valley and spread to adjacent areas. Its purpose was to heal women of psychoses and bodily ailments by identifying and appeasing the jinn. Today scientifically minded Muslims tend to deny the existence of these extraordinary spirits or explain them in psychological terms.

See also AMULETS AND TALISMANS; ARABIAN RELIGIONS, PRE-ISLAMIC; EVIL EYE.

Patrick O'Donnell and Juan E. Campo

Further reading: Eleanor Abdella Doumato, *Getting God's Ear: Women, Islam, and Healing in Saudi Arabia and the Gulf* (New York: Columbia University Press); Edward Westermarck, *Ritual and Belief in Morocco,* 2 vols. (New York: University Books, 1968).

jizya (Arabic: poll tax)

The *jizya* was a poll (or head) tax paid by non-Muslim subjects (DHIMMIS) to Muslim governments. The legal basis for this tax (Q 9:29), commands Muslims to "fight those who have previously received revelation who do not believe in God or in the Last Day and who do not forbid that which God and his Prophet have forbidden and who do not believe in the true religion, until they agree to pay the *jizya* in humility."

The legal texts that lay out the normative definitions of *jizya* are all from a period postdating the first century of Islam (ca. eighth century

C.E.), and so there has been great confusion as to what kinds of *jizya* were paid by non-Muslims in the earliest period. Because Egyptian papyri from this period have survived relatively abundantly, the situation of that province is best known during the first century of Islam. It appears that the term jizya in this period was not entirely fixed but that officials might call for a tax on the head or a tax on the land. The tax on the head is what would later come to be solely identified with the *jizya*. Thus, in normative discussions and in later times, the *jizya* tax was one imposed on all those non-Muslims who lived permanently within one of the Islamicate states. It could be imposed only on free, adult, able-bodied, sane men. While not a crushing tax, it was considered humiliating by some *dhimmi* elites and was onerous enough that it periodically posed a hardship for the *dhimmi* communities, as demonstrated especially by the Geniza documents found in CAIRO's Ben Ezra Synagogue, although those communities sometimes found ways to reduce the tax burden. It has often been argued that CONVERSION to Islam was at least in part under the pressure of the *jizya* tax.

The *jizya* had to be periodically adjusted, especially to take inflation into account, as when, between the end of the 17th and the middle of the 19th centuries, the *jizya* was increased sevenfold in Ottoman lands to account for the devastating inflation caused by the influx of New World bullion. While this created disturbances among the *dhimmi* populations, it probably reflected no more than the impact of inflation on the devaluation of the coinage. Additionally, the *jizya* was on a sliding scale. Thus, those at the top end in 1834 were responsible for 60 units of payment, while those at the bottom were responsible only for 15. In general, this spread appears typical of Ottoman *jizya* collection.

In Mughal India (1523–1857), AURANGZEB (d. 1707) imposed the *jizya* in 1679 after his great-grandfather AKBAR (d. 1605) had famously eliminated the tax as part of his general policy of toleration of all religions. Aurangzeb's policy of tightened central control and increasing religious rigor is credited, in part, with the subsequent breakup of the Mughal Empire under the pressure of separatist non-Muslim states and increased British influence. After his death, the *jizya* was not collected.

Today the *jizya* is nowhere in force. It was done away with in EGYPT by Khedive Said in 1855 and in the other Ottoman lands (the last significant territory in which it was practiced at all) by the Khatt-i-Humayun decree of 1856. In the latter part of the 20th century, militant groups such as the Islamic Group (al-Jamaa al-Islamiyya) of Egypt called for its reinstatement and began robbing Christian businesses towards this end; the state finally crushed these groups by the end of the 1990s. Mainstream Islamist groups, however, such as the MUSLIM BROTHERHOOD, have firmly rejected both the violence of these groups and the possibility of resurrecting *jizya*; they now embrace the logic of CITIZENSHIP with its notions of shared duties and rights for all.

See also CHRISTIANITY AND ISLAM; JUDAISM AND ISLAM; ISLAMISM; *KHARAJ*; MUGHAL DYNASTY; OTTOMAN DYNASTY; TANZIMAT.

John Iskander

Further reading: Daniel C. Dennett, Jr., *Conversion and the Poll Tax in Early Islam* (Cambridge, Mass.: Harvard University Press, 1950); S. D. Goitein, *A Mediterranean Society*, Vol. 2. (Berkeley: University of California Press, 1971); Jørgen Bæk Simonsen, *Studies in the Genesis and Early Development of the Caliphal Taxation System* (Copenhagen: Akademisk Forlag, 1988).

John the Baptist (early first century C.E.) *for Muslims, an exemplary prophet who appears in the Quran and many subsequent Islamic sources*
John the Baptist, the desert prophet who baptized JESUS (see, for example, Matt. 3; Mark 1; Luke 3), is known in Islamic tradition as Yahya ibn Zakariyya, meaning John the son of Zechariah.

Phrases such as *Baptist* and *Baptizer* are not used in reference to him in the QURAN. Rather, as has been and continues to be a common practice in naming people in the Muslim world, John is known as the son of his father. John is mentioned five times in the Quran. In Q 3:39 the ANGELS tell Zechariah, "God bids you rejoice in the birth of John, who shall confirm the word of God. He shall be princely and chaste, a prophet from among the righteous." In stating that John shall confirm the word of God, the Quran is referring to the affirming role that he was to have with respect to Jesus' life and message.

In the context of God's giving instructions and wisdom to ABRAHAM, the Quran lists John as one of many upright men, including such figures as Isaac, Jacob, Noah, DAVID, Solomon, Job, JOSEPH, MOSES, Aaron, and Zechariah (Q 6:83–87). In Q 19:7, God tells Zechariah that he should rejoice because he will be given a son, "and he shall be called John; a name no man has borne before him"; the uniqueness of John's name in this regard denotes for many Muslims his special role in the tradition. In one of the Quran's longest references to John (Q 19:12–15), God commanded John to, "'Hold fast to the book!' And we bestowed upon him wisdom while he was still a child, and grace, and purity. He was a godfearing man, honoring his father and mother, and neither arrogant nor rebellious. Blessed was he on the day he was born and the day of his DEATH; and may peace be on him when he is raised to life." Thus, John embodied many of the virtuous qualities that Muslims are to emulate in their own lives.

Also, Muslim interpreters believe that the scripture to which this passage refers is the TORAH, the sacred text of the Jews, reflecting the idea that John exists at an intersection between Judaism, Christianity, and Islam. In the Quran's 21st chapter, entitled "The Prophets," God recounts significant aspects of history and provides summaries of his relationships to various prophets and states: "And of Zechariah, who invoked his Lord, saying 'Lord, let me not remain childless, though of all heirs you are the best.' We answered his prayer and gave him John, curing his wife of sterility. They vied with each other in good works and called on us [i.e., God] in love and fear" (Q 21:89–90). These verses reaffirm the significant position John had in the line of prophets who preceded Muhammad. Even though there are a relatively small number of references to John in the Quran, they have been the basis of extensive discussions among Muslim scholars. There have been debates about John's chasteness and short biographies written about his life based on the New Testament and other Christian sources.

A church dedicated to John the Baptist was built by Christians on the site of a Roman temple in the ancient city of DAMASCUS. This shrine, said to contain his head, was subsequently incorporated into the grand Umayyad MOSQUE that now stands on the site.

See also CHRISTIANITY AND ISLAM; HOLY BOOKS; JUDAISM AND ISLAM; MARY; PROPHETS AND PROPHECY; UMAYYAD DYNASTY.

Jon Armajani

Further reading: John C. L. Gibson, "John the Baptist in Muslim Writings." *Muslim World* 45 (1955): 334–345; Geoffrey Parrinder, *Jesus in the Quran* (New York: Oxford University Press, 1977), 55–59; Jaafar Muhammad ibn Jarir al-Tabari, *The Ancient Kingdoms, The History of al-Tabari.* Vol. 4, Translated by Moshe Perlmann (Albany: State University of New York Press, 1987), 101–108; Ahmad ibn Muhammad al-Thalabi, *Arais al-majalis fi qisas al-anbiya, or "Lives of the Prophets,"* Translated by William M. Brinner (Leiden: E.J. Brill, 2002), 627–637.

Jordan (Official name: The Hashemite Kingdom of Jordan)

The state boundaries of Jordan were created by the British in the aftermath of World War I. Jordan gained formal independence from the British only in 1946. Although it has a small population of 6.2

million people (2008 estimate) and few natural resources of its own, Jordan sits at the center of a part of the Middle East that is important to the economic and political future of the entire region. In the west is ISRAEL and the occupied Palestinian territories; in the north is SYRIA; to the east is IRAQ; and SAUDI ARABIA borders Jordan to the east and south.

Jordan has been an important trade route linking Africa with West Asia. The Jordan River Valley and the area of the lowest point on earth, the Dead Sea, were sites of early human settlement dating back 8,000 years. Conquering peoples who entered Jordan early in its history were Assyrians, Greeks, and Romans. Jordan is home to some of the best-preserved archaeological sites of the Roman Empire, including Jarash, Umm Qais, and the amphitheater of the ancient city of Philadelphia in downtown Amman.

The greatest trading civilization that had its base in Jordan was that of the Nabateans. They began settling in southern Jordan in significant numbers in the third century B.C.E. The most enduring monument to Nabatean civilization is the city of Petra, which was carved into steep rock walls of river gorges in the first century B.C.E. At its height, Petra was populated by 20,000 people. Its multistoried rock-carved facades of monumental architecture were finally recognized in 2007 as a new wonder of the world and are visited by tens of thousands of tourists each year. The Nabateans eventually assimilated to Byzantine culture by the third century C.E. and used Greek instead of Aramaic as their literary language. Petra was largely destroyed and abandoned after an earthquake in 106 C.E.

Much of Jordan was uninhabited in the Byzantine period. The rise of Islam led to repopulation and a cultural revival in some areas conducive to rain-fed agriculture, such as the northern mountainous region. In medieval times, from the 11th century, both crusaders and Arab armies built castle fortresses on a line of mountain peaks from north to south. The castles at Ajloun, Karak, and Shobak are three of the best preserved today. How-

The Treasury, originally a royal Nabatean tomb (ca. first century B.C.E. to first century C.E.), Petra, Jordan (Juan E. Campo)

ever, much of the countryside outside the fortified mountain enclaves was uninhabited or merely the temporary seasonal resting place for migratory BEDOUIN tribes.

In the 19th century, Jordan was a backwater in the Ottoman Empire. It was governed from the provincial capital of DAMASCUS in Syria. The Ottoman authorities were unable to collect taxes from the townspeople in Ajloun, Salt, Karak, or Maan because of the military superiority of autonomous tribal bands who negotiated their own taxing arrangements with towns and villages in exchange for security. At the end of the century, the Ottomans began enforcing a more centralized taxing system and curbed the power of the tribes, first by military campaigns against them, and when that failed, by settling Circassians from the Caucasus region in tribal border areas such as the largely abandoned town of Amman. Increased security and the resulting upswing in regional commerce brought new immigrants to towns such as Irbid, Ajloun, Salt, and Karak. Syrian and Palestinian merchants from Damascus, Nablus, JERUSALEM, and Hebron settled branches of their families in the main Jordanian towns in order to expand their commercial ties.

Jordan is often described as the most preposterous of the newly mandated territories created by the British and French after World War I. Its jagged, straight-lined borders to the north, east, and south do not correspond to any natural geographical boundaries and seem arbitrary lines in the desert. In November 1920, Abd Allah, the son of Sharif Husayn ibn Ali (d. 1931) of MECCA, encamped in Maan with an armed group of 300 fighters intending to march on Damascus to assist in the defense of his brother Faysal's independent Arab kingdom declared in 1918. Instead, when he arrived in Amman in March 1921, the British offered to sponsor him as the emir (Arabic: *amir,* ruler) of Transjordan. Abd Allah accepted and later became the first king in the HASHIMITE DYNASTY that still rules Jordan today. Over the course of the 20th century, with the consolidation and longevity of state power, a Jordanian national identity has taken hold over a majority of the population.

One factor that has led to the partial success of national identity formation in Jordan is cultural homogeneity. Almost the whole population is Arab, with the exception of very small Circassian, Chechen, Kurdish, and Armenian communities. About 95 percent of Jordanians are Sunni Muslims who follow the HANAFI LEGAL SCHOOL, although this is changing. There are small groups of Alawis, Twelve-Imam Shia, and DRUZE. About 5 percent of Jordanians are Christians, mostly Greek Ortho-

dox. There are some Catholics, Maronites, and Protestants. Historically, institutionalized religion was weak in Jordan. At the beginning of the 19th century, there was hardly any functioning mosque or church of any significance in any town or village. The spread of formal religious structures began only during the 1920s with the establishment of Hashemite rule. Since the 1950s, the government has often allied itself with Islamist political forces such as the MUSLIM BROTHERHOOD in order to legitimize its authority. However, autonomous Islamist politicians who have gone against government policies have been severely repressed.

Jordan suffers from cataclysmic destabilizing events on its borders. It has been particularly affected by Israeli-Palestinian conflict. Although King Abd Allah secretly negotiated with Zionist leaders over the partition of PALESTINE, Jordanian troops led by a British commanding officer fought in the Jerusalem area in the 1948 war in Palestine. With the establishment of the state of Israel, Jordan annexed the West Bank of the Jordan River. By doing so, it immediately acquired a majority-Palestinian population and the largest number of the 750,000 to 800,000 Palestinians who either fled the fighting or were forced from their homes. King Abd Allah was assassinated by a Palestinian gunman on July 20, 1950, as he was entering the AL-AQSA MOSQUE in Jerusalem for Friday prayers. In the 1967 Arab-Israeli war, Israel occupied the West Bank, and 300,000 more Palestinian REFUGEES fled to the East Bank. Another 300,000 Palestinian refugees suddenly arrived in Jordan in 1991 after they were expelled from Kuwait at the end of the first Gulf War. As of December 2006, 1,858,362 Palestinians were officially registered with the United Nations Works and Relief Agency (UNWRA) as refugees in Jordan, and 328,076 of them lived in 10 refugee camps spread throughout the country. Jordan has by far the largest number of the 4.4 million Palestinians recognized by the UNWRA as refugees from 1948 and their descendants. It is estimated that from 60 percent to 80 percent of the Jordanian population is of Palestinian origin. The current reigning queen, Rania, is of Palestinian origin from Kuwait.

Much of the history of the modern state of Jordan since independence has been dominated by the figure of King Husayn who came to power when he was only 18 in May 1953 after his father Talal was forced to abdicate because of mental illness. The early years of his rule were marked by a resurgent opposition to foreign influence in Jordan. In elections held only a few weeks before Israel, France, and Britain invaded Egypt in 1956, Arab nationalists and communists won the majority of seats in parliament and were able to form a government. Husayn was forced to dismiss his British military advisers, but then exchanged British for U.S. patronage in 1957. The alliance with the United States was enduring and today Jordan is one of the largest recipients of U.S. foreign aid in the Middle East after Iraq, Israel, and Egypt.

The rule of King Husayn was seriously challenged by the rise of the PALESTINE LIBERATION ORGANIZATION (PLO) and Palestinian armed resistance organizations that were based in the refugee camps. After Palestinian militants hijacked three international airline carriers and flew them to an airfield near Zarqa in September 1970, the Jordanian army launched an all-out attack on the PLO armed presence in the camps and, by 1971, the PLO was forced to move its military and political headquarters to Beirut, Lebanon. In 1974 the ARAB LEAGUE recognized the PLO as the sole legitimate representative of the Palestinian people. King Husayn still claimed Jordanian sovereignty over the West Bank until 1988. During these years he maintained secret contacts with Israeli leaders. A full peace agreement with Israel was signed on October 26, 1994. King Husayn died of cancer on February 7, 1999, and was succeeded by his son Abdullah (b. 1962), the present monarch.

Jordan is witnessing a rapid demographic and economic transformation caused by the U.S. invasion of Iraq in 2003 with unpredictable consequences. Some reports put the number of Iraqis now resident in Jordan as high as 1.5 million or one-fifth of Jordan's entire population. Some of the Iraqi refugees are wealthy and billions of dollars have been poured into unproductive speculative investments such as the stock market and real estate. The rise in land and housing prices has hit Jordan's lower classes the hardest and caused overcrowding and the delay of marriages due to lack of suitable housing. The sudden influx of tens of thousands of poor Iraqi war refugees has overburdened the educational system and medical and social services. Many thousands of Iraqi refugee children have not been in school for two or more years, creating a potential generation of illiterates and unemployed who will be compelled to face the insecurity of the informal labor sector or fall into criminal activities. The poorest of the Iraqi refugees are beginning to move into the overcrowded low-income neighborhoods of East Amman and even into some of the Palestinian refugee camps causing social tensions as communities vie for scant public services and resources.

Jordan is quickly becoming a land of social contrasts. High-rise construction, the increase in the number of luxury hotels for tourism, and infrastructure modernization are occurring at an astonishing pace in areas such as West Amman, on the shores of the Dead Sea, and in Aqaba. U.S.-based fast food conglomerates, cafés, restaurants, nightclubs, and mega malls dot the landscape of West Amman with its villas and condos. Cities such as Zarqa or the neglected neighborhoods of East Amman that have not been the beneficiaries of priority public investment, the input of billions of recycled Iraqi war dollars, or the focus for the burgeoning tourist industry have suffered from a deterioration of housing stock, overcrowding, a lack of services, and serious environmental degradation. Unemployment and underemployment are rampant. Over 30 percent of the population lives below the poverty line and the thousands of undocumented Iraqi war refugees put even the best estimates in doubt. Yet despite these anomalies, the life expectancy of the average Jordanian of 78.5 years surpasses that of the average U.S. citizen by one year. Street crime, theft, and murders are rare occurrences. Jordan is also experimenting with democratic forms of political participation both at the state and local levels of government. Civil society is expanding and nongovernmental organizations are flourishing. The government promotes women's participation in government, business, and the public sphere. The LITERACY rates are among the highest in the region. The government has heavily invested in making Jordan a center for high-tech, medical, and professional services for the whole region. English has been introduced as a mandatory second language at all levels of the educational system. The challenge facing Jordan is how to achieve its developmental goals and not be sidetracked by unresolved conflicts on its borders that have serious consequences inside its own territory.

See also ALAWI; ARAB-ISRAELI CONFLICTS; ARMENIANS; CHRISTIANITY AND ISLAM; CRUSADES; DEMOCRACY; HUSAYN IBN ALI, SHARIF; ISLAMISM; OTTOMAN DYNASTY.

Garay Menicucci

Further reading: George Alan, *Jordan: Living in the Crossfire* (London: Zed Books, 2005); Joseph Massad, *Colonial Effects: The Making of National Identity in Jordan* (New York: Columbia University Press, 2001); Abd al-Raman Munif, *Story of a City: A Childhood in Amman* (London: Quartet Books, 1996); Eugene Rogan, *Frontiers of the State in the Late Ottoman Empire: Transjordan 1850–1921* (New York: Cambridge University Press, 1999); Jillian Schwedler, *Faith in Moderation: Islamist Parties in Jordan and Yemen* (New York: Cambridge University Press, 2006); Avi Shlaim, *The Politics of Partition: King Abdullah, the Zionists, and Palestine 1921–1951* (New York: Oxford University Press, 1998).

Joseph (Arabic: Yusuf) *the son of the Israelite patriarch Jacob and a Muslim prophet who, because of his brothers' jealousy, was sold to slavery and exiled in Egypt*

The longest segment of material about Joseph appears in sura 12 of the QURAN, which is named after Joseph, the son of Jacob (Arabic: Yaaqub). This sura's 111 verses constitute the Quran's longest continual narrative of one character's life. They relate Jacob's favoritism toward Joseph; his brothers' jealousy that compels Joseph be sold to slavery in EGYPT; Joseph's brother's deceitfulness toward their father Jacob; Joseph's handsomeness; the attempted seduction of Joseph by the wife of his Egyptian master; as well as Joseph's imprisonment, exoneration, and his interpretation of dreams, which led to his family's move to Egypt and their acceptance of Pharaoh's protection.

The sura about Joseph emphasizes the quranic theme that God can directly influence human affairs. It portrays God as playing a crucial role in directing the events in Joseph's and his family's lives. Joseph also exemplifies the powers associated with true prophets of God in that Joseph's prophetic dreams foretell future events. Joseph's life as a prophet embodies a pattern found in the lives of other quranic prophets: he is severely criticized and marginalized; finally, he is vindicated and rises to a position of great honor. As such, Joseph is one of many quranic prophets, the pattern of whose lives are precursors for the life of MUHAMMAD. The idea of Muhammad's life reflecting those of previous prophets such as Joseph's is strengthened by the belief of many Muslims that the sura about Joseph was revealed to Muhammad at the very time seventh-century skeptics of Muhammad challenged his knowledge of the narratives of the children of Israel. According to many Muslims, the detail and specificity of the sura provide a very persuasive response to this challenge.

Some of the best-known passages in this chapter portray Joseph as being so handsome that the women of Egypt cut their hands in their astonishment as they gazed at him. Some Muslims believe that this proverbial beauty is one of the rewards of heaven, where all men are as handsome as Joseph. Commentators have even asserted, "God allotted to Joseph two-thirds of (all) beauty and divided up the remaining third among humanity" (Thalabi 183). The Joseph story also attracted the attention of Sufi visionaries such as Muhyi al-Din IBN AL-ARABI (d. 1240), Jalal al-Din RUMI (d. 1273), and Jami of Herat (d. 1492). Persian and Turkish mystical poets in particular were drawn to the romance between Joseph and Zulaykha, the name given by commentators to the Egyptian's wife. Her desire for him was understood to symbolize the desire of the purified soul for union with God, the beloved.

The location of Joseph's remains is disputed. Pious Jews and Palestinians believe that they are located in the West Bank city of Nablus. This shrine has been the focus of conflict between Israelis and Palestinians; it suffered damage in 2000 during the al-Aqsa Intifada.

See also DREAMS; JUDAISM AND ISLAM; MAJNUN AND LAYLA; PROPHETS AND PROPHETHOOD.

Jon Armajani

Further reading: Shalom Goldman, *The Wiles of Women/ the Wiles of Men: Joseph and Potiphar's Wife in Ancient Near Eastern, Jewish, and Islamic Folklore* (Albany: State University of New York Press, 1995); G. R. Hawting and Abdul-Kader A. Shareef, *Approaches to the Quran* (London and New York: Routledge, 1993); John Kaltner, *Inquiring of Joseph: Getting to Know a Biblical Character through the Quran* (Collegeville, Minn.: Liturgical Press, 2003); Ahmad ibn Muhammad al-Thalabi, *Arais al-majalis fi qisas al-anbiya, or "Lives of the Prophets."* Translated by William M. Brinner (Leiden: E.J. Brill, 2002), 181–235.

Judaism and Islam

As Abrahamic religions, Judaism and Islam bear significant similarities that testify to a lengthy and complex history of dynamic interactions. Although it is widely perceived today that the relationship between these two religions is *essentially* one of conflict and opposition, closer examination reveals that there have been occasions of extended mutual accommodation and shared civilizational development in the past that cannot be easily dismissed. Indeed, scholars maintain that Judaism and Islam engaged in a "creative symbiosis," whereby each party benefited and changed as a result of its contacts with the other. It is also the case that in modern times national and geopolitical factors have been more important than religious ones. ARAB-ISRAELI CONFLICTS cannot be adequately explained in terms of the 12 centuries of Judeo-Muslim interaction that preceded the 20th-century conflicts. Moreover, though these modern conflicts have been horrific, they are of a limited scope, confined largely to a part of the Middle East region, directly involving only a minority of the world's total Muslim population.

FAMILY RESEMBLANCES

There are a number of key similarities that cluster together to support the view that Judaism and Islam form part of a family of religions, which may be called Abrahamic. The foremost of these is belief in a unique sovereign deity who governs creation. The commonest name for this deity in Islam, ALLAH, is historically related to one of the divine names in the Hebrew Bible, Elohim, and both names are related to a word root for god found in other Semitic cultures of the ancient Near East (for example, *el, il, ilu*). Both religions reject IDOLATRY, holding that God communicated to humanity in history through chosen prophets, a number of whom are shared by both religions. These revelations were captured in scriptures, or HOLY BOOKS. The primary scripture for Judaism is the TORAH of MOSES and for Islam it is the QURAN of MUHAMMAD. These scriptures, written in the sacred languages of Hebrew and Arabic, respectively, express key beliefs, ethical principles, sacred histories, and rules for worship and everyday life.

They also contain hymns of praise and thanksgiving. Hallowed written texts are complimented by a body of sacred oral texts in each religion—the Talmud (oral Torah) in Judaism and the HADITH (accounts of the actions and declarations of Muhammad and his Companions) in Islam. These oral traditions were collected in books and served as the basis of religious law (halakha and FIQH, respectively). They expanded upon the meanings of the written scriptures. The virtuosos of scriptural interpretation, law, and tradition in both religions were scholar-teachers known as rabbis in Judaism and as the ULAMA in Islam. Judaism and Islam also had similar eschatologies, anticipating that the dead would be resurrected and judged for their good and evil deeds, in accordance with the standards of belief and morality set forth in scripture. After JUDGMENT DAY the righteous in each religion are promised a place in paradise. Another important similarity is that each religion cherishes a holy land, comprised of sacred places where events described in scripture are believed to have occurred. In Judaism, the holy land is ISRAEL, and in Islam it is the Hijaz of western Arabia. The most sacred places in both religions are located in cities: JERUSALEM in Judaism and MECCA in Islam. Each of these cities is considered a cosmic center and focal point for worship and pilgrimage. Muslims also consider Jerusalem a holy city, after Mecca and MEDINA. Other points of resemblance can be added to this list, but it is important to note that there are significant differences among these family resemblances and these differences must be taken into account if the nature of Judeo-Islamic interrelationships is to be more fully comprehended.

QURANIC JUDAISM

The Quran portrays Judaism in two ways: as the ancient faith of Moses as revealed in the Torah and as that of the Jews living during the quranic era, which most scholars see as contemporaneous with the life of Muhammad (d. 632) in seventh-century Arabia. It construes the biblical figure ABRAHAM, who preceded Moses, as an exemplary prophet and monotheist (*hanif*), but not as the Jewish patriarch who had secured an exclusive covenant on their behalf. The Arabic terms used with reference to Jews in the Quran are *yahud* and its derivatives (18 times) and *Banu Israil* (Children of Israel [the descendants of Jacob], 43 times). Like the Hebrew Bible, the Quran recognizes the Jews as a special people chosen by God who were delivered from the afflictions of Pharaoh in EGYPT and given the Torah to keep (Q 45:16–17; 14:6). They subsequently lost God's blessing because of their disobedience and idolatry (Q 7:138–151). The Jews were also blamed for violating the Sabbath (Q 2:65) and persecuting prophets God had sent to them (Q 2:61, 87, 91), which echoes accusations against the Jews made in the New Testament. Stringent dietary rules were imposed on them because of their wrongdoing (Q 4:160). Moreover, the Quran accused them of distorting, concealing, and forgetting God's message (Q 4:46; 6:91). Similar accusations were levied against Christians, who were also called Children of Israel. Likewise, both Jews and Christians, because they were recipients of previous scriptures, were called PEOPLE OF THE BOOK. Some Quran verses indicate that at some point Muslim believers had engaged in warfare with People of the Book, defeating them and taking their property (Q 33:26–27). The people of the book are also to pay a tribute (*JIZYA*) when they are defeated (Q 9:29).

The function of the Quran's accounts about the Jews and their religion was, on the one hand, to illuminate the ancient genealogy of the religious ideas being promulgated in Muhammad's time and, on the other, to demonstrate how the Jews had strayed from their ancestral religion. This opened the door for Muslims (the "believers") to claim that they were now the people chosen to receive God's blessing, thanks to the call of Muhammad, the heir to the prophetic tradition of the past. Despite the criticisms the Quran levied against the Jews, it nevertheless recognized that there was also a righteous element among them

(Q 7:159; compare 28:52–54), which was understood by Muslim commentators to be a reference to Jews who had accepted Muhammad's message. Indeed, the Quran promised Jews and other believers a blissful afterlife in reward for their faith (Q 2:62; 4:162).

A BRIEF HISTORY OF THE JUDEO-MUSLIM SYMBIOSIS

Historical evidence for the history of the Jews in the centuries immediately preceding and following the emergence of Islam in the Middle East is limited largely to the Quran and early Muslim historiography, particularly Ibn Ishaq's biography of Muhammad (*Sirat rasul Allah,* mid-eighth century), al-Waqidi's history of Muslim military campaigns (*Kitab al-maghazi,* early ninth century), and al-Tabari's universal history (*Tarikh al-rusul wa'l-muluk,* early 10th century). Many scholars, including those working in Western academia, rely on these sources to reconstruct the history of relations between the two communities, as well as the Arabian origins of Islam itself. Some scholars have called the historicity of these sources into question, however, positing instead that the Quran and related accounts were not composed until the late eighth–early ninth century. Most, however, agree that Islamic sources do, in fact, provide witness to the early history of Islam, even though they may have been shaped by later concerns and biases. With respect to Judaism, the presence of biblical and post-biblical Judaic stories in the Quran and the histories indicates direct or indirect contacts with Jews when these texts were written, whether that occurred in the seventh century or later.

According to Muslim sources there were Jewish communities living in YEMEN and western Arabia (the Hijaz) when the Islamic movement began. Of particular importance were Jewish tribes in Yathrib, the city that would become known as Medina after the emigration (HIJRA) of Muhammad and his followers from Mecca to that city in 622. In the so-called Constitution of Medina, which scholars consider to be one of the earliest non-quranic Islamic documents, Jewish tribes in Medina were recognized as having their own religion (or judgment); those who agreed to follow Muhammad were considered to be on a par with the ANSAR and Meccan EMIGRANTS. According to Muslim accounts, Jewish groups in Medina refused to heed Muhammad's call and began to conspire with his opponents in Mecca. Muslim commentators indicate that it was in this context that the one-day Yom Kippur fast observed by Muhammad's followers in concert with the Jews was changed to the one-month fast of RAMADAN, signaling a break with the Jews. Likewise, Muhammad was instructed by God to change the prayer direction (QIBLA) from Jerusalem to Mecca. The escalating estrangement between Muslims and Jews in Medina ended with the destruction and expulsion of all the city's Jews by the time of Muhammad's death in 632. All non-Muslims would eventually be banned from living in the Hijaz region.

The Arab Muslim conquests of the wider Middle East and the establishment of a new empire that extended from North Africa to the Indus River valley during the late seventh and eighth centuries brought about a new order with new opportunities for subject peoples. Jews and Christians who submitted to Muslim rulers became "protected" (DHIMMI) members of the Islamicate polity who were obliged to pay the quranic *jizya* tax and observe other restrictions, but were otherwise allowed to pursue religious life under their own authorities. Evidence indicates that some Jews and Christians even participated with the Muslim armies in the conquests and settled into the new post-conquest towns and garrisons in Egypt and IRAQ. Jerusalem surrendered to the Arab invaders without resistance and Jews were allowed to return to the city after having been banned from it by the Byzantines. The uniting of lands formerly divided between the Byzantine and Persian empires into one great Islamicate *oikoumene* enhanced the integration of Jews living in the Mediterranean region with those living in the east. The key symbol for Jewish religious life was the dual Torah of Moses, oral and written, which gave meaning to their life in the diaspora and hope for messianic fulfillment. Muslim rulers encouraged the consolidation of leadership in the Jewish community under the Gaons, heads of the rabbinic academies in Iraq and PALESTINE, and the Exilarchs, political chiefs linked to the caliphal government.

Having *dhimmi* status assigned to them by Muslim authorities did not confine Jews to a single stratum of Islamicate society. They were actively involved in transregional trade networks and banking, often with the support and encouragement of the caliph. They also worked in menial or degrading trades and occupations such as weaving, tanning, blacksmithing, horse trading, working in public baths, jailers, and executioners. Indeed, S. D. Goitein's studies of 10th–11th-century CAIRO Geniza documents have shown that Jews worked in nearly every known occupation, ranging from high government office, education, medicine, and trade to the criminal professions. In Andalusia Jews participated in what has been called the *convivencia,* a coexistence with Muslims and Christians that led to the production of a rich Judeo-Arabic literary corpus, the translation and transmission of Arabic philosophy and science to medieval Europe, and the rise of such prominent Jewish intellectuals as Judah Ha-Levi (d. 1141) and Maimonides (d. 1204). Jewish converts were remembered in Islamic tradition for transmitting rabbinic traditions and adapting them to different Islamic textual genres, especially the hadith, *tafsir* (Quran commentary), legal texts, and stories about the Islamic prophets.

This is not to say that the history of the Judeo-Islamic symbiosis was perfectly harmonious. As part of an ongoing process of self-definition, Muslims engaged in anti-Judaic polemics, which Jews reciprocated. Jewish revolts were forcefully suppressed by Muslim rulers, and puritanical Muslim rulers occasionally ordered the persecution of their Jewish and Christian subjects. They also

did not hesitate to take actions against dissident Muslims, including Sunnis, as well as Shiis and sometimes even Sufis. Despite these more conflict-laden encounters, Goitein and other scholars of pre-modern Judeo-Muslim history have nevertheless asserted that the Judaism of today was largely formed in the context of Jewish-Muslim interaction in the Middle East during the Middle Ages. While this assertion begs further research, it is significant that in 1492, when Ferdinand and Isabella of Spain gave Jews the choice between converting to Christianity or expulsion, most of them migrated to lands that were under Muslim rule. Seeing the benefits to be gained from Jewish wealth and mercantile expertise, the rulers of the Ottoman Empire welcomed Sephardic immigrants from Spain and Ashkenazis from Europe. Bolstered by these immigrants from the west, Jewish communities in Istanbul, Edirne, Izmir, and Salonika grew and prospered significantly under the Ottomans. Although statistics are lacking, it is likely that the majority of the world's Jewish population lived under Muslim rule from the early seventh century until the fragmentation of the Ottoman Empire and the creation of the state of Israel in the 20th century.

The Judeo-Islamic symbiosis deteriorated greatly during the 18th century as the Ottoman and Persian Safavid empires succumbed to foreign incursions and internal disturbances. Muslim rulers were unable to provide adequate protection to Jewish communities, which became impoverished and vulnerable to attack by Christians, especially during the 19th century, when European anti-Semitism was imported into the region. European observers, including Jews, reported on the decrepit living conditions of Jewish communities in eastern lands compared to their improved status as educated citizens in Europe. As colonial powers vied for influence in the Ottoman Empire, they claimed the right to serve as protectors of religious minorities living in them. France and Russia intervened on behalf of Catholic and Orthodox Christians, respectively. Britain developed a special relationship with Ottoman Jewish communities. Former *dhimmi*s became agents who worked for the European colonial governments, which exacerbated interreligious tensions among Muslims and non-Muslims.

Strong nationalist currents in Europe coupled with growing anti-Semitic propaganda gave rise to the Zionist movement among European Jews in the late 19th century. The chief objective of the Zionists was to establish a homeland for Jews in Palestine, which had been part of the Ottoman Empire, but became a British mandate territory after World War I. The Zionist cause won limited British support and finally succeeded in creating a modern Jewish nation-state in 1948 in the aftermath of the first Arab-Israeli war. Israel was founded primarily by European Jews, many of whom had survived the horrors of the Holocaust, but, once created, it encouraged immigration of Jews from North Africa, the Arab Middle East, and IRAN. At the same time, nationalist currents in these regions victimized the Jews, or made them feel unsafe in the countries where they had lived for centuries. Muslims appropriated many of the anti-Semitic stereotypes that had circulated in Europe and used them to legitimate their harsh treatment of Jews. As a result, the Jewish populations of countries such as MOROCCO, Egypt, SYRIA, Iraq, Yemen, and Iran seriously dwindled. Small Jewish populations continue to exist in parts of North Africa, LEBANON, Syria, and Iran, but most Middle Eastern Jews have emigrated to Israel, Europe, or the Americas.

Today, Israel has achieved peace agreements with Egypt and Jordan, and it has friendly relations with TURKEY. Conflict continues, however, between Israelis and Palestinians, with radical Islamic groups becoming more influential in the last 20 years. Israel is also at war with Shii militias in Lebanon, especially HIZBULLAH. Despite these conflicts and the heated polemics exchanged between Israel's supporters and enemies, far-sighted Jews and Muslims are exploring new opportunities for DIALOGUE in North America and in Israel-Palestine. Such dialogue involves rediscovering the Judeo-Muslim symbiosis of former times as but one element in the articulation of a more peaceful *convivencia* in the 21st century.

See also ARAB-ISRAELI CONFLICTS; CHRISTIANITY AND ISLAM; CONVERSION; OTTOMAN DYNASTY; PROPHETS AND PROPHECY; SEPHARDIC JEWS.

Further reading: S. D. Goitein, *Jews and Arabs: Their Contacts through the Ages* (1974. Reprint, New York: Dover Publications, 2005); Bernard Lewis, *The Jews of Islam* (Princeton, N.J.: Princeton University Press, 1984); Maria Rosa Menocal, *The Ornament of the World: How Muslims, Jews, and Christians Created a Culture of Tolerance in Medieval Spain* (Boston: Little, Brown, 2002); Gordon D. Newby, *A History of the Jews of Arabia* (Columbia: University of South Carolina Press, 1989); F. E. Peters, *The Children of Abraham: Judaism, Christianity and Islam,* 2d ed. (Princeton, N.J.: Princeton University Press, 2006); Marilyn R. Waldman, *Muslims and Christians, Muslims and Jews: A Common Past, A Hopeful Future* (Columbus: The Islamic Foundation of Central Ohio, 1992); Steven W. Wasserstrom, *Between Muslim and Jew: The Problem of Symbiosis under Early Islam* (Princeton, N.J.: Princeton University Press, 1995).

Judgment Day

After belief in one god (ALLAH) the belief in a final judgment, or Judgment Day, is a fundamental tenet of ISLAM. On that day, which marks the end of the present world, all human beings will be resurrected and judged on an individual basis according to their righteousness or sinfulness. The righteous will be rewarded with a blissful life in PARADISE and sinners will experience the torments of the FIRE (hell).

Before Islam's appearance, belief in a final judgment had already become a widespread one in the Middle Eastern–Mediterranean region, as seen in the biblical and post-biblical writings of Jews and Christians. References to the "day of the Lord" when God would punish the wicked occur in many of the prophetic books of the Hebrew Bible (for example, Obad. 15; Amos 5:18–20; Zeph. 1:14–18). Isaiah uses the phrase "on that day" in referring to God's judgment (24:21). In the New Testament the proclamation of a final judgment is expressed frequently. The phrase "day of judgment" occurs in the Gospel of Matthew (10:15; 11:22, 24, and 12:36) and in several of the epistles (2 Pet. 2:9, 3:7; and 1 John 4:17), while the Pauline epistles use the phrase "day of our/the Lord Jesus Christ" (1 Cor. 1:8; 2 Cor. 1:14), indicating that Judgment Day is identified with the second coming of Jesus. The idea of a day of judgment also appears in extra-biblical religious literature, such as the Book of Enoch, the Book of Jubilees, the Revelation of Esdras, and the Apocalypse of 2 Baruch. Islamic visions of the endtimes developed their own distinctive character in a seventh-century milieu where beliefs in a last judgment were in wide circulation.

Judgment Day is explicitly mentioned in the QURAN. The most common renderings of this concept in Arabic are *yawm al-qiyama,* "resurrection day," and *yawm al-din,* "judgment day." Another common phrase, found especially in the Medinan chapters, is *al-yawm al-akhir,* "the last day." Synonyms for Judgment Day identified by commentators include *al-saa-a* "the hour," *yawm al-fasl,* "decision day," and *yawm al-hisab,* "day of accounting." According to the Quran only God knows when Judgment Day will come, but it may be very soon (Q 21:1) and happen suddenly (Q 16:77; 6:31). The signs of the approaching judgment are vividly portrayed in the Meccan suras: the seas will boil, mountains will move, the sun will darken, stars will fall, the fires of hell will be ignited, paradise will be brought near, the trumpet will be blown; and graves overturned (see, for example, Q 78; 81; 82). There is no set sequence for these events, except that they anticipate the resurrection of the dead, their gathering and standing before God (including angels and jinn), and the unfolding of the books containing the records of what individuals have done in their lives. Those given their book in the right hand will

attain paradise, while those who receive it in their left will go to the Fire. The Quran also speaks of a weighing of good deeds against bad on a scale (for example, Q 21:47). God will interrogate prophets and angels about what they and their people have done, and people will even be obliged to testify against themselves for not heeding God's signs (Q 6:130). The Quran also mentions the possibility of INTERCESSION, but only if God allows it (for example, Q 2:254; 10:3).

The Quran's depictions of Judgment Day and the AFTERLIFE inspired a large body of eschatological literature that encompassed the hadith, mysticism, THEOLOGY, PHILOSOPHY, and poetry. One of the issues addressed in this literature was whether there was a bodily resurrection, or whether the soul alone was resurrected. The consensus among most Sunnis and Shiis was that body and soul were conjoined for resurrection, although some maintained that the resurrected body would be different from the earthly one. Another issue was whether there was a preliminary judgment after DEATH, known as the "interrogation of the grave" or "the torture of the grave." According to this view, each human underwent a preliminary judgment in the grave and experienced a preview of his or her punishments or rewards until the final judgment was pronounced. There was also speculation about the place where the final judgment would occur. Many asserted that JERUSALEM was where this would happen. However, the Muslim theologian and mystic al-GHAZALI (d. 1111) likened the gathering of pilgrims at ARAFAT during the hajj to the gathering of the resurrected before God on Judgment Day.

See also ANGEL; ANTICHRIST; *AYA*; ESCHATOLOGY; FUNERARY RITES; HOLY BOOKS; MAHDI; PROPHETS AND PROPHECY; SOUL AND SPIRIT.

Further reading: Muhammad Abu Hamid al-Ghazali, *The Remembrance of Death and the Afterlife,* Kitab dhikr al-mawt wa-ma badahu, *Book XL of The Revival of the Religious Sciences,* Ihya ulum al-Din. Translated by T. J. Winter (Cambridge: The Islamic Texts Society, 1995);

T. O'Shaughnessy, *Muhammad's Thoughts on Death: A Thematic Study of the Quranic Data* (Leiden: E.J. Brill, 1969); Jane I. Smith and Yvonne Haddad, *The Islamic Understanding of Death and Resurrection* (Albany: State University of New York Press, 1981).

Junayd, Abu al-Qasim ibn Muhammad ibn al-Junayd al-Khazzaz al-Qawariri al-

(unknown–910) *leading Sufi master of Baghdad whose "sober" understanding of mystical experience won acceptance among conservative Sunni scholars*

Al-Junayd was from the city of BAGHDAD during the age of the ABBASID CALIPHATE. Although his writings are available today only in the form of letters and short treatises, he was often mentioned and quoted in the works of other Sufis. He had some knowledge of the legal sciences and it is reported that he was also respected by philosophers and theologians. The high regard in which he was held is indicated by the titles given to him by later writers: the Sayyid of the Religious Group and Supreme Shaykh. His uncle was another famous Sufi, Sari al-Saqati (d. ca. 867), a pious merchant who spoke of the mutual love between humans and God and of the spiritual stages on the way to God.

Scholars have commented on the difficulties posed by al-Junayd's work in terms of his obscure writing style, but they recognize that he was one of the first to speak about the challenges faced by Sufis in adhering to a life of ASCETICISM and devotion to God. He is also remembered for his explanation of the relation between *baqa* (abiding in God) and *fana* (annihilation in God). Instead of accepting the idea that annihilation was the end of self-existence, in contrast to the "intoxicated" Sufis, he stated that by God's grace, "My annihilation is my abiding," and continued to state paradoxically that God "annihilated me from both my abiding and my annihilation" (quoted in Sells 254). Because al-Junayd's thoughts about ecstasy and annihilation were considered moderate when compared with those of the "intoxicated" Sufis,

Sufi tradition placed him in the forefront of the "sober" Sufis. He taught that annihilation had three stages: (1) containing the lower self through the performance of self-less actions; (2) cutting oneself off from "the sweet desserts and pleasures of obedience;" and (3) attaining true existence in God by annihilation through ecstasy. His understanding of the nature of affirming God's unity (TAWHID) was also an important aspect of his spiritual teachings. Al-Junayd held that this affirmation had four forms: (1) proclamation by the common people that God was one; (2) fulfilling the duties of worship and following the sharia by the common people; (3) abolition of hopes and fears by the elect so as to allow them to experience perfect harmony in witnessing the reality of God; and (4) return of the elect to the original state of preexistence "as one was before one was," without outside attachments.

Mansur al-HALLAJ (d. 922) was one of al-Junayd's most famous disciples, but al-Junayd eventually rejected him because of controversial utterances he made while in spiritual ecstasy. His biographers say that al-Junayd made the pilgrimage to MECCA 30 times and that he died reciting the Quran. His tomb was located in western Baghdad, near those of his uncle Sari al-Saqati and the famous HADITH scholar and jurist Ahmad IBN HANBAL (d. 855). Many Sufi *tariqa*s (spiritual orders) subsequently included al-Junayd in the genealogies of spiritual masters that disciples must memorize when they are initiated into them.

See also ALLAH; ASCETICISM; *BAQA AND FANA*; BISTAMI, ABU YAZID AL-; COVENANT; SOUL AND SPIRIT; SUFISM; *TARIQA*.

Further reading: Christopher Melchert, "The Transition from Asceticism to Mysticism at the Middle of the Ninth Century C.E.," *Studia Islamica* 83 (1996): 51–70; Annemarie Schimmel, *Mystical Dimensions of Islam* (Chapel Hill: University of North Carolina Press, 1975); Michael Sells, *Early Islamic Mysticism: Sufi, Quran, Miraj, Poetic, and Theological Writings* (Mahwah, N.J.: Paulist Press, 1996), 251–265.

justice (Arabic: *adl, qist, haqq, sidq, ihsan*)

Justice is a fundamental principle concerned with the fair allocation of rewards and punishments, together with the rectification of wrongs. It is a key concept in the Abrahamic religions, where human beings are called to act in justice or righteousness, and where God is seen as its ultimate dispenser, especially on JUDGMENT DAY.

In Arabic one of the key words for justice is *adl*, a noun based on the verb *adala*, which means, among other things, to straighten or modify; to depart or deflect from one (presumably wrong) path to the other (presumably right one); to equalize; and to balance, weigh, or be in equilibrium. Among its numerous suggestive synonyms are *nasib* and *qist*, share; *haqq*, truth or justice; *qistas* and *mizan*, scale; and *taqwim*, straightening. Other synonyms imply the classical Greek virtue *sophrosyne*: temperance, harmony, self-mastery, and with respect to action: balance, proportionality, and judiciousness, or the Aristotelian principle of the (Golden) Mean between extremes. The semantically rich metaphorical image of the scale (*mizan*) is used in the QURAN with reference to divine justice on Judgment Day.

Justice is one of the foremost themes in the Quran. Indeed, it is part of the metaphysical rationale for creation: "God created the heavens and earth with what is true and just (*haqq*): to reward each soul according to its deeds. They will not be wronged" (Q 45:22). Humankind alone is responsible for whatever justice—or injustice (*zulm*)—is in the world (Q 10:44). Divine justice is more than a quid pro quo exchange, at least with regard to merit-based principles, for God "doubles any good deed and gives a tremendous reward of his own" (Q 4:40). The quranic concern for justice reiterates one of the fundamental demands (as "righteousness") made by God upon humans in revelations to the prophets of the Hebrew Bible. This continuity with earlier revelations might be inferred from the fact that "the Quran often refers to terms such as *adl* (equitable, just), *ihsan* (beneficence) [and] *maaruf* (a generally accepted good)

without defining them, as if the Quran assumes a pre-existing relationship to justice, equity and morality—a relationship that precedes the text" (quoted in Abou El Fadl 60).

Perhaps the best expression of the importance of justice in the Quran is:

> You who believe, uphold justice (*qist*) and be witnesses to God, even if it is against yourselves, your parents, or your close relatives. Whether the person is rich or poor, God can best take care of both. Do not follow your selfish desire, so that you can act justly. If you pervert or neglect justice, God is fully aware of what you do. (Q 4:135)

The call to justice is complemented by numerous admonitions against injustice (*zulm*) in the Quran.

Divine justice is by definition perfect, eternal, and ideal. People are urged to make every effort to approximate and reflect this metaphysical fact in their lives. Reward or punishment in the next life is allotted in accordance with the sincerity and strength of a person's efforts to follow this ideal, one reason for the association of justice with *ihsān*, beneficence or moral excellence, that is, doing the utmost good. The imperative of justice is both an individual and a collective obligation for Muslims, so that while we may distinguish between personal and social virtues, they are necessarily tied together.

MUHAMMAD (ca. 570–632), like the biblical prophets, was motivated by a strong sense of justice and protested the widespread inequity and oppression he found in Meccan society, where he had grown up. He sought to replace it with a new order and harmony within which the standards of justice would prevail. Whatever dimensions of justice were part of the BEDOUIN ethic of tribal manliness (*muruwwa*) in the *jahiliyya* (pre-Islamic Arabia), they appear to have precipitously declined in the time and place of Muhammad, hence the Meccan revelations of the Quran regarding the treatment of orphans and the plight of the poor. The Quran clearly evidences the urgency of addressing issues that fall under the rubric of socioeconomic or distributive justice, rebuking those who have greedily consumed their inheritance while having a greedy passion for wealth (Q 89:19–20). Moreover, the enshrinement of *zakat* (ALMSGIVING) as the third pillar of practice in Islam makes this duty integral to Muslim identity, effectively institutionalizing a "right" for the needy and deprived to a share in the community's wealth. In addition to this compulsory obligation, Muslims of sufficient means are expected to practice voluntary charitable giving (*sadaqa*). The Quran's ill-understood opposition to usury (*riba*) further illustrates the attempt to deal with problems of distributive justice.

Historically, questions of political justice were first broached in the Khariji opposition to the UMAYYAD CALIPHATE (661–750). The KHAWARIJ invoked the doctrine of *qadar* (power; FREE WILL, thus the corollary proposition that each individual is responsible for his or her acts) against the Umayyad rulers' attempt to legitimize their rule through the principles of IJMAA (consensus, agreement) and *bayaa* (oath of allegiance), fortified with the theological doctrine of *jabr* (lit., compulsion; predestination; here in the sense that Umayyad rule was seen as ordained by God). The absolute justice of God was one of the five tenets of Mutazili *kalam* (THEOLOGY), unremarkable in itself until we learn that it was bound up with debates over the nature of evil and injustice, including the metaphysical and ethical scope of man's free agency. The Mutazila even took to referring to themselves as the People of Justice (*adl*) and Unity (*tawhid*). The pursuit and realization of justice for the Mutazila was determined and constrained by the powers of reason (*aql*).

"The Father of Arab Philosophy" and Islam's first significant philosopher, Abu Yusuf Yaacub ibn Ishaq al-Kindi (d. ca. 866) held justice to be the central virtue owing to its balancing and coordinating functions vis-à-vis other (principally clas-

sical Greek) virtues, thereby demonstrating the integration of Peripatetic and Neoplatonic ideas into a distinctively Islamic PHILOSOPHY. Islam's first truly systematic philosopher, al-FARABI (ca. 870–950), envisioned the ideal Islamic polity portioning such goods as security, wealth, honor, and dignity according to a desert principle of distributive justice. Rational justice, formulated in terms of a social contract theory beholden to Plato's *Republic* and Aristotle's *Ethics*, as well as the Islamic sciences generally, was the center point of Ibn Sina's (Avicenna, 979–1037) political scheme to secure the common welfare from a pool of basic resources. For Muhammad IBN RUSHD (Averroës, 1126–98), justice was the sum and highest of all virtues of man as a citizen of the polity. Furthermore, it inheres in the fulfillment of responsibilities and duties in a social division of labor structured according to the standards and strictures of PHILOSOPHY (*falsafa*). While some virtues, such as wisdom and courage, are class-specific, justice was pertinent to all citizens, provided they performed the vocation for which they were fitted "by nature."

Justice in jurisprudential terms entails, in the first instance, equal treatment of all before the law (FIQH). With the SHARIA as lodestar (recalling, with Abou El Fadl, that the sharia "is God's will in an ideal and abstract fashion, but the *fiqh* is the product of the human attempt to understand God's will" [Abou El Fadl 32]), both ethics and law in Islam approach justice through the doctrinal formula of "commanding right and forbidding wrong" (*al-amr bi'l-maaruf wa'l-nahy an al-munkar*). In short, *fiqh* is a system of ethico-legal obligation formulated in imperative (*amr*) and prohibitive (*nahy*) terms, with all human actions exhaustively classified as mandatory (*fard* or *wajib*), encouraged (*mustahabb* or *mandub*), permissible (HALAL or *mubah*), discouraged (*makruh*), or forbidden (HARAM). Procedural justice in Islam tends toward personalism rather than corporatism and administrative principles insofar as trust is placed in the "just judge" or "just witness," trumping the judicial system as such. In other words, the status and personal qualities of juridical actors is paramount.

Exemplified in the works of Sayyid QUTB (1906–66), Muslim intellectuals typically concentrate on pressing questions of distributive justice, thus lacking the full historical compass and ethical range of prior philosophical and jurisprudential discussions. Most recently, Muslim scholars have persuasively argued for the relevance of Islamic conceptions of justice and jurisprudence to the ideals and values intrinsic to international HUMAN RIGHTS, such rights being the primary means for realizing and exploring principles of international justice. As Nigerian legal scholar Mashood Baderin writes, in principle, "the Sharia does not oppose or prohibit the guarantee of political and civil rights, liberal and democratic principles, or the liberty and freedom of individuals in relation to the State" (Baderin 167). This line of juridical thinking opens the door for interpreting Islamic law in accordance with modern legal and ethical notions of justice.

See also ALLAH; CRIME AND PUNISHMENT; ETHICS AND MORALITY; FATE; FIVE PILLARS; IBN SINA, ABU ALI AL-HUSAYN; INTERCESSION; MUTAZILI SCHOOL.

Patrick S. O'Donnell

Further reading: Khaled Abou El Fadl, *Speaking in God's Name: Islamic Law, Authority and Women* (Oxford: Oneworld, 2001); Mashood A. Baderin, *International Human Rights and Islamic Law* (New York: Oxford University Press, 2003); Michael Cook, *Commanding Right and Forbidding Wrong in Islamic Thought* (Cambridge: Cambridge University Press, 2000); Sohail H. Hashmi, ed., *Islamic Political Ethics: Civil Society, Pluralism, and Conflict* (Princeton, N.J.: Princeton University Press, 2002); Albert Hourani, *Arabic Thought in the Liberal Age: 1798–1939* (Cambridge: Cambridge University Press, 1983); Majid Khadduri, *The Islamic Conception of Justice* (1962. Reprint, Baltimore: Johns Hopkins University Press, 1983).

K

Kaaba

The Kaaba, also known as "the sacred house" (Q 5:2, 97) is the most holy place in Islam. A large cube-shaped building (approximately 50 feet high, 40 feet long, and 33 feet wide) made of cut stone, it is situated in the plaza of the Grand Mosque in MECCA. Its four corners point approximately to the four cardinal directions, with the famous BLACK STONE inserted in its eastern corner. The Kaaba is covered by a curtain and is empty inside, except for lamps and inscriptions. A large, ornately decorated door provides access to the interior. Opposite the Kaaba's northwest wall is the *Hijr*, a detached semi-circular walled area marking the place where HAGAR and Ishmael are believed to be buried. Nearby, opposite the northeast side, is the Station of ABRAHAM, and opposite the eastern corner the sacred well of ZAMZAM. Every day Muslims around the world face toward the Kaaba when they pray; it is their QIBLA, or PRAYER direction. Pilgrims who go to Mecca for the HAJJ and the UMRA assemble around it in concentric circles for prayer and must walk around it seven times counterclockwise to fulfill the required rites of pilgrimage. Muslim law also requires that an ANIMAL should be turned toward the Kaaba when it is slaughtered, and that a person should be laid in the grave facing toward it.

The age of the Kaaba is disputed and its early history shrouded by myths and legends. As is often the case with living holy sites, archaeological research is prohibited there. Based on Islamic textual evidence, most scholars (Muslims and non-Muslims) agree that the shrine was a place of worship even before the historical appearance of Islam in the seventh century. The QURAN describes it as "the first house established for humankind" (Q 3:96) and as "the ancient house" (Q 22:29). In the time of the JAHILIYYA (the era before MUHAMMAD), statues of gods and religious relics were kept in it; sacrifices and pilgrimage rituals were conducted there. Such evidence suggests that it did not differ significantly from other temples that had once been vital to the ancient civilizations of the Middle East, including that of Yahweh-Elohim in JERUSALEM.

The Quran states that Abraham and Ishmael first built it as a place for worship at God's command (Q 2:125–128). However, Islamic literary tradition embellished this brief quranic story by saying that the original Kaaba had been created at the beginning of time. According to one tradition, it was a building made of sapphires that God had sent down from PARADISE and placed on earth directly under his throne. He had an ANGEL bring Adam from INDIA, where he lived after being expelled from paradise, in order to perform the first pilgrimage rites. Other accounts credit Adam with being the first to actually build the Kaaba. According to this tradition, in the time of Noah, God raised it up to heaven when the great flood came. Abraham then later built a second Kaaba with his son at God's command and inaugurated the hajj rituals for all people to perform.

Muslim historical sources, such as Ibn Ishaq's *Life of the Prophet* (mid-eighth century), indicate that the Quraysh tribe rebuilt the Kaaba around the year 605, some five years before Muhammad began his career as a prophet. Muhammad was credited with having resolved a dispute among the QURAYSH clans over who would install the Black Stone, signaling his close association with the sanctuary and growing reputation as a leader. This building was destroyed during a civil war, then rebuilt and enlarged by Abd Allah ibn al-Zubayr (r. 683–692), an opponent of the UMAYYAD CALIPHATE who had gained control of Mecca. When the Umayyads took back control of the city, they restored it as it had been in Muhammad's time. In the ensuing centuries it has undergone numerous restorations and repairs, the latest by the government of Saudi Arabia near the end of the 20th century.

A cover (*kiswa*) of black cloth made in Saudi Arabia is placed over the Kaaba annually. It is embroidered in gold and silver thread with verses from the Quran. When the cover is replaced each year, the Saudi government places sections of the old one in its embassies, or gives them to foreign governments, international organizations, and important people. Also, many Muslims hang pictures of the Kaaba in their homes and businesses. In Egypt it is one of the motifs used in murals that people paint on the homes of hajjis, pilgrims who have gone to Mecca.

See also ADAM AND EVE; ARABIAN RELIGIONS, PRE-ISLAMIC; MOSQUE.

Further reading: Juan Eduardo Campo, *The Other Sides of Paradise: Explorations into the Religious Meanings of Domestic Space in Islam* (Columbia: University of South Carolina Press, 1991); G. R. Hawting, "The Origins of the Muslim Sanctuary in Mecca." In *Studies in the First Century of Islamic Society,* edited by G. H. A. Juynboll, 23–47 (Carbondale and Edwardsville: Southern Illinois University Press, 1982); F. E. Peters, *The Hajj: The Muslim Pilgrimage to Mecca and the Holy Places* (Princeton, N.J.: Princeton University Press, 1994), 3–19; Ahmad ibn Muhammad al-Thalabi, *Arais al-majalis fi qisas al-anbiya, or "Lives of the Prophets."* Translated by William M. Brinner (Leiden: E.J. Brill, 2002), 145–154.

kafir (Arabic: unbeliever, disbeliever; infidel; ungrateful)

Religions often provide maps for differentiating insiders from outsiders. In the monotheistic confessional religions of Christianity and ISLAM important distinctions are made between people on the basis of what they believe and do not believe. Moreover, these distinctions have a bearing on notions of salvation and a person's fate in the AFTERLIFE.

In Islam the word *kafir* and related words based on the Arabic root k-f-r are usually used to designate disbelievers or "infidels" (a Latin term originally used by medieval Christians), or those who fall outside the community of true people of faith (*muminin* and *muslimin*). This distinction is one of the essential ones used in the QURAN, where *kafir* or the plural *kafirun/kafirin* is used 134 times (its verbal cognates occur about 250 times; the verbal noun *kufr* [unbelief, infidelity] occurs 37 times). In many cases "disbeliever" is used polemically against the idolaters of Mecca who were opponents of MUHAMMAD (d. 632) and the early Muslim community (UMMA). It is a word that polarizes groups of people (distinguishing "us" versus "them"), helps create unity in the community against outsiders, and mobilizes insiders to take action accordingly. The kinds of action such polarization induces are diverse, including promoting adherence to quranic commandments and prohibitions, avoiding unbelievers, and taking defensive or offensive action (JIHAD) against them as enemies.

One of the earliest quranic statements on this subject is found in the sura known as *Al-Kafirun* (Q 109), which declares, "Say: O disbelievers! I do not worship what you worship, and you are not worshipping what I worship.... You have your religion (*din*) and I have my religion." These verses, which are traditionally associated with Muhammad's Meccan revelations, are often quoted in support of religious tolerance, but despite this interpretation, their effect is divisive. With the development of the early Muslim community, the Quran elaborated in more detail the identities of the disbelievers. They included those who practiced IDOLATRY, did not accept the absolute oneness of God, denied that Muhammad was a prophet, ignored God's commandments and "signs" (singular AYA), and rejected belief in a resurrection and final judgment. In some Medinan verses of the Quran, believing Muslims were instructed to avoid association with disbelievers (for example, Q 3:28, 118), but other Medinan passages actually called upon them to "exert" themselves or fight against them (for example, Q 2:190–193). Disbelievers were even declared to be the intimate friends of SATAN (Q 4:76). In the afterlife, moreover, disbelievers could expect to suffer severe punishment in the FIRE (for example, Q 8:50, 21:39).

The Quran referred to Jews and Christians as PEOPLE OF THE BOOK, or "those who have been given the book"; that is, members of religious communities who believed in God, his prophets, and the earlier scriptures of the TORAH and the GOSPEL. As a consequence of their proximity to Islam, Muslims were permitted to eat the meat of ANIMALS slaughtered by them, and Muslim men were permitted to marry their WOMEN. However, reflecting Muhammad's contacts with Jews and Christians after the HIJRA in 622, as well as divisions and opposition in MEDINA, the Medinan suras of the Quran began to query the People of the Book about why they did not believe God's

signs and why they concealed the truth when they should have known better (Q 3:70–71). Jews, as People of the Book, were condemned for their disbelief in God's signs and killing of some of the prophets, including JESUS (for example, Q 4:154–157). Christians were accused of *kufr* (unbelief) because they believed in the Trinity and Jesus as the son of God, which the Quran considered to be idolatry (for example, Q 5:73, 171). Above all, Jews and Christians were faulted for not believing in the prophethood of Muhammad, even though they believed in other prophets. Although they were usually regarded in a different light from the Meccan idolaters, some verses equated the People of the Book with the polytheists and promised them an eternity in hell, except for those who believed and did good works (Q 98).

Other meanings for words based on the Arabic root *k-f-r* are to reject the truth (for example, Q 35:14) and to be ungrateful, especially to God for his blessings (for example, Q 16:55; 30:34). The ideas of rejection and ingratitude, therefore, were linked in quranic discourse to that of disbelief.

The word *takfir*, based on the same Arabic root, was introduced in the post-quranic period with the meaning "to accuse another of disbelief and infidelity." This was first done by the KHAWARIJ, a sectarian group that accused any Muslim who committed a major sin of being a *kafir*. With the creation of Muslim empires comprised of large non-Muslim majorities, absolute condemnation of outsiders as disbelievers contradicted the priorities of maintaining the social order under Muslim rule. People of the Book, therefore, were given certain protections under Islamic law. According to the sharia, they were *dhimmi*s (protected peoples). This occurred not only in the Middle East, but also in South Asia, where Hindus were also considered *dhimmi*s under the rule of the DELHI SULTANATE and the MUGHAL DYNASTY. Accusations of infidelity were directed against non-Muslims living in lands that were not under Muslim control (*dar al-harb*) and against Muslims who in one way or another diverged from the normative beliefs and practices of the UMMA. Even though condemned in the HADITH, *kafir* became a polemical term used more by Muslim elites against other Muslims than against non-Muslims during the Middle Ages. Among those accused of unbelief were leading Muslim philosophers such as IBN SINA (d. 1037), "intoxicated" Sufis such as Mansur al-HALLAJ (d. 922), and members of various branches of the Shia.

Drawing on this tradition and promoting a rigid doctrine of absolute monotheism, the central Arabian revivalist Muhammad IBN ABD AL-WAHHAB (d. 1798) called any Muslim who failed to enact the requirements of believing in one God a *kafir.* This included Muslims who practiced fortune-telling, magic, astrology, wearing amulets, excessive mourning of the dead, Sufi shrine pilgrimage, and who followed Shii teachings about the Imams. The conquest of much of the Arabian Peninsula by the Saudis in alliance with the followers of Ibn Abd al-Wahhab's teachings, Saudi control of Islam's most sacred centers in Mecca and Medina, and OIL revenues have given significant weight to the influence of the Wahhabi understanding of Islam and disbelief well beyond the borders of SAUDI ARABIA.

In the modern period Islamist ideologists such as Abu al-Ala MAWDUDI (d. 1979) of Indo-Pakistan and Sayyid QUTB (d. 1966) of EGYPT have extended the polemics of unbelief to include condemnations of Western-style SECULARISM and the materialist understandings of society. They considered the 20th century to be Jahiliyya time, recalling the era that preceded Islam's appearance when unbelief prevailed. The main difference between the *jahiliyya* of ancient Arabia and today was that the modern *jahilyiya* was one when Muslim societies were being corrupted by Western laws and governments based on Western models that violated the SHARIA. Mawdudi and Qutb called upon a faithful corps of true Muslims, what Qutb called a "unique quranic generation," not only to reject the modern *jahiliya,* but to conduct jihad against it to bring about its destruction. They quoted the Quran in support of their radical ideology, especially the verse, "Those who judge not (or rule not) by what God has revealed are the *kafirs*" (Q 5:44). Even though rejected by most Muslims, this ideology was used by the Jihad Group of Egypt to justify the assassination of Egyptian president Anwar al-SADAT in 1981 and it inspired radical movements in many Muslim countries during the 1980s and 1990s. USAMA BIN LADIN used it in his fatwas and speeches against the United States and Israel, both of whom he accused of invading and occupying sacred Muslim lands.

Lastly, the term Kaffir is derived from *kafir.* It was originally used by Arabs for the indigenous peoples of Africa, then adopted by European slave traders. Eventually it became a racial slur, used particularly by whites in South Africa against the blacks.

See also APOSTASY; *BIDAA*; BLASPHEMY; CHRISTIANITY AND ISLAM; CRIME AND PUNISHMENT; *DHIMMI*; HERESY; JIHAD MOVEMENTS; JUDAISM AND ISLAM; PROPHETS AND PROPHECY; SHIISM; TAKFIR WA-HIJRA; WAHHABISM; ZIYARA.

Further reading: Peter Antes, "Relations with Unbelievers in Islamic Theology." In *We Believe in One God: The Experience of God in Christianity and Islam,* edited by Annemarie Schimmel and Abdoldjavad Falaturi, 101–111 (New York: Seabury Press, 1979); Toshihiko Izutsu, *Ethico-Religious Concepts in the Quran* (Montreal: McGill University Press, 1966); Marilyn Waldman, "The Development of the Concept of *kufr,*" *Journal of the American Oriental Society* 88 (1968): 442–455.

kalam See THEOLOGY.

Karbala

A shrine city in IRAQ, about 62 miles southwest of BAGHDAD, Karbala has an approximate population of 575,000. It is considered the holiest city to Shiis, after MECCA, MEDINA, JERUSALEM, and Najaf (site of the Imam Ali ibn Abi Talib's tomb). Karbala is a sacred space to the Shia because it is the DEATH and burial site of the third Imam, HUSAYN IBN ALI, grandson of the prophet Muhammad by his daughter, FATIMA (known by the Shia as al-Zahra, "the radiant one"), and cousin Ali ibn Abi Talib. On the 10th day (ASHURA) of the Islamic lunar month Muharram 61 A.H. (October 9–10, 680 C.E.) Husayn was killed along with most of the men of his household by the forces of Yazid, the son of Muawiya, founder of the Umayyad Caliphate (661–750). The WOMEN and CHILDREN in Husayn's company were taken into captivity. The Shia understand this event as MARTYRDOM (*shahada*), which is both the spiritual and moral center of their THEOLOGY and ritual life, giving force to doctrines of sanctification by martyrdom and the redemptive quality of suffering. The city grew up around the tombs of Husayn and his half-brother Abbas ibn Ali, who was also killed and buried at Karbala. It came to be known as *Mashhad al-Husayn* (the place of Husayn's martyrdom).

Husayn's shrine is a focus of Shii pilgrimage (ZIYARA) from all over the Muslim world, where pilgrims seek to obtain divine blessings (BARAKA) and saintly INTERCESSION (*wasila, shafaa*) by touching the sarcophagus (which now stands surrounded by an elaborate brass grill). Elderly Shiis often travel there waiting to die, as many Jews and Christians want to die and be buried in Jerusalem, or Hindus to be cremated in the Indian holy city of Varanasi (Banaras). The actual soil of Karbala is considered blessed, and Shiis carry a piece of Karbala with them, literally *turba Husayniyya* (or *mohr-i namaz*). This is a small light red or brown clay tablet made of Karbala soil, which symbolizes the blood of Husayn's martyrdom, on which Shiis rest their foreheads when performing *salat* (daily prayers). Symbolically, all space becomes transformed through ritual and religious material culture into Karbala, as Shiis often say, "every day is Ashura, and every place is Karbala."

The Shii UMMA invokes Karbala and renews its experience of the redemptive suffering of Imam Husayn by commemorating his "passion" and martyrdom annually with a cycle of rituals and

The Shrine of Imam Husayn in Karbala, Iraq
(AP Photos/Hussein Malla)

public demonstrations of devotion up to the 10th of Muharram (Ashura). Each country and culture of significant Shii population (the Twelvers, Ismailis, and Zaydis of Lebanon, Bahrain, and Yemen; the Twelvers of IRAN and IRAQ; and the Twelvers and Ismaili Bohras and Dawudis of northern INDIA, PAKISTAN, and BANGLADESH, as well as diverse transplanted communities of the Shia in North America and the Caribbean) demonstrate its devotion to Husayn's living memory by mourning him afresh every year wherever they are with public processionals (called *masiras*, or lamentation processions) and performances. These include leading Husayn's caparisoned HORSE (or displaying a representation of it), carrying such traditional items as mock coffins, poles topped by the five-fingered hand (representing the five members of the AHL AL-BAYT: Muhammad, Fatima, Ali, Hasan, and Husayn), displaying banners showing scenes from Husayn's life, and carrying scale models of the tomb of Husayn at Karbala (called *naql* or *darih*) on a palanquin; performing "passion plays" (*taaziya* in Iran or *shabih* in Iraq and Lebanon) reenacting the martyrdom at Karbala; participating in collective rites of self-flagellation (*latam*) using chains (*zanjir-zani*) and swords (*qumma-zani*) or, more recently, razor blades tapped on the forehead, and rhythmically beating the chest in unison (*sina-zani*). Celebrants set up a group of visual symbols for the events of Muharram, an *Imamzada*. There are performances of elegiac poetry and songs of devotion and veneration for Husayn and the *ahl al-bayt* in the home, and public recitals (*rawda-khani*) of the sufferings and martyrdoms of all the Imams, especially Husayn, at gatherings (*majlis/majalis*) in buildings known as *Husayniyyas* in Iran, Iraq, and Lebanon, *imambaras* in India, and *matams* in Bahrain. For many modern Sunni Muslims, particularly those in the West, Shii religious sensibility has always seemed extreme, even a bit frightening and repellent. Thus, some contemporary Shiis have moved away from Ashura rituals of "bloodletting" and even the bloodless flagellation of rhythmic chest beating, which function to evoke the "passion" and suffering of Imam Husayn, and have recently allowed the painless substitute of giving BLOOD to the Red Crescent (the Islamic equivalent of the Red Cross).

The ongoing impact of the events of Karbala and their annual commemoration during Ashura lie in Shiism's ideology of martyrdom, self-sacrifice, and redemptive suffering, and a strong directive toward community service and volunteerism. The moral example of Karbala, of resisting overwhelming evil even unto death, has illuminated Shii life experience through the centuries whether in the context of oppression of the minority Shii *umma* by the Sunni majority or its oppression by non-Muslim forces, as in Israel's invasions and bombings of southern Lebanon. Recent Shii religio-political movements, such as HIZBULLAH, continuously interpret their contemporary experiences of persecution and suffering within the trope of Husayn's passion and martyrdom at Karbala. Their sacrifice of blood and sweat, like Husayn's, is quite literal: "This is our Karbala, this is our Husayn, we live on, Karbala lives on in the Lebanese Resistance" (quoted in Deeb 159).

See also HOLIDAYS; HUSAYNIYYA; SHIISM.

Kathleen M. O'Connor

Further reading: Kamran Scot Aghaie, *The Women of Karbala: Ritual Performance and Symbolic Discourses in Modern Shii Islam* (Austin: University of Texas Press, 2005); Lara Deeb, *An Enchanted Modern: Gender and Public Policy in Shii Lebanon* (Princeton, N.J.: Princeton University Press, 2006); Elizabeth W. Fernea, *Guests of the Sheik: An Ethnography of an Iraqi Village,* (New York: Doubleday, 1989), 216–250; Syed Akbar Hyder, *Reliving Karbala: Martyrdom in South Asian Memory* (New York: Oxford University Press, 2006); Meir Litvak, *Shii Scholars of Nineteenth-Century Iraq: The Ulama of Najaf and Karbala* (New York: Cambridge University Press, 1998); Syed-Mohsin Naquvi, *The Tragedy of Karbala* (Princeton, N.J.: Mohsena Memorial Foundation, 1992); David Pinault, *Horse of Karbala: Muslim Devotional Life in India* (New York: St. Martin's Press, 2000); Vernon J. Schubel, "Karbala as Sacred Space among North American Shia: 'Every Day Is Ashura, Everywhere Is Karbala.'" In *Making Muslim Space in North America and Europe,* edited by Barbara Metcalf (Berkeley: University of California Press, 1996): 186–203.

Karimov, Islam Abdughanievich
(1938–) *president of Uzbekistan*

Islam Karimov came to power as first secretary of the Communist Party of Uzbekistan in 1989 and was named president of the Uzbek Soviet Socialist Republic in 1990. Shortly after Uzbekistan's independence from the Soviet Union in 1991, President Karimov declared himself victor in the state's first presidential election with 86 percent of the vote. He was reelected in 2000 with 91.9 percent of the vote, and a referendum in January 2002 extended what is supposed to be Karimov's final term to 2007 by amending the constitution to allow for presidential terms of seven years. Born in Samarkand, Karimov studied engineering and economics and began his career in the government in 1966, where he moved up through his work with the State Planning Committee. Nevertheless, he was considered a political outsider when Mikhail Gorbachev chose him for first secretary.

Since the collapse of the USSR Karimov has solidified his control over Uzbekistan. He has outlawed all significant secular and religious political parties and sent those opposition figures not in exile to prison. Since September 11, 2001, relations between the Karimov regime and the United States have grown stronger. With American troops now stationed in the country, Uzbekistan has been used as a staging ground for operations in neighboring AFGHANISTAN. This strategic relationship has lessened the outside pressure on Karimov to reform his increasingly repressive and authoritarian rule.

Islam Karimov, of course, is not anti-Islam, and his regime has supported mosque construction and shrine-restoration since independence. There is very little tolerance, however, for mosques or Islamic teachings outside of state control. In recent years, all opposition has been branded as "fundamentalist" and "extremist." For example, in 1997 when four policemen were killed in gang violence in the Fergana Valley, Islamic groups were blamed and mass arrests of Muslims took place. While some Islamic political groups do exist underground in Uzbekistan, their membership is very minimal.

See also CENTRAL ASIA AND THE CAUCASUS; COMMUNISM.

David Reeves

Further reading: Timothy J. Colton and Robert C. Tucker, eds., *Patterns in Post-Soviet Leadership* (Boulder, Colo.: Westview Press, 1995); Resul Yalcin, *The Rebirth of Uzbekistan: Politics, Economy and Society in the Post-Soviet Era.* (Reading, England: Ithaca Press, 2002).

Kashmir

A disputed land of spectacular mountains, green valleys, and beautiful lakes, Kashmir is divided between Indian and Pakistani rule. Indian Kashmir is a territory known officially as Jammu and Kashmir. The Pakistani part of Kashmir is divided into two regions known as Azad (Free) Jammu and Kashmir and the Northern Territories. Indian Kashmir consists of three provinces: Jammu, the Kashmir Valley, and Ladakh. China is located along its northern and eastern borders. It has an area of nearly 86,000 square miles, which is comparable to that of Minnesota in the United States. There are about 11 million people (2001 census) living in Indian Kashmir, of whom 65 percent are Muslims. This territory therefore has the largest percentage of Muslims among all of India's states and territories, with the exception of Lakshadweep (95.5 percent). Most Muslims reside in the Kashmir Valley proper, where they comprise about 95 percent of the population. They make up 44 percent of the population in Ladakh (Tibetan Buddhists are a 51 percent majority there) and 27 percent of the population in Jammu (Hindus comprise a 67 percent majority there). Sikhs are an important minority, especially in Jammu. In Azad Kashmir there are four million people; about 750,000 people live in the mountainous Northern Territories.

SUFISM has been an important aspect of Kashmiri religious life since the 14th century, and the majority of Kashmir's Muslims identify with Sunni Islam. Ismaili Shiis predominate in the Northern Territories, where they migrated centuries ago to escape persecution. There are also followers of TWELVE-IMAM SHIISM and the AHMADIYYA sect. Moreover, Kashmiri Islam developed infusions of folk, Hindu, and Buddhist elements. Kashmir's ethnic composition is diverse, consisting mainly of Turks, Mongols, Afghans, and Indo-Aryans.

Kashmir was home to competing Hindu and Buddhist regimes prior to the arrival of the first Muslims. Islamization occurred gradually over a number of centuries. Some accounts indicate that it may have occurred by conquest and forced conversion, others that it was accomplished through Sufi missionaries. Most likely a combination of different processes was involved. The first Muslims appear to have arrived as Turkish warriors imported from Afghanistan or Central Asia by local Hindu rulers during the 12th century. The European explorer Marco Polo (d. 1325) encountered "Saracens" (a medieval term for Arabs and Muslims) who worked as butchers in the Kashmir Valley. The Mongol conquests in the Middle East during the 13th and 14th centuries brought an influx of immigrants and refugees from Persia, Afghanistan, and Central Asia, many of whom were Sufis, ULAMA, and artisans. Bulbul Shah (also known as Sharaf al-Din), a member of the Suhrawardi Sufi Order, is said to have been responsible for the conversion of Rinchana, a Buddhist prince from Ladakh, to Islam early in the 14th century. Rinchana is recognized as being Kashmir's first SULTAN. A number of other Sufis and religious scholars immigrated from Herat, Khorasan, Samarqand, and BUKHARA. The artisans came from the same regions and introduced the crafts of paper making, papier-mâché, bookbinding, woodworking, and carpet weaving for which Kashmir is still known.

Local sultans provided support for religious scholars and mosques, thus laying the foundations for the creation of a permanent Muslim presence and ongoing influence over the local non-Muslim communities. One of the sultans, Sikandar (r. 1389–1413), was reported to have imposed the SHARIA on his subjects, destroyed Hindu temples, and forced them to convert to Islam, but these reports in the chronicles may have been exaggerated, as they were in chronicles about Muslim rulers in India. On the other hand Sikandar's heir, Zayn al-Abidin (r. 1420–70) was remembered for having abolished the JIZYA (a tax on non-Muslims) and supported temple-building projects. Hindu Brahmans, later known as Pandits, complained about the Islamic influence that was spreading through Kashmir, but they learned Persian, the administrative language, and accepted appointments as scribes and administrators in order to retain their higher status in the Hindu community. The confluence of Islamic and Hindu religious ideas did not occur among Brahmans and sultans, but among lower caste Hindus and Sufis. This is epitomized by the Rishi movement, which arose during the 15th century in rural Kashmir. The Rishis, who took their name from a Sanskrit word for the ancient sages of the Hindu Vedas, were closely identified with two local saint-poets—Lalla Ded, a female ascetic devoted to the Hindu god Shiva, and Shaykh Nur al-Din Nurani (d. 1438), a Sufi who considered Lalla Ded his teacher and a second RABIA AL-ADAWIYYA (the famed woman saint of Basra). Members of the movement were vegetarians, abstained from marriage, and often appeared as yogis. Their egalitarian outlook, spirituality, and charitable activities made them popular among the commoners. Nur al-Din's shrine at Charar-i Sharif, near the Kashmiri capital of Srinagar, was an important regional pilgrimage center until 1995, when it was destroyed in a clash between Kashmiri rebels and Indian troops.

In modern times Kashmir has become a flashpoint for conflict between INDIA and PAKISTAN that has cost dearly in terms of human suffering, loss of life, and economic damage. The Kashmiri conflict is a consequence of the 1947 partition of India into two states—India and Pakistan. One hundred years previously, in 1846, the British had established a Hindu monarchy to rule Kashmir by selling the right to rule to Gulab Singh (d. 1857) and his heirs, making them the Maharajas of Kashmir. Muslims were subject to excessive taxes in order to pay for the sale and fund the expenses of the government. At the time of partition Kashmiris were divided about what to do with their country. Some wanted to be joined to India, some wanted to be joined to Pakistan, others wished to remain independent. Maharaja Hari Singh (r. 1925–47), although inclined to remain independent, agreed to have his state incorporated into India and fled. This happened after thousands of Kashmiri Muslims had been massacred and Pakistan began allowing forces into the area to protect them. India responded by sending in its troops and registering a complaint at the United Nations against Pakistan's "aggression." Pakistan protested and assumed control of what it called Azad Kashmir. Subsequent mediation efforts to resolve the dispute between India and Pakistan concerning Kashmir's autonomy have failed. The Indian government under Jawaharlal Nehru's leadership negotiated with Shaykh Muhammad Abd Allah (d. 1982) and his National Conference, a Kashmiri secular nationalist organization, to grant Kashmir special territorial status in India. The Indian government removed him from office in 1953 and imprisoned him for 11 years because he would not surrender the right of Kashmiri self-determination.

Since 1987 there has been an escalation in violence as a result of the failure to arrive at an acceptable political solution to the Kashmiri question and economic stagnation. The bloodshed has been exacerbated by the growing strength of religious radicalism among Muslims and Hindus. Hindu nationalist organizations such as the Rashtriya Swayamsevak Sangh (RSS, National Volunteers Organization) and its political wing, the Bharatiya Janata Party (BJP, Indian People's Party), consider Muslims to be a threat to the nation and want Kashmir to be ruled by an Indian Hindu government. They refuse to allow any real autonomy to the Kashmiri Muslims. The government of Pakistan supported the emergence of an armed Kashmiri resistance, consisting of the secularist Jammu and Kashmir Liberation Front and the Islamist Hizb al-Mujahidin (Party

of Muslim Warriors). Another militant Islamist group seeking to bring an end to Indian rule in Kashmir is the Lashkar-i Tayyiba (Army of the Righteous), which was founded in Afghanistan in 1990, but is now based in Lahore. It has conducted attacks in India and Pakistan, as well as Kashmir. The violence has involved extensive human rights violations committed by all combatants, including armed attacks on civilians, torture, rape, "disappearances," and extrajudicial killings. War nearly broke out in 1999 between India, led by a newly elected BJP government, and Pakistan, led by a military dictator (Pervez Musharraf), when militants and Pakistani troops threatened to block the road connecting Srinagar to Ladakh at Kargil. The threat of a nuclear war between the two countries raised international concern. At the urging of the United States Pakistan withdrew its forces, thus diffusing the situation.

See also BUDDHISM AND ISLAM; HINDUISM AND ISLAM; HUMAN RIGHTS; JIHAD MOVEMENTS; NEPAL.

Further reading: Ainslie Embree, "Kashmir: Has Religion a Role in Making Peace?" In *Faith-Based Diplomacy: Trumping Realpolitik,* edited by Douglas Johnston, 33–75 (Oxford: Oxford University Press, 2003): Mohammad Ishaq Khan, "The Impact of Islam on Kashmir in the Sultanate Period." In *India's Islamic Traditions, 711–1750,* edited by Richard M. Eaton, 342–362 (Oxford: Oxford University Press, 2003); Raju G. C. Thomas, *Perspectives on Kashmir* (Boulder, Colo.: Westview Press, 1992).

Kazakhstan   *See* CENTRAL ASIA AND THE CAUCASUS.

Khadija bint Khuwaylid ibn Asad
(ca. 555–619) *prosperous merchant and first wife of Muhammad, she was the first to accept Islam*
A wealthy Meccan merchant of the QURAYSH tribe, Khadija owned a large caravan that traded goods in SYRIA. Around the year 595 she hired MUHAM-

MAD, well-known for his trustworthiness, to trade goods for her in Basra. It is reported that she sent Nafisa bint Umayya to propose marriage to the Prophet, who agreed to this, his first marriage. After marrying him (when her age was 40 and his was 25) she bore their sons al-Qasim and Abd Allah, and their daughters Zaynab, Ruqayyah, Umm Kulthum, and FATIMA. Only the daughters survived infancy.

Traditional accounts recall that after Muhammad received the first revelation of the QURAN, he sought refuge with Khadija, fearing that he had gone mad. She pacified and encouraged him, and consulted her cousin Waraqa ibn Nawfal, possibly a Christian, who affirmed Muhammad's prophethood. Offering Muhammad comfort and strength in his uncertainty and during his persecution, she is remembered for providing him with crucial moral and financial support.

Khadija was Muhammad's only wife at the time of their marriage. It was not until after her death that he married other women. She bore all his children except Ibrahim, son of Mariya al-Qibtiya. Khadija herself, a widow, was married twice before her marriage to the Prophet.

She shares the title of "mother of the believers," along with the other wives of the Prophet. In the HADITH she is remembered as an exemplary and ideal Muslim woman, as a pious and honorable wife and mother. She has been held in high esteem by both Sunnis and Shiis. Khadija died roughly nine years after the emergence of Islam, precipitating a crisis in the life of Muhammad and his early followers that led to the HIJRA to Medina about three years later in 622. She was buried in Mecca's main cemetery, Hajun. Muhammad continued to live in her house until the Hijra. During the reign of Muawiya, the first Umayyad caliph (r. 661–680), her house was converted into a MOSQUE and continued to be regarded as a shrine by pilgrims until destroyed by the Saudis in the 1980s.

See also AHL AL-BAYT; WOMEN.

Aysha A. Hidayatullah

Further reading: Leila Ahmed, *Women and Gender in Islam: Historical Roots of a Modern Debate* (New Haven, Conn.: Yale University Press, 1992); Muhammad ibn Ishaq, *The Life of Muhammad: A Translation of Ishaq's Sirat Rasul Allah.* Translated by A. Guillaume (London: Oxford University Press, 1955); Muhammad ibn Saad, *The Women of Medina.* Translated by Aisha Bewley (London: Ta-Ha Publishers, 1995); Denise A. Spellberg, *Politics, Gender, and the Islamic Past: The Legacy of Aisha bint Abi Bakr* (New York: Columbia University Press, 1994); Barbara Freyer Stowasser, *Women in the Quran: Traditions and Interpretation* (New York: Oxford University Press, 1994).

Khadir (Khidr, Khezr, Hizir) *legendary man believed to be immortal, to possess divine wisdom, and to have inspired Sufis*

At the time of Islam's appearance in the seventh century there was a large pool of myths and legends in the Middle East from which Muslims soon drew to enrich their understandings of the past, of life and death, and of the sacred. Khadir was a figure who seems to have been a kind of magnet for such stories in the early Muslim community. His name means "the green one," which gave rise to attempts to explain why a man would be associated with this color. Some accounts say it derives from belief that his color was a result of having gained immortality by drinking water from the miraculous spring of life. They also associated his color with plant life and fertility, and that the earth turned green wherever he stood or prayed. By some accounts he was among only four men believed to have ever attained immortality, the other three being Elijah, IDRIS, and JESUS. Stories that he lived on a distant island or at the meeting place of two seas and of his ability to assist people far from home made him a patron saint of sailors living on the shore of SYRIA or a deity for those traveling in the Indian Ocean region. An ambulance service in TURKEY today is named after him, in honor of his ability to assist others in time of need.

The Dutch scholar A. J. Wensinck proposed that elements in his story were related to the *Epic of Gilgamesh* of ancient Mesopotamia and to the Romance of ALEXANDER THE GREAT of the Late Antique era (third century to eighth century C.E.). All three story cycles involved heroic figures who traveled to the limits of the known world and uncovered hidden secrets. Khadir even appeared as a companion of Alexander in his quest for the spring of life in Arabic versions of the legend. Indeed, Khadir was famous in Islamic tradition for his knowledge of the unseen. So much so, in fact, that some Muslim scholars even ranked him among the prophets, thinking that his insights could have come only from a divine source. IBN ISHAQ (d. 767) included a chapter on Khadir in his collection of prophets' tales, equating him with the biblical prophet Jeremiah and relating how he interceded on behalf of the wayward Children of Israel with God. In PALESTINE and Syria Khidr is associated with the Christian Saint George for reasons that are not entirely clear.

Although Khadir was never mentioned in the QURAN, the majority of commentators identified him with an unnamed "servant" of God mentioned in its 18th chapter (Q 18:60–82). This passage was a legend about the journey of Moses to the meeting place of the two seas, which some commentators said was located between the seas of Byzantium and Persia (the Gulf)—perhaps in the Suez region. There he encountered one of God's servants (Khadir), who had been given the gift of God's mercy and knowledge. MOSES asked to travel with him so that he might acquire some of his knowledge. Khadir reluctantly agreed on the condition that Moses promise not to ask questions and be patient in his quest for knowledge. During their travels, Khidr, acting like the trickster known to the legends of the Native Americans, did three shocking things. He scuttled a boat in which they were sailing, he killed a young man without provocation, and he built a crumbling wall without charge. Moses lost his patience at each incident, much to Khadir's chagrin, and demanded an explanation. Exasperated at Moses's inability to grasp the meaning of his deeds, Khadir at last explained himself. He scuttled the boat because a tyrannical king was about to take it from its impoverished owners. He killed the youth because he was destined for a troubled life that would bring only grief to his faithful parents. Lastly, he built the wall to protect a buried treasure belonging to two orphans so that they had a means of support when they grew up. In each instance, Khadir demonstrated an uncanny knowledge about the future, which he attributed to God. Later commentators saw in the story the interplay of two kinds of knowledge. One, possessed by Moses, was knowledge of the material world and its apparent meanings. The other, possessed by Khadir, represented knowledge of the invisible world of the spirit and its deeper meanings.

Sufis have drawn inspiration from Khadir because of his knowledge of the unseen, his close relation to God, his capacity for travel, and his ability to flout conventions in order to teach deeper truths. He was an exemplary guide (*murshid* or *pir*) who could lead them to immortality, breaking their ties to the material world. Several mystics, including IBN AL-ARABI (d. 1240), claim to have met him and been initiated by him into the Sufi way. Among the Twelve-Imam Shia, Khadir is believed to have a close association with the 12th Imam, who is in Occultatation (GHAYBA). A mosque/shrine complex in Jamkaran, Iran (near the holy city of Qom), has become a popular pilgrimage site where people go to seek the assistance of both Khadir and the 12th Imam. Ismailis note that Khadir practices *tawil* (esoteric interpretation, Q 18:78) when he explains his troubling actions to Moses, thus affirming a key method used in interpreting scripture to arrive at its hidden (*batini*) meaning. Alawis in Turkey fast for three days in honor of Khadir. Many mosques in Muslim countries have been named after him. In addition to the shrine in Jamkaran, other shrines dedicated to Khadir exist on the island of Abadan (Iran) in the Persian Gulf, on Failaka Island off the coast of Kuwait, and in Sri Lanka at Kataragama, Bosra (Syria), Jerusalem, Iraq, and Samarkand (Uzbekistan). Not all Muslims accept Khadir as a SAINT or prophet, however. Sayyid QUTB (d. 1966), chief ideologist of militant Islam, argued that the connection between Khadir and the "servant" mentioned in the Quran was mere conjecture, and that the figure was to be understood in the literal sense as a righteous (*salih*) man, not a prophet or saint.

See also BATIN; BOAT; FOLKLORE; PROPHETS AND PROPHECY.

Further reading: Gordon Darnell Newby, *The Making of the Last Prophet: A Reconstruction of the Earliest Biography of Muhammad* (Columbia: University of South Carolina Press, 1989), 182–188; John Renard, *All the King's Falcons: Rumi on Prophets and Revelation* (New York: State University of New York Press, 1994), 83–86; Ahmad ibn Muhammad al-Thalabi, *Arais al-majalis fi qisas al-anbiya, or "Lives of the Prophets."* Translated by William M. Brinner, (Leiden: E.J. Brill, 2002), 361–382.

Khan, Inayat (1882–1927) *first Sufi leader to spread Sufism in America and Europe; founder of the Sufi Order of the West*

Inayat Khan was born in INDIA and grew up in a musical family. At the age of 12 he left home to pursue a life of MUSIC and devotion, traveling around India and working in various environments, such as serving as the court musician for the Nizam, or ruler, of Hyderabad. From there Khan was initiated into the Nizami branch of the CHISTI SUFI ORDER, a very popular order of Muslim mystics in India. Khan blended Hindu and Muslim philosophy, working under masters from both traditions. He was instructed to spread Sufism in the Americas and Europe, where he spent most of his adult years, and he left for New York in 1910. In his travels he aimed to bring universal harmony between East and West by introducing Sufi concepts.

Khan lectured for some time at Columbia University and then traveled across America attracting initiates. In New York he met Ora Ray Baker, whom he would marry in 1913 after moving to England. In 1916 Khan founded the Sufi Order in London and shortly after began a quarterly magazine, *Sufism*. In the 1920s Khan visited the UNITED STATES several times to tour the country, lecture, and continue to attract initiates. He died in 1927 in India. Following his death, Khan's son, Vilayat Khan (1916–2004), still a youth, was appointed leader of the order. However some initiates decided to accept the mentorship of the Sufi leader, Meher Baba (1894–1969). In the 1960s Vilayat Khan actively took over leadership of the Sufi Order of the West in America. The order sponsors a variety of activities, including healing seminars, retreats, and psychotherapy. Inayat Khan's teachings are available in several collections that bring together his essays and lectures, such as *The Heart of Sufism: Essential Writings of Hazrat Inayat Khan.*

See also EUROPE; NIZAM AL-DIN AWLIYA; SUFISM.

Mehnaz Sahibzada

Further reading: Wil van Beek, *Hazrat Inayat Khan: Master of Life, Modern Sufi Mystic* (New York: Vantage Press, 1983); Inayat Khan, *The Heart of Sufism: Essential Writings of Hazrat Inayat Khan* (Boston: Shambhala Publications, 1999); Franklin Lewis, *Rumi Past and Present, East and West: The Life, Teaching and Poetry of Jalal-al-Din Rumi* (Boston: Oneworld Publications, 2000); Jane I. Smith, *Islam in America* (New York: Columbia University Press, 1999).

kharaj (Arabic)

The *kharaj* was a tax levied by the Islamicate state, generally on the land, as opposed to a poll tax, or JIZYA. It was once thought that the distinction between the land tax and poll tax was clear cut and absolute; however, numerous historical studies have shown conclusively that, throughout Islamic history, the terms *kharaj* and *jizya* were used interchangeably. As it is formulated in the

Umayyad period (seventh to eighth centuries), however, it seems that the term *kharaj* was used to designate land conquered militarily rather than taken by treaty, and therefore to be permanently taxed at a rate higher than would apply to other lands. This would become especially important with increasing CONVERSION to Islam, which might have threatened the fiscal stability of the state. Until the modern period a tax on the land was the most important source of revenue for most Islamicate governments.

During and after the first Arab-Islamic conquests in the seventh century, conquered lands were sometimes distributed to the Muslim conquerors, and these lands were not subject to the *kharaj* but to the considerably lower taxation of *zakat,* technically alms, but collected as a tax from Muslim subjects. As the pace of conversion to Islam increased in the following centuries, it would have been financially ruinous to allow converts to pay the lower *zakat* rate rather than the higher rate originally paid by the conquered peoples. Therefore, it was likely in the third century of Islam, when Islamic law (the SHARIA) itself was entering its maturity and, coincidentally, conversion to Islam was increasing, that the jurists codified the definition of *kharaj* as a tax imposed on lands conquered militarily. In principle, such land would always be taxed at the higher rate, regardless of the religious disposition of its cultivator.

Nonetheless, the reality of taxation varied widely. Methods of computing the *kharaj* were inconsistent. The tax might be collected in produce or in money, and it often amounted to one-third of the land's income. Worse, perhaps, for the peasants was the leeway allowed, especially in times of weak central control, to the tax collectors, who could impose fees of their own, which might exceed the *kharaj* itself. In cases where the *kharaj* was overly burdensome, peasants might flee the land. Because the tax was generally levied on a collective body such as a village, however, it would not be easily reduced in case of disaster or

of flight from the land. In effect, the only way to escape the tax was to leave the land, but this did not reduce the tax that the remaining cultivators had to pay. While the rulers could cancel the land tax in times of famine or during failed harvests, they did so at their discretion.

Kharaj per se is no longer collected in Muslim countries, although farmers are still taxed by states. The end of *kharaj* is not very clearly demarcated in IRAN and INDIA. The British began to reform the tax system in the late 18th century in India, whereas *kharaj* in Iran continued to be collected into the 20th century. The Ottoman Empire abolished the *kharaj* and *jizya* in 1856 as part of the TANZIMAT reforms by which citizenship began to replace the communal model of societal organization.

See also AGRICULTURE; COLONIALISM; UMAYYAD CALIPHATE.

John Iskander

Further reading: Fred Donner, "Review of *Studies in the Genesis and Early Development of the Caliphal Taxation System," Journal of Near Eastern Studies* 51 (January 1992): 63–65; Ann Lambton, *Landlord and Peasant in Persia* (London: Oxford University Press, 1953); Hossein Modarressi Tabatabai, *Kharaj in Islamic Law* (Leiden: E.J. Brill, 1983); A. Ben Shemesh, *Taxation in Islam.* 3 vols. (Leiden: E.J. Brill, 1958, 1965, 1969).

Khawarij (Kharijites)

The Khawarij were the first sectarian movement in Islamic history. They emerged in 657 C.E. at the battle of Siffin, a site on the Euphrates between SYRIA and IRAQ, where the caliph ALI IBN ABI TALIB (d. 661) was fighting to assert his authority over the recalcitrant governor of Syria, Muawiya. After Ali's decision to arbitrate an end to the dispute, a group of his previous supporters withdrew from his ranks, taking as their watchword "Only God can judge" (i.e., God, not man, decides human affairs), and declaring their opposition to both

Ali and Muawiya's right to rule. Based on their decision to separate from the community of Muslims, this seceding faction came to be known as the Khawarij or, literally in Arabic, "those who go out." The Khawarij's initial opposition to Ali and Muawiya quickly developed into a more far-reaching protest against Muslim leadership in general and the corruption of Muslim society, and this protest took a very violent form. According to the Khawarij, those deviating from (Khariji) Islam became grave sinners whose Muslim status and life were forfeit. The Khawarij felt obliged to purge the community of sinners who jeopardized the spiritual good of the whole. The means of purifying the community became a subject of serious debate among Khawarij, leading to infighting and further sectarian splits. The most infamous subsect, the Azariqa, determined that the wives and children of grave sinners were subject to death. The most moderate subsect, the IBADIYYA, condemned grave sinners as HYPOCRITES but tolerated them within the community of Muslims. The Ibadiyya, then, were sectarian or heretical due to their beliefs, not their actions, which accounts for the fact that they are the only Khariji faction to survive until the present day.

While the diversity and radical independence of Khariji subsects prevents a clear articulation of their common beliefs and practices, they seem to have agreed on several key issues that distinguished them from Sunnis. First, they held a purist view of the CALIPH and the office he occupied: moral or religious infractions nullified a person's right to rule. At the same time, however, the Khawarij affirmed the equality of all believing men, permitting anyone to rise to the position of caliph, unlike the Sunnis who restricted the office to members of the tribe of Muhammad, the QURAYSH. Second, and related to the first, they rejected the idea that FAITH, not works, determined one's rightful membership in the community of believers. As a result, the community became the locus of charisma and purity, and the training ground for potential leaders.

Khariji uprisings throughout the seventh and ninth centuries served as a constant reminder of the limits to Sunni authority and legitimacy, which in turn provoked Sunni thought and propaganda, including discourse on the Khawarij. Some medieval Sunni sources portray the Khawarij as pious but well-intentioned Muslims whose moral zealotry compromised their ability to live peacefully within society; most maintain that Khariji piety and purity were a cover for more blatant political interests. By the year 1000 C.E., historical references to the Khawarij take on a generic meaning of "rebels." In modern Arab Muslim societies, the name Khawarij has been used to anathematize those who use religion to justify political violence, such as the assassins of Egyptian president Anwar al-SADAT (1918–81).

See also HERESY; *KAFIR*; SUNNISM; THEOLOGY.

Jeffrey T. Kenney

Further reading: Ignaz Goldziher, *Introduction to Islamic Theology and Law.* Translated by Andras and Ruth Hamori (Princeton, N.J.: Princeton University Press, 1981); Jeffrey T. Kenney, *Muslim Rebels: The Kharijites and the Politics of Extremism in Egypt* (New York: Oxford University Press, 2006); Michael G. Morony, *Iraq after the Muslim Conquest* (Princeton, N.J.: Princeton University Press, 1984); Julius Wellhausen, *The Religio-Political Factions in Early Islam.* Translated by R. C. Ostle and S. M. Walzer, edited by R. C. Ostle (New York: American Elsevier Publishing Company, 1975).

Khilafat Movement (also known as the Caliphate Movement)

The 1919–24 movement by Muslims in INDIA to advance the Ottoman SULTAN as the CALIPH (Arabic: *khalifa*) of all Muslims. This movement demonstrated Indian Muslim PAN-ISLAMISM, represented an attempt to mobilize the diverse body of Indian Muslims using the symbols of Islam and the ancient office of the CALIPHATE, and it served as the means by which Muslims came to participate in the Indian independence movement.

The caliph was the head of the Islamic community in Sunni Islam. Although some believe the office ended with the capture of BAGHDAD by the Mongols in 1258, throughout Islamic history there have been numerous attempts to revitalize the office, or at least to claim the caliph as a title. The Khilafat Movement represents a modern attempt to regenerate the ancient office in a time when Muslims were being threatened both by the downfall of the Ottomans, the last great Islamicate empire, and by Western COLONIALISM. By the end of World War I the British Empire stretched from Canada to Hong Kong, with most of the world's Muslims ruled by a European power. This had been the case for Indian Muslims since 1857, when the British brought the 300-year-old Mughal Empire to its final end. Thus, the Khilafat Movement was guided by Muslim elites whose immediate ancestors had ruled India for centuries.

Led by the brothers Muhammad Ali (d. 1931), his brother Shaukat Ali (d. 1938), Abul Kalam Azad (d. 1956), and Mukhtar Ahmad Ansari (d. 1936), among others, the movement successfully, albeit briefly, mobilized Indian Muslims, communities long separated from each other by sect, language, and region. It aimed to preserve the caliphate as the center of the Muslim world and to keep Arab lands and holy sites free from non-Muslim control. To this end, Khilafatists led delegations to Europe several times to press their demands; a number were imprisoned by the British on charges of conspiracy.

The movement received a major boost when Mohandas K. GANDHI (d. 1948), the leader of the Indian National Congress, took up the Khilafat cause in 1919 as part of the noncooperation movement against British rule. Noncooperation involved boycotting British goods, giving up political posts in the Anglo-Indian government, and, generally speaking, not cooperating with the mechanisms of British rule. Since Hindus dominated the Congress, adoption of the Khilafat cause did much to further Muslim-Hindu cooperation on an all-India scale and led to the belief that Indian self-government was in the best interest of India's Muslims.

Muslim-Hindu unity was not to last. Gandhi's suspension of noncooperation and factionalism, based on personal, religious, and ideological differences, ended the delicate Khilafat-Congress alliance in 1922. The final blow came when Mustafa Kemal ATATURK (d. 1938), the leader of the newly secular nation of TURKEY, abolished the caliphate in 1924. It is ironic that Indian Khilafatists were stressing Pan-Islamism at a time when most nations with Muslim majorities, Turkey included, sought to base their legitimacy along cultural and linguistic and not religious lines. Such "ethnolinguistic nationalism" characterized much of the Muslim world until the 1960s, perhaps dooming the Khilafat Movement to failure.

Kerry San Cherico

Further reading: Ali Abd Al-Raziq, "The Caliphate and the Bases of Power." In *Islam in Transition: Muslim Perspectives,* 2d ed., edited by John J. Donohue and John L. Esposito, 24–31 (New York and Oxford: Oxford University Press, 2007); L. Carl Brown, *Religion and the State: The Muslim Approach to Politics* (New York: Columbia University Press, 2000); Hamid Enayat, *Modern Islamic Political Thought* (1982. Reprint, London and New York: I.B. Tauris, 2005); Gail Minault, *The Khilafat Movement: Religious Symbolism and Political Mobilization in India* (New York: Columbia University Press, 1982).

Khoja   *See* AGA KHAN; ISMAILI SHIISM.

Khomeini, Ruhollah (Ayatollah Khomeini, Khumayni, Khomeyni) (1902–1989) *the most important Shii leader and jurist of the 20th century, founder of the Islamic Republic of Iran in 1979*

Ruhollah Khomeini was born in the central Iranian town of Khomein. He came from a family of Twelve-Imam Shii jurists that claimed to be *sayyid*s, descendants of the prophet MUHAMMAD

(d. 632) through the seventh Imam, Musa al-Kazim (d. 799). Khomeini's father was murdered shortly after he was born. He was raised by his mother and paternal aunt until both died when he was about 17. His elder brother Murtaza, a religious scholar, also cared for him and tutored him in Arabic grammar.

Khomeini began his EDUCATION in a government school, but he also attended a religious school (*maktab*) and memorized the QURAN while still a child. In 1920, with the encouragement of his brother, he went to the Shii MADRASA in Arak, a town near Isfahan, to study with Ayatollah Abd

Ayatollah Ruhollah Khomeini on the eve of his return to Iran in 1979 *(AP Photos)*

al-Karim Hairi Yazdi (d. 1936), one of the leading scholars in IRAN at the time. He and fellow students followed Ayatollah Hairi Yazdi to the Shii shrine city of Qom the following year. There he studied Islamic jurisprudence (FIQH), in addition to Quran commentary and HADITH, at the feet of leading Iranian religious scholars. In addition to his formal studies in Islamic law, he also immersed himself in the study of Gnostic mysticism (*irfan*), philosophy, ethics, and Persian poetry. He was known for his ability to quote for hours by heart from the works of Persian mystical poets such as JALAL AL-DIN RUMI (d. 1273), Saadi (d. ca. 1291), and Hafiz (d. ca. 1380). Under the guidance of Mirza Muhammad Ali Shahabadi (d. 1950) he became fascinated by the writings of the Andalusian Sufi MUHYI AL-DIN IBN AL-ARABI (d. 1240) and the Persian visionary Sadr al-Din Shirazi (also known as Mullah Sadra, d. 1641). The interest he showed for these subjects distinguished him from other students and teachers, who regarded such topics as secondary at best, after study of law and other traditional madrasa subjects. At the age of 27 Khomeini married Batul, the daughter of an ayatollah from Tehran. They had five CHILDREN—three daughters and two sons.

During the 1930s Khomeini completed his advanced studies and became a MUJTAHID in the Usuli tradition of Shii jurisprudence in Qom. This school of legal thought regarded the jurist as a living representative of the 12th Imam during his Occultation (GHAYBA), in contrast to the Akhbari School, which emphasized imitation (*taqlid*) of the Shii Imams and the traditions of the past. *Mujtahids* could exercise authority (*wilaya*) with respect to the needs of widows and orphans, the administration of pious endowments and religious institutions (mosques, shrines, madrasas), and the general welfare of the community. In general they were to uphold the Islamic ethical principle of "commanding the right and forbidding the wrong." Khomeini refrained from engaging overtly in politics at the time, deferring to senior leaders of the Shii religious establishment, some of whom were politically active, and others who felt that they should remain aloof from politics. However, his lectures on ethics and morality drew large audiences in Qom and also attracted the attention of the police. Observing that Islam was in decline and that Western influence was growing as a result of the modernizing reforms of REZA SHAH PAHLAVI (r. 1925–41), he sought to bring about the moral regeneration of Iranian society. His first book, *The Unveiling of Secrets (Kashf-i asrar)*, published in 1942, also signaled his interest in using his religious ideals to guide public life. In it he attacked secularist critics of the mullahs and traditional SHIISM. He declared that government must rule in accordance with Islamic law, which is founded upon reason. This book was written during World War II, when Reza Shah was overthrown and Iran was being occupied by British and Russian troops.

After the war Khomeini became one of the most respected mullahs in Qom. He continued to avoid politics out of deference to the leading ayatollah at the time, Sayyid Husayn Borujerdi (d. 1962), who favored reconciliation and unity among Muslims, including Sunnis. Khomeini only came out publicly against MOHAMMAD REZA PAHLAVI (r. 1941–79), the former shah's son and successor, and his supporters in 1963, after Borujerdi's death. Now a *marjaa al-taqlid,* or top-ranked AYATOLLAH, he was particularly angered by the growing influence of the United States in Iran as a result of the aid it extended to the shah's White Revolution. This was a comprehensive reform program, imposed by the government without popular consultation. It was intended to modernize Iranian economy and society, as well as make Iran into a close ally of the United States and a bulwark against Soviet expansion into the Middle East during the cold war years. The program featured land reform and the granting to women of the right to vote. Khomeini was arrested in June 1963 for speaking out against the shah at the Fayziya Mosque in Qom, which sparked violent anti-shah demonstrations. The

shah finally deported him in November 1964 after he protested against legal immunities that the shah had granted Americans working in Iran. Khomeini first went to Turkey, and then was allowed into IRAQ. He took up residence in the Shii holy city of Najaf, where the leading Shii madrasa was located.

While in exile Khomeini developed a network of support among Iranians living outside of Iran and students and colleagues in Iranian madrasas. He wrote a book on Shii *fiqh, Tahrir al-Wasila* (a commentary on an earlier *fiqh* manual by Abu Hasan al-Isfahani), which gave political meaning to traditional religious practices. In it he stated that Islam does not allow the separation of religion and politics. Inspired in part by the political activism of Ayatollah Muhammad Baqir al-Sadr (d. 1980), a leading Iraqi ayatollah in Najaf, and the Daawa Party, he developed the theory of Islamic theocracy, or "governance of the jurist" (*wilayat al-faqih* or *wilayat-i faqih*), delivered in the form of addresses to students at Najaf. These addresses were collected in the book *Islamic Government (Hukumat-i islami)* or *Wilayat-i faqih,* first published in 1970 and later translated into a number of languages including Arabic, Urdu, Turkish, French, and English. The key proposition in this book is that there is not only no division between Islam and politics but also that the political and religious spheres both fall under the authority (*wilaya*) of the supreme expert of *fiqh*—the *marjaa al-taqlid,* acting on behalf of the Hidden Imam, who was guided and inspired by God. Some scholars have proposed that Khomeini's ideology concerning this supreme leader was also inspired by his mystical thought, particularly the concept of the PERFECT MAN—a kind of philosopher-king who would lead others to moral perfection in a corrupt world, guided by an intimate knowledge of God's will. In essence the book constituted a condemnation of worldly political systems—monarchies, capitalist democracies, socialism, and COMMUNISM. Khomeini's vision was unique to Islamic history, for no jurist before him had stated that worldly government must be in the hands of one of the ULAMA.

The shah's government was increasingly hated by many Iranians, and the international community objected to its HUMAN RIGHTS abuses. Meanwhile, revolutionary currents were already circulating in the country due both to awareness of anticolonial revolutions in other countries in Africa and Asia and to the influence of leftist organizations. The spark that ultimately ignited Iran's revolutionary fire came in the form of a personal attack on Khomeini published in an Iranian newspaper on January 6, 1978. Demonstrations erupted in Qom, Tabriz, and swept across the country to the streets of Tehran, the capital. On September 24, 1978, the shah won the consent of SADDAM HUSAYN (d. 2006), then the Iraqi vice president, to have Khomeini deported from Iraq because of his role in stirring antigovernment demonstrations in Iran. Khomeini went to Paris, where he remained until the Shah fled Iran with his wife on January 15, 1979. The Grand Ayatollah returned triumphantly to Tehran on February 1 and was greeted by millions of cheering Iranians.

During the next 10 years, Ayatollah Khomeini sought to rule Iran in accordance with the principles set forth in his book on Islamic government. In effect he created a theocratic government with totalitarian leanings. In addition to being known as the *marjaa al-taqlid,* he was also officially designated as Iran's Leader of the Revolution (*rahbare inqilab*), or Supreme Leader (*rahbare muazzam*). He successfully transferred power into the hands of the Shii mullahs and eradicated or exiled his secular and religious opponents within a few months after his return. Khomeini also oversaw the drafting and implementation of a CONSTITUTION for the fledgling Islamic Republic before the end of his first year in office. The constitution allowed for a government consisting of legislative, executive, and judicial branches, but it placed these under the control

of religious authority. In November 1979 he gave his approval to the seizure of the U.S. embassy in Tehran by a group of students and revolutionaries, provoking a crisis in U.S.-Iranian relations that has continued until today. He also sought to spread the revolution to other countries, calling upon Muslims to rise up against monarchies and pro-Western governments.

Thinking that Iran's military defenses had been weakened by the revolution, Saddam Husayn invaded the country in September 1980. Under Khomeini's lead, the Iranians counterattacked, resulting in a costly nine-year war of attrition in which a million people lost their lives. Even as the war reached a stalemate in the late 1980s, Khomeini refused to negotiate peace with Iraq. The conflict did not end until after Khomeini's death.

In January 1988 Khomeini took his idea of "governance of the jurist" to what might be considered to be its most extreme limit. He proclaimed that the power of the Supreme Leader was absolute, and that his rulings could take precedence over any other Islamic laws, including those concerning prayer, fasting, and performing the hajj. Also, in a move to curb dissent and win popular support among Muslims at home and abroad, Khomeini issued a FATWA in February 1988 calling for the death of SALMAN RUSHDIE, the Indian author of The Satanic Verses, a controversial novel that retold the life of Muhammad and poked fun at religious dictators like Khomeini.

Ayatollah Khomeini died on June 3, 1989. He was buried in Tehran's Behesht-i Zahra cemetery, where his gold-domed tomb has become a shrine for Shii pilgrims. He was survived by one of his sons, Ahmad, also a MULLAH, who died in 1995. All of his daughters married into the families of merchants and Shii religious scholars. Some of his grandchildren also became mullahs.

See also AKHBARI SCHOOL; ETHICS AND MORALITY; GOVERNMENT, ISLAMIC; GULF WARS; POLITICS AND ISLAM; *SAYYID;* SATANIC VERSES; TWELVE-IMAM SHIISM; USULI SCHOOL.

Further reading: Ruhallah Khomeini, *Islam and Revolution: Writings and Declarations of Imam Khomeini.* Translated by Hamid Algar (Berkeley, Calif.: Mizan Press, 1981); Vali Nasr, *The Shia Revival: How Conflicts within Islam Will Shape the Future* (New York: W.W. Norton, 2007); Ali Rahnema, "Khomeini's Search for Perfection: Theory and Reality." In *Pioneers of Islamic Revival,* edited by Ali Rahnema, 64–97 (London: Zed Books, 2005).

khums   See SHIISM.

khutba   See SERMON.

Koran   See QURAN.

kufr   See KAFIR.

kuttab (Arabic: writing school)

A traditional Islamic QURAN school providing elementary levels of EDUCATION, the *kuttab* is also sometimes known as a *maktab,* though occasionally the two had separate functions. The *kuttab* curriculum consisted primarily of memorizing the Quran and learning the fundamentals of Islamic belief and practice. But it could also include study of Arabic grammar, Arabic or Persian classical poetry, and basic arithmetic. Instruction was centered on memorization through dictation, writing, and recitation, with little or no teaching time devoted to the meaning of the texts.

In the Middle Ages only a minority of boys from the ages of about four to 10 were given the opportunity to study at a *kuttab.* In most regions and periods, girls were excluded from attending, but this situation changed in the 19th and 20th centuries. Upper-class and elite families usually hired tutors to teach their children at home, but *kuttab*s were, by the early modern period, almost universally available to educate the poor and middle classes. A *kuttab* was often established as a charitable trust (*waqf*). The *kuttab* education could lead to further studies in the Islamic education system of *jami halqas,* or MOSQUE teaching circles, and MADRASAS, or institutions of higher learning for students who proved their ability. But most students probably ended their education after the *kuttab* and were left with little more than the ability to recite portions of complex literary Arabic they were unlikely to comprehend, in the case of Arabic and non-Arabic speakers alike. However, they would have been well prepared to perform their ritual duties as Muslims.

This institution developed very early in the Islamic period and spread widely in the wake of the Arab-Islamic conquests. It was important in all Islamicate lands, serving as the initial introduction to education as well as playing an important role in Islamization. The *kuttab* was a key feature of Islamicate civilization for many centuries; however, educational reforms from the mid-19th century to the present day have increasingly led to its decline. The functions of the *kuttab* were largely taken over by public, state-funded educational systems. In states where primary education was not universally provided until late in the 20th century, such as LIBYA, SAUDI ARABIA, and YEMEN, the *kuttab* remained the only source of education available in rural areas. The *kuttab* has been revived in some regions where the educational system has been completely secularized, for example, by Indian Muslims after partition (1947) and in ALGERIA during the 1930s. In some states, such as EGYPT and MOROCCO, the *kuttab* was modified and integrated into the national school system or it remains as an important alternative to the Islamic education provided in the public schools.

See also LITERACY.

Shauna Huffaker

Further reading: Ahmad Shalaby, *History of Muslim Education* (Beirut: Dar al-Kashshaf, 1954); Gregory

Starrett, *Putting Islam to Work: Education, Politics and Religious Transformation in Egypt* (Berkeley: University of California Press, 1998); Joseph S. Szyliowicz, *Education and Modernization in the Middle East* (Ithaca, N.Y.: Cornell University Press, 1973).

Kuwait   *See* GULF STATES.

Kyrgyzstan   *See* CENTRAL ASIA AND THE CAUCASUS.

L

Lat, al- *See* GODDESS.

Latin America

According to some scholars, Islam was first established in Latin America between the 11th and 12th centuries as a result of maritime contacts established by African Muslim sailors. The same scholars support the idea of a Muslim European influence in the 16th century stemming from the participation of *moriscos* (Andalusian Muslims who remained in Spain under Christian rulers after 1492) in the discovery and conquest of the continent. However, these first origins of Islam in Latin America are still debated. The first Muslim population to arrive of which we have specific data were the African Muslim slaves brought to the continent by the Dutch, French, and British colonial powers. Later on, in the 19th century, following the abolition of SLAVERY, the recruitment of indentured labor from INDIA and INDONESIA brought to Latin America a number of Indian and Indonesian Muslims, mainly to the present-day countries of Guyana, Suriname and Panama. Following this, in the last decades of the 19th century, Muslim and Christian Arabs from Greater SYRIA (the Mediterranean Levant) emigrated to and settled in Latin America as a consequence of both the devastating effects of the ongoing economic crisis of the Ottoman Empire and specific cases of religious persecution of Christian communities.

The Muslim community in Latin America today is small in size, diverse in character, and grouped in several countries. Although no exact statistics of the total Muslim population exist, it is estimated that the Muslim community constitutes less than 1 percent of the total population of Latin America. Suriname, Guyana, and Trinidad have the largest number of Muslims followed by Brazil and Argentina.

Although not the largest in number, Brazil has one of the strongest Muslim communities. Despite a number of African Muslim slaves who were brought to the country during the 17th and 18th centuries, the current Muslim community dates to the ARAB emigration in the last decades of the 19th century. It is concentrated mainly in the state of São Paulo, where the first mosque was established in 1950. In 1968 the Islamic Dawa Center of Latin America for the spread of Islam was founded.

Suriname has the largest Asian Muslim population, 26 percent of its total population. The Surinamese Muslim community originates from the indentured Indian and Indonesian labor brought by the Dutch and the British at the turn of the

20th century. The Indonesian identity of some members of the community is visible in specific practices that are linked to those in Indonesia, such as the orientation of their mosques facing west instead of east, following the practice of mosques in Indonesia, an issue that has created some controversy among Muslims in Suriname.

See also CANADA; COLONIALISM; *DAAWA*; UNITED STATES.

Maria del Mar Logrono

Further reading: Hisham Aidi, "Let Us Be Moors: Islam, Race and 'Connected Histories.'" *Middle East Report* 229 (Winter 2003): 42–53; S. A. H. Ahsani, "Muslims in Latin America: A Survey, Part I." *Journal of the Institute for Muslim Minority Affairs* 5 (1984): 454–463; Omar Hasan Kasule, "Muslims in Latin America: A Survey, Part II." *Journal of the Institute for Muslim Minority Affairs* 5 (1984): 464–467; Ali Kettani, *Muslim Minorities in the World Today* (New York: Institute of Muslim Minority Affairs, 1986); Ignacio Klitch and Jeffrey Lesser, "Introduction: Turko Immigrants in Latin America." *The Americas* 53 (July 1996): 1–14; Larry Luxner, "Muslims in the Caribbean." *Saudi Aramco World* (November–December 1987): 2–11.

law *See FIQH*; SHARIA.

law, international

In the 20th century the ways in which separate communities interact changed radically. Central to this change has been the growth and development of the modern nation-state, a process that began in 17th-century Europe with the Treaty of Westphalia (1648) and that reached its apex in the late 20th century. During the intervening centuries, the modern state replaced other kinds of political organization. Importantly, the development of the modern state coincided with the decline of explicitly religious authority in Europe and the rise of secular authority and the rule of law, giving rise to what is now called the modern state: an entity with fixed geographical borders and a government acting as the ultimate authority within that territory. As the modern state became the template for the entire world in the 20th century, a new body or regime of law was created to systematize the chaotic interactions among those states.

The modern system of international law rests on the authority of a series of international organizations, each having their origins in the creation of the United Nations (UN) in the wake of World War II (1945). Prior to the emergence of modern international law, interaction among political entities often took place on an ad hoc basis. Today, the UN, the World Trade Organization, the International Monetary Fund, and the World Bank oversee a system of law regulating economic, military, and diplomatic relations among states. In theory, international law is based on the equality of all states before the law. Each state must be independent—capable of making decisions free from external coercion—in order for international law to be effective and truly universal. The development of international law, however, raises serious questions about whether or not this is possible.

In this regard, there are three main points to keep in mind. First, the modern state developed in a particular setting—17th-century Europe—and its spread to other settings upset religious and political relationships and modes of organization in those areas. Second, the spread of the modern state often occurred through colonial relationships between European and non-European subjects. The construction of a free, stable, and truly independent state in this context has proved a difficult task, particularly given the tremendous dislocation of populations that accompanied the process. Finally, the idea of international law developed out of Anglo-American and European experiences in the wake of World Wars I and II, and addressed those parties' concerns. Many states that existed at the time and the many that have formed since the close of World War II were excluded from the negotiations that created the system of modern international law.

The vast majority of the conflicts confronting the world today, including ethnic conflict, religious violence, and the widening gap between developed and developing nations, reflect these problems. Many Islamist movements, for example, contest the authority of human-made law and of human sovereignty, both central to the concept of the modern state and to international law. Islamist movements, however, are certainly not alone in raising questions about the validity of international law. In many quarters of the world international law is a contested entity, far from the universally accepted regulatory system envisioned by 19th- and 20th-century American and European scholars and policymakers.

See also ARAB-ISRAELI CONFLICTS; CAMP DAVID ACCORDS; CITIZENSHIP; COLONIALISM; *DAR AL-ISLAM* and *DAR AL-HARB*; GULF WARS; ISLAMISM; HUMAN RIGHTS; JIHAD MOVEMENTS; TERRORISM.

Caleb H. Elfenbein

Further reading: Francis Anthony Boyle, *Foundations of World Order* (Durham, N.C.: Duke University Press, 1999); Richard A. Falk, *Unlocking the Middle East: The Writings of Richard Falk, An Anthology* (New York: Olive Branch Press, 2003); Wilhelm G. Grewe, *The Epochs of International Law* (New York: Walter de Gruyter, 2000); Majid Khadduri, *The Islamic Law of Nations: Shaybani's Siyar* (Baltimore: Johns Hopkins University Press, 1966); Majid Khadduri, The *Law of War and Peace in Islam* (Baltimore: Johns Hopkins University Press, 1955).

Laylat al-Qadr   See NIGHT OF DESTINY.

League of Arab States   See ARAB LEAGUE.

Lebanon (Official name: Lebanese Republic)

Lebanon is a small country of about 3.9 million people (2008 estimate) occupying a land of legendary beauty, which totals a little over 4,000 square miles at the eastern edge of the Mediterranean Sea. It is smaller than the state of Connecticut in the United States. Bordering ISRAEL on the south and SYRIA on the north and east, Lebanon comprises a narrow coastal plain that rises into the Lebanon Mountains, which parallel the sea and peak at the perennially snowcapped 10,131-foot Qurnat al-Sawda. Historically called "The Lebanon," these mountains drop on the east into the Beqaa Valley, which extends to the Anti-Lebanon Mountains at the eastern border. In general the coastline features a combination of rough shores, fine beaches, and ancient ports; the coastal plain is fertile and relatively humid; the Lebanon Mountains are rugged and lush; and the Beqaa is agricultural and relatively dry.

The population is about 60 percent Muslim and 40 percent Christian, with Shiis representing the largest Muslim group (1.2 million, 2005 estimate) and Maronites forming the largest Christian denomination (estimated between 800,000 and 900,000). Lebanon also has a significant DRUZE population. Arabic is the official language, though French, English, and Armenian are also spoken. The government has a democratically elected parliament, a president as chief of state, and a prime minister as head of state. The economy is about 67 percent service-based, 21 percent industry, and 12 percent agriculture, with substantial remittances also coming from large numbers of Lebanese living abroad.

Colonial empires throughout history have been attracted to the desirable location and natural habitat of Lebanon, and a striking legacy of Roman and native Phoenician ruins remains to the present. In the seventh century the Byzantine Empire lost control of what is now Lebanon to the rapidly expanding Islamicate empire, thereby setting the stage for the complex religious demographic that continues to exist today. In a succession of shifting reigns, the Crusaders seized the area in the 12th century, the Mamluks took control in the 13th century, and the Ottomans ascended to power in the 16th century. Facing oppression by the various conquering forces, marginalized religious groups (for example, Maronites, Shiis, and Druze) found refuge in the difficult terrain and remote heights of The Lebanon, thereby ensuring their ongoing participation in the diverse sectarian makeup of the population.

The Lebanon had been considered part of Greater Syria since ancient times, and, in the wake of World War I, in 1920, France received the mandate over much of Greater Syria. Later the same year the French established Greater Lebanon with its modern borders and with the capital at Beirut. Officially the Lebanese Republic, the country gained independence from France in 1943 with a government based on a confessional system of power sharing between its many religious sects. Per the last official census, from 1932, when Christians were the majority, the president is always a Maronite Christian, the prime minister a Sunni Muslim, and the speaker of parliament a Shii Muslim. While the demography has shifted and given rise to a Muslim majority, Lebanon's relatively high percentage of Christians continues to be unique among Arab countries.

Muslim sects include Sunnis, Twelve-Imam Shiis, Ismaili Shiis, Alawis, and Druze. Christian sects include Maronite, Greek Catholic, Roman Catholic, Greek Orthodox, Jacobite (Syrian Orthodox), Armenian Orthodox (Gregorian), Armenian Catholic, Assyrian (Nestorian), Chaldean, and Protestant. Large numbers of Palestinian refugees fled to Lebanon after the Arab-Israeli wars of 1948 and 1967, and southern Lebanon became an important base for the PALESTINE LIBERATION ORGANIZATION (PLO). Jews played an integral role in Lebanese society until they emigrated in large numbers under increasing pressures fomented especially by the Six-Day War of 1967 and the Israeli invasion of Lebanon in 1982, which ended PLO control in the south and gave rise to HIZBULLAH, a Lebanese Shii guerrilla and social welfare organization.

Underlying dissatisfactions with the sectarian power balance coupled with a long history of foreign meddling that was increasingly fueled by the Israeli-Palestinian conflict led to the Civil War of 1975–90. The brutality and chaos of this notorious war shattered any image of the tolerant pluralistic society for which Lebanon had been so well known. While resolution of the underlying causes of the war has remained elusive, substantial reconstruction was undertaken in Beirut, and Lebanon regained its attraction as a tourist destination in the late 1990s and early 2000s. This situation, however, began to deteriorate with the assassination of Rafiq Hariri, the former prime minister (1992–98, 2000–04), in February 2005 by unknown assailants. A hostage-taking incident at the Lebanese-Israeli border in summer 2006 resulted in a short-lived Israeli-Lebanese war that involved Hizbullah missile attacks on Israel and Israeli airstrikes and troop movements in Lebanon. The Lebanese infrastructure was seriously damaged, especially in the south. United Nations troops were introduced into the country to facilitate peace-keeping efforts in the war's aftermath.

See also ALAWI; ARAB-ISRAELI CONFLICTS; ARMENIANS; CHRISTIANITY AND ISLAM; COLONIALISM; CRUSADES; MAMLUK; OTTOMAN DYNASTY; SHIISM; SUNNISM.

Kenneth S. Habib

Further reading: Asad AbuKhalil, *Historical Dictionary of Lebanon* (Lanham, Md.: Scarecrow Press, 1998); Helena Cobban, *The Shia Community and the Future of Lebanon* (Washington, D.C.: American Institute for Islamic Affairs, 1985); Lara Deeb, *An Enchanted Modern: Gender and Public Piety in Shii Lebanon* (Princeton, N.J.: Princeton University Press, 2006); Philip Khuri Hitti, *Lebanon in History: From the Earliest Times to the Present*, 3d ed. (New York: St. Martin's Press, 1967); Michael Johnson, *Class and Client in Beirut: The Sunni Muslim Community and the Lebanese State, 1840–1985* (Atlantic Highlands, N.J.: Ithaca Press, 1986).

legal schools *See* FIQH; SHARIA.

Libya (Official name: Great Socialist People's Libyan Arab Jamahiriya [Peoples' Republic])

Libya is a North African country with an area of nearly 1.8 million square miles, comparable in size to the state of Alaska. It is bounded by the Mediterranean Sea to the north; EGYPT to the east; Niger, Chad, and SUDAN to the south; and TUNISIA and ALGERIA to the west. Most of the population (about 6 million, 2008 estimate) lives in a narrow belt near the coastline. About 97 percent are Berbers and Arabs, the rest being Europeans, Turks, and South Asians. Libyans, with the exception of a small number of Ibadi Muslims, are Sunnis (97 percent) who follow the MALIKI LEGAL SCHOOL like other North African Muslims. The northeastern part of the country is known as Cyrenaica, after the ancient Greek city of Cyrene. In Late Antiquity this region had a Jewish and Christian population. In 1948 there were about 38,000 Jews left in the country, almost all of whom have since migrated to ISRAEL. The modern capital is Tripoli, a city on the Mediterranean littoral.

Once part of the Greek, Roman, and Byzantine empires, the coastal region of Libya was incorporated into the Islamicate empire by Muslim armies that came from Egypt and Arabia during the reign of the third caliph, UTHMAN IBN AFFAN (r. 644–656). It obtained provincial status in various empires during the ensuing centuries, while the expanses of the Sahara and its oases were in the hands of ARAB and BERBER tribes and tribal confederacies. Libyan ports served as havens for pirates who raided Mediterranean shipping when governmental control was weak. Tripoli became part of the Ottoman Empire in 1551 and remained under intermittent Ottoman control until the Italian invasion of 1911. .

The Italians emulated France and other European powers by creating a colonial base in North Africa. They wanted Libya to be their Fourth Shore, part of a modern Roman Empire. Their ability to control land beyond the coast, however, met with strong resistance from tribal con-

federations led by the Sanusi Sufi Order. This order had been founded in Mecca in 1837 by an Algerian shaykh, Muhammad ibn Ali al-Sanusi (1787–1859), who claimed descent from the prophet MUHAMMAD through his daughter FATIMA. Because the order followed a simple form of SUFISM that lacked ecstatic rituals and promoted a strong work ethic, it won a wide following among BEDOUINS and Berbers. Centered in Cyrenaica, the order established a network of lodges for religious, educational, and social gatherings that stretched across the oases of the Sahara and into some of the northern cities. Although the Sanusi Sufis preferred to live a life of piety and study, they called for a jihad against foreign invaders, fighting the French in Chad, then the Italians in Libya. The French were able to defeat them, and later the Italians, but only after a guerrilla war that lasted for nearly 22 years. While the Sanusi leadership resided in exile in Egypt, the anticolonial war was fought by Bedouin led by tribal leaders such as Umar al-Mukhtar (1862–1931), a village Quran teacher. The Libyan resistance was quelled only when Italian forces, with the approval of Italian dictator Benito Mussolini, isolated the guerrillas in the mountains and blocked their access to civilian supporters. The conflict was a costly one for the Libyans—100,000 were placed in concentration camps and thousands died or were killed. In 1934 the Italians officially named their prize colony "Libya" after an ancient Greek name for the region of North Africa (based on the ancient Egyptian word LBW or RBW). During the 1930s the number of Italian colonials exceeded 100,000. Their control of Libya ended, however, in World War II as a result of Allied military victories in North Africa.

Britain, France, the United States, and the Soviet Union each had different ideas about what to do with Libya after World War II. In 1951, however, the United Nations General Assembly approved a resolution to grant Libya its independence as a kingdom under the rule of the Grand Sanusi, Sayyid Muhammad Idris (d. 1983). The kingdom was plagued by a poor educational system and a weak economy that depended on foreign aid from the United States. High-grade OIL was discovered in 1959, which eventually led to significant economic and social gains for the country.

In 1969 a group of Libyan officers lead by Captain (later Colonel) Muammar al-Qadhdhafi (b. 1943) deposed the monarchy in a bloodless coup while King Idris was out of the country. In its place they established the Libyan Arab Republic, which drew its inspiration from the ideals of secular Arab nationalism as espoused by President Jamal Abd al-NASIR of Egypt (r. 1954–70). The charismatic al-Qadhdhafi, a Bedouin, has revolutionized Libyan politics and society and has been the supreme leader in the country since the coup. He was once portrayed as an Islamic "fundamentalist" in the Western media because of his efforts to reintroduce Islamic law in the early 1970s. However in the mid-1970s he presented a new political ideology, called the Third Universal Theory, in his *Green Book*. His theory was conceived as an alternative to the "theories" of capitalism and Marxism, and it called for direct popular self-rule through networks of congresses and committees and the creation of a classless society. This theory provided the basis for renaming Libya the "Peoples' Republic" or "Republic of the Masses" (*Jamahiriyya*) in 1977. In reality the government has been an authoritarian one in which political parties are banned and has a record of serious HUMAN RIGHTS violations. Islam was not mentioned explicitly in his *Green Book,* although "religion" was discussed as a binding social and moral force. In his speeches, however, al-Qadhdhafi has portrayed Islam as an anticolonial religion based on the Quran and the use of IJTIHAD (reasoned legal judgment). He has condemned the traditional Islamic legal schools and Sufi orders as reactionary, and has even banned the Sanusis.

Under al-Qadhdhafi's leadership, economic and social conditions have improved significantly for most Libyans. From being one of the most destitute countries in the world it now has a poverty rate below 8 percent and one of the highest LITERACY rates in the Middle East (82.6 percent, 2003 estimate). Libya has improved its relations with its Arab and African neighbors and has been a strong supporter of anticolonial and advocacy movements of developing countries, including the PALESTINE LIBERATION ORGANIZATION and the Irish Republican Army. During the 1980s and 1990s it was viewed as a pariah state and a supporter of TERRORISM. U.S. president Ronald Reagan ordered a bombing of Libyan bases and al-Qaddhafi's residence in April 1986 after several military incidents in the Gulf of Sidra and suspected Libyan involvement in the bombing of a nightclub in West Berlin that killed two U.S. servicemen. The U.S. attacks may have precipitated the retaliatory bombing by Libya of Pan American Flight 103 over Lockerbie, Scotland, in which 270 people perished, including 37 American college students. In recent years, radical Islamist or JIHAD MOVEMENTS have not been able to establish a base in Libya and relations with the United States have improved as a result of the government's willingness to destroy its weapons of mass destruction and related facilities.

See also COLONIALISM; IBADIYYA; RENEWAL AND REFORM MOVEMENTS; SUFISM.

Further reading: Ali Abdullatif Ahmida, *The Making of Modern Libya: State Formation, Colonialization, and Resistance, 1830–1932* (Albany: State University of New York Press, 1994); Mahmoud Ayoub, *Islam and the Third Universal Theory: The Religious Thought of Muammar al-Qaddhafi* (London: KPI Limited, 1987); Dirk Vandewalle, *A History of Modern Libya* (Cambridge: Cambridge University Press, 2006).

literacy

Traditions of literacy have been fundamental to the growth and maintenance of Islamicate societies throughout the world. According to Sura 96 of the QURAN, often considered the first revelation delivered to MUHAMMAD by the angel GABRIEL,

Muhammad was commanded to read (*iqra*). The scriptural nature of Islam made literacy a primary vehicle for the dissemination of the faith, as well as a virtue for pious Muslims wanting to read the Quran and other religious texts.

As the Islamic religion spread beyond the Arabian Peninsula, Arabic, the language of the Quran, became a lingua franca for trade and government as well as religious EDUCATION and the literary arts. Prominent notables, as well as merchants and professionals, were careful to give their children the gift of literacy, at least in the Quran. Moreover, prominent institutions of learning, such as the House of Wisdom in BAGHDAD and al-AZHAR University in CAIRO, flourished at the height of the Islamicate empires.

Despite the rich legacy of literacy in Muslim lands, however, widespread literacy has been a more recent phenomenon, as in many other regions of the globe, as a result of the introduction of the printing press and, more recently, new electronic technologies. Modern governments in the Middle East have had varying success in spreading literacy in the postcolonial era. Reformers such as the Iraqi Sati al-Husri (1869–1967) proclaimed the importance of mass education for the success of the modern nation-state, while President JAMAL ABD AL-NASIR (d. 1970) expanded university education far beyond its traditional class boundaries in Egypt. Policies such as these did much to bring mass literacy closer to a reality for the modern Middle East.

However, many Muslim countries continue to struggle with literacy at the dawn of the 21st century. For example, among the largest Muslim populations in 2005, Indonesians had a literacy rate of 87.9 percent, but Pakistan's was 48.7 percent and Bangladesh's was 41.1 percent. The literacy rate among India's Muslim population was 59.1 percent. As of 2005 Egypt had a literacy rate of 55.6 percent, Sudan a rate of 59 percent, Iran a rate of 80 percent, and Saudi Arabia a rate of 79.4 percent. Jordan and Lebanon have been the most successful Arab nations in terms of literacy, reaching a rate of over 86 percent in 2005, while Israel had a rate of 96.9 percent. In TURKEY it was 88.3 percent. Although the majority of adults living in Muslim countries are literate, there is still much work to be done in a number of areas to achieve literacy rates that match those of top-tier countries of the world.

See also ADAB; ARABIC LANGUAGE AND LITERATURE; BOOKS AND BOOKMAKING; *KUTTAB*; MADRASA; ULAMA.

Nancy L. Stockdale

Further reading: Jack Goody, *The Interface between the Written and the Oral* (Cambridge: Cambridge University Press, 1987); Irfan Habib, Iqtidar Alam Khan, and K. P. Singh, "Problems of the Muslim Minority in India." *Social Scientist* 4 (June 1976): 67–72; Paul Lund, "Arabic and the Art of Printing." *Saudi Aramco World* 32 (March–April 1981): 20–35; Golnar Mehran, "Social Implications of Literacy in Iran." *Comparative Education Review* 36 (May 1992): 194–211; Brian V. Street, ed., *Literacy and Development: Ethnographic Perspectives* (London: Routledge, 2001).

literature   *See* AFRICAN LANGUAGE AND LITERATURE; ARABIC LANGUAGE AND LITERATURE; PERSIAN LANGUAGE AND LITERATURE; TURKISH LANGUAGE AND LITERATURE.

M

madhhab   *See* SHARIA.

Madina   *See* MEDINA.

madrasa

A place of EDUCATION for Muslim religious leaders and scholars. Islamic education began in the prophet MUHAMMAD's time, but centers of learning did not begin until after the first and second centuries of ISLAM. The most prominent of the earliest madrasas is EGYPT's al-AZHAR, which was opened under the Fatimids in 970 C.E. The opening in BAGHDAD of the Nizamiyya College in 1066 marked the beginning of the madrasa system. Many Nizamiyyas were opened afterward; the point of these madrasas and systems of madrasas in other regions was to create uniform opinion regarding Islamic law and THEOLOGY.

Compared to Jewish Yeshiva schools and Christian scriptural schools, madrasas concentrated on rote memorization of the QURAN, knowledge of correct ritual practice, and the deduction of legal points from the scriptures (*fiqh*), and, in fact, they eventually produced bodies of law. PHILOSOPHY, astronomy, and MATHEMATICS were also taught in medieval Iranian madrasas, but opposition grew in ARAB lands during this time against the study of philosophy, and, after the 14th century, Arab madrasas instead emphasized grammar and rhetoric as well as religious law. Fischer argues that after the 11th century, madrasas in the Arab world displayed little innovation, and intellectual freedom, instead focusing on repetition and commentary. Typically, a lecturer would dictate long quotations to his students, and then he would comment on meaning, content, and style.

At times friction between religion and government arose as scholarly opinions emanating from madrasas began to bear legal weight, because this legal aspect competed with other forms of AUTHORITY such as the court or the state. In 16th-century IRAN, the madrasa system maintained a much greater degree of independence from the state than in the Ottoman Empire, although Iranian rulers built madrasas and granted them endowments. Yet they were also privately supported, and were not absorbed into the state. The OTTOMAN DYNASTY, on the other hand, found it beneficial to control the madrasa system.

Modernizing forces in Europe in the 18th and 19th centuries brought about a new struggle, in which Europeans tried to free education from the church, and to reform education to be more relevant in the Industrial Age. A similar debate arose in the Middle East. In Iran during the 19th century, this resulted in the opening of secular profession schools, and, by the 20th century, Iranian madrasa students became an isolated yet still influential minority. The Ottomans reformed their institutions of higher learning before reforming the madrasa system for elementary students. In 1924 Ataturk's government in TURKEY eliminated the madrasa system in favor of secular education; however, Islamic education was reinstated in the late 1940s. In the second half of the 19th century in Egypt, Muslim Egyptians began to attend secular schools, and a movement arose in the late 19th to the early 20th century to modernize al-Azhar.

Madrasa education, although replaced to a great degree by the rise of systems of modern education, still exists all over the Muslim world. Fazlur Rahman notes that in contemporary Pakistan, madrasas teaching traditional interpretations of Islam flourish mainly in the countryside. He also argues that the more any given region in the Muslim world was affected by Western colonialism, the stronger the hold is in that region of traditional madrasa-style learning by the religious elite.

See also ALIGARH; DEOBAND; KUTTAB; ULAMA; ZAYTUNA MOSQUE.

Sophia Pandya

Further reading: Michael M. J. Fischer, *Iran: From Religious Dispute to Revolution* (Cambridge, Mass.: Harvard University Press, 1980); Fazlur Rahman, *Islam and Modernity: Translation of an Intellectual Tradition* (Chicago: University of Chicago Press, 1982); Charles Michael Stanton, *Higher Learning in Islam: The Classical Period, A.D. 700–1300* (Savage, Md.: Rowman and Littlefield Publishers, 1990).

Mahdi

Meaning "one who is rightly guided" in Arabic, the Mahdi is a messianic figure who, according to some Muslims, will return at the end of time to restore Islam to its original perfection.

Although the word *Mahdi* does not occur in the QURAN, it was used from the earliest days of Islam as an honorific title: the prophet MUHAMMAD was called the Mahdi, as was his son-in-law Ali, and his grandson AL-HUSAYN. However, it was not until the revolt led in the name of Ali's third son, Muhammad ibn al-Hanafiyya, against the UMAYYAD CALIPHATE (661–750 C.E.) that the term *Mahdi* began to refer to an expected ruler who would usher in JUDGMENT DAY.

Although eventually crushed, Ibn al-Hanafiyya's movement was instrumental in shaping the image of the expected Mahdi. Indeed, when his followers began insisting that their leader was not dead but rather hiding in a transcendent realm from which he would one day return to fill the world with JUSTICE, they initiated a doctrine that eventually became one of the central tenets of Shiism: the occultation (GHAYBA) and return (*rajaa*) of the Mahdi.

The doctrine of occultation and return was developed even further after the sudden death of Ismail ibn Jaafar (d. 762), who had originally been designated the seventh Imam. When Ismail was replaced by his younger brother, Musa al-Kazim, a small group of Shiis calling themselves the Ismailis refused to accept the new Imam and instead claimed that Ismail was alive and in occultation as the Hidden Imam, another term for the Mahdi. For the majority of Shiis, however, the line of Imams continued through Musa until the 12th Imam, Muhammad ibn al-Hasan (also known as MUHAMMAD AL-MAHDI), who himself went into final occultation in 941 C.E. as the Mahdi. Thus, by the middle of the 10th century, a complex apocalyptic theology concerning the Mahdi's second coming had become firmly entrenched in Shii THEOLOGY.

As the doctrine of the Mahdi developed in Shiism, the dominant Sunni law schools began to distance themselves from the idea, partly in an attempt to discourage what was becoming both a politically and a socially disruptive theology. And yet, to this day there exists a vigorous debate

The tomb of Muhammad Ahmad, the Sudanese Mahdi, in Omdurman, Sudan *(Juan E. Campo)*

among Sunni religious scholars over both the messianic function and the political role of the Mahdi. In fact, in the 18th and 19th centuries, a number of rebellions against the colonialist powers were led by Sunni Muslims who claimed to be the expected Mahdi, the most famous of whom was the Sudanese Mahdi, Muhammad Ahmad (d. 1885), whose forces managed to keep Britain and EGYPT at bay until 1898.

Nonetheless, it is among the Shia that the doctrine of the Mahdi has had its greatest development. Over the centuries, a number of Shii theologians have prophesied the Mahdi's imminent return, which, according to the traditions, will be heralded by civil wars, false prophets, earthquakes, and the abolition of Islamic law. In the 20th century, these messianic expectations were revived by the tumultuous events of the IRANIAN REVOLUTION OF 1978–1979, which was led by the Ayatollah RUHOLLAH KHOMEINI, whom some Iranians believed to be the expected Mahdi.

See also AHMEDIYYA; BAHAI FAITH; ESCHATOLOGY; ISMAILI SHIISM.

Reza Aslan

Further reading: Jassim M. Hussain, *Occultation of the Twelfth Imam* (London: The Muhammadi Trust, 1982); Moojan Momen, *An Introduction to Shi'i Islam* (New Haven, Conn.: Yale University Press, 1985); Abdulaziz A. Sachedina, *Islamic Messianism* (New York: State University of New York Press, 1981).

Mahdiyya movement

This revolutionary movement was launched in the SUDAN in 1881 by the religious reformer, Muhammad Ahmad, who claimed to be the MAHDI (the rightly guided messianic leader, whose just rule will usher in the end of the age). Like many other 19th-century JIHAD MOVEMENTS, the Mahdiyya had religious elements (fed by widespread eschatological expectations in the region) and political elements (based upon anticolonial sentiments directed toward Turco-Egyptian, and later British, dominance of the Sudan). Ahmad's followers succeeded in establishing an independent state, which implemented a government based upon classical Islamic institutions until its defeat by the British at Omdurman in 1898.

Upon revealing himself to be the long-awaited Mahdi in early 1881, Ahmad called upon Sudanese Muslims to make the HIJRA (emigration) from serving the infidels and to join him in establishing a just Islamic government. Those who answered this appeal were called ANSAR, in imitation of the Medinans who first aided the prophet MUHAMMAD. The Mahdi's jihad was tremendously successful, partially due to unrest within EGYPT that limited the Egyptian government's response and partially due to Ahmad's religious aura, which made Egyptian Muslim soldiers hesitant to fight him. However, shortly after establishing his state, the Mahdi died in 1885, leaving his disciple, Abdallahi, to succeed him as CALIPH. After putting down internal opposition, Abdallahi secured his authority over a broad expanse of territory roughly corresponding to the modern nation of the Sudan. However, the consolidation of British colonial power in Egypt led to an expedition by

Lord Kitchener that conquered the Mahdist state in 1898. Even in defeat, the Mahdists retained widespread popularity. Their descendants formed the Ansar party that pushed for Sudanese independence in the 1950s.

Further reading: Richard A. Bermann, *The Mahdi of Allah* (New York: MacMillan, 1932); P. M. Holt, *The Mahdist State in the Sudan* (London: Oxford University Press, 1958); Rudolf C. Slatin Pasha, *Fire and Sword in the Sudan: A Personal Narrative of Fighting and Serving the Dervishes, 1879–1895.* Translated by Major F. R. Wingate (London: Edward Arnold, 1896); Haim Shaked, *The Life of the Sudanese Mahdi* (New Brunswick, N.J.: Transaction Books, 1978).

Makka   *See* MECCA.

Majnun and Layla

Qays ibn al-Mulawwah, the "most famous of the famous" lovers, is a renowned ancient ARAB poet. Qays is also known by his nom de plume, Majnun, which means "the mad one" or "the one possessed." He was born in the Hijaz region of the Arabian Peninsula (in modern-day SAUDI ARABIA) during the latter half of the seventh century. Majnun is both a famous poet and a character in the Arabic romance associated with his name, namely, the Udhri love story of *Majnun Layla.* His life and love poetry are most fully recorded in a 10th-century multivolume work titled *Kitab al-Aghani,* or *Book of Songs,* produced by a Baghdadi courtier named Abu l-Faraj al-Isfahani.

There are several accounts of how Majnun and his beautiful beloved, named Layla bint al-Harish, fell in love, but the most oft-quoted one is that they fell in love when they were CHILDREN while tending to the flocks of their kin. What happens next between these two star-struck young people is legendary in the Islamic world. After a brief period of courtship between them, during which Majnun publicly serenades her and publicly recites what was then considered to be risqué poetry about his relation with the flirtatious Layla, her family veils her and bars him from seeing her. Afraid that he might lose her, Majnun then asks for her hand in marriage, but he is flatly refused by her father. After being summarily rejected, Majnun, despite numerous attempts by his kin to help him, becomes somewhat deranged and emotionally unstable. The biographical accounts describe how he starts to madly and aimlessly wander about and live with the beasts in the desert; at times, he wanders as far as the boundaries to SYRIA or YEMEN. Even after Layla is married to a wealthy man from another tribe, Majnun continues nostalgically to recall his beloved through his poetry. In the end, Majnun dies in a desert wilderness place remote from his tribal shelter and home. Appropriately, he is found dead by a fan of his verses who travels to Majnun's clan to hear and collect his poems. The burial lament for Majnun is attended by people from Layla's clan, including her father who repents his earlier harshness toward the youth.

Rather like a traveling folktale, the romance of *Majnun Layla* over time has crossed many cultural and linguistic boundaries, and it has spread throughout the Islamic world. It has been composed and recomposed in Persian, Arabic, Turkish, and Urdu literatures in the form of poetry, romance, and drama, and it has even been set to film. It has recently arrived in the West as well; in Germany it was made into a symphony and "Layla" is also a musical composition of Eric Clapton. Through its diffusion, the romance has undergone numerous changes, including acquiring new themes and motifs, as well as experiencing genre transformations. In the medieval Persian literary tradition, two famous authors who composed romance narratives celebrating these two lovers are Nizami (d. ca. 1217) and Jami (d. 1492). Indeed, part of the significance of the *Majnun Layla* romance (alternatively often known in non-Arabic literatures as *Layla Majnun*) is that it played an important role in the development of chronologically later genres, such as mystical Sufi literature, medieval Persian and Urdu love poetry and narratives, and, according to some scholars, medieval European romance.

See also FOLKLORE; PERSIAN LANGUAGE AND LITERATURE.

Ruqayya Yasmine Khan

Further reading: Michael Dols, *Majnun: The Madman in Medieval Islamic Society* (New York: Oxford University Press, 1992); Nizami, *The Story of Layla and Majnun.* Translated and edited by Rudolf Gelpke et al. (New York: Omega Publications, 1997).

maktab See KUTTAB.

Malamati Sufis

All Sufis seek to control the desires of the self (*nafs*), which prevent the individual from reaching God, but while many try to do so by devoting themselves to outward forms of worship, Malamatis reject outward display of their devotion, considering this too to be feeding the self's desire for acceptance by society. Malamati Sufism is not a clearly defined system of beliefs, but a set of practices and a psychology relating to the principle of refraining from actions that would gain the approval of society, including public performance of the prescribed forms of worship. Malamatis do not seek the approval of society, and they do not fear its blame. The Malamati Sufis base their beliefs on the Quranic verse: "They struggle in the path of God and fear not the blame of any blamer" (Q 5:54), and thus their name is derived from the Arabic word *malama*, meaning "blame."

As a consequence of their avoidance of public worship, Malamatis were often accused of not acting in accordance with religious law and condemned by orthodox authorities. Nevertheless, most Malamatis tried to live within the world, wearing clothing that did not attract attention and often working in the marketplace as artisans.

Though similar religious attitudes existed before the advent of Islam, Malamati Sufism in its Islamic form developed in the region of Khurasan in the ninth century, in part as a response to the extroverted asceticism of the Karramis. The first major figure of the Malamati movement was Hamdun al-Qassar (d. 884) of Nishapur, who taught the renunciation of the need to please people, which would lead to actions done in hypocrisy (*riya*). Malamatis did not participate in Sufi rituals such as DHIKR and *samaa* (musical audition), since in doing so their inner states might be revealed.

Because of the invisibility of Malamatis, it is difficult to discern any structured organization under that name and to determine the extent to which their influence spread. It seems likely, though, that the principles of Malamatism led some to purposely seek the blame of others by openly violating religious and social conventions, and these came to be known as Qalandars. The Naqshbandi order may also have been influenced by Malamatis, in its refusal of distinctive clothing and its preference for a silent *dhikr.* In Ottoman lands, Malamati principles were incorporated into the Malami and Hamzawi orders.

See also ASCETICISM; SUFISM.

Mark Soileau

Further reading: Annemarie Schimmel, *Mystical Dimensions of Islam* (Chapel Hill: University of North Carolina Press, 1975); Sara Sviri, "Hakim Tirmidhi and the Malamati Movement in Early Sufism." In *Classical Persian Sufism: From Its Origins to Rumi,* edited by L. Lewisohn (New York: Khaniqahi Nimatullahi Publications, 1993), 583–613; J. Spencer Trimingham, *The Sufi Orders in Islam* (Oxford: Oxford University Press, 1971).

Malaysia

The modern nation of Malaysia consists of the southern half of the Malay Peninsula and the states of Sarawak and Sabah on the northern coast of the island of Borneo. Each of the three components were British colonies, with Malaysia obtaining its independence in 1957. Sabah, Sarawak, and Singapore obtained their independence six years later and joined with Malaysia to create the Federation of Malaysia. At this time, the Sultanate of Brunei (also on Borneo) declined the invitation to join the federation. Singapore was expelled from the federation in 1965.

The present state of Malaysia covers 125,584 square miles, comparable to the area of the state of New Mexico. In 2008, it had a population of approximately 25.3 million. The country's people are ethnically diverse, with Malays constituting 50.8 percent, Chinese 23.8 percent, and Indians 7.1 percent. About 10 percent of the people, primarily residing in Sarawak, are indigenous people who have inhabited the land since prehistoric times. Religiously, the country is about 69 percent Muslim, with almost all Malays professing Sunni Islam. Most of Malaysia's Muslims, including immigrants from Indonesia, follow the SHAFII LEGAL SCHOOL, which was introduced in the 15th century. Islam is also the religion of many of the Indo-Pakistani community, and about one-third of the indigenous people of Sarawak. SUFISM has broad popularity in the country, and there is also a sizeable community of Shii Muslims. Buddhism is professed by about 20 percent of the people,

Sultan Salahuddin Abdul Aziz Shah Mosque in Kuala Lumpur, Malaysia—one of the largest in Southeast Asia
(J. Gordon Melton)

overwhelmingly Chinese. Most of the Indians are Hindus from southern INDIA. Christianity has made an impact primarily among the non-Malay half of the population, and now claims about 9 percent of the population.

From the first century C.E., Malaysia experienced migrations from both China and India and it became the home of kingdoms with Hindu and Buddhist roots. In the 15th century, following the opening of the port of Malacca on the peninsula's west coast, the first conversions to Islam were reported. Through the next century, Islam gradually replaced Buddhism as the dominant faith on the peninsula, and a set of states was established, each headed by a sultan. Islam's initial converts included some among the aristocratic class on the peninsula. It spread among this class over several centuries, often through marriage alliances.

Beginning in the 16th century, a variety of European colonial powers moved into the region. In 1511 the Portuguese seized Malacca. In the next century, the Dutch, in alliance with the sultan of Jahor, drove the Portuguese out. At the end of the 18th century, the British established their trading colony on the northern shore of Borneo and, in 1819, purchased Singapore from the sultan of Jahore, which they managed as an outpost to secure passage through the Straits of Malacca and the Singapore Straits. Shortly thereafter the British concluded a treaty with the Dutch guaranteeing the latter's hegemony in the East Indies (now INDONESIA).

Through the 19th century the British controlled the ports of Penang, Malacca, and Singapore into which they encouraged immigration from China and India to provide cheap labor for the tin mines and rubber plantations. Beginning in 1870 the British encouraged the formation of protectorates over the several sultanates on the Malaysian Peninsula and later in the northern half of Borneo (including Brunei). British rule was not welcomed by many Malays, including Muslim religious leaders who regarded the British as *kafirs* (disbelievers). The Japanese invaded

and occupied the region during World War II. After the war continuation of British colonial rule became increasingly untenable, which led to independence in stages through the 1950s and 1960s. With independence in 1957, Islam was named the state religion. The National Mosque (Masjid Negara), completed in 1965, serves as a symbol of Islam, the country's dominant faith.

Malaysia is a constitutional monarchy consisting of 13 states and one federal territory. Each state has a parliament and a chief minister. The chief ministers of nine of the states are hereditary rulers known as sultans who also oversee the Islamic affairs of their respective states. Every five years there is an election and one of them is selected as monarch. There are four states (Penang, Malacca, Sabah, and Sarawak) that are governed by chief ministers appointed by the government. There is also a national parliament elected by the people with the prime minister the highest elected official. Sarawak and Sabah have no designated head of Islam, but the king oversees the religious affairs of Penang and Malacca.

In 1965 a council for Islamic affairs was created. Operating out of the prime minister's office, it coordinates the efforts of the state councils, which advise the sultan on religious matters. The state and national legislatures have some power in legislating for the Muslim community. The constitution of Malaysia contains a provision affirming freedom of religion. At the same time, Islam is the official state religion. The practice of forms of Islam other than Sunni Islam is restricted significantly. Hari Raya Puasa (the end of the fasting season of RAMADAN), Hari Raya Qurban (the Feast of the Sacrifice at the end of the HAJJ pilgrimage), and the Prophet Muhammad's birthday (MAWLID) have been designated official national holidays. The issue of Muslims wishing to convert to another faith, primarily Buddhism or Christianity, has been a sensitive one in Malaysia. Ethnic Malays must overcome particularly difficult obstacles to leave the Islamic faith for another religion. In 2001 a High Court judge ruled that the constitution defined an ethnic Malay as "a person who professes the religion of Islam." There are few obstacles to anyone who wishes to convert from Buddhism or Christianity to Islam.

During the last decades of the 20th century and the early 21st century Malaysia has been dominated by the United Malays National Organization (UMNO), seen as the more moderate political party of the Muslim community. It is opposed by the Parti-Islam se-Malaysia (PAS), a more conservative group that has as its stated goal the transformation of Malaysia into an Islamic state that would adhere to sharia law, including its punishments, such as amputation and stoning.

See also BUDDHISM AND ISLAM; BUMIPUTRI; DAR UL-ARQAM; COLONIALISM; CRIME AND PUNISHMENT; ID AL-ADHA; SULTAN.

J. Gordon Melton

Further reading: R. W. Hefner, The Politics of Multiculturalism: Pluralism and Citizenship in Malaysia, Singapore, and Indonesia (Honolulu: University of Hawaii Press, 2001); J. A. Nagata, The Reflowering of Malaysian Islam: Modern Religious Radicals and Their Roots (Vancouver: University of British Columbia Press, 1984); Michael G. Peletz, Islamic Modern: Religious Courts and Cultural Politics in Malaysia (Princeton, N.J.: Princeton University Press, 2002); P. Sloane, Islam, Modernity, and Entrepreneurship among the Malays (New York: St. Martin's Press in association with St. Antony's College Oxford, 1999).

Malcolm X (Malcolm Little) (1925–1965)
Black nationalist, activist, and Muslim leader who advocated Black pride and separatism for African Americans

Malcolm Little, the future Malcolm X, was born in Omaha, Nebraska, and grew up primarily in Boston. His father, Earl Little, was a Baptist minister who openly supported the United Negro Movement and its leader, Marcus Garvey (1887–1940). Consequently the family endured frequent threats from white extremist groups. These threats even-

Malcom X *(Library of Congress)*

tually culminated in their father's murder. Later Malcolm's mother was institutionalized due to stress and mental illness, and, as a result, Malcolm was separated from his family and went to live with his half-sister, Ella, in Boston. Subsequently he entered a phase of crime, gambling, and drug abuse. In 1946 he was charged with robbery and imprisoned in Massachusetts. It was in this context that Malcolm was introduced to the NATION OF ISLAM. At the age of 22, he became a self-avowed member of the movement, passionately supporting its teachings, including the perception of whites as a "devil race," the need for black liberation and separatism, and the goal of displaying personal discipline through modest Islamic dress and eating habits. Malcolm left prison in 1952 and began working for Elijah Muhammad (1897–1975), the leader of the Nation of Islam. Malcolm idolized Elijah and soon took a leadership position within the Nation. During this time Malcolm exchanged the surname "Little," perceived as a "slave name," for the symbolic "X" to denote his lost African heritage. Soon he became a provocative public figure and militant spokesperson for the Nation of Islam. With Elijah Muhammad's health declining it appeared logical that Malcolm X would take over as head of the Nation. Jealousy among other group members led to insinuating rumors circulating about Malcolm. At the same time, some began to question Elijah Muhammad's character, with charges of adultery and hypocrisy leveled against him.

Under pressure from these charges, Malcolm was marginalized within the Nation and, in 1964, he formally announced he was leaving the organization to start his own group, Muslim Mosque, Inc. He also announced that he planned to travel through Africa and the Middle East and make a HAJJ, or pilgrimage, to MECCA, the Muslim holy city. Following this pilgrimage Malcolm underwent another phase of transformation. During his journey abroad he encountered white Muslims who openly embraced him, as well as the spectacle of Muslims of different skin colors and cultures praying in unity. With this new understanding of ISLAM Malcolm was forced to reconsider his separatist views and, upon his return to America, he adopted the name El Hajj Malik el-Shabazz to express his new identity. While giving a speech in Harlem on February 21, 1965, Malcolm was assassinated by three members of the Nation of Islam, leaving his wife, Betty Shabazz, a widow. Despite Malcolm's shifting views toward orthodox Islam near the end of his life, his charismatic leadership gave African Americans a model in expressing the right to feel anger and new viewpoints concerning white domination. Malcolm's ideologies, preserved in *The Autobiography of Malcolm X,* continue to influence ongoing debates concerning racial relations and African American identity.

See also AFRICAN AMERICANS, ISLAM AMONG; UNITED STATES.

Mehnaz Sahibzada

Further reading: Martha F. Lee, *The Nation of Islam: An American Millenarian Movement* (Syracuse, N.Y.: Syracuse University Press, 1996); Eric C. Lincoln, *The Black Muslims of America.* (Trenton, N.J.: Africa World Press, 1994); Clifton E. Marsh, *From Black Muslims to Muslims: The Transition of Separatism to Islam, 1930–1980* (Metuchen, N.J.: Scarecrow Press, 1984); Jane I. Smith, *Islam in America* (New York: Columbia University Press, 1999); Malcolm X, *The Autobiography of Malcolm X,* with the assistance of Alex Haley (London: Penguin, 2001).

Malik ibn Anas (ca. 708–795) *leading jurist of Medina and eponymous founder of the Maliki legal school*

Malik ibn Anas lived most of his life in MEDINA, the city of the prophet MUHAMMAD. In contrast to other early Muslim scholars, he is said to have left the city only in order to go on the hajj to Mecca. He specialized in the study of the HADITH and became famous for developing the idea that customary practice (SUNNA) of the Muslims of what Marshal G. S. Hodgson called "pristine" Medina should serve as a fundamental basis for Islamic law. Students traveled from great distances to study with Malik, and they carried his teachings, which were compiled in a book, the *Muwatta,* to the major centers of Islamic learning in EGYPT, IRAQ, North Africa, and ANDALUSIA (Spain). This book, whose title means "well-trodden path," is one of the most important sources for the study of the development of early Islamic legal tradition. It contains not only the hadith of Muhammad and his Companions, but also reports on the practices of Medina's inhabitants in later generations. Like the hadith collections of al-Bukhari (d. 870) and Muslim (d. 875), it is organized by subject, beginning with the FIVE PILLARS and followed by family law, business transactions, and criminal law. It also has chapters on miscellaneous subjects. Malik's opinions on legal matters were compiled later and became part of the tradition of the MALIKI LEGAL SCHOOL, which bears his name.

See also COMPANIONS OF THE PROPHET; SHARIA.

Further reading: Yasin Dutton, *The Origins of Islamic Law: The Quran, the Muwatta and Madinan Amal* (London: Routledge Curzon, 2002); Wael B. Hallaq, *The Origins and Evolution of Islamic Law* (Cambridge: Cambridge University Press, 2005).

Maliki Legal School

One of the four approved schools (sing.: *madhhab*) of Sunni Islamic law, the Maliki derives its name from the eighth-century scholar of MEDINA Malik ibn Anas (d. 795). Malik's text *Al-Muwatta* is one of the foundational legal tomes of the Maliki school. His approach places almost exclusive emphasis upon the QURAN, HADITH, and Medinese practice (*amal*) as sources of Islamic law. In contrast, Malik's near-contemporary Abu Hanifa (progenitor of the HANAFI LEGAL SCHOOL) drew upon personal reasoning (*ray*) in addition to the textual sources of the Quran and hadith in his legal formulations.

Highly respected as a scholar and collector of hadith, Malik passed on his knowledge to many students, who carried his doctrine throughout Muslim lands. In the decades after his death, Malik's teaching established a following in Qayrawan (modern TUNISIA), ANDALUSIA, (modern Spain), and Iraq. These locations later became centers of the nascent Maliki *madhhab* and were home to influential Maliki scholars such as the Tunisian Abd al-Salam Sahnun, and the Andalusians Yahya ibn Yahya al-Laythi and MUHAMMAD IBN RUSHD (Averroës). Maliki teaching later died out in Andalusia, due to the Christian *reconquista,* and it was supplanted by the SHAFII LEGAL SCHOOL in Iraq and Medina. However, the Maliki School would experience great success in North and WEST AFRICA, where it remains the dominant *madhhab* to this day.

The early Maliki insistence upon traditional Medinese practice gave the school a decidedly practical emphasis. This can be seen in the Maliki development of *istislah,* a procedure that gives precedence in some cases to a tangible human interest over a legal conclusion reached through strict analogical reasoning. However, Maliki jurists have always looked with suspicion upon the principle of *qiyas* (the use of analogy in legal judgments), unlike their brethren in the Hanafi and Shafii schools. The Maliki disinclination to use *qiyas* is such that Maliki jurists sometimes preferred to base their judgments upon weakly attested hadith rather than to employ analogy. While accepting the concept of IJMAA (scholarly consensus), Maliki scholars have frequently given preference to the *ijmaa* of Medina, since it was the city of the Prophet and his companions, as well as the home of Malik himself.

These particular emphases have led to distinct Maliki stances on matters such as inheritance law, marriage and divorce, and dietary restrictions. However, in most areas, Maliki law is surprisingly similar to the positions of the other Sunni legal schools. Like them, the Maliki *madhhab* has had to adapt to changing circumstances over time. Initially hostile to mystical practices, Malikis eventually learned to coexist with Sufi customs as the latter became widespread throughout North and West Africa. Many Muslims now adhere to both Maliki law and a Sufi order. The modern era has brought various innovative approaches and a heightened debate regarding the essence of Islamic law. Despite these new circumstances, the Maliki *madhhab* remains firmly established in African Islam, a situation that is unlikely to change in the foreseeable future.

See also FIQH.

Stephen Cory

Further reading: Jonathan E. Brockopp, *Early Maliki Law: Ibn 'Abd al-Hakam and His Major Compendium of Jurisprudence* (Leiden: E.J. Brill, 2000); Joseph Kenny, *The Risala: Treatise on Maliki Law of Abdallah Ibn Abi Zayd Al-Qayrawani (922–996)* (Islamic Edition Trust, 1992); Malik ibn Anas, *Al-Muwatta of Imam Malik Ibn Anas: The First Formulation of Islamic Law.* Translated and edited by Aisha Abdurrahmann Bewley. (The Islamic Classical Library Series, Kegan Paul Intl., 1989);

Mansour H. Mansour, *The Maliki School of Law: Spread and Domination in North and West Africa 8th to 14th Centuries* C.E. (Bethesda, Md.: Austin and Winfield, 1995).

mamluk

Mamluk means "thing possessed" in Arabic and is usually used to refer to a military slave. *Mamluks* were introduced into the Islamic lands by the Abbasid caliphs al-Mamun and al-Mutasim in the early ninth century C.E. Al-Mamun (r. 813–833) seized the throne after a civil war and, feeling he could not rely on the loyalty of the traditional army, he turned instead to slave troops. His younger brother, al-Mutasim (r. 833–842), spearheaded this project of acquiring slave soldiers, and he continued the process when he became CALIPH upon al-Mamun's death. Reliance upon a *mamluk* military elite is one of the unique characteristics of medieval and early modern Islamic government. It continued under the Ottoman sultans until the end of the 19th century.

Mamluks usually came from Central Asia or eastern Europe, where they were purchased as young boys who were either prisoners of war or sold into SLAVERY by their families who knew the potential for power and prestige that awaited them as *mamluks*. Upon their purchase the mamluks were converted to Islam, placed in a dormitory with fellow *mamluks*, and launched on an EDUCATION that included some religious instruction but focused primarily on the military sciences, in particular the cavalry. Upon "graduating" from this program the *mamluk* was manumitted, but he remained in a close bond of loyalty to his purchaser, a caliph, SULTAN, prince, or high *mamluk* officer. This bond was considered comparable to the relationship between father and son.

The strength and appeal of the *mamluk* system lay in the high military acumen of the *mamluks* and their complete loyalty and devotion to the ruler who had purchased and trained them. That this loyalty was essentially personal constituted the system's chief drawback. It therefore strengthened the rule of one caliph or sultan, but loyalty was not necessarily or easily transferred to his successor. With this in mind, hopefuls often spent their time as princes purchasing and training their own *mamluk* troops. The ability to pull off a smooth transition of power, however, depended not only on the strength of the prince's *mamluks* vis-à-vis his predecessor's but also on his ability to convince at least a few of these latter *mamluks* to swear an oath of loyalty to him. Thus a system initiated to strengthen the military and preserve the empire also brought with it real risks. Under the Abbasids, the *mamluk* Turkish commanders accrued more and more authority, on occasion even killing the caliph. Although this state of affairs was denounced by the ULAMA and political theoreticians, no ruler could circumvent his own need for *mamluks*.

Reflecting the overall strength and appeal of this system, in EGYPT and SYRIA *mamluks* ruled in their own right from 1250 to 1517, making their regime, rather aptly named the Mamluks, one of the longest and most durable Islamic regimes of the medieval period. The very nature of the system ensured that only the most capable rose to the highest positions of power, a characteristic that served all sides for many centuries.

See also ABBASID CALIPHATE; DELHI SULTANATE; JANISSARY.

Heather N. Keaney

Further reading: David Ayalon, *Gunpowder and Firearms in the Mamluk Kingdom: A Challenge to a Mediaeval Society* (London: F. Cass, 1978); ———, *Islam and the Abode of War: Military Slaves and Islamic Adversaries* (London: Variorum, 1994); Matthew S. Gordon, *The Breaking of a Thousand Swords: A History of the Turkish Military of Samarra* (A.H. 200–275/815–889 C.E.) (Albany: State University of New York Press, 2001); P. M. Holt, "The Structure of Government in the Mamluk Sultanate." In *The Eastern Mediterranean Lands in the Period of the Crusades*, edited by P. M. Holt, 44–61 (Werminster, England: Aris and Phillips, 1977).

Manat   *See* GODDESS.

Mappila   *See* INDIA.

maqam (Arabic: place, station)

Maqam has several meanings in Islamic religious contexts. In the most widespread sense it denotes a sacred place that commemorates a SAINT. Found in North Africa and the Middle East, such shrines consist of a domed building, inside of which is the saint's tomb. This tomb is enclosed by a screen, and often covered by layers of cloth brought as gifts by visitors and pilgrims seeking the saint's blessing (BARAKA). Disciples and members of the saint's family are often buried in the same chamber or nearby in the courtyard or adjacent buildings. Descendants of the saint, or his or her devotees, often serve as caretakers for the shrine. A *maqam* may be located in a crowded urban neighborhood, in a village, or in uninhabited areas. People visit it on the occasion of the saint's birthday (MAWLID), religious HOLIDAYS, or in connection with life-cycle rituals.

Muslims regard the Station (*maqam Ibrahim*) of ABRAHAM as one of the most important places inside the Grand Mosque of MECCA. In the QURAN it is called a PRAYER place (Q 2:125) and is located the northwest wall of God's house, the KAABA. Pilgrims perform prayers there after circumambulating the Kaaba. Commentaries and narratives about Mecca's mythic history affirm that it was originally a stone from PARADISE that Abraham stood upon to make his universal call to perform the HAJJ. It was believed that he left his footprint in it. Some commentators maintained that the Station of Abraham originally referred either to the larger sanctuary or to another location in the sacred territory surrounding Mecca.

The third meaning of *maqam* in Islam is a "station" on the mystical path to God. It was used as a technical term in the vocabulary of the Sufis. A station was attained by the intentional efforts of the mystic, in contrast to the HAL, which was a spontaneous gift from God. The spiritual seeker had to perfect each *maqam* before progressing to the next. The number, names, and sequence of stations varied greatly among Sufi authors and orders. They prescribed 4, 7, 50, 100, and even 1,000 stations. In the 11th century Al-Qushayri listed 50 stations starting with "repentance" and ending with "yearning," whereas al-Ansari's list of 100 began with "wakefulness" and ended with "unity." In a different vein, *The Conference of the Birds*, a Persian epic poem by Farid al-Din Attar (d. ca. 1220), depicted a mystical journey through seven valleys, each representing a *maqam* on the Sufi path: "seeking," "love," "knowledge," "detachment," "unity," "bewilderment," and "annihilation."

In Arab, Persian, and Turkish MUSIC, *maqam* refers to one of several different modes, or musical scales.

See also SUFISM; *WALI*.

Further reading: Farid Ud-Din Attar, *The Conference of the Birds* (New York: Penguin Books, 1984); Carl W. Ernst, *The Shambhala Guide to Sufism* (Boston: Shambhala, 1997); Ali ibn Uthman al-Hujwiri, *The Kashf al-Mahjub: The Oldest Persian Treatise on Sufism.* Translated by R. A. Nicholson (1959. Reprint, New Delhi: Taj Printers, 1997); Francis E. Peters, *The Hajj: The Muslim Pilgrimage to Mecca and the Holy Places* (Princeton, N.J.: Princeton University Press, 1994): 6–9, 16–17; Michael Sells, *Early Islamic Mysticism: Sufi, Quran, Miraj, Poetic and Theological Writings* (New York: Paulist Press, 1996), 102–103.

market   *See* BAZAAR.

martyrdom

Martyrdom (*shahada*) in Islam is intimately linked to the obligation of JIHAD ("struggle" for the FAITH). Traditionally, the martyr (Av. sing *shahid*), has several contexts of meaning in Islam. (1) The martyr can offer up his/her life to defend Islam and the Sunni UMMA, or majority religious community, from outward attack or persecution by unbelievers. (2) The martyr can be one of the dissenting minority of the Shia, whose watershed moment is the martyrdom of Imam Husayn, prophet MUHAMMAD's grandson along with members of his household on the 10th of Muharram, 61 A.H. (October 9–10, 680 C.E.) at KARBALA (in present-day IRAQ), commemorated ever afterward as simply, "Ashura," or "the Tenth," with communal rituals of "mourning," passion plays, and processions. (3) The martyr can die in defense of his/her own understanding/ interpretation of Islam in relation to the standards of faith articulated by the ULAMA, or jurists, and upheld by the Islamic state, as in the Sufi "martyrs" of the Middle Ages (AL-HALLAJ, d. 922 C.E., Ayn al-Qudat al-Hamadhani, d. 1131 C.E., RUZBIHAN BAQLI, d. 1209 C.E.) who were tried and executed for heresy due to making public theopathic statements, shathiyat, or expressions of temporary unity with God).

The original context for understanding "martyrdom" as a religious obligation in Islam is the Quran, which discusses the JIHAD incumbent on the early male disciples who were required to leave their homes in MECCA, emigrate with the prophet Muhammad to start the new community in MEDINA, and fight to defend the baby umma from the attacks of the pagan Meccans and struggles with rebellious tribes of the Arabian Peninsula. Jihad ("striving, exertion") fi sabil Allah ("in the way of God") is defined in the Quran in three ways: (1) struggle of leaving home, family, and property, and emigrating (HIJRA) to spread the faith (DAAWA) (Q. 4:95–100; 8:72–75; 9:20, 81, 87–89); (2) struggle against unbelievers during the Prophet's lifetime, such as the pagan Meccan "disbelievers" (kafirun) and "hypocrites" (munafiqun), and others (Jewish and Christian tribes) who rejected Islam, as well as those who did not "keep covenant" with the umma and with God after the Prophet's death, requiring the community to engage in the "wars of ridda" that brought the "backsliding" tribes back into the fold (Q. 9:13–16, 73; 25:52; 60:1; 66:9); and (3)

the witness to faith or "testifying" by the self-sacrifice of martyrdom (Q. 4:66, 74–78; 39:68–70). The Arabic root sh-h-d is resonant with multiple meanings, and its nominal form, shahada, meaning "witness to faith" (the first of the Five Pillars of Islamic ritual practice) also means "martyrdom." Thus, the Muslim who is killed in battle in defense of the umma or fights to the death resisting persecution of the religion of Islam is, at one and the same time, a "martyr" who is thereby "witnessing or testifying to the faith."

HADITH the Sira, or sacred BIOGRAPHY of the prophet Muhammad; and the TAFSIR (Quran commentary literature) all amplify the notion of martyrs and martyrdom, defining the rewards of the martyr, and portraying the state of martyrdom as so special that the warrior killed in battle wishes only to fall, so that he can return to be killed and killed yet again. The hadith list the prerogatives of the martyr: (1) his sins will be forgiven with the first rush of blood, (2) he will be shown his abode in PARADISE, (3) he will be dressed in the garment of belief, (4) he will be married to HOURIS (beautiful maidens/"spouses" who come to serve the martyr in paradise), (5) he will be protected against the torment of the grave, (6) he will be safe from the terror of the last judgment, (7) the crown of dignity, one ruby of which is better than this world, will be placed on his head, (8) he will be married to 72 wives from among the houris (another hadith mentions only two: "the blood of the martyr will hardly be dry on the earth when his two spouses will already be rushing to meet him [at the moment of death]"), (9) he will intercede for 70 of his relatives with God. The reward of paradise is promised, but its exact timing and location are not made clear; the martyrs are "near" God and are fed on the "fruits of paradise" but are not actually in paradise until the bodily resurrection. There is a compromise tradition that attempts to resolve the intermediate fate of the martyrs after DEATH and before the resurrection: the "souls" of the martyrs are in the "shape of white birds that feed on the fruits of paradise." Variants of this "bird" tradition state that the martyrs' souls are "like birds with God," "turned into green birds," "in the bellies of birds," or are "in the crops of green birds." These birds are said to "nestle in (golden) lamps that are hung (*muallaqa*) under the Throne of God," and their dwellings are near the "lote tree of the boundary."

In modern times, the definition of *shahid* has widened to include any personal/individual "sacrifice" for God's cause or "trial" sent by God resulting in death, such as dying abroad, dying from epidemic disease or natural disaster, in childbirth, by pleurisy or drowning, to protect one's family or property, and finally the jihadist "effort" of the ULAMA ("the ink of the scholars is of more value than the blood of the martyrs"). The widespread politicization of Islam after the 1960s has led to Shii ideologies of martyrdom linked to the political jihad of "revolution," as in the discourse of Ayatollahs Khomeini, Taliqani, and Mutahhari in Iran, or to guerrilla "resistance" movements that practice proactive martyrdom, as in HIZBULLAH in Lebanon. Models of Sunni martyrdom have also kept pace, inspired by such jihadist ideologues and organizations as HASAN AL-BANNA and SAYYID QUTB of al-Ikhwan al-Muslimun, or "MUSLIM BROTHERHOOD," in EGYPT; Abu al-Ala Mawdudi of JAMAAT-I ISLAMI in PAKISTAN, BANGLADESH, and northern INDIA; and HAMAS, which has religiously underwritten Palestinian intifada as an all-out civilian "resistance" specializing in martyrdom/SUICIDE bombings. Both Shii and Sunni jihadist ideologies of martyrdom are part of a multifront religious "struggle" against the hegemony of the West (whether interpreted as European colonial/postcolonial regimes, such as France in North Africa, Russia in AFGHANISTAN, Zionist Israel in the Arab Middle East, or active imperialist powers in the Muslim world today, principally the United States in its unilateral support for and interventions on behalf of ISRAEL and more recent military presence in Saudi Arabia and post 9/11 incursions in Afghanistan and IRAQ). Sunni and Shii jihadists define their task as resisting "secular" Western-style democracy and working for sharia-oriented governments and reinfusions of Islamic "values" in the Sunni *umma* throughout the Muslim Middle East, southeastern Europe, Central and South Asia, and Southeast Asia. Such postmodern Muslim "fighters" for the faith and "martyrs" for the *umma* now include women and children as well as the more traditional male "soldiers" for Islam. The "rewards" for these more tender martyrs seem focused on how they will be remembered in this world rather than on male-ordered definitions of "paradise." They are willing to expend their lives, using the power of their powerlessness, against what they perceive to be a more powerful, unjust, and oppressive enemy.

See also AFTERLIFE; JIHAD MOVEMENTS; SHIISM.

Kathleen M. O'Connor

Further reading: Sunni: David Cook, *Martyrdom in Islam* (New York: Cambridge University Press, 2007); Maher Jarrar, "The Martyrdom of Passionate Lovers. Holy War as a Sacred Wedding." In *Hadith: Origins and Developments,* edited by Harald Motzki (Burlington, Vt.: Ashgate/Variorum, 2004); Rudolph Peters, ed., *Jihad in Classical and Modern Islam, a Reader* (Princeton, N.J.: Markus Wiener, 1996); Christopher Reuter, *My Life Is a Weapon: A Modern History of Suicide Bombing* (Princeton, N.J.: Princeton University Press, 2004); David M. Rosen, "Fighting for the Apocalypse: Palestinian Child Soldiers." In *Armies of the Young: Child Soldiers in War and Terrorism* (New Brunswick, N.J.: Rutgers University Press, 2005). Shii: Mahmoud Ayoub, *Redemptive Suffering in Islam: A Study of the Devotional Aspects of 'Ashura' in Twelver Shi'ism* (The Hague: Mouton, 1978); Mehdi Abedi and Gary Legenhausen, eds. *Jihad and Shahadat: Struggle and Martyrdom in Islam* (Houston: Institute for Research and Islamic Studies, 1986); Kamran Scot Aghaie, *The Martyrs of Karbala: Shi'i Symbols and Rituals in Modern Iran* (Seattle: University of Washington Press, 2004); Ali Naqi Naqvi, *The Martyr of Karbala: English Translation of Allama Ali Naqi Naqvi's "Shaheed-e-insaniyat"* (Karachi: Islamic Culture and Research Trust/Muhammadi Trust of Great Britain and Northern Ireland, 1984); Lara Deeb, *An Enchanted Modern: Gender* and Public Piety in Shi'i Lebanon (Princeton, N.J.: Princeton University Press, 2006).

Mary (Arabic: Maryam) (late first century B.C.E.–early first century C.E.) *the mother of Jesus*

Mary is the only female figure mentioned by name in the QURAN, with a chapter named after her (Surat Maryam). She is the mother of JESUS (Ar. Isa) and a significant female exemplar of piety and purity in Islam in her own right. There are two chapters in the Quran that include her narrative in detail (Q 3:33–51 and 19:16-35), along with important mentions in other chapters (Q 4:171, 21:91, 66:11–12). Jesus is identified in Islam first and foremost as Isa ibn Maryam (Jesus son of Mary), as well as *ruh Allah* (spirit of God), *kalimat Allah* (word of God), and *al-masih* (Messiah). Aside from the Quran itself, other later sources for characterizations of Mary's life and role in Islam include Quran commentary literature (TAFSIR) and the genre of *qisas al-anbiya'* (stories of the prophets).

Mary's personal quality of *isma* (sinlessness) in Islam reflects her sinless conception by her mother, her ritual purity, which allowed her to serve in the Temple in JERUSALEM (normally a role restricted to men), and her virginity in conceiving Jesus. God is shown to have given Mary special favor. Mary is chosen and purified above all WOMEN in this world and has precedence over all other women in heaven. Her extraordinary personal devotion and piety led God to support her with miraculous provisions of summer fruit in winter and winter fruit in summer, allowing her to sustain her prayers in seclusion without outside labor.

Jesus is cast into Mary's womb as the "word" of God in three different senses according to Quran commentary: (1) creation of life by divine speech, that is, God says "be" and life "is"; (2) Jesus' prophetic mission is embodied in his "word," that is, the GOSPEL (Ar. *al-injil*); and (3) the communication of God's "word" to Mary, that is, the "annunciation" by the ANGEL. Despite Jesus' miraculous conception, Mary's experience of gestation and childbirth is documented in Islam as fully human. She experiences struggle and pain in laboring to give birth, during which God helps her with gifts of water and fresh dates. Mary returns to her people after the birth of Jesus and is miraculously defended by him. He speaks on her behalf in his cradle when she is accused of unchaste behavior in bearing a child while unwed.

Aside from Mary's importance as the mother of Jesus, she plays an ongoing role in Muslim piety as a model of pious devotion, sorrowing motherhood, and saintly (even "prophetic") inspiration. In SHIISM, the minority tradition in Islam, Mary is associated with the "mother of the Imams," FATIMA. Mary is believed by Twelver Shiis to have appeared to Fatima to console her in her last illness. Mary and Fatima are both understood in this theological context as a joint image of persecuted and holy motherhood, as their sons Jesus and Husayn are linked as the suffering, persecuted, and ultimately martyred leaders of the faithful. In the majority Sunni theological tradition, because of her righteousness, Mary is granted the ability to receive REVELATION and inspiration via the angel's transmission to her of the "word of God" (Jesus). She is even assigned some Sunni Quran commentary in the otherwise exclusively male function in Islam of prophethood (*nubuwwa*), since she received direct divine communication, as opposed to messengerhood (*risala*), or bringing a new scriptural revelation, a male-only function in Islam.

See also CHRISTIANITY AND ISLAM; JOHN THE BAPTIST; TWELVE-IMAM SHIISM.

Kathleen M. O'Connor

Further reading: Mahmoud Ayoub, *Redemptive Suffering in Islam: A Study of the Devotional Aspects of Ashura in Twelver Shi'ism* (The Hague: Mouton, 1978). Jane D. McAuliffe, "Chosen of All Women: Mary and Fatima in Qur'anic Exegesis," *Islamochristiana* 7 (1981): 19–28;

Jaroslav Pelikan, "The Heroine of the Qur'an and the Black Madonna." In *Mary through the Centuries: Her Place in the History of Culture* (New Haven, Conn.: Yale University Press, 1996); Aliah Schleifer, *Mary the Blessed Virgin of Islam* (Louisville, Ky.: Fons Vitae, 1998); Jane I. Smith and Yvonne Y. Haddad, "The Virgin Mary in Islamic Tradition and Commentary." *Moslem World* 79:3–4 (July–October 1989): 161–187; Barbara F. Stowasser, *Women in the Qur'an, Traditions and Interpretation* (New York: Oxford University Press, 1994); W. M. Thackston, trans. *The Tales of the Prophets of al-Kisa'i* (Boston: Twayne Publishers, 1978).

masjid *See* MOSQUE.

matam *See* HUSAYNIYYA.

mathematics

Mathematics occupied a prominent place on the scientific scene in the Arabo-Islamic empire. Although all works were translated into or written in Arabic, all ethnic and religious communities of the empire produced scholars who contributed to mathematics. The Arabo-Islamic scholars digested, commented on, summarized, and then built upon their predecessors' works regardless of their religion or ethnicity; their contributions to mathematics, regardless of its nature or size, were absolutely crucial for any further developments in the field. Translation of other works received its biggest thrust under the patronage of the Abbasid caliph al-Mamun (r. 813–833). Mathematical works were translated from sources such as Greek/Hellenistic, Persian, and Indian. A list of translators, translated books, and scholars was produced by Ibn al-Nadim (10th century) in his encyclopedic book *al-Fihrist.*

In the field of arithmetic, the Arabo-Islamic scholars identified Indian arithmetic as the most efficient, from which they borrowed and perfected Indian numerals, the decimal system, the place-value and the ideas of zero, fractions, root extractions, and associated operations. Later on, they integrated received and translated knowledge into a coherent body, which was then subject to further refinement.

The field of algebra was inaugurated by the work of al-Khawarizmi (ninth century). He introduced a complete terminology for solving arithmetical and geometrical problems through radicals, the idea of the unknown, the idea of equations, the first and second-degree equations, algorithmic solutions, and the demonstration of the solution formula. He actually gave his name to all systematic and step-by-step methods of solving problems, namely, the algorithms. Thabit ibn Qurra (d. 901) later gave a geometrical explanation of the equations of al-Khawarizmi. However, it was al-Khayyam (d. 1123) who elaborated a geometrical theory for equations of degree equal to or less than three. A full treatment of the solution of cubic equations was given two generations later by Nasiral-Din al-Tusi (d. 1274).

The Arabo-Islamic scholars added original contributions in all areas of the great Greek geometrical tradition, including laying the foundations of geometry, geometric constructions, geometric transformations, and projections. In addition, they established the connection between geometry and algebra. Finally, in trigonometry they devised trigonometric formulae for a triangle (these formulae were originally given for a sphere), and they defined and introduced the tangent function. These contributions found applications in astronomy, engineering, optics and MUSIC. Many of the works of the Arabo-Islamic mathematicians were translated into Latin after they entered Europe through trading contacts with Byzantium, Spain, and Sicily, and through interactions occasioned by the CRUSADES.

See also ANDALUSIA; SCIENCE.

A. Nazir Atassi

Further reading: Ibn al-Nadim, *The Fihrist of al-Nadim: A Tenth-Century Survey of Muslim Culture.* Translated by Bayard Dodge (New York: Columbia University Press, 1970); Roshdi Rashed, ed. *Encyclopedia of the History of Arabic Science.* Vol. 2, *Mathematics and the Physical Sciences* (London: Routledge, 1996).

Mawdudi, Abu al-Ala (Maudoodi)
(1903–1979) *leading Muslim revivalist thinker and founder of the Jamaat-i Islami movement in India-Pakistan*

Abu al-Ala Mawdudi was born in Awrangabad, INDIA, to a family claiming descent from Sufi saints of the Chishti order who had migrated to India from AFGHANISTAN in the 15th century. His father, Sayyid Ahmad Hasan, had close ties to the Mughal court before the dynasty was overthrown by the British in 1858. Later, Sayyid Ahmad and other members of Mawdudi family were among the first to be educated at the Muhammadan Anglo-Oriental College at ALIGARH, which was dedicated to providing Muslims with a modern Westernized EDUCATION in order to prepare them to participate in the colonial government of British India.

Mawdudi's thought benefited from a diversified educational career that began at home, where Sayyid Ahmad organized a traditional Islamic curriculum for him, consisting of Urdu and Persian learning, elementary Arabic, and tales drawn from Islamic history. Western learning was intentionally omitted by his parents, because they wanted him to have a solid grounding in Islamic tradition for a career as a religious scholar. His formal education began when he enrolled in a public school, where he was exposed to the natural sciences and other modern subjects. Mawdudi proved himself to be a gifted student of Arabic, and he demonstrated his skills in completing an Urdu translation of a work by the Egyptian modernist writer Qasim Amin (d. 1908) on the rights of women. At the age of 16 he was forced to give up schooling because of his father's failing health. To provide for himself and his family, he began a career as a writer. A few years later he moved to DELHI, where he continued to study Persian and Urdu literature, but he also immersed himself in the work of European philosophers and modern Muslim intellectuals. He sought to grasp the similarities and differences between traditional knowledge and modern thought. By the time he reached age 20, Mawdudi had developed close ties to leading ulama of the DEOBAND School and took up advanced studies in the traditional branches of Islamic learning, as well as SUFISM, rhetoric, logic, and PHILOSOPHY. He completed his formal studies in 1926 at the Fatihpuri MADRASA in Old Delhi, and he was certified to be one of the ULAMA. However, his career took a different turn, and his status as a religious scholar remained concealed from the public until after his death.

Mawdudi became a journalist and undertook involvement in various causes, eventually becoming one of India's leading Muslim political figures. He wrote briefly for a Delhi nationalist newspaper, but he was then appointed as editor for the official newspaper of the JAMIYYAT ULAMA-I HIND (Society of Indian Ulama), known as *Muslim* (later changed to *Jamiat*). In this position he wrote articles on issues important to Indian Muslims at the time, and he embarked on a life-long effort to promote the revival of Islam. His first major book was *Jihad in Islam,* a compilation of articles he wrote in 1925 to defend his religion against Hindu and British critics. During the 1920s Mawdudi supported the Indian nationalist movement and the KHILAFAT MOVEMENT, a campaign among Muslims in British India that ended when the CALIPHATE was officially abolished by the Turkish republic in 1924. He also supported the Hijra Movement (Tahrik-i Hijrat), which advocated Muslim emigration from India as long as it was ruled by non-Muslims, namely, the British.

Mawdudi moved to Hyderabad (Deccan), one of the last remaining centers of Muslim political power, in 1928. Declaring, "In reality I am a new Muslim," he soon became what would today be called an Islamist. The waning power of Muslim rule in Hyderabad and other parts of India led him to call for an end to British colonial rule, removal of indigenous cultural influences from the "true" Islam, separation of Muslims from Hindus, and a return to the original religion of Muhammad that he and other revivalists believed had prevailed during the Golden Age of Islam. In 1932 he bought the local journal *Tarjuman ul-Quran* (Interpreting the Quran) and began to publish editorials, essays, and books, hoping to motivate the Nizam (the local Muslim ruler) to initiate a reform of Islamic institutions. When this proved unsuccessful, he called upon Muslims across India to create a separate Muslim homeland, refute the nationalist ideals of the Congress Party (with its Hindu majority), and reject the ALL-INDIA MUSLIM LEAGUE, which was controlled by secular Muslims such as MUHAMMAD ALI JIN-NAH (1876–1948).

With the backing of the Muslim intellectual MUHAMMAD IQBAL (1877–1938) and others, he moved to the Punjab to direct the Dar al-Islam (House of Islam) communal project at Pathankot from 1938 to 1939. This was an area where Hindu, Sikh, and Ahmadiyya political groups were already active. Mawdudi planned to make Pathankot the launching pad for a modern Islamic revival and the creation of an Islamic government in India. He continued his *DAAWA* (calling) to stir Muslim elites throughout India to his cause through editorials in *Tarjuman ul-Quran,* books, pamphlets, and lecture tours. In 1939 he shifted the headquarters for his movement to the former Mughal capital of Lahore, where he officially launched the famous JAMAAT-I ISLAMI (Islamic Group), the leading Islamist organization in South Asia, in 1941. He began to publish his popular Urdu Quran commentary, *Tafhim al-Quran* (Understanding the Quran) in 1942. This multivolume work, like many of his writings, has been translated and circulated widely in Muslim communities.

When India was partitioned and PAKISTAN was created in 1947, the Jamaat-i Islami split into Pakistani and Indian branches, and Mawdudi remained in Pakistan. He was opposed to the new country's secular political leadership and worked for the drafting of a CONSTITUTION that he and his supporters hoped would lead to the establishment of an Islamic government. Part of his strategy involved lobbying to have the AHMADIYYA sect declared un-Islamic. The rioting this ignited led to his imprisonment and a death sentence in 1953, but he was eventually pardoned by the government. Mawdudi traveled widely between 1956 and 1974, visiting and lecturing in many Muslim countries and helping to establish an Islamic university in Medina and the MUSLIM WORLD LEAGUE. He remained leader of the Pakistani Jamaat-i Islami until 1972, and he is suspected of involvement in a coup against Pakistani prime minister Zulfikar Ali Bhutto (1928–78) in 1977. This brought General Muhammad Zia ul-Haq (1924–88) to power, who launched a series of measures to institute the SHARIA, to Mawdudi's great satisfaction. Mawdudi died while receiving medical treatment in Buffalo, New York, in 1979, and he was buried on the grounds of his house in Lahore.

Mawdudi was a contemporary of many leading figures of the Islamic revival of the 20th century, including HASSAN AL-BANNA (1906–49), SAYYID QUTB (1906–66), and Ayatollah RUHOLLAH KHOMEINI (1902–89). His understanding of Islam was deeply rooted in the religious and cultural experience of South Asian Muslims, including their traditions of Sufism and Sunni law, renewal, and reform, but his writings were translated and disseminated beyond India to Muslims in other parts of the world. Like many educated men of his time, he was also familiar with contemporary thought in the West, and he had direct experience with British colonial rule. His life was one of active involvement in the anticolonial and nationalist politics of his time, which gave shape to a modern Islamic revivalist ideology that still inspires many Islamic movements. His vision was rooted in belief in God's absolute sovereignty, which underpinned his call for all Muslims to join together to form a single UMMA (community) of believers modeled after that of Muhammad and his Companions in the seventh century. Ideally this Islamic state was to be one that transcended all national, ethnic, and racial boundaries, governed only by God's law, the sharia. Mawdudi was careful to say that he was not calling for the creation of a theocracy on the model of the medieval papacy in Europe. Rather, his Islamic state was to be a "theo-democracy" governed by a collective polity united in faith, acting as God's CALIPH on earth. The Jamaat-i Islam was to be the elite vanguard that would bring his utopian vision to fruition, and its participation in Pakistani politics was directed to this end. WOMEN and non-Muslims, however, held secondary or marginal status in Mawdudi's eyes, and he came to see Hindus, Sikhs, and Ahmadis as enemies of his cause. Although his movement has not engaged in overt militancy, his ideology is thought to have contributed to the radical jihadist doctrines of Sayyid Qutb and a number of radical Islamic movements that first emerged in the 1970s and 1980s.

See also CHISHTI SUFI ORDER; COLONIALISM; ISLAMISM; RENEWAL AND REVIVAL MOVEMENTS.

Further reading: Charles J. Adams, "Mawdudi and the Islamic State." In *Voices of Islamic Resurgence,* edited by John L. Esposito, 99–133 (New York: Oxford University Press, 1983); Abu Ala Maududi, *Towards Understanding Islam.* Translated by Khurshid Ahmed (Chicago: Kazi Publications, 1992); Seyyed Vali Reza Nasr, "Mawdudi and the Jamaat-i Islami: The Origins, Theory, and Practice of Islamic Revivalism." In *Pioneers of Islamic Revival,* 2d ed., edited by Ali Rahnema, 98–124 (London: Zed Books, 2005).

mawlid (Arabic: birthday; anniversary)

At the center of popular Muslim devotionalism from North Africa to Southeast Asia and in Muslim diaspora communities is the *mawlid,* or celebration of the birth or death anniversary of a holy person (WALI, SHAYKH, *pir*). Other words used

for this kind of popular celebration are variants such as *mulid* (Egypt), *mulud* (North Africa), *milad* or *id-i milad* (Middle East, Pakistan, India, Bangladesh); *mevlid* and *mevlut* (Turkey); as well as alternate terms like *mawsim* (or *musim,* literally "season"; North Africa), *urs* (literally "wedding," referring to the saint's mystical union with God; Pakistan, India, Bangladesh), *hawliyya* (Sudan and East Africa), *hol* (Malaysia), and *zarda* (Tunisia). They may occur at almost any time of the year, except during RAMADAN. The most widely celebrated *mawlid* is that of Muhammad the Prophet (d. 632), which occurs on the 12th day of Rabi al-Awwal, the third month on the Muslim lunar calendar. *Mawlids* have been celebrated since the 13th century, closely coinciding with the spread of Sufi brotherhoods (sing. TARIQA) and the establishment of non-Arab dynasties that sought legitimacy in the eyes of their subjects by patronizing popular saints and their shrines. *Mawlids* and the customs associated with them have been judged to be illicit innovations (sing. BIDAA) by literally minded Muslims—above all by proponents of WAHHABISM, who have prohibited them in Saudi Arabia and protested or violently attacked their celebration elsewhere.

Mawlids are usually centered at the shrine or tomb of the holy person who is honored by the holiday, or, as is the case with celebration of Muhammad's birthday (*mawlid al-nabi, mawlid al-rasul*), at a shrine containing his relics, or dedicated to one of his descendants, such as the mosque of Husayn near al-AZHAR Mosque in Cairo. The celebration may be a modest affair, confined to the neighborhood of the shrine, but the mawlids of the most famous saints now draw a million or more from great distances, who consider their journey to the shrine a pilgrimage (ZIYARA). Such celebrations may last up to a week or more, with the climax occurring on the eve of the last day. Though formal prayer is customarily performed at these shrines, celebrants engage in a wide range of activities. These include decorating the shrine, circumambulating the saint's tomb, leaving votive gifts, processions, animal sacrifice, circumcising boys, Quran recitation, all-night Sufi DHIKR sessions, devotional songs, feasting, dancing, tattooing, and acquisition of blessed souvenirs to take back home. Commercial activity as a rule is brisk at a *mawlid,* and special markets are set up for the larger ones. *Mawlid*s are often attended by non-Muslims. Moreover, the Coptic Christians of Egypt celebrate the *mawlid*s of their saints, as do Middle Eastern Jews theirs.

Mawlid also denotes a devotional song that praises Muhammad and celebrates the event of his birth, often embellished with legends. It is commonly performed in connection with the anniversary of his birth, other saints' holidays, and other celebratory occasions.

See also: ASHURA; AL-BADAWI, AHMAD; *BARAKA*; HOLIDAYS; *QAWWALI; SAYYID;* SUFISM.

Further reading: Nicholaas H. Biegman, *Egypt: Moulids, Saints, Sufis* (London: Kegan Paul International, 1990); P. M. Currie, "The Pilgrimage of Ajmer." In *Religion in India,* edited by T. N. Madan, 237–247 (Oxford: Oxford University Press, 1991); Carl W. Ernst and Bruce B. Lawrence, *Sufi Martyrs of Love: The Chishti Order in South Asia and Beyond* (New York: Palgrave Macmillan, 2002); Annemarie Schimmel, *And Muhammad Is His Messenger: The Veneration of the Prophet in Islamic Piety,* 144–158 (Chapel Hill: University of North Carolina Press, 1985); Nancy Tapper and Richard Tapper, "The Birth of the Prophet: Ritual and Gender in Turkish Islam." *Man,* New Series 22, no. 1 (March 1987): 69–92; Peter van der Veer, "Playing or Praying: A Sufi Saint's Day in Surat," *Journal of Asian Studies* 51, no. 3 (August 1992): 545–564.

Mecca (also Makkah)

A number of CITIES have been regarded as sacred centers in the history of religions. Varanasi (Banaras), Mathura, and Ayodhya in India are among those considered sacred by Hindus, Ise is sacred to the Japanese, and JERUSALEM is sacred to Jews, Christians, and Muslims. The most sacred city in Islam is Mecca, followed by MEDINA, Jerusalem, and, for the Shia, KARBALA and Najaf. Like these other cities, its special status as a holy city is based on events narrated in sacred history that are believed to have occurred there, its distinctive architectural landscape, and the complex of ritual practices that are performed there.

In Islamic sacred history, Mecca, which is known as "Ennobled Mecca" (Makka al-Mukarrama), is where Muslims believe that ABRAHAM and his son Ishmael built the KAABA and where Ishmael and his mother HAGAR are buried. It is the birthplace of MUHAMMAD (ca. 570–632) and where he received the early revelations of the QURAN. Indeed, another epithet for the city is "Dwelling Place of Revelation." Many of his wives and Companions were also born there, and it was the ancestral home of the Umayyad and Abbasid caliphs. According to accounts related by Muhammad ibn Abd Allah ibn Ahmad al-Azraqi (d. 837), who wrote a history of the city, it is called the "Mother of Towns" (*umm al-qura*) because it is where the CREATION of the earth began. His book also tells about how Adam traveled there from India, his home after being expelled from paradise, to be reunited with Eve and perform the first HAJJ rites, setting a precedent for performing these rites that would be reconfirmed in later times by Abraham and Muhammad.

Mecca is situated in a valley amidst the Sirat Mountains in the western region of the Arabian Peninsula known as the Hijaz. It is about 45 miles inland from the city of Jedda, which is located on the Red Sea coast. Its distinctive architectural landscape is defined by ritual spaces in the city, in the adjacent valley of Mina, and in the plain of Arafat. The ceremonial center of the urban ritual complex is the Sacred Mosque, where the Kaaba and the well of ZAMZAM are situated, and the concourse between the hills of Safa and Marwa, which is located on the northeastern side of the mosque. The Valley of Mina contains the three satanic pillars that are stoned by pilgrims at the conclusion of the hajj. About seven miles past

The Sacred Mosque in Mecca, as depicted in Ottoman ceramic tilework in the Sabil-Kuttab of Abd al-Rahman Katkhuda (18th century), Cairo, Egypt. The Kaaba is in the center, Safa and Marwa in the foreground, and the sacred mountains of Arafat and Light are in the background. *(Juan E. Campo)*

Mina is the plain of Arafat, which has a hillock called the Mount of Mercy and two mosques—Namira and Muzdalifa. The cave nearby in the Mount of Light is where Muhammad is said to have received his first revelation. There are many other sites in Mecca containing traces of past events in Islamic sacred history, but the passage of time, urban development, and the conservative nature of Saudi rule have combined to erase many of them.

The legendary holiness of the city of Mecca and the distinctiveness of its landscape are inex-tricably connected to an amalgam of ritual prac-tices and celebrations, which intensify during the annual hajj season. In addition to the five daily prayers, these rites include sevenfold circum-ambulation of the Kaaba, sevenfold "running" between Safa and Marwa, communal gatherings in Mina and Arafat, stoning Mina's three pillars, animal sacrifices and feasting during the ID AL-ADHA, and collecting water at the Zamzam well. The Quran is recited, sermons are delivered, and pilgrims pronounce special ritual phrases and petitions to God. During the hajj, pilgrims are also required to follow strict rules to maintain their bodily and spiritual purity, which heighten their awareness that they are in a sacred place permeated with BARAKA, God's grace and blessing. Assuming the condition of ritual purity, known as *ihram,* explicitly links pilgrims to the sacredness of the city, which is called *al-haram al-Makki,* the Meccan HARAM, or sacred precinct. This precinct is delimited by outlaying stations known as *miqats,* where pilgrims are supposed to enter their sacralized condition before entering the city to perform the hajj or UMRA. Since the seventh century non-Muslims have been forbidden from going to the city beyond these stations, further enhancing its holiness.

In the past, prior to the arrival of the Saudis in the 20th century, other religious activities were also conducted in Mecca. Ulama taught Islamic sciences, especially those related to the Quran, hadith, and law, in the arcades of the Sacred Mosque, and, after the 12th century, in as many as 23 madrasas (religious colleges). From the ninth century Muslim ascetics and Sufis traveled there as pilgrims, and also to study, teach, and engage in Sufi rituals. There were an estimated 59 hospices (*ribats*) built for the poor and Sufis in Mecca during the medieval period. Eventually almost all the Sufi *tariqas* would have lodges in Mecca, including the Qadiris, Naqshbandis, Khalwatis, Bedawis, Ahmadis (of the Idrisi tradition of Sufism), Fasis, and Sanusis—some surviving the anti-Sufism of Saudi WAHHABISM until the 1950s. Meccan natives had their own local festivals and ritual practices, even when they were not actually performing the hajj. In addition to marriage and funerary rites, they celebrated the prophet Muhammad's birthday (MAWLID), and several rituals during the month of Rajab that included parading decorated camels through the streets of the city, setting aside a day when only women were allowed into the Sacred Mosque, and the cleansing of the Kaaba. Another time of great celebration was the arrival of the *mahmal,* a camel-borne palanquin that accompanied the pilgrim caravans from Egypt, Syria, and Istanbul.

Mecca's success as a city has long depended on pilgrimage and the local and transregional economies driven by it. Scholars once thought that the city originally owed its growth to long-distance Arabian trade in spices in luxury goods, but this theory has been found to have serious flaws. Reliable archaeological and textual evidence from pre-Islamic Arabia is scanty, but evidence drawn from early Islamic texts indicates that before Islam Mecca was a shrine city that benefited from pilgrimage trade and the transport of local products to nearby settlements and towns. The ancient Kaaba housed idols and relics that were worshipped by peoples living in western Arabia, not just Mecca. The QURAYSH, the tribe to which Muhammad belonged, played a major role in governing the city, maintaining the shrine, and regulating the pre-Islamic pilgrimage. Muhammad and his followers abandoned it in 622 when the opposition of the Quraysh and other Meccan opponents became too much to bear, but he made its Sacred House (the Grand Mosque) the QIBLA (prayer direction) for his community shortly after arriving in Medina, and it has remained so for all Muslims through the centuries. Mecca's rulers, the Abd Shams clan of the Quraysh, launched attacks against the Muslims of Medina, but in 630 Muhammad triumphantly returned to take control of the city with very little loss of life.

Ever since Muhammad's time Mecca has been governed by Muslims, though it never served as the political capital for any of the Muslim caliphates or medieval sultanates. The Rashidun caliphs governed it from Medina and Kufa (632–661), then the Umayyads from Damascus (661–750), after defeating Abd Allah ibn al-Zubayr (d. 692), who had briefly occupied Mecca and attempted to make himself caliph. Umayyad rule was followed by Abbasids in Baghdad (750–1258), but Abbasid decline in the 10th century left the city vulnerable to attack by the Qarmatians, an Ismaili Shii sect. In 930 the Qarmatians actually plundered the city and seized the Kaaba's BLACK STONE. Mecca's distance from the centers of political power provided the Sharifs, a local aristocracy claiming descent from the AHL AL-BAYT through Muhammad's grandson Hasan (d. 669), with opportunities to maintain order and exercise power in the Hijaz region in varying degrees from the 10th century until the fall of the last sharif of Mecca to Saudi forces in 1924. His heirs were subsequently made the Hashemite kings of Transjordan (now JORDAN) and Iraq by the British. Meanwhile, the Fatimid and Ayyubid dynasties exercised what amounted to indirect control over Mecca between the 10th and 13th centuries, followed by the Mamluks (13th to 16th centuries), and the Ottomans (16th to 20th centuries). The largesse of these rulers, together with religious endowments (*waqf*s) established by pious individuals, were what provided the city with the infrastructure, financial resources, and even food supplies needed to serve its inhabitants and pilgrims through the centuries.

The creation of the Kingdom of SAUDI ARABIA in 1932 has inaugurated an era of epic change for Mecca. The Wahhabi outlook of the country has led to the eradication of many of its shrines and Sufi landmarks. The government, however, has been very careful to protect and improve the sites of the required hajj rituals to keep up with the growing numbers of pilgrims and win the good will of Muslims around the world. Within two years after taking control of the city in 1924, King ABD AL-AZIZ IBN SAUD (1880–1953) upgraded the electrical system of the Sacred Mosque, widened adjacent roads for the passage of automobiles, and built the city's first paved road. The Saudis conducted two major hajj building projects in 1955–78 and 1980–95. The latter construction phase is estimated to have cost $155 million, financed by the government from its oil revenues. The expansion and upgrading of the Sacred Mosque and adjacent neighborhoods has, however, led to the loss of much of the city's venerable architectural heritage, to the chagrin of architectural historians and cultural preservationists.

Commercial development of the precincts around the Sacred Mosque has resulted in the erection of luxury hotels, shopping malls, and high-rent residential complexes. As an indication of the importance Mecca has to the Saudi government, the governor of Mecca Province, which includes both Mecca and Jedda, is always a member of the royal family.

Because of Mecca's geography and climate, its population has been small for most of its history. An Ottoman census of its inhabitants in the early 16th century counted only 12,000, excluding merchants and soldiers. However, a recent census demonstrates how much the city has grown thanks to modern technologies, mechanized transport, and economic development. In 2004 it had an estimated population of 1.7 million. Likewise, the influx of pilgrims has grown at an astounding rate since the beginning of the 20th century. An estimated 83,000 pilgrims participated in the hajj of 1807; by the beginning of the 21st century over two million were thought to be performing the hajj annually. At other times of the year the *umra* now brings an additional 1.5 to 2 million pilgrims.

Even with all of the aspects of modernity that have become embedded in Mecca's sacred landscape, it continues to serve as a vital religious symbol in the everyday lives of Muslims everywhere. When they pray they face toward it, when they read the Quran they are reminded which of its chapters were revealed there, when they study the hadith they are studying the words of people who are believed to have been born there. The imagery of Mecca has been captured in poetry and art, and, more recently, on television and the Internet.

See also: ADAM AND EVE; ARABIAN RELIGIONS, PRE-ISLAMIC; COMPANIONS OF THE PROPHET; EMIGRANTS; GODDESS; HASHIMITE DYNASTY; SUFISM.

Further reading: Hamza Bogary, *The Sheltered Quarter: A Tale of a Boyhood in Mecca.* Translated by Olive Kenny (Austin: University of Texas Press, 1991); Richard F. Burton, *A Personal Narrative of a Pilgrimage to al-Madinah and Meccah.* 2 vols. (1855. Reprint, New York: Dover,

1964); Patricia Crone, *Meccan Trade and the Rise of Islam* (Princeton, N.J.: Princeton University Press, 1987); Suraiya Faroqhi, *Pilgrims and Sultans: The Hajj under the Ottomans* (London: I.B. Tauris, 1994); C. Snouck Hurgronje, *Mekka in the Latter Part of the Nineteenth Century: Daily Life, Customs and Learning, The Moslims of the East Indian Archipelago.* Translated by J. H. Monahan (Leiden: E.J. Brill, 1970); Richard T. Mortel, "Ribats in Mecca during the Medieval Period: A Descriptive Study Based on Literary Sources," *Bulletin of the School of Oriental and African Studies* 61, no. 1 (1998): 29–98; F. E. Peters, *Jerusalem and Mecca: The Typology of the Holy City in the Near East* (New York: New York University Press, 1986); ———, *Mecca: A Literary History of the Muslim Holy Land* (Princeton, N.J.: Princeton University Press, 1994); W. Montgomery Watt, *Muham-*

mad at Mecca (Oxford: Oxford University Press, 1953); Mai Yamani, *Cradle of Islam: The Hijaz and the Quest for Arabian Identity* (London: I.B. Tauris, 2004).

Medina (Arabic, city; al-Madina al-Munawwarah [the Radiant City], Madinat al-Nabi [City of the Prophet], Madinat al-Rasul [City of the Messenger])

Medina, which had a population of 918,889 in 2006, is located in Saudi Arabia, 210 miles north of Mecca and about 120 miles from the Red Sea coast. The UMMA, or religious community, was formally established in Medina after Muhammad's emigration from MECCA to Medina in 622 C.E. (called the HIJRA), which became the first year of the Islamic

Medina the Radiant. Traditional poster, with the Throne Verse from the Quran (Q 2:255) inscribed in the frame. The prophet Muhammad's mosque, encompassing his domed tomb, is shown in the center.

CALENDAR, 1 A.H. (*anno hijri,* or the year of the Hijra). It became the administrative center and capital of the growing Islamic empire in its initial period of expansion from the central province of Hijaz bordering the western coast of Arabia to encompass the Arabian Peninsula, Egypt, Syria, Iraq, and Iran by the end of the Rashidun Caliphate, 632–661. By the death of the fourth CALIPH, ALI IBN ABI TALIB (r. 656–661 C.E.), cousin and son-in-law of Muhammad, the capital would move to DAMASCUS under the UMAYYAD CALIPHATE, and later to BAGHDAD under the ABBASID CALIPHATE.

Medina's history during the lifetime of MUHAMMAD (ca. 570–632) is witnessed in part in the QURAN as well as other contemporaneous sources, the *maghazi* texts (which discuss Muhammad's battles), the HADITH (narratives of the Prophet's SUNNA, or customary words and deeds), and later hagiographical materials such as Muhammad ibn Ishaq's *al-Sira al-Nabawiyya,* or BIOGRAPHY of the Prophet. All of these texts mark the history of Muhammad's settlement in Medina, the growth of the first *umma,* and its spread to unite the Arabian tribes through battle and through treaty (and often diplomatic marriage between Muhammad and the daughter of another tribe). A history of intertribal conflict and warfare with the Jewish and pagan tribes of Medina, such as the Banu Aws and Banu Khazraj and their clients the Banu Nadir, Banu Qurayza, and Banu Qaynuqa, created a need for a strong and effective arbitrator and mediator, an opening Muhammad accepted in order to establish the Muslim community and Islam as a social and political as well as spiritual reality. According to the *Sira* of IBN ISHAQ, the Muslims and Jewish tribes of Medina signed an agreement, the "Constitution of Medina," which bound them to peaceful coexistence.

Medina's importance after its brief period as the political capital was primarily as a religious center in Islam, originating one of the four branches of Islamic law, namely, the Medinan school (*madhhab*) of MALIK IBN ANAS (ca. 715–796), and as the burial place of Muhammad, a number of the AHL AL-BAYT ("People of the House" of the Prophet), and early companions. These places became sites of pilgrimage in their own right, especially for Muslims who were visiting Mecca for the UMRA and the HAJJ. Thus all Sunni Muslims visit the Prophet's tomb and home MOSQUE in Medina when doing pilgrimage and Shii Muslims visit it for that reason and to visit the gravesites of several of the IMAMS. Medina is the second holiest city in Islam, second only to Mecca, due to its intimate connection with the Prophet and the foundation of the *umma.* The Prophet's mosque is in the eastern section of the city and a green dome tops the mausoleum. The mosque of the Prophet has been successively enlarged from its dimensions as his house and PRAYER place to an enormous complex with multiple MINARETS encompassing his tomb and permitting the approach of the enormous number of annual pilgrims who visit the site particularly during Ramadan and the annual hajj.

See also ANSAR; CITIES; COMPANIONS OF THE PROPHET; EMIGRANTS; JUDAISM AND ISLAM; ZIYARA.

Kathleen M. O'Connor

Further reading: Yasin Dutton, Malik ibn Anas, and Muhammad ibn Muhammad Ra'i, *Original Islam: Malik and the Madhhab of Madina* (New York: Routledge, 2007); Emel Esin and Haluk Doganbey, *Mecca the Blessed, Madinah the Radiant* (New York: Crown Publishers, 1963); Muhammad ibn Ishaq, *The Life of Muhammad: A Translation of Ishaq's Sirat Rasul Allah.* Translated by Alfred Guillaume (London: Oxford University Press, 1967); Michael Lecker, *Muslims, Jews and Pagans: Studies on Early Islamic Medina* (Leiden: E.J. Brill, 1995); Michael Lekker, "Muhammad at Medina, a Geographical Approach." *Jerusalem Studies in Arabic* 6 (1985): 29–62; Seyyed Hossein Nasr and Ali K. Nomachi, *Mecca the Blessed, Medina the Radiant: The Holiest Cities of Islam* (New York: Aperture Foundation, 1997); H. Rahman, "The Conflicts between the Prophet and the Opposition in Medina," *Der Islam* 62 (1985): 260–297; Muhammad ibn Saad, *The Women of Madina* (London: TaHa, 1995); Muhammad ibn Saad, *The Men of Madina* (London: TaHa, 1997); W. Montgomery

Watt, *Muhammad at Medina* (Oxford: Oxford University Press, 1956); ———, *Early Islam: Collected Articles* (Edinburgh: Edinburgh University Press, 1990); A. J. Wensinck, *Muhammad and the Jews of Medina* (Berlin: Adiyok, 1982).

Mernissi, Fatima (1940–) *Moroccan sociologist, writer, religious and political activist, and leading contemporary liberal Muslim intellectual*

Fatima Mernissi is a professor of sociology at the University of Mohammed V in Rabat, MOROCCO, having studied in Morocco, received a graduate degree from the Sorbonne, and a Ph.D. from Brandeis University. Most of her works constitute early milestones in Islamic feminism; she usually writes in French and many of her works have been translated into numerous other languages. Throughout much of her career, her main concern has been what she perceives as the oppressed status of WOMEN in majority Muslim cultures. Her most significant belief is that the marginalized status of Muslim women in virtually every aspect of life, including educational, economic, social, and religious, is contradictory to Islam's basic teachings. Mernissi maintains that the QURAN's pronouncements and MUHAMMAD's example require Muslims to implement equality, freedom, and liberty with respect to both genders and to socioeconomic domains. For Mernissi, the overriding reason for injustice in majority Muslim societies is because, throughout most of Islamic history, Muslim men have controlled the interpretation of Islam's texts and every other aspect of Islamic cultures. She asserts that the latter part of the 20th century constituted the first time that some Muslim women obtained the opportunity to retrieve Islam's original egalitarian teachings, to publicly critique Islamic societies, and to proclaim liberating paradigms for women and other marginalized groups based on those teachings.

Until the early part of the 21st century, Mernissi attempted to implement her vision for Islamic societies through her print publications, lectures, and nonelectronic political organizations. With increased use of the Internet and satellite television by many across the globe, Mernissi has utilized her Web site and her leadership in organizations such as *Synergie Civique* (Civic Synergy) and *Caravane Civique* (Civic Caravan) to promote DEMOCRACY and HUMAN RIGHTS. She envisions using satellite and other electronic means to spread her ideas in the future. The beauty and simple sophistication of Mernissi's vision and communication style coupled with the readily accessible venues for her work have been factors that have led to the popularity of her ideas inside and outside academic circles.

Jon Armajani

Further reading: Fatima Mernissi, *Dreams of Trespass: Tales of a Harem Girlhood* (New York: Perseus Publishing, 1995); ———, *Islam and Democracy: Fear of the Modern World* (New York: Perseus Publishing, 2002); ———, *Scheherazade Goes West: Different Cultures, Different Harems* (New York: Simon and Schuster, 2002); ———, *The Veil and the Male Elite: A Feminist Interpretation of Women's Rights in Islam* (New York: Perseus Press, 1992).

Mevlevi Sufi Order

The Mevlevi order is one of the most well known Sufi orders, due to its famous "whirling DERVISH" dance. It takes its name from the great 13th-century mystic poet JALAL AL-DIN RUMI, who is known in Turkish as Mevlana (from the Aratic *mawlana* = "our master"). Though Rumi's poetry was composed in Persian, the language of the Seljuk court, the order developed mostly in the Turkish context of the Ottoman Empire.

Rumi was born in Khurasan in 1207, and, shortly before the Mongol invasions, he migrated as a child with his father to Anatolia, which was then under Seljuk rule. They eventually settled in Konya, the Seljuk capital, where Rumi's father

Turkish children enact a Mevlevi *samaa* dance at a school in Nigde, Turkey. *(Juan E. Campo)*

secured a teaching position, which Rumi took over when his father died. Rumi was a respected teacher of Islamic sciences until his meeting with a mysterious figure named Shams, who inspired him to write his ecstatic poetry, and Shams introduced him to the whirling dance known as *samaa*. After his death in 1273, Rumi's circle of followers was organized into the Mevlevi order, the supervision of which was claimed by Rumi's descendants, who came to be called Chelebi. Rumi's son Sultan Walad (d. 1312) played an important role in the formation of the order, and his name was later incorporated into Mevlevi ritual.

Novices who were accepted into the order were initiated in a ceremony, after which they became known as *muhibb*. After a trial period of 1,001 days of service to the TEKKE (dervish lodge), another ceremony was held elevating the *muhibb* to the rank of dervish. Advanced dervishes could be appointed SHAYKHS, giving them the right to lead a *tekke*. Mevlevi dervishes wore a cloak (*khirka*) and a conical hat called a *sikke*. They were encouraged to learn the *samaa*, which involved a long period of instruction. The actual dance consists of repetitive counter-clockwise rotation with the right arm raised upward and the left downward, performed in four separate cycles to the accompaniment of music. The principal musical instruments used were the reed flute (*nay*) and a pair of small kettledrums (*kudum*).

The Mevlevi order came into prominence in the Ottoman period, spreading throughout Anatolia and to the Balkans and the ARAB lands. It benefited from the patronage of Ottoman SULTANS, and in one period the Chelebis were given the honor of girding new sultans with a sword at their enthronements. Some sultans were also said to be affiliated with the order. The Mevlevi order in general appealed to the upper classes and intellectuals. Mevlevi dervishes studied and produced art in the *tekkes,* and many famous Ottoman poets, composers, and calligraphers were Mevlevis. The order came to be known in Europe when travelers reported their observations of the whirling dance.

Mevlevi *tekke*s were closed along with those of all dervish orders in Turkey in 1925, and the *samaa* was prohibited. The central *tekke* at Konya, which houses the tomb of Rumi, was later opened as a museum. In 1953 the *samaa* was allowed to be performed in public, but as a cultural exhibition, rather than a religious ritual. Today, some Mevlevis continue the tradition in Turkey, but it has practically disappeared in the Balkans and Arab countries. The Mevlevi order has, however, influenced the ritual practices of other orders, such as the Jerrahis, who perform a similar *samaa*. The dance continues to be performed as a tourist spectacle, once a month in the Galata lodge in ISTANBUL, and annually in Konya at the commemoration of Rumi in December. In EUROPE and North America, the poetry of Rumi and Mevlevi rituals has attracted a new generation of spiritual seekers.

See also OTTOMAN DYNASTY; PERSIAN LANGUAGE AND LITERATURE; SELJUK DYNASTY; SUFISM.

Mark Soileau

Further reading: Ira Shems Friedlander, *The Whirling Dervishes* (New York: MacMillan, 1975); Talat Sait Halman and Metin And, *Mevlana Celaleddin Rumi and the Whirling Dervishes* (Istanbul: Dost, 1983); Franklin D.

Lewis, *Rumi: Past and Present, East and West* (Oxford: Oneworld, 2000).

mihrab

Mihrab is a term associated with the architectural vocabulary of MOSQUES, where it denotes the PRAYER niche and prayer orientation. *Mihrab* entered English usage through the accounts of 19th-century travelers whose objectives were to observe, describe, and catalogue Muslim behaviors and Islamic forms. To these European sensibilities familiar with the altars, chapels, and icons of churches, the concavity in the QIBLA wall of mosques stood out in what may have seemed rather stark interiors.

Mihrab with elaborate inlaid marble designs and inscriptions in the Sultan al-Nasir Hasan Mosque-Madrasa complex (14th century), Cairo, Egypt. *(Juan E. Campo)*

Located left of the minbar, the mihrab marked the position of prayers leaders and the direction of MECCA, and it held the promise of symbolic content. The religious emphasis was enhanced by rug dealers and collectors who, early in the 20th century, distinguished a type of rug with niche representations, dubbed "mihrab prayer rugs."

Most historical and contemporary mosques have mihrabs. In the past, these usually echoed the shape of the rounded niche that was the first form adopted for a mosque mihrab and that appeared in a series of state-sponsored monumental mosques of the early eighth century. Anatolian and Iranian mihrabs evince regional variations of this theme with their elaborate and gradated profiles, while 13th-century Ayyubid-Syrian ones are distinguished by geometric designs of inlaid marble. Today, some mihrabs are sculptural interpretations of the idea of the original; the mihrab of the King Faisal Mosque, ISLAMABAD, is an open book designed by the artist Gulgee. Mosques that omit the mihrab keep alive an historical controversy regarding the permissibility of mihrabs.

The mihrab has also generated a great deal of scholarly controversy among art/architectural historians and linguists who have attempted to fix its origins in a variety of architectural languages and contexts. However, the prevalence of the niche in late antique architecture, the continuing Arabic usage of the word in diverse ways, and even the appearance of mihrab in the QURAN (where none of its five occurrences means niche) have not supported such positivist efforts.

See also ARCHITECTURE.

Nuha N. N. Khoury

Further reading: Renata Holod and Hasan-Uddin Khan, *The Mosque and the Modern World* (London: Thames and Hudson, 1997); Nuha N. N. Khoury, "The Mihrab Image: Commemorative Themes in Early Islamic Architecture." *Muqarnas* 9 (1992): 11–28; Nuha N. N. Khoury, "The Mihrab: From Text to Form." *International Journal of Middle East Studies* 30 (1997): 1–27.

minaret (Arabic: *manara* "beacon," also *midhana* "place for making the call to prayer")

Many of the world's major civilizations have developed distinct forms or "languages" of religious ARCHITECTURE that have become emblematic for those civilizations and their dominant religious traditions. Examples include the pyramids of EGYPT and Mexico, the great Hindu temple towers of INDIA, Buddhist stupas (large hemispherical structures containing sacred relics of the Buddha), as well as the towers and spires found on many Christian churches and basilicas. For Islam, perhaps the most distinctive architectural form is the minaret, a tower where the ADHAN, or call to PRAYER, is performed. It stands within the sacred space of a MOSQUE. The minaret's antecedent is thought to have been the rooftop of MUHAMMAD's house-mosque in MEDINA, where BILAL, a former slave and one of the first Muslims, made the daily *adhan*. Later, in the wake of the early Arab conquests, churches seized from Christian opponents in SYRIA were converted into mosques and their towers were used for making the call to prayer.

The minaret as a specialized architectural form, however, did not develop until after the ninth century, especially in Sunni-majority regions of the Middle East. It became a very prominent religious signature on the Islamicate urban landscape. In addition to providing a place for making the *adhan,* the minaret informed people where the mosque was located and often symbolized the wealth and power of the individual or group who built and maintained it. In addition to mosques, it was also included in the architecture of medieval madrasas, Sufi hospices, and shrines. Minarets can be square or cylindrical in shape, or a combination of both. Most have an interior spiral staircase that leads to one or more balconies at the top, where the MUEZZIN stands to do the *adhan*. Many are made of stone, but wood, adobe, and concrete have also been used. They are often embellished with elaborate ARABESQUE designs, or bear Arabic inscriptions, but some have little decoration if any. Typically a mosque will have only one minaret, but imperial mosques often have two or more, indicating that their symbolic importance exceeds the practical purpose for performing the call to prayer. Minarets have been added to preexisting buildings, as was the case for the Aya Sofia Mosque in ISTANBUL, which had been the chief basilica for the Byzantine Empire until the city was taken by the Ottomans in 1453. The reverse happened in ANDALUSIA (Islamicate Spain), where the towering minaret La Giralda of Seville's Friday mosque was transformed into a bell tower after the city was captured by Christian armies in the 14th century. The same occurred at the Great Mosque of CORDOBA. Today, mosques in many Muslim countries are equipped with electronic sound systems for broadcasting the *adhan*, but the minaret has not been eliminated and continues to possess symbolic importance.

Different minaret styles have evolved in different parts of Islamdom, just as different kinds of church towers developed in lands with large Christian populations. These include the multistoried sculptured Mamluk minarets of 13th- to 16th-century CAIRO, which are topped by one or more bulblike decorations. North African and Andalusian minarets are square towers. Otto-

Mamluk (left) and Ottoman (center) minarets of Cairo, Egypt *(Juan E. Campo)*

man Turkish minarets have a simple design, like great pencils or rockets pointing heavenward. New minaret styles have been devised by modern architects, as can be seen at the magnificent Faysal Mosque in Islamabad, PAKISTAN, and the Islamic Cultural Center in New York City, UNITED STATES. Minarets were not used everywhere, however. Traditional mosques in EAST AFRICA, Kashmir, South India, and MALAYSIA did not have them. In the modern period minarets have become nearly universal. However, it is still possible to find mosques that lack them. This may be due to a variety of factors, including local tradition, building codes, lack of resources, or conscious decision by mosque governing boards to devote funds for other purposes.

Minarets have also gained a symbolic value beyond the limits of Islamic cultures and societies. They have been adapted for use in synagogue architecture, especially in Sephardic Jewish communities. They also hold a prominent place in romanticized Euro-American representations of the Middle East, particularly in popular art, cartoons, and the cinema. Minarets have even been used in the architecture of amusement parks, theaters, and shopping centers in EUROPE and the Americas.

See also CHRISTIANITY AND ISLAM; CITIES; SEPHARDIC JEWS.

Further reading: Doris Behrens-Abouseif, *The Minarets of Cairo* (Cairo: American University in Cairo Press, 1985); Jonathan Bloom, "The Minaret: Symbol of Faith and Power." *Saudi-Aramco World* 53, no. 2 (2002): 26–35; Omar Khalidi, "Import, Adapt, Innovate: Mosque Design in the United States," *Saudi-Aramco World* 53, no. 6 (2004).

minbar

The *minbar* is a seat raised on six or seven steps that is located against the QIBLA wall of MOSQUES. It is used by the IMAM to deliver the KHUTBA (sermon) on Fridays as it insures his visibility and allows his voice to be better heard by the assembly. At the end of the *khutba*, the imam descends from the *minbar*, turns to face the *qibla* wall (usually in front of the MIHRAB) and leads the assembled community in PRAYER. The association between the *minbar* and the imam's AUTHORITY is one reason it continues to be the most important element of mosques. Its importance was even greater in the past.

Historical sources inform us that the first *minbar* was created for the prophet MUHAMMAD's use at his mosque in MEDINA. A carpenter who observed the Prophet's fatigue during the Friday assemblies contrived a simple raised seat with steps that allowed the Prophet to sit while facing and addressing his followers. After the Prophet's death his successors (the first CALIPHS) used this seat but did not sit on the top step in honor of the Prophet's memory. This seat came to be known as the *minbar*, a term whose Arabic root signifies "amplification."

Art historians have attempted to fix the origins of the *minbar* by relating it to the pulpits of churches or the thrones of palaces. The role and importance of the mosque *minbar*, however, derives from its connection to the *khutba* and to the *khutba's* own political, social, and religious import. By extension, the *minbar* was related to the authority of the leadership that sponsored the *khutba* and protected Islam. Even when rulers no longer delivered it themselves, the *khutba* was given in their name and became the primary means of announcing and legitimating new rulers.

Since the *khutba* was delivered in the main or community mosques of towns and CITIES, the *minbar* itself became a marker of the presence of populations large enough to warrant a Friday mosque (some medieval geographers calculated the size of towns through the number of their *minbars*). It also marked the boundaries of towns, especially in situations where religious authorities allowed only one Friday mosque per city. For example, Hanafi law allows for multiple Friday mosques in a single city (which accounts for their numbers in Ottoman Constantinople) whereas the Shafii law allows only one (which accounts for the unique mosque of the city of Isfahan until its expansion in the 16th century). In time, rising populations and the consequent need for new mosques blurred the distinctions between Friday mosques and ordinary ones (*masjids*) so that now most *masjids* are also used on Fridays. Given its use, the form of the *minbar* has remained largely stable, but there are fine historical *minbars* of inlaid marble or wood, as well as new interpretations that update the general form.

Nuha N. N. Khoury

Further reading: Jonathan Bloom et al., *The Minbar from the Kutubiyya Mosque* (New York: Metropolitan Museum of Art 1998); Martin Frishman and Hasan-Uddin Khan, eds., *The Mosque: History, Architectural Development, and Regional Diversity* (New York: Thames and Hudson, 1994); Renata Holod and Hasan Uddin-Khan, *The Mosque and the Modern World: Architects, Patrons, and Designs since the 1950s* (London: Thames and Hudson, 1997).

miracle

Muslim THEOLOGY typically distinguishes between two types of miracle. One type is predicated only of the prophets, and is for the purpose of proving the authenticity of their prophetic mission. This is called a *mujiza*, literally, something the witness cannot imitate. The QURAN, believed by Muslims to be inimitable, is in this category. The other kind of miracle, in no way different in phenomenological or practical terms, is called a *karama*, and it is a gift, or a grace bestowed by God, generally to the saints (*awliya*). While theologians downplay the importance of this latter type of miracle, it is, of course, much more common and much more available to the public, and so it is widely attested and enormously popular.

In classical Islam, the belief in the saints, in their miracles, and in the social role played by holy men and WOMEN was largely taken for granted. With the institutionalization of Sufi orders, especially after the 13th century C.E., these holy people were often associated with specific orders, cherished and obeyed while alive, and venerated and supplicated after DEATH. The saints, living and dead, thus played an enormously important and well-recognized role in society, not least of which was their ability to work miracles of healing, fertility, INTERCESSION in times of need, and the countless other areas in which the saints could be of assistance.

There has always been a subculture that critiqued, limited, or sometimes utterly rejected this belief in nonprophetic miracles. The Mutazila, for whom reason was epistemologically crucial, denied the reality of nonprophetic miracles; since MUHAMMAD was the last prophet, this would mean that miracles no longer occurred. They lost most of their influence after the ninth century, and most subsequent critics of the belief in nonprophetic miracles came mainly from the intellectual line descending from TAQI AL-DIN AHMAD IBN TAYMIYYA (d. 1328), a Hanbali preacher, reformer, and intellectual of prodigious ability. Ibn Taymiyya himself did not deny the possibility of *karama*-type miracles, but he downplayed their importance by, on the one hand, encouraging Muslims to "pursue righteousness (*istiqama*), not miracles (*karama*)," while also suggesting that such miracles were for the novices, since those who have attained certainty (*yaqin*) do not need the affirmation of miracles. Because Ibn Taymiyya was scathingly critical of public veneration of saints' shrines, he effectively opposed the manner in which miracles were often sought and received, namely, by means of supplication to the saints at their tombs. Ibn Taymiyya's ideas had a very mixed reception during his life, but he gained renewed importance via the Wahhabi revivalist movement (18th century to the present) and the Salafi modernist reformers who evolved from the intellectual agitation of Sayyid JAMAL AL-DIN AL-AFGHANI (d. 1897). The 19th century—when imperialism brought Europe uninvited to much of the Islamic world—introduced the radical ideas of the Enlightenment, including the rejection of superstition and irrationality. This Enlightenment-inspired critique of "irrationality," the Salafi goal of stripping Islam of what the reformers considered non-Islamic accretions (a goal much in the spirit of the Protestant Reformation), and the puritanical model of the Wahhabis have combined in a very powerful way. At present, many Muslims regard nonprophetic miracles, saint veneration, and almost all practices associated with saints and their shrines to be both "un-Islamic" superstition and anti-modern. Thus, the more educated members of society reject a great deal of the old belief system, of which saints and miracles were integral parts, and consider their more sober and less exuberant form of religiosity to be more "Islamic" and more "rational." The world of miracles has thus been relegated, to a large extent, to that of "popular religion," or the religion of the lower classes.

Nonetheless, in countries such as EGYPT, MOROCCO, and INDONESIA, the belief in miracles, and in the saints who perform them, remains strong. Saints are expected to provide assistance, and stories confirming their miraculous activities abound. In many cases, even among the popular classes, the miracles of saints are combined with a great respect for modern science; a patient may see a doctor and also pray to the saint. Stories of saints performing miraculous surgeries of which doctors are at present incapable are not uncommon. Thus, for many, a world exists in which the miracle and the modern do not conflict but complement each other.

See also BARAKA; RENEWAL AND REFORM MOVEMENTS; SAINT; SALAFISM; TARIQA; WAHHABISM; WALI; ZIYARA.

John Iskander

Further reading: Carl W. Ernst, The Shambhala Guide to Sufism (Boston and London: Shambhala, 1997); Michael Gilsenan, Recognizing Islam: Religion and Society in the Modern Arab World (New York: Pantheon, 1982); Valerie Hoffman, Sufism, Mystics, and Saints in Modern Egypt (Columbia: University of South Carolina Press, 1995); Gregory Starrett, Putting Islam to Work: Education, Politics, and Religious Transformation in Egypt (Berkeley: University of California Press, 1998).

miraj   See NIGHT JOURNEY AND ASCENT.

Mohammedanism (Muhammedanism)

Mohammedanism is a term used by some scholars and religious officials, particularly those in EUROPE in the 18th, 19th and early 20th centuries, to identify Islam. There were previously many variants of the word, including Mahometanism, Mahometism, and Mahometry. Early in its usage, Mohammedanism (and other similar terms) often conveyed an explicitly hostile description of and attitude toward ISLAM. At other times, it was used because of an unwitting overemphasis on the role of the prophet MUHAMMAD or out of a desire to present information in a way that would make sense to Christian Europe.

Mohammedanism misrepresents Islam by implying that Muhammad is at the center of Islam, the object of worship guiding the community. Muhammad is indeed a central figure in the tradition, though only insofar as he served as a fully human conduit for God's word (QURAN) and as a model for pious and righteous behavior for the community. By focusing heavily on Muhammad, the idea of Mohammedanism as a conceptual category and descriptive term gave license to some 19th-century European scholars to claim Islam's inferiority to Christianity via criticism of Muhammad's behavior and its effect on Islam as a whole. This criticism, in contrast to the Christian idea of Christ's perfection, left Islam as merely a derivative form of Christianity and not, as Islam itself claims, its successor in the Abrahamic monotheisms.

Today, use of the term is limited almost wholly to new editions of older European and North American texts on Islam.

See also CHRISTIANITY AND ISLAM; ORIENTARISM.

Caleb Elfenbein

Further reading: Richard King, *Orientalism and Religion* (New York: Routledge, 1999); Edward Said, *Orientalism* (New York: Vintage Books, 1979).

Mohammad Reza Pahlavi (1919–1980)
the second and last shah of the Iranian Pahlavi dynasty

Mohammad Reza Pahlavi succeeded his father Reza Khan in 1941 and reigned until 1979, when he was overthrown in the popular revolution that ultimately led to the creation of the Islamic Republic of IRAN. As crown prince of Iran, Mohammad Reza lived a life of luxury that was very dissimilar to the ascetic habits of his father, REZA SHAH PAHLAVI (1878–1944). Though forced through military school in Iran and given a university EDUCATION in Switzerland, the young prince failed to display any leadership qualities and, as a result, was routinely reproached by his intimidating father as cowardly and weak. Nevertheless, after Reza Shah was compelled by the Allied forces to abdicate his throne in 1941, Mohammad Reza became the second shah of the Pahlavi dynasty.

Obliged to rely on the support of the United States and Britain to secure his AUTHORITY, Mohammad Reza continued the Western-inspired socioeconomic reforms of his father. At the same time, he retracted many of the religious restrictions—such as the outlawing of the VEIL—that had been imposed on Iran, and allowed the ULAMA greater religious freedom. Building on the massive accumulation of wealth that resulted from Iran's sale of OIL and natural gas, the new shah instituted a development and land distribution program he called the White Revolution in the 1960s, which not only privatized businesses and nationalized forests, but also for the first time gave WOMEN the right to vote.

Yet, because of his reliance on Western powers, Iran was increasingly required to comply with the political, strategic, and economic demands of its British and U.S. allies. When the shah unilaterally sold the rights to a quarter of the world's proven oil supply to the British Anglo-Iranian Oil Company, he unwittingly unleashed a resurgence of nationalist sentiment led by Iran's prime minister Muhammad Musaddiq (also spelled Mosaddeq, d. 1967) and his National Front Party. In 1953, riding a wave of anti-imperialist sentiment, Musaddiq's party forced Muhammad Reza Shah into exile and assumed control over the state. However, when Musaddiq moved ahead with his plans to nationalize Iran's oil, he was forcefully removed from power under a secret CIA (U.S./Central Intelligence Agency) operation codenamed AJAX, which reinstated Muhammad Reza as shah.

By the 1970s Mohammad Reza Shah, now propped up on the throne by the United States, had abolished the country's party system and effectively annulled its CONSTITUTION. The lack of political participation in the state, as well as the loss of national and religious identity in the face of Western cultural hegemony, led to waves of protests throughout the country, to which the shah responded ruthlessly through his dreaded secret police force, SAVAK (Organization for Intelligence and National Security). These repressive policies ultimately led to an alliance between Iran's clergy, its intellectuals, and its merchant class, headed by the shah's most vociferous critic, the Ayatollah RUHOLLAH KHOMEINI (d. 1989).

Although sent into exile in 1964, Khomeini continued promoting anti-imperialist activities against the monarchy until January 1979, when the shah was once again ousted from power. The political vacuum left behind by his departure was filled by Khomeini (r. 1979–89), who employed the language and symbolism of Iran's state religion, SHIISM, to implement his ideology of the *wilayat-i faqih* (the guardianship of the jurist), and inaugurate the Islamic Republic of Iran. One year later, in 1980, Mohammad Reza Pahlavi died in exile in Egypt.

See also COLONIALISM; IRANIAN REVOLUTION OF 1978–1979; POLITICS AND ISLAM; SECULARISM.

Reza Aslan

Further reading: Said Amir Arjomand, *The Turban for the Crown: The Islamic Revolution in Iran* (New York: Oxford University Press, 1988); Ryszard Kapuscinski, *Shah of Shahs* (New York: Harcourt Brace, 1985); Mohammad Reza Pahlavi, *The Shah's Story.* Translated by Teresa Waugh (London: Michael Joseph, 1980).

monotheism   *See* TAWHID.

moon

The moon (Arabic *qamar*) has assumed a distinctive importance in Islamic tradition. The appearance of the new or crescent moon (*hilal*) defines the beginning of each of the 12 lunar months in the Islamic CALENDAR. According to the SHARIA the *hilal* has to be seen with the naked eye in order for the first day of the month to be declared, although there are differences among the Muslim jurists about this matter. This practice, which is pre-Islamic in origin, is particularly important in identifying the beginning of the new year on the first day of Muharram, the beginning of the month of required fasting on the first day of RAMADAN, and the beginning of ID AL-FITR (the Feast of Fast-Breaking) after Ramadan on the first day of the 10th month of the Islamic calendar (Shawwal). Observation of the phases of the moon became an important topic in Islamic astronomy. There were also special prayers performed in the event of either a lunar or a solar eclipse.

The QURAN mentions the moon 26 times. One of its chapters, named "The Moon," describes the splitting of the moon as an event that precedes JUDGMENT DAY (Q 54), but this event was later claimed to be a miracle performed by MUHAMMAD (d. 632) in proving his prophethood to the unbelievers of Mecca. In other instances the moon is discussed as an aspect of God's CREATION, along with the sun and the stars, that submits to its creator (Q 22:18) and signifies one of God's blessings for humankind (Q 14:32–34). The moon is to be used as the basis of the calendar (Q 10:5). It also

appears in the story of Abraham's conversion to the worship of only one God, where he mistakes the moon for his lord (*rabb*), but then rejects this belief when he sees that it waxes and wanes in its rising and setting (Q 6:77). The Quran, moreover, explicitly prohibits worshipping both the sun and the moon (Q 41:37). In later Islamic poetry the full moon was often used as a metaphor for the beauty of the lover's face, as well as for Muhammad.

The crescent moon combined with a five- or six-pointed star has become an emblem for the Islamic religion, but only in recent times. They appeared together on early Islamic coinage, perhaps reflecting ancient Iranian, Roman, and Byzantine influences. They also occurred separately in a variety of secular and religious contexts on buildings and artifacts in Muslim lands during the medieval period. They did not have great iconographic importance until more recent centuries. The crescent and star symbol began to be used on military, imperial, and, later, national flags, first by the Ottomans in the 15th and 16th centuries, and subsequently by newly independent states in the Middle East, North Africa, South Asia, and Southeast Asia. These countries include Algeria, Azerbaijan, Malaysia, Mauritania, Pakistan, Tunisia, Turkey, and Uzbekistan. Since the 19th century the crescent-moon emblem has been used to decorate mosques and other religious buildings. Also, the U.S. Department of Veterans Affairs has accepted it as a symbol on gravestones of Muslim soldiers, making it comparable to the cross for Christians, the Star of David for Jews, the Wheel of Dharma for Buddhists, and the Sanskrit word Om for Hindus.

Some Christian evangelical organizations have claimed recently that Muslims are idolaters who actually worship a moon god. This is an unfounded assertion based on a mistaken interpretation of Muslim use of the lunar calendar instead of the solar calendar and of the crescent-star emblem. Muslims do not worship the moon or the crescent-star image in any way, as affirmed by the Quran itself.

See also CHRISTIANITY AND ISLAM; FLAG; HOLIDAYS; IDOLATRY; JUDAISM AND ISLAM.

Further reading: David King, "Science in the Service of Religion: The Case of Islam." *Impact of Science on Society* 159 (1990): 245–262; Paul Lunde, "Patterns of Moon, Patterns of Sun." *Saudi Aramco World* 55 (November–December 2004): 17–32; Annemarie Schimmel, *And Muhammad Is His Messenger: The Veneration of the Prophet in Islamic Piety* (Chapel Hill: University of North Carolina Press, 1985).

Morocco

Located on the northwestern tip of Africa, Morocco is a country roughly the size of California, with geographical features and a population size (34.3 million, 2008 est.) also similar to those of America's most populous state. Morocco's Atlantic coast stretches from the Strait of Gibraltar to the Canary Islands, and extends even further if one includes the Western Sahara (a disputed territory administered by the Moroccan government since 1975). The northern, eastern, and southern regions contain several mountain ranges, including the Rif, High Atlas, Middle Atlas, and Anti-Atlas. The country's climate is semi-arid, with deserts in the south and the east. Between the Middle Atlas and the Atlantic are Morocco's most fertile lands, including the Sebou valley, home to the cities of Meknes and FEZ. Along with Marrakech, these cities represent three of Morocco's four "imperial CITIES," with each serving as the country's capital at different historical periods. In the 20th century,

The town of Chefchaouen in Morocco's Rif Mountains, founded in the 15th century *(Federico R. Campo)*

these cities have been supplanted in importance by the Atlantic cities of Rabat and Casablanca, Morocco's modern capital and its major industrial center. Traditionally, Morocco's economy has been derived from agriculture, mineral wealth (phosphates, iron ore, manganese), and participation in the historical trans-Saharan caravan trade.

In ancient times, Morocco was loosely connected with the Roman Empire, but the area was conquered by the Arabs in the late seventh century. Morocco's indigenous peoples, the BERBERS, fought to maintain their autonomy, but they eventually adopted Islam. Early Moroccan dynasties ruled over the Western Sahara (the ALMORAVID DYNASTY, 1042–1147), central North Africa (the ALMOHAD DYNASTY, 1123–1269), or Islamic Spain (ANDALUSIA, both dynasties), and were led by Berber families who legitimized their reign through ARAB Islamic culture. Under Merinid rule (1248–1465), Fez became one of the glorious cities of Islam and a renowned center of learning. During the 16th century, political leadership passed to sharifian dynasties claiming descent from the prophet Muhammad (the Saadis, 1511–1659, and the Alawis, 1664–present). Under increasing pressure from Western powers, Morocco became a French protectorate in 1912, although the Alawi sultan was allowed to maintain his position under French control. Morocco achieved independence in 1956, after a long anticolonial struggle. The current king, Muhammad VI, rules over a constitutional monarchy that shares some limited power with a bicameral legislature, elected by the public.

The official language of Morocco is Arabic, although French is widely spoken, as are several Berber languages (Tamazight, Tachelhit, and Tarifit). The population is 99 percent Sunni Muslim, with a small number of Christians (mostly foreign) and Jews. Sufi movements have exerted extensive influence, with the largest orders being the Tijaniyya, Shadiliyya, and the Qadariyya. Tombs of Sufi saints, located throughout the country, represent pilgrimage sites and centers for annual festivals. The sharifian cult is based in the northern cities

of Fez and Mulay Idris, the latter named after the founder of Morocco's first Islamic dynasty. Moroccan Islam has traditionally followed Maliki religious law. ART, ARCHITECTURE, MUSIC, and culture combine Berber, Arab, and Andalusian themes, although the influence of European styles has become much more visible in recent years.

See also COLONIALISM; MALIKI LEGAL SCHOOL.

Stephen Cory

Further reading: Rahma Bourqia and Susan Miller, eds., *In the Shadow of the Sultan: Culture, Power and Politics in Morocco* (Cambridge, Mass.: Harvard University Press, 1999); Abdellah Hammondi, *Master and Disciple: The Cultural Foundations of Moroccan Authoritarianism* (Chicago: University of Chicago Press, 1997); James Miller and Jerome Bookin-Weiner, *Morocco: The Arab West* (Boulder, Colo.: Westview Press, 1998); C. R. Pennell, *Morocco since 1830: A History* (New York: New York University Press, 2001).

Moro National Liberation Front (MNLF)

This is one of several Muslim groups organized in the late 1960s in the PHILIPPINES after a massacre of Muslim military recruits and later attacks on Muslim communities committed by paramilitary groups called *ilaga* from 1970 to 1972. The MNLF was chaired by Nur Misuari with Abulkhayr Alonto as the vice chair. The MNLF trained and armed its soldiers in Sabah, MALAYSIA, with the strategic and financial help of members of the traditional Moro elite. Immediately following President Ferdinand Marcos's declaration of martial law in September 1972, the MNLF launched its first military offensive against the armed forces of the Philippines and thereafter seized territory in Mindanao and Sulu where they created revolutionary governing committees replacing the functions of the Manila government's political apparatus. The MNLF demanded secession from the Philippines in favor of an independent Moro state in Mindanao, Sulu, and Palawan. Seeing itself as the legitimate representative of the Moro people, the MNLF sought international recognition as the sole representative of the Moro nation (Bangsamoro). Meanwhile, one of the leaders of the MNLF, Salamat Hashim, educated in Cairo's AL-AZHAR University and influenced by the Islamic movements in the Middle East during JAMAL ABD AL NASIR's presidency, grew concerned that the leadership of the MNLF was rapidly progressing toward Marxist-Maoist politics and away from an Islamic orientation. Thus, he split from the MNLF to organize the Moro Islamic Liberation Front (MILF). Although the MNLF and the MILF signed a unity pact in 2001, the MNLF continues to be plagued by factional divisiveness fomented to some degree by the Philippine government. In December 1996 the Final Peace Agreement was signed between the Philippine government and the MNLF. In the same year, Misuari ran in the gubernatorial race for the Autonomous Region of Muslim Mindanao (ARMM) and won. However, Misuari is currently imprisoned and charged with rebellion.

Tara Munson

Further reading: Cesar A. Majul, *The Contemporary Muslim Movement in the Philippines* (Berkeley: Mizan Press, 1985); Thomas M. McKenna, *Muslim Rulers and Rebels: Everyday Politics and Armed Separatism in the Southern Philippines* (Berkeley: University of California Press, 1998); Najeeb M. Saleeby, *The History of Sulu* (Manila: Bureau of Science, Division of Ethnology Publications, 1908).

Moses (scholars debate his historicity; some place him ca. 13th century B.C.E.) (Arabic: Musa) *biblical leader who freed Israelites from slavery in ancient Egypt and received the Torah on Mount Sinai; considered an exemplary prophet in Judaism and Islam*

Moses is one of the most prominent people in the Bible and the QURAN. In both HOLY BOOKS he is portrayed as a man called by God to lead the people of ISRAEL from enslavement under the

Mount Sinai, Egypt *(Juan E. Campo)*

Egyptian pharaoh and deliver God's revelations to them. Jews refer to the Hebrew Bible as the TORAH (instruction or law) of Moses, and consider their Talmud (study or learning) to be the oral Torah of Moses. For them, he is both a prophet and a rabbi, or teacher. Moses is mentioned more than any other Hebrew prophet in the New Testament. Christians also hold him in high esteem as a lawgiver, and they have drawn parallels between him and JESUS, whom they also call the "second Moses."

Muslim understandings of Moses are based in the Quran and the Islamic scriptural commentaries (sing. TAFSIR). He is also mentioned in the hadith and in the "stories (qisas) of the prophets" literature. All of these sources presume contexts in which biblical and post-biblical accounts about Moses were in wide circulation among the Arabs, even before Muhammad's time (i.e., prior to the seventh century). His name is mentioned in the Quran more than any other prophet—136 times, not counting indirect references to him. It occurs in chapters associated with both the Meccan and Medinan phases of Muhammad's life, with the lengthiest narratives in Q 7, 18, 20, and 26. The stories are told so as to let the reader/listener draw parallels between events in the life of Moses and that of MUHAMMAD (see, for example Q 20:99).

They include accounts about God's selection of both as his prophets, how both came into confrontation with their enemies as a result of their belief in one God, how they received holy books from God (the Torah and the Quran, respectively), and how they experienced rejection by their own people. There is also a parallel drawn between the deliverance of Moses and the Israelites from Egypt and the emigration (HIJRA) of Muhammad and his followers from Mecca to Medina. Just as the pharaoh and his people were drowned in the sea, the enemies of the Muslims were also threatened with defeat and destruction. The Quran is clearly seeking to underscore the validity of Muhammad's status as a prophet by making these parallels. It is also showing how the Jews, through their disobedience, have broken their COVENANT with God, and that it has been transferred to Muhammad and his followers (Q 7:168–170).

Biblical events involving Moses also mentioned in the Quran are his being cast away on the waters as an infant by his mother to save his life (Q 20:37–40); his killing of the Egyptian (Q 28:15); his escape to Midyan (Q 28:22–28); his calling by a fire and a divine voice coming from a tree (rather than a bush) by Mount Tur (Sinai, Q 28:29–30); his performing signs and wonders before pharaoh's court (Q 7:104–109); his 40-day sojourn in the wilderness, where he received the tablets from God at the mountain (Q 7:144–145); and the Israelites' disobedience of his brother Aaron (Harun) and worship of the golden calf (Q 7:148–149; 20:85–91). A story mentioned in the Quran but not in the Bible is his journey to the "meeting place of the two seas" and encounter with a mysterious "servant of God," identified by later commentators as KHADIR (the green one), who is more knowledgeable than Moses (Q 18:60–82). Moses then travels with Khadir to acquire some of his wisdom, but shows himself to be a less than adept student. The stories of the prophets tradition elaborates on this and other narratives about Moses, including the building of a temple for God and the deaths of both Aaron and Moses in the wilderness. In accounts concerning Muhammad's NIGHT JOURNEY AND ASCENT, Muhammad enters the sixth heaven and encounters Moses there with his people. The biblical prophet declares that Muhammad is more honored in God's eyes than he, and weeps because more of Muhammad's community (UMMA) will enter paradise than of his. Later in the story, Moses helps Muhammad negotiate with God to reduce the number of daily prayers Muslims are required to perform from 50 to five.

Over time Shiis and Sufis developed their own distinctive understandings concerning the body of narratives connected with Moses. The Shia see in the relationship of Moses with his brother Aaron a prefiguration of Muhammad's relationship with ALI IBN ABI TALIB (d. 661), his cousin, son-in-law, and the first Shii Imam. They also include Moses among the prophets through whom the authority of the Imams was transmitted in the generations preceding that of Muhammad and his cousin Ali. In ISMAILI SHIISM, Moses is counted as one of seven "speaking" prophets (the others are Adam, Noah, Abraham, Jesus, Muhammad, and Muhammad ibn Ismail), who revealed God's law for all believers to obey; whereas Aaron is one of seven of seven "silent" prophets who convey the hidden truths of God's revelation to a select group of believers. Sufis, for their part, have looked to Moses's encounter with God at Sinai as an exemplary mystical experience, and they saw in his success in splitting the sea and overcoming the 40 years of trial in the desert a model for those seeking inspiration to pursue the mystic's path to unity with God. Jalal al-Din RUMI (d. 1273) taught that Moses and pharaoh were contending spiritual impulses embodied in each person, suggesting that those guided by the light of Moses will discover that Sinai, the place of the encounter with God, can be found in their own hearts.

During the 20th century the story of Moses's confrontation with pharaoh has been invoked by Islamists to justify their opposition to "disbelieving" secular regimes and tyrannical rulers.

Sayyid QUTB (d. 1966) and JIHAD MOVEMENTS in Egypt condemned JAMAL ABD AL-NASIR (d. 1970) and ANWAR AL-SADAT (d. 1981), both presidents of Egypt, for being equivalents to the unbelieving pharaoh who opposed Moses; members of the Jihad Group assassinated al-Sadat for being a disbeliever. During the IRANIAN REVOLUTION OF 1978–79, government troops were cautioned not to "kill Moses [members of the Islamic opposition] for the sake of pharaoh [the Shah's regime]." In other words, they were not to kill the Islamic revolutionaries and their masses of supporters. A well-known revolutionary poster of the time showed Ayatollah RUHOLLAH KHOMEINI standing over a fallen shah, with the phrase "For every pharaoh there is a Moses" inscribed over the Ayatollah's head, thus identifying the revolution's foremost leader with the prophet.

See also IMAM; ISLAMISM; JUDAISM AND ISLAM; KAFIR; PROPHETS AND PROPHECY.

Further reading: Gilles Kepel, *Muslim Extremism in Egypt: The Prophet and the Pharaoh.* Translated by Jon Rothschild (Berkeley: University of California Press, 1985); John Renard, *All the King's Falcons: Rumi on Prophets and Revelation* (Albany: State University of New York Press, 1994): 67–86; Ahmad ibn Muhammad al-Thalabi, *Arais al-majalis fi qisas al-anbiya, or "Lives of the Prophets."* Translated by William M. Brinner (Leiden: E.J. Brill, 2002): 278–414; Robert Tottoli, *Biblical Prophets in the Quran and Muslim Literature* (Richmond, England: Curzon Press, 2002); Brannon Wheeler, *Moses in the Quran and Islamic Exegesis* (London: Routledge, 2002).

Moslem   See ISLAM.

mosque (Arabic: *masjid,* ritual prostration place)

A HADITH that proclaims the entire world a mosque indicates that Muslims may pray anywhere as long as certain rules are observed. Chief among these is correct orientation toward MECCA, the QIBLA. An object placed in front of the person at PRAYER insures the integrity of the *qibla* by acting as a barrier (*sutra*) between this person and passersby. Ritual purity is required for the person and the prayer area. One way of insuring it is to reserve a cloth or rug exclusively for prayer. By conforming to these rules, Muslims can fulfill prayer obligations several times a day (the number varies among sects but is often five). These individual acts of prayer then create a mosque every time they take place regardless of the availability of buildings created specifically for this purpose. The absence of liturgical rituals in ISLAM also makes mosque buildings unnecessary, though they have always existed in large numbers and varied forms.

The phrase *masjid juma* (Friday mosque) or *masjid jami* ("collective" or community mosque) refers to mosques used for required group prayers on Fridays. The historical forerunner of these mosques is considered the mosque built by MUHAMMAD at MEDINA. In the past, the *jami* was distinguished by the presence of a MINBAR and was always associated with cities. These were the first mosques to acquire monumental form, a process that began in 705–715.

Mosques quickly acquired a standard set of forms and elements. The earliest ones were divided into two parts, a covered prayer hall and an open courtyard. The far wall of the prayer hall is the *qibla* wall. A niche MIHRAB marks the center of this wall in proximity to the *minbar,* with the two defining an important area (*maqsura*) often covered with a dome. ABLUTION fountains (*maydaa*) appear in or at the edges of the courtyard. Tall towers (MINARETs) mark mosques visually and transmit their presence audibly in as much as the call to prayer (ADHAN) is sometimes transmitted from them. This basic template was always subject to variation according to location, population, and sectarian divergences; and books of mosque rules became a prominent genre in the Middle Ages. Historically, the only constants were the

Sultan Hasan Mosque (left, 14th century) and al-Rifai Mosque (right, 19th century), Cairo, Egypt. Both mosques contain tombs for rulers; the Sultan Hasan Mosque also once housed four madrasas. *(Juan E. Campo)*

close association between Friday mosques and urban areas populated by Muslims and the role of mosques in announcing the presence of Islam in the land. Mosques were usually funded privately by rulers, wealthy patrons, and various social groups and organizations. Great mosques tended to legitimize the leaders, demonstrating simultaneously their piety, their wealth, and their power.

In many Muslim countries, mosques are connected to tombs and shrines for important rulers and holy people. Muhammad's mosque in Medina as an exemplary representation of this, for it also contains his tomb, as well as that of other impor-

tant members of the early Muslim community. His mosque also exemplifies the social function of the mosque, for it served as a communal meeting place. People went there both to pray and to discuss social and religious matters. Soon after the early Islamic conquests of the seventh and eighth centuries, the mosque became an identifying element of Muslim presence. It also became an important educational center, a function that contributed to the creation of the MADRASA (religious college) by the 11th century.

The most highly esteemed mosques in the Muslim world are the Grand Mosque in Mecca,

Muhammad's mosque in Medina, and the AQSA MOSQUE in JERUSALEM. The Shia would also add the mosque-tombs of their Imams, such as those of ALI IBN ABI TALIB (d. 661) in Najaf (Iraq) and HUSAYN IBN ALI IBN ABI TALIB (d. 680) in KARBALA (Iraq). Contemporary mosques are designed to accommodate new social requirements and environments, although they continue some of the older roles played by mosques. They are seldom combined with shrines any more, but they continue to serve educational as well as ritual purposes. Mosque building continues to be an important undertaking in modern Muslim societies, even among Muslims who have migrated to EUROPE and North America.

See also ARCHITECTURE; BAZAAR.

Nuha N. N. Khoury

Further reading: Martin Frishman and Hasan Uddin Khan, eds., *The Mosque: History, Architectural Development, and Regional Diversity* (New York: Thames and Hudson, 1994); Oleg Grabar, *The Formation of Islamic Art* (New Haven, Conn.: Yale University Press, 1973); Renata Holod and Hasan Uddin-Khan, *The Mosque and the Modern World: Architects, Patrons, and Designs since the 1950s* (London: Thames and Hudson, 1997); David McCauley, *The Mosque* (New York: Houghton Mifflin, 2003).

moulid See MAWLID.

Mudejar

Muslims residing willingly as subjects of a Christian kingdom of the Iberian Peninsula (*see* ANDALUSIA) were known as Mudejars. The phenomenon of Mudejarism emerged with the Christian capture of Muslim territories, for example Toledo (1085), and concluded with the decrees of compulsory conversion to Christianity (1501, 1515, 1526). The Spanish term *mudéjar* derives from an Arabic verb connoting inter alia the taming of wild animals. Mudejarism differs conceptually from the Quranic status of DHIMMI (protected peoples) that Muslims accorded non-Muslim "PEOPLE OF THE BOOK" residing in Islamic territories. Whereas Islamic law protected non-Muslims, the Mudejars could be disenfranchised and enslaved with impunity.

The survival of Mudejar culture and institutions depended upon whether the capture was accomplished through negotiated surrender or military defeat, the ratio of Muslim to Christian populations, the competing interests of the monarchy and the papacy, and economic exigencies. For instance, during the conquest of the Balearic Islands, the Muslims of Menorca refused to surrender and were enslaved. In Aragon, Navarre, Castile, and Portugal, however, many Mudejars capitulated following negotiations between local Muslim rulers and the Christians. In theory, these treaties safeguarded Mudejar property, customs, and institutions provided they swore loyalty to the monarchy and paid an annual capitulation tax. In practice, however, Mudejar rights were often curtailed.

Congregational MOSQUES were confiscated and converted into churches. In Aragon, the Crown appointed Islamic judgeships and judicial rulings could be overturned in a higher Christian court. In Navarre and especially Valencia, where the Mudejar majority constituted an indispensable economic "royal treasure," Muslims were banned from emigration to Islamic territories. Papal council edicts ordering the use of distinguishing clothing for Muslims (Fourth Lateran Council, 1215) and prohibiting the call to PRAYER and Muslim pilgrimages (Council of Vienna, 1311) were applied in Castile and Aragon, but rarely enforced in Valencia. Increasingly from the 13th century, Mudejars were confined to ghettos (*aljama*s).

Mudejar institutions declined as the supply of competent teachers of Arabic and the Islamic sciences diminished. In response, the Mudejars developed strategies of cultural resistance. Isa ibn Jubayr of Segovia translated the QURAN and an abridged SUNNA into Romance (Latin-derived languages) for the Mudejars who no longer understood Arabic. Mudejars banned from travel abroad wrote to Muslim jurists (MUFTIS) to seek legal opinions (FATWAS) regarding how to preserve Islam under Christian rule. Mudejar jurists and preachers urged the strict application of Islamic ritual purity and morality codes in everyday life. Such strategies also challenged uncompromising judges such as MUHAMMAD IBN RUSHD (d. 1122), who condemned the Mudejars for remaining in non-Muslim territory.

Under the patronage of Christian monarchs, Mudejars collaborated in the translation schools that transmitted classical and Islamic knowledge to western Europe. Mudejar architects, artisans, and institutions left their cultural imprint on the Iberian Christian kingdoms. Mudejar ARABESQUE decorations and brickwork appear in churches and palaces built in Spain and Portugal and in the Americas from the 16th century. Following the royal decrees of compulsory conversion to Christianity, Mudejars came to be known as Moriscos.

See also ARCHITECTURE; CHRISTIANITY AND ISLAM.

Linda G. Jones

Further reading: John Boswell, *The Royal Treasure: Muslim Communities under the Crown of Aragon in the Fourteenth Century* (New Haven, Conn.: Yale University Press, 1977); Robert I. Burns, *Islam under the Crusaders: Colonial Survival in the Thirteenth-Century Kingdom of Valencia* (Princeton, N.J.: Princeton University Press, 1973); L. P. Harvey, *Islamic Spain, 1250 to 1500* (Chicago: University of Chicago Press, 1990); Khaled Abou el Fadl, "Islamic Law and Muslim Minorities: The Juristic Discourse on Muslim Minorities from the Second/Eighth to the Eleventh/Seventeenth Centuries." *Islamic Law and Society* 1, no. 3 (November 1994): 141–187.

muezzin (Arabic: *muadhdhin*)

The muezzin is the man who performs the daily call to PRAYER (ADHAN). His counterpart in a church would be a bell ringer. According to Islamic tradition the first muezzin was BILAL IBN RABBAH (d. ca. 641), one of the COMPANIONS OF THE PROPHET known for his beautiful voice. Eventually the muezzin became part of the staff employed in a MOSQUE. In the early days he would do the call from any high point in the mosque so that people in the surrounding neighborhoods could hear that prayer time had arrived. When the MINARET became a standard feature of mosque ARCHITECTURE, the muezzin would climb its winding stairs to the top to do his job. Muezzins were also hired to accompany caravans that traveled to MECCA for the HAJJ. In modern times they use a public address system without having to climb up the minaret, and people can now also hear their calls to prayer via radio, television, and portable electronic devices.

Further reading: Barry Hoberman, "The First Muezzin." *Saudi Aramco World* 34 (July–August 1983): 2–3; Scott L. Marcus, *Music in Egypt: Experiencing Music, Expressing Culture* (Oxford: Oxford University Press, 2007): 1–15.

mufti

A mufti is a Sunni Muslim trained in Islamic law, the SHARIA, who has the AUTHORITY to issue formal legal opinions called FATWAS. This person's counterpart in Shii contexts is called a *MUJTAHID*. The opinions given by a mufti are informed by the QURAN, the SUNNA, and legal tradition. They can be solicited by individuals or government officials and political authorities. This function appeared early in the Muslim community when it determined that it must strive to apply the legal prescriptions of the Quran and sunna to the daily needs of the newly emerging Islamic religious and political order in the Middle East. Unlike a judge (*qadi*), a mufti's ruling was not necessarily tied to a court case, nor was it final. Rather, it had to contend with advisory opinions issued by other muftis. However, the decisions of muftis were collected in books and played an instrumental role in the development of the Islamic legal tradition. At first muftis were paid by donations from private individuals, but their decisions could often have a bearing on public life. By the 14th century, they were included in government ruling councils, together with the SULTAN and provincial governors. During the era of the OTTOMAN DYNASTY (15th–20th centuries) it became a formal government office, also known as *shaykh al-Islam,* and was regarded as the highest-ranking position in the land for religious affairs. The mufti of ISTANBUL oversaw the MADRASAS in the capital city and provided advisory opinions based on the SHARIA to the sultan and his court. With the appearance of secular nation-states based on European civil codes, the functions of muftis became more diversified. In some cases, their functions were limited to issues of family law (for example, marriage, divorce, and inheritance). Some states, such as EGYPT, TUNISIA, Oman, and PAKISTAN, have designated an official known as the Grand Mufti, who is responsible for overseeing the religious affairs of the country. Some countries with Muslim minority populations also have such officials, but they are regarded as leading representatives of the Muslim community to state authorities, rather than as sources of advisory rulings based on the sharia. These countries include Russia, France, and ISRAEL/PALESTINE.

See also FIQH, IJTIHAD; SHAYKH; ULAMA.

Further reading: Muhammad Khalid Masud, Brinkley Messick, and David S. Powers, *Islamic Legal Interpretation: Muftis and Their Fatwas* (Cambridge, Mass.: Harvard University Press, 1996); Brinkley Messick, "The Mufti, the Text, and the World: Legal Interpretation in Yemen," *Man* 21, no. 1 (March 1986): 102–119; R. C. Repp, *The Mufti of Istanbul: A Study in the Development of Ottoman Learned Hierarchy* (London and Atlantic Highlands, N.J.: Ithaca Press, 1986).

Mughal dynasty (1526–1858)

The Mughals were a Sunni dynasty that ruled much of INDIA between the 16th and 19th centuries. The name Mughal is a variant of Mongol, as the empire's founder, Babur (r. 1483–1530), claimed descent from the Mongol ruler Genghis Khan, as well as TAMERLANE. Babur became the ruler of a small territory in Central Asia at a young age. He soon set about enlarging his territory, leading raids and expeditions throughout the region. In 1504 he captured Kabul and established a kingdom in present-day AFGHANISTAN. In 1505 Babur made his first forays into India. Over the years, these forays grew from raids into serious attempts at conquest, and in 1526 Babur defeated the ruler of the DELHI SULTANATE at Panipat, near DELHI. Establishing his imperial seat at Agra, Babur continued his conquest of northern India.

Babur was succeeded by his eldest son, Humayun (r. 1530–40, 1555–56), but Babur's other sons tried to seize the throne. Sher Khan Suri, a leader of the Pashtun tribe in present-day Afghanistan, took advantage of the brothers' rivalry, defeating the Mughal army and declaring himself ruler. Humayun was forced to seek refuge in Persia (present-day IRAN). After Sher Khan's death in 1545, Babur's sons again sought control of the empire; aided by Bayram Khan, one of Babur's soldiers, Humayun finally succeeded in winning back the territory his father had left him, and established his capital at Delhi. He was succeeded by his son AKBAR (r. 1556–1605), one of the empire's greatest rulers. With the help of Bayram Khan, Akbar extended the empire until it included most of the subcontinent north of the Godavari River in South India.

To govern this vast area, Akbar developed an efficient bureaucracy. He also worked to integrate the Muslim and Hindu population of his empire (*see* HINDUISM AND ISLAM), introducing policies based on religious toleration. He abolished the *JIZYA,* the tax imposed on non-Muslim adult males, and he included Hindus as well as Muslims in his administration. Although Akbar's policies were designed to unify the empire, his support of different theological ideas made some of his Muslim subjects uneasy, and his declaration that he was the final interpreter of Islamic law alarmed the ULAMA, or religious leaders. Akbar also supported architecture and the arts, integrating Muslim and Hindu traditions to create a distinctive Mughal style.

Akbar's heir, Jahangir (r. 1605–28), lacked his father's administrative and military abilities. During Akbar's reign, European powers became an increasing presence in India, with Portuguese, English, and Dutch merchants establishing trading posts such as Bombay, Goa, and Calcutta. Jahangir's son, Shah Jahan (r. 1628–58), initially launched a fresh wave of conquest, capturing parts of the Deccan and halting the Portuguese in Bengal. He then turned much of his energy to building projects, including the Taj Mahal, built as a tomb for his beloved wife, Mumtaz Mahal, who died in 1631 while giving birth to her 14th child. Under Shah Jahan, Delhi became one of the great cities of the Muslim world. However, his lavish expenditures drained the imperial treasury, while trade fell increasingly into the hands of European powers. In 1658 his son AURANGZEB (r. 1658–1707) seized the throne, imprisoning his father and having his brothers killed.

Aurangzeb ruled with a reformer's zeal. An intensely devout Sunni Muslim, he declared SHARIA, or Islamic law, the law of the land, and strictly enforced regulations against drinking, gambling, and prostitution. He reinstated the *jizya*, or tax on non-Muslims, while abolishing all taxes not authorized by Islamic law. The reintroduction of the *jizya* meant that the tax burden fell most heavily on the empire's Hindu population, while the abolition of other taxes reduced the empire's revenues overall. Although he succeeded in capturing the sultanates of Bijapur and Golconda, he was unable to subdue the Marathas, a

Taj Mahal (17th century), built by Shah Jahan in memory of his wife, Mumtaz Mahal, Agra, India *(Juan E. Campo)*

Hindu tribal confederacy in the Deccan. Over the course of Aurangzeb's long reign, uprisings were common; his sons were all imprisoned for instigating rebellions. By the time he died, after ailing for almost 50 years, the empire was in decline.

The empire was soon under attack from both without and within. Aurangzeb's death was followed by a series of struggles for the throne. Between 1707 and 1719, the empire had five rulers. In 1739 Persian leader Nadir Shah invaded from the northwest, defeating the Mughal army and sacking Delhi. His successor made regular attacks on India. At court, the disputed successions and brief reigns led to chaos within the administration, and various regions began to rule as independent states. The British also took advantage of the fractured empire, pressing for—and receiving—trade privileges.

At the same time, the British and French extended their hostilities in Europe to the Indian subcontinent. Soon both the British East India Company and its French counterpart, the Compagnie des Indes, were supporting contenders for power in various Indian states. By the mid-1700s, although the Mughals still ruled in name, the English East India Company was effectively the main power in India. The last Mughal emperor, Bahadur Shah Zafar II, was tried for sedition by the British in 1857 and exiled to Burma. The English East India Company was abolished and India became a British colony, governed directly by parliament.

See also CHISHTI SUFI ORDER; COLONIALISM.

Kate O'Halloran

Further reading: William Dalrymple, *The Last Mughal: The Fall of a Dynasty, Delhi, 1857* (New York: Random House, 2006); John F. Richards, *The Mughal Empire* (Cambridge: Cambridge University Press, 1993); Annemarie Schimmel, *The Empire of the Great Mughals: History, Art, and Culture* (New Delhi: Oxford University Press, 2005).

Muhajirun *See* EMIGRANTS.

Muhammad (Arabic: praiseworthy)

(ca. 570–632) *historic founder and prophet of Islam*

Recognized as both a prophet and a statesman, Muhammad delivered the QURAN to the people of MECCA and MEDINA and created a religious community that would grow into a great civilization after his death. He is beloved by Muslims, who follow his example in their spiritual and worldly affairs.

Recognizing Muhammad as God's messenger (*Rasul Allah*) is a central requirement of Islam, as reflected in the second part of the SHAHADA, or Muslim testimony of faith. He lived in the western part of the Arabian Peninsula during the sixth and seventh centuries, when the major empires of the time, Byzantium and Persia, were being weakened by warfare and internal strife. But Muhammad's importance in the history of religions and civilizations extends far beyond his land and time. His major contribution is the QURAN, the Islamic holy book, which Muslims believe he received from God during the last 23 years of his life. Muhammad's own words and deeds (the HADITH) are known to Muslims everywhere, and they have given a distinctive stamp to the spiritual, moral, cultural, social, and political contours of their lives.

His full name is Abu l-Qasim Muhammad ibn Abd Allah al-Hashimi al-Qurashi. The first part of his name, which means "Qasim's father," indicates that he had a son named al-Qasim; Abd Allah ("servant of God") was Muhammad's father, a member of the clan of Hashim of the QURAYSH tribe. Sources say that Qasim died when he was only two years old. Muhammad has traditionally been known by numerous other names, too, including *Ahmad* ("most praiseworthy"), *al-Mahmud* (a variant of Muhammad), *al-Mustafa* ("chosen one"), and *al-Amin* ("trustworthy one"). In addition to calling him God's Messenger, Muslims also know him reverently as *al-Nabi* ("prophet") and *al-Habib* ("beloved"). They believe that he is a descendant of ABRAHAM and Ishmael, two major figures in the Hebrew Bible. He is also recognized

An Ottoman *hilya,* or word-portrait of Muhammad's physical appearance, based on the description attributed to Ali ibn Abi Talib. It is embellished with Quran verses and the names of the first four caliphs.

in the Quran (Q 33:40) as the Seal of the Prophets (*khatam al-nabiyyin*), which, according to Islamic belief, means that he is the last one to bring God's word to humankind.

The main source for knowing about Muhammad's life is a BIOGRAPHY known as the *Sira* (also known as *Sirat Rasul Allah*), written in the middle of the eighth century by MUHAMMAD IBN ISHAQ (d. 767) and later edited by Ibn Hisham. This book weaves oral history and legendary accounts into a grand heroic narrative. The Quran is also a source for biographical information, but it contains mainly indirect references to events in his

life, except for the last 10 years in Medina. Scholars have obtained additional information from the hadith, but both Muslims and non-Muslims suspect that some, if not many, of the assertions were invented after Muhammad's death. There is scant knowledge about Muhammad's childhood, even the exact year of his birth is uncertain. It is generally agreed that he was born in MECCA to a family belonging to the clan of the Banu Hashim, a branch of the powerful Quraysh tribe that dominated the city in the late sixth century. This was the chief city of western Arabia and it was home to a major temple, the KAABA, where Arabian gods and goddesses were worshipped and where sacred relics were housed. The Quraysh tribe profited from its being a pilgrimage center for people living in the region.

MUHAMMAD IN MECCA

Muhammad's father died before his birth, and, in accordance with Arab custom, he was nursed by a Bedouin woman, Halima. According to early biographical lore, he was taken aside by two men dressed in white (identified as angels in some accounts), who opened his belly and purified his heart with snow, an event that was taken as a sign that he was destined to become a prophet. Muslim commentators also associated it with the chapter of the Opening of the Breast in the Quran (Q 94). Muhammad's mother Amina died when he was six years old, so he became a dependent of his paternal grandfather, Abd al-Mutallib. Then, when his grandfather died two years later, he was cared for by his paternal uncle, Abu Talib. As a youth, Muhammad became involved in Mecca's caravan trade, which brought him into contact with peoples living in other parts of the Arabian Peninsula and Syria. As an adult his career was bolstered by marriage to KHADIJA (d. 619), a wealthy Meccan businesswoman who was about 15 years older than he. She was to bear all his children—several daughters, including FATIMA (d. 633), and two sons, both of whom died in infancy. Known for his honesty, Muhammad mediated a dispute that erupted when the leading tribes of Mecca fell into a dispute when rebuilding the Kaaba about who would place the sacred BLACK STONE in its southern corner. He had the stone placed on a large cloth and instructed representatives of the different factions to join in lifting the cloth and carrying it to the shrine. Then he took the stone and placed it in the corner of the temple himself, thereby resolving the crisis.

Muhammad's career as a prophet did not begin until later in life, around the year 610, when he was about 40 years old. Accounts say that he would go into the mountainous wilderness outside Mecca on retreats. It was during a retreat to Hira, a cave in a nearby mountain, that he had a vision of the angel GABRIEL (the Quran indicates the vision was of God himself) and received the first quranic revelations, which commanded, "Recite in the name of your lord who created, created humans from a clot of congealed blood. Recite, and your lord is most generous, who taught by the pen, taught humans what they did not know" (Q 96:1–2). Muhammad was reportedly profoundly shaken by this encounter and sought reassurance from Khadija and Waraqa ibn Nawfal, a male relative of hers familiar with Jewish and Christian scriptures. They convinced him that the REVELATION was truly from God. When Muhammad made his revelations public, he was suspected of being a soothsayer inspired by spirits known as jinn. But a message he received from God confirmed for him that this was not the case (Q 52:29). Rather, he was God's prophet sent to remind people in clear Arabic speech that they should worship God alone, follow "the straight path," and give up their pagan ways. He also warned them that they would be accountable on JUDGMENT DAY for their disbelief, at the same time promising that those who had true faith and performed good deeds need not fear—they would be rewarded in PARADISE. In addition to their beliefs, therefore, Muhammad warned his listeners that God would judge them on moral grounds, especially for their treatment of the poor and the weak. The early chapters of the

Quran that he communicated to his listeners were delivered in a terse, energetic style, as if to signal the urgency of his message. Later chapters were more prosaic, featuring elaborated descriptions of the AFTERLIFE, moral teachings, and stories about former prophets and the fates of those who failed to heed them. Many of these prophets' stories were drawn from the Jewish and Christian Bible, and from post-biblical narratives that circulated orally among the peoples of the Middle East. Although the Quran tells us very little about Muhammad's life, these tales about earlier prophets, especially ABRAHAM and MOSES, were indirect commentaries on key moments in his own career—his encounters with God, his struggles against idolatry and persecution, and his mission to win believers.

The early sources also maintain that Muhammad went on a miraculous journey from Mecca into heaven one night, mounted on a winged animal and guided by Gabriel. This legendary event, known as the NIGHT JOURNEY AND ASCENT, appears to be mentioned briefly in the Quran (Q 17:1), but the story was continually elaborated in the following centuries along the lines of other-world journeys mentioned in pre-Islamic Jewish and Christian literatures, where the journeys were undertaken by holy figures like Enoch and Paul. According to Islamic accounts, Muhammad visited different levels of heaven, where he met holy figures such as Adam, JESUS, JOHN THE BAPTIST, JOSEPH the son of Jacob, IDRIS (probably Enoch), Moses, and Abraham. Finally, after visions of paradise and the fires of hell, he encounters God and receives the instructions for performing the five daily prayers. Muhammad then returned to Mecca.

The sources indicate that Muhammad's message was heeded by individuals from a cross-section of Mecca's society, starting with his own family—his wife Khadija, paternal cousin ALI IBN ABI TALIB (d. 661), and members of the clans of his mother and father. When he began to preach in public, he won followers like ABU BAKR (d. 634), a merchant, and members of the most powerful branches of the QURAYSH tribe, such as UMAR IBN AL-KHATTAB

(d. 644) and UTHMAN IBN AFFAN (d. 656). These four men were to become the first four caliphs, or successors to Muhammad, after his death in 632. Many of the converts were young Arabs of modest social standing, including women. There were also freedmen and slaves such as BILAL IBN RABBAH (d. 641), an Ethiopian, who would become the first MUEZZIN for the community. Muhammad's early prophetic pronouncements, together with the growth of a religious movement that appealed to diverse members of Meccan society, stirred vehement opposition among the wealthy and powerful, especially the leading clans of the Quraysh. They felt that he was not only attacking their religious and tribal values, but he was also threatening their lucrative pilgrimage businesses. By 615 their ire appears to have become so intense that Muhammad was obliged to dispatch a group of his followers to Ethiopia for protection under that country's Christian rulers. This was called the first Islamic HIJRA (emigration). Back in Mecca, believers were subjected to verbal attacks, ostracism, and an unsuccessful boycott.

Muhammad's position became especially tenuous when his uncle Abu Talib and his wife Khadija both died in 619, leaving him without his two most respected guardians. He began to search for new allies outside of Mecca, and finally found them in Yathrib, an agricultural settlement about 275 miles north of Mecca. In his negotiations Muhammad agreed to serve as a mediator between the two leading tribes in the town, the Aws and the Khazraj, in exchange for their conversion to Islam and permission to migrate there with his followers. His followers quietly began to leave Mecca. Barely escaping a plot against his life, Muhammad joined the rest of the Muslim emigrants, about 70 in number, in Yathrib around September 24, 622. This was the second Hijra, but the one that would be forever remembered by Muslims as *the* Hijra, which was later proclaimed to mark the first year on the Muslim lunar CALENDAR. Yathrib eventually became known as the City (*madina*) of God's Prophet, or simply MEDINA.

MUHAMMAD IN MEDINA

After his arrival, Muhammad recruited his followers to help him build his house, which became the main mosque for the early Muslim community (UMMA), and Islam's second most sacred mosque after that of Mecca. He also established a covenant, the so-called Constitution of Medina, that affirmed the mutual rights and obligations of the EMIGRANTS (*muhajirun*) from Mecca and Muhammad's Medinan converts, the "Helpers" (ANSAR). It affirmed the legal status of Jews and non-Muslim Arab members in Medina, and prohibited any alliances with the community's enemies. It also declared that any disputes were to be resolved by referring them to God and Muhammad. The chapters of the Quran that are traditionally ascribed to this period of Muhammad's career reflect the changing fortunes of the young community. They continue to affirm and expand upon key themes from the Meccan period, but they also contain rules and guidelines for the faithful concerning worship, almsgiving, family law, relations with non-Muslims, and incitements to act in defense of the community against its enemies.

Soon after arriving in Medina, Muhammad was drawn into open warfare with his opponents in Mecca, the Quraysh and their allies. He also had to contend with opposition from Jewish tribes in Medina, namely, the Banu Nadir and the Banu Qurayza, who refused to recognize his authority as prophet and formed secret alliances with the Quraysh. In 624 skirmishes with Meccan caravans led to the Battle of Badr, which ended in victory for the Muslims. This was a momentous event for the young community, in which, according to the Quran, 3,000 angels were sent to help the faithful (Q 3:123–125). Another clash at Uhud in 625 ended in a nearly disastrous defeat for the Muslims and the wounding of Muhammad. The Meccans assembled a large force of 10,000 warriors (a probable exaggeration) in April 627 and laid siege to Medina for about a month. The confrontation, known as the Battle of the Ditch, ended with the withdrawal of the Meccan forces and the alleged extermination of Banu Qurayza males because some of them conspired with the Quraysh against Muhammad. The Muslims and the Quraysh negotiated a peace in 628 that allowed Muslims to go to Mecca the following year for the UMRA, or "lesser" pilgrimage. A minor infraction of the treaty was used by Muhammad to justify an attack on Mecca, the city of his birth. It fell to Muslim forces with minimal loss of life in January 630. One of the factors contributing to their triumph was the conversion of Abu Sufyan, the leader of Muhammad's Quraysh opponents. Muhammad then launched a campaign to destroy the idols worshipped in Mecca and the surrounding towns, but some reports say that he exempted pictures of Jesus and Mary that had been kept inside the Kaaba with other idols. Even though Mecca was now under Muslim rule, Muhammad declared that he preferred to keep his home in Medina.

During this phase in Muhammad's career he established alliances with Arabian tribes, which included their conversion to Islam. He also ordered successful attacks on oases and towns along the roads that led northward into Syria and Iraq. In 627–28 Byzantine forces defeated the Persians who had been the main power in the region. This created a situation that Arab Muslim forces would take advantage of after Muhammad's death to defeat both the Byzantines and the Persians and create a new empire in their place.

Muhammad performed a "farewell HAJJ" to Mecca in 632. Muslim commentators say that it was on this occasion when he pronounced the following verse from the Quran: "Today I perfected your religion (*din*) for you, perfected my grace for you, and desired that Islam be your religion" (Q 5:2). According to the account furnished by Ibn Ishaq in the *Sira,* Muhammad instructed the faithful on how to perform the rites of the hajj and gave a sermon in which he stated, "Time has completed its cycle and is as it was on the day God created the heavens and the earth" (Ibn Ishaq, p. 651). After completion of the hajj he returned to Medina, where he suddenly fell ill and died in the lap of Aisha, his wife, on June 8, 632. He was buried by his Companions in his house, where his grave is now marked by the Green Dome of his mosque in Medina.

MUHAMMAD'S LEGACY

The Quran lays the foundations for Muslim understandings of Muhammad. It not only places him in the ranks of former prophets known to the Bible and the Arabs, but it also sets him apart from them at a higher rank. It declares him to be the Seal of the Prophets "who has knowledge of everything" (Q 33:40), which Muslims interpret to mean that he is the last of the prophets to bring God's word to humankind. Muhammad is called *al-nabi al-ummi* (Q 7:158), which has been widely understood by Muslims as an affirmation of his being an "unlettered prophet" who received his religious knowledge only from God and not from human sources. Additionally, the Quran calls him the "beautiful model" (*al-urwa al-hasana*) for those who hope for God and the last day" (Q 33:21).

Muhammad is believed to excel in the qualities of moral excellence and physical perfection, serving as the example for others to emulate through his SUNNA, as recorded in the hadith. All of the Islamic schools of law regard the sunna as one of the "roots" of FIQH (jurisprudence), second only to the Quran. In addition to countless biographies written about him, a sizeable body of Islamic literature concerned with detailing his virtues, known as the *shamail,* was composed by Muslim writers, one of the most prominent of whom was Qadi Iyad (d. 1149), a Maliki jurist in Andalusia and Ceuta. The Shia venerate Muhammad both as the last prophet and as the father of the Imams. He is one of the five members of the People of the House (AHL AL-BAYT), together with Fatima, his daughter, Ali, his cousin and son-in-law, and their sons Hasan and Husayn. All of the Sufi brotherhoods traced their spiritual lineage to Muhammad. Moreover, those influenced by IBN AL-ARABI (d. 1240) and Islamic Neoplatonism, identified the Prophet's beauty and excellence with the doctrine of the PERFECT MAN, the first thing God created, and his last messenger, who mediated between himself and his creation.

Since the l2th–13th century Muslims have celebrated the anniversary of Muhammad's birth and death, known as the Prophet's MAWLID, although religious conservatives have condemned this holiday as an illegitimate innovation (BIDAA). His mosque in Medina became a major shrine shortly after his death, and most pilgrims who go to Mecca still visit it during their journey. It is considered to be the second most holy place after Mecca. The pious believe that blessing the Prophet and visiting his grave will win them his intercession on Judgment Day. Muhammad has been praised in poetry and songs, including modern compositions recorded by leading performing artists. Many Muslims claim to have had visions of him in their DREAMS, thus giving whatever the dream revealed validity. Turkish calligraphers have assembled Quran verses and hadiths about the Prophet to create verbal portraits known as hilya, which people display in mosques and homes in order to imbue them with divine blessing (BARAKA). In the face of growing Euro-American influence and Christian missionary activities, modern Muslim writers have portrayed Muhammad variously as a unique symbol of Islamic civilization, a revolutionary hero, and a brilliant politician and military strategist.

Muhammad has usually been judged harshly by non-Muslims, especially in Europe and North America. With some exceptions, authorities in the medieval Latin church regarded him as a magician, false prophet, power-hungry charlatan, and hedonist. Crusaders depicted Muhammad as a pagan god, while Dante Alighieri (d. 1321), the famous Italian poet, consigned Muhammad and Ali to the level of hell reserved for heretics. The legacy of these medieval views has continued until the present. In the Age of Reason he was seen as an imposter, and even as the Antichrist in some polemical works. During the 18th century some scholars began to regard him in a more favorable light. One of the most positive non-Muslim

interpretations written during this period was that of the Victorian historian and essayist Thomas Carlyle (d. 1881). His book *On Heroes, Hero Worship, and the Heroic in History* (1859) included an essay that refuted the medieval stereotypes about Muhammad and portrayed him instead as a thoughtful and upright man of religion. Nevertheless, negative views have persisted, as made evident in William Muir's *Life of Mahomet* (1858), which explained Muhammad's experiences as a result of epileptic seizures. More recently, Salman Rushdie's fictional portrayal of Muhammad as a doubt-ridden man in his book Satanic Verses (1987) and derogatory cartoon images of him published in a Danish newspaper (2006) sparked widespread controversy and protest around the world. Such incidents will no doubt arise on occasion. At the same time, however, Muslim and non-Muslim scholars in North America and Europe are contributing to the growing body of knowledge about Muhammad's role in early Islamic history and the significance of his standing in Muslim devotional life in different times and places. Inter-religious DIALOGUE between Muslims and non-Muslims is also contributing to less polemical understandings of Islam's prophet.

See also ADAB; ARABIAN RELIGIONS, PRE-ISLAMIC; COMPANIONS OF THE PROPHET; HASHIMITE DYNASTY; HOLIDAYS; HYPOCRITES; IDOLATRY; JUDAISM AND ISLAM; MOHAMMEDANISM; PBUH; PEOPLE OF THE BOOK; PROPHETS AND PROPHECY; REVELATION; SATANIC VERSES; SAYYID: SHIISM; SUFISM.

Further reading: Ali S. Asani, Kemal Abdel-Malik, and Annemarie Schimmel, *Celebrating Muhammad: Images of the Prophet in Popular Muslim Poetry* (Columbia: University of South Carolina Press, 1995); Muhammad Husayn Haykal, *The Life of Muhammad*. Translated by Ismail R. Faruqi (Indianapolis: American Trust Publications, 1976); Muhammad ibn Ishaq, *The Life of Muhammad: A Translation of Ibn Ishaq's Sirat Rasul Allah*. Translated by Alfred Guillaume (Oxford: Oxford University Press, 1955); Ibn Kathir, *The Life of the Prophet Muhammad*. Translated by Trevor Le Gassick

(Reading, England: Garnet Publishing, 1998); F. E. Peters, *Muhammad and the Origins of Islam* (Albany: State University of New York Press, 1994); ———, *A Reader on Classical Islam* (Princeton, N.J.: Princeton University Press, 1994, 44–98); Maxime Rodinson, "A Critical Survey of Modern Studies of Muhammad." In *Studies on Islam,* edited by Merlin Swartz, 23–85 (New York: Oxford University Press, 1981); ———, *Muhammad.* Translated by Anne Carter (New York: New Press, 2002); Annemarie Schimmel, *And Muhammad Is His Messenger: The Veneration of the Prophet in Islamic Piety* (Chapel Hill: University of North Carolina Press, 1985); Barbara Stowasser, *Women in the Quran: Traditions and Interpretation* (Oxford: Oxford University Press, 1994); W. Montgomery Watt, *Muhammad: Prophet and Statesman* (London: Oxford University Press, 1961).

Muhammad Ali dynasty

This dynasty was founded by Muhammad Ali Pasha (r. 1804–48) when he was appointed governor of EGYPT by the Ottoman SULTAN in gratitude for his help in defeating the French forces in Egypt. Muhammad Ali was determined to both modernize Egypt and establish an independent dynasty there. A man of amazing drive and ambition, he achieved both. He was succeeded by his descendants Abbas (r. 1848–54), Said (r. 1854–63), Ismail (r. 1863–79), Tawfiq (r. 1879–92), Abbas II (r. 1892–1914), Husayn Kamil (r. 1914–17), Fuad (r. 1917–36), and Faruq (r. 1936–52).

Muhammad Ali is considered the father of modern Egypt; he set Egypt on the path of rapid modernization and industrialization, forces that were then continued by his successors. His grandson, Ismail, once expressed his conviction to Europeanize Egypt, stating: "My country is no longer in Africa, it is now in Europe." Ismail encouraged the development of a European-educated Egyptian elite while at the same time holding on to a traditional and autocratic view of his own authority. He was granted the title of khedive from the Ottoman sultan, which conveyed a form of royalty, and was given permission to expand his own army and issue his own currency. Ismail used the greater freedom in economic affairs to fund his ambitious development projects. In the process, however, he drove Egypt into bankruptcy. In 1876 the British took over the Egyptian economy and were drawn further into Egyptian affairs when they forcefully put down the popular Urabi revolt in 1882. Under British occupation access to free EDUCATION was restricted and Egyptian industry was neglected while cotton production increased for export to English factories. Egypt had not become a part of Europe, but it had become a part of a European empire and was forced to develop in ways that benefited the colonizer more than the colonized.

In 1922 Britain declared Egypt independent, and London elevated the status of the Egyptian ruler to king. But the British undermined the idea

Muhammad Ali Mosque (19th century), Cairo Citadel, Egypt *(Juan E. Campo)*

of both independence and kingship by retaining responsibility for communications and for defense of Egypt as well as foreign affairs within Egypt. Although a parliament and CONSTITUTION were also established, the effectiveness of both was limited as the monarchy, the parliament, and the British were in a continuous tug-of-war for control of Egyptian affairs. The king looked to the British to support him against the reforming efforts of the parliament, ultimately undermining his authority and hindering the development of the country. Moreover, the king and the parliament, made up of Western-trained elites, were cut off from the majority of the people. Caught in their own power struggles, they failed to address the real and growing needs of the Egyptian people. Egypt was crippled by social injustices and huge economic disparities. The personal excesses of King Faruq only confirmed the people's perception that the government was corrupt and irreligious. The final blow to the old regime came with the military catastrophe of 1948 when the Egyptian army (along with those of Syria and Jordan) was soundly defeated by the new state of ISRAEL.

Political disorder and social disarray continued until popular riots broke out in January 1952. A few months later the government fell in a military coup d'état led by JAMAL ABD AL NASIR. Three days later King Faruq was forced to abdicate and compelled to go into exile. There was no violence; he set sail from Alexandria on the royal yacht and spent the remainder of his life on the French Riviera. In 1953 the monarchy was officially abolished and Egypt was declared a republic.

The Muhammad Ali dynasty transformed Egypt, laying the foundations for the governmental infrastructure and administration that are still the basis for Egyptian government today. However, the dynasty also encouraged some of the ideological and economic rifts that continue to plague Egyptian society.

See also ABDUH, MUHAMMAD; COLONIALISM; RENEWAL AND REFORM MOVEMENTS.

Heather N. Keaney

Further reading: Joel Beinin and Zachary Lockman, *Workers on the Nile: Nationalism, Communism, Islam and the Egyptian Working Class, 1882–1954* (Princeton, N.J.: Princeton University Press, 1987); Arthur Goldschmidt, Jr., *Modern Egypt: The Formation of a Nation-State* (Boulder, Colo.: Westview Press, 1991); Afaf Lutfi al-Sayyid Marsot, *Egypt's Liberal Experiment: 1922–1936* (Berkeley: University of California Press, 1977); Robert L. Tignor, *Modernization and British Colonial Rule in Egypt, 1882–1914* (Princeton, N.J.: Princeton University Press, 1966); P. J. Vatikiotis, *The History of Modern Egypt: From Muhammad Ali to Mubarak,* 4th ed. (Baltimore: Johns Hopkins University Press, 1991).

Muhammad al-Mahdi (868; disappeared 874 C.E.) *the 12th and last Imam in Twelver Shiism, considered by the majority of Shiis to be the Mahdi*

Immediately upon becoming the 12th IMAM at the age of six, Muhammad ibn al-Hasan (as he was originally known) was taken away and hidden by the Shia in an attempt to save him from imprisonment at the hands of the ABASSID CALIPHATE. Thus, for the first few years of his imamate, Muhammad was represented in the community by his agents who claimed to be in contact with the young Imam and who spoke for him on matters of law and religion. This period from 874 to 941 became known as the Lesser Occultation, so called to differentiate it from the Greater Occultation that occurred when, according to his agents, Muhammad ibn al-Hasan left the earth, ceased communication with his followers, and became Muhammad al-Mahdi: the Hidden Imam who will return at the end of time to restore justice on earth and usher in the JUDGMENT DAY.

See also GHAYBA; MAHDI; SHIISM; TWELVE-IMAM SHIISM.

Reza Aslan

Further reading: Jassim M. Hussain, *Occultation of the Twelfth Imam* (London: The Muhammadi Trust, 1982); Abdulaziz A. Sachedina, *Islamic Messianism* (New York: State University of New York Press, 1981).

Muharram

The month in which the Shia celebrate the death of the third imam, HUSAYN IBN ALI IBN ABI TALIB. The first month in the Islamic CALENDAR, Muharram is most famous for the Shii commemoration that takes place during its first 10 days and culminates in the festival of ASHURA on the 10th day of the month. It is on Ashura that al-Husayn's martyrdom at KARBALA (680)—the defining moment in the development of SHIISM—is remembered through ritual acts of communal mourning such as *taziyeh* performances and *matam* processions.

Taziyeh is a passion play, performed almost entirely in verse, which recounts in dramatic form the final moments of al-Husayn and his followers at Karbala. Although considered the only indigenous drama in the Islamic world, the *taziyeh* is not so much a theatrical production as it is ritualized mourning. Just as in the Christian passion plays, which commemorate the death of Christ, the audience at a *taziyeh* participate fully in the performance by weeping loudly and beating themselves on the chest in mourning for the fallen martyrs at Karbala.

Matam refers to self-flagellation, either with chains on the back or with blows to the forehead, where a small incision has been made to encourage bleeding. Although *matam* is not universally performed, it is meant to be a public and communal activity. Indeed, it is as much a form of proselytization as it is an act of devotion. And while it may appear to be a ghastly and bloody spectacle to some, according to most participants it is a nearly painless activity that leaves no permanent disfigurement. The most important aspect of *matam* is not feeling pain but shedding blood as a symbol of sacrifice.

Muharram activities such as *taziyeh* and *matam* not only allow the Shia to physically and emotionally connect themselves to the martyrdom of al-Husayn, but they also foster a continued self-assessment of one's commitment to the ideals of Shiism, particularly with regard to the pursuit of justice and morality against tyranny and evil. Nevertheless, one should not think that Muharram is sacred only to the Shia. All Muslims celebrate the first day of Muharram as the Islamic New Year, and Sunni Muslims consider Ashura a day of blessings and spiritual renewal.

Reza Aslan

Further reading: Heinz Halm, *Shi'a Islam: from Religion to Revolution* (Princeton, N.J.: Markus Wiener, 1997); David Pinault, *Horse of Karbala: Muslim Devotional Life in India* (New York: Palgrave, 2001); Vernon Schubel, *Religious Performance in Contemporary Islam* (Columbia: University of South Carolina Press, 1999).

mujaddid   See RENEWAL AND REFORM MOVEMENTS.

mujahid (pl. *mujahidin*)

Literally, "one who strives in the path of God," the Arabic term often refers to those who undertake holy war on behalf of Islam. The plural, *mujahidin,* has been applied in the modern era to a number of groups leading revivalist or anticolonial movements. Examples include the *mujahidin* led by Shah Wali Allah and Sayyid Ahmad Brelwi in South Asia during the 18th and 19th centuries, or the JIHAD movements of WEST AFRICA and the Mahdist MOVEMENT in the SUDAN during the same time period.

Technically, jihad (in the sense of war) can be launched only against disbelievers who resist or repress the practice of ISLAM. However, in the mid-20th century, Islamists such as SAYYID QUTB (d. 1966) redefined the term KAFIR (disbeliever) to include professing Muslim political leaders who fail to implement Islamic law and whose practice of Islam is deemed to be insufficient by the Islamists. As a result, radical organizations claiming to be *mujahidin* have increasingly attacked secular Muslim leaders, intellectuals, or writers, along with the usual colonial or neocolonial targets. In their pursuit of war, these groups undertake terrorist actions while justifying their deeds in quranic terms.

Such activity has dramatically increased since the mid-1970s. *Mujahidin* groups led Afghan resistance to the Soviet invasion during the 1980s, supported the 1978 Iranian revolution and sought to export that revolution to other Middle Eastern sites, assassinated secular leaders in EGYPT and other locations, resisted Russian authorities in CHECHNYA and Israeli authorities in PALESTINE, launched terrorist operations throughout the world, including the attacks of September 11, 2001, and kidnapped/executed Westerners in combat zones such as LEBANON and IRAQ. Moderate Muslims reject such interpretations of jihad, often emphasizing the primacy of the so-called greater jihad (a peaceful struggle against unrighteousness in one's own life and one's community). However, the *mujahidin* recruit warriors and gain support for their actions by tapping into considerable Muslim resentment toward Western power and excesses as well as fears regarding threats to their faith from Western influences. It is clear that the struggle over the interpretation of jihad will be a major issue within the Muslim world for years to come.

See also AFGHAN MUJAHIDIN.

Stephen Cory

Further reading: J. J. G. Jansen, *The Neglected Duty: The Creed of Sadat's Assassins and Islamic Resurgence in the Middle East* (New York: Macmillan, 1986); Gilles Kepel, *Jihad: The Trail of Political Islam.* Translated by Anthony Roberts (Cambridge, Mass.: Harvard University Press, 2002); Barry Rubin and Judith Colp Rubin, eds. *Anti-American Terrorism and the Middle East: A Documentary Reader* (Oxford: Oxford University Press, 2002).

Mujahidin-i Khalq (The People's Religious Warriors, or People's Mujahidin; also Mojahedin-e Khalq; acronym: MEK)

Officially known as the Sazman-i Mujahidin-i Khalq-i Iran (People's Mujahidin Organization of Iran, acronym PMOI), the MEK is a group of Shii Muslim-Marxist revolutionaries that arose during the 1960s to oppose the regime of MUHAMMAD REZA SHAH PAHLAVI of IRAN (r. 1953–79). It was one of several anti-shah movements that objected to his authoritarian rule and his strong pro-American stance. The real catalyst for this opposition was the White Revolution, launched in 1963, which imposed modernization from the top down in the country with significant support from the UNITED STATES. The MEK's membership consisted of many college-educated young men recruited from the urban middle class. It conducted several attacks against the government in the 1970s, but declined in strength as a result of internal feuding and successful government countermeasures.

The movement was revitalized in the aftermath of the IRANIAN REVOLUTION OF 1978–79, when the new Islamic Republic of Ayatollah RUHOLLAH KHOMEINI (r. 1979–89) was being created. Its leader was Masud Rajavi (b. 1947), a former student who had been imprisoned by the shah, and who subsequently was denied the right to run for the presidency of the Islamic Republic by Khomeini. As a consequence, the group organized antigovernment demonstrations, followed by a campaign of bombing attacks against Khomeini's allies, killing dozens of people, including the Iranian president, prime minister, chief justice, and members of parliament. Khomeini's government responded with force, killing and executing nearly 10,000 of its members between 1981 and 1985. Surviving members fled to France and then to IRAQ, which was engaged in a bloody war of attrition against Iran at the time. SADDAM HUSAYN (r. 1979–2003) gave Rajavi and his MEK sanctuary and supported its armed terrorist operations against Iran, even after the war's end in 1988. Indeed, in 1997 it was designated a terrorist organization by the United States, as well as by Canada and several European countries. Masud Rajavi has been superceded by his wife Miryam Rajavi (b. 1953), one of the founding members of the movement. She was elected to share joint leadership with her husband in 1985, and then became its secretary general in 1989. After the fall of Husayn's regime in 2003, MEK came under the control of U.S. armed forces in Iraq. French security agents raided MEK properties in France in 2003, fearing that the organization was attempting to set up a new base in that country. Several members burned themselves to death in protest.

The MEK's original ideology was based on a modern Marxist interpretation of traditional Shii concepts and symbols, paralleling ideas espoused by Iranian intellectual and visionary ALI SHARIATI (d. 1977). In its propaganda Islamic terms such as TAWHID (monotheism), JIHAD, MUJAHID, and *shahid* (martyr) were reconfigured to mean "egalitarianism," "liberation struggle," "freedom fighter," and "revolutionary hero," respectively. UMMA, the idea of the ideal Muslim community of believers, was interpreted to mean "dynamic classless society," an idea that is a cornerstone of Marxist ideology. The movement's ideology has changed considerably as the political dynamics of the Middle East have changed and Marxism has fallen out of fashion. It now presents itself as an enemy of the religious fanaticism of the Islamic Republic of Iran. Maryan Rajavi is known as president-elect of the National Council of Resistance of Iran, in which MEK holds a dominant position.

See also COMMUNISM; POLITICS AND ISLAM; TERRORISM.

Further reading: Ervand Abrahamian, *The Iranian Mojahedin* (New Haven, Conn.: Yale University Press, 1989); Nikki R. Keddie and Farah Monian, "Militancy and Religion in Contemporary Iran." In *Fundamentalisms and the State: Remaking Polities, Economies, and Militance,* edited by Martin E. Marty and R. Scott Appleby, 511–538 (Chicago: University of Chicago Press, 1993); Nicola Pedde, "Role and Evolution of the Mojahedin-e Kalgh." *Vaseteh: Journal of the European Society for Iranian Studies* 1, no. 1 (2005): 113–123.

mujtahid

Among the Shia, the *mujtahid* is synonymous with the FAQIH: an expert in Islamic jurisprudence. However, in the absence of the Imams, the *mujtahid* has the ability to issue legal decisions by means of employing IJTIHAD, or independent juristic reasoning.

Ijtihad has long been a cause of strife in Islamic law. Because many legal scholars considered it to be based on little more than the personal opinion of the jurist, *ijtihad* ceased to be a major source of the SHARIA in the traditional Sunni schools by the 10th century. And yet, even within the Shia schools there existed a fervent debate over the validity of the *mujtahid* to use individual reasoning or rational conjecture to make legal decisions about those issues in which the QURAN and the SUNNA are silent. The AKHBARI SCHOOL, for instance, utterly rejected the use of *ijtihad,* and required all jurisprudence to be based on the traditions of the Prophet, the Imams, and the previous jurists. However, the USULI SCHOOL, whose position eventually became the dominant ideology in SHIISM, encouraged the use of *ijtihad* in the formation of Islamic jurisprudence, thereby elevating the position of the *mujtahid* to "the deputy of the Hidden Imam," or MAHDI.

Today, there are so many qualified *mujtahid*s in the world that only those who have attained the highest level of scholarship and who can boast the greatest number of followers, are truly free to practice *ijtihad* and issue authoritative legal declarations (fatwa), which the Shia are obliged to follow. At the top of this order of *mujtahid*s are the AYATOLLAHS, whose authority on legal issues is unmatched in the Shia world. Indeed, it was precisely this religious and political authority that allowed the Ayatollah RUHOLLAH KHOMEINI to impose his leadership upon the social, political, and economic forces that led to the IRANIAN REVOLUTION OF 1978–1979. Currently, only a handful of authoritative ayatollahs exist, primarily in IRAN and IRAQ, though their religious and political leadership over the world's Shiis is still formidable.

Reza Aslan

Further reading: Moojan Momen, *An Introduction to Shi'i Islam* (New Haven, Conn.: Yale University Press,

1985); Joseph Schacht, *An Introduction to Islamic Law* (Oxford: Clarendon, 1964); Linda Walbridge, *The Most Learned of the Shi'a* (London: Oxford University Press, 2001).

mullah (molla)

A mullah is a title for a Muslim religious authority, a member of the ULAMA. It is based on the Arabic *mawla*, which can mean "master," "slave," or "client." In early Islamic history a *mawla* often referred to a non-Arab Muslim who had become a client of an Arab tribe or had been a slave and was manumitted (freed). It later gained wide and varied usage in Muslim lands. It is, for example, the basis for the Turkish epithet for JALAL AL-DIN RUMI, Mevlana (our master), and for the South Asian title for religious leaders and Sufis, *mawlawi* (my master). In IRAN and other eastern lands in the Muslim world it especially became a title of respect for religious authorities, or Muslim clerics, qualified to teach, preach, and officiate at rituals, as well as interpret Islamic law. Such individuals usually would wear distinctive cloaks and turbans as signs of their status. In Safavid Iran (16th and 17th centuries) the most respected religious office that one of the ulama could occupy was that of *mullabashi* (chief mullah). A female mullah would be called a *mullabaji* (sister-mullah). During the colonial period the prestige associated with the title began to decrease. The British, for example, coined the derogatory name "mad mullah" to insult Muslim leaders who took up arms against them in INDIA and EAST AFRICA in the 19th century. But the title has also lost respect among many contemporary Muslims themselves, who make mullahs the butts of their jokes and apply the title to shady characters and religious fanatics.

See also AUTHORITY; MEVLEVI SUFI ORDER; SAFAVID DYNASTY.

Further reading: Said. A. Arjomand, "The Office of Mulla Bashi in Shiite Iran," *Studia Iranica* 57 (1983):

135–146; Patricia Crone, *Slaves on Horses: The Evolution of the Islamic Polity* (Cambridge: Cambridge University Press, 1980).

Mullah Sadra (1571–1640) *Iranian philosopher, theologian, and mystic who became the leading teacher of what is known as the School of Isfahan*

Born in Shiraz, IRAN, during the SAFAVID DYNASTY and educated in the imperial capital of Isfahan, Mullah Sadra is perhaps the most influential philosopher/theologian in SHIISM. His genius lay in his ability to synthesize the philosophy of Aristotle and ABU ALI AL-HUSAYN IBN SINA (Avicenna) with the theological principles of Shiism and the metaphysics of SUFISM. The result was a profoundly influential theory that all living beings share in the essence of Being, though in different degrees. Therefore, although humanity boasts the highest degree of Being, we are all connected to the rest of CREATION at the core of our existence. Mullah Sadra's metaphysics were most clearly expounded in his monumental work, *The Four Journeys,* in which he divided the spiritual path into a fixed number of degrees or stages, which ultimately lead to enlightenment and sainthood.

For his unorthodox views, Mullah Sadra was condemned as a heretic by the leading ULAMA of his time. However, his school of theosophical Shiism and his ability to unite disparate philosophies into a single metaphysical theory proved so popular, particularly among the AKHBARI SCHOOL, that his theories ultimately formed the foundation of Shii THEOLOGY.

Reza Aslan

Further reading: F. E. Peters, *Aristotle and the Arabs* (New York: New York University Press, 1968); Roy Mottahedeh, *The Mantle of the Prophet: Learning and Power in Modern Iran* (New York: Simon and Schuster, 1985); Mullah Sadra, *The Metaphysics of Mullah Sadra* (Texas: Global Publications Associations, 1992).

munafiqun *See* HYPOCRITES.

murid

This is an aspirant or disciple associated with a Sufi order, who has sworn allegiance to a Sufi master (MURSHID or SHAYKH). This term, derived from the Arabic root *irada*, or desire, is generally used to describe those who participated in *tariqas* (Sufi orders) from approximately the 12th to the 15th centuries throughout Islamdom. This period is characterized by SUFISM's organization into hierarchical structures, with each Sufi master guiding his *murid*s along a certain method or path of mystical knowledge, which he in turn had learned from his master and the long *silsila* or chain of mystical teachers before him. *Murid*s typically would undergo initiation ceremonies, in which they would be presented with a cloak or a hat. Expected to memorize the names of all previous masters in the *silsila* of his *tariqa*, the *murid* also prepared to learn its particular mystical teachings, so that he in turn could transmit them to others when he would become a master. The word *murid* is still used today in a similar way, characterizing the relationship of one who is under the guidance of a Sufi master.

Many manuals were written expressing the correct relationship between the master and his disciple, which was one of complete surrender reflecting divine hierarchy, and in particular the Islamic emphasis on surrender to God. It was said that the *murid* should be as passive as a corpse being washed. Feminine imagery is found in medieval Sufi literature as well, with advice that this submission should be as a bride to a bridegroom, and a description of the Sufi master as nourishing his *murid* like a mother does a child.

Sophia Pandya

Further reading: Carl W. Ernst, *Shambhala Guide to Sufism* (Boston: Shambhala, 1997); Margaret Malamud, "Gender and Spiritual Self-Fashioning: The Master-Disciple Relationship in Classical Sufism." *Journal of the American Academy of Religion* 64 (1996): 89–117; J. Spencer Trimingham, *The Sufi Orders in Islam* (Oxford: Clarendon Press, 1971).

Muridi Sufi Order (Muridiyya)

A Sufi order established among the Wolof tribe of Senegal in Touba around 1886 by the shaykh AHMADU BAMBA (1850–1927). Originally an offshoot of the QADIRI SUFI ORDER, the order produced its own rituals and litanies and developed a unique emphasis upon the value of hard work, which would become a hallmark of the Muridiyya. Disciples were taught to obey their shaykhs, renounce worldly pleasures, and devote themselves to productive occupations. Over time, the Muridiyya became an economic force in the region, particularly due to their cultivation and sale of peanuts.

Muridiyya independence could be viewed as resistance to the French colonial regime, a fact that increased their attractiveness to the Wolof and caused French administrators to view them with suspicion. For this reason, colonial authorities twice exiled Bamba from Senegal, hoping to diminish his popularity. When this failed, the French attempted to co-opt the Muridiyya, finally establishing a modus vivendi with the group in recognition of their stabilizing influence. The Muridiyya attracted Wolof from all different social strata, emphasizing the development of a community that transcended normal societal divisions. Bamba's religious knowledge, integrity, and humble piety, when combined with his organizational abilities, helped him to create an order that provided much-needed structure for a Senegalese society disrupted by colonial domination. Bamba eventually won the confidence of French authorities by demonstrating a lack of interest in temporal authority and by cooperating with them in tangible ways.

Following the shaykh's death in 1927, the Muridiyya continued this policy of cooperation with political authorities, despite internal succession disputes that threatened to divide the order. This fact, coupled with their economic prosperity, emphasis upon the disciplines of character and hard work, resistance to radicalizing influences (such as WAHHABISM), and ability to adjust to changing circumstances (such as the Senegalese ground-nut crisis), have made the Muridiyya a dynamic and important influence in Senegalese society and beyond.

Further reading: Lucy E. Creevey, "Ahmad Bamba 1850–1927." In *Studies in West African Islamic History*, Vol. 1, edited by John Ralph Willis (London: Frank Cass, 1979); Christopher Harrison, *France and Islam in West Africa, 1860–1960* (Cambridge: Cambridge University Press, 1988); Donald B. Cruise O'Brien, *The Mourides of Senegal: The Political and Economic Organization of an Islamic Brotherhood* (Oxford: Oxford University Press, 1971); David Robinson, *Paths of Accommodation: Muslim Societies and French Colonial Authorities in Senegal and Mauritania, 1880–1920* (Athens: Ohio University Press, 2000).

Murjia

Murjia is a movement that began during early Islam that emphasizes faith and confession of FAITH, significantly more than acts. The Arabic root of *murjia* means "to defer judgment" and in the case of the Murjia it refers to the obligation that Muslims should have to defer judgment of a person's ultimate fate, regarding whether they will live eternally in heaven or hell, to God. In sharp contrast, traditionalist Sunni Muslims believe that Muslims must have faith in God *and* act in accordance with God's commandments in order to be granted eternal life in heaven. The Murjia worldview, however, was based on Quran 9:106 and similar verses, "There are some . . . whose ultimate destinies are deferred to God's judgment. He may punish or pardon them, for God is all-knowing and all-wise." The Murjia maintained that Muslims should not lose their status as believers because of any actions—this status

was affirmed by their very faith. Yet, the Murjia condemned people who violated God's dictates as aberrant believers who may ultimately be forgiven or punished by God. Thus, according to the Murjia, decisions regarding the final moral status of these and other acts were deferred to divine judgment.

Murjia espoused the belief that faith is made up of knowledge and public confession of God, God's prophets, and their messages to humanity. That is, they described beliefs and the public affirmation of them as a complete and indivisible whole. They had a broad understanding of who is Muslim; they considered all Muslims—except those whom Muslim consensus excludes—to be true believers. Beginning in the eighth century, one political dimension of the Murjia movement was manifested as they vigorously advocated the equality of non-Arab converts to Islam. Through its ties with the HANAFI LEGAL SCHOOL, aspects of Murjia doctrine have lingered, despite the opposition of traditionalist Sunnis.

See also MUTAZILI SCHOOL; THEOLOGY.

Jon Armajani

Further reading: Michael A. Cook, *Early Muslim Dogma: A Source-Critical Study* (Cambridge: Cambridge University Press, 2003); Henry Corbin, *History of Islamic Philosophy* (New York: Kegan Paul International, 1993); Tilman Nagel, *The History of Islamic Theology from Muhammad to the Present* (Princeton, N.J.: Markus Weiner Publishers, 2000); W. Montgomery Watt, *The Formative Period of Islamic Thought* (Edinburgh: Edinburgh University Press, 1973); A. J. Wensinck, *The Muslim Creed: Its Genesis and Historical Development* (New Delhi: Oriental Books Reprint Corporation, 1979).

murshid

This is a Sufi guide, also known as SHAYKH (Arabic), or *pir* (Persian), who serves as the spiritual master of a Sufi. The *murshid* traced his spiritual AUTHORITY through a *silsila*, or chain of spiritual transmission, which included all of the former *murshid*s of that particular order back to the initial founder, and sometimes as far back as the prophet Mohammad. Typically, the Sufi order would be named after the initial founder of the spiritual lineage. A *murshid* would be expected to maintain the particular mystical teachings that were passed on to him by his predecessors and to instill them in turn in his disciples.

The relationship between the *murshid* and his disciples was the key to their spiritual progress. First, they had to swear allegiance to the *murshid* in an initiation ceremony (*bayaa*) in which often they would receive a hair cut. The *murshid* would then present them with a hat or cloak, symbolizing their new status. After joining the Sufi order, complete submission and obedience to the *murshid* was expected. In fact, many manuals on the correct behavior of disciples exist, with advice on subjects such as the proper way to sit in the presence of one's Sufi master.

See also ADAB; TARIQA.

Sophia Pandya

Further reading: Carl W. Ernst, *Shambhala Guide to Sufism* (Boston: Shambhala, 1997); J. Spencer Trimingham, *The Sufi Orders in Islam* (Oxford: Clarendon Press, 1971).

Musa *See* MOSES.

music

With the rise of ISLAM in the seventh century and its rapid spread throughout West Asia and North Africa, the sounds associated with this swiftly growing religion traveled far and traversed many cultures. Following the ascent of the ABBASID CALIPHATE in 750 the ensuing golden age of the Islamic Empire was known for its intellectual pursuits, intercultural exchange, and developments in SCIENCE, PHILOSOPHY, and the arts. With all of these interrelated cultural forces at work, the production of music and musical knowledge was extraordinary. An invaluable contribution of this period is by Abu l-Faraj al-Isfahani (d. 967), a musician of Persian origin who studied in BAGHDAD and produced the monumental *Kitab al-aghani al-kabir* (The great book of songs), which comprises 24 volumes and nearly 10,000 pages in modern print editions. During this time, performers and scholars of diverse backgrounds greatly influenced the development of music in the region and often were patronized by or belonged to the court. State support of music continued with the rise of the OTTOMAN DYNASTY in the 14th century, which again, was multiethnic in nature, and included important musical contributions from Turks, Arabs, Greeks, and Armenians of Muslim, Christian, and Jewish religious beliefs.

While music has flourished within Muslim-governed societies, it also has been opposed and censored on religious grounds in different ways. At issue is the extent to which, if at all, Islam allows or embraces music. The QURAN does not directly reference the censorship of music, while the HADITH can be understood to support suppression or allowance. This debate has been fueled by the affective power and popular appeal of listening (*samaa*) to music in addition to the relationship of music to poetry and dance, which have their own attractions. SUFISM frequently has been at the center of this tension as it can involve the use of music in especially mystical ways. Examples of Sufi music include the song of praise (*madh*), song honoring MUHAMMAD (*madih al-nabi*), and remembrance ceremony (DHIKR) involving Quranic recitation, music, and dance. Of particular interest are the call to prayer (ADHAN) and Quranic recitation (*qiraa*), which are practiced throughout the Islamic world. While they are not considered music, they can sound

Drums on display at a shop in Marrakesh, Morocco *(Federico R. Campo)*

very musical and follow traditional theoretical models of music theory. In particular, the ornamental style (*tajwid*) of Quranic recitation is especially melodic, elaborate, and vocally artistic. The resulting combination of Quranic text conveyed in beautiful voice can produce ecstatic responses in listeners, and indeed, major MUEZZINS often enjoy a huge fan base and even hold starlike status.

Music in the world of Islam is as diverse as the Muslim cultures that have given rise to it. Even in the case of AFGHANISTAN, where the TALIBAN applied Islam to destroy music, a musical revival is underway with the new Islamic government. At present, we can find examples of Islamic musical expression ranging from the very traditional to rock and rap. In the future we can expect a musical panorama increasingly reflective of the various areas of the world where Muslims have made their homes.

See also QAWWALI; UMM KULTHOUM.

Kenneth S. Habib

Further reading: Henry George Farmer, *The Science of Music in Islam,* 2 vols. (1925–66. Reprint, Frankfurt: Institute for the History of Arabic-Islamic Science, 1997); Kristina Nelson, *The Art of Reciting the Qur'an* (Austin: University of Texas Press, 1985); Amnon Shiloah, *Music in the World of Islam* (Detroit: Wayne State University Press, 1995); Lawrence E. Sullivan, ed. *Enchanting Powers: Music in the World's Religions* (Cambridge, Mass.: Harvard University Press, 1997).

Muslim *See* ISLAM.

Muslim Brotherhood (Arabic: al-Ikhwan al-Muslimun; also known as the Society of Muslim Brothers)

The first modern city-based Islamist movement with mass appeal in the Arab world was the Muslim Brotherhood. Founded in 1928 by HASAN AL-BANNA (1909–49), an Egyptian school teacher, in the Suez Canal Zone city of Ismailiya, it subsequently created hundreds of branches and spin-off organizations throughout EGYPT, and subsequently in LIBYA, PALESTINE, JORDAN, SYRIA, SUDAN, YEMEN, and KUWAIT. It developed close contacts with Wahhabis in SAUDI ARABIA that continue to the present day. Splinter groups have arisen elsewhere in the region, and it served as the basis, directly or indirectly, from which a number of more radical Islamic movements have arisen. Today the Muslim Brotherhood is an especially influential religiopolitical force in Egypt, the Sudan, and Jordan.

Egypt was a protectorate of Great Britain when al-Banna established the Muslim Brotherhood. At the time there was a limited degree of Egyptian self-rule under a monarchy and national legislature, but the people desired complete independence from foreign occupation and a more democratic government. Al-Banna appealed to this widespread anticolonial sentiment and combined it with a call for moral renewal in accordance with an idealized Islam of the Quran and the *salaf,* the esteemed first generations of Muslims. He had been inspired by the teachings of JAMAL AL-DIN AL-AFGHANI (d. 1897), MUHAMMAD ABDUH (d. 1905), and MUHAMMAD RASHID RIDA (d. 1935), leaders in the modern Islamic reform movement that was sweeping many Muslim countries. Al-Banna was particularly troubled by the growing influence European secular values were having on Egypt's Muslim youth and the inability of the traditionalist ULAMA to counteract this influence. He saw this development as more of a threat than British military occupation of his country. In the 1930s

another issue in which he developed great interest was the fate of Palestine under British rule and the success of the Zionist movement. Al-Banna gave speeches about these matters in coffeehouses in Cairo and Ismailiya that attracted large audiences, from among whom he recruited the first members of the Muslim Brotherhood.

In addition to educating people about Islam, the Brotherhood engaged in political activity and provided social services to the needy. Reflecting the diverse sources from which he formed his vision of the Brotherhood's mission, al-Banna declared his new organization to be "a Salafiyya message, a Sunni way, a Sufi truth, a political organization, an athletic group, a cultural-educational union, an economic company, and a social idea" (quoted in Voll, 362). He strove to keep the Brotherhood from being associated with ulama and secular Egyptian political parties. At the time of al-Banna's assassination in 1949, its membership is estimated to have reached 500,000 active members, not to mention many more sympathizers and supporters. After the Free Officers secured Egypt's independence in 1953, membership dropped significantly, and the organization soon came into conflict with the new Arab nationalist government of JAMAL ABD AL-NASIR (r. 1953–70).

The Brotherhood's success in winning popular support was in large part due to its leadership and its ability to promote its message of Islamic renewal through a tightly knit organizational structure. It was like a mini-state, headed by a General Guide (MURSHID), Guidance Council, and Consultative Assembly. This governing body worked through a network of units charged with technical operations and coordination of activities at the local level. The operational units were concerned with teaching and outreach (DAAWA) to students, professionals, labor, peasants, and the wider UMMA, or Muslim community. It also had committees charged with financial oversight, provision of legal and social services, issuance of legal opinions (sing. FATWA), and policymaking. A section for women, known as the Muslim Sisters, was established in the 1940s, although this was not as successful as the Brotherhood in recruiting members. An independent Syrian branch of the Brotherhood was created in the 1930s by Mustafa al-Sibai (1915–64), a Syrian who had studied in Egypt and met al-Banna. Egyptian members had visited Palestine and Transjordan during the 1930s, but the first independent Jordanian branch did not officially open until 1946, headed by Abd al-Latif Qurah (d. 1953), a Jordanian. In 1948 the Brotherhood recruited volunteers to fight in Palestine against the Israelis, reflecting their concern for pan-Arab causes. Sudanese who had studied in Cairo established the first branches in the Sudan in the late 1940s, but the official headquarters of the Sudanese Muslim Brotherhood did not open until 1954. Perhaps the most prominent leader to arise from this branch was Hasan al-Turabi (b. 1932), who had joined the Brotherhood as a student and rose to prominence in the organization in the 1960s and 1970s. He became the chief ideologist of the Sudanese National Islamic Front, the Brotherhood's political party, in the 1980s.

From the beginning, the Brotherhood made effective use of the print media to spread its message. In Egypt it launched several periodicals in the 1930s, then took over *al-Manar* (Lighthouse), the Islamic reformist magazine, when its chief editor Rashid Rida died in 1935. In 1942 it began publishing a weekly magazine called *al-Ikhwan al-Muslimin*, which was replaced by a daily newspaper of the same name in 1946. This publication was shut down when the Brotherhood was banned by the government in 1948. From 1951 to 1956 it published *al-Daawa* magazine, which was also banned, but allowed to resume in 1976, until banned again by the government in 1981. Since the 1980s the Brotherhood has published a weekly periodical known as *Liwa al-Islam* (Banner of Islam), and it has also been able to disseminate its ideology through numerous books and other oppositional newspapers, even when its official publications have been banned.

In a development that proved to be a significant one with respect to its status in the eyes of Egyptian authorities, the Brotherhood formed a JIHAD unit (known as the "secret apparatus") designed to defend the organization against police crackdowns and to attack the British during World War II. After the war it conducted a campaign of terror that included attacks on the British, government officials, popular cinemas, and Egyptian Jews. This cycle of violence culminated with the assassination of Egypt's prime minister, al-Nuqrashi Pasha, in 1948, followed by the government's retaliatory assassination of al-Banna in 1949. The jihad unit was also implicated in an attempt on the life of President Nasir in 1954, which resulted in widespread arrests and executions of key members of the Brotherhood. One of those imprisoned at this time was SAYYID QUTB (1906–66), a former literary critic and recent Muslim Brotherhood convert, whose experience and torture in prison shaped his vision of a united Islamic struggle against modern IDOLATRY and corruption. Two of the major works he wrote at this time were a multivolume Quran commentary and *Maalim fi'l-tariq* (Milestones). He became the foremost ideologist of the Brotherhood after al-Banna's death, and his ideas have inspired numerous new radical Islamist movements since the 1970s in many Muslim countries.

A great resurgence of ISLAMISM swept through Middle Eastern lands when many of the newly independent national regimes were unable to meet the expectations of their people and turned to secular authoritarianism to stay in power. Democratic impulses that had emerged earlier in the 20th century were stifled. The defeat of Arab armies in the 1967 Arab-Israeli war in particular served as a catalyst for the popular turn to religion. Egyptian president ANWAR AL-SADAT (r. 1970–81), Nasir's successor, took advantage of this religious turn to consolidate his power against Nasirite loyalists and leftists, releasing members of the Brotherhood from prison and allowing Islamic student groups to become active on university campuses. Although the leadership of the Muslim

Brotherhood now favored implementing Islamic law through peaceful participation in the political process, more radical Islamist groups arose, incited by the ideology of Qutb and the success of Ayatollah Khomeini's Islamic revolution in Iran (1978–79). One of these radical organizations, the Jihad Group, assassinated al-Sadat in October 1981, because of their anger at his increasingly oppressive rule and the peace agreement he had signed with ISRAEL. In Syria, meanwhile, the Muslim Brotherhood had become the most serious domestic threat to the government of Hafiz al-Asad and the ruling BAATH PARTY. In 1982 it led a popular uprising in the city of Hama, which was quelled violently by Syrian troops, resulting in the loss of thousands of lives. It has never recovered from this blow. Syrian and Egyptian members or former members of the Muslim Brotherhood carried its ideology to Saudi Arabia, where it became combined with WAHHABISM. This fusion of radical Islamic jihadist ideas influenced USAMA BIN LADIN (b. 1957) and others, who used them to recruit followers to fight against the Soviets in AFGHANISTAN, as well as other Arab governments, and to conduct terrorist attacks against U.S. and European interests. In Palestine, former members of the Muslim Brotherhood created HAMAS in 1987. This was an Islamist organization opposed to Yasir Arafat's secular PALESTINE LIBERATION ORGANIZATION. Moreover, Hamas sought to engage in a jihad to bring the illegal Israeli occupation of the Palestinian homeland. At the same time, however, the nonviolent tactics of the mainline branches of the Muslim Brotherhood have allowed it to successfully compete in legislative elections in both Egypt and Jordan, despite having to face periodic restrictions and government crackdowns.

See also ARAB-ISRAELI CONFLICTS; COLONIALISM; GHAZALI, ZAYNAB AL-; JIHAD MOVEMENTS; RENEWAL AND REFORM MOVEMENTS.

Further reading: Nazih N. Ayubi, *Political Islam: Religion and Politics in the Arab World* (London: Routledge, 1991); Gilles Kepel, *Muslim Extremism in Egypt: The Prophet and the Pharaoh*. Translated by Jon Rothschild (Berkeley: University of California Press, 1985); Richard P. Mitchell, *The Society of the Muslim Brothers* (Oxford: Oxford University Press, 1993 [1969]); John O. Voll, "Fundamentalism in the Sunni Arab World: Egypt and the Sudan." In *Fundamentalisms Observed,* edited by Martin Marty and R. Scott Appleby, 345–402 (Chicago: University of Chicago Press, 1991).

Muslim ibn al-Hajjaj, Abu al-Husayn *See* HADITH.

Muslim League *See* ALL-INDIA MUSLIM LEAGUE.

Muslim Public Affairs Council (MPAC)

Founded as the Political Action Committee of Southern California in 1986, the Muslim Public Affairs Council assumed its present name in 1988. It is an American Muslim advocacy organization that works with city, state, and national officials to promote issues involving the civil and HUMAN RIGHTS of Muslims and other minorities in the UNITED STATES. Its early leadership developed from members of the Islamic Society of Southern California, one of the first MOSQUES established in Los Angeles, California. This center has played an active role in the public sphere and interfaith dialogue since the 1980s. One of MPAC's founding members was Maher Hathout, an Egyptian physician who has become a leading spokesman for Muslims in the United States since he arrived in 1971. He is currently the senior adviser to the MPAC board of directors. MPAC's executive director since about 1990 has been Salam al-Maryati (b. 1960), who was born in BAGHDAD, Iraq, and came to the United States with his family in 1964. He holds a bachelor's degree in biochemistry from the University of California at Los Angeles and a master's degree in business administration from the University of California at Irvine. His wife, Laila al-Maryati, is a practicing physician and founder of the Muslim Women's League. Both are active MPAC leaders, American citizens, and spokespersons on Muslim affairs in the United States. They have each testified before Congress and, in 1998, at the request of Hillary Rodham Clinton, they organized a White House celebration of ID AL-FITR (the Fast-Breaking Feast).

Citing the QURAN, MPAC identifies its vision in terms of what it considers to be the Islamic values of mercy, justice, peace, human dignity, freedom, and equality. Its mission is to work in cooperation with public institutions in the United States and to prepare American Muslims for leadership in the public sphere. In addition to promoting the interests of American Muslims and involvement in civil liberties education and advocacy, MPAC has also been engaged in combating anti-Islamic sentiments (Islamophobia) in the United States, working with public officials and the law in helping to secure the country from TERRORISM, and strengthening ties to Muslims in other parts of the world. It has offices in Washington, D.C., and Los Angeles, as well as chapters in New York, Ohio, Iowa, Kansas, and Arizona. Its organization includes departments assigned to build relations with Congress, the media, the community, and to combat hate crimes. MPAC has issued several books and policy papers dealing with human rights, Muslim identity, terrorism, and counterterrorism. Every year since 2001 it has convened a national conference for discussion of these and related issues, and it has welcomed nationally recognized politicians and media commentators as guest speakers. MPAC issues press releases regularly that address current events, including condemnations of acts of Islamic terrorism as well as calls for an equitable solution to the Israeli-Palestinian conflict and for interfaith harmony. The organization has been attacked by some groups and individuals because of its promotion of Muslim issues in the American public sphere, but these attacks have been offset by the organization's interfaith activities

and by the bridges it has built to a wide variety of community agencies and minority groups, including African Americans, Japanese Americans, and Korean Americans.

See also COUNCIL ON AMERICAN-ISLAMIC RELATIONS.

Further reading: Aslam Abdullah and Ghasser Hathout, *American Muslim Identity: Speaking for Ourselves* (Los Angeles: Multimedia Vera International, 2003); Zahid H. Bukhari, Sulayman S. Nyang, et al., *Muslim's Place in the American Public Square* (Lanham, Md.: Altamira Press, 2004).

Muslim Students Association

The Muslim Students Association (MSA) was founded by 75 foreign students studying in the UNITED STATES and CANADA, at a conference convened in January 1963 at the University of Illinois at Champaign-Urbana. It has since become the largest Muslim organization in North America, with chapters at many if not most North American colleges and universities. These chapters are composed of undergraduate and graduate students, domestic and foreign, enrolled at the host institutions. Depending on how student organizations are instituted at each school, they typically have faculty advisers and build cooperative relationships with other campus groups. MSA chapter funding comes from local fund-raising activities, and chapters often qualify for partial funding by campus student associations. The national organization's policy on funding states that the MSA rejects donations from foreign sources; it also opposes funding from any one donor who may therefore seek to gain undue influence on a chapter. Because the MSA emphasizes the ideal of achieving Muslim unity, it accepts members without regard to nationality, ethnicity, or Islamic religious affiliation. Nevertheless, it bears a strong Sunni reformist stamp in its portrayal of Islam and its membership, with many of its leaders being from South Asia. This has led to the creation of

Women members of the Muslim Students Association at a campus Ramadan *iftar* meal *(Juan E. Campo)*

the MSA Persian-Speaking Group (MSAPSG), which appeals to Shii students with ties to Iran.

MSA chapters are encouraged to join the MSA national network, which is divided into U.S. and Canadian chapters. These chapters are subdivided into geographical regions: eastern, central, and western regions for the United States; eastern and western ones for Canada. Each region holds its own "national" conference, in coordination with MSA national. The MSA national organization is governed by a general secretariat, with its headquarters in Plainfield, Indiana. Women hold visible leadership roles at both the chapter and the general secretariat levels. In 2007 MSA adopted a logo that shows two nested crescent moons, together with symbols and colors of the U.S. and Canadian flags. The word *salam* is written in Arabic inside the logo, which MSA interprets as referring both to "peace" and the customary expression of greeting exchanged by Muslims: *al-salamu alaykum* "peace be upon you."

Until the 1990s the MSA looked for inspiration to the Islamist reformism embodied in the writings of SAYYID QUTB (d. 1966) and ABU AL-ALA MAWDUDI (d. 1979), which are now seen as too radical by most members. Today, in promoting the ideals of religious identity and unity among Muslim college students, the MSA affirms a list of values that helps define its place in American society and contributes to combating anti-Muslim prejudice in North America, especially since the September 11, 2001, attacks at the World Trade Center and the Pentagon. These values include sincerity, knowledge, patience, truthfulness, moderation, tolerance, and forgiveness. The secretariat and the campus chapters hold conferences and meetings to help realize these values. One of the major activities they undertake is organizing an Islam Awareness Day or Week, which features films, guest speakers, and exhibits to educate non-Muslims about Islam. During RAMADAN MSA chapters sponsor "fastathons" to raise funds for charities and evening interfaith *iftar* meals, which mark the end of the daily fast. Many participate in interfaith events throughout the year that foster mutual understanding and acceptance in the campus community as a whole, especially among Jewish, Christian, and Muslim students. The MSA also engages in outreach through the Internet.

An indication of the remarkable success that MSA has experienced since it was founded are the nonstudent Islamic organizations it has inspired. These include the Islamic Society of North America (ISNA), created in 1981, with which it still maintains an affiliation. Professional organizations have also been established by former MSA members, such as the Islamic Medical Association of North America (IMANA), the Association of Muslim Social Scientists (AMSS), and the Association of Muslim Scientists and Engineers (AMSE).

See also COUNCIL ON AMERICAN-ISLAMIC RELATIONS; *DAAWA*; DIALOGUE; ISLAMISM; MUSLIM PUBLIC AFFAIRS COUNCIL; RENEWAL AND REFORM MOVEMENTS.

Further reading: Geneive Abdo, *Mecca on Main Street: Muslim Life in American after 9/11* (Oxford: Oxford University Press, 2007); Kambiz GhaneaBassiri, *Com-*

peting Visions of Islam in the United States: A Study of Los Angeles (Westport, Conn.: Greenwood Press, 1997); Jane Smith, *Islam in America* (New York: Columbia University Press, 1999).

Muslim World League (Arabic: Rabitat al-Alam al-Islami)

The Muslim World League is a pan-Islamic organization founded in 1962 to promote the unity of the UMMA (the universal Muslim community). Although it describes itself as a "cultural organization" for Muslims, it was created by a group of Muslim political leaders, intellectuals, and experts opposed at the time to the widespread influence of secular Arab nationalism and the spread of COMMUNISM and socialism in Muslim lands during the cold war period after World War II. Saudi king FAYSAL IBN ABD AL-AZIZ (r. 1964–75) was instrumental in its formation, it receives a substantial amount of its funding from SAUDI ARABIA, and its headquarters is in Mecca. Its governing council, which must be led by a Saudi citizen, is composed of Sunni religious authorities reflecting strong Wahhabi and Islamist outlooks, such as those espoused by the MUSLIM BROTHERHOOD and ABU AL-ALA MAWDUDI's JAMAAT-I ISLAMI. There are no Shii Muslims or liberal Muslims in the organization. In contrast to the ORGANIZATION OF THE ISLAMIC CONFERENCE, which was founded in 1969 as a body of Muslim nation-states, the Muslim World League has been primarily concerned with promoting the implementation of the SHARIA and conducting DAAWA (religious outreach) activities. It hosts meetings during the annual HAJJ and, to meet its objectives, it has created a Fiqh Council, a World Supreme Council for Mosques, councils for relief and charitable activities, as well as for religious EDUCATION and memorization of the Quran. The league's chief publication is the *Muslim World League Journal,* which is issued in English.

See also PAN-ISLAMISM; WAHHABISM; WORLD MUSLIM CONGRESS.

Further reading: Mozammel Haque, "The Role of Rabitat al-Alam al-Islami in the Promotion of Islamic Education," *Islamic Quarterly* 6, no. 1 (1992): 58–63; Jacob Landau, *The Politics of Pan-Islam: Ideology and Organization* (Oxford: Oxford University Press, 1990).

mutaa   *See* TWELVE-IMAM SHIISM.

Mutazili School

The first truly doctrinal school of THEOLOGY (*kalam*) in Islam, the Mutazili School flourished from the eighth to the 11th centuries. Its comparative rationalist orientation influenced discussions within classical Islamic PHILOSOPHY, and made decisive contributions to the development and intellectual sophistication of *ilm al-kalam* (science of theology). In fact, the rationalist approach and doctrines of Mutazili theology impacted a variety of Islamic sciences. In our own time, historical and theoretical treatments of Mutazili theology have affected the tenor and tone of modernist and postmodernist Muslim discourse in general and Islamic liberalism in particular: from the Indonesian scholar Harun Nasution to such diverse figures as the late FAZLUR RAHMAN, MUHAMMED ARKOUN, FATIMA MERNISSI, and Hassan Hanafi.

The school's name is derived from an Arabic verb meaning "to withdraw, stand aside" (*itazala*), here in the sense of "those who separate themselves." The following traditional account elaborates: AL-HASAN AL-BASRI (642–728), an ascetic Sufi who belonged to the generation of pious Muslims (*tabiun*) after the COMPANIONS OF THE PROPHET MUHAMMAD, argued that humans have been accorded free will and thus possess moral and spiritual responsibility for their behavior. This viewpoint, propagated by the Qadariyya, opponents of the UMAYYAD CALIPHATE, allowed them to hold the CALIPH accountable for his acts. Technically, *qadar* meant "divine decree" or "predestination," but for the Qadariyya and the

Mutazila after them, it referred to the fact that God has endowed man with a metaphysical and ethical power through his acts such that "determination" (*qadar*) is in reference to the essence of human action. This is in stark contrast to the Jabriyya (or Mujbira), who upheld the notion of divine "compulsion"—*jabr*—to account for the ultimate power or true attribution of what *appears* to be human agency. Tradition has it that when al-Hasan was asked whether a grave sinner (*fasiq*) should be classified as a believer or disbeliever, his hesitant or unsatisfactory response was the occasion for one Wasil ibn Ata (d. 748) to dissent from the consensual view that such a sinner was either a *mumin* (believer) or KAFIR (disbeliever). Wasil proclaimed the sinful Muslim was rather in an "intermediate state," thereby effectively "separating" himself or "withdrawing" from al-Hasan's circle of scholars and students. Amr ibn Ubayd (d. 761), another of al-Hasan's disciples, joined Wasil after the death of their teacher.

Mutazili theology was systematized in schools that developed in Basra and BAGHDAD, although members of the respective schools were not always confined to these geographic locales. From the earliest period in Basra we note Abu al-Hudhayl (d. ca. 849–850), while the Baghdad branch was guided by Bishr ibn al-Mutamir (d. 825). Under the Abbasid caliph al-Mamun (r. 813–833), a *mihna* (inquisition) was instituted in the early ninth century on behalf of a specific tenet of Mutazili doctrine, namely, the notion of a "created" (rather than "eternal") QURAN. While not instigated by the Mutazila themselves, the *mihna* required the regime's judges to publicly assent to the notion that God's speech—the Quran—was created, a position conspicuously contrary to popular belief, as vigorously espoused by AHMAD IBN HANBAL (780–855), a leader among the "people of HADITH" (*ahl al-hadith*). Ibn Hanbal refused assent and consent to this demand and suffered

imprisonment as a result, not to be released until some years later when the caliph al-Mutawakkil (r. 847–861) renounced the *mihna*.

Mutazili *mutakallimun* (theologians) entertained questions later definitive of the agenda of Islamic theology: whether the Quran is created or eternal; the nature and scope of free will and moral responsibility; the problem of theodicy (i.e., how to reconcile God's goodness with the evil that is part of the human condition or, put differently: Did God create evil?); how to interpret and understand the attributes of God (as enshrined in *al-asmaa al-husna,* the 99 NAMES OF GOD); and the role of reason (*aql*) vis-à-vis God's revelations or the understanding of God's will.

In the 10th century the "Basran" school is defined largely by Abu Ali al-Jubbai (d. 915) and his son, Abu Hashim ibn al-Jubbai (d. 933). Of the "Two Masters," it was the son who was to have the greater influence in this school, clearly evidenced in the work of the "last great thinker of [this] school of thought" (Martin and Woodward, p. 35), qadi Abd al-Jabbar (d. 1025). Among those worthy of mention in the Baghdad school are Abu al-Husayn al-Khayyat (d. ca. 913) and Abu al-Kasim al-Balkhi (d. 929).

Mutazili theology faced implacable opposition from Hanbali and Zahiri traditionalists (*ahl al-sunna*), on the one hand, and from the ASHARI school (founded by a former Mutazili, Abu al-Hasan al-Ashari) and Maturidi theologians on the other. The end of its golden age is coincident with the arrival of the Seljuks, first in Persia and then IRAQ, by the middle of the 11th century. Nevertheless, the Mutazila persevered for two more centuries, its school disappearing with the Mongol conquest in the 13th century.

As far back as Abu al-Hudhayl, Mutazili theology was distinctive for its articulation and advocacy of five fundamental principles (*al-usl al-khamsa*): (1) The absolute unity, uniqueness, and oneness of God (TAWHID): While a basic tenet of Muslim belief, Mutazili theology is distinctive in the manner in which it spells out the nature of divine transcendence in relation to God's attributes so as to avoid the Scylla of ANTHROPO- PHISM and the C[...] concrete meani[...] his essence, an[d...] metaphorical te[...] God. By way o[f...] meted out by G[...] free will or choi[ce...] between good a[nd...] errors ascribed t[...] which is not th[e...] (e.g., the illness [...] is said to warran[t...] intriguingly fron[...] independent (i.e[...] TION) use of reas[on...] of at least some [...] as well as knowi[ng...] and evil actions. [...] there are basic an[d...] conduct apart fro[m...] be sure, there are [...] motivated exclusi[vely...] has graciously acce[pted...] prophets to tell us wh[...] await us in the next life [...] us to achieve the former [...] detailing various laws and du[...] our disposition to act rightly and so merit[...] mate reward" (Leaman, pp. 164–165). God is just by definition, meaning he is constrained by the rules of justice. Thus we do what is right and good because, objectively speaking, it *is* right and good, not simply or only because God has commanded us to do it. (3) The "promise and the threat" (*al-wad wa al-waid*). In reference to Judgment Day, God promises recompense to those who obey him and threatens punishment for those who disobey him. Those guilty of grave sin (e.g., murder) who die without repentance will suffer the torments of hell. (4) The theory of an "intermediate state" (*al-*

manzila bayna l-manzilaytan). As discussed above, a grave sinner was classified as neither believer [...] but was said to be in an interme- [...]ween these categories, hence also [...]etween the views of the Khawarij [...]nd the MURJIA (Murjiites). (5) The [...]ressed to all Muslims for ". . . com- [...]and forbidding wrong." This is an [...] personal and public. The Mutazila [...]lytical treatment of this topic, as [...]an "underlying homogeneity of [...]ace and time." All the same, their [...] subject has been characterized as [...] "heroic." [...]ns, the Mutazila employed their [...]lectical rationalist skills on behalf [...]lation and the interpretation of [...]erstood their employment of rea- [...] the endeavor to provide a correct [...] the divine will. This assumes we [...] first and fundamental obligation [...]er of reason so as to know God, [...] the truth of his existence. The [...]y on the cosmological argument, [...]s begun to exist and in fact does [...]ndence on a God that transcends [...]f that which he has created. Our [...]ning should prompt us to ask [...]order of why something, rather [...]ts. Persistence and trust in the [...]hould lead us to a belief in the [...] of God's existence and eventu- ally [...] appreciation of his attributes.

With good reason, later Mutazilis called themselves the "People of Divine Unity and Justice" (*ahl al-adl wa l-tawhid*).

See also ABBASID CALIPHATE; TWELVE-IMAM SHIISM.

Patrick S. O'Donnell

Further reading: Binyamin Abrahamov, *Islamic Theology: Traditionalism and Rationalism* (Edinburgh: Edinburgh University Press, 1998); Michael Cook, *Commanding*

Right and Forbidding Wrong in Islamic Thought (Cambridge: Cambridge University Press, 2000); Josef van Ess, *The Flowering of Muslim Theology* (Cambridge: Cambridge University Press, 2006); Oliver Leaman, *An Introduction to Classical Islamic Philosophy* (Cambridge: Cambridge University Press, 2002); Richard C. Martin and Mark R. Woodward (with Dwi S. Atmaja), *Defenders of Reason: Mu'tazilism from Medieval School to Modern Symbol* (Oxford: Oneworld, 1997); Harry Austryn Wolfson, *The Philosophy of Kalam* (Cambridge, Mass.: Harvard University Press, 1976).

mysticism   *See* ASCETICISM; SUFISM; *TARIQA*.

N

nabi *See* PROPHETS AND PROPHETHOOD.

nafs *See* SOUL AND SPIRIT.

namaz *See* PRAYER.

names of God (Arabic: *al asma al-husna,* the most beautiful names)

Muslims believe in one God, but know him by 99 "most beautiful" names that attest to different divine qualities. The QURAN states, "The most beautiful names belong to God (ALLAH) so call on him by them; but shun such men as use profanity in his names: for what they do, they will soon be requited" (Q 7:180). Moreover, a HADITH from Abu Hurayra (d. 678), the close companion of the Prophet, asserts, "God has 99 names, one hundred minus 1, and whoever memorizes them will enter paradise." The first verse of the Quran, known as the BASMALA, states three of these names: "In the name of God (Allah), the most compassionate (*al-Rahman*), the most merciful (*al-Rahim*)." This verse begins all but one of the Quran's chapters. Other names attest to the divine qualities of omnipotence (*al-Qadir*), omniscience (*al-Alim*),

gentleness (*al-Latif*), righteousness (*al-Barr*), and kindness (*al-Rauf*). Muslims have speculated about God's hundredth name, which some believe is hidden and that only God knows it.

The 99 names come from three sources: (1) directly from the Quran (as in the *basmala* and Q 59:22–24); (2) names derived indirectly from the Quran (for example, *al-Basit* Expander [of hearts], Q 2:245); and (3) traditional names of God that are not found in the Quran in any form (for example, *al-Adl* The Just). Muslim theologians have divided the 99 names into two groupings. One involves differentiating between the Names of the Essence (such as God's own name, Allah, which is the supreme name, and *al-Rahman*) from the Names of the Qualities (such as *al-Barr*).

All of God's names are incorporated into the lives of Muslims in a wide variety of ways. They appear as first and/or last names of persons preceded by the word *Abd* (Servant of . . .), such as Abd Allah (Servant of God), Abd al-Salam (Servant of Peace), or Abd al-Jabbar (Servant of the Powerful). God's names are recited in the required daily prayers, during meditations involving PRAYER BEADS, and Sufi DHIKR rituals. They are printed on posters for display in mosques, homes, and businesses. One of the most popular religious songs in modern times is "Asma Allah al-husna"

الرحمن	الغفار	البصير	الحسيب	الحق	الحي	الظاهر	الجامع
Al-Rahman Most Compassionate	Al-Ghaffar The Forgiver	Al-Basir The All Seeing	Al-Hasib The Reckoner	Al-Haqq The Truth	Al-Hayy The Ever-Living	Al-Zahir The Manifest	Al-Jami The Gatherer
الرحيم	القهار	الحكم	الجليل	الوكيل	القيوم	الباطن	الغني
Al-Rahim The Merciful	Al-Qahhar The Subduer	Al-Hakam The Judge	Al-Jalil The Majestic	Al-Wakil The Disposer of Affairs	Al-Qayyum The Self-Existing by Whom all Subsist	Al-Batin The Hidden	Al-Ghani The All-Sufficient
الملك	الوهاب	العدل	الكريم	القوي	الواجد	الوالي	المغني
Al-Malik The King	Al-Wahhab The Bestower	Al-Adl The Just	Al-Karim The Generous	Al-Qawi The Most Strong	Al-Wajid The Self-Sufficient	Al-Wali The Protector	Al-Mughni The Enricher
القدوس	الرزاق	اللطيف	الرقيب	المتين	الماجد	المتعالي	المانع
Al-Quddus The Most Holy	Al-Razzaq The Provider	Al-Latif The Gentle	Al-Raqib The Watchful	Al-Matin The Firm One	Al-Majid The Glorified	Al-Mutaali The Most Exalted	Al-Mani The Preventer of Harm
السلام	الفتاح	الخبير	المجيب	الولي	الواحد	البر	الضار
Al-Salaam The Peace	Al-Fattah The Opener, The Judge	Al-Khabir The All Aware	Al-Mujib The Responsive	Al-Wali The Protector	Al-Wahid The One	Al-Barr The Benign	Al-Darr The Afflicter
المؤمن	العليم	الحليم			الاحد	التواب	النافع
Al-Mumin The Granter of Security	Al-Alim The All-Knowing	Al-Halim The Forbearing			Al-Ahad The One and Only	Al-Tawwab The Granter and Accepter of repentance	Al-Nafi The Benefiter
المهيمن	القابض	العظيم			الصمد	المنتقم	النور
Al-Muhaymin The Protector	Al-Qabid The Withholder	Al-Azim The Incomparingly Great			Al-Samad The Eternal	Al-Muntaqim The Avenger	Al-Nur The Light
العزيز	الباسط	الغفور	الواسع	الحميد	القادر	العفو	الهادي
Al-Aziz The Mighty	Al-Basit The Expander	Al-Ghafur The Forgiving	Al-Wasi The All-Embracing	Al-Hamid The Praiseworthy	Al-Qadir The Omnipotent	Al-Afuww The Pardoner	Al-Hadi The Guide
الجبار	الخافض	الشكور	الحكيم	المحصي	المقتدر	الرؤوف	البديع
Al-Jabbar The Compeller	Al-Khafid The Abaser	Al-Shakur The Appreciative	Al-Hakim The Wise	Al-Muhsi The Reckoner	Al-Muqtadir The Powerful	Al-Rauf The Most Kind	Al-Badi The Originator
المتكبر	الرافع	العلي	الودود	المبدئ	المقدم	ملك الملك	الباقي
Al-Mutakabbir The Majestic	Al-Rafi The Exalter	Al-Aliyy The Most High	Al-Wadud The Loving One	Al-Mubdi The Originator	Al-Muqaddim The Expediter	Malik-al-Mulk Owner of the Kingdom	Al-Baqi The Everlasting
الخالق	المعز	الكبير	المجيد	المعيد	المؤخر	ذو الجلال والاكرام	الوارث
Al-Khaliq The Creator	Al-Muizz The Bestower of Honor	Al-Kabir The Most Great	Al-Majid The Most Glorious	Al-Muid The Restorer to Life	Al-Muakhkhir The Delayer	Dhu-al-Jalali wa-al-Ikram Possessor of Majesty and Honor	Al-Warith The Ultimate Inheritor
الباري	المذل	الحفيظ	الباعث	المحيي	الاول		الرشيد
Al-Bari The Maker	Al-Mudhill The Humiliator	Al-Hafiz The Preserver	Al-Ba'ith The Resurrector	Al-Muhyi The Giver of Life	Al-Awwal The First		Al-Rashid The Guide
المصور	السميع	المقيت	الشهيد	المميت	الآخر	المقسط	الصبور
Al-Musawwir The Shaper	As-Sami The All-Hearing	Al-Muqit The Sustainer	Al-Shahid The Witness	Al-Mumit The Causer of Death	Al-Akhir The Last	Al-Muqsit The Just	Al-Sabur The Patient One

Remember Me and I will remember you (Quran 2:152)

الله

ALLAH

The Most Beautiful Names belong to Allah; invoke Him by them (Quran 7:180)

The 99 names of God

("God's most beautiful names"), composed by the Egyptian musician Sayyid Makkawi (1924–1997). Recitations of God's names have also been posted as audio files on the Internet.

See also PRAYER; THEOLOGY.

Jon Armajani

Further reading: Abu Hamid Muhammad ibn Muhammad al-Tusi al-Ghazali, *The Ninety-Nine Beautiful Names of God.* Translated by David B. Burrell and Nazih Daher. (Cambridge: Islamic Texts Society, 1995); Mujtaba Musavi Lari and Hamid Algar, *God and His Attributes* (Qom, Iran: Foundation of Islamic C.P.W., 2000); Fazlur Rahman, *Major Themes of the Quran* (Minneapolis: Bibliotheca Islamica, 1994); Muhammad ibn Abd al-Wahhab, *Kitab al Tawhid: Essay on the Unicity of Allah or What Is Due to Allah from His Creatures.* Translated by Ismail al-Faruqi. (Al-Ain, United Arab Emirates: Zayed Welfare Centre for the New Muslims, 1990).

Naqshbandi Sufi Order

The Naqshbandiyya Sufis constitute one of the world's most prominent Sufi orders and are known best for their active engagement in worldly affairs and their rejection of outward signs of religious devotion. The order is named after a 14th-century mystic and Sufi SHAYKH named Baha al-Din al-Naqshbandi, born in 1317 in the village of Qasr al-Arifan near BUKHARA in Central Asia. As an infant he was taken under the tutelage of a prominent Sufi master. In his youth he experienced visionary revelations and before the age of 20 was recognized as a brilliant Islamic scholar. He is said to have received training through the spirit—*ruhaniyat*—of earlier masters of the lineage, and by the mysterious Khidir, a special agent of God known to Islamic tradition. Baha al-Din died in 1389 and was buried in his birthplace.

Through the endowments of successive rulers of Bukhara, a *khanqah* (Sufi hospice), MADRASA, and MOSQUE were added to his tomb site, quickly making the area a major learning and pilgrimage center. By the end of the 15th century the Naqsh-bandis had become the dominant Sufi order in Central Asia, creating a strand of religious and cultural continuity and political influence across the geographically and culturally disparate Sunni strongholds of the Ottoman Empire, Central Asia, and INDIA.

The Naqshbandi Sufis consider themselves guardians of the practices of MUHAMMAD and his Companions, and trace their lineage back to ABU BAKR (d. 634), the first CALIPH. This, they claim, informs their highly distinctive practice of silent—as opposed to vocal—DHIKR (repeated invocation in the name of Allah), a practice they believe was first given to Abu Bakr by God.

Another distinctive characteristic of the Naqshbandi order, made definitive in the 15th century by Kwaja Nasiruddin Ubayd Allah Ahrar, is the primacy given to the establishment of SHARIA in Muslim societies. With Ahrar, Naqshbandi engagement with political establishments became characterized by the shaykhs' involvement with political rulers in concerns of both spiritual and mundane importance in order to cause these leaders to establish and enforce the sharia laws.

One of the great Naqshbandi innovators, Shaykh AHMAD SIRHINDI (1564–1624), contributed substantially to the diffusion of the order by establishing the Naqshbandiyya-Mujaddidiyya lineage in India. Another major leader of the Naqshbandis was Khalid Shahrazuri, a 19th-century Kurd from present-day northern Iraq, who initiated a new lineage, the Khalidis. The Khalidi branch was influential in the 19th-century Ottoman Empire, and it continues to be so in contemporary TURKEY.

The Naqshbandis of Central Asia were actively involved in resisting Russian colonization in the 19th century. Since the 1990s many communities in the former republics of Soviet Central Asia have been seeking to reconstruct their religious traditions, which involves recovering Naqshbandi traditions and histories. In Uzbekistan, for example, a recent resurgence of interest in Sufi heritage has involved an efflorescence of hagiographic materials that figure prominently in a reconstruction of the history of Naqshbandis in the region. Today branches of the Naqshbandi Sufi Order exist in Turkey, Bosnia, SYRIA, PAKISTAN, India, BANGLADESH, AFGHANISTAN, INDONESIA, MALAYSIA, Turkmenistan, Uzbekistan, China, Britain, and the Americas.

See also HAQQANI, MUHAMMAD NAZIM AL-; RENEWAL AND REFORM MOVEMENTS; SHAMIL; SUFISM.

Megan Adamson Sijapati

Further reading: Arthur F. Buehler, *Sufi Heirs of the Prophet: The Indian Naqshbandiyya and the Rise of the Mediating Sufi Shaykh* (Columbia: University of South Carolina Press, 1998); Elisabeth Ozdalga, ed., *Naqshbandis in Western and Central Asia: Change and Continuity* (Istanbul: Curzon Press, 1999); Vernon Schubel, "Post-Soviet Hagiography and the Reconstruction of the Naqshbandi Tradition in Contemporary Uzbekistan." In *Naqshbandis in Western and Central Asia: Change and Continuity,* edited by Elisabeth Ozdalga, 73–87 (Istanbul: Curzon Press, 1999).

Nasser, Gamal Abdel   *See* NASIR, JAMAL ABD AL-

Nasir, Jamal Abd al- (Gamal Abdel Nasser) (1918–1970) *charismatic president of Egypt from 1954 to 1970*

Jamal Abd al-Nasir was born on January 15, 1918. The son of a lower-middle-class postal official, Abd al-Nasir served with distinction in the 1948 Arab-Israeli war. As a lieutenant colonel in the Egyptian army, he was the leader of the Free Officers, a group of mainly young officers in the military from the lower or lower middle classes. The Free Officers successfully overthrew King Farouk on July 23, 1952, and established the Revolutionary Command Council, which became the ruling political group of EGYPT. Abd al-Nasir was elected president in 1956.

Abd al-Nasir was a strong nationalist, and his secular policies quickly alienated him from the MUSLIM BROTHERHOOD. In 1954, after an assassination attempt, Abd al-Nasir promptly purged the organization, imprisoning its members and hanging its leaders. While successful in the short run in disabling the Muslim Brotherhood as an effective organization, the purges contributed to the growth and development of Islamist movements in Egypt and throughout the world—Islamists such as SAYYID QUTB (d. 1966), who even today remains influential, were able to write and lay the ideological groundwork for radical ISLAMISM. Abd al-Nasir, however, remained immensely popular, especially among lower- and middle-class urban workers and rural dwellers in Egypt and in the wider Arab world.

Abd al-Nasir accomplished a major achievement in reforming the EDUCATION system by making it free for all Egyptians. This would eventually backfire, however, as universities later became a hotbed for breeding Islamic opposition. Abd al-Nasir's economic policies carried a socialist bent to them, and another one of his achievements was reforming land laws, limiting the size of land holdings for large landowners and redistributing acreage to the lower classes; however, while certain of his economic policies were popular with many Egyptians, his regime became increasingly autocratic as time passed. Ruling during the height of the cold war, Abd al-Nasir leaned toward the Soviet Union, which provided financial support for the construction of the Aswan Dam in 1964. One of his most visible legacies, the Aswan Dam introduced electricity to much of rural Egypt but also created major environmental problems.

In 1956 Abd al-Nasir received wide acclaim in Egypt and throughout the Arab world for seizing the Suez Canal from Britain, and his popularity quickly swelled as a symbol of pan-Arab nationalism. As Abd al-Nasir's status across the Arab world increased, he sought to capitalize on his notoriety by pursuing a foreign policy increasingly international in scope. In 1958 Egypt and Syria agreed to form the United Arab Republic (UAR), theoretically merging the two countries into a single, united Arab country. However, the UAR quickly dissolved in 1961 after just three years. Further, Abd al-Nasir became involved in the North YEMEN civil war in 1962, but this also ended in failure, and Egyptian troops were recalled in 1967.

By far the most significant foreign policy failure, however, was the disastrous defeat in the 1967 Arab-Israeli war, which for many discredited the Egyptian and pan-Arab nationalisms that Abd al-Nasir had helped popularize, and spawned a swelling in the ranks of Islamist movements as some sought a viable alternative to nationalism. Nonetheless, Abd al-Nasir remained an immensely popular figure until his death in 1970; his funeral is estimated to have drawn some five million attendees. He was succeeded in office by ANWAR AL-SADAT (d. 1981), his vice president.

See also ARAB-ISRAELI CONFLICTS; COLONIALISM; POLITICS AND ISLAM; SECULARISM.

Joshua Hoffman

Further reading: Ghada Hasem Talhami, *Palestine and Egyptian National Identity* (New York: Praeger, 1992); James Jankowski, *Nasir's Egypt, Arab Nationalism, and the United Arab Republic* (Boulder, Colo.: Lynne Reinner Publishers, 2002); Gilles Kepel, *Muslim Extremism in Egypt: The Prophet and the Pharaoh.* Translated by Jon Rothschild (Berkeley: University of California Press, 2003); Gamal Abdel Nasir, *The Philosophy of the Revolution* (Washington, D.C.: Public Affairs Press, 1955); P. J. Vatikiotis, *Nasir and His Generation* (London: C. Helm, 1978).

Nasr, Seyyed Hossein (1933–)
internationally known Iranian-American Muslim philosopher whose writings examine Islamic science, philosophy, and Sufi mysticism

Born in Tehran, IRAN, Nasr completed his preparatory education at the Peddie School in New Jersey, and his undergraduate education in physics at the Massachusetts Institute of Technology. At Harvard he received his master's degree in geology and geophysics and his Ph.D. in the history of SCIENCE under the direction of Bernard Cohen, H.A.R. Gibb, and Harry Wolfson. After returning to Iran, he held academic appointments at the University of Tehran as professor, dean and vice chancellor, and he served as president of Aryamehr University and later chief of the cultural bureau for the empress of Iran, Farah Diba (b. 1938). Since leaving Iran permanently, following the IRANIAN REVOLUTION OF 1978–79, he has held professorships at the University of Utah, Temple University, and George Washington University.

Central to Nasr's thought is the idea that, beginning with the Enlightenment, PHILOSOPHY and even the great quest for knowledge itself, has become separated from the sacred. This separation has led to the tragic plight of modern humans who have tried to find truth in purely scientific-technical endeavors. This has caused a gap between science, religion, and philosophy with the result that people seek their origins in incomplete Darwinism, denigrate religion to mere belief, and demean philosophy to analysis of language and scientific claims. Nasr's philosophy attempts to remedy these failings by taking a holistic approach to these three disciplines.

In his early scientific studies, Nasr encountered a chasm between his need for a complete scientific understanding of the world and his deep devotion to Islam as well as to perennial philosophy. His explorations into the QURAN regarding cosmic and human origins, geology, oceanography, and medicine led him to advocate that real science is *sapientia*, knowledge engendering wisdom. He points out that a number of the great Islamic philosophers, such as al-Kindi (d. 866), IBN RUSHD (d. 1198), and IBN SINA (d. 1037), were also scientists and physicians. Furthermore, philosophers inspired by SUFISM, such as IBN AL-ARABI (d. 1240), MULLA SADRA (d. 1640), and al-Suhrawardi (d. 1191), connect the task of philosophy to the experience of the divine. Nasr's comparative philosophy shows that the aim of philosophy from Plato (d. ca. 348 B.C.E.) in Greece to Shankara (ca. ninth century C.E.) in India to Confucius (d. 479 B.C.E.)

in China was to unify knowledge as a sacred quest for the truth. Finally the world's great religions as reflected in HOLY BOOKS, such as the Hindu Vedas, the Bhagavad Gita, the Bible, and the *Daodejing* (*Tao te Ching*), all illuminate a path to divinity through a spiritual philosophy, seeking to unify humans, nature, and God.

Nasr was the youngest philosopher ever honored by the Library of Living Philosophers and the first Muslim. He has exerted considerable influence in efforts to revive Islamic philosophy in Europe and the Americas with his discussion of philosophers after Ibn Rushd. He has profoundly influenced scholars worldwide who are seeking to reunderstand Islamic philosophy and the sacred nature of knowledge.

See also CREATION; SECULARISM; THEOLOGY.

Judy Saltzman

Further reading: Lewis Hahn, Randall Auxier, and Lucien W. Stone, Jr., eds., *The Philosophy of Seyyed Hossein Nasr* (Chicago: Open Court Publishing, 2001); Seyyed Hossein Nasr, *Islamic Philosophy from Its Origins to the Present* (Albany: State University of New York Press, 2006); ———, *Science and Civilization in Islam* (Cambridge, Mass.: Harvard University Press, 1970); ———, *Philosophy and the Plight of Modern Man* (London: Longmans, 1976); ———, *Knowledge and the Sacred* (Albany: State University of New York Press, 1989); ———, *Religion and the Order of Nature* (Oxford: Oxford University Press, 1996).

Nation of Islam

This indigenous African-American Muslim community of the Nation of Islam (NOI) began in 1930, when racism and violence against blacks were still widespread in the UNITED STATES. Although the shadowy figure of W. D. Fard (also known as Fard Muhammad, Wallace D. Fard, Wali Fard Muhammad, et al.) was the original impetus of the community's distinctive black THEOLOGY and eschatological message, its true founder and leader for many decades until his death was Elijah Muhammad, born Elijah Poole (1897–1975), in Sandersville, Georgia. In 1923 he married Clara Evans, who later came to be known in the NOI as Sister Clara Muhammad, and settled in Detroit, where, in the early 1930s, he became acquainted with W. D. Fard and his already established Temple of Islam. By 1934 Fard had disappeared and Elijah Muhammad became the sole leader of the new community known as the Nation of Islam.

Combining use of the Bible and later the QURAN, Elijah Muhammad preached a message of modern black prophecy that emphasized themes of the chosenness and salvific destiny of the "Blackman," doing his own revisionist history on racist American attitudes toward the "Negro" or "colored man" since the Civil War (1861–65). Possible Islamic sources for these teachings have been found by scholars of SUFISM and Islamic sectarian theologies (SHIISM, AHMADIYYA, and even DRUZE teachings), all of which espouse varying notions of the divinity within, cyclic prophecy, ongoing revelation, messianism in the Islamic figure of the MAHDI, and millennialism in the imminent coming of the Last Judgment and reversal/overthrow of the present corrupt world order. Several of these ideas exist on the margins of Islamic sectarianism and are strongly disavowed by the Sunni Muslim majority, particularly notions of modern prophecy, ongoing revelation, and human (in this case, black) divinity. These doctrines have made the NOI universally rejected by the American Sunni community since its origins, although there are more recent signs of a rapprochement with the larger world Muslim UMMA, or religious community.

The NOI has frequently been categorized in purely secular political or sociological terms as black nationalism and not as a religious community. This community certainly has played a large role in paralleling, stimulating, and critiquing various civil rights and sociopolitical activism movements in America: the National Association for the Advancement of the Colored People (NAACP), Marcus Garvey's Universal Negro Improvement

Association (UNIA), the Black Power movement (1966–75), and Dr. Martin Luther King, Jr.'s Civil Rights movement (1955–68). However, the NOI is best understood as a religious organization with strong sociopolitical aims and its fits better into the Islamic term, *umma,* or Muslim religious community, with its implications of individual and social identity, economic relations, and political order ideally guided by divine law, the SHARIA. It is clearly, by its own admission, not part of the Sunni *umma,* but that does not exclude it from the larger communal and theological diversity of Islam.

According to the theological discourse of the founder, Elijah Muhammad, conveyed primarily through speeches/sermons and eventually recorded as written works, such as *Message to the Blackman in America,* the "Blackman" (a key term in NOI discourse) is the original first human, made in the divine image and therefore himself partaking in divinity. His original nature makes him/her the prototype of all people of color (black, brown, red, yellow, symbols for all non-Caucasian people of the world). Being the original, the "Blackman" is therefore the good, the beautiful, and the blessed, thus negating the antiblack, derogatory, and racist connotations of such American designations as "Negro" and "colored," as well as derogatory colloquial slurs. NOI theology treats seriously the question of the origin of evil in the world, particularly the evils suffered by persecuted peoples, such as the African people's history of enslavement at the hands of Europeans, the horrors of the Middle Passage (described in NOI terms as prefiguring the Nazi Holocaust of World War II), and the persecution and denigration of their descendants in post–Civil War America to the present. Elijah Muhammad's answer to the question of cosmic and human evils experienced by the Blackman is to posit a gnostic demiurge, the evil Yakub, who is understood as a proximate source of the world's evils, not God, but a powerful and malign force setting up this present world order in which "White is right" and all people of color are tormented and lost. He is the

white creator, the mad scientist, who has caused the present-day evils of racism, persecution, poverty, unjust imprisonment, and despair (whether referring to slavery itself or being caught up in the belly of the Beast, devoured by American police, courts, and prisons). The ultimate purpose of this demiurge and the immediate evils endured by the Blackman is their spiritual reclamation, or, as Elijah Muhammad put it, their "resurrection from the mentally dead."

The future and ultimate destiny of the community's members is to serve as agents of salvation, overturning the devil's work (meaning initially Yakub, and in history, all white evildoers and persecutors of people of color). NOI theology of the end times draws upon a biblical reference (Ezekiel 1:15–18) to the prophetic vision of the divine chariot with flaming wheels, known in Jewish mysticism as Merkavah, and recast in Elijah Muhammad's exegesis (as expressed in *The Fall of America* and *The Theology of Time*) as the "Mother Plane." This teaching brings modern American awareness of the atomic age to the notion of "heaven," envisioning a celestial JUDGMENT DAY and redemption as literally heavenward or extraterrestrial. NOI members in this vision await their apocalypse, which will destroy the corrupt present order of society but redeem the righteous, namely, all people of color who have suffered and fought oppression and injustice. It will take them via a spaceship—the Mother Plane—to freedom and bliss. Interestingly, this NOI motif of the Mother Plane gained wide (if unacknowledged) currency after Elijah Muhammad's death through the popular culture venue of P-Funk (a pop American music genre during the 1970s that defined groups formed under the aegis of George Clinton). P-Funk (and the Mothership) has since achieved a rebirth and reissue, increasing the popular currency and longevity of Elijah's apocalyptic teachings in the "sampling" of Islamic Hip Hop and artists such as Public Enemy, Arrested Development, Brand Nubian, X-Clan, and others.

Elijah Muhammad's greatest social emphases included the need for the community to become socially and economically self-sufficient and independent of the cycle of post–Civil War urban and rural poverty, drugs, and violence, as well as dependence on government welfare that he felt was leaching the strength and motive force from the community. He implemented strong directives throughout the NOI (which had a great impact on nonmembers in the African-American community as well) to adopt a healthful lifestyle through a change in diet and nutrition, which he advocated in his two-volume *How to Eat to Live*. This book taught the virtues of abandoning the nutritional habits of "soul food," which had its origins among blacks in the American South and was associated with the culture of black rural poverty. Muhammad's health agenda included prohibiting alcohol, smoking, and drugs (for their economic and health consequences, as well as the traditional Islamic one, that person cannot be spiritual aware, ritually prepared, or morally responsible if she or he is impaired by alcohol or drugs). Followers were expected to follow these standards in their conduct, as well as dress and comport themselves in public and private in a way that bolstered self-respect and respect for the community by nonmembers, white or black. Male community members still follow the dress code and style established by the founder in the 1930s—the blue or gray business suit, white shirt with red bow-tie. Female members model themselves on the modified veil and long full dress worn by the founder's wife, "Sister" Clara Muhammad (d. 1972). Elijah Muhammad further advocated that the community achieve economic self-sufficiency and independence from white business and government aid through his philosophy of "buy Black": be self- or community-employed, create and foster NOI product lines (such as household, health-care, and hygiene products; homemade food products; and the community newspaper, *Muhammad Speaks*), and support local black business (which had been rig-orously discouraged or eliminated by large-scale white competition in the 1930s), keeping black dollars inside the black community. The last and, perhaps, most important item in his social/religious agenda was the founding of a NOI school system as an alternative to the U.S. K–12 public system. Such school systems taught basic literacy and history of the world and of the Blackman according to NOI cosmology discussed above.

The community came to its greatest public and media notice during the civil rights era of the 1960s, when MALCOLM X served as chief lieutenant for Elijah Muhammad and as public relations spokesperson for the NOI. His charismatic speaking style carried the message of the NOI to universities across America as well as in media interviews with famous journalists and television personalities of the day, such as Mike Wallace's 1959 documentary *The Hate That Hate Produced*. The NOI charted a more verbally militant and aggressive stance in relation to white America than the parallel Christian civil rights leader, Martin Luther King, Jr. (1929–68), and it came under much negative public, media, government/law enforcement attention. It is now well documented in recently declassified FBI documents that the then director of the FBI, J. Edgar Hoover, pursued a long-standing campaign of harassment and media disinformation against the NOI in order to discredit the organization and, if possible, to disband it. One of the issues the NOI has pursued throughout its history until the present day is a strong prison outreach and conversion ministry, tied to rehabilitation in the NOI community upon release. As seen in Malcolm X's own AUTOBIOGRAPHY, this activity has had a significant impact on prison populations and improved their constitutional religious rights to freedom of worship.

Both a sex scandal associated with Elijah Muhammad's behavior within the community and Malcolm's public remarks on the death of President John F. Kennedy in 1963 about "chickens coming home to roost" caused Malcolm X to be censured. In 1964 he broke away from the community and converted to Sunni Islam while undertaking the HAJJ ritual to Mecca in 1964. After his return he adopted the appropriate Islamic title El-Hajji (one who has accomplished Hajj), which he added to his chosen Sunni name. In 1965 Malcolm X was assassinated and the NOI's founder, Elijah Muhammad, died.

After its original prophet and revelator died, the NOI experienced a sea change. First the son of the founder, Wallace D. Muhammad (b. 1933–2008), assumed leadership and directed the community away from the founder's teachings toward the world Sunni majority. His decision was implemented by adopting the ritual pillars of traditional Islamic practice (the witness to faith, five daily prayers, fasting through the month of RAMADAN, formal almsgiving, and pilgrimage to MECCA) and rigorous education in the fundamentals of Arabic, as well as the study of the Quran. He adopted an Islamic version of his birth name, Warith Deen Muhammad, and named his organization, which included most of the former members of the NOI, the American Muslim Mission. The remnant of the NOI that maintained allegiance to the founder's theology followed the leadership of his chief lieutenant at the time of Elijah's death, LOUIS FARRAKHAN (born Louis Eugene Walcott in 1933), who continued the fundamental style and approach of the founder while de-emphasizing the agenda of political separatism and national land reparations to African-American descendants of slaves. He focused NOI attention on continuing Elijah Muhammad's programs of socio-spiritual reeducation and economic self-sufficiency. Through his speeches, writings (*Torchlight*), and the renamed NOI newspaper, *The Final Call,* he continues to lead the community and has placed increased stress on study and use of the Quran in his teachings. Although a charismatic speaker who has led some noteworthy social efforts, such as the Million Man March in Washington, D.C., in 1995, he has been widely criticized for ANTI-SEMITISM, sexism, and racism in many of his public statements.

The Nation of Islam clearly displays significant features that place it firmly within American social and religious pluralism and the psychology and sociology of minority and persecuted groups. American characteristics of the NOI, its offshoots (the Nation of Five Percenters) and parallels (the Ansaaru Allah Community) include an identity defined positively by race (positively for blacks and negatively for whites); an aggressive defense of the disadvantaged, oppressed, harassed urban poor, and a strong rehabilitative appeal to and recruitment of prison populations. It has also maintained a secret discourse in its internal theology wedded to a paranoid and conspiracy-minded attitude to the public sphere and media-makers of America, especially its governmental powers (police, the courts, the prison system, even in a larger sense the welfare system).

Although NOI teachings include a spectrum of biblical and esoteric Christian teachings, it also displays significant Islamic features drawn from the deep wells of theological and sectarian diversity within the larger history of Islam, as well as increasing reference to and use of the Quran. The Islamic characteristics of the NOI and other parallel Black Muslim theologies include: contemporary and ongoing REVELATION and prophetic presence (first, W.D. Fard, and then Elijah Muhammad); charismatic and divinely inspired AUTHORITY; experiential wisdom and teachings of mysticism, coded initiant-only language designed to reveal to the like-minded and conceal from the outsider the inner truths of the community (as in Sufi and Shii exegesis and other esoteric venues, such as the Islamic occult sciences); political militancy, social defiance, and economical activism (in line with Islamic jihadist and activist movements) without actually coming to violence or outright warfare (its "war" is social and symbolic, and the victory pragmatic and immediately practical); and finally the holistic concept of the Muslim *umma,* or the religious community, which is also ideally a social, economic, and political community, with its universal quest for the just Muslim society.

As a final note, the NOI and other parallel groups have often been labeled collectively "Black Muslims." These include such related communities as the Moorish Science Temple (begun before the NOI in 1913 in Newark, New Jersey, by Noble Drew Ali, born Timothy Drew), the Five Percent Nation of Gods and Earths, or Five Percenters (an offshoot of the NOI started in 1964 by ex-NOI member Clarence "Pudding" 13X, born Clarence Jowars Smith, killed in 1969), and the Ansaaru Allah Community (an apocalyptic and theologically eclectic community founded by Isa Muhammad, aka Malachi Z. York, born Dwight York ca. 1935). The term *Black Muslim* was coined by an early scholar on the NOI, C. Eric Lincoln in 1961 and came to be commonly associated with various sectarian African-American Muslim communities, but particularly the Nation of Islam. This usage was intended to distinguish the Nation of Islam from the immigrant, expatriate, and white convert population of the American Sunni majority who have tended to claim "Moslem" or "Muslim" for themselves.

See also AFRICAN AMERICANS, ISLAM AMONG; SUNNISM.

Kathleen M. O'Connor

Further reading: Claude Andrew Clegg, III, *An Original Man: The Life and Times of Elijah Muhammad* (New York: St. Martin's Press, 1998); Robert Dannin, "Islands in a Sea of Ignorance." In *Black Pilgrimage to Islam* (New York: Oxford University Press, 1995); E. U. Essien-Udom, *Black Nationalism: A Search for Identity in America* (New York: Dell Publishing, 1962); Matthias Gardell, *In the Name of Elijah Muhammad: Louis Farrakhan and the Nation of Islam* (Durham, N.C.: Duke University Press, 1996); C. Eric Lincoln, *The Black Muslims In America* (Boston: Beacon Press, 1961); Malcolm X and Alex Haley, *The Autobiography of Malcolm X* (1965. Reprint, New York: Ballantine Books, 1992); Aminah Beverly McCloud, *African American Islam* (New York: Routledge, 1995); Kathleen M. Moore, *Al-Mughtaribun: American Law and the Transformation of Muslim Life in the United States* (Albany: State University of New York Press, 1995); Elijah Muhammad, *Message to the Blackman in America* (1965. Reprint, Newport News, Va.: United Brothers Communications Systems, 1992); Sonsryea Tate, *Little X: Growing Up in the Nation of Islam* (Knoxville: University of Tennessee Press, 2005); Richard Brent Turner, *Islam in the African-American Experience* (Bloomington: Indiana University Press, 1997).

Navruz (Persian: new day; Nawruz, Nowruz, Nevruz)

Navruz is the ancient Persian New Year's holiday, traditionally celebrated in IRAN and neighboring countries from Turkey to Uzbekistan at the time of the spring equinox (around March 21). Originally, it was an ancient Zoroastrian festival that was adopted by the Persian kings before Islam's appearance in the seventh century C.E. It was celebrated widely in Middle Eastern cultures as a public holiday. It is now celebrated over a period of 12 to 14 days in late March by people who have grown up in Persianate cultures and households, regardless of religious affiliation. This includes the majority of Sunni and Shii Muslims, Christians, and Jews living in Iran, or in communities influenced by the Persian cultural heritage.

Navruz is a time for family visits and exchanging gifts. The home has become one of the main centers for celebrating it. After people do a thorough housecleaning, they set up the *haft-sin* (seven food items beginning with the letter "s") with a mirror and candles on a table in a common area where visitors can see it. An older custom is to place these items on a carpet or cloth that has been spread on the ground. Seven is considered a lucky number and the food items placed on the table are said to be auspicious for the coming year, representing good health, happiness, prosperity, fertility, and long life. There is some variation among the symbolic items displayed, but they often include *sabzi* (green sprouts), *sib* (apples), *samanu* (a sweet, creamy pudding), *sir* (fresh garlic), *sumaq* (a sour berry used in Persian cuisine), *sirkeh* (vinegar), and *sinjid* (oleaster, or jujube fruits). It is also common to put a book of wisdom on the *haft-sin* table. It might be the Quran, the Bible, the Zoroastrian *Avesta,* the Persian epic poem *Shahnama,* or a collection of poetry by Hafiz (d. ca. 1380). Fortunes are often divined at this time by reading randomly selected passages from one of these books. Other auspicious objects placed on the table may include flowers, coins, nuts and sweets, a basket of painted eggs, and a goldfish in a bowl. In Afghanistan a dish consisting of seven kinds of fruits and nuts is prepared instead of the *haft-sin.*

Navruz is also an occasion for public celebrations. On the last Wednesday of the old year people set bonfires in the streets or parks and take turns jumping over them, celebrating the increased spring daylight and the good things connected with it. Like Halloween in America, children wearing shrouds representing the spirits of the dead go door to door, banging on pots and pans and collecting treats. This is related to a tradition of driving away the forces responsible for causing bad luck. A clown named Hajji Firuz sings and dances in the streets announcing the arrival of the New Year. People customarily wear new clothes for this popular holiday. The end of the holiday period is marked by a picnic and disposal of green sprouts that were grown for this occasion.

Even though Navruz is not an Islamic holiday, it nonetheless has taken on Islamic associations in the past, especially among the Shia. According to

Navruz *haft-sin* display in a Persian home *(Venus Nasri)*

tradition it is the anniversary of God's COVENANT with Adam and his offspring at the beginning of creation, Abraham's destruction of the idols of his community, Muhammad's designation of ALI IBN ABI TALIB (d. 661) as his successor, and the future appearance of the Hidden Imam, who will do battle with the Dajjal (ANTICHRIST).

See also CALENDAR; CHILDREN; HOLIDAYS; SHIISM.

Further reading: Najmieh Batmanglij, *New Food for Life: Ancient Persian and Modern Iranian Cooking and Ceremonies,* 3d ed. (Washington, D.C.: Mage Publishers, 2004), 384–391; Mary Boyce, "Iranian Festivals." In *Cambridge History of Iran.* Vol. 3, Part 2, *The Seleucid, Parthian, and Sasanian Periods,* edited by Ehsan Yarshater, 792–815 (Cambridge: Cambridge University Press, 1983); Bess A. Donaldson, *The Wild Rue: A Study of Muhammadan Magic and Folklore in Iran* (London: Luzac, 1938), 120–123.

Nepal

Nepal is a small country (approximately 54,362 sq. miles, slightly larger than the state of Arkansas) located along the southern region of the Himalayan range. It shares a border to the east, south, and west with INDIA and to the north with the Tibetan region of CHINA. It has three distinct geographic zones—the Himalayan range in the northern region, the foothills and Kathmandu Valley in the central region, and the Terai plains in the southern region. It is home to the highest peak in the world, Mt. Everest, and it is the birthplace of the Buddha. Its population is approximately 29.5 million (2008 est.) and is a complex and heterogeneous mix of both Indo-European and Tibeto-Burman ethnic groups and languages, and of various tribes and castes, each with their own distinct languages and cultural traditions. In the late 18th century, the Gorkha king Prithvi Narayan Shah consolidated the territories of what is today Nepal. With the exception of the period of Rana rule from 1846 to 1951, descendants of the shah king have ruled Nepal as a Hindu state throughout most of the country's history. Since 1951 Nepal's form of government has changed several times, most notably from a Hindu monarchy to a multiparty democracy and constitutional monarchy in 1991, then to an absolute monarchy in 2002, and most recently to a parliamentary democracy achieved in April 2006 after months of mass protests led by the country's seven political parties and the Maoists. Since 1996 Nepal has suffered from a Maoist insurgency that has resulted in the deaths of over 10,000 Nepali people.

According to the 2001 Nepali government census, Hindus constitute 80 percent of Nepal's population, Buddhists 11 percent, and Muslims 4.2 percent. The majority of Nepali Muslims live in the Terai region, with small populations also in the Kathmandu Valley and the western hill regions. There are numerous mosques and madrasas in the Terai, including a prominent Ahl-e Hadis (People of the Hadith) MADRASA in the southern district of Kapilvastu. In the Kathmandu Valley there are seven mosques, the two largest of which are the Kashmiri Taqiyya and the Nepali Jame Masjid (Friday Mosque), and several madrasas, which impart a mixture of Islamic and government curriculum. Nepali Muslims are of varying ethnic and cultural backgrounds, primarily Kashmiri, North Indian, Tibetan, Newari, and Nepali, and they retain distinct cultural identities as such. Most Nepali Muslims are Sunni and of primarily Deobandi, Barelwi, Ahl-e Hadith, or TABLIGHI JAMAAT affiliation.

Though an eighth-century Arabic text entitled *Hudud al-alam* (Boundaries of the world) mentions the import of musk from Nepal, suggesting that there may have been early trade links between Nepalis and Arab tradesmen, the earliest historical evidence of Muslim presence in Nepal comes from an inscription recording an invasion in 1349 from the east by the Muslim sultan Shams ad-din Ilyas of Bengal, which destroyed the royal Hindu temple of Pashupatinath and the Buddhist stupa Swayambunath. In the late 15th and early 16th-centuries Kashmiri Muslim traders of woolen goods became the first Muslims to settle in Nepal when they were permitted to migrate there during the reign of Ratna Malla in Kantipur (now Kathmandu). Oral history tells us that the first Muslim to settle in Nepal was a 16th-century Kashmiri *faqir* (DERVISH) by the name of Miskeen Shah who, through his magical powers, convinced the king to give him land to establish a MOSQUE. This is corroborated by records indicating that a Muslim SAINT who entered Kathmandu in 1524 built the first mosque in Nepal, which today is called the Kashmiri Taqiyya, the mosque of Nepal's Kashmiri Muslim population and the site of the saint's *dargah* (shrine). In the 17th century Muslims from India began migrating to Nepal, and they were given royal permission to build a mosque in Kathmandu, the Nepali Masjid, which today serves as a major center of Muslim social and devotional activity in the Kathmandu Valley. The kings of Nepal's Malla Dynasty (13th–18th centuries) were influenced by the style of the Muslim imperial courts at DELHI and emulated their imperial portraiture style, adopted Persian words into Nepali language, and struck their own imperial coins modeled after those of the Delhi courts. Following the Indian Revolt of 1857, significant numbers of Indian Muslims migrated to various parts of Nepal. Many Muslims in the Terai are descendants of Indians who migrated to the region in the 17th through 19th centuries.

Though the relationship between the Muslim minority and Hindu majority in Nepal has been a historically peaceful one, in September 2004 Nepali Muslims became the target of religious violence following the murder of 13 Nepali workers in Iraq, marking the second major incident of anti-Muslim violence in the country's history. Mosques, madrasas, and Muslim homes and businesses throughout Nepal suffered heavy damage. This tragedy led to the establishment of the National Muslim Forum, an organization of Muslim leaders from throughout Nepal that aims to bring together Nepali Muslims across ethnic, regional, and sectarian differences into a united forum. Many of its leaders are also members of Nepal's largest Islamic organization, Islami Sangh Nepal, which conducts Islamic education programs throughout the country, oversees Kathmandu's Islamic library and the Al-Hira Educational Society, and publishes *Paigham,* a quarterly Muslim journal in Urdu. It also publishes *Madhur Sandesh,* a monthly Muslim magazine in Nepali.

See also BARELWI, SAYYID AHMAD; BUDDHISM AND ISLAM; DEOBAND; HINDUISM AND ISLAM; KASHMIR.

Megan Adamson Sijapati

Further reading: Hamid Ansari, "Muslims in Nepal," *Journal of Muslim Minority Affairs* 2, nos. 2–3, (Winter 1980–Summer 1981): 138–158; Mollica Dastider, *Religious Minorities in Nepal: An Analysis of the State of Buddhists and Muslims in the Himalayan Kingdom* (New Delhi: Nirala Publication, 1995); Marc Gaborieau, "Muslim Minorities in Nepal." In *The Crescent in the East: Islam in Asia Major* edited by Raphael Israeli, 79–101 (London: Curzon Press, 1982).

New Zealand

New Zealand, also called Aotearoa by the Maori, its original inhabitants, is an island nation in the South Pacific, separated from Australia by the Tasmanian Sea. It consists of two main islands and a number of smaller ones. Its land area is approximately 103,000 square miles, making it about the same size as Japan. It is home to some four million people. The Maori people constitute about 14 percent of the population. Their hegemony over Aotearoa was challenged early in the 19th century by the arrival of the British. Europeans had become aware of New Zealand's existence in the 17th century and Captain James Cook (1728–79) had rediscovered it in 1769.

The Maori had originally settled Aotearoa in the 9th century C.E. In 1642 Abel Tasman (ca. 1603–59), a Dutch sea captain, named it New Zealand. Then Captain Cook surveyed the islands and produced an initial map. The establishment of British colonial settlements in the early decades of the 19th century led to conflict with the Maori natives, which was settled in 1840 with the signing of the Treaty of Waitangi that established the island nation. Over the next century immigrants from Great Britain came to be the single largest element of New Zealand's population and they brought the different forms of Christianity then dominant in their homeland with them.

A few Muslims arrived in New Zealand through the first half of the 20th century, but most lived there as alien residents rather than seeking citizenship. They have since immigrated to the country from across the Muslim world. By 1979, when an initial national organization, the Federation of Islamic Associations of New Zealand (FIANZ) was formed, there were only some 1,700 Muslims, but the community experienced a relatively rapid growth in the latter part of the 20th and early 21st centuries. By 1986 there were more than 2,500 permanent residents with increasing numbers coming from Fiji and South Asia. By the end of the century the community had grown to more than 14,000, and in the first decade of the 21st century the Muslim population reached an estimated 20,000.

Interestingly, of the Muslim residents, less than half were born in New Zealand, with about one-third of the community arriving from Asia and about one-fourth from various Pacific islands, especially Fiji. Within the country, the largest concentration of Muslims is to be found in Auckland. Because of the nature of the community, mosques tend to be multiethnic.

FIANZ emerged out of earlier local associations, the first formed in Auckland in the 1950s. It provides guidance on matters such as dating of religious observances and providing religious education to Muslim children, as well as speaking to the wider public on national issues. FIANZ seeks to build a positive image of Islam in New Zealand and prints basic literature for those inquiring about the faith.

See also AUSTRALIA.

J. Gordon Melton

Further reading: Christopher van der Krogt, "Islam." In *Religions of New Zealanders,* edited by Peter Donovan, 186–205 (Palmerston North, N.Z.: Dunmore Press, 1990); William Shepard, "Muslims in New Zealand." In *Muslim Minorities in the West, Visible and Invisible,* edited by Yvonne Haddad and Jane I. Smith, 233–254 (Walnut Creek, Calif.: AltaMira Press, 2002).

Night Journey and Ascent (Arabic: *al-isra wal-miraj*)

The story of MUHAMMAD's night journey (*isra*) to JERUSALEM and eventual meeting with God above the seventh heaven is told throughout the Muslim world in many venues: Egyptian street-side illustrated pamphlets, Friday SERMONS, Persian illuminated manuscripts, Pakistani pilgrimage busses, Swahili and Hausa poetry. It is based on events narrated in the HADITH collections and Ibn Ishaq's eighth-century BIOGRAPHY (*sira*) of Muhammad. Muslims attribute the night journey to the QURAN (Q 17:1): "Glory to the one who took his servant on a night journey from the sacred place of prayer to the furthest place of prayer upon which we have sent down our blessing, that we might show him some of our signs. He is the All-Hearing, the All-Seeing." Traditionally an earlier episode in Muhammad's life, the opening of his breast by GABRIEL, who cleans his heart of all impurity in preparation for his role as messenger of God, is appended to the night journey story. Muslims consider as further proof texts of the story Quran Sura 94, which depicts the opening of Muhammad's breast, and Q 53:1–18, which contains visions associated with the heavenly ascent.

According to the most widely known version of the story, after being woken from sleep in the mosque at MECCA, Muhammad rides to Jerusalem on the back of the mythical steed called BURAQ, a creature depicted as a horse with the head of a woman. In Jerusalem he prays at the furthest (*aqsa*) MOSQUE, sometimes understood to be the heavenly mosque, and then ascends to heaven (*miraj* literally means "ladder"). During his ascent through the heavens with Gabriel, Muhammad meets former prophets—Adam, John the Baptist, JESUS, JOSEPH, Enoch (IDRIS), Aaron, MOSES, and ABRAHAM—who each acknowledge his remarkable status. As his journey continues the visions of the punishments suffered by the inhabitants of hell and the rewards of the blessed in PARADISE reflect major eschatological themes in the Quran. After being advised by Moses during his descent from the highest heaven to ask God for a reduction in number of prayers, Muhammad eventually returns to his UMMA with the five daily prayers.

While there is debate in the Muslim world as to whether Muhammad's journey took place in body or spirit, it represents a mandate for Muhammad's superiority in status over the former prophets as the Seal of the Prophets. Many Muslims celebrate the Night Journey and Ascent every year on the 27th of Rajab (the seventh month on their CALENDAR). Sufis, in particular, understand this story as a model of human devotion to God and, conversely, God's devotion to his creation, to be emulated in their own spiritual quests for union with the divine. Among the most famous Sufis who are said to have undertaken an ascent to heaven are ABU YAZID BISTAMI (ninth century) and RUZBIHAN AL-BAQLI (d. 1209).

See also ANGEL; AQSA MOSQUE; DOME OF THE ROCK; PRAYER; SUFISM.

Margaret Leeming

Further reading: Annemarie Schimmel, *And Muhammad Is His Messenger: The Veneration of the Prophet in Islamic Piety* (Chapel Hill: University of North Carolina Press, 1985); Michael Sells, *Early Islamic Mysticism: Sufi, Quran, Miraj, Poetic, and Theological Writings* (Mahwah, N.J.: Paulist Press, 1996); Abu Abd al-Rahman Sulami, *Subtleties of Ascension: Early Mystical Sayings on the Prophet Muhammad's Night Journey, the Isra wa Miraj*. Translated by Frederick Colby (Louisville, Ky.: Fons Vitae, 2007).

Night of Destiny (Arabic: Laylat al-Qadr; Persian: Shab-i Qadr/ Shab-e Qadr; alternate meaning: Night of Power)

If RAMADAN is the most sacred Islamic month, Laylat al-Qadr is the most sacred night in that month. The Arabic word *qadr* can mean both destiny and power; Muslim commentators have differed over which is the correct meaning. The phrase occurs in Sura 97 of the QURAN, which is called al-Qadr. The first verse in this chapter states, "Indeed we have revealed it on the Night of al-Qadr . . . the Night of al-Qadr is better than a thousand months" (Q 97: 1, 3). Some commentators have identified this passage with the event of Muhammad's receiving the Quran in its entirety via angels who brought it down to him from heaven. This belief seems to contradict earlier accounts, which hold that the Quran was revealed gradually during the last 23 years of Muhammad's life. To reconcile the two views Muslim commentators have proposed that the ANGELS first brought it down on one night from the Preserved Tablet (God's heavenly book) to the lowest level of heaven and that from there GABRIEL revealed it gradually to MUHAMMAD in MECCA and MEDINA. Still others say that the event refers only to Muhammad's first REVELATION at the Mountain of Light Hira outside of Mecca. Euro-American Islamic studies scholars have pointed out that the celebration of a single moment of revelation may have been inspired by pre-Islamic Jewish and Christian traditions of revelation, such as the revelation of the TORAH at Mount Sinai and the birth of JESUS. Shiis have added yet another level of meaning to this night, for they believe it is also when FATIMA (ca. 605–633), Muhammad's daughter and mother of the imams, was born, and when ALI IBN ABI TALIB (d. 661) was martyred.

The holiday falls on one of the last odd-numbered nights in Ramadan; Sunnis usually observe it on the 27th and Shiis on the 23rd. Devout Muslims customarily go to mosques to celebrate it, spending the entire night there in PRAYER and listening to Quran recitations. Some even go on retreat for up to 10 days at the end of Ramadan.

According to the HADITH, prayer and performing good deeds on this night will win God's forgiveness for past sins. Many Muslims also believe that on this night each year God decrees all that will happen in the year to come, in keeping with the meaning of *qadr* as "destiny."

See also FATE; MARTYRDOM; PROPHETS AND PROPHETHOOD.

Further reading: S. D. Goitein, "Ramadan: The Muslim Month of Fasting." In *Studies in Islamic History and Institutions* edited by S. D. Goitein, 90–100 (Leiden: E.J. Brill, 1966); Michael Sells, *Approaching the Quran: The Early Revelations* (Ashland, Oreg.: White Cloud Press, 1999): 100–103.

Nizam al-Din Awliya (Nizam ud-Din Auliya) (1243–1325) *renowned Sufi saint of the Chishti order in India who is credited with inspiring the spread of Chishti teachings throughout South Asia*

Nizam al-Din Awliya was born in 1243 in Badaon, a settlement east of DELHI, INDIA, to which his grandfather had migrated from BUKHARA in Central Asia. His father died when Nizam al-Din was five years old and his mother, whom he revered as a model of piety, raised Nizam al-Din and his sister in abject poverty. As the son of a SAYYID, Nizam al-Din received religious EDUCATION in his youth from teachers in Badaon and was quickly recognized as a brilliant student in the QURAN, HADITH, and FIQH. In his late youth he moved to Delhi with his mother, where he visited the *khanqah* (Sufi hospice) of Shaykh Farid ad-Din Ganj-i Shakar (1173–1265), known commonly in India as Baba Farid, of the CHISHTI SUFI ORDER. He immediately impressed Shaykh Farid and joined his *khanqah* to become his pupil. At the early age of 23 he was appointed as Shaykh Farid's *khalifa* (successor), making him the fourth Chishti SHAYKH of the Sultanate period in India, after which he was directed to settle in Delhi to spread the Chishti teachings as part of the larger flowering of Chishti *khanqahs* throughout India.

Nizam ad-Din became a legend during his own lifetime, known for his charisma, his passionate desire for God, and his belief that the ultimate essence of Sufism was service to humanity. His *khanqah* on the outskirts of Delhi served in part as a local charity center in which he worked to alleviate poverty. Unlike most other Sufis of his time, Nizam ad-Din was celibate and unmarried. He fasted regularly, both out of concern for the needs of the poor as well as for his own spiritual practice, and he integrated a schedule of personal prayerful solitude with an active cultivation of community prayer and devotion in his *khanqah*. His *khanqah* attracted people from all segments of Indian society, and *samaa* assemblies—gatherings of ecstatic devotional MUSIC performance—were held regularly there despite controversy in the Sultanate surrounding the practice. He eschewed involvement in the politics of the Sultanate, most notably evidenced in his refusal to accept land grants from the sultans and invitations to their court.

Nizam al-Din's renown stems largely from the remarkable historical record provided by the Indo-Persian poet Amir Hasan Sijzi, who recorded his conversations. This record, entitled *Fawaid al-fuad* (Morals for the heart), was begun in 1308 and completed almost 14 years later. It was a popular contemporary text prior even to its completion, and its panegyrics helped to launch the popularity of the shaykh. Nizam al-Din's popularity spread further through the poetry of Amir Khusraw (d. 1325), a STUDENT of the shaykh and the most celebrated and widely read of the Persian poets of India. He is also the subject of a Chishti hagiography called *Siyar al-awliya* (Lives of the saints), written 30 years after his death in 1325. Contemporary *khanqahs* throughout South Asia trace their roots back to Nizam al-Din Awliya, and to the present day South Asian Muslims and Hindus visit his tomb in Ghiyathpur, a suburb of Delhi, to receive blessings.

See also ASCETICISM; DELHI SULTANATE; PERSIAN LANGUAGE AND LITERATURE; QAWWALI; SUFISM.

Megan Adamson Sijapati

Further reading: Nizam al-Din Awliya, *Morals for the Heart*. Recorded by Amir Hasan Sijzi and translated by Bruce Lawrence (New York: Paulist Press, 1992); Muneera Haeri, *The Chishtis: A Living Light* (Oxford: Oxford University Press, 2000); Khaliq A. Nizami, *The Life and Times of Shaikh Nizam ud-Din Auliya* (Delhi: Idarah-i Adabyat-i Delli, 1991).

Nizari   *See* ISMAILI SHIISM.

nomad   *See* BEDOUIN.

Nowruz   *See* NAVRUZ.

Nusayri   *See* ALAWI.

O

oil

When the first oil well was drilled in 1859 in Titusville, Pennsylvania, oil, which is also called petroleum, was used primarily for illumination. The single most significant incentive to develop the oil industry was the arrival of the motorcar, run on gasoline, at the turn of the 20th century. Today, oil is used in producing a variety of products besides gasoline, including asphalt, explosives, fertilizers, jet fuel, medicines, paints, plastics, rubbers, waxes, and others. Because it is a resource that is in high demand throughout the world, oil plays a significant role in international economics and politics.

The UNITED STATES is the largest consumer of oil, accounting for 25 percent of world oil consumption in 2007. CHINA is a distant second, at about 8 percent, and Japan third, at 6.5 percent. As of 2004, 57 percent of total proven oil reserves are located in countries bordering the Persian Gulf, with about one-fourth of the world's proven oil reserves in SAUDI ARABIA alone. IRAQ, IRAN, Kuwait, and the United Arab Emirates are the countries with the second, third, fifth, and sixth largest proven oil reserves, respectively. Other countries with high proven oil reserves include LIBYA and Nigeria, which are the ninth and 10th largest.

At first, the oil resources of countries with Muslim majority populations were under direct or indirect outside control; for example, Iraq and Kuwait were under British colonial control, and Iran was under British and Russian influence. Saudi Arabia, while an independent kingdom, conceded development and control of its oil resources to American petroleum companies. Therefore, oil resources in such countries were directly controlled by a number of foreign companies. In exchange for these concessions over control of their oil production, the host countries received a percentage of the revenue generated. Initial attempts to seize control by the host countries were met with failure—in 1951 Muhammad Musaddiq (d. 1967), the prime minister of Iran, nationalized the British-owned oil company in charge of Iran's oil, but in 1953 a coup instigated by the United States ousted Musaddiq and put a pro-U.S. leader, MUHAMMAD REZA PAHLAVI, back into power. He quickly offered oil concessions to the West. However, with the formation of the ORGANIZATION OF PETROLEUM EXPORTING COUNTRIES (OPEC) in 1960 and the widespread nationalization of domestic oil resources in the 1970s, oil-producing countries gained control over their oil production and price setting.

After the 1973 Arab-Israeli war, the main oil-producing states found themselves with revenues vast enough to assure them a clear position of influence throughout the Muslim world. Saudi Arabia, in particular, found itself in a position to export its conservative Wahhabi form of Islam through international development and charity projects, supporting international Islamic associations, and even distributing Wahhabi texts in mosques and madrasas throughout the world. Oil also provides an incentive for immigration to oil-producing countries, particularly in the Gulf, where annually millions of foreigners from all over the world go to work in the oil industry and remit money back to their home countries.

Oftentimes foreign policies from within and without oil-producing countries are heavily influenced or dictated by the need for cheap oil. In 1996, for example, the TALIBAN came to power in AFGHANISTAN, and were at first supported by the United States, in part because a huge pipeline project was at the time under negotiation between the Taliban and UNOCAL, a major American oil company.

Oil was also a crucial factor in the two GULF WARS between the United States and Iraq. In August 1990 Saddam HUSAYN (r. 1979–2003), the Iraqi president, ordered the invasion of Kuwait largely because of concerns that Kuwait was undermining oil prices. In January 1991 the United States led a coalition to drive Iraq out of Kuwait, a decision heavily influenced by the concern of the administration of George H. W. Bush that Saddam Hussein would seize control of Saudi oilfields. Further, in March 2003, the administration of George W. Bush also invaded Iraq. One of the primary reasons for this decision was the belief that, by seizing control of the country with the second largest proven oil reserves, the United States could weaken Saudi Arabia's leverage over oil pricing and exercise greater control over access to the world's major petroleum resources. Further, the Bush administration sought to ensure U.S. energy security and protect American consumers from the prospect of rising oil prices.

Historically, oil prices have widely fluctuated. Two major oil crises, the first engendered by the 1973 OPEC oil embargo and the second by the IRANIAN REVOLUTION OF 1978–79, drove oil prices up sufficiently high to damage Western economies. As of 2006 oil prices reached record highs at $75 per barrel, largely caused by demand for motor fuel in the United States, damage caused by Hurricane Katrina to American oilfields, rebel attacks in Nigeria that damaged the country's oil output, the virtual collapse of Iraq's oil industry following the American invasion, fears of a U.S. strike on Iran, and increasing demand by rapidly industrializing countries. In 2008, oil prices exceeded $150 per barrel, then began a rapid decline.

See also ARAB-ISRAELI CONFLICTS; GULF STATES; ISLAMISM; MADRASA; WAHHABISM.

Joshua Hoffman

Further reading: Norman J. Hyne, *Nontechnical Guide to Petroleum Geology, Exploration, Drilling, and Production* (Tulsa, Okla.: Penn Well Corp., 2001); Oystein Noreng, *Oil and Islam: Social and Economic Issues* (Chichester, N.Y.: J. Wiley and Sons, 1997); Francisco Parra, *Oil Politics: A Modern History of Petroleum* (London and New York: I.B. Tauris, 2004); Ian Rutledge, *Addicted to Oil: America's Relentless Drive for Energy Security* (New York: Palgrave Macmillan, 2005); Tobey Shelley, *Oil: Politics, Poverty, and the Planet* (New York: Palgrave Macmillan, 2005).

Oman   *See* GULF STATES.

Organization of Petroleum Exporting Countries (OPEC)

OPEC is an international body consisting of 11 countries, the purpose of which is to coordinate its members' oil-producing and selling policies. Founded in 1960 by IRAN, IRAQ, Kuwait, SAUDI ARABIA, and Venezuela, it has since expanded to include Qatar, INDONESIA, LIBYA, the United Arab Emirates, Nigeria, and ALGERIA. Today the OPEC countries account for 40 percent of world OIL production. Initially the stated goal of OPEC was to nationalize and gain control of its members' oil resources, which at the time were held primarily by American, British, and Dutch transnational corporations, including British Petroleum, Exxon, Texaco, and others.

By 1973 many of the OPEC countries had made progress in seizing control of their oil resources. However, it was not until the outbreak of the 1973 Arab-Israeli war that OPEC's international power became visibly apparent, when, led by its Arab members, OPEC doubled the price from $2.55 to $5.09 per barrel, and the Arab countries imposed an embargo on the United States because of its close ties with ISRAEL. Between 1973 and 1978 OPEC raised the price three times. However, OPEC's unity began to fray in 1980 when war broke out between Iraq and Iran, two of its most important members. Falling demand meant lower prices from 1983 onward, and the flooding of the market in 1986 by Kuwait and Saudi Arabia, aimed at weakening Iran, brought the price down. Leading up to the 1990–91 Gulf War, SADDAM HUSAYN (r. 1979–2003) urged OPEC to push world oil prices up, but the disunity among OPEC countries failed to bring that into effect. As oil prices continued to drop, OPEC coordinated a scaling back of oil production beginning in 1998.

In mid-2004 OPEC announced that its members had little excess pumping capacity, indicating that it was losing influence over oil prices. Faced with record oil prices in 2006 OPEC members declared their inability to increase output in order to drive prices down, leading some to speculate that the organization's power may be waning. However, although OPEC countries have accounted for an average of 40 percent of world oil production since 1970, the amount of proven world oil reserves under their control is much higher, at around 69 percent. This implies increased OPEC production as a proportion of total world production over the long term.

See also ARAB-ISRAELI CONFLICTS; GULF WARS.

Joshua Hoffman

Further reading: Jahangir Amuzegar, *Managing the Oil Wealth: OPEC's Windfalls and Pitfalls* (London and New York: I.B. Tauris, 2001); Nathan J. Citino, *From Arab Nationalism to OPEC: Eisenhower, Kind Saud, and the Making of U.S.-Saudi Relations* (Bloomington: Indiana University Press, 2002); Dag Harald Claes, *The Politics of Oil-Producer Cooperation* (Boulder, Colo.: Westview Press, 2001).

Organization of the Islamic Conference (OIC)

The OIC is an international body composed of 57 member states, most of which have Muslim majorities. There are also 13 states and organizations that have observer status, including the ARAB LEAGUE, the United Nations, the Russian Federation, Thailand, and the MORO NATIONAL LIBERATION FRONT of the Philippines. In June 2007 the United States announced that it would be sending a special envoy to OIC meetings. INDIA, with the world's second largest Muslim population, has expressed a desire to obtain observer status, but this has been blocked by Pakistan, its chief rival in South Asia.

The OIC was established in Rabat, MOROCCO, in September 1969. Its aims are to promote cooperation among Muslim countries and to serve as a collective voice for Muslim interests on the world scene. In the aftermath of World War II several new transregional power blocs of nation-states were created. These included the bloc of Western capitalist countries led by the United States and western European countries, the bloc of communist countries led by the Soviet Union and China, the nonaligned countries (such as India, INDONESIA, and EGYPT), as well as international organizations such as the United Nations and the Arab League. Although newly decolonized Muslim countries had long been aware of the pan-Islamic notion of a united community (UMMA) of the faithful, they lacked a means by which to establish a common bond or collectively exert their influence in global affairs in the 20th century. This situation changed considerably when the secular Arab nationalist movement under the leadership of JAMAL ABD AL-NASIR (d. 1970) lost its credibility as a result of the shocking victory of Israel over Egypt, Jordan, and Syria in the 1967 Arab-Israeli war. At the same time many governments in Muslim countries feared the spread of socialism and COMMUNISM, especially among newly urbanized populations and youth.

Saudi king FAYSAL IBN ABD AL-AZIZ (d. 1975), a life-long opponent of the secular Arab nationalist movement and communism, spearheaded an international effort to promote solidarity among Muslim countries and create an international organization with a specifically Islamic identity. The loss of JERUSALEM to Israel and a failed attempt to burn down the AQSA MOSQUE by an Australian evangelical Christian in August 1969 helped King Faysal convince enough Muslim leaders to convene a summit meeting in Rabat in 1969. This led to several follow-up meetings and finally a charter issued in February 1972. It had 25 founding member states, including Pakistan, Malaysia, Turkey, Iran, Indonesia, Afghanistan, Chad, and Niger, in addition to SAUDI ARABIA and Morocco.

The OIC, which has its main headquarters in Jeddah, Saudi Arabia, resembles the UN in its organization. It has a permanent Secretariat and five standing committees that specialize in social, cultural, economic, and financial affairs. There are also a number of other OIC subsidiary institutions and affiliates located in several Muslim countries, ranging from Turkey to Uganda, Bangladesh, and Malaysia. These organizations include universities, a research center, media organizations, a chamber of commerce, a FIQH academy, and even a

sports federation for the Islamic Solidarity Games. The OIC has held 10 summit meetings for heads of state since 1969, plus three extraordinary sessions. The last of the extraordinary sessions, convened in 2005, dealt with the controversial cartoons of MUHAMMAD that were published in Danish newspapers in September of that year. In addition to the summit meetings the OIC also holds annual meetings for the foreign ministers of member states. Recent meetings have been held in Karachi (2007), Baku (2006), Sanaa (2005), Istanbul (2004), and Tehran (2003).

The work of the OIC has centered on political matters rather than on religious affairs, and Saudi influence is significant. The OIC has sought to have a voice in resolving ARAB-ISRAELI CONFLICTS, the Iraq-Iran war of 1980–88, the Bosnian crisis, the status of KASHMIR, and recent issues pertaining to the threat of Islamic radicalism, the Israeli-Lebanese war of 2006, the reconstruction of AFGHANISTAN, and Darfur. On the issue of the U.S. occupation of IRAQ and its consequences, it has recently resolved to affirm the territorial integrity and sovereignty of Iraq, calling for greater participation by neighboring countries and international agencies in its reconstruction. It has also condemned terrorist attacks on civilians. On specifically religious affairs, its most important achievement has been to establish quotas for the number of pilgrims each country can send for the annual HAJJ to MECCA.

See also ARAB-ISRAELI CONFLICTS; BOSNIA AND HERZEGOVINA; FEDERATION OF ISLAMIC ORGANIZATIONS; GULF WARS; PAN-ISLAMISM.

Further reading: Robert R. Bianchi, *Guests of God: Pilgrimage and Politics in the Islamic World* (Oxford: Oxford University Press, 2004); Golam W. Choudhury, *Islam and the Contemporary World* (London: Indus Thames, 1990); Saad S. Khan, *Reasserting International Islam: A Focus on the Organization of the Islamic Conference and Other Islamic Institutions* (Karachi: Oxford University Press, 2001).

Orientalism

The study of the East ("the Orient"), especially the "Islamic East," by European and American scholars during the 19th and 20th centuries is known as Orientalism. The ancient Greeks made an initial differentiation between themselves in the "Occident" (West) and the peoples of the Orient, which meant anywhere east of themselves, from Asia Minor to the eastern Mediterranean lands and beyond. They also assigned qualities to this basic geographic division—Westerners (meaning themselves) were democratic, rational, and civilized, while Easterners were despotic, irrational, and barbaric. During the Middle Ages this differentiation was adopted by western Europeans and invested with religious meaning through their reading of the Bible. Europeans claimed that they were descended from Noah's favored son Japheth, while Asians and Africans were descended from Shem and Ham, Noah's less-favored sons. In the aftermath of the medieval CRUSADES some church scholars began to investigate Islamic religion, but they did this mainly in order to defend Christianity, or to convert Muslims, whom they often called Saracens or Moors (in ANDALUSIA). There was a great deal of interest in the Arabic translations of and commentaries about Aristotle, which formed the underpinnings of medieval scholastic theology. Europeans were also very interested in Arabic scientific literature (medicine, MATHEMATICS, physics, astronomy, and chemistry/ALCHEMY). These works were translated into Hebrew and Latin at centers of learning in Spain and Italy, and subsequently carried to centers of learning in France, England, and elsewhere in Europe.

The cumulative tradition of scholarly study of Islam and the peoples and cultures of Muslim lands, which would later call itself Orientalism, did not develop noticeably in Europe until the late 18th and early 19th centuries. This study was stimulated by several factors: commitment to the study of human history and cultures based on Enlightenment rationalism rather than theology; the exploration and colonization of the Americas, Asia, and Africa by newly emerging European powers (Spain, Portugal, the Netherlands, France, and England); and discovery of ancient civilizations in the Middle East and Asia and decipherment of their languages. One of the first Orientalists in the modern sense of the word was Baron Silvestre de Sacy (1758–1838), a Parisian scholar of Arabic and other "living oriental languages" who advised the French Foreign Ministry, and became the first president of the Société Asiatique (founded in 1822). Many of Europe's leading Orientalist scholars studied under him and regarded him as the pioneer in their field. In INDIA the leading promoter of Orientalist research was William Jones (1746–94), an employee of the English East India Company with expertise in Arabic, Persian, and Hebrew who founded the Asiatic Society of Bengal in 1784. This scholarly organization furnished Europe with English translations of religious and philosophical literature written in Arabic, Persian, Sanskrit, and other South Asian languages. It also served as a model for the Royal Asiatic Society of Great Britain and England (established in 1824). Other societies specializing in Orientalist studies were formed throughout Europe and in North America where the American Oriental Society was established in 1842.

Monuments in lands newly colonized by European powers and manuscripts obtained from major centers of Islamic learning such as ISTANBUL, CAIRO, and DELHI provided Orientalists with substantial amounts of "raw" material for reconstructing and studying the languages, religions, histories, and peoples of Asia/the Orient. They published scholarly journals, reference grammars, indexes, dictionaries, and, above all, critical editions and translations of Arabic, Persian, Turkish, and Sanskrit texts. Much of what they wrote (excluding the Sanskritic materials) concerned Islamicate cultures and, above all, ISLAM—its scriptures, laws, doctrines, mysticism, and history. Moreover, Orientalists, despite their scholarly abilities, often stereotyped these cultures as static, despotic, inferior, and effeminate, usually attributing these defects to Islam or race. Although there were exceptions, as a group they wanted to clearly differentiate their own European civilization and Christianity—the religion with which they most closely identified by heritage if not by personal conviction—from "Islamic civilization" or "Islamic society" and Islam.

Among the key Orientalist scholars to emerge in the late 19th and early 20th centuries were Edward W. Lane (d. 1876), Richard Burton (d. 1890), W. Robertson Smith (d. 1894), and William Muir (d. 1905) in England; Ernest Renan (d. 1892), Jean Sauvaget (d. 1950), and E. Levi-Provincal (d. 1956) of France; Julius Wellhausen (d. 1918), Theodor Noeldeke (d. 1930), Carl Becker (d. 1933), and Carl Brockelman (d. 1956) of Germany; Reinhart Dozy (d. 1883), Arent J. Wensinck (d. 1939), and C. Snouck Hurgronje (d. 1943) of the Netherlands; Leone Caetani (d. 1935) and Giorgio Levi Della Vida (d. 1967) of Italy; Miguel Asin Palacios (d. 1944) of Spain; Ignaz Goldziher (d. 1921) of Hungary; and Henri Lammens (d. 1937) of Belgium. By the 1950s the fields of Oriental and Islamic Studies had become firmly established in major universities in Europe and North America: Cambridge, Oxford, Edinburgh, London, Paris, Leiden, Berlin, Leipzig, St. Petersburg, Harvard, Yale, Princeton, Chicago, and Los Angeles. It should be noted, however, that in North America the term 'Oriental' pertained more to the Far East rather than the Middle/Near East.

Orientalist scholarship regressed during the 1960s and 1970s, becoming a marginal field while academic interest was drawn to modern topics such as nationalism, economic development, social change, educational reform, secular politics, and postcolonialism. Growth in the number and size of universities in the United States, coupled with the strategic challenges posed by the cold war between the countries of the Western bloc led by the United States against the Communist bloc countries led by the Soviet Union and the People's Republic of China, gave rise to area studies programs in many major American universities. These areas included that of the Middle East (from Egypt to Iran) and North Africa (from Morocco to Egypt), which had become a strategically important region, particularly because of its OIL. Some scholars began to point out Orientalism's shortcomings at this time, while recognizing how it had shaped the ideas and knowledge many educated Europeans and Americans had about Islam and the Middle East.

The most forceful criticism of Orientalism was made by Edward Said (1935–2003), a Palestinian-American intellectual who had become a leading scholar of comparative literature and literary criticism at Columbia University. In his path-breaking 1978 book, *Orientalism,* he argued that it was not just a field of objective research, but a formation of knowledge interlinked with political power that had given Europeans and (more recently) Americans the means by which to justify and perpetuate domination over non-European peoples, especially those living in the Middle East. Said supported his argument by showing how Euro-American scholars, travel writers, and journalists had been deeply implicated in the colonization and governance of Muslim lands, and how their writings had shaped Western biases in the aftermath of colonial rule. Though the book does not lack critics, Said and his supporters have been able to document how Orientalist stereotypes about "the Arab" and "the Muslim" were revived again and again in the aftermath of the 1967 Arab-Israeli war, the Iranian hostage crisis of 1979–80, the SALMAN RUSHDIE affair of 1988, the ongoing Palestinian-Israeli conflict, the 1990 Gulf War, and, most recently, the global "war on terror" launched by the United States after the attacks of September 11, 2001, which had been perpetrated by members of the radical Islamist organization AL-QAIDA. A good deal of this war has been conducted on Muslim lands, including IRAQ and AFGHANISTAN, which created a new context for reviving old Orientalist stereotypes and developing new ones. Said's critique of Orientalism has been embraced in various degrees by specialists in other areas of study, including postcolonial studies, literary criticism, gender studies, film studies, and ethnic studies.

See also ARAB-ISRAELI CONFLICTS; ARABIAN NIGHTS; CHRISTIANITY AND ISLAM; COLONIALISM; GULF WARS; TERRORISM; WOMEN.

Further reading: Zachary Lockman, Contending Visions of the Middle East: The History and Politics of Orientalism (Cambridge: Cambridge University Press, 2004); Alexander L. Macfie, Orientalism: A Reader (New York: New York University Press, 2001); Maxime Rodinson, Europe and the Mystique of Islam. Translated by Roger Veinus (London: I.B. Taurus, 1988); Edward Said, Orientalism (1978. Reprint, New York: Random House, 2003).

Osama bin Ladin   See USAMA BIN LADIN.

Oslo Accords

The Oslo Accords, or Declaration of Principles, became the foundational documents for an attempted peace between ISRAEL and the Palestinians in the 1990s. Signed in 1993 by Israel and the PALESTINE LIBERATION ORGANIZATION (PLO), the decrees initiated a hopeful era of negotiations, but they failed ultimately to forge a lasting peace.

Initiated by Norway's foreign minister, Johan Jørgen Holst, the negotiations that resulted in the Oslo Accords were conducted in secret. Signed privately on August 20, 1993, the world watched with some disbelief a public handshake of approval between Israeli prime minister Yitzhak Rabin and the leader of the PLO, YASIR ARAFAT, hosted by U.S. president Bill Clinton on the White House Lawn on September 13, 1993. By signing the documents, Israel recognized the PLO as the legitimate representative of the stateless Palestinian people, and the PLO renounced violence against Israel and asserted the Jewish state's right to exist.

The contents of the Oslo Accords served as the framework for a subsequent transitional period of rule over the territories of the West Bank and Gaza Strip, occupied by Israel in 1967. In the documents, Israel agreed to withdraw from parts of the Occupied Territories, and a newly created Palestinian Authority (PA) assumed self-rule over parts of the territories in place of the Israeli military. The West Bank and Gaza Strip were divided into Areas A, B, and C, with A regions under the control of the Palestinian Authority, B regions under Palestinian civil and Israeli military control, and C regions under full Israeli control. The map of these regions, however, was significantly fragmented; nevertheless, at the height of the PA's authority in the late 1990s, the majority of Palestinians in the Occupied Territories lived under some form of Palestinian civil rule.

Many of the most contentious issues of the Israel-Palestine conflict, including the expansion of Israeli settlements in the Occupied Territories, the issue of the status of JERUSALEM, and the fate of Palestine's massive refugee population were purposely left out of the agreement. According to the Oslo Accords, final status talks, including issues pertinent to these topics, were to begin no later than May 1996. However, despite further diplomatic efforts from 1994 until 2000, the final status talks promised by the Oslo Accords were not held. Furthermore, the dissolution of the Palestinian Authority in the wake of the al-Aqsa intifada of 2000 and Israel's dramatic response to it have rendered the Oslo Accords obsolete.

See also AQSA MOSQUE; ARAB-ISRAELI CONFLICTS; REFUGEES.

Garay Menicucci

Further reading: William L. Cleveland, A History of the Modern Middle East (Boulder, Colo.: Westview Press, 2000); Walter Laqueur and Barry Rubin, The Israel-Arab Reader: A Documentary History of the Middle East Conflict, 6th ed. (New York: Penguin Books, 2001).

Ottoman dynasty (1299–1922)

The Ottoman dynasty ruled over an empire in the Middle East and Balkans (southeastern EUROPE) between the 14th and 20th centuries. It takes its name from Osman (also spelled Uthman, r. 1281–1326), a warrior who led a Turkish principality in the period following the demise of the Anatolian Seljuk Sultanate (1077–1307). Ottoman control was consolidated in western Anatolia and extended to the Balkans under Osman's successors Orhan I (r. 1326–62) and Murad I (r. 1362–89), and was extended eastward under Bayezid I (r. 1389–1402). It was under Mehmed II (r. 1444–46, 1451–81) that the Ottomans conquered Constantinople, the last bastion of the Byzantine Empire, in 1453. With Constantinople (ISTANBUL) as its capital, the Ottoman Empire continued to consolidate politically, administratively, and legally.

The empire reached its apogee in the 16th century. Sultan Selim I (r. 1512–20) conquered EGYPT and assumed control over the holy cities of MEDINA and MECCA and as far south as YEMEN. His successor, Suleyman I (known as "the Magnificent," r. 1512–66), conquered Hungary, and even besieged Vienna in 1529. Their successes were due in part to a strong infantry, known as the Janissaries. But these successes were followed by military defeats in confrontations with the empire's main rivals—the Austrians in Europe and the Safavids of IRAN—in the late 16th century. The Ottoman Empire had been built on military conquests, and when expansion was checked, the empire began to decline. The 18th century was marked by confrontations with the empire's new rival, Russia, and a complex web of political relationships developed between the empire and European powers.

Confronted with the military superiority of the West, the Ottomans began to institute modernizing reforms in the 19th century. The empire's first constitution was enacted in 1876, but it was soon repealed by Abd al-Hamid II (r. 1876–1909), who preferred autocratic rule. The constitution was reenacted in 1908 in response to the Young Turk Revolution, and Abd al-Hamid II was deposed in 1909. The empire had come to be dominated by the European powers, and the decision to side

Sultan Ahmed Mosque (early 17th century), Istanbul, Turkey (*Juan E. Campo*)

with the Germans in World War I brought about disastrous peace terms at the end of hostilies. With the British occupying Istanbul, MUSTAFA KEMAL ATATURK led a nationalist resistance, which eventually won independence and overthrew the Ottoman regime. The last of the Ottoman sultans, Mehmed VI (d. 1926), was deposed in 1922. His successor, Abd al-Majid II, continued to hold the title of CALIPH until this position was abolished in 1924. From the ashes of the Ottoman Empire modern Turkey emerged under the leadership of Ataturk (r. 1923–38). The Ottoman household has continued to survive to the present day, but it lacks any political authority. The current head of the House of Osman, Ertugrul Osman (b. 1912), lives in New York City.

Sunni Islam was the official religion of the Ottoman Empire, with the HANAFI LEGAL SCHOOL as the basis of state law. The Ottomans also allowed Shafii law to prevail in areas where it had significant followings, such as Egypt, Syria, the Hijaz (western Arabia), and among the Kurds. Through conquests and population resettlements, Sunni Islam was brought to the Balkans. The Ottomans were generally opposed to SHIISM, but they allowed some degree of latitude to the Alawis of Anatolia and Syria (where they are also known as Nusayris) and Twelve-Imam Shii religious authorities in southern IRAQ, particularly in the 19th and early 20th centuries. Another form of Islam that flourished in Ottoman lands was that of the Sufi brotherhoods (sing. *TARIQA*), especially those of the NAQSHBANDIS, BEKTASHIS, MEVLEVIS, and Khalwatis.

The empire, above all the capital Istanbul, also featured a multiethnic mix of peoples and religions. The Ottomans incorporated the *millet* system under their system of government, allowing different groups of Orthodox Christians, ARMENIANS, and Jews to practice their religions under their own leadership in different localities throughout the empire. Each community also maintained its own schools. When SEPHARDIC JEWS were expelled by the Christian rulers of Spain in 1492 the Ottoman sultan Bayezid II (r. 1481–1512) issued a decree inviting them to immigrate to the Ottoman realm, and large numbers took advantage of the opportunity. However, whatever harmony had existed between religious communities and ethnic groups deteriorated with the rise of nationalisms and Ottoman repressions against rebelling minorities in the 19th and 20th centuries. The most violent of these was directed against the Armenians in the closing years of the empire during World War I (1915–17).

During the six centuries of its existence, the Ottoman Empire developed a unique culture shared by the variety of peoples under its sway, and arts such as literature, music, and architecture flourished. Since the demise of the empire this culture has been replaced by a series of ethnic and linguistic national cultures. Nevertheless, traces of the Ottoman synthesis can still be found in the culinary traditions shared by peoples living in the Balkans, Turkey, and the lands bordering the eastern Mediterranean, where stuffed vegetables (dolmas), skewered kabobs, yoghurt dishes, baklava, and "Turkish" coffee are favorite items on the menu.

See also ALAWI; BOSNIA AND HERZEGOVINA; CALIPHATE; CHRISTIANITY AND ISLAM; CONSTITUTIONALISM; FOOD AND DRINK; JANISSARY; JUDAISM AND ISLAM; MUHAMMAD ALI DYNASTY; SELJUK DYNASTY; SAFAVID DYNASTY; TANZIMAT; *TEKKE*; TURKISH LANGUAGE AND LITERATURE.

Mark Soileau

Further reading: Halil Inalcik, *The Ottoman Empire: The Classical Age 1300–1600.* Translated by Norman Itzkowitz and Colin Imber (New York: Praeger Publishers, 1973); Norman Itzkowitz, "The Ottoman Empire: The Rise and Fall of Turkish Domination." In *The World of Islam: Faith, People, Culture,* edited by Bernard Lewis, 273–300 (London: Thames and Hudson, 1976); Cemal Kafadar, *Between Two Worlds: The Construction of the Ottoman State* (Berkeley and Los Angeles: University of California Press, 1995); Stanford Shaw and Ezel Kural Shaw, *History of the Ottoman Empire and Modern Turkey.* 2 vols. (Cambridge: Cambridge University Press, 1976).

P

painting**painting**   *See* ART; CALLIGRAPHY.

Pakistan (Official name: Islamic Republic of Pakistan; Urdu/Persian: Land of the Pure, also an acronym for five homelands of its people—Punjab, Afghania, Kashmir, Sindh, and Baluchistan)

Pakistan is a South Asian country. It has an area of 307,374 square miles, comparable in size to the states of Texas and Virginia combined. It is bordered by the Arabian Sea to the south, INDIA and KASHMIR to the east, CHINA to the north, and IRAN and AFGHANISTAN to the west. The Indus River transects the country from the Himalayas in the north to the Arabian Sea.

Pakistan was created as a homeland for Indian Muslims through the partition of the Indian subcontinent following independence in 1947 from British imperial rule. Its population is approximately 172.8 million (2008 estimate) and its capital is Islamabad. Ninety-seven percent of Pakistan's population is Muslim, which makes it the second largest Muslim country after Indonesia. (India has the second largest Muslim population overall, but it is not a Muslim-majority country.) About 80 percent of Pakistani Muslims are Sunnis and follow the HANAFI LEGAL SCHOOL. Pakistan's Shii minority are predominantly followers of TWELVE-IMAM SHI-ISM, although it also has a small Ismaili population. It is also home to a large number of members of the AHMADIYYA sect, although they are legally considered to be non-Muslims by the government. There are also relatively small numbers of Christians (about 1 percent), Hindus, and Parsis (Zoroastrians) in the country. Pakistan became the first Muslim nation to elect a woman as head of state when Benazir Bhutto became prime minister in 1988. She was reelected in 1993 but was assassinated during her third campaign for this office in 2007.

The idea that Muslims in the Indian subcontinent needed their own autonomous political identity was first articulated in the early 1930s by the influential poet-philosopher MUHAMMAD IQBAL (d. 1938). By 1940 fears of an imminently independent India that would be dominated by a Hindu majority compelled the ALL-INDIA MUSLIM LEAGUE to enact the Pakistan Resolution, and, under the leadership of MUHAMMAD ALI JINNAH (1876–1949), who envisioned Pakistan as a liberal democratic state for Muslims, the Muslim League worked alongside the Hindu-dominated, but secularist, Indian National Congress for independence from the British.

When Pakistan was created on August 14, 1947, Jinnah became its first governor-general. In 1949 the Objectives Resolution was passed stating that the constitution of Pakistan would be based on democratic and Islamic principles. This paved the way for the 1956 Constitution, which provided for a parliamentary form of government, though it was soon followed by a period of martial law. In the civil war of 1971, the eastern region of Pakistan became the independent state of BANGLADESH.

In 1977 Prime Minister Zia-ul-Haq (r. 1977–88) introduced strict Islamic codes that included obligatory Islamic *zakat* taxes, SHARIA courts, enforcement of Islamic punishments, partial elimination of bank interest, and Islamic-oriented revisions of school curriculum. Since then, major debates and periods of political instability have continued to center around the appropriate role of Islam and Islamic law in the state. Though sharia remains the guiding paradigm for Pakistan's legal system—interpreted and implemented to varying degrees province by province—Pervez Musharraf, who took power by force in 1999, was a moderate on issues of the role of Islam in the state. He was driven from office by popular opposition in 2008 and the new government also holds moderate religious views.

Since the partition of the Indian subcontinent, Pakistan has had strained relations with its neighbor India. A major point of dispute has been the contested boundaries of KASHMIR, which led most recently to the Kargil war in 1999. In 1998, the same year that India tested nuclear devices, Pakistan became the world's seventh country to develop nuclear capabilities, and tension between the two countries took on a new dimension with the possibility of nuclear confrontation.

Pakistan has been home to or has supported a number of Islamist movements and organizations. The JAMAAT-I ISLAMI, founded by ABU AL-ALA MAWDUDI (d. 1979) in India, has been active in Pakistani affairs since the country's creation. Privately managed mosques and madrasas (Islamic schools) have provided the majority of educational opportunities in the country as well as a base for independent, and often oppositional, Islamist organizations. During the 1980s Pakistan cooperated with the United States and other coun-

tries in helping the AFGHAN *MUJAHIDIN* conduct a guerrilla war against Soviet forces that occupied Afghanistan in 1978. Millions of Afghans came to Pakistan as REFUGEES to escape the turbulence in their native land, and the refugee camps in eastern Pakistan provided fertile ground for recruiting fighters. The Pakistani intelligence service (ISI) later gave aid to the TALIBAN, a radical Islamist organization that ruled most of Afghanistan from 1996 to 2001. Since 2001 the Pakistani government has supported the United States in its anti-terrorism efforts in a military campaign against the Taliban and al-Qaida hideouts along the Afghan-Pakistani border.

See also ALL-INDIA MUSLIM LEAGUE; CRIME AND PUNISHMENT; JAMIYYAT AL-ULAMA-I ISLAM; MADRASA.

Megan Adamson Sijapati

Further reading: Husain Haqqani, *Pakistan: Between Mosque and Military* (Washington, D.C.: Carnegie Endowment for International Peace, 2005); Mohammad Asghar Khan, ed., *Islam, Politics, and the State: The Pakistan Experience* (London: Zed Books, 1985); Soofia Mumtaz, Jean-Luc Racine, and Imran Anwar Ali, eds., *Pakistan: The Contours of State and Society* (New York: Oxford University Press, 2002).

Palestine

Since Roman times, the term Palestine has referred to a region in the eastern Mediterranean rich in spiritual and historical significance. It is historically diverse in religions and ethnicities, a characteristic that has contributed to the modern Palestinian experience as one of conflict, struggle, and controversy. Palestine is claimed as sacred space by Jews, Christians, and Muslims and is often referred to as the "Holy Land." As the focus of both spiritual longing and political contest for many centuries it has drawn world attention far beyond its borders, particularly in the past 100 years following the emergence of modern nationalism in Palestine.

Arabs constituted a majority in Palestine from the seventh century C.E., and, with the exception of the Crusader era (11th–13th centuries), the people of Palestine, known as Palestinians, were ruled by leaders who confessed Islam until 1917. Under the Ottoman Empire Palestine was governed as a part of the Greater Syria province, which included the current nations of SYRIA, JORDAN, LEBANON, ISRAEL, and the Occupied Territories (Gaza and the West Bank).

Like their European neighbors and Middle Eastern contemporaries, the people of Palestine began to engage with serious issues of modern nationalism in the 19th century, a process that developed rapidly with the emergence of Zionism in the 20th century. As in nations such as Iraq and Egypt, Palestinians were proud of their Arab heritage, and many embraced ideas of pan-Arabism. However, their specific residence in Palestine marked them as distinct from Arabs in other countries, and the trauma of wide-scale displacement in the wake of the creation of the state of Israel in 1948 gave Palestinians a particularly heightened need for a clearly articulated national identity.

In the 20th century Palestinians have endured tremendous upheavals and conflicts. Under the British who occupied Palestine under a League of Nations mandate (1917–48), Palestinian Arabs formed a strong national identity in response to the growing Zionist movement, but found themselves increasingly cast out of the nascent state apparatus of the proposed Jewish state. When that goal was realized with the creation of Israel, hundreds of Palestinian villages were destroyed, and Palestinians were faced with a massive diaspora of REFUGEES counting in the millions. The Israeli-Arab war of 1967 resulted in Israel's occupation of the West Bank and Gaza, expanding the population of displaced Palestinians and strengthening the nationalism of Palestinians demanding a state of their own.

Although the creation of a Palestinian nation-state has yet to be achieved, Palestinians constitute a nation with a specific national identity. This identity has been heightened by the loss of Palestine to an Israeli state, which asserts nationalism opposed to an Arab presence in its borders. Two *intifadas*, or uprisings, against Israeli occupation have been mounted (1987–93, 2000–present), but Palestinians still struggle for national recognition. Although Palestinians have expressed their national identity in terms of secular politics by agencies such as the PALESTINE LIBERATION ORGANIZATION (PLO), as well as by the religiously grounded ideologies of the Islamic Resistance Movement (HAMAS), an unquestionable tenant of both has been the belief in a unique Palestinian nationalism distinct from larger pan-Arabist ideologies.

In the absence of an official census, it is estimated there are about 10.5 million Palestinians in the world today (2006 estimate), about half of whom live in neighboring Middle Eastern countries, the Americas, and elsewhere—many as refugees. About 3.6 million reside in the occupied West Bank and Gaza territories and another 1.3 million are Israeli citizens (2004 estimate). The Palestinian territories are governed by the Palestinian National Authority, a branch of the PLO established after the OSLO ACCORDS in 1994. Its first head of state was YASIR ARAFAT (d. 2004), and it is now led by Mahmoud Abbas (b. 1935). Its legislative branch is the Palestinian Legislative Council, an elective body with 132 seats.

See also ARAB-ISRAELI CONFLICTS; COLONIALISM; DOME OF THE ROCK; HUSAYNI, AMIN; JERUSALEM; OTTOMAN DYNASTY.

Nancy Stockdale

Further reading: Rashid Khalidi, *Palestinian Identity* (New York: Columbia University Press, 1998); Walter Laqueur and Barry Rubin, *The Israel-Arab Reader: A Documentary History of the Middle East Conflict.* 6th ed. (New York: Penguin Books, 2001); Edward W. Said, *The Question of Palestine* (New York: Vintage, 1992); Tom Segev, *One Palestine, Complete: Jews and Arabs under the British Mandate* (New York: Metropolitan Books/Henry Holt, 2000).

Palestine Liberation Organization (PLO)

The Palestine Liberation Organization is the national liberation movement of the Palestinian people. It was originally founded in East JERUSALEM in May 1964 at the behest of Egyptian president JAMAL ABD AL-NASIR (d. 1970) and other Arab leaders who attended a summit meeting in Cairo in January of that year. The PLO was originally headed by a functionary of the ARAB LEAGUE, Ahmad Shuqayri, but it was taken over at a meeting of the Palestine National Congress in Cairo in October 1968 by the largest Palestinian guerrilla organization Fatah (Palestine National Liberation Movement). YASIR ARAFAT (d. 2004), the leader of Fatah, was chosen as chairman of the PLO Executive Committee and he remained in that position for more than three decades. According to its 1964 charter, the PLO was conceived as a secular organization whose purpose was to reclaim the Palestinian homeland from Jewish Zionists through popular armed struggle (JIHAD). While asserting the Arabness of the Palestinian national ideal, it promised citizenship to Palestinian Jews.

The PLO evolved into a full Palestinian government in exile with a representative parliament (the Palestine National Council), a cabinet (the PLO Executive Committee), and departments that replicated ministries such as planning, social affairs, and information. The PLO also encompassed armed guerrilla organizations (for example, Fatah, the Popular Front for the Liberation of Palestine, the Democratic Front for the Liberation of Palestine, and al-Saiqa), as well as unions and mass organizations for women, workers, students, and writers. The PLO became a coordinating body for Palestinian military forces (the Palestine Liberation Army) in Arab countries and guerrilla organizations. It maintained significant military forces in JORDAN until 1970 and then in LEBANON until the forced withdrawal of PLO fighters after the Israeli invasion of the country in 1982. The PLO was totally eclipsed as a significant military threat to ISRAEL by the defeat in 1982 and a series of Israeli assassinations of leading members of the PLO in the 1980s, including two of the original founders of Fatah, Khalil al-Wazir (Abu Jihad) and Salah Khalaf (Abu Iyad).

Shortly after Fatah gained ascendancy in the PLO in 1968, the organization achieved unprecedented diplomatic recognition in the international arena and especially in the United Nations. In 1969 the UN General Assembly first affirmed the right of "the people of PALESTINE" to "self-determination." In 1970 a General Assembly resolution affirmed that the Palestinians were victims of "colonial and alien domination" and were therefore entitled to restore their rights "by any means at their disposal." The PLO international diplomatic initiatives were capped in 1974 by the first full-fledged debate on the Palestine question in the UN since 1947 and Chairman Arafat was invited to New York that October to address the General Assembly. In 1975 the General Assembly set up a permanent committee for exercising the rights of the Palestinians to self-determination and the UN Secretary General is still bound to report to this committee to this day.

The Palestinian uprising in the West Bank and Gaza in 1988, known as the *intifada,* bolstered the international consensus for the creation of an independent Palestinian state led by the PLO. However, after the first Gulf War in 1991, the PLO gave up its strategy of UN diplomacy. Chairman Arafat and Israeli prime minister Yitzak Rabin (d. 1995) signed the OSLO ACCORDS on the lawn of the White House on September 13, 1993. In exchange for U.S. recognition and Israel's allowing Arafat to set up a restricted Palestinian Authority in the West Bank and Gaza, the PLO favored the United States instead of the UN as the arbiter of Palestinian national legitimacy. However, the Oslo Accords did not recognize an independent Palestinian sovereign entity and described the Palestinian negotiating partner as the "PLO team" within a Jordanian-Palestinian delegation to a Middle East peace conference. There were no enforcement mechanisms within the agreement that would compel Israel to abide by the terms of the West Bank and Gaza withdrawal clauses.

As the terms of the Oslo Accords were never implemented, the Palestinians in the West Bank and Gaza once again rose up in the fall of 2000. Israeli military forces besieged PLO chairman Arafat's headquarters in the West Bank town of Ramallah. They decimated the administrative infrastructure of the Palestinian Authority, including its police forces. Israeli leaders called for the expulsion of Arafat from the West Bank and the PLO diminished as a significant political force for a negotiated settlement to the Israeli-Palestinian conflict that became increasingly militarized and violent. The PLO remains as a symbolic shell for Palestinian national aspirations. It remains to be seen if it can be revived as a meaningful political structure for implementing a future Palestinian sovereign state.

See also ARAB-ISRAELI CONFLICTS; HAMAS; REFUGEES.

Garay Menicucci

Further reading: Helena Cobban, *The Palestinian Liberation Organisation: People, Power and Politics* (Cambridge: Cambridge University Press, 1984); David Hirst, *The Gun and the Olive Branch: The Roots of Violence in the Middle East* (New York: Thunder's Mouth/Nation Books, 2003); Graham Usher, *Palestine in Crisis: The Struggle for Peace and Political Independence after Oslo* (London: Pluto Press, 1995).

pan-Islamism (pan-Islam)

One of the responses Muslim leaders had to the colonization of their lands by European powers in the 19th century was what Europeans called pan-Islamism. This was an attempt to forge a modern Islamic political unity (*ittihad-i Islam*) based not on nationality, ethnicity, or geography, but on membership in the UMMA, the universal community of Muslims. Although this idea has its roots in memories of Islamic unity in the foundational era of MUHAMMAD (d. 632) and the first caliphs, it was more directly inspired by 19th-century nationalist movements among Slavs, Greeks, and others.

The pan-Islamist idea first took hold during the 1870s in the lands of the Ottoman Empire, which had been losing territory to the Russian and Austro-Hungarian empires since the 17th century. It was promoted by Sultan Abd al-Hamid II (r. 1876–1909) and supported by the Islamic reformer/activist JAMAL AL-DIN AL-AFGHANI (1838–97) and later by Said Nursi (1878–1960). The Ottomans had already initiated extensive administrative reforms, the TANZIMAT, aimed at modernizing the state and limiting the influence of traditional Islamic authorities and other opponents. As part of his pan-Islamist program Abd al-Hamid revived the symbolic importance of the CALIPHATE in an effort to win the support of Muslims even beyond the boundaries of the Ottoman Empire, where he sought to convince Muslims that he was upholding the faith on their behalf. He also built a new railway that carried pilgrims to the sacred cities of MEDINA and MECCA from Istanbul, the Ottoman capital, and other locations along its path. In the 1870s al-Afghani traveled to Afghanistan and other Muslim lands, including Iraq, India, Iran, and Russia to promote the pan-Islamist cause. Al-Afghani returned to Istanbul from his mission in 1892, where he died a few years later.

Abd al-Hamid's efforts on behalf of Muslim unity enjoyed little success. He encountered strong opposition from a well-organized coalition of secularist reformers known as the Young Turks, who succeeded in forcing him to leave the throne in 1909. Pan-Islamism was also undermined by other nationalist currents that were stirring in Ottoman lands and India, and it failed to rally non-Sunni Muslim minorities like the Shia. British support for the Hashimites in the Arabian Hijaz helped end Ottoman control and paved the way for Saudi conquest in the 1920s. Abd al-Hamid's own authoritarian character was also detrimental. Pan-Islamism was used to rally Muslim support for the Ottoman alliance with Germany against Britain, France, and

Russia in World War I, but, by so doing, it fueled efforts by France and Britain to break up its empire after the war. They wanted to prevent pan-Islamism from taking hold in Sunni Muslim lands and threatening their own imperialist designs. Even the caliphate was officially abolished by the new Turkish republican government in 1924.

Despite the failure of Abd al-Hamid's brand of pan-Islamism, the ideal of Muslim political unity continued to arise periodically in the 20th century. It is evident in the Indian KHILAFAT MOVEMENT of 1919–24 and international Islamic bodies such as the MUSLIM WORLD LEAGUE (founded in 1962) and the ORGANIZATION OF THE ISLAMIC CONFERENCE (founded in 1969). Iraq's SADDAM HUSAYN attempted to invoke pan-Islamist sympathies to rally support against the international coalition of powers that opposed his occupation of Kuwait in 1990–91. It has also been an aspect in the ideology of some Islamist movements such as the early JAMAAT-I ISLAMI and HIZB UT-TAHRIR. The assertion that radical Islamist organizations are pan-Islamist in orientation is an exaggerated one, however, since most operate in relation to the political landscapes of specific nation-states (for example, Egypt, Pakistan, Afghanistan, etc.)

See also COLONIALISM; HASHIMITE DYNASTY; ISLAMISM; OTTOMAN DYNASTY.

Further reading: Nikki R. Keddie, "Pan-Islam as Proto-Nationalism," *Journal of Modern History* 41, no. 1 (March 1969): 17–28; Saad S. Khan, *Reasserting International Islam: A Focus on the Organization of the Islamic Conference and Other Islamic Institutions* (Karachi: Oxford University Press, 2001); Jacob Landau, *The Politics of Pan-Islam* (Oxford: Oxford University Press, 1990).

paper *See* BOOKS AND BOOKMAKING.

paradise (Arabic: *janna*; Persian: *firdaws*)

Islamic beliefs about paradise are based partly on biblical motifs found in the book of Genesis and in later Jewish and Christian writings. They also reflect indigenous Arabian ideas and some Persian influence. Muslims conceive of paradise as a verdant GARDEN of bliss where people are able to meet with loved ones, God, the ANGELS, and other spiritual beings. Paradise is the primordial garden of ADAM AND EVE, where the first human beings met with God, the angels, and SATAN. In this best of possible worlds the first two humans went without thirst and ate the fruits of the garden until Satan tempted them to eat fruit from the one tree that God had forbidden to them (Q 2:35–36; 20:117–123). When they did this, God expelled them into the lower world of mortal existence. When Adam repented for what he had done, God forgave him and promised that he and his kind would be able to return to it in the AFTERLIFE if they are judged to have been among the righteous after the resurrection. Islamic lore also indicates that the perfumed plants and precious jewels that people enjoy in this world originated in paradise and that God allowed Adam to enjoy them in his worldly existence. One jewel that originated in paradise was the BLACK STONE, originally a white sapphire that some early Muslim writings say GABRIEL gave to Adam. (It later turned to black because of human impurity.) Even the KAABA is said to have come from paradise.

The afterlife paradise is described in great detail in the QURAN and other Islamic writings. According to the Quran it is a great, gated garden or park that is permeated by the scent of musk, camphor, and ginger. It is graced with fountains, and abundant rivers of water, milk, honey, and wine flow through it (Q 47:15). Its inhabitants wear luxurious clothing and dwell in beautiful mansions furnished with couches, carpets, and household goods made of gold and silver (Q 9:72; 35:55–58; 88:10–16). There they gather with loved ones and the angels, and they are served food and drink by handsome youths and beautiful young women (sing. HOURI) (Q 43:71; 76:15–22). The specially blessed will even be able to meet with God, though theologians and Quran commentators debated whether or not they would actually be able to see him. HADITH literature describes paradise as having eight gates, each named after a different virtue. Some accounts speculate that there may actually be eight paradises, not just one. Each one would have its own name, taken from the Quran, such as *dar al-salam* (House of Peace), *jannat al-khuld* (Garden of Eternity), and *jannat Adin* (the Garden of Eden). The hadith also elaborate on the nature of life in paradise: people will have beautiful bodies, they will never age, and they will be able to enjoy carefree sexual relations. The quranic paradise is the exact counterpart of hell, which is a multileveled realm of FIRE, pain, and suffering.

Ideas of paradise inspired rulers, writers, artists, and architects, enriching the heritage of Islamicate civilization. The grand mosque of DAMASCUS, the Alhambra palace in GRANADA (Spain), and royal garden pavilions in Iran were decorated with paradisal motifs. The capital of the ABBASID CALIPHATE (8th–14th centuries), BAGHDAD, was regarded as an earthly paradise, as reflected in its alternate name, *Madinat al-Salam* (City of Peace), alluding to *dar al-salam,* one of the quranic names of paradise. Persian and Turkish manuscripts depicting Muhammad's NIGHT JOURNEY AND ASCENT include scenes of paradise and the fire. The garden grounds of the exquisite Taj Mahal of Mughal India (17th century) were designed according to the four-garden (*chahar bagh*) plan of Persian royal gardens, wherein the waterways represented the four rivers of paradise. Also, many Muslim homes and palaces bear inscriptions and decorations that create a symbolic relationship between the abodes of this world and those of the afterlife.

See also ESCHATOLOGY; HOUSES; MARTYRDOM; PERSIAN LANGUAGE AND LITERATURE.

Further reading: Sheila Blair and Jonathan M. Bloom, eds., *Images of Paradise in Islamic Art* (Hanover, N.H.: Hood Museum of Art, Dartmouth College, 1991); Juan Eduardo Campo, *The Other Sides of Paradise: Explora-*tions into the Religious Meanings of Domestic Space in Islam (Columbia: University of South Carolina Press, 1991); Muhammad Abu Hamid al-Ghazali, *The Remembrance of Death and the Afterlife, Kitab dhikr al-mawt wa-ma badahu, Book XL of The Revival of the Religious Sciences, Ihya ulum al-din.* Translated by T. J. Winter (Cambridge: Islamic Texts Society, 1995).

pbuh

The four letters *p-b-u-h* combine to form an acronym for the phrase "Peace be upon him," which is the English rendering of the Arabic *alayhi al-salam.* It is used in English-language Islamic publications and written texts whenever mention is made of MUHAMMAD as the prophet (*nabi* or *rasul*) of ISLAM. It is not used by non-Muslims or in Western scholarship about Muhammad and Islam.

Invoking peace on another is the signature greeting used by Muslims. According to the QURAN, ANGELs use it when greeting the blessed in PARADISE (for example, Q 16:32) and people should use it in greeting God's servants (Q 27:59). The peace blessing is also invoked by the Quran for the prophets, including ABRAHAM, MOSES, Aaron, and Elias (for example, Q 37:109, 114, 120, 130, 181). It is required in the performance daily prayers, when the peace blessing is recited for the Prophet (*nabi*) Muhammad, the person performing the prayer, and believers in general.

The peace blessing (*salam*) for Muhammad as the prophet of Islam is an abbreviated rendering of an Arabic formula known as the *tasliyya.* It consists of the invocation *salla Allah alayhi wa sallam* (May God bless him and grant him peace), which is used with reference to Muhammad (and other prophets) in Arabic-language Islamic texts, publications, sermons, recitations, and speeches. There are several variations on this formula used in everyday speech, including the popular expressions "Bless the Prophet!" (*salli ala al-nabi*) and "Bless the beauty of the Prophet!" (*salli ala jamal* al-nabi), as well as "May blessing and peace be upon him" (alayhi al-salat wal-salam). Invoking blessing and peace upon Muhammad is considered to be an expression of devotion that is endorsed by the Quran, which states, "God and the angels bless the Prophet. O you believers! Bless him and greet him with peace" (Q 33:56). In Islamic popular religion calling for blessing and peace upon Muhammad is believed to bring God's blessing (BARAKA) and repel evil from the person using it. Some Muslims believe it will win those who use it Muhammad's INTERCESSION on JUDGMENT DAY. Such phrases are recited in Sufi DHIKR rituals and included in amulets that are worn on the body or displayed in homes, businesses, and vehicles.

See also AFTERLIFE; AMULETS AND TALISMANS; PROPHETS AND PROPHECY.

Further reading: Constance E. Padwick, *Muslim Devotions: A Study of Prayer-Manuals in Common Use* (1961. Reprint, Rockport, Mass.: Oneworld, 1996), 152–166, 220–232.

People of the Book (Arabic: *ahl al-kitab;* alternately "those who have been given the book" [*alladhina utu al-kitab*])

Muslims believe that their religion is related to that of the Jews and Christians through the HOLY BOOKS God has revealed in human history to his prophets. This belief is evident when they call Jews and Christians "People of the Book," signifying that they understand the QURAN to be related to the TORAH of MOSES, the Psalms (*Zabur*) of DAVID, and the GOSPEL of JESUS. All three holy books have their origin in a single divine source—God. As Muslims encountered new people they also used this designation for Zoroastrians of IRAN, Sabians (identified with the Mandeans of southern IRAQ or the Yazidis of northern Iraq/southeastern TURKEY), Hindus, Buddhists, and Sikhs. In the light of the historical evidence the use of this designation, therefore, was somewhat flexible, especially out-

side the Middle East. In terms of the SHARIA the People of the Book held special legal status under Muslim rule. As the people granted protection (*ahl al-dhimma,* or *dhimmi*s), Jews and Christians enjoyed minority legal status that allowed them to have their own religious authorities and follow their own religious laws, as long as they paid the JIZYA tax (irregularly enforced), remained loyal to the state, and did not attempt to convert Muslims or otherwise undermine the religion of the state—Islam.

The source for the labeling Jews, Christians, and others as People of the Book is the Quran, where the phrase occurs 31 times (plus an additional 21 times in the alternative phrasing). It occurs predominantly in the chapters that Muslim tradition ascribes to the MEDINA period of MUHAMMAD's career, between 622 and 632. This was when he and his followers had to negotiate their relations as a religious minority with other religious and social groups, as reflected in the so-called Constitution of Medina. A number of quranic verses depict relations of the faithful Muslims (*muminin*) with others in terms of the commonalities of their belief in one God and his prophets, as reflected in Q 29:46–47 and 3:64, 84. Many of the passages, however, reflect adversarial relations between the three Abrahamic religions, based largely on the assertion that Jews and Christians did not recognize Muhammad as a prophet and that some of them had joined with the idolaters and disbelievers (for example, Q 2:105, 109). This latter charge was connected with the Jewish anticipation of a messianic savior and the Christian belief in JESUS as the son of God, as stated in sura 9 Repentance, where some of the most polemical statements against the People of the Book are to be found. There believers are urged, "Fight those who have been given the Book who do not believe in God and the Last Day, who do not forbid what God and his prophet have forbidden, and do not follow the true religion until they pay the *jizya* tax with their own hands. They are contemptible" (Q 9:29).

The designation of non-Muslims as People of the Book has experienced a revival in recent decades. Progressive and modern-minded Muslims have invoked its egalitarian connotations to further their efforts at interreligious DIALOGUE and greater religious and cultural pluralism. On the other hand, radical Islamist movements have drawn from the more polemical verses in the Quran concerning the People of the Book to justify attacking and subjugating them. For many Muslims the concept today is primarily an aspect of the heritage of the past, one that must give way to modern SECULARISM, nationalism, and the construction of individual identities that differ from those of confessional religious communities.

See also CHRISTIANITY AND ISLAM; *DHIMMI*; HINDUISM AND ISLAM; IDOLATRY; JUDAISM AND ISLAM; *KAFIR*; UMMA.

Further reading: Ali S. Asani, "'So That You May Know One Another': A Muslim American Reflects on Pluralism and Islam." *Annals of the American Academy of Political and Social Science* 588 (July 2003): 40–51; Abd al-Aziz Sachedina, "Jews, Christians and Muslims According to the Quran." *Greek Orthodox Theological Review* 31 (1986): 87–105; Zeki Saritoprak and Sydney Griffith, "Fethullah Gülen and the People of the Book: A Voice from Turkey for Interfaith Dialogue." *Muslim World* 95, no. 3 (2005): 329–340.

Perfect Man (Arabic: *al-insan al-kamil*)

The concept of the Perfect Man, or Universal Man, was most fully developed by the great 12th–13th century Sufi mystic and teacher MUHYI AL-DIN IBN AL-ARABI (d. 1240). According to Ibn al-Arabi, humanity and the cosmos are two separate but intimately connected constructions of the same Universal Spirit (God), like two mirrors facing each other. The Perfect Man, therefore, is that individual who, in embarking on the Sufi path toward self-annihilation, or *fana,* discards his own qualities and attributes and enters fully into the qualities and attributes of God. In doing so the Perfect

Man fully realizes his oneness with the Universal Spirit, becoming the medium through which God is made manifest. As "the copy of God," to quote Ibn al-Arabi's disciple, Abd al-Karim al-Jili (d. ca. 1423), the Perfect man's individuality is merely his "external" form, while his "inward" reality is the universe itself. Although SUFISM considers all prophets and messengers, as well as the imams and the *pirs* (Sufi shaykhs), to be representatives of the Perfect Man, the paradigm of this unique being for all Sufis is none other than MUHAMMAD (d. 632) himself.

See also BAQA AND FANA; CREATION; MULLA SADRA; THEOLOGY.

Reza Aslan

Further reading: Titus Burckhardt, *An Introduction to Sufi Doctrine* (Wellingsborough, England: Aquarian Press, 1976); Annemarie Schimmel, *And Muhammad Is His Messenger* (Chapel Hill: University of North Carolina Press, 1985); Idries Shah, *The Sufis* (New York: Anchor, 1964).

Persia   *See* IRAN.

Persian Gulf   *See* GULF STATES; GULF WARS; IRAN; IRAQ; SAUDI ARABIA.

Persian language and literature

Persian (also known as Farsi) is one of the leading languages, together with Arabic and Turkish, known to the Islamicate cultures and civilizations. It has been the medium for writing history, poetry, PHILOSOPHY, SCIENCE, and religious literature among Persian-speaking peoples in the Middle East and Central and South Asia for more than one thousand years. Today it is estimated that there are more than 100 million Persian speakers. It is an official language in IRAN, AFGHANISTAN, and Tajikistan, but there are also sizeable Persian-speaking populations in Azerbaijan, Uzbekistan, and

Turkmenistan. Many of the Iranian immigrants in North America and EUROPE also continue to speak Persian.

Persian is classified as an Indo-European language by linguists, which means that it is historically related both to the languages of North INDIA and PAKISTAN (including Sanskrit, Hindi, and Urdu) and to those of Europe and the Americas (including English, German, Spanish, and French). It is written in the Arabic script with an additional four letters to convey consonants that are not found in Arabic (p, ch, zh, and g). Although there are thousands of Arabic loanwords in Persian, it is not classified as a Semitic language because of its sentence structure, grammar, and native vocabulary. The kinship of Persian with Euro-American languages can be readily seen in words like *pedar* (English father, Spanish *padre,* and French *père*), *madar* (English mother, Spanish *madre,* and French *mère*), and *dar* (English door, German *Tür*). The Arabic equivalents to these words are quite different: *abu* or *walid, umm* or *walida,* and *bab.*

The Persian language has evolved in three chief stages. The earliest to have left textual evidence is known as Old Persian, the official language of the Achaemenid Empire that ruled Iran from ca. 539 to ca. 330 B.C.E. It has been found only in royal inscriptions written in cuneiform characters adapted from the civilizations of ancient Mesopotamia. The eastern branch of this language included Avestan, which was the ancient language of the sacred texts of the Zoroastrian religion. Old Persian was replaced by Middle Persian after the fall of the Achaemenids. It was written in what is known as the Pahlavi script (adapted from Aramaic) and used during the reign of the Sasanian dynasty of Iran and adjacent lands between 224 C.E. and 651 C.E., although many Middle Persian texts were written later during the early centuries of Islam. Middle Persian was used in the writing of Zoroastrian literature, wisdom texts, and court poetry. Modern Persian (also called New Persian), the language still used today, emerged in the aftermath of the conquests of Persian lands by Arab armies in the seventh and eighth centuries. It overlapped with Middle Persian and expressed the colloquial dialect. It was (and still is) written in Arabic script, with the earliest Modern Persian texts dating back to the 10th century. The interaction of Persian and Arabic speakers resulted in the appropriation of hundreds of Arabic loanwords into Modern Persian, but only a few Persian words have survived in the Arabic language.

Many of the major scholars who arose during the era of the ABBASID CALIPHATE (750–1258) were Persian, or of Persian descent, but they wrote mostly in Arabic. These included the historian and Quran commentator Muhammad ibn Jarir al-Tabari (838–923), and a number of major collectors of Sunni hadith: Muhammad al-Bukhari (810–870), Abu Dawud (818–888), and IBN MAJA (824–887). The foremost Arabic grammarian Sibawayh (d. ca. 793), the philosopher IBN SINA (979–1037), the noted astronomer and geographer ABU RAYHAN AL-BIRUNI (d. 1051), and the renowned Sunni theologian and mystic ABU HAMID AL-GHAZALI (1058–1111) were all Persians who wrote mostly if not entirely in Arabic. One's reputation as a scholar of religion, history, and the fine arts in general depended upon one's command of Arabic at this time.

The roots of an indigenous Persian literary tradition have been traced to poetic passages in Middle Persian Zoroastrian hymns and the oral traditions of the *gosans*, Persian minstrels, like Barbad and Sarkash. It was further influenced by Indian literature during the Sasanian era. Traces of these literary traditions survived both in Modern Persian and Arabic translations. The weakening of Abbasid hegemony and the emergence of Turkish dynasties in eastern Islamicate lands during the 10th and 11th centuries led to a Persian-language literary renaissance. Turkish rulers patronized Persian court poets who composed works that praised them, extolled courtly life, and told tales that interwove romantic and heroic themes. Modern Persian, with deep vernacular roots, thus became the language of "high" Persianate culture in Iran, Afghanistan, Central Asia, and later in Ottoman Turkey and North India. Among the foremost literary works of this era was the epic *Shahnamah* (Epic of kings), composed by Firdawsi at the beginning of the 11th century. It drew upon legends of the ancient kings of Persia, and related tales of the heroic prince Rustam, the demonic king Zahhak, and the lovers Bizhan and Manizhah, as well as Zal and Rudabah. Altogether this work tells 62 stories in 60,000 rhyming couplets and it remains a favorite among Iranians to this day. Nasir-i Khusraw (1003–88), an Ismaili missionary, wrote poetry about his experiences and commentaries on his times, as well as an account of his pilgrimage to Egypt and Mecca. Another noteworthy work of Persian literature was the *Khamsa* (Quintet) of Nizami (1141–1209), which retold some of the heroic and romantic stories of the *Shahnamah,* the Arabic romance of MAJNUN AND LAYLA, and incorporated poetic reflections on philosophical and religious themes. Nizami had a great influence on the subsequent development of Persian poetry.

Other major poets whose verses are still memorized by Persian speakers are Sanai (d. 1130), Saadi (d. 1292), and Hafiz (d. 1390). Although Persian poetry did not hesitate to draw upon Arabic poetic conventions, a distinctive genre developed by this group of writers was that of the GHAZAL, a short lyrical poem that sought to evoke aesthetic and emotional responses in the reader or listener. It was especially concerned with the feelings of love, separation, and union. Many of the poems composed by these men reflect the influence of SUFISM, making for some ambiguity with respect to the meaning of the metaphors used. Was the poem about worldly love or divine love? Was the beloved a handsome boy or beautiful girl, or was he/she God? Poets played with these ambiguities, but the meanings of the poetic imagery were also determined by the setting and the audience. The most significant composers of Sufi verse in Persian were Farid al-Din Attar (d. ca. 1230) and JALAL AL-DIN RUMI (1207–73). Attar wrote

several books of mystical poetry, the most famous of which was *Mantiq al-tayr* (The conference of the Birds), a collection of didactic stories set in the frame of the pilgrimage of a flock of birds (representing the human soul) to their divine king, SIMURGH. Rumi's most famous works were *Diwan-i Shams-i Tabriz,* a collection of *ghazal*s and quatrains composed in honor of his spiritual master and friend, Shams-i Tabriz, and the *Mathnawi* (also known as the *Masnavi*), a poem consisting of rhyming couplets dealing with themes of separation and union with God, conveyed through quranic imagery, prophet and saint stories, and metaphors drawn from everyday life. At 40,000 verses in length, Rumi's *Diwan* is thought to be the longest work of Persian poetry. His *Mathnawi* has been called by the scholar-poet Abd al-Rahman Jami (1414–92) and others "the Quran in the Persian tongue." It is held in the highest esteem by speakers of Persian and Turks, and is familiar to readers around the world, including the United States, through many translated editions. One of the last of the great Persian mystical writers was Jami of Herat (now in Afghanistan), whose most famous collection of poems, *Haft awrang* (Seven thrones) expanded upon the symbolism of romantic legends developed by Nizami and other Persian poets to probe the hidden realities of the world and of mystical experience. It had a significant influence on later Sufi writings in both Iran and INDIA.

A significant body of Persian literature was produced in India, starting with the reign of the DELHI SULTANATE (1211–1526) and continuing through that of the MUGHAL DYNASTY (1526–1857). It included histories, mystical texts, philosophical works, and, of course, poetry. The Mughal emperor AKBAR (r. 1556–1605) commissioned the translation of Hindu epics into Persian, and his great grandson DARA SHIKOH (1615–59) translated the Hindu *Upanishad*s, and wrote several works on mystical and philosophical topics. The first great Persian poet to emerge in India was Amir Khusraw of Delhi (1253–1325), a court poet and member of the CHISHTI SUFI ORDER. He was a composer of *ghazal*s and was inspired by the stories of the *Shahnamah* and Nizami's *Khamsa*. In addition, he wrote historical poems in honor of his royal patrons and collected the sayings of the Chishti saint NIZAM AL-DIN AWLIYA (1238–1325). The large number of Persian historical, mystical, and secular works produced in India contributed significantly to the shaping of the modern Urdu literary tradition. One of the major figures who marked the linkage of these two South Asian literary traditions was Mirza GHALIB (1797–1867), who wrote poetry and prose in both languages.

Critics have observed that Persian literature declined in quality after Jami. Whether or not this is the case, Western influence and the development of print culture in the 19th and early 20th centuries revolutionized it. New generations of writers have emerged who have shown great creativity and promoted the exploration of radical new ideas and visions. One of the most prominent of these literary figures was Nima Yushij (1897–1960), who combined his knowledge of the classical Persian poetic heritage and his familiarity with Russian and French poetics. His ideas met with resistance from traditionalists, but he also inspired others to engage in individualistic styles of literary expression. This, together with increased literacy, opened the door for female writers, the foremost of whom was Furugh Farrukhzad (1935–67). Two of the leading writers of fiction of Nima's generation were Muhammad Ali Jamalzadah (1892–1997) and Sadiq Hidayat (1903–51), each of whom specialized in crafting the modern Persian short story. Many Iranian writers, dramatists, and filmmakers were caught up with the Islamic Revolution of 1978–79, but when the government of the shah turned into a theocracy under the rule of mullahs, a number of liberal, independently minded artists went into exile in Europe and the United States. This created a tradition of Iranian diaspora literature, much of which is now written in English and French rather than Persian. Other authors have emerged in Iran since the 1970s, some writing in support of the government's Islamization policies, others choosing to work on secular themes around the margins of government censorship, under the threat of possible imprisonment.

See also ALPHABET; ARABIC LANGUAGE AND LITERATURE; CINEMA; IRANIAN REVOLUTION OF 1978–1979; SAFAVID DYNASTY; TURKISH LANGUAGE AND LITERATURE.

Further reading: Farid ud-Din Attar, *Conference of the Birds.* Translated by Afkham Darbandi and Dick Davis (London: Penguin Books, 1984); Carl W. Ernst, *The Shambhala Guide to Sufism* (Boston: Shambhala Publications, 1997); Reuben Levy, *An Introduction to Persian Literature* (New York: Columbia University Press, 1969); Jalal al-Din Rumi, *The Masnavi, Book One.* Translated by Jawid Mojaddedi (Oxford: Oxford University Press, 2004); Annemarie Schimmel, *Mystical Dimensions of Islam* (Chapel Hill: University of North Carolina Press, 1975); Marianna Shreve Simpson, *Persian Poetry, Painting and Patronage: Illustrations in a Sixteenth-Century Masterpiece* (Washington, D.C.: Smithsonian Institution, 1998); Ehsan Yarshater, ed., *Persian Literature* (Albany, N.Y.: Bibliotheca Persica, 1988).

pesantren   *See* INDONESIA; *KUTTAB*; MADRASA.

pets   *See* ANIMALS.

petroleum   *See* OIL.

Philippines (Official name: Republic of the Philippines)

The Philippines is a country in Southeast Asia comprised of 7,107 islands. The two largest islands are Luzon and Mindanao. Between Mindanao and Luzon are several smaller islands collectively called the Visayas. MALAYSIA and INDONESIA are the nearest neighbors to the south, and CHINA lies to the north. The population of the Philippines is 96 million (2008 estimate), roughly 81 percent of whom are Roman Catholic, about 5 percent are Muslims (known locally as Moros), and the rest practice Protestantism, Buddhism, and indigenous religions. The Muslims are Sunnis, most of whom follow the SHAFII LEGAL SCHOOL and belong to different ethnic groups, including the Maranao, the Maguindanao, the Iranun, the Tausug, the Yakan, the Sama, the Sangil, the Kaagan, the Kolibugan, the Palawan, and the Molbog. Muslim communities are among the most impoverished in the Philippines, lagging in median annual income compared to other provinces and regions.

Prior to the Spanish establishment of a settlement in Cebu in 1565, most of the islands were locally organized into independent *barangays* (villages and districts), each headed by a chieftain. Islam arrived in the Philippines in the 13th century through Muslim merchants traveling through the Malay Archipelago toward China. According to genealogical studies of elite Muslim families in Sulu and Mindanao, Islam became established after Muslim religious leaders from neighboring islands intermarried with the ruling elite in Sulu and Mindanao. By the mid-1500s there were already two sultanates (territories ruled by sultans) flourishing in Mindanao and Sulu, and Manila already had extensive contact with the sultanates of Sulu and of Borneo. Additionally, the sultanate of Maguindanao reached its peak during the mid-1600s after the Spanish had already begun colonizing the Philippines. Although most of Luzon and the Visayas were Christianized by Spain, Mindanao managed to remain independent until it was conquered and pacified by the Americans. In 1898 Spain ceded the Philippines to the United States after the Spanish-American War.

The Philippines was granted its independence from the United States on July 4, 1946. It maintains close ties with the United States. Muslims in the Philippines were galvanized into organizing resistance movements in the late 1960s, renewing debates about the place of Muslims in a largely Catholic country that bore strong colonial imprints. The MORO NATIONAL LIBERATION FRONT (MNLF) and the Moro Islamic Liberation Front (MILF) continue to challenge the Philippine government's national integrity. In 1976 the Tripoli Agreement was signed between the MNLF and the Philippine government, providing autonomy to 13 provinces, and creating Islamic courts and banks for Muslim Filipinos. The Autonomous Region of Muslim Mindanao (ARMM) was created in 1983 by the Republic Act 6734, in which 4 of the 13 provinces were incorporated into the ARMM. Every presidency since the Tripoli Agreement has attempted to implement parts of the agreement, but not the whole, and thus hostilities continue between the MNLF and the Philippine government. Malaysia is also brokering a peace agreement between the MILF and the Philippine government.

See also CHRISTIANITY AND ISLAM; COLONIALISM; ISLAMISM.

Tara Munson

Further reading: Jose Abueva, ed., *The Making of the Filipino Nation and Republic* (Quezon City: University of the Philippines Press, 1998); Cesar A. Majul, *Muslims in the Philippines* (Quezon City: University of the Philippines Press, 1973).

philosophy (Arabic: *falsafa*)

Perhaps the best characterization of Islamic philosophy is both generous and vague: it is the tradition of philosophy that arose out of classical Islamicate culture. One virtue of such a circular definition is its capacity to accommodate contesting portraits of the philosophical tradition drawn with one eye toward illustrating or proving different theories in the field of Islamic studies. What is more, most definitions of Islamic philosophy will exclude recognition of the rational approaches, methods, and arguments—hence a philosophical temperament—found in varying degrees in the Islamic sciences, such as dialectical THEOLOGY (*kalam*), rules for legal reasoning in Islamic jurisprudence (FIQH), as well as quranic exegesis (TAFSIR). And whatever their polemical positions toward philosophy qua philosophy, Muslim theologians (mutakallimun) were well versed in the arts of dialectical reasoning. No less a theologian than ABU HAMID AL-GHAZALI (1058–1111), author of *The Incoherence of the Philosophers* (ca. 1095), ardently defended the utility of Aristotelian logic for theology. Indeed, "his arguments against philosophy are themselves philosophical" (Leaman 2002: 27).

Islamic philosophy proper begins under the auspices of the ABBASID CALIPHATE in the ninth century. Its origins are principally Greek, although it was transmitted largely by Christian scholars translating philosophical and other works into Arabic (with some of these from Syriac translations of Greek manuscripts). Of lesser but not insignificant impact was the rendering of Indian and Persian literature likewise into Arabic.

Many of the ULAMA did not welcome works of Peripatetic (Aristotelian and Pseudo-Aristotelian) and Neoplatonic provenance into the circle of Islamic sciences. The theologian Abu Said al-Sirafi (d. 979), for instance, argued that the conventionality of language meant interpretative principles must be unique to each language, thus Greek logic may be applied to works in Greek, but it is wholly inappropriate for the analysis of texts, say, in Arabic. In general, Greek philosophy was perceived as a challenge if not threat to the integrity of the traditional Islamic sciences. MUHAMMAD IBN RUSHD (Averroës) (1126–98), a preeminent Islamic philosopher, viewed philosophy and theology (kalam) as distinct yet compatible and alternative routes to the same truth(s). Nevertheless, for Ibn Rushd, philosophy alone leads to certitude owing to its reliance on the formal logic of Aristotle. According to Ibn Rushd, philosophy does not deny the assent to quranic truth provided by the rhetorical and dialectical methods of the Islamic sciences, for such sciences are well suited to the spiritual pedagogical needs of the masses. Philosophy, on the other hand, is not for the common man, but is rather the prerogative of an elite in possession of that rare combination of virtue and wisdom (hikma).

Philosophy flourished in the Islamic world from the ninth to the 12th centuries. It met with considerable opposition from two formidable figures: al-Ghazali and TAQI AL-DIN AHMAD IBN TAYMIYYA (1263–1328), the former arguably Islam's greatest theologian, the latter a notable Hanbali jurist and theologian. Their main contention was that the absolute truth of divine revelation could in no way depend on the consent of the aql ("reason") of the philosophers for its definitive confirmation. In other words, the revealed will and law of prophetic tradition is more than mere allegory or metaphor, and in the end, the demonstrative syllogism of philosophy cannot account for revealed truth. In brief, al-Ghazali and Ibn Taymiyya proffered arguments against those philosophers who subscribed to the view that religion was intended for the salvation of unsophisticated believers, whose piety could not compensate for their lack of philosophical acumen. For their part, most Islamic philosophers, commencing with the Quran, were intensely devoted to what we now term hermeneutic investigation. One presumption of such scrutiny being the sacred veracity of revealed texts.

A distinction is frequently drawn between *falsafa* and *hikma* ('wisdom'), and theology and mysticism (SUFISM) have often fallen under the rubric of *hikma*, hence the categorical boundaries between philosophy, theology, and mysticism are blurred when considering a philosopher like Shihab al-Din Suhrawardi (1154–91) or a Sufi like MUHYI AL-DIN IBN AL-ARABI (1165–1240). In addition, and in spite of ABU ALI AL-HUSAYN IBN SINA's (Avicenna) (979–1037) enshrinement of this distinction as one between *al-hikmat al-mashriqiyya* (Oriental philosophy) and Aristotelian thought, most philosophers conceived of their enterprise as exemplifying *hikma*.

Abu Yusuf Yaqub ibn Ishaq al-Kindi (d. after 866), Islam's earliest philosopher of note, argued there was no inherent contradiction or even antagonism between the philosophical heritage of the Greeks and God's revelations. Al-Kindi's conclusion, however, found few adherents, as *kalam* and *falsafa* developed relatively independent of each other, marked by periods of fertile conflict and constructive engagement. Intriguingly, a philosophical disposition is at the core of Mutazili theology, as the MUTAZILI SCHOOL represents a species of theological rationalism in which reason (*aql*) is accorded pride of place in the determination of God's will as revealed in the prophetic traditions, the Quran, and hadith. ABU NASR AL-FARABI (ca. 870–950) is the tradition's first truly systematic philosopher and logician, having penned a distinguished work of Islamic political philosophy inspired by several Platonic dialogues. Disagreeing with al-Sirafi, al-Farabi stressed the fundamental differences between the logic of philosophy and the rules of grammar, with grammar unable to provide the logical constraints for reasoning in language, nor was it sufficient for explaining the kinds of reasoning employed in the Islamic sciences.

Ibn Sina was a first-rate logician and the tradition's greatest Neoplatonic philosopher. His impact on medieval Christian theology and philosophy was profound, as was his influence on European science and literature. Indeed, he is responsible for articulating the metaphysical vocabulary appropriated by St. Thomas Aquinas (d. 1274). Like Ibn Sina before him, Ibn Rushd was a polymath, yet unlike his predecessor, he was deeply involved in public life, first as a judge of Seville and later as chief judge of Cordoba, while also serving as the sultan's physician. For Ibn Rushd, philosophy and religion converge on the same truths, revelations speaking through narrative, allegory, symbol, analogy, and metaphor, while philosophy communicates with the logical consistency, coherence, and conceptual clarity evidenced in the certitude attained by syllogistic demonstration, a method befitting the exalted reasoning of the philosophers.

There appears to be consensus among many contemporary Muslim intellectuals that Islamic philosophy reached its quintessential expression in the work of Muhammad ibn Ibrahim al-Qawami al-Shirazi, better known as MULLAH SADRA (ca. 1572–1640). This is in consonance with the historical observation that since the 12th century, the cultivation of Islamic philosophy has taken place largely on Shii soil, especially its Persian precincts. In the modern period, something of Islamic philosophy persists in the writings of JAMAL AL-DIN AL-AFGHANI (1838–97) and MUHAMMAD ABDUH (1849–1905), although their output, together with that of MUHAMMAD RASHID RIDA (1865–1935) and SAYYID QUTB (1906–66), is more aptly seen as the product of Muslim intellectuals rather than the musings of philosophers. Still, our time knows something of Islamic philosophy in the precious few works of the Indo-Pakistan poet-philosopher MUHAMMAD IQBAL (1877–1938), while SEYYED HOSSEIN NASR (b. 1933) remains the best-known and most prolific contemporary Muslim philosopher.

See also AFTERLIFE; ALLAH; CREATION; FATE; REVELATION; SOUL AND SPIRIT.

Patrick S. O'Donnell

Further reading: Peter A. Adamson and Richard C. Taylor, eds., *The Cambridge Companion to Arabic Philosophy* (Cambridge: Cambridge University Press, 2005); Majid Fakhry, *A History of Islamic Philosophy*, 3d ed. (New York: Columbia University Press, 2004); Lenn E. Goodman, *Islamic Humanism* (New York: Oxford University Press, 2003); Oliver Leaman, *A Brief Introduction to Islamic Philosophy* (Oxford: Polity Press, 1999); ———, *An Introduction to Classical Islamic Philosophy* 2d ed. (Cambridge: Cambridge University Press, 2002); Seyyed Hossein Nasr and Oliver Leaman, eds., *History of Islamic Philosophy* (London: Routledge, 2001).

pilgrimage   *See* HAJJ; *UMRA; ZIYARA.*

Pillars of Islam   *See* FIVE PILLARS.

pir   *See* SHAYKH.

politics and Islam

In the medieval period the religious establishment of Sunni Islam had for the most part come to a position of mutual cooperation with the government and refrained from direct involvement in the political realm. However, the rise of European powers in the 18th century and the corresponding waning of Ottoman power encouraged several Islamic revivalist movements that managed to take over political power as well. Among these were the Wahhabi movement that allied with the tribe of Muhammad ibn Saud in Arabia (and which still holds power down to the present day) and the Mahdist movement in SUDAN that was brought to an end by the British in 1898.

Although European colonial powers were aware of the potential threat of a religiously motivated and pan-Islamic political movement, it never fully materialized. Instead the anti-imperialist efforts in Muslim lands and indeed the political landscape as a whole were dominated by other secular ideologies such as pan-Arabism, nationalism, and socialism. However, it was the failure of these ideologies to deliver on their promises, combined with continuing economic hardships, and a series of events—most notably the defeat of the ARAB states by ISRAEL in 1967, the OIL crisis of 1973, and the IRANIAN REVOLUTION OF 1978–1979—that helped to transform the ideal of Islam into not only a viable political option, but also—for some—into the only solution for the dilemmas facing Muslim-majority countries and the world at large.

This is not to say there is any consensus on what the exact relationship should be between Islam and politics. Muslim intellectuals and scholars still debate to what extent *din wa-dawla* (religion and government) accurately describes Islam itself or what is the appropriate relationship between religion and government. While some argue for a separation of religion and government, others believe Islam should shape government and law.

Although many political parties believe Islam supports democratic values and try to come to power through democratic processes, they have yet to be successful. This in turn has stirred up debate about the possibility of an Islamic DEMOCRACY. At the conceptual level, Islam is neither more nor less compatible with democracy than any other religion; the debate has to do with the ways in which historical and cultural factors shape how Islam and politics are practiced and understood in Muslim societies. A popular revolution brought an Islamic government to power in Iran in 1979, and the development of representative government there has been encouraging; nonetheless, that country is currently facing tensions between the reformers elected by the people, and the unelected council of religious leaders that has the power to veto any law or policy that they feel conflicts with Islam. In many Muslim countries, however, people have never been given the opportunity to debate the role of religion in politics.

Attempts to form religiously based political parties have been thwarted by the largely secular and military-based regimes that dominate Muslim countries from North Africa to South Asia. When an Islamic party won elections in ALGERIA in 1992 the existing regime refused to step down and a bloody civil war ensued. The Egyptian government prevented a potentially similar outcome by outlawing Islamic parties and arresting their leaders. In TURKEY the military has used various means to ensure that its usually more secular point of view is taken into account by the members of parliament. In Asia, Islamic political parties struggle to work within the very limited freedoms that exist. All of this has only increased the popular appeal of Islamic groups as a solution to political oppression, government corruption, and economic stagnation.

With apparently limited options, some Islamic militant groups, especially in EGYPT, Algeria, and, most recently, INDONESIA have turned to acts of TERRORISM to destabilize and overthrow existing regimes. It is important to remember, however, that resorting to violence is in many ways a direct result of being cut off from participating in the political process.

See also ABD AL-RAZIQ, ALI; AUTHORITY; CALIPHATE; COLONIALISM; CONSTITUTIONALISM; INDIA; GOVERNMENT, ISLAMIC; HAMAS; IRAQ; ISLAMISM; JAMAAT-I ISLAMI; MUSLIM BROTHERHOOD; NASIR, JAMAL ABD AL-; PAKISTAN; RENEWAL AND REFORM MOVEMENTS; SECULARISM; WAHHABISM.

Heather N. Keaney

Further reading: Joel Beinin and Joe Stork, eds., Political Islam: Essays from Middle East Report (Berkeley: University of California Press, 1997); L. Carl Brown, Religion and State: The Muslim Approach to Politics (New York: Columbia University Press, 2000); Edmund Burke III and Ira Lapidus, eds., Islam, Politics, and Social Movements (Berkeley: University of California Press, 1988); Dale F. Eickelman and James Piscatori, Muslim Politics (Princeton, N.J.: Princeton University Press, 2004).

polytheism See IDOLATRY.

pork See DIETARY LAWS.

prayer

There are two main forms of prayer in Islam. Liturgical prayer (salat), one of Islam's FIVE PILLARS, is the primary form of public worship, requiring the believer to pray in Arabic, the language of divine speech, drawn from the QURAN. Salat must be performed facing toward the KAABA in MECCA (the QIBLA direction, because it is believed by Muslims to be God's sacred "house") five times daily: dawn (fajr), noon (zuhr), afternoon (asr), sunset (maghrib), and night (isha). Each time of prayer is preceded and announced by the call to prayer (ADHAN) summoning believers to the MOSQUE (Q 50:39–41). The number and times of salat are not fully set in the Quran, but became established during Prophet

MUHAMMAD's lifetime based on his SUNNA (customary behavior), as recorded in the HADITH. The quintessential prayer gesture is the prostration (sujud) in which the believer first bows from a standing position, kneels, and leans forward touching forehead to the ground. Muslims are defined in the Quran as "those who prostrate themselves" (Q 48:29), and the mosque is the "place of prostration" (masjid). Since prayer involves no sitting, mosques traditionally are open spaces having no seating or pews, only carpeting or matting on which to stand, kneel, and prostrate, along with a pulpit (MINBAR) for Friday noon sermons, and a niche (MIHRAB) indicating the direction of prayer (qibla).

In order to be ready to pray, the believer must be ritually pure, requiring ABLUTION of the hands, arms, face, and feet (wudu), or a full bath (ghusl) after menses or sexual relations (Q 5:6, 9). The dress code for prayer requires modesty, minimally for men covering from navel to knees, and for WOMEN from neck to ankles, usually including a scarf covering the hair. Liturgical prayer in Islam can be performed in any clean location. Thus, Muslims can do salat in their homes, at their jobs, in the street, as well as in the conventional location of the mosque. Salat can be performed alone or in a group organized in rows led by an

Men and women at noon prayer in the Sultan Hasan Mosque, Cairo, Egypt (Juan E. Campo)

IMAM (prayer leader). Although all prayer times are considered obligatory, attending the Friday (*jumaa*) noon prayer time is considered especially meritorious; men are particularly encouraged to participate collectively in this prayer at the mosque. Although the Prophet's hadith encourages Muslim women to pray in the home, women are not forbidden from praying at the mosque. When they join men in the mosque, prayer is traditionally sexually segregated, women praying behind the men, or to one side, in a balcony or other separate space. The reason given is to prevent inappropriate sexual distraction from prayer. Some mosques in the West or in more liberal Islamic communities no longer practice sexual segregation in prayer.

The second form of prayer is personal prayer (*duaa*), which is voluntary and additional to the five times daily *salat* prayers. Personal prayer allows believers to be creative and spontaneous in their own native language instead of the Arabic of formal prayer (only about 10 percent of Muslims around the world are native Arabic speakers). The believer can ask for specific needs or wants from God on their own behalf or on behalf of family and community. Believers have often used prayers from collections authored by devout believers and scholars and handed down from generation to generation as prayer manuals. Although Islam has no formal system of INTERCESSION—no priesthood or formal hierarchy to mediate between believers and God—it does have a strong popular tradition of informal intercession (*wasila*, Q 5:34, 17:57) via holy persons, places, and objects. There are prayers for blessings on Muhammad and his immediate family, the Sufi SAINTs, and Shii Imams; local pilgrimage (ZIYARA) and prayers offered at the birth and DEATH places and tombs of holy persons; and objects that convey divine blessing (BARAKA) such as quranic prayers written, embroidered, and carved functioning as AMULETS AND TALISMANS.

See also ADHAN; BASMALA; ID AL-ADHA; PBUH; PRAYER BEADS.

Kathleen M. O'Connor

Further reading: Seyyed Hossein Nasr, ed., *Islamic Spirituality: Foundations* (New York: Crossroad, 1987); Seyyed Hossein Nasr, Hamid Dabashi, and Seyyed Vali Reza Nasr, eds., *Shiism: Doctrines, Thought, and Spirituality* (Albany: State University of New York Press, 1988); Jacob Neusner, Tamara Sonn, and Jonathan E. Brockopp, *Judaism and Islam in Practice: A Sourcebook* (London: Routledge, 2000); Constance E. Padwick, *Muslim Devotions: A Study of Prayer-Manuals in Common Use* (1961. Reprint, Rockport, Mass.: Oneworld, 1996); Muhammad A. Rauf, *Islam: Creed and Worship* (Washington, D.C.: The Islamic Center, 1974); John Renard, *Seven Doors to Islam: Spirituality and the Religious Life of Muslims* (Berkeley: University of California Press, 1996).

prayer beads

Muslims use prayer beads like a Catholic rosary as a devotional aid to count recitations performed during private worship. Known as the *subha, tasbih,* or *misbaha,* prayer beads are widely used by Muslims from all parts of the Islamic world. Use of beads in prayer and devotional practices began as early as the ninth century. The *subha* is composed of either a short single string of beads or a long strand divided into three groups separated by larger marker beads with a short handle at the end. The beads are most often arranged in groups of 11, 33, or 99 but the number may vary if the handle or marker beads are intended to be included in counting. In practice 100 beads must be counted in reciting the 99 NAMES OF GOD, most of which are mentioned in the QURAN, and his essential name ALLAH. Prayer beads are also used in other recitation practices such as repetitions of the phrase *la ilaha illa allah,* (there is no god but God). Sufis often employ prayer beads in their recitation practices.

All Muslims are encouraged to constantly have the name of God on their lips, and some choose to always keep a set of beads in their hand for this purpose. Some scholars historically discouraged the use of prayer beads based on reports in the HADITH. In these reports MUHAMMAD (d. 632) encouraged using the joints of the fingers to count recitations, though using pebbles and knots in a string are also mentioned as acceptable. In modern times Wahhabi scholars and some other Muslims have renewed the debate by denouncing the use of prayer beads as BIDAA, a religious innovation introduced after the time of Muhammad. Nevertheless prayer beads remain an important part of worship for many Muslims.

See also DHIKR; PRAYER; SUFISM; WAHHABISM.

Shauna Huffaker

Further reading: Daniel da Cruz, "Worry Beads." *Saudi Aramco World* 19 (November–December 1968): 2–3; Samuel M. Zwemer, "The Rosary in Islam." *Muslim World* 21 (1931): 329–343.

prayer rug   *See* PRAYER.

predestination   *See* FATE.

prophets and prophethood

Belief in prophets and prophethood is a primary feature in the Abrahamic religions of Judaism, Islam, and Christianity. Prophets are virtuosos in divine-human communication. In Islam there are two main terms for prophet: (1) messenger (sing. *rasul,* pl. *rusul*), the bringer of a message or revelation sent from God via ANGELS (implying that the transmitter of the message is not the source and revelation is not a human product, but divine speech, Q 16:2), and (2) the older Jewish term *navi* prophet, or in Arabic *nabi* (pl. *nabiyin* or *anbiya*)—a law bringer who mediates a specific covenantal relation with God and conveys the binding quality of divine law upon the community of believers. Prophets as law-bringers are sent by God to every people, conveying God's message in language they can understand (Q 30:47). This was later interpreted to mean an Arabic revelation to the Arab people, a Hebrew revelation to

the Jewish people, and a Greek revelation to the Christian people (Muslims were familiar with the Greek-speaking Christians of Byzantium).

In Islamic belief, the prophetic tradition begins with the forefather of humanity, Adam, with whom God is said to have formed a preexisting COVENANT (Q 7:172). Islamic tradition accepts, and the QURAN details, the ongoing covenantal legacy of Jewish and Christian prophets and revelations, including three chief scriptures: (1) Jewish TORAH (Arabic: *tawrat,* encompassing Torah, Naviim, and Ketuvim [Pentateuch, Prophets, and Writings, except Psalms]), (2) *Zabur* (the Psalms of DAVID), and (3) Christian *Injil* ("Gospel," implicitly the whole of the New Testament). In addition to MUHAMMAD, the full list of prophets mentioned in the Quran includes: Adam, Alyasa (Elisha), Ayyub (Job), Daud (David), Dhu al-Kifl (Ezekiel), Hud, Ibrahim (ABRAHAM), IDRIS (Enoch), Ilyas (Elijah, Elias), Isa (JESUS), Ishaq (Isaac), Ismail (Ishmael), Luqman, Lut (Lot), Musa (MOSES), Nuh (Noah), Salih, Shuayb (Jethro), Sulayman (Solomon), Yunus (Jonah), Uzeir (Ezra), Yahya (JOHN THE BAPTIST), Yaqub (Jacob), and Yusuf (JOSEPH). Although revelations appear to be plural (even if only by virtue of inevitable errors in transmission by earlier human communities), the prophets in Islam are all understood to be equal, with no difference between one and another (Q 2:135–140; 2:285). Belief in the prophets without distinction brings reward (Q 4:152).

Female figures with some of the "prophetic" gifts deserve some mention here. MARY, mother of Jesus, is the only female figure to have a chapter of the Quran named for her (Q 19). She does not fully fit the category of prophet, which otherwise seems a completely male category. She does, however, receive divine messages via an angelic messenger of the "word of God" (*kalimat Allah*), which God breathes into her in the divine conception of Jesus (Q 3:45; 4:171). She is credited in Islam with extraordinary holiness, herself immaculately conceived, and is a "receiver/transmitter" of the "Word of God" via her son, Jesus. However, she has no prophetic ministry, she does not bring a new religion,

The Tree of the Prophets, showing Adam at the base of the trunk and Muhammad at the top, just under the moon, which proclaims God as the light of heaven and Earth. The lower trunk and branches include prophets mentioned in the Quran, while the upper branches have leaves bearing the names of the first four caliphs.

Prophethood (*nubuwwa*) is a fundamental aspect of Islamic teaching and belief, as reflected in the SHAHADA, which declares Muhammad God's messenger (*rasul Allah*). It is understood in Islamic tradition to have a variety of associative qualities and attributes. A prophet (1) is divinely elected; (2) possesses knowledge of the unseen (*al-ghayb*) through divine inspiration (*wahy*) and dream visions (*ruya*); (3) is often rejected and persecuted by his own people; (4) has extraordinary moral virtue or sinlessness (*isma*), which still allows human fault, but not intentional wrongdoing; (5) displays truthfulness and probity, thus his leadership can be trusted (as in Muhammad's nickname, *al-Amin*, the trustworthy) and the revelations he brings cannot be doubted; (6) is simultaneously a warner of the coming JUDGMENT DAY and a bringer of glad tidings (Q 6:48) about the blessings of the AFTERLIFE; and (7) stands as a witness (*shahid*) to God of the righteousness of his community on Judgment Day.

Individual prophets can also have special gifts from God that function as "signs" (sing. AYA) and "proofs" (*bayyinat*) in support of their prophetic mission. Some signs are supernatural or miraculous abilities, like Solomon's command of the winds and the jinn (Q 34:12–13; 38:34–39), Moses's magical ability to overcome the Pharaoh's priests (for example, Q 7:104–126; 20:65–73), and Jesus's extraordinary healing abilities and power to animate a bird made of clay and raise the dead (Q 3:49). Other prophetic qualities are interior principles, such as Abraham's being *hanif* (a pre-Islamic monotheist) and *khalil Allah* (the "friend of God," Q 4:125); Moses's quality of near communion with God at the burning bush, making him *kalim Allah* ("one to whom God spoke," Q 4:164); and Muhammad's being regarded as both the lover and beloved of God (*habib Allah*) by later Islamic tradition.

Prophecy is said to be kin to illumination, as God's essence is light, and He sheds that light on the world through REVELATION (Q 24:35). In HADITH and mystical literature, Muhammad and the Shii Imams are said to be composed of divine light (*nur muhammadi*) or to be a pillar of light

nor is she a law-bringer. There is a history of theological debate about her status, and the question of the possibility of a woman being a prophet. For the Shia, FATIMA al-Zahra ("the Radiant"), the historic mother of Muhammad's only male descendants (Hasan and Husayn) attains an almost transcendent theological role as Fatima Fatir ("Creator," one of the divine attributes), the cosmic progenetrix of the Imams. In the Shii tradition (whether Twelver or Ismaili) theologically she occupies a role similar to Mary for the Sunni tradition, the indirect vehicle/receiver of divine "revelation."

between earth and heaven, signaling their revelatory function. The color green has long been associated with Muhammad's family and, in a larger sense, the community of Islam, where it is frequently found in both Islamic religious flags and the state flags of Muslim countries. Islamic mystics have reflected on the emanation of God's light in the color green as a metaphor for the resurrection. Just as the green growth of living vegetation comes out of the dry earth, and as humanity was originally formed as "vegetation" from the earth, so the body will grow from the earth again at the resurrection (Q 71:17–18).

Finally, one last special quality associated with prophecy is the Islamic doctrine of "seal of prophets" (Q 42:24, *khatim al-nabiyin* or *khatim al-anbiya*). The Sunni majority interpret "seal of prophets" to mean the closure of prophetic function and they assign that title solely to Muhammad. However, minority Muslim opinion (among some Sufis and Shiis) interprets "seal" to be the seal on the King's (God's) treasure-house that validates or preserves its contents for future reopening and use, implying an open-ended, even cyclic understanding of prophecy and the possibility of future prophets and revelations from God. This notion of ongoing "prophecy" has been embraced by some modern Muslim sectarian groups who have been very influential in the spread of Islam in North America, especially among African Americans during the 20th century (for example, GHULAM AHMAD (d. 1908) and the Qadiri branch of the AHMADIYYA community and their impact on Elijah Muhammad, "Prophet" to the NATION OF ISLAM, as well as Isa Muhammad, founding theologian and "revelator" of the Ansaru Allah Community).

See also AHL AL-BAYT; ANGEL; *BIDAA*; BLASPHEMY; DREAMS; FLAG; GABRIEL; HERESY; HOLY BOOKS; IMAM; NIGHT OF DESTINY; PERFECT MAN; SAINT; SHIISM; WOMEN.

Kathleen M. O'Connor

Further reading: Muhammad ibn Ishaq, *The Life of Muhammad: A Translation of Ishaq's Sirat Rasul Allah.* Translated by Alfred Guillaume (London: Oxford University Press, 1967); Muhammad ibn Abd Allah al-Kisai, *The Tales of the Prophets (Qisas al-anbiya)*. Translated by W. M. Thackston, Jr. (1978. Reprint, Chicago: KAZI Pubs, 1997); Martin Lings, *Muhammad: His Life Based on the Earliest Sources* (1983. Reprint, Rochester, Vt.: Inner Traditions, 2006); Jane D. McAuliffe, "Mary and Fatima in Quranic Exegesis," *Islamochristiana* 7 (1981): 19–28; Gordon Darnel Newby, *The Making of the Last Prophet* (Columbia: University of South Carolina Press, 1989); Geoffrey Parrinder, *Jesus in the Quran*; Annemarie Schimmel, *And Muhammad Is His Messenger: The Veneration of the Prophet in Islamic Piety* (Chapel Hill: University of North Carolina Press, 1985); Brannon M. Wheeler, *Moses in the Quran and Islamic Exegesis* (London: Routledge, 2002); Brannon M. Wheeler, *Prophets in the Quran: An Introduction to the Quran and Muslim Exegesis* (New York: Continuum, 2002).

puberty rites   *See* CHILDREN; CIRCUMCISION.

purdah

A Persian and Urdu word meaning *curtain*, purdah most commonly refers to practices of sexual segregation by Muslims and Hindus in the Indian subcontinent (INDIA, PAKISTAN, BANGLADESH). This separation of the sexes may be organized spatially, delegating separate areas for men and WOMEN in HOUSES or in public spaces. A barrier such as a screen or curtain may divide joint spaces, or different rooms in a building (or separate buildings altogether) may be assigned to each sex. The practice of purdah may also make use of women's garments, such as head scarves or the BURQA. Muslim practices of purdah are intended as a safeguard against illicit sexual contact between members of the opposite sex. Muslims in India likely assimilated the practice from Hindu customs that preceded the emergence of Islam in the area, although those bear significant historical differences from Muslim adaptations.

Muslim practices of purdah most likely developed as a way of enforcing the sexually modest behavior recommended in the QURAN and SUNNA. For example, quranic verses 24:30–31 call upon men and women to "lower their gaze" away from objects of sexual desire. Purdah practices in the subcontinent are mostly concentrated among members of the upper classes, thus frequently indicating elevated social status. It is important to note that practices of purdah vary significantly according to the surrounding social and cultural milieu, and they must be understood within their specific historical and cultural contexts.

See also HAREM; VEIL.

Aysha A. Hidayatullah

Further reading: Sitara Khan, *A Glimpse through Purdah: Asian Women—the Myth and the Reality* (Staffordshire, England: Trentham Books, 1999); Ruby Lal, *Domesticity and Power in the Early Mughal World* (Cambridge: Cambridge University Press, 2005); Hanna Papanek, "Purdah: Separate Worlds and Symbolic Shelter." In *Separate Worlds: Studies of Purdah in South Asia,* edited by Hanna Papanek and Gail Minault, 3–53. (Columbia, Mo.: South Asia Books, 1982).

purity and impurity   *See* ABLUTIONS; CIRCUMCISION; DIETARY LAWS; *HALAL.*

Q

Qadari School *See* MUTAZILI SCHOOL; THEOLOGY.

qadi *See* CRIME AND PUNISHMENT; *FIQH*; SHARIA.

Qadiri Sufi Order

The Qadiri *TARIQA* is one of the oldest and most widespread of the Sufi orders. It is named after ABD AL-QADIR AL-JILANI, a pious Hanbali jurist who lived in BAGHDAD in the 11th and 12th centuries. Abd al-Qadir was a Sufi ascetic and popular preacher, but he did not establish a formal Sufi organization in his lifetime. The development of the order that bears his name occurred in the centuries after his death, beginning with the efforts of his sons and other followers in IRAQ, with Baghdad as the center of their activity. A 14th-century biography credits his sons with spreading the Qadiri order throughout Islamdom, but it is more likely that it did not really begin to spread until the 14th century. Stories about Abd al-Qadir's miraculous powers gained wide circulation. Individual Qadiri shaykhs trained disciples, drawing from the teachings, meditation techniques, and ritual practices that were in circulation among other Sufi groups. Eventually the order acquired a more formal hierarchy and system of rituals and techniques, but it retained enough flexibility to adapt to different cultural environments. It traced its spiritual genealogy from Abd al-Qadir back to MUHAMMAD, through ALI BIN ABI TALIB (d. 661) and a number of other prominent Sufis and descendants of Muhammad's household.

The first branches outside of Iraq may have been in SYRIA, EGYPT, and YEMEN, and the Mongol invasions of the 13th and 15th centuries probably helped the order spread eastward to IRAN, AFGHANISTAN, and INDIA and westward to North Africa. The first branches in India were in the northwest and the Deccan, and they were favored by Muslim ruling elites in cities and towns. Among the most prominent Indian Qadiris were Muhammad Ghawth of Uchch (d. 1517), credited with introducing the order in India, and Miyan Mir (d. 1635), who was attributed with healing powers and claimed to be in spiritual contact with Abd al-Qadir. He later became the teacher of the Mughal prince DARA SHIKOH (d. 1659), who was deeply interested in both Muslim and Hindu mysticism. The Qadiris also established branches in Central Asia, China, and Southeast Asia, where they still exist. In Iraq the Ottoman Turks lavishly restored the shrine of Abd al-Qadir in 1535, but the order did not found any hospices in Istanbul, the Ottoman capital, until the 17th century. From there they established branches in Anatolia and southeastern Europe. In 1925 the new republican government of Mustafa Kemal ATATURK (d. 1938) officially banned the Qadiri order, as well as all other *tariqas,* in TURKEY. To the west, the Qadiris spread from MOROCCO southward into Mauritania and WEST AFRICA in the 18th and 19th centuries. Among the most prominent members to arise in that region were al-Mukhtar ibn Ahmad al-Kunti (d. 1811), a revered teacher and saint who inspired USMAN DAN FODIO (d. 1817), the founder of the SOKOTO CALIPHATE in Nigeria. The most famous Algerian Qadiri leader was ABD AL-QADIR AL-JIZAIRI (d. 1883), who led the resistance against French colonial expansion in North Africa until he surrendered in 1847. In the early 20th century a Turkish Qadiri branch joined with a branch of the RIFAI SUFI ORDER to form the Qadiri-Rifai Sufi Order, which now has branches in North America, Bosnia, and AUSTRALIA.

See also ASCETICISM; HANBALI LEGAL SCHOOL; OTTOMAN DYNASTY; SUFISM.

Further reading: Bradford G. Martin, *Muslim Brotherhoods in 19th Century Africa* (Cambridge: Cambridge University Press, 2003); S. A. A. Rizvi, *A History of Sufism in India.* 2 vols. (New Delhi: Munshiram Manoharlal, 1978–1983); J. Spencer Trimingham, *The Sufi Orders in Islam* (Oxford: Oxford University Press, 1971).

al-Qaida (also al-Qaeda; Arabic: the base, foundation)

The most infamous of the radical Islamic organizations to emerge in the late 20th/early 21st century is al-Qaida. It gained worldwide notoriety for the suicide attacks conducted by 19 of its members against the World Trade Center in New York City and the Pentagon in Washington, D.C., on September 11, 2001, that resulted in the immediate deaths of 2,974 civilians and rescue workers, plus countless other victims in the United States and abroad in the aftermath of the attacks. The effects of this catastrophe were still being felt globally nearly a decade later.

Al-Qaida's beginnings date back to the mid-1980s amidst the chaos caused by the Soviet Union's 1979 occupation of AFGHANISTAN and the civil war that ensued there when the Soviets finally left in 1989. Al-Qaida's founding members were drawn from young ARAB volunteers who wanted to assist the AFGHAN MUJAHIDIN in their fight against the Soviet military and its Afghan communist allies. They created the Arab *Mujahidin* Services Bureau (*Maktab al-khadamat li'l-mujahidin al-Arab,* MAK) in 1984, based in Peshawar, PAKISTAN. Its leaders were USAMA BIN LADIN (b. 1957), one of the wealthy sons of Muhammad bin Ladin (1906–67), SAUDI ARABIA's leading building contractor, and Ayman al-Zawahiri (b. 1951), a surgeon who came from a prominent Egyptian family of doctors, politicians, and scholars. Al-Zawahiri was a leader in the Jihad Group that had assassinated Egyptian president ANWAR AL-SADAT in 1981; in the 1980s he was seeking to reconstitute the group in exile after serving time in prison. Bin Ladin and al-Zawahiri had both been inspired by the radical Islamic ideology of SAYYID QUTB (d. 1966), a leading member of the MUSLIM BROTHERHOOD who had been executed in 1966 for conspiring against Egyptian president JAMAL ABD AL-NASIR (r. 1953–70). Another person who had greatly influenced the Arab *Mujahidin,* especially bin Ladin, was Abd Allah Azzam (1941–89), a charismatic Palestinian member of the Muslim Brotherhood and an advocate of global JIHAD and MARTYRDOM. He had first met bin Ladin while serving as imam at the King Abd al-Aziz ibn Saud University mosque in Jeddah, SAUDI ARABIA, during the early 1980s. He subsequently became an effective recruiter of Arab volunteers to fight in Afghanistan.

The Afghan *Mujahidin* and their Arab allies, funded by Saudi Arabia and the UNITED STATES through the Pakistani intelligence agency (ISI), considered the Soviet withdrawal from Afghanistan a God-given victory. The Arab jihadists, who had set up a training camp in Afghanistan during the war against the Soviets, dreamed of creating an Islamic state, but their hopes were dashed when civil war erupted among the heavily armed Afghan guerrilla factions. In August 1988 Azzam, bin Ladin, al-Zawahiri, and fellow Arab jihadists secretly met to form what they called "the Military Base" (*al-qaida al-askariyya*), an armed organization that evolved into the international terrorist group that attacked the United States in 2001. Bin Ladin was considered a hero by many young Saudis, but he was regarded with suspicion by Saudi authorities. In particular they were concerned about his opposition to the large influx of U.S. forces into Saudi Arabia at the time of the 1990 Gulf War against Iraq. As a consequence of Saudi opposition, al-Qaida's chief base of operations shifted from Afghanistan to SUDAN in 1992 at the invitation of the new Islamist government that had established itself there in a 1989 coup. Al-Qaida had limited success in Sudan, although it was in this period that bin Ladin began to publicize his hatred for the "Crusader-Jewish alliance" and the House of Saud. Under pressure from EGYPT, Saudi Arabia, and the United States, the Sudanese government expelled bin Ladin and associates from the country in 1996. Al-Qaida returned to Afghanistan, where it found safe haven under the auspices of the TALIBAN, a group of young militants who were emerging as the most dominant of the factions fighting in the Afghan civil war. The close relationship between the Taliban and al-Qaida lasted until 2001, when a U.S.-led international coalition invaded the country as a consequence of this relationship and its connection with the 9/11 attacks. Until that time, al-Qaida's encampments in Afghanistan provided training in guerrilla warfare and terrorist tactics to thousands of young jihadists coming mainly from the Middle East and Asia.

The ideology espoused by al-Qaida's leadership was drawn essentially from two sources: (1) the anti-Western jihadism of Sayyid Qutb as interpreted by Azzam and al-Zawahiri, and (2)

the puritanical reformism of MUHAMMAD IBN ABD AL-WAHHAB (d. 1791). The first formed in reaction to the secular authoritarianism of Abd al-Nasir's Egypt in the 1950s and 1960s, the second in conjunction with the establishment of Saudi rule in the Arabian Peninsula, together with funding made possible by that country's vast OIL revenues. The radical agenda of al-Qaida seeks the establishment of Islamic government based on the SHARIA through an elite vanguard of true believers engaging in jihad. However, its leaders have called upon all Muslims to participate in this struggle. Al-Qaida's ideology has been further shaped by the perception that it was Islam that had brought about the defeat of the Soviets in Afghanistan and that it would ultimately triumph over its remaining enemies, especially the United States and ISRAEL. The public declarations of bin Ladin and al-Zawahiri also list specific grievances for which they seek revenge. These include the corruption and immorality of the Saudis and other pro-U.S. rulers, the Israeli occupation of PALESTINE, the 1982 Israeli invasion of LEBANON, the stationing of U.S. troops in the land of Islam's two holy mosques (in Mecca and Medina), the deaths of Iraqi civilians caused by the U.S.-led embargo of the 1990s, and, most recently, the U.S.-led occupation of IRAQ.

Al-Qaida is a loosely knit organization, likened to clusters of grapes, a business consortium, or a network. Funded by governments and private donors, it disseminates its ideas through the Internet and has had some success in recruiting followers at the grass-roots level. Its organizational structure and outreach program have allowed it to operate on a global scale and elude detection of its centers of operation by American and other intelligence agencies. Although its exact size is impossible to gauge at this time, it is known to have gained its recruits from a volatile mix of idealistic young Muslims, drifters, and militant opponents of pro-U.S. governments such as Saudi Arabia, Israel, Egypt, Pakistan, and Afghanistan. Fifteen of the 19 hijackers on 9/11 were from Saudi Arabia. The 9/11 attacks were preceded by coordinated suicide bombings (seen as an al-Qaida trademark) against the American embassies in Kenya and Tanzania in August 1998, and against the USS *Cole,* a destroyer docked in the Yemeni port of Aden, in October 2000. After the U.S.-led coalition's 2003 invasion of Iraq, young Sunnis from various countries were recruited to form the "al-Qaida in Mesopotamia Group," a jihadist guerrilla organization under the leadership of Abu Musab al-Zarqawi (1966–2006), a Jordanian militant who had been marginally involved in the Afghan jihad. This group, though small in size, attacked U.S. troops and is suspected of having fomented Sunni-Shii conflict through a campaign of suicide bombings and assassinations, causing many civilian casualties. It also claimed responsibility for the bombing of a luxury hotel in Amman, Jordan, in 2005. Although Zarqawi is known to have been in communication with al-Zawahiri, there is no evidence of a direct chain-of-command connection between the two organizations. In addition, deadly public transportation bombings in Madrid in 2004 and London in 2006 were allegedly conducted by local al-Qaida cells, but no direct connection has been established. Most likely they were carried out by individuals who had been inspired by al-Qaida's propaganda. A group called al-Qaida in the Islamic Maghrib, which appears to be a spin-off from the Armed Islamic Group, has conducted bombings in ALGE-RIA to deadly effect since 2006. Al-Qaida has also been linked to terrorist attacks in Indonesia and the Philippines.

Al-Qaida's notoriety and continued existence has generated much controversy around the world between Muslims and non-Muslims, and among Muslims themselves, about the nature of its relation to Islam. Even though more is now known about the organization than in the past, a body of politicians, scholars, religious leaders, and editorialists persists in equating its ideology and use of violence with Islam as a whole, both in the distant past and in the current post–cold war period. This understanding has had an impact on policymak-ing, security measures, and military planning domestically and internationally. The chief defect in this line of thought is that it overlooks both the great diversity of forms Islam has assumed historically as well as the widespread rejection of al-Qaida's ideology and tactics by governments of Muslim-majority countries and ordinary Muslims. Another group of politicians, scholars, religious leaders, and editorialists has persisted in minimizing or denying any connection with Islam at all. While this denial may help temporarily deflect criticism and suspicion from Islam and Muslims, the vast majority of whom have nothing to do with al-Qaida and its spin-offs, it nevertheless fails to give serious consideration to the fact that al-Qaida's leaders and membership believe themselves to actually be good Muslims seeking to defend Islam and the wider Muslim UMMA from their enemies. Between the two extremes of polemics and apologetics there are more balanced understandings that are conducive to a better assessment of the nature of Islamic radicalism, the actual threat al-Qaida poses, and how to best proceed to counteract that threat. The report of the 9/11 Commission, for example, found, "most Muslims prefer a peaceful and inclusive vision of their faith . . . [and] are repelled by mass murder and barbarism whatever their justification." But it also concluded that bin Ladin and other Islamists "draw on a long tradition of extreme intolerance within one stream of Islam (a minority tradition)" that was "further fed by grievances stressed by bin Ladin and widely felt throughout the Muslim world."

See also ABD AL-RAHMAN, UMAR; ARAB-ISRAELI CONFLICTS; EUROPE; GULF WARS; ISLAMISM; JIHAD MOVEMENTS; PAN-ISLAMISM; WAHHABISM.

Further reading: Rohan Gunaratna, *Inside Al Qaeda: Global Network of Terror* (New York: Columbia University Press, 2002); Raymond Ibrahim, *The Al Qaeda Reader* (New York: Random House, 2007); National Commission on Terrorist Attacks upon the United States, *The 9/11 Commission Report: Final Report* (New

York: W.W. Norton, 2004); Osama bin Laden, *Messages to the World: The Statements of Osama bin Laden*, edited by Bruce Lawrence and translated by James Howarth (New York: Verso, 2005); Michael Wolfe and the Producers of Belief Net, eds., *Taking Back Islam: American Muslims Reclaim Their Faith* (Emmaus, Pa.: Rodale, 2002); Lawrence Wright, *The Looming Tower: Al-Qaeda and the Road to 9/11* (New York: Random House, 2006).

Qajar dynasty

The Qajar dynasty, which ruled IRAN from 1796 to 1925, was originally composed of a loose tribal federation in the northwest territories of Iran until 1796, when a SHAYKH named Agha Muhammad Khan defeated his rival shaykhs and declared himself the first Qajar shah of Iran. Although Khan was assassinated a year after taking power, his descendants managed to unify the country under a strong, centralized government, putting an end to the tribal warfare and civil strife that had gripped Iran for centuries.

Under the Qajar shahs, Iran went through an intense process of modernization and Westernization in nearly every sector of society. At the same time, the Qajars encouraged the blossoming of a distinctly Persian literary and artistic tradition, and they promoted a high level of philosophical and theological creativity unmatched in the rest of the Middle East at the time.

Despite these successes, however, the Qajar shahs were unable to escape the Anglo-Russian rivalry that dominated most of the 19th century. Consequently, they were powerless to keep Iran from being partitioned into British and Russian zones of influence. The loss of national sovereignty and the plundering of the country's natural resources by foreign powers led a coalition of merchants, clerics, and intellectuals in 1906 to force the Qajar shah, Mozaffar al-Din (r. 1896–1907), to accept a CONSTITUTION that created an elected parliament, or Majlis, transforming Iran into a constitutional monarchy. Yet, the constitution-

alists were promptly repressed by Russia, who feared that the rising sense of nationalism in Iran would compromise their political and economic interests in the region. Using the might of their Cossack forces, the Russians, with the support of the British, propped up a succession of weak-willed shahs on the Qajar throne. However, with the outbreak of World War I, the Russians and British recognized the need for strong leadership in Iran. As a result, they encouraged a coup d'état by the commander of the Cossack Brigade, REZA SHAH PAHLAVI (r. 1925–41), who, in 1925, put an end to the Qajar dynasty by declaring himself the first Pahlavi shah of Iran.

See also COLONIALISM; DEMOCRACY.

Reza Aslan

Further reading: Hamid Algar, *Religion and State in Iran: 1795–1906* (Berkeley: University of California Press, 1969); A. K. S. Lambton, *Qajar Persia* (London: I.B. Tauris, 1987); Hasan-e Fasai, *History of Persia under Qajar Rule.* Translated by Heribert Busse (New York: Columbia University Press, 1972).

Qalandar *See* DERVISH.

Qaramatians *See* ISMAILI SHIISM.

Qatar *See* GULF STATES.

qawwali

Qawwali is a form of Islamic MUSIC that has recently gained popularity in Europe and the Americas by the pioneering efforts of the late great Pakistani singer Ustad Nusrat Fateh Ali Khan (1948–97), but its roots are over 600 years old. *Qawwali* music is devotional music, traditionally sung by South Asian Sufi singers at religious festivals and Sufi shrines. A typical *qawwali* group has a lead singer, a few back-up singers, a harmonium player, a *tabla* player, and a chorus of men singing and clapping. The rhythmic drive of *qawwali* is powered by the clapping and the percussion, and this provides a dynamic backdrop to the searching and soulful singing associated with *qawwali*. *Qawwali* incorporates within its structure the classical music forms of *raag* (melody) and *taal* (rhythm).

Qawwali is the music of the South Asian Sufis, especially those belonging to the CHISHTI SUFI ORDER, who ultimately seek a complete spiritual union with God. Unlike orthodox Islam, SUFISM uses poetry and music in order to induce a mystical experience. The lyrics sung in *qawwali* include praises of God and MUHAMMAD, and they often employ metaphoric language and symbolic imagery in order to illustrate the pain of separation and the ecstasy of reunion. The poet is often characterized as the spurned and dejected lover, tirelessly searching for the Beloved/God. Thus, these Sufi compositions are profound on a number of levels; a mundane reading of the poetry paints a picture of a lover gone mad separated from the beloved, while a more symbolic reading illuminates the pain an individual soul feels when alienated from God. This is evident in the following lyrics from a poem by Bulhe Shah (d. 1758) of the Punjab:

> *Falling in love with you*
> *Was like taking a sip of poison*
> *Come my healer, forsaken, I am sad*
> *For your love has made me dance like mad*

(trans. Kartar Singh Dugal)

In addition to Bulhe Shah, *qawwali* singers use the compositions of other renowned South Asian medieval mystical poets in their songs, such as Amir Khusrow (d. 1325), Kabir (15th century), Guru Nanak (d. 1539), and Shah Husayn (d. 1599). The range of languages represented in *qawwali* is indicative of the great cultural and geographical diversity that Sufism seeks to incorporate. These languages include Persian, Arabic, Punjabi, Urdu, Hindi, Braj Basha, and Rajasthani.

See also MAJNUN AND LAYLA; SOUL AND SPIRIT.

Varun Soni

Further reading: Vikas Bhushan and Varun Soni, "Intoxicated Spirit: Nusrat Fateh Ali Khan and the Art of *Qawwali*," *Sufi* 44 (1999): 8–12; Regula Burckhardt Qureshi, "The Mahfil-e Sama: Sufi Practice in the Indian Context," *Islam and the Modern Age* 17 (1986): 133–166; Regina Burckhardt Qureshi, "Sama in the Royal Court of Saints: The Chishtiyya of South Asia." In *Manifestations of Sainthood in Islam,* edited by Grace Martin Smith and Carl W. Ernst, 111–127 (Istanbul: Editions Isis, 1994); Hiromi Lorraine Sakata, "The Sacred and the Profane: Qawwali Represented in the Performances of Nusrat Fateh Ali Khan," *The World of Music* 36, no. 3 (1994): 86–99.

qibla

The *qibla* is the Arabic term for the direction all Muslims face when they pray—toward the KAABA in MECCA. In MOSQUES the *qibla* is indicated by the MIHRAB, a concave niche located in the wall that faces Mecca, usually to the left of the pulpit (MINBAR) inside the main prayer hall. In addition to serving as the orientation for daily PRAYER, the *qibla* is also the direction toward which the dead are oriented when they are buried, and animals are turned toward it when sacrificed in accordance with Muslim DIETARY LAWS. Conversely, observant Muslims *avoid* facing the *qibla* when they relieve themselves, and they avoid sleeping or sitting with their feet toward it so as not to insult the holiness of Islam's most sacred place.

Orientation in prayer had become a practice among Jews and Christians in the Middle East well before Islam's appearance in the seventh century. Ancient Jews, the Israelites, faced toward the temple on Zion in JERUSALEM. Later, the Holy Ark containing the scrolls of the TORAH was placed in front of the synagogue wall that faced Jerusalem, so that worshippers prayed toward both the Torah and

Jerusalem. In a parallel manner, Christian churches were built with the altar on the eastern side, oriented toward the rising sun. Such practices are still common among Orthodox Jews and Christians.

Islamic accounts differ about which direction Muhammad prayed when he still lived in Mecca before the HIJRA to MEDINA in 622. Some say he faced toward the Kaaba, others say that he faced toward Syria (probably Jerusalem). Later sources tried to reconcile these two different accounts by saying that he prayed on the south side of the Kaaba facing northward, which allowed him to face both that shrine and Jerusalem at once. The decisive moment, however, came after the emigration to Medina, where the first *qibla* recognized by the new Muslim community was Jerusalem. Then, perhaps as a result of the failure of Jews in Medina to recognize Muhammad as their prophet, the following revelation was received: "Therefore we shall turn you toward a *qibla* that will please you. Turn your face toward the Sacred Mosque; wherever you may be, turn your face toward it" (Q 2:144). At this point in their early history, Muslims began to make a clear break with Jews and Christians, setting the course for Islam's emergence as a distinct religious tradition. Later commentators maintained that in changing the prayer direction Muhammad was simply returning to the original *qibla* of ABRAHAM.

The QURAN, together with the HADITH and community consensus, established the Kaaba as the *qibla* for Islam. In theory, therefore, as conquest, trade, and travel took Muslims far away from Mecca, the *qibla* lines of orientation from all directions would converge at one point in Mecca, as long as one allowed for the curvature of the earth. In reality, however, *qibla* directions varied, even within the same city, like medieval CAIRO. The *qibla* of the Great Mosque in CORDOBA, Spain, faced south rather than southeast. This may have been because the builders were emulating the *qibla* of the UMAYYAD CALIPHATE (r. 661–750) far to the east in Damascus, SYRIA, where mosques face to the southward to Mecca. Orientation of other mosques may be affected by the natural or urban landscape, or imprecise mathematical calculations. Despite, and perhaps because of, such variations, and with the benefit of advances in MATHEMATICS and SCIENCE between the ninth and 14th centuries, Muslim astronomers and geographers went to great lengths to calculate the exact *qibla* from a given locality. Syrian astronomer Shams al-Din al-Khalili (14th century) finally found the trigonometric formula for determining the exact *qibla* from any longitude and latitude on the surface of the earth, and *qibla* compasses were developed soon thereafter. Based on these methods, Muslims living in the mainland United States and Canada have determined that their prayer direction is to the northeast.

Muslims have consulted each other and religious scholars to determine the *qibla* when they are not in a mosque. Now they are posting signs and using modern devices to do this, too. Hotel rooms in some Muslim countries have signs indicating the prayer direction, and satellite-guided *qibla* compasses can be found on passenger aircraft, such as those owned by Saudi Arabian Airlines. *Qibla* compasses are also widely available for purchase, and they can be programmed in digital watches, cellular phones, and computers.

See also FUNERARY RITUALS.

Further reading: David A. King, "Architecture and Astronomy: The Ventilators of Medieval Cairo and Their Secrets," *Journal of the American Oriental Society* 104, no. 1 (1984): 97–133; ———, *Astronomy in the Service of Islam* (Aldershot, England: Varorium, 1993); Nuha N. N. Khoury, "The Mihrab: From Text to Form," *International Journal of Middle East Studies* 30 (1998): 1–27; F. E. Peters, *Muhammad and the Origins of Islam* (Albany: State University of New York Press, 1994), 207–209.

qiyas *See* FIQH.

al-Quds *See* JERUSALEM.

Quran (Arabic: recitation, reading)

The Quran is the sacred scripture of ISLAM. Muslims believe it contains the infallible word of God as revealed to MUHAMMAD the Prophet in the Arabic language during the latter part of his life, between the years 610 and 632 in the Western calendar. They also hold that it is the last of a sequence of revealed books delivered to humankind through history, but, because previous scriptures, particularly the TORAH and GOSPEL, had become corrupted, it is the most perfect of all revelations. Through recitation, worship, exegesis, and the art of CALLIGRAPHY, Muslims have made it part of daily life wherever they are.

The Quran is about the same length as the Christian New Testament. It consists of 114 chapters called suras. These chapters are organized roughly by length, from longest to shortest, excepting the opening one, the FATIHA, which is a short prayer asking for God's guidance and blessing. There is no logical or narrative connec-

Page from an Arabic Quran manuscript showing the first verses of sura 39, Maghribi script (North African Style) 13th–14th century. (*Art Resource/The Metropolitan Museum of Art*)

tion between one chapter and the next, which makes it a challenge for beginners to read without guidance. The Quran's structure contrasts with that of the first books of the Hebrew Bible and the New Testament's Gospels and Book of Acts, which follow a narrative sequence (from creation to the destruction of the Jerusalem Temple and the return from exile in the former, and the ministries of Jesus and his disciples in the latter). Corresponding to beginning with the Fatiha, the Quran ends with two short chapters known as the "protecting" ones (Q 113 and 114), because they ask God's protection from evil.

To facilitate memorization and recitation of the sacred text, Islamic tradition has given each of the Quran's chapters a distinctive title. In a few cases the title assigned is indicative of the chapter's content, such as the sura of Yusuf (Q 12), which tells the story of the biblical JOSEPH, the son of Jacob. Likewise for the chapters named for MARY (Q 19) and Noah (Q 71), which include versions of the Bible stories about these figures, as well as the sura of The Cave (Q 18), which contains a story about a group of youths who escape persecution for their beliefs by hiding in a cave. A number of chapters in the latter part of the Quran have names that identify them with events associated with the end of the world and JUDGMENT DAY, such as The Resurrection (Q 75), The Tidings (Q 78), The Folding Up (Q 81), Splitting Apart (Q 82), and The Earthquake (Q 99). The names of other chapters are derived from the mysterious letters with which some of them begin, such as Q 9 Qaf, Q 20 Ta-Ha, and Q 36 Ya-Sin. Most chapters, including many of those already mentioned, obtain their titles from a unique word or name that occurs in them. Thus, Q 2 is called al-Baqara (The Cow), a word that occurs only in this chapter (verses 67–69, 71). Sura 16 is named The Bee (*nahl*) after the bee mentioned only in verse 68, and sura 96 is entitled The Blood Clot (*alaq*) because this word occurs in verse 2 and nowhere else in the Quran.

Each chapter in the Quran is divided into verses (sing. AYA). The Quran has more than 6,200 verses that vary in length from one letter (Q 50:1) or word (Q 89:1) to several sentences (Q 5:40). All chapters but one (Q 9) begin with the BASMALA, a liturgical citation of God's name, but only in the first sura is it counted as a verse. Other oft-cited verses in the Quran have also acquired their own names, such as the Throne Verse (Q 2:255), the Light Verse (Q 24:35), and the Sword Verse (Q 9:5). Verses in the shorter chapters, many of them counted among the early revelations received by Muhammad, often share an end-rhyming pattern of prose known as *saj,* but in the longer chapters they usually do not rhyme. The physical divisions between verses are usually marked by circles or florets in Quran manuscripts, but in modern print editions they are numbered due to the influence of the modern Euro-American practice of numbering verses in print editions of the Bible.

Manuscript and print editions of the Quran also show other kinds of organization. One of these is to distinguish chapters revealed when Muhammad lived in MECCA (610–622 C.E.) from those associated with the Medinan phase of his career (622–632 C.E.). The classification of Meccan and Medinan suras can usually be found at the head of each sura, next to its title. However, Muslim commentators and jurists have also recognized that a chapter classified as Medinan may contain Meccan verses in it, which suggests editing of the quranic text at some time after it was first composed. To facilitate memorization and recitation of the entire Quran, Muslims have also divided it into 30 portions (sing. *juz*) of equal length, which they have further subdivided into two equal parts (sing. *hizb*). The markings for these divisions can be found in Quran manuscripts and in most printed editions in Arabic.

Muslims believe that the Quran, the speech of God, provides guidance in all matters of FAITH, action, and the attainment of eternal salvation. In support of this belief, the Quran declares,

That is the book in which there is no doubt,
a proper guide for those who fear God, who

believe in the unseen, perform prayer, and disburse (in charity) what he has granted to them. (It is the book) of those who believe in what has been revealed to you (Muhammad), what was revealed before you, and who are certain about the hereafter. They are the ones who are guided rightly by their lord and who are prosperous. (Q 2:2–5)

The Quran's leading theme is the declaration that there is only one all-powerful, all-knowing, and merciful God (ALLAH) who alone created the universe and governs all that is in it. Another theme is that as the creator of human beings, God makes his will known to them through signs and revelations delivered by prophets sent throughout history in order to guide them to salvation and warn them away from damnation. The Quran tells this religious history by referring to biblical stories about figures such as ABRAHAM, Joseph, MOSES, DAVID, and JESUS and how their communities, called the PEOPLE OF THE BOOK, often rejected them. In doing so it placed Muhammad directly or indirectly among these former prophets and identified its message with theirs. Indeed, Muslims have regarded the Quran as the culmination of these earlier revelations, correcting the errors that people have introduced to them. In addition to biblical figures, the Quran also mentions Arabian prophets such as Salih (Q 7:73–79) and Shuayb (Q 7:84–93).

In the Quran the theme of salvation is linked to the idea that human beings are divided into believers and disbelievers, the righteous and the wrongdoers, who are all to be held accountable for their beliefs and actions at the end of the world on JUDGMENT DAY, when all the dead will be resurrected. Those judged to be among the righteous will be rewarded with a blissful life in paradise, and sinners will suffer the agonies of the hell-fire. The Quran provides graphic descriptions of the blessings and punishments that people will receive in the AFTERLIFE, and, like the Bible, it also gives an accounting of the rewards and punishments people have experienced in history because of their belief or disbelief. In several chapters linked to the Medinan period of Muhammad's life, the Quran calls upon believers to fight "in the path of God" against disbelievers and PEOPLE OF THE BOOK opposed to them, which has led non-Muslims to conclude that violence and hatred are significant themes in the Quran. Although some Muslims have chosen to interpret their scripture in this limited way, it is also important to point out that many Muslims do not accept this understanding, pointing to verses that uphold the values of peaceful coexistence and acceptance of religious and cultural differences. Moreover, some modern commentators and reformers have argued that the more militant verses in the Quran pertained only to specific circumstances faced by Muhammad and his small community in their struggle for survival in MEDINA, and that they were not intended to be universally applicable.

The themes of God's oneness, REVELATION, prophecy, individual accountability, and the Last Judgment would mean little if they were not connected to a code of ETHICS AND MORALITY that links individuals to society. The Quran calls upon people to perform acts of charity, especially for orphans and the needy, and oppose greed, oppression, and wrongdoing. It also affirms family life by legislating on matters of marriage, ADULTERY, DIVORCE, and inheritance. The pre-Islamic Arabian practice of slaying infant girls was prohibited, as was usury and gambling. The Quran also provides rules governing worship, lawful and prohibited FOOD AND DRINK, relations with non-Muslims, as well as the division of the spoils of war. Although the number of legislative verses, found mainly in the Medinan suras, is small in comparison with nonlegislative ones, the Quran is one of the fundamental "roots" of the SHARIA, or Islamic law.

The Quran's accounts of prophets before Muhammad attribute miraculous signs to them. It states that people of Muhammad's time challenged him to produce similar wonders, to which the Quran replies, "Is it not sufficient that we have revealed to you (Muhammad) the book that is recited to them? In that there is a mercy and reminder for a people who believe" (Q 29: 50–51). From this and similar declarations the ULAMA developed the doctrine of the Quran's miraculous nature, or inimitability (ijaz). They said it was miraculous because its language and style could not be replicated in ordinary human speech, its chapters and verses were uniquely arranged, it spoke of past and future events of which Muhammad had no knowledge, it revealed God's names and attributes, its laws and commandments were universal in application, and, unlike other HOLY BOOKS, it has remained unaltered since it was revealed to Muhammad. Some Muslims today assert that the Quran also speaks to modern scientific theories, such as those concerning the origin of the universe and the genetic code. Such beliefs have been contested by non-Muslims and Euro-American scholars, as well as skeptical Muslims. Nevertheless, the consensus reached by many Muslims through the ages has been that the Quran is Muhammad's chief MIRACLE and proof of the truth of his prophethood.

Belief in the Quran's miraculous nature, taken together with a desire to place its origins on a par with Jewish belief in the revelation of the Torah on Mt. Sinai and Christian belief in Jesus as the word of God incarnate, has inspired the belief held by many Muslims that the angel GABRIEL revealed the entire Quran to Muhammad on the NIGHT OF DESTINY (laylat al-qadr), one of the last nights in the month of RAMADAN. This belief, not stated by the Quran itself, is in tension with the view endorsed by Islamic historical sources that the Quran was revealed piecemeal during Muhammad's life, between 610 C.E. and 632 C.E., and that it was collected into a physical book (mushaf) only after his death. Early commentaries and Islamic historical sources support this understanding of the Quran's early development, although they are unclear in other respects. They report that the third CALIPH,

UTHMAN IBN AFFAN (r. 644–656) ordered a committee headed by Zayd ibn Thabit (d. ca. 655), Muhammad's scribe, to establish a single authoritative recension of the Quran. Uthman reportedly had divergent versions, which were being used in different parts of the early Muslim community, destroyed. To avoid disputes, everyone was to use a single version of the Quran, known as the Uthmanic codex, its technical name, which Muslims believe to be the canonical version used today. The first copies were sent from Medina to the cities of Mecca, DAMASCUS, Basra, and Kufa (the latter two are in Iraq).

Islamic sources indicate that during Muhammad's lifetime his Companions had both memorized the revelations and written them on palm branches, stone tablets, and the shoulder blades of animals. They also state that there was a pre-Uthmanic version of the Quran in the hands of his predecessor ABU BAKR (r. 632–634), which had been collected out of a concern that the verses would be lost or forgotten when Muhammad's Companions died. Abu Bakr's copy was passed on to Hafsa, one of Muhammad's widows and daughter of the caliph UMAR IBN AL-KHATTAB (r. 634–644). This was probably one of the main copies used in the creation of Uthman's codex. Nevertheless, evidence from coins, early inscriptions, and texts tells us that there continued to be non-Uthmanic versions of the Quran circulating in the Muslim community after the seventh century. A 10th-century source (Abu Dawud al-Sijistani, d. 929) indicates that there were as many as 28 codices at that time. Moreover, because early Arabic manuscripts of the Quran were often written without vowels and markings to differentiate consonants, variant "readings" of the Uthmanic codex arose in the far-flung lands of the Arab Muslim empire. At the apex of the ABBASID CALIPHATE (10th century), the consensus was that there were seven authorized readings. The standard edition printed today was first published in 1923 in CAIRO; it is based on the eighth-century "reading" of Kufa in IRAQ. The numbering of verses in the Cairo edition has become the standard for most modern printings of the Quran.

The Quran holds a place of primary importance in the history of Islam and in the daily life of Muslims. It is considered a foundational document in matters of EDUCATION, law, THEOLOGY, and history. Children begin their religious education by learning how to read and recite it in Arabic, believed the unadulterated language of God's revelation. All Muslims must memorize short chapters of the Quran in order to perform their daily prayers. Some choose to memorize the entire book. The ulama have had to go even greater lengths to gain advanced levels of expertise in its language and rhetoric. Indeed, a work of religious scholarship would be considered inadequate if it were to omit quranic quotations. Consequently, a sizeable body of literature about the Quran has been produced through the centuries by ulama working in the major centers of Islamic learning. Perhaps the most important genre of writings concerning the Quran is that of TAFSIR, or scriptural exegesis. This Islamic "science" has helped Muslims both maintain the integrity of God's revelations in their original language and make them a part of their lives in times and places quite distant from seventh-century Arabia, even in modern Europe and the Americas.

The artful recitation of the Quran, known as *tajwid* and *tartil,* is another way in which the Quran has been incorporated into the life of the Muslim community. The Quran can be recited by individuals in order to gain divine blessing (BARAKA) and forgiveness, but recitations are also performed on formal occasions such as at large assemblies and during funerals and mourning rites. Quran reciters can attain a reputation comparable to that of opera stars, and several countries hold national Quran recital competitions. Recorded recitations of the Quran are available in all the electronic media, making it possible for Muslims to listen to them at home, work, or while traveling. In addition to artful recitation, the Quran is also quoted in Friday sermons, and quranic phrases have even entered everyday speech, especially in countries where Arabic is the native language.

Complementing the art of recitation is that of CALLIGRAPHY. Great care was taken in rendering the sacred text of the Quran in writing. The cursive Arabic script lends itself to a wide variety of forms and styles, from the simplest to the most complex, as is evident in the countless Quran manuscripts that have been produced through the centuries. Prior to the modern period the most magnificent manuscripts were created by professional calligraphers at the behest of rulers and wealthy patrons. Although today most people have printed editions of the Quran, small numbers of handwritten copies of the Quran continue to be produced. During the Middle Ages the calligraphic rendering of verses and chapters from the Quran was carried from the medium of paper to that of ARCHITECTURE. Beautiful quranic inscriptions can still be seen on great Islamic monuments in Egypt, Palestine, Turkey, Iran, Central Asia, and India. Examples are the mosques of al-AZHAR and Sultan Hasan in Cairo, the DOME OF THE ROCK in Jerusalem, the Sultan Ahmad and Suleymaniye mosques of ISTANBUL, the Shaykh Lutfallah Mosque of Isfahan, the Tilakari madrasa of Samarkand, the Qutb Minar of Delhi, and Agra's Taj Mahal. Quranic calligraphy continues to be an important part of modern mosque design, too. Muslims also place artfully rendered verses from the Quran in the form of posters and wall hangings in their homes, schools, places of work, and even cars and trucks. Copies of the entire *mushaf* can be found displayed in these locations, although sometimes it is kept in a colorful box for protection from the elements.

See also ALMSGIVING; AMULETS AND TALISMANS; ARABIAN RELIGIONS, PRE-ISLAMIC; ARABIC LANGUAGE AND LITERATURE; BOOKS AND BOOKMAKING; *KAFIR*; PROPHETS AND PROPHECY.

Further reading: Farid Esack, *The Quran: A User's Guide* (Oxford: Oneworld Publications, 2005); Jane Dam-men McAuliffe, ed., *The Cambridge Companion to the Quran* (Cambridge: Cambridge University Press, 2006); Kristina Nelson, "The Sound of the Divine in Everyday Life." In *Everyday Life in the Middle East,* edited by Donna Lee Bowen and Evelyn A. Early, 257–261 (Bloomington: Indiana University Press, 2002); Abu Ammaar Yasir Qadhi, *An Introduction to the Sciences of the Quran* (Birmingham, England: Al-Hidaayah Publishing and Distribution, 1999); Fazlur Rahman, *Major Themes of the Quran* (Minneapolis: Bibliotheca Islamica, 1980); Michael Sells, *Approaching the Quran: The Early Revelations* (Ashland, Oreg.: White Cloud Press, 1999); W. Montgomery Watt and Richard Bell, *Introduction to the Quran* (Edinburgh: University of Edinburgh Press, 1970).

Quraysh

The tribe that dominated MECCA when MUHAMMAD (ca. 570–632) was born was the Quraysh. It was composed of 10 main clans. The Banu Hashim clan was the one to which Muhammad belonged. Another clan, the Abd Shams, was more wealthy and powerful. Both branches played very important roles in the first centuries of Islamic history.

The Quraysh profited from control of the holy sites in Mecca and the caravans that traveled to YEMEN and SYRIA. They were also responsible for taking care of pilgrims who came to worship at the KAABA, the leading temple in Mecca. Muslim historians claimed that the Quraysh were descendants of ABRAHAM and Ishmael, the builders of the Kaaba. According to these accounts, the Quraysh became dispersed for about seven centuries after the time of Ishmael. Qusayy, one of Muhammad's ancestors, reunited the tribe in Mecca. He claimed the right to take care of the Kaaba and feed and water pilgrims. In the history of religions it is very common for a particular family or clan to be in charge of operating holy places, and Mecca was no exception. When Qusayy died, his sons took control and divided the city into quarters in which the different tribes and clans were to reside. One of his grandsons, Hashim, was Muhammad's great grandfather. He was known for his involvement in the caravan trade and was responsible for providing FOOD AND DRINK to pilgrims. His descendants are called the Banu Hashim, the sons of Hashim. Muhammad's grandfather, Abd al-Muttalib, followed in his father's footsteps, but he was also said to have been involved in organizing a successful defense of Mecca when it was threatened by an army from Yemen. This event was mentioned in sura 105 of the QURAN, entitled *Al-Fil* (The Elephant) because these animals were used in the army of the invaders. Abd al-Muttalib is also remembered for having discovered the sacred well of ZAMZAM, next to the Kaaba.

The Quraysh gave Muhammad his first converts and his first opponents. They also participated in the founding of the Islamicate civilization that flourished in lands between the Atlantic Ocean and eastern Iran during the Middle Ages. In the Quran they were included among both the believers (*muminun*) who are promised paradise and the disbelievers (*kafirun*) who are threatened with damnation. The first four caliphs to succeed Muhammad as leaders of the community, known as the Rashidan, were all of the Quraysh: ABU BAKR (r. 632–634), UMAR IBN AL-KHATTAB (r. 634–644), UTHMAN IBN AFFAN (r. 644–655), and ALI IBN ABI TALIB (r. 655–661). Leading women in Muhammad's life were from the same tribe—his wives KHADIJA, Hafsa, and AISHA. Most of the EMIGRANTS who participated in the HIJRA in 622 were from the Quraysh. Moreover, according to the Quran commentaries, the Arabic language of the Quran was said to have been in their dialect. The members of Muhammad's family who are considered the ideal Imams by the Shia are, of course, also members of the Banu Hashim clan. On the other hand, powerful members of the Abd Shams persecuted Muhammad and his followers. They plotted against his life, organized armies to fight him after he took up residence in Medina, and prevented him and his followers from fulfilling their pilgrimage obligations. In 630 the leader of the Abd Shams, Abu Sufyan (d. 653), converted to Islam and surrendered Mecca to Muhammad and his army, allowing the holy city to be taken peacefully. Later, the sons of Abu Sufyan and other members of the Abd Shams clan founded the UMAYYAD CALIPHATE (661–750) in DAMASCUS. This dynasty was eradicated by members of the Banu Hashim clan who claimed descent from Muhammad's paternal uncle Abbas. They established the ABBASID CALIPHATE that ruled Islamicate civilization until they were destroyed by Mongol invaders in 1258. Indeed, according to medieval Islamic political writings, one of the qualifications for a person to be CALIPH was that he be a male of Quraysh descent.

The legacy of the Quraysh lives on today. All the Sufi orders claim spiritual descent from Muhammad through either Ali or Abu Bakr. Many Shii religious authorities are considered to be blood relatives of Muhammad, which makes them members of the Banu Hashim. The kings of MOROCCO and JORDAN claim to be his heirs, as reflected in the official name of Jordan, which is called the Hashimite Kingdom. Also, BEDOUIN tribes living in the vicinity of Mecca today still claim to be of the Quraysh.

See also AHL AL-BAYT; AUTHORITY; COMPANIONS OF THE PROPHET; *FITNA*; HASHIMITE DYNASTY; *KAFIR*; SHIISM; SUFISM.

Further reading: Patricia Crone and Martin Hinds, *God's Caliph: Religious Authority in the First Centuries of Islam* (Cambridge: Cambridge University Press, 1986); Marshall G. S. Hodgson, *The Venture of Islam: The Classical Age of Islam*. Vol. 1 (Chicago: University of Chicago Press, 1974); F. E. Peters, *Muhammad and the Origins of Islam* (Albany: State University of New York Press, 1994).

Qurtuba   *See* CORDOBA.

qutb   *See* WALI.

Qutb, Sayyid (1906–1966) *leading ideologue of the Muslim Brotherhood*

Sayyid Qutb is widely considered today to be one of the founders and intellectual forebears of modern Islamist movements. Qutb was born and raised in the Egyptian village of Musha, where he was educated from a young age in the QURAN, having memorized it by age 10. His early career ranged from being a teacher for the Ministry of Public Instruction to an author, literary critic, and journalist. He was at first actively involved in nationalist politics, and for a time was a firm supporter of the Wafd Party. In 1948 he went to the UNITED STATES to study the American EDUCATION system, receiving a master's degree from Colorado State College of Education (now University of Northern Colorado) in 1950.

While in the United States Qutb witnessed what he considered to be the immorality, sexual promiscuity, and materialism of the United States and the West, and this partially impelled him into his career as an Islamist. Upon returning to EGYPT in 1951, Qutb joined the MUSLIM BROTHERHOOD, where he was an outspoken critic of Egyptian president JAMAL ABD AL-NASIR (r. 1953–70) and his regime, becoming the organization's key ideologue and filling the vacuum left by the DEATH of the HASAN AL-BANNA, the Muslim Brotherhood's founder, in 1949. Under Qutb, the Muslim Brotherhood became more radical than it had been under his predecessor. After the attempted assassination of Nasir in 1954, Qutb, along with other members of the Muslim Brotherhood, was imprisoned, and he himself was tortured. While in prison Qutb wrote his two most important works: *In the Shade of the Quran,* a commentary on the Quran, and *Signposts on the Road* (often shortened to *Signposts* or *Milestones*; Arabic: *Maalim fi al-tariq*).

In *Signposts,* Qutb vigorously attacked the Nasir regime, its SECULARISM, and the social inequalities that he believed were perpetuated by it. Although *Signposts* is clearly a scathing polemic aimed largely at the Egyptian government, it has been widely translated and remains an enormously influential text well past his lifetime and well beyond Egypt's national borders. Qutb set forth many of the ideas and themes that would recur in the ideologies of a wide variety of subsequent Islamist thinkers, from the assassins of Egypt's president ANWAR AL-SADAT (r. 1970–81) all the way to USAMA BIN LADIN (b. 1957). Part of the appeal of *Signposts* stems from its novel evocation of traditional and familiar Islamic symbols and application of them to the modern world, including, for example, a reinterpretation of the term *JAHILIYYA*. Qutb redefined the meaning of the term, which originally meant the "age of ignorance" before Islam, and he applied it to the modern period, when he accused secular and Muslim rulers of governing in blatant opposition to God's will and making a mockery of the traditional, "pure" Islam. Qutb also rejected Nasir's secular Egyptian and Arab nationalism based on national borders and language, and indeed rejected all modern political systems, including COMMUNISM, socialism, and DEMOCRACY. Instead, Qutb called for a JIHAD to be led by a unique Islamic vanguard to establish a single Islamic polity, based on his interpretation of the early Islamic community of Muhammad that encompassed all Muslims, regardless of nationality or language. *Signposts* offered a blueprint for how to bring this revolution about.

Qutb was released from prison in 1964, but he was rearrested in 1965, tried, and executed by hanging in 1966. Although many today regard Qutb as an Islamic "fundamentalist" intent on bringing back "original" Islam, Qutb's ideas and ISLAMISM itself are in reality a distinctly modern phenomenon—they are a response to the rapid urbanization, population growth, Westernization, and widespread poverty that characterize the modern world in many countries. Further, there is little about Qutb's ideas that Muslims even 20 years before him would have recognized; his application of *jahiliyya* to modern life, his ideas about political revolution, and many other aspects of Qutb's thought would have been inconceivable before his time.

See also JIHAD MOVEMENTS; RENEWAL AND REFORM MOVEMENTS.

Joshua Hoffman

Further reading: John Calvert and William Shepard, *A Child from the Village* (Syracuse, N.Y.: Syracuse University Press, 2004); Gilles Kepel, *Muslim Extremism in Egypt: The Prophet and the Pharaoh.* Translated by Jon Rothschild (Berkeley: University of California Press, 2003); Sayyid Qutb, *Milestones.* Translated by Ahmad Zaki Hammad (Indianapolis: American Trust Publications, 1993); William Shepard, *Sayyid Qutb and Islamic Activism: A Translation and Critical Analysis of Social Justice in Islam* (Leiden: E.J. Brill, 1996).

R

Rabia al-Adawiyya (Rabia al-Basriyya, Rabia al-Qaysiyya) (ca. 717–801) *legendary female Muslim mystic and saint, considered to be one of the first Sufis*

What is known about Rabia al-Adawiyya is culled from many different hagiographic sources spanning several centuries, and it is not easy to separate fact from legend. Indeed, Rabia's legend has developed over time, but she is most famous for her ascetic lifestyle, weeping over her separation from God, for whom she developed a profound love.

Born in Basra during the Abbasid era, she was most likely influenced by her socioreligious milieu. Basra housed a school for WOMEN ascetics at a time when an impulse for ASCETICISM was increasing. Basra was also the home of the renowned ascetic al-HASAN AL-BASRI (642–728), with whom Rabia was often associated in legend, although the two probably never met. However, there is no reason to doubt the accounts of her contemporary al-Jahiz (d. 868) regarding her association with other female mystics and her ascetic lifestyle. According to some sources, Rabia was a slave of the al-Atik clan until freed by her master when he recognized her great spiritual attainment. She then dedicated her life to the continuous worship of God.

It is interesting to note the different ways in which Rabia's figure has been constructed and reinterpreted over the centuries, as those who told her stories shaped and reshaped her legacy. For example, al-Jahiz's stories of Rabia simply portrayed a self-denying ascetic from his community, who was known for refusing all worldly things. Her love was for God alone; she would not marry, nor let the promise of PARADISE or fear of the FIRE distract her from him. Approximately four hundred years later the Persian mystic Farid al-Din Attar depicted Rabia as possessing miraculous powers and a biting wit, in addition to her deep piety. In one story he described her as capable of flying in the sky on her carpet, and in another as illuminating the darkness with her fingers, which one night shone like lanterns. When she was making a pilgrimage to MECCA, the KAABA miraculously came to her. She was also often credited for her sarcastic rebukes of male disciples for being too worldly. A 1963 Egyptian film portrayed her as a beautiful young slave girl forced to perform Oriental dances by her master, but she then discovered God and dedicated her life to preaching and PRAYER. The famed Egyptian vocalist UMM KULTHOUM (d. 1975) recorded the songs for this movie. More recently, the Egyptian feminist writer Leila Ahmed has depicted her as a social rebel whose example has inspired Muslim women to free themselves from the limitations of their biological roles, and whose legend reflects countercultural understandings of gender.

Her devotees believe that her tomb is located on JERUSALEM's Mount of Olives in a 17th-century MOSQUE near a church that memorializes the place of JESUS's ascent into heaven. A modern mosque named in her honor has been built in a suburb of CAIRO, Egypt.

See also ABBASID CALIPHATE; SLAVERY; SUFISM.

Sophia Pandya

Further reading: Annemarie Schimmel, *My Soul Is a Woman.* Translated by Susan H. Ray (New York: Continuum International Publishing Group, 1997), 34–37; Michael Sells, *Early Islamic Mysticism: Sufi, Quran, Miraj, Poetic, and Theological Writings* (Mahwah, N.J.: Paulist Press, 1996), 151–170; Margaret Smith, *The Life and Work of Rabia and Other Women Mystics in Islam* (1928. Reprint, Oxford: Oneworld Publications, 1994); Abu Abd al-Rahman al-Sulami, *Early Sufi Women (Dhikr an-niswa al-mutaabbidat as-sufiyyat).* Translated by Rkia E. Cornell (Louisville, Ky.: Fons Vitae, 1999).

Rahim *See* BASMALA; NAMES OF GOD.

Rahman *See* BASMALA; NAMES OF GOD.

Rahman, Fazlur (1919–1988) *noted liberal Muslim intellectual, whose wide-ranging writings examined the Quran, Islamic history, philosophy, education, and politics*
Born in what is now PAKISTAN, Rahman earned a master's degree in Arabic from Punjab University in Lahore, Pakistan, in 1942 and a doctorate in Islamic PHILOSOPHY from Oxford University in 1949, where he studied under the noted Orientalist scholar, Hamilton A. R. Gibb (1895–1971).

Subsequently, he held academic positions at Durham University, McGill University, Pakistan's Central Institute of Islamic Research, the University of California-Los Angeles, and the University of Chicago, where he served until his death.

According to Rahman, the idea of socioeconomic JUSTICE is one central notion within the Quranic message. Rahman maintained that the most significant problems that emerged during Islam's medieval period were (1) religious and political hierarchies that perpetuated socioeconomic oppression and (2) educational systems that emphasized rote memorization and discouraged critical thinking.

According to Rahman, the QURAN, as well as the examples set by MUHAMMAD and the early Islamic community, requires majority-Muslim countries to institute democratic political systems. For example, Rahman believed that Muhammad and the early Islamic community governed their affairs by means of *shura* (consultation) and *IJMAA* (consensus) with the equality and freedom of all Muslims before God functioning as shared principles among early Muslims. Concomitantly, Rahman asserted that God has endowed human beings with a unique capacity to reason (*aql*) that can provide them with tremendous insight and good judgment as they democratically govern themselves. At the same time, modern Islamic educational systems must contribute to Islam-based democracies by encouraging critical thinking and immersing students in diverse academic disciplines. Rahman's main religious and political opponents were Pakistani Islamists who were members of the organization JAMAAT-I ISLAMI led by Sayyid Abu al-Ala Mawdudi. The most significant influence of Rahman's life and work is evident in some American colleges and universities where many of his former students teach; his long-term impact on Islamic political and educational systems remains to be seen.

See also DEMOCRACY; EDUCATION; ORIENTALISM; RENEWAL AND REFORM MOVEMENTS.

Jon Armajani

Further reading: Frederick Denny and Earle Waugh, eds., *The Shaping of an American Islamic Discourse: A Memorial to Fazlur Rahman* (Atlanta, Ga.: Scholars Press, 1998); Fazlur Rahman, *Islam* (Chicago: University of Chicago Press, 1979); ———, *Islam and Modernity: Transformation of an Intellectual Tradition* (Chicago: University of Chicago Press, 1990); ———, *Prophecy in Islam: Philosophy and Orthodoxy* (1958. Reprint, Chicago: University of Chicago Press; Midway Reprint, 2003); ———, *Revival and Reform in Islam: A Study of Islamic Fundamentalism,* edited by Ebrahim Moosa (Oxford: Oneworld, 2000).

Ramadan (also Ramazan; *Puasa* in Indonesia and Malaysia)

Ramadan is the ninth month of the Islamic CALENDAR—a time of obligatory FASTING for all able Muslims, and an important time for commemorating Islamic sacred history. The month-long fast is the fourth pillar of Islam and requires abstaining from all food, drink, and sexual activity during daylight hours. At the end of each day, the fast is broken with a light meal called *iftar* (breakfast). It is a month that fosters communal solidarity and individual piety. MOSQUE attendance increases at this time, and many Muslims fulfill their charitable obligations. In addition to ritual fasting, daily PRAYER, and acts of charity, observant Sunni Muslims also perform supererogatory prayers known as *tarawih* at night throughout the month. The Shia do not accept this form of prayer.

The onset of the month-long fast is determined visually when the new moon is sighted at the end of the eighth month, Shaaban. Similarly, the month ends with the sighting of the new moon of the 10th month, Shawwal, and the three-day feast of ID AL-FITR (the breakfast feast). First occurring during the summer on the pre-Islamic Arabian solar calendar, Ramadan became a lunar month with the advent of Islam, advancing 11 or 12 days each year relative to the solar calendar.

APPROXIMATE RAMADAN STARTING DATES 2008–2013

2008	September 1
2009	August 21
2010	August 11
2011	August 1
2012	July 20
2013	July 9

Ramadan is esteemed to be the holiest month of the year. This is partly because of its connection with the revelation of the QURAN. Muslims maintain that the entire holy book was revealed to MUHAMMAD on the NIGHT OF DESTINY (*Laylit al-Qadr*), which falls during the last few days of the month. To facilitate memorization and recitation, the Quran has been divided into 30 equal parts, one for each day of this month. People are encouraged to gather to listen to nightly recitations of the Quran and improve their own knowledge and memorization of the scripture. Also, it is widely held that God is most receptive to people's prayers at this sacred time, especially in the last few days of the month. Another reason for the month's special status is its historical connection with the first victory of Muslims against their Meccan enemies at Badr in 624, two years after the HIJRA (emigration) to MEDINA. The chapter of the Quran that has the most detailed instructions for the fast, *al-Baqara* (Q 2, The Cow), is one that is thought to have been revealed at this time. Some Euro-American historians of religion have plausibly argued, based on critical readings of the Quran and early Islamic historical texts, that the connection of Ramadan observances with both the revelation of a holy book and victory over enemies is patterned after pre-Islamic fasting and feasting traditions, especially Jewish observance of Yom Kippur and Passover, which are connected with the revelation of the TORAH to Moses and deliverance from the pharaoh of EGYPT.

Other events in Islamic sacred history that occurred during Ramadan include the death of KHADIJA (Muhammad's first wife) in 619, the birth of FATIMA (Muhammad's daughter and mother of the Shii Imams), the assassination of ALI IBN ABI TALIB (the fourth CALIPH and first Shii IMAM) in 661, and the MARTYRDOM of Ali al-Rida (the eighth Shii Imam) in 818.

Even though the month of fasting affirms the universal community of all Muslims, individual Muslim cultures observe Ramadan in a variety of ways that are shaped by local tradition. There are distinctive food traditions with respect to dishes and sweets eaten in the evening and pre-dawn hours. In North Africa a favorite recipe for breaking the fast is a creamy soup called *harira,* made of meat, chickpeas, lentils, tomatoes, and fresh herbs. Turks prepare a tripe soup served with a pocket bread called *ramadan pide* (pita). *Ramadaniyya,* a dessert made of dried fruits that have been soaked overnight, is a favorite in the Arabian Peninsula. Southeast Asian Muslims prepare special meat curry dishes and *dodol,* a dessert made of sugar, rice flour, and coconut milk.

Aside from different food traditions, Muslims have other ways of celebrating the month. In Egypt these include decorating streets and houses with colorful lanterns. In many Muslim countries special evening television programs are offered. Ramadan celebrations in many countries have become more commercialized in recent years, with luxury hotels offering expensive *iftar* banquets featuring popular entertainers. Since the 1980s in the United States, Ramadan has become the one Muslim holiday of which non-Muslims have become aware. Community newspapers publish features about how it is observed by the local Muslim population, including traditional food recipes. Since the terrorist attacks on September 11, 2001, Muslim organizations have participated increasingly in interfaith activities, including community *iftar* dinners with Christians and Jews. The White House has also honored this holy Islamic month by holding *iftar* dinners.

See also ALMSGIVING; CUSTOMARY LAW; FIVE PILLARS; FOOD AND DRINK; HOLIDAYS; JUDAISM AND ISLAM.

Further reading: Sarah Gauch, "Fasting Days, Festive Nights: Ramadan in Cairo," *Saudi Aramco World* 53 (January–February 2002): 60–65; S. D. Goitein, "Ramadan: The Muslim Month of Fasting." In *Studies in Islamic History and Institutions,* edited by S. D. Goitein, 90–100 (Leiden: E.J. Brill, 1966); Angelika Neuwirth, "Three Religious Feasts between Narratives of Violence and Liturgies of Reconciliation." In *Religion between Violence and Reconciliation,* edited by Th. Sheffler, 49–82 (Beirut/Würzburg: Erbon Verlag in Kommission, 2002).

Rashid Rida, Muhammad (1865–1935)
Islamic reformer and modernist

Muhammad Rashid Rida was born in Tripoli, SYRIA (present-day LEBANON), on September 23, 1865, to a family that claimed descent from MUHAMMAD. He was educated first in a traditional religious school and then at the National Islamic School in Tripoli. The curriculum at this school combined instruction in Islamic doctrine and law with European languages and the natural sciences. Here Rida learned to view SCIENCE, technology, and some European political ideas positively. During the same period Rida became convinced, through study of the medieval theologians AL-GHAZZALI (1058–1111) and IBN TAYMIYYA (1263–1328), that many contemporary Muslim religious practices and orders were unacceptable corruptions (sing. BIDAA) of ISLAM. He condemned Sufi rituals and popular saints festivals in particular. He was a prolific writer, producing several books, and worked most of his life as editor of the magazine *Al-Manar* (The beacon), which he founded in 1898. Rida is one of the most important and influential intellectuals who, through his writings, strove to reconcile Islam with modernity.

As a young man, Rida was deeply impressed by the Salafi reform movement founded in CAIRO by JAMAL AL-DIN AL-AFGHANI (1838–97) and his student MUHAMMAD ABDUH (1849–1905). Both men argued that Muslims needed to unify against external threats and internally reinvigorate Islam in order to resist COLONIALISM and Western domination. They encouraged Muslims to base their actions on the Quran and SUNNA and to abandon any traditional religious practices not supported by these texts. Together with their call to reopen the door to IJTIHAD, or reinterpretation of Islamic law in light of reason, these assertions undermined the leadership role of the traditional ULAMA. Upon the death of al-Afghani, Rida moved to Cairo to work with Muhammad Abduh, where he expanded access to Salafi thought through his magazine.

Rida was especially concerned about the backwardness he perceived in Muslim societies, which permitted them to be dominated by the European powers. In response to the challenges of World War I, and the breakup of the Ottoman Empire, Rida promoted a program of religious, political, and social reform that differed somewhat from that of his predecessors. Modern EDUCATION, in Rida's view, was sorely needed to enable the ARAB peoples to adopt positive elements of European civilization, including adoption of modern technical advances. He argued for the restoration of the CALIPHATE as a remedy for corrupt regimes who cooperated with the colonial powers. Rida later moved away from PAN-ISLAMISM toward pan-Arabism and is considered by some an early proponent of Arab nationalism. Rida reinterpreted the ideas of the early reformists and passed them on to succeeding Muslim intellectuals. Different aspects of his ideas have appealed to both secular modernists in Arab countries and Islamist activists.

See also ISLAMISM; RENEWAL AND REFORM MOVEMENTS; SALAFISM; SECULARISM.

Shauna Huffaker

Further reading: Albert Hourani, *Arabic Thought in the Liberal Age: 1798–1939* (1962. Reprint, Cambridge: Cambridge University Press, 1983), 222–244; Malcom H. Kerr, *Islamic Reform: The Political and Legal Theories of Muhammad Abduh and Rashid Rida* (Berkeley: University of California Press, 1966); Muhammad Rashid Rida, *The Muhammadan Revelation*. Translated by Yusuf DeLorenzo (Alexandria, Va.: Al-Saadawi Publications, 1996); Emad Eldin Shahin, *Through Muslim Eyes: M. Rashid Rida and the West* (Herndon, Va.: International Institute of Islamic Thought, 1993).

Rashidun   *See* ABU BAKR; ALI IBN ABI TALIB; CALIPH; UMAR IBN AL-KHATTAB; UTHMAN IBN AFFAN.

rasul   *See* PROPHETS AND PROPHETHOOD.

rawza khavani   *See* ASHURA.

ray   *See* IJTIHAD.

Refah Partisi (Turkish: Welfare Party)

The Refah Partisi (RP) is the name of an Islamist political party that operated in TURKEY from 1983 to 1998. Soon after the Republic of Turkey was founded in 1923, its first president MUSTAFA KEMAL ATATURK (d. 1938) pushed through a series of reforms aimed at breaking the hold of Islam over the state and society. Historically, Turkey's strong military has been a staunch defender of these secularist policies, and successive efforts to ease restrictions on Islamic education and worship starting in the 1950s have been met with military coups and the disbanding of political parties oriented toward Islam. When single-party rule ended in 1950, the new Democrat Party began easing restrictions that had been imposed on Islamic EDUCATION and worship, but it was closed following the military coup of 1960.

The first explicitly Islamic parties (the National Order Party in 1971 and the National Salvation Party in 1980) were formed under the leadership of Necmettin Erbakan (b. 1926), but they were closed in the succeeding military coups.

Erbakan was himself banned from politics following a 1980 coup, but in 1983 Islamists regrouped under a new party—Refah—of which Erbakan took control when his ban was lifted in 1987. The party grew steadily in strength, sweeping the local elections of 1994 and gaining important mayorships, including ISTANBUL and Ankara. In the parliamentary elections of 1995, Refah won 21.4 percent of the vote, a plurality, pressing other parties to join it to form a coalition. After much political wrangling, Refah managed to form a government in 1996, with Erbakan as the country's first Islamist prime minister.

Refah's success stemmed from its effective appeal to a segment of the Sunni population, which felt Turkey's secular attitude had repressed Islam, but also to its populist and anticorruption discourse, and to its strong grass-roots organization, which distributed food and other basic necessities to the poor. Erbakan sought closer ties with countries such as IRAN and LIBYA, and it openly supported the religious brotherhoods, which had been outlawed since 1925. These and other reform measures met with opposition from the military and the secular media, and, in 1997, under heavy pressure from the military, Erbakan resigned as prime minister. The Refah Party was closed in 1998, and Erbakan was again banned from politics.

Some Refah members resurfaced in the Fazilet (Virtue) Party, with a more Western orientation, focusing on DEMOCRACY, civil rights, and entrance into the European Union, but, despite its more moderate approach, Fazilet also ran into problems with the secularist forces, especially over the issue of WOMEN wearing headscarves. In 2001 Fazilet was also closed down, after which a split occurred in its ranks. The younger, more moderate faction formed the AKP (Justice and Development Party). Refah Party members have subsequently worked with the Fazilet (Virtue) Party and the AKP (Justice and Development) Party, the latter of which won a majority of parliamentary seats in the 2002 election, and it was able to form a government with Recep Tayyip Erdogan (b. 1954) as prime minister.

See also GOVERNMENT, ISLAMIC; HUMAN RIGHTS; ISLAMISM; POLITICS AND ISLAM; SECULARISM.

Mark Soileau

Further reading: Marvine Howe, *Turkey Today: A Nation Divided over Islam's Revival* (Boulder, Colo.: Westview Press, 2000); David Shankland, *Islam and Society in Turkey* (Huntingdon, U.K.: Eothen Press, 1999).

refugees

Civilians who are forced to flee their homes to escape violence or persecution are known as refugees. Several major refugee migrations are known in the history of Islam before the modern era. These include the flight of Muslims to SYRIA and EGYPT in the west and INDIA in the east to escape the onslaught of the Mongol armies that invaded the Middle East in the 13th century, and again in the 14th and 15th centuries. These refugees contributed significantly to religious, intellectual, and social life in the countries where they made their new homes. Another significant refugee population consisted of Jews and Muslims who were driven out of Spain by the European Christian armies of the *Reconquista* in the 14th and 15th centuries. Most of these refugees settled in North Africa, EGYPT, and lands in the east Mediterranean basin. In the 19th century sizeable Muslim refugee populations were created as a result of the Crimean War (1853–56) and the British suppression of the Sepoy Rebellion in northern India in 1857.

Like many other parts of the world, lands with sizeable Muslim populations in the Middle East and South Asia witnessed massive population displacements in the 20th century, resulting in the creation of millions of refugees and significant disruptions to economic, social, political, religious, and personal networks. Ottoman massacres of Armenian Christians in the early part of the century forced survivors of that minority community to flee to Syria, LEBANON, PALESTINE, and Egypt. In 1947 the partition of India led to unparalleled cross-migrations of Muslims from India to PAKI-STAN and Sikhs and Hindus from Pakistan to India. It is estimated that more than 10 million people were involved in this bi-directional exodus of civilians fleeing outbreaks of violence. The 1947 partition also led to the creation of Kashmiri refugee populations composed mainly of Muslims and Hindus, and of Bihari Muslims who moved to West Pakistan (now BANGLADESH) to escape communal violence. Later, in 1971, the war for the liberation of Bangladesh from West Pakistan involved widespread violence against civilians and to the creation of refugee camps for Biharis, who opposed independence from West Pakistan.

One of the longest lasting unsettled refugee crises in the world is that of the Palestinians. According to the UN Relief and Works Agency for Palestine Refugees in the New East (UNRWA), 914,000 Palestinians lost their homes between June 1946 and May 1948, as a result of the Arab-Israeli conflict. These people and their descendants, numbering by 2002 over 4 million, are officially considered refugees by UNRWA. However, only a fraction of them, approximately 1.3 million Palestinians, currently live in UNRWA-administered refugee camps in Gaza, the West Bank, JORDAN, Lebanon, and Syria. Existing in crushing poverty, Palestinian refugees in these camps face serious health problems and limited options for EDUCATION and employment. In addition, those living in Gaza and the West Bank come under nearly constant physical threat from the ongoing violence between Israeli soldiers and Palestinian resistance fighters, and they often face further displacement with the continued establishment of Israeli settlements in the occupied territories. Unlike all other refugees in the world, Palestinian refugees are not protected by the UN's Refugee Convention (1951) because some of them receive direct assistance from UNRWA. Thus, the millions who are not living under the direct influence of UNRWA receive no protection, while those under the watch of UNRWA receive merely basic assistance.

Afghan nationals comprise another population that has suffered massive population displacement, both internal and external. Prior to the U.S. invasion of AFGHANISTAN in late 2001 following the September 11, 2001, attacks, over 5 million Afghans had become refugees as a result of more than 25 years of civil war and foreign invasion. Four million of those refugees sought sanctuary in neighboring countries, such as IRAN and Pakistan, while another million lived displaced within Afghanistan itself, making Afghans the largest refugee population it the world today. In 2001 all six of Afghanistan's neighbors have closed their borders to further refugees. At the same time, hundreds of thousands of Afghans have been encouraged to return to their homes. Unfortunately the instability that remains in Afghanistan makes a viable resettlement nearly impossible in most regions of the country.

Perhaps the fastest growing refugee population today consists of Iraqis, Muslims and non-Muslims, as a consequence of the U.S. occupation of the country in 2003 and the civil war that erupted there in 2006. It is estimated that as of September 2007 nearly 2.3 million had fled their homes for safer parts of IRAQ (United Nations High Commissioner for Refugees, UNHCR). These are called "internally displaced persons." Another 2.5 million have fled to other countries in the region, especially JORDAN, Syria, Iran, TURKEY, Lebanon, and Egypt (UNHCR 2007). The assets these refugees were able to take with them have quickly dwindled, posing serious social, political, and economic challenges for the host countries. About 100,000 Iraqis have moved to countries in Europe, the United States, and Canada (UNHCR 2007). Prior to the U.S.-led invasion of 2003, over 2 million Kurds had been displaced from their homes in Iraq and Turkey, and over 100,000 Marsh Arabs were displaced from their traditional homelands in southern Iraq by the government forces of SADDAM HUSAYN (d. 2006). One of the staggering human costs of war in the Middle East, its dramatic refugee crises can be expected to expand should conflict in the region continue.

Other significant refugee populations in Muslim-majority countries at the dawn of the 21st century include over 4.5 million displaced Sudanese (with at least 475,000 forced abroad in the past decade). In recent years as many as one million of these have come from the region of Darfur, where an ethnic civil war erupted in 2003. They have combined with internal refugees from conflict in Chad to form an estimated refugee population in that country of nearly one-half million. There is also a large refugee population in Somalia, as a result of civil war and foreign invasions. Approximately 150,000 Sahrawis from Spanish Sahara live as refugees in the Algerian desert pending resolution of the status of Western Sahara, now claimed by Morocco. The Bosnian war of 1992–95 created more than a million internal refugees, but with the end of the war, many of the displaced have returned to their homes.

See also Arab-Israeli conflicts; Armenians; Bosnia and Herzegovina; Gulf Wars; Hijra; human rights; Israel; Kashmir; Sudan; Taliban.

Nancy L. Stockdale

Further reading: Michael R. Fischbach, *Records of Dispossession: Palestinian Refugee Property and the Arab-Israeli Conflict* (New York: Columbia University Press, 2003); Patricia A. Omidian, *Aging and Family in an Afghan Refugee Community* (New York: Garland Publications, 1996); United Nations High Commissioner for Refugees, *The State of the World's Refugees: Human Displacement in the New Millennium* (Oxford: Oxford University Press, 2006); *World Refugee Survey, 2007* (Washington, D.C.: U.S. Committee for Refugees and Immigrants, 2007).

renewal and reform movements

All the major movements that have defined Islam in the contemporary world have been based on Islamic concepts of renewal and reform. These concepts draw inspiration from the Quran and the foundational moments in Islam's history—seventh-century Medina under the leadership of Muhammad and his Companions. However, the shape and content of the contemporary Islamic movements are varied and they should be understood in relation to the historical experience of Muslim peoples since the 18th century. This experience includes the political and economic weakening of Muslim empires, European colonialism and colonial warfare, Christian missionary activity in Muslim lands, and the introduction of Euro-American secularism, political ideologies, institutions, and laws. Other important factors include improved regional and global interconnectedness made possible by mechanized transportation, the development of print cultures and the modern media, and the rise of nationalist movements and the modern nation-state. Islamic renewal and reform movements, also known as revival movements, have been responsible for significant changes in the spheres of education, law, politics, and society. In some cases they have succeeded in winning control of the state, but more often they have adapted to different kinds of political systems, working to bring about gradual change from within. They have also given rise to radical Islamism and jihad movements seeking to bring about rapid revolutionary change through violence.

IDEOLOGICAL FOUNDATIONS

The Quran depicts Islam not as something that originally appeared in the time of Muhammad, but as a way to salvation that God delivered in former times to Adam and other prophets such as Abraham and Moses and their communities. Islamic salvation history, however, like that of the Bible, narrates how people have strayed from the path, disobeying God and his prophets. The Quran's revelation, therefore was a "reminder" (*dhikr*) or "guidance" (*huda*) for people of Muhammad's time to heed; in other words, to change their ways, or reform their belief and conduct accordingly. Moreover, the Quran holds people accountable for correcting wrongs, as when it declares,

"Let there be a community among you that calls people to the good and commands what is right and forbids what is wrong" (Q 3:104). Likewise, it says, "Indeed, God will not change what is in a people until they change what is in themselves" (Q 13:11). Such declarations have been used by Muslims in later times to call for individual moral correction in accordance with what is understood to be God's Law (the SHARIA) and, circumstances permitting, to advocate collective moral, religious, and social reform. The quranic term that is used most commonly today with respect to the idea of reform is *islah*. It is related to a term for reconciliation and peacemaking (*sulh*), as well as to the idea of doing what is good. In its verbal form it can also mean "to restore" and "to renew," and those who engage in such action are the "restorers" or "reconcilers" (*muslihun*). *Islah* was not widely used in the sense of "reform" until the modern reform movements of the 19th and 20th centuries.

The Arabic term most commonly used for renewal is *tajdid*. Unlike *islah,* this word is not found in the Quran. Rather, proponents of Islamic renewal cite a HADITH found in later collections (Abu Dawud, ninth century). This hadith states, "At the beginning of each century God will bring forth for this community (UMMA) a person who will renew its religion." Different "renewers" (sing. *mujaddid*) have been acclaimed in Islamic history. These include the Umayyad caliph Umar II (r. 717–720), Sunni theologian and mystic AL-GHAZALI (d. 1111), Hanbali jurist IBN TAYMIYYA (d. 1327), Egyptian Sunni scholar Jalal al-Din al-Suyuti (d. 1505), Indian mystic and reformer AHMAD SIRHINDI (d. 1625), and Iranian jurist and revolutionary Ayatollah RUHOLLAH KHOMEINI (d. 1989). The idea of a "renewer" is primarily encountered in Sunni Islam; it is eclipsed in SHIISM by belief in the MAHDI. Nevertheless, there have been important religious reform movements in Shii communities, too.

The establishment of the ABBASID CALIPHATE in the eighth century and the subsequent consolidation of orthodox SUNNISM also contributed significantly to the shaping of Islamic reform-

ism and renewal. Pro-Abbasid Sunni historians portrayed the UMAYYAD CALIPHATE as illegitimate, accusing it of being too worldly and un-Islamic, the implication being that the Abbasids were the legitimate restorers of the true religion of the prophet MUHAMMAD. Developments during the first century of Abbasid rule led not only to the establishment of the major Sunni legal schools, but also to the articulation of the fundamental principles of belief. Rather than Abbasid political authorities, however, it was the religious scholars, the ULAMA, who became the official arbiters of the sharia and Islamic teachings. Though every Muslim in theory was responsible for leading people on the path of religious and ethical correctness, the ulama claimed priority. This is reflected in the list of *mujaddids* named above, all but one of whom (Umar II) had expertise in the religious sciences.

MODERN RENEWAL AND REFORM MOVEMENTS

Although Islamic movements of this type differ in organization, ideology, and even objective, there are nevertheless characteristics that many of them share. These include (1) promoting a "return" to the "straight path" of religion based on the Quran and SUNNA, which are regarded as universally valid; (2) looking to the righteous community of the first Muslims (the *salaf*) for inspiration; (3) and reforming traditional practices and beliefs that are considered to be innovations (sing. BIDAA) or deviations from cherished Islamic principles established by the Quran, Muhammad, and the *salaf*. Islamic studies scholars also point out that reformers and revivalists have not only been critical of rulers, but also of "traditionalist" religious authorities who rely too much on "imitation" (*taqlid*) at the expense of essential Islamic principles. In order to validate their break with traditionalists and imitators and adapt the Quran and Sunna to changing circumstances, reformers call for the use of IJTIHAD, an approved method of jurisprudence (FIQH) that allows for the use of individual legal reasoning when explicit guidance is not offered by the Quran and Sunna. Although conservative ulama have regarded this method of legal reasoning cautiously, preferring the conventions of legal tradition, it has been accepted as one of the methods of *fiqh,* to greater or lesser degree, since the ninth century. Islamic studies scholars have also asserted that renewers and reformers do not really wish to simply return to the Golden Age of the past, but that they actually seek to invoke the past in order to bring about a better present and future. This claim has validity, but it overlooks movements that idealize "pristine" Islam to such an extent that it leads to religio-political extremism, oppressive laws, armed violence, and human rights violations that actually undermine the prospects for improved conditions in the present and future.

Two main types of renewal and reform movements have arisen in Islamicate lands since the 18th century. One of these, sometimes called the "modernist movement," has sought to initiate change by interpreting the Quran and the sunna in ways that help Islamicate societies more readily adapt modern European learning and political liberalism. This trend is visible among Egyptian and Ottoman ulama who had become familiar with European SCIENCE and society during the colonial era, including Rifaa Rafi al-Tahtawi (d. 1873), JAMAL AL-DIN AL-AFGHANI (d. 1897), and MUHAMMAD ABDUH (d. 1905). Islamic modernism was spearheaded in INDIA by SAYYID AHMAD KHAN (d. 1898) in the wake of the successful British suppression the 1857 Sepoy revolt. However, whereas al-Afghani's modernism assumed an overtly anticolonial coloring, Ahmad Khan was attempting to bridge the gap between Muslims and the British in order to win a more favorable place for them in the colonial administration. Abduh, initially sympathetic to al-Afghani's views, later took a more gradualist approach to reform, which won him the support of the British authorities who governed EGYPT in the late 19th and early 20th centuries. Ahmad Khan's modernism paved the way for the Muslim leadership that emerged in

the Indian independence movement in the 20th century. It went in two directions, however. One group of modernists joined to promote the creation of an independent PAKISTAN, while another supported the cause of the Indian National Congress, which wanted to create a united Indian nation. Said Nursi (d. 1960) was one of the most important leaders of Islamic reformism in TURKEY, but he eventually clashed with ATATURK (d. 1938), who promoted a strong secular brand of Turkish nationalism, and he was exiled from the country. Other important modernist reform movements arose in North Africa, IRAN, and INDONESIA.

Muslim modernists assert that many of the core principles of Western science and morality originated in Islamicate civilization. Reform, therefore, was a matter of reviving what they defined as the original Islamic heritage that had become corrupted by popular ignorance and backward-thinking ulama. They thought that this was the best way to protect their cultures from colonial domination by European powers. Their efforts were aimed at educated Muslims who were tempted to abandon their Islamic heritage to follow the European secular path promoted by Muslim rulers seeking to rapidly modernize their armies and governments with the help of foreign advisers and legal codes. Many of the modernists turned their attention to educational reform and took advantage of print culture to disseminate their ideas.

The second type of renewal and reform movement in Islam is that which directly attacks beliefs and practices in Muslim societies that are believed to be un-Islamic; it opposes or resists Euro-American influence and reasserts core Islamic values. This kind of movement, sometimes called "revivalist," seeks to achieve its ends partly through doctrinal education (DAAWA) in the Quran and sunna, and partly through overt political action aimed at Islamizing secular governments and pressing them to uphold the sharia. This brand of renewal also employs armed JIHAD to achieve its aims. One of the earliest and best known of these movements was the one initiated by Muhammad IBN ABD AL-WAHHAB (d. 1792) in Arabia, which was directed against what he regarded to be un-Islamic practices such as shrine visitation, folk magic, and Shii veneration of their Imams. The Wahhabis (who call themselves the *muwahhidun* "Unitarians") assisted in the creation of Saudi Arabia and subsequently benefited from the vast oil revenues reaped by that country in the latter part of the 20th century. Revivalist reformism directed against aspects of popular Sufism and the esoteric doctrines and mystical teachings of IBN AL-ARABI (d. 1240) emerged among members of the NAQSHBANDI SUFI ORDER, which was based in India and spread afar from there. Among its early proponents were Ahmad Sirhindi, Shah Wali Allah (d. 1762), and Ghulam Ali (or Abd Allah Dihlavi, d. 1824). Reform-minded Sufi groups and leaders subsequently conducted armed attacks against European colonizers as well as against un-Islamic practices in their own societies. In India these included the movement of AHMAD BARELWI (d. 1831), which also attacked Sikhs, and the FARAIZI MOVEMENT. Russian imperial expansion in the Caucasus was opposed by the Naqshabandi shaykh SHAMIL (d. 1871). Similar movements of non-Naqshabandi reformist Sufis, combined with renewalist elements, arose in West Africa to create new states. They opposed Anglo-Egyptian expansion in the SUDAN and Italian colonization of LIBYA.

During the 20th century both the modernist and the revivalist versions of renewal and reform continued to develop. The shift from colonial regimes to nation-states led to new challenges, adaptations, and forms, which became embedded in the nation-state, as in Saudi Arabia, Libya before 1969, and Iran (after 1979). These included peaceful participation in national politics, as in Pakistan, Sudan, Lebanon (especially after 1993), Jordan, Turkey, and Iraq (after 2003) as well as opposition to secular or authoritarian governments, as in Egypt, Palestine, Iran (before 1979), and Iraq (before 2003). The relationship between these movements and established governments often changes with the political climate in the country.

A good example of this is the MUSLIM BROTHERHOOD, considered to be the first modern Islamic mass movement. Created in 1928 by HASAN AL-BANNA (d. 1949), an Egyptian schoolteacher, as an Islamic renewal organization emphasizing religious education and social welfare projects, it opposed both traditional ulama and British colonial rule. It participated in the nationalist movement that finally succeeded in wining independence for Egypt in 1952, but it fell into disfavor with JAMAL ABD AL-NASIR (d. 1970) and the "Free Officers," who wanted to establish a government based on secular Arab nationalism rather than the sharia. The Muslim Brotherhood conspired against Abd al-Nasir and was harshly suppressed by the Egyptian government in the 1950s and 1960s. However, after Egypt's shocking defeat in the 1967 Arab-Israeli war, it began to regain influence and was allowed some degree of freedom in the 1970s. Since that time its fortunes have fluctuated depending on the amount of opposition the Egyptian government is willing to tolerate, but it has been able to elect supporters to the Egyptian parliament. The Muslim Brotherhood also exemplifies two other characteristics of contemporary renewal and reform movements. One of these is transnationalism—offshoots have established themselves in many Muslim-majority Arab countries. The other is that its oppositional aspect, including the jihadist doctrines of its chief ideologue SAYYID QUTB (d. 1966), has given rise to more radical Islamic movements, such as the Jihad Group that assassinated Egyptian president ANWAR AL-SADAT in 1981, HAMAS in PALESTINE, and even AL-QAIDA.

The modernist type of Islamic renewal and reform also continues to develop, as reflected in the writings of figures such as FAZLUR RAHMAN, Muhammad Said al-Ashmawi, MUHAMMAD ARKOUN, FATIMA MERNISSI, Abdullahi An-Naim, KHALID ABU FADL, Abd al-Karim Soroush, Shireen Ebadi, FETHULLAH GÜLEN, Tariq Ramadan, NASR HAMID ABU ZAYD, Maher Hathout, Muhammad Shahrur,

Mamadiou Dia, and Amina Wadud. These individuals come from many different backgrounds and they address a wide range of issues, including religious tolerance and pluralism, DEMOCRACY, HUMAN RIGHTS, social justice, gender equality, and the problem of religious violence. However, this dimension of reformism in Islam remains highly individualistic, lacking organization, financing, and mass appeal in most cases. It is at a disadvantage with respect to the power and influence of ulama, radical Islamic groups, and authoritarian governments. Indeed, many (but not all) of these thinkers live in Europe and North America, where a number have held academic appointments in universities and research institutes.

See also ALIGARH; DAAWA; ETHICS AND MORALITY; PAN-ISLAMISM; POLITICS AND ISLAM; RASHID RIDA, MUHAMMAD; SALAFISM; SHARIATI, ALI; WAHHABISM.

Further reading: Albert Hourani, *Arabic Thought in the Liberal Age: 1798–1939* (1962. Reprint, Cambridge: Cambridge University Press, 1983); Farouq Jahanbakhsh, *Islam, Democracy and Religious Modernism in Iran, 1953–2000: From Bazargan to Soroush* (Boston: E.J. Brill, 2001); Charles Kurzman, *Liberal Islam: A Sourcebook* (Oxford: Oxford University Press, 1998); Fazlur Rahman, "Revival and Reform in Islam." In *The Cambridge History of Islam,* edited by P. M. Holt, Ann K. S. Lambton, and Bernard Lewis, Vol. 1, 632–642 (Cambridge: Cambridge University Press, 1970); Ali Rahnema, ed., *Pioneers of Islamic Revival* (1994. Reprint, London: Zed Books, 2005); John O. Voll, "Renewal and Reform in Islamic History: *Tajdid* and *Islah.*" In *Voices of Resurgent Islam,* edited by John L. Esposito, 32–47 (Oxford: Oxford University Press, 1983).

resurrection   *See* AFTERLIFE; DEATH; ESCHATOLOGY; JUDGMENT DAY.

revelation
Communication of knowledge by words, visions, and inspiration from sacred, supramundane beings to humans is known as revelation. It usually involves disclosure of a truth, or set of truths, that has been previously hidden or unknown. Revelation is a phenomenon recognized by many if not all religious systems.

In Judaism, Christianity, and Islam revelation is most commonly associated with prophets—individuals chosen by God to deliver his word to humans. Jewish rabbinic tradition regards the written and oral TORAH as a revelation "given" by God to MOSES and accepted by the community of Israel above all nations. Moreover, the written Torah bears witness to God's actions in the history of the Hebrews, from the covenant times of the patriarchs and the events in EGYPT and Sinai to the building of the temple in Jerusalem and its destruction by the Babylonians. Christian tradition holds the Old Testament (the Hebrew Bible or written Torah) to be a preliminary revelation, but it considers Christ (JESUS), the son of God, the most perfect and complete revelation of God to humanity. The New Testament bears witness to this and is itself considered to be the product of divine inspiration. Also, the last book of the New Testament, known as *The Revelation to John* (or *The Apocalypse of John*), contains visions about the future revealed to John by Christ.

In Islamic belief the QURAN is the final, most perfect revelation from God. It was preceded by revelations delivered to former prophets in the course of human history, but in its final form it embodies the speech of God revealed (literally "sent down") to MUHAMMAD on different occasions between 610 and 632 while he was living in both MECCA and MEDINA. The terms used for this revelation are based on the Arabic root n-z-l (*tanzil* and *nuzul*), which connotes downward movement. Muslim scholars developed a genre of exegetical literature called *asbab al-nuzul* that sought to identify the different historical "occasions" when revelation came to Muhammad, often situations involving interactions with human, rather than divine, interlocutors. Although there are tensions between the divine and human elements involved in revelation, the Quran and the earlier revelations of the Torah, Psalms, and the GOSPEL are all believed to be earthly manifestations of a heavenly book, known as "the mother of the book" (*umm al-kitab*), "the preserved tablet" (*al-lawh al-mahfudh*), and "the hidden writing" (*kitab maknun*). Muslims believe that the Quran was not sent down directly in the form of a physical book of scripture, but that it was God's speech, recited (or read) to Muhammad. Only after Muhammad died, according to conventional accounts, was it assembled in the form of book.

Although some of the revelations Muhammad had were of a visual nature, most were verbal. Passages in the Quran suggest that Muhammad had a vision of God (Q 53:1–18). Others suggest that GABRIEL was the conveyor of revelation, which has become the conventional belief. According to the HADITH, on some occasions Muhammad saw Gabriel approach as a young man and repeated what he heard the ANGEL say. The accounts of Muhammad's first revelation provided by the *Sira* of IBN ISHAQ (d. 767) and Tabari's history (late ninth century) relate that while on retreat in a mountain cave near Mecca he saw a supramundane being, identified as Gabriel, who commanded him to recite the first lines of Sura 96. When Muhammad expressed reluctance to recite, the angel throttled and pressed upon him until he accepted the call. After this he fled to his wife KHADIJA who, together with her cousin Waraqa bin Nawfal, confirmed the authenticity of his revelatory experience. Subsequent experiences of revelation were less dramatic. The hadith relate that instead of a vision Muhammad heard a sound like a bell ringing or the buzzing of bees before hearing the revealed message. He also received revelation in the form of inspiration (*wahy*). Although the sayings of Muhammad contained in the hadith are not "revelations" per se, one group of them, known as "sacred hadith," contained divine statements not found in the Quran that are credited to Muhammad as the transmitter, unlike quranic verses. The counterpart of quranic revelations that

"descended" upon Muhammad or were inspired in him was his famed NIGHT JOURNEY AND ASCENT, an event during which he is said to have seen and conversed with a number of former prophets, angels, and God himself. The instructions for the five daily prayers were given to him according to conventional accounts of this event.

Although Muslims consider the Quran a unique revelation, it is not the only kind of revelation that has been claimed in Islamic history. Shii ULAMA have attributed to their Imams the ability to receive inspiration from God when a matter arose that was not addressed in the Quran or Sunna. They called this kind of inspiration *ilham*, and sometimes *wahy*, a lesser kind of revelation than that received by Muhammad. JAAFAR AL-SADIQ (d. 765), the sixth IMAM, is credited with stating,

> A messenger (*rasul*) is one who sees an angel who comes to him with the message from his lord. He speaks with him just as one of you would speak with your companion. And the prophet (*nabi*) does not see the angel but revelation (*wahy*) descends upon him and he sees (the angel) in a vision . . . and the speaker (the imam) hears the voice but does not see anything (adapted from Momen 150).

The Shii Imams are also identified with the "signs" (*ayat*) of God mentioned in the Quran (for example, Q 29:49–50; 36:46). This suggests that they embody revelation.

A further elaboration of notions of revelation occurred within the circles of the Sufis, the virtuosos of Islamic mysticism. Many acknowledged that saints could receive divine inspiration, called *ilham*, but that this differed in kind and degree from the kind of revelation received by prophets (*wahy, tanzil*). In contrast to the Shia, some held the view that this inspiration was meant for the individual rather than the community as a whole, though most saints were looked to as authorities and examples to be emulated by their disciples and the wider community of their devotees. One of the most prominent Sufi visionaries who claimed to have such revelations was IBN AL-ARABI (d. 1240), one of whose most important works is entitled *The Meccan Revelations (al-Futuhat al-Makkiyya)*. At the beginning of this book he wrote,

> The essence of what is included in this work comes from what God inspired in me while I was fulfilling circumambulations of [God's] house (the KAABA), or while I was contemplating it while seated in its holy precincts (adapted from Ibn al-Arabi 8).

Ibn al-Arabi also claimed that a vision of Muhammad inspired him to write another of his major works, *The Bezels of Wisdom*. Visions and dreams of Muhammad are widely attested in Sufi literature, as well as popular lore. Among the most desired goals of Sufis, moreover, was to obtain a vision and intimate experience of God through their spiritual discipline and God's grace-acts, much as Muhammad had been able to do. In addition to inspiration (*ilham*), they also spoke of revelation in terms of "unveiling" or "illumination" (*kashf*), but, in doing so, they sometimes also posited equivalence between prophets and saints. The Persian mystic RUZBIHAN BAQLI (d. 1209), a contemporary of Ibn al-Arabi, spoke of messengers, prophets, angels, and saints as all being God's lovers to whom God unveiled himself and revealed not only secret knowledge and wisdom, but even his essence and divine attributes. Claims to have such divine knowledge sparked negative reactions from conservative religious authorities, who had the authority to level charges of innovation (*BIDAA*), BLASPHEMY, or even APOSTASY against the visionaries and their proponents.

See also ANGEL; *AYA*; *FIQH*; HOLY BOOKS; PROPHETS AND PROPHECY; SUFISM.

Further reading: Ruzbihan Baqli, *The Unveiling of Secrets: Diary of a Sufi Master*. Translated by Carl W. Ernst (Chapel Hill, N.C.: Parvardigar Press, 1997); William A. Graham, *Divine Word and Prophetic Word in Early Islam* (The Hague: Mouton, 1977); Ibn al-Arabi, *The Meccan Revelations*. Vol. 1. Edited by Michel Chodkiewicz and translated by William C. Chittick and James W. Morris (New York: Pir Press, 2002); Moojan Momen, *An Introduction to Shii Islam* (New Haven, Conn.: Yale University Press, 1985), 148–160; F. E. Peters, *Muhammad and the Origins of Islam* (Albany: State University of New York Press, 1994); Fazlur Rahman, *Major Themes of the Quran* (Minneapolis: Bibliotheca Islamica, 1994).

Reza Shah Pahlavi (also known as Reza Khan and Reza Shah) (1878–1944) *founder of the Iranian Pahlavi dynasty, he reigned as shah from 1925 to 1941*

By the beginning of the 20th century the tide of popular discontent and nationalist aspirations in IRAN began to focus on the weak and corrupt rule of the QAJAR DYNASTY, which had forfeited most of its power and influence over the state to Russia and Britain. The deteriorating situation ultimately led to a coup d'état that abolished Qajar rule and ultimately led to the crowning of Reza Khan in 1925 as the first shah (Persian: king) of the Pahlavi dynasty.

Reza Shah Pahlavi was a strong-willed and impatient man. Born in poverty, he received no formal education. Like so many poor Iranians of his time he had no choice but to seek his fortunes in the military. Joining the Cossack Brigade as a teenager, he quickly rose through its ranks to become a deeply feared and respected commander of what was in truth little more than the Qajar shah's personal bodyguards. He was, therefore, in an opportune position to seize control of the throne after the fall of the Qajars, first as minister of war in the transitional government that ruled from 1921 to 1925, and then as shah from 1925 to 1941.

Heavily influenced by the European-inspired reforms of Turkey's MUSTAFA KEMAL ATATURK (d. 1938), Reza Shah instituted a series of sweeping changes in Iran. He adopted Western-based legal and EDUCATION reforms, mandated a Western dress code, and abolished the wearing of the VEIL. He created a strong central government by destroying the old fiefdoms that had divided the country internally and he limited the AUTHORITY of Iran's Shii religious institutions by controlling the tithes that functioned as their primary source of wealth. The shah's reforms sparked Iran's economy and reignited its sense of national sovereignty, making Iran one of the most stable and formidable powers in the Middle East. Yet, because of his lasting distrust of the British and Russians, Reza Shah Pahlavi chose not to assist the Allies in their fight against German forces during World War II. As a result, in the closing year of the war, the Allied forces reoccupied Iran, forced his abdication, and replaced him on Iran's throne with his son, MOHAMMAD REZA PAHLAVI (r. 1944–79).

Reza Aslan

Further reading: Amin Banani, *The Modernization of Iran* (Stanford, Calif.: Stanford University Press, 1961); Cyrus Ghani, *Iran and the Rise of Reza Shah* (London: I.B. Tauris, 1998); Homa Katouzian, *State and Society in Iran: The Eclipse of the Qajars and the Emergence of the Pahlavis* (London: I.B. Tauris, 2000).

ridda See APOSTASY.

Rifai Sufi Order

The Rifai Sufi Order takes its name from Ahmad al-Rifai (1106–82), a Shafii legal scholar and mystic from the marshlands of southern IRAQ. He was a contemporary of ABD AL-QADIR AL-JILANI (d. 1166), the eponymous founder of the QADIRI SUFI ORDER, and disciples claimed he was from the household of MUHAMMAD, the Prophet. Details about al-Rifai's life are sketchy, other than that he was raised by his paternal uncle, Mansur, after the death of his father. Mansur had initiated a DERVISH order called the Rifaiyya, which Ahmad led

after his uncle's death. He was 28 years old at the time. His tomb in the village of Umm Ubayda in southern Iraq had become a large dervish hospice by the time IBN BATTUTA visited it in the mid-14th century. The famed Rifai Mosque in CAIRO is also thought to contain his remains, but because this is a late-19th century MOSQUE, it most likely contains the remains of one of his descendants or a Rifai shaykh.

As has often been the case for Islamic organizations, it was Ahmad's disciples who developed the order's rituals, rules, and doctrines. They also established branches throughout the Middle East and southeastern Europe. It remained the most widespread order in Sunni ARAB lands until the 15th century, when it was superseded by the Qadiri order. The Ottoman SULTAN Abd al-Hamid II (d. 1918) renewed its importance as part of his effort to promote PAN-ISLAMISM. Today the most prominent Rifai branches are in IRAQ, SYRIA, PALESTINE, EGYPT, TURKEY, Bosnia and Herzegovina, Albania, Bulgaria, and Greece. There are branches in coastal cities of INDIA, especially Surat, where it is the most important Sufi order. Several branches have also been established in the United States, including in California and New York.

According to a 16th-century source, the Rifais credited their founder with teaching about five stages (*maqamat*) of spiritual development: pious circumspection (*waraa*), worship (*taabud*), love (*mahabba*), mystical insight or gnosis (*maarifa*), and unity with God (TAWHID). The Rifai order is most famous for its ecstatic rituals, which included riding lions, snake-handling, walking on fire, eating glass, and piercing the body with hooks, swords, and skewers. The shaykh of the order purifies the wounds of the dervishes with his spittle. The absence of bleeding is taken as a demonstration of the SAINT's miraculous powers. Such practices came to be widely condemned in the Muslim community only in the 19th and 20th centuries, when political authorities, liberals, and Wahhabi-minded reformers denounced such practices as un-Islamic innovations. Nevertheless, they are still conducted among some Rifai groups today.

See also AHL AL-BAYT; BADAWI, AHMAD AL-; BIDAA; MAQAM; MAWLID; MIRACLE; SUFISM.

Further reading: Frederick De Jong, *Turuq and Turuq-Linked Institutions in Nineteenth-Century Egypt* (Leiden: E.J. Brill, 1978); John S. Trimingham, *The Sufi Orders in Islam* (Oxford: Oxford University Press, 1971); Peter Van Der Veer, "Playing or Praying: A Sufi Saints Day in Surat." *Journal of Asian Studies* 51, no. 3 (August 1992): 545–564.

rosary   *See* PRAYER BEADS.

ruh   *See* SOUL AND SPIRIT.

Rumi, Jalal al-Din (Mawlana, Arabic: Our Master) (1207–1273) *Persian Sufi master and mystical poet who lived much of his life in Konya, Turkey*

Mawlana Jalal al-Din Rumi is perhaps the most famous Sufi poet, and he is one of the most cherished poets in Persian literature, due to the beauty and exuberance of his voluminous poetry, which has inspired Muslims for centuries and, more recently, spiritual seekers in EUROPE and the Americas.

Jalal al-Din was born in Balkh (in modern-day AFGHANISTAN) in 1207, but when still a child migrated with his father to Anatolia (known in Islamic history as Rum, hence the name Rumi), shortly before the Mongol invasions. They settled in Konya, which was then the capital of the SELJUK DYNASTY of Rum (1077–1307), and Rumi's father secured a position as a teacher of Islamic sciences. When his father died, Rumi took over the position, and was widely respected. In 1244 his life changed when he met a wandering DERVISH named Shams al-Din Tabrizi (d. 1248), and the two

became inseparable friends. Under the influence of Shams, Rumi was inspired to write exuberant mystical poetry and was introduced to the ecstatic whirling dance known as *samaa* (Arabic: audition). Many of his verses were in fact composed while Rumi was whirling in *samaa*. After Shams died, Rumi found similar spiritual friendships with a goldsmith named Salah al-Din Zarkub (d. 1258), and later Husam al-Din (d. 1284–85), with whose inspiration Rumi began to compose the verses that would become his most famous work, the *Mathnawi*. Rumi died in Konya in 1273. His life was described in hagiographical works not long after his death, such as Aflaki's *Manaqib al-arifin* (The virtues of the gnostics).

Rumi's most important works include a large collection of short lyric poems called *Divan-i*

Tomb of Jalal al-Din Rumi in Konya, Turkey *(Juan E. Campo)*

Shams-i Tabriz, dedicated to Shams al-Din Tabrizi and totaling over 35,000 lines of poetry, and a collection of rhymed couplets called the *Mathnawi-i maanawi* (also known as the *Masnavi*), which includes more than 25,000 lines of Persian verse. Rumi's lectures and conversations were collected in a work called *Fihi ma fihi* (In it is what is in it). Important themes in Rumi's poetry include the spiritual quest, the search for the inner significance of words and practices, the unity of existence, and especially divine love.

After Rumi's death, his followers formed the MEVLEVI SUFI ORDER, which eventually became famous as the "whirling dervishes" for its standardized version of Rumi's ecstatic *samaa*. The order also perpetuated Rumi's memory through recitation of, and commentary on, the *Mathnawi*. Rumi's poetry has been immensely popular throughout the Muslim world, especially in Turkey and Iran. He has also recently enjoyed great popularity in Europe and the Americas due to translations and interpretations of his poetry in an accessible free verse style. Rumi's poetry of love continues to touch people everywhere.

See also DHIKR; PERSIAN LANGUAGE AND LITERATURE; SUFISM; TURKEY.

Mark Soileau

Further reading: Franklin D. Lewis, *Rumi Past and Present, East and West* (Oxford: Oneworld, 2000); Jalal al-Din Rumi, *The Masnavi, Book One.* Translated and edited by Jawid Mojaddedi (Oxford: Oxford University Press, 2004); Annemarie Schimmel, *The Triumphal Sun: A Study of the Works of Jalaloddin Rumi* (London: East-West Publications, 1978).

Rushdie, Salman (1947–) *award-winning author who was forced into hiding from 1989 to 1998 due to a death sentence issued by Ayatollah Khomeini*

Salman Rushdie is an acclaimed novelist and critic who became a household name after his 1988 novel, *The Satanic Verses*, drew protests from numerous Muslims and Muslim groups because of its treatment of MUHAMMAD, his wives, and companions. Ayatollah RUHOLLAH KHOMEINI (d. 1989), IRAN's conservative religious leader, pronounced a FATWA (legal opinion) in 1989 that sentenced Rushdie to death, and, as a result, Rushdie was forced into hiding from 1989 to 1998. As of this writing, Rushdie lives in the UNITED STATES, dividing his time between Los Angeles, Atlanta, and New York City.

Rushdie was born to Muslim parents in Bombay, INDIA, and educated at the Cathedral School there. In 1961 he left India to attend Rugby, a prestigious boarding school in England. Rushdie then attended King's College, Cambridge, where he wrote a paper on Muhammad and the origins of Islam for the first part of his history examinations. Early literary influences on Rushdie included the Arabic classic *The Thousand and One Nights* (also known as the ARABIAN NIGHTS) and the Urdu (an Indian language which is the official language of Pakistan) poet Faiz Ahmed Faiz (d. 1984), a family friend.

Rushdie's first novel, *Grimus* (1975), a variation of the medieval Sufi (mystic) poet Farid al Din Attar's *The Conference of the Birds,* was a commercial and critical failure. His second novel, *Midnight's Children* (1981), about the lives of 1,001 children born at the stroke of midnight on India's independence from Britain, won him critical acclaim, including the 1981 Booker Prize. In that book Rushdie's satirical portrayal of India's leader Indira Gandhi resulted in a lawsuit that was resolved when a sentence considered particularly hurtful by Gandhi was omitted from subsequent editions of the novel. His third novel, *Shame* (1983), satirized Pakistani politics (and politicians such as Zulfikar Ali Bhutto [d. 1979] and General Zia al Haqq [d. 1988]) in the way that its predecessor had satirized Indian politics. Clearly, Rushdie knew much about Islam, Muslims, and South Asian politics and culture.

The Satanic Verses (1988) was Rushdie's fourth novel, and it dealt with the theme of migration, of being brown in England, and the multiple identities that come with being Asian in London. The main character is Gibreel Farishta (which translates from Urdu as "the Angel GABRIEL"). It is this character who assumes the persona of the angel Gabriel and has a series of dreams that begin in the second chapter of the book, "Mahound." Mahound (a name for the prophet Muhammad in medieval Christian polemic against Muslims) is an orphan, a businessman living in a city named Jahilia, who through revelation begins to preach a religion named "Submission," which represents Islam. In another chapter, Gibreel also has a series of encounters with another character, an exile, known simply as "the imam," who represents Khomeini.

The book was first banned in India on October 5, 1988, at the urging of several Indian Muslim politicians. Subsequently, the book was banned in South Africa (November 24, 1988), burned publicly in Bradford, England (January 14, 1989), and protested against in Islamabad, PAKISTAN (where six people died during a riot on February 12, 1989) and Bombay (with 12 people killed in a riot on February 24, 1989). On February 14, 1989, Khomeini pronounced his death sentence on Rushdie. While distancing itself from Khomeini's death sentence, the 11th session of the Islamic Law Academy of the MUSLIM WORLD LEAGUE (held in MECCA from February 10 to 26, 1989) issued a statement declaring Rushdie an apostate and recommending that he be prosecuted in a British court and tried in absentia under the SHARIA laws of an Islamic country.

On the whole, North American responses were much more muted and peaceful than in other countries. To take the case of Toronto, the city with Canada's largest population of Muslims, there was a deliberate effort made by various Muslim communities to keep the protests nonviolent. The protests in Toronto, as well as in major American cities such as Los Angeles and New York, were not used for political purposes, in the way that they were used in, for example, IRAN or India. No Muslim leaders in North America used the book as an occasion to develop or consolidate their own power. Many Muslims in the UNITED STATES and CANADA felt hurt by the book. Unlike in some other countries, such as Pakistan, there was also some sympathy and tolerance for Rushdie in North America, and, in fact, a small number of Muslims did not want the book to be banned.

During his time in hiding, Rushdie became quite a celebrity, but he was still able to publish a number of works. These included a children's story written for his son, *Haroun and the Sea of Stories* (1990); a collection of nonfiction, *Imaginary Homelands* (1991); a collection of short stories, *East, West* (1994); and a novel, *The Moor's Last Sigh* (1995). Rushdie's marriage to the novelist Marianne Wiggins also ended during his time in hiding. Changes in the governments of both Iran and Britain led to an end to the fatwa, announced on September 24, 1998, in a joint statement issued by the foreign ministers of Iran and Britain. Since coming out of hiding, Rushdie has written four other novels; *The Ground Beneath Her Feet* (1999), *Fury* (2001), *Shalimar the Clown* (2005), and *The Enchantress of Florence* (2008).

In 2000 Rushdie moved from London to New York City. He continues to write and has published several short pieces on Islam. These are collected in his second anthology of nonfiction, *Step Across This Line* (2002). In 1993 he was awarded the Booker of Bookers for *Midnight's Children*. In 2005, Iranian leader Ayatollah Ali Khamenei reaffirmed the *fatwa* that called for Rushdie's death. In 2006 Rushdie accepted a teaching position at Emory University, where his official archive will be housed. In 2008, he won the Best of the Booker for *Midnight's Children*.

See also APOSTASY; EUROPE; JAHILIYYA; SATANIC VERSES.

Amir Hussain

Further reading: Lisa Appignanesi and Sara Maitland, eds., *The Rushdie File* (London: Fourth Estate, 1989); Roger Y. Clark, *Stranger Gods: Salman Rushdie's Other Worlds* (Montreal: McGill–Queen's University Press,

2001); Michael M. J. Fischer and Mehdi Abedi, *Debating Muslims: Cultural Dialogues in Postmodernity and Tradition* (Madison: University of Wisconsin Press, 1990); Amir Hussain, "Misunderstandings and Hurt: How Canadians Joined Worldwide Muslim Reactions to Salman Rushdie's *The Satanic Verses.*" *Journal of the American Academy of Religion* 70, no. 1 (March 2002): 1–32; Mohammad Hashim Kamali, *Freedom of Expression in Islam* (Cambridge: Islamic Texts Society, 1997).

S

sacrifice   *See* ID AL-ADHA.

sadaqa   *See* ALMSGIVING.

al-Sadat, Muhammad Anwar (1919–1981) *president of Egypt from 1970 to 1981*

Muhammad Anwar al-Sadat served as Egyptian president from September 28, 1970, until his assassination on October 6, 1981. Sadat was born into a poor family, one of 13 brothers and sisters. He graduated from the Royal Military Academy in 1938, was involved in the Free Officer Movement, and its efforts to oust the British from EGYPT and nationalize the Suez Canal. Sadat served in various prominent positions in the government of JAMAL ABD AL-NASIR, including as vice president from 1964.

In 1973 Sadat, along with SYRIA, launched the Yom Kippur War (October War) with ISRAEL, which succeeded in regaining parts of the Sinai Peninsula and garnered much popularity for him domestically. On November 19, 1977, Sadat became the first Arab leader to officially visit Israel when he met Prime Minister Menachem Begin and spoke before the Knesset in JERUSALEM. This visit ultimately resulted in the 1978 CAMP DAVID ACCORDS, which stipulated that Egypt recognize Israel and secured American economic aid for Egypt, which

continues today. Sadat pursued economic policies that were more favorable to capitalism and outside trade than those of his predecessor, Jamal Abd al-Nasir. Sadat was immensely popular in the West—he graced the cover of the November 28, 1977, issue of *Time* magazine and received the 1978 Nobel Peace Prize.

Sadat styled himself as the "believer president," praying regularly and publicly, and initially he enjoyed a cordial relationship with Muslim and Islamist organizations. From the beginning of his presidency, Sadat sought to downplay the socialism of the Abd al-Nasir period and encouraged antisocialist elements in Egypt. This included permitting the public expression of Islamic opposition, releasing many of the activists imprisoned by Abd al-Nasir, and allowing the MUSLIM BROTHERHOOD to publish magazines and organize in MOSQUES and universities—this actually backfired, providing a forum for Islamist activists to express themselves. Further, Sadat's trip to Jerusalem, recognition of Israel, and economic policies soured his relationship with the Islamic opposition, spurring the growth of Islamist movements such as AL-TAKFIR WAL HIJRA and Islamic JIHAD. Under the threat of growing opposition, Sadat changed his stance, and, in September 1981, he cracked down on Muslim organizations and student groups, with arrests totaling nearly 1,600. These purges added fuel to the fire, and, on October 6, Sadat was assassinated in CAIRO during a parade commemorating the 1973 war. The assassin was Khalid Islambouli, a member of Islamic Jihad. It could be said that the Islamist movement in Egypt reached its maturity under Sadat's presidency.

Joshua Hoffman

Further reading: Kirk J. Beattie, *Egypt during the Sadat Years* (New York: Palgrave, 2000); Raymond A. Hinnebusch, *Egyptian Politics under Sadat: The Post-Populist Development of an Authoritarian-Modernizing State* (Boulder, Colo.: Lynne Rienner Publishers, 1988); Anwar El Sadat, *In Search of Identity: An Autobiography* (New York: Harper and Row, 1978).

Saddam Hussein   *See* HUSAYN, SADDAM.

Safavid dynasty

The Safavid dynasty ruled IRAN from 1501 to 1722, and it was the first to institute Shii Islam as the official state religion. Although the founder of the Safavid dynasty was likely Safi ad-Din Ishaq (b. ca. 1252), head of a mysterious paramilitary Sufi order in Gilan called the Safawiyya, it was not until one of Safi ad-Din's heirs, a 15-year-old boy named Ismail (d. 1524), defeated the rival tribes in IRAN and declared himself shah in 1501 that the Safavid dynasty was born.

Shah Ismail was a charismatic figure who proclaimed TWELVE-IMAM SHIISM the official state religion and declared a brutal JIHAD against Sunni Islam both within his lands and in the neighboring Ottoman Empire. The young king was unmoved by arguments against the legitimacy of a Shii state in the absence of the Hidden Imam, simply declaring himself to be the long-awaited MAHDI. Safavid extremism ended under Ismail's successors, but the ideological and religious nature of the state he had founded continued throughout the Safavid era, so that SHIISM is to this day the state religion of Iran.

The Safavid state flourished for two centuries after Ismail's death, reaching its zenith at the end of the 16th century under the reign of Shah Abbas I (r. 1587–1629). Abbas not only created a strong bureaucratic state backed by a powerful military force, but he also turned his capital, Isfahan, into one of the most prosperous and resplendent cities in the Middle East. Indeed, many of Islam's greatest and most lasting contributions to architecture, the arts, and the sciences were developed in Isfahan under Safavid patronage.

By the beginning of the 18th century, however, a number of internal and external factors resulted in a massive decline in the state's economy. Uprisings throughout Iran ultimately led to the destruction of the Safavid dynasty in 1722, but it was not until 1773 and the ascension of Nadir Shah as the first ruler of the Afsharid dynasty that the Safavid state ceased to exist.

See also QAJAR DYNASTY; SUFISM; USULI SCHOOL.

Reza Aslan

Further reading: Marshal Hodgson, *The Venture of Islam.* Vol. 3 (Chicago: University of Chicago Press, 1974); Charles Melville, ed., *Safavid Persia* (London: I.B. Taurus, 1996); Roger Savory, *Iran under the Safavids* (Cambridge: Cambridge University Press, 1983).

sahaba   *See* COMPANIONS OF THE PROPHET.

sahur   *See* RAMADAN.

saint

The Arabic word usually translated as saint, WALI, refers primarily to the quranic verse 10:62: "Indeed, on the friends of God (*awliya Allah*) there is no fear, neither shall they grieve." Two words derived from *walī* are generally taken to refer to sainthood, *wilaya* and WALAYA. Medieval Muslim scholars, as well as contemporary observers of Islam, have debated which of these two terms is the most appropriate, for they can be understood to have different meanings: *wilaya* connotes power, while *walaya* generally indicates closeness. While Muslim scholars have differed as to whether the saints are known by their closeness to God or their power, the saints in fact should be understood to be very special people who combine these two attributes. "Saint," then, connotes both friend and protector. One who is a saint is close to God. God protects the saint and gives the saint power (BARAKA). Just as God is the patron of the saint, dispensing power to him or her, so, too, the saint has power and acts as a patron.

There is no generally recognized churchlike structure in Islam to recognize or canonize saints, which means that the saints emerge relatively organically from their environments. This does not mean, however, that one becomes a saint spontaneously, or without effort. On the contrary, it is clear that individuals have often striven to be

Popular religious poster showing an assembly of leading Chishti saints, shown with their shrines in India

considered saints, and it is also clear that saints are made, or at least come to be widely recognized, by the actions and efforts of their followers.

The great scholar of SUFISM, Abu al-Qasim al-Qushayri (d. 1072), defined the saint as "first, someone whose affairs are taken over by God, and, second, as someone whose worship of God is constant without any defect of rebellion" (Hoffman, 109). People may become saints after long years of discipline and ASCETICISM, or they may reach that state in an immediate, overwhelming experience of the divine that takes over the person's intellect. At the level of the average believer, however, the defining characteristic of saints is the ability to work miracles, known as *karamat,* through their blessing power (*baraka*). This power to work miracles is a sine qua non for saints, much as it is in Christianity.

The saints are thus special people, often hidden or obscured from the attention of others during their lives, who have a special closeness to God that allows them to act as intercessors on behalf of the believers, providing them access to the power and grace of God. Most often the deceased saint has a shrine to which people make visitation (ZIYARA), and to which people come annually for a local or regional saint festival (MAWLID). This shrine, known variously as a MAQAM, *qubba, darih,* or *dargah,* contains the body and relics of the saint. It is also believed to contain the saint's *baraka.*

The reality of saints, and especially their veneration, has been under strenuous attack in the Islamic world for over a century. RENEWAL AND REFORM MOVEMENTS of the 18th, 19th, and 20th centuries have objected to the practices associated with saint veneration. The Wahhabis, who emerged in the Arabian Peninsula in the 18th century, destroyed all the saints shrines they found, a practice that is continued by the modern Saudi state through some of its charitable arms. For them, saint veneration risked compromising the Islamic belief in the oneness of God, thus constituting IDOLATRY, or *SHIRK*: the greatest sin of Islam. In the 19th and 20th centuries, many Muslim reformers came to see saint veneration as archaic superstition that had to be eliminated if

Muslims were ever to become modern, which most Muslims agree is a necessity. In the SALAFISM movement, especially during the time of MUHAMMAD RASHID RIDA (d. 1935), these two strands of thought largely merged, leading to the present situation in which saint veneration is often the province of the less educated and less sophisticated. The dominant discourse, which is largely a modernist one, has come to look down upon saint veneration and intercession as being both un-Islamic and backwards. This does not mean that saints or their cults are disappearing. It does mean, however, that many Muslims, and particularly those who are intellectually and politically active, will, for the foreseeable future, perceive the saints to be an aspect of "folk" or "popular" Islam rather than the integral part of Islam that they were for a millennium.

See also AHL AL-BAYT; AL-BADAWI, AHMAD; BIDAA; MIRACLE; SUFISM; WAHHABISM; ZAYNAB BINT ALI IBN ABI TALIB.

John Iskander

Further reading: Vincent Cornell, *Realm of the Saint: Power and Authority in Moroccan Sufism* (Austin: University of Texas Press, 1998); Gerald T. Elmore, *Islamic Sainthood in the Fullness of Time: Ibn al-Arabi's Book of the Fabulous Gryphon* (Leiden: E.J. Brill, 1999); Valerie J. Hoffman, "Muslim Sainthood, Women, and the Legend of Sayyida Nafisa." In *Women Saints in World Religions,* edited by Arvind Sharma, 107–144 (Albany: State University of New York Press, 2000); Lamin Sanneh, "Saints and Virtue in African Islam: An Historical Approach." In *Saints and Virtues,* edited by John Stratton Hawley, 127–143 (Los Angeles: University of California Press, 1987).

Saladin (Al Malik al Nasir Abu'l Muzaffar Yussuf ibn Ayyub, better known by his title, Salah al-Din) (1138–1193) *Muslim soldier and leader of Kurdish descent, who became the ruler of Egypt and Syria and led the Arab Muslim jihad against the Crusaders*

Saladin was born in Takrit, north of BAGHDAD in Iraq, where his father was governor. But Saladin's family transferred their loyalty to Nur al-Din ibn Zangi, the ruler of Aleppo and DAMASCUS. Saladin began his career as a member of the military machine marshaled by Nur al-Din to combat the Christian crusaders in the latter half of the 12th century. Nur al-Din's first task was to unify the Muslims and it was with this aim that Saladin was sent as part of an expeditionary force to defeat the Shii Fatimid rulers of EGYPT. The campaign was successful and shortly thereafter Saladin was recognized as the ruler of Egypt. In this role, Saladin undertook numerous building projects to fortify the country's defenses, most notably the citadel that still has a prominent place on the CAIRO skyline.

Saladin's ambitions placed him in conflict with Nur al-Din, but before they could settle the matter in battle, Nur al-Din died in 1174. Saladin spent the next 12 years continuing Nur al-Din's program of unifying the Muslim princes of SYRIA and PALESTINE, this time under his own AUTHORITY and leadership. Once he had accomplished this—either by treaty or by force—Saladin focused his efforts on expelling the crusaders from the region.

He began his offensive campaign with a decisive victory in 1187 at the Battle of Hattin. Saladin then led his troops in retaking, with little resistance or bloodshed, most of the CRUSADE cities and fortresses. Saladin's primary objective, however, was JERUSALEM, which he besieged in 1189. Unable to adequately defend themselves, the city's inhabitants quickly came to terms with Saladin, who allowed them to ransom themselves as prisoners of war. This action stood in sharp contrast to the crusader conquest of the city almost a century earlier. Indeed Saladin was famous for his generosity and honor. He often allowed crusader prisoners to go free with the simple promise not to take up arms against him again—a promise that was not always kept.

The highpoint of Saladin's career came with restoration of the Muslim holy places in Jerusalem. The last years of his life were spent battling the Christian forces in the Third Crusade, which ended in stalemate. Richard the Lion-Heart led many reinforcements from Europe to Palestine through the crusader stronghold of Tyre, securing cities on the coast but never gaining a foothold inland nor entering Jerusalem. Although Richard requested to meet

Saladin on many occasions, Saladin always refused, stating: "Kings meet together only after the conclusion of an accord, for it is unthinkable for them to wage war once they know one another and have broken bread together." They eventually did sign a five-year peace treaty, but they never met, as Richard left immediately thereafter for England. Saladin died a few months later in 1193 in Damascus.

In European sources Saladin is regarded as a worthy opponent of generous and noble character. In Muslim sources he is praised for his commitment to unifying Muslims, waging JIHAD against the crusaders, and strengthening Sunni Islam in all the territories under his control by enforcing justice and supporting religious institutions. His descendants formed the Ayyubid dynasty that ruled SYRIA and Egypt until 1250.

See also CHRISTIANITY AND ISLAM.

Heather N. Keaney

Further reading: Francesco Gabrieli, *Arab Historians of the Crusades* (Berkeley: University of California Press, 1957); H. A. R. Gibb, *The Life of Saladin* (Oxford: Clarendon Press); Malcolm Cameron Lyons and D. E. P. Jackson, *Saladin: The Politics of the Holy War* (Cambridge: Cambridge University Press); Amin Maalouf, *The Crusades through Arab Eyes.* Translated by Jon Rothschild (1984. Reprint, Cairo: The American University in Cairo Press, 1990).

Salafism (Arabic: al-Salafiyya)

Salafism refers to a cluster of different Sunni RENEWAL AND REFORM MOVEMENTS and ideologies in contemporary Islam. The term is based on the Arabic word *salaf*—the pious ancestors of the Islamic UMMA, also known as *al-salaf al-salih* (the righteous ancestors). Salafists consider these ancestors to be the Muslims who had lived during early centuries of Islam, especially the Companions of the prophet Muhammad (until 712), their Successors (the *tabiin*) in the second generation (until 796), and then the Successors of the Successors in the third (until 855). Although some scholars mistakenly trace Salafism back through the centuries to these first generations, it is actu-

ally a modern phenomenon. Since the latter part of the 19th century, when they first appeared, Salafists have used the print and later the electronic media to promote their message that Islam, as well as Muslim society, is in crisis, having been corrupted from within by backward-thinking ULAMA, SUFISM, and spurious innovations (sing. BIDAA). Moreover, they maintained that Islam was being threatened from without by Western COLONIALISM and SECULARISM. In order to meet these challenges, Salafists have sought to restore Islam to what they believe is its ideal, pristine form. Their reading of the past, however, has been shaped by their present circumstances and concerns.

Salafists are in general agreement that bringing back the true Islam means to stop blindly following the rulings of the ulama of the traditional Sunni law schools and look instead only to the QURAN, the SUNNA of the prophet Muhammad, and the example of the *salaf*. They have had radically different opinions about how to do this, however—a fact often overlooked by journalists and scholars. The modernist branch of the Salafis, first established in EGYPT by JAMAL AL-DIN AL-AFGHANI (d. 1897) and MUHAMMAD ABDUH (d. 1905), have seen the Quran and sunna in the light of reason, seeking in them spiritual inspiration and general ethical principles, as they believe the first Muslims had done. They have also accepted the authority of these sources in matters of worship, like prayer, almsgiving, fasting, and the HAJJ. Matters not dealt with in the Quran and sunna are to be decided by the application of IJTIHAD (independent human judgment), which they were convinced would provide the community with the vitality needed to adapt to modernity. The other branch of Salafism is that of the followers of WAHHABISM in Saudi Arabia. Indeed, they often prefer to be known as Salafis rather than Wahhabis, which is a derogatory term usually used by outsiders. They read the Quran as the literal word of God, and maintain that it, together with the sunna, should be the basis of the SHARIA (sacred law), which is to be strictly followed in all matters. They accept *ijtihad*, but interpret it conservatively. Wahhabi

Salafis are also vehemently opposed to SHIISM, as well as Sufism.

These two branches of Salafism, the modernist and the Wahhabist, have evolved in different and complex ways during the 20th and early 21st centuries. The modernists have emphasized reforms that were intended to reconcile religion with SCIENCE and modernity. They have called for modernizing the educational system (but still keeping Islamic subjects in the curriculum), creating democratic governments, and liberating WOMEN from shackles of tradition. In promoting these ideals, Salafists portrayed the Islam's civilizational heritage as superior to that of the West, redefining traditional concepts in conformity with their progressive outlook. In their publications consultation between a ruler and his advisors (*shura*) became parliamentary DEMOCRACY, the consensus of jurists in matters of law (*IJMAA*) became public opinion, and swearing allegiance to a ruler (*bayaa*) became the right to vote.

Although modernist Salafism was opposed by traditionalist Sunni ulama, it spread rapidly from Egypt to other Arab countries, and eventually to non-Arab ones. In ALGERIA it was promoted by Abd al-Hamid ibn Badis (d. 1940), a religious scholar and a leader of the resistance against the French colonialists. A Tunisian Salafist, Abd al-Aziz al-Thaalibi (d. 1944), founded the Destour Party, which sought to create a constitutional democracy in that country. Salafism also developed roots in MOROCCO. As part of their political activism, Salafists in these countries campaigned against Sufi orders, which they thought were detrimental to their reformist agenda. In INDONESIA the Muhammadiyah reformist movement was founded in 1912 by Ahmad Dahlan (d. 1923), a Javanese scholar who had been influenced by Abduh. Egyptian Salafism has also been credited with influencing the religious outlook of the MUSLIM BROTHERHOOD and the JAMAAT-I ISLAMI in Indo-Pakistan, although the influence of the DEOBAND school was greater in the case of the latter.

Wahhabi Salafists are closely allied to Saudi rulers and, unlike the modernist Salafis, they have become embedded in the authoritarian government of Saudi state that was created by ABD AL-AZIZ IBN SAUD (d. 1953) in the first decades of the 20th century. They control the judiciary and education, and are in charge of strictly enforcing public morality in accordance with their conservative understanding of the sharia. This official Wahhabi Salafism, because it is so closely tied to a regime that holds great wealth from its OIL revenues and because millions of pilgrims visit MECCA and Medina each year, has had widespread influence on Muslims around the world. Its rigid ideology of rule by religious law has inspired violent Sunni JIHAD MOVEMENTS like Hamas in Palestine, Egyptian Islamists, the Taliban in Afghanistan, and similar groups elsewhere. The close connection of Wahhabi Salafism with the Saudi state, however, has also undermined its legitimacy in the eyes of many, including Saudi dissidents. These critics and opponents view the royal family as authoritarian, corrupt, and materialistic, and resent its close ties with the United States and its allies. Some of these opponents have been pushing for gradual democratization and greater respect for HUMAN RIGHTS, like modernist Salafis have done elsewhere. Others, however, have embraced what some have called neo-Wahhabism, and call for the violent overthrow of the Saudi state and the establishment of one that they maintain truly conforms to the sharia. The seizure of the Grand Mosque in Mecca in 1979 was an early manifestation of this militant trend. It also contributed to the shaping of Usama bin Ladin's worldview and the creation of al-Qaida's global terrorist network in the 1980s and 90s.

See also COMPANIONS OF THE PROPHET; IBN ABD AL-WAHHAB, MUHAMMAD; ISLAMISM; AL-QAIDA; RASHID RIDA, MUHAMMAD; SAUDI ARABIA; USAMA BIN LADIN.

Further reading: Asad Abukhalil, *The Battle for Saudi Arabia: Royalty, Fundamentalism, and Global Power* (New York: Seven Stories Press, 2004); Malcolm H. Kerr, *Islamic Reform: The Political and Legal Theories of Muhammad Abduh and Rashid Rida* (Berkeley: University of California Press, 1966); Charles Kurzman, *Modernist Islam, 1840–1940: A Sourcebook* (Oxford:

Oxford University Press, 2002); Madawi al-Rasheed, *Contesting the Saudi State: Islamic Voices from a New Generation* (Cambridge: Cambridge University Press, 2007); Itzchak Weismann, *Taste of Modernity: Sufism, Salafiyya, and Arabism in Late Ottoman Damascus* (Leiden: E.J. Brill, 2001).

salam   *See* ISLAM; PBUH.

salat   *See* PRAYER.

samaa   *See* MUSIC; QAWWALI.

Sanusi Sufi Order   *See* LIBYA; RENEWAL AND REFORM MOVEMENTS.

Satan

In ISLAM the devil is called both Satan (Arabic *shaytan*) and Iblis. These names occur in the QURAN and throughout Islamic religious literature. The two names developed out of pre-Islamic beliefs about evil beings and demons that circulated in Middle Eastern Zoroastrian, Jewish, and Christian communities. Zoroastrianism, which was the state religion of IRAN prior to the Islamic conquests of the seventh century, held that the universe was locked in a struggle between two supreme beings and their armies of angels and demons. The two deities are Ahura Mazda (Lord Wisdom), the benevolent creator god of goodness, light, and knowledge, and Angra Mainyu (Ahriman), the god of evil, darkness, and ignorance. At the end of time, with human assistance, Angra Mainyu and his minions would be defeated and goodness would reign. Scholars think that the Zoroastrian idea of an evil adversary of the good creator god may have influenced the theologies of other religions in the Middle East, including Judaism and Christianity.

The Hebrew word *satan* (accuser) occurs a number of times in the Old Testament, usually in reference to a human who acts as an adversary or accuser (for example, 1 Samuel 29:4). It is in the later books, however, that the word is used for a supramundane being, particularly in Job 1–2 and Zechariah 3. There he is depicted as an angelic member of God's heavenly court who raises accusations against human beings because of their sins. These books of the Hebrew Bible were written between the sixth and fifth centuries B.C.E., at the time of the Babylonian Captivity of the Jews of the Kingdom of Judah (586–537 B.C.E.) and the reign of Persian Achaemenid dynasty (648–330 B.C.E.). This dynasty supported Zoroastrianism and allowed Babylonian Jews to return to JERUSALEM to rebuild their temple that the Babylonians had destroyed in 586, providing an opportunity for Zoroastrian beliefs to influence Jewish ones. The association of Satan with the serpent in the story of ADAM AND EVE does not occur in the Hebrew Bible; this association was made in later Christian writings. Satan as the enemy of God makes his first appearance in the Christian New Testament in the Gospels and the Book of Revelation. These writings identify him as a "tempter" (Matthew 4:3), "the prince of demons" (Matthew 12:24), and "the evil one" (1 John 5:18). He is also called the devil (*diabolos* accuser; for example, Matthew 4:1), which is the word used for Satan in the Septuagint, the Greek translation of the Hebrew Bible. The Book of Revelation calls Satan the "ancient serpent" and "the devil," who will first be bound by the ANGEL of God for a thousand years, thrown into hell for a thousand years, then released in the last days before the Final Judgment (Rev. 20).

The two main stories involving Satan in the Quran are the ones about his rebellion against God and about his temptation of Adam and Eve in PARADISE. In the first of these (related in Q 2:34; 7:11; 15:31; 17:61; 18:50; 20:116; 38:74), God commands the angels to prostrate themselves to Adam when he is created. Satan refuses, unlike the others, and is expelled from paradise for his disobedience. Now called an ungrateful disbeliever (KAFIR), God allows him to become an enemy and a deceiver of humanity until the JUDGMENT DAY. The righteous, however, will be able to successfully resist his efforts to misguide and harm them. This story is not in the Bible, but a version of it can be found in pre-Islamic writings that circulated among Middle Eastern Jews and Christians after the first century C.E. In the second story (Q 7:19–25), Satan seduces Adam and his wife into disobeying God and eating fruit from the Tree of Immortality in paradise. They follow his advice and realize that they have disobeyed their creator. God punishes them by expelling them from paradise. At the end of the story, the Quran warns people, "Do not let Satan seduce you as he did when he caused your parents to be expelled from paradise, stripping their garments so as to expose their private parts. Indeed, he and his tribe (of demons) will watch you where you cannot see them. We have made demons (literally satans) the intimate companions of those who do not believe" (Q 7:27). The quranic story of the fall of Adam does not mention the serpent of the ancient biblical one. Nonetheless other versions of the story in Islamic literature tell how a female serpent helps Satan sneak into paradise by letting him hide in her mouth.

When Islam appeared in the seventh century, stories and doctrines about the devil within monotheistic belief systems had spread to many parts of the Middle East and they had become more elaborate. It is not surprising, therefore, to find that Satan is mentioned in the Quran and that Islamic understandings of him have drawn upon biblical and post-biblical traditions, combined with ancient Arabian beliefs in demons and spirits. Satan's Islamic name, Iblis, was derived from *diabolos,* the term used in the Septuagint. The word *devil* in English is likewise based on this Greek word. Although no longer an accuser in God's heavenly court, the quranic Satan is a tempter, a deceiver, and an enemy of humans. He sneaks around and lies in wait to attack people on God's "straight path" (Q 7:16–17). Satan is also associated with defilement caused by pork, wine, gambling, and divination, which make people become violent, forget God, and neglect PRAYER (Q 5:91–92). The Quran suggests that he is an angel, but it also clearly states that he was one of the Jinn (Q 18:50), lesser spirits capable of both

good and evil known to Arabs before the Islamic era. Muslim commentators affirm that he is the chief of the jinn, pointing to the verse in which he declares that he is made of fire like them, not of clay like humans (Q 7:11). Some commentators, seeking to harmonize the two different quranic understandings, say that he was once an angel named Azazil who became Iblis after being cursed for his disobedience. Others speculate that he was originally a youthful JINNI who was captured in a battle with the angels and raised by them.

In Islamic religious thought Satan only has the power that God allows him to have. God alone has power over all things. What agency Satan is allowed is limited to the earthly sphere of human affairs, and humans have the capacity to reject him. This means, for example, that when modern Iranian leaders refer to the United States as the Great Satan in SERMONS, speeches, and political demonstrations, they are using a trope that identifies the United States with disbelief, deception, and diversion from God's path, while recognizing that the U.S. government is still under God's power and capable of being opposed by righteous people. Sufis, those pursuing a mystical experience of God, have generally regarded Satan in the same light as other Muslims, and they have identified him with the lower self (*nafs*) that hinders seekers from finding God or the Truth. A few, however, have taught that even Satan could be seen in a positive light. MANSUR AL-HALLAJ (d. 922), Ahmad al-Ghazali (d. 1226), and Farid al-Din Attar (d. ca. 1220) saw Satan as the perfect monotheist, for he alone refused to bow to Adam, which he saw as an act of idolatry. The ULAMA rejected such views. The famous Sufi master JALAL AL-DIN RUMI (d. 1273) supported the view of the ulama, pointing out that Satan's disobedience was the result of his failure to recognize that Adam had been brought to life with God's breath and was formed according to his image. Therefore bowing down to him when he was created would not be IDOLATRY, but a way of worshipping God.

Muslims are cognizant of Satan's existence in their ritual life. A Quran recital usually begins with the prayer formula, "I seek refuge in God from the reviled Satan," followed by the BASMALA. The word "reviled" (*rajim*) literally means "pelted with stones." Indeed, the stoning of three pillars in Mina that represent Satan is one of the concluding rituals of the annual HAJJ. It is linked to the story of Abraham's near sacrifice of his son, when Abraham repelled Satan with stones for trying to persuade him to disobey God. Millions of pilgrims perform this ritual each year when they go to MECCA.

See also ABRAHAM; ALLAH; CREATION; SATANIC VERSES; WOMEN.

Further reading: Peter J. Awn, *Satan's Tragedy and Redemption: Iblis in Sufi Psychology* (Leiden: E.J. Brill, 1983); Fazlur Rahman, *Major Themes of the Quran* (Minneapolis, Minn.: Bibliotheca Islamica, 1980); Ahmad ibn Muhammad al-Thalabi, *Arais al-majalis fi qisas al-anbiya, or "Lives of the Prophets."* Translated by William M. Brinner (Leiden: E.J. Brill, 2002): 43–57; Alford T. Welch, "Allah and Other Supernatural Beings: The Emergence of the Quranic Doctrine of *Tawhid.*" *Journal of the American Academy of Religion* 47 (1979): 733–758; T. J. Wray and Gregory Mobley, *The Birth of Satan: Tracing the Devil's Biblical Roots* (New York: Palgrave Macmillan, 2005).

Satanic Verses

Euro-American Islamic studies scholars in the 20th century coined the term *Satanic Verses* for certain verses Muslim sources say SATAN attempted to have MUHAMMAD include in the QURAN. A number of respected early Quran commentaries and historical writings provide testimonies about this incident, including Said ibn Jubayr (d. 714,), Ikrima (d. 723), al-Suddi (d. 745), Ibn Ishaq (d. 767), al-Waqidi (d. 823), and al-Tabari (d. 923). Although they differ in detail, these accounts state that when Muhammad was still preaching in MECCA, Satan deceived him into delivering "false" revelations that recognized the existence of Allah's three daughters. After reciting Q 53:19–20 ("Have you seen al-Lat, al-Uzza, and another, Manat, the third?"), Muhammad reportedly said, "Indeed, these are the exalted cranes/the exalted maidens (*gharaniq*), and their intercession is desired." (The double meaning of *gharaniq* here may have been a rhetorical device, or it may indicate that the cranes were symbols for the goddesses. Birds in Middle Eastern lore are ANIMALS that link heaven and earth.) By mentioning the three goddesses, Muhammad appears to admit that they had the power to act for the benefit of those who worshipped them. This has been seen as an effort to appeal to members of the QURAYSH who were unhappy with Muhammad's attacks against their gods and goddesses. The historical reports go on to say that Muhammad later realized he had made a mistake and repudiated the verses in question. They also indicate that he received a subsequent revelation in which God declares that Satan was responsible for his error, and that he (God) had allowed it to happen as a test of faith (Q 22:52–54).

Muslim scholars increasingly rejected the historical truth of this incident and their views have prevailed until the present time among most Muslims. The first generations of scholars opposed to the veracity of the Satanic Verses incident included such notable Quran commentators as Abu Bakr ibn al-Arabi (d. 1148), Fakr al-Din al-Razi (d. 1210), and Ibn Kathir (d. 1373). They argued that the incident portrayed Muhammad as a flawed prophet, one who made a mistake by recognizing that there were other deities besides God and who could not tell the difference between the word of God and the word of Satan. The correct doctrine in their view, which was gaining widespread acceptance, was that God had made all prophets, including Muhammad, incapable of error and free of sin. Muhammad, therefore, could never have been misled by Satan and would never have endorsed IDOLATRY. The attribution of infallibility (*isma*) to Muhammad affirmed the truth of the Quran and Muhammad's SUNNA, both of which had already become essential bases of Islamic law (*FIQH*). Moreover, the doctrine was reinforced by the popular veneration for Muhammad and other Muslim holy men and women connected with the spread of SUFISM.

In 1988 the award-winning Indian author SALMAN RUSHDIE (b. 1947) published an English-language novel entitled *The Satanic Verses,* which sparked a controversy of global proportions. It aggravated relations between Muslims and non-Muslims, as well as between pious Muslims and secular ones, since Rushdie was himself a Muslim more by heritage than conviction. The book was not so much about Muhammad and the Satanic Verses incident per se, but it did contain passages that were interpreted to be blasphemies against the Prophet and his wives. Demonstrations against the book irrupted in Bradford, England (January 14, 1989), Bombay, Islamabad, PAKISTAN (February 12), and INDIA (February 24). In IRAN, AYATOLLAH RUHOLLAH KHOMEINI issued a FATWA (advisory ruling based on the SHARIA) on February 14, 1989, that called for his death. Khomeini exploited the incident to revitalize Iranian popular support for his revolutionary government, which was just ending a long, costly war with Iraq. He may also have been personally offended by derogatory passages in Rushdie's book that talk about a puritanical "IMAM," Khomeini himself. As a consequence, Rushdie was forced to go into hiding for nearly 10 years. Khomeini died in 1989, but the fatwa was reaffirmed by the Iranian government in 2005. Rushdie, meanwhile has kept busy with writing more novels and making numerous public appearances.

See also BLASPHEMY; GODDESS; *TAFSIR*.

Further reading: Shahab Ahmed, *The Problem of the Satanic Verses and the Formation of Islamic Orthodoxy* (forthcoming); Lisa Appignanesi and Sara Maitland, eds., *The Rushdie File* (London: Fourth Estate, 1989); Salman Rushdie, *The Satanic Verses* (London: Viking Penguin, 1988); W. Montgomery Watt, *Muhammad at Mecca* (Oxford: Oxford University Press, 1953).

Saudi Arabia (Official name: Kingdom of Saudi Arabia)

Named after the dynasty that rules it, Saudi Arabia is one of the most powerful nations in the Middle East. It is has an area of 756,785 square miles (about one-fifth the size of the United States), a population of 28.1 million people (2008 estimate), and the world's largest OIL reserves. The birthplace of Islam, the home of MECCA and

MEDINA, the two holiest cities in Islam, and host to millions of pilgrims every year, Saudi Arabia has great religious importance within the Muslim world. It also occupies a position of geographic importance, bordering both the Persian Gulf and the Red Sea, as well as IRAQ, JORDAN, and Kuwait to the north, Oman and YEMEN to the south, and Qatar and the United Arab Emirates to the east. Saudi Arabia occupies most of the Arabian Peninsula. Along the Red Sea coast lie the regions of Hijaz and Asir. Much of the center of Saudi Arabia is an arid rocky plateau known as the Najd. Along the Persian Gulf coast lies the Hasa Plain. Other important regions include the deserts of Al-Nafud, Al-Dahna, and the Rub al-Khali. Saudi Arabia's major cities are Mecca and Medina in the Hijaz, Riyadh in the Najd, and the tri-city region of Dammam, al-Khubar, and Dharan along the Gulf coast in the east. Its indigenous population is overwhelmingly Arab, but it has a significant number of foreign workers from all over the world, including the United States. The state religion is based on a puritanical form of Sunni Islam known as WAHHABISM, but there is a sizeable Shii minority population of about 11 percent (2005 estimate) in the eastern region of the country, along the Gulf coast.

Because much of the Arabian Peninsula consists of desert, the first permanent settlements in the region were along the coasts of the Red Sea and the Persian Gulf. These towns soon became active in trading between the rich civilizations of Egypt to the west and the Tigris-Euphrates region to the east, which brought prosperity to some areas, particularly along the southwestern coast. As the development of camel caravans increased trade across the peninsula, urban centers also appeared in the interior regions. Outside the cities, most inhabitants of the region were nomadic tribes. The northern area, where the archaeological site of Madam Salih is located, was once home to the Nabateans, an ancient Arab trading culture that extended northward into Jordan.

About 613 C.E., Muhammad ibn Abd Allah first began preaching the message of Islam in

Mecca. By the time of his death in 632, an Islamic empire was in its first stages of development, with its center in Medina. However, as the empire expanded, its capital was moved, first to DAMASCUS under the UMAYYAD CALIPHATE, then to BAGHDAD under the ABBASID CALIPHATE. As the Islamic empire lost power, the Hijaz, or western area of Arabia where Mecca and Medina are located, fell under MAMLUK rule from about 1250 to 1517, followed by the OTTOMAN DYNASTY. During most of this period the Hijaz was important to Arabia's foreign rulers, both as the birthplace of Islam and as an important source of revenue from pilgrims making the HAJJ. It was locally ruled by the Sharifs, a dynasty claiming descent from Muhammad. Neither the foreign nor the local rulers, however, tried to exert their authority over the Najd, which was occupied by nomadic tribes.

It was in the Najd that Islamic reformer MUHAMMAD IBN ABD AL-WAHHAB (d. 1792) began preaching, urging a return to a more austere form of Islam. One of his early supporters was a local ruler, Muhammad ibn Saud (d. 1765). Ibn Saud offered lbn Abd al-Wahhab his protection, and adopted his vision of Islam. Ibn Saud and his successors, leading Wahhabi military forces in JIHAD, began to unite the tribes of the Najd, eventually conquering almost all of the Arabian Peninsula.

This first Saudi state was short-lived, but in 1902 ABD AL-AZIZ IBN SAUD captured Riyadh; from there he expanded the areas under his control. In 1932 these areas were unified as the Kingdom of Saudi Arabia, with Abd al-Aziz as king. Since his death in 1953, the kingdom has been ruled by his sons: Saud (r. 1953–64); Faysal (r. 1964–75); Khalid (r. 1975–82): Fahd (r. 1982–2005), and Abd Allah (r. 2005–   ). Members of the royal family hold most of the major ministries and provincial governorships. The king, who is also known as the Servant of the Two Holy Mosques (in Mecca and Medina), also appoints members of the Consultative Council (Majlis al-Shura), the closest thing the country has to a legislature; political parties are banned. The Basic Law of the country is the SHARIA, as interpreted by the HAN-BALI LEGAL SCHOOL, the tradition that inspired the Wahhabi movement. The Quran is said to be the constitution. Religious affairs are managed by the ULAMA, especially by the Al al-Shaykh, descendants of Ibn Abd al-Wahhab. They continue to lend legitimacy to the government, and provide it advice and guidance in affairs of state. Strict religious law is enforced in the courts and by the *mutawwaa*, Wahhabi public morality police. Public criticism of the government or royal family is generally not permitted. King Abd Allah, the current ruler, is seen as favoring reforms that are balanced with a respect for Saudi tradition, and he has continued the cautious reform program he began as crown prince.

In 1933 King Abd al-Aziz granted Standard Oil of California (SOCAL) the concession to prospect for oil in the kingdom. Its discovery in Dhahran in 1938 significantly changed the young nation from an underdeveloped desert region to one of the world's wealthiest countries. Much of the kingdom's development only began after World War II and was carried out by the American oil concession, renamed in 1944 as the Arabian American Oil Company (Aramco, now known as Saudi Aramco). In 1960 Saudi Arabia was one of the founding members of OPEC (ORGANIZATION OF PETROLEUM EXPORTING COUNTRIES), which coordinates the petroleum policies of member nations. In 1973 it participated in an oil embargo against the United States and the Netherlands because of their support for Israel in the 1973 Arab-Israel war. Oil revenues increased significantly as a result. Petroleum and petroleum products today make up 90 percent of Saudi Arabia's exports; the nation is the world's largest oil exporter. Despite its vast oil wealth, Saudi Arabia faces economic challenges. The economy is heavily dependent on oil. To diversify the economy, the government is encouraging the development of industries in the private sector. It is hoped that this will also reduce the country's high unemployment rate. In 2005 Saudi Arabia joined the World Trade Organization (WTO); it is hoped that membership will help attract foreign investment to Saudi Arabia. Its oil wealth has also made it possible to project its influence and conservative Islamic doctrines around the world.

During the cold war years, Saudi Arabia developed a close relationship with the United States as a bulwark against the spread of Soviet influence and leftist movements in the Middle East. It played a leading role in the creation of the MUSLIM WORLD LEAGUE (founded in 1962) and the ORGANIZATION OF THE ISLAMIC CONFERENCE (founded in 1969), both of which exist to promote global Muslim unity. It has also taken a strong stand against the spread of revolutionary Iranian Shiism in the Gulf region, and supported Iraq in its 1980–88 war with Iran. In 1990–91, however, Saudi Arabia joined a large international coalition of forces, led by the United States, to expel Iraq from neighboring Kuwait. It also joined with the United States and Pakistan in the 1980s to aid the AFGHAN MUJAHIDIN in their war against the Soviet Union, which had occupied AFGHANISTAN in 1978.

Saudi Arabia has made great strides toward educating its people, both men and WOMEN, since the 1970s. It has 20 public universities and more than 24,000 schools. Many members of the royal family and the middle class have received their college educations abroad in the United States and Britain. At the same time, Saudi Arabia has had to balance its conservative Islamic tradition, based on sharia law, with internal pressure for reform. Several domestic opposition movements have developed, while others are based abroad. These groups have called for a variety of reforms, particularly with regard to democratization, HUMAN RIGHTS reform, and social justice. The lives of Saudi women are strictly controlled, but in 1990 a number of university women publicly protested the ban that prohibits women from driving. In 2008 the government agreed to some changes in rights for women, including a decree that allows women to enter a hotel without a chaperone; the government has also agreed to lift the driving ban, but no official decree has yet been issued.

Saudi Arabia must also deal with the question of religious violence and TERRORISM. In 1979 a group of rebels, following a Saudi they believed to be the promised MAHDI, seized the Sacred Mosque in Mecca after the *hajj* and called for an end to Saudi rule. They were opposed to the sweeping modernization programs that the government had launched in the 1970s. The rebels could be removed only by force, with significant loss of life. The event left the Saudi kingdom greatly shaken. Later, in September 2001, many of the hijackers involved in the attacks on New York and Washington were Saudi nationals. USAMA BIN LADIN, the leader of the AL-QAIDA organization that conducted these attacks, was the son of the country's foremost contractor, Muhammad bin Ladin (d. 1967), who had founded the company that built much of Saudi Arabia's modern infrastructure. Although Usama had assisted the Saudi government in Afghanistan in the 1980s, he was stripped of his Saudi nationality in 1994 because of his opposition to the government's close relationship with the United States. In particular, he was opposed to the stationing of U.S. troops in the Muslim holy land. Beginning in 2003 suicide bombers and militants suspected of having links to al-Qaida carried out, or attempted to carry out, a number of attacks in Saudi Arabia; most of those killed were Saudi nationals.

See also BEDOUIN; COMMUNISM; FAYSAL IBN ABD AL-AZIZ AL-SAUD; GULF STATES; GULF WARS; HASHIMITE DYNASTY; RENEWAL AND REFORM MOVEMENTS; SHIISM.

Juan E. Campo and Kate O'Halloran

Further reading: Paul Aarts and Gerd Nonneman, eds., *Saudi Arabia in the Balance: Political Economy, Society, Foreign Affairs* (New York: New York University Press, 2006); Christine Moss Helms, *The Cohesion of Saudi Arabia: Evolution of Political Identity* (Baltimore, Md.: Johns Hopkins University Press; London: Croom Helm, 1981); Madawi al-Rasheed, *A History of Saudi Arabia* (Cambridge: Cambridge University Press, 2002); Mai Yamani, *Changed Identities: The Challenge of the New Generation in Saudi Arabia* (London: Royal Institute of International Affairs, 2000); Ayman al-Yassini, *Religion and State in the Kingdom of Saudi Arabia* (Boulder, Colo.: Westview Press, 1985).

sawm See FASTING.

say   *See* HAJJ; UMRA.

sayyid (seyyed)

One of the most important titles of honor given to a man in a Muslim society is that of *sayyid,* for a woman it is *sayyida.* In Arabic it has been used since pre-Islamic times to signify that someone has high status and dignity, a "lord" or "master" (alternately, "lady" or "mistress") and is nearly synonymous with the term *sharif.* Ancient ARAB tribal chieftains were known as *sayyids,* but its most widespread use in Islam has been with reference to the AHL AL-BAYT, those regarded as members of Muhammad's family and their direct descendants. According to the hadith, Muhammad (d. 632) referred to members of his family by this title. Over time it was used particularly for descendants of HUSAYN IBN ALI (d. 680), while *sharif* was used primarily for descendants of Husayn's brother Hasan. People claiming descent from the *ahl al-bayt* have migrated throughout Muslim lands, where their families have multiplied. In Shii societies *sayyids* qualify to receive a special tax payment from the faithful known as the *khums.* Respected Sufi masters were also known as *sayyids,* or, in popular usage *sidi* ("my lord"). The tombs of *sayyids,* men and women, have become pilgrimage shrines in many countries. In recent times that term has come to be used more loosely as a title of respect in Middle Eastern societies. The Andalusian nobleman and warrior, Rodrigo Diaz de Vivar (d. 1099), was known as El Cid, based on the Arabic *al-sid.* Romances were written about him in Latin and Spanish, and an epic film starring Charlton Heston as the title character premiered in 1961.

See also HONOR AND SHAME; SAINT; SHIISM; ZIYARA.

Further reading: Michael Gilsenan, *Recognising Islam: Religion and Society in the Modern Middle East* (London: Croom Helm, 1982).

Sayyid Qutb   *See* QUBT, SAYYID.

school   *See* AZHAR, AL-; EDUCATION; *KUTTAB*; MADRASA; STUDENT; UNIVERSITY.

science

During ancient and medieval times, sciences (or hard sciences) were indistinguishable from PHILOSOPHY. Therefore, sciences hereafter are taken to mean intellectual endeavors outside the fields of THEOLOGY and literature. Sciences flourished in the Arabo-Islamic empire since the ninth century. The most significant thrust came from a movement of translation of other scientific and philosophical traditions into Arabic. CALIPHs and high officials were usually the sponsors of this movement, and of scholarship in general. Prominent among them is the Abbasid caliph al-Mamun (ninth century), who commissioned the building of the famous library and translation house of Bayt al-Hikmah in BAGHDAD. Other famous centers of learning and scholarship in the empire were Gundishapur and Harran, DAMASCUS, CAIRO, and CORDOBA.

Although all scientific works were translated into or written in Arabic, all ethnic (Greeks, Anatolians, Syriacs, Persians, Arabs) and religious (Christians, Jews, Sabians, Muslims) communities of the empire produced scholars who contributed to sciences. Taking the term Arabo-Islamic to denote belonging to a political entity rather than to a religious, ethnic, or linguistic entity, these scholars will be referred to hereafter as the Arabo-Islamic scholars. Scientific and philosophical works were translated from the Greek, Syriac, Sanskrit and Persian languages by such scholars as Ishaq ibn Hunayn (d. ca. 911), Thabit ibn Qurra (d. 901), the Banu Musa brothers (ninth century), al-Khawarizmi (d. ca. 850), and AL-BIRUNI (d. 1048).

The contribution of the Arabo-Islamic scholars to the genesis of modern sciences constitutes a passionately debated topic of research (see Huff and Sabra), and in many encyclopedias of science and its history, the Arabo-Islamic scholars are credited only with preserving Greek learning for European medieval scholars. However, the debate is slightly misguided because the work of any scholar should be studied with reference to his/her own culture, and not only to how it impacted modern culture and sciences.

Because of its importance to religious duties (for example, calculating the QIBLA and prayer times), astronomy held a prominent place on the scientific scene. Rulers sponsored the construction of observatories and large observation instruments and employed scientists such as al-Battani (d. 929), al-Khayyam (d. 1123), and al-Tusi (d. 1274) to construct astronomical tables and keep time. In medicine and pharmaceutics the *Qanun* of IBN SINA (Avicenna, d. 1037) continued to serve as a major reference until the 18th century. All across the empire, public hospitals were constructed to cure the ill and train new doctors. In MATHEMATICS al-Khawarizmi inaugurated a new science, algebra. In optics Ibn al-Haytham (d. 1039) was the first to use the experimental method in science. Trying to transform cheap metals into gold, Arabo-Islamic alchemists such as Jabir ibn Hayyan discovered new substances and devised ways for making them. Scientific teaching was mainly dispensed from private homes and hospitals where teachers would certify that a student "read" (studied) this or that major book with him.

See also ALCHEMY.

A. Nazir Atassi

Further reading: Toby E. Huff, *The Rise of Early Modern Science: Islam, China, and the West,* 2d ed. (London: Cambridge University Press, 2003); Roshdi Rashed, ed., *Encyclopedia of the History of Arabic Science* (London: Routledge, 1996); A. I. Sabra, *Optics, Astronomy and Logic: Studies in Arabic Science and Philosophy* (Hampshire, England: Variorum, 1994).

secularism

Secularism denotes a relationship between religion and the state born out of modern Anglo-Atlantic conceptions of social, religious and political AUTHORITY. Although it has become a prominent political idea worldwide, it is important to note that secularism is rooted in a particular context and reflects both the theological developments and the predominance of a scientific outlook toward political, economic, and social organization that developed in medieval, Renaissance, and Enlightenment EUROPE. Thus, while secularism has made its way into political and religious ideas

across the world, its exact meaning in those different contexts is sometimes difficult to discern.

There are two dominant models and understandings of secularism in contemporary Western European and North American societies. One, the strict disestablishment of religion, is found in the UNITED STATES and stresses that the state may not ally itself with any particular religious tradition. In this case, it is important to note, however, that individual decisions made by the government often reflect the tradition in which most law- and policymakers have been shaped, namely, Christianity. The second model, found in particular in France and TURKEY, is often called laicism. In it, the state oversees and regulates religion, working to enforce a privatized understanding of religion, thus removing religion from public visibility. These two models reflect the history of the different rationales for secularism: on the one hand, the protection of religion from the hands of the state and, on the other hand, the protection of the state from the hands of religion.

During the 19th century and into the 20th century, colonized societies in the Middle East and South Asia began to grapple with the issue of secularism, often as a result of legal, economic, and political reforms instituted by colonial authorities and sympathetic local elites. Vigorous debates surrounded the effects of these secular reforms, debates that had a tremendous influence on the character of modern states that emerged from colonial control in the early to mid-20th century, such AS SYRIA, IRAQ, EGYPT, and INDIA.

Many of the conflicts that have racked these states since independence, from the partition of India/PAKISTAN to conflicts between Islamists and both nominally secular and self-consciously Islamic states throughout the Middle East, have resulted in part from disagreements about the proper role of religion—in general or in regard to specific traditions—in the public sphere. Today, many opponents of secularism stress the historic particularity of secularism's origins, thus raising questions about the portability of the idea from its original context, dominated by Christianity, to non-Christian societies. Furthermore, and perhaps most importantly, disputes about the nature of secularism reflect different definitions of religion and cannot be reduced to political, economic, or social variables.

See also COLONIALISM; REFORM AND RENEWAL MOVEMENTS; THEOLOGY; WESTERNIZATION.

Caleb Elfenbein

Further reading: Owen Chadwick, *The Secularization of the European Mind in the 19th Century* (Cambridge: Cambridge University Press, 1975); Louis Duprié, *Passage to Modernity* (New Haven, Conn.: Yale University Press, 1993); Albert Hourani, *Arabic Thought in the Liberal Age 1798–1939* (Cambridge: Cambridge University Press, 1962).

Seljuk dynasty

With roots in the steppes of Central Asia, the Seljuk dynasty came to control much of the Middle East and Central Asia from the 11th to the 13th centuries. It largely relied on bands of nomadic Turkmen warriors for its fighting force and on Persian officials for its administration.

The early Seljuk clan was part of the ancient Oghuz tribal group of steppe nomads in Central Asia, out of which arose in the 10th century an individual named Seljuk, who was probably the first of his group to convert to Islam. His sons and grandsons were successful raiders, who, through skillful military operations, expanded their territory over much of IRAN by the mid-11th century.

In 1055 Seljuk's grandson Toghril (d. 1063) entered BAGHDAD, overthrew the Buyid prince, and was consequently proclaimed SULTAN by the Abassid CALIPH. This recognition by the caliph of a separate sultan created an important division between spiritual authority and secular rule. In addition, the military power of the Sunni Seljuks, by halting the spread of SHIISM in the region, ensured the dominance of SUNNISM in the central Islamic lands.

Toghril was succeeded by his nephew Alp Arslan (d. 1073), who named as his VIZIER the capable administrator Nizam al-Mulk (d. 1091). Together they were successful in consolidating Seljuk power

in Anatolia. However, as conflicts arose over succession, the empire was gradually weakened over the next century. A branch of the Seljuk dynasty based in Konya maintained power in Anatolia until the beginning of the 14th century.

While the Seljuk dynasty held AUTHORITY due to military might, it was also a great supporter of the arts, especially ARCHITECTURE. Many MOSQUES and MADRASAS were built during their reign, which was also marked by a distinctive style of tomb architecture with cylindrical bases and conical roofs that resemble a certain type of tent in Central Asia. Notable scholars such as AL-GHAZALI (d. 1111) and Umar Khayyam (d. 1123) flourished during the Great Seljuk Empire, and the mystic poet JALAL AL-DIN RUMI (d. 1273) composed his poetry in the Anatolian Seljuk capital of Konya. The period of Seljuk rule also saw the formation of the first major DERVISH orders.

See also ABBASID CALIPHATE; TURKEY.

Mark Soileau

Further reading: Claude Cahen, *Pre-Ottoman Turkey* (London: Sidgwick and Jackson, 1968); Marshall G. S. Hodgson, *The Venture of Islam.* Vol. 2: *The Expansion of Islam in the Middle Periods* (Chicago: University of Chicago Press, 1974); Tamara Talbot Rice, *The Seljuks in Asia Minor* (London: Thames and Hudson, 1961).

Sephardic Jews

Sephardic Jews are the descendants of those Jews who settled in Iberia (Spain) before it was under Roman control and remained there until the expulsion of 1492, experiencing periods of economic prosperity and cultural flourishing alternating with those of persecution and forced conversions.

Sephardic Jews remember the Convivencia (Spanish, "living together") in al-Andalus as a golden age, marked by poetry, PHILOSOPHY, ARCHITECTURE, and religious tolerance. This era ended with the Almohad takeover of 1147, when many Jews were forced to convert to Islam. During the Christian reconquest, Jews faced increasing massacre and forced conversion from 1391 through the Inquisitions of 1478–1834. By the time of the expulsion in 1492, three categories of Jews had emerged: *conversos* (Sp., "converts"), *marranos* (Sp., derogatory term for crypto-Jews, who converted while maintaining Jewish practices in secret), and those who refused to convert. Some emigrants established Portuguese-speaking communities in Western Europe, while most resettled in the Ottoman Empire, where they continued to speak Arabic and Ladino.

The Ottoman SULTAN welcomed this mass immigration of talented Sephardic Jews, whose connections to Europe and allegiance to the Ottomans made them exceptional diplomats, translators, and purveyors of European medicine and military technology. Sephardic communities, such as those of Salonika and Istanbul, were famous for their printing presses and academies. Their magnificent yeshivas and synagogues are distinct from Ashkenazic buildings, and in fact the synagogue service and unique rituals also reflect local customs and Islamic influences.

The decline of Ottoman Jewry accompanied the decline of the empire itself. The TANZIMAT reforms of 1839 attempted to curtail foreign intervention by bringing minorities under the control of the central government. However, the Damascus Affair of 1840, in which the Syrian Jewish community was charged with a blood libel, provoked international Jewish defense efforts and increased demands by Britain and France for Ottoman reforms. This international solidarity was the catalyst for the Alliance Israélite Universelle, begun in 1860 by liberal French Jews. This program introduced Eastern Jews to Western ideas and values in an attempt to achieve full citizenship for the Jews of the Ottoman Empire. The Sephardic community split between supporting the alliance and adopting the Zionist position that emancipation was possible only within a Jewish state.

After the victors of World War I split apart the former Ottoman Empire, the majority populations persecuted the Sephardic ethnic and religious minorities. World War II decimated the Sephardic community. Those few who survived emigrated primarily to ISRAEL, France, and North America in the following years. Each community shows evidence of maintaining a distinct Sephardic cultural and religious identity while at the same time assimilating into the broader community.

See also ANDALUSIA; ALMOHAD DYNASTY; ISTANBUL; JUDAISM AND ISLAM; OTTOMAN DYNASTY; REFUGEES.

Jessica Andruss

Further reading: Shlomo Deshen and Walter P. Zenner, eds., *Jews among Muslims: Communities in the Precolonial Middle East* (New York: New York University Press, 1996); Daniel J. Elazar, *The Other Jews: The Sephardim Today* (New York: Basic Books, 1989); Jane S. Gerber, *The Jews of Spain: A History of the Sephardic Experience* (New York: The Free Press, 1992); Norman A. Stillman, *The Jews of Arab Lands in Modern Times* (New York: Jewish Publication Society, 1991).

scripture *See* HOLY BOOKS.

sermon

Islam developed three homiletic traditions: the *khutba* (sermon), pious exhortation (*mawiza, waaz,* or *tadhkir*), and homiletic storytelling (*qasas*).

The *khutba* belongs to a larger genre of public oratory that predates ISLAM and was performed in a variety of ceremonial contexts, including official receptions, war declarations, and wedding speeches. In Islam, the canonical or liturgical sermon (*khutba shariyya*) forms a prescribed part of ritual observances, notably the Friday congregational PRAYER, the two feast days, and communal rogations for rainfall. It also became customary to perform liturgical sermons during other festivals and to exhort JIHAD.

Islamic legal sources stipulate that the canonical sermon comply with the liturgical conditions that MUHAMMAD reportedly instituted in the seventh century. For example, on Fridays, the *khutba* must precede the communal prayer, but in all other rituals the prayer comes first. After the call to prayer, the preacher (*khatib*) should arise, grasp a sword or staff (pre-Islamic symbols of authority), and ascend the pulpit steps right foot first. He pronounces two sermons standing, but must sit and pause briefly in between them. He should initiate both sermons with liturgical formulae of praise to God, the Muslim profession of faith, and invocations of blessings upon the Prophet. The first sermon should contain admonitions and counsel relevant to the occasion, while the second "qualifying" sermon features prayers on behalf of the Prophet, the ruler, and the community. The *khutba* is often delivered in rhymed prose, believed to enhance its affective and persuasive power. Today, in most Islamic countries, the state determines the content of the "official" Friday and festival *khutbas*.

Exhortatory preaching assemblies (*majlis* or *maqamat al-waaz*) varied in performance styles and ritual environments and were not subject to the same liturgical conditions as the canonical sermon. Exhortatory preachers crafted their sermons from scriptural recitation, HADITH sayings, Sufi ceremonial litanies praising God, personal admonitions, and preexisting homiletic literature. Morality, the remembrance of DEATH, and JUDGMENT DAY were the most common themes. Preachers delivered exhortatory sermons during Sufi ceremonies, as erudite homilies in MADRASAS, as part of feast day celebrations and funerals, and as regular public moral instruction. Itinerant and "free" preachers coexisted uneasily with those appointed by the authorities to preach.

Religious storytelling (*qasas*) developed from quranic tales of the prophets and the People of Israel and from the so-called stories of the prophets genre of exegetical narratives embellishing the scriptural stories. Liturgical and exhortatory preachers sometimes incorporated them into their sermons. Independent storytellers preached on roadsides and in cemeteries and held storytelling assemblies in mosques, where they read stories to the public. Socially, storytelling served to edify and exhort the faithful to imitate the prophets' moral examples. The religious authorities sometimes censured the storytellers as a public nuisance for narrating fraudulent hadith to an unsuspecting audience.

See also CEMETERY; *DHIKR*; PROPHETS AND PROPHECY.

Linda G. Jones

Further reading: Jonathan Berkey, *Popular Preaching and Religious Authority in the Medieval Islamic Near East* (Seattle and London: University of Washington Press, 2001); Patrick D. Gaffney, *The Prophet's Pulpit: Islamic Preaching in Contemporary Egypt* (Berkeley: University of California Press, 1994). Ibn al-Jawzi, *Kitab al-qussas w'al-mudhakkirin* (*The Book of Storytellers and Popular Preachers*). Edited and translated by Merlin L. Swartz (Beirut: Dar al-Machreq, 1986); Linda G. Jones, "The Boundaries of Sin and Communal Identity: Muslim and Christian Preaching and the Transmission of Cultural Identity in Medieval Iberia and the Maghreb (12th to 15th Centuries)." Ph.D. dissertation (unpublished), University of California, Santa Barbara, 2004.

Seveners *See* ISMAILI SHIISM.

Shaarawi, Huda (1879–1947) *pioneering Egyptian feminist leader*

Born into an elite family in upper EGYPT, Shaarawi was raised in CAIRO. Although her father, a prominent government official died when she was four, she continued to lead a privileged childhood. She was instructed along with her only brother in all subjects but Arabic, which was deemed inappropriate for a young girl. As a result Shaarawi became fluent in Turkish and French and had memorized the QURAN by the age of nine. However, she also became conscious from an early age of differences in gender norms. She was married at the age of 13 to her paternal cousin, Ali Shaarawi, but months later a dispute led to a seven-year separation. This period served as a crucial developmental time, allowing her to continue her studies with foreign tutors. She also met Eugénie Le Brun, a French woman who became her mentor and began attending her weekly salon, where Islamic modernist ideas concerning WOMEN were discussed. Shaarawi was exposed to new ideas about veiling, seclusion, EDUCATION for girls, and Egyptian family law, known as the personal status codes.

In 1900 she was reconciled to her husband and resumed married life. After the birth of two children she dedicated the next several years to raising her son and daughter. However, in 1909 Shaarawi entered a new period of activism and leadership. She founded a secular women's philanthropist organization dedicated to providing medical care to poor women and CHILDREN, and she organized a series of lectures for and by women. Five years later she founded two additional organizations similarly aimed at meeting the needs of different classes of women: the Women's Refinement Association and the Ladies Literary Improvement Society. The activities of these years prepared her well for her next role as leader in the nationalist struggle for independence. In 1919 she organized the first women's demonstration against British rule. She worked closely with her husband and other leaders of the nationalist Wafd Party, and she was named president of the party's Women's Central Committee. However, upon the granting of limited independence from Britain and the establishment of a constitution in 1923, Sharawi and other women activists were disappointed. Their demands for suffrage were not met, nor were women's rights significantly improved under the new constitution.

Thereafter her activism became more markedly feminist in character, and the same year she helped to found the Egyptian Feminist Union (EFU). At the end of her return journey from an international women's conference, which she attended as the EFU delegate, she publicly removed her face veil as an act of protest. This remains the act for which she is best known in Egypt today. In some ways, the EFU served to reflect secular Egyptian nationalism as Christian and Muslim middle- and upper-class women worked together to achieve common aims. Their concerns included securing women's rights to participate at all levels of Egyptian politics as well as in the labor market and the educational system, and demanding reforms to the personal status codes. The members of the EFU continued to participate in the struggle for full independence from Britain. Shaarawi remained especially interested in providing health care to poor women and children throughout her life, as evidenced by the work of the EFU and her private philanthropy.

Shaarawi utilized various methods to advance her feminist causes, including founding two jour-

nals, the French language *L'Egyptienne* in 1925 and the Arabic language *Al-Misriyya* in 1937. She was also a strong supporter of international women's rights movements, serving on the executive board of the International Woman Suffrage Alliance for many years. She was instrumental in founding the Arab Feminist Union in 1945, and she served as that organization's first president. She remained an ardent Egyptian nationalist throughout her life and was awarded the state's highest decoration in 1947, the year she died. Shaarawi's legacy is widely respected in EGYPT today. She is remembered for having laid the foundation for women to lead more publicly productive lives.

See also HUMAN RIGHTS; SECULARISM.

Shauna Huffaker

Further reading: Leila Ahmed, *Women and Gender in Islam* (New Haven, Conn.: Yale University Press, 1992); Margot Badran, *Feminists, Islam and the Nation: Gender and the Making of Modern Egypt* (Princeton, N.J.: Princeton University Press, 1995); Huda Shaarawi, *Harem Years: The Memoirs of an Egyptian Feminist (1879–1924)* (London: Virago Press, 1986).

Shaarawi, Muhammad al- (1911–1998)
Muslim teacher and television preacher

Al-Shaykh al-Shaarawi became famous in the 1970s as a master of QURAN commentary on television. It was not so much the profundity of his exegesis that was attractive as it was the simplicity of his style, which made his ideas accessible to the wider public. By the time he died in 1998, he had developed a huge following, where his sermons were broadcast on television both in Egypt and across the Arabic-speaking world.

Shaarawi played an important part in the a wave of religious revival in Egypt in the 1970s. During the previous period, until the death of JAMAL ABD AL NASIR in 1970, Egypt's government had been intent on modernization and secularization, which led to attempts to domesticate and restrict the public role of religion. At the same time, Nasir had ample reason to fear the challenge posed by Islamists, especially those in the MUSLIM

BROTHERHOOD and its offshoots, and so he kept them and their activities on a short leash. Much of this changed with the coming of ANWAR AL-SADAT (r. 1970–81) to power, although he was not solely responsible for the change by any means. A reform-minded Islamist movement had been important in Egypt since the founding of the Muslim Brotherhood in 1928, and it was only Nasir's combined charisma and autocracy that kept their activities suppressed, especially after 1954. Sadat released many of the members of the Muslim Brotherhood from the prison camps where Nasir had placed them, and he encouraged the Islamist movements to broaden their power base and attack the leftists, which Sadat saw as buttressing his own authority against the legacy of his predecessor. Shaarawi benefited from all of this, even though he was never exactly an activist, and it seems he was never a member of the Muslim Brotherhood. Sadat, as a means of encouraging the kind of Islam that he thought politically beneficial, provided "moderate" Islamists such as Shaarawi access to a large popular audience, thereby doing much to shift the national discourse onto a more religious basis.

Shaarawi was closely allied to the Saudi Arabian elite, having taught in that country for much of the 1960s and 1970s. His beliefs, while not extreme, tended toward the literalism and dogmatism of the Islamists. Since his death, a great deal of debate and controversy has arisen in Egypt surrounding efforts by his son to ensure that his father is revered as a SAINT and miracle worker, and that his tomb is visited in an annual pilgrimage. Many of Shaarawi's most devoted followers consider this a sacrilege, and it is hard to imagine that Shaarawi would have been pleased with the controversy. Nonetheless, there is now a saint's shrine over Shaarawi's place of burial, and an annual saint's festival or MAWLID takes place there in early June, to which singers of religious songs and believers from Egypt and elsewhere come to pray, to join in the sacred and secular aspects of the festival, and to honor Shaarawi in their own way.

See also ISLAMISM; SERMON.

John Iskander

Further reading: Johannes J. G. Jansen, "The Preaching of Shaykh as-Shaarawi: Its Political Significance." In *Proceedings of the 14th Congress of the Union Européenne des Arabisants et Islamisants.* (Budapest, 29th August–3rd September 1988, 1995); ———, "Shaykh al-Shaarawi's Interpretation of the Quran." In *Proceedings, Union européenne des arabisants et islamisants:* 10th Congress, Edinburgh, 9–16 September 1980, edited by Robert Hillenbrand; Hava Lazarus-Yafeh, "Muhammad Mutawalli al-Sha`rawi—A Portrait of a Contemporary `Alim in Egypt." In *Islam, Nationalism, and Radicalism in Egypt and the Sudan,* edited by Gabriel Warburg and Uri M. Kupferschmidt, 281–297 (New York: Praeger, 1983).

Shabazz, el-Hajj Malik el-   *See* MALCOLM X.

Shadhili Sufi Order

The Shadhili Sufi Order is one of the oldest Sufi orders, known for promoting orthodoxy and propriety as the means to achieve an internal union with the divine. This important strand of Sufi thought is attributed to the Moroccan mystic Abu al-Hasan Ali al-Shadhili (d. 1258) who lived and taught in TUNISIA and EGYPT. No writings from al-Shadhili survive and it was his immediate successors, especially Ahmad ibn Ata Allah al-Iskandari (d. 1309) who recorded his teachings. Though considered to be a Sufi way, or TARIQA, the Shadhiliyya Sufis never formed a centralized organization; rather, throughout its history many branches have emerged with weak links to one another, but all claiming spiritual descent from the founder and adhering to his teachings. Around the turn of the 13th century SUFISM increasingly began to be practiced in institutional settings, which emphasized establishing life-long relationships to a single master. It is in this context that the Shadhiliyya movement arose and spread.

In contrast with other more emotional and ascetic strands of Sufi thought, al-Shadhili taught that each member of the *tariqa* could best achieve mystical and spiritual fulfillment through living an exemplary, but ordinary life. The individual should seek complete devotion and gratitude to God by transforming his heart through performing ritual duties such as pilgrimage, PRAYER, and fasting. For example, al-Shadhili performed the *HAJJ* to MECCA every two years, and he promised to protect and assist any of his followers who accompanied him. Equally important is living a full work and family life within the larger Muslim community. This sober and pragmatic approach to Sufism has made this movement attractive to middle- and upper-class Muslims to the present day.

Few Sufi *tariqas* have had as widespread an influence as the Shadhiliyya. Shadhiliyya movements rapidly spread throughout Egypt and across North Africa, and they reached IRAN during its first century. Though it was initially associated with elites in urban settings, subsequent leaders from around the Islamic world transformed the orientation of the movement leading to the development of popular movements with mass appeal. Subsequently, Shadhiliyya movements appeared in West and EAST AFRICA and the islands of the Indian Ocean. Today new branches of the Shadhiliyya continue to form and attract new followers such as the Burhaniya Disuqiyah, founded by Shaikh Muhammad Uthman Abdu (d. 1983) in the SUDAN, which subsequently spread to Egypt and SYRIA. The 20th century has also seen Shadhiliyya branches established in new regions of the world such as EUROPE, North America, and South Asia.

Shauna Huffaker

Further reading: Vincent Cornell, *Realm of the Saint: Power and Authority in Moroccan Sufism* (Austin: University of Texas Press, 1998); Michael Gilsenan, *Saint and Sufi in Modern Egypt* (Oxford: Oxford University Press, 1973); Muhammad ibn Abi al-Qasim Ibn al-Sabbagh, *The Mystical Teachings of al-Shadhili: Including His Life, His Prayers, Letters, and Followers.* Translated by Elmer Douglas (Albany: State University of New York Press, 1993); Annemarie Schimmel, *Mystical Dimensions of Islam* (Chapel Hill: University of North Carolina Press, 1975); J. Spencer Trimingham, *The Sufi Orders in Islam* (Oxford: Oxford University Press, 1971).

shafaa See INTERCESSION.

Shafii, Muhammad ibn Idris al- (767–820)
leading legal theorist and eponymous founder of the Shafii Legal School

Known as the "father of Muslim jurisprudence" (*FIQH*), al-Shafii was born in the area of Gaza in PALESTINE to an ARAB family that claimed descent from the prophet MUHAMMAD (ca. 570–632). He grew up in MECCA and is reported to have become skilled in archery and the composition of Arabic poetry. He studied HADITH and law with MALIK IBN ANAS (d. 795) in MEDINA for 10 years. Biographical sources report that al-Shafii became involved with a pro-Shii group in Yemen and was brought to BAGHDAD, the flourishing capital of the ABBASID CALIPHATE for punishment. The caliph HARUN AL-RASHID (r. 786–809) reportedly pardoned him as a result of the intercession of al-Shaybani (d. 804), a leading Hanafi jurist who had also studied with Malik. Al-Shafii stayed in IRAQ to study *fiqh* with al-Shaybani and the other early founders of the HANAFI LEGAL SCHOOL, but then he moved to Fustat (later part of CAIRO) in EGYPT. Maliki jurists there rejected him because he was critical of Maliki legal theory, having been influenced by the teachings of both the Hanafis and AHMAD IBN HANBAL (d. 855). Indeed, he may even have been murdered there by a Maliki faction. He was buried in Cairo's Southern Cemetery, where his mosque-tomb has become a major shrine. A *MAWLID* (saint festival) is held there annually, and devotees are known to bring letters to him requesting his intercession in legal matters. The legal school that bears his name developed into one of the leading ones in Islamdom during the Middle Ages and continues to prevail in EAST AFRICA, parts of Yemen, South INDIA, INDONESIA, and MALAYSIA.

Al-Shafii's major writings are the *Risala* (Treatise) and *Kitab al-umm* (Book of Guidance). In these and shorter works he laid the groundwork for what would become the prevailing system of Islamic jurisprudence. On the one hand, he rejected the Maliki position that law had to be based on the living example of the community in Medina. On the other, he strongly opposed the Hanafi school's acceptance of reasoned opinion (*ray*) in legal reasoning because it was too arbitrary. Indeed, some rationalists wanted to bypass the hadith altogether. Instead, al-Shafii argued that all law should be derived from revelation, especially the QURAN and the SUNNA of Muhammad, as witnessed by the hadith. Rather than completely reject independent legal reasoning, he allowed for the use of analogical reasoning (*qiyas*), but subordinated it to REVELATION. It could be conducted only when it was based on the literal meaning of the Quran and hadith. This provided jurists some flexibility in applying legal precedents based on revelation to new situations. For example, while the Quran explicitly forbids the consumption of grape wine (*khamr*), the ban on other alcoholic beverages, such as other kinds of wine and hard liquor, was legitimized by arguing on the basis of an analogy that, like grape wine, they have an intoxicating effect. Al-Shafii's legal theory contributed significantly to the development of Islamic jurisprudence, which remains in effect today for many Muslims.

See also IJTIHAD; SHAFII LEGAL SCHOOL; SHARIA.

Further reading: Norman Calder, *Studies in Early Muslim Jurisprudence* (New York: Clarendon Press, 1993); Wael B. Hallaq, *A History of Islamic Legal Theories* (Cambridge: Cambridge University Press, 1997); Muhammad ibn Idris al-Shafii, *Islamic Jurisprudence: Shafii's Risala.* Translated by Majid Khadduri (Baltimore: Johns Hopkins University Press, 1961).

Shafii Legal School

Of the four main Sunni legal schools (sing. *madhhab*), one of the largest and most widespread, after that of the Hanafis, is the Shafii Legal School. It dates to the ninth century and bears the name of its founder, MUHAMMAD IBN IDRIS AL-SHAFII (767–820). Drawing on al-Shafii's concept of the four "roots" of Islamic jurisprudence (*usul al-FIQH*), this school emphasizes the priority of REVELATION based on the Quran and HADITH over local custom and human reasoning. It was also a strong proponent of ASHARI SCHOOL of theology against Mutazili rationalist theology.

It began with al-Shafii and his circle of students in Fustat, Egypt, but the tradition first became systematized as a school in BAGHDAD after al-Shafii's death. The founding theorist of the Shafii School there was Ibn Surayj (d. 918), a prominent jurist from Shiraz, Iran, who had become interested in al-Shafii's ideas via students of the Egyptian scholar Ibrahim Muzani (d. 877), who had studied under al-Shafii. Although the school had early branches as far west as ANDALUSIA, it flourished mainly in Egypt, Syria, Iraq, Mecca and Medina, Yemen, and Iran during the medieval period. Its major rival in these lands was the HANAFI LEGAL SCHOOL. In Khurasan (northeastern Iran), Shafii-Hanafi rivalry became very intense, but in most regions, the legal schools generally agreed to coexist and agree to disagree. In some places the Sunni schools actually shared the same MADRASA, where each had its own wing for teachers and students. Examples include the mosque-madrasa complexes of al-Nasir Muhammad (r. 1285–1341) and Sultan Hasan (1347–61) in CAIRO. The Shafii School also had a prayer station next to the KAABA in Mecca, alongside those of the other Sunni schools, but all were destroyed when the Saudis gained control of Mecca in the early 20th century. Among the most famous members of the Shafii School were the scholars and mystics such as Abu al-Qasim Abd al-Karim al-Qushayri (d. 1074), Abu Ishaq al-Shirazi (d. 1083), ABU HAMID AL-GHAZALI (d. 1111), and Fakhr al-Din al-Razi (d. 1209).

Turkish rulers such as the Seljuks of Iran and Iraq (1038–1194), the Seljuks of Anatolia (1077–1307), and the Ottomans (1281–1922) favored the Hanafi School, pushing the Shafiis out to the outer limits of Islamdom. As a consequence of this gradual process, the Shafii School now prevails in East Africa, parts of Yemen, South India, INDONESIA, and MALAYSIA. Many Shafiis, however, still travel to Egypt to study Shafii law at AL-AZHAR University in Cairo, not far from where Imam al-Shafii is buried.

See also SHARIA.

Further reading: Richard W. Bulliet, Islam: *The View from the Edge* (New York: Columbia University Press,

1994); Wael B. Hallaq, *The Origins and Evolution of Islamic Law* (Cambridge: Cambridge University Press, 2005); Christopher Melchert, *The Formation of the Sunni Schools of Law* (Leiden: E.J. Brill, 1997).

Shah, Idries (1924–1996) *popular writer and teacher who introduced Sufism to the West as a form of self-realization*

Born in Simla, INDIA, to an Afghan father and a Scottish mother, Shah came to England as a teenager, studied at Oxford, and subsequently traveled extensively. Following his father's death in 1969, Shah became known as the leader of the Sufis, or Islamic mystics. Shah spent most of his adult career in England enthusiastically introducing SUFISM to Western audiences, while teaching and writing books that emphasized the psychological dimensions of Sufism. Shah has authored over 30 titles, and most popular are his books on Sufi wisdom stories and folktales. Shah's purpose was to dispel Western myths about Sufism while educating the public about Islamic mysticism. In his texts, he does not claim to be part of any particular Sufi order, nor does he promote a belief in ISLAM. In this respect he is a nontraditional Sufi. Shah's work is popular in the UNITED STATES. It has been translated into 12 languages and is used in various academic disciplines, including psychology, anthropology, and religious studies. Shah's books, including *The Sufis* (1964), *Tales of Dervishes: Teaching Stories of the Sufi Masters over the Past Thousand Years* (1967), and *Learning How to Learn: Psychology and Spirituality in the Sufi Way* (1978), earned him the admiration of numerous writers and poets, and his home and center in England routinely catered to upper-class gatherings. In 1970 the BBC produced and televised a documentary, *Dreamwalkers,* focusing on Shah and Sufism. Shah won numerous awards, including several first prizes from UNESCO (United Nations Educational, Scientific, and Cultural Organization) and was the director of studies for the Institute for Cultural Research in London from 1966 until his death. Shah's followers, organized as the Society for Sufi Studies, remain critical of traditional Sufi practices that emphasize forms they believe are in conflict with the modern world.

Mehnaz Sahibzada

Further reading: Franklin Lewis, *Rumi Past and Present, East and West: The Life, Teaching and Poetry of Jalal-al-Din Rumi* (Boston: Oneworld Publications, 2000); Idries Shah, *The Sufis* (London: Octagon Press, 1977); Jane I. Smith, *Islam in America* (New York: Columbia University Press, 1999); L. F. Rushbrook Williams, ed. *Sufis Studies: East and West* (New York: E.P. Dutton, 1973).

shahada (Arabic: testimony, witnessing)

The *shahada* is the first of the FIVE PILLARS OF ISLAM. It is a formulaic "testimony" or "witness" of one's Islamic FAITH—that "there is no god but God and MUHAMMAD is his messenger"—and affirmation of membership in the community (UMMA) of Muslims. Usually pronounced in Arabic (*ashhadu an la illah illa Allah wa ashhadu Muhammad rasul Allah*), this formula proclaims belief in the unity of God and in the prophetic status of Muhammad. It also expresses a rejection of IDOLATRY and implicitly accepts the missions of other prophets (it does not say Muhammad is the *only* messenger). Also known as the "two *shahada*s" and the *kalima,* it is based on quranic themes, but its wording occurs only in a fragmentary form in the QURAN (see Q 2:163, 255 and 48:29). Variations of the two parts of the formula occur separately on late seventh-century Islamic coins and building inscriptions, but the familiar wording concerning both God and Muhammad that is now used in Islamic ritual probably did not become firmly established until the early or mid-eighth century (by 750).

Muslims are obliged to pronounce the *shahada* repeatedly throughout their lives. It is recited when a baby is born, in the calls to PRAYER, and in daily prayers. Anyone who wishes to convert to Islam must pronounce it sincerely before witnesses. A dying person should turn toward MECCA and recite it, but if he or she is unable to do so, others may recite it instead. The Shia have modified the *shahada* by adding "Ali is the friend of God" (*Ali wali Allah*), which affirms their belief in the preeminence of ALI IBN ABI TALIB (d. 661) as their first IMAM, in addition to their belief in God and his prophet. The *shahada*, especially the first part, is frequently used by Sufis in their DHIKR rituals. It is also a frequent subject in Islamic CALLIGRAPHY, where it is drawn in a variety of beautiful and elaborate styles. It is frequently displayed in Islamic buildings, especially in MOSQUES and shrines, but it may also be posted in homes and businesses. AMULETS AND TALISMANS designed to insure God's blessing and protection also make use of the *shahada*.

The concept of witnessing in Islam encompasses several additional aspects. In the Quran's statements about JUDGMENT DAY, evildoers will be condemned on the testimonies of virtuous people who bear witness against them (for example Q 4:41, 159). Witnessing is also required by the SHARIA in certain cases of civil and criminal law: financial transactions, wills, divorce, and execution for adultery. However, the most important meaning of *shahada*, aside from being the first pillar of Islam, is that of MARTYRDOM. The idea of giving up one's life for God and religion is considered to be a form of bearing "witness" to one's faith. The Islamic concept was influenced by early Christianity, in which the Greek term *martyr* (witness) was used for Christians who were tortured and killed by Roman authorities. Martyrdom is a doctrine found in both Sunni and Shii Islam, but it has achieved an especially rich significance within TWELVE-IMAM SHIISM.

See also ADHAN; CRIME AND PUNISHMENT; FUNERARY RITUALS; SUNNISM.

Further reading: Constance Padwick, *Muslim Devotions: A Study of Prayer-Manuals in Common Use* (London: SPCK, 1961); Andrew Rippin, *Muslims: Their Religious Beliefs and Practices*. 2d ed. (London: Routledge, 2001).

shahid   *See* MARTYRDOM.

shame   *See* HONOR AND SHAME.

Shamil (1786–1871) *North Caucasus Muslim resistance leader*

Shamil was born around 1786 into a noble family from the Avar people of southern Daghestan. From the 1830s to 1859, Shamil was able to unite many of the ethnically and linguistically diverse peoples of the North Caucasus (areas now within CHECHNYA and Dagestan in Russia and northeastern Azerbaijan) to fight against the encroaching Russian Empire. Shamil was a religious, political, and military leader. Under the banner of *ghazawat* (the Caucasian variant of JIHAD), Shamil and his followers (MURIDS) were able to inflict great damage on and hold off the Russian army over the course of a decades-long war, setting up a fledgling Islamic state in areas under their control. Shamil's power derived as much from religious AUTHORITY as from military prowess, and he was able to convert his religious authority, based as the leader of the local NAQSHABANDI SUFI ORDER, into political and military power by transforming the hierarchical religious structure of the Sufi brotherhood into a political movement and state structure. Shamil sought to implement strict adherence to Islamic law, and he claimed to be chosen by God to lead his people.

Shamil successfully employed guerrilla tactics to keep the Russians at bay until the Russians deployed nearly 500,000 troops and decimated Shamil's fighters and demoralized the local population using scorched earth tactics. He surrendered to the Russians in 1859, but he was uncharacteristically treated magnanimously and sent to live in exile in the Russian city of Kaluga. After much correspondence, he was allowed to make the pilgrimage to MECCA, and he died in 1871 in MEDINA. With Shamil's surrender, the resistance to the Russians collapsed, only to flair up again whenever Russian control was weak. To this day, Shamil is held in great esteem by the population of the North Caucasus, and his name and authority are evoked by those leading the current fight in Chechnya.

See also CENTRAL ASIA AND THE CAUCASUS; RENEWAL AND REFORM MOVEMENT.

David Reeves

Further reading: Moshe Gammer, *Muslim Resistance to the Tsar: Shamil and the Conquest of Chechnia and Daghestan* (London: Frank Cass, 1994); Anna Zelkina, *In Quest for God and Freedom: The Sufi Response to the Russian Advance in the North Caucasus* (New York: New York University Press, 2000).

sharia (Arabic: path to a source of water; also Persian and Urdu: *shariat*)

Sharia is the law of Islam based on God's sovereign commandments and prohibitions as conveyed by the QURAN, and on the SUNNA of Muhammad and his Companions, as embodied in the HADITH. It is often identified with another concept of Islamic law—jurisprudence (FIQH). Thus, it can be defined as both the infallible revealed law of God *and* the fallible, ongoing efforts undertaken by human beings, particularly the ULAMA and Muslim judges, to interpret REVELATION and apply it to particular sociohistorical contexts. Like the understanding of revealed law in rabbinic Judaism, Muslims have for centuries seen the sharia as a process wherein jurists and judges debated legal rulings and interpretations in their efforts to apply revelation to all areas of human conduct. They thought that sharia should be relevant not only to matters of worship, but also to family life, DIETARY LAWS, business transactions, CRIME AND PUNISHMENT, warfare, dress, hospitality, and even the exchange of greetings. Also, just as following a path to water (the literal meaning of sharia) entails the nourishment of the body, following God's sharia promises material and spiritual benefits to Muslims. It is the way to win God's blessing in this world and salvation in the AFTERLIFE. In actual practice, the sharia has undergone a complex history of development, interacting with other legal traditions and local CUSTOMARY LAW. One of the chief duties of Muslim ruler was to uphold the sharia, while the ulama and judges had the responsibility of studying it, teaching it, and interpreting it. The centers for their activities were the madrasas and the courts in all the major cities found in lands under Muslim rule.

Historically, the sharia has become embodied in different traditions of Islamic jurisprudence known as *madhhabs* (schools, ways). In Sunni Islam there are four *madhhabs*: the Malikis, the Hanafis, the Shafiis, and the Hanbalis. These schools are not religious sects with different theological doctrines, however. Since the 10th–11th century all four have accepted a system of jurisprudence based on four "roots" (*usul al-fiqh*). Two of these are based in revelation—the Quran and sunna. Two are based on methods of interpreting revelation—IJMAA (consensus) and *qiyas* (analogical reasoning). To a greater or lesser degree all schools have allowed for the derivation of individual legal opinions based on reason (IJTIHAD), but reason has often been circumscribed by the forces of tradition and imitation (*taqlid*) of the legal authorities of the past. Though the Shia have tended to follow a more devotional form of Islam wherein the Imams are held in higher esteem than the law, they have also developed their own legal traditions. These bear close resemblance to the Sunni legal traditions. The legal tradition in TWELVE-IMAM SHIISM is known as the Jaafari Legal School, named after JAAFAR AL-SADIQ (d. 765), the sixth Imam. It developed two chief branches: the AKHBARI SCHOOL and the USULI SCHOOL. The Ismaili Shia, though often known for their esoteric interpretations of Islam, also follow the sharia, but under the guidance of their Imam and his agents. In the distant past there were extremist Shii sects, the GHULAT, which were believed to have claimed that the sharia had been abrogated.

Today, the sharia is understood in Muslim nations variously as a *basis* for law within the framework of a predominantly secular legal system modeled after those of western Europe and Britain, or as applicable to only limited areas of law, especially marriage, divorce, and inheritance law. This is one of the results of colonial rule in Muslim lands during the 19th and 20th centuries. Where it has occurred—in countries such as Libya, Egypt, Jordan, Bahrain, Pakistan, and Malaysia—a system of dual courts exists to accommodate the two traditions of law. Alternately, in countries such as Saudi Arabia and Iran the sharia stands in ideological *opposition* to Euro-American secular law.

However, even in these countries, it is not the only law of the land. Creating governments exclusively based on the sharia is a major tenet of today's Islamist movements, both radical and gradualist. In non-Muslim countries some jurists and legislators have proposed limited adoption of certain elements of the sharia for Muslim immigrants and citizens, but such suggestions have met with public outcries. The public perception of the sharia in Europe and North America, as well as among non-Muslim minorities in Muslim lands, is that it is an inflexible, tyrannical system of medieval rules. Muslim reformers and modernists, on the other hand, argue that this is incorrect, that the sharia's perceived faults are the result of corrupt or poorly educated Muslim authorities, as well as the indirect effects of COLONIALISM. To counteract negative interpretations of the sharia, they are reexamining its foundations and history, in order to bring it into greater conformity with universal notions of JUSTICE, HUMAN RIGHTS, and gender equality.

See also ABOU EL-FADL, KHALID; ALLAH; HANAFI LEGAL SCHOOL; HANBALI LEGAL SCHOOL; ISLAMISM; MADRASA; MALIKI LEGAL SCHOOL; RENEWAL AND REFORM MOVEMENTS; SHAFII LEGAL SCHOOL; SHIISM.

Further reading: Ahmad Atif Ahmad, *Structural Interrelations of Theory and Practice: A Study of Six Works of Medieval Islamic Jurisprudence* (Leiden: E.J. Brill, 2006); Laleh Bakhtiar, ed., *Encyclopedia of Islamic Law: A Compendium of the Major Schools* (Chicago: Kazi Publications, 1996); Wael B. Hallaq, *A History of Islamic Legal Theories: An Introduction to Sunni usul al-fiqh* (Cambridge: Cambridge University Press, 1999); Fazlur Rahman, *Islam*, 2d ed. (Chicago: University of Chicago Press, 1979), 100–116; Bernard Weiss, *The Spirit of Islamic Law* (Athens: University of Georgia Press, 1998); Muhammad Qasim Zaman, *The Ulama in Contemporary Islam: Custodians of Change* (Princeton, N.J.: Princeton University Press, 2002).

Shariati, Ali (1933–1977) *Islamic modernist, ideologue of the Iranian Revolution of 1978–1979*

Ali Shariati is widely considered one of the most important social thinkers of 20th-century IRAN. Shariati combined ideas from existentialism and Marxism with Islamic ideas from the QURAN, HADITH, and Shii tradition. His goal was to transform Islam from a set of rules for the individual to follow into a progressive ideology that could change society.

Shariati was born in the village of Mazinan in northeastern Iran. His father, Muhammad Taqi Shariati, was a reformer who worked to bring educated young Iranians back to Islam by explaining how the ideals of Islam were connected to the contemporary world. To advance his ideas, he founded the Center for the Spread of Islamic Teachings in Mashhad. Shariati went to school in Mashhad but also studied with his father and was deeply influenced by his teachings. In 1949 Shariati trained to become a teacher. After several years as a teacher he enrolled in the University of Mashhad, graduating in 1960 with a B.A. in French and Persian literature. He then went to Paris to pursue graduate studies and received a Ph.D. in 1964 from the Sorbonne. One of Shariati's teachers there was the noted French Catholic scholar of Islamic Studies, Louis Massignon (d. 1962), whom he credited for inspiring his inner transformation in those years.

Shariati had also become an anti-shah activist. In 1957 he was arrested for taking part in a rally supporting the National Front, a political group that opposed the government of MOHAMMAD REZA SHAH PAHLAVI (r. 1941–79). While in Paris, he participated in the anti-shah student movement. He was named the editor of the newspaper of the Congress of the National Front, *Iran-i azad* (Free ban), and he also contributed articles to the Algerian revolutionary newspaper *Al-Mujahid*.

In France, while he was influenced by thinkers such as Jean-Paul Sartre and Albert Camus, he also criticized their rejection of traditional religion. Rather than seeing religion as the "opiate of the people," as Karl Marx described it, he believed that the only way nations such as Iran could counteract Western imperialism was through a strong cultural identity that was supported by religious traditions.

In 1964, when Shariati returned to Iran, he was arrested and imprisoned for his antigovernment activities in France. After his release, he began teaching at the University of Mashhad. His lectures there quickly became popular, attracting listeners from outside the university. The government, seeing his popularity as a threat, engineered his dismissal from the university. In 1967 Shariati joined other religious reformers in Tehran at the Husayniya-yi Irshad, which offered lectures, discussions, seminars, and publications on religious subjects—the name commemorates the martyrdom of the Prophet's grandson Husayn ibn Ali, the third IMAM of TWELVE-IMAM SHIISM, at KARBALA in 680 C.E.

Shariati's lectures, in which he tried to explain the problems of Muslim societies in the light of Islamic principles, soon made him the most popular instructor at the Husayniya-yi Irshad. Young people were drawn to his new interpretation of Islam and its role in society. By 1973 the government began to view his classes as a threat. Shariati was again arrested and jailed. He was released from jail in March 1975, but his freedom was restricted. He was prohibited from teaching or publishing, and he was required to stay in his home town of Mazinan. After two years of virtual house arrest, Shariati was given permission to travel to Europe. In June 1977 he went to England. On June 19 he was found dead in his brother's house in Southampton, England. The official cause of death was given as a heart attack. However, many of Shariati's supporters suspect involvement by the Iranian secret police in his death. Shariati was buried in DAMASCUS, Syria, near the tomb of ZAYNAB BINT ALI, the sister of the third imam, Husayn.

In his lectures and writing, Shariati opposed following tradition simply because it was tradition, and he held that IJTIHAD (independent thought) was not just for the experts but for every individual. In the revolution that toppled the shah's regime in 1979, portraits of Shariati were carried by demonstrators along with portraits of Ayatollah RUHOLLAH KHOMEINI (d. 1989). In the aftermath of the revolution, the moderate, inclusive teachings of Shariati were drowned out by the fundamentalist teachings of Khomeini and other clerics. However, he is still viewed as an important contributor to the Islamic revolution in Iran.

See also EUROPE; *HUSAYNIYYA*; IRANIAN REVOLUTION OF 1978–1979; MUJAHIDIN-I KHALQ; POLITICS AND ISLAM.

Kate O'Halloran

Further reading: Michael Fischer, *Iran: From Religious Dispute to Revolution* (Cambridge, Mass.: Harvard University Press, 1980); Ali Rahnema, "Ali Shariati: Teacher, Preacher, Rebel." In *Pioneers of Islamic Revival,* edited by Ali Rahnema, 208–250 (New York: Zed Books, 2005); Malise Ruthven, *Islam in the World* (Oxford: Oxford University Press, 2006); Abulaziz Sachedina, "Ali Shariati: Ideologue of the Iranian Revolution." In *Voices of Resurgent Islam,* edited by John L. Esposito (New York: Oxford University Press, 1983); Ali Shariati, *Man and Islam.* Translated by Ghulam F. Fayez (Mashhad, Iran: University of Mashhad Press, 1982); ———, *Marxism and Other Western Fallacies: An Islamic Critique.* Translated by R. Campbell (Berkeley, Calif.: Mizan Press, 1980); ———, *On the Sociology of Islam.* Translated by Hamid Algar (Berkeley, Calif.: Mizan Press, 1979).

shaykh (sheik, sheikh)

Shaykh is an honorific title used for AUTHORITY figures and holy men in Islamic societies. Originally applied specifically to older men with gray hair in kin-based ARAB tribal societies, it has come to enjoy wider use in Arab and non-Arab Muslim cultures. It is a title of respect for members of the ULAMA who have mastered the religious sciences (QURAN, *TAFSIR*, HADITH, and *FIQH*) and for administrators of religious institutions such as MOSQUES and MADRASAS. It has also been given to masters in SUFISM who have guided their disciples on the path to spiritual enlightenment and union with the divine Beloved (God). Sufi shaykhs are also often deeply venerated and credited with having miraculous powers. Indeed, mystical writings and poetry speak of how a shaykh can reflect the otherworldly light of God and his prophet MUHAMMAD. Sufi maxims also teach that anyone following the mystical path without a shaykh to guide him actually has SATAN for a shaykh, which implies that such a seeker will ultimately be led astray. Female Sufi leaders and spirit mediums are called by the feminine form of this word—*shaykha*. Since the 15th century, the most highly esteemed Muslim scholars and mystics have been recognized by the honorific title *shaykh al-Islam* (Shaykh of Islam). It was also used as an official title in the Ottoman Empire for a high-ranking religious scholar appointed by the SULTAN. Based in Istanbul, he functioned as a MUFTI, issuing advisory rulings based on the SHARIA regarding issues of state as well as private matters.

The term continues to be used in modern contexts in a variety of ways. For example, Muslim authorities in SAUDI ARABIA who are descended from MUHAMMAD IBN ABD AL-WAHHAB (1703–92), the founder of the Wahhabi sect, are called *Al al-Shaykh* (Family of the Shaykh) in his honor. The rulers of Arab nations in the Persian Gulf region (Kuwait, Qatar, the United Arab Emirates, and, until recently, Bahrain) are called shaykhs and their countries are known as *shaykhdoms*. Whether the term applies to a tribal authority, religious scholar, Sufi master, revivalist leader, or head of state, its bearer is due respect and deference by others, especially those with lower status. The equivalent to *shaykh* in Persian is *pir,* with a comparable range of meanings, but especially in Sufi contexts. It is used in eastern Muslim lands such as IRAN, PAKISTAN, and INDIA.

See also GULF STATES; *MURSHID;* OTTOMAN DYNASTY.

Further reading: Robert A. Fernea, *Shaykh and Efendi: Changing Patterns of Authority among the El Shabana of Southern Iraq* (Cambridge, Mass.: Harvard University Press, 1970); Leonard Lewisohn, trans., "Hasan Palasi's Encounter with Shaykh Khujuji." In *Windows on the House of Islam: Muslim Sources on Spirituality and Religious Life,* edited by John Renard, 375–383 (Berkeley: University of California Press, 1998); George Makdisi, *The Rise of Colleges: Institutions of Learning in Islam and the West* (Edinburgh: University of Edinburgh Press, 1971).

shaytan   *See* SATAN.

Shiism

In studying the history of religions, scholars have noted that religious traditions as a rule develop alternative movements and sectarian expressions. Judaism, which has had alternative forms in the past, today has Orthodox, Reform, and Conservative branches. Christianity, known for having many sects and denominations throughout its history, today has Roman Catholic, Orthodox, and Protestant branches. Hindu devotionalism, known as *bhakti,* is characterized by a threefold division into traditions centered on the gods Vishnu and Shiva, and the Goddess (Devi). The Buddhist community, or *sangha,* developed three major doctrinal traditions—Theravada, Mahayana, and Vajrayana. Islam, though often identified with the ideal of a unified community of all believers known as the UMMA, is no different. The primary division it has is the one that exists between SUNNISM, the majority tradition, and Shiism, an umbrella term for the minority tradition.

The term *Shiism* is used by modern scholars of Islamic Studies to describe not one but several important Islamic sectarian traditions and movements that have appeared in Islam's history. It is based on the Arabic word *shia,* which means party or faction, and it was first used with reference to the group of Muslims who favored the candidacy of ALI IBN ABI TALIB (d. 661) and his descendants as the legitimate successors to the prophet MUHAMMAD, the leader of the Muslim community, upon his sudden death in 632. This group was called *shiat Ali,* the party of Ali. Unlike other men in the early Muslim community, Ali was Muhammad's closest male relative, his paternal cousin and son-in-law by marriage to his daughter FATIMA. He staked his claim as a candidate for leadership on the basis of kinship, and, according to the Shia, Muhammad's declaration at GHADIR KHUMM that Ali was the master (*mawla*) of those who also regarded Muhammad as their master. However, many of the influential members of the community favored choosing a leader on the basis of reputation and the consensus of leading males. This view prevailed at the time of Muhammad's death, and Abu Bakr (r. 632–634) became the first CALIPH (successor to the Prophet) of the Muslim community. This consensual understanding of legitimate AUTHORITY eventually became identified with the Umayyad and Abbasid Caliphates, and the Sunni branch of Islam.

In 656 Ali finally became the caliph after the assassination of UTHMAN IBN AFFAN (r. 644–656), the third caliph, and he established his capital in the city of Kufa in IRAQ. Ali's legitimacy, however, was contested by his Meccan rivals. He successfully defeated three of his major opponents—AISHA (Muhammad's widow) and Talha and al-Zubayr (respected COMPANIONS OF THE PROPHET)—at the Battle of the Camel in southern Iraq. He was then forced to confront Muawiya ibn Abi Sufyan (d. 680), the leader of the Umayyad clan of the QURAYSH. Ali and Muawiya fought until the conflict was settled by arbitration at Siffin, which left some of Ali's supporters, known as the KHAWARIJ (separatists), discontented. One of them assassinated Ali in Kufa in 661. Ali's son Hasan agreed to recognize Muawiya as the next caliph, and Muwawiya founded the UMAYYAD CALIPHATE with Damascus as its capital in 661. Consequently, Ali's second son, Husayn, launched a campaign to win back the caliphate, but he was killed in 680, together with many of his supporters, by an Umayyad army at KARBALA while traveling to join his supporters in Kufa.

The historical split between Sunnis and Shiis can therefore be traced to what was originally a political dispute over succession to leadership in the Muslim community. However, much of what scholars know about this period of Islamic history is based on accounts told from Sunni points of view that prevailed several centuries later. Scholars, therefore, have an incomplete understanding of Shiism's development in the early period. During the ninth century the Shia began to maintain that Ali and his heirs, known as the Imams, had suffered martyrdom at the hands of unjust and corrupt Sunni Muslim rulers. The unfortunate outcome of Shii political expectations and Shii belief in the just cause of their Imams eventually evolved into the distinctive Shii belief in sanctification through the deaths of the infallible Imams and belief in a messianic redeemer, known as the IMAM MAHDI, who would come in the endtimes. The shift in the worldview of the Shii movement occurred gradually between the seventh and 10th centuries, and it was probably influenced by Jewish and Christian beliefs in MARTYRDOM and messianic redemption circulating in the Middle East at the time.

The fate of the Imams, coupled with a history of periodic persecution, led many Shii groups to develop a doctrine that allowed for pious concealment, known as *taqiyya*, of their true Shii identity for self-protection. ASHURA, the commemoration of the death of Husayn at Karbala during Muharram, the first month in the Islamic lunar year, began to be observed as the most important Shii holiday during the 10th century, under the protection of the Shii Buyid dynasty that ruled in the name of the Abbasid caliph. In addition to belief in the return of a hidden imam in the endtimes, most of the Shia also maintained that the Imams would intercede for the righteous on JUDGMENT DAY. Another identifying trait of Shiism that developed in this period was devotion to Muhammad and his descendants through Ali and Fatima, known as the People of the House (AHL AL-BAYT). Sunnism also has held the prophet Muhammad's family in high regard, but its understanding of Islam has given greater importance to the SHARIA. In the Sunni understanding of the sharia, it is Muhammad and his Companions who have precedence, rather than his family per se.

An estimated 12 to 15 percent of the world's Muslim population today belongs to the Shii branch of Islam, equal to between 156 and 195 million adherents (out of a total of around 1.3 billion Muslims). Almost all Shiis belong to one of three major sects, basically distinguished from each other according to which Imams they recognize and which they do not. Each tradition has also developed its own specific doctrines, rites, and concepts of authority (for details, see entries for each tradition). The largest tradition is known as TWELVE-IMAM SHIISM, and its followers are called the Twelvers, the Ithnaashariyya, and the Imamis. They recognize Musa al-Kazim (d. 799), the son of JAAFAR AL-SADIQ (d. 765) as the seventh Imam,

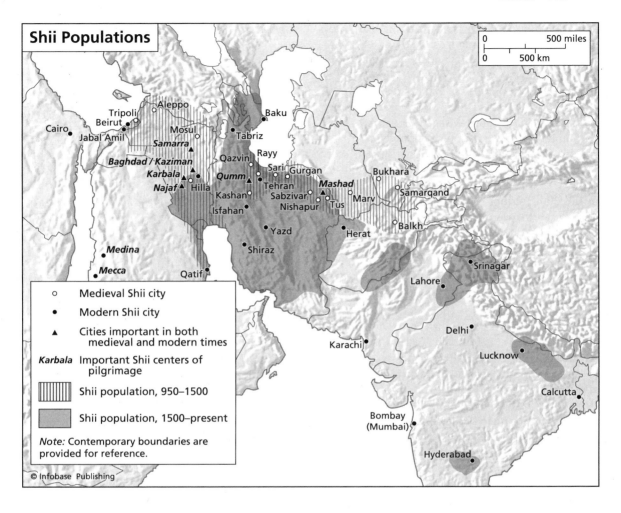

Shii Populations

Legend:
- ○ Medieval Shii city
- ● Modern Shii city
- ▲ Cities important in both medieval and modern times
- *Karbala* Important Shii centers of pilgrimage
- ||||| Shii population, 950–1500
- ▓ Shii population, 1500–present

Note: Contemporary boundaries are provided for reference.

© Infobase Publishing

and they believe that the 12th Imam, MUHAM-
MAD AL-MUNTAZAR (b. 868), entered concealment
as a boy in 874. His concealment will end only
when God allows, just before Judgment Day. The
Twelve-Imam Shia follow their own legal tradition, which is divided into Akhbari (traditionalist) and Usuli (rationalist) Schools. They now
comprise an estimated 90 percent of the world's
Shii population, and they are majorities in IRAN
(89 percent), Iraq (60 percent), Bahrain (70 percent), and Azerbaijan (85 percent). There are also
Twelve-Imam Shii minority populations in Lebanon, eastern Saudi Arabia, Kuwait, Qatar, United
Arab Emirates, AFGHANISTAN, Tajikistan, PAKISTAN,

and INDIA, as well as sizeable immigrant communities in Europe and the United States.

The second sect Shii is known as ISMAILI SHIISM
(also called the Seveners and the Sabiyya). The
Ismailis recognize Ismail (d. 760), Jaafar al-Sadiq's
first son, as the rightful seventh Imam instead of
Musa al-Kazim, as claimed by the Twelve-Imam
Shia. The FATIMID DYNASTY that ruled in North
Africa and Egypt from 909 to 1171 claimed to be
caliph-imams descended from Ismail, and they
gave rise to the two major Ismaili sects known as
the Mustalis and Nizaris. Fatimid missionaries,
known as *dais*, spread the doctrines of Ismaili Shiism to YEMEN, Syria, Iran, and India. Because of

persecution and also to facilitate their search for new converts, they practiced *taqiyya,* assuming Sunni, Twelve-Imam Shii, Sufi, and even Hindu guise, depending on the context. Mongol invasions in the 13th century contributed to a wide dispersion of the Ismailis, with sizeable communities in India and Pakistan. These are known as the Khojas, who belong to the Nizari sect, and the Bohras, who belong to the Mustali sect. Indian Ismailis migrated to East Africa in the 19th century, as well as to England and North America in the 20th century. Although precise figures are lacking, recent estimates have placed the size of the Ismaili population today at around 15 million, or about one-tenth the size of the Twelve-Imam Shii population.

The third major Shii sect is known as ZAYDI SHIISM. The Zaydis believe that Zayd ibn Ali, who was killed in a revolt against the UMAYYAD CALIPHATE in 740, was the fifth Imam instead of Muhammad al-Baqir (d. 731), whom the Twelve-Imam Shia recognized as the fifth. After Zayd's death, Zaydi missionaries established a following in the Caspian region and later Yemen. The Zaydis favored outward opposition to corrupt rulers, and they did not practice *taqiyya* to the same degree as the other Shii sects. They also rejected the idea of a messianic Mahdi. Holding concepts of leadership similar to those of the Sunnis, they accepted the legitimacy of the first caliphs and adhered closely to the SHAFII LEGAL SCHOOL, one of the four major Sunni schools. Their theology, on the other hand, was strongly influenced by the MUTAZILI SCHOOL, which was rejected by most Sunnis. Zaidi communities in the Caspian region converted to Twelve-Imam Shiism by the 16th century, but the Yemeni Zaidis still exist, to about 36 percent of that country's population, or about 8 million (2007 estimate).

Other forms of Shiism existed in the past and to the present day. The GHULAT (extremists) were heterodox sectarian movements that emerged in Islam's first centuries. The earliest of these was associated with a semi-historical Jewish convert, Abd Allah ibn Saba al-Himyari of seventh-century Iraq, who asserted that Ali had never died and would return as a messiah. Other beliefs that

were associated with the *ghulat* include ANTHROPOMORPHISM, transmigration, and belief in prophets after Muhammad. Some *ghulat* beliefs, however, were accepted as orthodox Shii doctrine, such as the belief in the concealment and messianic return of the last Imam. The Alawis (or Alevis) are members of a Shii sect that believes that Ali is divine. They are found in Syria, Lebanon, Turkey, and southeastern Europe. In addition, there are religious communities that have roots in Shiism, but evolved into separate religious traditions, such as the DRUZE religion, which developed from Ismaili missionary activities in the 11th century. Moreover, the BAHAI FAITH, now regarded as a universal religion, appeared first as a Shii sect in 19th-century Iran.

Although Shii communities have accepted political quietism, legitimated by the doctrine of *taqiyya,* in the face of persecution by other Muslims through much of their history, there have been significant moments when they have engaged in overt political activity and militancy. In addition to early anti-Umayyad movements and involvement in the Abbasid revolution in the eighth century, Shii activism is also evident in the Ismaili Qarmatian and Fatimid movements of the 10th century, and the SAFAVID DYNASTY, which made Twelve-Imam Shiism the state religion of Iran in the 16th century. A Shii dynasty known as the Bahmanids ruled the Deccan region of India between 1347 and 1526, and the Lucknow region of northern India was ruled by Shii Nawabs between 1732 and 1856. Such governments encouraged the celebration of Shii devotional activities and gave strong support to Shii ULAMA. Shii authorities began to support anticolonial movements in late 19th-century Iran, which spawned more radical Shii activism in the 20th century, not only in Iran, but also in Lebanon, Iraq, and the wider Persian Gulf region. This is evident in the rise of the DAAWA PARTY in Iraq, the establishment of the Islamic Republic of Iran in 1979 under the leadership of Ayatollah RUHOLLAH KHOMEINI (d. 1989), and the formation of HIZBULLAH in southern Lebanon in response to the Israeli invasion of 1982. Moreover, SUICIDE bombings against civilian and military targets began to be used by radical Shii groups at this time, which legitimated this tactic in terms of the Shii concept of martyrdom. The removal of the Baathist regime of SADDAM HUSAYN in Iraq in 2003 by the United States and Great Britain inadvertently gave political Shiism more power in Iraq and the wider Middle East, leading some observers to speak of a modern "Shia revival" that will significantly reshape the region for years to come.

See also AGA KHAN; AKHBARI SCHOOL; ALAWI; ASSASSINS; *BATIN*; BOHRA; *DAAWA*; *FITNA*; GULF WARS; HERESY; HOLIDAYS; USULI SCHOOL.

Further reading: Kamran Scot Aghaie, ed., *The Women of Karbala: Ritual Performance and Symbolic Discourses in Modern Shii Islam* (Austin: University of Texas Press, 2005); William C. Chittick, ed., *A Shiite Anthology* (Albany: State University of New York Press, 1981); Farhad Daftary, *A Short History of the Ismailis* (Edinburgh: Edinburgh University Press, 1998); Heinz Halm, *Shia Islam: From Religion to Revolution* (Princeton, N.J.: Marcus Wiener Publishers, 1997); S. H. M. Jafri, *The Origins and Early Development of Shia Islam* (London: Longman, 1979); Etan Kohlberg, ed., *Shiism* (Burlington, Vt.: Ashgate, 2003); Reinhold Loeffler, *Islam in Practice: Religious Beliefs in a Persian Village* (Albany: State University of New York Press, 1988); Moojan Momen, *An Introduction to Shii Islam: The History and Doctrines of Twelver Shiism* (New Haven, Conn.: Yale University Press, 1985); Matti Moosa, *Extremist Shiites: The Ghulat Sects* (Syracuse, N.Y.: Syracuse University Press, 1988); Sayyed Hossein Nasr, Hamid Dabashi, and Seyyed Vali Reza Nasr, eds., *Shiism: Doctrines, Thought, and Spirituality* (Albany: State University of New York Press, 1988); Vali Nasr, *The Shia Revival: How Conflicts within Islam Will Shape the Future* (New York: W.W. Norton, 2007).

shirk

Shirk is the heretical act of accepting other deities in addition to God. *Shirk* is the worst form of disbelief in ISLAM because the SHAHADA, which is the most important statement of belief (i.e., "There is no God but God, and MUHAMMAD is the messenger of God"), affirms the Muslim notion of the one and only God. The *talbiya*, recited typically during the HAJJ, reinforces this idea, "You have no associate." The QURAN contains five occurrences of *shirk* and, in only two of these cases, the word is used in terms of forbidding people to ascribe partners to God (Quran 31:13 and 35:14). In the other three (Quran 34:22; 35:40; 46:4), the Quran rejects the belief that any other deities were God's partners during creation.

Two types of people to whom the quranic proclamations on *shirk* were directed were polytheists (primarily those living in the Arabian Peninsula during the seventh century) and Christians. The pre-Islamic polytheists may have worshipped hundreds of deities arranged around the KAABA and, according to Muslims, they were one group toward which Islam's message of God's unity and universal sovereignty was directed. On the surface, it would seem that the Quran's antipolytheistic message may have also been directed toward Christians, although this case is more ambiguous. For instance, according to the Quran there are disbelievers who say God is the "third of three" (5:73) and that "God is the Christ, son of Mary" (5:72), while these disbelievers worship JESUS and MARY as two deities in addition to God (5:116). Yet, the Quran identifies Christians as one of the PEOPLE OF THE BOOK who received God's message before Muhammad, and, as such, Muslims recognize Christians as monotheists, whose worldview teeters dangerously close to polytheism. Finally, members of the Wahhabi movement, Islamists with roots in the worldviews of MUHAMMAD IBN ABD AL-WAHHAB (1703–92), expanded the notion of *shirk* to include as heretics Sufis, the Shia, those who supported Western interests, and virtually anyone else who disagreed with the Wahhabi's interpretation of Islam. *Shirk* and related notions of God's oneness continue to be central in Islamic belief and practice.

See also CHRISTIANITY AND ISLAM; IDOLATRY; JAHILIYYA; SUFISM; WAHABBISM.

Jon Armajani

Further reading: David Adams Leeming, *Jealous Gods and Chosen People: The Mythology of the Middle East* (New York: Oxford University Press, 2004); G. R. Hawting, *The*

Idea of Idolatry and the Emergence of Islam: From Polemic to History (Cambridge: Cambridge University Press, 1999); Muhammad Ibrahim Hafiz Ismail Surty, *The Quranic Concept of* al-Shirk (London: Ta-Ha Publishers, 1982); Muhammad ibn Abd al-Wahhab, *The Book of Tawheed* (Riyadh, Saudi Arabia: International Islamic Publishing House, 1998).

shrine   *See* MAWLID; SAINT; *WALI.*

Simurgh (Simorgh)

The Simurgh is a gigantic mythological bird mentioned in Persian literature. It has been identified with the *anka,* a legendary bird in Arabian tales, Garuda, the winged mount of the Hindu god Vishnu, and the phoenix, a mythological fire bird that Greeks and Romans believed had first appeared in ancient Egypt. Pre-Islamic and Islamic textiles, metalwork, ceramics, and illustrated manuscripts from IRAN and INDIA feature depictions of it.

Ancient Iranian texts say that Simurgh was immortal and lived in the Tree of Knowledge; other Persian texts say that it could live for 1,000 years. It is described as having brilliant plumage and the power to bestow fertility in the land and good health among human beings. According to Firdawsi's SHAHNAMA (the Persian *Epic of Kings,* composed in the late 10th century), Simurgh lived in the Alburz Mountains of northern IRAN. When Zal, the albino child of a Persian warrior, was abandoned there by his father, Simurgh, a female bird, raised him as one of her own offspring. Zal returned to his people as an adult, bearing a golden feather Simurgh had given him to use in case he needed her help. Zal married Rudabe, a beautiful princess, and when she was suffering a painful childbirth, Zal used the feather to call upon Simurgh's assistance. The bird saved both the mother and child, and Zal's son grew up to become the great Persian hero Rustam.

The Simurgh is also featured in Farid al-Din Attar's Persian-language Sufi poem, *Conference of the Birds* (*Mantiq al-tayr*), written in the 13th century. There it is portrayed as an ideal king (a metaphor for God) living in far-off China to whom a flock of different kinds of birds are called to journey. After overcoming spiritual obstacles and passing through seven valleys, which represent stages in the mystical quest for the divine, a party of 30 birds finally arrives at Simurgh's palace, only to discover that the king they seek is really the God reflected in their inner hearts. Attar here makes a play on the name Simurgh, which can also mean "thirty birds" in Persian.

See also ANIMALS; MAQAM; PERSIAN LANGUAGE AND LITERATURE; SUFISM.

Further reading: Farid ud-Din Attar, *Conference of the Birds.* Translated by Afkham Darbandi and Dick Davis (London: Penguin Books, 1984); Vesta Sarkhosh Curtis, *Persian Myths* (Austin: University of Texas Press, 1993).

sin   *See* CRIME AND PUNISHMENT; JUDGMENT DAY; THEOLOGY.

Sipah-i Sahaba   *See* JAMIYYAT ULAMA-I ISLAM.

sira   *See* BIOGRAPHY; FOLKLORE.

Sirhindi, Ahmad (1564–1624) *Naqshbandi Sufi shaykh of the late Mughal period in India who adamantly argued against Indian Sufi trends of pantheistic mysticism, advocating instead the implementation of sharia*

Shaykh Ahmad Sirhindi was born in Sirhind, in east Punjab, INDIA, in 1564. In his youth he received a traditional religious education from his father, the Sufi shaykh Abd al-Ahad, and he continued his religious training as an adolescent with teachers in Sialkot, India. His remarkable level of scholarship gained him an invitation to the Mughal emperor Akbar's court in Agra, where he assisted Abu al-Fazl, the court historian and minister. In 1599 he went to DELHI, where he met Khwajah Abd al-Baqi, the first Naqshbandi SAINT to come to India, soon after which he was initiated into the NAQSHBANDI SUFI ORDER. He quickly became a *pir* and a prolific writer on points of doctrine of the Naqshbandi branch of SUFISM.

Though his central concern was with Sufi thought on issues of religious renewal, prophecy, and sainthood, he is best known for advocating the strict implementation of SHARIA by the state and the purification of ISLAM from what he viewed as Hindu accretions. He established the Naqshbandi Sufi lineage in India by founding the subbranch of the Mujaddidin, and he was named "the renewer of the second millennium" by his followers.

Sirhindi's famous collection of letters, known as *Maktubat-i imam-i rabbani,* is today a classic of Indo-Muslim literature, though at the time of publication it was proscribed by the Mughal emperor AURANGZEB. Sirhindi's ideas were received by 17th-century Muslims with both enthusiasm and hostility. He sharply denounced the eclectic pluralism of Emperor Akbar's *din-i-ilahi,* and his continued criticism of the inadequate role given to Islam in the politics of the state led to his brief imprisonment by Emperor Jahangir in 1619 in the Fort of Gwalior. Sirhindi condemned forms of Sufism that cultivated what he saw as extremism equivalent to the pantheistic mysticism of IBN AL-ARABI, and he attributed such trends to Hindu influence. From the informed perspective of his own mystical experiences, Sirhindi argued that at the final stages of mystical experience, which are understood by other schools of Sufi thought as annihilation, *fana* (see BAQA AND FANA), and ultimate union with God, the truth emerges that God cannot be comprehended intuitively. Hence, he argued that humans can know God only through His REVELATION, and this can take place only through human submission to SHARIA, the Muslim legal code based on revelation.

Sirhindi's arguments necessitated his vociferous and uncompromising attitude toward Hinduism and marked the shifting of Indian Muslim attitudes away from tolerance of Hinduism to the attitudes of strict nontolerance so characteristic of Aurangzeb's reign. Sirhindi is interpreted by modern historians as the individual largely responsible for initiating Sunni revivalism in the subcontinent by his persuasive arguments against the pluralistic and pantheistic trends of his time. Sirhindi died in 1624, and he is believed to be buried in the vicin-ity of his mosque in Sirhind, which is a sacred place of pilgrimage for Indian Muslims.

See also HINDUISM AND ISLAM; MUGHAL DYNASTY.

Megan Adamson Sijapati

Further reading: Muhammad Abdul Haq Ansari, *Sufism and Shariah: A Study of Shaykh Ahmad Sirhindi's Effort to Reform Sufism* (Leicester, England: The Islamic Foundation, 1986); Yohanan Friedmann, *Shaykh Ahmad Sirhindi: An Outline of His Thought and a Study of His Image in the Eyes of Posterity* (Montreal and London: McGill-Queen's University Press, 1971).

siyam   See FASTING.

slavery

Islam does not abolish the practice of slavery, but it does place certain limitations upon it. The QURAN delineates rights and restrictions for slave holders, such as granting them the right to engage in sexual relations with their slave girls, while maintaining that Muslims must treat "those whom your right hand possesses" with kindness and equity. Slaves are allowed to marry with their owners' permission, are provided a degree of protection for their lives and property, and are held accountable for their actions. The Quran encourages the release of slaves as a meritorious act and Muslims are required to free their slaves to receive forgiveness for certain sins.

In the HADITH and Islamic legal manuals, slavery is envisioned as an exceptional condition. Individuals may be enslaved as prisoners of war or may be born into slavery. Although free Muslims are not allowed to be enslaved, a slave who becomes a Muslim is not automatically released from bondage. Slaves possess a dual nature: As property, they may be bought and sold, and they are subject to their owners; but as persons they may profess faith in Islam, own property, earn money, marry, obtain an EDUCATION, or purchase their own freedom. In terms of religious obligations, Islamic law recognizes a slave's inherent limitations. Many religious obligations are optional for slaves, subject to the amount of liberty that their masters grant them. For some infractions, the penalties for slaves are actually lighter than those for free individuals. The law prescribes freedom for certain slaves upon their master's DEATH, such as the *umm walad,* who has borne her master's child, or the *mudabbar,* to whom he has promised liberation.

Slavery in the Islamic world has historically been milder than the plantation slavery practiced in the Americas in the 18th and 19th centuries. While forced labor in fields and mines is not unknown, Islamic slavery has tended to favor domestic servants, often treated as members of the family, or slave armies, preferred owing to their personal loyalty to the SULTAN. In fact, slaves sometimes rose to positions of extensive authority. In slave dynasties, such as the medieval Egyptian Mamluks, soldiers originally from the slave class actually oversaw governments. On the other hand, Islamic slavery was not without its brutal episodes. Muslim slave traders in Africa were notable for their harshness and for disregarding legal niceties by including free Muslims among their victims.

During the modern era, Muslim countries took steps to abolish slavery, largely in response to pressure from European nations. Modernist Muslim scholars reinterpreted the Quran to support the abolition of slavery. They argued that Muhammad (d. 632) tolerated a practice (slavery) that God intended to phase out over time as contrary to the basic quranic principles of liberty and equality. However, many Muslim elites resisted abandoning a privilege granted them in Islamic law, and slavery has been difficult to eliminate in the Islamic world. It continues to be practiced in rural areas and under repressive Islamist governments, such as in SUDAN.

See also HAREM; HUMAN RIGHTS; JANISSARY; *MAMLUK.*

Stephen Cory

Further reading: Humphrey J. Fisher, *Slavery in the History of Muslim Black Africa* (New York: New York University Press, 2001); Murray Gordon, *Slavery in the Arab World* (New York: New Amsterdam, 1992); Bernard Lewis, *Race and Slavery in the Middle East: A* *Historical Enquiry* (Oxford: Oxford University Press, 1992); Shaun E. Marmon, ed., *Slavery in the Islamic Middle East* (Princeton, N.J.: Marcus Weiner, 1999).

Sokoto Caliphate

The Sokoto Caliphate was a 19th-century Islamic state in Hausaland (modern-day northern Nigeria), founded by the preacher and jihadist Shehu USMAN DAN FODIO (1754–1817). The Shehu withdrew from and launched JIHAD against the sultanate of Gobir in 1804, in direct imitation of the prophet MUHAMMAD's jihad against the Arabs of MECCA. Spreading throughout Hausaland, dan Fodio's jihad gained widespread support among Fulani tribesmen and led to the establishment of the largest independent African state during the 19th century. The city of Sokoto in northwestern Nigeria was designated capitol of the Fulani state, which united a region that had been divided among city-states for hundreds of years. Dan Fodio established a systematic government, with ultimate AUTHORITY in the hands of a CALIPH, and local authority divided between emirs, who were responsible for governing specific regions (or emirates). The first caliph was Dan Fodio's son and military commander, Muhammad Bello, who succeeded his father in 1817. An electoral college made up of prominent officials chose later caliphs from among the Shehu's descendants.

Government in the CALIPHATE of Sokoto was based upon a classical Muslim model, a hierarchical system of authority, with ministries and titles derived from Islamic history. Islamic law (SHARIA) was held to be the law of the land, interpreted according to the MALIKI LEGAL SCHOOL. Supported by an active commercial network and thriving agricultural production, the caliphate was fairly prosperous for much of the century. Boasting a number of accomplished scholars, the Sokoto administration placed an emphasis upon education, which even extended to women at times (for instance, the Shehu's daughter, Nana Asm'u, was a famous scholar who promoted EDUCATION for WOMEN). Despite its decentralized government, the state held together largely due to its prosperous and efficient administrative structure and out of respect for the Shehu's teaching and the authority of his family. During the last decade of the 19th century, however, the Sokoto Caliphate was exposed to growing pressure from French colonial power to the north and British power to the south. It was eventually conquered by Sir Frederick Lugard, who established British authority over the region in 1903.

See also COLONIALISM; JIHAD MOVEMENTS; WEST AFRICA.

Stephen Cory

Further reading: R. A. Adeleye, *Power and Diplomacy in Northern Nigeria, 1804–1906* (London: Longman Group Limited, 1971); H. A. S. Johnston, *The Fulani Empire of Sokoto* (London: Oxford University Press, 1967); Beverly B. Mack and Jean Boyd, *One Woman's Jihad: Nana Asma'u, Scholar and Scribe* (Bloomington: Indiana University Press, 2000); Ibraheem Sulaiman, *The Islamic State and the Challenge of History* (London: Mansell Publishing, 1987).

Somalia   *See* EAST AFRICA.

song   *See* MUSIC; QAWWALI.

soul and spirit

The life force that animates the body is commonly known as the soul or spirit. Comparative study shows that beliefs about the soul and spirit vary widely, based on different ideas about what a human being is and how humans are believed to be related to the wider universe in both its physical and metaphysical aspects. Native classifications for the life force and its related aspects can become quite complex and contradictory—even within a single culture or religious tradition. It has become associated with notions of breath, the heart, mind, reason, BLOOD, and body. The English word *soul* is old Germanic in origin and is thought to have originally been a translation of the ancient Greek word *psych*, which means "life," "spirit," or "consciousness." These meanings are connected

with the idea of the life breath, as is the term *spirit*, which is derived from Latin. In many religions the soul or spirit is believed to be separate from the body, having a preexistence and an afterlife and being able to leave the body temporarily during sleep, trances, or states of ecstasy. It is also often believed to be connected with beings such as sacred ancestors, deities, and a universal spirit or cosmic energy.

Islamic beliefs about the soul and spirit were first expressed in the Quran and later elaborated and systematized by theologians, philosophers, and mystics. These beliefs differ, beginning with a significant shift less than two centuries after Muhammad's death in 632. Nevertheless, a degree of learned consensus was reached by theologians and traditionalists by the 10th century. The differing views about the soul and spirit can be attributed in part to variations of belief among local Muslim communities, sects, and movements but are also the results of several other factors. These include the heritage of indigenous pre-Islamic beliefs in Arabia and the wider Middle East, the Muslim reception of Jewish and Christian doctrines, and the influence of the ideas of Hellenistic PHILOSOPHY and Neoplatonism, especially after Greek texts were translated into Arabic during the ABBASID CALIPHATE, particularly between the eighth and 10th centuries.

The two key Arabic terms for soul and spirit in Islam are, respectively, *nafs* and *ruh,* both of which are derived from Arabo-Semitic terms for "breath" or "respiration," a requirement for life. The Hebrew cognates are *nefesh* and *ruah,* which occur in the Bible. Both Arabic words occur in the Quran with equivalent meanings but also with meanings that differ. *Nafs* often denotes the "self" and is used reflexively with reference to humans, the JINN, God, and SATAN. It is also used in the sense of "person." Thus, the Quran states that it is God "who created you from a single person [*nafs*] and made from her, her mate, that he might find rest in her" (Q 7:189). *Nafs* is a feminine noun in Arabic, so this verse indicates that men and women originated in a single feminine *nafs* (person). In several contexts the Quran gives *nafs* negative meanings; it connotes greed and desire. For example, the Quran attributes to JOSEPH the declaration, "Selfishness [*nafs*] incites evil" (Q 12:53), and promises, "As for the one who fears standing before his lord and prevents the self [*nafs*] from desire, indeed the garden [of paradise] will be the place of refuge" (Q 79:40–41). It also states that each person [*nafs*] will taste death (Q 3:185) and will be held to account on JUDGMENT DAY (Q 74:38).

The Islamic concept of spirit, as distinct from *nafs*, is often expressed by the word *ruh*. It occurs 21 times in the Quran in contexts involving themes of CREATION and REVELATION. In contrast to *nafs* it can be treated as either a masculine or feminine noun, and unlike *nafs*, which refers to the human being as an individual person, *ruh* is closely identified with God. For example, after forming Adam from clay, God brought the first human being to life by breathing his spirit (*ruh*, Q 32:9) into formed clay or mud. In a similar manner, MARY conceived JESUS after receiving the breath of God's spirit (Q 66:12). In one instance, Jesus is identified with the spirit (Q 4:171), and in three other verses, God is said to have strengthened Jesus with the holy spirit (*ruh al-qudus*, Q 2:87, 253; 5:110). The holy spirit is also credited with bringing God's true revelation to Muhammad (Q 16:102). The association of the spirit with revelation is also evident in Q 97, where it is said to have descended with the angels on the NIGHT OF DESTINY. Commentators later connected this sura with the occasion of Muhammad's receiving of the first revelation of the Quran and identified the spirit of revelation with the angel GABRIEL. Outside of the Quran, the hadith continue to use *ruh*, to mean the "human spirit."

Ibn Qayyim al-Jawziyya (d. 1350), a noted Hanbali jurist and theologian, is often credited with summarizing the key points of orthodox doctrine concerning the human soul, which he identified with the spirit. Reflecting post-quranic views, he maintained that while the body is mortal, the soul is created and immortal. It infuses the body like water in roses or fire in charcoal. Ibn Qayyim employed quranic phrases to ascribe to the embodied soul (*nafs*) three different charac-

teristics: it incites a person to do evil, upbraids a person for wrongdoing, and instills blissful tranquility that will lead to salvation. In other words, each person possesses a lower self or soul that inclines her or him to sin and wrongdoing and a higher one that inclines to the good and virtuous. The orthodox maintained, in opposition to some philosophers and mystics, that the soul had a material quality that received its own individual characteristics. Upon DEATH the soul is separated from the body and takes on a life of its own, with the ability to hear and see, in anticipation of the Final Judgment. It was widely held that the angel of death came to extract the soul from the body at a person's appointed time, which could be easy or difficult, depending on how the deceased had lived his or her life. Souls of prophets and martyrs go to PARADISE. The souls of other people enter a transitory state (*barzakh*) during which they might travel and have visions of paradise and the FIRE. Eventually they return to body to undergo the "interrogation of the grave," when they are asked about their faith by angels known as Munkir and Nakir. Afterward, the soul is believed to remain near the body and suffer or sleep until the resurrection, when it is reunited with the body again. Belief in the presence of the souls and spirits of the dead near the body is widely held and is reflected in FUNERARY RITUALS and burial practices. In many Muslim societies, people believe that the souls of the dead can be encountered in DREAMS, and they have the power to help or harm the living. There are also beliefs and rituals connected with spirit possession in different Muslim cultures.

Muslim philosophers and mystics did not always accept the doctrines about the soul and spirit that were taught by the ULAMA. They formed their understandings by combining Islamic belief, sometimes minimally, with ideas derived from Hellenistic philosophy and personal experience. Thus, philosophers like al-Kindi (d. ca. 870), a native of Iraq, maintained that the soul was immaterial and immortal. Abu Bakr Muhammad al-Razi (d. ca. 925), a Persian physician and philosopher familiar with the writings of Plato (d. ca. 347 B.C.E.), argued that the soul was one of five eternal elements in the universe, along with God, matter, time, and space. God allowed the soul to fulfill its desire to become embodied in matter but gave it a degree of his own intelligence in order to help maintain order in the universe and eventually find its way back to its primordial state of existence. AL-FARABI (d. ca. 950) and IBN SINA (d. 1037) adopted the Neoplatonist concept of cosmic CRE-ATION through a sequence of emanations beginning with God, the uncreated Being and First Cause, followed by intellects, and the material world—the lowest level of creation. The human soul, embed-ded in material existence, had different faculties, some that linked it to the worlds of ANIMALS and plants, and others, especially the faculty of reason, that could incline it to engage in ethical actions and eventually lift it to the eternal light world of pure intellect. Only an elect few could ever hope to attain this level of existence, however, and souls unable to live virtuous lives were condemned to an eternity of suffering.

Similar currents of thought were pursued by Sufi thinkers and visionaries. Many held that humans were a compound of soul, spirit, and body and drew a particularly sharp distinction between the lower soul (nafs), which chained the seeker to the transient world of the baser passions, sin, and blameworthy actions, and the heavenly spirit that linked people to God. Sufis strove to discipline their "selfish" impulses and purify themselves of negative qualities and attachments in order to strengthen their higher spirit (ruh) and experience abidance in, or unity with, God, the Beloved. They also spoke of the heart as a soul-mirror that was capable of becoming a reflection of God through ascetic prac-tices. Expressing patriarchal cultural bias, they often portrayed the lower soul and the material world as a woman. MUHYI AL-DIN IBN AL-ARABI (d. 1240), how-ever, identified the nafs with God's essence (DHAT). A 13th-century masterwork of Sufi literature, Farid al-Din Attar's Mantiq al-tayr (Conference of the birds), portrayed the process of overcoming worldly attachments and experiencing perfection in God as an epic journey of a flock of soul-birds across seven valleys to the palace of their king, the SIMURGH. Only a select few reached their goal. Another mystic who

wrote in Persian verse, JALAL AL-DIN RUMI (d. 1273), spoke of the higher soul as a falcon striving to free itself of the world and ascend to its heavenly home. Likewise, he wrote that humans occupied a place in creation between angels and animals, the for-mer possessing pure intellect, the latter possessing pure sensuality. By following the intellect, humans could surpass the angels, and by succumbing to the senses, they could fall lower than the animals. Life was a struggle between these contending aspects of human nature.

It was in philosophy and mysticism that Mus-lim understandings of the nature of the soul and spirit were most fully developed before the mod-ern era. In modernity these understandings have become more widely known than ever before, thanks to the publication of printed editions and translations of Islamic texts dealing with these subjects. At the same time, however, contempo-rary Muslim understandings have been affected by modern scientific ideas and Enlightenment rationalism. SALAFISM and WAHHABISM have played a major role in limiting speculation on such spiri-tual matters to the Quran, hadith, and the consen-sus of traditionally minded ulama.

See also ADAM AND EVE; ALLAH; ASCETICISM; BAQA and FANA; ETHICS AND MORALITY; ISMAILI SHIISM; MARTYRDOM; SUFISM; THEOLOGY.

Further reading: William C. Chittick, The Sufi Path of Love: The Spiritual Teachings of Rumi (Albany: State University of New York Press, 1983), 27–41, 173–193; Marsha K. Hermansen, "Shah Wali Allah's Theory of the Subtle Spiritual Centers (Lataif): A Sufi Model of Person-hood and Self-Transformation." Journal of Near Eastern Studies 47, no. 1 (1988): 1–25; Leor Halevi, Muhammad's Grave: Death Rites and the Making of Islamic Society (New York: Columbia University Press, 2007); Duncan B. MacDonald, "The Development of the Idea of Spirit in Islam." Muslim World 32 (1932): 24–42, 153–168; Michael E. Marmura, "Islamic Concepts of the Soul." In Death, Afterlife, and the Soul, edited by Lawrence E. Sul-livan, 223–231 (New York: Macmillan Publishing Com-pany, 1989); Jane I. Smith and Yvonne Y. Haddad, The Islamic Understanding of Death and Resurrection (Albany: State University of New York Press, 2002).

Spain · *See* ANDALUSIA.

stoning *See* CRIME AND PUNISHMENT.

student

The acquisition of knowledge is considered a religious duty in ISLAM. A famous HADITH states "seek knowledge even in China," which means seek knowledge throughout the world. This duty is also evidenced by the Arabic word for student, *talib,* which means a person who requests.

A well-developed educational system was an integral part of Islamic civilization from very early in its history. In primary schools, known as *KUTTAB,* students were taught basic literacy and memorized the QURAN. Physical beatings were used to keep order and discourage laziness. Talented students were encouraged to continue their EDUCATION at MOSQUE schools and the colleges of Islamic law, the MADRASA, and were often supported by stipends provided by a *waqf,* or charitable endowments. Classes at these centers were organized in teaching circles, known as the *halqa.* As a student advanced in the system the curriculum increasingly included analysis of the material discussed, though mastery and memorization of classic texts remained the foundation of an Islamic education. The system was built around personal relationships to individual mentors and lines of scholarly descent. Once a student had mastered a text, he was said to have received an *ijaza,* or authorization to teach the text to others. Students might travel thousands of miles to study with a famous scholar or to attend a well-known school like AL-AZHAR in EGYPT or ZAYTUNA MOSQUE in Tunisia.

This well-developed system was thrown into decline as the result of changes and reforms adopted in the 19th and 20th centuries. If the education of the traditional Islamic world had been focused on religious knowledge, during this period students began to be perceived as opportunities to create future model subjects. In the context of COLONIALISM, educational opportunities for students were shaped to suit the needs of the colonizer. For example, the Dutch East Indies government began to offer education to Indonesian CHILDREN only in the 1850s after they determined that educated Indonesians could administer the colony more cheaply for the Dutch. Under the French regime in North Africa limits were placed on education as seen in the program of acculturation that denied to Algerian students instruction in Arabic or Islamic subjects. As early as 1839, the Ottoman Empire was sending students to new Western-style schools to create efficient bureaucrats and teach Ottoman values, which included loyalty to the state. Similarly, newly independent states in Muslim lands saw students as future model citizens, and scholars built on the foundations of mass education systems left to them by the colonizers.

However, states are not always successful in their efforts to shape their citizenry. As is the case all over the world, students have played an important part in public demonstrations and political uprisings. Iranian students were very active participants in the IRANIAN REVOLUTION OF 1978–1979. In Egypt, student activists from various organizations regularly demonstrate for a variety of causes from protesting HUMAN RIGHTS abuses to demanding increased Islamization of government. Despite regional differences, students in many Muslim countries continue to play an important role in religious, social, and political affairs.

See also ALIGARH; DEOBAND; RENEWAL AND REFORM MOVEMENTS; TALIBAN.

Shauna Huffaker

Further reading: Afshin Matin-Asgari, *Iranian Student Opposition to the Shah* (Costa Mesa, Calif.: Mazda Publishers, 2001); George Makdisi, *The Rise of the Colleges* (Edinburgh: Edinburgh University Press, 1981); Selcuk Aksin Somel, *The Modernization of Public Education in the Ottoman Empire 1839–1908: Islamization, Autocracy and Discipline* (Leiden: E.J. Brill, 2001); Bill Williamson, *Education and Social Change in Egypt and Turkey* (London: Macmillan Press, 1986).

subha *See* PRAYER BEADS.

Subud (abbreviation for the Sanskrit phrase *Susila Buddhi Dharma*)

Subud is one of the more successful new Islamic-inspired spiritual movements to emerge in INDONESIA in the 20th century. It was founded by Muhammad Subuh Sumohadiwidjojo (1901–87), who began to receive messages from a spiritual source as a teenager. This culminated in 1925 when he received a REVELATION concerning the *latihan kejiwaan,* the basic spiritual practice of Subud. During this initial period, he studied with various teachers, including some Sufi leaders. He worked with the *latihan* for the next few years and also went through a period of spiritual/mystical growth. It would be eight years later, however, before others began to practice the *latihan.* Thus 1933 is generally accepted as the beginning date of the movement, which slowly spread through the country. Initially Bapak (as his followers came to call him) named the small group that was gathering around him *Ilma Kasunyatan.*

The group's spiritual practice, *latihan,* involves a gathering of members for about half an hour twice a week. Sitting with others of their own sex (men and WOMEN practice separately), they wait for a spontaneous impulse to act. Some begin to move, others will utter sounds. These movements and utterances vary widely. Members go through the *latihan* as a catharsis-like experience, often accompanied with the reception of some personal guidance. Depending on their life situation at any given moment, the immediate impact may be positive or negative.

After more than a decade, Bapak introduced the term *Subud* to the movement, occasioned by the development of a more stable organization in 1947. The new name is derived from three Sanskrit words (*Susila Buddhi Dharma*) that carry the essence of the movement—following the will of God, or the power of the life force that works both within us and without. To outsiders, Subud appears to be a completely new religion; members, however, do not see it as such, and Bapak noted that Subud lacks a holy book, formal teaching, and sacred formula. Rather, it is a process of surrendering to God and receiving inspiration. Subud was limited to Indonesia until the 1950s, when some followers of Western spiritual teacher George Gurdjieff (d. 1949) identified Bapak as the person their teacher had described as the coming prophet of consciousness. They invited Bapak to England in 1956 and a number of Gurdjieff's students identified with him. In 1957, as she began to participate in the movement, actress Eva Bartok (d. 1998) experienced a much publicized physical healing. The Institute for the Comparative Study of History, Philosophy and the Sciences at Coombes Springs, England, founded by John G. Bennett (d. 1974), became the point from which Subud initially spread in the West.

Subud did not allow proselytizing or advertising to assist the spread of the movement and Bapak also counseled against charging membership fees. However, as the movement spread, a periodical, *Subud News,* was launched in 1959, and a publishing house, Dharma Book Company, founded. Today, the movement is headed by the International Subud Committee, headquartered in the Indonesian island of Bali, with Western headquarters in the United States. Its charitable arm, Susila Dharma International, has NGO (nongovernmental organization) status with the United Nations. Subud groups are now found in some 70 countries on every continent.

See also HINDUISM AND ISLAM; SUFISM.

J. Gordon Melton

Further reading: Eva Bartok, *Worth Living For* (New York: University Books, 1959); John G. Bennett, *Concerning Subud* (New York: University Books, 1959); Antoon Geels, *Subud and the Javanese Mystical Tradition* (Richmond, England: Curzon, 1997); Robert Lyle, *Subud* (Kent, England: Humanus, 1983); Matthew Barry Sullivan, *Living Religion in Subud* (London: Subud Publications International, 1990).

Sudan (Republic of the Sudan; Jumhuriyat al-Sudan; Al-Sudan)

Sudan is the largest country in Africa with an area of 2,505,810 sq. km (slightly more than one-quarter the size of the United States) and an estimated population of 40.2 million in 2008. It is located in northeastern Africa, bordering the Red Sea. It is bordered by EGYPT to the north and LIBYA on the northwest. Other neighbors include Eritrea, the Central African Republic, Chad, the Democratic Republic of the Congo, Ethiopia, Kenya, and Uganda. The Nile River and its tributaries flow from south to north through the country. A large majority of the people of Sudan are Sunni Muslims (70 percent) located mainly in the north of the country. About 5 percent are Christian; they are located mainly in the south and in the capital, Khartoum. About 25 percent of the population follow traditional African religions. About half of the people of Sudan—primarily those living in the northern two-thirds of the country—consider themselves Arabs. The southern part of the country is home to a number of indigenous African groups, including the Dinka (8 percent), Nuba (6 percent), Nuer (4 percent), and Fur (3 percent). The official language of Sudan is Arabic, but more than 100 other languages are spoken, especially in the south; most of them belong to the Afro-Asiatic, Niger-Congo, and Nilo-Saharan language families. Sudan's major cities include Khartoum (the capital), Omdurman, Port Sudan, and Kassala.

Sudan has been inhabited for thousands of years. By about 4000 B.C.E. people had settled in villages along the Nile, farming and raising animals. The area was conquered by Egypt some time after 2600 B.C.E. A new civilization developed, heavily influenced by Egypt. Around 500 C.E. Coptic missionaries converted the rulers of northern Sudan—then known as Nubia—to Christianity. By the mid-600s, Egypt was conquered by ARAB Muslims. As time passed, many Arabs migrated to Nubia. Eventually, the Christian kingdoms of northern Nubia came under Muslim control. Around 1504, the FUNJ SULTANATE was founded in central Sudan. The king converted to Islam and spread the new religion through much of the rest of Sudan.

In 1820 Muhammad Ali (r. 1805–48), the ruler of Egypt, attacked Sudan, bringing the Funj Sultanate to an end. By 1821 Sudan was under Egyptian control. In 1881 a Sudanese Muslim religious teacher named Muhammad Ahmad declared that he was the MAHDI, a messianic guide appointed by God. Over the next few years, he led a successful revolt against the Egyptian rulers. Then, in 1898, Egyptian and British forces joined to suppress the revolt. An agreement was made to place Sudan under joint British-Egyptian rule; however, the British appointed a governor-general to Sudan, and most important officials were British.

In 1956, after years of nationalist struggle, Sudan became an independent nation. However, the north and south were distinctly different in terms of ethnic background, religion, and language, leading to a series of civil wars. The first civil war ended in 1972 with the establishment of autonomy for the south. However, civil war broke out again in 1983. In that same year, president Jaafar Nimeiri (r. 1969–85), declared the introduction of SHARIA, or Islamic law, for the entire country, regardless of religious affiliation. This proclamation stemmed from the growing prominence of the MUSLIM BROTHERHOOD, an Islamic activist movement originating in Egypt that established a branch in Sudan in the 1950s. Hasan al-Turabi (b. 1932) reorganized it and renamed it the National Islamic Front in 1985. A more radical Islamist regime was established in 1989, after a coup led by General Umar al-Bashir, who was allied with al-Turabi. In addition to gaining control of the government, the Islamists also controlled the civil service, professional syndicates, and the economy. Meanwhile, the civil war continued for some two decades, leading to the displacement of more than 4 million people and the deaths of some 2 million more, many of them as a result of famine. A peace agreement was signed in 2005.

In 2003, a separate conflict broke out in the western region of Darfur, whose population is largely black African Muslims. Pro-government Arab militias known as the Janjaweed are accused of ethnic cleansing against non-Arabs. The conflict has displaced nearly 2 million people and caused an estimated 200,000 to 400,000 deaths. It has also brought instability to other countries in the region, including Chad and the Central African Republic.

Sudan's economy is booming, thanks to oil production and rising oil prices. However, the nation is suffering from two decades of civil war in the south, the conflict in Darfur, and a lack of basic infrastructure, leaving much of the population living in poverty.

See also ARAB; COLONIALISM; COPTS AND THE COPTIC CHURCH; EAST AFRICA; MUHAMMAD ALI DYNASTY; REFUGEES.

Kate O'Halloran

Further reading: John L. Esposito and John O. Voll, eds., *Makers of Contemporary Islam* (Oxford: Oxford University Press, 2001); Carolyn Fluehr-Lobban, *Islamic Law and Society in the Sudan* (London: F. Cass, 1987); John O. Voll, ed., *Sudan: State and Society in Crisis* (Bloomington: Indiana University Press, 1991).

Sufi Movement

The Sufi Movement, a representative of the CHISHTI SUFI ORDER, emerged following the death of India-born INAYAT KHAN (1892–1927), who had founded the SUFI ORDER INTERNATIONAL in 1910 in the UNITED STATES. Khan initiated a woman, Rabia Martin, and designated her as his successor. His choice was, however, rejected by Khan's family and his growing European following. Khan died at a relatively young age and had not written a will. Seizing upon this circumstance (and the fact that his son/successor was still a minor), the European members rejected Martin's leadership and organized the Sufi Movement. They chose Mehboob Khan (1887–1948), Inayat's brother, as their new leader. He would be succeeded in 1948 by a cousin, Mohammad Ali Khan (1881–1958), then by Musharaff Khan (1895–1967), and then by Fazal Inayat Khan (1942–90). Fazal resigned leadership in 1982.

After Fazal Khan's resignation, a collective leadership tried to assume control, but it soon met with dissent so deep that it split the movement. Hidayat Inayat Khan (b. 1917) soon emerged as the leader of the largest part of the Sufi Movement. He shared leadership with Murshida Shahzadi. Hidayat, one of the sons of Hazrat Inayat, finally became the sole leader of the movement in 1993.

Hidayat Inayat Khan was only 10 years old when his father passed away in 1927. From his father he inherited a love of MUSIC. He studied at the Ecole Normale de Musique and eventually became a professor in the Music School of Dieulefit, Drome, France, and conducted an orchestra in Haarlem, Holland. He wrote numerous compositions, including both secular music and a collection of Sufi hymns, and was a founding member of the European Composers' Union.

The Sufi Movement resembles the Sufi Order International, headed by Hazrat Inayat's elder son, Vilayat Inayat Khan, and it is organized in five divisions to focus on universal worship, community, healing, symbology, and esoteric activity. The movement has spread across EUROPE to CANADA and the United States. Members meet weekly for DHIKR (worship) and classes.

J. Gordon Melton

Further reading: *The Gathas* (Katwijk, Netherlands: Servire, 1982); Fazal Inayat Khan, *Old Thinking: New Thinking* (New York: Harper and Row, 1979); Hidayat Inayat Khan, *Sufi Teachings* (Victoria, Canada: Ecstasis Editions, 1994).

Sufi Order International

The Sufi Order International is a religious organization whose primary aim is to promote the universalist Sufi teachings of INAYAT KHAN (1882–1927) and his son, Pir Vilayat Khan (b. 1916). Inayat Khan was a renowned Indian musician who became a disciple of Abu Hashim Madani, a Sufi master from a branch of the famed CHISHTI SUFI ORDER in INDIA. Before his DEATH, Madani asked Khan to bring SUFISM to the West. Khan arrived in the UNITED STATES in late 1910 and both taught Sufism and performed music in eastern and western coastal cities before traveling to EUROPE and Russia to organize formal Sufi centers. The seeds of future division were sown at this time, as different disciples (MURIDS) were placed in charge of national centers in Europe and North America. The American leader, Rabia Martin, having been rejected by the members of Khan's family, led the American followers into a relationship with Indian teacher Meher Baba.

In 1926 Khan named his 11-year-old son, Vilayat, to be his successor as head of the Sufi Order. Following his father's death in 1927, Vilayat studied philosophy, psychology, and music in Paris and Oxford and began intensive meditation training under various Sufi masters in the Middle East and India. He eventually emerged as a legitimate successor to his father's work, though much of the European following had reorganized as the SUFI MOVEMENT, under Maheboob, Inayat Khan's brother. However, Vilayat rebuilt the Sufi Order and eventually reinstated it in the United States during the 1960s. His efforts in California were helped by Murshid Samuel Lewis (1896– 1971), an eclectic teacher who had received initiation into several Sufi orders during a lifetime of spiritual seeking. Lewis brought his group of students into the Sufi Order in 1968, but some of those students left the order in 1977 over disagreements with Vilayat's regulations and formed the Sufi Islamia Ruhaniat Society.

Over the past 40 years, Pir Vilayat Khan has become an internationally recognized spiritual teacher who gives frequent public lectures and participates in various religious congresses, interfaith dialogues, meditation camps, and New Age expositions in the United States, western Europe, and India. Pir Vilayat and Pir Zia, his son and successor, were invited to attend the UN Peace Summit for world spiritual and religious leaders in 2000.

The Sufi Order International's teachings generally consist of the writings of Hazrat Inayat Khan and their further elaboration by Pir Vilayat and Pir Zia. All three Khans teach the essential unity of spiritual ideals across religious traditions. Pir Vilayat seeks to establish in his initiates a "stereoscopic consciousness" that cultivates simultaneous awareness of everyday human reality and the most elevated levels of the Divine Being. He emphasizes that the realm of ordinary perception both reveals and veils a sublime reality that is unfolding itself within and through human life. The universe is evolving, in other words, toward a Chardin-like Omega point. In books such as *Toward the One* and *Awakening: A Sufi Experience,* Pir Vilayat synthesizes prayer,

meditation, and breathing methods from different spiritual traditions with traditional Sufi practice with the intention of helping disciples experience the underlying unity of all things in the Divine Ground. All of Pir Vilayat's teachings comprise a natural outgrowth of his father's intention to foster tolerance and mutual understanding between East and West and between the different branches of the Beni Israel traditions.

The present-day teaching work of the Sufi Order International includes seminars and retreats that focus on spiritual healing arts, meditation practices, the spirituality of music, esoteric studies, and universal dances of peace. The Sufi Order International is headquartered in France and the North American headquarters are at the Abode of the Message, a residential Sufi community founded in 1975 in New Lebanon, New York. There, the former Shaker colony houses Omega Publications and its retail outlet, Wisdom's Child Bookstore, and Sacred Spirit Music. The Abode of the Message hosts an annual program of spiritual retreats, the healing arts center, and ongoing classes in DHIKR (a traditional Sufi chanting practice), DERVISH whirling, and universal worship. This latter liturgy was developed by Inayat Khan and draws on elements of the world's major religions.

Additional teaching centers exist in large cities throughout the United States and EUROPE, with center and branch leaders appointed by the president of the order. The Hope Project is a charitable program, active in India.

On February 4, 2000, Pir Zia Inayat Khan received the teaching mantle of Pir Vilayat in an investiture ceremony at Hazrat Inayat Khan's tomb in Delhi, India. He was also elevated to the presidency of the Sufi Order in North America, although Pir Vilayat remains chairman of the board of directors. Pir Zia divides his time between the Abode of the Message, India, and Europe. He is particularly interested in creating stronger ties with established Sufi orders in the Middle East and Asia and with helping Sufism as a tradition to move in a more universal direction. Pir Zia is committed to his grandfather's vision of building Universal temples that honor all religions. The Universal is currently developing an institute designed to promote and implement its vision of a humanity that is tolerant, just, and unified in spirit, if not in the particulars of traditional beliefs and practices.

The Sufi Order International is not recognized as a traditional Islamic Sufi order, because its membership is open to people of all faiths and it does not promote traditional Islam. Most of its members are white, middle-class Europeans and Americans, many of whom have been affiliated with the order since the 1970s. The order is a prototypical New Age religion, with its eclectic embrace of traditional religious practices, its desire to synthesize science and religion, its expectation of a dawning New Age of spiritual unity, and its interest in both Eastern and Western methods of psychological, physical, and spiritual healing.

J. Gordon Melton

Further reading: Pir Vilayat Inayat Khan, *Awakening: A Sufi Experience* (New York: Jeremy P. Tarcher/Putnam, 1999); ———, *The Message in Our Time: The Life and Teaching of the Sufi Master, Pir-o-Murshid Inayat Khan* (San Francisco: Harper and Row, 1978); ———, *Toward the One* (1974. Reprint, New York: Harper and Row, 1995).

Sufism

The mystical traditions of Islam are known by the general term Sufism. This term, which was first coined at the end of the 19th century by British scholars in India, refers to the Islam of inward vision and individual religious experience, but it also encompasses an assortment of outwardly oriented doctrines, practices, social organizations, and literary works that spans many centuries, regions, and cultures.

The Arabic term on which the word Sufism is based is *tasawwuf,* and the individual who follows this brand of Islam is called a Sufi. Both terms have been derived from the Arabic word for wool (*suf*), unrefined material from which the garments worn by ascetics in the Middle East were made. Sufis, however, proposed other etymologies for the term, including the word *safa* "to be or become pure" and *suffa,* in reference to the bench on which poor, pious members of Muhammad's community in Medina were accustomed to sit when they gathered in his mosque. Sufis referred to themselves in other terms as well, such as *abid* (slave, devotee), *zahid* (ascetic), DERVISH or *faqir* (impoverished ascetic); *arif* (knower of spiritual truth), *salik* (spiritual traveler), and *ashiq* (lover). They also made differentiations between spiritual masters, called shaykhs, *pirs,* or *murshids* (guides), and their disciples, known as *murids* (seekers). A Sufi saint was known as a WALI or friend of God.

Although European scholars once claimed that Sufism had been mostly borrowed from Eastern Christian mysticism or Buddhism, the Sufis themselves considered Muhammad as their forerunner and the exemplar for spiritual and moral excellence. They also looked to the most pious members of the early Muslim community. Such men were known not only for piety, but also for their ability to achieve closeness to God through renunciation of worldly attachments. Historically, Sufism began with individual ascetics living in Iraq and Iran during the eighth and ninth centuries. During the 10th and 11th centuries, Sufi adepts began to organize into groups of masters and their disciples that developed into mystical orders known as *tariqas* or "paths," each with its own distinct doctrines, practices, and spiritual genealogy (*silsila*), which all members had to study and memorize. Sufis met in mosques, homes, and madrasas, but their chief centers were hospices and retreat centers known as *khanqahs, ribats, tekkes,* and *zawiyas.* These usually contained tombs of former shaykhs and members of the order, and often became popular shrines that would attract devotees from near and far seeking blessings (BARAKA) from the saint. Conservative ulama would intermittently attack Sufis for such practices, considering saint veneration in particular to be a form of IDOLATRY (*shirk*) or at best a corrupt innovation (BIDAA). They also condemned the Sufi DHIKR, an ecstatic form of ritual chanting and rhythmic movement that Sufis practiced during their assemblies, as well as the *samaa,* a musical form of *dhikr,* such as that performed by members of the MEVLEVI SUFI ORDER, also known as the Whirling Dervishes. Sufis for their part criticized jurists for being too concerned with their reputations and the letter of the law. Nevertheless, a degree of consensus was reached between the ULAMA and mystics as reflected in the writings of ABU QASIM AL-JUNAYD (d. 910), Abu al-Qasim al-Qushayri (d. 1074), and ABU HAMID AL-GHAZALI (d. 1111), who promoted what was called "sober" Sufism as opposed to the "intoxicated" Sufism of figures such as ABU YAZID AL-BISTAMI (d. ca. 875) and MANSUR AL-HALLAJ (d. 922). Indeed, it was common for jurists and scholars to also be members of the brotherhoods. Even one of Sufism's strongest critics, TAQIY AL-DIN IBN TAYMIYA (d. 1328), a follower of the literalist HANBALI LEGAL SCHOOL, was reported to be a member of the QADIRI SUFI ORDER.

The growth of Sufism was partly a reaction against the worldly orientation taken by the Muslim community in the wake of the conquest of Middle Eastern lands in the seventh and eighth centuries, as well as against political violence and official corruption. Sufis benefited from the mystical traditions of Christianity, Hinduism, and Buddhism, and they subsequently played a significant role in the indigenization of Islam among the peoples living in lands governed by Muslim rulers. They carried Islam via trade routes into sub-Saharan Africa, INDIA, Central Asia, southeastern Europe and the Caucasus, and Southeast Asia. Among the leading Sufi orders that arose and spread across Islamdom were the Qadiris, Suhrawardis, Rifais, Kubrawis, Shadhilis, Mevlevis, Naqshbandis, and Bektashis. The most famous of the Sufi orders in India is that of the Chishtis. Each of these orders was named after its founding Sufi master, and many of them enjoyed the patronage of rulers and wealthy merchants.

Sufis have played a significant role in Islamic RENEWAL AND REFORM MOVEMENTS. Two orders that were especially active in this were the NAQSHBANDI SUFI ORDER and the Khalwatis. The Naqshbandis, under the leadership of AHMAD SIRHINDI (d. 1624) and Shah Wali Allah (d. 1762) in India, spread reformist ideas throughout Asia and Ottoman lands during the 17th and 18th centuries. Among the leading Naqshbandi teachers in the Middle Eastern region were Taj al-Din ibn Zakariya (d. 1640) in

Mecca, Murad al-Bukahri (d. 1720), and Abd al-Ghani al-Nablusi (d. 1731) in the Levant and Syria, and Khalid al-Baghdadi (d. 1827) in Kurdistan and among Ottoman authorities. The Khalwati brand of reformism was initiated by Mustafa al-Bakri (d. 1748), a student of al-Nablusi, and his leading disciple in Egypt, Muhammad al-Hifnawi (d. 1767). Their reformist teachings were well received among the ulama and Sufis alike, and, in concert with Naqshbandi teachings, they sparked the establishment of new reform-minded Sufi orders in ALGERIA, TUNISIA, SUDAN, and the Arabian Peninsula.

Sufis also were involved in leading armed opposition to the forces of European colonial powers that penetrated and occupied Muslim lands in the 19th and 20th centuries. Between 1830 and 1847, ABD AL-QADIR AL-JAZAIRI (d. 1883), a Qadiri Sufi shaykh inspired by Naqshbandi reformism, led Algerian tribes in a JIHAD against the French. Outbreaks of resistance continued after Abd al-Qadir's deportation, culminating in the great Algerian revolt of 1871, which resulted in a strengthening of the French stranglehold on the region. A Sammani Sufi shaykh named Muhammad Ahmad (d. 1885), proclaimed to be the promised MAHDI, led a tribal coalition against Ottoman-Egyptian troops and established a Mahdist state in northern Sudan in 1885. British forces put an end to his regime in 1898, but Mahdist partisans have continued to play a prominent role in Sudanese religious and political affairs to this day. Another reformist Sufi order, the Sanusis, established a network of lodges throughout much of LIBYA and the central Sahara region during the 19th century. From 1901 to 1914 they led unsuccessful campaigns against French expansion into Chad, then against the Italians in Libya from 1911 to 1932.

Despite the active involvement of Sufi orders in such resistance movements, Muslim modernists such as JAMAL AL-DIN AFGHANI (d. 1897) and MUHAMMAD ABDUH (d. 1905) have blamed Sufi ideas and practices for making the UMMA vulnerable to foreign domination. The Sufis have also incurred the wrath of the Wahhabis of Saudi Arabia, and today they are vulnerable to attack wherever Wahhabi influence is strong. Sufism is banned in Saudi Arabia, and Sufi orders have also been banned from Shii IRAN, where they had flourished for centuries. Sufi theosophy, known as *irfan,* has been embraced in Iran, and has had a significant influence on Iranian religiosity. Ayatollah RUHOLLAH KHOMEINI (d. 1989) was an enthusiastic student of this brand of Islamic mysticism. Meanwhile, Sufism has found new devotees in Europe and the Americas among spiritual seekers. Many, including those not affiliated with any form of organized Sufism, enjoy reading translations of the mystical poetry of JALAL AL-DIN RUMI (d. 1273) and watching Mevlevis perform their *samaa* dances on stage in concert halls and churches.

See also ABD AL-QADIR AL-JILANI; ASCETICISM; BAWA MUHAIYADDEEN FELLOWSHIP; CHISHTI SUFI ORDER; COLONIALISM; AL-HASAN AL-BASRI; IBN AL-ARABI, MUHYI AL-DIN; MULLAH SADRA; *MURID; MURSHID;* MUSIC; RABIA AL-ADAWIYYA; SHAYKH; *TARIQA;* WAHHABISM; *ZIYARA.*

Further reading: Carl W. Ernst, *Shambhala Guide to Sufism* (Boston: Shambhala, 1997); Carl W. Ernst, ed., *Teachings of Sufism* (Boston: Shambhala, 1999); Ahmet Karamustafa, *God's Unruly Friends: Dervish Groups in the Islamic Later Middle Period* (Oxford: Oneworld, 2006); Javad Nurbakhsh, *Sufi Women,* 2d ed. (New York: Khaniqahi Nimatullahi, 1990); John Renard, *Friends of God: Islamic Images of Piety, Commitment, and Servanthood* (Berkeley: University of California Press, 2008); Annemarie Schimmel, *Mystical Dimensions of Islam* (Chapel Hill: University of North Carolina Press, 1975); Abu Abd al-Rahman al-Sulami, *Early Sufi Women (Dhikr al-niswa al-mutabbidat al-sufiyyat).* Translated by Rkia E. Cornell (Louisville, Ky.: Fons Vitae, 1999); J. Spencer Trimingham, *The Sufi Orders of Islam* (Oxford: Oxford University Press, 1971); John O. Voll, *Islam: Continuity and Change in the Modem World* (Boulder, Colo.: Westview Press, 1982).

suicide

A nearly universal aspect of human existence addressed by religion is that of DEATH and its meaning. In Islam, the most widely accepted view is that death is a matter that lies in God's hands—he determines all things and is the giver of both life and death. Suicide, the willful taking of one's own life is therefore often considered to be morally wrong and an offense against God in Islam. In Arabic, it is called *intihar* and *qati nafs.* Muslims believe that suicide victims will be punished in the AFTERLIFE. They base this view partly on the Quran, but mainly in the HADITH and the consensus of Muslim jurists and theologians. Religious tradition aside, suicide is a phenomenon that occurs for a variety of different reasons—psychological, sociological, and political. Since the 1980s it has become an urgent matter in many countries because of the marked increase in the number of incidents in which Muslims have conducted deadly attacks on military and civilian targets that also involved the loss of the attacker's life. In many cases explosives are strapped to the attacker's body or placed in a vehicle driven by him (or her). They have therefore been called by their proponents and opponents "suicide bombings," "suicide attacks," and more recently "martyrdom operations." AL-QAIDA's assaults on the World Trade Center and the Pentagon on September 11, 2001, are the most infamous suicide attacks executed in recent years, involving the deaths of nearly 3,000 people. Although religious ideology has been involved in these attacks, the degree to which it has been a decisive factor is highly disputed.

Suicide was not a significant issue in the Quran and hadith, and only became so among Muslims relatively recently. Nevertheless, the issue was addressed in Islamic tradition. The most relevant verses in the Quran are Q 4:29–30 and 2:195. These verses are ambiguous in their meaning, however. The former, dated to the Medinan period, includes the command, "Do not kill yourselves. . . . Whoever does that in enmity and wrongfully, we will roast him in the FIRE." Traditional commentators have said that this can be either an injunction against suicide, or against Muslims killing each other. The second passage occurs in a section of Q 2 (also dated to the Medinan period) concerning warfare; it states, "Spend [of your wealth?] on God's behalf and do not throw [yourselves] into danger." Commentators disagree about what this means. Does it mean that Muslims should not go into battle unless they have enough provisions, or are they being instructed to keep fighting for the cause, lest God punish them for giving up or retreating? Or, is it actually a prohibition of suicide? The clearest condemnations of suicide, however, are to be found in the major hadith collections, some of which devoted chapters to the subject. In one hadith, Muhammad declares, "Whoever strangles himself will repeat this deed in the Fire, and whoever kills himself by stabbing his own body with some weapon will repeat his deed in the Fire" (al-Bukhari, *Sahih,* quoted in Rozenthal). This hadith and others promise that God will punish suicide victims severely in the afterlife.

Apart from statements in the Quran and hadith, the subject of suicide was also debated by FIQH specialists. They discussed it in relation to whether FUNERARY RITUALS should be held for suicide victims. The conservative view was that such rites should not be performed, but others were more lenient, taking into consideration cultural practice and the emotional states of the bereaved. Franz Rosenthal, a leading Islamic Studies scholar, has identified other questions raised in medieval *fiqh* literature. These include the liability of those who unknowingly contributed to the commission of a suicide and the status of the legally stipulated bridal gift when a prospective bride kills herself. Suicidal themes also arise in love poetry and Sufi literature, where the lover perishes in the absence of the beloved, or becomes self-annihilated, as a moth perishes when drawn to the flame. The morality of euthanasia only became a topic for jurists in the modern period, with most ruling that it should be considered a form of suicide.

In discussions of JIHAD warfare, as David Cook has found, Muslim jurists discussed whether going to battle against a superior force should be considered suicide. Most ruled that it is not, depending on the intent of the soldier, the necessity for resorting to such desperate measures, and whether the act is performed on behalf of the community or for self-glorification. These discussions invariably dovetailed into discussions of MARTYRDOM (SHAHADA). Although martyrdom achieved a high degree of symbolic importance in SHIISM, focused on the figure of HUSAYN IBN ALI (d. 660) and the battle of KARBALA, it was also discussed by Sunni jurists. In the case of both traditions, martyrs were considered to have been specially blessed—they were exempted from stipulated burial procedures (washing of the corpse and enshroudment) and promised a higher rank in PARADISE than ordinary believers.

Today, debates over suicide attacks committed by Muslims in places like LEBANON, ISRAEL/PALESTINE, IRAQ, AFGHANISTAN, or in the U.S. on 9/11 reflect a wide spectrum of views among both Muslims and non-Muslims. The most simplistic and ideologically motivated positions taken in these debates attribute the attacks to what is claimed to be Islam's essentially violent nature, irregardless as to context, or justify them as forms of communal self-defense. More careful treatments of the subject explain it in relation to several contextual factors, some giving more emphasis to religion than others. Those identifying religion as a significant explanatory factor maintain that it is a relatively recent phenomenon in Islam, and point to the specific Islamist ideologies and groups that underpin it.

On the other hand, Robert A. Pape of the University of Chicago has conducted a systematic study of all cases of suicide terrorism that occurred around the world from 1980 through 2003. He documented a total of 315 incidents in this period and found that there was little connection between them and the Islamic religion per se. Indeed, the largest number of attacks (76 out of 315) by a single group was conducted by the Tamil Tigers, a Marxist-Leninist nationalist movement in Sri Lanka with no connection to Islam. Only about half of the attacks were conducted by Islamist groups. Instead, Pape has argued that suicide TERRORISM is primarily a response to foreign occupation, rather than being a phenomenon of ISLAMISM, and that it has several specific characteristics, including 1) desire to achieve national liberation of a homeland from occupation by a foreign power ruled by a democratic government; 2) the identity of the occupier differs significantly from that of the occupied (in terms of culture, religion, language, etc.); 3) suicide attacks are conducted by organized groups, rather than by random, irrational individuals; and 4) because terrorist groups learn from each other; there is a tendency for it to spread. Foreign occupation will only increase the incidence of suicide bombings over time and make terrorist recruitment efforts more successful. Pape recommends that the U.S. cease to use military coercion against foreign countries, let these countries exercise more autonomy, help strengthen them with non-military economic assistance, and keep a military force trained and ready to handle any major crises that cannot be resolved by other means.

At the time of this writing (summer 2008), it is not clear which course U.S. policy makers will pursue in the years to come, although the most vocal policymakers and media voices continue to favor military occupation, as witnessed in Iraq and Afghanistan. Governments in many Muslim-majority countries are seeking either to eradicate oppositional Islamic groups where they are able, or apply a combination of pressures and incentives to prevent them from engaging in armed violence, including suicide attacks. Other governments appear to favor the use of suicide attacks when they serve their national strategic interests.

See also HAMAS; HIZBULLAH; JIHAD MOVEMENTS.

Further reading: Jonathan E. Brockopp, "The 'Good Death' in Islamic Theology and Law," in idem, ed., *Islamic Ethics of Life: Abortion, War, and Euthanasia* (Columbia: University of South Carolina Press, 2003), 177–193; David Cook, *Martyrdom in Islam* (Cambridge: Cambridge University Press, 2007); David Cook and Olivia Allison, *Understanding and Addressing Suicide Attacks: The Faith and Politics of Martyrdom Operations* (Cambridge: Cambridge University Press, 2007); Bernard K. Freamon, "Martyrdom, Suicide, and the Islamic Law of War: A Short Legal History," in *Fordham International Law Journal* 27 (2003), 299–369; Haim Malka, "Must Innocents Die? The Islamic Debate over Suicide Attacks," in *Middle East Quarterly* 10, no. 2

(Spring 2003), on http://www.meforum.org/ article/530; Robert A. Pape, *Dying to Win: The Strategic Logic of Suicide Terrorism* (New York: Random House, 2005); Franz Rosenthal, "On Suicide in Islam," in *Journal of the American Oriental Society,* 66 (July–Sept. 1946): 239–259, reprinted in idem, *Muslim Intellectual and Social History: A Collection of Essays* (Aldershot, Hampshire, U.K.: Varorium, 1990).

sultan

In Arabic the term *sultan* generally means "power" or "AUTHORITY," but starting in the 10th century C.E. increasingly it also came to be an official title designating the *person* who holds power and authority. Although the title could refer to a provincial governor or prince, it could also serve as the title of the ruler of an entire region or empire.

This was the case when the Shii Buyids seized control of BAGHDAD in 945 C.E. The Buyids allowed the ABBASID CALIPHATE to continue as the symbolic and religious head of the Muslim community while their own leader took over all real military and political authority under the title of sultan. Although this division of authority did not form a part of the early Islamic ideals, both the caliph and political theorists accommodated themselves to the realities of the situation. They concluded that because the Buyids upheld Islamic law (SHARIA), the chaos and violence that would likely ensue in an attempt to overthrow them was not worth the risk. At the same time, however, they tried to put limits on the devolution of power by insisting that only the caliph could confer the title of sultan. The Buyids and those who came after them accepted this and eagerly sought this statement of investiture from the caliph for the legitimacy that it bestowed. In return the sultan promised to defend the lands of Islam from external threats, while ensuring justice internally. In this way Muslim theorists adopted a more Persian-inspired model of government in which religion and government are seen as brothers that mutually support each other.

When the Seljuk Turks defeated the Buyids in 1055 the caliph did not regain any of his authority under the new regime, but the defeat did bring the two wings of government under one Sunni umbrella. It was during the Seljuk period that the ideal government of the sultanate was spelled out by Nizam al-Mulk (d. 1092), the VIZIER to the sultan Alp Arslan and Malikshah. Whereas the caliph was primarily a religious figurehead, the sultan should defend Islam from external attack, ensure internal justice by upholding sharia and supporting religious leaders, and develop "civilization" by maintaining roads, MOSQUEs, schools, BAZAARs, and other infrastructure.

In the 12th century the Abbasid Caliphate was able to regain some of its power, but only within Iraq, while the rest of the empire was divided up among regional sultans. When Baghdad was destroyed by the Mongols in 1258 even these minimal gains came to an end. Although a survivor of the Abbasid house was proclaimed caliph in CAIRO, authority for the Islamic heartlands remained in the hands of the MAMLUK sultans of Cairo and, after them, the Ottoman sultans in ISTANBUL.

When Islam spread to South and Southeast Asia most rulers continued to use titles derived from the local languages, but they also adopted the title of sultan, which conveyed the authority and legitimacy of a Muslim ruler. In the modern period some monarchies continue to use the title of sultan, such as the Sultanate of Brunei and the Sultanate of Oman.

See also ISLAMIC GOVERNMENT; OTTOMAN DYNASTY.

Heather N. Keaney

Further reading: Heribert Busse, "The Revival of Persian Kingship under the Buyids." In *Islamic Civilization 950–1150,* edited by D. S. Richards, 47–69 (London: Bruno Cassirer, 1973); Carole Hillenbrand, "Islamic Orthodoxy or Realpolitik? Al-Ghazali's Views on Government," *Iran: Journal of the British Institute of Persian Studies* 26 (1988): 81–94; Ann Lambton, *State and Government in Medieval Islam* (Oxford: Oxford University Press, 1981); Roy Mottahedeh, *Loyalty and Leadership in an Early Islamic Society* (Princeton, N.J.: Princeton University Press, 1980); Nizam al-Mulk, *The Book of Government or Rules for Kings (Siyasat-namah or Siyar al-muluk).* Translated by Hubert Drake (New Haven, Conn.: Yale University Press, 1960).

sunna (Arabic: custom, tradition, precedent; pl. *sunan*)

In Islam the body of idealized precedents for religious and moral behavior that go with the QURAN is known as the sunna. It is one of the four "roots" of Islamic law (FIQH). First systematized in the ninth and 10th centuries, the sunna was based on the exemplary words and actions of MUHAMMAD (ca. 570–632), Islam's prophet, as reported in the HADITH. In addition to its collective meaning, the term *sunna* can also mean an individual precedent found in the hadith.

In order to authenticate the hadith, which are narratives that were first transmitted orally and then compiled in books, Muslims developed a tradition of critical inquiry that assessed individual hadiths according to the reliability and continuity of the reported sequence (isnad) of individuals said to have transmitted it. Sunni Muslims hold the hadith collections of al-Bukhari (d. 870) and Muslim ibn al-Hajjaj (d. 875) to be the most authentic (sahih) ones, but there are others from which they derive the sunna, too.

As an example of how a sunna can be conveyed by a hadith, let us examine the following hadith from al-Bukhari's collection: Zayd ibn Aslam's father said, "I saw UMAR IBN AL-KHATTAB kiss the [Black] Stone and say, 'If I had not seen God's Messenger kiss you, I would not have kissed you'" (Sahih, Kitab al-hajj). This hadith informs us, according to a reliable witness, that Muhammad kissed the BLACK STONE of the Kaaba while performing the hajj and that the second caliph, Umar (r. 634–644) also did it, because he saw Muhammad perform the action. The sunna to be drawn from this is one that instructs Muslims that they are permitted to kiss the Black Stone when they perform the HAJJ, based on the precedent set by Muhammad and confirmed by his companion Umar. This practice is not mentioned in the Quran, so it constitutes an elaboration of the Quran's rulings concerning the hajj. A single sunna may be supported by one hadith, as in this case, or many. Conversely, a single hadith may authorize more than one sunna, depending on the content of the report.

In the early decades of Islamic history, the idea of the sunna had a broad range of meanings that became narrower with the passage of time and the consolidation of Islamic belief and tradition. In the Quran, prophets are represented as exemplary figures and Muhammad is called the "beautiful model" (al-uswa al-hasana) for those "who hope for God and the last day" (Q 33:21). The Quran also repeatedly urges believers to "obey God and his messenger" (for example, Q 5:92; 8:20, 46). However, it does not associate the term sunna with Muhammad's words and deeds. Rather, the Quran uses sunna in two senses: (1) with reference to the wrongful ways of peoples of earlier generations (for example, Q 3:137; 8:13; 18:55), and (2) with the rightful way of God's judgments (Q 33:60–62; 40:85). After Muhammad's death, Muslims found that God's laws and prohibitions as stated in the Quran were often too general to give guidance in real-life situations, even in matters of worship, such as PRAYER and ALMSGIVING. While many Muslims continued to follow their own tribal customs and judges relied on individual legal opinion, the piety-minded advocated reliance on accounts of Muhammad's life (sira) and the good example of his Companions and their heirs ("the successors") in MECCA and MEDINA, as well as those who had migrated with them to the cities and towns of Syria and Iraq. Contending notions of legal precedent and correct religious practice gave rise to a variety of living local traditions, or "precedents" (sunan) to be emulated.

The efforts of ARAB Muslim rulers to consolidate their power and centralize the administration of the newly conquered lands also prompted efforts to standardize the diffused community's traditions and laws. Some claimed that the "living" sunna of Medina was identical with that of Muhammad, a position that was conveyed in the teachings of MALIK IBN ANAS (d. 795), the eponym of the MALIKI LEGAL SCHOOL. Because Muslims living elsewhere in Islamdom did not favor elevating the practice of Medinan Muslims above their own, they found that reliance on the exemplary authority of Muhammad and other individuals in the early Islamic community as transmitted in

the hadith, not the living example of Medinese Muslims, was an especially suitable alternative. This led to the creation of a vast body of hadith, including fabricated ones. Modern scholars have argued that these hadith embodied not only the sunna of Muhammad, the early caliphs, and the Companions, but that they also gave legitimacy and religious sanction to pre-Islamic Arab practices (sunan) that continued to be followed in the broader Muslim community during the first centuries of Islamic history. The elevation of the hadith also appealed to newly converted non-Arab Muslims in Iran and elsewhere who could not claim to embody the "living" sunna of Muhammad and his Companions. This may be why so many of the collectors of hadith, such as al-Bukhari, al-Tirmidhi (d. 892), and ibn Maja (d. 892), were Persians by heritage. However, it was MUHAMMAD IBN IDRIS AL-SHAFII (d. 820), the eponym of the SHAFII LEGAL SCHOOL, who most forcefully argued that the sunna be grounded in hadith rather than in the living practice of Muslims. Along with the Quran it became the basis for jurisprudence recognized by all the major Islamic legal schools (sing. madhhab). Moreover, both the Quran and the sunna have come to be seen as forms of REVELATION from God, which is analogous to the Jewish rabbinic belief in both the written and oral Torah of MOSES. The Quran embodies God's word, Muhammad's sunna is inspired by God. Any practice or belief that could not be validated by the Quran and sunna was liable to be condemned as an unauthorized "innovation" (BIDAA), especially by Muslims with a highly literalistic understanding of their religion.

The distinction between Sunni and Shii Muslims hinges in part on their different understandings of the sunna. The Shia define it in relation to Muhammad and his household (the AHL AL-BAYT), particularly as embodied in the hadith (or akhbar) of ALI IBN ABI TALIB (d. 661) and the other sacred Imams descended from him. Indeed, their name is a shortened form of the phrase "faction of Ali" (shiat Ali), the first IMAM. Starting in the ninth/10th century, Muslims who followed the sunna of Muhammad and his Companions instead of the Shii Imams saw themselves as the People of the Sunna (*ahl al-sunna*), or People of the Sunna and Community (*ahl al-sunna wa'l-jamaa*). They eventually became known simply as the Sunnis.

Since the 18th century many Islamic RENEWAL AND REFORM MOVEMENTS have called for a rejection of "innovation" and a return to the Quran and sunna. Although found in several of the Sufi orders, such as that of the Naqshbandis, it is expressed most clearly in the revivalism of the Wahhabis, the MUSLIM BROTHERHOOD, the JAMAAT-I ISLAMI, the TABLIGHI JAMAAT, and groups inspired by them. On the other hand, Muslim modernist reformers have questioned the reliability of the hadith and sunna, arguing that they be either rejected or carefully circumscribed. Instead, many propose following general ethical principles based on the Quran, in harmony with reason, modern SCIENCE, HUMAN RIGHTS, religious pluralism, DEMOCRACY, and gender equality. This trend is represented by figures such as SAYYID AHMAD KHAN (d. 1898), MUHAMMAD ABDUH (d. 1905), and ALI ABD AL-RAZIQ (d. 1966), and more recently by thinkers such as FAZLUR RAHMAN (d. 1988), Muhammad Shahrur (b. 1938), and FATIMA MERNISSI (b. 1940).

See also COMPANIONS OF THE PROPHET; ETHICS AND MORALITY; SHARIA; SHIISM.

Further reading: Daniel Brown, *Rethinking Tradition in Modern Islamic Thought* (Cambridge: Cambridge University Press, 1996); Yasin Dutton, *The Origins of Islamic Law: The Quran, the Muwatta, and the Madinan Amal* (London: Routledge Curzon, 2002); Wael B. Hallaq, *The Origins and Evolution of Islamic Law* (Cambridge: Cambridge University Press, 2005); G. H. A. Juynboll, "Some New Ideas on the Development of Sunna as a Technical Term in Early Islam," *Jerusalem Studies in Arabic and Islam* 10 (1987): 97–118; Fazlur Rahman, *Islam*, 2d ed. (Chicago: University of Chicago Press, 1979), 43–84.

Sunnism

Sunnism was the last of the major traditions of Islam to be clearly articulated. In fact, it is possible to think of Sunnism as comprising the broad swath of Muslims who did not incline toward the other two early traditions, SHIISM and Kharijism. The KHAWARIJ broke with the rest of Muslims over the question of whether the sinner could be considered a Muslim. They defined the community narrowly, and they were initially disposed to fight those with whom they disagreed; the consensus among Muslims grew that this position was too extreme and the Khawarij eventually became a tiny sect with few adherents. Shii identity formed around a dispute over the leadership of the community, but it fairly quickly culminated in a belief that the leadership of the community was no mere matter of human preference, but rather formed part of a divinely inspired plan for the salvation of the community.

The Sunnis, then, are those Muslims who eventually united in a belief that only God knows the hearts, and so judgment should be left to God—thus rejecting Khariji extremism—and that the leadership of the community as it emerged historically was part of God's plan, thus rejecting the heart of Shii claims about legitimate leadership; subsequent leadership would not be considered very significant theologically because the Sunni orthodoxy that eventually emerged held that the CALIPH, while theoretically necessary for the existence of an Islamic state, was less important than the CALIPHATE as an institution. Finally, it was held that the scholars (ULAMA) were the keepers of the community's morals, not the caliphs.

The term *sunni* is an abridgement of *ahl al-sunna wa'al-jamaa*, meaning the people of the prophetic tradition and community. This refers to the focus, especially dating from the ninth century, on the collection of accounts of the prophet Muhammad, the SUNNA, and following in the path of that sunna. All Muslims accept the primacy of the QURAN, but the Sunnis place a unique emphasis on the sunna of Muhammad.

Today, Sunnis make up some 85 percent of Muslims worldwide. The sunni legal schools have traditionally been the means by which Sunni Muslims actually learned the specifics of their Islam. The importance of these schools has broken down in the 20th century, causing contemporary Sunnism to break with its traditional educational and intellectual roots in a way that has not happened as noticeably in Shiism. This has led to some problems facing contemporary Sunni Islam, especially because the most vigorous intellectual leadership, that of the Islamists, has not, in the main, come from the ulama class but rather from those educated in the modern methods, especially the hard sciences. In this respect, then, it could be argued that Sunnism finds itself in a real crisis of identity and direction quite similar to the period of crisis that European Christianity endured after the Protestant Reformation began in the 16th century.

Some tensions exist between Sunnis and Shiis, especially in regions where sizeable populations of both sects exist, such as PAKISTAN, IRAQ, and LEBANON. But on the whole, these differences are submerged in the larger contexts of agreement, whether they be religious, nationalistic, or ethnic. Where these differences are reemerging, such as in IRAQ after the American invasion, the divisions reflect at least in part the failure of nationalism to provide an effective source of cohesion.

John Iskander

Further reading: Patricia Crone, *God's Rule* (New York: Columbia University Press, 2004); Qasim Zaman, *Religion and Politics under the Early 'Abbasids: The Emergence of the Proto-Sunni Elite* (Leiden: E.J. Brill, 1997); Qasim Zaman, *The Ulama in Contemporary Islam: Custodians of Change* (Princeton, N.J.: Princeton University Press, 2002).

suq *See* BAZAAR.

sura *See* QURAN.

Syria (Official name: Syrian Arab Republic)

Syria is one of the most important countries in the Middle East in terms of its size and its role in Middle East regional politics. Its population is rapidly changing as a result of a high birth rate (2.24 percent in a 2007 estimate) and a dramatic influx of REFUGEES due to violent conflict along its borders with IRAQ, LEBANON, and ISRAEL. The official population was about 19.8 million in 2008,

but this number does not account for the UNHCR estimate of more than one million Iraqi war refugees residing in Syria with little prospect of return to their home country. In addition, Syria is home to more than 400,000 Palestinian refugees who came to Syria in four major waves of forced migration: in 1948, 1967, 1973, and after the expulsion of the PALESTINE LIBERATION ORGANIZATION (PLO) from Lebanon in 1982.

Syria's current land area of 185,180 square kilometers (about the size of North Dakota) is home to some of the world's oldest civilizations. The Euphrates River flows across northeastern Syria. The ancient city of Hamoukar was recently discovered in northeast Syria near the shores of the Euphrates. It may have been settled by humans as early as 8,000 years ago. The ancient kingdoms of Ebla (southwest of Aleppo) and Mari (on the Euphrates) developed cuneiform writing, a precursor to our modern alphabet. Ebla was so prosperous that "no fewer than seventeen varieties of wheat were raised" and "Ebla was in a condition to feed more than 18 million people" (Batatu, p. 92). These early empires were succeeded by the Hittites at Ugarit in the northern coastal region (1600–1200 B.C.E.), the Persians (539–333 B.C.E.), the Greeks (333–64 B.C.E.), and the Romans (64 B.C.E.–395 C.E.). In the 200s, Queen Zenobia conquered most of EGYPT and Asia Minor. She built the sprawling city of Palmyra in the eastern Syrian desert before being defeated by the Romans in 272 C.E. Today Palmyra is one of Syria's most spectacular archaeological sites.

Syria is also a land of diverse religious traditions. The majority of the population is Sunni Muslim (74 percent). Syria was conquered by Muslim armies from the Arabian Peninsula in 634 C.E., two years after the death of MUHAMMAD (ca. 570–632). The capital of the first Islamic empire of the Umayyads (634–750) was DAMASCUS. Other religious sects within the Islamic tradition that are prevalent in Syria include the ALAWI, DRUZE, Shii, Ismaili, and Yazidi (16 percent). From the 1200s through the 19th century, Sufi Islam was the dominant form of religious practice among Muslims. Sufis were organized into religious orders, and devotees prayed together in a *zawiyah,* or Sufi lodge. Up until the 18th century even the smallest Syrian village had its own *zawiyah.* SUFISM had a precipitous decline as a practice in the 19th century. As Syria's urban population began to rapidly increase and the Ottoman authorities in ISTANBUL exerted centralizing reforms on its ARAB provinces, institutionalized Sunni Islam prevailed over more heterodox popular forms of religious expression. Most of the more than 1 million war refugees who have fled IRAQ for Syria since 2003 are Shii. The shrine of Sayyida Zaynab south of Damascus is a major pilgrimage site for Iraqi, Iranian, and Lebanese Shiis. Zaynab was the daughter of the Shii martyr Ali and the granddaughter of the prophet Muhammed. Many Iraqi Shiis now live in the crowded slum areas adjacent to the shrine.

Christianity has flourished in Syria from the earliest times and Christians now make up about 10 percent of the population. Aramaic was the language of early Christianity in Syria and is still used in liturgy in the ancient village of Maaloula with its Mar Sergius Church dating back to the third century C.E. Syria was part of the Byzantine Empire from 395 to 632 C.E. during which time most of the population converted. The Byzantines imposed their own Greek-speaking clergy on the local population, creating a schism. Syrians adopted Islam gradually and the majority of the population may not have become Muslim until the 10th or 11th centuries. The main Christian denominations in Syria today are Greek Orthodox, Syrian Orthodox, Armenian Orthodox, Syrian Catholic, Armenian Catholic, Maronites, and a variety of smaller Protestant sects. Damascus, Aleppo, and Kamishli near the border with TURKEY still have very small Jewish communities. The Jewish quarter in the old city of Damascus dates back to pre-Christian times.

In the modern period, Syria has suffered from foreign domination and COLONIALISM. From 1516 to 1916, Syria was a province of the Ottoman Empire. The last years of the empire were particularly harsh. The Ottoman sultan Abdul Hamid II (1876–1909) stepped up forced conscription—even among Syria's Christians, who had formerly been exempt from military service. An economic recession and the collapse of traditional handicraft industries caused by the flooding of local markets with cheap European industrial goods created a wave of peasant and urban lower-class migration to South America and the UNITED STATES. The repressive policies of Abdul Hamid gave rise to a growing opposition movement among Syria's newly educated professional class who sought promotion of the Arabic language in the educational system and government administration. After Abdul Hamid was deposed by the Young Turk Movement in 1909, some members of the Syrian opposition began calling for complete independence. The nascent Arab nationalist movement was ruthlessly crushed by the Turkish military authorities during World War I. In 1915 and 1916, 33 Arab nationalists were publicly hanged in the main squares of Beirut and Damascus.

Syria's present borders are the result of colonial partition sponsored by the British and French in the Sykes-Picot Agreement of 1916. Under the terms of the agreement, Syria was placed under French role as a mandate of the League of Nations. ARAB armies led by Faysal Husayn, son of the Sharif of MECCA, entered Damascus in 1918 and declared an independent Arab kingdom. At the same time, French military forces landed in Syria and Lebanon. Faysal's government was militarily defeated by the French in 1920, and the country was placed under foreign military rule. The ruthlessness of French military and economic policies radicalized the Syrian population. In 1925 and 1926, the Syrians rose in a massive revolt beginning in the Druze mountainous areas in the south, then encompassing much of the countryside and eventually reaching the urban centers of Damascus and Aleppo. To crush the armed revolt, the French employed their foreign legion, aerial bombardment, and even the use of napalm. Almost a third of the Syria population became homeless.

The French mandate left a legacy of a bifurcated body politic that plagued Syria for the rest of the 20th century. The French relied on large absentee landowners, wealthy merchants, and urban notables as their collaborators in administering Syria. The disenfranchised middle class and educated professionals were blocked from advancing their own interests. Increasingly, those who were not the beneficiaries of French political and economic patronage turned to new political movements with radical anticolonialist ideologies. These two political forces would wrestle for control of Syria's governmental apparatus for the first 30 years of Syria's existence as an independent state after World War II. The dominant ideology of the patriotic Syrian bourgeoisie was Arab nationalism that espoused a reversal of the colonial partition of Arab lands by the Sykes-Picot Agreement, Arab political sovereignty over its own territory, and the adoption of Arab cultural policies that recognized the significance of Islam as the majority religious tradition in the region. Every anticolonialist popular movement that emerged in Syria in the 20th century clung to some variant of Arab nationalism as a basic political principle. The Communist Party of Lebanon and Syria, founded in 1928, was one of the new uncompromising anticolonialist political movements. By the 1950s, it became one of the largest and best organized communist parties in the Arab world.

Another of the radical Arab nationalist parties that emerged during the period of the French mandate was the BAATH PARTY, founded in 1939 by two schoolteachers, one Greek Orthodox and the other Sunni Muslim. In addition to adhering to a basic policy of Arabism, unity, and political independence, the party also advocated a vague notion of socialism that would evolve in time to include land reform, state ownership of key economic institutions such as banks, and state regulation of the private sector. The Baath finally came to power in 1966. From the 1950s through 1970s, the leadership of the Syrian Baath Party was almost exclusively composed of members of professions: professors, schoolteachers, doctors, lawyers, and military officers—the very people who had been thwarted from achieving political power and economic advancement by the old ruling classes of landowners, merchants, and urban notables. In a military coup in 1970, one Alawi air force officer, Hafiz al-Asad, prevailed over all other factions in the Baath Party and became president of Syria until his death in 2000. He was succeeded by his son Bashar al-Asad who remains the Syrian president in 2008.

Syria became a key player in Arab regional politics. It is a frontline state in the ARAB-ISRAELI CONFLICTS. Syrian volunteers fought in the 1948 war in Palestine and, at its conclusion, Syria served as one of the countries of refuge for Palestinian refugees. ISRAEL occupied the Syrian Golan Heights in 1967 and expelled most of the population. More of the Golan was occupied in 1973. Today there are only about 20,000 Syrians, mostly Druze, left in the Israeli occupied part of the Golan Heights. The occupied territory has also been populated by about 20,000 Israeli settlers. Israel declared the unilateral annexation of the Golan Heights in 1981.

Syria was a key Middle East regional ally of the Soviet Union during the years of the cold war. The USSR supplied the country with MIG fighter jets and missile systems in order to defend itself, but Syria was never allowed to achieve military parity with Israel. When Israel mounted a full-scale invasion of Lebanon in June 1982 and the Syrian air force challenged Israeli jets bombing its antiaircraft missile defense systems along its border with Lebanon, a third of the entire Syrian air force was destroyed in only a few hours. Since 1982 Syria has supported Palestinian factions who have rejected peace proposals that fall short of full Palestinian national sovereignty in the West Bank and Gaza. Syria has opposed regional peace initiatives that are bilateral in nature and ignore the issue of Syrian sovereignty over the Golan Heights. At the same time, Syria has conducted secret negotiations with Israel through third-party intermediaries and has shown flexibility over proposals for limiting Syria's return to full sovereign control of the Golan by having any future peace agreement monitored by international peacekeeping forces, including those of the United States, and installing electronic early warning systems.

Syria has played a pragmatic role in Arab regional politics. It has been cautious in nurturing its relations with SAUDI ARABIA and the GULF STATES. Over the years Saudi Arabia has supplied

Syria with an abundance of military and economic aid for its role as a confrontation state with Israel. Syria maintained an historic enmity for the regime of SADDAM HUSAYN in Iraq and fostered good relations with IRAN after the Islamic Revolution in 1979. Syria participated in the U.S.-sponsored military coalition in the First Gulf War after Iraq invaded Kuwait in 1990. Syria has not supported the U.S. occupation of Iraq after 2003 and its economy has suffered from the sudden influx of hundreds of thousands of war refugees. Syria has been intricately involved in the long-running civil war in Lebanon. Syrian troops were invited into Lebanon by the government as a buffer force in 1975 and remained there until 2005. Since the end of the Syrian military presence, one of its main exports to Lebanon has been a cheap labor force that has been terribly exploited.

Syria is a multisectarian, multiethnic society that is rich in cultural diversity. It has become a largely secular society and its people in cities such as Damascus, Aleppo, and Latikiya are decidedly cosmopolitan. Syria has one of the highest LITERACY rates in the Arab world. The country is noted for its contributions to Arab CINEMA culture, TV, music, Arabic literature, and publishing. The once-thriving theater scene in Baghdad has now moved to Damascus. Damascus and Aleppo are important centers for artistic creativity, museums, and galleries. Syria is wired, and Internet cafes are cropping up everywhere. The nation has its own distinctive cuisine renowned throughout the Arab world, of which *kibab halabi* (skewered meat from Aleppo) is only one of its most famous dishes. Café society is lively in Damascus, Aleppo, and elsewhere. Syria's archaeological wonders serve as a boon for scholars and tourists.

See also ARMENIANS; CHRISTIANITY AND ISLAM; CRUSADES; IBN TAYMIYYA; MUSLIM BROTHERHOOD; OTTOMAN DYNASTY; UMAYYAD CALIPHATE.

Garay Menicucci

Further reading: Hanna Batatu, *Syria's Peasantry, the Descendants of Its Less Rural Notables, and Their Roles* (Princeton, N.J.: Princeton University Press, 1999); James Gelvin, *Divided Loyalties: Nationalism and Mass Politics in Syria at the Close of Empire* (Berkeley: University of California Press, 1998); Raymond Hinnebusch, *Syria: Revolution from Above* (London: Routledge, 2001); Hugh Kennedy, *The Great Arab Conquests* (Cambridge, Mass.: Da Capo Press, 2007), 66–97; Tabitha Petran, *Syria* (London: Ernest Benn Ltd., 1972).

T

taawiz   *See* AMULETS AND TALISMANS.

taaziya   *See* ASHURA; MUHARRAM.

Tablighi Jamaat

The Tablighi Jamaat is a transnational Muslim reform movement founded in the early 20th century in colonial INDIA. Although it is one of the largest of such organizations in the world, its lack of institutional hierarchy and structure makes systematic study of the Tablighi Jamaat's membership and program quite difficult. The picture that emerges from the small body of literature that does exist is that of a "revivalist" movement looking to precipitate societal reform through a HADITH-based program of personal piety, and a program of *tabligh* (offering guidance) to wayward Muslims. What distinguishes the Tablighi Jamaat from many Islamist movements, which often also base programs of reform on a mythico-historical community of Muhammad (d. 632) and his Companions, is that state power is anathema to the Tablighi program.

The Tablighi Jamaat, however, is not at all apolitical—in fact, the movement's central principles are themselves political in that they deal with issues of AUTHORITY (God versus the material state). While many scholars confuse a rejection of the modern state with a lack of political vision, the Tablighi Jamaat's political outlook is simply a rejection of modern political organization. This is particularly true internationally. Although many of its scholars understand the Tablighi Jamaat to be apolitical, the movement's aversion to state affairs stems from the tension between two vastly different political visions.

The Tablighi Jamaat seeks the creation of a parallel authority to the state that does not entail any direct involvement with it, including active or open opposition. Avoiding the state-centered identity that is characteristic of modern political organization, the Tablighi Jamaat preaches fealty to Islam above all else—being Muslim trumps all other identities, including family and nation-state. In this sense, the principles that govern the Tablighi Jamaat resemble those of AL-QAIDA. The Tablighi Jamaat, however, offers an alternative vision of how transnational revivalist movements can work toward reform. In light of the tremendous amount of attention given to "Islamist" and "Jihadist" movements, which are not limited to al-Qaida, the Tablighi Jamaat points to an important alternative, nonviolent method of political organization and authority.

See also RENEWAL AND REFORM MOVEMENTS; TERRORISM.

Caleb Elfenbein

651

Further reading: Gilles Kepel. "*Foi et pratique*: Tablighi Jama'at in France." In *Travellers in Faith,* edited by Muhammad Khalid Masud, 188–205 (Boston: E.J. Brill, 2000); Muhammad Khalid Masud, "The Growth and Development of the Tablighi Jama'at in India." In *Travellers in Faith,* edited by Muhammad Khalid Masud, 3–43 (Boston: E.J. Brill, 2000); Barbara Metcalf, "Islam and Women: The Case of the Tablighi Jama'at." *Stanford Humanities Review* 5, no. 1 (1995): 1–9.

tafsir

Religions with HOLY BOOKS or scriptures require ongoing traditions of interpretation and commentary (exegesis) that contribute to preserving the sacredness of those books and adapting them to the changing social and historical circumstances of the communities that possess them. Commentary is a way of making the texts meaningful to new generations of adherents. This can be seen in the histories of Judaism and Christianity, where biblical commentary has been a significant meaning-making activity, especially with regard to matters of law and tradition in the former and theological doctrine in the latter. Hindus, Buddhists, Jains, Confucians, and Taoists have also produced significant bodies of commentary literature for their sacred texts.

In Islam, QURAN commentary is one of the foremost subjects of classical Islamic learning and one of largest genres of Islamic religious literature, second perhaps only to BIOGRAPHY. It is generally known as *tafsir,* an Arabic term meaning "discovery of something hidden," but probably adapted from an Aramaic or Syriac term (*peshar, pashshar*) used earlier by Jews and Christians in relation to their own commentary traditions. Another term, *tawil* ("returning to the beginning," "interpretation"), was once used synonymously with *tafsir,* but eventually was understood with reference to the elucidation of the Quran's hidden (BATIN) or esoteric meanings, which could only be known by a select few. This approach to commentary was embraced especially by the Sufis and Shii ULAMA.

Tafsir, on the other hand, became more closely associated with the elicitation of the "plain" or exoteric meanings of the Quran. More elaborate classifications of *tafsir* have been proposed that include both of these aspects. For example, the sixth Shii Imam JAAFAR AL-SADIQ (d. 765) is credited with proposing a four-tiered model of Quran interpretation, according to 1) literal meaning (*ibara*); 2) allegorical meaning (*ishara*); 3) subtle and symbolic meanings (*lataif*); and 4) higher spiritual meanings (*haqaiq*).

Typically, commentaries are organized in accordance with the chapters (suras) in the Quran, proceeding sequentially verse by verse. Topics addressed in standard books of *tafsir* include whether the chapter or verse was revealed in Mecca or Medina, the reasons for revelation (*asbab al-nuzul*), grammar and vocabulary, rhetoric, variant readings for consonants and vowels (debated because of the lack of vowel and consonant markings in early manuscripts of the Quran, and because of regional differences), and legal implications of the verse and whether it had been abrogated by another verse (*al-nasikh wa'l-mansukh*). Commentators (known as *mufassirun*) in the early centuries included narratives, called *Israiliyyat,* drawn from a wider body of lore circulating among different communities in the Middle East to expand upon quranic narratives, such as those concerning ADAM AND EVE, ABRAHAM, MOSES, and other biblical figures. Likewise, this was done with regard to stories about events in the life of MUHAMMAD, such as accounts of his first revelations and his NIGHT JOURNEY AND ASCENT. Through the centuries, commentators also discussed the benefits and blessings to be accrued from reciting certain chapters and verses. A special subgroup of commentaries focused only on the small number of verses that concern legal matters (*ahkam*), such as worship, family, business, and warfare. There were also commentaries written by Sufis, the mystics of Islam, that focused on select verses considered to be of import for their spiritual teachings and insights. The Shia, for their part, also developed their own exegetical traditions, based on the authority of their Imams. Shii commentaries pointed out hidden and allegorical references to the Imams, while identifying Sunnis with the disbelievers and evildoers mentioned in the Quran.

Muslims traditionally have distinguished between two types of commentary. The one recognized by the more traditionally minded is based on authoritative lines of transmission from earlier generations, starting with that of the Muhammad and his Companions, as conveyed in the HADITH. Some include the Quran's self-commentaries as an authority in this tradition. This is known as *al-tafsir bi'l-mathur,* or *al-tafsir bi'l-riwaya.* The second major type of commentary is *al-tafsir bi'l-ray,* or commentary that has been guided more by individual opinion than by traditional authority. This type is regarded with suspicion by those who prefer to abide by prophetic tradition, and reflects differences between parties like the Hanbalis and the Hanafis, or the people of hadith and the MUTAZILI SCHOOL. In order to better accommodate commentaries of this nature, some scholars drew a further distinction between "praiseworthy" works written by scholars who had a solid grasp of the traditional Islamic sciences and the Arabic language and "objectionable" works written primarily on the basis of personal opinion by scholars who were considered to be unqualified. In any case, even the most tradition-bound of commentators still exercised his own reasoned judgment in interpreting the Quran, and was subjectively influenced by his personal circumstances, social milieu, and events of his time. A third type of commentary identified by scholars of the Islamic commentary tradition is *al-tafsir bi'l-ishara* (commentary based on allegorical allusion), which is concerned with the deeper, hidden meanings of the Quran. It is a kind of *tawil,* as explained above.

Leading Medieval Commentaries. The historical formation of the quranic commentary tradition is a subject of some disagreement among scholars. Abd

Allah ibn Abbas (d. 688), Muhammad's paternal cousin, is remembered by Muslims as the father of *tafsir,* but Sunni tradition credits 10 of the Companions and 10 of their Successors as establishing this area of Islamic learning. The Companions identified in this regard include, aside from Ibn Abbas, the first four Sunni caliphs (especially ALI IBN ABI TALIB [D. 661]), Abd Allah ibn al-Zubayr (d. 692), Anas ibn Malik (d. ca. 709), and the famed warrior Amr ibn al-As (d. ca. 663). Nearly all of the Successors are said to have been students of Ibn Abbas, and they included Ikrima (d. 723), al-Hasan al-BASRI (d. 728), and Ali ibn Abi Talha (d. 737). Some modern Islamic studies scholars, however, maintain that this genealogy of *tafsir* was a pious fiction, and that the tradition did not develop until the early 9th century.

The foremost scholar of quranic exegesis during the medieval period was Ibn Jarir al-Tabari (d. 923), a Persian who achieved renown during the era of the ABBASID CALIPHATE for the breadth of his knowledge in the areas of hadith, history, FIQH, and the quranic sciences. His *tafsir,* the *Jami al-bayan an tawil ay al-Quran* (The Compendium of Clarity Concerning the Exegesis of the Verses of the Quran), is an encyclopedic work that gathers a substantial body of comments and opinions about the meanings of quranic verses that were known up to his time. Modern print editions of this commentary number as many as 30 volumes. Al-Tabari's commentary is considered to be foundational for succeeding generations of *mufassirun* and is part of the *tafsir bi'l-mathur* tradition of exegesis. Other major commentaries in this group include those of Abu 1-Layth al-Samarqandi (d. 983), Abu Ishaq al-Thaalabi (d. 1035), Abu Muhammad al-Baghawi (d. 1122, an abridgment of al-Thaalabi's commentary), IBN KATHIR (d. 1373, an abridgment of al-Tabari's commentary); Jalal al-Din al-Suyuti (d. 1505), and the Zaydi Shii jurist Muhammad bin Au al-Shawkani (d. 1834) of Yemen.

One of the foremost commentaries in the *tafsir bi 'i-ray* tradition is Mahmud ibn Umar al-Zamakhshari's *Al-Kashshaf an haqaiq al-tanzil wa uyun al-aqawil fi wujuh al-tawil* (The Unveiler of the Subtle Truths of Revelation and Essences of Discussions Concerning Aspects of Exegesis, 12th century), which approaches the Quran with a focus on its grammar, philology, and literary qualities. Al-Zamakhshari was a Hanafi jurist from Persia, and like al-Tabari, he excelled in his command of Arabic. Even though his commentary reflects Mutazili influence, it nevertheless holds high esteem among Sunni scholars. An abridged version of it, *Anwar al-tanzil* (The Lights of Revelation), was composed by al-Baydawi (d. 1286) and became a popular text in Sunni madrasas. It is short and relatively easy to use. Another commentary based on those of al-Zamakhshari and al-Baydawi, but with all traces of Mutazilism removed, was that of the Hanafi scholar Abu al-Barakat al-Nasafi (d. 1310). Fakhr al-Din al-Razi's *Mafatih al-ghayb* (Keys to the Unseen, published in eight large volumes), written in the late 12th/early 13th century, represents a more theological and scientific approach to interpreting the Quran. Al-Razi was an expert in Ashari theology, and wrote his *tafsir* under its influence, but added significant scientific and philosophical insights drawn from Greek, Persian, and Indian sources, as well as Arabic ones. A pious man by nature, he nevertheless favored reason over unquestioning reliance on traditional sources, and he maintained that nature itself provided proof of God's existence. A later *tafsir*, written in the 16th century, was Jalal al-Din al-Muhalla and Jalal al-Din al-Suyuti's *Tafsir al-Jalalayn* (The Commentary of the Two Jalals). Along with al-Baydawi's commentary, it was widely used in madrasas and has become a popular *tafsir* because of its brevity and simplicity.

The Shia consider their Imams to be the most learned and qualified to engage in quranic commentary, not the Companions and their Successors. Among the Twelve-Imam Shia, a further distinction is made between commentaries written before the Great Occultation (*ghayba*) of the 12th Imam in 941 and those that came later. Two early commentaries are attributed to the sixth and eleventh Imams, Jaafar al-Sadiq and Hasan al-Askari (d. 874). The leading commentaries of the later period were Abu Jaafar al-Tusi's (d. 1066–67) *Al-Tibyan fi tafsir al-Quran* (The Clarification in Quran Commentary) and Abu Ali al-Fadl al-Tabarsi's (d. 1154) *Majmaa al-bayan li-tafsir al-Quran* (The Confluence of Elucidation for Quran Commentary), both of which took a more moderate attitude toward Sunnism than early Shii commentaries and reflect Mutazili influence.

Like the Shiis, especially the Ismailis, Sufis looked for the hidden, allegorical, and moral meanings of the Quran, although a number of them also treated its grammatical, historical, and legal aspects. Perhaps the most notable early Sufi commentary was Sahl al-Tustari's (d. 896) *Kitab fahm al-Quran* (Book of Understanding the Quran), compiled by his disciples. Al-Tustari, a Persian who spent his last years in Basra (Iraq), provided commentary for about 1,000 verses of the Quran, including lore about the prophets, stories and teachings of earlier Sufis, moral advice, instructions for his disciples, and anecdotes about his personal life. He included little of the standard kinds of commentary found in the works of al-Tabari, al-Zamakhshari, and Ibn Kathir. His work was especially influential in ANDALUSIA (Islamicate Spain), where it contributed to the formation of Muhyi al-Din ibn al-Arabi's (d. 1240) mystical thought. Ibn al-Arabi himself is credited with having written a partial commentary consisting of some 66 volumes, but it has been lost. Commentaries by him and his disciples on specific sections of the Quran have survived, however, and significant parts of his other major works, including *Al-Futuhat al-Makkiyya* (Meccan Revelations), contain large amounts of exegetical material. Other Sufi commentaries include those of Abu Abd al-Rahman al-Sulami (d. 1021), Abd al-Karim al-Qushayri (d. 1072), Ruzbihan BAQLI (d. 1209), and Rashid al-Din al-Maybudi (d. 1135).

Modern Commentaries. Print editions of medieval *tafsir* books enjoy widespread circulation today, reflecting continuity with the past. Those of al-Tabari, Ibn Kathir, the two Jalals, and al-Baydawi are especially popular among Sunnis, as are medieval commentaries focusing on quranic laws. Moreover, some modern editions of the Quran are published with abbreviated commentary drawn from these sources in the margins. Some modern interpreters rely on the traditional commentaries, but proponents of Islamic renewal and reform have composed new works of *tafsir,* seeking to adapt their understandings of the Quran to the challenges and opportunities offered by modernity. Others have proposed new principles for interpreting the word of God, a development that has caused some consternation among traditionally minded Muslims.

The first of the modern commentaries is *Tafsir al-Manar* by MUHAMMAD RASHID RIDA (d. 1935) and MUHAMMAD ABDUH (d. 1905), first published in installments in *Al-Manar* (The Beacon), a periodical that embodied the modernist program of Abduh and his students. This work, although it only treated select passages of the text, was a modern version of the *tafsir bi'l-ray* approach to commentary. Rashid Rida claimed that it was written without consulting the classical books of *tafsir* so as ensure its compatibility with modern thought and science. The miraculous elements were minimized for the sake of underscoring the Quran's rationality. The Indian reformer SAYYID AHMAD KHAN (d. 1898) had proposed a similar approach to the Quran earlier in response to the downfall of the MUGHAL DYNASTY in 1857 at the hands of the British. The scientific approach to *tafsir* became even more pronounced in the works of Tantawi Jawhari (d. 1940), an Egyptian scholar, Abd al-Hamid ibn Badis (d. 1940), an Algerian scholar and nationalist, and Muhammad Husayn Tabatabai (d. 1982), an Iranian Shii scholar. Other *tafsirs* written to demonstrate the Quran's agreement with modern rationality were those of Mustafa Maraghi (d. 1952) and Mahmud Shaltut (d. 1963), both disciples of Abduh and shaykhs of al-Azhar in Egypt. Several English translations of the Quran

have appeared with modernist commentary, such as those of Yusuf Ali (d. 1953) and Muhammad Asad (d. 1992). These include references to Abduh and Rashid Rida, but also make overt use of classical Sunni commentaries and the hadith. An unfinished Urdu commentary by ABU AL-KALAM AZAD (d. 1958) also took a modernist approach—one that emphasized religious pluralism, particularly among Muslims and Hindus, and was inspired by European history of religions scholarship.

Modern Quran commentaries have also been written by two of the leading ideologists of ISLAMISM—SAYYID QUTB (d. 1966) of the Egyptian MUSLIM BROTHERHOOD and ABU AL-ALA MAWDUDI (d. 1979) of Pakistan's JAMAAT-I ISLAMI. Qutb's commentary, *Fi zilal al-Quran* (In the Shade of the Quran, 6 volumes) was written in Egypt during his years of imprisonment and torture for alleged conspiracy against Jamal Abd al-Nasir's government in the 1950s and 60s. In it he constructed a religio-political vision of the righteous struggle (JIHAD) of God's true believers against the anti-Islamic West and the forces of disbelief and tyranny at work within Muslim society, which he called the "Jahiliyya society," thus drawing a parallel between the present day and the era of "ignorance" that prevailed when Islam first appeared in the seventh century. Qutb let his own response to the Quran dominate his commentary, paying scant attention to older commentators and methods. Mawdudi's Urdu commentary, *Tafhim al-Quran* (Understanding the Quran, 6 volumes), began to be written in 1942, just before India's partition, and was not completed until 1972. Mawdudi's interpretation, unlike that of Qutb, was not shaped by imprisonment, but by his involvement in partition and post-partition politics, first in India, then in Pakistan. In his reading of the Quran he offered a vision of a perfect, universal Islamic society governed by God's law. Although opposed to European powers and secular values, he took a more gradualist, democratic approach than did Qutb to political action, believing in the eventual establishment of an Islamic "theo-democracy."

A long list of contemporary Muslim scholars have proposed new approaches to relating the Quran to modern life and have taken up that task of interpretation according to a limited set of themes. Most of them come from a new Muslim intelligentsia, rather than the ranks of the ulama, reflecting the democratization of Islamic learning and the fragmentation of traditional AUTHORITY. Some of them received some or all of their education in Western-style schools and universities, or have held academic appointments in Europe and North America. These include FAZLUR RAHMAN (d. 1988), MUHAMMAD ARKOUN (b. 1928), NASR HAMID ABU ZAYD (b. 1943), KHALID ABOU EL FADL (b. 1963), Abd al-Karim Soroush (b. 1945), Muhammad Shahrur (b. 1938), Aisha Abd al-Rahman (d. 1999), and Amina Wadud (b. 1952). Several of these scholars have focused on specific literary themes or linguistic characteristics of the Quran, as well as the comparative study of the concrete historical situations within which different suras were composed. Others have been more concerned with finding new ways to think about quranic law and ethics, as seen in light of contemporary topics such as human rights, women's rights, social justice, inter-religious dialogue, and pluralism. Such undertakings, along with the continued study of classical books of *tafsir* and the mobilization of quranic ideas in the service of radical Islamist ideologies, attest to the pivotal importance that the Quran has held and continues to hold in the eyes of Muslims around the world. They also serve as an indication of the critical importance *tafsir* in its many forms has acquired in adapting the Quran to the changing social and cultural circumstances experienced by Muslims through history.

See also ARABIC LANGUAGE AND LITERATURE; COMPANIONS OF THE PROPHET; FATIHA; IMAM; ISMAILI SHIISM; MADRASA; SALAFISM; SUFISM; TWELVE-IMAM SHIISM.

Further reading: Mahmoud M. Ayoub, *The Quran and Its Interpreters.* 2 vols. (Albany: State University of New York Press, 1984, 1992); Meir M. Bar-Asher, *Scripture and Exegesis in Early Imami Shiism* (Leiden: E.J. Brill, 1999); John Burton, "Quranic Exegesis." In *Religion, Learning and Science in the Abbasid Period,* edited by M. J. L. Young, J. D. Latham, and R. B. Serjeant, 40–55 (Cambridge: Cambridge University Press, 1990); Farid Esack, *The Quran: A User's Guide* (Oxford: Oneworld, 2005), 121–146; Helmut Gätje, *The Quran and Its Exegesis: Selected Texts with Classical and Modern Muslim Interpretations.* Translated by Alford T. Welch (Berkeley: University of California Press, 1976); Jane Dammen McAuliffe, "The Tasks and Traditions of Interpretation." In *The Cambridge Companion to the Quran,* 181–210 (Cambridge: Cambridge University Press, 2006); Abu Ammar Yasir Qadhi, *An Introduction to the Sciences of the Quran* (Birmingham, U.K.: Al-Hidaayah Publishing and Distribution, 1999); Andrew Rippin, ed., *Approaches to the History of the Interpretation of the Quran* (Oxford: Clarendon Press, 1988); Kristin Z. Sands, *Sufi Commentaries on the Quran in Classical Islam* (London: Routledge, 2006); Stefan Wild, "Political Interpretation of the Quran." In *The Cambridge Companion to the Quran,* edited by Jane Danimen McAuliffe (Cambridge: Cambridge University Press, 2006), 273–290.

tahara *See* ABLUTION; CIRCUMCISION; DIETARY LAWS.

tajdid *See* RENEWAL AND REFORM MOVEMENTS.

Tajikistan *See* CENTRAL ASIA AND THE CAUCASUS.

tajwid *See* QURAN.

takfir *See* KAFIR.

Takfir wa'l-Hijra

Takfir wa'l-Hijra is the popular name for a militant Islamist organization operating in EGYPT during the 1970s. Led by Shukri Mustafa, an agronomy

STUDENT from Asyut and a MUSLIM BROTHERHOOD activist, al-Takfir wa'l-Hijra formed out of the prison debates that divided Islamists who had been incarcerated by the regime of Egyptian president JAMAL ABD AL-NASIR (1918–70). Mustafa was jailed in 1967 during one of the many crackdowns on the Muslim Brotherhood, which Nasir viewed as a threat to his political control of EGYPT. Subjected to harsh mental and physical abuse while incarcerated, the Muslim Brotherhood split into two distinct and often antagonistic factions: the moderates, who believed that peaceful activism (preaching, teaching, publishing, charity) was the best way of surviving and working toward the Islamist ideal, and the militants, who regarded the then-current society as corrupt, un-Islamic, and in need of a kind of radical purification that simple activism could not effect.

While in prison, Mustafa took charge of one of the militant subfactions, the Society of Muslims (later labeled al-Takfir wa'l-Hijra by the Egyptian press), and, upon his release in 1971, he returned to Asyut, where he preached and gained a following. One of the distinctive features of the Society of Muslims was its commitment to separate itself from society, both spiritually and physically. For a time, some members lived in the hills surrounding Asyut; even those residing in the suburbs of CAIRO created a communal existence in isolation from the corrupting influences of what was deemed secular Egypt. Eventually the activities of the group became known to the press, which depicted Shukri and his followers as social and religious misfits. Of particular media interest was the accusation that members had abducted young women to serve as their wives. Religious officials also weighed in against the society, declaring its members to be extremists along the lines of the KHAWARIJ, an early radical Islamic sect.

When a competing Islamist group attempted to entice a number of Shukri's members away from the society in 1976, Shukri declared that any defector would be considered an apostate and subject to the ultimate punishment: DEATH. A subsequent public brawl with this competing group led the government to arrest a number of society members, though Shukri escaped and went into hiding. It was at this time that the media came to refer to the Society of Muslims as al-Takfir wa'l-Hijra or Excommunication and Emigration, because of the group's decision to condemn fellow Muslims as unbelievers (pronounce the Takfir) and to separate itself from the community (perform a HIJRA). In an effort to pressure the government to free his followers, Shukri ordered the kidnapping of Shaykh Muhammad al-Dhahabi, an ex-religious official and one of the earlier critics of the Society. After the government refused to negotiate, the Takfir organization executed Shaykh al-Dhahabi and mass arrests followed. At his trial, Shukri leveled a scathing critique of Egypt's religious and political authorities and justified the use of violence. Several leaders, including Shukri, were sentenced to death and later executed; many others were given lengthy prison terms.

See also ISLAMISM; JIHAD MOVEMENTS.

Jeffrey Kenney

Further reading: Gilles Kepel, *Muslim Extremism in Egypt* (Berkeley: University of California Press, 1985); Emmanuel Sivan, *Radical Islam,* enlarged ed. (New Haven, Conn.: Yale University Press, 1990).

talaq   *See* DIVORCE.

Taliban (Pashto: "students"; also Taleban)

The most notorious Afghan Islamic movement to appear in the last decade of the 20th century was the Taliban. Composed of Pushtun (the dominant ethnic group in AFGHANISTAN) students and fighters who had been recruited from Afghan madrasas (schools) and refugee camps in PAKISTAN, it surprised the world in 1996 by defeating veteran AFGHAN MUJAHIDIN militias and seizing control of Kabul, Afghanistan's capital. Under the leadership of Mullah Muhammad Umar (b. ca. 1959), the Taliban government, known as the Islamic Emirate of Afghanistan, became a brutal regime based on an inflexible code of strict Islamic rulings. It formed an alliance with AL-QAIDA, the Arab terrorist organization led by USAMA BIN LADIN (b. 1957) and his deputy Ayman al-Zawahiri (b. 1951), and it was suspected of complicity in the September 11, 2001, terrorist attacks on the United States. Taliban rule was effectively ended by a U.S.-led invasion known as Operation Enduring Freedom in November 2001.

The Taliban movement developed during the 10-year Soviet occupation of Afghanistan (1979–89) and the chaotic civil war that broke out among Afghan mujahidin warlords when the Soviets were forced to withdraw. Some five million Afghans had to flee their country during these troubled times, most of them going to neighboring Pakistan. There, a generation of Afghan refugee children grew up knowing little of the world around them but conflict and poverty. They were indoctrinated with radical Islamic ideology in schools founded in both Afghanistan and Pakistan by the JAMIYAATUL ULAMA-I ISLAM (JUI), a powerful Pakistani Islamist organization with links to the reformist tradition of DEOBAND. JUI ULAMA were Sunnis affiliated with the HANAFI LEGAL SCHOOL, but the curriculum in their madrasas promoted a combination of Wahhabi conservatism and jihadism, a militant form of Islam. Wahhabi influence became especially strong in these schools because the Pakistani government had allowed them to receive Saudi funding. The Taliban also obtained military training and combat experience by joining with older Afghan veterans in their war against the Soviets.

The youthful, STUDENT-based movement won widespread support among Afghan Pushtuns living in Kandahar by offering an Islamic alternative to the corruption and wanton violence of rival Afghan militias. Starting in 1994 the Taliban also began to receive significant support in arms and cash from the government of Pakistan through its Inter-Services Intelligence Directorate (ISI), that

country's counterpart to the Central Intelligence Agency (CIA) of the United States. Pakistan had long been a major supporter of different Afghan militias, and at that time it believed that its strategic and commercial interests in the region would be best served by backing this newly formed Islamist movement. The Taliban would never have been able to gain control over most of Afghanistan without this support. Their regime, however, was not recognized by most of the world's nations. Only Pakistan, SAUDI ARABIA, and the United Arab Emirates had done so by 1998.

The Taliban government quickly earned international condemnation for the harsh measures it took to impose its narrow understanding of Islam on the country. Allied with the JUI, which operated madrasas and jihadist training camps, it persecuted and killed thousands of Hazaras (Afghan Shiis) and threatened other non-Pushtun ethnic groups in the country. It prevented Afghan girls from going to school and WOMEN from working outside the home, and even required them to wear burqas whenever they went out, or else they could be publicly beaten. Women were also denied adequate medical care. Meanwhile men were obliged to grow long, untrimmed beards and attend mosques for prayer. In its anti-Westernism and antimodernism, it banned television, films, music, and even kite flying. Violators and opponents of the regime were subject to harsh Islamic punishments, including death by stoning. The violence committed by the government against its own people was effectively captured in *The Kite Runner,* an award-winning novel by Khaled Hosseini (a film version appeared in 2007), an Afghan immigrant physician and writer living in the United States. The world was also horrified when in 2001 the Taliban destroyed two famed colossal images of Buddha in Bamyan that had survived for 15 centuries. The Taliban considered them to be pagan idols.

When the Taliban came to power in 1996 they cautiously agreed to allow Usama bin Ladin to establish new bases and training camps in the country. Bin Ladin, who had helped the Afghan *mujahidin* fight the Soviets in the 1980s, returned there with his family and followers in 1996 after being driven out of SUDAN as a result of pressure by Saudi Arabia, Egypt, and the United States on the Sudanese government. The Saudi government attempted to have the Taliban arrest and place him in their custody, but, instead, the Taliban retained their alliance with him and used al-Qaida fighters in their operations against opponents in the country. Bin Ladin, in turn, used Afghanistan as a base to declare JIHAD against the United States and ISRAEL, and to condemn the Saudi government for allowing foreign "unbelievers" to occupy the land of Islam's two holiest mosques—those of Mecca and Medina. When al-Qaida bombed U.S. embassies in Nairobi, Kenya, and Dar es Salaam, Tanzania, in 1998, the United States retaliated with cruise missile attacks on two al-Qaida camps in Afghanistan. The U.S. attack did not inflict much damage, but it strengthened al-Qaida's position, allowing it to move forward with plans that led to the bombing of the USS *Cole* in Yemen (2000) and the 9/11 attacks on the mainland United States in 2001. A core group of Taliban fighters and their leaders survived the U.S.-led invasion of November 2001 and retreated to remote regions along the Afghan-Pakistani border, from which they have launched attacks on the new Afghan government and coalition forces. By 2006 they had regained enough strength, with the help of income derived from opium production, to increase the number and effectiveness of attacks against their enemies. It is thought that Mullah Umar still serves as a Taliban leader.

See also BURQA; ISLAMIC GOVERNMENT; ISLAMISM; MADRASA; REFUGEES; RENEWAL AND REFORM MOVEMENTS; TERRORISM; WAHHABISM.

Further reading: Steve Coll, *Ghost Wars: The Secret History of the CIA, Afghanistan, and Bin Laden, from the Soviet Invasion to September 10, 2001* (New York: Penguin, 2004); Khaled Hosseini, *The Kite Runner* (New York: Riverhead Books, 2003); Peter Marsden, *The Taliban: War and Religion in Afghanistan* (London: Zed Books, 2002); Ahmed Rashid, *Taliban: Militant Islam, Oil, and Fundamentalism in Central Asia* (New Haven, Conn.: Yale University Press, 2000); Lawrence Wright, *The Looming Tower: Al-Qaeda and the Road to 9/11* (New York: Random House, 2007).

Tamerlane (Timur, Timur-e Lang)

(1336–1405) *great Mongol ruler who built an empire based in Central Asia, but whose armies devastated many Middle Eastern and Indian cities*

Tamerlane, born the son of a nomadic chief, rose to become one of the great empire builders of history. By the time of his death, his kingdom stretched from INDIA and Central Asia into Russia and TURKEY, and threatened CHINA. He helped the main CITIES of his native land (now Uzbekistan), BUKHARA and Samarkand, become prosperous trading centers along the Silk Road, but the peoples of the Middle East and India suffered as a result of his destructive conquests.

Genghis Khan (1167–1227) invaded Central Asia in 1219 and 1220, and the khan's second son, Chagatai (d. 1241), was given the territory to govern. Tamurlane, born into the Barlas tribe, would, as he rose to power, claim descent from the great khan through Chagatai. As a young man, he was wounded with an arrow, and he would have limited use of one arm and leg as a result. His Westernized name means "Timur the Lame."

Putting his own physical problems aside, however, in the 1360s Tamerlane began to take control of the lands inhabited by his tribe's neighbors, and, by 1369, he took control of all the territory formerly ruled by Chagatai. He assumed sovereign powers and established his capital at Samarkand. He almost immediately began to add territory to his empire. Largely self-educated, he gradually became a most capable general and developed shrewd political skills. He invited the peoples he conquered into his rule and integrated them into his army. He pushed into India in the 1290s and after the turn of the century moved westward through Persia into Turkey. One of his great victories was over his fellow Muslims, the Ottomans, at Ankara in 1402.

Tamerlane emerged at a time when the HANAFI LEGAL SCHOOL was the dominant form of ISLAM in Central Asia. He included Hanafi scholar Abd al-Jabbar Khwarazmi among his prominent advisers, but he largely distanced himself from the majority of the scholarly community. Instead he seemed to favor the Sufis. For example, he honored Sayyid Baraka, a Sufi shaykh who resided in Tirmidh, and allowed his burial in his own tomb, the Gur-e Amir. While using Islam to unite his empire (much of it carved out from Islamic lands), he did not impose his faith on conquered lands. He was known for his inclusion of Shii Muslims and even Christians in his army.

Economically, his early goal was to make the Silk Road the exclusive connecting link between China and Europe. His rise to power coincided with the emergence of the Ming dynasty (1368–1644) in China. Toward the end of his life, he decided to move against China and restore the former Yuan rulers. In the winter of 1404–05, he launched another expedition, but his age caught up with him and he died along the way before entering Ming territory. His body was returned to Samarkand and buried at the Gur-e Amir.

Tamerlane became the fountainhead of the Timurid dynasty, which maintained power in Central Asia until the Uzbek leader Muhammad Shaybani (ca. 1451–1510), emerged out of Kazakhstan and conquered Tamerlane's former capital. Subsequently, the Uzbeks became the dominant force in the surrounding area, now called Uzbekistan. About the same time, Tamerlane's lineage would establish itself in India through Babur (r. 1526–30), founder of the MUGHAL DYNASTY (1526–1857).

See also CENTRAL ASIA AND THE CAUCASUS.

J. Gordon Melton

Further reading: Samuel Adrian M. Adshead, *Central Asia in World History* (New York: St. Martin's Press, 1993); Beatrice Forbes Manz, *The Rise and Rule*

of Tamerlane, Cambridge Studies in Islamic Civilization (Cambridge: Cambridge University Press, 1989); Justiin Marozzi, *Tamerlane: Sword of Islam, Conqueror of the World* (London: HarperCollins, 2004).

Tanzeem-e Islami (Tanzim-i Islami; Urdu: The Islamic Group)

Tanzeem-e Islami is a Pakistani Islamic revitalization movement founded in 1975 by Israr Ahmad (b. 1932). He was a teenager in the years following World War II when the partition of PAKISTAN from INDIA took effect. He attended King Edward Medical College in Lahore and during the years leading to his graduation in 1954 he associated with the JAMAAT-I ISLAMI, the Islamic renewal organization founded by ABU AL-ALA MAWDUDI (1903–79). During these years he not only absorbed Mawdudi's thought, but he also became familiar with the work of MUHAMMAD IQBAL (1877–1938), who had in 1930 initially proposed the establishment of Pakistan as a Muslim state separate from Hindu India.

Following his graduation, Ahmad worked with the Jamaat-i Islami, which sought to build a revitalized Islam through influencing students and social elites. However, in 1957, following Mawdudi's decision to enter fully into electoral politics, Ahmad withdrew. While launching a career as a physician, he also became an independent religious teacher and pursued advanced work in Islamic studies, completed in 1965 at the University of Karachi.

In 1967 Ahmad authored "Islamic Renaissance: The Real Task Ahead," a tract in which he articulated his basic notion that revitalizing Islam should be pursued by instilling the true FAITH and certitude in individual Muslims, especially the intelligentsia, which could be accomplished by propagating Muslim teachings combining contemporary language and the best scholarship. One problem that needed to be addressed was the seeming dichotomy between modern SCIENCE and Islam. Ahmad abandoned his medical practice in

1971 and, the following year, he founded the first of several organizations to pursue his approach to Islamic renewal, including the Markaz-i Anjuman Khuddam ul-Quran in Lahore. This organization sought to promote the study of the Quran and propagate its teachings so as to foster a return to the true Islam. He founded Tanzeem-e Islami three years later.

Ahmad began with Mawdudi's understanding that Islamic thought should be implemented not just in one's personal life, but also in the larger world of the social, cultural, juristic, political, and economic realms. Tanzeem-e Islami teaches that a Muslim should develop sincere faith, live in obedience to Muslim law (SHARIA), and make an effort to propagate the teachings to all humanity. The ultimate goal is to place Islam over all human-constructed systems (from government to science). Any Sunni Muslim may join Tanzeem-e-Islami. Membership involves offering a pledge of obedience to the organization's Amir (leader), currently Hafiz Akif Saeed. That pledge operates within the realm of obedience to the sharia.

Tanzeem-e Islami has emerged as a strong conservative force within Pakistan. It has opposed the development of modern secular curriculum at Pakistani universities, the Pakistani government's friendly relations with the United States (and especially the sending of troops to IRAQ), and the influx of Western values and vices into Pakistan. While primarily active in Pakistan, Tanzeem-e Islami has developed affiliates based in the Indo-Pakistani Muslim communities in North America and Europe.

See also ISLAMISM; RENEWAL AND REFORM MOVEMENTS.

J. Gordon Melton

Further reading: Israr Ahmad, *Rise and Decline of the Muslim Ummah.* Translated by S. Ansari (London: Ta-Ha,1986); Tanzeem-e-Islami Web site. Available online. URL: http://www.tanzeem.org/. Accessed December 19, 2005.

tanzil   *See* REVELATION.

Tanzimat

The term *Tanzimat* (plural of *tanzim* = "ordering") refers to the series of reforms designed to reorganize and modernize the Ottoman state, which were introduced under Sultan Abd al-Majid (r. 1839–61) and continued under Abd al-Aziz (r. 1861–76), and more generally to this period in Ottoman history. Earlier reforms had been attempted during the Tulip Period (1718–30), when military defeats had convinced Ottoman intellectuals of the need for adopting European technologies. After the French Revolution (1789), Selim III (r. 1789–1807) initiated a series of military, economic, political, and diplomatic reforms, and interaction with Europe continued to develop during the process. These reforms were elaborated under Mahmud II (r. 1808–39). The Tanzimat reforms drew on these earlier attempts, and they were prompted by military defeats resulting in the independence of Greece and the autonomy of EGYPT. Confronted with the economic and military superiority of EUROPE, the Ottomans felt an increased need for modernization.

Abd al-Majid acceded to the throne as SULTAN in 1839, and he named as his foreign minister Mustafa Rashid Pasha, a diplomat with experience in Europe. Rashid Pasha urged the sultan to approve an imperial decree known as the Gulhane Edict, which Rashid Pasha read publicly in 1839. This decree constituted a quasi-constitutional document outlining a replacement of traditional economic, legal, and educational institutions with modern ones, many of them derived from Europe, which many Ottomans saw as representing progress. It called for reforms in tax collection and military conscription, provided for the formation of councils of representatives at the provincial level and of secular schools, and ensured some rights and protections for citizens of all classes and religious communities. This gesture of equality to Christian and Jewish minorities was meant to curb the threat of separatism by promoting a kind of patriotism known as Ottomanism. The edict also included some limitations on the arbitrary powers of the sultan. This document served partly to show the European powers, which were increasingly becoming a dominating force in Ottoman politics, that progress was being made.

The reforms were not entirely successful, due in part to opposition from conservatives, who objected to the imposition of non-Muslim institutions, and to conflicts with the European powers. After the Crimean War (1853–56), reforms continued with the promulgation of another imperial edict in 1856, which revised the rights of the 1839 decree, and lasted until the end of Abd al-Aziz's reign through the efforts of the reformist viziers Fuad Pasha and Ali Pasha. In 1876, the empire's first CONSTITUTION was promulgated under Sultan Abd al-Hamid, but it was soon suspended and the parliament established under its terms was abolished by this sultan, who saw it as a challenge to his own absolute authority.

Besides these specific reforms, the Tanzimat era saw a general increase in European influence, secularization, and liberal ideals based on the individual, as well as the continued growth of nationalist sentiment, particularly in the Balkans. It was also during this period that important technological advances, which were to have an impact on the social and political fabric of society, began to take hold, especially the railroad, telegraph, and newspapers. The Tanzimat period highlighted the problem of the compatibility of ISLAM with modern Western civilization, which was to continue to be an issue until the end of the empire and the founding of the Republic of Turkey in 1923.

See also OTTOMAN DYNASTY; SECULARISM; WESTERNIZATION.

Mark Soileau

Further reading: Bernard Lewis, *The Emergence of Modern Turkey* (New York: Oxford University Press, 1968); Niyazi Berkes, *The Development of Secularism in Turkey* (Montreal: McGill University Press, 1964); Roderic H. Davison, *Reform in the Ottoman Empire 1856–1876* (Princeton, N.J.: Princeton University Press, 1963).

taqiyya *See* SHIISM.

taqlid *See* AKHBARI SCHOOL; IJTIHAD; RENEWAL AND REFORM MOVEMENTS; SHARIA.

taqwa

Taqwa is an Arabic term that describes attitudes of piety, reverence, and good judgment in Islam that are related to worshipping and obeying God. Muslims believe *taqwa* is a characteristic that God bestows upon Muslims who desire to submit themselves to God, "Those who are rightly guided will be given greater guidance by him and he will provide them with *taqwa*" (Quran 47:17). *Taqwa* entails that Muslims strictly observe ISLAM's legal codes, showing beneficence toward other people, while respecting peace and the sanctity of human life. At times, the meanings of *taqwa* and *iman* (FAITH) overlap. For example, Quran 2:197 reflects, in part, the relationship between *taqwa, iman,* and the HAJJ, "Make provisions for the journey, and the best provision is *taqwa*." In this sense, reverence to God is equated with faith, meaning that if a Muslim believes in God as she or he makes the hajj, that person's physical and spiritual needs will be met through God's steadfastness. Muslims also interpret this passage as suggesting that God will provide for them consistently as they pursue life's journey.

Taqwa is also the capacity of good judgment that God instills in faithful Muslims, "When the disbelievers fostered a sense of honor in their hearts, a sense of pagan honor, God sent down tranquility on his apostle and the believers, and imposed on them the command to act in accordance with *taqwa* for they were deserving and worthy of it" (Quran 48:26). Muslims believe that *taqwa* enables them (1) to properly understand the meanings of the QURAN, HADITH, and SHARIA without misconstruing or misapplying them and (2) to make the correct moral judgments both as individuals and as a community. Muslims are obliged to fulfill all their ritual duties (such as the

FIVE PILLARS of Islam) with a sense of *iman* and *taqwa*, since without these spiritual and psychological characteristics, the performance of these duties are meaningless.

Jon Armajani

Further reading: Jane Dammen McAuliffe, Joseph Ward Goering, and Barry Walfish, eds., *With Reverence for the Word: Medieval Scriptural Exegesis in Judaism, Christianity, and Islam* (New York: Oxford University Press, 2003); Fazlur Rahman, *Major Themes of the Quran* (Minneapolis: Bibliotheca Islamica, 1994); Yassin Roushdy, *Allah: The Divine Nature* (London: Dar al-Taqwa, 1999); Mohamed Taher, ed., *Encyclopedic Survey of Islamic Culture*. Vol. 11, *Islamic Thought: Growth and Development* (New Delhi: Anmol Publications, 1998).

tarawih See RAMADAN.

tariqa (Arabic: path, way)

The term *tariqa* carries several meanings within Sufi rhetoric. One use is as a metaphor for the individual's inner journey to God, which was outwardly reflected in the Sufi practice of travelling to other lands to seek mystical knowledge. SUFISM itself was seen as a *tariqa,* or path through one's soul toward the Divine. On this path, the wayfarer passes through various stations, or *maqamat,* such as repentance and trust in God. The *tariqa* is also described as constituting the second part in the three essential parts of Islamic religious life, the first being SHARIA (the outer laws of Islam), and the third being either *marifa* (mystical gnosis) or HAQIQA (truth).

The term *tariqa* has also come to mean a course or method of religious study, which was institutionalized in a Sufi establishment called a *tariqa,* or Sufi order. Various types of these orders existed and still exist in most areas of the Middle East, and, depending on the region, they were also known as *tekkes, zawiyas,* and *dar-gahs*. J. Spencer Trimingham has categorized the stages of Sufism's development, and he describes the second stage, from the 13th century to the 15th century, as the Tariqa phase. This phase is characterized by the organization of Sufism into hierarchical structures, with an emphasis on the relationship between Sufi masters and their disciples. The Sufi master of each *tariqa* traced his spiritual lineage through a *silsila,* or chain of transmission, and thus the source of his mystical knowledge through chains of past Sufi masters. Key figures often found in these *silsila*s include ABU AL-QASIM AL-JUNAYD (d. 910) and ABU YAZID AL-BISTAMI (d. ca. 875), all lineages ultimately begin with the prophet MUHAMMAD. Through these genealogical trees, masters and ultimately their MURIDs, or disciples, would derive recognized legitimacy. Prominent *tariqa*s, named after their respective founders, included the Suhrawardi, QADIRI, RIFAI, CHISHTI, NAQSHBANDI, MEVLEVI, and BEKTASHI. Sufi orders or lodges first appeared between the 11th and 13th centuries, somewhat before Trimingham's *tariqa* phase, and many are still active today.

Other scholars have noted the social, economic, and political functions of *tariqa*s. These mystical brotherhoods created new ways in which to form communal identity other than on the basis of ethnicity and tribal kinship. The sometimes diverse background of the *tariqa* members allowed for some orders to play community peacekeeping roles. The *tariqa* sites served as community burial grounds, schools, and places in which ritual dancing, chanting, vigils, and processions took place. The surrounding land possessed by certain *tariqa*s was sometimes used for agricultural purposes, thus helping to financially provide for its members. At times, local rulers would try to get support, military or otherwise, from a given *tariqa,* and some *tariqa*s found it beneficial indeed to lend their backing in this way, thus wielding political influence themselves and sometimes receiving gifts such as land endowments. These Sufi orders are commonly associated with conversions of non-Muslims to Islam, but some scholars such as Carl Ernst cast doubt upon the veracity of *tariqa* missionary activities.

Although Sufism was originally an antinominal response to the power held by Islamic religious leaders who had systematized Islam in ways that Sufis considered to be dogmatic and devoid of spiritualism, the *tariqa* system ultimately created and maintained an alternate religious vision and system of transmitting knowledge. This, in turn, maintained tradition and served in part as a conservative force.

See also BAGA AND FANA; DHIKR; MURID; MUNSHID; RENEWAL AND REFORM MOVEMENTS; SAINT; ZIYARA.

Sophia Pandya

Further reading: Carl W. Ernst, *Sufism* (Boston: Shambhala, 1997); Michael Gilsenan, *Saint and Sufi in Modern Egypt* (Oxford: Clarendon Press, 1973); Annemarie Schimmel, *Mystical Dimensions of Islam* (Chapel Hill: University of North Carolina Press, 1975); J. Spencer Trimingham, *The Sufi Orders in Islam* (Oxford: Clarendon Press, 1971).

tasawwuf   *See* SUFISM.

tashbih   *See* ANTHROPOMORPHISM.

tasliyya   *See* PBUH.

tawaf   *See* HAJJ; UMRA.

tawil   *See* TAFSIR.

tawhid (Arabic: to proclaim God as one; monotheism)

Monotheism is the belief in one god, or in a god's essential oneness. It is an English term that was first coined in the 17th century to distinguish Christian, Jewish, and later Islamic beliefs about God from the beliefs of those belonging to other religions, especially those described as being polytheistic (believing in more than one god). Scholars of the comparative history of religions have recognized that monotheistic belief has taken different forms in human history, and they have proposed a variety of technical terms to describe these different forms: monolatry (worshipping one god), monism (belief that a single being unites all beings in the universe), deism (belief in a single god who does not intervene in his creation), unitarianism (belief that god is absolutely one), trinitarianism (belief that god has three aspects or "persons," as in Christianity), and pantheism (belief that god and the universe are identical). *Tawhid* is the Arabic word that Muslims today most commonly equate with the English term "monotheism," but the historical range of connotations and meanings *tawhid* has taken in Islamic theological, philosophical, and mystical discourses is greater than this simple translation would otherwise suggest.

The idea of the oneness of God (ALLAH) is clearly expressed in the first part of the Islamic testimony of faith, the SHAHADA—"There is no god but God" which is repeated by Muslims throughout their lives and in the daily calls to prayer. It is also one of the Quran's most fundamental messages. Q 112 states that he is one (*ahad*), he does not beget, and he has no equal. Other verses declare, "your God is one God" (Q 18:110; 21:108; 39:4), while others stress that he has no partner (*sharik*; Q 6:163; 17:111) and condemn polytheists (*mushrikin*)—those who claim that God does indeed have partners. Although the Quran attributes this message to all of God's prophets, it is especially associated with ABRAHAM, who is the figurehead of the *hanif* religion, a kind of primordial monotheism that preceded that of Jews and Christians. The importance of acknowledging belief in one God is reiterated in the hadith.

Tawhid served as a starting point for Muslim THEOLOGY (known as *kalam*), which was concerned with the issue of God's oneness, especially as it pertained to his attributes. The most prominent theological school to articulate Islamic monotheistic theology was that of the Mutazila, who called themselves the People of Justice (*adl*) and Divine Unity (*tawhid*). They argued on behalf of God's absolute unity and transcendence, and they denied the reality of any human attributes ascribed to him by the Quran (such as his hearing, seeing, knowing, etc.). To recognize these attributes as anything other than metaphors, they thought, would compromise God's essential unity. They also argued that the Quran, as God's speech, was created in time, which they thought would counter any tendency to believe that it possessed its own godliness, like Christ, who was called the Word of God in the Gospel of John. The doctrine that the Quran was created, however, was firmly refuted by scriptural literalists such as AHMAD IBN HANBAL (d. 855) and by the ASHARI SCHOOL of theology, which argued that (1) God's attributes were real, even if we do not know how they are so; and (2) the Quran was God's speech and therefore eternal and uncreated as he is. Asharis did not feel that they had compromised the idea of his uniqueness in taking this position, which has been the dominant one in Sunni theology since the 12th century. *Tawhid* is also the foremost of the theological doctrines espoused in TWELVE-IMAM SHIISM, which adopted most of the Mutazili doctrines.

In SUFISM, the mystical tradition of Islam, the fundamental doctrine of *tawhid* was recognized and given new meaning. For the mystics, who sometimes called themselves "the affirmers of God's unity" (*muwahhidun*), confessing "there is no god but God" was an external aspect of faith that as Muslims they had to embrace, along with God's law, the sharia. Their objective, however, was to proceed to a special sense or awareness that allowed them to discover that there was nothing real or true in the world *but* God in his oneness. ABU AL-QASIM AL-JUNAYD (d. 910) spoke of how God's assistance was needed to annihilate the self and abide in union with him. He also identified four aspects of *tawhid*: one for the common people in accordance with belief in one God, one for devout Muslims who are outwardly doing

what God commanded and prohibited, and two for spiritual virtuosos who transcend the first two aspects and calmly bear witness to the divine reality, and then become immersed in God's unity, as they were before they ever existed. Following previous Sufi teachers, the Persian writer Farid al-Din Attar (ca. 12th–13th century) identified *tawhid* in his allegorical poem, *The Conference of the Birds*, as a stage where the seeker sees God and the world as one on his journey to spiritual self-annihilation. Sufis also eroticized their idea of mystical oneness by identifying it with the union of the lover with the beloved after suffering painful separation.

Doctrines concerning God's unity (and unity with him) were embedded not just in matters of worship, theology, and the spirit, but also in matters of the world. Muslims addressed issues connected with defining their identities in relation both to alternative understandings of Islam and to their relations with non-Muslims. Concern with *tawhid* helped Muslims set themselves apart as a single community (*umma*) from those who did not acknowledge God's oneness, especially idolaters and disbelievers, and to connect themselves to those whom they considered to be PEOPLE OF THE BOOK (Jews, Christians, Zoroastrians, and others). *Tawhid* gave birth to periodic REFORM AND RENEWAL MOVEMENTS, as exemplified in the "unitarian" movement of IBN TUMART (d. 1130), who had studied theology and mysticism in Baghdad, and then established the ALMOHAD DYNASTY that ruled Spain and North Africa from 1123 to 1269. Much later, on the cusp of the modern era, the Arabian preacher MUHAMMAD IBN ABD AL-WAHHAB (d. 1792) made *tawhid* a cornerstone in his campaign to reform Islam in the Arabian Peninsula and to eradicate what he considered to be the idolatrous beliefs and practices of the people, especially Shiis and Sufis. His puritanical, literalist understanding of Islam became the official ideology of SAUDI ARABIA. In the early 20th century, the Egyptian modernist theologian MUHAMMAD ABDUH (d. 1905) revived Mutazili understandings of divine unity based on reason to argue against traditional ways of thought and demonstrate the compatibility of what he thought of as true Islam with modern science. SAYYID QUTB (d. 1966) of Egypt and the modern Indo-Pakistani reformist ABU AL-ALA MAWDUDI (d. 1979) both conceived of *tawhid* as a process that unified society in complete submission to God, against modern forms of idolatry and disbelief, including the secular nation-state. Their ideologies inspired many Islamic reform and radical movements in the late 20th and early 21st centuries. The ideology of *tawhid* as the principle that should unite all human endeavors into an ideal social order has also been espoused by leading revolutionary thinkers in Iran, such as ALI SHARIATI (d. 1977) and Ayatollah Mahmud Taleqani (d. 1979).

See also ADHAN; ANTHROPOMORPHISM; *BAQA AND FANA*; MUTAZILI SCHOOL; *SHIRK*.

Further reading: Natana J. DeLong-Bas, *Wahhabi Islam: From Revival to Reform in Global Jihad* (Oxford: Oxford University Press, 2004); Madeleine Fletcher, "Almohad Tawhid: Theology Which Relies on Logic," *Numen* 38 (June 1991): 110–127; Toshihiko Izutsu, *God and Man in the Koran: Semantics of the Koranic Weltanschauung* (Tokyo: Keio Institute of Cultural and Linguistic Studies, 1964); Fazlur Rahman, *Major Themes of the Quran* (Minneapolis: Bibliotheca Islamica, 1980); Michael Sells, *Early Islamic Mysticism: Sufi, Quran, Miraj, Poetic and Theological Writings* (Mahwah, N.J.: Paulist Press, 1996); W. Montgomery Watt, *The Formative Period of Islamic Thought* (Edinburgh: University of Edinburgh Press, 1973).

taxation *See* ALMSGIVING; *JIZYA*; *KHARAJ*.

tekke (Turkish rendering of Arabic *takiyya* "place of support," "place of rest")

Many terms are used to refer to the meeting places of DERVISHES—*tekke, dargah, zawiya, asitane, khanqah, ribat*—often interchangeably, but sometimes with distinctions as to size, type, or function. The term *tekke* (Turkish rendering of the Arabic *takiyya*) is most often used for lodges in the Ottoman or Turkish context, and especially for those of Sufi orders that were strongly influenced by Turkish culture, such as the Mevlevis and the Bektashis.

Dervish lodges can be linked historically to the frontier outposts set up during periods of Islamic expansion, when dervishes were involved in conquests. Many were located strategically on important roads or mountain passes or in recently conquered towns and cities. Once non-Muslim lands were conquered, dervish life was organized into stable orders and the structure of the lodges came to reflect this.

In general, the dervish lodge consisted of a communal residence for dervishes and/or a meeting place for dervishes who live elsewhere. Some lodges also served other functions such as providing lodging for travelers and feeding the poor. Most *tekke*s were linked to a particular Sufi order and were designed for the particular practices of that order. While the lodges varied widely in size and facilities, many included the tomb of the founding SAINT and later *shaykh*s, a MOSQUE, space for rituals such as the DHIKR and *samaa,* cells for solitary PRAYER, rooms for dervishes and for the SHAYKH, guest rooms, bathrooms, a kitchen, and storage rooms. Many lodges were supported by agricultural production and included stables for animals. Most lodges were administered by pious endowments known as *waqf*s. In addition to activities related to the day-to-day maintenance of the lodge and to Sufi rituals, some *tekke*s also served as centers for the study and production of arts, especially MUSIC and CALLIGRAPHY. Their primary purpose, however, was the spiritual EDUCATION and training of dervishes.

See also SUFISM; *TARIQA*.

Mark Soileau

Further reading: Raymond Lifchez, ed., *The Dervish Lodge: Architecture, Art, and Sufism in Ottoman Turkey* (Berkeley and Los Angeles: University of California Press, 1992); Annemarie Schimmel, *Mystical Dimensions of Islam* (Chapel Hill: University of North Carolina

Press, 1975); J. Spencer Trimingham, *The Sufi Orders in Islam* (Oxford: Clarendon Press, 1971).

terrorism

Terrorism is today used to describe many different kinds of violence. As a result, the meaning of the word *terrorism* is highly contested. Most individual states, and much of the international community in the form of international organizations and law, define terrorism as the use of illegal force by non-state actors. This definition focuses attention on the violence of nonstate actors—often understood by those who carry out such violence as resistance to a particular AUTHORITY or past violent activity perpetrated by that authority—at the expense of attention to violence perpetrated by the state.

Rather than focusing on the causes that lead to violent resistance, discussions of terrorism are often limited to questions about the legitimate use of force. However, a more general definition of the term emerges from understanding the dynamics of the conflicts thought to include terrorism or violent resistance: the use of violence against nonmilitary targets in order to create an environment of fear and intimidation for the purposes of achieving a desired end. This definition avoids a judgment of validity of one kind of violence over another, state and non-state, legitimate and illegitimate, for example, and focuses instead on the use of a particular kind of violence and means of achieving a desired end.

Since the 1970s, in Western media and public imagination terrorism has become increasingly synonymous with ISLAM. From the 1972 killing of Israeli Olympic athletes at the hands of Palestinian gunmen in Munich, Germany, to the events of September 11, 2001, images creating the impression of an essential link between violence and Islam have been ubiquitous. This is not to say that the word *terrorism* has not been used to describe violence in other parts of the world throughout this time, such as in Northern Ireland, South Africa, and the Oklahoma City bombing in the United States (to name just a few cases). None-theless, terrorism and Islam, in the eyes of some western European and North American commentators, are inextricably linked; the overemphasis of the concept of JIHAD as "holy war" in interpreting Islam, among both Muslims and non-Muslims, also contributes to this image. It is essential to note, however, that the Arabic term for terrorism, *irhab,* is a recent addition to the Arabic language. It does not appear in the QURAN nor is it found in any HADITH. The relationship between terrorism and Islam, then, must be understood in the contexts in which violence is termed terrorism.

The kind of violence generally called terrorism is not particular to any religious tradition or political system. In the previous two decades, violence against nonstate actors has been perpetrated by Christians, Jews, Muslims, Buddhists, and Hindus as well as by nonbelievers and adherents of local religious traditions, all living in varied political systems. At the same time, members of all religious traditions and citizens in states with different political systems have denounced violence of this nature as inimical with the tradition or system in question. When thinking about terrorism, then, it is more useful to focus on the fact of violence and the kinds of violence at work as well as the dynamics in which the violence is found than it is on whether or not such force is legitimate according to a given tradition.

See also ARAB-ISRAELI CONFLICT; GULF WARS; HAMAS; HIZBULLAH; AL-QAIDA; SUICIDE.

Caleb Elfenbein

Further reading: Giovanna Borradori, *Philosophy in a Time of Terror* (Chicago: University of Chicago Press, 2003); Mark Juergensmeyer, *Terror in the Mind of God* (Berkeley: University of California Press, 2003).

testimony   *See* SHAHADA.

theology

The systematic study and teaching of religious beliefs about God by experts who hold those beliefs as members of a religious community is a basic definition of theology. This subject is most commonly identified with Christianity, where it was once regarded as the "queen of the sciences." In addition to treating the nature of God, theology also involves learned reflection about humanity, CREATION, and God's relation to both. Jews and Muslims developed their own theological traditions, often in conversation with Christians, but they have not as a rule given theology the same prominence that Christians have. Jewish rabbis and the Muslim ULAMA have been more concerned with religious practice and jurisprudence, for which ample evidence can be found in the talmudic writings and FIQH literature of each group respectively.

Kalam (Arabic: speech) is the term used for Islamic theology. It is more correctly translated as "dialectical theology," because the writings in this area of Islamic learning were originally composed as a set of pro and con arguments concerning disputed matters of doctrine. In a theological treatise it was customary for a theologian, known as a *mutakallim,* to make a theological claim, and then rationally to defend its truth against rival views by pointing out their logical contradictions and substantive errors. Modern Islamic studies scholars differ among themselves about the origins of *kalam.* Some think it was influenced by Greek PHILOSOPHY and Christian theology. Others say it originated within the Muslim community as a result of religio-political disputes that occurred in the seventh and eighth centuries. Most likely the formation of *kalam* was due to both, beginning within the Muslim community, then developing as a result of increased contact with Middle Eastern traditions of Greek philosophy and Christian theology. Irrespective of the origins of the Islamic theological tradition, all its practitioners based their arguments on revelation—the QURAN and HADITH.

Muslim theologians, Sunnis and Shiis, were concerned with a common set of issues: the status of sinners, God's unity (TAWHID), God's JUSTICE, predeterminism versus human free will, the created-

ness of the Quran, and ESCHATOLOGY. Additionally, the Shia were concerned with defending doctrines concerning the unique qualities of their Imams, as well as their redemptive role in human history and eschatology. The earliest known theological traditions appeared in Iraq. These included the MURJIA (from the Arabic *irjaa,* to suspend judgment) of the seventh century, who maintained that a Muslim could not be condemned as a disbeliever (KAFIR), no matter how serious the transgression committed. The Murjia were opposed to the KHAWARIJ (secessionists) who felt that even the CALIPH could be condemned and killed as an unbeliever for offenses against God's law. Another early group were the Qadaris, eighth-century proponents of the doctrine of human free will and responsibility against the predeterminists, who argued that God (ALLAH) was the cause of all acts. Qadari doctrines were adopted later by the MUTAZILI SCHOOL, which flourished in Iraq during the early ABBASID CALIPHATE. The Mutazilis took a rationalist approach to theological issues, but they grounded their arguments in revelation nevertheless. Their doctrines about the createdness of the Quran and metaphorical nature of God's attributes (for example, his seeing, hearing, and knowing) inflamed Sunni traditionists, such as AHMAD IBN HANBAL (d. 855), who considered any diminution of God's power and divinity to be heretical. For them, the Quran was uncreated and God's attributes were real, not figures of speech.

Abu al-Hasan al-Ashari (d. 935), a former student of Mutazilism, took up the traditionist cause and conducted a refutation of Mutazili truth claims, using their own methods, combined with philosophical reasoning. The ASHARI SCHOOL of *kalam* that bears his name became the leading Sunni tradition of theology, providing faith with a rational basis for defense against philosophers, innovators, heretics, and the theological claims of other Abrahamic religions. It affirmed the unity of God and the reality of his attributes, the eternal nature of the Quran, and God's omnipotence—his power to determine all things, whether good or evil. Prominent thinkers of the Ashari tradition include Abu Bakr al-Baqillani (d. 1013), Imam al-Haramayn al-Juwayni (d. 1085), ABU HAMID AL-GHAZALI (d. 1111), and Fakr al-Din al-Razi (d. 1209). Despite its defense of Sunni doctrine, it was viewed with suspicion by literal-minded jurists nevertheless, especially Ibn Hanbal's followers. An important exception was IBN TAYMIYYA (d. 1328), who used *kalam* arguments to uphold the Hanbali view that all true knowledge about God was to be found in the Quran and hadith. The Maturidi tradition of *kalam,* named after Abu Mansur Muhammad al-Maturidi (d. 935), arose as a rival to the Asharis in eastern Islamic lands. Its adherents held views similar to those of the Asharis, but in time they accepted free will and human responsibility for deeds. Unlike the Asharis, many of whom were members of the SHAFII LEGAL SCHOOL, Maturidis belonged exclusively to the HANAFI LEGAL SCHOOL. Mutazilism, the oldest of the three major *kalam* traditions, entered a decline in the 10th century from which it was unable to recover. Its key doctrines, however, were accepted as principles of faith in Twelve-Imam Shiism.

Theological topics were also addressed in Islamic philosophy, as well as in esoteric Shii and Sufi writings. Unlike the theologians, Muslim philosophers did not limit themselves to the Quran and hadith in making their arguments. Instead they maintained that knowledge could also be acquired from non-Islamic sources, particularly "the ancients"—meaning Greek philosophers such as Plato, Aristotle, and their heirs, the Neoplatonists. The god of the Islamic faith, Allah, became known to Muslim philosophers as the "Necessary Being" and the "First Cause." Among the first Muslim thinkers to articulate a philosophical understanding of God, creation, and humanity was al-Kindi (d. 866), known as the "Philosopher of the Arabs." Other leading philosophers include AL-FARABI (d. 950), IBN SINA (d. 1037), and IBN RUSHD (d. 1198). A number of these thinkers became known to medieval Christian theologians. Ibn Rushd, known in Europe as

Averroës, had a major influence on the theology of Thomas Aquinas (d. 1274) and other Christian scholastic theologians. These men wrote on a variety of topics, including MATHEMATICS and SCIENCE, but it was their views on theological subjects that provoked the ulama, especially those who were experts in *kalam.* Their most controversial teachings included (1) the world was eternal, not created; (2) God had knowledge of universals, but not the particulars of his creation; and (3) the human soul was immortal, and therefore not subject to resurrection. All of these ideas were opposed to traditionist doctrines in Islam based on the revelation. After the 12th century, the philosophical tradition survived in the speculative teachings of SHIISM and SUFISM, but it was never held in high esteem among traditional ulama and the madrasa system of higher Islamic learning.

In the modern period aspects of dialectical theology have been taken up again by Muslim reformers such as SAYYID AHMAD KHAN of India (d. 1898), who called for a rationalist "modern theology" (*kalam*) in conformity with science, and MUHAMMAD ABDUH of Egypt (d. 1905), who drew upon Mutazili forms of argumentation in *Risalat al-tawhid* (Epistle on Unity). Mutazilism more recently has contributed to the thinking of FAZLUR RAHMAN (d. 1988), MUHAMMAD ARKOUN (b. 1928), and NASR HAMID ABU ZAYD (b. 1943). On the other hand, radical Islamist movements and ideologues reject medieval rationalist theology, espousing views that they claim to be based on a literal reading of the Quran and hadith (often influenced by modern secular ideologies nonetheless). They propose to defend Islam against its enemies at home and abroad through creation of Islamic governments that enforce the SHARIA, which they believe will resolve the injustices and crises faced by Muslim societies in the modem world. In this regard, some scholars have compared ISLAMISM to the Liberation Theology espoused by Catholic priests and intellectuals in Latin America in the second half of the 20th century. If there is an underlying theological claim in the Islamist movements, it is that the only legitimate government is that which recognizes the absolute unity and sovereignty of God. In their view submission to Islamic rule offers believers a way to salvation in this world and in the afterlife. Where attempts at establishing such theocratic governments have been made, however, the record is less than impressive thus far. They have usually resulted in totalitarian rule and gross violations of individual HUMAN RIGHTS.

See also ANTHROPOMORPHISM; *BATIN*; BRETHREN OF PURITY; DIALOGUE; FATE; *FITNA*; HASAN AL-BASRI; HERESY; IBN AL-ARABI, MUHYI AL-DIN; IMAM; ISLAMIC GOVERNMENT; *KUFR*; MULLA SADRA; RENEWAL AND REFORM MOVEMENTS.

Further reading: Frederick M. Denny, *An Introduction to Islam,* 3d ed. (1994. Reprint, Upper Saddle River, N.J.: Pearson Education, 2006), 164–186; Sayyed Hossein Nasr and Oliver Leaman, eds., *History of Islamic Philosophy* (London: Routledge, 1996); F. E. Peters, *A Reader on Classical Islam* (Princeton, N.J.: Princeton University Press, 1994), 358–412; Fazlur Rahman, *Islam.* 2d ed. (Chicago: University of Chicago Press, 1979); Josef van Ess, *The Flowering of Muslim Theology* (Cambridge, Mass.: Harvard University Press, 2006); W. Montgomery Watt, *Islamic Philosophy and Theology* (Edinburgh: Edinburgh University Press, 1962); Harry A. Wolfson, *The Philosophy of Kalam* (Cambridge, Mass.: Harvard University Press, 1976).

Thousand and One Nights See ARABIAN NIGHTS.

Timbuktu

Timbuktu is a West African city renowned as a "city of scholars" during medieval times. Its fame extended to Europe, where it became fabled as a city of mystery and wealth, due to its connections with the historic caravan trade in gold. In the 19th century, Timbuktu became the destination of European explorers, who sought to confirm its glorious reputation. However, the small, provincial town they discovered largely disappointed them.

Located near the Niger River (in modern-day Mali) and along several important caravan trade routes, Timbuktu achieved its fame during the ascendancy of the Songhay dynasty (1468–1591). However, the city always maintained a degree of autonomy, perhaps developed during its early history as a self-governing town. From 1325, the empire of Mali ruled Timbuktu. Yet, the city's inhabitants asserted their independence whenever possible, finally breaking free of Malian sovereignty in 1433. It may have been this penchant for independence that led the Songhay founder, Sunni Ali, to treat Timbuktu harshly after he conquered the city in 1468. However, later Songhay leaders showed more favor to Timbuktu, and it developed as a bustling commercial center and home for a renowned line of Maliki religious scholars.

The city's golden age was brought to an abrupt end when Moroccan armies, sent by the sultan Ahmad al-Mansur (r. 1578–1603), brought down the Songhay dynasty in 1591. Once again, the autonomy of Timbuktu led to harsh treatment by the new conquerors, who rounded up the leading religious authorities and took them to Marrakesh in chains. Following this disaster, Timbuktu lost its centrality as a "city of scholars," undoubtedly due to the decline of the caravan trade, which was also severely disrupted by the Moroccan invasion. In the following centuries, Timbuktu would be eclipsed by other cities as centers of West African Islamic scholarship. Nevertheless, its love for autonomy remained, as seen in the rise of a resistance movement to the jihadist al-Hajj UMAR TAL, who attempted to control the city in 1862. A counter-JIHAD, led by Timbuktu scholar Ahmad al-Bakkai, laid siege to Umar's capital at Hamdullahi, bringing an end to his state. However, the establishment of French colonial authority in 1894 once again put Timbuktu under the authority of outside powers. Since the achievement of Mali's independence in 1960, and with the caravan trade all but eliminated, the city has survived mostly as a tourist attraction.

See also COLONIALISM; MOROCCO; WEST AFRICA.

Further reading: R. A. Adeleye, *Power and Diplomacy in Northern Nigeria, 1804–1906* (London: Longman Group Limited, 1971); Beverly B. Mack and Jean Boyd, *One Woman's Jihad: Nana Asma'u, Scholar and Scribe* (Bloomington: Indiana University Press, 2000); Elias N. Saad, *Social History of Timbuktu: The Role of Muslim Scholars and Notables, 1400–1900* (Cambridge: Cambridge University Press, 1983); Ibraheem Sulaiman, *The Islamic State and the Challenge of History* (London: Mansell Publishing, 1987).

Tirmidhi, Abu Isa Muhammad al-   *See* HADITH.

Torah (Hebrew: instruction, teaching; Arabic: *Tawrat*)

The Torah is the Jewish holy book, believed to have been revealed to MOSES on Mount Sinai. The written Torah consists of the first five books of the Hebrew Bible (known to Christians as the Old Testament): Genesis, Exodus, Leviticus, Numbers, and Deuteronomy. Many Jews use the term in an expanded sense with respect to the entire Hebrew Bible (including the books of the prophets and other writings) and the oral Torah of Moses, also known as the Talmud (Hebrew: study). The Torah is mentioned explicitly 18 times in the QURAN, in addition to a number of indirect references. On the basis of statements in the Quran, Muslims agree that it is the holy book of the Jews revealed to Moses on Mount Sinai, and that it is why they consider Jews to be PEOPLE OF THE BOOK (for example, Q 5:44, 68). Sometimes referred to as the "tablets" (Q 7:145, 150, 154), the Torah is seen as a COVENANT between God and the Children of Israel, who, following the biblical and quranic theme, violate its commandments (Q 2:63–64, 83–85). The Quran declares that they will be punished on

JUDGMENT DAY for this, as well as suffer burdensome restrictions in this life, such as the Jewish DIETARY LAWS. The Quran also alleges that Jews and other People of the Book have changed or corrupted God's word (for example, Q 4:46; 5:12–13), which Muslims used to support the doctrine that the Quran is the uncorrupted REVELATION. Later commentators asserted that the Jews had changed the Torah in order to conceal references to MUHAMMAD, believed by most Muslims to be the final prophet. The existence of different translations of the Torah was used to support allegations that it had been corrupted or distorted. This meant, in part, that even though the Torah must still be regarded as a sacred scripture, its laws were not binding for Muslims. In medieval GRANADA Jews involved in court cases before a Muslim judge were allowed to swear by it, thus attesting to its sacred status in the eyes of the SHARIA nonetheless. Muslims as a rule know the Torah only on the basis of what is said in the Quran, commentaries, and hadith literature. Nevertheless, Hunayn ibn Ishaq (d. 873), the well-known Christian translator of Greek philosophical works, translated it from the Greek into Arabic, and Saadia (d. 940), the head of the Jewish community in IRAQ, translated it into Arabic from the Hebrew. These translations, however, were not read widely by Muslim scholars. It is noteworthy that the Masoretic text of the Hebrew Bible, which has all the diacritical markings for correct pronunciation, was assembled during the early centuries of Muslim rule, and completed in the rabbinic academies of Iraq and Palestine during the 10th century C.E.

See also HOLY BOOKS; JUDAISM AND ISLAM; PROPHETS AND PROPHECY.

Further reading: Camilla P. Adang, *Muslim Writers on Judaism and the Hebrew Bible: From Ibn Rabban to Ibn Hazm* (Leiden: E.J. Brill, 1996); Jane D. McAuliffe, "The Quranic Context of Muslim Biblical Scholarship." *Islam and Christian-Muslim Relations* 7 (1996): 141–158; Brannon M. Wheeler, "Israel and the Torah of Muhammad." In *Bible and Quran: Essays in Scriptural Intertextu-*

ality, edited by John C. Reeves, 61–85 (Atlanta: Society for Biblical Literature, 2003).

tradition   *See* CUSTOMARY LAW; HADITH; *IJMAA*; *IJTI-HAD*; SHARIA; SUNNA.

travel

Muslims have traveled the world for centuries to visit holy sites and search for knowledge. Travel has played an important role in the Islamic world. Natural inclinations to travel have been reinforced with Islamic traditions inciting Muslims to journey for knowledge and pilgrimage. A central tenet of ISLAM has been the HAJJ, the annual pilgrimage to MECCA. As one of the FIVE PILLARS of Islam, many Muslims over the generations have made the journey to fulfill their religious duty and strengthen their commitment to the FAITH. Large annual pilgrimage caravans would be formed and sponsored by local rulers to help pilgrims make their way to their destination. This tradition has been a powerful unifying force for the Islamic community, drawing together Muslims from diverse regions for a common purpose.

The prophet MUHAMMAD (d. 632) also urged his followers to travel in search of knowledge, "even as far as China" and many Muslims wandered from MOROCCO to China and beyond in their quest for deeper insight and spiritual wisdom. Gradually, a mobile network of religious scholars (ULAMA) developed throughout the Islamic world. Educated men such as IBN BATTUTA (d. 1377) would travel from one center of learning to another, listening to lectures, attending classes, and gaining employment as teachers, judges, and bureaucrats. A literary genre of travel accounts developed, attesting to the popularity of this activity. This network has been damaged in the modern period, when colonial powers established hard nationalist borders in a world that had been more porous. With the imposition of controls such as passports and visas, the traditions of traveling across the Islamic world became more limited, although this has been partially offset by technological advances such as the train and the airplane. Nonetheless, the tradition of travel remains an important tenet of Islam as Muslims continue to make the hajj in the millions and Islamic scholars from everywhere flock to study in the Islamic universities of CAIRO, DAMASCUS, FEZ, and Saudi Arabia.

See also BOAT; CAMEL; COLONIALISM; HORSE; *TARIQA*.

Eric Staples

Further reading: Dale Eickelman and James Piscatori, eds., *Muslim Travelers* (Princeton, N.J.: Princeton University Press, 1996); F. E. Peters, *The Hajj* (Princeton, N.J.: Princeton University Press, 1996); Hamilton A. R. Gibb, *The Travels of Ibn Battuta 1325–1354*, 5 vols. (Cambridge: Hakylut Society at the University Press, 1954–2000); Ian R. Netton, *Seek Knowledge: Thought and Travel in the House of Islam* (Richmond, England: Curzon Press, 1996).

truth   *See* HAQIQA; PHILOSOPHY.

Tunisia (Official name: Tunisian Republic)

The northernmost country in Africa, Tunisia juts out into the Mediterranean Sea, bordered on the west by ALGERIA and on the south by LIBYA, forming a link between three different cultures: sub-Saharan Africa to the south, EUROPE and the Mediterranean region to the north, and the Maghreb, the countries of northwestern Africa. Tunisia has a population of about 10.5 million people (2008 estimate) and an area of about 63,000 square miles (163,610 sq. km), slightly larger than the state of Georgia. The people of Tunisia include Berbers, Arabs. Europeans, and other groups. The vast majority of the population—some 98 percent—are Sunni Muslims, most of whom follow the MALIKI LEGAL SCHOOL. Others, claiming Turkish ancestry, follow the HANAFI LEGAL SCHOOL. A small number of Tunisians, living mainly on Jerba Island, belong to the IBADIYYA sect of Islam. The official language is Arabic, but French is often used, especially in commerce. In the millennia since it was first settled, Tunisia has been used as a regional center by a series of conquerors. including the Romans, Arabs, Ottomans, and French.

With its jagged coastline, fine harbors, and location in the central Mediterranean, near important shipping routes, Tunisia was settled around 1100 B.C.E. by the Phoenicians. By about the sixth century B.C.E. the city-state of Carthage, near the present-day capital of Tunis, had become an important power, dominating the western Mediterranean. This led to a series of wars with Rome and resulted in Carthage's destruction in 146 B.C.E. The region was incorporated into the Roman Empire, and, except for a brief period of conquest by the Vandals, it remained under Roman rule until it was conquered by Arabs in the seventh century C.E. The indigenous Berbers converted to Islam, and immigrants from other parts of the Islamic empire—including Andalusian Muslims and Jews—led to Tunisia becoming a center of ARAB culture and learning. Tunis was the capital of the early Shii FATIMID DYNASTY (909–1073) and of the Sunni Hafsid dynasty (1228–1574). It was also home to the ZAYTUNA MOSQUE-University, one of the oldest and most important centers of learning in Sunni Islam. Several North African Sufi groups established branches there, including the Qadiris, Rahmanis, and the Tijanis. In 1570–74 Tunisia was incorporated into the Ottoman Empire. Although the Ottomans ruled the region until the 19th century, Tunis was virtually independent.

During the 19th century, trade with Europe increased, and many foreign merchants established permanent homes in Tunisia. This also led to increased European interest in the region. By the late 1800s, France and Italy were both vying for control in Tunisia. In 1881 a French army occupied Tunisia, which became a French protectorate. During World War II Tunisia came under French Vichy rule, and some of the major battles of the North African campaign were fought in Tunisia.

A nationalist movement had developed in Tunisia as early as 1920, but only after the end of World War II did France begin to heed the call for independence. Tunisia was recognized as an independent state in 1956. Habib Bourguiba (1903–2000), who had led a radical pro-independence faction, became its first president.

Bourguiba dominated Tunisia's political and cultural life for 31 years. He quickly enacted a controversial measure, the Personal Status Code, which gave WOMEN in Tunisia full citizenship rights and challenged some traditional Muslim practices. The code banned such traditions as secret divorce, polygamy, and women wearing the *HIJAB*. It also introduced compulsory free EDUCATION and reformed the judicial system, replacing the former Islamic, Christian, and Jewish courts with a uniform secular court system. To further reduce the power of the ULAMA. Bourguiba nationalized the lands that had belonged to religious endowments. Today, the government controls and subsidizes mosques and pays the salaries of prayer leaders; it also pays the salary of the Grand Rabbi of the Jewish community in Tunisia.

Despite Bourguiba's attempts to repress political Islam, an Islamic revival group, the nonviolent Islamic Tendency Movement (MTI), developed in Tunisia in the 1970s. It was made up of Muslims who were unhappy both with the secular state as envisaged by Bourguiba and with the reversals suffered by Arab peoples as a result of the ARAB-ISRAELI CONFLICTS. It was inspired by the ideology of the MUSLIM BROTHERHOOD and led by RASHID GHANNOUSHI (b. 1941), a charismatic philosophy professor with degrees from Zaytuna University and the University of Damascus, and Abd al-Fattah Muru. a lawyer. In 1988 the MTI changed its name to the Renaissance Party (Hizb al-Nahda) and called for a return to Islamic values and a more democratic political process. The party was able to pressure the government to make some concessions, but it ceased to be an effective political force by 1989 because of measures taken by the government against it.

Bourguiba's foreign relations also provoked some unrest. His foreign policy was generally pro-Western; for example, during the Arab-Israeli War of June 1967, Bourguiba declined to break off relations with the United States, despite pressure to do so. In 1987, after more than three decades in power, Bourguiba was declared mentally unfit to rule. Prime Minister Zine el Abidine Ben Ali replaced him as president. Since then, Ben Ali has been elected president four times, in 1989, 1994, 1999, and 2004.

Tunisia's economy has shown steady growth, with a diverse economy, healthy exports, renewed growth in tourism, agricultural production, and strong trade links with Europe. Industries include petroleum, mining (particularly phosphate and iron ore), tourism, and textiles.

See also BERBER; COLONIALISM; ISLAMISM; OTTOMAN DYNASTY; SECULARISM.

Kate O'Halloran

Further reading: Francois Burgat and William Dowell, *The Islamic Movement in North Africa,* 2d ed. (Austin: Center for Middle Eastern Studies, University of Texas at Austin, 1997); Mohamed Elhachmi Hamdi, *The Politicization of Islam: A Case Study of Tunisia* (Boulder, Colo.: Westview Press, 2000); Kenneth Perkins, *A History of Modern Tunisia* (Cambridge: Cambridge University Press, 2004).

Turkey (Official name: Republic of Turkey)

Europeans have used forms of the name "Turkey" to refer to the dominant presence of Turkish peoples and states in Anatolia since the time of the CRUSADES; however, the Turkish form *Türkiye* has been used officially only since the foundation of the present Republic of Turkey in 1923. The country today comprises the peninsula known as Anatolia (Asia Minor) and the southeastern tip of the Balkan Peninsula (Europe), which are separated by the Bosphorus strait, on both sides of which sits the city of ISTANBUL. It shares borders in the northwest with Greece and Bulgaria; in the east with Georgia, Armenia, and Iran; and in the south-southeast with Syria and Iraq. Because of its unique geographical position and the historical movement of peoples and ideas between Asia and Europe, Turkey has often been called a bridge between East and West.

Turkey occupies an area of 301,303 square miles, which makes it comparable in size to Texas. It is bordered by the Black Sea to the north; Bulgaria and Greece to the northwest; the Aegean Sea to the west; the Mediterranean Sea, Syria, and Iraq to the south; Iran, Azerbaijan, and Armenia to the east; and Georgia to the northeast. Turkey's population was estimated at 71.9 million in 2008, and is made up predominantly of those of Turkish ethnicity, though there is a large Kurdish minority (est. 20 percent), as well as smaller numbers of Arabs, Laz, Greeks, Armenians, Jews, and other ethnic groups. The population is predominantly Muslim (mostly Sunni, but with a substantial number of Alevis and some Shiis), along with a small number of Christians and Jews. The official language is Turkish.

The influx of Turkish-speaking peoples into Anatolia gained impetus after the Seljuk victory over Byzantine forces at Manzikert in 1071. Their dominance over the land was then ensured by powerful states set up by the Seljuks and later by the Ottomans. While the Ottomans subsequently gained control over much of the Middle East and the Balkans, Anatolia remained the heartland of the Turkish population, though with large populations of Greek and Armenian Christians and non-Turkish Muslims, such as the Kurds, also inhabiting the area.

When the Ottoman Empire was dissolved after World War I, a Turkish national movement led by MUSTAFA KEMAL ATATURK (d. 1938) succeeded in founding the Republic of Turkey, the borders of which were delineated by the Treaty of Lausanne (1923). Through an exchange of populations with Greece, there resulted an overwhelming Muslim majority in Turkey, including the large Alevi minority. In addition, the new republic's nationalist policies sought to build a strong Turkish identity, which involved attempts at assimilating non-Turkish Muslim peoples such as the Kurds.

As Turkey's first president, Ataturk pushed through a series of reforms designed to modernize and Westernize the country, a process that affected state institutions, legal codes, education, women's rights, language, and even dress. Adopting a policy of SECULARISM, Ataturk's government reduced the role of ISLAM in political and social life by abolishing the CALIPHATE and closing the DERVISH lodges, among other measures. Turkey has been a representative DEMOCRACY since the first multiparty elections were held in 1950, though its powerful military staged coups in 1960 and 1980, when it was felt politicians were departing from the principles laid down by Ataturk. Since 1980 Turkish politics has been dominated by center-right parties. In 1996 Necmettin Erbakan (b. 1926) became Turkey's first Islamist prime minister. Though his REFAH PARTY was soon forced to close by the staunchly secular military, members of this party later formed the Justice and Development Party (AKP), which controlled a majority of parliament seats in 2006.

Turkey's economy is dominated by agriculture, industry, and commerce sectors, and it is in a process of rapid modernization. With its long Mediterranean coastline and abundance of historic sites, Turkey is also a major tourist destination. In recent decades Turkey has faced problems such as economic instability, marked by rampant inflation, and mass migrations of people from rural areas to urban centers such as Istanbul, Ankara, and Izmir. Issues that are presently debated in Turkey include the possibility of Turkey being admitted into the European Union, and the role of Islam in social and political life.

See also ALAWI; ARMENIANS; CHRISTIANITY AND ISLAM; EUROPE; JANISSARY; MEVLEVI SUFI ORDER; OTTOMAN DYNASTY; SELJUK DYNASTY; WESTERNIZATION.

Mark Soileau

Further reading: Bernard Lewis, *The Emergence of Modern Turkey* (New York: Oxford University Press, 1968); Adil Ozdemir and Kenneth Frank, *Visible Islam in Modern Turkey* (New York: Palgrave Macmillan, 2000); Hugh Poulton, *Top Hat, Grey Wolf and Crescent: Turkish Nationalism and the Turkish Republic* (London: Hurst, 1997); Erik J. Zurcher, *Turkey: A Modern History* (London: I.B. Tauris, 1997).

Turkish language and literature

Turkish is the official language of the Republic of TURKEY, and it is also spoken among Turkish minorities in surrounding countries such as Cyprus, Syria, Greece, and Bulgaria. It is a member of the Altaic branch of the Ural-Altaic family, which also includes Mongolian. It is part of the Turkic subbranch, so it is related to many languages of Central Asia, such as Uzbek, Kazakh, and Kyrgyz, but it is most closely related to Azeri and Turkmen. Like other languages of this family, Turkish is marked by the features of agglutination (multiple suffixes are added to roots, often producing very long words) and vowel harmony (suffix vowels are either front or back, according with the vowels of root syllables).

When the Turks converted to ISLAM, they adopted the Arabic ALPHABET, and the Turkish language absorbed many Arabic words. Through contact with IRAN, Persian vocabulary and grammatical structures also entered Turkish. By the time the Turks had migrated to Anatolia and the Ottoman Empire was established, such foreign elements came to dominate the written court language, though the spoken language of the common people was less affected. After the Republic of Turkey was founded in 1923 a series of language reforms were introduced, intended to promote progress and influenced by the Turkish nationalist movement. In 1928 the Arabic alphabet was officially replaced with a modified Latin alphabet, which was thought to be more suitable to the Turkish language which and also established a link with the Western world. Attempts were also made to remove many Arabic and Persian elements, and new words based on Turkic roots were created to replace them.

The earliest written Turkish is found in the form of inscriptions on stone monuments in Mongolia dating from the eighth century C.E. Artistic production in the language, however, was predominantly in oral form, including epics such as that of Dede Korkut, which were later written down. A comparative dictionary of Turkic dialects was prepared in the 11th century by Kashgarli Mahmud. Written literature began to proliferate in the Islamic era, and many early works were of a religious nature, such as the mystical poetry of YUNUS EMRE, Ashik Pasha, and Kaygusuz Abdal, along with religious and mystical prose works. During the Ottoman period (14th–18th centuries), poets such as Pir Sultan Abdal, Karacaoglan, and Erzurumlu Emrah continued to compose works in vernacular Turkish, while in Ottoman court circles a sophisticated literature developed, heavily influenced by classical Persian poetry, and represented by such poets as Baki, Fuzuli, Nedim, Nefi and Shaykh Galib. During the TANZIMAT reform period of the 19th century, European literature began to exert an influence on the form and subject matter of Ottoman literature, and it was in this period that the Turkish novel began to develop as a genre. Inspired by the French Revolution, Ottoman writers developed an Ottoman patriotism, best exemplified by the works of Namik Kemal (1840–88). After the 1908 revolution, this sentiment developed into a Turkish nationalist movement, which was reflected in the literature of the period, especially in the short stories of Omer Seyfettin (1884–1920).

Literature after the foundation of the Republic of Turkey in 1923 dealt with themes relevant to the period: progress, the promotion of Turkish culture, the recent war of independence, and the gap between Ottoman intellectuals and rural Turks. Notable writers from this period included the novelists Halide Edip Adivar (1884–1964) and Yakup Kadri Karaosmanoglu (1889–1974). The poet Nazim Hikmet (1902–63) broke from metrical conventions while dealing with social themes, and he is credited with modernizing Turkish poetry. Writing about everyday life in a simple style, Orhan Veli Kanik (1914–50) is one of the many popular poets of modern Turkish literature. Many Turkish novelists have had their works translated into English, most notably Aziz Nesin (1915–95), Yashar Kemal (1922–   ). In 2006 the novelist Orhan Pamuk (b. 1952) was awarded the Nobel Prize in literature.

See also ARABIC LANGUAGE AND LITERATURE; OTTOMAN DYNASTY; PERSIAN LANGUAGE AND LITERATURE.

Mark Soileau

Further reading: Walter G. Andrews, et al., eds., *Ottoman Lyric Poetry: An Anthology* (Austin: University of Texas Press, 1997); Geoffrey Lewis, *The Turkish Language Reform: A Catastrophic Success* (Oxford: Oxford University Press, 1999); Kemal Silay, ed., *An Anthology of Turkish Literature* (Bloomington: Indiana University Turkish Studies, 1996); Talal Sait Halman, ed., *Contemporary Turkish Literature: Fiction and Poetry* (Rutherford, N.J.: Fairleigh Dickinson University Press, 1982); Nermin Menemencioglu and Fahir Iz, eds., *The Penguin Book of Turkish Verse* (New York: Penguin, 1978).

Turkmenistan See CENTRAL ASIA AND THE CAUCASUS.

Twelve-Imam Shiism (also called Twelver Shiism, Ithnaashari Shiism, and Imami Shiism)

SHIISM is the leading sectarian alternative to Sunni Islam. The largest of the three major Shii traditions is Twelve-Imam Shiism (the other two being ISMAILI SHIISM and ZAYDI SHIISM). Its name is based on belief that 12 male descendants from the family of Muhammad (d. 632), starting with ALI IBN ABI TALIB (d. 661) and ending with the MAHDI Muhammad al-Muntazar (entered concealment in 874), are Imams—exemplary authorities for the community and focal points for religious devotion.

It is estimated that the Shia as a whole constitute between 12 percent and 15 percent of the total Muslim population today (1.3 billion, 2008 estimate), or between 156 million and 195 million adherents. The largest Twelver populations are located in IRAN and IRAQ, where there are about 58.9 million (90 percent, est. 2007) and 17 million (60–65 percent, est. 2007) adherents, respectively. Twelvers are also majorities in Azerbaijan (85 percent) and Bahrain (70 percent); they are large minorities in LEBANON (30 percent), Kuwait (25 percent), the United Arab Emirates (16 percent), SAUDI ARABIA (15 percent), AFGHANISTAN (19 percent), Tajikistan (5 percent), PAKISTAN (18–20 percent), and INDIA (2–5 percent). In addition, since the latter part of the 20th century, small immigrant communities of Twelver Shii Muslims have arisen in Europe, the United Kingdom, the United States, and Canada. Although Twelvers have often avoided overt involvement in politics, and developed religious doctrines to make this permissible, their understanding of Islam changed significantly in the latter part of the 20th century, leading to what some scholars have called a "revival" of political Shiism.

BEGINNINGS

The historical roots of Twelve-Imam Shiism date back to the crisis that confronted the early Muslim community in Medina when Muhammad died in 632, before succession to leadership had been clearly determined. Arabian society was strongly patrilineal, but Muhammad had no sons to succeed him. The consensus of leading members of the UMMA was that Muhammad's successor, or CALIPH, should be ABU BAKR (r. 632–634), one of his closest companions and a respected member of the community. However, a minority favored Ali, Muhammad's paternal cousin and son-in-law. Ali's backers became known as his *shia* (party or faction), which is the basis of the English term "Shiism." They also became known as the Alids. According to Shii accounts and the hadith, shortly before his death Muhammad had identified Ali as the "master" (*mawla*) of those who had also regarded Muhammad as their master. Even though Ali became the caliph in 655, his reign was troubled by civil wars and the strong opposition of the Umayyad clan of Mecca and Damas-

cus. Ali was assassinated by a disgruntled former supporter, one of the KHAWARIJ, thereby setting a pattern for MARTYRDOM that would eventually profoundly shape Shii thought and worship. Muslim factions in the Hijaz and southern Iraq continued to agitate for a male descendant of Muhammad's family to claim leadership of the *umma,* and a number arose and were defeated. Foremost among these was Ali's son Husayn, who was killed by Umayyad forces at KARBALA in southern Iraq in 680, together with most of his male supporters. This event solidified martyrdom for a just cause as a key component of Shii piety.

Another significant stage in the development of Twelve-Imam Shiism occurred during the imamate of JAAFAR AL-SADIQ (ca. 699–765), the great-grandson of Husayn. A highly respected scholar in Medina, he lived when the Abbasid Revolution overturned the UMAYYAD CALIPHATE and then turned against Shii partisans who had been their allies against the Umayyads. Jaafar was reportedly imprisoned several times by the Abbasid caliph al-Mansur (r. 754–775) and chose to distance himself from anti-Abbasid politics as a consequence. Despite difficulties, he won a wide following as both a scholar and a proponent of political quietism, which developed into the doctrine of *taqiyya,* or pious concealment of one's Shii beliefs in the face of persecution or punishment. He has also been credited with affirming his father Muhammad al-Baqir's idea of *nass*, the divinely inspired designation of an Imam by his predecessor, as a way to resolve conflicting claims to Alid leadership. To further enhance this idea and elevate the Imams to a position as leading authorities in matters of religion, the doctrine of the infallibility (*isma*) of the Imams was also asserted during Jaafar's time. Additionally, Shii tradition remembers him as an expert in FIQH (jurisprudence). Consequently, the Twelver tradition of law is known as the Jaafari School. Succession to Jaafar became confused when his designated heir, Ismail, predeceased him in 755. Those remaining loyal to Ismail recognized his infant son Muhammad as the next Imam and became known as the Ismailis. Twelve-Imam Shiism, however, stemmed from the Shia who recognized Musa al-Kazim (d. 799), one of Jaafar's surviving sons, as the seventh Imam.

The culminating stage in the foundational period of Twelve-Imam Shiism began with the Imamate of Hasan al-Askari (r. 868–874), the 11th Imam and a descendant of Musa al-Kazim. According to Shii accounts he was kept under close watch by the Abbasids for most of his life in Samarra, the Abbasid capital at that time. He communicated with his followers through his agents. When he died Shii historians say his followers split up into as many as 15 sects. Some of these maintained that the imamate had ended with Hasan and that he had gone into occultation (GHAYBA), or concealment. Some said that one of his future descendants would arise as the Mahdi. The sect that was to become that of the Twelvers, however, maintained that Hasan actually had a young son, Muhammad, whom he had designated as the 12th Imam. After a brief appearance at the age of five, Muhammad entered occultation in 874. As the Hidden Imam, he maintained contact with his followers through his representatives until 941. This period is known as that of the Lesser Occultation. The period of his Greater Occultation started in 941 and continues to the present day. Although still alive during this second phase, the 12th Imam is no longer in direct communication with his representatives. Also known as al-Hujja (the proof), al-Qaim (the one who will arise), al-Muntazar (the awaited one), and the Mahdi, Twelvers believe he will be sent one day by God as a messianic redeemer who will inaugurate the rule of justice in anticipation of the final resurrection and Judgment Day. Meanwhile, authority in the Shii community was exercised through the descendants of the Imams, known as *sayyids,* and Twelver Shii ulama.

BELIEFS AND DOCTRINES

The Twelve-Imam Shia believe that the Quran is the revealed word of God, but unlike Sunnis they have tended to read it for hidden meanings that support Shii beliefs. They largely reject Sunni hadith collections because they contain many hadiths transmitted by AISHA and other COMPANIONS OF THE PROPHET, whom they reject as illegitimate authorities. Instead, they look to the hadith (or *akhbar*) of the Imams for guidance, which they have brought together in collections by Muhammad al-Kulayni (d. 939), Muhammad ibn Babuya (d. 991), and Muhammad al-Tusi (d. 1067). Another important Shii hadith collection is *Bihar al-anwar* (The Sea of Lights) by Muhammad Baqir Majlisi (d. 1699). The Shia also hold a 10th-century collection of Ali's speeches, prayers, and writings known as *Nahj al-balagha* (The Summit of Eloquence) in high esteem.

Twelve-Imam Shiism has five fundamental religious tenets (*usul al-din*).

(1) *TAWHID* (Unity of God). Like Sunnis, Twelver Shiis believe that there is only one God. Unlike most Sunnis, they believe that God's attributes and names have no reality apart from God's essence. They assert that God does not have a physical form, and they consider anthropomorphic references to his appearance and actions as metaphorical, with no independent reality.

(2) *Nubuwwa* (Prophethood). Like Sunnis, Twelvers recognize Muhammad as the last of many prophets who have brought God's revelations to humanity through the ages. According to a hadith, there have been 124,000 such prophets, only a few of whom are mentioned in the Quran, such as Adam, Abraham, Moses, and Jesus. They are all believed to be infallible and sinless.

(3) *Maad* (Resurrection). Twelvers, like Sunnis, believe that there will be a resurrection, or return, of all humanity on Judgment Day, when God will reward and punish everyone based on their faith and deeds.

(4) *Imama.* In contrast to the Sunnis, Twelvers believe in 12 divinely inspired Imams descended from Muhammad through his daughter Fatima and her husband Ali ibn Abi Talib, counted as the first Imam. Apart from Muhammad, the Imams are

considered to be the best of men and the foremost members of the *ahl al-bayt* (Muhammad's descendants). Indeed, they are thought to embody a divine light that is identical to the light that God used to create the universe. Such beliefs indicate that the Shia have developed a complex imamology, or set of doctrines concerning the Imams. The key doctrines include *nass* (divinely inspired designation by the previous Imam), *isma* (infallibility and sinlessness), *ilm* (knowledge of God's revelation and the law), *walaya* (expertise in spiritual guidance), *ghayba* (occultation of the 12th Imam), and *rajaa* (return of the 12th Imam before Judgment Day). The Imams also epitomize ideas of Martyrdom (*shahada*) and righteous suffering, which open the way to salvation for the Shii community.

(5) *Adl* (Divine Justice). Twelve-Imam Shia accept an understanding of God's JUSTICE that closely resembles that of the MUTAZILI SCHOOL. They consider it to be a rationally based attribute of God, associated with his wisdom. Because of this, he is essentially good, and nothing evil or profane can be attributed to him. Humans, therefore are fully accountable for their disobedience and evil deeds. On the other hand, the ASHARI SCHOOL, the leading proponents of Sunni THEOLOGY, argued that God could not be compelled to always act justly and that ultimately he was the sole creator of all actions done by humans, whether good or bad.

LAW, MYSTICISM, AND RELIGIOUS PRACTICE

Like Sunnis, Twelve-Imam Shia believe that religious law is based on God's commandments and prohibitions as conveyed by the Quran and hadith. They also accept a notion of consensus (*IJMAA*) in their jurisprudence. Unlike the Sunnis, they give greater weight to human reasoning or intelligence (*aql*) in deriving law from God's revelations, whereas the Sunnis only allow for a more limited use of analogical reasoning (*qiyas*). The Shii tradition of *FIQH* (jurisprudence), known as the Jaafari School in honor of Jaafar al-Sadiq,

formally developed after the 12th century, which was well after the major Sunni schools had formed. Basing their authority on the assertion that they were representatives of the Hidden Imam, they have given considerable weight to both the hadith of the Imams and to reasoning, which caused a split between traditionalist ulama, known as the AKHBARI SCHOOL, and the rationalists, known as the USULI SCHOOL. The Usuli School, which emphasizes the importance of *ijtihad* (individual legal judgment based on reason) has prevailed in Iran, and it is the school to which the Ayatollah RUHOLLAH KHOMEINI (d. 1989) and other leading Iranian ULAMA belong. On points of practical law, Shii jurisprudence is similar to that of the Sunnis, with minor variations. A significant exception in this regard is its recognition of the institution of temporary marriage, known as *mutaa*, which is allowed mainly in Shii Iran and rejected by Sunnis. On the other hand, Shii *fiqh* makes divorce in regular marriages more difficult than in Sunni law.

Running counter to its legal and theological rationalism, Twelve-Imam Shiism has also embraced mysticism, particularly in the form known as *irfan* (theosophy, gnosticism). The Shii ulama opposed organized *tariqa* SUFISM, which adversely affected its popularity in Shii communities, but many of the Persian-speaking ulama were drawn to the ecstatic poetry of JALAL AL-DIN RUMI (d. 1273), Hafez (d. 1390), and Jami (d. 1492), together with the illuminationist philosophy of Shihab al-Din Suhrawardi (d. 1191), which inspired members of the neo-Platonic school of Isfahan. The two leading mystical thinkers in this school were Mir Damad (d. 1631) and MULLA SADRA (d. 1640). Ayatollah Khomeini, the ideologist and leader of the IRANIAN REVOLUTION OF 1978–1979, was a student of *irfan*, and wrote several commentaries and books on the subject.

Twelver Shiis practice the so-called FIVE PILLARS of worship with some variations. They pronounce the SHAHADA, but are allowed to add the phrase "and Ali is God's friend" at the end. They are permitted to combine the five daily prayers into three (morning, afternoon, and evening), and, in remembrance of the events of Karbala, they are expected to touch a small block made of earth from Karbala with their foreheads during prostrations in daily prayer, rather than the prayer rug. In addition to giving alms in charity, they also pay an annual tax of one-fifth of their net income, called the *khums,* for the benefit of the ulama, descendants of Muhammad, orphans, and other needy individuals. They also are required to perform the hajj if they are able, as are Sunnis. Other obligatory acts include defensive JIHAD (for men) and calling on people to do what is good and avoid what is evil. However, in situations where their safety and security are in danger, the Shia are encouraged to practice *taqiyya,* which allows them to conceal their Shii beliefs from Sunnis and others who might harm them.

POPULAR DEVOTIONALISM

The most visible characteristic of Twelver religiosity through the centuries has been individual and communal attachment to the 12 Imams, FATIMA, Muhammad, and other descendants of the holy family. This is reflected in the cycle of religious holidays that commemorate the martyrdom of the Imams each year, as well as in ritual performances, and sacred art and architecture. The most prominent ritual practices commemorate the martyrdom of Husayn during ASHURA; they involve lamentations, poetic eulogies, passion plays, sermons, processions, self-flagellation and mutilation, and pilgrimage (ZIYARA) to Husayn's shrine in Karbala, Iraq. A pilgrim who has gone there is honored by being called *karbalai*—as a person who has gone to Mecca for the hajj is called *hajji.* The tombs of other Imams and their descendants are also the objects of pilgrimage, including those of women, such as Sayyida ZAYNAB, the sister of Husayn, in Damascus, and the Fatima Maasuma, sister of Imam Rida, the eighth Imam, in Qumm. Additionally, the Shia have constructed special ritual centers for local performances of Ashura observances that are known variously as *husayniyyas, imambarahs, imambargas,* and *taaziyakhanas.*

POLITICAL SHISM AND REFORM

While religious traditionalism and popular devotion to the Imams remain important aspects of Twelve-Imam Shiism in the late 20th and early 21st centuries, it, like SUNNISM, has also been affected by the far-reaching impact of religious reform movements and political activism. Among the ulama political activism became significant in the late 19th century as popular opposition to concessions made to the British by the shah led to the Tobacco Revolt of 1892, which was legitimated by a fatwa from Hujjat al-Islam Mirza Shirazi. The ulama were also active in the Constitutional Revolution of 1905–11, standing both for and against limiting the shah's power with a constitutional monarchy. In addition to anti-imperialism, several leading Shii ulama criticized Shii traditionalism and promoted PAN-ISLAMISM and religious reform as a way for Muslims to meet the challenges of COLONIALISM and modernity. Leading reformer-activists during this period included JAMAL AL-DIN AL-AFGHANI (d. 1897) and Hadi Najmabadi (d. 1902). Iranian ulama as a whole supported the establishment of the Pahlavi dynasty in the 1920s, even though they ended up opposing its secular modernization policies and efforts on behalf of women. Their opposition intensified in the 1960s when MUHAMMAD REZA SHAH (PAHLAVI) (r. 1941–79) launched his modernization program, known as the White Revolution. Religious and secular opposition alike coalesced around the figure of Khomeini and led to the IRANIAN REVOLUTION OF 1978–79, which ended the Pahlavi dynasty and established a new government based on Khomeini's ideology of Islamic government (*wilayat al-faqih*), much to the dismay of Iranian democrats and leftist parties. Khomeini's revolutionary Shii message and the Shii liberation theology of ALI SHARIATI (d. 1977) energized Islamic movements and Shii communities in much of the Middle East and South Asia. Even though Khomeini favored building bridges with Sunni Muslims with respect to law and doctrine, his success was seen as a political threat by Sunni leaders in Saudi Arabia, Bahrain, and Iraq. Indeed, these governments, together with that of Pakistan undertook repressive measures against Shii organizations and subjects, and Iraq entered into an eight-year war of attrition with Iran in 1980–88, supported by an alliance of Sunni Arab governments. At the same time, although Shii militant and political organizations favored the establishment of Islamic governments based on the SHARIA, many did not accept Iranian-style rule by the mullahs.

In Iraq, Shii authorities had cooperated with the Ottomans in the 19th century to promote tribal settlement and agricultural development, one result of which was conversion of many of these Arab tribes to Shiism. Iraqi Shiis joined with Sunni tribes in 1920 to oppose the British occupation and mandate authority that they established at the end of World War I. The revolt failed, and the British retaliated by giving the Sunnis political dominion of the country and engaging in policies designed to alienate Arab Shii ulama from their Iranian co-religionists. The rise of socialist and Marxist movements in Iraq and Iran attracted urban Shii youth, especially after World War II and the end of British colonial influence. The Iraqi Shii clergy, experiencing a decline in status, regarded leftist movements and secular nationalism with suspicion and countered by organizing their own religio-political parties and movements, the foremost of which are the DAAWA PARTY and the Supreme Council for Islamic Revolution in Iraq. These organizations were persecuted by Saddam Husayn's Baathist government, and many of their leaders were imprisoned and executed.

Lebanon became another center of Twelve-Imam Shii political activism, particularly through the influence of a young Iranian Shii mullah from Najaf, Musa al-Sadr (d. 1978), who won Lebanese Shii support among those who had become disenchanted with secular Arab nationalist and leftist movements. In 1975 he formed the Amal militia, which became a Shii fighting force in the Lebanese civil war and which trained other Islamic militias, including the Revolutionary Guards of Iran. Another Shii militant organization, HIZBUL-LAH, superseded Amal in the 1980s and remains a leading force in Lebanese politics today. In addition to its militancy and political strength, which were inspired by Khomeini's success in Iran, it has also become active in providing needed social services and financial aid to Lebanese Shiis. It operates one of the major Arabic language satellite television stations in the Middle East. However, several governments, including those of the United States and Israel, regard it as an Islamic terrorist organization.

When the United States and coalition forces overthrew the Baathist government of Saddam HUSAYN in 2003, they created conditions that made it possible for Iraq's Shii majority to establish the Arab world's first modern Shii state, which is now in the hands of competing, and sometimes clashing, political parties. The wider Middle East region as a consequence is witnessing significant Shii political activism and Iranian influence, as well as violent confrontations with Sunni governments and Islamist groups such as AL-QAIDA and the TALIBAN. These conflicts are already spilling beyond the Middle East to Afghanistan and Pakistan, and they are likely to complicate efforts to stabilize the region for years to come.

See also AUTHORITY; *BATIN*; COLONIALISM; COMMUNISM; CONSTITUTION; FADLALLAH, MUHAMMAD HUSAYN; GHADIR KHUMM; GULF STATES; GULF WARS; *HUSAYNIYYA*; IMAM; MUJAHIDIN-I KHALQ; POLITICS AND ISLAM; RENEWAL AND REFORM MOVEMENTS; *SAYYID; TAFSIR*.

Further reading: Kamran Scot Aghaie, ed., *The Women of Karbala: Ritual Performance and Symbolic Discourses in Modern Shii Islam* (Austin: University of Texas Press, 2005); Said Amir Arjomand, *The Shadow of God and the Hidden Imam: Religion, Political Order, and Societal Change in Shiite Iran from the Beginning to 1890* (Chicago: University of Chicago Press, 1987); William C. Chittick, ed., *A Shiite Anthology* (Albany: State University of New York Press, 1981); Heinz Halm, *Shia Islam: From Religion to*

Revolution (Princeton, N.J.: Markus Wiener Publishers, 1997); S.H.M. Jafri, *The Origins and Early Development of Shia Islam* (London: Longman, 1979); Etan Kohlberg, ed., *Shiism* (Burlington, Vt.: Ashgate, 2003); Reinhold Loeffler, *Islam in Practice: Religious Beliefs in a Persian Village* (Albany: State University of New York Press, 1988); Mansoor Moaddel, "Shia Islamic Societies." In *The Oxford Handbook of Global Religions,* edited by Mark Juergensmeyer, 447–463 (Oxford: Oxford University Press, 2006); Moojan Momen, *An Introduction to Shii Islam: The History and Doctrines of Twelver Shiism* (New Haven, Conn.: Yale University Press, 1985); Yitzhak Nakash, *The Shiis of Iraq* (1994. Reprint, Princeton, N.J.: Princeton University Press, 2003); Sayyed Hossein Nasr, Hamid Dabashi, and Seyyed Vali Reza Nasr, eds., *Shiism: Doctrines, Thought, and Spirituality* (Albany: State University of New York Press, 1988); Vali Nasr, *The Shia Revival: How Conflicts within Islam Will Shape the Future* (New York: W.W. Norton, 2007); David Pinault, *The Shuites: Ritual and Popular Piety in a Muslim Community* (New York: St. Martin's Press, 1992).

U

ulama (also *ulema*; Arabic: plural of *alim*, "possessor of knowledge")

The chief religious authorities in Islam are the ulama. In addition to scholars and teachers, they include jurists, judges, preachers, imams (prayer leaders), market inspectors, and advisers to rulers. The ulama view themselves as the heirs of the prophet MUHAMMAD (ca. 570–632) in matters of religious law (SHARIA) and tradition, the masters of the QURAN and HADITH, and moral guardians of the community of believers. They support their claims to religious AUTHORITY by invoking the Quranic injunction, "Obey God, the Prophet, and *those who have authority among you*" (italics added, Q 4:59). They are not a priesthood, however, since they do not conduct sacramental rites on behalf of the laity. Nor do they administer a "church" or congregation like priests and ministers do in Christianity. Rather, the ulama are more like Jewish rabbis; they advise people about God's commandments and prohibitions, and they issue opinions and judgments in matters of dispute or legal necessity. Their status varies greatly, from being half-literate caretakers at village mosques to being highly esteemed scholars patronized by the powerful and wealthy in the major urban centers of Islamdom.

In Sunni Islam, which embodies the majority of Muslims, there is no central religious authority like a Roman Catholic pope or Orthodox Christian patriarch. Rather, the authority of Sunni ulama is built upon a web of relations that extends from the mosque or MADRASA (religious college) to the palace, marketplace, BAZAAR, neighborhood, household, and across entire regions from North Africa and ANDALUSIA to India and beyond. Only in the era of Ottoman rule was an official ranking recognized, focused on the figure of the MUFTI. This office became decentralized with the collapse of the Ottoman Empire after World War I. Shii ulama differ from Sunni ulama; their authority is based on belief in the infallibility of the Imams, venerated descendants of Muhammad's household (AHL AL-BAYT). As a consequence, Shii ulama, particularly in TWELVE-IMAM SHIISM, have developed a centralized hierarchy since the 18th century, with the top ranks held by senior jurists known as *ayatollahs*. The most highly ranked of these, determined by consensus of the ulama on the basis of the jurist's knowledge and reputation, is the *marjaa al-taqlid* (source of imitation). Shii ulama, like their Sunni counterparts, also depend on extensive networks of support and patronage.

More is known about the ulama than any other social group in Islamic history, thanks to the voluminous amount of biographical literature that they created over the centuries. Studies of this literature have shown that ulama were recruited from different walks of life, but they were usually supported by the ruling class, wealthy merchants and landholders, who earned merit for their generosity. After obtaining a primary EDUCATION at a KUTTAB or at home (if the father was himself a scholar), a would-be scholar went to a madrasa to study with a master teacher, or select group of scholars, of the Islamic sciences. Students (sing. *talib,* seeker) traveled far from home and often attended several different madrasas, which served as pathway for upward mobility. The hadith-based notion of "seeking knowledge, even in China" has been a guiding dictum for learning in Islamic tradition. The madrasa, an institution that originated in the 10th–11th century, was usually associated with a particular tradition of Islamic law (*madhhab*)—Hanafi, Shafii, Maliki, or Hanbali for Sunnis, and Jaafari for Shiis. Some madrasas included teachers of more than one legal tradition.

The main subject taught was Islamic jurisprudence (FIQH), together with quranic studies, hadith and hadith criticism, as well as a variety of secondary subjects (for example, Arabic grammar, rhetoric, logic, dialectical THEOLOGY, and history). For their lessons, students congregated around their teachers, forming circles (sing. *halqa*) to study their books with them and hear their commentaries. When a session was completed they would form their own study circles to discuss their lessons further and assist each other in memorizing the texts and commentaries. When a student mastered a book, he would receive a certificate (*ijaza*) from his teacher, which usually would qualify the student to teach the book to others. Students, therefore, could collect several certificates in their course of study, and move into the ranks of the ulama based on the knowledge of the Islamic sciences they had acquired in madrasas at the feet of their teachers. Although WOMEN were

excluded from the medieval madrasa system, the biographical dictionaries mention that some were included among the ulama nevertheless. They were known especially as scholars and teachers of hadith, and usually they gained their expertise at home from male scholars in their families.

Through the centuries the ulama were able to establish a sphere of authority for themselves in religious matters without undue interference from the state, despite the fact that they often depended on rulers for patronage and protection. They did this by granting legitimacy to them and maintaining close relations with the populace. The ulama often endorsed popular customs and religious devotionalism, or remained neutral. The evidence indicates that most accepted Sufi ideas, such as ABU HAMID AL-GHAZALI (d. 1111), and were even members of Sufi brotherhoods, such as AHMAD SIRHINDI (d. 1624). The antipathy of the ulama to aspects of SUFISM and popular saint veneration has been exaggerated by modern scholars of Islamic studies, and was limited to a relatively small number of literalists, such as TAQI AL-DIN AHMAD IBN TAYMIYYA (d. 1328) and MUHAMMAD IBN ABD AL-WAHHAB (d. 1792), until the 20th century.

The establishment of colonial regimes by European powers during the 19th and 20th centuries, followed by the emergence of new nation-states in Muslim lands, contributed significantly to undermining the authority of the traditional ulama. These governments established secular laws and legal systems that emulated those of western Europe, effectively displacing the ulama in that area. The opening of schools based on modern curricula undermined the preeminence of the ulama in the area of education and produced a literate public who could study Islamic texts themselves, or appropriate new forms of secular and techno-scientific knowledge from post-Enlightenment Europe. These developments helped compel ulama in different regions to engage in Islamic reform programs, as exemplified by the efforts of JAMAL AL-DIN AL-AFGHANI (d. 1897), MUHAMMAD ABDUH (d. 1905), MUHAMMAD

RASHID RIDA (d. 1935), and the DEOBAND movement in Indo-Pakistan. Despite these efforts, the ulama found themselves blamed for the intellectual backwardness and political weakness of their societies by secular Muslims, on the one hand, and advocates of political Islam like SAYYID QUTB (d. 1966) and ABU AL-ALA MAWDUDI (d. 1979), on the other. Even though the ulama were abolished in TURKEY in the 1920s and became little more than government employees in countries such as EGYPT, they have undergone a significant transformation in a number of countries recently, as exemplified by their influence in SAUDI ARABIA and their involvement in Pakistani politics and the rise of the TALIBAN in Afghanistan. The clearest example of this trend is that of IRAN, where Shii ulama under the leadership of Ayatollah RUHOLLAH KHOMEINI (d. 1989) established a revolutionary Islamic government in 1979, an event unprecedented in the history of Islam. The U.S.-led invasion and occupation of IRAQ in 2003 gave Shii ulama in that country, many with links to neighboring Iran, an opportunity to take a leading role in religious and political affairs.

See also AYATOLLAH; BIOGRAPHY; COLONIALISM; HISBA; IJMAA; IJTIHAD; IMAM; ISLAMISM; MULLAH; OTTOMAN DYNASTY; PAKISTAN; RENEWAL AND REFORM MOVEMENTS; SECULARISM; SHAYKH; STUDENT.

Further reading: Jonathan P. Berkey, *Transmission of Knowledge in Medieval Cairo: A Social History of Islamic Education* (Princeton, N.J.: Princeton University Press, 1992); R. Stephen Humphreys, *Islamic History: A Framework for Inquiry.* Rev. ed. (Princeton, N.J.: Princeton University Press, 1991), 187–208; Joseph A. Kechechian, "The Role of the Ulama in the Politics of an Islamic State." *International Journal of Middle East Studies* 18 (1986): 53–71; Ira M. Lapidus, *Muslim Cities in the Later Middle Ages* (Cambridge, Mass.: Harvard University Press, 1967); Mojan Momen, *An Introduction to Shii Islam* (New Haven, Conn.: Yale University Press, 1985); Stephen Sharot, *A Comparative Sociology of World Religions: Virtuosos, Priests, and Popular Religion* (New York: New York University Press, 2001),

Muhammad Qasim Zaman, *The Ulama in Contemporary Islam: Custodians of Change* (Princeton, N.J.: Princeton University Press, 2002).

Umar ibn al-Khattab (586–644)
(r. 634–644) *second Muslim caliph, established the political structure of the Islamic empire*

A member of the Adi clan of the QURAYSH tribe, Umar ibn al-Khattab was born in MECCA. Initially an opponent of Muhammad, he converted to ISLAM in about 615. He went on to become one of Muhammad's closest advisers, accompanying him to MEDINA in 622 during the HIJRA. He became the Prophet's father-in-law when Muhammad married his daughter, Hafsa. After Muhammad's death in 632 Umar supported ABU BAKR (r. 632–634) to succeed him; he himself succeeded Abu Bakr shortly afterward, becoming the second of the four Sunni "rightly guided" caliphs, or Rashidun, which include UTHMAN IBN AFFAN (r. 644–655) and ALI IBN ABI TALIB (r. 656–661). Umar was the first caliph to adopt the title Amir al-Muminin, or commander of the faithful.

Under Umar's rule, the Islamic state expanded from a local principality to a major power. He continued the military campaigns begun by Abu Bakr, resulting in the conquest of SYRIA, PALESTINE, EGYPT, IRAQ, and IRAN. Umar established guidelines for administering these new conquests. He left the conquered peoples in possession of the land and did not require them to serve in his army or attempt to convert them to Islam; in return, they paid tribute to the government. As governors and administrators, Umar appointed skillful managers who were loyal to him. He also established garrison cities to administer the newly conquered territory; they included Basra, at the head of the Persian Gulf; Kufa, on the Euphrates River; and Fustat, later to become CAIRO, just below the Nile Delta. He instituted the empire's judiciary, set up a postal system, and introduced a system of taxes to finance the state. Umar is also credited with instituting the use of the Islamic CALENDAR. In

644, Umar was assassinated by a slave who had a personal grudge against him. Umar is said to have appointed a committee to choose the next CALIPH; they named Uthman as his successor.

See also COMPANIONS OF THE PROPHET.

Kate O'Halloran

Further reading: Hugh Kennedy, *The Prophet and the Age of the Caliphates* (London: Longman, 1985); Wilferd Madelung, *The Succession to Muhammad: A Study of the Early Caliphate* (Cambridge: Cambridge University Press, 1997).

Umar Tal (Al-Hajj Umar) (1797–1864)
Tijani Sufi shaykh who launched jihad to reform Islamic practice and resist French colonial expansion in West Africa during the mid-19th century

Born in Futa Toro (in modern-day Senegal), Umar Tal joined the Tijani Sufi order at the age of 18. As a young man, Umar departed his homelands for an extended pilgrimage to MECCA and the eastern Islamic lands. While in Mecca, Umar studied under the Tijani SHAYKH Muhammad al-Ghali, who appointed him as the representative for the order in WEST AFRICA. After three years in the east, Umar returned to West Africa, staying in Sokoto for some six years. In 1838 he settled in Futa Jallon (Senegal), where he established a reputation as a holy man and mystic.

By 1849 the local tribal authorities in Futa Jallon became concerned by the large number of the shaykh's followers and his increasing vehemence in preaching Islamic revival. Forced to leave the region, Umar retreated to Dinguiray, where he established a community. In imitation of the prophet MUHAMMAD, Umar declared that his flight had been his own *HIJRA* and he began to recruit warriors and assemble weapons in preparation for JIHAD against the ungodly rulers who opposed his message. During the next 15 years, Umar and his followers launched countless attacks upon surrounding communities, resulting in a state of some 150,000 square miles in the region of modern-day Guinea, Mali, and Mauritania. In 1862 he conquered Hamdullahi on the Bani River and sacked TIMBUKTU. However, tribal resistance led to a siege of Hamdullahi, in which Umar and his followers were trapped for some eight months before he ordered the town to be burned and fled to the nearby cliffs of Bandiagara. Here he died mysteriously in February 1864. The empire that he established, bequeathed to his son, Ahmadu, collapsed into civil war, and Ahmadu was finally driven out of Nioro in 1891, effectively ending Umarian AUTHORITY in the region. Despite the short duration of the state he established, al-Hajj Umar's jihad was one of a number of similar reform movements that revived Islam and resisted the spread of French colonial authority in 19th-century West Africa.

See also RENEWAL AND REFORM MOVEMENTS.

Stephen Cory

Further reading: John H. Hanson, *Migration, Jihad, and Muslim Authority in West Africa* (Bloomington: Indiana University Press, 1996); B. O. Oloruntimehin, *The Segu Tukulor Empire* (London: Longman Group, 1972); David Robinson, *The Holy War of Umar Tal* (Oxford: Oxford University Press, 1985); John Ralph Willis, *In the Path of Allah: The Passion of al-Hajj 'Umar* (London: Frank Cass, 1989).

Umayyad Caliphate (661–750)

The Umayyad Caliphate was a Sunni dynasty that expanded the area of Islamic rule and developed a distinct Islamic culture. During the years of Umayyad rule, the Islamic state changed from a coalition of Arab tribes to a centralized empire that stretched from present-day Pakistan to the Atlantic Ocean and included the Arabian Peninsula, IRAN, EGYPT, much of North Africa, and the Iberian Peninsula. This vast area was held together by an Islamic culture that included a common language and coinage. At the same time, the CALIPHATE created permanent divisions within the Muslim community, or UMMA.

The Umayyads came to power in the turbulent period following the death of UTHMAN IBN AFFAN

(r. 644–655), the third CALIPH, and the accession of ALI IBN ABI TALIB (r. 656–661). Uthman's cousin, Muawiya, who was governor of SYRIA, refused to recognize Ali as caliph. Civil war broke out between supporters of Ali and Muawiya; Ali was assassinated, and Muawiya declared himself caliph. Muawiya was a member of the Umayyad family, the wealthiest and most powerful branch of the QURAYSH in MECCA. Muawiya moved the capital of the Islamic state from MEDINA to DAMASCUS, Syria. He also changed the caliphate in fact, if not in principle, to a dynasty by naming his son as his successor, thus setting a precedent for the caliphate passing from father to son.

Under the Umayyads, the process of Islamic expansion began again. Parts of Egypt that had fallen under Byzantine control were retaken. Umayyad armies moved west across North Africa to the Atlantic coast. In 711 they crossed the Strait of Gibraltar and began the conquest of ANDALUSIA (Spain); soon, the entire Iberian Peninsula was under Muslim control. Their advance into Europe was finally stopped in 732 at the Battle of Tours, when Charles Martel of France won a decisive engagement against a Muslim raiding force. In the east, the expansion continued, eventually reaching as far as the borders of present-day INDIA.

As the Umayyads increased the extent of their empire, they set in place systems to unite the disparate peoples of the empire. Abd al-Malik (r. 685–705) declared Arabic the official language of the empire. Up to this time, local government had been conducted in the local language; now, all government business was conducted in Arabic. The Umayyads introduced a common coinage throughout the empire, called dinars. The common currency made it easier to conduct business between different parts of the empire. The Umayyads also spread Islamic religious architecture throughout the empire. When a region was conquered, a MOSQUE was built for communal prayer and to give thanks to God. Although these mosques were built from local materials, they eventually featured the same essential elements: a MINARET, a MIHRAB, and an ablution fountain. The introduction of a common language, currency, and religious architecture helped develop a distinctive Islamic culture.

After about 90 years of Umayyad rule, the empire faced serious internal challenges. By 732, the armies were making fewer conquests. This stopped the flow of captured wealth into the economy. At the same time, many non-Muslims within the empire had converted to Islam. As a result, they paid less in taxes, decreasing a steady source of revenue. The divisions within Islam itself also came to the fore. Muslims who had supported Ali as caliph because of his family ties to Muhammad were known as *shiat Ali,* "party of Ali," or the Shia (*see* SHIISM). They saw the Umayyads as usurpers who had seized the caliphate from the rightful head of the Muslim community. This internal conflict was exploited by the Abbasids, who claimed the caliphate based on the descent of Abbas, Muhammad's uncle. In 747 this dissension led to rebellion against the Umayyads; in 750 the Umayyad caliphate was overthrown, and the ABBASID CALIPHATE began.

See also ARABIC LANGUAGE AND LITERATURE; *FITNA.*

Kate O'Halloran

Further reading: Hugh Kennedy, *The Prophet and the Age of the Caliphates* (Harlow, England: Longman, 2003); Wilferd Madelung, *The Succession to Muhammad: A Study of the Early Caliphate* (Cambridge: Cambridge University Press, 1999).

umma (Arabic: community, nation, tribe, people)

In each of the three Abrahamic religions the idea of an overarching community of the faithful holds great importance alongside doctrines of individual responsibility before God. The foremost concept of such a community in Judaism is that of Israel, or the people of Israel (Bene Yisrael). In Christianity it is the church (*ekklesia*). Muslims feel that they are united into a single community, or *umma,* by a shared system of Islamic beliefs and practices concerning a single, all-powerful and merciful god—ALLAH, who revealed himself in the QURAN, the holy book delivered by the prophet Muhammad in the seventh century C.E. They view the *umma* as a joining of all believers, without regard to sect, caste, class, ethnicity, gender, or nationality. The Muslim *umma* stands in contrast to communities that are founded on such social divisions, and it is opposed to those founded on disbelief (*kufr*) and IDOLATRY (*shirk*). It is close, however, to other communities believed to be founded on prophetic revelation—the PEOPLE OF THE BOOK, among whom the Jews and Christians are foremost.

The concept of the *umma* was been formed during three phases of Islamic history: (1) the age of the first community in MEDINA under Muhammad's leadership; (2) the age of the caliphates and their successor states; and (3) the modern age of European COLONIALISM and nation-states. Of these three, that of the Medinan phase is the one that has been most idealized by Muslims. Indeed, it is so significant that the year of the creation of this original *umma* in Medina under Muhammad's leadership in 622 C.E. was selected to be year one on the Islamic lunar CALENDAR. The exemplary nature of this community is conveyed by the Medinan chapters of the Quran, the HADITH, and the biographies of Muhammad and his Companions. Much of what the ULAMA determined to be the SUNNA (body of precedents) of Islam is based on traditions (the hadith) about what Muhammad and his followers said and did in that era.

In the Quran the word *umma* occurs 62 times in chapters dated to both the later Meccan and Medinan periods of Muhammad's life. It is used with reference to all humankind (Q 2:213) and to different groups and subgroups, including the People of the Book, who have in one way or another gone astray (for example, Q 23:52–54). Above all, however, it refers to Muhammad's community, the Muslims. It is called a "middle" community (Q 2:143) and the "best" community, whose members are obliged not only to believe in God, but also to uphold his laws, "commanding the right and forbidding the wrong" (Q 3:110). Aside from the Quran, another important early source for information about the *umma* is a collection of documents known as the Constitution of Medina, found in early Islamic sources such as MUHAMMAD IBN LSHAQ's *Sirat rasul Allah* (Life of the Prophet of God, mid-eighth century). This document, issued after the HIJRA in 622, establishes the community in political terms, affirming social solidarity among the Meccan EMIGRANTS and the Arab clans of Medina (ANSAR), and regulating relations with outsiders. It also set forth terms for peaceful coexistence with the Jews of Medina.

During the era of the caliphates (seventh to 13th century), and in the ensuing centuries of Islamic empires and states, the ideal of the exemplary Muslim community of Medina became firmly established, particularly among Sunni Muslims. The initial pluralism of the Medinan community reflected in the Constitution of Medina became even more pronounced and diversified after Muhammad's death, with the extraordinary expansion of Islamic rule outside the Arabian Peninsula toward Spain (ANDALUSIA) in the west and the INDUS River valley in the east. The imperial *umma* came to include not only Arab Muslims, but also clients and converts from many different ethnic, social, and religious backgrounds. Among the converts were former Jews, Christians, and Zoroastrians, as well as members of diverse ethnic groups such as Persians, Africans, Kurds, Turks, Circassians, Asians, and various European peoples. Required Islamic ritual practices—the SHAHADA, PRAYER, ALMSGIVING, FASTING, and the HAJJ—fostered communal unity. The status of Arabic as the sacred language and the leading means of transmitting religious knowledge also contributed. During this era of great Islamic cultural achievement, the Muslim *umma* overlapped with the *dar al-Islam* (House of Islam)—territories ruled by Muslims, where the SHARIA was observed. Worldly authority was wielded by the ruling elites, while the ulama wielded authority in religious matters, especially the law. Non-Muslims in the *dar al-Islam* remained the majority in most regions until the 12th or 13th century. They were legally "protected" people under Islamic law, known as *ahl al-dhimma,* or simply *dhimmis.*

Although Muslims developed local loyalties and identities wherever they lived, and the *dar al-Islam* was beset by intracommunal tensions and conflicts that led to political fragmentation, the ideal of the communal solidarity of believers endured. It even withstood invasions by crusaders and Mongols and sectarian challenges posed by the KHAWARIJ and the Shia. The Shia especially became a significant political threat to the ideal of a unified *umma* between the 10th and 12th centuries. They held that the community had gone astray after Muhammad's death in 632, and they asserted that its moral virtue and authenticity could be fully restored only under the leadership of the Imams, divinely inspired descendants of the Prophet's household (*AHL AL-BAYT*). Nevertheless, the major branches of SHIISM have sought ways to negotiate coexistence with SUNNISM throughout much of their history, and efforts at rapprochement continue to the present day. The *umma* ideal took root outside the Middle East in sub-Saharan Africa, India, and beyond. This more globalized aspect of communal solidarity was embodied in transregional networks involving the movement of goods, people, and ideas, as reflected in the biographies of famous Muslim scholars, Sufis, warriors, and travelers such as IBN BATTUTA (1304–77).

The third phase in the development of the concept of the *umma,* that of European colonialism and the modern nation-state, began in the 18th century and continues to the present. During this time the last vestiges of transregional Muslim political rule were wiped away with the fall of the MUGHAL DYNASTY in 1857 and of the OTTOMAN DYNASTY in 1922. The title of caliph was discontinued, the authority of the ulama was weakened,

and the *dar al-Islam* as a large contiguous territory under centralized Muslim government became but a memory. The colonial era saw many Muslim lands ruled by non-Muslims, and, even with independence, the governments and laws of newly created nation-states, with few exceptions, emulated the secular policies of Europe. The *umma* ideal, however, did not disappear. Islamic RENEWAL AND REFORM MOVEMENTS, inspired and led by men such as JAMAL AL-DIN AL-AFGHANI (d. 1897), MUHAMMAD ABDUH (d. 1905), and MUHAMMAD RASHID RIDA (d. 1935). The renewal of the unity of the *umma,* particularly in the face of secular and leftist political currents during the cold war era, was a factor that led to the creation of international bodies such as the MUSLIM WORLD LEAGUE (1962) and the ORGANIZATION OF THE ISLAMIC CONFERENCE (1969). It is also evident in the formation of transnational DAAWA movements such as the TABLIGHI JAMAAT, launched in the 1920s, and support given by Muslim organizations and states for Muslim victims of conflicts, political persecution, and natural disasters around the world. Cooperation among Muslim states with SAUDI ARABIA in the organization of the hajj is another way in which the *umma* ideal is affirmed today. Local and global ties among Muslims in the modern era have also been strengthened by both mechanized forms of transportation and the print and electronic media.

Restoring the *umma* ideal in a more political sense is a foundational aspect of radical Islamist ideology, as expressed in the writings of SAYYID QUTB (d. 1966) and ABU AL-ALA MAWDUDI (d. 1979), and is embraced by radical JIHAD MOVEMENTS, many of which want to unify Muslims against secular regimes and create theocratic governments based on the sharia. This message is used by HAMAS to rally Muslims against Israel and by USAMA BIN LADIN to justify the terrorist attacks of al-Qaida.

See also CALIPHATE; COMPANIONS OF THE PROPHET; CONVERSION; CRUSADES; *DAR AL-ISLAM* AND *DAR AL-HARB*; *DHIMMI*; ISLAMIC GOVERNMENT; PAN-ISLAMISM; SUNNISM; *TAWHID*.

Further reading: Abdullah al-Ahsan, *Umma or Nation? Identity Crisis in Contemporary Muslim Society* (Leicester, England: Islamic Foundation, 1992); Frederick Mathewson Denny, "The Meaning of *Ummah* in the Quran," *History of Religions* 15, no. 1 (1975): 35–70; Dale F. Eickelman and James Piscatori, *Muslim Politics* (Princeton, N.J.: Princeton University Press, 1996), 141–155); R. Stephen Humphreys, *Islamic History: A Framework for Inquiry.* Rev. ed. (Princeton, N.J.: Princeton University Press, 1991), 92–98, 255–283; C. A. O. Nieuwenhuijze, "The Ummah: An Analytic Approach," *Studia Islamica* 10 (1959): 5–22; F. E. Peters, *The Children of Abraham,* 2d ed. (Princeton, N.J.: Princeton University Press), 41–66; David Waines, *An Introduction to Islam,* 2d ed., 175–184 (Cambridge: Cambridge University Press, 2003).

Umm Kulthoum (Umm Kulthum) (1904–1975) *famed Egyptian singer*

First a provincial religious singer, Umm Kulthoum became one of the most prominent artists in the 20th-century ARAB world. Her childhood in the Nile Delta village of Tammay al-Zahayra laid the foundation for her career: She studied Quranic recitation from age five and joined her family's local performances of songs narrating the Prophet's life. In the 1920s she established herself in CAIRO by singing an increasingly romantic repertory in elite homes and MUSIC halls.

By the 1930s she was performing this repertory with a growing instrumental ensemble. Her performances were distinguished by skills she had developed through quranic recitation and her religious repertory—correct pronunciation, breath control, melodic ornamentation, and varied vocal timbres. She excelled in improvising and communicating poetic meaning. As her commercial recordings, radio airplay, and musical films boosted her popularity, she ensured her success through business acumen and artistic control.

The work of outstanding poets and composers, her songs appealed to changing popular sensibilities. Thus, the 1940s featured her singing two contrasting groups of songs: accessible romantic songs in colloquial Arabic and denser *qasidah* compositions in formal Arabic, including several on religious themes (e.g., "Wulid al-Huda" and "Nahj al-Burda"). Following the 1952 revolution in Egypt, she recorded numerous patriotic songs and the radio program (later film) *Rabia al-Adawiyya.* She married in 1954.

Her final years were distinguished by her response to the war of June 1967. She offered fund-raising concerts in EGYPT, the Arab world, and Europe to rebuild the Egyptian military. These concerts reinvigorated the sexagenarian's career, intensified her fan base across the Arab world, and solidified her image in national and regional memory as a patriotic figure—an image persisting long after her death in Cairo on February 3, 1975.

While romantic texts dominate her output of roughly 300 songs, her career's trajectory reveals a commitment to religious projects and a return to her beginnings with her 1960s plan to record the Prophet's life story, including quranic recitation. Having established a popular, yet respectable, platform by singing romantic songs, she repeatedly used it to disseminate serious religious songs to an extraordinarily wide audience.

See also CINEMA; WOMEN.

Laura Lohman

Further reading: Virginia Danielson, *The Voice of Egypt: Umm Kulthum, Arabic Song, and Egyptian Society in the Twentieth Century* (Chicago: University of Chicago Press, 1997); Michal Goldman, *Umm Kulthum: A Voice like Egypt* (Waltham, Mass.: Filmmakers Collaborative, 1997); Laura Lohman, "'The Artist of the People in the Battle': Umm Kulthum's Concerts for Egypt in Political Context." In *Music and the Play of Power in the Middle East, North Africa and Central Asia,* edited by Laudan Nooshin (Aldershot, U.K.: Ashgate Press, 2008).

umra (Arabic)

The *umra* is the lesser pilgrimage to MECCA. Unlike the HAJJ, it is not obligatory for most Muslims, even though the QURAN declares, "Complete the *umra* and the hajj for God" (Q 2:196). It is thought that the *umra* was celebrated before Islamic times during the spring month of Rajab, the seventh month, as a local Meccan ritual that involved ANIMAL sacrifice. During the early Islamic era, it was changed. Thus, in contrast to the hajj, it can be done at any time of the year, and consists of ritual practices that are confined to the Sacred Mosque area only. The journey to Mina and ARAFAT is not involved, nor is animal sacrifice required. Islamic law, however, permits combining the *umra* with the hajj. According to the HADITH, performing the *umra* temporarily absolves one of any sins committed beforehand, while performing the hajj earns one a place in PARADISE.

The basic components of this pilgrimage are: (1) declaration of intention (*niyya*); (2) ritual purification and wearing two white seamless garments (*ihram*); seven circumambulations (*tawaf*) of the KAABA; (3) touching the BLACK STONE; (4) prayer at the Station of ABRAHAM; (5) running seven times between the hills of Safa and Marwa next to the Sacred Mosque; and (6) a ritual hair cut or shaving of the head. Pilgrims also pronounce the *talbiyya* ("At your service, O Lord, at your service!") and other invocations during these rites. Many take a drink of water from the ZAMZAM well. For WOMEN, the *umra* does not require either the distinctive *ihram* garments or the shaving of the head.

Since the last decades of the 20th century millions of pilgrims have participated in the *umra* annually. Many prefer to do it during RAMADAN, an especially holy month in the Islamic CALENDAR.

See also ABLUTION.

Further reading: Laleh Bakhtiar, *Encyclopedia of Islamic Law: A Compendium of the Major Schools* (Chicago: ABC International Group, 1996), 165–202; F. E. Peters, *The Hajj: The Muslim Pilgrimage to Mecca and the Holy Places* (Princeton, N.J.: Princeton University Press, 1994), 129–134.

unbeliever   *See* APOSTASY; *KAFIR*.

United Arab Emirates   *See* GULF STATES.

United States

The history of Islam in the United States goes back to the 18th century, but significant growth of the community does not begin until the late 19th century. Immigration increased throughout the 20th century, until the Muslim community became the fastest growing religious community (both by immigration and conversion) in the United States today. Current census figures of Muslims in America are difficult to estimate. Negative media exposure to sectarian African-American Muslim communities since the civil rights era and to immigrant and expatriate Muslim communities since September 11th have made many Muslims reluctant to reveal religious information in census surveys. Census figures assessing the size of the Muslim community in the United States vary greatly, starting as low as 3 to 4 million and others ranging as high as 6 million to 7 million. The greatest concentrations (by virtue of the number of MOSQUES) are located in California, New York, and Michigan, followed by Pennsylvania, Texas, Ohio, Illinois, and Florida. In addition to those Muslims who are actively religious and practice to varying degrees, there are also those who may best be identified as "cultural" or "secular" Muslims, reflecting the modern evolution of ISLAM as an ethnic or cultural identity but not as a belief or practice.

The earliest Muslim immigrants came to the United States beginning in the late 19th century from the predominantly Arabic-speaking Middle East (LEBANON, SYRIA, JORDAN, Palestinian Authority, and ISRAEL), becoming small merchants and factory laborers with the strongest settlement in New York and the Midwest. Muslim immigration declined during the periods of World War I and II (1914–18, 1939–45), but continued to grow in between and afterward. Changes in U.S.

immigration law in 1965, particularly the end of the Asian Exclusion Act of 1924, increased the momentum of Muslim immigration, particularly from South Asia, East and Southeast Asia, Eastern Europe, and the Soviet Union, primarily coming from and settling in urban areas. Conflict throughout the Muslim Middle East and Central Asia since the late 1960s (post-1967 war between ISRAEL and the Arab states, the Lebanese civil war [1975–90], Iranian Revolution [late 1970s], Iran-Iraq war [1980–88], Iraq-Kuwait/Gulf war [1990–91], Afghanistan civil war [1978–present], and U.S.-Iraq war [2003–present]) have stimulated immigration of sectarian and other Muslim minorities to America, particularly Shii populations, resulting in a higher than world average (20 percent rather than 10 percent) in relation to the world Sunni Muslim majority. In addition to immigrants, large numbers of Muslim professionals and students arrived to secure advanced training or degrees from all parts of the Muslim world, and they have added their cultural, ethno-linguistic, and theological diversity to the Muslim community in America for periods from as short as five to as long as 20 years.

The American Muslim community reflects the theological as well as ethnic and linguistic diversity of the world Muslim UMMA, or religious community, including established Sufi orders and new Sufi teachers and groups, as well as a large number of new indigenous Islamic groups and sectarian offshoots. The presence and example of the American Muslim immigrant and expatriate community has stimulated a growing number of converts to Islam throughout the 20th century to the present, particularly among African Americans. Immigrant Muslims have struggled to maintain Islamic identity and life ways in a non-Muslim majority environment through their commitment to the five pillars of practice (SHAHADA/witness to FAITH, *salat*/PRAYER, *zakat*/ALMSGIVING, *sawm*/fasting, HAJJ/pilgrimage) and the categories of HALAL/

Islamic Center of Southern California in Los Angeles *(J. Gordon Melton)*

Islamic Center of America, a leading mosque for Shii Muslims in Dearborn, Michigan *(J. Gordon Melton)*

permitted and HARAM/forbidden behavior (such as abstaining from alcohol and pork, both of which are endemic to many work and social settings in American culture).

Basic Islamic religious roles and institutions, such as the mosque (*masjid*) and IMAM (religious teacher and leader), have adapted to American society to fill a wider range of social functions than they cover traditionally in the larger Muslim world, taking on "parish"-style responsibilities for CHILDREN's and adult continuing EDUCATION, community/youth social events, marriage/family counseling, and neighborhood/media liaison. Traditional Islamic gender coding has also adapted,

bringing Muslim girls and WOMEN into public and coeducation schooling, into the workforce, into mosque governance, and, ultimately, into the public discourse of forming Islamic thought through taking on the authority to interpret religious texts, such as the QURAN and HADITH. Muslim boys and men have been correspondingly affected by American society in many of the same ways, but with greater access to heterosexual contact outside of marriage in the context of "dating." Muslim parents are still more conservative in the standards set for daughters than for sons, and although often disapproving of sons' dating, will turn a blind eye to it, whereas daughters engaging

Islamic Society of Salt Lake City, Utah *(J. Gordon Melton)*

in the same behavior may bring shame on not only themselves but also their families.

African-American Muslims, although not separate from the immigrant and expatriate Muslim community, have a different history of entering Islam, and have evolved many new indigenous forms of Islam not found in the larger Muslim world. East and West African Muslims came to the New World (the Caribbean, South America, and North America) as slaves to the British, French, Spanish, and Dutch colonies from the 16th through the mid-19th centuries. After the Civil War (1860–65) most African Muslim ex-slaves in the United States returned to their countries of origin, although there is testimony from their descendants of settlement by African Muslims and their families in the coastal islands of Georgia and the Carolinas into the mid-20th century. The

rise and growth of the African-American Muslim community cannot be directly traced to the descendants of those African Muslims from the slave era except as an issue of awareness among modern African Americans of Islam as a religion of African origin offering an alternative to post-slavery Christianity.

Although conversion to Islam among African Americans has been overwhelmingly to the Sunni tradition, new and sectarian communities have received far more public and media recognition since the civil rights era. One such sectarian group, the AHMADIYYA Community, whose missionizing (DAWA) efforts have been highly successful among African Americans, came to America early in the 20th century. SUFISM has also had a strong, but as yet not fully charted history among African Americans. The development of new African-American Muslim communities includes the Moorish Science Temple, beginning in 1913 and led by Noble Drew Ali; the NATION OF ISLAM, beginning in the early 1930s and led by Elijah Muhammad, and two of the most recent coming out of New York, the Five Percent Nation of Gods and Earths, beginning in the 1960s as a youth off-shoot of the Nation of Islam and led by Clarence "Pudding" 13X, and the Ansaaru Allah Community, beginning in 1970 and led by Isa Muhammad. All of these communities share a commitment to a black theology and strong apocalyptic tone, which set them apart from the mainstream of Islam in America and the world Muslim UMMA.

The later history of the Nation of Islam reflects a growing trend toward adopting the Sunni tradition by the majority of African-American Muslims. Warith Deen Muhammad (d. 2008), after the death of his father, Nation of Islam founder Elijah Muhammad, led the majority of the community toward the Sunni mainstream by directing them to learn Arabic, practice the five pillars, and join the world Sunni *umma,* renaming it first the World Community of al-Islam in the West and finally the American Muslim Mission. Relations between the African-American and immigrant/expatriate Muslim communities have sometimes been strained to the extent that African-American Muslims have formed their own movements or mosques in a parallel history to formation of black churches in response to post–Civil War racism. The character of the African-American Sunni majority is as complex and diverse as the immigrant and expatriate Sunni community in America, marked by as many theological differences as the immigrant community is by multiple ethnolinguistic identities. However, both immigrant and African-American communities are part of one *umma* and share in its common challenge of following the "straight path" (Q.1:6) in America.

The experience of the American Muslim community as a whole since the September 11, 2001,

Islamic Community Center of Tempe, Arizona, designed to resemble the Dome of the Rock in Jerusalem *(Juan E. Campo)*

attacks has been stressful, with immediate effects including personal attacks, property vandalism of mosques and Islamic centers, and random hate crimes. Long-term negative attention to the American-Muslim community continues from the press, law enforcement, and government organizations; and Muslims (as well as Arab Americans and others of Middle Eastern background) continue to encounter religiously, ethnically, and culturally motivated harassment on the street, in schools, and in the workplace. Many American Muslims are frightened of ongoing prejudice and its consequences to the future of the community, but they have begun to organize themselves through such networks and ISNA (ISLAMIC SOCIETY OF NORTH AMERICA) and CAIR (COUNCIL OF AMERICAN-ISLAMIC RELATIONS), in cooperation with other civic organizations like the ACLU (American Civil Liberties Union) to resist situations of religious discrimination through disseminating accurate information to the public about Islam and the Muslim community. In spite of these difficulties, Muslims in increasingly larger numbers are continuing to immigrate to the United States seeking political and religious freedom and economic opportunity, and Americans are continuing to convert to Islam for its positive sense of personal identity, communal cohesion, and family values.

See also BAWA MUHAIYADDEEN FELLOWSHIP; CANADA; MALCOLM X; MUSLIM PUBLIC AFFAIRS COUNCIL; MUSLIM STUDENTS ASSOCIATION; WEBB, ALEXANDER RUSSELL.

Kathleen M. O'Connor

Further reading: Robert Dannin, *Black Pilgrimage to Islam* (New York: Oxford University Press, 2002, and E-book); Sylviane A. Diouf, *Servants of Allah: African Muslims Enslaved in the Americas* (New York: New York University Press, 1998); Ron Geaves, Theodore Gabriel, Yvonne Y. Haddad, and Jane I. Smith, eds., *Islam and the West Post 9/11* (Burlington, Vt.: Ashgate Publishing, 2004); Michael A. Gomez, *Black Crescent: The Experience and Legacy of African Muslims in the Americas* (New York: Cambridge

University Press, 2005, and E-book); Yvonne Y. Haddad and Jane I. Smith, eds., *Muslim Communities in North America* (Albany: State University of New York Press, 1994, and E-book); Yvonne Y. Haddad, Jane I. Smith, and Kathleen M. Moore, *Muslim Women in America: The Challenge of Islamic Identity Today* (New York: Oxford University Press, 2006, and E-book); Aminah Beverly McCloud, *African American Islam* (New York: Routledge, 1995); Larry Poston, *Islamic da'wah in the West: Muslim Missionary Activity and the Dynamics of Conversion to Islam* (New York: Oxford University Press, 1992); Carolyn Moxley Rouse, *Engaged Surrender: African American Women and Islam* (Berkeley: University of California Press, 2004, and E-book); Jane I. Smith, *Islam in America* (New York: Columbia University Press, 1999).

university

While the content and form of instruction has dramatically changed with the introduction of Western-style universities in the 19th and 20th centuries, higher EDUCATION in the Islamic world has had a long and venerable history. Important institutions of learning associated with MOSQUES such as al-AZHAR in EGYPT, al-Zaytuna in Tunisia, and al-Qarawiyyin in MOROCCO arose during the ninth and 10th centuries, preceding the development of universities even in Europe. The MADRASA, or school of Islamic law, was the primary teaching institution. Additional institutions such as the *khanqah* or *zawiya*, two kinds of Sufi institutions, later came to supplement the education available from the madrasa. For information on any of these traditional institutions of higher learning, please see relevant encyclopedia articles, as this entry will address the development of Western-style learning in the Islamic world.

Increasing European dominance and encounters with COLONIALISM led leaders in Muslim lands to undertake educational reform. Technical training schools, usually schools of medicine or ones focused on military skills, were founded during the first half of the 19th century. With the introduction of Western-style institutions such

as these, often with help from European experts, the way was paved for the establishment of other colleges or faculties. These institutions often contributed to the early founding of a national university, as in the Ottoman Empire (1900), EGYPT (1906), SYRIA (1924), and IRAN (1934). Elsewhere, as in South Asia, the colonial governments themselves founded universities. The first three universities in the region were founded in British INDIA in 1857, with three additional universities established before the end of the century, including one in Lahore. Missionaries, too, played a role in founding universities, specifically in LEBANON in 1864 and 1875. However, the balance of Muslim-majority countries did not witness the establishment of Western-style universities until the postwar period, for example, INDONESIA and MALAYSIA (1949), LIBYA (1955), IRAQ (1956), SAUDI ARABIA (1957), and Kuwait (1960).

All of these universities were modeled on Western-style teaching methods and university curricula, and in some cases they offered instruction only in Western languages. In the 1970s a movement began to establish Islamic universities, or to "Islamize" teaching at existing universities. At Saudi Arabia's Islamic University of MEDINA, traditional subjects are taught by Western teaching methods. The First World Conference on Muslim Education in MECCA, held in 1977, prompted Malaysia and PAKISTAN to begin the process of founding specifically Islamic universities, and BANGLADESH and Niger followed. Soon after, JORDAN, MOROCCO, ALGERIA, TUNISIA, and other states introduced courses in Islamic culture into their required university curricula. Independently, the textbooks and curricula of Iranian universities were "Islamized" following the 1979 revolution.

See also ABDUH, MUHAMMAD; ALIGARH; *KUTTAB*; RENEWAL MOVEMENTS; SECULARISM; WESTERNIZATION.

Shauna Huffaker

Further reading: H. H. Bilgrami and Syed Ali Ashraf, *The Concept of an Islamic University* (Cambridge: Cambridge University Press, 1985); George Makdisi, *The Rise of the*

Colleges (Edinburgh: Edinburgh University Press, 1981); Seyyed Hossein Nasr, *Islamic Science* (London: World of Islam Festival Publishing Co., 1976); Joseph S. Szyliowicz, *Education and Modernization in the Middle East* (Ithaca, N.Y.: Cornell University Press, 1973).

urf   *See* CUSTOMARY LAW.

urs   *See* MAWLID.

Usama bin Ladin (Osama Binladen, Usama Binladin, Ussamah Bin Ladin, Oussama Ben Laden, Ussamah Bin Ladin) (1957–   ) *Islamic militant, head of al-Qaida network that attacked the New York World Trade Center and the Pentagon on September 11, 2001*

Usama bin Muhammad bin Awad bin Ladin became involved in the Afghan JIHAD after the Soviet Union (USSR) invaded AFGHANISTAN in 1979. In 1988, with a group of other jihadists, he founded the AL-QAIDA network to train soldiers for an ongoing jihad after the end of the fighting in Afghanistan. It is believed that bin Ladin has funded or masterminded a number of terrorist attacks around the world, including the September 11, 2001, attacks on the World Trade Building in New York and the Pentagon in Washington, D.C.

Bin Ladin was born in Riyadh, SAUDI ARABIA, one of 54 children of Muhammad Awad bin Ladin (1906–1967), a businessman who had made a fortune in the construction business. Muhammad had come to Saudi Arabia in the 1920s as a poor immigrant from YEMEN and was hired as a laborer by the Arabian American Oil Company (Aramco, now known as Saudi Aramco) in the 1930s, rising to become an independent contractor for Aramco and eventually developing close ties to the Saudi royal family. His construction company, known as the Muhammad Bin Ladin Organization (now known as the Saudi Binladin Group), was respon-

Usama bin Ladin, leader of al-Qaida   *(AP Photos)*

sible for building many of the kingdom's first roads and renovating the holy sites in MECCA and MEDINA. Usama's mother, Alia, came from a Syrian family that may have belonged to that country's ALAWI community. Usama's parents divorced when Usama was four or five years old and his mother then married Muhammad al-Attas; the couple had four children, raising Usama in Jeddah with his stepbrothers and stepsister. He frequently joined in family gatherings with half-siblings on his father's side of the family, and was included in the list of heirs to the Bin Ladin family fortune. Among his favorite pastimes was raising and riding horses.

Usama attended Al-Thaghr Model School, an elite secondary school in Jeddah, and is remembered by his teachers as having been an average student. It was there, when he was 15 years old, that he experienced a religious and political awakening. The school boasted a Western-style curriculum, but Usama's conversion occurred in an after-school study group conducted by a physical education instructor who was a member of the Syrian branch of the MUSLIM BROTHERHOOD. Usama had been raised as a devout Sunni Muslim, but he now became extremely pious compared to his friends and other members of his family. He refused to wear Western dress outside school, began fasting twice a week, prayed frequently, memorized chapters from the Quran, and grew strict with his younger brothers and sister. He became more aware of, and concerned about, the Muslim world, particularly with regard to the situation in PALESTINE. It is thought had he had actually been recruited into the Muslim Brotherhood at this time, and started the reading the books of SAYYID QUTB (d. 1966), his brother Muhammad Qutb (b. 1915), and the medieval Hanbali jurist and theologian TAQI AL-DIN IBN TAYMIYYA (d. 1328). Usama graduated from Al-Thaghr in 1976, then enrolled at King Abd al-Aziz ibn Saud University in Jeddah, where he majored in business administration. He also became involved in the family construction business.

In December 1979, Soviet troops invaded AFGHANISTAN. Like many other Muslims, bin Ladin was shocked and angry. An acquaintance of bin Ladin's, a Palestinian scholar named Abd Allah Azzam (1941–1989), moved to Pakistan to join the Afghan resistance. He made frequent trips to Peshawar, the headquarters of the resistance. He also often returned to Jeddah, where he stayed in bin Ladin's home and held meetings to recruit young Saudis to join the Afghans. Bin Ladin soon started raising funds for the anti-Soviet jihad; eventually, he went to Afghanistan and became a *mujahid* himself. This is when he and Ayman al-Zawahiri (b. 1951), an infamous Egyptian jihadist, co-founded the Arab Mujahidin Services Bureau, the predecessor of al-Qaida.

In 1988, with a group of other Afghanistan war veterans, bin Ladin founded al-Qaida al-

Askariya (the military base). The goal of the new organization was to act as a training system for *mujahidin*. In 1990, after the Soviets pulled out of Afghanistan, bin Ladin returned to Saudi Arabia, where he was seen as a hero of the jihad. Then, later that same year, IRAQ invaded Kuwait. Because he opposed the presence of U.S. troops in Saudi Arabia, bin Ladin offered the Saudi king his own figures, trained in Afghanistan, to drive the Iraqis out of Kuwait. When the king refused his offer, bin Ladin criticized the Saudi royal family for their dependence on the U.S. military. In 1992 bin Ladin moved to SUDAN, where he set up a new base for *mujahidin* operations. His continued criticism of the Saudi king led to his being stripped of his Saudi passport and citizenship.

On December 29, 1992, a bomb exploded at a hotel in Aden, Yemen; two people were killed. It is believed that this was the first bombing attack in which bin Ladin was involved. Since then, he has been implicated in funding or masterminding attacks in Somalia and New York in 1993, in Saudi Arabia in 1995, in Kenya and Tanzania in 1998, against the USS *Cole* in 2000, and in the September 11, 2001, attacks in New York and Washington, D.C.

In 1996 bin Ladin was expelled from Sudan; returning to Afghanistan, he became a supporter of the TALIBAN regime there. After the September 11 attacks, the United States led an international coalition to invade Afghanistan, ousting the Taliban government; however, bin Ladin was not captured. He has been indicted in U.S. courts on a number of charges connected with different attacks, although he has not been charged in connection with the September 11 attacks. Many claims have been made since 2001 about bin Ladin's whereabouts, but his location remains unknown.

See also GULF WARS; OIL; SALAFISM; TERRORISM; WAHHABISM.

Juan E. Campo and Kate O'Halloran

Further reading: Peter Bergen, *The Osama Bin Laden I Know: An Oral History of al-Qaeda's Leader* (New

York: Free Press, 2006); Steve Coll, *The Bin Ladens: An Arabian Family in the American Century* (New York: Penguin Press, 2008); Raymond Ibrahim, ed., *The Al Qaeda Reader* (New York: Doubleday, 2007); Osama bin Laden, *Messages to the World: The Statements of Osama bin Laden.* Edited by Bruce Lawrence, translated by James Howarth (New York: Verso, 2005); Lawrence Wright, *The Looming Tower: Al-Qaeda and the Road to 9/11* (New York: Vintage Books, 2006).

Usuli School

The Usuli School is a tradition of jurisprudence (FIQH) in TWELVE-IMAM SHIISM that has its roots in the 10th century, when different Sunni and Shii legal theories were being formally constituted. Its name comes from the Arabic word *usul,* which means "roots" or "foundations," of law, but in the case of the Shia, it was used with special reference to a type of legal theory that recognized the use of human reason (*aql*) and unrestricted legal reasoning (*IJTIHAD*) by qualified ULAMA. The forerunner for the rationalist approach to *fiqh* within Shii circles was the scholar Muhammad ibn al-Hasan al-Tusi (905–1066/67) of Khurasan and Baghdad, but the tradition was first fully elaborated in the teachings of al-Muhaqqiq al-Hilli (d. 1277), who lived most of his life in the town of Hilla in southern IRAQ, and his student Allama al-Hilli (d. 1325).

When the SAFAVID DYNASTY (1501–1722) established Shiism as the state religion in IRAN, *usuli* jurists, who came to be known as *mujtahids* because of their preference for *ijtihad,* promoted the view that ordinary Shiis should without question follow the authority of a living jurist before that of a dead one. Additionally, the *mujtahids* claimed that they were deputies of the messianic 12th IMAM, the MAHDI. These doctrines gave qualified jurists far-reaching authority among the Shia, especially in Iran and Iraq. They also set them apart from the Sunni ulama, who admitted only limited use of *ijtihad* and could not claim to be agents of a hidden messiah. However, the

Usulis also provoked a reaction among traditionist ulama among the Shia, who feared that the fundamental principles of Shiism, based on the QURAN and the teachings (*akhbar*) of the Imams, would be undermined by unrestricted Usuli rationalism. These traditionally minded ulama formed what is called the AKHBARI SCHOOL of Shii jurisprudence. The Usulis and Akhbaris engaged in factional disputes with each other at the madrasas of Iran and Iraq, even in distant Mecca, in the early 19th century. The Usulis emerged triumphant by the middle of the century, and soon organized themselves into a hierarchy of religious experts, from ordinary mullahs and *akhunds* at the bottom to grand ayatollahs at the top. The supreme AYATOLLAH, determined by reputation and networks of relations with BAZAAR merchants, was known as the *marjaa al-taqlid* (source of imitation), whose legal rulings were considered to be the most binding by other Shiis. The political mobilization of Usuli ulama became apparent in the late 19th century, when Mirza Hasan al-Shirazi called for a boycott of the British tobacco monopoly in 1891–92. Ayatollah RUHOLLAH KHOMEINI (d. 1989) and the ulama who founded the revolutionary Islamic Republic of Iran in 1979 were all Usulis. Indeed, Khomeini's ideology of government by the jurist (*wilayat al-faqih*), encompassing the political as well as the religious spheres, marked the logical culmination of the Usuli idea that supreme authority was vested in the person of the leading *mujtahid.* Outside of Iran, Usulis today have large followings among the Shia of Lebanon, Iraq, Bahrain, Pakistan, and India.

See also FATWA; MADRASA; MULLAH.

Further reading: Robert Gleave, *Inevitable Doubt: Two Theories of Shi'i Jurisprudence* (Leiden: E.J. Brill, 2000); Mier Litvak, *Shii Scholars of 19th-Century Iraq: The Ulama of Najaf and Karbala* (Cambridge: Cambridge University Press, 1998); Mojan Momen, *An Introduction to Shi'i Islam* (New Haven, Conn.: Yale University Press, 1985).

Usman Dan Fodio (Uthman ibn Fudi) (1754–1817) *religious reformer and founder of the Sokoto Caliphate in northeastern Nigeria*

Born to a distinguished scholarly family during the late 18th century, Usman established himself as a respected scholar and teacher in the Hausa kingdom of Gobir. An adherent of the QADIRI SUFI ORDER, Usman preached a radical message of reform that attracted a large following during the 1780s and 1790s. When the sultan of Gobir attacked his followers in 1804, Usman imitated the example of MUHAMMAD by leaving Gobir on a HIJRA, establishing an Islamic state and declaring holy war (JIHAD) against his persecutors. In the ensuing years, Usman's armies united much of Hausaland under his authority. At his death in 1817, Usman's son Muhammad Bello (d. 1837) succeeded him as CALIPH in the new capital city of Sokoto, which he had helped design. The Sokoto caliphs effectively organized their territories into a coherent state that maintained its independence until the British colonized the region in 1903.

Although he founded the largest independent state in Africa during the 19th century, Usman was primarily a religious teacher and spiritual example. A prolific writer on religious topics, he was also an accomplished poet, composing poems in both Arabic and his native Fulfide. In his later years, Usman was regarded as a SAINT, and people sought him out for spiritual power. After his death, Usman's tomb became a pilgrimage site, and stories of his miraculous works added to the luster of his image as a holy man.

See also RENEWAL AND REFORM MOVEMENTS; SOKOTO CALIPHATE; WEST AFRICA.

Stephen Cory

Further reading: Remi Adeleye, *Power and Diplomacy in Northern Nigeria, 1804–1906: The Sokoto Caliphate and Its Enemies* (New York: Humanities Press, 1971); Mervyn Hiskett, *The Sword of Truth: The Life and Times of the Shehu Usman Dan Fodio,* 2d ed. (Evanston, Ill.: Northwestern University Press, 1994); Murray Last, *The Sokoto Caliphate* (London: Humanities Press, 1967).

Uthman ibn Affan (ca. 580–656) *third Muslim caliph*

Uthman ibn Affan was the third of the four Sunni "rightly guided" caliphs, or Rashidun, along with ABU BAKR (r. 632–634), UMAR IBN AL-KHATTAB (r. 634–644), and ALI IBN ABI TALIB (r. 656–661). A member of the Umayyad clan of the QURAYSH tribe of MECCA, he inherited his father's business and became a wealthy trader before converting to ISLAM. After his conversion, he became Muhammad's son-in-law. On the death of Umar ibn al-Khattab, the committee charged with electing a successor named Uthman CALIPH. This angered the supporters of Ali, who was both Muhammad's son-in-law and his cousin and was thus a blood relative of the Prophet.

As caliph, Uthman continued the expansion of the empire begun by Abu Bakr and Umar ibn al-Khattab. He also defeated attempts by the Byzantines to recover some of their lost territory. Uthman centralized the administration of the CALIPHATE, dividing it into 12 provinces, each with a governor, chief judge, and tax collector. Some of these administrative positions, including the governorships of four provinces, were given to members of Uthman's own Umayyad family. Many saw this as nepotism. Objections were also raised to one of Uthman's other projects: compiling the definitive text of the QURAN. Until that time, the Quran had been an oral text, memorized and recited by followers of Muhammad. Uthman formed a committee to collect all versions of the Quran, both oral and written, and to prepare a definitive written version of the text. Some of Uthman's opponents saw this as religious innovation and an attempt to control the text of the Quran. Combined with economic difficulties resulting from mismanagement of the empire's finances, these issues led to widespread discontent. In 656 Uthman was assassinated in his

home. A civil war erupted over who should succeed him as caliph. Thus, Uthman's death marked
an important turning point in Islamic history, as it
signalled the beginning of open conflict within the
Islamic community.

See also COMPANIONS OF THE PROPHET.

Kate O'Halloran

Further reading: Hugh Kennedy, *The Prophet and the Age of the Caliphates* (London: Longman, 1985); Wil-ferd Madelung, *The Succession to Muhammad: A Study of the Early Caliphate* (Cambridge: Cambridge University Press, 1997).

Uzbekistan   *See* CENTRAL ASIA AND THE CAUCASUS.

Uzza, al-   *See* GODDESS.

V

veil

Veil is the most common English translation of the Arabic word HIJAB (a word whose many meanings also include "cover" or "screen"), most frequently understood as the head scarf worn by some Muslim WOMEN. The matter of the veil is a highly contentious and controversial one. There is much historical evidence indicating that the practice of veiling is not peculiar to ISLAM, and nothing in the QURAN explicitly or unequivocally requires it of women. Muslim proponents of the *hijab* often refer to Quranic verses 24:30–31, which direct both Muslim men and women to dress and interact modestly, and also instruct women not to display their beauty except to their husbands and close relatives. The word *hijab* does not appear here; rather the reference is to the draping of *khumur*—a type of covering over the hair worn by some women in seventh-century Arabia—over the chest. Nor does the word appear in verse 33:59, which instructs women to cover their persons using *jalabib* (loose cloaks). During the time of the prophet MUHAMMAD (d. 632) only the women of his own family, who were held to unique standards of modesty, veiled themselves. Muslims continue to debate today both the issue of whether the Quran prescribes a specific type of covering of women's bodies or rather modest clothes for women in general as well as the stringency of that prescription.

Colonial discourses in the Euro-American and Muslim worlds have played a significant role in constructing images and perceptions about the veil. The history of Western colonization in Muslim countries recounts European manipulation of the veil as a symbol of Islam's backward and barbaric nature and as evidence of the necessity for occupying and civilizing Muslim societies. In turn, Muslim resistance to COLONIALISM has often reconfigured the veil as a symbol of its religio-national essence. Some assumptions about the veil within Euro-American feminist discourse have also tended to oversimplify its meanings for Muslim women. In all cases, debates on the veil have tended to ignore the agency of Muslim women and the rich, varied expressions of their veiling, which, to name only a few, may include statements about a woman's class standing, her religious or national identification, or even her resistance to Western modes of sexuality.

See also BURQA; PURDAH.

Aysha A. Hidayatullah

Further reading: Leila Ahmed, *Women and Gender in Islam: Historical Roots of a Modern Debate* (New Haven, Conn.: Yale University Press, 1992); Fadwa El Guindi, *Veil: Modesty, Privacy and Resistance* (Oxford, U.K.:

702

Berg, 1999); Aysha Hidayatullah, "Islamic Conceptions of Sexuality." In *Sexuality and the World's Religions,* edited by David W. Machacek and Melissa M. Wilcox, 255–292. (Santa Barbara, Calif.: ABC-CLIO, 2003).

vizier

The Arabic word *wazir* (Persian *vazir*) appears in the QURAN referring to Aaron as MOSES' *wazir,* or "helper." With the establishment of the ABBA-SID CALIPHATE in the eighth century C.E. and the ongoing formalization of government structures, the vizier became an official government position. The vizier was usually appointed directly by the CALIPH, personally responsible to him, and second only to him in AUTHORITY. Thus he was the servant of the ruler, not the state.

The vizier was in charge of the civil administration, especially the collection of taxes. Government was divided into the "men of the pen" and the "men of the sword," and the vizier was the head of the former. At his appointment he was given, among other things, a golden inkpot symbolizing his role as the top of the bureaucratic machinery of the state. Viziers often clashed with the head of the military branch, the *amir al-umara,* particularly over the distribution of revenues.

Perhaps the biggest factor in determining the power and prestige of the vizier was his own ambition and personality compared with that of the ruler and the rival leaders in the military. The vizier was vulnerable to the personal whims of the ruler and many a vizier came to an untimely and violent end. On the other hand, caliphs often played only symbolic roles and sultans were primarily military men, leaving the vizier as the effective head of the government. The office of the vizierate reached its greatest level of power in the medieval period under the Seljuk vizier Nizam al-Mulk (1018–92).

During the Abbasid period the viziers came from a few influential families, or they rose through the ranks of the secretaries and were usually non-Arab. Often the vizierate could remain within an influential family for several generations. Under the Fatimids the vizier was at first in charge of the civil administration, but in 1074 the position was taken over by a military man who combined the traditional authority of the vizier with that of the *amir al-umara* (or *amir al-djuyush*) and basically assumed all real authority from the Fatimid caliphs. In the Ottoman period the vizier often began life as a slave (MAMLUK), working his way up and thus owing complete loyalty to the ruler who had aided his advancement. While this may have ensured loyalty to the ruler, it often came at the cost of doing what was in the best interests of the state. During the late 18th and 19th centuries, as the Ottomans tried to reform the government in order to keep up with Western Europe, there were efforts to transform the vizierate into a position similar to that of prime minister, but these efforts were ultimately thwarted by the rulers, who insisted that ministers report to them directly rather than to the vizier.

See also FATIMID DYNASTY; OTTOMAN DYNASTY; SELJUK DYNASTY.

Heather N. Keaney

Further reading: Carter V. Findley, *Ottoman Civil Official-dom* (Princeton, N.J.: Princeton University Press, 1989); S. D. Goitein, *The Origin of the Vizierate and Its True Character* (Leiden: E.J. Brill, 1968); C. L. Klausner, *The Seljuk Vezirate: A Study of Civil Administration, 1055–1194* (Cambridge, Mass.: Harvard University Press, 1973); Ann Lambton, *State and Government in Medieval Islam* (Oxford: Oxford University Press, 1981); Yaacov Lev, *State and Society in Fatimid Egypt* (Leiden: E.J. Brill, 1991).

W

Wahhabism (Arabic: Wahhabiyya)

Named after its founder, MUHAMMAD IBN ABD
AL-WAHHAB (d. 1792), Wahhabism is the most
important form of militant Islamic reformism to
arise in the Arabian Peninsula. The designation
was first coined with derogatory connotations by
Muslim opponents and observers in Europe and
North America. It refers to a set of doctrines and
practices *and* to a sectarian movement comprised
of those who embrace them. Allied to the clan
of the Al Saud from the Najd in central Arabia,
the Wahhabis, who prefer to call themselves the
muwahhidun (unitarians, or those who affirm
the unity of God), played an essential role in the
formation of the modern state of SAUDI ARABIA.
They have had a significant impact on the ways
Muslims understand and practice their religion in
many parts of the world today.

Ibn Abd al-Wahhab was educated by his father
and other ULAMA in the HANBALI LEGAL SCHOOL,
which was the chief school followed by the tribal
communities of the Najd. His thinking was also
shaped by his encounters with reformist scholars
in Mecca and Medina, and by his antipathy for
local religious practices associated with SAINT
shrines, SHIISM, and folk medicine. Around 1740
he began to proclaim publicly his reformist message about what he believed to be the true Islam.

Basing his ideas on a literal reading of the Quran
and hadith, his teaching affirmed the absolute
oneness of God (TAWHID), adherence to the SUNNA
of the prophet Muhammad, and performance of
basic duties of Islamic worship (prayer, almsgiving, fasting, and hajj). Performance of the FIVE
PILLARS alone was not sufficient in his opinion,
however. Any belief or practice that fell outside
this narrow definition of Islam was held suspect
as an illegitimate innovation (BIDAA) or IDOLATRY
(SHIRK) that could put a Muslim, even an observant Muslim, outside the bounds of the faith. Ibn
Abd al-Wahhab also called upon Muslims to reject
belief in intercession of saints and Shii Imams; he
wanted them to cease practices such as praying to
the dead and the JINN, performing votive sacrifices,
worshipping sacred trees, and building shrines.
Indeed, a hallmark of Wahhabi religiosity is the
destruction of domed tombs and the burial of the
dead in unmarked graves. The sectarian character
of Wahhabism was not based only upon rejection
of local religious practices that were linked to Shiism and SUFISM, however. It also was opposed to
key doctrines held by most Sunni ulama, such as
adherence (*taqlid*) to the cumulative tradition of
jurisprudence (*FIQH*), recognition of the sunna of
the COMPANIONS OF THE PROPHET and the four first
caliphs on a par with that of Muhammad, and

Abd al-Aziz's Wahhabi army (the Ikhwan) on the march in eastern Arabia, 1911 *(Courtesy of the Saudi Information Office)*

acceptance of a Muslim's faith on the basis only of declaration of the SHAHADA and performance of the Five Pillars of worship, without regard to other beliefs and practices.

Many in the Najd did not readily embrace Ibn Abd al-Wahhab's condemnation of their dearly held traditional beliefs and practices, including many in his own home town, which had expelled him. Others, however, appear to have been open to the doctrinal and legal simplicity of his message. Without doubt, his reformist agenda benefited greatly from the alliance that he entered with Muhammad ibn Saud (d. 1765), the head of the clan of the Al Saud of Diriyya, a settlement located near the oasis town of Riyadh. The Saudi SHAYKH supported the preacher's campaign to realize his reformist vision through proselytization (DAAWA) and warfare (JIHAD), in exchange for obtaining the right to collect *zakat* (alms) and obtain religious legitimation for Saudi rule throughout the Najd. The first Saudi state, which was created in 1744 and lasted until 1818, was one governed both by the Wahhabi understanding of the sharia and tribal custom. It survived the deaths of both Muhammads, and the alliance between the religious and the political was carried on by their heirs, who extended Saudi-Wahhabi rule to the Shii region of Hasa in the east (1780) and to the holy cities of Mecca and Medina (1803–04) in the west. Their jihad depended on the recruitment of young warriors who came from settlements that had accepted Saudi-Wahhabi rule and were attracted to the cause of Islam and the promise of booty. Additional raids were conducted into Iraq, where the Shii holy city of KARBALA was pillaged and the shrine of Husayn ibn Ali (d. 680) was destroyed, and Syria. In 1814 Ottoman authorities retaliated by invading the Najd, destroying Diriyya, and taking the Saudi leader, Muhammad ibn Saud's great grandson Abd Allah, to Istanbul, where he was executed in 1818.

A second, weakened Saudi state based in Riyadh subsequently arose and lasted until 1891, when it was brought down by a rival tribal confederacy led by the Rashidis of Hail. The third Saudi-Wahhabi state was created by Abd al-Aziz ibn Saud (1880–1953), who used his clan's alliance with the Wahhabis to establish the Kingdom of Saudi Arabia in 1932 and place it under sacred law, the sharia. Ibn Saud had relatives among the Al al-Shaykh, descendants of Ibn Abd al-Wahhab, and he had been educated in religious matters by them. When the Saudis retook Riyadh in 1902, the Wahhabis swore allegiance to Ibn Saud and proclaimed him their IMAM, or community leader. Among his strongest supporters were the *mutawwaa*, teachers and ritual specialists who had been propagating Wahhabi doctrines and practices through madrasas in the oasis settlements of the Najd since the 18th century. In exchange for supporting Ibn Saud, they claimed the authority to enforce the sharia and punish violators. They stood in the forefront of a revival of the Wahhabi brand of Islam that swept across the Arabian Peninsula under Ibn Saud's leadership. They had also indoctrinated a new fighting force known as the Ikhwan (Brotherhood), recruited from BEDOUIN tribes that had been recently settled in villages under the supervision of the *mutawwaa* and Wahhabi ulama. The Ikhwan were fierce fighters who treated the populations of towns that opposed them brutally. They destroyed any shrines and tombs that offended their puritanical religious sensibilities. After the conquest of the Hijaz (western Arabia), however, they rebelled against Ibn Saud, who successfully defeated them with the backing of Wahhabi ulama. In the rebellion's aftermath, he centralized his control over the country and reasserted Saudi authority in political affairs. The Saudi wars of expansion came to an end with the establishment of the Kingdom of Saudi Arabia in 1932.

Wahhabism has developed in two different directions since the kingdom was founded. On the one hand, it has become the official religion of a rapidly modernizing Islamic state, bolstered by OIL wealth. Major decisions are made only after consultation with the Supreme Council of the Ulama, who claim the right to issue legal opinions and judgments on the basis of *ijtihad* (independent legal reasoning), rather than legislative law. Family and political ties continue to bind the Al Saud to the Al al-Shaykh, who hold the portfolios for the ministries of religious affairs and justice. In addition, the *mutawwaa* serve the state as religious police, operating as a branch of the Ministry of the Interior. They strictly enforce conformity to the staunch moral conservatism of their sect, including gender segregation, dress codes, the bans on alcohol and gambling, and censorship of books, magazines, television, videos, and music. Religious courts sentence defendants to death who have been found guilty of major moral crimes such as adultery, drug trafficking, and murder. Saudi state Wahhabism is also often criticized for the intolerant attitude it holds for other religions and other forms of Islam.

The second direction that Wahhabism has taken, particularly among the younger generations since the 1970s, is sometimes called neo-Wahhabism, or SALAFISM. It has been shaped by oppositional Islamist ideologies espoused by groups such as the MUSLIM BROTHERHOOD and radical jihadist organizations. Proponents of this type of Wahhabism condemn Saudi government corruption and injustice and seek to radically transform other Muslim societies to bring them under the rule of their concept of the sharia, even through violence. This kind of Wahhabism is epitomized by USAMA BIN LADIN (b. 1957) and AL-QAIDA. Both kinds of Wahhabism have achieved global influence as a result of oil, the print and electronic media, mass education, labor migration, regional and international conflicts, and disenchantment with corrupt and authoritarian governments.

See also ISLAMISM; JIHAD MOVEMENTS; POLITICS AND ISLAM; RENEWAL AND REFORM MOVEMENTS.

Further reading: Michael Cook, "On the Origins of Wahhabism." *Journal of the Royal Asiatic Society* 3, no. 2 (1992): 191–202; Natana J. DeLong-Bas, *Wahhabi Islam: From Revival and Reform to Global Jihad* (Oxford: Oxford University Press, 2004); Joseph A. Kechechian, "The Role of the Ulama in the Politics of an Islamic State: The Case of Saudi Arabia." *International Journal of Middle East Studies* 18 (1986): 53–71; Madawi al-Rasheed, *Contesting the Saudi State: Islamic Voices from a New Generation* (Cambridge: Cambridge University Press, 2007); ———, *A History of Saudi Arabia* (Cambridge: Cambridge University Press, 2002); Ayman al-Yassini, *Religion and State in the Kingdom of Saudi Arabia* (Boulder, Colo.: Westview, 1985).

wahy *See* REVELATION.

walaya

The Arabic word *walaya* comes from a root meaning "to be near." The related concept of *wilaya*, generally referring to guardianship or the AUTHORITY that derives from it, has a range of meanings in Islamic law, politics, Shii cosmology, and SUFISM. *Wilaya* can thus mean legal guardianship, the administration of a province, a province itself, or the sainthood of a Sufi SAINT (*wali*) or a Shii IMAM.

The form *walaya* is often used in Shiism as an alternative vocalization of *wilaya,* to refer to the spiritual authority thought to reside with the Imams, and it is thus closely tied to the question of succession after the death of the prophet MUHAM-MAD, which is the central point on which Shiis differ from Sunnis. Shiis believe that Muhammad designated as his successor his son-and-law and cousin ALI IBN ABI TALIB when he announced at the oasis of Ghadir Khumm: "For whomever I am the authority (MAWLA), Ali is his authority." Thus, for Shiis, the spiritual and political authority of the Muslim community should have passed to Ali. Though political authority was assumed by three CALIPHS before it came to Ali, and after his murder it was claimed by Muawiya and his descendants, Shiis believe spiritual authority, and especially esoteric knowledge of the QURAN, passed directly to Ali, and from him to his sons Hasan and Husayn. *Walaya* then passed to Husayn's son and continued in a line of descent for another eight generations (in the dominant Twelver Shiism). These 12 figures are known as *Imam*s (leaders), who served as representatives of God on earth. The 12th Imam, AL-MAHDI, disappeared leaving no heirs, though he is still thought to maintain a spiritual presence.

Some Shii scholars distinguish between *wilaya* (the authority of the Imams) and *walaya,* which refers to devotion and loyalty to the Imam, which is incumbent on Shiis, and is even considered a pillar of faith.

See also FIVE PILLARS; TWELVE-IMAM SHIISM; *WALI*.

Mark Soileau

Further reading: 'Allamah Sayyid Muhammad Husayn Tabataba'i, *Shi'ite Islam.* Translated by Seyyed Hossein Nasr (Albany: State University of New York Press, 1975); Said Amir Arjomand, *The Shadow of God and the Hidden Imam* (Chicago: University of Chicago Press, 1984); Abdulaziz Abdulhussein Sachedina, *The Just Ruler (al-sultan al-'adil) in Shi'ite Islam: The Comprehen-sive Authority of the Jurist in Imamite Jurisprudence* (New York: Oxford University Press, 1988).

wali

In Arabic, *wali* (plural *awliya*) means someone who is near, a supporter, a guardian, or a friend, but most often refers to a SAINT in the Islamic world. In this sense, the word is often used in the expression *wali ALLAH*—"Friend of God." Saints are found in almost all Islamic countries, but their status as saints is usually not official, since ISLAM has no official process of canonization. Islamic saints are those who are recognized as such by the people, usually because they are considered holy and/or able to perform MIRACLES. They inspire feelings of reverence in people, and their help is sought in times of need. This is true for both living and dead saints.

While there have been examples of WOMEN saints in Islam, the majority have been men. They can be of a number of different types of histori-cal figures: mystics, ascetics, founders of dervish orders, poets, martyrs, warriors, or descendants of the Prophet. Most saints are, however, associated in some way with SUFISM. While their appeal is mostly to common people, Muslim scholars such as al-Tirmidhi, Hujwiri, and IBN AL-ARABI have made them the subject of much study, devising elaborate hierarchies of saints. Saints are thought to be endowed with the blessing (BARAKA) of God, which they can transmit to ordinary humans through contact and which is often thought to be manifested in miraculous acts (*karamat*), such as flying, changing form, multiplying food, healing the sick, and foretelling future events. Legendary accounts of the lives of many saints have been col-lected in hagiographies (*manakib*). While many people believe in the literal truth of such miracles, Sufis often focus on their esoteric meanings. Saints are thought to maintain their power after their DEATHS, inspiring believers to make pilgrim-ages (*ziyarat*) to their graves, where they may ven-erate the saint by praying, circumambulating the tomb, sacrificing ANIMALS, and leaving offerings. Pilgrims seek the saint's blessing, intercession in fulfilling personal requests of God such as healing and fertility, or a mystical experience.

Though some literalist Muslims, influenced by the writings of the jurist TAQI AL-DIN AHMAD IBN TAYMIYYA (d. 1328), are opposed to such veneration on the grounds that Islam does not allow human INTERCESSION between an individual and God, saints throughout the Islam world continue to inspire the admiration of Muslims.

See also MARTYRDOM; MIRACLE; PRAYER; PROPHETS AND PROPHETHOOD; *WALAYA*

Mark Soileau

Further reading: Farid al-Din Attar, *Muslim Saints and Mystics: Episodes from the Tadhkirat al-Auliya* ("Memorial of the Saints"). Translated by A. J. Arberry (New York: Arkana, 1990); Michael Gilsenan, *Saint and Sufi in Modern Egypt: An Essay in the Sociology of Religion* (Oxford: Clarendon Press, 1973); Bernd Radtke and John O'Kane, *The Concept of Sainthood in Early Islamic Mysticism: Two Works by Al-Hakim al-Tirmidhi* (Richmond, U.K.: Curzon Press, 1996); Grace Martin Smith and Carl W. Ernst, *Manifestations of Sainthood in Islam* (Istanbul: Isis Press, 1993).

Webb, Alexander Russell (1846–1916)
American journalist and publisher who was an early spokesman for Islam in the United States

Alexander Russell Webb, one of the earliest known American converts to Islam, was born in Hudson, New York, near the end of the Second Great Awakening, a period of renewed interest in religion, spirituality, and social activism. His father, Alexander Nelson Webb, was a leading journalist of the time. Webb was raised a Presbyterian but found the church uninspiring and left it while still a young man.

Like his father, Webb became a journalist, working for several newspapers in St. Louis, Missouri, including the *Missouri Morning Journal* and the *Missouri Republican*. While in St. Louis, Webb

became involved in the Theosophical Society, a group that worked to promote the study of world religions, including Hinduism, Buddhism, and Zoroastrianism. He developed an interest in spirituality and religions other than Christianity.

In 1887 President Grover Cleveland named Webb the American consul to the Philippines, based in Manila. Although Catholicism was the dominant religion in the Philippines at the time, Webb encountered some Muslim merchants from India and began reading about Islam, including the writings of members of the ALIGARH movement, formed to promote modern EDUCATION among Muslims in India. In 1888 Webb produced a pamphlet in which he declared his conversion to Islam; he adopted the name Mohammed Alexander Russell Webb.

Over the next few years, Webb corresponded with Muslim scholars in India, including Ghulam Ahmad (d. 1908), the leader of the AHMADIYYA Muslims. In 1892 he resigned his position as consul and traveled around India, studying and raising money for an effort to spread Islam in the United States. When he returned to the United States in February 1893, he set up the American Mission in New York, dedicated to spreading knowledge about Islam. The center, which was the first mosque in America, included a library and reading room and offered lectures on Islamic doctrines and customs. He also set up a publishing arm, the Oriental Publishing Company, which published his writings, including his major work, *Islam in America.* In May 1893 he published the first issue of *Moslem World*; designed to "spread the light of Islam in America," it was the earliest Islamic missionary periodical in the United States, lasting only until November 1893.

In September 1893 the World's Parliament of Religions, the first formal gathering of representatives of both Eastern and Western spiritual traditions in the United States, was held in Chicago. Webb gave two speeches at the parliament: "The Influence of Islam upon Social Conditions" and "The Spirit of Islam." Dubbed by the press "the

Yankee Mohammedan," Webb also spoke about Islam in private homes and at public speaking engagements around the country. Webb's mission and publishing center lacked sufficient funding, and, by 1896, he ended the mission and moved to Rutherford, New Jersey, where he again worked as a journalist. In 1901, in recognition of his advocacy of Islam in general and his defense of Turkey in particular, Webb was named honorary Turkish consul to New York. He traveled to Istanbul where Sultan Abdulhamid II (r. 1876–1909) gave him the third Order of Medjidie and the Medal of Merit, as well as the honorific title of Bey. Webb died on October 1, 1916.

See also CONVERSION; *DAAWA*; MOHAMMEDANISM; UNITED STATES.

Kate O'Halloran

Further reading: Umar F. Abd-Allah, *A Muslim in Victorian America: The Life of Alexander Russell Webb* (New York: Oxford University Press, 2006); Mohammed Alexander Russell Webb, *Yankee Muslim: The Asian Travels of Mohammed Alexander Russell Webb* (Rockville, Md.: Wildside Press, 2006); Mohammed Alexander Russell Webb, *Islam in America: A Brief Statement of Mohammedanism and an Outline of the American Islamic Propaganda* (New York: Oriental Publishing, 1893).

West Africa

ISLAM entered West Africa within the first decade after the death of the prophet MUHAMMAD (d. 632), when Muslim armies set out westward from EGYPT. The first ARAB expeditions were launched across the Sahara in the eighth century, although no permanent Muslim presence seems to have been established in sub-Saharan Africa until 200 years later. That presence was brought about through the efforts of Muslim traders, who engaged in business along the lucrative Saharan caravan routes, and who introduced their FAITH to West African businessmen and tribal chiefs.

In the late 11th century, the West African kingdom of Ghana is said to have converted to Islam through the influence of the Berber ALMORAVID DYNASTY. By the 14th century Muslim chiefs ruled over the Kingdom of Mali, the best known of whom, Mansa Musa (r. 1307–32), made the pilgrimage to MECCA in 1324. The rise of Islamic influence in West Africa continued under the Songhay dynasty, which ruled over vast domains centered on the Niger River during the 15th and 16th centuries. The Songhay (Songhai) Empire included TIMBUKTU, known as the "city of scholars," a location renowned throughout the region for Islamic jurisprudence.

By the 18th century, West Africa was impacted by European colonial expansion. European pursuit of raw materials, gold, and slaves stimulated Islamic revival movements that resulted in the "JIHAD states" of West Africa during the 18th and 19th centuries. The leaders of these states emphasized Islamic education and sought to purify society, replacing non-Islamic practices with laws and cultural norms deemed to be more faithful to Islam. During this period, Islam was transformed from the religion of the political and religious elite to becoming the faith of the masses. SUFI orders such as the Qadiriyya and the Tijaniyya were also instrumental in popularizing the Islamic faith by creating a synthesis between African cultural practices and Islamic principles.

Ironically, European colonial rule instituted changes during the late 19th and early 20th centuries that also aided the spread of Islam. The influence of Muslim religious leaders expanded as they gained credibility for their heroic resistance to colonial repression. In addition, the creation of new urban centers consisting of people uprooted from traditional tribal life caused many seekers to turn to Islam for identity and comfort. During the postcolonial era, the MALIKI LEGAL SCHOOL continues to dominate West African Islam and the many Sufi orders are also very influential. Revivalist movements originating in the Middle East have increasingly influenced West Africans. Such influences have frequently heightened tensions with Christian communities in many African states, sometimes leading to interfaith violence. The continent's largest country, Nigeria, has been particularly plagued by conflict between its Christian majority and sizeable Muslim minority population.

As the 21st century opens, West African Muslims face the critical challenges of uniting Muslims from many backgrounds and persuasions, maintaining peaceful coexistence with non-Muslims, and helping their societies overcome crippling problems such as poverty, underdevelopment, and corrupt governments.

See also CHRISTIANITY AND ISLAM; COLONIALISM; EAST AFRICA; MURIDI SUFI ORDER; QADIRI SUFI ORDER; SOKOTO CALIPHATE; UMAR TAL.

Stephen Cory

Further reading: J. F. Ade Ajayi, Michael Crowder, ed., *History of West Africa*. 2 vols. (London: Longman, 1987); Louis Brenner, *Muslim Identity and Social Change in Sub-Saharan Africa* (Bloomington: Indiana University Press, 1993); Peter B. Clark, *West Africa and Islam* (London: Arnold, 1982); Mervyn Hiskett, *The Development of Islam in West Africa* (London: Longman, 1984).

West Bank   *See* PALESTINE.

Westernization

The process of Westernization is generally, although not exclusively, associated with changes as postcolonial and developing nations move from more traditional political, social, and economic systems of organization to models mirroring Western, primarily western European and North American, societies and the institutions that developed there in the 17th, 18th, and 19th centuries. These changes include industrialization, the move toward capitalism, the development of parliamentarianism, the growth of state bureaucracies, and a new, increasingly private role for religion.

Beginning in the late 19th century, Muslim societies experienced heightened interaction with Western powers and ideas, most notably through the latter's colonial activities in the Middle East and North Africa, as well as in South and Southeast Asia. Among other effects of this contact was the initiation of reform efforts in Muslim societies, most notably the Ottoman Empire. Intellectually and politically, Ottoman officials, regional governors, and intellectuals worked to reconcile modern Western ideas of EDUCATION, economics, law, the family, and SCIENCE with an Islamic framework. Many of the same issues with which these figures grappled in the 19th century continue to inform debate today.

Many disputes surrounding the idea and phenomenon of Westernization focus on the origins of its constitutive elements and the degree to which they are transferable to non-Western societies. Some of the most widely felt and passionate debates about the meaning of Westernization and its effects have taken place in societies with majority Muslim populations. In many cases, these debates center on whether or not modernization can be distinguished from Westernization, that is, whether it is possible to integrate modern scientific, religious, political, social, and economic ideas while at the same time protecting aspects of local identities and institutions.

In both IRAN and EGYPT, for example, serious attempts have been made to distinguish technological, military, economic, religious, social, and political changes from outright adherence to Western ideas and norms. The association of many of these ideas and institutions with COLONIALISM and imperialism has inspired strenuous efforts to distinguish modernization from Westernization, with the latter most often tied to the onset of social and moral decay. Modernization, on the other hand, refers to the use of modern science and technologies and is generally accepted by Islamists and other critics of Westernization. In fact, many urban Islamists have a background in the modern natural sciences, reflecting a perceived distinction between the cultural effects of Westernization, generally seen as destructive, and the technological and economic benefits of modernization. Governments, too, have been forced to make this distinction in order to garner legitimacy in the eyes of their citizens.

See also MUSTAFA KEMAL ATATÜRK; RUHOLLAH KHOMEINI; MUHAMMAD MUHAMMAD ALI DYNASTY; SECULARISM.

Further reading: Talal Asad, *Genealogies of Religion* (Baltimore: Johns Hopkins University Press, 1993); 'Abdullah Ahmed Na'im, *Toward an Islamic Reformation* (Syracuse, N.Y.: Syracuse University Press, 1990).

wilayat al-faqih   *See* KHOMEINI, RUHOLLAH.

wine   *See* DIETARY LAWS.

women

The earliest Islamic exemplars for women are the wives, daughters, and women companions of MUHAMMAD (ca. 570–632). The wives of Muhammad, known as "Mothers of the Believers," were witnessed by the two earliest and most authoritative Islamic sources, the QURAN and HADITH. Further, they were significant transmitters of the oral record of Muhammad's life (the hadith) and the experiences of the early Muslim community. The women of his household are "causes of revelation" (*asbab al-nuzul*) in the Quran in several specific contexts: (1) the definition of modesty required of Muhammad's wives is the first use of the term HIJAB (usually translated as "VEIL"), in this instance not meaning a garment but rather a physical barrier or screen between the private women/children's quarters of Muhammad's household and the public areas where non-kin male visitors might approach (Q 33:53); (2) the prescription of casting an outer garment (*jilbab*) over their person when outside the home (Q 33:59); (3) Muhammad's wives are "not like other women" and must keep a higher standard of public modesty, domestic seclusion, voluntary charity, and supereroga-

tory piety (Q 33:28–34); and (4) the case of AISHA BINT ABI BAKR and accusations of sexual misconduct, which became the occasion for the Islamic code of witnesses required for accusations against a woman (Q 24:4–5, 11–20, 23–26). The standards set for Muhammad's household, of Islam's foremost prophet, become the ideal standard for Muslim women thereafter. Expectations regarding modesty, domestic seclusion, and piety based on this household, which later became applied to all Muslim women, are being questioned by modern interpreters of Islamic tradition. Precisely because the standards set for Muhammad's wives were extraordinarily high, and their social situation unlike that of any other Muslim woman, many modern Muslim women have challenged traditional legal interpretations of Islamic sources (the Quran and hadith) and see them as inappropriate legal exemplars for modern Muslim women's behavior. Although adherence to the traditional values of female modesty continues, the precise forms of that adherence vary widely from veiling in diverse forms to "modest dress" (long sleeves/hems, loose clothing), to modesty of behavior and attitude rather than dress.

Aside from the social role and spiritual example of such historical figures as Muhammad's

Turkish women invite American visitors to join them at a park in Istanbul. *(Juan E. Campo)*

wives and daughters and the female saints of the Islamic traditions, women have played an important theological role in Islam. Women of the *ahl al-bayt* ("People of the House" of the Prophet) are sources for sectarian theology in Islam. Although Muhammad had no living sons, his daughter FATIMA (d. 632 C.E.), married to his cousin Ali ibn Abi Talib (d. 661), became the mother of his grandsons, Hasan and Husayn. The claim to prophetic charisma by the Shiat Ali ("Party of Ali") through these grandsons, makes Fatima, called al-Zahra (the "luminous"), and the wives/daughters of the early Shii Imams of central importance to Shii martyrology (based on the drama annually commemorated among the Shia of Imam Husayn's martyrdom at KARBALA in 680 C.E.). The other most significant figure in Islamic theology is MARY, the blessed virgin of Islam. She is the only woman to have a chapter of the Quran named after her (Surat Maryam, Q 19:16–40) and to have important narratives of the quranic text devoted to her role as the mother of JESUS, the last great prophet in Islam before Muhammad (Q 33:33–47).

Muslim women's traditional importance in Islamic society has always been and continues to be the ground and foundation of the Islamic family. Social values strongly reinforce orientation toward marriage and CHILDREN as the normative pattern based on Muhammad's own example. Childrearing and early education and socialization of children are among women's most important tasks in Islamic societies worldwide. Although traditionally excluded from public male dominant institutions of Islamic learning, Muslim women have always been privately involved in study and oral transmission of Islamic source texts (Quran and hadith, narratives about the prophets, etc). In modern times, they have entered into both secular and religious forms of EDUCATION with enthusiasm supporting their long-standing role as family educators and moral exemplars, and as training for professional careers in the workplace outside the home.

Women have also been ritually active in performing the FIVE PILLARS of Islamic practice (witness to FAITH, five daily prayers, fasting during RAMADAN, almsgiving, and pilgrimage to Mecca) and they have been centrally involved in the social and familial aspects of commemorating the two most important festival occasions in the Islamic lunar calendar (the Feast of Sacrifice [ID AL-ADHA] at the closure of HAJJ, and the Feast of Breaking the Fast [ID AL-FITR] at the end of the month of Ramadan. Although discussion of women's ritual lives is brief before modern times, the study of the medieval textual record as well as the growing anthropological and sociological record beginning in the 19th century bear witness to the complexity and fervor of women's devotions whether in the context of formal institutional practice (the Pillars) or in the wide diversity of "popular" or folk practices throughout Muslim lands (folk healing, shrine pilgrimages, etc.). Even those areas that, because of women's unique biology, dictate adaptations or restrictions in ritual practice (such as the requirement to suspend fasting while menstruating and continue it later in the year) are understood by many women as a special challenge and spiritual opportunity, part of their "greater JIHAD," or struggle for the faith.

The most important issues that Muslim women have addressed throughout the 20th century and into the 21st are diverse struggles to maintain Islamic identity while adapting to modernity. Muslim women have struggled to advance women's social, educational, and professional status in Islamic countries throughout the world, and they have struggled to maintain and affirm their Islamic identity in the face of growing secularization and WESTERNIZATION. One of their responses to this struggle has been the re-veiling movement. Veiling has become, perhaps more than any other single issue, the defining "women's question" in the last 40 years. Although unveiling and the adoption of various forms of Western dress among the educated middle and upper classes since the 1930s became a visible benchmark of modernity (along with women's education, right to vote, entering the workplace, etc.), the re-veiling movement, which began in the 1970s, has become a worldwide phenomenon expressing a new response to modernity. It also expresses a transnational form of Islamic feminism that has been marked by the entry of women into all public spheres of Islamic life, including formal religious learning (Quran interpretation) and ritual leadership of the community (as women imams, or leaders of mixed male-female prayer in the mosque). The symbol that had in the past meant public invisibility has become a politicized expression of Islamic identity, which ensures perfect public respectability and supports the entry of Muslim women fully into contemporary public life.

See also ADULTERY; BIRTH RITES: CIRCUMCISION; COMPANIONS OF THE PROPHET; DIVORCE; HOUSES; MERNISSI, FATIMA; RABIA AL-ADAWIYYA; SHAARAWI, HUDA AL-; *ZIYARA*.

Kathleen M. O'Connor

Further reading: Khaled Abou El-Fadl, *Speaking in God's Name: Islamic Law, Authority and Women* (Oxford, U.K.: Oneworld Publications, 2001); Lila Abu-Lughod, *Veiled Sentiments: Honor and Poetry in a Bedouin Society* (Berkeley: University of California Press, 1986); Kamran Scott Aghaie, *The Women of Karbala: Ritual Performance and Symbolic Discourses in Modern Shi'i Islam* (Austin: University of Texas Press, 2005); Leila Ahmed, *Women and Gender in Islam, Historical Roots of a Modern Debate* (New Haven, Conn.: Yale University Press, 1992); Laleh Bakhtiar, *Shariati on Shariati and the Muslim Woman: Who Was Ali Shariati? For Muslim Women: The Islamic Modest Dress, Expectations from the Muslim Woman, Fatima Is Fatima and Guide to Shariati's Collected Works* (Chicago: KAZI Publications, 1996); Asma Barlas, *"Believing Women" in Islam, Unreading Patriarchal Interpretations of the Qur'an* (Austin: University of Texas Press, 2002); Marjo Buitelaar, *Fasting and Feasting in Morocco: Women's Participation in Ramadan* (Oxford, U.K./Providence: Berg, 1993); Miriam Cooke, *Women Claim Islam: Creating Islamic Feminisms through Literature* (New York: Routledge, 2001); Lara Deeb, *An Enchanted Modern: Gender and Public Piety in Shi'i Lebanon* (Princeton, N.J.: Princeton University Press, 2006); Eleanor A. Doumato, *Getting God's Ear: Women, Islam, and Healing in Saudi Arabia and the Gulf* (New York: Columbia University Press, 2000); John L. Esposito with Natana J. DeLong-Bas, *Women in Muslim Family Law*, 2d ed. (Syracuse, N.Y.: Syracuse University Press, 2001); Joyce B. Flueckiger, *In Amma's Healing Room: Gender and Vernacular Islam in South Asia* (Bloomington: Indiana University Press, 2006); Gavin R. G. Hambly, ed., *Women in the Medieval Islamic World: Power, Patronage, and Piety* (New York: St. Martin's Press, 1998); Camille A. Helminski, ed., *Women of Sufism: A Hidden Treasure, Writings and Stories of Mystic Poets, Scholars and Saints* (Boston: Shambhala, 2003); Muhammad H. Kabbani and Laleh Bakhtiar, eds., *Encyclopedia of Muhammad's Women Companions and the Traditions They Related* (Chicago: KAZI Publications, 1998); Beverly B. Mack and Jean Boyd, *One Woman 's Jihad: Nana Asma'u, Scholar and Scribe* (Bloomington: Indiana University Press, 2000); Fedwa Malti-Douglas, *Medicines of the Soul: Female Bodies and Sacred Geographies in a Transnational Islam* (Berkeley: University of California Press, 2001, and online); Sachiko Murata, *The Tao of Islam: A Sourcebook on Gender Relationships in Islamic Thought* (Albany: State University of New York Press, 1992); Mohammad Akram Nadwi, *al-Muhaddithat: The Women Scholars of Islam* (Oxford, U.K.: Interface Publications, 2007); Catharina Raudvere, *The Book and the Roses: Sufi Women, Visibility, and Zikir in Contemporary Istanbul* (London: I.B. Tauris, 2003); Denise A. Spellberg, *Politics, Gender, and the Islamic Past: The Legacy of 'A'isha bint Abi Bakr* (New York: Columbia University Press, 1994); Barbara F. Stowasser, *Women in the Qur'an, Traditions, and Interpretation* (New York: Oxford University Press, 1994, and online); Pieternella van Doorn-Harder, *Women Shaping Islam: Reading the Qur'an in Indonesia* (Champaign: University of Illinois Press, 2006); Aminah Wadud, *Inside the Gender Jihad: Women's Reform in Islam* (Oxford, U.K.: Oneworld Publications, 2006); Mai Yamani, ed., *Feminism and Islam: Legal and Literary Perspectives* (New York: New York University Press, 1996); Sherifa Zuhur, *Revealing Reveiling: Islamist Gender Ideology in Contemporary Egypt* (Albany: State University of New York Press, 1992).

World Muslim Congress (World Islamic Congress)

The World Muslim Congress (WMC, *Mutamar al-Alam al-Islami*), established for the purpose of world peace and unity among Muslims, emerged following its first conference in 1926 after being founded by a group of distinguished leaders from the World of Islam gathering in MECCA and hosted by King ABD AL-AZIZ IBN SAUD of SAUDI ARABIA. In 1931 the WMC became further institutionalized when rules and regulations were created and approved by its second International Islamic Conference in Jerusalem, convened by AMIN AL-HUSAYNI, Grand Mufti of JERUSALEM, to secure foreign Muslim support for the ARAB struggle against the British Mandate and Zionism. Following the creation of PAKISTAN, a majority Muslim state, on August 14, 1947, prominent members of the World of Islam gathered once again in order to revive the WMC. The partitions of both INDIA and PALESTINE and aims to promote solidarity among Pakistanis and Arab Muslims against INDIA and ISRAEL provided the impetus for this revival, which was achieved in February 1949 at the third WMC in the capital of Pakistan at the time, Karachi. The revitalization continued during a larger, fourth conference, held in Karachi in February 1951 when cooperation among Muslim countries and citizens became a focal point of the organization under the leadership of its president, Amin al-Husayni. In 1962 a fifth conference was held in BAGHDAD in which members agreed upon a constitution, set up committees, and established regional branches for the WMC.

The WMC currently represents one of the oldest international nongovernmental Muslim organizations. Since its establishment in 1926 the organization has succeeded in founding a World Muslim News Agency and an International Muslim Development Bank as part of its drive for unity. Additionally, the organization has supported Muslims worldwide, such as Filipino and Bosnian Muslims, as well as other causes such as KASHMIR and Palestine. In 1987 the organization witnessed two milestone moments with the completion of its headquarter complex in Karachi and the receipt of Japan's notable Niwano Peace Prize. It was also awarded the Templeton Foundation Award. Currently, the WMC maintains its base in Karachi in addition to holding offices in Geneva, Jeddah, and Vienna. The organization possesses consultative status with the UN through its Economic and Social Council (ECOSOC) and the United Nations Children's Fund (UNICEF) and it also maintains observer status with the ORGANIZATION OF THE ISLAMIC CONFERENCE (OIC) based in Jeddah.

See also ARAB-ISRAELI CONFLICTS; ARAB LEAGUE; PAN-ISLAMISM; POLITICS AND ISLAM.

Fahad A. Alhomoudi

Further reading: Anita L. P. Burdett, *Islamic Movements in the Arab World, 1913–1966.* 4 vols. (Slough, England: Archive, 1998); Martin Kramer, *Islam Assembled: The Advent of the Muslim Congresses* (New York: Columbia University Press, 1985).

writing *See* ALPHABET; BOOKS AND BOOKMAKING; CALLIGRAPHY.

wudu *See* ABLUTION.

wuquf *See* ARAFAT; HAJJ.

Y

Yahya *See* JOHN THE BAPTIST.

Yathrib *See* MEDINA.

Yemen

Since the pre-Islamic era, Yemen (*al-Yaman*) has been defined as the southwestern part of the Arabian Peninsula; it has acquired a progressively narrower geographical definition in modern times. Since 1992 historical boundaries have come substantially within the Republic of Yemen, which resulted from the unification of the People's Democratic Republic of South Yemen and the Yemen Arab Republic. Yemen borders the Arabian Sea, Gulf of Aden, and Red Sea, between OMAN and SAUDI ARABIA, thus occupying a strategic location on one of the world's most active shipping lanes. It is one of the poorest countries in the ARAB world, with its economic fortunes mostly dependent upon oil reserves. Yemen has a total area of 527,970 square kilometers, nearly twice the size of the state of Nevada, and although mostly desert, possesses a varied terrain and climate, which supports agriculture in the temperate mountainous region. These conditions have proven ideal for the cultivation of coffee, fruits, nuts, and the mildly narcotic *qat* plant.

Unlike other inhabitants of the Arabian Peninsula who have historically been nomadic or semi-nomadic, Yemenis have led a mostly sedentary existence in small villages and towns scattered throughout the highlands and coastal regions. Yemen's population of 23 million (2008) is predominantly Arab, with some Afro-Arab and South Asian ethnic minorities. The national language is Arabic, spoken in several regional dialects, and Yemen is considered to be a homeland of the South-Semitic branch of languages. Accounting for approximately half the total population, the north and northwest are chiefly ZAYDI SHIA by religious persuasion, with small minorities adhering to ISMAILI SHIISM and Judaism; however, SUNNISM of the SHAFII LEGAL SCHOOL has been making its mark on the capital city of Sanaa since the 1970s. The Shafii school is predominant in the south and southeast, with a renowned center of scholarship in the city of Tarim; SUFISM has also been simultaneously prevalent in this region. In recent history, Islamic RENEWAL AND REFORM MOVEMENTS have exercised a considerable influence upon religious attitudes throughout the country, especially under the auspices of the Islah political party.

Traditionally, Yemeni towns were contained within the territory of an individual tribe (*qabila*), with the exception of Sanaa, the population of which distinguished itself by the greater significance it attached to adherence of the SHARIA. Tribal divisions and subdivisions are headed by a SHAYKH, who, as arbiter of customary law and intertribal relations, continues to be recognized as an official mediator by the Republic of Yemen. Especially in the north and northwest, this social structure overlaps with a system of social ranks, composed of status groups graded according to ancestry and professional activity. Until the emergence of the modern state, the descendants of the Prophet (SAYYID) including the Zaydi IMAM, took their place at the top of the hierarchical order. This social order has been weakened by such factors as the founding of a republican regime, increased social mobility, and urbanization.

Yemen is one of the oldest centers of civilization in the Middle East. Between the ninth century B.C.E. and the sixth century C.E., it formed part of the kingdoms of Minaea, Saba, Himyar, Qataban, Hadramawt, and Awsan, which controlled the lucrative spice trade. It was known to Romans as Arabia Felix because of the riches its trade generated; Caesar Augustus attempted to annex it in 24 B.C.E., but the expedition failed. Persian and Abyssinian kings were more successful and Yemen was incorporated into the Sassanid and Abyssinian empires in the sixth and early seventh centuries C.E. The attempt of Abraha, the Abyssinian governor of Yemen, to conquer MECCA in the renowned "year of the Elephant" (570), was memorialized in the QURAN. Muslim historians have traditionally asserted that, in 628, Badhan, the Sassanid governor of Sanaa, embraced Islam and the whole country immediately followed suit. However, modern historians argue that Islamization proceeded over at least three centuries, beginning when CALIPHS exerted their control over Yemen through official representatives, such as governors and judges. During the era of the Rightly Guided Caliphs, Yemen provided the vast majority of manpower for the Islamic conquests. With the breakup of the ABBASID CALIPHATE after the 10th century, Yemen came under the control of the imams of various Zaydi dynasties, who established a theocratic political structure that survived until modern times.

Zaydi dominance was interrupted during the 11th and 12th centuries by the Sunni Ayyubid and Rasulid dynasties of EGYPT, who controlled much of southern Yemen. By the end of the 16th century and again in the 19th century, Yemen fell under the rule of the Ottoman Empire, while facing intermittent resistance from Zaydi forces. Northern Yemen became independent of the Ottoman Empire in 1918, and the Yemen Arab Republic was formed in 1962. Notable literary and political figure Muhammad Mahmud al-Zubayri (d. 1965) championed the cause of Yemeni independence, and he continues to be regarded as a national hero. The British, who had occupied the southern port city of Aden since 1839, withdrew in 1967 from what became the People's Democratic Republic of South Yemen, which officially subscribed to communism in 1970. The two countries were formally united as the Republic of Yemen on May 22, 1990. A southern-based and Saudi-supported secessionist movement was quickly subdued in 1994 by forces loyal to President Ali Abdullah Salih (b. 1942). The bombing of the USS *Cole* in 2000 and the 2002 attack on the French oil tanker *Limburg* have drawn attention to the activities of alleged AL-QAIDA associates in Yemen, and recent Zaydi rebel attacks have occurred in the northwest.

See also ARABIC LANGUAGE AND LITERATURE; IMAM; SHAFII LEGAL SCHOOL; ZAYDI SHIISM.

Gregory Mack

Further reading: Robert D. Burrowes, *Historical Dictionary of Yemen* (Lanham, Md.: Scarecrow Press, 1995); Werner Daum, ed., *Yemen: 3000 Years of Art and Civilization* (Innsbruck and Frankfurt am Main: Pinguin-Verlag, 1988); Paul Dresch, *A History of Modern Yemen* (New York: Cambridge University Press, 2000); Brinkley M. Messick, *The Calligraphic State* (Berkeley: University of California Press, 1993).

Yunus Emre (late 13th to early 14th centuries) *Turkish mystical poet*

Yunus Emre is perhaps the most well-known Turkish poet, not only because he was the first major representative of Anatolian Turkish poetry, but also because of the sheer beauty and sincerity of his poems, and the continuing relevance they have today.

Little historical information exists on the life of Yunus Emre, though a note on a manuscript collection of his poetry suggests that he died in 1320 or 1321. This places him during the turbulent period after Mongol invasions had weakened the Seljuk Empire and Turkish principalities were vying for control over various parts of Anatolia. Several places in TURKEY claim to have been the birthplace of Yunus, and even more claim to bear his grave; it is likely that this is due to his immense popularity and to the existence of other poets going by the name Yunus and writing in his style, which also complicates attributing specific poems to him. Bektashis consider him to have been a Bektashi, but he is also respected by most other DERVISH orders in Turkey. His poetry includes references to Tapduk Emre as his spiritual master.

Yunus Emre's poems have been collected in a *Divan,* though the various manuscripts show discrepancies in their content. He is also the author of a poetic work entitled *Risalat al-nushiyya,* which is dated to 1307–08. The language of his poems is generally simple and close to that of the common people. Motifs are drawn from nature and from classical Sufi poetry, and themes include the poet's relationship with God (the Friend), the transitoriness of life, and especially mystical love. Most of his poems, because of their form and mystical content, are considered *ilahi*s (mystical hymns), and many have been sung in the ceremonies of dervish orders. A well-known example of Yunus's poetry is translated here in part by Talat Halman:

> I am not at this place to dwell,
> I arrived here just to depart.
> I'm a well-stocked peddler, I sell
> To all those who'll buy from my mart.
>
> I am not here on earth for strife,
> Love is the mission of my life.
> Hearts are the home of the loved one;
> I came here to build each true heart.
>
> My madness is love for the Friend,
> Lovers know what my hopes portend;
> For me duality must end:
> God and I must not live apart.

As the first major Turkish poet, Yunus Emre influenced later poets writing in that language, and he laid the foundation for the development of Turkish mystical poetry. He continues to inspire modern Turkish poets today, and his hymns continue to be read and recited and to be sung in the ceremonies of almost all dervish orders in Turkey. Yunus has served as the subject of films, plays, and an oratorio, and he is commemorated annually in festivals.

See also BEKTASHI SUFI ORDER; MUSIC; SELJUK DYNASTY; TURKISH LANGUAGE AND LITERATURE.

Mark Soileau

Further reading: Talat Halman, ed., *Yunus Emre and His Mystical Poetry* (Bloomington: Indiana University Turkish Studies, 1981); Grace Martin Smith, *The Poetry of Yunus Emre, a Turkish Sufi Poet* (Berkeley and Los Angeles, University of California Press, 1993).

Yusuf   *See* JOSEPH.

Z

zahir *See* BATIN; TAFSIR.

zakat *See* ALMSGIVING.

Zamzam

A feature of many sacred places and pilgrimage centers is the water source. Practically, it provides water for the people and ANIMALS who reside in or frequent the site. However, the water from this source is also used in ritual activity, such as performing ABLUTIONS and other purification rites. Often, its significance is woven into the mythology and sacred history of the site. For Muslims the most sacred water source is the well known as Zamzam. It is situated within the courtyard of the Sacred Mosque in MECCA, near the corner of the KAABA, which contains the BLACK STONE. Pilgrims performing the HAJJ and UMRA (the lesser pilgrimage) customarily drink water from the well, although this is not a required part of pilgrimage rituals. Those who do that believe the water is full of blessings (BARAKA) and has healing power. Many take vials of Zamzam water home with them, or they soak cloth in it that will be used as burial shrouds. It is also mixed with

rosewater and used in the ritual cleansing of the Kaaba twice each year, during RAMADAN and during the hajj season.

The source of the water for Zamzam is subterranean runoff from the sporadic rains that come between October and March. Since Mecca is located at the low point of a narrow valley, water collects in the aquifer about 90 feet below the surface that feeds the well through springs. Without this vital source, and other wells in the area, the town would not have flourished through the centuries as it has. Zamzam's importance, however, is also recognized and magnified in Islamic traditional literature. Although never mentioned in the QURAN, other early Islamic lore, such as Ibn Ishaq's *Sira,* an early BIOGRAPHY of MUHAMMAD (written in the eighth century), explains that the well originated in the days of ABRAHAM, when he left HAGAR and Ishmael, his wife and son, there. (He would later return to join his son in building the Kaaba.) Ishmael, perhaps an infant at the time, thirsted for water. Hagar left him and went to search of it, praying and running in desperation—an event commemorated whenever pilgrims "run" between the hills of Safa and Marwa next to the Sacred Mosque during the hajj and *umra.* At last Hagar's prayers were answered and the water came forth from the earth beneath her son. Some accounts say that it was the ANGEL GABRIEL who actually opened the well head. In time, the well fell into disuse and was forgotten. According to Muslim accounts, Zamzam was rediscovered by Muhammad's grandfather, Abd al-Muttalib, who found precious golden objects and weapons in it. These were removed and the well was reopened for use by pilgrims. Providing water and food to pilgrims, a prestigious service, remained the monopoly of Muhammad's family for generations thereafter. In later centuries it became a lucrative business for the Zamzamis, a class of water carriers who served the needs of pilgrims.

Today Zamzam is no longer a well in the traditional meaning of the word. The government of SAUDI ARABIA has been engaged in significant renovation and expansion projects throughout the Haram area, including Zamzam. It has installed pumps, filtering systems, and public taps to make sure that Zamzam water is potable and that it is readily available to the millions of pilgrims who come to Mecca each year. Zamzam water is bottled and distributed to pilgrims, and there are even free Zamzam water dispensers and public faucets at convenient locations in and around the Sacred Mosque. To monitor these efforts and help conserve the water supply, a Zamzam Studies and Research Center was recently created under royal decree within the Saudi Geological Survey.

Zamzam has also taken on modern commercial and political significance. In 2002 an Iranian soft drink company began to market a beverage called Zamzam Cola. It became a popular drink that year, especially among pilgrims in Mecca, as an alternative to Pepsi and Coca-Cola. At the time, many Muslims boycotted these drinks to protest Israeli attacks against Palestinians and the anticipated U.S. and British invasion of IRAQ, which occurred in March 2003. In Saudi Arabia, the government consulted with religious authorities and decided to ban the import of the drink because it felt that the commercial use of the

name zamzam was improper. The Iranian company continues to produce the beverage, however, and has distributed it as far away as Great Britain.

Further reading: G. R. Hawting, "The Disappearance and Rediscovery of Zamzam and the Well of Mecca," *Bulletin of the Society of Oriental and African Studies* 43 (1980): 44–54; Muhammad ibn Ishaq, *The Life of Muhammad: A Translation of Ibn Ishaq's Sirat Rasul Allah.* Translated by Alfred Guillaume (Oxford: Oxford University Press, 1955); F. E. Peters, *The Hajj: The Muslim Pilgrimage to Mecca and the Holy Places* (Princeton, N.J.: Princeton University Press, 1994).

Zaydi Shiism

Also known as Fiver Shiism, the Zaydi tradition of SHIISM is today found mainly in YEMEN, where Zaydis are estimated to be about 36 percent of the population (Yemen's total population was estimated at 23 million in 2008). In keeping with other branches of Shiism, it traces its heritage to the AHL AL-BAYT—the household of the prophet Muhammad (ca. 570–632). Its name is derived from that of Zayd ibn Ali (d. 740), the son of Ali Zayn al-Abidin (d. 714) and grandson of HUSAYN IBN ALI, who was killed at Karbala in 680. According to Zaydi doctrine he is the fifth Imam, instead of Muhammad al-Baqir (d. 731), who is considered to be the fifth in TWELVE-IMAM SHIISM. Known for his religious knowledge, Zayd became embroiled in anti-Umayyad politics, and he was considered by his followers to be a Shii IMAM because of his descent and because he led a revolt against the Umayyads. He received only nominal support from other Shii factions in Arabia and Iraq, partly because he refused to condemn ABU BAKR (r. 632–634) and UMAR IBN AL-KHATTAB (r. 634–644), the first two caliphs. Zayd was killed by Umayyad troops in a skirmish in Kufa in 740. The Syrians dismembered his body—the head was presented to the CALIPH in Damascus and the body was crucified, then later burned and the ashes thrown into the Euphrates. His movement, however, did not die.

Zaydi missionaries succeeded in winning converts in the Caucasus region, near the Caspian Sea, where two rival branches of the sect became established: the Qasimis (named after al-Qasim ibn Ibrahim, d. 860) and the Nasiris (named after al-Hasan ibn Ali al-Nasir li'l-Haqq, d. 917). The founders of these groups had both been successful Zaydi missionaries, respected for their knowledge of the religious sciences and law. Only some of the later leaders of these communities felt qualified to call themselves Imams, however. Those who fell short in these qualifications were known as "inviters" (sing. *dai*) and "commanders" (sing. *amir*). During the 12th century, Zaydi influence declined due to factionalism and the rise of ISMAILI SHIISM. Nevertheless, a Zaydi presence survived in the Caucasus area until the 16th century, when the last remnants converted to Twelve-Imam Shiism.

Zaydi Shiism has had a longer history in Yemen. It was first brought there from the Caucasus region by al-Hadi ila al-Haqq al-Mubin (the Guide to Clear Truth, d. 911), the grandson of al-Qasim ibn Ibrahim. Al-Hadi won the loyalty of tribal groups in the vicinity of the city of Saada, which is still the center of Zaydi Shiism. He and his heirs were buried in the city's main mosque. Several Zaydi sects appeared, differing over leadership and theological issues. The popularity of SUFISM in 14th-century Yemen forced the Zaydis to define their views toward this other expression of Islamic devotion and piety. Most of their leaders attacked Sufism because they thought it ran counter to the SHARIA; they also did not like anti-Shii views held by the Sufis. Later, Sufi support for Ottoman rule in Yemen led to further animosities. Nevertheless, in the 17th century the Zaydi Imams became powerful enough to establish a dynasty, known as the Qasimis, who ruled Yemen intermittently from 1650 to 1962, depending on their strength.

Even though the Zaydis call their leaders Imams, their concepts of legitimate AUTHORITY have tended to be closer to those of the Sunnis than to those of the Twelve-Imam Shia and the Ismailis. Zaydi Imams claim descent from Muhammad through Ali and Fatima, but they acquire their position by their abilities, instead of being designated by their predecessors, and they do not claim infallibility or secret knowledge. They recognize the legitimacy of the first caliphs and their tradition of law resembles that of the Sunnis, especially Shafii FIQH in later centuries. On the other hand, Zaydis have generally followed, after some disputation, the theological views of the MUTAZILI SCHOOL, including belief in God's oneness and justice, human free will, and denial of ANTHROPOMORPHISM.

See also DAAWA; UMAYYAD CALIPHATE.

Further reading: Heinz Halm, *Shiism*. Translated by Janet Watson (Edinburgh: University of Edinburgh Press, 1992); Wilferd Madelung, *Religious Schools and Sects in Medieval Islam* (London: Varirum Reprints, 1985); Brinkley Messick, *The Calligraphic State: Textual Domination and History in a Muslim Society* (Berkeley: University of California Press, 1996); G. vom Bruck, "The Zaydi Sadah of the Yemen: The Temporalities of Religious Tradition," *Oriente Moderno* 18 (1999): 393–411.

Zaynab bint Ali ibn Abi Talib (627–682)
granddaughter of Muhammad widely venerated by Shii Muslims

Commonly known as Sayyida (or Sitt) Zaynab, Zaynab bint Ali ibn Abi Talib was the granddaughter of MUHAMMAD and, as a witness to the Battle of KARBALA, played a seminal role in the history and development of SHIISM. She is now an important role model for many Shii Muslims (especially women) in both their political and their personal lives.

Sayyida Zaynab was born to FATIMA, the daughter of Muhammad, in Medina in 627. Her father Ali became the fourth CALIPH (r. 656–661) after Muhammad's death and is considered by

Shii Muslims as the first Imam. Sayyida Zaynab's brothers Hasan and Husayn met violent deaths like their father and are recognized as the second and third Imams, respectively. At an unknown age she married Abd Allah ibn Jaafar, with whom she had five children.

The most significant event in Sayyida Zaynab's life was certainly her presence in 680 at the Battle of KARBALA, in present day IRAQ, where a much larger Umayyad army overwhelmed Husayn's forces. As the sole surviving adult, Sayyida Zaynab was transported, along with the head of Husayn, first to Kufa and then to DAMASCUS, where the caliph Yazid I (r. 680–683) made them examples of the fate of rebels. Sayyida Zaynab is remembered for having publicly and eloquently defended the honor of Husayn, his companions, and AHL AL-BAYT (Muhammad's family) generally, in front of her captors. Sources say that upon returning to MEDINA, she educated the nascent Shii community about what happened at Karbala and led them until the fourth Imam, Ali ibn Husayn Zayn al-Abidin (658–713), matured. She also is remembered for having initiated many of the rituals that are now part of the annual commemoration of Husayn's MARTYRDOM known as ASHURA, which occurs in Muharram, the first month of the Islamic calendar.

There is some dispute about Sayyida Zaynab's final resting place. Both CAIRO and Damascus are home to large shrines in her name that host pilgrims and tourists from all over the Muslim world. Pilgrims often appeal to Sayyida Zaynab to intercede with God on their behalf. They hope that as a woman who suffered much in her life she will understand their suffering and help them with issues ranging from business matters to illnesses to efforts to become pregnant.

Each year Sayyida Zaynab's MAWLID festival in Cairo draws tens of thousands of Sunni and Shii Muslims. This stands in contrast to her Damascus shrine, which is more dominantly Shii and shows significant Iranian influence both architecturally and in the population it attracts. Since the late 1970s, Sayyida Zaynab has become an important figure for political activists, especially in IRAN and LEBANON. The patience, piety, and forthrightness in the face of oppression that she exhibited during her life are seen by many as ideal characteristics for a modern Shii woman seeking to live a truly Islamic life.

See also HUSAYN IBN ALI; INTERCESSION; SAINT; WOMEN; *ZIYARA*.

Michelle Zimney

Further reading: Kamran Scot Aghaie, ed., *The Women of Karbala: Ritual Performance and Symbolic Discourses in Modern Shii Islam* (Austin: University of Texas Press, 2005); Lara Deeb, *An Enchanted Modern: Gender and Public Piety in Lebanon,* (Princeton, N.J.: Princeton University Press, 2006).

Zaytuna Mosque

The oldest and largest MOSQUE in Tunis, TUNISIA, the Zaytuna was completed by the Aghlabid amir Ibrahim bin Ahmad in the 860s, building upon the site of an earlier Umayyad mosque constructed in 732. Building materials, including some 200 marbled columns, were taken from the nearby ruins of Carthage. Over the centuries, the mosque was expanded by the Zirids, who built the galleries, the crypt, and the dome in the 10th century; the Hafsids, who constructed the library in the 15th century; and the Ottomans, who built the current minaret in the 19th century.

The Zaytuna mosque served as the central structure in the old medina of Tunis, around which SUQS and guild-shops were constructed. The mosque included a UNIVERSITY, which provided an advanced EDUCATION in the religious sciences and related subjects by some of the leading local ULAMA. Many well-known scholars and administrators of the premodern era studied at the Zaytuna, which became a focal point of debate between Westernizing reformers and traditional ulama in the 19th century. With the establishment of the French protectorate in 1881, the Zaytuna experienced STUDENT unrest and repeated demands for reform. Following Tunisian independence in 1956, the Zaytuna became part of the Tunisian public education system and its library was integrated into the National Libraries of Tunisia.

See also WESTERNIZATION.

Stephen Cory

Further reading: Robert Brunschvig, *La Berbérie orientale sous les Hafsides des origins á la fin du XVe siècle* (Paris: Adrien Maisonneuve, 1940–1947); Ahmad Fikri, *Masdjid al-Zaytuna, al-djami' fi Tunis* (Cairo: 1953); Muhammad b. 'Uthman al-Hasha'ishi, *Djami' al-Zaytuna* (Tunis: 1974); Georges Marçais, *L'architecture musulmane d'Occident: Tunisie, Algérie, Maroc, Espagne et Sicilei* (Paris: Gouvernement Général de l'Algérie, 1955).

zikr   *See* DHIKR.

zina   *See* ADULTERY.

ziyara (Arabic; Persian and Urdu: *ziyarat*)

Pilgrimages are religious journeys to holy places that involve encounters with supramundane beings, such as a god, saint, ancestor, relic, or another sort of spiritual being. They also bring people, many of them strangers, into relationship with each other. Pilgrimage traditions exist in many of the world's cultures and religion. In addition to Islam, they also have been an important part of religious life for the followers of the Christian, Hindu, and Buddhist religions, in which pilgrimages are made to hundreds of holy sites by millions of people each year.

One of the major forms of pilgrimage in Muslim lands is the *ziyara,* which in Arabic literally means "visit" and "visitation." Islamic law requires that all Muslims who are able perform the HAJJ pilgrimage at least once in their lives to MECCA. This is one of Islam's FIVE PILLARS. The UMRA, or lesser pilgrimage to Mecca, is one that is recommended, but not required. These two pilgrimages are accepted by all of the Muslim legal schools. *Ziyara* is the term usually used for voluntary pilgrimages to other Muslim shrines. They are very popular and are found, with a few important exceptions, in all Muslim communities. Like Mecca, these other sites are focal points of BARAKA (blessing and grace) where communications between humans and the divine are believed to be especially effective. Unlike Mecca, however, shrines are sacred because they are believed to contain the physical remains or relics of a holy man or woman. Some *ziyara* shrines are transregional, drawing pilgrims from near and far, others are more local. Pilgrims frequent these sites for many reasons—in quest of a cure, fertility, forgiveness, consolation, success in business or school, resolution of a dispute, fulfillment of a vow, participation in Sufi devotions and *dhikrs,* or joining with others in a carnivalesque celebration of the holy person's anniversary (MAWLID or urs). Key ritual activities performed during shrine pilgrimages include decoration of the tomb with flowers, lights, pictures, calligraphy, and cloth coverings, circumambulation of the tomb, touching and kissing the tomb, votive offerings, formal PRAYER (*salat*) and voluntary petitions (*dua*), Quran recitation, ceremonial processions, animal sacrifice, distribution of food, and ALMSGIVING. Other activities that may be found include musical performances, *dhikrs,* and circumcisions. Pilgrims include a cross-section of society, including many women. Where it is possible, such as sites in INDIA and EGYPT, non-Muslims also join in, either as pilgrims, local celebrants, or vendors.

The sacred *ziyara* site par excellence for Muslims is the mosque-tomb of Muhammad in MEDINA. Although it is not part of the hajj, visiting the Prophet's mosque and praying there is considered to be highly meritorious before or after performing the hajj or *umra.* Indeed, according to an oft-quoted hadith, Muhammad promised, "Whoever visits my grave (or house), deserves

Pilgrims visit the tomb of the wife of the Chishti saint Bakhtiar Kaki in Mehrauli, New Delhi, India. *(Juan E. Campo)*

my intercession." The high esteem in which this pilgrimage is held is also reflected in the murals painted on the houses of Egyptian pilgrims, which often display images of Muhammad's mosque in Medina next to images of the KAABA in Mecca. Another major pilgrimage shrine connected with Muhammad is the Noble Sanctuary in JERUSALEM, where he is believed to have traveled during his NIGHT JOURNEY AND ASCENT.

There are literally hundreds of other pilgrimage shrine sites connected with prophets and saints (known as *walis*). Some of these have ancient pre-Islamic origins, but most began to noticeably appear in Muslim communities only between the 13th and 15th centuries, with some developing as recently as the late 20th century. Many of the most prominent are identified with descendants of Muhammad's family, the AHL AL-BAYT. These include the tombs of HUSAYN IBN ALI, Zaynab, and Nafisa in Cairo. The most important shrines visited by the Shia are those of the Imams and their descendants, especially ALI IBN ABI TALIB in Najaf (Iraq), Husayn in KARBALA, the Kazimayn (the seventh and ninth Imams Musa al-Kazim and Muhammad al-Taqi) in a north Baghdad suburb, Ali al-Hadi and Hasan al-Askari (the 10th and 11th Imams) in Samarra (Iraq), al-Rida (or Reza, the eighth Imam) in Mashhad (Iran), and his sister Fatima in Qumm. In recent years the shrine of ZAYNAB BINT ALI IBN ABI TALIB, in Damascus has attracted large numbers of Shii pilgrims. Major pilgrimage shrines connected with Sufi saints include those of Mum al-Din Chishti in AJMER (India), Baba Farid al-Din Ganjshakar in Pakpattan (Pakistan), Hajji Bektash and JALAL AL-DIN RUMI in Turkey, AHMAD AL-BADAWI in Tanta (Egypt), and Moulay Idris in Morocco. The shrine of Sunan Giri, also known Raden Paku, a legendary warrior saint who is known for having won many converts, is one of the major pilgrimage sites in INDONESIA.

Although *ziyara* has become a widely accepted practice among the Shia, its acceptability as a religious practice has been debated by Sunni Muslims for centuries. Many of the ULAMA and Sufis have approved it, or at least said it was permissible. Those who favored a strict interpretation of the Quran and the sunna believed that it was a form of BIDAA (innovation) and should be avoided or forbidden. Critics also say that it is a form of IDOLATRY (*SHIRK*). Among the foremost proponents of this opinion in the medieval era was Taqi al-Din IBN TAYMIYYA (d. 1328). His views were revived in the puritanical reformism of MUHAMMAD IBN ABD AL-WAHHAB (d. 1792) and the Wahhabi brand of Islam that swept through the Arabian Peninsula in the 18th century and then was established as the reigning Islamic ideology of the Kingdom of SAUDI ARABIA in the 20th. Wahhabi warriors led a raid in 1801 on Karbala in southern Iraq, killing several thousand and desecrating the shrine of Husayn. In 1804 they plundered the mosque of Muhammad in Medina and prevented pilgrims from visiting it. When they retook Medina in 1925 they destroyed hundreds of shrines belonging to members of Muhammad's family, his Companions, and prominent scholars. Today the only pilgrims allowed into the country are those who are going for hajj or *umra.* Outside of Saudi Arabia, shrine visitation is opposed by Muslims who have been influenced by Wahhabi teachings, by reform-minded Muslims, and by some secularized Muslims who see such practices as antiquated. Nevertheless, for many Muslims, visiting the shrines of the holy dead remains an important part of their religious life.

See also DHIKR; INTERCESSION; MIRACLE; SAINT; WALI.

Further reading: Anne H. Betteridge, "Muslim Women and Shrines in Shiraz." In *Everyday Life in the Muslim Middle East.* 2d ed., edited by Donna Lee Bowen and Evelyn A. Early, 276–289 (Bloomington: Indiana University Press, 2002); P. M. Currie, *The Shrine and Cult of Muin al-Din Chishti of Ajmer* (Oxford: Oxford University Press, 2007); Muhammad Umar Memon, *Ibn Taymiya's Struggle against Popular Religion* (The Hague: Mouton, 1976); Yitzhak Nakash, *The Shiis of Iraq* (Princeton, N.J.: Princeton University Press, 1994), 163–184; Christopher S. Taylor, *In the Vicinity of the Righteous: Ziyara and the Veneration of Muslim Saints in Late Medieval Egypt* (Leiden: E.J. Brill, 1999).

zuhd   *See* ASCETICISM.

BIBLIOGRAPHY

I. General Reference Works and Atlases

Esposito, John, ed. *Oxford Encyclopedia of the Modern Islamic World*. 4 vols. Oxford: Oxford University Press, 1995.

Gibb, H. A. R. et al., eds. *Encyclopaedia of Islam*. 2d ed. Leiden, Netherlands: E.J. Brill, 1960–2004.

Gibb, H. A. R. et al., eds. *Shorter Encyclopaedia of Islam*. Leiden, Netherlands: E.J. Brill, 1953.

Joseph, Suad, ed. *Encyclopedia of Women and Islamic Cultures*. 5 vols. Leiden, Netherlands: E.J. Brill, 2006.

Kennedy, Hugh, ed. *An Historical Atlas of Islam*. 2d ed. Leiden, Netherlands: E.J. Brill, 2002.

Martin, Richard C., ed. *Encyclopedia of Islam and the Muslim World*. 2 vols. New York: Macmillan Reference, 2004.

McAuliffe, Jane Dammen, ed. *Encyclopaedia of the Quran*. 5 vols. Leiden, Netherlands: E.J. Brill, 2001–06.

Nanji, Azim A., ed. *The Muslim Almanac: A Reference Work for the History, Faith, Culture and Peoples of Islam*. Detroit: Gail Research, 1996.

Newby, Gordon D. *A Concise Encyclopedia of Islam*. Oxford: Oneworld, 2002.

Nicolle, David. *Historical Atlas of the Islamic World*. New York: Checkmark Books, 2003.

Robinson, Francis. *Atlas of the Islamic World since 1500*. New York: Facts On File, 1982.

Ruthven, Malise, and Azim Nanji. *Historical Atlas of Islam*. Cambridge, Mass.: Harvard University Press, 2004.

II. The Quran

The leading English translations of the the Quran are: M.A.S. Abdel Haleem, *The Quran* (Oxford: Oxford University Press, 2005); Abdullah Yusuf Ali, *The Holy Quran* (Brentwood, Md.: Amana Corp., 1987); Ahmed Ali, *Al-Quran: A Contemporary Translation* (Princeton, N.J.: Princeton University Press, 1988); A. J. Arberry, *The Koran Interpreted: A Translation* (New York: Macmillan, 1964); N. J. Dawood, *The Koran*. 5th rev. ed. (New York: Penguin Books, 2006); and Mohammed Marmaduke Pickthall, *The Meaning of the Glorious Koran* (New York: New American Library and Mentor Books, n.d.).

Cragg, Kenneth. *Readings in the Quran*. London: Collins, 1988.

Esack, Farid. *The Quran: A User's Guide*. Oxford: Oneworld Publications, 2005.

Gätje, Helmut. *The Quran and Its Exegesis: Selected Texts with Classical and Modern Interpretation*. Translated by A. T. Welch. Oxford: Oneworld, 1996.

Izutsu, Toshiko. *Ethico-Religious Concepts in the Quran*. Montreal: McGill-Queen's University Press, 2002.

Kasssis, Hanna E. *A Concordance of the Quran*. Berkeley: University of California Press, 1983.

Lawrence, Bruce. *The Quran: A Biography*. New York: Atlantic Monthly Press, 2007.

McAuliffe, Jane Dammen, ed. *The Cambridge Companion to the Quran*. Cambridge: Cambridge University Press, 2006.

Osman, Fathi. *Concepts of the Quran: A Topical Reading*. Los Angeles: MVI Publications, 1997.

Qadhi, Abu Ammaar Yasir. *An Introduction to the Sciences of the Quran*. Birmingham, England: Al-Hidaayah Publishing and Distribution, 1999.

Rahman, Fazlur. *Major Themes of the Quran*. Minneapolis: Bibliotheca Islamica, 1980.

Sells, Michael. *Approaching the Quran: The Early Revelations*. Ashland, Ore.: White Cloud Press, 1999.

Stowasser, Barbara F. *Women in the Quran: Traditions and Interpretation*. Oxford: Oxford University Press, 1989.

Watt, W. Montgomery, and Richard Bell. *Introduction to the Quran*. Edinburgh: University of Edinburgh Press, 1970.

III. Islamic Religion, Anthologies, and Islamic Studies

Abou El Fadl, Khalid et al. *The Place of Tolerance in Islam*. Boston: Beacon Press, 2002.

Baghawi, Husayn, as expanded by Wali al-Din al-Khatib al-Tabrizi. *The Niche for Lamps (Mishkat al-masabih)*. Translated by James Robson. 4 vols. Lahore: Sh. Muhammad Ashraf, 1964–1966.

Bakhtiar, Laleh. *Encyclopedia of Islamic Law: A Compendium of the Major Schools*. Chicago: Kazi Publications, 1996.

Cook, Michael. *Forbidding Wrong in Islam: An Introduction*. Cambridge: Cambridge University Press, 2003.

Denny, Frederick Mathewson. *An Introduction to Islam*. 3d edition. Upper Saddle River, N.J.: Pearson/Prentice Hall, 2006 (1994).

Elias, Jamal. *Islam*. Upper Saddle River, N.J.: Prentice Hall, 1999.

Endress, Gerhard. *An Introduction to Islam*. Translated by Carole Hillenbrand. New York: Columbia University Press, 1988.

Ernst, Carl W. *The Shambhala Guide to Sufism*. Boston: Shambhala Publications, 1997.

Foltz, Richard C., Frederick M. Denny, and Azizan Baharuddin, eds. *Islam and Ecology: A Bestowed Trust*. Cambridge, Mass.: Harvard University Press, 2003.

Goldziher, Ignaz. *An Introduction to Islamic Theology and Law*. Translated by Andras and Ruth Hamori. Princeton, N.J.: Princeton University Press, 1981.

Leaman, Oliver. *An Introduction to Medieval Islamic Philosophy*. Cambridge: Cambridge University Press, 1985.

Lewis, Bernard. *The Political Language of Islam*. Chicago: University of Chicago Press, 1988.

Lockman, Zachary. *Contending Visions of the Middle East: The History and Politics of Orientalism*. Cambridge: Cambridge University Press, 2004.

Martin, Richard C. *Islamic Studies: A History of Religions Approach*. 2d ed. Upper Saddle River, N.J.: Prentice Hall, 1996.

Martin, Richard C., ed. *Approaches to Islam in Religious Studies*. Tucson: University of Arizona Press, 1985.

Mernissi, Fatima. *The Veil and the Male Elite: A Feminist Interpretation of Women's Rights in Islam*. Translated by Mary Jo Lakeland. Reading, Mass.: Addison-Wesley, 1991.

Momen, Moojan. *An Introduction to Shii Islam: The History and Doctrines of Twelver Shiism*. New Haven, Conn.: Yale University Press, 1985.

Nasr, Seyyed Hossein. *Ideals and Realities of Islam*. Boston: Beacon Press, 1972.

———. *Science and Civilization in Islam*. Cambridge, Mass.: Harvard University Press, 1968.

Nasr, Seyyed Hossein, Hamid Dabashi, and Seyyed Vali Reza Nasr, eds. *Shiism: Doctrines, Thought, and Spirituality*. Albany: State University of New York Press, 1988.

Nicholson, Reynold A. *The Mystics of Islam*. London: Routledge & Kegan Paul, 1979.

Peters, Francis E. *A Reader on Classical Islam*. Princeton, N.J.: Princeton University Press, 1994.

Pinault, David. *The Shiites: Ritual and Popular Piety in a Muslim Community*. New York: St. Martin's, 1992.

Qaradawi, Yusuf al-. *The Lawful and Prohibited in Islam (Al-Halal wa'l-haram fi'l-Islam)*. Indianapolis: American Trust Publications, n.d.

Rahman, Fazlur. *Islam.* 2d edition. Chicago: University of Chicago Press, 1979.

Renard, John. *101 Questions and Answers on Islam.* Mahwah, N.J.: Paulist Press, 2004.

———. *Windows on the House of Islam: Muslim Sources on Spirituality and Religious Life.* Berkeley: University of California Press, 1998.

Rippin, Andrew. *Defining Islam: A Reader.* London: Equinox, 2007.

Schimmel, Annemarie. *And Muhammad Is His Messenger: The Veneration of the Prophet in Islamic Piety.* Chapel Hill: University of North Carolina Press, 1985.

———. *Mystical Dimensions of Islam.* Chapel Hill: University of North Carolina Press, 1975.

Trimingham, J. S. *The Sufi Orders of Islam.* Oxford: Oxford University Press, 1971.

van Ess, Josef. *The Flowering of Muslim Theology.* Cambridge, Mass.: Harvard University Press, 2006.

Waines, David. *An Introduction to Islam.* 2d edition. Cambridge: Cambridge University Press, 2003.

Watt, W. Montgomery. *Islamic Philosophy and Theology.* Edinburgh: Edinburgh University Press, 1967.

Wheeler, Brannon M., ed. *Teaching Islam.* Oxford: Oxford University Press, 2005.

Williams, John Alden. *The Word of Islam.* Austin: University of Texas Press, 1994.

Winter, Tim, ed. *The Cambridge Companion to Classical Islamic Theology.* Cambridge: Cambridge University Press, 2008.

IV. Historical Studies

Ahmed, Leila. *Women and Gender in Islam.* New Haven, Conn.: Yale University Press, 1991.

Berkey, Jonathan P. *The Formation of Islam: Religion and Society in the Near East, 600–1800.* Cambridge: Cambridge University Press, 2003.

Bulliet, Richard W. *Islam: The View from the Edge.* New York: Columbia University Press, 1994.

Daftary, Farhad. *A Short History of the Ismailis.* Princeton, N.J.: Marcus Wiener, 1998.

Esposito, John, ed. *The Oxford History of Islam.* Oxford: Oxford University Press, 1999.

Hallaq, Wael B. *The Origins and Evolution of Islamic Law.* Cambridge: Cambridge University Press, 2005.

Haykal, Muhammad Husayn. *The Life of Muhammad (Hayat Muhammad).* Translated by Ismail R. al-Faruqi. Indianapolis: American Trust Publications, 1976.

Hodgson, Marshall G. S. *The Venture of Islam: Conscience and History in World Civilization.* 3 vols. Chicago: University of Chicago Press, 1974.

Hourani, Albert. *A History of the Arab Peoples.* Cambridge, Mass.: Harvard University Press, 1991.

Humphreys, R. Stephen. *Islamic History: A Framework for Inquiry.* Rev. ed. Princeton, N.J.: Princeton University Press, 1991.

Ibn Ishaq, Muhammad. *The Life of Muhammad.* Translated by A. Guillaume. Oxford: Oxford University Press, 1955.

Keddie, Nikki R., and Beth Baron, eds. *Women in Middle Eastern History: Shifting Boundaries in Sex and Gender.* New Haven, Conn.: Yale University Press, 1991.

Kennedy, Hugh. *The Prophet and the Age of the Caliphates: The Islamic Near East from the Sixth to the Eleventh Century.* London: Longman, 1986.

Lapidus, Ira M. *A History of Islamic Societies.* 2d ed. Cambridge: Cambridge University Press, 2002.

Mernissi, Fatima, *Women and Islam: An Historical and Theological Enquiry.* Translated by Mary Jo Lakeland. Oxford: Basil Blackwell, 1991.

Metcalf, Barbara D. *Islamic Revival in British India: Deoband, 1860–1900.* Princeton, N.J.: Princeton University Press, 1982.

Nasr, Seyyed Hossein, and Oliver Leaman, eds. *History of Islamic Philosophy.* London: Routledge, 2001.

Peters, Francis E. *Muhammad and the Origins of Islam.* Albany: State University of New York Press, 1994.

Rodinson, Maxim. *Muhammad.* Translated by Anne Carter. London: I.B. Taurus, 2002.

Schacht, Joseph, and C. E. Bosworth, eds. *The Legacy of Islam.* Oxford: Oxford University Press, 1974.

Trimingham, J. S. *The Influence of Islam upon Africa.* New York: Praeger, 1968.

Watt, W. Montgomery. *Muhammad, Prophet and Statesman.* Oxford: Oxford University Press, 1964.

V. Islam in the Modern World

Beinen, Joel, and Joe Stork, eds. *Political Islam: Essays from Middle East Report.* Berkeley: University of California Press, 1997.

Blank, Jonah. *Mullahs on the Mainframe: Islam and Modernity among the Daudi Bohras.* Chicago: University of Chicago Press, 2001.

Brown, L. Carl. *Religion and the State: The Muslim Approach to Politics.* New York: Columbia University Press, 2001.

Cook, Miriam, and Bruce B. Lawrence, eds. *Muslim Networks from Hajj to Hip Hop.* Chapel Hill: University of North Carolina Press, 2005.

Donohue, John J., and John L. Esposito, eds. *Islam in Transition: Muslim Perspectives.* 2d ed. Oxford: Oxford University Press, 2007.

Eickelman, Dale, and James Piscatori. *Muslim Politics.* Princeton, N.J.: Princeton University Press, 1996.

Eickelman, Dale, and James Piscatori, eds. *The New Media in the Muslim World: The Emerging Public Sphere.* Bloomington: Indiana University Press, 2003.

Enayat, Hamid. *Modern Islamic Political Thought.* Austin: University of Texas Press, 1982.

Ernst, Carl W. *Following Muhammad: Rethinking Islam in the Contemporary World.* Chapel Hill: University of North Carolina Press, 2003.

Esposito, John L. *Unholy War: Terror in the Name of Islam.* Oxford: Oxford University Press, 2002.

Esposito, John L., and John O. Voll. *Islam and Democracy.* Oxford: Oxford University Press, 1996.

Geertz, Clifford. *Islam Observed: Religious Development in Morocco and Indonesia.* Chicago: University of Chicago Press, 1971.

Hourani, Albert. *Arabic Thought in the Liberal Age, 1798–1939.* Cambridge: Cambridge University Press, 1983.

Kurzman, Charles, ed. *Liberal Islam: A Sourcebook.* New York: Oxford University Press, 1998.

Loeffler, Reinhold. *Islam in Practice: Religious Beliefs in a Persian Village.* Albany: State University of New York Press, 1988.

Marsden, Magnus. *Living Islam: Muslim Religious Experience in Pakistan's North-West Frontier.* Cambridge: Cambridge University Press, 2005.

McCloud, Aminah Beverly. *African American Islam.* London: Routledge, 1995.

Meyer, Ann Elizabeth. *Islam and Human Rights: Tradition and Politics.* 4th edition. Boulder, Colo.: Westview Press, 2007.

Mitchell, Richard. *The Society of the Muslim Brothers.* Oxford: Oxford University Press, 1969.

Mottahedeh, Roy P. *The Mantle of the Prophet: Religion and Politics in Iran.* Oxford: Oneworld, 2000.

Naqash, Yitzhak. *The Shiis of Iraq.* Princeton, N.J.: Princeton University Press, 1994.

Nasr, Seyyed Vali Reza. *Mawdudi and the Making of Islamic Revivalism.* Oxford: Oxford University Press, 1996.

———. *The Shia Revival: How Conflicts within Islam Will Shape the Future.* London: W.W. Norton, 2007.

Rahman, Fazlur. *Islam and Modernity: The Transformation of an Intellectual Tradition.* Chicago: University of Chicago Press, 1984.

Rahnema, Ali, ed. *Pioneers of Islamic Revival.* 2d edition. London: Zed Books, 2005.

Rashid, Ahmed. *Taliban: Militant Islam, Oil and Fundamentalism in Central Asia.* New Haven, Conn.: Yale University Press, 2001.

Ruthven, Malise. *Islam in the World.* 3d edition. Oxford: Oxford University Press, 2006.

Said, Edward W. *Covering Islam: How the Media and the Experts Determine How We See the Rest of the World.* New York: Random House, 1997.

Smith, Jane I. *Islam in America.* New York: Columbia University Press, 1999.

Webb, Gisela, ed. *Windows of Faith: Muslim Women Scholar-Activists in North America.* Syracuse, N.Y.: Syracuse University Press, 2000.

Zaman, Muhammad Qasim. *The Ulama in Contemporary Islam: Custodians of Change.* Princeton, N.J.: Princeton University Press.

VI. Islam and Other Religions

Assayag, Jackie. *At the Confluence of Two Rivers: Muslims and Hindus in South India.* New Delhi: Manohar, 2004.

Bulliet, Richard W. *The Case for Islamo-Christian Civilization.* New York: Columbia University Press, 2006.

Cohen, Mark R. *Under Crescent and Cross: The Jews in the Middle Ages.* Princeton, N.J.: Princeton University Press, 2008.

Cragg, Kenneth. *Jesus and the Muslim: An Exploration.* London: George Allen and Unwin, 1985.

Eaton, Richard M., ed. *India's Islamic Traditions, 711–1750.* Oxford: Oxford University Press, 2003.

Gilmartin, David, and Bruce B. Lawrence. *Beyond Turk and Hindu: Rethinking Religious Identities in Islamicate South Asia.* Gainesville: University Press of Florida, 2000.

Goitein, Shlomo D. *Jews and Arabs: A Concise History of Their Social and Cultural Relations.* New York: Dover Publications, 2005.

Graham, William A. *Beyond the Written Word: Oral Aspects of Scripture in the History of Religions.* Cambridge: Cambridge University Press, 1987.

Hussain, Amir. *Oil and Water: Two Faiths, One God.* Kelowna, Canada: Copper House, 2006.

Levtzion, Nehemiah, ed. *Conversion to Islam.* New York: Holmes and Meier, 1979.

Lewis, Bernard. *The Jews of Islam.* Princeton, N.J.: Princeton University Press, 1987.

McAuliffe, Jane Dammen. *Quranic Christians: An Analysis of Classical and Modern Exegesis.* Cambridge: Cambridge University Press, 1991.

Menocal, Maria Rosa. *The Ornament of the World: How Muslims, Jews, and Christians Created a Culture of Tolerance in Medieval Spain.* Boston: Little, Brown, 2002.

Peters, Francis E. *Islam: A Guide for Jews and Christians.* Princeton, N.J.: Princeton University Press, 2005.

VII. Islam and the Arts

Blair, Sheila S., and Jonathan M. Bloom. *The Art and Architecture of Islam, 1250–1800.* New Haven, Conn.: Yale University Press, 1995.

———. *Islamic Arts.* London: Phaidon Press, 1997.

Ettinghausen, Richard, and Oleg Grabar. *The Art and Architecture of Islam, 650–1250.* New York: Viking Penguin, 1987.

Grabar, Oleg. *The Formation of Islamic Art.* New Haven, Conn.: Yale University Press, 1973.

Nelson, Kristina. *The Art of Reciting the Quran.* Cairo: American University in Cairo Press, 2001.

Schimmel, Annemarie. *Calligraphy and Islamic Culture.* New York: New York University Press, 1990.

VIII. Internet Resources

There are many sites on the Web that focus on Islam, but they are of varying quality, and, like other Web sites, they are prone to disappear or change their URLs. Some are scholarly, many are devotional or seek to explain the religion from the point of view of Muslim believers. The following is a list of useful, well-organized sites that have been maintained and updated for several years.

Encyclopaedia of Islam, online edition. This site includes the entire second edition of this major reference work, with revisions, plus installments for the new third edition. Access by subscription.
URL: www.brillonline.nl/subscriber/uid=3144/advanced_search?authstatuscode=202

Encyclopaedia of the Quran, online edition. This includes the entire reference work, with updates and revisions. Access by subscription.
URL: www.brillonline.nl/subscriber/uid=3144/advanced_search?authstatuscode=202

Encyclopaedia of Women and Islamic Cultures, online edition. The entire reference work, with updates and revisions. Access by subscription.
URL: www.brillonline.nl/subscriber/uid=3144/advanced_search?authstatuscode=202

Index Islamicus. Online version of scholarly literature in the fields of Islamic and Middle Eastern Studies, as well as the wider Muslim world. Searchable data base. Access by subscription.
URL: www.md3.csa.com/ids70/advanced_search.php?SID=aa7153a015406126f28dac82b93940a2

Islamicity. A very large Muslim site, loaded with text, audio, and video files. Includes sections on the Quran, hadith, history, and links to Muslim organizations and countries.
URL: www.islamicity.com/default.shtml

Islam Online. Another exhaustive Muslim site, loaded with text, as well as audio and video files.
URL: http://www.islamonline.net/English/index.shtml

Islamic Studies, Islam, Arabic and Religion: An award-winning site covering many facets of Islam and Muslim life, created by Prof. A. Godlas, an Islamic Studies scholar. Includes links for the Quran, hadith, law, Shiism, and Sufism.
URL: www.arches.uga.edu/~godlas/

The Muslim Women's Home Page: Very useful collection of information about Islamic understandings of women as expressed by Muslims themselves.
URL: www.jannah.org/sisters/index.html

Saudi Aramco World. Online version of the bimonthly publication on Islamic and Arab culture, history, and geography. Back issues go all the way to 1960. Very informative articles for general readers and students.
URL: www.saudiaramcoworld.com/about.us/

The Shia Home Page. Web site created by Shii Muslims, the minority branch of Islam, to explain their doctrines and practices.
URL: www.shia.org/

INDEX

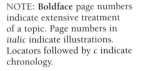